The 2000-2001 Official PFA

FOOTBALLERS FACTFILE

Edited by
Barry J Hugman

Assistant Editors
Peter Lovering
and Roy Grant

Photographs by
Colorsport

Queen Anne Press

The Official PFA Footballers Factfile
is produced in association with
www.soccer-files.com
email: admin@sports-files.com
telephone: 01844 339909

First published in Great Britain in 2000 by
Queen Anne Press
a division of Lennard Associates Limited
Mackerye End, Harpenden
Hertfordshire AL5 5DR

A CIP catalogue record for this book
is available from the British Library

ISBN 1 85291 626 5

PFA Awards photograph on p 384: Allsport UK

Typeset and designed by
Typecast (Artwork & Design)
8 Mudford Road
Yeovil, Somerset BA21 4AA

Printed and bound in Great Britain by
Butler & Tanner, London and Frome

Acknowledgements

Now into its sixth year, the *Factfile* continues to expand and reach out, not only as a media tool, and invaluable to those in the game, but as a part-work which, in due course, will cover the season-by-season record of every player's complete career and should be of interest to all who follow this great game of ours. As a book with a heavy workload, I would once again like to express my thanks to **Gordon Taylor**, the chief executive, and all those at the PFA, including **Brendon Batson** and **Garry Nelson**, who are genuinely supporting and helping to establish the Factfile. Their help is much appreciated.

Also, I am exceedingly grateful to all those at the Premier League, such as **Mike Foster**, **Adrian Cook** and **Jonathan Hargreaves** for their help in establishing good, solid, and reliable information, especially regarding player appearance stats. That gratitude also extends to **Sandy Bryson** of the Scottish FA. I would also like to thank **Debbie Birch and Louise Standing** of the Football League for all of their help in the past.

This year, the text of the player profiles was edited by a team led by **Peter Lovering**. Peter has been involved in the production of sports books for more than a decade and is the author of *Chelsea: Player by Player*. He received invaluable assistance from **Trevor Bugg** and **Ian Nannestad**, who have both contributed to the *Factfile* for several years, and **Matthew Hancock**, a young sports journalist with a bright future. On the stats front, **Roy Grant** once again diligently kept note of all player appearances, subs and goals on a weekly basis and, along with help from **Michael Featherstone**, collated heights, weights, birthplaces, birthdates, while double checking all statistical data. Regarding international appearances from junior to senior level across many countries, **Ian Nannestad**, who is looking after that material on the new player website, *soccer-files.com*, which covers every player to make a league appearance since 1946, gave it his best shot. He was lucky to be able to call upon **David Barber** (English FA), **Ceri Stennett** (official FA of Wales statistician), and **Marshall Gillespie** (editor of the Northern Ireland Football Yearbook). At this juncture, I would like to thank **Ron Hockings**, the author of several books on international football and a leading specialist on the subject, for all of his help prior to this edition. Others who gave their time were **Alan Platt**, **Jenny Hugman**, and many Premier and Football League members up and down the country.

For the sixth year, **Jonathan Ticehurst**, managing director of Windsor Insurance Brokers' Sports Division, has thrown his weight behind the *Factfile*, both financially and vocally. His and Windsor's support, as with the *British Boxing Board of Control Yearbook*, is greatly appreciated.

For details provided on players, I have listed below, in alphabetical order, the names of the "team", without whose help this book would not have been possible to produce. Once again, I thank every one of them for all the hard work they put in.

Audrey Adams *(Watford):* Producer and statistician for BBC Radio Sport and a Watford supporter since the days of Cliff Holton, Audrey was the club statistician for the *Ultimate Football Guide*.

Geoff Allman *(Walsall):* A university lecturer by trade, he saw his first ever game in February 1944, Walsall versus Wolves. Has written for Walsall's programme for over 30 seasons and, at one time or another, has provided articles for more than half of the clubs currently in the Premiership and Football League. Geoff is also a Methodist local preacher and press officer.

Stuart Basson *(Chesterfield):* Saw his 1998 *Who's Who, Lucky Whites and Spireites,* become Yore Publications fastest-selling book to date. A contributor to the *Factfile* since its inception, Stuart hopes to complete a Chesterfield FC history in the next couple of years, and is starting work on a broader history of football in north-east Derbyshire.

Ian Bates *(Bradford):* Has followed City since 1951 and refereed in amateur football up until 1995-96. A member of the AFS, this is the first publication that Ian has been involved in.

David Batters *(York City):* A supporter since 1948, David is the club historian and a contributor to the matchday programme. Is the author of *York City, the Complete Record 1922-1990*, and the compiler of *Images of Sport - York City FC*. Commentates on matches for York Hospital Radio and is a member of the AFS.

Harry Berry *(Blackburn Rovers):* Author of the club centenary history, *A Century of Soccer* and other books on Rovers, and co-author of the *Preston North End* history, along with several books on athletics.

Eddie Brennan *(Sunderland):* A season ticket holder at the Stadium of Light, and a former contributor to the *Carling Ultimate Football Guide*, Eddie has been a regular supporter since 1976.

Jim Brown *(Coventry City):* The club's official statistician and contributor to the programme, he also pens a column for the local newspaper answering readers' queries.

Mark Brown *(Plymouth Argyle):* Helped on the *PFA Factfile* profiles by his wife Nicola, Mark has been supporting the club for over 25 years, having been introduced to them at the tender age of five by his Argyle mad family. Follows most of their games, whether home or away, and is a member of the travel club.

Trevor Bugg *(Hull City):* A supporter of the Tigers for over 30 years, Trevor is a major contributor to Hull City's much respected matchday programme.

Graham Caton *(Bournemouth):* Into his sixth year with the *Factfile*, Graham is a committed Cherries' supporter who has always enjoyed collating facts and figures relating to the club.

Wallace Chadwick *(Burnley):* A supporter for over 30 years, he has seen all the extremes in the period from the great days of the '60s, including the championship of all four divisions and a narrow escape from relegation to the Conference. Wallace is a regular contributor to the Clarets' programme.

Gary Chalk *(Southampton):* A member of the hagiology group of Saints' historians committed to the collection and dissemination of accurate information on the history of Southampton FC. Currently the club's official co-historian and statistician, and co-authored *Saints: A Complete History 1885-1987* and *The Alphabet of the Saints 1992* with Duncan Holley.

Dennis Chapman *(Manchester City):* Now retired, Dennis has followed City since 1937-38. Has worked on several publications, including the *FA Carling Premier League: The Players* and the *Ultimate Football Guide*. Possesses possibly the largest collection of City programmes, the earliest being 1902-03, and has been a life member of the Association of Football Statisticians since 1980. Also contributes and updates the statistical section of the club's official Handbook.

Paul Clayton *(Charlton Athletic):* Paul wrote a regular feature in the club programme between 1993 and 1998, having previously written other articles for the now defunct Charlton Athletic magazine and Valiants' Viewpoint (Supporters' Club newsletter/fanzine). He has also provided the Charlton statistics for a number of publications, including the *Ultimate Football Guide*, since 1987, along with the Charlton player information for the *Factfile* since its inception in 1995. A member of the AFS, he is a long-standing season ticket holder at the Valley and rarely misses a game, home or away, despite living in Wiltshire.

Grant Coleby *(Exeter City):* A member of both Exeter City's Supporters' Club and the Association of Football Statisticians, Grant has been the official contributor to the Factfile since its inception.

Eddie Collins *(Nottingham Forest):* A Forest supporter since 1956, and a member of the Associated Football Statisticians, this is the first publication he has been involved in.

David Copping *(Barnsley):* A life-long Barnsley fan who has commentated on hospital radio for many years before moving on to the club's videos, David has also written regularly in the matchday programme during the past 12 seasons. Is currently working on player profiles for a unique new player-based internet site.

Frank Coumbe *(Brentford):* Has not missed a competitive Brentford game since December 1977, a club record. He has also been the Bees' statistician for this publication since it began, and acted in a similar capacity for the *Ultimate Football Guide* until its demise. If you require any information on Brentford players during the last 20 years, then Frank's your man.

Ken Craig *(Colchester United):* Ken, who continues to produce the monthly newsletter, *U's from 'ome*, for all United fans living away from home, has recently celebrated 25 years of supporting the club. He is now looking forward to the next 25 years!

Peter Cullen *(Bury):* As Bury FC's official historian, and a life-long fan, Peter completed *Bury FC: The Official History* – a 324 page book charting the club's 115 years to date – which was the first complete history of the Shakers ever to be published.

John Curtis *(Scunthorpe United):* A life-long Scunthorpe fan who has seen all of United's league matches, home and away, for the past eight seasons, John is currently deputy sports editor of the *Scunthorpe Evening Telegraph*, and a former editor of the matchday programme for four years.

Carol Dalziel *(Tranmere Rovers):* Has been watching Tranmere for over 30 years, is a regular contributor to the matchday programme, and operates the club's electronic scoreboard.

Denise Dann *(Aston Villa):* In her own words, Denise is a mad, crazy Villa supporter, who follows them up and down the country without fail. Her only previous football work was to help me with the club's profiles required for the *Premier League: The Players* publication. She is helped by her husband, Paul.

Gareth Davies *(Wrexham):* Assists in the much acclaimed club programme, the editor of which, **Geraint Parry**, also helped on heights and weights, etc, for this publication. Gareth has written and published the *Coast of Soccer Memories*, the centenary history of the *North Wales Coast FA (1995)*, and co-authored with Ian Garland the *Who's Who of Welsh International Soccer Players (1991)*. Also heavily involved in Wrexham, *A Complete Record 1872-1992*, written by Peter Jones. His most recent work, co-authored with Peter Jones, is *The Racecourse Robins*, an A-Z of all Wrexham players, both past and present. With dedicated research, this book is among the best of its kind ever produced.

David Downs *(Reading):* The official club historian and statistician, now employed full-time by Reading FC as its education and welfare officer, he claims to be the oldest player to have scored a goal at the Madejski Stadium, when playing for the Office Staff XI versus the Programme Printers XI. Has made numerous television and radio appearances, usually connected with football, and also had a short-lived career as a Tarzanogram! Co-authored *The Definitive Reading FC, 1896-1998.*

Ray Driscoll *(Chelsea):* A life-long Blues' fan, born and bred two miles away from Stamford Bridge – he still has to pinch himself to make sure that he has not dreamed the last few seasons at Chelsea, although he was saddened by the departure of Ruud Gullit. Is a contributor to many football books, and also wrote articles for the *Euro '96* programmes.

Mark Evans *(Leeds United):* Has supported United for over 30 years and describes his association with the club as one of the loves of his life. The Leeds' statistician for the *Ultimate Football Guide* for nearly nine years, he was also involved in my two editions of the *FA Carling Premiership: The Players.*

Keith Evemy *(Fulham):* A regular supporter, both home and away, since 1943, Keith missed Fulham's only previous post-war honour, the Second Division championship in 1948-49, being away on military service. Has contributed to the club programme for more than 20 years, the 1998-99 season's success was the sweeter for having waited so long.

Colin Faiers *(Cambridge United):* A 40-year-old chartered accountant, Colin, a fan for over 30 years, is the recognised club statistician and currently writes the historical features for the programme.

Harold Finch *(Crewe Alexandra):* The club historian has just completed 66 seasons of supporting the Alex, being the programme editor for over 40 years, and still contributes a regular page in the matchday programme. Harold is the author of The Images of Sports publication, *Crewe Alexandra FC – A Pictorial History of the Club.*

Mick Ford and **Richard Lindsey** *(Millwall):* Mick has been a life-long supporter of Millwall from childhood, through army service, and now back in civilian life 46 years later. Brought up in the New Den area, but now living in Worcester, he goes to all the home games and most of the away fixtures, and has a formidable collection of memorabilia which he adds to when attending many programme fairs right across the country. And, as a full badge licence holder, he likes to cast an eye over the team performance. Meanwhile, his Factfile partner, Richard, the author of *Millwall: The Complete Record*, continues to help estaablish the Millwall FC Museum at the New Den.

Paul Godfrey *(Cheltenham Town):* Paul first watched football as a toddler when his father was on the committee of the local Cheltenham club, St Marks CA, prior to graduating to Town in the late 1970s and continuing to watch them both during and after his studies at Oxford University. He has so far spent ten seasons as the club's programme editor, and between October 1990 and February 2000 every home and away first-team match. Is currently writing for the *Gloucester Citizen* newspaper, while working on the *Official History of Cheltenham Town FC.*

Dave Goody *(Southend United):* A season ticket holder and life-long Blues' fan, Dave is the co-author of *Southend United: The Official History of the Blues*, and a recently published *Potted Shrimps: A Southend United Encyclopedia.* Having collected programmes and memorabilia from the whole of the club's history, he will shortly be co-authoring *The Archive Photograph Series: Southend United FC* with the noted football author, Peter Miles.

Frank Grande *(Northampton Town):* Author of *The Cobblers, A History of Northampton Town FC* and a *Who's Who* on the club, he has now written a fourth book titled *The Centenery History of Northampton Town.* Has contributed a regular column to the club programme for the past 20 seasons.

Roy Grant *(Oxford United):* Formerly assistant secretary at Oxford United, as well as being the club programme editor and statistician, he also handled the clubline telephone service. In the past, a contributor to the *Official Football League Yearbook* and the *Ultimate Football Guide*, he has supported United from boyhood.

Michael Green *(Bolton Wanderers):* Despite being a fanatical Newcastle United supporter, Michael covers Bolton for the Factfile and his excellent efforts are much appreciated. Having a yearning to get involved in the area of freelance journalism, preferably concerning football or popular entertainment (music, films etc), he hopes to go full time sooner or later. Has recently formed a band called Pub Monkey with some friends, playing lead guitar, and is looking to gig in the Bolton area soon.

Roger Harrison *(Blackpool):* Life-long supporter who has seen the Pool play every other league side both home and away, and joint programme editor and club statistician, Roger also contributes to other publications, including *Rothmans* and the *Ultimate Football Guide.*

Richard and **Janey Hayhoe** *(Tottenham Hotspur):* Now the proud parents of Holly (a future Spurs' fan), Janey and Richard were again happy to put the club's biographies together for the *Factfile* despite their exta duties. With George Graham now in charge at White Hart Lane, things can only get better.

Des Hinks *(Stockport County):* A Hatter's fanatic for 36 years, Des independently runs County's ClubCall line, the official website, as well as editing and producing the club's award-winning reserve team match programme.

Ray Hugman *(Luton Town):* Looking to build himself a career in writing, Ray, who lives in Hatfield and has supported Queens Park Rangers since a lad, enjoys watching his football at Luton these days. He is especially interested in assessing and analysing player skills throughout a match.

Mike Jay *(Bristol Rovers):* Mike, the club's official historian and programme contributor, has now had three books published on Bristol Rovers, namely *The Complete Record (1883-1987)*, *Pirates in Profile, a Who's Who of Players (1920-1994)*, and *Bristol Rovers FC Images of England Photographic History*. Is currently working in conjunction with Stephen Byrne on a detailed history of the club which is due to be published next year.

Chris and **Darran Jennison** and **Rob Ringsell** *(Wimbledon):* Chris has been supporting the Dons for over 25 years and was aided on the player pen portraits for the *Factfile* by her husband, Darran. Both are season ticket holders in the family stand, where they sit with their two sons. Her brother Rob Ringsell, who was also involved, is currently working for DVLA and is looking forward to the club being promoted at the end of the coming season.

Colin Jones *(Swansea City):* A fan since the early 1960s and a contributor to the club programme during the last six years. Played non-league football, before being involved in training and coaching.

Andrew Kirkham *(Sheffield United):* A Blades' supporter since 1953, and a regular contributor to the club programme and handbook since 1984, Andrew is a member of the AFS and 92 club. Was also a contributor to *Sheffield United: The First 100 Years*, while January 2000 saw the publication of *A Complete Record of Sheffield United Football Club, 1889-1999*, of which he was the co-author.

Geoff Knights *(Macclesfield Town):* Having arrived in the Macclesfield area in the late 1980s following a career move, Geoff rarely misses a match these days whether it be home or away. Describing himself as an ordinary supporter who stands on the terraces, and one who enjoys the friendly atmosphere of a small club, he keeps very detailed stats on the club which are often used in response to media enquiries. As a former senior manager for a clearing bank, his experience of writing staff appraisals came in useful when describing players for the *Factfile*.

Geoffrey Lea *(Wigan Athletic):* Editor of the matchday programme, Geoff has been an Athletic supporter for over 25 years, first watching the club during their non-league days. And, as the matchday reporter for Clubcall, he has worked for local radio stations following the club's progress. Was also the club statistician for the *Ultimate Football Guide*.

Bob Lonkhurst *(Arsenal):* A life-long Gunners' supporter, having had trials with the club as a 16-year-old goalie, Bob is a regular visitor to Highbury, and has a keen interest in the youth team. Is also a successful boxing author, with a large collection of boxiana, being a contributor to two magazines and the author of *Man of Courage,* the story of the ring legend, Tommy Farr. Pat Rice, the former Arsenal star, also helped out with information.

John Lovis *(Torquay United):* A supporter since 1955, and a regular contributor to the club programme, he was also United's statistician for the *Ultimate Football Guide*.

Gordon Macey *(Queens Park Rangers):* Gordon has been following QPR for nearly 40 years and is now recognised as the club's official historian and statistician. A life-long member of the AFS, and the author of the successful *Complete Record of Queens Park Rangers* published by Breedens, his third book on the club was published in August 1999. His "daytime" job involves a large amount of overseas travel, which gives him the opportunity to watch football (and ice hockey) in a number of different countries.

Steve McGhee *(Derby County):* A collector of Derby memorabilia and a fan since 1969. Earlier involved in a bi-monthly historical magazine on County, he also compiled the club section for the *Ultimate Football Guide*.

Richard Mackey *(Swindon Town):* Having supported the club from boyhood, Richard joined Town as the marketing and press officer on leaving Cardiff University with a BA (Hons) in 1977. Is now with the Carling Premier League, managing the press office.

John Maguire *(Manchester United):* A one-club man for the *Factfile* since its inception in 1995, John has been working on several sports related topics over the past 12 months, including a new booklet on Manchester United based around Rudyard Kipling's famous 'IF'. He jokes, 'if working with Kipling doesn't get me a best seller, nothing will'! A member of the AFS, he thanks Sports Pages for their continued support.

Carl Marsden *(Oldham Athletic):* Carl has followed the Latics since 1983 and first became seriously involved as a founder member of the 'Stop the Rot' campaign aimed at reversing the club's slide down the divisions. As well as producing an independent Oldham Athletic e-zine that can be found on the internet at *www.oafc.co.uk*, he is also a regular contributor to the *Beyond the Boundary* fanzine.

Wade Martin *(Stoke City):* For many years a major contributor to the club programme, as well as writing *A Potters Tale* and the *Master Potters'* series of books.

Tony Matthews *(West Bromwich Albion):* Official statistician and curator of Albion, his publications include, *the complete records of Aston Villa, Birmingham City, WBA, Wolves, Walsall and Stoke City.* Has also compiled *Who's Whos* on the first four clubs listed above, plus Manchester United, and currently contributes to several programmes.

Paul Morant *(Leyton Orient):* Paul, a 30-year-old insurance messenger who works in the City of London, has been supporting Orient for 22 years, and travels to all games, whether home or away – even attending reserve and youth-team matches where possible.

Ian Nannestad *(Lincoln City):* A past contributor to the Imps' programme and co-author of the *Who's Who of Lincoln City, 1892-1994* publication.

Adrian and **Caroline Newnham** and **Tim Carder** *(Brighton & Hove Albion):* Adrian and Caroline are life-long supporters of the Albion who actually met through football. They have been heavily involved in the successful campaign which saw the Seagulls return to Brighton and Hove this season, as well as being active in the efforts to secure a permanent home for the club at Falmer. Adrian was also the editor of the Albion fanzine, *Scars and Stripes*. Tim is chairman of both the Supporters' Club and the Albion Collectors and Historians' Society. Along with Roger Harris, he co-authored *Seagulls: The Story of Brighton and Hove Albion FC*, and *Albion A-Z: A Who's Who of Brighton and Hove Albion FC*. He is also a respected local historian on matters ranging far beyond the Albion.

John Northcutt *(West Ham United):* Has supported the Hammers since 1959 and is the co-author of West Ham books, *The Complete Record* and the *Illustrated History*. A regular contributor to the club programme and was the club adviser to the *Ultimate Football Guide*.

Richard Owen *(Portsmouth):* A life-long supporter and official club historian, Richard performs a number of jobs for the club as a labour of love. As a regular contributor to the matchday programme for the past 22 years, he has missed only a handful of away games in 24 years, while watching Pompey on 104 league grounds. An avid programme collector, with almost a complete set of post-war Portsmouth home and away issues, he co-published the *Pictorial History of Portsmouth FC* in 1998 before compiling *A Team Collection*, which featured every team picture of the club since 1888.

Brian Pead *(Liverpool):* Brian, who can be reached on 0208 302 6446, has authored several books on Liverpool FC, hundreds of articles, and is the writer for BBC's Extra Time, involving Liverpool's matches. His website address is www.liverpoolfchistorian.com.

Steve Peart and **Dave Finch** *(Wycombe Wanderers):* A former programme editor of the club and a supporter for over 20 years, Steve put together the player profiles, while the club statistics were supplied by Dave, the official Wycombe statistician. Both were authors of *Wycombe Wanderers 1887-1996 – The Official History*, published in 1996.

Steve Phillips *(Rochdale):* A Dale fan of over 30 years standing, he is the club's official statistician and author of *The Survivors: The Story of Rochdale AFC*.

Terry Phillips *(Cardiff City):* Chief soccer writer for the *South Wales Echo* since 1994, and a sports journalist for nearly 30 years – *Kent Evening Post* (1970-1977), *Derby Evening Telegraph* (1977-1986), *Gloucester Citizen* (1986-1994) – Terry has previously covered clubs at all levels, including Brian Clough's Nottingham Forest, Derby County, Gillingham, and Gloucester City.

Andrew Pinfield *(Halifax Town):* Andrew is a life-long supporter of Halifax who follows the Shaymen home and away without fail. Is also the club's assistant commercial manager and programme editor.

Kevan Platt *(Norwich City):* Kevan has supported the Canaries for over 30 years and has been employed by the club in various full-time capacities since 1980, witnessing at first hand the enormous swings in fortune during that period. Currently City's programme editor and press officer, he also co-edits the official handbook, and is a keen statistician, keeping detailed records of all the club's representative sides. Now the club secretary, despite his official role, he remains a fan, and can still be witnessed leaping to his feet in celebration when surrounded by the gathered media within the press box.

David Prentice *(Everton):* Everton correspondent for the *Liverpool Echo* since 1993 and author of a club history five years earlier, when he was reporting both Everton and Liverpool for the *Daily Post*, he completed his Mersey set when reporting on Tranmere Rovers for three years from 1990.

Mike Purkiss *(Crystal Palace):* Having supported Palace since 1950 and produced stats on them since 1960, Mike is the author of the *Complete History of Crystal Palace, 1905-1989*, was the club statistician for the *Ultimate Football Guide*, and also contributed to *Premier League: The Players*.

Mike Renshaw *(Sheffield Wednesday):* Has followed Wednesday for over 40 years and is a great supporter of European soccer. Also produced the club section for the *Ultimate Football Guide*.

Mick Robinson *(Peterborough United):* Another life-long fan, for a number of years Mick has contributed to the club programme and was the joint editor of the *Official Peterborough History*. Was also club statistician for the *Ultimate Football Guide*.

Phil Sherwin *(Port Vale):* As Vale's statistician, Phil works on a number of other publications and has contributed to the club programme for 19 years. A fan since 1968, he follows them home and away.

Derrick Slasor *(Middlesbrough):* First saw the Boro play in December 1946 and, as managing director of Trapezium Transport Services, is well known in the area for sponsoring various club activities.

Mike Slater *(Wolverhampton Wanderers):* The Wolves' contributor to the *Factfile* since its inception, Mike wrote a book on the club's history called *Molineux Memories*, which he published in 1988. Well-known as the eight-time compiler of the *Brain of Wolves' Quiz*, he also produced a booklet in 1996 containing all of Wolves' competitive results and record against every other club.

Andy Sleight *(Barnet):* Andy covered the Bees' emotional campaign for Metro, Hayters, and ClubCall alongside his commitments as the club's programme editor.

Gordon Small *(Hartlepool United):* Having supported United since October 1965, experiencing two promotions, two relegations, and several close calls, with 1999-2000 being one of the better seasons with the club reaching the Play-Offs, Gordon was the club statistician for the *Ultimate Football Guide*. He also brought out the *Definitive Hartlepool United FC* book last year.

Dave Smith *(Leicester City):* A regular columnist in the programme, co-author of *Fossils & Foxes* and the *Foxes Alphabet*, he assists with several other club handbooks.

Gerry Somerton *(Rotherham United):* The deputy sports editor of the *Rotherham Advertiser*, who co-edits the matchday programme and is the club's official historian, Gerry has followed Rotherham for over 50 years. Has also published two best-selling books on the club, works on a part-time basis for BBC Radio Sheffield, and has provided information for the *Factfile* since its inception.

Paul Stead *(Huddersfield Town):* A regular supporter, both home and away, and a season ticket holder at the McAlpine Stadium, Paul took over *Factfile* duties from his brother, Richard. Also contributed to the *Ultimate Football Guide*.

David Steele *(Carlisle United):* A programme contributor for over a decade, as well as producing more general historical articles, David has now profiled well over 150 ex-Carlisle players.

Richard Stocken *(Shrewsbury Town):* A supporter for over 40 years and a collector of club programmes and memorabilia, Richard has been an annual contributor to the *Ultimate Football Guide* and other publications.

Bill Swann *(Newcastle United):* A supporter since the Jackie Milburn days of the early 1950s, and a long-term shareholder in the club along with his wife and three children, he is a keen collector of memorabilia connected with the club, and a member of the AFS. Has now consolidated his information on club matches, teams, scorers, and players into a database for easy access and analysis. Also assisted in the production of the club's volume in the Complete Record series, and is now in his fifth year as a contributor to the *Factfile*. His 14-year-old son Richard, also a Newcastle fanatic, supplied much of the 'anorak' information for the player biogs.

Alan Tait *(Scottish clubs):* A regular contributor to Tony Brown's ultimate *Scottish League* book, and a compiler of statistics appertaining to that country, Alan is currently working on a project, probably still several years down tbe road, that will give line-ups for all Scottish League matches since 1890.

Colin Tattum *(Birmingham City):* Colin has reported the fortunes of Birmingham City and west midland clubs for the *Birmingham Evening Mail* and *Sports Argus* newspapers for almost a decade. A native of the second city, he also covers the national side.

Paul Taylor *(Mansfield Town):* A Mansfield Town supporter for over 30 years, Paul has contributed to many publications over the last few years, and co-authored the club's centenary history, published in 1997, with Jack Retter. On Jack's untimely death last year, he was invited to take over the roles of club historian and Supporters' Club president from his friend.

Richard and **Sarah Taylor** *(Notts County):* Richard (father) is a member of the AFS, and a life-long fan in a family of County supporters; while Sarah (daughter) is a student who has been an avid follower of the team for over ten years, and rarely misses a game.

Les Triggs *(Grimsby Town):* Became involved with the statistical side of the club when asked to assist with Town's centenary exhibition in 1978. A retired librarian, Les, who first saw the Mariners in a wartime league match, is the co-author of the Grimsby Town volume in the *Complete Record* series and was the club statistician to the *Ultimate Football Guide* from its inception.

Roger Triggs *(Gillingham):* Has written three books on the club, *Gillingham FC - A Chronology 1893-1984, Priestfield Profiles 1950-1988* and the centenary publication, *Home of the Shouting Men*, which he co-authored with Andy Bradley. Also a feature writer in the programme since 1975.

Frank Tweddle *(Darlington):* As Darlington's official historian and statistician, Frank, a supporter for over 40 years, has contributed articles to the club programme for the last 25 seasons. He is also the author of *Darlington's Centenary History* published in 1983 and soon *The Definitive Darlington 1883-2000*, along with producing work for various other football publications. Is a member of the 92 club and the AFS.

Paul Voller *(Ipswich Town):* A Town supporter since 1963-64, Paul works at the ground on matchdays and is a member of the supporters' management committee. Other publications worked on include the *FA Carling Premier League: The Players* and the *Ultimate Football Guide*.

Richard Williams *(Chester City):* A supporter of the Blues for over 20 years after being taken to his first match at the tender age of four by his Dad, he has been a regular matchday programme contributor for nearly half of that time. In this, his debut season in writing for the *PFA Factfile*, Richard, who is a personal loans advisor for a large financial company and is married with one daughter (Jessica), would like to thank John Martin for putting his name forward to Barry Hugman.

Tony Woodburn and **Martin Atherton** *(Preston North End):* Both North End fans for over 30 years, Tony (statistics) and Martin (text) provide statistical and historical information on the club for the permanent Preston North End collection being established at the National Football Museum at Deepdale, as well as writing for the club programme and, of course, the *Factfile*. Tony is a member of the Association of Football Statisticians, the 92 club, and the Scottish 38 club, whilst Martin is the principal researcher for the University of Central Lancashire's Deaf United project, investigating the history, social, and cultural aspects of deaf football in Britain.

David Woods and **Tony Ticktum** *(Bristol City):* A regular supporter since 1958, and a shareholder in both the old club and the re-vamped 1982 organisation, David has been involved with four books on City, the latest being *Bristol City – The Modern Era* published by Desert Island Books. Is a life member of the AFS and a member of the 92 club. Other interests include rugby, tennis, cricket, badminton, speedway, geology, history, photography and reading. Played for his school at rugby, but became secretary of Bristol Casuals AFC (the side formed by Bristol City supporters) in 1966 when they came together as one of the founder members of the Bristol and District SFL, making 100 appearances for them before hanging up his boots in 1972. A shareholder at Ashton Gate, Tony first watched City at the end of the last war and, as a talented inside-forward, played for RAF Fassberg during his National Service in Germany before demob and turning out for a top local Bristol club, De Veys, between 1955 and 1957. His other passions include cricket, boxing, music, gardening, reading and walking. He first worked on the *Factfile* last year, assisted with the publication, *Bristol City – The Modern Era*, and hopes one day to have the pleasure of seeing his beloved City win a league title, as he saw very little of their last success in 1954-55.

Finally, on the production side of the book, my thanks go to Jean Bastin, of Typecast (Artwork & Design), for her patience and diligent work on the typesetting and design, which again went far beyond the call of normal duty and was much appreciated. She was ably supported by Nina Whatmore (Orchard Design).

Forewords

Once again I am extremely pleased to give the PFA's full endorsement and recommendation to Footballers' Factfile. In this modern age of such tremendous interest in the professional football game, and its high profile, it is nice to have at hand the definitive book on statistics and profiles for every one of our members playing in first team football throughout the Premier League and Football League in England and Wales last season.

The book clearly reflects the changing face of English football, and its cosmopolitan nature, with the English leagues having more foreign players than any other league in the world. Euro 2000 showed that the game is in as good a quality position as ever before, especially with the football displayed by countries such as France, Holland and Portugal, in particular.

There was consolation for England's early exit with our first competitive victory against Germany since 1966, and we did score five goals in three games. If it's any consolation, way back in 1988 after losing all three games in the European Championships, two years later we were good enough to reach the semi-finals of the World Cup and unlucky to go out on penalties, against Germany, of course!

I hope that with the financial investment in Academies and coaching, and an appreciation of the necessary skills for success on the international stage emphasising technique, possession football and flair, that we can copy our past with qualification for the World Cup in 2002.

The publication has been sponsored by Windsor Insurance Brokers, the key figures in our industry with regard to the protection of players against injury, and written by Barry Hugman, whose record in this field is unsurpassed. Barry has a team of over 90 people who provide him with the invaluable aspects of local information that gives this book such credibility, and makes it a must for every enthusiast, administrator and commentator on our great game.

Gordon Taylor,
Chief Executive, The Professional Footballers' Association.

There is no doubt in my mind that the Footballers' Factfile goes from strength to strength as the years go by. Barry Hugman and his research team are to be congratulated, yet again, on this season's publication, which I see on the desk or in the bookcase of almost everybody connected with the game today.

The Windsor Insurance Group continues its close association with professional football that was first established over 25 years ago. Together, with the Professional Footballers' Association, we manage the Players Permanent Disablement Fund, whereby every registered player in the English leagues receives an insurance benefit if his career is ended through injury or sickness. The level of benefit is continually reviewed and was increased significantly in recent times.

Our close links with the Professional Footballers' Association, and the clubs, leagues, and national associations, give us a unique position from which we can offer advice on insurance related matters to all in football. And, we are more than happy to continue to support and again lend our name as sponsors to this excellent publication.

Jonathan Ticehurst,
Managing Director of the Sports Division, Windsor Insurance Brokers Limited.

Editorial Introduction

Following on from last year's edition, the *Factfile* portrays the statistical career record of every FA Carling Premiership and Nationwide League player who made an appearance in 1999-2000, whether it be in league football, the Football League Cup (Worthington Cup), FA Cup (Sponsored by AXA), Charity Shield, European Cup, UEFA Cup, Auto Windscreens Shield, or in the Play Offs. Not included are Inter-Toto Cup, other than West Ham's final home and away legs against Metz, or Welsh Cup matches. It goes beyond mere statistics, however, with a write up on all of the 2,300 plus players involved, and also records faithfully last season's playing records separately by club.

The work falls into three sections, all inter-relating. Firstly, the main core, PFA Footballers' Factfile: A-Z (pages 9 to 356); secondly, Where Did They Go? (pages 357 to 360); lists all players shown in the previous edition of the *Factfile* who either moved on or did not play in 1999-2000; and thirdly, FA Carling Premiership and Nationwide League Clubs: Summary of Appearances and Goals for 1999-2000 (pages 361 to 383). Below is an explanation on how to follow the *PFA Footballers' Factfile*.

As the title suggests, all players are listed in alphabetical order and are shown by Surnames first, followed by full Christian names, with the one the player is commonly known by shown in **bold.** Any abbreviation or pseudonym is bracketed.

Birthplace/date: You will note that several players who would be predominately classified as British, were born in places like Germany and India, for example. My book, *Premier and Football League Players' Records*, which covers every man who has played league football since the war, has, in the past, used the family domicile as a more realistic "birthplace". But, for our purposes here, I have reverted to that which has been officially recorded.

Height and Weight: Listed in feet and inches, and stones and pounds, respectively. It must be remembered that a player's weight can frequently change and, on that basis, the recorded data should be used as a guide only, especially as they would have been weighed several times during the season.

Club Honours: Those shown, cover careers from the Conference and FA Trophy upwards. For abbreviations, read:- European Honours: EC (European Cup), ESC (European Super Cup), ECWC (European Cup Winners' Cup). English Honours: FAC (FA Cup), FLC (Football League Cup), CS (Charity Shield), FMC (Full Members Cup, which takes in the Simod and Zenith Data sponsorships), AMC (Associated Members Cup - Freight Rover, Sherpa Van, Leyland DAF, Autoglass and Auto Windscreens), AIC (Anglo-Italian Cup), GMVC (GM Vauxhall Conference), FAT (FA Trophy), FAYC (FA Youth Cup). Scottish Honours: SPD (Scottish Premier Division), S Div 1/2 (Scottish Leagues), SC (Scottish Cup), SLC (Scottish League Cup). Welsh Honours: WC (Welsh Cup). Please note that medals awarded to P/FL, FLC, and AMC winners relate to players who have appeared in 25%, or over, of matches, while FAC, EC, and ECWC winners medals are for all-named finalists, including unused subs. For our purposes, however, Charity Shield winners' medals refer to men who either played or came on as a sub. Honours applicable to players coming in from abroad are not shown, but the position will be reviewed in future editions.

International Honours: For abbreviations, read:- E (England), NI (Northern Ireland), S (Scotland), W (Wales) and Ei (Republic of Ireland). Under 21 through to full internationals give total appearances (inclusive of subs), while schoolboy (U16s and U18s) and youth representatives are just listed. The cut-off date used for appearances was up to and including 9 June, except for the countries competing in Euro 2000, which finished on 2 July.

Player Descriptions: Gives position and playing strengths and, in keeping the work topical, a few words on how their season went in 1999-2000. This takes into account, in a positive fashion, key performances, along with value to the team, injuries, honours, and other points of interest, etc. To allow for play off and international input to be included, and the publication date to be maintained, the cut-off date used was 12 July. Transfers, however, are shown as stop press if they took place after 20 May, the cut-off date used by the Football and Premier Leagues to produce the close season retained and free transfer lists. The decision was taken on the grounds that the May/June Registration and Transfer booklets would not be available until after going to press.

Career Records: Full appearances, plus substitutes and goals, are given for all Carling Premiership and Nationwide League games and, if a player who is in the book has played in any of the senior Scottish Leagues, his appearances with the club in question will also be recorded at the point of signing. Other information given, includes the origination of players (clubs in the non-leagues, junior football, or from abroad), registered signing dates (if a player signs permanently following a loan spell, for our purposes, we have shown the initial date as being the point of temporary transfer. Also, loan transfers are only recorded if an appearance is made), transfer fees (these are the figures that have been reported in newspapers and magazines and should only be used as a guide to a player's valuation), and a breakdown of matches by P/FL (Premiership and Football League), PL (Premier League), FL (Football League), FLC (Football League Cup), FAC (FA Cup), and Others. Other matches will take in the Play Offs, Anglo-Italian Cup, Auto Windscreens Shield, Charity Shield, and any major European competition. All of these matches are lumped together for reasons of saving space. Scottish appearances for players on loan to P/FL clubs in 1999-2000 are shown at the point of transfer and do not include games following their return to Scotland. That also applies to players transferred from England to Scotland.

Career statistics are depicted as
Appearances + Substitutes/Goals

Whether you wish to analyse someone for your fantasy football team selection or would like to know more about a little-known player appearing in the lower reaches of the game, the *PFA Footballers' Factfile* should provide you with the answer.

Barry J. Hugman, Editor, PFA Footballers' Factfile

PFA Footballers' Factfile : A-Z

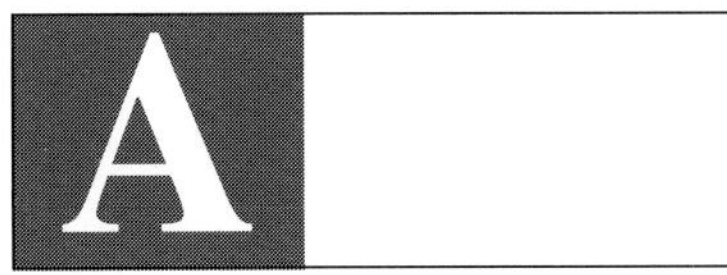

ABBEY Benjamin (Ben) Charles
Born: London, 13 May 1978
Height: 5'7" Weight: 11.0
Ben joined Oxford last October from Dr Martens side Crawley Town for a £35,000 fee. He was that league's top scorer in 1998-99 with 35 goals but didn't have much opportunity to break into the Oxford side last season. Very quick, he is on the small side for a striker but gets into some good positions, which saw him score his only Oxford goal in the FA Cup success over Morecambe. Much watched by a number of clubs prior to his move, Ben has yet to start a game for United, making 12 substitute appearances.
Oxford U (£30,000 from Crawley T on 29/9/1999) FL 0+10 FAC 0+1/1 Others 0+1

ABBEY George Peterson
Born: Port Harcourt, Nigeria, 20 October 1978
Height: 5'10" Weight: 10.10
This promising right back signed for Macclesfield in August 1999 from Nigerian club FC Sharks after earning a contract with some impressive performances in pre-season friendlies. He has a distinctly individual style of play and had to try to mould his skills into the team pattern. He displayed his potential with a "Man of the Match" award on his full debut against Swansea. Appearances became restricted due to competition for places in the defence, but he still performed enthusiastically when called upon.
Macclesfield T (Signed from Sharks FC, Port Harcourt, Nigeria on 20/8/1999) FL 12+6 FLC 1 FAC 0+2

ABBEY Nathanael (Nathan)
Born: Islington, 11 July 1978
Height: 6'1" Weight: 12.0
Nathan agreed a new contract with Luton in the 1999 close season, after the departure of Kelvin Davis to Wimbledon, and started the new season as the club's first-choice goalkeeper. He retained his place in the starting line-up until February but after a dip in form, certainly not helped by barracking from a section of Luton fans, he was finally rested by his manager. A very good shot stopper, Nathan possesses proficient handling skills in the air, and he will be hoping to build on his return to league action as a second-half substitute in the final game of the season. However, he was out of contract in the summer and at the time of writing it seemed likely that this able young 'keeper would be starting the new season elsewhere.
Luton T (From trainee on 2/5/1996) FL 34+1 FLC 3 FAC 5 Others 2

ABBEY Zema
Born: Luton, 17 April 1977
Height: 6'1" Weight: 12.11
The appropriately named Mr Abbey moved to Cambridge's Abbey Stadium last February from non-league Hitchin. Best described as a striker with a physical presence, he is good in the air and holds the ball up well. With his first-team appearances limited, Zema returned to Hitchin until the end of the season. He is the brother of Luton's Nathan Abbey.
Cambridge U (Signed from Hitchin T on 11/2/2000) FL 2+6

ABIODUN Ayodeji **Opeyemi (Yemi)**
Born: Clapton, 29 December 1980
Height: 5'11" Weight: 10.9
A small and sprightly forward, Yemi made his first-team debut for Southend in the opening game of the 1999-2000 season, and proved himself to be a handful for defenders with his lightning pace. With more senior players coming into the team, and an ankle ligament injury ruling him out for a while, Yemi featured only a few more times. He will hope that the new season will see more regular outings.
Southend U (From trainee on 2/7/1999) FL 1+2 FLC 1+1

ABLETT Gary Ian
Born: Liverpool, 19 November 1965
Height: 6'1" Weight: 12.7
Club Honours: Div 1 '88, '90; CS '88, '95; FAC '89; '95
International Honours: E: B-1; U21-1
Gary was still recovering from knee trouble at the start of 1999-2000 and it was not until October that he began playing for Birmingham City's reserves. A cool left-footed central defender, he failed to break into the first team at St Andrews and in December he joined Wycombe on loan to help a defence missing three regular central defenders. His class was immediately obvious, with his composure and excellent distribution particularly impressive, and his four outings included a game at left back. Freed by City last January, he signed for Blackpool after a brief trial with Scunthorpe but, despite his experience, he was unable to prevent the Seasiders from being relegated. He was released in the 2000 close season.
Liverpool (From apprentice on 19/11/1983) FL 103+6/1 FLC 10+1 FAC 16+2 Others 9
Derby Co (Loaned on 25/1/1985) FL 3+3 Others 2
Hull C (Loaned on 10/9/1986) FL 5
Everton (£750,000 on 14/1/1992) F/PL 128/5 FLC 12 FAC 12/1 Others 4
Sheffield U (Loaned on 1/3/1996) FL 12
Birmingham C (£390,000 on 21/6/1996) FL 96+8/1 FLC 13 FAC 7/1 Others 1
Wycombe W (Loaned on 3/12/1999) FL 4
Blackpool (Free on 10/1/2000) FL 9+1/1 Others 2

ABOU Samassi
Born: Gagnoa, Ivory Coast, 4 April 1973
Height: 6'0" Weight: 11.6
International Honours: France: U21
For all his abundant talent this tall striker found himself out of the running for a first-team spot at West Ham last season, but he showed dazzling skills after joining Walsall on loan in October. His distribution was at times a delight but he had no luck at all with his finishing and his overall form seemed to decline in wet conditions. The France U21 international returned to Upton Park at the end of his loan spell having started seven games and made one substitute appearance. He was released in the summer.
West Ham U (£300,000 from Cannes, France on 3/11/1997) PL 14+8/5 FLC 2+1/1 FAC 3+3
Ipswich T (Loaned on 3/12/1998) FL 5/1
Walsall (Loaned on 1/10/1999) FL 7+1
Kilmarnock (Loaned on 18/2/2000) SL 5+5

ACHTERBERG John
Born: Utrecht, Holland, 8 July 1971
Height: 6'1" Weight: 13.8
John began the 1999-2000 campaign as first-choice 'keeper for Tranmere but as the season wore on he found himself sharing the position with rising star Joe Murphy. Even when dropped, his commitment never faltered and he persevered with his game in the Pontins League side, returning to first-team duties even better than before. John has a calm approach, excellent handling skills and good distribution. Despite the disappointment of missing out on a place in the team for the Worthington Cup final, John signed a new three-year contract for Rovers towards the end of the campaign.
Tranmere Rov (Free from PSV Eindhoven, Holland on 22/9/1998) FL 48+2 FLC 7+1 FAC 2

ADAMS Neil James
Born: Stoke, 23 November 1965
Height: 5'8" Weight: 10.12
Club Honours: Div 1 '87, Div 2 '91
International Honours: E: U21-1
Neil returned to Oldham in July 1999 but had a disappointing time at Boundary Park in 1999-2000. After an uncomfortable spell in midfield he switched to a wing-back role in October but, although he retained his place through to February, he rarely achieved the form he is capable of. His season ended early when he limped off in the home game with Bristol Rovers after aggravating an old injury and had to have an operation to remove a screw that had previously been inserted in his foot.
Stoke C (Signed on 1/7/1985) FL 31+1/4 FLC 3 FAC 1 Others 3
Everton (£150,000 on 7/7/1986) FL 17+3 FLC 4+1/1 Others 5+1
Oldham Ath (Loaned on 11/1/1989) FL 9
Oldham Ath (£100,000 on 21/6/1989) F/PL 93+36/23 FLC 13+2/1 FAC 10+2/2 Others 1+1
Norwich C (£250,000 on 17/2/1994) P/FL 164+18/25 FLC 16+1/4 FAC 7/1
Oldham Ath (Free on 6/7/1999) FL 29/2 FLC 2 FAC 2/1 Others 1

ADAMS Stephen (Steve) Marc
Born: Plymouth, 25 September 1980
Height: 6'0" Weight: 11.10
Having played in the FA Cup and Auto Windscreens Shield during the previous

campaign, this highly rated young defender made his league debut for Plymouth at Mansfield on the final day of the 1999-2000 season, his first as a professional. He produced a comfortable and authoritative display in defence and, if he continues with the form he showed, he should be one to watch in the new season. Steve was offered a new contract in May.

Plymouth Arg (From trainee on 6/7/1999) FL 1 Others 0+1

ADAMS Tony Alexander
Born: Romford, 10 October 1966
Height: 6'3" Weight: 13.11
Club Honours: Div 1 '89, '91; PL '98; FLC '87, '93; FAC '93, '98; ECWC '94; CS '98
International Honours: E: 64; B-4; U21-5; Yth

For the second successive season the long-serving Arsenal captain was plagued by injuries in 1999-2000. A double hernia operation followed by foot, back and groin injuries caused Tony to miss many games at both club and international levels. He is a dominant centre back, totally committed yet composed when in possession, and when he was fit his outstanding leadership qualities, both on the field and in the dressing room, were vital to the Gunners' success. A man who will not tolerate a drop in effort or workrate, he led by example, particularly in the UEFA Cup away legs at Barcelona and Lens. Recognised throughout the game as the country's finest motivator, he is expected to succeed Alan Shearer as England captain, fitness permitting. He added seven full caps to an already impressive total but injury restricted him to a single appearance against Portugal in the Euro 2000 finals. A good all-round player, Tony gets forward whenever he can. His height and strength make it possible for him to score goals from boot and head, particularly from set pieces.

Arsenal (From apprentice on 30/1/1984) F/PL 464+4/31 FLC 58+1/5 FAC 46+1/6 Others 47/4

Tony Adams

ADAMSON Christopher (Chris)
Born: Ashington, 4 November 1978
Height: 5'1" Weight: 11.0

Third in line for the goalkeeping spot at West Bromwich, Chris joined Halifax on loan at the start of the 1999-2000 season for his second spell in the Third Division. The loan was necessary because the Shaymen had only one recognised 'keeper in the form of Tony Parks. He impressed during his stay at the Shay, the highlight being an outstanding display in the 1-0 victory at Rochdale, and played against Albion in the Worthington Cup. Following an injury to Alan Miller and the transfer of Phil Whitehead (to Reading), Chris arrived back at the Hawthorns to find himself number one in a struggling West Bromwich side. It was a very demanding situation and he was eventually replaced by new signing Brian Jensen. Still young enough to prove his worth, he is a very capable 'keeper and commands his area well.

West Bromwich A (From trainee on 2/7/1997) FL 12 FAC 1
Mansfield T (Loaned on 30/4/1999) FL 2
Halifax T (Loaned on 1/7/1999) FL 7

ADEBOLA Bamberdele (Dele)
Born: Lagos, Nigeria, 23 June 1975
Height: 6'3" Weight: 12.8

Dele began 1999-2000 alternating between the starting line-up and the substitutes' bench for Birmingham City and then suffered a hairline fracture of the leg that kept him out for several weeks. He formed an excellent partnership with Isiah Rankin when the latter arrived on loan from Bradford last January, and scored five times in a run of six games to propel the Blues into contention for a play-off spot. He is a strong, pacy striker with a powerful shot and good aerial ability.

Crewe Alex (From trainee on 21/6/1993) FL 98+26/39 FLC 4+3/2 FAC 8+2/3 Others 10+1/2
Birmingham C (£1,000,000 on 6/2/1998) FL 70+28/25 FLC 7+2/3 FAC 1+1/1 Others 1+2/1

AGGREY James (Jimmy) Emmanuel
Born: Hammersmith, 26 October 1978
Height: 6'3" Weight: 13.6

The lanky defender's chances were restricted at Torquay last season owing to the good form at the back of Alex Watson, Wayne Thomas and Lee Russell. Jimmy proved to be a valuable member of the Gulls' squad, though, as he was involved in more than half of their 1999-2000 fixtures. He never let the side down when called upon to play, and is very much one for the future.

Fulham (Free from Chelsea juniors on 2/7/1997)
Airdrieonians (Free on 30/6/1998)
Torquay U (Free on 22/10/1998) FL 44+8 FLC 2 FAC 4+1 Others 4

AGNEW Stephen (Steve) Mark
Born: Shipley, 9 November 1965
Height: 5'10" Weight: 11.9
Club Honours: Div 1 '96

With two years of his three-year contract with York to run, Steve turned down a move to Carlisle after being allowed to play for the Cumbrians in two 1999 pre-season friendlies. He was eventually recalled to first-team duty by York in October, but the classy midfielder then suffered a series of injury set-backs. He returned for the last couple of months of the season and played an important part in the club's revival that saw them move clear of trouble near the bottom of the Third Division.

Barnsley (From apprentice on 10/11/1983) FL 186+8/29 FLC 13/3 FAC 20/4 Others 6+1
Blackburn Rov (£700,000 on 25/6/1991) FL 2 FLC 2
Portsmouth (Loaned on 21/11/1992) FL 3+2 Others 2
Leicester C (£250,000 on 9/2/1993) F/PL 52+4/4 FLC 4+1 FAC 2 Others 2
Sunderland (£250,000 on 11/1/1995) P/FL 56+7/9 FLC 4 FAC 2+1/1
York C (Free on 10/7/1998) FL 39+3/2 FLC 1 FAC 3

AGOGO Manuel (Junior)
Born: Accra, Ghana, 1 August 1979
Height: 5'10" Weight: 11.7

This speedy Sheffield Wednesday striker had loan spells with four different clubs during the first half of the 1999-2000 season. He began the campaign with Oldham but started only two games for the Latics and struggled to make much impact. He joined Chester in September and was arguably the best player to appear for the club during the campaign. He scored six goals in ten appearances during his three-month stay at the Deva, a highly creditable achievement in difficult circumstances, and all of them were special. Chester were not in a position to make the transfer permanent and in November Junior moved on to Second Division Chesterfield. He again demonstrated his lightning pace and eye for goal but, despite hitting the post in the last few minutes of his final appearance, against Brentford, he was unable to lift the gloom at Saltergate by finding the net. December saw a return to the Third Division with Lincoln. He scored on his debut against Shrewsbury and looked sharp but in subsequent matches he found it difficult to get into the game. Following his return to Hillsborough Junior decided to turn his back on English football and pursue a modelling career in America through his mother's agency. He starred for MLS club Chicago Fire in their pre-season fixtures, only to be transferred to Colorado Rapids in April.

Sheffield Wed (Signed from Willesden Constontaine on 8/10/1996) PL 0+2 FAC 0+1
Oldham Ath (Loaned on 18/7/1999) FL 2
Chester C (Loaned on 3/9/1999) FL 10/6
Chesterfield (Loaned on 11/11/1999) FL 3+1
Lincoln C (Loaned on 17/12/1999) FL 3/1

AGYEMANG Patrick
Born: Walthamstow, 29 September 1980
Height: 6'1" Weight: 12.0

Patrick spent three months on loan at Brentford to further his development at the start of 1999-2000, his first season as a professional with Wimbledon. A striker whose awkward style makes it difficult for the opposition, he was mostly used by the Bees as a substitute, coming on to run at and unsettle defences. Brentford were keen to extend the loan until the end of the season but no deal could be agreed.

Wimbledon (From trainee on 11/5/1999)
Brentford (Loaned on 18/10/1999) FL 3+9 FAC 1

AINSWORTH Gareth
Born: Blackburn, 10 May 1973
Height: 5'9" Weight: 12.5

A player with a wealth of experience in the lower divisions, Gareth made only two appearances for Wimbledon during the 1999-2000 campaign owing to a groin injury. Although both were from the subs' bench, he did score two goals against Newcastle, securing a point with an injury-time equaliser. Gareth is an exciting winger who has pace and an eye for goal. He will certainly be a major asset for Wimbledon during the coming season if he can stay fit and should be a first choice in Terry Burton's line-up.

Preston NE (Signed from Northwich Vic, via Blackburn Rov YTS, on 21/1/1992) FL 2+3 Others 1/1
Cambridge U (Free on 17/8/1992) FL 1+3/1 FLC 0+1
Preston NE (Free on 23/12/1992) FL 76+6/12 FLC 3+2 FAC 3+1 Others 8+1/1
Lincoln C (£25,000 on 31/10/1995) FL 83/37 FLC 8/3 FAC 2 Others 4/1
Port Vale (£500,000 on 12/9/1997) FL 53+2/10 FLC 2/1 FAC 2
Wimbledon (£2,000,000 on 3/11/1998) PL 5+5/2

AISTON Samuel (Sam) James
Born: Newcastle, 21 November 1976
Height: 6'1" Weight: 12.10
Club Honours: Div 1 '96
International Honours: E: Sch

This tall, skilful left winger did not make a senior appearance for Sunderland in 1999-2000. He started the season on loan at Stoke, but never really had a run in the first team and returned to the North-east after a two-month stay at the Britannia Stadium. Sam joined Shrewsbury on loan in December and played in ten league games. He is a favourite of Town manager Kevin Ratcliffe, who had twice signed him on loan while at Chester. He soon became very popular at Gay Meadow thanks to his direct style on the left, especially when he gained greater match fitness. Any possibility of a permanent move was ended, however, when he returned to Sunderland after sustaining an injury at Carlisle.

Sunderland (Free from Newcastle U juniors on 14/7/1995) P/FL 5+15 FLC 0+2 FAC 0+2
Chester C (Loaned on 21/2/1997) FL 14 FLC 1 Others 2
Chester C (Loaned on 27/11/1998) FL 11 Others 1
Stoke C (Loaned on 6/8/1999) FL 2+4 FLC 1
Shrewsbury T (Loaned on 24/12/1999) FL 10

AKINBIYI Adeola (Ade) Peter
Born: Hackney, 10 October 1974
Height: 6'1" Weight: 12.9
International Honours: Nigeria: 1

In a season containing many disappointments for Bristol City fans, none was more keenly felt than the club's decision to sell Ade to Wolves last September for a £3.2 million fee, a record for a deal between Football League clubs, with another £250,000 payable if Wolves were promoted. He arrived at Molineux shortly after the £6 million sale of Robbie Keane. Failure to adequately replace their ace goalscorer cost City dear, as without his electric pace and strength on the ball goals became scarce and all chance of a promotion push was virtually gone by the time of manager Tony Pulis's mid-season departure for more ambitious Portsmouth. A powerful striker, though not always effective in the air, Ade is fast and aggressive, and has an instinct for getting into scoring positions. There were signs by the end of the season that his link-up play was improving, too. Ade started slowly at Wolves and was guilty of an awful miss at Sheffield United before getting off the mark in his fourth game at Crystal Palace. This was the first of four consecutive matches in which he scored, and a hat-trick against Grimsby in November made it a run of eight goals in nine. He made his debut for Nigeria against Greece the same month but failed to win a place in the squad for the African Nations' Cup finals after a confusing saga that unsettled him a little. Ade scored a cracker versus Queens Park Rangers in January, but was sent off at home to Forest a month later and following that the goals dried up for him. It was a relief for all concerned when he took his Wolves total to 16 with a brace against Barnsley in April, his first goals for over two months.

Norwich C (From trainee on 5/2/1993) P/FL 22+27/3 FLC 2+4/2 FAC 1+2 Others 0+1
Hereford U (Loaned on 21/1/1994) FL 3+1/2
Brighton & Hove A (Loaned on 24/11/1994) FL 7/4
Gillingham (£250,000 on 13/1/1997) FL 63/28 FLC 2 FAC 2/1 Others 0+1
Bristol C (£1,200,000 on 28/5/1998) FL 47/21 FLC 5/4 FAC 1
Wolverhampton W (£3,500,000 on 7/9/1999) FL 36+1/16

Ade Akinbiyi

ALCIDE Colin James
Born: Huddersfield, 14 April 1972
Height: 6'2" Weight: 13.10

After he had missed the start of Hull's 1999-2000 campaign with a groin injury and a hamstring strain, the big striker's season took off with a memorable equaliser against Liverpool in the Worthington Cup at Anfield after City had been two down. Following earlier links to Carlisle and Halifax, the Tigers accepted York's £80,000 bid in November but Colin's physical strength was sorely missed. An effective target man, he holds the ball up well and has good touch for a player of his size. He scored on his Minstermen debut to seal a win over Shrewsbury, but he was then troubled by injuries before returning to the squad in the closing weeks of the campaign.

Lincoln C (£15,000 from Emley on 5/12/1995) FL 105+16/27 FLC 7+2/2 FAC 3+3/2 Others 3+1
Hull C (Loaned on 4/2/1999) FL 5/1
Hull C (£50,000 on 10/3/1999) FL 22+2/3 FLC 3+1/2 FAC 0+2
York C (£80,000 on 23/11/1999) FL 9+6/2 Others 1

ALDRIDGE Martin James
Born: Northampton, 6 December 1974
Height: 5'11" Weight: 12.1

This experienced striker made a handful of appearances for Blackpool as a substitute in the early part of the 1999-2000 campaign and then spent last October on loan with Port Vale. He made his debut for the Vale in front of over 31,000 fans at Manchester City, coming on as a substitute at half time, and made two further appearances from the bench before returning to Bloomfield Road. He was loaned out again in January, this time to Conference high-fliers Rushden & Diamonds. Tragically, Martin was involved in a car accident near Wellingborough while returning from the Diamonds' home fixture with Northwich Victoria and he died on Sunday, 30 January at the Radcliffe Infirmary in Oxford. All the players, staff and supporters at Bloomfield Road sadly miss him.

Northampton T (From trainee on 27/8/1993) FL 50+20/17 FLC 1+2 FAC 1+1/1 Others 5+2/4
Oxford C (Free on 22/12/1995) FL 46+26/19 FLC 8+4/3 FAC 2+2
Southend U (Loaned on 23/2/1998) FL 7+4/1
Blackpool (Free on 3/8/1998) FL 19+8/7 FLC 2+1/2 FAC 1/1
Port Vale (Loaned on 28/9/1999) FL 0+3

ALDRIDGE Paul John
Born: Liverpool, 2 December 1981
Height: 5'11" Weight: 11.7

This uncompromising young midfield player came up through the ranks at Tranmere and made his bow in senior football when he came on as a substitute at Swindon last April. He went on to make three further appearances from the subs' bench to gain a taste of first-team football after signing full professional terms for the Prenton Park club towards the end of the 1999-2000 season. A former pupil of Liverpool's Blue Coat School, Paul learnt his trade in the Pontins League. He is the son of Rovers' manager John Aldridge.

Tranmere Rov (From trainee on 24/3/2000) FL 0+4

ALEXANDER Gary George
Born: Lambeth, 15 August 1979
Height: 5'11" Weight: 13.0

A first-choice striker at Exeter in 1999-2000, Gary joined the Devon club on loan from West Ham for the full season. He

developed an instant rapport with the fans, as his 19 goals made him the club's leading scorer. His vision and awareness were there for all to see. Gary became the first loanee to be voted City's "Player of the Year" since George Foster in 1982. He was the subject of a £200,000 bid from Rushden & Diamonds in March.
West Ham U (From trainee on 6/7/1998)
Exeter C (Loaned on 19/8/1999) FL 37+16 FLC 1 FAC 3/1 Others 4/2

Gary Alexander

ALEXANDER Graham
Born: Coventry, 10 October 1971
Height: 5'10" Weight: 12.7
Club Honours: Div 2 '00

Preston's experienced right back finished the 1999-2000 season with a career total of over 450 games to his credit, having been ever-present in the league as North End captured the Second Division championship and missed only the Auto Windscreens Shield game against Hartlepool. Despite a rough patch in March, Graham was well worth his place in the PFA award-winning Second Division team for his sterling work both in defence and in attack, where he poses a real danger with thunderbolt free kicks and shots on the run. His abilities in this area allowed him to finish as the club's second-top scorer for the season, helped by eight penalties, all of them in a spell of 18 games.
Scunthorpe U (From trainee on 20/3/1990) FL 149+10/18 FLC 11+1/2 FAC 12/1 Others 13+3/3
Luton T (£100,000 on 8/7/1995) FL 146+4/15 FLC 17/2 FAC 6+1 Others 6+2
Preston NE (£50,000 on 25/3/1999) FL 56/6 FLC 5/1 FAC 6/3 Others 3

ALEXANDERSSON Niclas
Born: Halmstad, Sweden, 29 December 1971
Height: 6'2" Weight: 11.8
International Honours: Sweden: 44

This hard-working right-sided midfield player was one of the few successes in a very disappointing 1999-2000 season for Sheffield Wednesday. Despite the club's relegation worries he performed consistently well in the centre of the park, where his skilful play and unselfishness were well to the fore. Niclas was again a regular for Sweden during the season, scoring goals against Bulgaria and Luxembourg last September and appearing in all three games in the Euro 2000 finals.
Sheffield Wed (£750,000 from Gothenburg, Sweden, via Halmstad, on 9/12/1997) PL 73+2/8 FLC 4+1/2 FAC 8/2

ALJOFREE Hasney
Born: Manchester, 11 July 1978
Height: 6'0" Weight: 12.1
International Honours: E: Yth

Last season was something of a stop-start one for Hasney. Having begun the campaign as a regular on the substitutes' bench, he made a few starts for Bolton, but his chances were limited due to the excellent form of Robbie Elliott and Mike Whitlow. When he did figure during the season, he was sometimes switched away from his more accustomed left-back role to play in the midfield area, where he acquitted himself very well. Composed and comfortable on the ball, this promising young player has proven himself to be a very bright prospect, although his chances at the Reebok have been limited due to the overall quality of the Wanderers squad. He was released during the summer. Stop Press: Hasney was reported to have signed for Dundee United at the beginning of July.
Bolton W (From trainee on 2/7/1996) P/FL 6+8 FLC 4+2 FAC 0+2

ALLARDYCE Craig Samuel
Born: Bolton, 9 June 1975
Height: 6'3" Weight: 13.7

Craig forced his way into the Mansfield side at the tail end of 1998-99, but was never a first-team regular last season, featuring in only a handful of matches. A tall, sturdy central defender in the same mould as his father, Sam of Bolton Wanderers fame, he was overlooked for much of the time in favour of loan signings Leigh Bromby and Jonathan Fortune. The writing was on the wall and at the beginning of April he was allowed to move to Boston United on a free transfer.
Preston NE (From trainee on 16/7/1993) FL 0+1 (Free to Macclesfield T on 16/4/1994)
Blackpool (Free from Northwich Vic on 20/9/1994) FL 0+1 (Freed on 23/11/1996)
Chesterfield (Free from Chorley on 26/3/1998) FL 0+1
Peterborough U (Free on 6/8/1998) FL 4 (Free to Welling U on 5/11/1998)
Mansfield T (Free on 22/12/1998) FL 7+3 FLC 0+2

ALLEN Bradley James
Born: Romford, 13 September 1971
Height: 5'8" Weight: 11.0
International Honours: E: U21-8; Yth

Released by Charlton at the close of the 1998-99 campaign, Bradley joined Grimsby Town as a replacement for the departed Lee Nogan. Starting last season as a first-choice striker alongside Lee Ashcroft, Bradley soon found himself relegated to the subs' bench as manager Alan Buckley favoured the partnership of Ashcroft and Jack Lester. Called into action on a regular basis, however, he always added a new dimension to the Grimsby attack, with a natural instinct for goal that in terms of goals per minute on the pitch made him the most prolific scorer in the squad, often of vital late match-saving goals. His efforts to reclaim his regular first-team spot following Lester's departure were somewhat frustrated by a broken toe

Niclas Alexandersson

sustained in the 0-3 defeat at Carrow Road, and the return of Daryl Clare from loan and Ashcroft's recovery from injury meant that, when fit again, Bradley had to be satisfied with a place on the bench once more. A firm favourite with the Grimsby Town faithful, he could well take over the mantle of Lester as the King of Blundell Park in the future.

Queens Park R (From juniors on 30/9/1988) F/PL 56+25/27 FLC 5+2/5 FAC 3+2 Others 1
Charlton Ath (£400,000 on 28/3/1996) FL 30+10/9 FLC 3+1/2 FAC 0+2 Others 1+1
Colchester U (Loaned on 24/2/1999) FL 4/1
Grimsby T (Free on 12/7/1999) FL 12+19/8 FLC 0+4 FAC 0+2/1

ALLEN Christopher (Chris) Anthony
Born: Oxford, 18 November 1972
Height: 5'11" Weight: 12.2
International Honours: E: U21-2

This wide midfield player began the 1999-2000 season back at Oxford but failed to make the first team and moved to Stockport on a monthly contract in October on the recommendation of assistant manager Dave Moss, who had previously worked with him at the Manor Ground. Chris produced some promising displays in his early games at Edgeley Park but was unable to maintain this form and dropped out of the side in February. A quick and lively left winger, he was released by the club in the summer.

Oxford U (From trainee on 14/5/1991) FL 110+40/12 FLC 11+2/4 FAC 5+5/1 Others 5+3
Nottingham F (Loaned on 24/2/1996) PL 1+2/1
Nottingham F (£300,000 on 3/7/1996) F/PL 17+8 FLC 2/1 FAC 1/1
Luton T (Loaned on 28/11/1997) FL 14/1
Cardiff C (Loaned on 22/10/1998) FL 3+1 Others 1
Port Vale (Free on 8/3/1999) FL 2+3/1
Oxford U (Free on 18/8/1999)
Stockport Co (Free on 29/10/1999) FL 10+6 FAC 0+1

ALLEN Graham
Born: Bolton, 8 April 1977
Height: 6'1" Weight: 12.8
International Honours: E: Yth

Graham featured regularly for Tranmere Rovers in the opening two months of the 1999-2000 campaign but he was then absent through injury for lengthy spells that caused him to miss the squad for the Worthington Cup final with Leicester. His preferred position is at right back, where he is a sound and uncompromising defender who is eager to join in with attacking moves. He is one of the more underrated members of John Aldridge's team, and showed his value to the side when performing competently as a striker when called upon in an emergency.

Everton (From trainee on 10/12/1994) PL 2+4
Tranmere Rov (Free on 28/8/1998) FL 62+3/5 FLC 6+2 FAC 1

ALLEN Rory William
Born: Beckenham, 17 October 1977
Height: 5'11" Weight: 11.2
Club Honours: FLC '99
International Honours: E: U21-3

Rory became the most expensive player in Portsmouth's history when he signed from Tottenham for a £1 million fee in the summer of 1999. He got off to a good start at Fratton Park, scoring at Wolves in the second game of the 1999-2000 season, but then injured his right ankle in mid-September. Returning to fitness in early December, he then fractured the other ankle in his comeback match against Sheffield United and this kept him out of action until the last few weeks of the season, when he made a handful of appearances from the subs' bench. Rory showed considerable ability as an out-and-out striker after arriving at Pompey with a reputation as a hard worker who was accurate in front of goal.

Tottenham H (From trainee on 28/3/1996) PL 10+11/2 FLC 3+3/2 FAC 1
Luton T (Loaned on 26/3/1998) FL 8/6
Portsmouth (£1,000,000 on 16/7/1999) FL 10+5/3 FLC 0+1

ALLISON Wayne Anthony
Born: Huddersfield, 16 October 1968
Height: 6'1" Weight: 12.6
Club Honours: Div 2 '96

The big striker found himself starting down the pecking order at Huddersfield at the start of last season under new manager Steve Bruce, and was regularly on the substitutes' bench. Wayne was often brought on to cause mayhem in opposing defences with his aerial prowess and unselfish play, but in September he was transferred to Tranmere for a £300,000 fee. He was an immediate success at Prenton Park and finished the season as leading scorer with 19 league and cup goals, his one disappointment being that a brief appearance for Huddersfield in an early-season Worthington Cup tie caused him to miss Rovers' amazing run in the competition and a Wembley appearance. A powerful, competitive player, Wayne is good in the air, excellent at holding the ball up and leads the line well. He quickly became a favourite of the Tranmere crowd and his all-action style was an inspiration to his colleagues. He finished the campaign as Rovers' club captain.

Halifax T (From trainee on 6/7/1987) FL 74+10/23 FLC 3/2 FAC 4+1/2 Others 8+1/3
Watford (£250,000 on 26/7/1989) FL 6+1
Bristol C (£300,000 on 9/8/1990) FL 149+46/48 FLC 4+5/2 FAC 12+1/5 Others 6+2/2
Swindon T (£475,000 on 22/7/1995) FL 98+3/31 FLC 9/3 FAC 7/2 Others 3
Huddersfield T (£800,000 on 11/11/1997) FL 71+3/15 FLC 3+1/2 FAC 6/2
Tranmere Rov (£300,000 on 3/9/1999) FL 40/16 FAC 4/3

ALLOTT Mark Stephen
Born: Manchester, 3 October 1977
Height: 5'11" Weight: 12.6

This young Oldham striker featured regularly in the first half of 1999-2000 but finished the season on the transfer list after failing to reach agreement on a new contract. Excellent at holding the ball up, Mark performed will in a linking role between midfield and attack and netted ten goals during the campaign.

Oldham Ath (From trainee on 14/10/1995) FL 70+30/20 FLC 3+2/2 FAC 6+4 Others 1+1

ALLOU Anoh **Bernard**
Born: Ivory Coast, 19 June 1975
Height: 5'8" Weight: 10.4
International Honours: France: U21-24

Bernard had a disappointing 1999-2000 season with Nottingham Forest, appearing in the starting line-up on just three occasions. A wide midfield player who arrived at the City Ground with a string of French U21 caps, he will be looking to revive his career in 2000-01.

Nottingham F (Free from Grampus 8, Japan on 22/3/1999) P/FL 1+5/1 FLC 2+2/1

ALLSOP Daniel (Danny)
Born: Australia, 10 August 1978
Height: 6'1" Weight: 12.0
International Honours: Australia: U23-7; Yth

Danny was once again on the fringes of the Manchester City first team last season, as he had been in 1998-99, before dropping out of contention. He was named as a substitute for the first 15 matches but was used only in the four Worthington Cup games against Burnley and Southampton and then in three league games, usually late on. The Australian striker has a powerful physique, which serves him well when chasing through-balls or battling for possession, but a place in the starting line-up at City remained tantalisingly out of reach. He moved to Notts County on loan last November to cover for injuries to the Magpies' regular strike force. Danny scored within two minutes of his debut for Notts against Gillingham but appeared only twice more before returning to Maine Road. He was again loaned out in February, this time to Wrexham as manager Brian Flynn sought to add punch to his attack. At the time the Robins appeared to be in free fall towards the relegation zone but Danny helped produce a remarkable transformation in the club's fortunes and led them towards safety. He scored twice on his debut at Oxford and then netted decisive strikes against Luton and Brentford, but he unfortunately suffered damage to his medial ligaments at Griffin Park and failed to recover before the end of the season. Danny was a regular member of the Australia U23 squad before his injury and will be hoping to recover in time for the Olympic Games tournament in the autumn.

Manchester C (£10,000 from Port Melbourne, Australia on 7/8/1998) FL 3+25/4 FLC 0+7/1 Others 1+1/1
Notts Co (Loaned on 5/11/1999) FL 3/1
Wrexham (Loaned on 25/2/2000) FL 3/4

ALMEIDA Marco Antonio
Born: Lisbon, Portugal, 2 February 1979
Height: 6'1" Weight: 12.2
International Honours: Portugal: U21

A Portuguese U21 international centre back, Marco joined Southampton in the summer of 1999 on a year-long loan from Sporting Lisbon with a view to a permanent move later. However, after initial success as a substitute in pre-season matches, he was left in the reserves, occasionally occupying a place on the bench for first-team games. After he had made just one substitute appearance, against Arsenal in September, his chances became increasingly limited as manager Dave Jones opted for more experienced defenders. Marco, hungry for first-team football, returned to Portugal in December 1999.

Southampton (Loaned from Sporting Lisbon, Portugal on 27/7/1999) PL 0+1

ALOISI John
Born: Adelaide, Australia, 5 February 1976
Height: 6'0" Weight: 12.13
International Honours: Australia: 12; Yth

Coventry's Australian striker had a miserable season in 1999-2000. With Darren Huckerby's departure in August, he looked set for a first-team place, only for Robbie Keane to arrive a week later. Then, when Keane's first-choice partner, Noel Whelan, was injured the following week, John scored as a substitute against Manchester United – only to be injured himself two games later against Leeds after finding the net again. The injury to his hamstring seemed innocuous for some weeks, but he ended up missing the rest of the season. It was a desperate shame for John, who had shown his predatory instinct for goal in 1998-99, netting 22 times for Portsmouth and the Sky Blues. A player with an astute football brain, he will be looking to make a similar impact in 2000-01.

Portsmouth (£300,000 from Cremonese, Italy on 8/8/1997) FL 55+5/25 FLC 6/3 FAC 1
Coventry C (£650,000 on 18/12/1998) PL 10+13/7 FAC 0+2

ALSOP Julian Mark
Born: Nuneaton, 28 May 1973
Height: 6'4" Weight: 14.0
Club Honours: Div 3 '00

Despite finding the net in the league on only three occasions during the 1999-2000 season, Julian did record the fastest-ever hat-trick by a Swans player when he scored three goals in just four minutes at the Vetch Field against Cwmbran Town in October in a Welsh Premier Cup tie. He is a difficult striker to handle in the penalty area, and his effectiveness was highlighted when non-league Rushden & Diamonds reportedly offered £100,000 for his services prior to transfer deadline day. The former demolition worker missed the last three league matches and the promotion run-in after damaging knee ligaments against Torquay. Although he won a Third Division championship winners' medal, Julian turned down a new contract in May, amid interest from ten clubs. Stop Press: He was reported to have signed for Cheltenham at the beginning of July.

Bristol Rov (£15,000 from Halesowen on 14/2/1997) FL 20+13/4 FLC 2/1 FAC 1/1 Others 2
Swansea C (Loaned on 20/1/1998) FL 5/2
Swansea C (£30,000 on 12/3/1998) FL 73+12/14 FLC 4+2 FAC 6+1/1 Others 5

AMANKWAAH Kevin
Born: Harrow, 19 May 1982
Height: 6'1" Weight: 12.0
International Honours: E: Yth

This young wing back was one of the many starlets who broke through from Bristol City's much-acclaimed academy last season. After coming on as a substitute in the 1-1 home draw at Oldham in March, he made his full debut the following week in a 1-0 home win over Brentford. He immediately impressed with his dribbling skills when going forward and with his ability to cross the ball. While his tackling was assured, defensively he took some time to settle, but the more he played the better his positional sense became. At Wembley in the Auto Windscreens Shield final he produced one of the highlights of City's season with a tremendous tackle in the dying minutes to prevent a certain goal. Kevin was capped by England at U17 level when he came on as a substitute against Luxembourg last April.

Bristol C (Trainee) FL 4+1 Others 0+1

AMBROSETTI Gabriele
Born: Italy, 7 August 1973
Height: 5'11" Weight: 11.8

A talented left-sided midfielder, Gabriele followed a well-worn path when he joined Chelsea in the second week of the 1999-2000 season. Like Gustavo Poyet and Bjarne Goldbaek before him, he had impressed the Blues' hierarchy when playing against Chelsea in a European Cup-Winners' Cup tie – so much so that the London club made determined efforts to secure his signature, fending off Serie A giants Perugia and Lazio in the process. Gabriele opened his Chelsea goalscoring account with a delightful left-footed angled drive which completed the Blues' nap hand against Galatasaray in the Champions' League in Istanbul. He is exceptionally fast (his nickname at Vicenza was "Spidi Gabriele") and, having clinched his signing, Chelsea boss Gianluca Vialli described him as "the Italian Ryan Giggs", a tag he has successfully overcome as he has established a firm reputation of his own. Like Roberto Di Matteo, Gabriele is an Italian who has scored the winning goal in a Wembley cup final; he hit the only goal of the game for Brescia against Notts County in the Anglo-Italian Cup final in 1994.

Chelsea (£3,500,000 from Vicenza, Italy on 20/8/1999) PL 9+7 FLC 1 FAC 0+1 Others 1+4/1

AMPADU Patrick **Kwame**
Born: Bradford, 20 December 1970
Height: 5'10" Weight: 11.10
Club Honours: AMC '94
International Honours: RoI: U21-4; Yth

Kwame had a much better season for Leyton Orient in 1999-2000 than he had in 1998-99, and managed to stay injury free for the majority of the campaign. He is a good passer of the ball who manages to create attacks with decisive through-balls, and can also break them up with his fierce tackling, which unfortunately earned him some harsh bookings. Although only captain Dean Smith equalled the midfielder's total of appearances for the O's last season, he was one of three players released by the club at the end of the campaign. Stop Press: Kwame was reported to have signed for Exeter at the end of June.

Arsenal (From trainee on 19/11/1988) FL 0+2
Plymouth Arg (Loaned on 31/10/1990) FL 6/1 Others 1
West Bromwich A (£50,000 on 24/6/1991) FL 27+22/4 FLC 6+1 FAC 1 Others 5/1
Swansea C (£15,000 on 16/2/1994) FL 128+19/12 FLC 8+1/1 FAC 5+1/1 Others 16/1
Leyton Orient (Free on 30/7/1998) FL 69+3/1 FLC 8 FAC 4+1/1 Others 1

ANDERSEN Trond
Born: Kristiansand, Norway, 6 January 1975
Height: 6'2" Weight: 12.8
International Honours: Norway: 8; U21; Yth

Trond was signed by the then Wimbledon manager Egil Olsen from Norwegian club Molde shortly after the start of the 1999-2000 campaign and proved to be adaptable and consistent during what was a difficult season for the Dons. Although he also played in defence, he probably made more of an impact in midfield as a defensive holding player. One of Olsen's more successful signings, Trond hardly missed a match and showed good qualities throughout: he was impressive both in the air and in his tackles, ran for 90 minutes and competed for the ball with great spirit. Trond appeared regularly for Norway during the run-up to the Euro 2000 finals, but although he made the final 22 he failed to add to his total of caps during the tournament.

Wimbledon (£2,500,000 from Molde, Norway on 9/8/1999) PL 35+1 FLC 2 FAC 2

Trond Andersen

ANDERSON Iain
Born: Glasgow, 23 July 1977
Height: 5'8" Weight: 9.10
Club Honours: Div 2 '00
International Honours: S: U21-14

Signed from Toulouse last February as cover for Lee Cartwright, the ex-Dundee winger became an instant hit with the Preston fans and earned a Second Division championship medal. Able to play on either flank, but more effective on the right, the nippy ball-player could easily have scored a hat-trick at Burnley, before coming up with the winner in successive home games against Luton and Wrexham. Both Iain and the Deepdale faithful are hoping his move can be made permanent over the summer, so that his scintillating runs and powerful shooting can become a regular part of the Preston North End attack during the coming season.

Dundee (From juniors on 10/8/1994) SL 90+36/15 SLC 3+5 SC 6+3/2 Others 6+1/2 (Signed by Toulouse on 28/7/1999)
Preston NE (Loaned from Toulouse on 18/2/2000) FL 11+1/2

ANDERSON Ijah Massai
Born: Hackney, 30 December 1975
Height: 5'8" Weight: 10.6
Club Honours: Div 3 '99

Ijah is an experienced Brentford left back and the Bees' longest-serving player. He is a fine example to the club's younger professionals, being hard working and sound in the tackle and possessing good attacking skills. He made an impressive start to the 1999-2000 season but then suffered a pulled thigh muscle which it took him three months to fully recover from. The Bees' form dipped in his absence and his importance to the squad was further shown last March when the club offered, and he accepted, an extension to his contract that should keep him at Griffin Park until 2003.

Southend U (Free from Tottenham H juniors on 2/8/1994)
Brentford (Free on 31/7/1995) FL 153+4/4 FLC 15/1 FAC 4+3 Others 8+1

Darren Anderton

ANDERTON Darren Robert
Born: Southampton, 3 March 1972
Height: 6'1" Weight: 12.5
Club Honours: FLC '99
International Honours: E: 27; B-1; U21-12; Yth

Another long mid-season lay-off due to injury wrecked the versatile Tottenham midfielder's chances of re-establishing himself in the England squad in 1999-2000 and frustratingly prevented him from rediscovering his true form with any consistency. At his most influential in the role of a creative play-maker in the centre of midfield, Darren is a cultured, pacy player who always uses the ball intelligently. When he returned from injury in January, he looked sharp in the games against Leeds and Arsenal, standing out as a determined attacker going forward and with a gritty edge to his game when trying to regain possession. His tremendous right foot failed to net anywhere near Darren's average of ten goals per season, but he did manage to hit the back of the net against Southampton in March and Wimbledon in April. Again taking responsibility for penalty kicks, Darren fired home from the spot in the final game of the season at home to Sunderland, Tottenham's only penalty of the campaign. After much speculation, Spurs secured his services for another season with a one-year extension to his existing contract.

Portsmouth (From trainee on 5/2/1990) FL 53+9/7 FLC 3+2/1 FAC 7+1/5 Others 2
Tottenham H (£1,750,000 on 3/6/1992) PL 184+17/28 FLC 20/4 FAC 20+1/4

ANDREASSON Marcus
Born: Sweden, 13 July 1978
Height: 6'4" Weight: 12.2

After playing for Bristol Rovers in their second league match of the 1999-2000 season at Gillingham, this young central defender decided after 12 months in England to go home to Sweden. Marcus joined Kalmar for the remainder of the season and then remarkably moved back to Rovers on transfer deadline day, returning with a mop of curly hair which made him unrecognisable to his team-mates and Rovers' fans from his earlier spell at the club. His original squad number of 15 having been given to Vitalijs Astafjevs, Marcus was handed the number 36 shirt, thus becoming the first player to have two different squad numbers with the same team in one season. Marcus, whose height and pace are his strongest assets, made his second appearance of the season nearly eight months after the first when he stepped in for injured Steve Foster in the thrilling 3-3 home draw with Stoke City.

Bristol Rov (Free from Osters IF, Sweden on 28/7/1998) FL 10+1 FLC 2

ANDRESEN Martin
Born: Norway, 20 February 1977
Height: 5'11" Weight: 11.12
International Honours: Norway: U21; Yth

A £1.8 million signing from Norwegian club Stabaek in October 1999, Martin arrived at Wimbledon with two claims to fame: a goalscoring midfield player who has represented Norway at U21 level, he is also reputed to be Norway's sexiest man! Martin prefers to play on the right side of midfield, but the Dons' fans had only limited opportunities to see what he is capable of. He made a very impressive appearance as a substitute at home to Liverpool towards the end of the season, scoring a consolation goal in a 2-1 defeat. This gave the supporters cause for optimism, but Martin will miss the start of the Dons' 2000-01 campaign, as he has been loaned to Norwegian club Molde.

Wimbledon (£2,000,000 from Stabaek, Norway on 8/10/1999) PL 4+10/1 FLC 0+1 FAC 1

ANDREWS John Henry
Born: Cork, 27 September 1978
Height: 6'1" Weight: 12.8

Formerly with Grantham Town, John joined Mansfield, initially as a trialist, in October 1999. With several impressive reserve-team displays to his credit, he was plunged into first-team action a couple of weeks later following the 2-5 drubbing at Macclesfield and did enough during the ensuing weeks to be offered a contract. A right-sided or central defender who reads the game and tackles well, he improved as the season wore on, securing a regular place in the side.

Coventry C (From trainee on 15/5/1997. Free to Shepshed Dynamo during 1998 close season)
Mansfield T (Free from Grantham T on 21/10/1999) FL 29+1/1 Others 2

ANDREWS Keith Joseph
Born: Dublin, 13 September 1980
Height: 5'11" Weight: 11.5

A busy midfielder who joined the professional ranks at Wolves in 1997, Keith was given a squad number early in the 1999-2000 season when named among the substitutes at Queens Park Rangers. He had two brief tastes of first-team action in March, coming on as a substitute in successive games at Swindon and at home to Crewe, though his time at senior level amounts to only five minutes to date.

Wolverhampton W (From trainee on 26/9/1997) FL 0+2

ANGEL Mark
Born: Newcastle, 23 August 1975
Height: 5'10" Weight: 11.10

Basically a permanent reserve at the Hawthorns, Mark made just four first-team appearances for West Bromwich during 1999-2000 (three of them as a substitute) and when the curtain came down he found himself surplus to requirements under his third different manager at the club, Gary Megson. He has the necessary commitment and a certain amount of skill, but despite some impressive displays in the second team he was unable to mount a serious challenge to the regular members of the Baggies' midfield and will now be hoping to gain first-team football elsewhere. During the season Mark had a trial with Hartlepool United.

Sunderland (From Walker Central on 31/12/1993)
Oxford U (Free on 9/8/1995) FL 40+33/4 FLC 4+4 FAC 4+2 Others 2+1/1
West Bromwich A (Free on 2/7/1998) FL 4+21/1 FLC 0+1 FAC 1+1

ANGELL Brett Ashley Mark
Born: Marlborough, 20 August 1968
Height: 6'2" Weight: 13.11
Club Honours: Div 2 '00

This experienced striker began the 1999-2000 season on the transfer list at Stockport and after featuring in the opening matches he was loaned to Notts County last December. He was needed to help overcome an injury crisis at Meadow Lane, where he proved to be an instant success, scoring a hat-trick in his first game against Bournemouth, thus becoming the first Magpies player to score three times on his debut for the club since Fred Smith back in 1934. Brett added another two against Burnley in the new year but a permanent transfer failed to materialise after Notts announced they were unwilling to meet his wage demands. His effectiveness in the air, ability to hold the ball up and instinct for finding goalscoring positions more than compensate for a certain lack of pace and mobility. In February Brett joined Preston on loan until the end of the season; he made his first three appearances for the club from the bench, scoring twice in the home defeat by Colchester. He claimed the winner on his full debut at Bournemouth, and followed this up with two on his full home debut against Oxford. He contributed a total of eight goals to North End's Second Division championship effort and was rewarded with a winners' medal. Stop Press: It was reported at the end of June that Brett had signed for relegated Walsall.

Portsmouth (From trainee on 1/8/1986)
Derby Co (£40,000 from Cheltenham T on 19/2/1988)
Stockport Co (£33,000 on 20/10/1988) FL 60+10/28 FLC 3 FAC 3/1 Others 8/4
Southend U (£100,000 on 2/8/1990) FL 109+6/47 FLC 7+1/4 FAC 3/2 Others 9+1/10
Everton (£500,000 on 17/1/1994) PL 16+4/1 FLC 0+1
Sunderland (£600,000 on 23/3/1995) FL 10 FLC 1/1
Sheffield U (Loaned on 30/1/1996) FL 6/2
West Bromwich A (Loaned on 28/3/1996) FL 0+3
Stockport Co (£120,000 on 19/8/1996) FL 122+4/50 FLC 16+3/7 FAC 7/4 Others 4+1/1
Notts Co (Loaned on 9/12/1999) FL 6/5
Preston NE (Loaned on 24/2/2000) FL 9+6/8

ANSELIN Cedric
Born: Lens, France, 24 July 1977
Height: 5'9" Weight: 11.4
International Honours: France: Yth

Having completed his move to Carrow Road from Bordeaux for a fee of £250,000 in May 1999 following an initial three-month loan stint, Cedric has become the "darling" of the Norwich fans. Technically gifted, he is a clever passer of the ball, preferring to unlock defences with his vision rather than trying to take on his direct opponent. Nominally a wide right-sided midfield player, he is probably better suited to playing just behind the front men, where his creativity would be best utilised. He started the 1999-2000 campaign as a regular, but an injury sustained against Crewe in mid-September interrupted his season and he will be hoping to steer clear of fitness problems in 2000-01.

Norwich C (£250,000 from Bordeaux, France on 25/3/1999) FL 22+4/1 FLC 2 FAC 1

ANSELL Gary Scott
Born: Ilford, 8 November 1978
Height: 5'10" Weight: 12.0

After impressing during Barnet's build-up to the 1999-2000 season, Gary earned himself a one-year contract with the club, but he was ultimately unable to recapture that scintillating level of form once the campaign was under way. Signed from non-league Barking, Gary proved to be an effective front runner with a predator's eye for goal, but these attributes were largely confined to Barnet's second string. In his debut against Bournemouth in the Worthington Cup he was employed as a right-sided midfielder, yet in his later outings he was utilised as an extra attacking option. Loaned to Hayes in September 1999, he was out of contract in the summer.

Barnet (Signed from Barking on 17/8/1999) FL 0+3 FLC 0+1

ANTHONY Graham John
Born: South Shields, 9 August 1975
Height: 5'8" Weight: 10.8

Graham was considered to be the best passer of the ball at Carlisle in 1999-2000, and he earned a "star man" verdict for his creative midfield skills in the games against Halifax in October and Mansfield in January. However, he was less conspicuous in the latter part of the season as the side battled against relegation. Graham was not retained at the end of the campaign, so began the search for his sixth league club.

Sheffield U (From trainee on 7/7/1993) FL 0+3 FLC 1 Others 2
Scarborough (Loaned on 1/3/1996) FL 2
Swindon T (Free on 26/3/1997) FL 3
Plymouth Arg (Free on 7/8/1997) FL 5 FLC 2
Carlisle U (Free on 26/11/1997) FL 58+11/2 FLC 1+2 FAC 1 Others 6+1/1

ANTHROBUS Stephen (Steve) Anthony
Born: Lewisham, 10 November 1968
Height: 6'2" Weight: 13.0

Signed on a "free" from Crewe Alexandra in the summer of 1999, Steve had a great debut for Oxford, scoring a goal at Stoke in United's opening-day victory. However, "Bus" sadly managed only one other goal throughout the season to end with just two goals from 34 starts (plus 13 substitute appearances). An effective target man, he had shown his capabilities in pre-season, scoring a few goals, but as the campaign progressed he spent more and more time using his height and heading ability to help out his under-pressure defence. He always gave everything and his workrate never dipped but, although he made a valuable contribution to the team, goals remained elusive. Stop Press: Steve was called up by Barbados for their World Cup qualifying games in the middle of July.

Millwall (From juniors on 4/8/1986) FL 19+2/4 FLC 3 Others 1
Wimbledon (£150,000 on 16/2/1990) F/PL 27+1 FLC 1 FAC 2
Peterborough U (Loaned on 21/1/1994) FL 2
Chester C (Loaned on 26/8/1994) FL 7
Shrewsbury T (£25,000 on 8/8/1995) FL 60+12/16 FLC 4+1 FAC 5+3/1 Others 7+2/1
Crewe Alex (£75,000 on 24/3/1997) FL 53+8/9 FLC 2+1
Oxford U (Free on 1/7/1999) FL 25+11/2 FLC 4 FAC 3+1 Others 2+1

APPLEBY Matthew (Matty) Wilfred
Born: Middlesbrough, 16 April 1972
Height: 5'8" Weight: 11.12

Having appeared as a sweeper for Barnsley in 1998-99, Matty found himself switched to a roving midfield role by new manager Dave Bassett in 1999-2000. The move was a success and he proved an asset to the team in his new position. He also scored his first goals for the Oakwell club when he netted twice in the 6-0 thrashing of Portsmouth last August and added another against Grimsby in the new year. Matty is comfortable on the ball, works hard to close the opposition down and reads the game well – all useful skills for a midfield player.

Newcastle U (From trainee on 4/5/1990) F/PL 18+2 FLC 2+1 FAC 2 Others 2+2
Darlington (Loaned on 25/11/1993) FL 10/1 Others 1
Darlington (Free on 15/6/1994) FL 77+2/7 FLC 2 FAC 4 Others 8/3
Barnsley (£200,000 on 19/7/1996) F/PL 114+6/5 FLC 9+2 FAC 5+2 Others 3

APPLEBY Richard (Richie) Dean
Born: Middlesbrough, 18 September 1975
Height: 5'9" Weight: 11.4
Club Honours: Div 3 '00
International Honours: E: Yth

Although he was a regular member of the Swansea first team at the start of the 1999-2000 season, a heel injury in October followed by a sending-off against Cwmbran Town in a Welsh Premier Cup tie in December saw Richie placed on the transfer list. He is an extremely talented ball player on his day but, despite being taken off the transfer list in February, he made only one further appearance in the starting line-up, although he was used as a substitute on a number of occasions. A vital squad member, the wing back or midfielder won a Third Division championship winners' medal.

Newcastle U (From trainee on 12/8/1993) Others 2
Ipswich T (Free on 12/12/1995) FL 0+3 Others 1
Swansea C (Free on 16/8/1996) FL 87+18/11 FLC 4+3 FAC 5+1/2 Others 3+3/1

APPLETON Michael Antony
Born: Salford, 4 December 1975
Height: 5'9" Weight: 12.4
Club Honours: Div 2 '00

Preston's record signing had an in-and-out season in 1999-2000, disrupted by an early cartilage injury which saw him out of action for ten weeks. The energetic midfielder regained a regular first-team place when he returned to fitness, playing his 100th game for the club in the FA Cup tie at Everton in January, but he was then relegated to the substitutes' bench for a spell. Restored to the starting line-up for the win at Bristol Rovers in mid-April after a ten-game absence, Michael immediately demonstrated that he had lost none of his ability to tackle ferociously and contribute vast amounts of work in all areas of the field. He also chipped in with four goals during the season, and his efforts earned him a Second Division championship medal.

Manchester U (From trainee on 1/7/1994) FLC 1+1
Lincoln C (Loaned on 15/9/1995) FL 4 Others 1
Grimsby T (Loaned on 17/1/1997) FL 10/3
Preston NE (£500,000 on 8/8/1997) FL 65+24/7 FLC 6+1/1 FAC 8+1/1 Others 6+1/1

ARBER Mark Andrew
Born: Johannesburg, South Africa, 9 October 1977
Height: 6'1" Weight: 12.11

This left-sided centre back matured into an outstanding prospect with Barnet in 1999-2000 and was a virtual ever-present during his first full league campaign. His aerial prowess provided the Bees with an extra option at set-piece situations and he netted their opening goal of the campaign at Chester. In fact, Mark's assured displays at the heart of the Bees' rearguard during the opening months of the season led to speculation about an imminent move to QPR. The suspension that followed his dismissal in the home match against Brighton in March proved to be a blessing in disguise because, after his short break from first-team duties, he returned with renewed vigour and weighed in with an outstanding

four goals in the closing six games of the term.
Tottenham H (From trainee on 27/3/1996)
Barnet (£75,000 on 18/9/1998) FL 78+2/8 FLC 2 FAC 1 Others 5/1

ARDLEY Neal Christopher
Born: Epsom, 1 September 1972
Height: 5'11" Weight: 11.9
International Honours: E: U21-10
The former England U21 international made his debut for Wimbledon at the age of 18 after coming up through the Dons' youth team. An excellent crosser of the ball and a danger at set pieces, Neal did not make his first start of the 1999-2000 season until mid-December but was usually part of the match-day squad during the second half of the campaign. He really shone out in the closing matches of a difficult season with his "never say die" attitude and the 100 per cent commitment that he showed on the pitch. He has a strong rapport with the fans, who will be hoping to see him feature in the team regularly in 2000-01. He scored Wimbledon's only penalty of the campaign, securing a 2-1 win against Leicester in March, but he will always be remembered for his devastation on realising that Wimbledon had been relegated after the final whistle blew in the last match at Southampton.
Wimbledon (From trainee on 29/7/1991) F/PL 149+30/12 FLC 19+3/5 FAC 21+3/1

ARENDSE Andre
Born: Capetown, South Africa, 27 June 1967
Height: 6'4" Weight: 11.5
International Honours: South Africa: 38; (ANC '96)
Andre, a South African international goalkeeper, joined Oxford in the summer of 1999 from Fulham for a small fee. Although he had been unable to break into the Cottagers' strong side, he started the new season as first choice at the Manor Ground but ended up alternating with Paul Lundin as the Oxford management tried to decide which of the two they preferred. A tall, imposing figure, Andre lost his place after he was called up for international duty for the African Nations' Cup finals in the new year. A good shot stopper, he was sidelined towards the end of the season with a shoulder injury and then could not displace on-loan Derby 'keeper Richard Knight. Still first choice for the *Bafana Bafana*, he won five more caps in the African Nations' Cup finals, when South Africa took third place, and also appeared in the US Nike Cup matches during the summer.
Fulham (Signed from Capetown Spurs, South Africa on 7/8/1997) FL 6 FLC 2 FAC 1 Others 1
Oxford U (£30,000 on 16/7/1999) FL13 FLC 4 FAC 1+1

ARMSTRONG Alun
Born: Gateshead, 22 February 1975
Height: 6'1" Weight: 11.13
Club Honours: Div 1 '98
Alun was regarded as an exciting young prospect when he arrived at Middlesbrough from Stockport in February 1998, but sadly, like the previous campaign, 1999-2000 was not a season that the popular striker will remember with any great fondness. His injuries were slow to heal and what should have been the birth of a new era for him fizzled out like a damp squib. A meagre total of appearances and a solitary goal against West Ham just about summed up his season and no doubt left him contemplating what might have been. He moved to Huddersfield on loan on transfer deadline day and was quickly thrust into action alongside Clyde Wijnhard against Crewe. Alun was unable to maintain his record of scoring on his debut for every new club and also failed to find the net in his subsequent appearances for the Terriers, although he created a favourable impression with his accurate passing and ability to create space for himself. Although he made great efforts to revive his career, he still has a mountain to climb and his future is now somewhat uncertain.
Newcastle U (From trainee on 1/10/1993)
Stockport Co (£50,000 on 23/6/1994) FL 151+8/48 FLC 22/8 FAC 10+1/5 Others 7
Middlesbrough (£1,500,000 on 16/2/1998) P/FL 10+19/9 FLC 3
Huddersfield T (Loaned on 23/3/2000) FL 4+2

Chris Armstrong

ARMSTRONG Christopher (Chris) Peter
Born: Newcastle, 19 June 1971
Height: 6'0" Weight: 13.3
Club Honours: Div 1 '94; FLC '99
International Honours: E: B-1
Although 1999-2000 had looked as though it would be an indifferent season for Chris, the agile and tenacious striker once again ended up as Tottenham's top league scorer, largely due to a really fine run of form after Christmas. It was a satisfying achievement for both player and manager alike, George Graham having urged the Tottenham fans to give Chris time and encouragement. Chris paid Graham back for his patience and support with some impressive displays, coming up with the winning goals in games against Derby County in October, Liverpool in January and Coventry City in February. Whether with his head or clinical right foot, Chris proved to his critics that he still has much to offer. This was acknowledged by the interest shown in the former Crystal Palace striker by rival Premiership clubs including Leicester, who reportedly wanted him as a replacement for the departed Emile Heskey. With five goals more than Heskey during the season, Chris could prove an attractive option for many sides.
Wrexham (Free from Llay Welfare on 3/3/1989) FL 40+20/13 FLC 2+1 FAC 0+1 Others 5+1/3
Millwall (£50,000 on 16/8/1991) FL 11+17/5 FLC 3+1/2 FAC 0+1 Others 0+1
Crystal Palace (£1,000,000 on 1/9/1992) F/PL 118/45 FLC 8/6 FAC 8/5 Others 2/1
Tottenham H (£4,500,000 on 30/6/1995) PL 114+14/46 FLC 15/10 FAC 9+5/4 Others 3

ARMSTRONG Steven **Craig**
Born: South Shields, 23 May 1975
Height: 5'11" Weight: 12.10
The burly defender started the 1999-2000 season at left back for Huddersfield, with his decisive tackling a feature of some solid defensive displays. Often used to link down the flanks, he pushed forward with great purpose. Craig later proved to be equally at home in central defence, showing great awareness complemented by some quality passing and effective headwork. With a good eye for a shot at goal, he became an important member of the first team as Steve Bruce's side chased a play-off place.
Nottingham F (From trainee on 2/6/1992) P/FL 24+16 FLC 6+2/2 FAC 1
Burnley (Loaned on 29/12/1994) FL 4
Bristol Rov (Loaned on 8/1/1996) FL 4
Bristol Rov (Loaned on 28/3/1996) FL 9+1
Gillingham (Loaned on 18/10/1996) FL 10 FLC 2 Others 1
Watford (Loaned on 24/1/1997) FL 3
Watford (Loaned on 14/3/1997) FL 12
Huddersfield T (£750,000 on 26/2/1999) FL 50+2/1 FLC 5+1 FAC 1

ARMSTRONG Gordon Ian
Born: Newcastle, 15 July 1967
Height: 6'0" Weight: 12.11
Club Honours: Div 3 '88
Used variously at left back, as part of a three-man central defence or in midfield, Gordon was usually a solid if unspectacular performer and an effective captain for the first two-thirds of Burnley's 1999-2000 season. The signing of Ian Cox and manager Stan Ternent's preference for attacking wing backs then left Gordon on the sidelines, although he remained club captain. As he is now no longer the obvious first choice in any position, it is difficult to see him regaining a regular place, although his leadership qualities would certainly be useful in the event of Steve Davis's absence.
Sunderland (From apprentice on 10/7/1985) FL 331+18/50 FLC 25+4/3 FAC 19/4 Others 18+1/4
Bristol C (Loaned on 24/8/1995) FL 6
Northampton T (Loaned on 5/1/1996) FL 4/1 Others 1
Bury (Free on 16/7/1996) FL 49+22/4 FLC 5+2/2 FAC 2+1 Others 1+1
Burnley (Free on 27/8/1998) FL 62/3 FLC 1 FAC 3+1

ARMSTRONG Joel
Born: Chesterfield, 25 September 1981
Height: 5'11" Weight: 12.7
Chesterfield appear to have discovered another fine goalkeeping prospect! This promising youngster has yet to graduate from the club's academy scheme but made his first-team debut in the 4-1 win at Rotherham in the Auto Windscreens Shield last January, and followed that up with three league games after relegation became a certainty. Joel proved unflappable, earning the confidence of his defence. He is agile and quick witted and, despite an apparent lack of height for his position, he is willing to come off his line to command the penalty area. Joel was Chesterfield's "Young Player of the Year".
Chesterfield (Trainee) FL 3 Others 1

ARMSTRONG Paul George
Born: Dublin, 5 October 1978
Height: 5'10" Weight: 10.12
International Honours: RoI: U21-2
This ball-playing midfielder's appearances for Brighton were restricted by an ankle injury during the early part of 1999-2000. Paul failed to make the impact that the previous season's performances promised, and was released in May 2000. A product of Albion's youth team, he had the misfortune of being substituted after coming on as a sub during the 2-0 defeat at Hull in February. Paul was released during the summer.
Brighton & Hove A (From trainee on 10/7/1997) FL 33+20/2 FLC 0+1 FAC 1 Others 1

ARNISON Paul Simon
Born: Hartlepool, 18 September 1977
Height: 5'10" Weight: 10.12
One of several players released by Newcastle manager Bobby Robson, Toon's reserve-team captain jumped at the offer of a loan spell with Hartlepool, his home-town club, in March 2000. With his preferred right-back position already adequately filled, Paul was played in midfield and turned in several good performances that showed he was totally committed to the club. He was soon signed on permanent contract and finished the 1999-2000 season as a useful squad member.
Newcastle U (From trainee on 1/3/1996)
Hartlepool U (Free on 10/3/2000) FL 5+3/1 Others 2

ARNOTT Andrew (Andy) John
Born: Chatham, 18 October 1973
Height: 6'1" Weight: 13.2
After he lost his way in the latter stages of 1998-99, it was clear that Andy's days at Brighton were numbered. His Albion involvement last term was limited to one start, in the Worthington Cup tie at Gillingham, and one appearance as a substitute in Division Three. It was no surprise when he was loaned to Colchester United in October, with Warren Aspinall moving the other way, and the swap deal was made permanent a month later. The remainder of Andy's season was disrupted by injuries, particularly a hernia problem, which severely restricted his appearances for his new club but he gave glimpses of what can be expected next season, if he has more luck with his fitness. Fully fit, he would certainly add strength and aggression to the U's squad.
Gillingham (From trainee on 13/5/1991) FL 50+23/12 FLC 2+3 FAC 10+2/1 Others 3+2
Leyton Orient (£15,000 on 25/1/1996) FL 47+3/6 FLC 2 FAC 2 Others 1
Fulham (£23,000 on 17/6/1997) FL 0+1 Others 0+2
Brighton & Hove A (£20,000 on 23/10/1998) FL 27+1/2 FLC 1 FAC 1 Others 1
Colchester U (Free on 24/9/1999) FL 4+8

ARPHEXAD Pegguy Michel
Born: Abymes, Guadeloupe, 18 May 1973
Height: 6'2" Weight: 13.5
Club Honours: FLC '00
The popular understudy to Tim Flowers in the Leicester goal in 1999-2000, Pegguy continued to perform exceptionally whenever called upon. His ever-growing cult status at Filbert Street was enhanced further by his role in two crucial penalty shoot-outs as the Foxes battled through in the two domestic cup competitions. His save from Fulham's Geoff Horsfield rounded off an unlikely comeback by City in the Worthington Cup quarter-final, then another save in the sudden-death stages against Arsenal earned a famous FA Cup victory. Pegguy finished the season between the sticks for City when Tim Flowers suffered a back problem and, as usual, looked assured and highly capable. He picked up a Worthington Cup winners' medal after being on the bench for the win over Tranmere at Wembley.
Leicester C (Free from Lens, France on 20/8/1997) PL 17+4 FLC 4 FAC 3+1

ARTELL David John
Born: Rotherham, 22 November 1980
Height: 6'2" Weight: 13.9
A very promising Rotherham central defender who increased in strength during the 1999-2000 season, David gained his first senior experience when he took over from Paul Dillon in the closing minutes of October's visit to promotion rivals Swansea. Otherwise, he was a vital member of the successful reserve team that lifted the Pontins League Division One title, while still a regular in the Millers' youth squad.
Rotherham U (From trainee on 1/7/1999) FL 0+1

ASABA Carl Edward
Born: London, 28 January 1973
Height: 6'2" Weight: 13.4
The 1999-2000 season proved most frustrating for this big and powerful Gillingham striker but ultimately provided a successful conclusion. He was initially sidelined with a groin injury suffered in the heartbreaking 1998-99 Wembley play-off against Manchester City, the problem requiring a series of operations before he was able to recover full fitness. He eventually returned for the Gills' reserve team last February and he made his first-team comeback in the FA Cup sixth-round tie against Chelsea at Stamford Bridge. However, after just a handful of games he then suffered a hamstring injury that put him out of action for a further month, and it was only during the final weeks of the season that he appeared regularly in the starting line-up. Even so, Carl made a significant contribution to the club's promotion campaign, hitting a hat-trick against Cardiff in early May and making the team for the Second Division play-off final against Wigan when the Gills earned a historic victory and promotion to Division One for the first time ever.
Brentford (Free from Dulwich Hamlet on 9/8/1994) FL 49+5/25 FLC 5 FAC 4 Others 7/2
Colchester U (Loaned on 16/2/1995) FL 9+3/2
Reading (£800,000 on 7/8/1997) FL 31+2/8 FLC 7+2/4 FAC 3/1
Gillingham (£600,000 on 28/8/1998) FL 47+5/26 FAC 1+1 Others 9/2

ASHBEE Ian
Born: Birmingham, 6 September 1976
Height: 6'1" Weight: 13.7
International Honours: E: Yth
Consistent and versatile, Ian appeared in all of Cambridge's league games in 1999-2000. He gamely filled holes in defence before forming a crucial midfield partnership with Paul Wanless, and added power and gritty determination to the side. A vital member of the squad, he is always one of the first names on the team sheet.
Derby Co (From trainee on 9/11/1994) FL 1
Cambridge U (Free on 13/12/1996) FL 111+10/6 FLC 4 FAC 11 Others 3+1

ASHBY Barry John
Born: Park Royal, 2 November 1970
Height: 6'2" Weight: 13.8
Club Honours: FAYC '89
This robust Gillingham player once again proved to be one of the top defenders in the Second Division in 1999-2000. Having signed a new contract in the summer of 1999, he went on to produce a series of consistent performances and capped a fine season by contributing one of the goals in the play-off semi-final second leg against Stoke. Barry is a composed and reliable central defender who is good both in the air and on the ground.
Watford (From trainee on 1/12/1988) FL 101+13/3 FLC 6 FAC 4 Others 2+1
Brentford (Signed on 22/3/1994) FL 119+2/4 FLC 11 FAC 9/1 Others 11+1
Gillingham (£140,000 on 8/8/1997) FL 122/4 FLC 7 FAC 11/1 Others 9/1

ASHCROFT Lee
Born: Preston, 7 September 1972
Height: 5'10" Weight: 11.10
International Honours: E: U21-1
Following a frustrating first season with Grimsby, Lee established himself as a vital part of the Mariners' strike force in 1999-2000. He developed a high degree of mutual understanding with fellow striker Jack Lester, the pair constituting an attacking partnership that caused problems for many First Division defences. As the season progressed Lee started to recapture the scoring skills that made him Town's record signing. Following Lester's departure for Nottingham Forest, Lee had hardly had time to strike up a new strike partnership with

Bradley Allen when both were sidelined with injuries sustained in the away game at Norwich in February. He eventually returned to first-team action having been out of the side for most of March.

Preston NE (From trainee on 16/7/1991) FL 78+13/13 FLC 3 FAC 5 Others 6+2/1
West Bromwich A (£250,000 on 1/8/1993) FL 66+24/17 FLC 2+3 FAC 3+1/1 Others 8+3
Notts Co (Loaned on 28/3/1996) FL 4+2
Preston NE (£150,000 on 5/9/1996) FL 63+1/22 FLC 4 FAC 5/5 Others 2+1
Grimsby T (£500,000 on 12/8/1998) FL 52+9/15 FLC 7/2 FAC 1

ASHER Alistair Andrew
Born: Leicester, 14 October 1980
Height: 6'0" Weight: 11.6

This promising Mansfield defender was presented with the Stags' "Youth Team Player of the Year" award for the 1998-99 season immediately before making his first-team debut in the game against Carlisle last August when he came on as a substitute for the injured Bobby Hassell. Alistair deservedly retained his place at right back for two months until displaced by the returning Hassell, but later returned to the side in a more central defensive position. He is cool under pressure and his accurate passing and crossing of the ball were an asset to the side. Alistair's rapid progress was confirmed when he was voted the Mansfield "Player of the Year".

Mansfield T (From trainee on 23/6/1999) FL 29+6 FAC 0+1 Others 1+1

Alistair Asher

ASHTON Jonathan (Jon) Frank
Born: Plymouth, 4 August 1979
Height: 5'11" Weight: 12.0

The 1999-2000 season was a frustrating one for the former YTS trainee. Given a new contract in the 1999 close season by Plymouth manager Kevin Hodges, he started the campaign in his familiar position of right back, but a string of niggling injuries restricted his appearances. Jon will be looking to return to the fine form of 1998-99, but it seems unlikely that it will be to the Pilgrims' benefit, as he was released at the end of the season. Stop Press: He was reported to have signed for Exeter during the summer.

Plymouth Arg (From trainee on 29/7/1997) FL 27+7 FLC 1+2 FAC 5 Others 2

ASKEY John Colin
Born: Stoke, 4 November 1964
Height: 6'0" Weight: 12.2
Club Honours: GMVC '95, '97; FAT '96
International Honours: E: SP-1

Macclesfield's longest-serving player with some 600 appearances, "Gentleman John" is equally at home on the wing or as a forward and spent roughly fifty per cent of his time in each position during the 1999-2000 season. He achieved his highest tally of goals in a season since becoming a league player, and was Macclesfield's second-highest scorer with 15 goals. John holds the ball up effectively, and is still a very skilful player who always makes intelligent use of possession. He made his 100th league appearance during the season, and in January was appointed joint coach with Steve Wood on the appointment of Peter Davenport as manager. Although he is now at the veteran stage, last season was probably the most successful of his distinguished career and he fittingly gained the supporters' "Player of the Year" award.

Macclesfield T (Free from Milton U during 1987-88) FL 105+12/25 FLC 7+1/2 FAC 6/1 Others 2

ASPIN Neil
Born: Gateshead, 12 April 1965
Height: 6'0" Weight: 13.10
Club Honours: AMC '93

Following his 410 games for Port Vale, the vastly experienced defender was a rock in the centre of the Darlington defence in 1999-2000, often alongside the equally seasoned Steve Tutill. However, Neil suffered a series of niggling problems that limited his involvement. Notably, he picked up a knee injury at Chester in January while a recurring hamstring problem ruled him out of the play-off semi-finals. Despite his dominance in the air, Neil is still looking for his first Darlington goal.

Leeds U (From apprentice on 6/10/1982) FL 203+4/5 FLC 9/1 FAC 17 Others 11
Port Vale (£200,000 on 28/7/1989) FL 343+5/3 FLC 20 FAC 24 Others 18
Darlington (Free on 13/7/1999) FL 29 FLC 1 FAC 2 Others 2

ASPINALL Warren
Born: Wigan, 13 September 1967
Height: 5'9" Weight: 12.8
Club Honours: AMC '85, '97; Div 3 '99
International Honours: E: Yth

A vastly experienced, combative midfielder, Warren was brought to Colchester by Mick Wadsworth in 1998-99 to add experience and a competitive edge to United's struggle against relegation. He very quickly established himself as team captain and a firm favourite of the fans, but it all went wrong early last season with Wadsworth's sudden departure. Despite a match-winning two-goal performance in Steve Whitton's first game in charge against Reading, Warren went on loan to Brighton in October in exchange for Andy Arnott, the move eventually becoming permanent. Warren, who had been Brighton manager Micky Adams's first signing when he was in charge at Brentford back in 1997, was to be a frequent member of the Seagulls' midfield and scored his first goal for the club in the 1-0 win at Carlisle United. His experience and never-say-die attitude proved invaluable during the closing stages of the campaign, when he often came on as a late substitute to steady the nerves of his team-mates. Although he was released at the end of the season, Warren's proven abilities are likely to attract a number of enquiries from lower-division clubs.

Wigan Ath (From apprentice on 31/8/1985) FL 21+12/10 FLC 1 FAC 2+3/2 Others 1+5/2
Everton (£150,000 on 4/2/1986) FL 0+7 FLC 0+1 Others 0+2
Wigan Ath (Loaned on 6/2/1986) FL 18/12 Others 2/2
Aston Villa (£300,000 on 19/2/1987) FL 40+4/14 FLC 4/2 FAC 1+1
Portsmouth (£315,000 on 26/8/1988) FL 97+35/21 FLC 8+3/3 FAC 4+5/2 Others 6+1/2
Bournemouth (Loaned on 27/8/1993) FL 4+2/1
Swansea C (Loaned on 14/10/1993) FL 5 Others 1
Bournemouth (£20,000 on 31/12/1993) FL 26+1/8 FLC 4 FAC 1 Others 1
Carlisle U (Free on 8/3/1995) FL 99+8/12 FLC 8/3 FAC 6 Others 10+1/1
Brentford (£50,000 on 21/11/1997) FL 41+2/5 FLC 4 FAC 1+1 Others 2
Colchester U (Free on 9/2/1999) FL 22/5 FLC 2
Brighton & Hove A (Free on 24/9/1999) FL 19+12/3 FAC 3 Others 2

ASTAFJEVS Vitalijs
Born: Riga, Latvia, 3 April 1971
Height: 5'11" Weight: 12.5
International Honours: Latvia: 66

This experienced midfield player, Latvia's most capped international and current captain, played in England last September for his former club, Skonto Riga, in the preliminary round of the Champions' League against Chelsea. Having come to the attention of Bristol Rovers when he was recommended to them by the Latvian national manager, Gary Johnson, the former Cambridge United coach, Vitalijs joined the club in January after winning an appeal to the Employment Department for a work permit. He was introduced to English league football initially as a substitute for the final 11 minutes of Rovers' 3-1 defeat of Wrexham which saw them go top of the Second Division. The skilful midfielder appeared for Latvia against Romania three days later, then scored his first goal for Rovers at Oldham Athletic on 26 February. Unfortunately, in the same match he was stretchered off with an ankle ligament injury but he returned to play an important part in Rovers' drive for promotion and win a further cap against Finland at the beginning of June.

Bristol Rov (£150,000 from Skonto Riga, Latvia on 28/1/2000) FL 13+3/2

ATHERTON Peter
Born: Orrell, 6 April 1970
Height: 5'11" Weight: 13.12
International Honours: E: U21-1; Sch

Sheffield Wednesday's club captain performed solidly during the 1999-2000 season. He was mostly used in his favoured position in the centre of the defence, although he can also play at full back and in a holding midfield role. Peter leads the team by example, always giving 100 per cent for the cause whatever the circumstances. His strengths are his tackling and anticipation, and with a little extra height and better distribution he would be a really top-class defender. Stop Press: Peter was reported to have joined Bradford in early July.

Wigan Ath (From trainee on 12/2/1988) FL 145+4/1 FLC 8 FAC 7 Others 12+1
Coventry C (£300,000 on 23/8/1991) F/PL 113+1 FLC 4 FAC 2
Sheffield Wed (£800,000 on 1/6/1994) PL 214/9 FLC 16 FAC 18

ATKINS Mark Nigel
Born: Doncaster, 14 August 1968
Height: 6'0" Weight: 13.2
Club Honours: PL '95
International Honours: E: Sch

Fighting off interest from Walsall and Sheffield United, York signed Mark at the start of the 1999-2000 season on a short-term contract. Sitting in front of the City defence, he played in the first 12 league and cup games before his release in November. An experienced and versatile player, he netted on his debut in the opening game against Swansea, and also in a defeat at Barnet. A week after leaving Bootham Crescent, he joined his home-town club, Doncaster Rovers.

Scunthorpe U (From juniors on 9/7/1986) FL 45+5/2 FLC 3+1 FAC 5 Others 6+1
Blackburn Rov (£45,000 on 16/6/1988) F/PL 224+33/35 FLC 20+2/4 FAC 11+3 Others 17+2/1
Wolverhampton W (£1,000,000 on 21/9/1995) FL 115+11/8 FLC 12+1/2 FAC 11+1 Others 2/1
York C (Free on 5/8/1999) FL 10/2 FLC 2

ATKINSON Brian
Born: Darlington, 19 January 1971
Height: 5'10" Weight: 12.5
International Honours: E: U21-6

Unfortunately, Brian was again dogged by injury problems in 1999-2000, his fourth season with Darlington, after a relatively injury-free 1998-99 campaign. His main problem in the new year was a stomach strain. Undoubtedly his ability to keep the ball under pressure in midfield was missed as he played in all but two cup games up until the end of January.

Sunderland (From trainee on 21/7/1989) FL 119+22/4 FLC 8+2 FAC 13/2 Others 2+3
Carlisle U (Loaned on 19/1/1996) FL 2 Others 1
Darlington (Free on 10/8/1996) FL 122+13/6 FLC 9 FAC 8+1/2 Others 5+1/1

ATKINSON Graeme
Born: Hull, 11 November 1971
Height: 5'8" Weight: 11.3
Club Honours: Div 3 '96

Having failed to take him to Mansfield during the previous campaign, new Rochdale boss Steve Parkin finally got his man in the 1999 close season. Graeme made an immediate impact in his second spell at Spotland, scoring on his debut and netting four times in the first ten games. Playing wide on the left up front or in midfield, he was a key player in Dale's tremendous start to the new season. He also figured at left back, especially after Rochdale adopted a 5-3-2 formation late in the campaign. Graeme was a Dale fixture until April when he damaged knee ligaments at Peterborough.

Hull C (From trainee on 6/5/1990) FL 129+20/23 FLC 6+3/2 FAC 4+1/1 Others 9
Preston NE (Signed on 7/10/1994) FL 63+16/6 FLC 5/1 FAC 2+1 Others 5/2
Rochdale (Loaned on 12/12/1997) FL 5+1
Brighton & Hove A (Free on 5/3/1998) FL 16 FLC 1
Scunthorpe U (Free on 2/11/1998) FL 0+1
Scarborough (Free on 18/2/1999) FL 15/1
Rochdale (Free on 1/7/1999) FL 32+8/5 FLC 2 FAC 3/1 Others 4+1

AUSTIN Dean Barry
Born: Hemel Hempstead, 26 April 1970
Height: 5'11" Weight: 12.4

An experienced right-sided Crystal Palace defender, Dean had a consistent season in 1999-2000 despite the Eagles' off-the-field problems. His determination and speed were assets to the team, and he enjoyed a short spell as club captain when Simon Rodger was injured. He scored two goals, both of which came when he joined the attack at set pieces. He was released in the summer.

Southend U (£12,000 from St Albans C on 22/3/1990) FL 96/2 FLC 4/1 FAC 2 Others 7
Tottenham H (£375,000 on 4/6/1992) PL 117+7 FLC 7+2 FAC 16+1
Crystal Palace (Free on 8/7/1998) FL 62+3/3 FLC 8 FAC 1

AUSTIN Kevin Levi
Born: Hackney, 12 February 1973
Height: 6'0" Weight: 14.0

Kevin joined Barnsley from Lincoln City under the Bosman ruling in the summer of 1999. He began the 1999-2000 campaign in the left-back position and was settling in comfortably when he had the misfortune to rupture his achilles tendon last August while playing in a Worthington Cup tie against his old club, the injury putting him out of action for the whole of the season. Kevin's strengths are his speed, power and a certain versatility, for he can also play at centre back if required. He will be hoping to recover full fitness in time for the start of 2000-01 and finally link up with the Trinidad and Tobago national squad, whose interest was put on hold following his injury.

Leyton Orient (Free from Saffron Walden on 19/8/1993) FL 101+8/3 FLC 4/1 FAC 6 Others 7
Lincoln C (£30,000 on 31/7/1996) FL 128+1/2 FLC 9 FAC 6 Others 4
Barnsley (Free on 5/7/1999) FL 3 FLC 2

AVDIU Kemajl
Born: Kosovo, 22 December 1976
Height: 5'10" Weight: 11.7

Frustrated by a lack of first-team appearances the previous season, Bury's pacy Croatian striker was again largely ignored by Neil Warnock throughout the first half of 1999-2000. Although he was frequently named among the list of substitutes, Kemajl seldom joined the action and it took a change of manager in December before opportunities finally arrived. He made a highly impressive full league debut at home to Wrexham on the right wing, showing plenty of pace and good skills on the ball and working hard to get back and cover in defence as well. Unfortunately, he failed to maintain that promise in subsequent appearances, struggled to achieve any real consistency and was unable to add a finishing touch in front of goal to his game. Kemajl was released on a free transfer in May.

Bury (Free from Esbjerg, Denmark on 28/8/1998) FL 8+19/1 FLC 0+2 Others 0+1
Partick Thistle (Loaned on 30/3/1999) SL 6/1

AWFORD Andrew (Andy) Terence
Born: Worcester, 14 July 1972
Height: 5'10" Weight: 12.0
International Honours: E: U21-9; Yth; Sch

This solid and reliable Portsmouth defender was used in five different positions during the 1999-2000 season, but wherever he played he showed a calm and focused approach. Andy netted a rare goal, only his third in 11 seasons of senior football, when he headed home a corner in the 3-2 defeat by West Bromwich Albion last November but missed several games towards the end of the season with niggling injuries. Andy is now approaching 300 Football League appearances for Pompey, and his strengths are his excellent distribution and an ability to read the game well.

Portsmouth (From trainee on 24/7/1989) FL 291+20/3 FLC 29+1 FAC 17 Others 12

AXELDAHL Jonas Michael
Born: Holm, Sweden, 2 September 1970
Height: 5'11" Weight: 11.7

Jonas guested for Ipswich during their pre-season tour of Sweden in 1999 and returned to England with the team for an official trial. As a result of this he was offered, and accepted, a one-year contract. He was seen as a player who could cover for the existing strikers and keep them on their toes as it was felt that a lack of firepower in the later stages of the previous season had contributed to the club's failure to gain an automatic promotion place. Jonas is predominantly right footed but has good mobility and his game seems to suit playing as a foil to a big front man. He was used mainly as a substitute at first-team level and was unable to open his account for the club, but he was a prolific scorer for the reserves, notching 20 goals. He was released in the summer.

Ipswich T (Free from Foggia, Italy on 31/7/1999) FL 1+15 FLC 0+3 FAC 0+1

AYRES James Martin
Born: Luton, 18 September 1980
Height: 6'3" Weight: 13.0

A commanding central defender who makes excellent use of his height in both penalty areas, James joined Luton as a schoolboy, and progressed from YTS hopeful to captain of the Luton youth team, playing a key role as the side won the Division Two championship of the South East Counties League in 1999. Very strong in the air and a useful extra striker, he scores regularly from set pieces and, although he had only one first-team outing in 1999-2000, in the Auto Windscreens Shield at Oxford in December, he looks set for a bright future.

Luton T (From trainee on 9/2/1999) Others 1

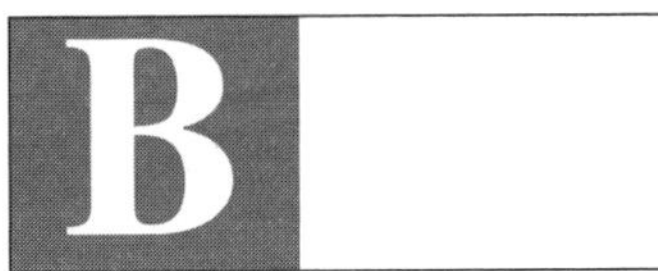

BABAYARO Celestine
Born: Kaduna, Nigeria, 29 August 1978
Height: 5'8" Weight: 11.0
Club Honours: FLC '98; ESC '98; FAC '00
International Honours: Nigeria: 24; U23 (OLYM '96); Yth (World-U17 '93)

Chelsea finally competed in the European Cup last season, 44 years after pulling out of the inaugural tournament, and Celestine created a piece of club history by notching the Blues' first goal in the competition. He latched on to a clever lay-off by fellow substitute Tore Andre Flo to smash home a sweet drive with his "swinger" right foot from the edge of the box against plucky Latvian side Skonto Riga. "Baba's" only other goal of the season also came in the Champions' League: a diving header in the second-phase match against Feyenoord which opened the floodgates for a comprehensive Chelsea victory. Celestine returned to Nigeria in January to take part in the African Nations' Cup finals and played in all six games for the Eagles, who eventually lost out on penalties to Cameroon in the final of the competition. Unfortunately, he missed vital FA Cup and Champions' League matches as a result of his international call-up, but forced his way back into the first team, dislodging young Jon Harley, who had proved to be a very capable deputy in his absence. An athletic and aggressive player, Celestine was mostly used at left back in 1999-2000 following the injury to Graeme Le Saux, although he is equally comfortable on the left of midfield. In either role he likes to get forward, although he sometimes displays a surprising lack of self-confidence when faced by opposition full backs. He gained an FA Cup winners' medal at Harley's expense when Vialli opted for his greater experience for the 1-0 victory over Aston Villa at Wembley.

Chelsea (£2,250,000 from Anderlecht, Belgium on 20/6/1997) PL 57+4/3 FLC 4+1 FAC 5+1 Others 23+3/3

BABB Philip (Phil) Andrew
Born: Lambeth, 30 November 1970
Height: 6'0" Weight: 12.3
Club Honours: FLC '95
International Honours: RoI: 33; B-1

After failing to win a place in Liverpool's first team in 1999-2000, this experienced defender crossed the Mersey to spend a month on loan at Tranmere Rovers last January. He started brightly, but as his spell at Prenton Park wore on his form faded and the loan was not extended when his month was up. On his day Phil is a stylish player, strong in the tackle and with excellent distribution. He was recalled to the Republic of Ireland team for a friendly against the Czech Republic at the end of February, adding a further cap against Scotland before touring the US for the Nike Cup matches in the summer. Phil was out of contract at Anfield in the summer. Stop Press: It was reported at the beginning of July that he had moved to Sporting Lisbon.

Millwall (From trainee on 25/4/1989)
Bradford C (Free on 10/8/1990) FL 73+7/14 FLC 5+1 FAC 3 Others 3+1
Coventry C (£500,000 on 21/7/1992) PL 70+7/3 FLC 5/1 FAC 2
Liverpool (£3,600,000 on 1/9/1994) PL 124+4/1 FLC 16 FAC 12 Others 12+2
Tranmere Rov (Loaned on 21/1/2000) FL 4 FLC 1 FAC 2

BACON Daniel (Danny) Stephen
Born: Mansfield, 20 September 1980
Height: 5'10" Weight: 10.12

A YTS youngster who is very highly thought of at Field Mill, Danny missed most of the previous season with a broken leg but forced his way into the Mansfield first team in 1999-2000 on his return to full fitness. He looked to be in for a long spell in the team until shin splints forced him out of action just before Christmas. When this problem failed to clear even after an operation, a second operation was required, further delaying his comeback. He likes to play up front and has scored many goals for the youth teams, and it looks as though, given the chance, he may repeat that success for the senior team.

Mansfield T (From trainee on 5/1/2000) FL 6+2/2 FAC 0+1

Walid Badir

BADIR Walid
Born: Kafr Kasm, Israel, 12 March 1974
Height: 6'0" Weight: 12.11
International Honours: Israel: 23

Walid arrived at Wimbledon just prior to the start of the 1999-2000 season in a £900,000 deal with Israeli club Hapoel Petach Tikva. A big, strong defensive midfielder, he likes to push forward whenever he can. His appearances during his first season with the Dons were somewhat limited owing to the large number of midfield options open to the manager, but he did have the satisfaction early in his Wimbledon career of scoring against Manchester United and silencing the Old Trafford crowd. Walid, one of only two Arabs to represent Israel, added a further six caps during the season and scored three goals, including two in the 4-1 defeat of Russia last February. His combative presence in midfield is likely to be useful for some of the tough away trips the Dons will face in the First Division.

Wimbledon (£900,000 from Hapoel Petach Tikva, Israel on 5/8/1999) PL 12+9/1 FLC 3 FAC 0+1

BAIANO Francesco
Born: Naples, Italy, 24 February 1968
Height: 5'7" Weight: 10.7
International Honours: Italy: 2

Although Francesco, a former Italian international attacking midfielder whose range of creative passes is a feature of his game, was in the Derby team for the first three matches of the 1999-2000 season, his subsequent appearances tended to be as a substitute as Jim Smith looked for a different blend in the middle of the park. After he had expressed a desire to return with his family to Italy, his contract, due to expire in June 2000, was cancelled by mutual consent on 9 November, allowing him to take up an offer from Serie B club Ternana. His skills will be missed at Pride Park but the move was probably the best outcome for both parties. The player has expressed a wish to further his career by moving into coaching after retirement.

Derby Co (£1,500,000 from Fiorentina, Italy, via Napoli, Empoli, Parma, Avelino and Foggia, on 8/8/1997) PL 52+12/16 FLC 6 FAC 5/3

BAILEY Alan
Born: Macclesfield, 1 November 1978
Height: 5'9" Weight: 11.12

After failing to make the grade with Manchester City, Alan moved on a free transfer to Stockport last August. A series of niggling injuries hindered his progress at Edgeley Park and it was not until mid-November that he had a decent run in the first team. He had a great game for County against his old colleagues at Maine Road last December, scoring the equaliser then winning the penalty which Tony Dinning converted to give the Hatters a 2-1 victory over their more illustrious neighbours. Alan also netted in the following Saturday's FA Cup tie with Grimsby before again succumbing to injuries: he missed the last few months of the season with hamstring trouble. A pacy striker who holds the ball up well, he will be hoping to return to full fitness in time for the start of the 2000-01 campaign.

Manchester C (From trainee on 2/7/1997) Others 0+1
Macclesfield T (Loaned on 29/1/1999) FL 5+5/1
Stockport Co (Free on 4/8/1999) FL 5+9/1 FLC 0+1 FAC 1/1

BAILEY John Andrew
Born: Lambeth, 6 May 1969
Height: 5'8" Weight: 10.8

This Bournemouth midfield player had a most frustrating time in 1999-2000 when he missed virtually the whole of the season due to persistent back problems. He was restricted to just two appearances from the subs' bench last September and will be hoping to make a full recovery in time for the 2000-01 campaign. John is a tireless worker on the right or in the centre of midfield when fully fit, fierce in the tackle and capable of surging forward runs.

Bournemouth (£40,000 from Enfield on 5/7/1995) FL 136+13/6 FLC 11+2 FAC 9+1 Others 11+1/1

BAIRD Andrew (Andy) Crawford
Born: East Kilbride, 18 January 1979
Height: 5'10" Weight: 12.6

This talented young Wycombe striker was mostly restricted to outings from the subs' bench in the early part of the 1999-2000 season and it was not until the end of November that he was given a decent run in the starting line-up. He scored five times during the campaign, the low tally being partly as a result of his unselfish play, but scored a couple of crackers in the end-of-season games against Gillingham and Cambridge. Andy kicks well with either foot and is much admired for his strength, speed and high workrate.

Wycombe W (From trainee on 18/3/1998) FL 45+15/10 FLC 1+4/1 FAC 6/2 Others 2

BAKALLI Adrian
Born: Brussels, Belgium, 22 November 1976
Height: 6'3" Weight: 13.6

This big, blond Belgian's strong physical presence was a welcome, if only occasional, addition to the Watford midfield during the 1999-2000 season. Signed from Molenbeek in January 1999, Adrian made his Premiership debut at Leicester last August and also came on during the home match with Newcastle in November; otherwise he was a regular in the reserves apart from a brief absence with a thigh strain during January.

Watford (£100,000 from RWD Molenbeek, Belgium on 19/1/1999) PL 0+2

BAKER Matthew (Matt) Christopher
Born: Harrogate, 18 December 1979
Height: 6'0" Weight: 12.8

Having been sidelined for over 15 months due to a snapped medial ligament and damaged cruciate ligament in the same knee, this promising young goalkeeper was promoted to Hull City's subs' bench in the opening weeks of the 1999-2000 season. He was called upon on three occasions, the highlight coming against Liverpool at Anfield in the Worthington Cup following Lee Bracey's sending-off. Previously associated with Leeds United, Matt was on schoolboy forms at Elland Road at the same time as their East Riding-based England U21 'keeper, Paul Robinson. He was released at the end of the season.

Hull C (From trainee on 16/7/1998) FL 0+2 FLC 0+1 Others 1

BAKER David **Paul**
Born: Newcastle, 5 January 1963
Height: 6'1" Weight: 14.2

Twelve years after his last appearance in a Carlisle shirt, this vastly experienced and powerful striker made a surprise return to Brunton Park in August 1999. He scored in his first two appearances and was rewarded with a contract as player-coach. Though his playing role later diminished, Paul showed touches of class as well as an enthusiasm for the fray that belied his years and long career in the lower divisions. His coaching duties increased after Christmas, but he was released at the end of the campaign despite helping to secure the club's survival in the Football League.

Southampton (£4,000 from Bishop Auckland on 1/7/1984)
Carlisle U (Free on 2/7/1985) FL 66+5/11 FLC 4/1 FAC 3 Others 2+1
Hartlepool U (Free on 31/7/1987) FL 192+5/67 FLC 12/4 FAC 16/6 Others 16/5
Motherwell (£77,500 on 1/8/1992) SL 5+4/1 SLC 1
Gillingham (£40,000 on 7/1/1993) FL 58+4/16 FAC 5/1 Others 2
York C (£15,000 on 1/10/1994) FL 36+12/18 FLC 2+2/2 FAC 3 Others 5+1/1
Torquay U (£25,000 on 19/1/1996) FL 30/8 FLC 2/3
Scunthorpe U (£15,000 on 4/10/1996) FL 21/9 FAC 3/5 Others 2
Hartlepool U (Signed on 27/3/1997) FL 25+10/9 FLC 2/1 Others 0+1
Carlisle U (Free on 26/8/1999) FL 12+5/2

BAKER Steven (Steve) Richard
Born: Pontefract, 8 September 1978
Height: 5'10" Weight: 11.11
International Honours: RoI: U21-4

A stylish full back who defends well and attacks with purpose, Steve joined Huddersfield on loan from Middlesbrough on the eve of the 1999-2000 season. Unfortunately, his stay at the McAlpine Stadium was cut short by a hamstring injury after three appearances. On transfer deadline day in March he was loaned to Darlington and went straight into the side in the right-back slot. However, after just two impressive displays he was injured and he appeared in only three more games. Steve's spell with the Quakers came to a painful conclusion when he was carried off on a stretcher after coming on as a substitute in the last game of the season at home to Lincoln.

Middlesbrough (From trainee on 24/7/1997) P/FL 6+2 FLC 2+2 FAC 0+1
Huddersfield T (Loaned on 6/8/1999) FL 3
Darlington (Loaned on 23/3/2000) FL 4+1

BAKKE Eirik
Born: Sogndal, Norway, 13 September 1977
Height: 6'2" Weight: 12.9
International Honours: Norway: 8; U21; Yth

Amid all the speculation and dealings of the 1999 close season, Eirik appeared to slip in at Elland Road unnoticed, completing a £1.75 million move from Songdal of Norway after a week's trial. What a signing! Bought by Leeds as one for the future, he was on the substitutes' bench at first but made his full debut against Newcastle in September and started two more games the following month. His big chance came when David Batty was injured at the end of November and he looked as though he'd been in the side for years. Eirik impressed immediately and his involvement and effectiveness grew as the season progressed. A strong and powerful midfielder, he has a fine first touch, and goes past opponents, using his strength and skill, almost at will. His first three goals for the club came in the FA Cup, but his first league goal was worth the wait. Picking up a through-ball on the edge of the Wimbledon box, he controlled the ball and flicked a curler past Neil Sullivan with the outside of his right foot. Eirik is an excellent deputy for Batty, and all at Elland Road will be happy that he will be at Leeds for a long time to come. He added six more caps during the season, appearing in all three of Norway's games in the Euro 2000 finals in the summer, and looks set to be a regular in the national team for the foreseeable future.

Leeds U (£1,000,000 + from Sogndal, Norway on 13/7/1999) PL 24+5/2 FLC 2 FAC 3/4 Others 9+1/2

BALDRY Simon Jonathan
Born: Huddersfield, 12 February 1976
Height: 5'10" Weight: 11.6

The right winger came on as a substitute in Huddersfield's local derby against Barnsley in October and promptly scored the winner. He then kept his place with some solid all-round displays, including a "Man of the Match" performance against Ipswich Town, only for a thigh injury to put him on the sidelines. Often called from the bench to add pace down the wing, Simon is a vital member of the squad whose strong crossing and defensive qualities are also highly prized.

Huddersfield T (From trainee on 14/7/1994) FL 44+41/4 FLC 3+3 FAC 1+1 Others 1+2/1
Bury (Loaned on 8/9/1998) FL 0+5

BALL Kevin Anthony
Born: Hastings, 12 November 1964
Height: 5'10" Weight: 12.6
Club Honours: Div 1 '96, '99

One of the saddest events of last season for all Sunderland supporters was the departure in December of the inspirational "Bally", who had served the club magnificently in defence and midfield for nine and a half years. In July 1999 a tremendous crowd of 27,506 had turned out at the Stadium of Light for Kevin's testimonial against Sampdoria, and although he did not begin the season as one of Peter Reid's first-choice players he remained club captain and an important squad member. Following sporadic appearances as a substitute, one of which saw him score his last Sunderland goal in a Worthington Cup tie at Wimbledon in October, Kevin joined First Division Fulham shortly before Christmas. Fulham manager Paul Bracewell signed his former Sunderland team-mate to perform the holding midfield role but unfortunately things didn't work out as planned. Kevin had obviously done a great job in helping Sunderland into the Premiership the previous season but the defensive outlook which resulted in the team scoring just three goals in the last 13 away matches caused Fulham to lose out even on a play-off position. Kevin always gave 100 per cent but a lack of creativity in midfield was

largely responsible for a disappointing ninth place at the end of the season.
Portsmouth (Free from Coventry C juniors on 6/10/1982) FL 96+9/4 FLC 8+1 FAC 8 Others 6
Sunderland (£350,000 on 16/7/1990) P/FL 329+10/21 FLC 23+3/4 FAC 16 Others 7/2
Fulham (£200,000 on 9/12/1999) FL 15+3 FAC 2

BALL Michael John
Born: Liverpool, 2 October 1979
Height: 5'10" Weight: 11.2
International Honours: E: U21-7; Yth; Sch
After he had been called up to Kevin Keegan's full England international squad for a trip to Hungary at the end of the previous season, the 1999-2000 campaign was a big disappointment for Michael. His most consistent run of matches – seven – ended in November and for the rest of the season he struggled to convince Walter Smith he was worth a starting place in a full-strength Everton side. At his best a sharp tackler and a good distributor, and blessed with a solid temperament, he too often failed to live up to the high standards he had set himself. The England left-back position has been a problem one for a succession of national coaches and at one time Michael looked set to progress naturally into the berth, but although he added two early-season caps for England at U21 level he was left out of the squad for the European Championships in Slovakia during the summer. It is to be hoped that he will enjoy the first real break of his young football career in the summer, and return next season refocused and ready to re-establish himself on the Premiership stage.
Everton (From trainee on 17/10/1996) PL 73+19/5 FLC 6+2 FAC 5+1

BALMER Stuart Murray
Born: Falkirk, 20 September 1969
Height: 6'0" Weight: 12.11
Club Honours: AMC '99
International Honours: S: Yth; Sch
As Wigan's acting captain, Stuart led the Latics out at Wembley in the Second Division play-off final against Gillingham at Wembley last May. He was once again a virtual ever-present at the heart of the defence in 1999-2000, and his coolness, powerful heading and timely tackles were a real asset to the promotion push. Stuart scored two league goals during the campaign, including the winner at Wycombe. The away game at Gillingham in April marked his 300th Football League match. The dominant centre back has completed a century of games in two seasons at Wigan.
Glasgow Celtic (From juniors in 1987)
Charlton Ath (£120,000 on 24/8/1990) FL 201+26/8 FLC 15 FAC 9+1 Others 11+1
Wigan Ath (£200,000 on 18/9/1998) FL 77/3 FLC 5 FAC 7 Others 11/1

BAMBER Michael (Mike) John
Born: Preston, 1 October 1980
Height: 5'7" Weight: 10.2
This youngster spent the majority of the 1999-2000 season playing in the Macclesfield reserve team. Initially employed as a full back but later in midfield, he put in some excellent performances, using his considerable pace to great advantage. Mike made what must have been one of the shortest first-team debuts ever seen when he came on from the bench for the last 21 seconds of Macc's last home game of the campaign against Rochdale. He will be hoping for a proper chance to prove himself during the coming season.
Macclesfield T (Free from Blackpool juniors on 16/12/1999) FL 0+1

BANGER Nicholas (Nicky) Lee
Born: Southampton, 25 February 1971
Height: 5'9" Weight: 11.6
A striker who can also play in midfield, Nicky started the 1999-2000 season with Oxford. In the summer he had decided against taking up the offer made to him by United but he had returned to the Manor Ground after being unable to secure a new club. However, after making just one start during the opening weeks of the campaign he was not given a new long-term deal and moved north to join Dundee in the Scottish Premier League.
Southampton (From trainee on 25/4/1989) F/PL 18+37/8 FLC 2+2/3 FAC 0+2 Others 1
Oldham Ath (£250,000 on 4/10/1994) FL 44+20/10 FLC 6/1 FAC 2+1 Others 0+1
Oxford U (Free on 24/7/1997) FL 41+22/8 FLC 6+2/1 FAC 3

BANKOLE Ademola (Ade)
Born: Abeokuta, Nigeria, 9 September 1969
Height: 6'3" Weight: 12.10
Ade, or George, as he is sometimes called, joined Queens Park Rangers in the summer of 1998, becoming the club's third-choice goalkeeper. He wasn't seen in the first team in 1998-99 and the form of Lee Harper and Ludo Miklosko meant that his opportunities were again very restricted last season. Although he was selected as substitute 'keeper when Miklosko was injured, Ade made only one appearance, coming on in the home game against Tranmere in October when Harper pulled a muscle. Later in the season he went on loan to Leyton Orient and then to Bradford, but didn't make a first-team appearance for either club.
Doncaster Rov (Free from Shooting Stars, Ibadan, Nigeria on 30/11/1995)
Leyton Orient (Free on 27/12/1995)
Crewe Alex (Free on 25/9/1996) FL 6 FLC 1
Queens Park R (£50,000 on 2/7/1998) FL 0+1

BANKS Christopher (Chris) Noel
Born: Stone, 12 November 1965
Height: 5'11" Weight: 12.2
International Honours: E: SP-2
Awarded a deserved benefit match against Aston Villa during the 1999-2000 season, Chris remained a tremendous servant to Cheltenham throughout the campaign. Returning to the Football League after a ten-year absence, he was one of the first Cheltenham players to settle at the higher level. Chris missed just five matches all season, and his central defensive partnership with Mark Freeman was a key feature of the Robins' successful campaign. A superb reader of the game who makes up for his lack of real pace with vision and positional sense, Chris is also comfortable bringing the ball out of defence and is a valuable character around the dressing room. He has signed an extended contract at Whaddon Road and states that his remaining ambition is to score another Football League goal, believing that he might then be able to claim some sort of record for the length of time between goals – his last was for Exeter City in 1990.
Port Vale (From juniors on 3/12/1982) FL 50+15/1 FLC 3+3 FAC 4 Others 8+4
Exeter C (Free on 24/6/1988) FL 43+2/1 FLC 2 FAC 1 Others 2 (Free to Bath C during 1989 close season)
Cheltenham T (Free on 11/8/1994) FL 41+1 FLC 2 FAC 2 Others 2

BANKS Steven (Steve)
Born: Hillingdon, 9 February 1972
Height: 6'0" Weight: 13.2
Despite being an excellent goalkeeper, Steve was another player who found his chances of first-team football at Bolton were limited in 1999-2000 due to the overall quality of the Wanderers squad. Vying for the goalkeeping spot with class players such as Jussi Jaaskelainen and Keith Branagan was always going to be difficult for Steve, and so it proved. He spent almost all of the season on the subs' bench due to the exceptional form (especially in the second half of the campaign) of Jaaskelainen. Steve did get a run in the starting line-up during January and he performed quite well during this time. However, once Jaaskelainen got back into the team and had his exceptional run, it became obvious that he had established himself as the first-choice 'keeper. Having said that, it must be very reassuring for Sam Allardyce to have such a talented group of 'keepers in his squad, and if Steve can get the chance to play in the first team again he may yet claim the position for good.
West Ham U (From trainee on 24/3/1990) Others 1
Gillingham (Free on 25/3/1993) FL 67 FAC 7 Others 2
Blackpool (£60,000 on 18/8/1995) FL 150 FLC 13 FAC 8 Others 10
Bolton W (£50,000 on 25/3/1999) FL 11 FLC 4 FAC 2 Others 3

BARACLOUGH Ian Robert
Born: Leicester, 4 December 1970
Height: 6'1" Weight: 12.2
Club Honours: Div 3 '98
International Honours: E: Yth
Though normally a left wing back, Ian moved successfully to a more central role for Queens Park Rangers when needed in 1999-2000 due to injuries to other players. He was one of six men to be given the captain's armband during the season. While he is not noted for his goalscoring – he has netted only once during his Rangers career – Ian made regular attacking runs forward and is a positive influence on the team. He has also gained the respect of the fans with his attitude towards the game.
Leicester C (From trainee on 15/12/1988) FAC 1 Others 0+1
Wigan Ath (Loaned on 22/3/1990) FL 8+1/2
Grimsby T (Loaned on 21/12/1990) FL 1+3
Grimsby T (Free on 13/8/1991) FL 1
Lincoln C (Free on 21/8/1992) FL 68+5/10 FLC 7/1 FAC 4 Others 7

Mansfield T (Free on 6/6/1994) FL 47/5 FLC 7 FAC 4 Others 4
Notts Co (Signed on 13/10/1995) FL 107+4/10 FLC 5+1/1 FAC 8 Others 2
Queens Park R (£50,000 on 19/3/1998) FL 94+2/1 FLC 6 FAC 3

BARDSLEY David John
Born: Manchester, 11 September 1964
Height: 5'10" Weight: 12.2
International Honours: E: 2; Yth

David is a vastly experienced defender who appeared regularly for Blackpool in the 1999-2000 campaign, mostly taking the right-back position. He is still adept at sending long balls down the flanks beyond the opposition full backs, but was unable to prevent the Seasiders from being relegated at the end of the season. David was released during the summer.

Blackpool (From apprentice on 5/11/1982) FL 45 FLC 2/1 FAC 2
Watford (£150,000 on 23/11/1983) FL 97+3/7 FLC 6/1 FAC 13+1/1 Others 1
Oxford U (£265,000 on 18/9/1987) FL 74/7 FLC 12 FAC 5 Others 3
Queens Park R (£500,000 on 15/9/1989) F/PL 252+1/4 FLC 20/1 FAC 19 Others 3/1
Blackpool (Free on 3/7/1998) FL 64 FLC 5 FAC 1 Others 4

BARKER Christopher (Chris) Andrew
Born: Sheffield, 2 March 1980
Height: 6'0" Weight: 11.8

This young Barnsley left back made his Football League debut against Tranmere last September and went on to take full advantage of Kevin Austin's injury to establish himself as a regular in the first-team line-up in 1999-2000. Chris took time to settle in, but went on to produce a series of accomplished displays and did so well that he won the club's "Young Player of the Year" award at the end of the season. He has a cultured left foot and good passing ability.

Barnsley (Signed from Alfreton on 24/8/1998) FL 28+1 FLC 4 FAC 1 Others 0+1

BARKER Richard (Richie) Ian
Born: Sheffield, 30 May 1975
Height: 6'0" Weight: 13.5
International Honours: E: Yth; Sch

Richie signed for Macclesfield in the 1999 close season and, in contrast to his introduction at Brighton, soon became a favourite with the supporters. He scored on his debut against Northampton, and regularly found the net in the first half of the season. In September Richie created a club record by scoring in five consecutive league matches. He damaged his ankle ligaments at the end of November but quickly came back and, although not fully fit, played through the pain barrier to help the team. Unfortunately, he struggled to regain his early-season form and had a goal drought over several weeks. He suffered a recurrence of the ankle injury during March, which kept him out for the remainder of the season. He is a strong and hard-working forward and looks to take advantage of goalscoring opportunities at all times. He fitted into the Macclesfield side well, finishing the season as top scorer on 17 goals. The £500,000-rated striker was reported to have attracted interest from such as Norwich, Stoke, Wigan, Bristol Rovers, Stockport, Peterborough and Rushden & Diamonds. Richie capped a fine first season at Moss Rose by being included in the PFA award-winning Third Division team.

Sheffield Wed (From trainee on 27/7/1993. Free to Linfield on 22/8/1996)
Doncaster Rov (Loaned on 29/9/1995) FL 5+1 Others 0+1
Brighton & Hove A (Free on 19/12/1997) FL 48+12/12 FLC 1+1/1 FAC 1/1 Others 1
Macclesfield T (Free on 5/7/1999) FL 35/16 FLC 2 FAC 2 Others 1/1

BARKER Simon
Born: Farnworth, 4 November 1964
Height: 5'9" Weight: 11.7
Club Honours: FMC '87
International Honours: E: U21-4

The evergreen midfielder was only a squad player with Port Vale in 1999-2000. Simon had his best game of the campaign on the season's opening day in a goalless draw at one of his old clubs, Blackburn, but only started a further three games, being deemed surplus to requirements by the manager. A skilful player on his day with an astute football brain, he expressed a wish to move into coaching and left Vale Park on a free transfer in November 1999.

Blackburn Rov (From apprentice on 6/11/1982) FL 180+2/35 FLC 11/4 FAC 12 Others 8/2
Queens Park R (£400,000 on 20/7/1988) F/PL 291+24/33 FLC 29+2/5 FAC 22+1/3 Others 7
Port Vale (Free on 11/9/1998) FL 26+6/2 FLC 1

BARLOW Martin David
Born: Barnstaple, 25 June 1971
Height: 5'7" Weight: 10.3

Martin returned to the Plymouth ranks last March, following a double operation on a groin injury in June 1999. He made his first start against Chester, but unfortunately lasted only 15 minutes before another injury took its toll. Argyle's longest-serving player, he will be looking to get fit for the start of the new campaign. The Pilgrims will be pleased to welcome back the control and passing skills of their most experienced midfielder.

Plymouth Arg (From trainee on 1/7/1989) FL 277+32/24 FLC 9+1/2 FAC 17 Others 17+1

BARLOW Stuart
Born: Liverpool, 16 July 1968
Height: 5'10" Weight: 11.0
Club Honours: AMC '99

Wigan's top scorer for the second successive season, Stuart netted 23 goals in total in 1999-2000. His acceleration and ball control again proved a constant menace to Division Two defenders. He created a club record by scoring in six successive matches in October and November, his total tally including a hat-trick in the 4-1 victory at Preston. His terrific form in the first half of the season saw him bag 21 goals by the turn of the millennium. Although his goals dried up from January onwards (due in part to an ankle operation), he returned for the play-off final against Gillingham at Wembley, coming off the bench to score what looked as though it would be the winning goal. A popular player among the fans, Stuart has since been linked with moves to Reading, Bolton and Huddersfield.

Everton (Free from Sherwood Park on 6/6/1990) F/PL 24+47/10 FLC 3+5/1 FAC 4+3/2 Others 0+2
Rotherham U (Loaned on 10/1/1992) Others 0+1
Oldham Ath (£450,000 on 20/11/1995) FL 78+15/31 FLC 5+1 FAC 6+1/1 Others 1
Wigan Ath (£45,000 on 26/3/1998) FL 72+11/40 FLC 6/3 FAC 5/3 Others 9+3/6

BARMBY Nicholas (Nick) Jonathan
Born: Hull, 11 February 1974
Height: 5'7" Weight: 11.3
International Honours: E: 15; B-2; U21-4; Yth; Sch

A typically clinical goal at Leeds in May took Nick into double figures for a single season for the first time. But it was the quality of his overall performances as much as his goals which marked the 1999-2000 season as his most successful in an Everton jersey. Employed largely as a left-sided midfielder, Nick combined deftness of touch with vision and a voracious appetite for hard work. He also displayed his versatility, regularly switching to the right flank and occasionally operating in the centre. His performances were regularly of the highest class and he was one of the driving forces behind a much-improved season for Everton. A sparkling hat-trick at Upton Park in February, the first of his professional career, was one high point of his season and another came with his recall to the full England squad. After appearing in the friendly games with Brazil, the Ukraine and Malta he made the final 22 for Euro 2000 and added two further caps when coming on from the subs' bench during the tournament.

Tottenham H (From trainee on 9/4/1991) PL 81+6/20 FLC 7+1/2 FAC 12+1/5
Middlesbrough (£5,250,000 on 8/8/1995) PL 42/8 FLC 4/1 FAC 3/1
Everton (£5,750,000 on 2/11/1996) PL 105+11/18 FLC 2+3/3 FAC 12/3

BARNARD Darren Sean
Born: Rintein, Germany, 30 November 1971
Height: 5'9" Weight: 12.3
International Honours: E: Sch. W: 12

Darren was moved to a role on the left side of midfield by new Barnsley manager Dave Bassett and responded with some fine performances and a career-best total of 15 league and cup goals. He was always a threat to opposition defences when moving forward and his crossing and powerful shooting were used to good effect in a high-scoring team. A dead-ball specialist who shared the penalties with Craig Hignett, he had the misfortune to have a vital spot kick saved in the play-off final against Ipswich, but like the true professional he is Darren vowed to put the disappointment behind him. He continued to be part of the Wales international set-up and was an ever-present during the season, adding a further six caps to his total.

Chelsea (£50,000 from Wokingham T on 25/7/1990) F/PL 18+11/2 FLC 1+1 FAC 1+1
Reading (Loaned on 18/11/1994) FL 3+1
Bristol C (£175,000 on 6/10/1995) FL 77+1/15 FLC 4/1 FAC 6 Others 6/1
Barnsley (£750,000 on 8/8/1997) P/FL 91+11/19 FLC 13+1/3 FAC 7/2 Others 3

BARNES Paul Lance
Born: Leicester, 16 November 1967
Height: 5'11" Weight: 13.6

When Bury's veteran striker went off with a hamstring injury after just twenty minutes of last season's opening game against Gillingham, it signalled the start of what was to be a frustrating, injury-hit campaign for Paul. That particular injury kept him out for six weeks as Bury tried to nurse him slowly back to fitness. Sadly, he seemed to get a few games in and score the odd goal only to then suffer another injury, a bout of flu over Christmas and an ankle injury in February bringing further lay-offs. Still a good finisher, a willing worker and a proven goalscorer, Paul also assisted on the coaching side with the youth team during the second half of the season.

Notts Co (From apprentice on 16/11/1985) FL 36+17/14 FAC 0+1 Others 4+6/5
Stoke C (£30,000 on 23/3/1990) FL 10+14/3 FLC 0+2 Others 3+1/2
Chesterfield (Loaned on 8/11/1990) FL 1 FAC 1/1
York C (£50,000 on 15/7/1992) FL 147+1/76 FLC 10/5 FAC 5 Others 16/4
Birmingham C (£350,000 on 4/3/1996) FL 15/7
Burnley (£350,000 + on 6/9/1996) FL 63+2/30 FLC 5 FAC 5/1
Huddersfield T (Signed on 16/1/1998) FL 13+17/2 FLC 0+3 FAC 1+1
Bury (£40,000 on 15/3/1999) FL 19+19/4 FLC 0+1 FAC 2 Others 1

BARNES Philip (Phil) Kenneth
Born: Sheffield, 2 March 1979
Height: 6'1" Weight: 11.1

Phil began the 1999-2000 season as first-choice 'keeper for Blackpool after some impressive performances in pre-season games but then lost his place after just three matches. He later suffered an injury in a reserve game and did not return to first-team action until last March. He is a good shot stopper with a safe pair of hands and will be looking to find regular first-team action in the coming season.

Rotherham U (From trainee on 25/6/1997) FL 2
Blackpool (£100,000 on 22/7/1997) FL 14 FLC 1 Others 2

BARNES Steven (Steve) Leslie
Born: Harrow, 5 January 1976
Height: 5'4" Weight: 10.9

The 1999-2000 season proved to be a frustrating one for Steve, as his progress at Barnet was hindered by a seemingly endless spate of injuries. Ruled out at the start of the campaign with a knee injury, he was restricted to the fringes of the first team until Darren Currie's suspension in late October provided him with an opportunity to showcase his talents. During his quartet of appearances, Steve showed both an incisive and industrious edge to his game as he shuttled down the left flank. Unfortunately, despite some flawless displays, when Currie was eligible to return Steve was sent back to the anonymity of the reserves, thus denying him the settled sequence of first-team outings that he so clearly craved. After spending another couple of months sidelined with the same injury, Steve was loaned to Welling United and he netted a couple of goals in the Wings' spirited, yet ultimately fruitless, bid to stave off the threat of relegation from the Conference. The diminutive winger was released by Barnet during the close season.

Birmingham C (£75,000 from Welling U on 9/10/1995) FL 0+3 FLC 0+1 Others 0+1
Brighton & Hove A (Loaned on 23/1/1998) FL 12
Barnet (Free on 22/10/1998) FL 4+11 FAC 0+1

BARNESS Anthony
Born: Lewisham, 25 March 1973
Height: 5'10" Weight: 13.1
Club Honours: Div 1 '00

Although he was given the Charlton number two shirt at the start of the 1999-2000 season, injury prevented Anthony from playing in the first few games, and when he was fit again he had to be content with the substitutes' bench until he regained his first-team place in February. After a couple of indifferent performances he quickly got back to his best form and retained his place in the side for the rest of the season, playing an important role in Charlton's march to the First Division championship. A good defender, equally comfortable in either full-back berth, he gets forward whenever possible and likes to make runs into the opposing penalty area, where he will put in a cross or try for goal himself. Anthony was released during the summer. Stop Press: It was reported at the beginning of July that he had signed for Bolton Wanderers.

Charlton Ath (From trainee on 6/3/1991) FL 21+6/1 FLC 2 FAC 3 Others 1+1/1
Chelsea (£350,000 on 8/9/1992) PL 12+2 FLC 2 Others 2+1
Middlesbrough (Loaned on 12/8/1993) Others 1
Southend U (Loaned on 2/2/1996) FL 5
Charlton Ath (£165,000 on 8/8/1996) P/FL 83+13/3 FLC 5 FAC 3+1 Others 1+1

BARNETT David (Dave) Kwame
Born: London, 16 April 1967
Height: 6'1" Weight: 13.12
Club Honours: AMC '95; Div 2 '95

This solid centre back was signed by Lincoln in the summer of 1999 to add strength to a depleted defence. In addition to his qualities as a defender, he also contributed a useful supply of goals during 1999-2000 from set-piece moves. He had five different partners in the centre of defence in the first half of the season as the Imps struggled to overcome their horrendous injury problems. Dave was dropped in the middle of January and was then loaned to Conference club Forest Green Rovers in February. He was one of a number of Nationwide League players selected to represent the Cayman Islands in a World Cup qualifier against Cuba early in 2000 but was then ruled ineligible at the last minute, having already flown out to the Caribbean. At the end of the season he was made available on a free transfer.

Colchester U (Signed from Windsor & Eton on 25/8/1988) FL 19+1 FLC 2 FAC 3+2 Others 3 (Freed in June 1988)
West Bromwich A (Free from Edmonton Oilers, Canada on 13/10/1989)
Walsall (Free on 17/7/1990) FL 4+1 FLC 2 (Free to Kidderminster Hrs on 1/10/1990)
Barnet (£10,000 on 29/2/1992) FL 58+1/3 FLC 5 FAC 3 Others 5
Birmingham C (£150,000 on 20/12/1993) FL 45+1 FLC 1 FAC 5 Others 8
Dunfermline Ath (Free on 18/7/1997) SL 21/1 SLC 3 SC 2
Port Vale (Free on 20/3/1998) FL 34+2/1 FAC 1
Lincoln C (Free on 28/7/1999) FL 20+2/3 FLC 1 FAC 3/1 Others 1

BARNETT Jason Vincent
Born: Shrewsbury, 21 April 1976
Height: 5'9" Weight: 11.6

Jason signed a new contract with Lincoln in the summer of 1999 but unluckily suffered a toe injury on the first day of the new season. He played the first 45 minutes of the following match but then underwent an operation and was out of action until February. He eventually won his first-team place back and finished 1999-2000 as a regular in the Imps' starting line-up. He was mostly used as an attacking right back but also occasionally appeared as part of a three-man central defence.

Wolverhampton W (From trainee on 4/7/1994)
Lincoln C (£5,000 on 26/10/1995) FL 139+9/3 FLC 6 FAC 7 Others 8

BARR William (Billy) Joseph
Born: Halifax, 21 January 1969
Height: 5'11" Weight: 10.8

Billy's 1999-2000 season ended in February with a bad injury in Carlisle's game with Shrewsbury. Until then he had featured in the majority of United's matches either at full back or in central defence. He was perhaps more comfortable in the latter role, but was always a hard-working performer who did all that could be expected of him. The injury will sideline the Cumbrians' former captain until Christmas but Billy will have to recover away from Brunton Park as he was released in May.

Halifax T (From trainee on 6/7/1987) FL 178+18/13 FLC 8+1/2 FAC 11+1/2 Others 14+3
Crewe Alex (Free on 17/6/1994) FL 73+12/7 FLC 2 FAC 4 Others 8+1
Carlisle U (Free on 18/7/1997) FL 88+3/3 FLC 7+1 FAC 2 Others 4

BARRAS Anthony (Tony)
Born: Billingham, 29 March 1971
Height: 6'0" Weight: 13.0

This stout-hearted central defender made an impact after joining Walsall from Reading during the 1999 pre-season for a trial period and was signed more permanently in September. His timely interventions and command in the air earned him the "Man of the Match" award in his debut game against Swindon on the opening day of the new campaign and he also showed his worth in snatching vital goals. In the early part of the season he scored in three successive games and he also headed a fine equaliser against Wolves in January.

Hartlepool U (From trainee on 6/7/1989) FL 9+3 FLC 2 FAC 1 Others 1
Stockport Co (Free on 23/7/1990) FL 94+5/5 FLC 2 FAC 7 Others 19+1
Rotherham U (Loaned on 25/2/1994) FL 5/1
York C (£25,000 on 18/7/1994) FL 167+4/11 FLC 16/2 FAC 10/1 Others 8+1/1
Reading (£20,000 on 19/3/1999) FL 4+2/1
Walsall (£20,000 on 16/7/1999) FL 19+5/4 FLC 4/1 FAC 1

BARRASS Matthew (Matt) Robert
Born: Bury, 28 February 1980
Height: 5'11" Weight: 12.0

One of a number of Bury-born youngsters to be given their chance by the Shakers during the season, this promising defender was undoubtedly the pick of the bunch. Matt made his Football League debut under the management of Neil Warnock in an away game at Bristol Rovers in November, but went on to gain a regular place at right back during the second half of the campaign under new boss Andy Preece. Strong in the tackle and good in the air, Matt signed an extended two-year contract in February and the only blip on an otherwise highly successful season for the defender was a harsh dismissal in waterlogged conditions at home to Blackpool in April.

Bury (From trainee on 19/5/1999) FL 24+1/1 FLC 0+1 Others 1

BARRETT Adam Nicholas
Born: Dagenham, 29 November 1979
Height: 5'10" Weight: 12.0

Having returned from a scholarship in the USA, Adam gained a 12-month contract with Plymouth after impressing in the reserves in the latter stages of 1998-99. He became a firm favourite with the Home Park faithful last season after some commanding performances at the heart of the defence. A left-sided defender who is towering in the air and also a confident passer of the ball, the former Leyton Orient trainee is dangerous at set plays, as was shown by his winning goal against high-flying Swansea in April. Already a regular Pilgrim, Adam is definitely one to watch for the future.

Plymouth Arg (Free from USA football scholarship on 13/1/1999) FL 38+5/3 FLC 2 FAC 6+1 Others 1

BARRETT Daniel (Danny) Thomas
Born: Bradford, 25 September 1980
Height: 6'0" Weight: 11.12

A young player of great promise who emerged from Chesterfield's academy scheme, Danny has yet to settle on his best position. He can operate in central defence, on the right of midfield or up front, which is where he made his first-team debut against Notts County in the Spireites' penultimate game of 1999-2000. He has good balance, vision and positional awareness, and when he was given his chance by caretaker boss Nicky Law he seized it with both hands, coming off the bench to set up a goal for David Reeves with a lovely flick-on, and proving a handful for the County defence.

Chesterfield (From trainee on 2/7/1999) FL 0+2

BARRETT Graham
Born: Dublin, 6 October 1981
Height: 5'10" Weight: 11.7
Club Honours: FAYC '00
International Honours: RoI: U21-5; Yth (UEFA-U16 '98); Sch

Graham is an exciting young Arsenal striker for whom a bright future is predicted. A member of the Republic of Ireland U16 team that won the European title in 1998, he made his debut at U21 level against the Czech Republic in February, adding a further cap against Greece and also appearing in the three Toulon Tournament fixtures during the summer break. He played regularly in both the U19 and reserve teams at Highbury last season, and made his senior debut when he came on as a substitute in the Premiership game at Leicester early in December.

Arsenal (From trainee on 14/10/1998) PL 0+2

BARRETT Paul David
Born: Newcastle, 13 April 1978
Height: 5'11" Weight: 11.5
International Honours: E: Yth

This industrious Wrexham midfield player was in and out of the first team during 1999-2000, his first full season with the club. Paul was enjoying a spell of good form when he suffered a knee injury in the 4-1 defeat at Oxford last February and as a result minor surgery was required to clear some floating bone near the cartilage. He can play on either flank, bringing aggression and enthusiasm to the side. Although he is not a regular goalscorer, he netted twice during the season, at Wycombe last August and at Scunthorpe in February.

Newcastle U (From trainee on 20/6/1996)
Wrexham (Free on 24/3/1999) FL 25+3/2 FAC 1+1 Others 1

BARRETT Scott
Born: Ilkeston, 2 April 1963
Height: 6'0" Weight: 14.4
Club Honours: GMVC '92; FAT '92

Scott was Leyton Orient's regular first-choice goalkeeper in 1999-2000. Although now in the veteran stage, he is still very agile and is a good shot stopper. Scott held off the challenge of Ashley Bayes for most of the season, only losing his place in the closing weeks. His form warranted another year's contract, and Scott will be aiming to regain his place during the new season.

Wolverhampton W (Signed from Ilkeston T on 27/9/1984) FL 30 FLC 1 FAC 1 Others 3
Stoke C (£10,000 on 24/7/1987) FL 51 FLC 2 FAC 3 Others 4
Colchester U (Loaned on 10/1/1990) FL 13
Stockport Co (Loaned on 22/3/1990) FL 10 Others 2
Gillingham (Free on 14/8/1992) FL 51 FLC 7 FAC 4 Others 4
Cambridge U (Free on 2/8/1995) FL 119 FLC 6 FAC 7 Others 3
Leyton Orient (Free on 25/1/1999) FL 49 FLC 2 FAC 1 Others 3

BARRICK Dean
Born: Hemsworth, 30 September 1969
Height: 5'9" Weight: 12.0
Club Honours: Div 3 '96

After being frozen out of the first-team picture at Bury for nine months, Dean earned a call-up at left back against Wycombe Wanderers last September but, despite always being a reliable defender, was unable to command a regular place over the months that followed. He also suffered a bad groin injury, in an FA Cup replay at Cardiff in November, which needed surgery, and after a lengthy spell on the sidelines was then sent off in his comeback game in the reserves in January. To compound his ill-luck, upon gaining another first-team call-up, he suffered a particularly nasty injury in Bury's 1-0 win at Chesterfield in March, fracturing his eye socket in two places and breaking his nose.

Sheffield Wed (From trainee on 7/5/1988) FL 11/2
Rotherham U (£50,000 on 14/2/1991) FL 96+3/7 FLC 6 FAC 8 Others 5/1
Cambridge U (£50,000 on 11/8/1993) FL 90+1/3 FLC 7/1 FAC 7/1 Others 6
Preston NE (Signed on 11/9/1995) FL 98+11/1 FLC 7+1/1 FAC 5 Others 6
Bury (Free on 3/7/1998) FL 28+9/1 FLC 5+2 FAC 1+1
Ayr U (Loaned on 19/2/1999) SL 11 SC 2

BARRON Michael James
Born: Chester le Street, 22 December 1974
Height: 5'11" Weight: 11.9

The club's "Player of the Year" in the previous two seasons, Hartlepool's popular captain had another impressive campaign in 1999-2000. He led by example to help take Pool to their first-ever appearance in the end-of-season play-offs. A dependable central defender who occasionally operates in midfield, Michael continues to play every game to the best of his ability and is someone who always likes to be involved. He has been an automatic first-team choice for three years, and is a player who has typically made fast recoveries whenever he has been out injured.

Middlesbrough (From trainee on 2/2/1993) P/FL 2+1 FLC 1 Others 3+3
Hartlepool U (Loaned on 6/9/1996) FL 16
Hartlepool U (Free on 8/7/1997) FL 110+1/1 FLC 5 FAC 4 Others 10

BARRY Gareth
Born: Hastings, 23 February 1981
Height: 6'0" Weight: 12.6
International Honours: E: 2; U21-4; Yth

This rising star had another great season for Aston Villa in 1999-2000 and already seems to be destined for a long and successful career in top-class football. Gareth broke into the first team last September and remained an essential member of the side through to the end of the season, going on to appear in the starting line-up for the FA Cup final against Chelsea. He was predominantly used in the centre of Villa's defence alongside Gareth Southgate and Ugo Ehiogu but also had a short spell in the left-back position when Alan Wright was injured. He is developing into a very composed defender with anticipation beyond his years. He also continued his rapid progress in the England set-up, captaining the U18s last autumn then recording a further U21 appearance against Yugoslavia in March before going on to make his full international debut, appearing as a substitute against the Ukraine and Malta in the run-up to Euro 2000. It seems only a matter of time before he becomes a fixture in the England defence.

Aston Villa (From trainee on 27/2/1998) PL 58+6/3 FLC 8 FAC 8 Others 3

BARRY-MURPHY Brian
Born: Cork, Ireland, 27 July 1978
Height: 6'0" Weight: 12.4
International Honours: RoI: U21-6; Yth

A strong-running left-sided midfielder

signed from Cork City shortly before the start of the 1999-2000 season, Brian made his Preston debut as a substitute at Wrexham in the Worthington Cup three weeks later. After appearing for the Republic of Ireland U21s against Yugoslavia and Malta he was unfortunately sidelined by a cartilage operation in October. When fit again, he made unwanted history on his full debut against Wrexham in the Auto Windscreens Shield when he became the first player sent off under the experimental "10-yard" rule, having earlier been booked. A second cartilage operation to his other knee meant he had to wait until the last game of the season at Bristol City to get his first taste of league action, appearing as a late substitute.
Preston NE (Free from Cork C on 3/8/1999) FL 0+1 FLC 0+1 Others 1

BART-WILLIAMS Christopher (Chris) Gerald
Born: Freetown, Sierra Leone, 16 June 1974
Height: 5'11" Weight: 11.6
Club Honours: Div 1 '98
International Honours: E: B-1; U21-16; Yth
This vastly experienced Nottingham Forest player appeared in five different positions in 1999-2000 and excelled in every one, further underlining his value to the squad by captaining the team in Riccardo Scimeca's absence. Chris is essentially a midfielder with great awareness and tremendous stamina. He netted eight times in league and cup games for the Reds, including five from the penalty spot.
Leyton Orient (From trainee on 18/7/1991) FL 34+2/2 FLC 4 Others 2
Sheffield Wed (£275,000 on 21/11/1991) F/PL 95+29/16 FLC 14+2/4 FAC 9+3/2 Others 1+3/2
Nottingham F (£2,500,000 on 1/7/1995) F/PL 137+7/13 FLC 12/1 FAC 13/2 Others 7+1

BARTON Warren Dean
Born: Stoke Newington, 19 March 1969
Height: 6'0" Weight: 12.0
International Honours: E: 3; B-3
Signed by Kevin Keegan for what was then a record British fee for a defender, Warren has now completed five years at Newcastle under four different managers. Although he was initially a cornerstone of the side, his career had stuttered somewhat for a couple of years, but through diligent application, hard work and commitment he re-established himself in 1999-2000 and by the end of a very successful season his was one of the first names on the team sheet. A wholehearted player who always gives of his best, Warren's professional, energetic, all-action style enables him to play in various positions, but last season saw him used on the right flank, primarily as a full back or wing back depending on the defensive formation used. His experience and reliability have allowed him to become a leader on the field, and his liking for racing down the wing allied to his crossing ability enable him to quickly turn defence into attack. He was sent off for the first time in his life at Coventry, but apart from the subsequent suspension he was a regular in the side, earning his place with his consistently high standard of play. Warren hopes to move into management at the end of his playing career, and to that end he became the first Newcastle player to take the UEFA "B" coaching badge, planning to take the "A" qualification next year, but the move into management may be deferred a while yet if he maintains the form he showed last season. Meanwhile he is gaining early experience by running regular coaching sessions for local youngsters.
Maidstone U (£10,000 from Leytonstone on 28/7/1989) FL 41+1 FLC 0+2 FAC 3/1 Others 7
Wimbledon (£300,000 on 7/6/1990) F/PL 178+2/10 FLC 16/1 FAC 11 Others 2
Newcastle U (£4,500,000 on 5/6/1995) PL 111+19/4 FLC 10/1 FAC 18+2 Others 14+2

BARTRAM Vincent (Vince) Lee
Born: Birmingham, 7 August 1968
Height: 6'2" Weight: 13.4
Vince put in some impressive performances as Gillingham's goalkeeper in the 1999-2000 season. He suffered a slight dip in form in September when on-loan Anthony Williams replaced him for a few games but otherwise he was a near-ever-present as the Gills battled their way to promotion via the play-offs. Tall and agile, he has a safe pair of hands and shows good command in the air.
Wolverhampton W (From juniors on 17/8/1985) FL 5 FLC 2 FAC 3
Blackpool (Loaned on 27/10/1989) FL 9 Others 2
Bournemouth (£65,000 on 24/7/1991) FL 132 FLC 10 FAC 14 Others 6
Arsenal (£400,000 on 10/8/1994) PL 11 FLC 0+1
Huddersfield T (Loaned on 17/10/1997) FL 12
Gillingham (Free on 20/3/1998) FL 96 FLC 4 FAC 8 Others 10

BARWICK Terence (Terry) Patrick
Born: Sheffield, 11 January 1983
Height: 5'11" Weight: 10.12
A first-year trainee at Scunthorpe, Terry was rewarded for a string of excellent displays in the juniors and reserves in 1999-2000 by being called into the first-team squad for the final game of the season at home to Burnley. He started on the substitutes' bench but came on at half time and produced a mature performance in the second period, not looking out of place in Division Two. A tough-tackling midfielder whose strengths are winning the ball and passing it, he was part of the Scunthorpe juniors squad that got to Wembley in April and should have a bright future in the game.
Scunthorpe U (Trainee) FL 0+1

BASHAM Michael (Mike)
Born: Barking, 27 September 1973
Height: 6'2" Weight: 13.9
Club Honours: AMC '94
International Honours: E: Yth; Sch
Once again, Mike's progress was hindered by a succession of injuries in 1999-2000; however, following a series of accomplished displays, he remains the most cultured central defender on Barnet's books. During the club's pre-season schedule he was sidelined with a knee injury, and then a recurring ankle knock prevented him from establishing himself in the side's central defensive trio. Yet the former England youth international was able to exhibit signs of his outstanding ability in the latter stages of the campaign, when he was allocated the role of the polished centrepiece in the Bees' backline. He laboured ceaselessly to regain his fitness and when his opportunity arose he effortlessly assimilated into the line-up that attained a coveted play-off place. His aspirations of featuring in the post-season drama appeared to be somewhat ill-fated when he suffered a severe laceration to the forehead in the club's final league match at Underhill against Leyton Orient. However, after requiring 14 stitches to his deep wound, he returned to the side and his impeccable distribution and awareness brought a sense of calm to the Bees' defence.
West Ham U (From trainee on 3/7/1992)
Colchester U (Loaned on 18/11/1993) FL 1
Swansea C (Free on 24/3/1994) FL 27+2/1 FAC 6 Others 8+2
Peterborough U (Free on 18/12/1995) FL 17+2/1 FLC 1 FAC 0+1
Barnet (Free on 5/8/1997) FL 66+1/2 FLC 1 FAC 0+1 Others 6+1

BASHAM Steven (Steve) Brian
Born: Southampton, 2 December 1977
Height: 5'11" Weight: 12.0
Club Honours: Div 2 '00
After a sensational loan spell at Deepdale in 1998-99, Steve opted to leave Southampton and sign permanently for Preston during the summer of 1999, but a groin operation meant he was not fully fit for the start of the season. A versatile goalscorer, with two quick feet and an ability to get in front of his marker, he soon opened his account, his first start bringing a goal at Wrexham in the Worthington Cup, and in all he scored three times in five games before a knee injury put him out again. His bad luck did not end there, for when returning to fitness he turned his ankle, and he did not start another game until February. He will be looking to relaunch his Preston career next season, and once more become a major threat to opposition defences, having failed to score again after 1 September, although he did end the season with the consolation of a Second Division championship medal.
Southampton (From trainee on 24/5/1996) PL 1+18/1 FLC 0+1
Wrexham (Loaned on 6/2/1998) FL 4+1
Preston NE (£200,000 on 5/2/1999) FL 26+15/12 FLC 1+1/1 FAC 0+1

BASS Jonathan (Jon) David
Born: Weston super Mare, 1 January 1976
Height: 6'0" Weight: 12.2
International Honours: E: Sch
This hard-working Birmingham City defender once again found it impossible to dislodge Gary Rowett from the right-back position in 1999-2000. He was one of several fringe players given an outing in the Worthington Cup game at Exeter last August and had two brief runs in the first team in the autumn thanks to the Blues' dreadful injury problems. He moved on loan to Gillingham on transfer deadline day in a bid to gain regular first-team action and had a fine debut for the Gills against Colchester. Jon retained his place until Adrian Pennock was fit again, then made a few more

appearances from the subs' bench before returning to St Andrews.
Birmingham C (From juniors on 27/6/1994) FL 60+7 FLC 7+1 FAC 5
Carlisle U (Loaned on 11/10/1996) FL 3
Gillingham (Loaned on 23/3/2000) FL 4+3

BASSINDER Gavin David
Born: Mexborough, 24 September 1979
Height: 5'8" Weight: 11.1
This former Barnsley trainee made his debut in senior football last September in the Worthington Cup tie against Stockport County but failed to break into the first team again and eventually moved on a free transfer to Mansfield at the beginning of March, initially on trial. After an outing for the reserves he was given a contract until the end of the season, with a lengthier contract on offer. Gavin was awarded the match sponsor's "Man of the Match" award on his debut against Macclesfield. He is a more than useful right-sided player who is equally at home in either defence or midfield. Gavin was not offered a new contract when his trial period ended in May.
Barnsley (From trainee on 7/7/1998) FLC 1
Mansfield T (Free on 10/3/2000) FL 1+3

BASTOW Darren John
Born: Torquay, 22 December 1981
Height: 5'11" Weight: 12.0
As he looked ahead to 1999-2000, Darren was aiming to continue his fine form from the previous season, when he became Plymouth's youngest-ever goalscorer. He started in the early games of the campaign, and also spent a week's trial at Premiership Derby County. He returned to Argyle to score back-to-back goals against Brighton and Southend in November but, due to lack of form and fitness, his last appearance in the first team was at Swansea in December. Despite his more recent disappointments, the young midfielder has shown that he is capable of playing at a higher level.
Plymouth Arg (From trainee on 13/1/1999) FL 28+14/3 FLC 2 FAC 6+2/1 Others 1

BATES James (Jamie) Alan
Born: Croydon, 24 February 1968
Height: 6'2" Weight: 14.0
Club Honours: Div 3 '92, '99
This tall and commanding central defender was again a tower of strength at the back for Wycombe in the 1999-2000 season. He scored his first goal for the Chairboys when blasting home a free kick against Scunthorpe last January but then sustained ankle ligament damage in the next match that kept him out of action until April. Jamie produced a number of match-saving performances, particularly away from home, where he seemed to soak up the pressure from opposition strikers with ease.
Brentford (From trainee on 1/6/1987) FL 399+20/18 FLC 37+3/3 FAC 20+1/2 Others 44/1
Wycombe W (Free on 25/3/1999) FL 39+2/1 FLC 4 FAC 5

BATTERSBY Anthony (Tony)
Born: Doncaster, 30 August 1975
Height: 6'0" Weight: 12.7
Lincoln's joint record signing found it difficult to get into the Imps' first team at the start of the 1999-2000 season and was loaned to Northampton in September. The timing of the move was unfortunate as shortly after his arrival at Sixfields manager Ian Atkins left the club. A big striker who is able to hold the ball up effectively and lay it off accurately to his colleagues, Tony made only three appearances for the Cobblers, all as a substitute, and was on the field for a total of just 45 minutes, but still managed to score one of the goals in a 3-0 win over Torquay. New manager Kevin Wilson decided not to pursue the option of a permanent move and Tony returned to Sincil Bank after a month. He was finally given his chance by Lincoln in January and responded with three goals in three games before dropping back into the reserves. Although he still has another year of his contract to run, the club informed him at the end of the season that he could leave on a free transfer.
Sheffield U (From trainee on 5/7/1993) FL 3+7/1 FLC 1+1 Others 2+1/1
Southend U (Loaned on 23/3/1995) FL 6+2/1
Notts Co (£200,000 on 8/1/1996) FL 20+19/8 FLC 1 FAC 0+3 Others 4
Bury (£125,000 on 3/3/1997) FL 37+11/8 FLC 3+1/1 FAC 2
Lincoln C (£75,000 on 8/8/1998) FL 42+13/10 FLC 2/1 FAC 2/1 Others 3/1
Northampton T (Loaned on 24/9/1999) FL 0+3/1

Tony Battersby

BATTY David
Born: Leeds, 2 December 1968
Height: 5'8" Weight: 12.0
Club Honours: Div 2 '90, Div 1 '92; CS '92
International Honours: E: 42; B-5; U21-7
When David O'Leary brought David back to Leeds from Newcastle United in December 1998, it was like the return of the Prodigal Son. Looked upon as a vital part of a mainly young side, David began the 1999-2000 season in style, his tactical moves proving invaluable. He constantly made himself available for the ball, and his fierce tackling, his approach to the game and, above all, his experience made him a key figure in the Leeds line-up. He was an ever-present at the start of the season, but in late November he had to leave the field in the game against Southampton. Amid media stories of a heart problem, David then spent the rest of the season on the sidelines trying to overcome a calf injury. His influence was sorely missed, never more so than towards the end of the campaign, when his presence could have proved invaluable both for Leeds and for England in the European Championship. United can only hope he makes a full recovery in time for the coming season.
Leeds U (From trainee on 3/8/1987) F/PL 201+10/4 FLC 17 FAC 12 Others 17
Blackburn Rov (£2,750,000 on 26/10/1993) PL 53+1/1 FLC 6 FAC 5 Others 6
Newcastle U (£3,750,000 on 2/3/1996) PL 81+2/3 FLC 6 FAC 9/1 Others 16
Leeds U (£4,400,000 on 9/12/1998) PL 26 FLC 2 Others 4

BAYES Ashley John
Born: Lincoln, 19 April 1972
Height: 6'1" Weight: 13.5
International Honours: E: Yth
Ashley joined Leyton Orient on a free transfer under the Bosman ruling from Exeter in June 1999. He was unlucky to find Scott Barrett in such fine form, and spent much of the season on the subs' bench after being first choice at his previous clubs. When called upon, he didn't let the side down, and his personal highlight was a penalty save at Grimsby in the Worthington Cup. Ashley finished the season as first choice and will be hoping to hold off Scott's challenge in 2000-01.
Brentford (From trainee on 5/7/1990) FL 4 FLC 5 FAC 2 Others 1
Torquay U (Free on 13/8/1993) FL 97 FLC 7 FAC 9 Others 6
Exeter C (Free on 31/7/1996) FL 127 FLC 6 FAC 8 Others 4
Leyton Orient (Free on 5/7/1999) FL 17 FLC 2 FAC 1 Others 1

BAYLISS David (Dave) Anthony
Born: Liverpool, 8 June 1976
Height: 5'11" Weight: 12.4
Rochdale's longest-serving player, Dave regained his position in the centre of the defence at the start of the 1999-2000 season. He then suffered an injury that kept him out for a couple of months, but regained his place when Keith Hill and Mark Monington were injured. Dave turned in some top-class performances, netting spectacular goals into the bargain. A volleyed winner against Chester in February was particularly memorable.
Rochdale (From trainee on 10/6/1995) FL 119+17/6 FLC 8 FAC 4+3 Others 10+1

BAZELEY Darren Shaun
Born: Northampton, 5 October 1972
Height: 5'10" Weight: 11.7
Club Honours: Div 2 '98
International Honours: E: U21-1
Darren surprisingly left promoted Watford in the summer of 1999, remaining in Division One with Wolves. It was also strange that Wolves should have signed a right back, as they had two good players contesting that place. However, Darren often performed on the right of midfield,

and showed his attacking flair by scoring the Wolves goal in two successive pre-season friendlies. He made a steady start competitively, though he did shine at Ipswich in November. By January he was the only ever-present, and one of his typically accurate crosses created a goal at Walsall. He was a good team player and produced consistently sound displays, yet he was capable of the spectacular, too, making a good run, then cutting in to score with a neat, low shot against Tranmere. In the next home match Darren netted from outside the area with a curling left-foot shot, although he missed an easy chance to equalise at Norwich in April. He ended the season with a 100 per cent appearance record and was on the field throughout Wolves' 51 matches.
Watford (From trainee on 6/5/1991) FL 187+53/21 FLC 13+5/2 FAC 12+1/3 Others 9+1/1
Wolverhampton W (Free on 13/7/1999) FL 46/3 FLC 2 FAC 3

BEADLE Peter Clifford William James
Born: Lambeth, 13 May 1972
Height: 6'1" Weight: 13.7
Peter began the 1999-2000 season as a first choice in the Notts County team but quickly lost his place to Duane Darby and was then restricted to outings from the subs' bench before moving on to Bristol City in October. A big, strong target man who leads the line well, he received an unenthusiastic welcome from the City fans, who well remembered his match-winning goal for Bristol Rovers at Ashton Gate four years earlier. Peter was never going to win over all his critics, but he did enough to impress the more sensible supporters as he formed a partnership with Tony Thorpe that helped turn the Robins' season around in the new year. His four goals in the Auto Windscreens Shield went a long way to taking City to the final, allowing the club to generate much-needed revenue following the massive loss of the previous season.
Gillingham (From trainee on 5/5/1990) FL 42+25/14 FLC 2+4/2 FAC 1+1 Others 1
Tottenham H (£300,000 on 4/6/1992)
Bournemouth (Loaned on 25/3/1993) FL 9/2
Southend U (Loaned on 4/3/1994) FL 8/1
Watford (Signed on 12/9/1994) FL 12+11/1 FLC 1
Bristol Rov (£50,000 on 17/11/1995) FL 98+11/39 FLC 2+1 FAC 5/2 Others 7+1/1
Port Vale (£300,000 on 6/8/1998) FL 18+5/6 FLC 2 FAC 1
Notts Co (£250,000 on 18/2/1999) FL 14+8/3 FLC 1+3
Bristol C (£200,000 on 19/10/1999) FL 22+3/6 FAC 3 Others 4+2/4

BEAGRIE Peter Sydney
Born: Middlesbrough, 28 November 1965
Height: 5'8" Weight: 12.0
International Honours: E: B-2; U21-2
This talented player had a great 1999-2000 season in midfield for Bradford City, his vast experience proving invaluable to the Premiership new boys. He is a great favourite of the club's supporters with his dazzling runs down the wing, superb crossing ability and willingness to help out with defensive duties. Peter showed he could find the net, too, scoring with a 30-yard drive against Leeds and contributing two goals to the vital 3-0 win over Wimbledon towards the end of the season. In January it was reported that he had agreed a one-year extension to his current contract which was due to expire in the summer.
Middlesbrough (From juniors on 10/9/1983) FL 24+9/2 FLC 1 Others 1+1
Sheffield U (£35,000 on 16/8/1986) FL 81+3/11 FLC 5 FAC 5 Others 4
Stoke C (£210,000 on 29/6/1988) FL 54/7 FLC 4 FAC 3/1
Everton (£750,000 on 2/11/1989) F/PL 88+26/11 FLC 7+2/3 FAC 7+2 Others 5+1/1
Sunderland (Loaned on 26/9/1991) FL 5/1
Manchester C (£1,100,000 on 24/3/1994) F/PL 46+6/3 FLC 8/1 FAC 4+1/1
Bradford C (£50,000 on 2/7/1997) P/FL 104+8/19 FLC 9/3 FAC 5
Everton (Loaned on 26/3/1998) PL 4+2

BEALL Matthew John
Born: Enfield, 4 December 1977
Height: 5'7" Weight: 10.12
Matthew was an important part of the Leyton Orient midfield during the early stages of 1999-2000. He lost his place owing to injury and the form of the other midfielders at the club but remained a valuable member of the squad. Despite his lack of height, he is an excellent tackler; he uses the ball well, and also has a good engine that allows him to get from box to box. Matthew, who followed O's boss Tommy Taylor to Brisbane Road from Cambridge, can also play at right back, if required.
Cambridge U (From trainee on 28/3/1996) FL 73+8/7 FLC 2 FAC 6/2 Others 1+1
Leyton Orient (Signed on 26/10/1998) FL 43+13/3 FLC 2 FAC 6 Others 3

BEARD Mark
Born: Roehampton, 8 October 1974
Height: 5'10" Weight: 11.3
Southend United's 1998-99 "Player of the Year", Mark once again gave his full commitment to the cause last season, regardless of the position he was asked to fill. His immense stamina and strong tackling made him ideal as a wing back, a position that he made his own for the majority of the campaign. However, it was with some reluctance that manager Alan Little released Mark in May. He felt Martyn Booty, Gary Cross and Tom McDonald could fill the right-wing-back berth.
Millwall (From trainee on 18/3/1993) FL 32+13/2 FLC 3+1 FAC 4/1
Sheffield U (£117,000 on 18/8/1995) FL 22+16 FLC 2+1 FAC 2+2
Southend U (Loaned on 24/10/1997) FL 6+2 Others 1
Southend U (Free on 6/7/1998) FL 74+4/1 FLC 1 FAC 2 Others 1

BEASANT David (Dave) John
Born: Willesden, 20 March 1959
Height: 6'4" Weight: 14.3
Club Honours: Div 4 '83, Div 2 '89; Div 1 '98; FAC '88; FMC '90
International Honours: E: 2; B-7

Dave Beasant

This veteran Nottingham Forest goalkeeper seemed to improve as the 1999-2000 campaign wore on. He came into the first team last December when Mark Crossley was dropped and kept his place for the rest of the season. Big, strong and brave, he provided a fine example for the club's younger professionals. He became the oldest player to appear in the Football League for the Reds when he played against Port Vale at the City Ground on 29 April 2000 at the age of 41 years 39 days, breaking Sam Hardy's record set some 76 years previously.

Wimbledon (£1,000 from Edgware T on 7/8/1979) FL 340 FLC 21 FAC 27 Others 3
Newcastle U (£800,000 on 13/6/1988) FL 20 FLC 2 FAC 2 Others 1
Chelsea (£725,000 on 14/1/1989) F/PL 133 FLC 11 FAC 5 Others 8
Grimsby T (Loaned on 24/10/1992) FL 6
Wolverhampton W (Loaned on 12/1/1993) FL 4 FAC 1
Southampton (£300,000 on 4/11/1993) PL 86+2 FLC 8 FAC 9
Nottingham F (Free on 22/8/1997) P/FL 94 FLC 6+1 FAC 5

BEATTIE James Scott
Born: Lancaster, 27 February 1978
Height: 6'1" Weight: 12.0
International Honours: E: U21-5

For James, 1999-2000 was a season of unfortunate injuries. A groin operation at the end of the previous campaign was followed by a fall on the eve of the new season which kept him out of the Southampton side for nearly two months. When fit again, the powerful striker found competition for places stronger; with manager Dave Jones adopting a 4-5-1 system away from home, chances were limited. When he plays, he is good in the air and has great physical presence, while his passion makes him popular with the Southampton fans. He added a further U21 cap when appearing against Poland last September.

Blackburn Rov (From trainee on 7/3/1995) PL 1+3 FLC 2 FAC 0+1
Southampton (£1,000,000 on 17/7/1998) PL 30+23/5 FLC 2+3/1 FAC 2+1

BEAUCHAMP Joseph (Joey) Daniel
Born: Oxford, 13 March 1971
Height: 5'10" Weight: 12.11

A winger who, at his most effective, is capable of opening up the best defences with a mixture of skill and pace, Joey had a slightly disappointing season for Oxford in 1999-2000, scoring only six times as defenders sought to cut out his crosses and make things difficult for him after his previous successful seasons in the Second Division. Joey's best game was against Bristol City when he hit a brace in United's biggest win of the season. He also scored the winner when United caused a shock at Everton in the Worthington Cup. He was a virtual ever present until early March when he suffered a groin injury that limited him to just one substitute appearance in the last 12 matches – his longest spell of injury in all his time at the Manor Ground.

Oxford U (From trainee on 16/5/1989) FL 117+7/20 FLC 6+1/2 FAC 8/3 Others 5+1
Swansea C (Loaned on 30/10/1991) FL 5/2 Others 1
West Ham U (£1,000,000 on 22/6/1994)
Swindon T (£850,000 on 18/8/1994) FL 39+6/3 FLC 7+2/1 FAC 2 Others 4
Oxford U (£75,000 on 4/10/1995) FL 169+23/35 FLC 21/8 FAC 10+3/1 Others 1+4

BEAUMONT Christopher (Chris) Paul
Born: Sheffield, 5 December 1965
Height: 5'11" Weight: 11.12

Chris has made a discernible improvement to his game in each season with Chesterfield, and 1999-2000 was no exception. Despite playing in a struggling side he performed reliably and with distinction in a variety of positions in defence and midfield, confirming his value to the Spireites as a utility player.

Rochdale (Free from Denaby U on 21/7/1988) FL 31+3/7 FLC 0+1/1 FAC 2/1 Others 2
Stockport Co (£8,000 on 21/7/1989) FL 238+20/39 FLC 14+3/3 FAC 15/2 Others 34+2/7
Chesterfield (£30,000 on 22/7/1996) FL 128+16/6 FLC 11+3 FAC 7+2/1 Others 6

BEAVERS Paul Mark
Born: Blackpool, 2 October 1978
Height: 6'3" Weight: 13.5

A big and powerful young striker whose physical presence makes him a handful for most opposition defences, Paul joined Oldham on a free transfer in August 1999 after impressing at Boundary Park while on loan during 1998-99. He struggled with a series of niggling injuries and, apart from a few games early on, he rarely featured for the Latics before eventually joining Hartlepool on loan on transfer deadline day. Unfortunately, he did not have the best of times back in his native North-east and was unable to become the goalscorer Pool manager Chris Turner was looking for.

Sunderland (From trainee on 14/4/1997)
Shrewsbury T (Loaned on 7/12/1998) FL 2 Others 1
Oldham Ath (Signed on 25/3/1999) FL 10+1/2 FLC 0+1 Others 0+1
Hartlepool U (Loaned on 23/3/2000) FL 2+5 Others 1

BECK Mikkel Venge
Born: Aarhus, Denmark, 4 May 1973
Height: 6'2" Weight: 12.9
International Honours: Denmark: 19

The Danish international striker was unable to make much impression at Derby in 1999-2000, his first full season with the club, and was rarely included in the starting line-up. His most effective performance was as a substitute at Southampton in October when he salvaged a point in injury time and gave a display which seemed to show that he had got over his initial self-confessed inability to settle at the club. At his best he is a highly accomplished player, as he proved during his time at Middlesbrough, but it seemed in the best interests of all concerned when he joined Nottingham Forest on loan in November as a replacement for the departed Ian Wright. He scored just once in five games for the Reds but was beginning to forge a promising partnership with Stern John when he was recalled to Pride Park. Mikkel later spent two months on loan at Queens Park Rangers and his experience was of considerable value to the club while their first-choice strikers were unavailable. During his spell at Loftus Road he made ten appearances and scored four goals, having taken on responsibility for penalty kicks in the absence of the club's usual penalty-taker. In April the hard-working striker moved back to Denmark for a third loan spell, this time with Aalborg BK. His form attracted the attention of the Danish team manager and he was recalled to the national team against Sweden the same month, going on to make the squad for the Euro 2000 finals, where he added further caps against France and the Czech Republic.

Middlesbrough (Free from Fortuna Cologne, Germany, via Kolding and B1909, on 13/9/1996) F/PL 66+25/24 FLC 14+2/5 FAC 5+3/2
Derby Co (£500,000 on 26/3/1999) PL 11+7/2 FLC 2/1 FAC 0+1
Nottingham F (Loaned on 12/11/1999) FL 5/1
Queens Park R (Loaned on 11/2/2000) FL 10+1/4

BECKETT Luke John
Born: Sheffield, 25 November 1976
Height: 5'11" Weight: 11.6

Luke's total of 14 goals in Chester's 1999-2000 relegation season could well have been doubled in more favourable circumstances. An ever-present during a traumatic campaign, he will have benefited from his experiences. He gave 100 per cent effort in every game, and finished as the Blues' top scorer for the second season in a row. Reported as a target for several First Division clubs, Luke is likely to make an immediate return to the Football League, and seems destined to play at a higher level. Stop Press: He signed for Chesterfield in the middle of June, with the fee to be decided by a tribunal.

Barnsley (From trainee on 20/6/1995)
Chester C (Free on 11/6/1998) FL 70+4/25 FLC 5/5 FAC 4/2 Others 1

BECKHAM David Robert Joseph
Born: Leytonstone, 2 May 1975
Height: 6'0" Weight: 11.12
Club Honours: FAYC '92; PL '96, '97, '99, '00; FAC '96, '99; CS '96, '97; EC '99
International Honours: E: 34; U21-9; Yth

David is a supremely talented midfielder, with a sublime range of passing and shooting skills, yet in 1998-99 the Manchester United star's life seemingly oscillated between triumph and disaster almost on a daily basis. After his marriage to Spice Girl Victoria Adams in Dublin in the summer of 1999, the back pages continued to portray him as either a hero or a villain, depending on the particular writer's point of view, during the following season. Apart from a weekly barrage of insults from rival supporters, there was a £50,000 fine for breaking a club curfew before a key European game, occasions when more column inches were devoted to his "petulant" behaviour than to the team's actual performance on the pitch, his wife's misinterpreted quotes about how it would be more advantageous if he played for a London side, and then a bust-up with Sir Alex Ferguson after he missed a training session to look after his poorly son Brooklyn. Quite how David manages to stay on an even keel amid such hyperbole is one of life's great mysteries; but despite it all he remains, quite simply, the most outstanding English footballer of his generation. To illustrate the point, he started the season with his now mandatory free-kick "special", with Arsenal the victims in the Charity Shield opener at Wembley. Although he waited another 18 games to register his next competitive goal, against Zagreb in the Champions' League, he took the runner-up spot behind Rivaldo in the "European Footballer of the Year" award. Despite being sent off against Necaxa in the World Club Championship in Brazil in January, and the FA extending him an invitation to explain his supposed petulance on the pitch in October, the hard facts were that David had gone 520 minutes in the Premiership without even receiving a yellow card. Although the media circus continued to link his name with a possible £25 million move to Arsenal or Inter Milan, both David and United dismissed the stories out of hand. Insisting that he was happy to stay at Old Trafford for the rest of his career, he was even looking forward to the day when he might captain the side. Once again playing wide on the right of midfield, where his inviting crosses posed a constant threat, he came to the fore as the season reached its exciting finale but, while his goals against Leicester, Bradford and West Ham kept United in line for another Premiership title, his brilliant solo effort in the European Cup quarter-final against Real Madrid at Old Trafford wasn't enough to prevent their elimination from the competition. Also a fixture in the England line-up, he was one of the few successes of the Euro 2000 campaign, laying on both goals against Portugal and providing Alan Shearer with the winner against Germany. David's talents were again recognised by his fellow professionals, who included him in the PFA award-winning Premiership team.

Manchester U (From trainee on 29/1/1993) PL 158+17/35 FLC 5+2 FAC 16+2/5 Others 51+2/9
Preston NE (Loaned on 28/2/1995) FL 4+1/2

David Beckham

BEDEAU Anthony (Tony) Charles Osmond
Born: Hammersmith, 24 March 1979
Height: 5'10" Weight: 11.0

The pacy Torquay striker continued his improvement with some fine goals throughout 1999-2000. His partnership with Eifion Williams caused many defences problems, especially away from home. Tony missed some games later in the season through a close family bereavement, and also damaged ankle ligaments. A seasonal tally of 17 goals more than doubled his career total. Despite obvious interest from clubs at a higher level, Tony pledged his future to the Gulls by signing a contract in May that ties him to Plainmoor until the summer of 2002. Wimbledon, Ipswich and Stoke are reported to be following his development with interest.

Torquay U (From trainee on 28/7/1997) FL 83+37/31 FLC 5+1/1 FAC 6+3/1 Others 0+8

BEECH Christopher (Chris)
Born: Congleton, 5 November 1975
Height: 5'10" Weight: 11.12
International Honours: E: Yth; Sch

After playing in the first few games of the 1999-2000 season, his second at Rotherham, this left-footed defender was ruled out of action by an injury and failed to regain his place. However, Chris skippered the reserve team to Pontins League Division One championship success. He can always be relied upon to give of his best, with his great attitude and dogged defending ability real assets.

Manchester C (From trainee on 12/11/1992)
Cardiff C (Free on 7/8/1997) FL 46/1 FLC 2 FAC 6
Rotherham U (Free on 30/6/1998) FL 29+1 FLC 4

BEECH Christopher (Chris) Stephen
Born: Blackpool, 16 September 1974
Height: 5'11" Weight: 11.12

Starting the 1999-2000 season, his second with the Terriers, Chris faced intense competition for a place in the Huddersfield team but he was to make a central midfield role his own. Barring minor injuries, he was a regular fixture alongside Kenny Irons and, with his tireless workrate a key factor, Town seemed to play more fluently with him in the side. Good in the air, as he showed with his brilliant winning goal at Manchester City, and an intelligent passer of the ball, he was rightly rewarded with a new contract. A skilful, attacking player, he is a natural goalscorer, a brace against Crewe at the McAlpine in March taking him into double figures for the season, and his finishing made an invaluable contribution to his club's push for promotion.

Blackpool (From trainee on 9/7/1993) FL 53+29/4 FLC 4+4 FAC 1 Others 3+3/2
Hartlepool U (Free on 18/7/1996) FL 92+2/23 FLC 5/1 FAC 3/1 Others 3/1
Huddersfield T (£65,000 on 27/11/1998) FL 47+5/11 FLC 4/1 FAC 2/2

BEESLEY Mark Anthony
Born: Ormskirk, 5 December 1980
Height: 5'10" Weight: 11.2

Mark's first involvement with Preston's first team came when he sat on the bench twice last September, before making his debut as a late substitute against Hartlepool in the Auto Windscreens Shield. A fine goalscoring prospect, he formed an effective strike force with Mark Wright in the reserves and youth team, and this partnership was introduced to the senior side when Beesley made his league debut – again as a late sub – at Oxford alongside Wright. Neither looked out of place but, although there were considerable hopes for their partnership at first-team level, Mark was released during the close season.

Preston NE (From trainee on 26/6/1999) FL 0+1 Others 0+1

BEESLEY Paul
Born: Liverpool, 21 July 1965
Height: 6'1" Weight: 12.6

This experienced and dependable central defender joined Blackpool from Port Vale during the 1999 close season but had to wait until November to make his debut for the club after suffering a pre-season injury. Paul appeared regularly in the Seasiders' first team until last February but rarely featured after that.

Wigan Ath (Free from Marine on 22/9/1984) FL 153+2/3 FLC 13 FAC 6 Others 11
Leyton Orient (£175,000 on 20/10/1989) FL 32/1 FAC 1 Others 2/1
Sheffield U (£300,000 on 10/7/1990) F/PL 162+6/7 FLC 12+1 FAC 9+2/1 Others 3/1
Leeds U (£250,000 on 2/8/1995) PL 19+3 FLC 5+1 FAC 5 Others 2+2
Manchester C (£500,000 on 7/2/1997) FL 10+3
Port Vale (Loaned on 24/12/1997) FL 5
West Bromwich A (Loaned on 12/3/1998) FL 8
Port Vale (Signed on 28/8/1998) FL 33+2/3 FAC 1
Blackpool (Free on 2/7/1999) FL 15+3 FAC 1 Others 3

BEETON Alan Matthew
Born: Watford, 4 October 1978
Height: 5'11" Weight: 11.12

This left-sided Wycombe defender had the misfortune to contract meningitis in the 1999 close season on the eve of the club's trip to Ireland but thankfully made a quick recovery. He made a number of appearances last autumn when deputising for Chris Vinnicombe at left back but then dropped out of contention in the second half of the season. Alan is competitive, pacy and capable of making useful runs down the left flank.

Wycombe W (From trainee on 1/7/1997) FL 36+16 FLC 4+1 FAC 5+2

BEHARALL David Alexander
Born: Jarrow, 8 March 1979
Height: 6'0" Weight: 11.12

One of the few local lads in the Newcastle squad and a product of the club's School of Excellence, David is a tall, slim centre back who is a sound defender and comfortable on the ball, and is considered a fine prospect for the future. Having made his debut the previous season, he had high hopes of mounting a serious challenge for a regular place in the first team in 1999-2000 after signing a new four-year contract in the summer, but his start to the campaign was disrupted by knee and hamstring injuries. When fit again David had to take his place in line behind the club's many other central

defenders whose greater experience was important as Newcastle battled to climb away from the relegation zone, so his season was spent patiently learning his trade from the sidelines. He made only two substitute appearances, both in the early traumatic stages of the campaign, against Wimbledon and at Old Trafford, although he made the bench on three further occasions.
Newcastle U (From trainee on 4/7/1997) PL 4+2

BELGRAVE Barrington
Born: Bedford, 16 September 1980
Height: 5'9" Weight: 11.0
Previously with Norwich before joining Plymouth in the 1999 close season, Barrington has blistering pace and likes to get into the thick of the action. He made the majority of his Pilgrim appearances from the substitutes' bench but, after impressing in reserve fixtures, made his first start in November at Cheltenham. A lively striker, Barrington was given the chance to gain experience in non-league football on loan before being released at the end of the season.
Plymouth Arg (Free from Norwich C juniors on 28/7/1999) FL 2+13 FLC 0+1 FAC 0+2

BELL Leon Earl
Born: Hitchin, 19 December 1980
Height: 5'7" Weight: 9.7
Although he did not receive the public acclaim that his meteoric progress deserved, Leon's inaugural season in the professional ranks at Barnet in 1999-2000 proved to be highly successful. Restricted to the fringes of the first team during the opening months of the campaign, Leon toiled honestly at the training ground to improve both his fitness and awareness and, as a result, his confidence on the pitch visibly blossomed. During the latter stages of the term, Leon registered a succession of impressive performances for Barnet's second string and was duly rewarded with a brief substitute appearance in the club's final league match of the season at Rochdale. A right-sided midfielder, Leon combines thoughtful distribution with abrasive tackling, and looks set to make an impact next season.
Barnet (From trainee on 2/7/1999) FL 0+1

BELL Michael (Mickey)
Born: Newcastle, 15 November 1971
Height: 5'9" Weight: 11.4
After he broke his leg at the Hawthorns in 1998-99 the good form of Jim Brennan kept Mickey from reclaiming a regular first-team berth at Bristol City last season until his rival departed to Nottingham Forest early in the campaign. This £150,000 signing from Wycombe Wanderers in the 1997 close season took the opportunity to fully establish himself once more and reforged his partnership with Brian Tinnion down the left to earn himself a new four-year contract. Despite not scoring as many goals as in previous campaigns, Mickey still posed a considerable threat at dead-ball situations. Excellent when going forward, he was selected as a member of the PFA award-winning Second Division team.
Northampton T (From trainee on 1/7/1990) FL 133+20/10 FLC 7+1 FAC 5/1 Others 9+2/1
Wycombe W (£45,000 on 21/10/1994) FL 117+1/5 FLC 5 FAC 9/2 Others 3+1
Bristol C (£150,000 on 2/7/1997) FL 111+2/20 FLC 8 FAC 6 Others 6

BELLAMY Craig Douglas
Born: Cardiff, 13 July 1979
Height: 5'9" Weight: 10.12
International Honours: W: 10 U21-8; Yth; Sch
A dreadful cruciate ligament injury sustained in a pre-season friendly at Southend ruled this talented Welsh international out of the Norwich line-up for all but the final two weeks of the 1999-2000 campaign. After he had netted 19 times the previous season hopes were high that Craig would fire the Canaries into promotion contention as well as playing a full part in Wales's Euro 2000 qualifying efforts, but it was not to be. However, in his four end-of-season appearances for Norwich, the first two as a substitute, he confirmed that he had lost none of his ability, scoring twice, and he then made his international comeback in the prestige friendlies against Brazil and Portugal. A natural goalscorer and a determined character, Craig has the talent to go on to be one of the country's top players. He is quick and has an instinct for being in the right place at the right time when chances are created, while his clinical finishing in one-on-one situations is of the very highest quality.
Norwich C (From trainee on 20/1/1997) FL 70+13/32 FLC 6/2 FAC 1

Franny Benali

BENALI Francis (Franny) Vincent
Born: Southampton, 30 December 1968
Height: 5'10" Weight: 11.0
International Honours: E: Sch
Southampton's long-serving left-sided defender is equally at home as a left back or a central defender. He was probably more effective last season in a central position, where he was used on a number of occasions by new manager Glenn Hoddle. Franny seems to improve with experience – he has now spent more than 13 years at the Dell – and is a cool customer when the chips are down.
Southampton (From apprentice on 5/1/1987) F/PL 269+33/1 FLC 24+7 FAC 21 Others 3+1

BENGTSSON Robert
Born: Goteborg, Sweden, 4 June 1968
Height: 5'10" Weight: 12.0
This experienced defender joined Barnsley during the Swedish domestic close season on a three-month loan deal. He made two first-team appearances in cup games as a replacement at right back for the ineligible John Curtis, but otherwise found his opportunities very limited. In his brief spell at Oakwell he showed himself to be an accomplished performer but he found it difficult to settle in South Yorkshire and made an early return to Scandinavia.
Barnsley (Free from Vastra Frolunda, Sweden on 9/11/1999) FLC 1 FAC 1

BENJAMIN Trevor Junior
Born: Kettering, 8 February 1979
Height: 6'2" Weight: 13.2
If the 1998-99 season was good for Trevor, the 1999-2000 season was excellent. The Cambridge forward carried on as before, forming an impressive partnership with Martin Butler. Then, after Martin's departure in January, he took on the role of United's main striker. Powerfully built, he broke a club scoring record when he netted in eight consecutive appearances in March and April and finished the season as the Us' leading goalscorer. Trevor's abilities were recognised at the end of the season when he was invited to train with the England U21 squad. The main question for United fans is whether the club can hold on to this proven goalscorer in the coming season. Leicester, Chelsea and Ipswich have all reportedly expressed an interest.
Cambridge U (From trainee on 21/2/1997) FL 96+27/35 FLC 7+3/4 FAC 9+1/5 Others 3/2

BENNETT Frank (Frankie)
Born: Birmingham, 3 January 1969
Height: 5'7" Weight: 12.1
Frankie recovered from the knee injuries which had kept him out of action for most of the previous season to finally regain full fitness in 1999-2000. He made some early-season substitute appearances for Bristol Rovers in an unaccustomed right-wing-back role, which he seemed to enjoy, and then joined Third Division Exeter City in February, initially on loan. He made eight appearances for City, playing in his usual right wing position, and scored in the Devon derby with Plymouth Argyle at St James Park but, although he was offered a contract for the rest of the season, he opted to join Gloucestershire-based club Forest Green

Rovers in March to assist their efforts to retain their Conference status.

Southampton (£7,500 from Halesowen T on 24/2/1993) PL 5+14/1 FLC 1+2 FAC 0+1
Shrewsbury T (Loaned on 25/10/1996) FL 2+2/3
Bristol Rov (£15,000 on 22/11/1996) FL 15+29/4 FLC 1+2 FAC 0+2 Others 3+1/2
Exeter C (Free on 3/2/2000) FL 8+1/1

BENNETT Gary Ernest
Born: Manchester, 4 December 1961
Height: 6'1" Weight: 13.0
Club Honours: Div 3 '88

Although he started Darlington's first game of 1999-2000, his second season with the Quakers, Gary went on to make only three further starts during the campaign. Otherwise, he concentrated on the coaching side of his role at the club. He coached the reserve team to promotion to the Pontins League First Division, as well as victory in the Durham Challenge Cup final. He was out of contract at the end of the season.

Manchester C (Free from Ashton U on 8/9/1979)
Cardiff C (Free on 16/9/1981) FL 85+2/11 FLC 6/1 FAC 3
Sunderland (£65,000 on 26/7/1984) FL 362+7/23 FLC 34+1/1 FAC 17+1 Others 21/1
Carlisle U (Free on 16/11/1995) FL 26/5 Others 5/1
Scarborough (Free on 2/8/1996) FL 86+2/18 FLC 6/3 FAC 4 Others 3
Darlington (Free on 8/7/1998) FL 30+4/4 FLC 1 FAC 3/1 Others 1

BENNETT Ian Michael
Born: Worksop, 10 October 1971
Height: 6'0" Weight: 12.10
Club Honours: Div 2 '95; AMC '95

The Birmingham goalkeeper missed the first six weeks of the 1999-2000 campaign after suffering a broken finger in training. He then made a sensational return to the first team in the Worthington Cup tie against Newcastle United last October, when he saved Alan Shearer's penalty and helped the Blues to a shock 2-0 win over the Premiership outfit. He retained his place for a further six games before being dropped, and it was not until the new year that he was able to displace Kevin Poole as first-choice 'keeper. Ian then succumbed to the St Andrews injury hoodoo when he fractured his left thumb in a freak training accident that kept him out for the rest of the season. He is a highly rated shot stopper with superb reflexes and considered one of the best 'keepers in the Nationwide League.

Newcastle U (Free from Queens Park R juniors on 20/3/1989)
Peterborough U (Free on 22/3/1991) FL 72 FLC 10 FAC 3 Others 4
Birmingham C (£325,000 on 17/12/1993) FL 208 FLC 26 FAC 14 Others 11

BENNETT Thomas (Tom) McNeill
Born: Falkirk, 12 December 1969
Height: 5'11" Weight: 11.8

This Stockport midfielder missed the first half of the 1999-2000 campaign after contracting a serious virus during the close season and then struggling with a calf injury. He was loaned to First Division strugglers Walsall in December and his dynamic midfield play was a key factor in a run of three wins and a draw in five games. Tom was restored to County's first team when he returned to Edgeley Park but, despite winning three "Man of the Match" awards in seven games, he was allowed to rejoin the Bescot Stadium club for a second loan period on transfer deadline day. He captained the side when Adrian Viveash was injured and played a major part in the late-season win over West Bromwich, scoring one goal and setting up the other with a powerful shot. A classy, influential player, he is one of the men Walsall desperately want to hold on to in the hope of making an immediate return to Division One.

Aston Villa (From apprentice on 16/12/1987)
Wolverhampton W (Free on 5/7/1988) FL 103+12/2 FLC 7 FAC 5+2 Others 3+1
Stockport Co (£75,000 on 23/6/1995) FL 105+5/5 FLC 20/2 FAC 10 Others 6+1
Walsall (Loaned on 30/12/1999) FL 4/1
Walsall (Loaned on 23/3/2000) FL 7/2

BENT Junior Antony
Born: Huddersfield, 1 March 1970
Height: 5'6" Weight: 10.9

Junior is a fast and exciting winger who began the 1999-2000 campaign as a regular in the Blackpool line-up. He later spent time on the substitutes' bench, regularly coming on to run at opposition defences, but finished the season playing mainly with the reserves. His only goal came against Colchester last January, when he scored from eight yards after being set up by on-loan man Rob Matthews.

Huddersfield T (From trainee on 9/12/1987) FL 25+11/6 FLC 1 FAC 3+1/1 Others 4
Burnley (Loaned on 30/11/1989) FL 7+2/3
Bristol C (£30,000 on 22/3/1990) FL 142+41/20 FLC 10+3/1 FAC 12+3/2 Others 7+3
Stoke C (Loaned on 26/3/1992) FL 1
Shrewsbury T (Loaned on 24/10/1996) FL 6
Blackpool (Signed on 29/8/1997) FL 64+39/5 FLC 4+1/1 FAC 2+3 Others 6+1

BENT Marcus Nathan
Born: Hammersmith, 19 May 1978
Height: 6'2" Weight: 12.4
International Honours: E: U21-2

A striker with an eye for goal, Marcus began the 1999-2000 season with Port Vale, the club he had joined the previous February, but for some reason he never really hit it off there. He began the campaign on the left-hand side of midfield but then a sending-off at Chester in the Worthington Cup disrupted his progress. Upon his return he was again in and out of the side, managing just the one goal, against Grimsby when playing up front, before he moved to Sheffield United for £250,000, a fee that rose to £300,000 on appearances. Signed by Adrian Heath shortly before his resignation, Marcus quickly became a hit with the United fans. Fast, with good ball control and the ability to beat a man, and a good header of the ball, he blossomed under the guidance of Neil Warnock, adding an increased workrate to his other attributes, and he soon became the

Tom Bennett

focus of interest for Premiership clubs. He scored goals with both head and feet, including a hat-trick – the first of his career – in the 6-0 defeat of West Bromwich. He also scored the winning goal in the penalty shoot-out against Rushden & Diamonds. He is still only 22 years old, and the club look to him for many goals next season.

Brentford (From trainee on 21/7/1995) FL 56+14/8 FLC 7/1 FAC 8/3 Others 5+1/1
Crystal Palace (£150,000 + on 8/1/1998) P/FL 13+15/5 FLC 0+2 FAC 0+1
Port Vale (£375,000 on 15/1/1999) FL 17+6/1 FLC 1
Sheffield U (£300,000 on 28/10/1999) FL 32/15 FAC 3/1

Marcus Bent

BERESFORD David
Born: Middleton, 11 November 1976
Height: 5'5" Weight: 11.4
International Honours: E: Yth; Sch

The speedy Huddersfield winger's only taste of first-team football with the Terriers last season was a brief appearance as a substitute against Notts County in the second round of the Worthington Cup. He joined Preston on loan in December as cover for Lee Cartwright but the North End fans were to see little of the trickery and accurate crossing of which he is capable in his role on the right of midfield. An exciting player who likes to get forward to support the strikers, David made his debut against Blackpool, but unfortunately had to be substituted at half time because of a hamstring injury. He made only one more start for Preston, although he was also used as an occasional substitute, and returned to the McAlpine Stadium before the end of his second month without having had much chance to impress.

Oldham Ath (From trainee on 22/7/1994) P/FL 32+32/2 FLC 3+3 FAC 0+1 Others 3
Swansea C (Loaned on 11/8/1995) FL 4+2
Huddersfield T (£350,000 on 27/3/1997) FL 24+9/3 FLC 1+3 FAC 1+1
Preston NE (Loaned on 17/12/1999) FL 1+3 FAC 0+1 Others 1

BERESFORD John
Born: Sheffield, 4 September 1966
Height: 5'7" Weight: 12.0
Club Honours: Div 1 '93
International Honours: E: B-2; Yth; Sch

After missing almost the entire 1998-99 season with a serious cruciate ligament injury, the Southampton left back found himself out of favour at the Dell after appearing as a substitute on the opening day of the 1999-2000 season. Having cleared the air with manager Dave Jones in early October, John joined First Division club Birmingham on loan and made his debut for the Blues at Walsall. Unfortunately, he was one of the many players to suffer the St Andrews injury jinx last season, for within 24 hours he had fallen down the stairs at home and damaged a cartilage in his knee. The injury required surgery and he returned to the south coast. John did not return to first-team action until January, when he played as a substitute against his former club, Newcastle United. After just one further substitute appearance, injury was again to plague him for the remainder of the season. When fully fit, John is a highly accomplished performer who defends resolutely yet possesses the skill and pace of a winger, and he can also operate in midfield if required.

Manchester C (From apprentice on 16/9/1983)
Barnsley (Free on 4/8/1986) FL 79+9/5 FLC 5+2/2 FAC 5/1
Portsmouth (£300,000 on 23/3/1989) FL 102+5/8 FLC 12/2 FAC 11 Others 2
Newcastle U (£650,000 on 2/7/1992) F/PL 176+3/3 FLC 17 FAC 17+1/1 Others 17+1/4
Southampton (£1,500,000 on 6/2/1998) PL 11+6
Birmingham C (Loaned on 7/10/1999) FL 1

BERESFORD Marlon
Born: Lincoln, 2 September 1969
Height: 6'1" Weight: 13.6

The Middlesbrough goalkeeper must have been pleased when the 1999-2000 season ended, for it must surely have been one of the most difficult of his career. He waited patiently for the almost ever-present Mark Schwarzer to leave the door to the first team open – even slightly ajar might have been sufficient – but it remained tightly shut. Marlon's only opportunity came against Aston Villa in February and he will no doubt wish to forget that game, having been beaten four times just when he needed a clean sheet to help him in his quest for a first-team run. A capable shot stopper noted for his exemplary distribution, Marlon has the experience and resilience to bounce back but the big Aussie seems set to resist everything that is thrown at him, and while the club benefits from having two such fine 'keepers competing for a place in the side it is frustrating for the number two who has to bide his time in the wings.

Sheffield Wed (From trainee on 23/9/1987)
Bury (Loaned on 25/8/1989) FL 1
Northampton T (Loaned on 27/9/1990) FL 13 Others 2
Crewe Alex (Loaned on 28/2/1991) FL 3
Northampton T (Loaned on 15/8/1991) FL 15
Burnley (£95,000 on 28/8/1992) FL 240 FLC 18 FAC 20 Others 16
Middlesbrough (£500,000 on 10/3/1998) P/FL 8 FLC 3

BERG Henning
Born: Eidsvell, Norway, 1 September 1969
Height: 6'0" Weight: 12.7
Club Honours: PL '95, '99, '00
International Honours: Norway: 73

A solid central defender whose timing and judgement are always impeccable, Henning found his position as Jaap Stam's regular partner in the Manchester United back four under severe pressure at the start of the 1999-2000 season when Sir Alex Ferguson signed Mikael Silvestre from Inter Milan in September. Despite having played in all of United's first 15 games, he was forced to wait patiently in the wings as the Frenchman virtually made the position his own. Henning deputised for Stam in the World Club Championship match against South Melbourne in Brazil at the turn of the year, but there was still no joy when the team returned home to continue their quest for domestic and European honours. Although at times he even had difficulty commanding a regular place on the bench, Henning was given another chance to shine in the Champions' League encounter with Fiorentina at Old Trafford which secured United's place in the quarter-finals. That match proved to be a major turning point in his fortunes as he became a central figure in United's bid to land both the Premiership and the European Cup. He scored his only goal of the campaign against Sunderland at Old Trafford in April and ended the season with his third Premiership winners' medal. A regular for Norway, he added a further ten caps but appeared in only one of their three games in a rather dismal Euro 2000 tournament for the Scandinavians.

Blackburn Rov (£400,000 from Lillestrom, Norway on 26/1/1993) PL154+5/4 FLC 16 FAC 10 Others 9
Manchester U (£5,000,000 on 12/8/1997) PL 49+16/2 FLC 3 FAC 7 Others 22+5/1

BERGER Patrik
Born: Prague, Czechoslovakia, 10 November 1973
Height: 6'1" Weight: 12.6
International Honours: Czech Republic: 38; Czechoslovakia: 2; Yth (UEFA-U16 '90)

Patrick enjoyed his finest season in Liverpool's colours in 1999-2000. Featuring on the left of midfield, he increased his workrate and improved the defensive aspects of his game. He is potentially a world-class midfielder, his only weakness being his tendency to drift inside too often, which can mean that Liverpool lack width, and can be vulnerable down the flank. Patrick's contribution to the Liverpool cause was magnificent last season, particularly in terms of the number of goals he scored, his highest since joining the club from Borussia Dortmund in 1996. He is a key weapon in midfield and his brilliant goals against Leeds, Wimbledon and Manchester United were among the highlights of Liverpool's season. He has improved the defensive side of his game and is likely to be a cornerstone of next season's team. He played a further six times for his country during 1999-2000, scoring goals against Bosnia-Herzegovina last September and Israel in April.

Liverpool (£3,250,000 from Borussia Dortmund, Germany, via Slavia Prague, on 15/8/1996) PL 83+28/25 FLC 7+2/2 FAC 4+2 Others 13+1/4

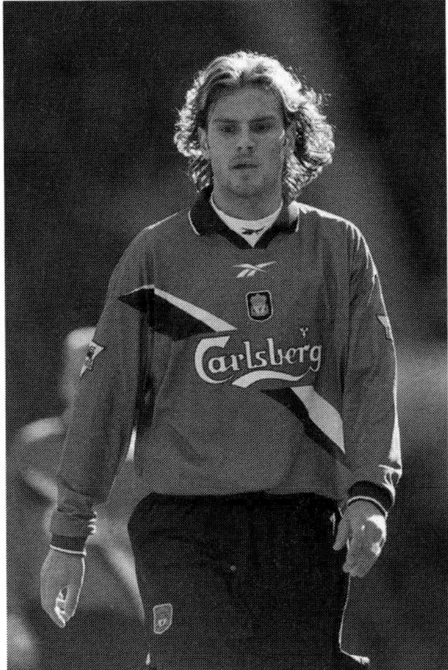

Patrik Berger

BERGERSEN Kent
Born: Oslo, Norway, 8 February 1967
Height: 5'10" Weight: 10.8

This classy Stockport midfield man was described by his manager, Andy Kilner, as "the best technical player at the club" but struggled to cope with the physical side of the English game at times during the 1999-2000 season. He arrived after spending the summer with Norwegian club Stromsgodset but after featuring regularly for the Hatters in the autumn he dropped out of the first-team squad. Very comfortable on the ball and able to operate on either flank, Kent will benefit from a full pre-season programme and should prove an asset to the club in 2000-01.

Raith Rov (Signed from Valerengen, Norway on 29/11/1996) SL 6/1 (Free to Panionios on 16/1/1997)
Stockport Co (Free from Stromsgodset, Norway on 10/9/1999) FL 10+7 FAC 1

BERGKAMP Dennis
Born: Amsterdam, Holland, 18 May 1969
Height: 6'0" Weight: 12.5
Club Honours: PL '98; CS '98
International Honours: Holland: 79

On his day, Dennis is a genuine world-class striker with the ability to destroy any defence. He started the 1999-2000 season fully fit, in contrast to the previous year when he was still suffering from the demands of that summer's World Cup. His freshness was evident as he scored in both of Arsenal's opening two league games. Although he continued to turn in good performances, niggling injuries then caused him to miss a number of matches during mid-season, but on his return he formed an effective partnership with fellow striker Thierry Henry. Dennis became very much a creator of chances for team-mates, but he still scored crucial goals later in the season, in particular a great strike to give Arsenal a 1-0 victory over Lens in the home leg of the semi-final of the UEFA Cup. Still a regular at international level, he added a further 11 caps during the season, appearing in all of his country's games in the Euro 2000 finals, when Holland reached the semi-finals.

Arsenal (£7,500,000 from Inter Milan, Italy, via Ajax, on 3/7/1995) PL 140+7/57 FLC 14/8 FAC 16/7 Others 17/6

BERGSSON Gudni
Born: Reykjavik, Iceland, 21 July 1965
Height: 6'1" Weight: 12.3
Club Honours: Div 1 '97
International Honours: Iceland: 77

"The Iceman" was a revelation last season, putting in performances of such quality and consistency for Bolton that it was hard to believe at times that he is now in his mid-thirties. He was out of contract in the summer and was expected to return to Iceland to take up a career as a lawyer. If he does so, it will be a monumental blow to the Wanderers, and the club seemed certain to try everything in their power to stop him quitting the game for good. Operating mainly as a central defender in 1999-2000, although he also occasionally covered the right-back berth, Gudni struck up a phenomenal pairing with Mark Fish at the centre of Bolton's defence, creating one of the most solid and feared pairings in the First Division. They proved to be the perfect foils to each other; while he does not possess Fish's electric pace, Gudni's awareness, positioning and reading of the game are second to none, and he had what must have been his most successful season to date in a Bolton shirt. Gudni also has the knack of chipping in with the odd vital goal or two, such as the winner away to Port Vale last February. While he will admit to not being one of the club's biggest names (such as Eidur Gudjohnsen and Claus Jensen), his team-mates would disagree, since Gudni was voted the "Players' Player of the Year" last season.

Tottenham H (£100,000 from Valur, Iceland on 15/12/1988) F/PL 51+20/2 FLC 4+2 FAC 2+2 Others 5+1
Bolton W (£115,000 on 21/3/1995) P/FL 158+7/13 FLC 22+1/1 FAC 8 Others 5+2

BERKLEY Austin James
Born: Dartford, 28 January 1973
Height: 5'10" Weight: 11.6

Shrewsbury's "Player of the Year" the previous season, Austin had a disappointing 1999-2000 campaign. The left-sided mid-field player made 28 starts, but seemed to struggle to make an impact going forward. It was a very difficult season at Shrewsbury and Austin's creativity appeared to suffer. He can usually be relied upon to net one or two spectacular goals, but finished the season empty handed. He was one of a number of players released by the club in May. Stop Press: Austin was reported to have signed for Barnet in mid-June.

Gillingham (From trainee on 13/5/1991) FL 0+3 Others 0+3
Swindon T (Free on 16/5/1992) FL 0+1 FLC 0+1 Others 3+1/1
Shrewsbury T (Free on 29/7/1995) FL 152+20/12 FLC 5+2 FAC 6+1 Others 11/1

BERNAL Andrew (Andy)
Born: Canberra, Australia, 16 July 1966
Height: 5'10" Weight: 12.5
International Honours: Australia: 14

Although he continued to give a series of combative performances all along the Reading back line in 1999-2000, Andy's season was greatly hampered by injury, and after six seasons' service with the club he was not offered a new contract because of a persistent foot problem. He did not play after February, and the high points of his campaign came when he scored his first goals for the club for four years – one against Yeovil in the FA Cup, and another against Leyton Orient in the Auto Windscreens Shield. Andy was released in the summer.

Ipswich T (Free from Sporting Gijon, Spain on 24/9/1987) FL 4+5 Others 0+2
Reading (£30,000 from Sydney Olympic, Australia on 26/7/1994) FL 179+8/2 FLC 17+2 FAC 14/1 Others 6/1

BERNTSEN Thomas (Tommy)
Born: Oslo, Norway, 18 December 1973
Height: 6'2" Weight: 12.8

This experienced Lillestrom central defender joined Portsmouth on loan last November during the Norwegian winter break. He appeared as a substitute against Manchester City at Maine Road and then made the starting line-up for the home game with Birmingham, but then suffered a hamstring injury and returned to Scandinavia at the end of the month.

Portsmouth (Loaned from Lillestrom, Norway on 1/11/1999) FL 1+1

BERRY Paul Andrew
Born: Warrington, 6 December 1978
Height: 5'9" Weight: 10.8

Paul followed Macclesfield's Damien Whitehead from Warrington Town of the North Western Trains League to the league ranks when he joined Chester last August. As he found his feet in the higher sphere, Paul was regularly included among the Blues' substitutes. He made his debut when coming off the bench at Torquay, with his goal securing the ultimately doomed Blues' first point of their relegation season. It is to be hoped that Paul displayed enough of his undoubted ability to earn another chance in the league.

Chester C (Signed from Warrington T on 17/8/1999) FL 0+9/1 FLC 0+2 FAC 0+1

BERRY Trevor John
Born: Haslemere, 1 August 1974
Height: 5'7" Weight: 11.2
Club Honours: AMC '96
International Honours: E: Yth

Trevor is the second-longest-serving member of the Rotherham squad behind Paul Hurst. His goals in 1999-2000 were fewer than he would have hoped, but this tricky right winger always makes them something special, thanks to his talent for finding the net with spectacular efforts. Trevor had a good run in the first team in the first half of the season, but then had to settle for a place on the substitutes' bench as the Millers battled towards promotion. Sometimes asked to play as an orthodox striker, United's man of Surrey invariably gives his best whenever required.

Aston Villa (£50,000 from Bournemouth juniors on 3/4/1992)
Rotherham U (£20,000 on 8/9/1995) FL 121+41/20 FLC 3+2 FAC 9+3/3 Others 9+2/1

BESWETHERICK Jonathan (Jon) Barry
Born: Liverpool, 15 January 1978
Height: 5'11" Weight: 11.4

Given his opportunity due to Paul Gibbs's injury, Jon had an outstanding first full season with Plymouth in 1999-2000. His confident displays as an attacking left wing back impressed many. A tough tackler and fine crosser of the ball on the run, "Bessie" provided many goalscoring opportunities for his team-mates, including three at Torquay in the Devon derby in March. His superb form was confirmed when he was named in the Opta Index Third Division "Team of the Season". Jon has also been rewarded with a new contract.

Plymouth Arg (From trainee on 27/7/1996) FL 62+7 FLC 1 FAC 11 Others 2

BETSY Kevin Eddie Lewis
Born: Seychelles, 20 March 1978
Height: 6'1" Weight: 11.12
International Honours: E: SP-1

Apart from a couple of early-season appearances as a substitute, this highly rated striker was not given a chance to prove himself in the Fulham first team in 1999-2000 despite the catalogue of injuries to the club's other strikers. Kevin spent a month on loan at Bournemouth last September but, although he showed touches of skill, he started only once for the Cherries and returned to Craven Cottage when his loan period was up. In November he was loaned to Hull (whose assistant boss, John McGovern, had been his manager at Woking) following Colin Alcide's move to York. With Hull's ranks including Jamaican internationals, Kevin's exotic birthplace seemed apt yet he also has relatives in nearby Gilberdyke. Returning to Fulham before the end of his loan, he has proved to be a versatile player who can also operate at wing back and as a wide midfielder. Although treading water for much of the season, his many admirers among the Craven Cottage crowd will be hoping that 2000-01 proves more rewarding.

Fulham (£80,000 + from Woking on 16/9/1998) FL 1+8/1 FLC 0+1 FAC 0+1 Others 1
Bournemouth (Loaned on 3/9/1999) FL 1+4
Hull C (Loaned on 26/11/1999) FL 1+1 Others 1

BETTNEY Christopher (Chris) John
Born: Chesterfield, 27 October 1977
Height: 5'10" Weight: 11.4

Signed by Chesterfield from Sheffield United during the 1999 close season on a three-month contract, this pacy winger showed good touches without ever stamping his influence on a game. He turned down an extended contract and joined Rochdale, initially on trial, in November. His speedy play on the right wing soon made him a favourite with the crowd, and earned him a contract to the end of the season. With Dale operating with only one wide player, he alternated in the side with Graeme Atkinson for a time, often starting on the bench. Chris had fewer opportunities after Dale changed to a wing-back system. He was released in May.

Sheffield U (From trainee on 15/5/1996) FL 0+1
Hull C (Loaned on 26/9/1997) FL 28+2/1 FLC 2 Others 1
Chesterfield (Free on 3/7/1999) FL 7+6 FLC 3
Rochdale (Free on 5/11/1999) FL 12+12 FAC 0+1 Others 3+2

BETTS Robert
Born: Doncaster, 21 December 1981
Height: 5'10" Weight: 11.0

The captain of Coventry's successful youth team, Robert was given his chance at senior level as a substitute towards the end of last season. Coventry signed him from Doncaster Rovers, for whom he had first appeared in the Football League as a 15-year-old. He is the grandson of former Manchester United, Stoke, Coventry and West Bromwich warhorse Maurice Setters and shows his grandfather's tenacity in the tackle. A great future is predicted for a young man once described by Gordon Strachan as a "natural leader". He made his City debut as a substitute at West Ham and came on again the following week at Newcastle.

Doncaster Rov (Trainee) FL 2+1
Coventry C (From trainee on 23/12/1998) PL 0+2

BEWERS Jonathan
Born: Kettering, 10 September 1982
Height: 5'9" Weight: 10.2
International Honours: E: Yth; Sch

Jonathan is one of several bright prospects on Aston Villa's books and was given his Premiership debut at Tottenham last April when he came on as a substitute for Mark Delaney in the closing minutes. He had an excellent 1999-2000 campaign with Villa's youth team, appearing at full back, in the centre of defence and in midfield at various points in the season. A regular in the England U16 team in 1998-99, he appeared for the U17s in Luxembourg last April and is clearly one to watch for the future.

Aston Villa (From trainee on 16/9/1999) PL 0+1

BHUTIA Bhaichung
Born: Gangtok, Sikkim, India, 15 December 1976
Height: 5'8" Weight: 10.2
International Honours: India: 40

The arrival of this pint-pot forward, who is the captain of the Indian international team, was heralded as a real scoop when Bury finally obtained a work permit for him last September. Bhaichung made his debut against Cardiff City at Gigg Lane in October, although a general lack of fitness coupled with the need to adjust to English football meant that he found himself utilised as a substitute for much of the time. Skilful on the ball and a chaser of lost causes, he proved to be an excellent finisher at reserve-team level but managed just two goals in the first team. His first goal came against Chesterfield at Gigg Lane on 15 April and the general feeling at Bury is that there is much more to come next season from Bhaichung.

Bury (Signed from East Bengal, India on 29/9/1999) FL 6+8/2 FAC 1+3

[BICA] DI GIUSEPPE Marcos
Born: San Paulo, Brazil, 12 March 1972
Height: 6'4" Weight: 12.7

This Brazilian striker arrived at Sunderland for a two-week trial last September. Nicknamed "Bica", the stylish forward made an impressive start at the Stadium of Light with a goal for the reserves against Manchester United and appeared as a substitute for the first team against Walsall in a 5-0 away Worthington Cup win, scraping the crossbar with a thunderous drive from 25 yards. However, Peter Reid decided not to extend Marcos's loan period and he moved on, joining Walsall on trial. He played for the last 14 minutes of the 1-0 win at West Bromwich on 16 October but was released soon after sitting on the bench as a non-playing substitute for the next match at Portsmouth, having also appeared in three reserve games.

Sunderland (Free from Sport Boys, Callao, Peru on 21/9/1999) FLC 0+1
Walsall (Free on 12/10/1999) FL 0+1

BIGNOT Marcus
Born: Birmingham, 22 August 1974
Height: 5'10" Weight: 11.2
International Honours: E: SP-1

Since moving to Crewe from Kidderminster in 1997, Marcus has proved to be a versatile defender. Having made occasional appearances earlier in the season, he was restored to the starting line-up against Bolton last October and held his place until early March, when he sustained a shoulder injury against Portsmouth which forced him to miss all the remaining games. Usually employed at right back, he is a pacy player who competes enthusiastically for every ball but he has yet to score his first goal for the club.

Crewe Alex (£150,000+ from Kidderminster Hrs on 1/9/1997) FL 93+2 FLC 8 FAC 3

BILLY Christopher (Chris) Anthony
Born: Huddersfield, 2 January 1973
Height: 5'11" Weight: 11.8

Bury's versatile utility player enjoyed a much more consistent season in 1999-2000 than he had in the previous twelve months and was again employed in a mixture of defensive and midfield positions to much effect. After suffering an early-season ankle injury Chris managed to stay largely clear of further knocks and seldom missed a game. He also increased his goalscoring contribution, grabbing five goals during the season, including a spectacular long-range shot against Wigan and a satisfying goal in the final fixture against his former club Notts County.

Huddersfield T (From trainee on 1/7/1991) FL 76+18/4 FLC 8+2 FAC 5 Others 15+2/2

Plymouth Arg (Signed on 10/8/1995) FL 107+11/9 FLC 5 FAC 8/1 Others 5+1
Notts Co (Free on 2/7/1998) FL 3+3 FLC 2
Bury (Free on 17/9/1998) FL 67+6/4 FLC 1 FAC 4/1 Others 1

BIMSON Stuart James
Born: Liverpool, 29 September 1969
Height: 5'11" Weight: 11.12

Stuart recovered from a knee operation during the 1999 summer break only to miss the start of the new season with a fresh injury. When he recovered fitness he was often out of favour at Lincoln, and after Christmas he lost his place to teenage prospect Paul Mayo. The left back and corner specialist had a disappointing 1999-2000 season: having begun the campaign by signing a new contract, he finished it open to offers as a free transfer.

Bury (£12,500 from Macclesfield T on 6/2/1995) FL 36 FLC 5 Others 3
Lincoln C (Free on 29/11/1996) FL 65+13/3 FAC 5+1 Others 5+1/1

BIRCHAM Marc Stephen John
Born: Wembley, 11 May 1978
Height: 5'10" Weight: 12.4
International Honours: Canada: 10; U23-1

Marc, still only 22, is a product of the excellent Millwall youth policy. A strong-tackling midfield player, he was enjoying an excellent 1999-2000 season until an injury at Bury in January put him out for the rest of the campaign. His normal position was full back but he seemed most at home in the centre of midfield, where he formed an excellent partnership with Tim Cahill. He plays with total commitment, has real appetite for the game and is devoted to the Millwall cause. His performances for the Lions earned him international recognition with Canada, whose manager saw Marc as the player he needed in centre midfield. He was called upon on several occasions including the CONCACAF Gold Cup, which he was sadly forced to sit out through injury. He was greatly missed by his club during his absence so it is hoped that he will recover fully for next season.

Millwall (From trainee on 22/5/1996) FL 51+9/1 FLC 2+1 FAC 2+1 Others 3+1

BIRD Anthony (Tony)
Born: Cardiff, 1 September 1974
Height: 5'10" Weight: 12.8
Club Honours: Div 3 '00
International Honours: W: U21-8; Yth

Despite showing impressive form in the early-season Worthington Cup matches, Tony was unable to claim an automatic place in the Swansea side during the 1999-2000 season. He joined non-league Merthyr in January on loan and scored on his debut against Atherstone. Placed on the transfer list at the Vetch Field, he did, however, make a return to the first team towards the end of the season, playing an important role in the Swans' promotion squad with regular appearances from the substitutes' bench. He won a Third Division championship winners' medal, but was released in May. Stop Press: Tony was reported to have signed for league newcomers Kidderminster Harriers in early June.

Cardiff C (From trainee on 4/8/1993) FL 44+31/13 FLC 8/2 FAC 4+1/1 Others 12+4/3 (Free to Barry T in January 1996)
Swansea C (£40,000 on 8/8/1997) FL 51+35/18 FLC 5+2/1 FAC 2+1 Others 3+3/3

BIRMINGHAM David Paul
Born: Portsmouth, 16 April 1981
Height: 5'6" Weight: 10.0

This young defender joined Portsmouth in the summer of 1999 after recovering from a badly broken leg. He was promoted to the first-team squad after a series of excellent performances for the youths and reserves, making his debut in senior football as a substitute at Bolton last March and then appearing in the starting line-up for the visit to Ipswich. David is a pacy player who is courageous in the tackle and works hard. He missed the last few weeks of the 1999-2000 season as he required an operation to remove a surgical pin that had been inserted into his leg when it was broken.

Portsmouth (Free from Bournemouth juniors on 4/8/1999) FL 1+1

BISHOP Ian William
Born: Liverpool, 29 May 1965
Height: 5'9" Weight: 10.12
International Honours: E: B-1

Ian began the 1999-2000 season on the subs' bench for Manchester City and started in only two of the club's first nine games. However, he came into the team for the match at Walsall in mid-September and didn't look back. He is a creative midfielder of genuine class who is prepared to hold the ball before playing perceptive passes to the wings and through the middle. Hugely experienced, Ian was also a calming influence on his colleagues in the middle of the pitch and it is a measure of his importance to the team that many of City's best results were achieved when "Bish" was on form. An injury in late November that caused him to miss three games interrupted what was otherwise an unbroken run until March, when City manager Joe Royle began to rotate his squad. Ian bagged both goals in the 2-1 win against Port Vale in October and also scored twice in the FA Cup. He has accepted a one-year extension to his contract and will be able to finish his career in the Premiership.

Everton (From apprentice on 24/5/1983) FL 0+1
Crewe Alex (Loaned on 22/3/1984) FL 4
Carlisle U (£15,000 on 11/10/1984) FL 131+1/14 FLC 8/1 FAC 5/1 Others 4
Bournemouth (£35,000 on 14/7/1988) FL 44/2 FLC 4 FAC 5 Others 1
Manchester C (£465,000 on 2/8/1989) FL 18+1/2 FLC 4/1 Others 1
West Ham U (£500,000 on 28/12/1989) F/PL 240+14/12 FLC 21+1/1 FAC 22+1/3 Others 4+1/1
Manchester C (Free on 26/3/1998) FL 50+18/2 FLC 2+2 FAC 3+1/2 Others 0+1

BLACK Kingsley Terence
Born: Luton, 22 June 1968
Height: 5'9" Weight: 11.2
Club Honours: FLC '88; FMC '92; AMC '98
International Honours: E: Sch. NI: 30; B-3; U21-1

Once again Kingsley had to struggle for a place in the Grimsby midfield in 1999-2000 as a result of the club's rich supplies of talent in that area. Coming back into the side as a replacement for young Adam Buckley, he became first choice on the left flank. Ever the consummate professional, he can always be relied upon to give of his utmost in providing a service to the strikers and putting in some telling balls from free kicks. On recapturing his regular place on the left of midfield he played a vital role in the Mariners' climb from the relegation zone to a comfortable mid-table position before being released in the summer.

Luton T (From juniors on 7/7/1986) FL 123+4/26 FLC 16+2/1 FAC 5+1/2 Others 3+2/1
Nottingham F (£1,500,000 on 2/9/1991) F/PL 80+18/14 FLC 19+1/5 FAC 4 Others 4+2/1
Sheffield U (Loaned on 2/3/1995) FL 8+3/2
Millwall (Loaned on 29/9/1995) FL 1+2/1 FLC 0+1
Grimsby T (£25,000 on 16/7/1996) FL 87+49/8 FLC 14 FAC 5+2 Others 2+5/1

BLACK Michael James
Born: Chigwell, 6 October 1976
Height: 5'8" Weight: 11.8
Club Honours: FAYC '94
International Honours: E: Sch

Michael moved north to Tranmere in the summer of 1999 after developing through the ranks at Highbury. He made his debut for Rovers when he came on as a late substitute in the opening game of the 1999-2000 season against Bolton, but apart from a handful of starts most of his senior experience was from the subs' bench. He registered his only goal with a neat strike in the 4-0 Worthington Cup win over Barnsley in November. He is a skilful winger with excellent ball control and a good cross who makes up for his lack of inches with his strength and determination. Michael is expected to establish himself as a regular in the Tranmere team during the 2000-01 season. He is the elder brother of Arsenal's Tommy Black.

Arsenal (From trainee on 1/7/1995) Others 0+1
Millwall (Loaned on 3/10/1997) FL 13/2 Others 1
Tranmere Rov (Free on 14/7/1999) FL 7+15 FLC 1+4/1

BLACK Thomas (Tommy) Robert
Born: Chigwell, 26 November 1979
Height: 5'7" Weight: 11.4

Tommy is the younger brother of Michael Black, formerly with Arsenal and now with Tranmere Rovers. He joined Arsenal as a trainee in the summer of 1996, and is another product of the club's successful youth scheme. He is a former England schoolboy trialist, and has played regularly in the Gunners' U19 and reserve teams for the past two seasons. A hard-working winger with an eye for goal, Tommy was loaned to Carlisle early in the 1999-2000 campaign and displayed pace and good control as he turned in some effective performances for the club. His only goal came in Carlisle's 4-2 victory over Plymouth, one of their best displays of the season. Hopes of a more permanent deal were dashed when he was recalled to Highbury, and he made his Arsenal debut in the Worthington Cup tie at Middlesbrough last November. The following month he joined Bristol City on loan, and his all-action style made him an instant favourite with the fans who witnessed his sparkling debut in the home game against Wycombe Wanderers. Unfortunately, all thought of a permanent move to the West Country was thwarted by the high price Arsenal wanted for his transfer, and after making four appearances, which included a spell in a striking role, he returned to Highbury.

Arsenal (From trainee on 3/7/1998) PL 0+1 FLC 1
Carlisle U (Loaned on 25/8/1999) FL 5/1
Bristol C (Loaned on 17/12/1999) FL 4

BLACKBURN Christopher (Chris) Raymond
Born: Crewe, 2 August 1982
Height: 5'7" Weight: 10.8

The Chester trainee had his first taste of senior action at the tender age of 17 years and 12 days when he came on as a substitute for the vastly experienced Shaun Reid at Rotherham in August 1999. Chris took a further chance to display his potential when starting, and scoring, in a Cheshire FA Senior Cup defeat by Macclesfield in November.

Chester C (Trainee) FL 0+1

BLACKMORE Clayton Graham
Born: Neath, 23 September 1964
Height: 5'8" Weight: 11.12
Club Honours: FAC '90; ECWC '91; ESC '91; PL '93; Div 1 '95
International Honours: W: 39; U21-3; Yth; Sch

This experienced left back came to Notts County in July 1999 after being released by Barnsley. He produced some superb form for the Magpies in the early part of 1999-2000 but then faded from the scene in the second half of the season. At his best Clayton is a strong-tackling and skilful left-sided midfielder who can also fill in as a left wing back. He was released during the summer.

Manchester U (From apprentice on 28/9/1982) F/PL 150+36/19 FLC 23+2/3 FAC 15+6/1 Others 19/4
Middlesbrough (Free on 11/7/1994) P/FL 45+8/4 FLC 4+2 FAC 4+1 Others 1
Bristol C (Loaned on 1/11/1996) FL 5/1
Barnsley (Free on 26/2/1999) FL 4+3 FAC 1
Notts Co (Free on 20/7/1999) FL 21/2 FLC 4/2 FAC 1 Others 0+1

BLACKWELL Dean Robert
Born: Camden, 5 December 1969
Height: 6'1" Weight: 12.7
International Honours: E: U21-6

Dean has been a consistent performer for Wimbledon in recent seasons but the Dons were robbed of his services for the majority of the 1999-2000 campaign owing to injuries. Even when he was back in action at the end of the season, it was only because of an injury crisis in defence and, although he played in the matches, he trained only occasionally. A commanding centre half who wins more than his fair share of headers and tackles, Dean would fit comfortably into any Premiership side when fully fit. A one-club player, he has been a loyal servant to Wimbledon and is respected by the club and the fans alike. Having gone through the whole of the 1998-99 season without being booked, Dean was ironically sent off in Wimbledon's opening game of 1999-2000 at Watford.

Wimbledon (From trainee on 7/7/1988) F/PL 175+24/1 FLC 19 FAC 22+1 Others 1
Plymouth Arg (Loaned on 15/3/1990) FL 5+2

BLACKWOOD Michael
Born: Birmingham, 30 September 1979
Height: 5'10" Weight: 11.10

The young Aston Villa striker had his first taste of senior football when he went on loan to Chester early in the Deva club's 1999-2000 relegation campaign. Although the Blues were struggling, Michael made a favourable impression, often showing some nice touches of Premiership potential, and confirmed that he is one to watch. He was released by Villa in the summer. Stop Press: Michael was reported to have signed for Second Division Wrexham at the end of June.

Aston Villa (From trainee on 14/4/1998)
Chester C (Loaned on 3/9/1999) FL 9/2

BLAKE Mark Antony
Born: Nottingham, 16 December 1970
Height: 5'11" Weight: 13.0
International Honours: E: U21-9; Yth; Sch

Mark joined Mansfield last August as a non-contract player after being released by Walsall in the summer, having missed the whole of the 1998-99 season through injury. He got his chance in Town's midfield in the third game of the season, at a time when his tough tackling and measured distribution were sorely needed, and some impressive displays were enough for him to be offered full-time terms by the Stags' management. A first-team regular thereafter, he scored with a spectacular long-range effort in the FA Cup at Bristol City in October and repeated the feat at Macclesfield a few days later.

Aston Villa (From trainee on 1/7/1989) FL 26+5/2 FLC 1+1 FAC 2 Others 2
Wolverhampton W (Loaned on 17/1/1991) FL 2
Portsmouth (£400,000 on 5/8/1993) FL 15 Others 4+1
Leicester C (£360,000 on 24/3/1994) P/FL 42+7/4 FLC 4 Others 3
Walsall (Free on 23/8/1996) FL 51+10/5 FLC 2 FAC 0+4 Others 2+2/1
Mansfield T (Free on 13/8/1999) FL 40+3/1 FLC 1 FAC 1/1 Others 2

BLAKE Nathan Alexander
Born: Cardiff, 27 January 1972
Height: 5'11" Weight: 13.2
Club Honours: WC '92, '93; Div 3 '93, Div 1 '97
International Honours: W: 15; B-1; U21-5; Yth

Nathan has been unable to recapture the form that made him such a dependable goal-scorer during his time with Bolton since moving to Blackburn in October 1998, finding it difficult to make much of an impact in a struggling side. He was in and out of the Rovers line-up in 1999-2000 and never really built up any momentum. His undoubted pace and power were rarely seen to any great effect, and as his confidence ebbed away his finishing suffered, but he deserves credit for regularly getting into goalscoring positions. An early goal against Tranmere confirmed his strengths as he dummied and then ran powerfully before finishing clinically. Although being sent off against Ipswich, he provided Rovers' best moment of the season when he scored the only goal in the FA Cup tie at Anfield. He made four international appearances for Wales.

Cardiff C (Free from Chelsea juniors on 20/8/1990) FL 113+18/35 FLC 6+2 FAC 10/4 Others 13+2/1
Sheffield U (£300,000 on 17/2/1994) P/FL 55+14/34 FLC 3+1/1 FAC 1 Others 1
Bolton W (£1,500,000 on 23/12/1995) F/PL 102+5/38 FLC 10+1/8 FAC 6/2
Blackburn Rov (£4,250,000 on 30/10/1998) P/FL 26+13/6 FLC 2 FAC 5+2/2

Nathan Blake

BLAKE Noel Lloyd George
Born: Jamaica, 12 January 1962
Height: 6'1" Weight: 14.2

Noel assumed the role of manager at Exeter after Peter Fox left the club in January 1999. Although he played only a handful of games last season, Noel's experience and presence in his familiar centre-back berth paid off as City immediately stopped haemorrhaging goals. Although not initially interested in the job, he fought off competition from 150 applicants to earn the contract to be in charge of the Grecians in 2000-01.

Aston Villa (Signed from Sutton Coldfield T on 1/8/1979) FL 4
Shrewsbury T (Loaned on 1/3/1982) FL 6
Birmingham C (£55,000 on 15/9/1982) FL 76/5 FLC 12 FAC 8
Portsmouth (£150,000 on 24/4/1984) FL 144/10 FLC 14/1 FAC 10/2 Others 5/1
Leeds U (Free on 4/7/1988) FL 51/4 FLC 4+1 FAC 2 Others 4

Stoke C (£175,000 on 9/2/1990) FL 74+1/3 FLC 6 FAC 3+1 Others 4+1
Bradford C (Loaned on 27/2/1992) FL 6
Bradford C (Free on 20/7/1992) FL 38+1/3 FLC 2+1 FAC 5/1 Others 4
Dundee (Free on 10/12/1993) SL 52+2/2 SLC 2 SC 5 Others 3
Exeter C (Free on 18/8/1995) FL 132+10/10 FLC 6 FAC 6 Others 3+2

BLAKE Robert (Robbie) James
Born: Middlesbrough, 4 March 1976
Height: 5'9" Weight: 12.6

Robbie began the 1999-2000 season on the transfer list at Bradford City after failing to agree a new contract and it was not until the end of September that he made the starting line-up for a Premiership match. He was in and out of the side after this until the closing weeks of the season, when a run of superb form saw him back in contention for a regular place in the team. Although his preferred role is as a striker, he was mostly employed on the right side of midfield.

Darlington (From trainee on 1/7/1994) FL 54+14/21 FLC 4+2/1 FAC 3+1 Others 3+1/1
Bradford C (£300,000 on 27/3/1997) P/FL 76+30/26 FLC 5+3/2 FAC 5/1

BLATHERWICK Steven (Steve) Scott
Born: Hucknall, 20 September 1973
Height: 6'1" Weight: 14.6

Steve seized the chance of a regular first-team place with Chesterfield last season with some determined, bullish displays at the heart of the defence. His greatest asset is his power in the air, which makes him a difficult opponent in either penalty box. Chesterfield were relegated despite a pretty good "goals against" record, due in no small part to Steve's presence.

Nottingham F (Free from Notts Co juniors on 2/8/1992) FL 10 FLC 2 FAC 1 Others 2
Wycombe W (Loaned on 18/2/1994) FL 2 Others 1
Hereford U (Loaned on 11/9/1995) FL 10/1 Others 2
Reading (Loaned on 27/3/1997) FL 6+1
Burnley (£150,000 on 18/7/1997) FL 16+8 FLC 5 FAC 1+1 Others 3
Chesterfield (Loaned on 18/9/1998) FL 2
Chesterfield (£50,000 on 1/12/1998) FL 43+5/1 FLC 2 FAC 1 Others 5/2

BLOOMER Matthew (Matt) Brian
Born: Grimsby, 3 November 1978
Height: 6'0" Weight: 13.0

Despite Grimsby's increasing injury problems in the middle of the back line last season, this young central defender was restricted to a couple of appearances as a substitute towards the end of the campaign. The likely departure of Mark Lever in the close season may mean more opportunity for Matt in 2000-01.

Grimsby T (From juniors on 3/7/1997) FL 0+6 Others 0+1

BLOOMER Robert (Bob) Stephen
Born: Sheffield, 21 June 1966
Height: 5'10" Weight: 12.7

This central midfield player returned to the Football League in 1999-2000 with Cheltenham eight years after leaving it when he was released by Bristol Rovers. Bob played in the opening match of the season but was not called upon to start another game after that, his subsequent appearances being from the substitutes' bench. Nevertheless, Bob is regarded as an important member of the Robins' squad, although he sees his future in coaching. His vast experience was put to good use helping the club's younger players, and his first-class attitude rubs off on the rest of the squad. For example, he played in every reserve-team game during the season as Cheltenham lifted the Optimum Interiors Central Conference title. A hard-working midfield player who can also cover defensive positions, Bob has been awarded a further year's contract at the club.

Chesterfield (From juniors on 21/8/1985) FL 120+21/15 FLC 2+2 FAC 5+1 Others 9+1/1
Bristol Rov (£20,000 on 22/3/1990) FL 11+11
Cheltenham T (Free on 15/8/1992) FL 1+10 FLC 0+2 Others 0+1

BOA MORTE Luis Pereira
Born: Lisbon, Portugal, 4 August 1977
Height: 5'10" Weight: 11.5
Club Honours: PL '98; CS '98, '99
International Honours: Portugal: U21

Although he started the 1999-2000 season as an Arsenal player, Luis's only appearances for the club were from the substitutes' bench in the Charity Shield and against Derby and Sunderland in the Premiership in August. He then jumped at the chance to join his younger brother Bruno Leah at Southampton later that month. A forward of enormous potential, he made an unlucky start by being sent off in his debut at Middlesbrough in early September. Employed as a squad player, Luis spent the majority of the season on the bench, but when used he showed his power and pace to good effect; probably his best performance came against Bradford City at the Dell when he ran himself into the ground with his non-stop sprints down the left. He is a player with a bright future and without doubt a full international appearance for Portugal will follow.

Arsenal (£1,750,000 + from Sporting Lisbon, Portugal on 25/6/1997) PL 6+19 FLC 3/2 FAC 2+3/1 Others 2+4/1
Southampton (£500,000 + on 27/8/1999) PL 6+8/1 FLC 0+2 FAC 1

BOATENG George
Born: Nkawkaw, Ghana, 5 September 1975
Height: 5'9" Weight: 11.7
International Honours: Holland: U21-18

This former Dutch U21 skipper moved to Aston Villa from their Midlands rivals Coventry City in the summer of 1999 for a £4.5 million fee. He began 1999-2000 playing in a wide midfield role for Villa and took some time to fit in with his new club's style of play. However, the team was reshuffled last December following the injury to Dion Dublin and George was switched to a holding role in the centre of midfield. He was a revelation from then onwards, producing some outstanding displays in the second half of the campaign as the team went on to reach the FA Cup final. George received a runners-up medal for his efforts against Chelsea and will be aiming to make this the first of many honours in the English game. He is ideally suited to the central midfield slot, having both tremendous energy and a ferocious tackle. His other talents include accurate distribution, the ability to support his attack and a fine shot.

Coventry C (£250,000 from Feyenoord, Holland, via Excelsior, on 19/12/1997) PL 43+4/5 FLC 3/1 FAC 8/1
Aston Villa (£4,500,000 on 22/7/1999) PL 30+3/2 FLC 7/1 FAC 5

George Boateng

BOERTIEN Paul
Born: Haltwhistle, 21 January 1979
Height: 5'10" Weight: 11.2

The young left wing back continued to make good progress in Derby's reserve side in 1999-2000 while occasionally featuring on the bench for the first team. Unfortunate in that his position is so well covered by others at Pride Park, thus reducing his immediate opportunities, he was loaned to Crewe Alexandra for a month in February, although he was restricted to just two appearances for the Gresty Road club. One of several very good youngsters at Derby, while not the quickest of players, he overcomes this by his ability to read the game and intercept opposition passes.

Carlisle U (From trainee on 13/5/1997) FL 16+1/1 FLC 0+2 FAC 1 Others 1
Derby Co (£250,000 on 25/3/1999) PL 0+3 FLC 0+1
Crewe Alex (Loaned on 11/2/2000) FL 2

BOGIE Ian
Born: Newcastle, 6 December 1967
Height: 5'8" Weight: 12.0
International Honours: E: Sch

The skilful midfield player was used sparingly by Port Vale in 1999-2000 despite his ability to put his foot on the ball and change moves in an instant. Ian began the season on the transfer list but, with no takers, he knuckled down to win a first-team place and had a four-game run in September and October. Unfortunately, a niggling groin strain hampered his progress and, apart from a further short run of four games, that was all he had to show for the season. He was released on a free transfer in April and returned to live in the North-east.

Newcastle U (From apprentice on 18/12/1985) FL 7+7 FLC 0+1 FAC 1+2 Others 3/1
Preston NE (Signed on 9/2/1989) FL 67+12/12 FLC 3+1 FAC 3 Others 4+1
Millwall (£145,000 on 16/8/1991) FL 44+7/1 FLC 1 FAC 2 Others 3
Leyton Orient (Signed on 14/10/1993) FL 62+3/5 FLC 2 FAC 2 Others 8+1
Port Vale (£50,000 on 23/3/1995) FL 133+21/9 FLC 9/1 FAC 8+2/2 Others 8

BOHINEN Lars
Born: Vadso, Norway, 8 September 1969
Height: 6'0" Weight: 12.10
International Honours: Norway: 48

By his own admission, Derby's Norwegian international midfield player will be glad to see the back of the 1999-2000 season. He started the campaign as a regular in the first team, but a knee operation in September kept him out for three months, this being his second operation to remove loose cartilage. Midway through the season, he was transfer listed and though he later returned to the fold a hamstring injury towards the end of the season meant his on-field activity was limited to helping the reserves pick up their league title. Lars prefers to play on the right side of midfield and, while possessing a wide range of creative passing, does seem to struggle with the more physical aspects of life in the Premiership.

Nottingham F (£450,000 from Young Boys of Berne, Switzerland, via Valergengen and Viking, on 5/11/1993) F/PL 59+5/7 FLC 7+1/2 FAC 2/1 Others 1
Blackburn Rov (£700,000 on 14/10/1995) PL 40+18/7 FLC 3+2/1 FAC 2+1/1
Derby Co (£1,450,000 on 27/3/1998) PL 46+8/1 FLC 2 FAC 3

BOLAND William (Willie) John
Born: Ennis, Ireland, 6 August 1975
Height: 5'9" Weight: 11.2
International Honours: RoI: B-1; U21-11; Yth; Sch

The Irish-born midfielder found it difficult to adjust to Second Division football after joining Cardiff from Coventry during the 1999 close season. It was obvious that Willie is a talented player, but he struggled to adapt to life outside the Premiership. He was committed and always trained hard, but little seemed to go right for him. He wasn't helped by being labelled on his arrival as "Cardiff's most expensive signing ever", which inevitably created unrealistic expectations. However, he showed that he is a fighter and finished the season looking strong, with his ability beginning to shine through. At his best, Willie rarely wastes a pass, has good movement, gets forward and can score goals, and Cardiff will be looking to get the most out of him during his second season at Ninian Park.

Coventry C (From juniors on 4/11/1992) PL 43+20 FLC 6+1 FAC 0+1
Cardiff C (Free on 24/6/1999) FL 20+8/1 FLC 3 FAC 1+2 Others 1

BOLDER Adam Peter
Born: Hull, 25 October 1980
Height: 5'8" Weight: 11.0

Although his only first-team experience going into the 1999-2000 season was a thirty-minute appearance as a substitute the previous January, Adam was to enjoy a truly meteoric rise during the campaign. A graduate of Hull's Centre of Excellence who had signed his first professional contract in the summer, he broke into the City first team in December and held his place as the Tigers went on their best run of the season. The tenacious right-sided midfielder was so impressive that he was given an improved two-and-a-half-year contract in March. It was to run for only a couple of weeks, however, as cash-strapped Hull then accepted Derby's bid for the youngster, who thus teamed up again with ex-Tiger Andy Oakes and fellow East Riding exile Lee Morris. A talented all-round sportsman, Adam also excelled at rugby union and judo as a boy, while his brother Chris is a trainee at Hull.

Hull C (From trainee on 9/7/1999) FL 18+2 Others 2+1
Derby Co (Signed on 3/4/2000)

BOLLAND Paul Graham
Born: Bradford, 23 December 1979
Height: 5'11" Weight: 11.0

This promising Notts County midfielder was in and out of the first team during 1999-2000 but showed steady improvement and scored his first goal in senior football with a cracking 15-yard shot in the 2-1 defeat at Chesterfield towards the end of the season. He produced a series of mature displays that belied his youth and will be hoping to establish himself as a regular in the Notts team in 2000-01. Paul is a hard-working and competitive player whose best position is in the centre of midfield.

Bradford C (From trainee on 20/3/1998) FL 4+8 FLC 2
Notts Co (£75,000 on 14/1/1999) FL 30+8/1 FLC 0+3 FAC 1 Others 0+1

BONALAIR Thierry
Born: Paris, France, 14 June 1966
Height: 5'9" Weight: 10.8
Club Honours: Div 1 '98
International Honours: France: U21

Thierry appeared regularly in the Nottingham Forest first-team squad in the first half of 1999-2000, scoring one of the goals in the 2-0 win at Port Vale last October, but featured only twice after the dismal 3-1 defeat by Huddersfield the following month. His contract was due to end in the summer but he left Forest by agreement last April with the intention of returning to France and opening up a restaurant.

Nottingham F (Free from Neuchatel Xamax, Switzerland, via Nantes, Auxere and Lille, on 17/7/1997) P/FL 58+13/5 FLC 6+2 FAC 1

BONNER Mark
Born: Ormskirk, 7 June 1974
Height: 5'10" Weight: 11.0

A gutsy, tenacious midfield player, Mark was one of the few successes of Cardiff's relegation season in 1999-2000. As the battle to avoid the drop intensified, he seemed to become stronger, more alert and even more committed to the cause. He is the kind of character the Bluebirds will need as they aim to bounce back to the Second Division at the first attempt. Named Cardiff's "Most Improved Player" by the supporters in recognition of his strong finish to the season, he certainly earned the respect of the Ninian Park faithful. It was Cardiff manager Billy Ayre who gave Mark his league debut when they were both at Blackpool, and Ayre will want to see the midfielder start the coming season as he ended the last. However, he didn't score a league goal – something he wants to put right in 2000-01.

Blackpool (From trainee on 18/6/1992) FL 156+22/14 FLC 15+3 FAC 11 Others 10+3/1
Cardiff C (Free on 17/7/1998) FL 50+6/1 FLC 4 FAC 2 Others 1
Hull C (Loaned on 8/1/1999) FL 1/1

BONNOT Alexandre (Alex)
Born: Paris, France, 31 July 1973
Height: 5'8" Weight: 11.4

The French midfield player confirmed his standing as a regular member of the Watford first-team squad by signing a two-year contract at the beginning of the 1999-2000 season. Alex's workrate and firm tackling belie his slight build, and he is a skilful and accurate passer of the ball. With Micah Hyde injured, he played in Watford's first two matches but was then mainly confined to the substitutes' bench until November, when he suffered what turned out to be a protracted back injury. After going back to France for treatment, Alex returned to the fray, making another four starts but usually being named as a sub.

Watford (Free from SCO Angers, France on 10/11/1998) P/FL 8+8

BOOK Steven (Steve) Kim
Born: Bournemouth, 7 July 1969
Height: 5'11" Weight: 11.1
International Honours: E: SP-3

An ever-present in the Cheltenham goal in 1999-2000, Steve held off the challenge of new signing Shane Higgs throughout the season. As was the case for many of Cheltenham's players, the opening-day defeat against Rochdale was his Football League debut, made, belatedly, at the age of 30. A confident and cheerful character, Steve's strengths are superb reflexes and shot-stopping ability. Like many lower-division goalkeepers, he is not so strong on crosses, although his tendency to punch rather than catch served him well in terms of clearing danger from the penalty area. Steve has also worked to improve his distribution, which assisted in providing a number of goals, such as the one scored by Martin Devaney against Torquay in March. Although he ultimately ended on the losing side, his save at Southend on the last day of the season was quite outstanding. He also saved penalties against Leyton Orient and Rochdale.

Cheltenham T (Signed from Forest Green Rov on 23/7/1997) FL 46 FLC 2 FAC 2 Others 2

BOOTH Andrew (Andy) David
Born: Huddersfield, 6 December 1973
Height: 6'0" Weight: 13.0
International Honours: E: U21-3

This Sheffield Wednesday striker found his place in the team under threat following the arrival of Gilles de Bilde and Gerald Sibon in the summer of 1999. However, although he failed to make the squad for the opening game against Liverpool, Andy soon forced his way back into contention and by September he had regained his place in the starting line-up. He then missed most of the second half of the campaign with injury before returning for the last few games. He is good in the air and works hard for the team but still needs to improve his goals-per-game ratio.

Huddersfield T (From trainee on 1/7/1992) FL 109+14/54 FLC 6+1/3 FAC 8/3 Others 12+1/4
Sheffield Wed (£2,700,000 on 8/7/1996) PL 107+8/25 FLC 8/1 FAC 8+1/4

Andy Booth

BOOTY Martyn James
Born: Kirby Muxloe, 30 May 1971
Height: 5'8" Weight: 11.2

Martyn's excellent 1999-2000 season for Southend was curtailed in January by injury, and the defence suffered as a consequence. Strong at either full back or centre half, Martyn was very consistent and his distribution from the back was always evident, as was his good sense of timing in the tackle. Southend will be hoping that he can recapture his top form in the new season.

Coventry C (From trainee on 30/5/1989) FL 4+1 FLC 2 FAC 2
Crewe Alex (Free on 7/10/1993) FL 95+1/5 FLC 6 FAC 8/1 Others 13
Reading (£75,000 on 18/1/1996) FL 62+2/1 FLC 10+1 FAC 7/1
Southend U (Free on 7/1/1999) FL 46+2 FLC 2 FAC 1

BORBOKIS Vassilios (Vass)
Born: Serres, Greece, 10 February 1969
Height: 5'11" Weight: 12.0
International Honours: Greece: 2

The former Sheffield United right wing back had a disappointing season at Derby in 1999-2000, losing his place in the starting eleven to the improved form of Rory Delap. On the occasions he did appear he still displayed great pace on overlapping runs and good distribution, though the defensive side of his game left something to be desired at times. His most effective performance was probably at Southampton, where his crosses helped Derby snatch two injury-time goals to earn a 3-3 draw. Vass asked for a transfer in December and at the end of the month he moved, for a nominal fee, back to his home country, joining PAOK Salonika.

Sheffield U (£900,000 from AEK Athens, Greece, via Apollon, on 9/7/1997) FL 55/4 FLC 9/3 FAC 9/1 Others 1/1
Derby Co (£600,000 + on 12/3/1999) PL 9+7 FLC 3/1 FAC 1

BOSHELL Daniel (Danny) Kevin
Born: Bradford, 30 May 1981
Height: 5'11" Weight: 11.10

This highly rated Oldham youngster made his league debut in February when he came on as a substitute in the home game with Gillingham and went on to make the starting line-up for the last few games of the 1999-2000 season. A midfield play-maker with an elegant style and a good range of passing, he is being mentioned as a potential successor to John Sheridan in the Latics' team. He came close to finding the net at Luton when he hit the bar with a free kick and, having scored regularly for the reserve and youth teams, he seems certain to hit his first goal in senior football before too much longer.

Oldham Ath (From trainee on 10/7/1998) FL 4+4

BOSNICH Mark John
Born: Sydney, Australia, 13 January 1972
Height: 6'2" Weight: 14.2
Club Honours: FLC '94, '96; PL '00
International Honours: Australia: 17; U23; Yth

A superb goalkeeper with a safe pair of hands and a flair for pulling off the spectacular, Mark finally rejoined Manchester United from Aston Villa in the summer of 1999 in a deal that had been football's worst-kept secret. While the prospect of replacing Peter Schmeichel was a daunting challenge, Mark said that he was actually relishing it. Not that it was ever going to be easy, particularly when he sustained a hamstring injury against Leeds at Old Trafford after just four games of the new campaign, which prompted Sir Alex Ferguson to rush out and sign Massimo Taibi from AC Milan. When he was then relegated to third-choice 'keeper behind Taibi and Rai van der Gouw for a short spell, there was speculation about a possible move to Spanish side Real Zaragoza. Coping admirably with the pressure, Mark came back to play a prominent role in United's continuing quest for honours. Safe and dependable, his performance against Palmeiras in the Intercontinental final in November was hailed as "inspiring" by Sir Alex and "world class" by United's skipper and match winner, Roy Keane. Although he suffered more hamstring problems in his next match against Everton in December, and went through another "sticky" patch in March, when Sir Alex preferred van der Gouw for the key European matches against Bordeaux, it just made him even more determined to fight for his place. With another world-class performance against Real Madrid in the Bernabeu in April under his belt, by the season's end Mark had re-established himself as the Reds' undisputed number one, his contribution to a successful season being rewarded with a Premiership winners' medal. He also added to his international experience with a further cap for Australia against Hungary last February. However, he suffered a considerable set-back when United signed the French international goalkeeper, Fabien Barthez, from Monaco during the summer, and he would appear to have little long-term future at Old Trafford.

Manchester U (Free from Sydney Croatia, Australia on 5/6/1989) FL 3
Aston Villa (Free on 28/2/1992) F/PL 179 FLC 20+1 FAC 17 Others 11
Manchester U (Free on 7/7/1999) PL 23 FLC 1 Others 11

BOSSU Bertrand (Bert)
Born: Calais, France, 14 October 1980
Height: 6'7" Weight: 14.0

Towering well over six feet, the teenage Frenchman spent the majority of the 1999-2000 campaign appearing in Barnet's youth team. An imposing figure between the posts, he was given an opportunity to appear in the reserves following a knee injury to Danny Naisbitt and his overall game improved as a result of the added experience. Bert's Bees' debut occurred in the highly charged play-off match at Peterborough, when he replaced the injured Lee Harrison in the closing minutes.

Barnet (Signed from RC Lens, France on 21/10/1999) Others 0+1

BOULD Stephen (Steve) Andrew
Born: Stoke, 16 November 1962
Height: 6'4" Weight: 14.2
Club Honours: Div 1 '89, '91; PL '98; ECWC '94; FAC '98; CS '98
International Honours: E: 2; B-1

A commanding former England centre back, Steve joined Sunderland in July 1999 from Arsenal for £400,000. Some eyebrows were raised when Peter Reid chose to offer a player in his mid-thirties a two-year contract, but the signing looked to be a masterstroke as Sunderland raced to third place by Christmas, thanks in no small part to the ex-Gunner, who formed a solid partnership with Paul Butler at the heart of the Black Cats' defence. Steve was immediately installed as team captain upon arrival and his positional sense, aerial dominance, experience and ability to organise and cajole his fellow defenders more than compensated for his advancing years. Unfortunately for Sunderland, a torn hamstring sustained against Leeds in January was to sideline Steve until March, a period when the Black Cats suffered their most barren run of the season. Although he returned as a substitute against Everton, and steadied defensive nerves as the team picked up their first win of 2000, a troublesome toe injury was to keep Steve out for the rest of the season.

Stoke C (From apprentice on 15/11/1980) FL 179+4/6 FLC 13/1 FAC 10 Others 5
Torquay U (Loaned on 19/10/1982) FL 9 FAC 2
Arsenal (£390,000 on 13/6/1988) F/PL 271+16/5 FLC 33/1 FAC 27+2 Others 18+6/2
Sunderland (£500,000 on 9/7/1999) PL 19+1 FAC 2

Steve Bould

BOULDING Michael Thomas
Born: Sheffield, 8 February 1975
Height: 5'10" Weight: 11.4

A former tennis professional signed by Mansfield in the summer of 1999 from local Sheffield team Hallam, Michael is a pacy and persistent left-sided attacking player who was used mainly as a substitute during 1999-2000. He scored a cracking 25-yarder at Shrewsbury in October to open his goal account for the Stags and had a short run in the team thereafter. Strangely, when seemingly on a scoring run, he was dropped from the side and returned to the subs' role, although he later returned to the first eleven when Tony Lormor was injured. During his first season in league football Michael showed that he is not afraid to take opponents on, using his pace to cause them trouble.

Mansfield T (Signed from Hallam FC on 2/8/1999) FL 16+17/6 FLC 1+1 FAC 0+1 Others 1

BOUND Matthew Terence
Born: Melksham, 9 November 1972
Height: 6'2" Weight: 14.6
Club Honours: Div 3 '00

A strong left-sided central defender, Matthew was placed on the Swansea transfer list last October after turning down offers of a new contract. The three league matches he missed during the 1999-2000 season were as a result of a sending-off at Exeter in an Auto Windscreens Shield tie. His central defensive partnership with Jason Smith was arguably the best in the Third Division last term. Matthew was also included in the PFA divisional team and he deservedly earned a championship winners' medal.

Southampton (From trainee on 3/5/1991) F/PL 2+3
Hull C (Loaned on 27/8/1993) FL 7/1
Stockport Co (£100,000 on 27/10/1994) FL 44/5 FLC 1 FAC 3/1 Others 3/1
Lincoln C (Loaned on 11/9/1995) FL 3+1 Others 1
Swansea C (£55,000 on 21/11/1997) FL 116/4 FLC 6/1 FAC 7 Others 7/2

BOWEN Jason Peter
Born: Merthyr Tydfil, 24 August 1972
Height: 5'7" Weight: 11.0
Club Honours: AMC '94
International Honours: W: 2; B-1; U21-5; Yth; Sch

Jason was Cardiff's joint-top scorer last season with 17 goals, 12 of which came in the league, finishing the campaign level with Kevin Nugent. Jason's pace and movement mark him out as a player of real quality, but he is not a natural central striker and proved more of a danger when he played wide on the right or made runs from just behind the front two. He emerged with considerable credit from what was a disappointing season for the Bluebirds.

Swansea C (From trainee on 1/7/1990) FL 93+31/26 FLC 6+1/2 FAC 9+2/1 Others 15+3/8
Birmingham C (£350,000 on 24/7/1995) FL 35+13/7 FLC 4+6/2 FAC 1+4 Others 2/2
Southampton (Loaned on 2/9/1997) PL 1+2
Reading (£200,000 on 24/12/1997) FL 12+3/1 FLC 1+1 FAC 5
Cardiff C (Free on 12/1/1999) FL 42+14/14 FLC 4/2 FAC 5+1 Others 1

Jason Bowen

BOWEN Mark Rosslyn
Born: Neath, 7 December 1963
Height: 5'8" Weight: 11.11
Club Honours: EUFAC '84
International Honours: W: 41; U21-3; Yth; Sch

Released by Charlton in the summer, Mark was recruited by Wigan on a monthly contract at the start of the 1999-2000 season because of injuries in the left-back position. His vast experience and calmness under pressure coupled with his good passing ability saw him play the opening seven league games, and he was never on the losing side in his two months with the Latics. When he was released at the start of December Mark went to Reading on trial but played just one game, an Auto Windscreens Shield tie against Leyton Orient. He did reasonably well but could not agree terms with the club and left after only a week. He then accepted a position in new Wales manager Mark Hughes's backroom staff, taking up a role as coach to the U21 side.

Tottenham H (From apprentice on 1/12/1981) FL 14+3/2 FAC 3 Others 0+1
Norwich C (£97,000 on 23/7/1987) F/PL 315+5/24 FLC 34/1 FAC 28/1 Others 17/1
West Ham U (Free on 10/7/1996) PL 15+2/1 FLC 3 (Free to Shimizu SP, Japan on 17/3/1997)
Charlton Ath (Free on 16/9/1997) P/FL 36+6 FAC 3 Others 3
Wigan Ath (Free on 6/8/1999) FL 7 FLC 3
Reading (Free on 3/12/1999) Others 1

BOWER Mark James
Born: Bradford, 23 January 1980
Height: 5'10" Weight: 11.0

New manager Terry Dolan's first signing, Mark joined York on loan from Bradford City in February 2000. A promising left-footed defender, he impressed in the centre of the Minstermen's back line as they pulled themselves to safety in the Third Division. Mark also found time to score in a home win over Lincoln. It seems unlikely that he will make a permanent move to Bootham Crescent, as Bradford offered him a two-year contract in May.

Bradford C (From trainee on 28/3/1998) FL 1+2
York C (Loaned on 16/2/2000) FL 15/1

BOWLING Ian
Born: Sheffield, 27 July 1965
Height: 6'3" Weight: 14.8

Having started the 1999-2000 season in the treatment room recovering from the broken arm he suffered at the end of the previous term, Ian returned to the Mansfield goal in November but was ruled out once more after being injured again in January. One of three Town players who required surgery to the left knee, he progressed well at first but then required a second operation to remove fibrous tissue. An excellent shot stopper who does not let the side down, he will be hoping for better fortune in 2000-01. He was out of contract in the summer.

Lincoln C (£2,000 from Gainsborough Trinity on 23/10/1988) FL 59 FLC 3 FAC 2 Others 4
Hartlepool U (Loaned on 17/8/1989) FL 1
Bradford C (Loaned on 25/3/1993) FL 7
Bradford C (£27,500 on 28/7/1993) FL 29 FLC 2 FAC 2+1 Others 1
Mansfield T (Free on 11/8/1995) FL 170 FLC 8 FAC 9 Others 8

BOWMAN Robert (Rob) Alexander
Born: Durham City, 21 November 1975
Height: 6'1" Weight: 12.10
Club Honours: FAYC '93
International Honours: E: Yth (UEFA-U18 '93)

An attacking full back, Rob was allocated the Carlisle number two shirt at the start of the 1999-2000 campaign, but medical

problems delayed his seasonal debut until October. Even then his appearances were restricted as further injuries kept him out of the side for much of the campaign. All in all, it was a disappointing end to his time at Brunton Park, as Rob was released in May. With Premiership and European experience from his time at Leeds, Rob will be determined to fulfil his undoubted potential elsewhere.
Leeds U (From trainee on 20/11/1992) PL 4+3 FLC 0+1 Others 1
Rotherham U (Free on 21/2/1997) FL 13
Carlisle U (Free on 14/8/1997) FL 42+4/2 FAC 2 Others 2

BOWRY Robert (Bobby) John
Born: Hampstead, 19 May 1971
Height: 5'9" Weight: 10.8
Club Honours: Div 1 '94
Bobby made only a handful of first-team appearances during 1999-2000 due to the quality of the Millwall midfield. He is a neat passer of the ball who gets forward quickly from midfield and, although his opportunities last season were limited, when he was given a start he usually put in a sound performance. Bobby made his 125th appearance for Millwall during the course of the campaign.
Queens Park R (Signed on 8/8/1990)
Crystal Palace (Free from Carshalton on 4/4/1992) F/PL 36+14/1 FLC 10 FAC 1
Millwall (£220,000 on 5/7/1995) FL 125+14/5 FLC 9 FAC 6 Others 4

BOWYER Lee David
Born: London, 3 January 1977
Height: 5'9" Weight: 10.6
International Honours: E: U21-13; Yth
Lee became the country's most expensive midfielder when he was signed by the Leeds manager of the time, Howard Wilkinson, in 1996. It has proved to be money well spent. Lee's consistent dynamic performances in the heart of the Leeds midfield last season increased speculation that England recognition was just around the corner. He reaped dividends from the hard work he put in, becoming one of the best all-round midfielders in the Premiership. His goal-scoring ability has never been in doubt, and his form continued during the last campaign. Two long-range goals at Partisan Belgrade in the UEFA Cup were followed by another excellent one from a distance against Newcastle. There were also superb goals from within the box against Leicester and Manchester City. Yet following his well documented court appearance, he seemed to be under pressure and missed relatively easy chances against Manchester United and Middlesbrough. However, his performance and goal against Slavia Prague were a testament to his professionalism. When he is on his game, he is one of the best all-action, combative midfield players in the country, though this can see him unjustifiably earn a booking from time to time. He should have a big future in the game.
Charlton Ath (From trainee on 13/4/1994) FL 46/8 FLC 6+1/5 FAC 3/1 Others 2
Leeds U (£2,600,000 on 5/7/1996) PL 119+6/21 FLC 5+1/1 FAC 14/3 Others 15/5

BOXALL Daniel (Danny) James
Born: Croydon, 24 August 1977
Height: 5'8" Weight: 11.6
Club Honours: Div 3 '99
International Honours: RoI: U21-8
This talented Brentford right back has good ball control and is at his best when pushing forward out of defence. Danny was a regular in the Bees' back four in 1999-2000 until suffering a cruciate ligament injury at Luton last February that kept him out of action for the rest of the campaign. He added to his total of Republic of Ireland U21 caps with appearances against Croatia and Malta.
Crystal Palace (From trainee on 19/4/1995) F/PL 5+3 FLC 1+1
Oldham Ath (Loaned on 21/11/1997) FL 6 Others 1
Oldham Ath (Loaned on 27/2/1998) FL 12
Brentford (Free on 9/7/1998) FL 62+1/1 FLC 6 FAC 4 Others 5

BOYCE Emmerson Orlando
Born: Aylesbury, 24 September 1979
Height: 5'11" Weight: 11.10
Another cultivated graduate of Luton's youth programme, Emmerson is a talented right back or central defender who established himself in the club's first team during the second half of the 1999-2000 season. He is strong in the tackle, defends well and possesses a deadly shot, while his commanding ability in the air and great pace enable him to come forward in support of his forwards. He also passes the ball well, and scored his first senior goal for Luton in Town's 2-1 defeat at home by Bournemouth in February. After signing a new contract tying him to the club until 2002, he continued to impress and, as one of Luton's most rapidly improving young players, will be looking to secure a regular spot in the starting line-up next season.
Luton T (From trainee on 2/4/1998) FL 24+7/1 FLC 2 FAC 0+2 Others 2

BOYD Adam Mark
Born: Hartlepool, 25 May 1982
Height: 5'9" Weight: 10.12
Young Adam signed his first professional contract early in the 1999-2000 season after impressing Hartlepool manager Chris Turner. An attacking midfielder or striker, he was not rushed into first-team football, but was given the chance to gain experience with a number of substitute appearances. With so much expected of him, he did not let the club down. Adam opened his goalscoring account against Shrewsbury in February, winning the game with a superb 20-yard shot from an acute angle in the last minute.
Hartlepool U (From trainee on 20/9/1999) FL 0+4/1 Others 0+2

BOYD Walter
Born: Jamaica, 1 January 1972
Height: 5'11" Weight: 11.10
Club Honours: Div 3 '00
International Honours: Jamaica
Brought up in the ghettoes of Kingston, Walter has been labelled as Jamaica's most enigmatic and controversial player. A member of the Reggae Boyz' 1998 World Cup squad in France, he made two sub appearances in the finals. After an unsuccessful trial at West Bromwich in 1997, he joined Swansea in October 1999 from Arnett Gardens. He had an electrifying Swans debut against Rotherham and scored both goals in a 2-0 win. However, six weeks later he was sent off in a record-breaking 57 seconds after coming on as a substitute. Walter initially struggled to get to grips with the style of football, but his quickness off the ball in and around the penalty area was a constant threat to the opposition. He finished equal top goalscorer with seven goals and won a Third Division championship winners' medal. Stop Press: Walter won a surprise recall to the Jamaica national team at the beginning of July, appearing in friendly matches against Cuba and Barbados.
Swansea C (Free from Arnett Gardens, Jamaica on 11/10/1999) FL 21+6/7 FAC 1+1 Others 1

Walter Boyd

BOYLAN Lee Martin
Born: Chelmsford, 2 September 1978
Height: 5'6" Weight: 11.6
International Honours: RoI: Yth
Lee joined Exeter on loan from Swedish club Trelleborgs in November 1999. He made eight appearances with his only goal coming in the Devon derby defeat of Torquay. Unfortunately, his loan was not extended beyond the first two months. Lee was previously a colleague of fellow Grecian loanee Gary Alexander at West Ham.
West Ham U (From trainee on 7/7/1997) PL 0+1 (Free to Trelleborgs, Sweden during 1999 close season)
Exeter C (Free on 11/11/1999) FL 3+3/1 FAC 2

BRABIN Gary
Born: Liverpool, 9 December 1970
Height: 5'11" Weight: 14.8
International Honours: E: SP-3
The burly, big-hearted midfielder was rewarded for his crucial part in Hull City's 1998-99 "Great Escape" with an improved contract – including some coaching duties –

in the summer. Having missed much of the 1999 pre-season with illness and an ankle injury, "Brabs" took a while to recapture his best form, then suffered a neck injury around the turn of the year. He was an influential member of the squad, but it seemed that his previous disciplinary record preceded him as, in addition to being sent off twice in particularly doubtful circumstances, Gary was fined and received a further ban from the FA after an incident against Macclesfield Town.

Stockport Co (From trainee on 14/12/1989) FL 1+1 Others 1+1
Doncaster Rov (£45,000 from Runcorn on 26/7/1994) FL 58+1/11 FLC 2 FAC 2 Others 4
Bury (£125,000 on 29/3/1996) FL 5
Blackpool (£200,000 on 30/7/1996) FL 50+13/5 FLC 7+1 FAC 2 Others 2+2
Lincoln C (Loaned on 11/12/1998) FL 3+1 Others 1
Hull C (Free on 8/1/1999) FL 58/7 FLC 4 FAC 3 Others 1

BRACE Deryn Paul John
Born: Haverfordwest, 15 March 1975
Height: 5'8" Weight: 10.12
Club Honours: WC '95
International Honours: W: U21-8; Yth

Deryn is a popular Wrexham full back who loves to be involved in the thick of the action and always gives everything he has. His first-team opportunities were restricted in 1999-2000 by a series of injuries and the large squad at the Racecourse. He was released by the club in the summer.

Norwich C (From trainee on 6/7/1993)
Wrexham (Free on 28/4/1994) FL 79+9/2 FLC 6 FAC 5 Others 7

BRACEY Lee Michael Ian
Born: Barking, 11 September 1968
Height: 6'2" Weight: 13.6

After three years as Ipswich goalkeeper Richard Wright's unused understudy, Lee was brought to Hull in the summer of 1999 to replace Andy Oakes. With unbelievable bad luck, he suffered a nightmare start to his career with the club. He was harshly sent off three times – against Macclesfield in the league, at Liverpool in the Worthington Cup (having lost 0-8 on his last visit to Anfield ten years earlier) and in a reserve game at Hartlepool – leading to a six-match ban. The experienced 'keeper also conceded crucial penalties in three consecutive games. But for four cup outings, his only senior involvement after early October was one league game.

West Ham U (From trainee on 6/7/1987)
Swansea C (Free on 27/8/1988) FL 99 FLC 8 FAC 11 Others 10
Halifax T (£47,500 on 17/10/1991) FL 73 FLC 2 FAC 1 Others 2
Bury (£20,000 on 23/8/1993) FL 65+2 FLC 4 FAC 2 Others 1
Ipswich T (£40,000 on 5/8/1997)
Hull C (Free on 5/7/1999) FL 10 FLC 4 FAC 3 Others 1

BRADBURY Lee Michael
Born: Isle of Wight, 3 July 1975
Height: 6'2" Weight: 13.10
International Honours: E: U21-3

Lee began the 1999-2000 season at Crystal Palace and was an ever-present in the first-team squad in the early games. However, a Football League ruling that the final instalment of his transfer fee must be paid to Manchester City forced the Eagles to sell him to his first club, Portsmouth, last October. He settled down quickly at Fratton Park, scoring on his debut against Walsall, but then had a long barren spell. However, new manager Tony Pulis persisted with him and he was rewarded with a cracking hat-trick in just seven minutes against Swindon last March. Lee is a big, bustling striker, strong on the ball and with a tremendous workrate.

Portsmouth (Free from Cowes on 14/8/1995) FL 41+13/15 FLC 1+2 FAC 4/2
Exeter C (Loaned on 1/12/1995) FL 14/5
Manchester C (£3,000,000 + on 1/8/1997) FL 34+6/10 FLC 6/1
Crystal Palace (£1,500,000 on 29/10/1998) FL 28+4/6 FLC 3+1/1 FAC 1/1
Birmingham C (Loaned on 25/3/1999) FL 6+1 Others 1+1
Portsmouth (£380,000 on 14/10/1999) FL 35/10 FAC 1

Lee Bradbury

BRADLEY Shayne
Born: Gloucester, 8 December 1979
Height: 5'11" Weight: 13.2
International Honours: E: Sch

Yet to start a first-team match for Southampton having come through the trainee ranks at the Dell, Shayne made a single substitute appearance last season at Everton before being loaned to Exeter City in September. A bustling striker, full of running on and off the ball, he donned a City shirt nine times, and scored his first senior goal in a 4-1 win at Shrewsbury. His Premiership experience was in evidence as he acquitted himself well in Division Three. However, his lack of opportunities at Southampton, where the likes of Kevin Davies and James Beattie take precedence, could prevent him from establishing himself at the highest level.

Southampton (From trainee on 16/1/1998) PL 0+4
Swindon T (Loaned on 25/3/1999) FL 6+1
Exeter C (Loaned on 17/9/1999) FL 6+2/1 FAC 1

BRADSHAW Carl
Born: Sheffield, 2 October 1968
Height: 5'11" Weight: 11.11
Club Honours: AMC '99
International Honours: E: Yth

Carl proved his versatility once again in 1999-2000 by playing for Wigan in a number of defensive positions. The club captain has now completed a century of games for the Latics. An experienced, tough-tackling campaigner, he prefers the right-back position, but his season was hampered by hamstring injuries. When he was in the side, Carl proved both consistent and reliable with wholehearted commitment. His only league goal came from the penalty spot at Reading, where he had also scored the previous season.

Sheffield Wed (From apprentice on 23/8/1986) FL 16+16/4 FLC 2+2 FAC 6+1/3 Others 1
Barnsley (Loaned on 23/8/1986) FL 6/1
Manchester C (£50,000 on 30/9/1988) FL 1+4 FAC 0+1 Others 0+1
Sheffield U (£50,000 on 7/9/1989) F/PL 122+25/8 FLC 10+1/2 FAC 12+1/3 Others 4
Norwich C (£500,000 on 28/7/1994) P/FL 55+10/2 FLC 6+1/1 FAC 2
Wigan Ath (Free on 6/10/1997) FL 87+6/8 FLC 5/1 FAC 5 Others 7+1/1

BRADSHAW Gary
Born: Hull, 30 December 1982
Height: 5'6" Weight: 10.6

Although he received offers from Leeds United, Blackburn Rovers, Sheffield Wednesday and Aston Villa, this young local lad returned to Hull in the summer of 1999 having turned down the offer of a YT contract with Newcastle United. Following four years at City's Centre of Excellence, Gary had been associated with the Premiership giants since the age of 13. An England U16 and U15 trialist – he also made the final 32 for the National Academy at Lilleshall in 1997 – his return to his roots appears a wise move as he was playing first-team football by the following March. A diminutive forward, his tricky ball skills quickly caught admiring eyes. Definitely one to watch. Gary's immediate impact was rewarded with the Tigers' "Young Player of the Year" award.

Hull C (Trainee) FL 5+7

BRADSHAW Mark
Born: Ashton under Lyne, 7 September 1969
Height: 5'10" Weight: 12.0
International Honours: E: SP-1

Mark's appearances for Halifax in 1999-2000 were limited somewhat with the arrival at the start of the season of Mark Jules. Injuries and suspensions did not help the former warehouse manager as he spent most of the campaign on the substitutes' bench. He went out on loan to Nuneaton in the Conference during March, where he teamed up with former Shaymen Dave Hanson, Andy Thackeray, Jon Brown and Steve Prindiville. Mark then returned to the Shay and forced his way back into the first team. The popular left back was offered a new contract at the end of the season.

Blackpool (From trainee on 9/12/1987) FL 34+8/1 FLC 3/1 FAC 5+1 Others 1+2 (Free to Stafford R during 1991 close season)

York C (Loaned on 16/4/1991) FL 0+1
Halifax T (Free from Macclesfield T on 18/5/1995) FL 58+8/5 FLC 3 FAC 2+1 Others 1/1

BRADY Garry
Born: Glasgow, 7 September 1976
Height: 5'10" Weight: 11.0
International Honours: S: Yth; Sch

Garry arrived at Norwich on loan from Newcastle United just prior to transfer deadline day last March, making his debut at Queens Park Rangers three days later. The former Tottenham man quickly impressed City fans with his clever footwork and accurate distribution, trademarks of his White Hart Lane upbringing. A natural passer of the ball, he works hard to create space for himself both when in possession and when making himself available to team-mates. An excellent striker of the ball, his first telling contribution in a Norwich shirt was to deliver a free kick on to Lee Marshall's head in the 13th minute of his debut at Loftus Road.

Tottenham H (From trainee on 9/9/1993) PL 0+9 FAC 1+1
Newcastle U (£650,000 on 15/7/1998) PL 3+6 FAC 2+1
Norwich C (Loaned on 22/3/2000) FL 6

BRADY Matthew (Matt) John
Born: Marylebone, 27 October 1977
Height: 5'11" Weight: 11.10

After failing to make the grade at Barnet, Matt drifted off to Ryman League club Boreham Wood before his career was resurrected by Wycombe manager Lawrie Sanchez last November. He made the starting line-up for the first time at Preston last January, when he scored from close in, and added another opportunist goal in the next game against Wrexham before it was decided to rest him until the last few games of the season. Matt was mostly used in an attacking role on the left of midfield, from where he was able to curl in dangerous crosses and occasionally drift in to find space inside the box. Having made such a promising start at Adams Park, he will be looking to establish himself in the first team in the 2000-01 season.

Barnet (From trainee on 3/7/1996) FL 2+8 (Free to Boreham Wood on 6/11/1998)
Wycombe W (Loaned on 11/11/1999) FL 4+3/2 Others 0+1

BRAMBLE Titus Malachi
Born: Ipswich, 21 July 1981
Height: 6'1" Weight: 13.10

This young Ipswich centre back's progress last season was hampered by a series of niggling injuries and he did not make any first-team appearances for the club. He went to Colchester on loan at the turn of the year in a bid to gain some much-needed match fitness, his arrival coinciding with the start of the unbeaten run which took United clear of relegation danger. A hugely promising player with terrific physical attributes, Titus sadly played only two matches for the U's before he picked up another injury which virtually ended his season.

Ipswich T (From trainee on 24/8/1998) FL 2+2 FAC 0+1
Colchester U (Loaned on 29/12/1999) FL 2

BRAMMER David (Dave)
Born: Bromborough, 28 February 1975
Height: 5'10" Weight: 12.0

A dynamic Port Vale midfield player who gives everything and covers every blade of grass for the cause, Dave was effective in a largely defensive role in 1999-2000 but unfortunately this was to the detriment of his attacking play, with the result that he did not figure among the scorers all season. He was sent off in the final minute at Sheffield United, which ruined his ever-present record up to that time, but he then picked up a leg injury at Grimsby Town in February which meant that he was ruled out until the final game of the season. Dave was surprisingly transfer-listed at the end of the season.

Wrexham (From trainee on 2/7/1993) FL 118+19/12 FLC 6+2 FAC 8+2/1 Others 13+2/1
Port Vale (£350,000 + on 24/3/1999) FL 38 FLC 2

BRANAGAN Keith Graham
Born: Fulham, 10 July 1966
Height: 6'0" Weight: 13.2
Club Honours: Div 1 '97
International Honours: RoI: 1; B-1

Keith was one of three very strong 'keepers in the Bolton squad last season, and because of this he didn't figure in the first team as often as he has done in previous campaigns. The excellent form of Jussi Jaaskelainen meant that the Finn was considered to be the Wanderers' first-choice 'keeper for the majority of the season, leaving Keith and Steve Banks to fight it out for the 'keeper's position on the substitutes' bench. Keith started the season in the team, but an ankle injury sustained in the home game against Huddersfield gave Jaaskelainen the chance he needed to establish himself in the starting line-up. When Keith returned to full fitness, he was unable to regain his place. A lack of first-team chances late on in the season prompted him to go to Ipswich on loan, as cover for Richard Wright.

Cambridge U (From juniors on 4/8/1983) FL 110 FLC 12 FAC 6 Others 6
Millwall (£100,000 on 25/3/1988) FL 46 FLC 1 FAC 5 Others 1
Brentford (Loaned on 24/11/1989) FL 2 Others 1
Gillingham (Loaned on 1/10/1991) FL 1
Bolton W (Free on 3/7/1992) P/FL 214 FLC 33 FAC 10 Others 6
Ipswich T (Free on 7/4/2000)

BRANCH Graham
Born: Liverpool, 12 February 1972
Height: 6'2" Weight: 12.2

Mainly a left-sided player employed either as a winger or wing back, though occasionally used as an out-and-out striker, Graham was one of Burnley's most improved players of the 1999-2000 season. Fast, skilful and determined, his only weakness is an occasional lack of accuracy with the final ball. At his best going forward, he nevertheless performed competently on his outings at left back, his lack of natural defensive skills being sometimes compensated for by the solidity of the middle three at the back. He is capable of spectacular goals but is perhaps sometimes over-ambitious in his scoring attempts.

Tranmere Rov (Free from Heswall on 2/7/1991) FL 55+47/10 FLC 4+8/1 FAC 1+2 Others 2+1
Bury (Loaned on 20/11/1992) FL 3+1/1 Others 1
Wigan Ath (Loaned on 24/12/1997) FL 2+1
Stockport Co (Free on 31/7/1998) FL 10+4/3 FLC 1
Burnley (Free on 31/12/1998) FL 45+19/4 FLC 2 FAC 0+3 Others 1

BRANCH Paul **Michael**
Born: Liverpool, 18 October 1978
Height: 5'10" Weight: 11.7
International Honours: E: U21-1; Yth; Sch

Prior to joining Wolves in November 1999 the speedy forward had not been able to fulfil his youthful promise, largely due to injuries, his three Everton goals being back in 1996-97. He came initially on loan, missing a good opening on his debut at Tranmere. At home to Manchester City he showed fine opportunism to score twice in the first half, and he further endeared himself to the crowd with his sheer hard work, running himself into the ground at Blackburn. This was his last scheduled appearance, but a permanent transfer was agreed, with Wolves paying a fee of £500,000, rising to £625,000. Branch continued to impress, except when missing an important spot kick in a penalty shoot-out with Sheffield Wednesday in the FA Cup. He responded a few days later against Queens Park Rangers, flicking the ball over the goalkeeper then heading it in. He scored a controversial goal against Forest, playing on when their goalkeeper had attempted to kick the ball out of play following an injury. Michael seemed to be unaware of this, and was taken off a few minutes later. He showed signs of fatigue and was given a two-day rest from training in April. The following Saturday he quickly found a bit of space and centred accurately for Allan Nielsen to score the winner against Blackburn. The Barnsley match in April was his tenth, including two as a substitute, without a goal, but he showed his ability in setting up two for Ade Akinbiyi that day.

Everton (From trainee on 24/10/1995) PL 16+25/3 FLC 0+1 FAC 1+2
Manchester C (Loaned on 29/10/1998) FL 4
Wolverhampton W (£500,000 + on 25/11/1999) FL 25+2/6 FAC 2

BRANDON Christopher (Chris) William
Born: Bradford, 7 April 1976
Height: 5'7" Weight: 10.3

Arguably the "find" of the 1999-2000 season in Division Three, Chris is a tricky right-footed midfield player who was signed by Torquay from Unibond League side Bradford Park Avenue after impressing in pre-season friendlies. He scored a number of quite spectacular goals, and is seen as a major key to United's future progress. The former Sheffield United trainee reportedly considered a return to Yorkshire at the end of the campaign following interest from Halifax.

Torquay U (Free from Bradford PA on 5/8/1999) FL 41+1/5 FLC 2 FAC 4/1 Others 2

BRANSTON Guy Peter Bromley
Born: Leicester, 9 January 1979
Height: 6'0" Weight: 13.12

Guy started the 1999-2000 season on Leicester's books but was loaned to Lincoln shortly afterwards to provide cover after the Imps suffered a spate of injuries. A tall, strong central defender, he found it difficult to settle into a team going through a run of bad results and returned to Filbert Street after a month. In October he had another loan spell at Rotherham and impressed sufficiently to earn a permanent contract. He helped bring solidity to the Millers' defence and played a leading role in their promotion to the Second Division, his obvious will to win making him something of a cult hero with the club's fans. Very good in the air at both ends of the pitch, Guy weighed in with a handful of vital goals, which were invariably celebrated with his distinctive "stomp". He has made rapid progress since his move to Millmoor, and is still young enough to go all the way to the top.

Leicester C (From trainee on 3/7/1997)
Colchester U (Loaned on 9/2/1998) FL 12/1 Others 1
Colchester U (Loaned on 7/8/1998) FL 0+1
Plymouth Arg (Loaned on 20/11/1998) FL 7/1 Others 1
Lincoln C (Loaned on 10/8/1999) FL 4 FLC 2
Rotherham U (£50,000 on 15/10/1999) FL 30/4 Others 2

BRASS Christopher (Chris) Paul
Born: Easington, 24 July 1975
Height: 5'10" Weight: 12.6

The arrival of Mitchell Thomas pushed Chris out of contention for a regular place in Burnley's defence in 1999-2000. On his few first-team appearances he never let the side down and looked as solid as ever, but the back three looks settled and his chances are likely to stay limited barring injuries and suspensions. An accomplished, determined central defender who can also operate at right back, he is certainly too good a player to languish in the reserves, and it has to be wondered if his future may not lie away from Turf Moor.

Burnley (From trainee on 8/7/1993) FL 120+14/1 FLC 8+1 FAC 6+1 Others 8+2
Torquay U (Loaned on 14/10/1994) FL 7 FAC 2 Others 1

BRAYSON Paul
Born: Newcastle, 16 September 1977
Height: 5'4" Weight: 10.10
International Honours: E: Yth

The diminutive striker made only a handful of appearances for Reading in 1999-2000, mainly as a second-half substitute, and was once again unable to conjure up a first-team goal for the Royals. After refusing the opportunity to join Conference club Woking on loan, Paul moved to Cardiff in March for the remainder of the season. The bright and chirpy Geordie was determined to reproduce his goalscoring form with Reading's reserve team in the Second Division and got off the mark in a 2-1 win at Oldham. A quick, skilful forward, he gained a Welsh Cup runners-up medal during his spell at Ninian Park and Cardiff were evidently impressed by his contribution, as they opened negotiations to sign him on a free transfer during the close season.

Newcastle U (From trainee on 1/8/1995) FLC 1+1
Swansea C (Loaned on 30/1/1997) FL 11/5
Reading (£100,000 on 26/3/1998) FL 15+26/1 FLC 0+2 FAC 1+1 Others 2
Cardiff C (Loaned on 16/3/2000) FL 7+2/1

BRAZIER Matthew (Matt) Ronald
Born: Leytonstone, 2 July 1976
Height: 5'8" Weight: 11.6

Matt was described as the "People's Signing" after he joined Cardiff from Fulham for £100,000 in the 1999 close season. He had had a successful loan spell at Ninian Park in 1998-99 and the City fans were delighted to have him back. He plays on the left side, usually as a winger, but can also operate as a wing back or in midfield. Unfortunately, he found it difficult to live up to such inflated expectations and at times looked somewhat lightweight. He undoubtedly has talent but seemed rather frustrated as the Bluebirds' relegation season unfolded. Still part of manager Billy Ayre's plans, he will be hoping for a far better season in 2000-01.

Queens Park R (From trainee on 1/7/1994) P/FL 36+13/2 FLC 3+2/1 FAC 3
Fulham (£65,000 on 20/3/1998) FL 4+5/1 FAC 2+1 Others 1
Cardiff C (Loaned on 28/8/1998) FL 11/2
Cardiff C (£100,000 on 9/7/1999) FL 20+10/1 FLC 1+3/1 FAC 3/1 Others 1

BREACKER Timothy (Tim) Sean
Born: Bicester, 2 July 1965
Height: 6'0" Weight: 13.0
Club Honours: FLC '88
International Honours: E: U21-2

Tim, a right back, was in and out of the Queens Park Rangers side in 1999-2000 owing to injury. The main problem was a leg injury he picked up in December, which kept him out for the rest of the campaign. The high spot of his season was scoring his second goal for the club in the home win over Sheffield United. When fit, Tim is normally the first choice for the right-wing-back berth, but he had strong competition for it last term.

Luton T (From apprentice on 15/5/1983) FL 204+6/3 FLC 22+2 FAC 21 Others 7
West Ham U (£600,000 on 12/10/1990) F/PL 229+11/8 FLC 20+1 FAC 27+1 Others 7
Queens Park R (Loaned on 2/10/1998) FL 2
Queens Park R (Free on 10/2/1999) FL 31+1/2 FLC 2 FAC 2

BREBNER Grant Iain
Born: Edinburgh, 6 December 1977
Height: 5'10" Weight: 12.0
Club Honours: FAYC '95
International Honours: S: U21-17; Sch

Probably Tommy Burns's best signing for Reading, Grant was surprisingly sold to Hibernian for £400,000 by Burns after the third game of the 1999-2000 season. He had already shown his ability by scoring and making chances from midfield, and will always be remembered as the first player to score a league goal at the Madejski Stadium. He signed a five-year contract at Hibs and became a regular in their first team.

Manchester U (Free from Hutchinson Vale BC on 17/3/1995)
Cambridge U (Loaned on 9/1/1998) FL 6/1
Hibernian (Loaned on 26/2/1998) SL 9/1
Reading (£300,000 on 15/6/1998) FL 38+3/10 FLC 4/1 FAC 1

BRECKIN Ian
Born: Rotherham, 24 February 1975
Height: 6'0" Weight: 12.9
Club Honours: AMC '96

Ian's was probably one of the first names on the Chesterfield team sheet last season. A groin injury robbed the side of his calm, commanding defending for some vital games, but he gradually played his way back to the sort of form that has brought scouts to watch him. Spireites fans will hope that he signs another contract in the summer but, given the club's recent plight, he must be fancied to improve himself by moving on. Ian was voted the Chesterfield players' "Player of the Year".

Rotherham U (From trainee on 1/11/1993) FL 130+2/6 FLC 6 FAC 5 Others 11
Chesterfield (£100,000 on 25/7/1997) FL 121+4/4 FLC 11 FAC 5/1 Others 5

BREEN Gary Patrick
Born: Hendon, 12 December 1973
Height: 6'2" Weight: 12.0
International Honours: RoI: 30; U21-9

Gary is a skilful, right-footed central defender who likes to bring the ball out of defence and is also very good in the air. After a mixed season in 1998-99 he again failed to make the Coventry starting line-up as a centre back at the beginning of 1999-2000. The form of Paul Williams and Richard Shaw meant his only appearances in the first two months were as a right back, a position he is known to dislike. Shaw's injury in November gave him his chance at centre back and he played well alongside Williams for 16 games. It was all-change, however, after a 3-0 defeat at Leeds in which Colin Hendry made his first appearance, and Gary was once again out of favour. He was recalled for the Middlesbrough game in April and showed himself to be solid at the back and dangerous at near-post corners. He appeared regularly for the Republic of Ireland during the season, missing just one game and adding a further ten caps.

Maidstone U (Free from Charlton Ath juniors on 6/3/1991) FL 19
Gillingham (Free on 2/7/1992) FL 45+6 FLC 4 FAC 5 Others 1
Peterborough U (£70,000 on 5/8/1994) FL 68+1/1 FLC 6 FAC 6 Others 6/1
Birmingham C (£400,000 on 9/2/1996) FL 37+3/2 FLC 4 FAC 1
Coventry C (£2,400,000 on 1/2/1997) PL 79+6/1 FLC 6+1 FAC 9

BRENNAN James (Jim) Gerald
Born: Toronto, Canada, 8 May 1977
Height: 5'9" Weight: 12.5
International Honours: Canada: 14 (Gold Cup 2000); U23-1

This Canadian international wing back began the 1999-2000 season in tremendous form for Bristol City and it was no surprise that his exciting attacking play attracted the attention of higher-division clubs. In late October he was transferred to Nottingham Forest and he immediately established himself as a regular in the Reds' line-up. Jim has all the attributes required of an attacking full back: great pace, an excellent cross and a good shot. He also appeared regularly for

Canada during the season and was a member of the team that surprisingly defeated Colombia in the final of the CONCACAF Gold Cup last February.
Bristol C (Free from Sora Lazio, Canada on 25/10/1994) FL 51+4/3 FLC 6 FAC 1
Nottingham F (£1,500,000 on 29/10/1999) FL 22+3 FAC 3

BRESLAN Geoffrey (Geoff) Francis
Born: Torquay, 4 June 1980
Height: 5'8" Weight: 11.0
Geoff was in and out of the Exeter line-up in 1999-2000, as he made almost as many appearances from the substitutes' bench as he did in the starting line-up. When he did play, Geoff's touch on the ball and passing ability created numerous chances. He netted for the only time last season in the Auto Windscreens Shield area semi-final defeat of Brentford.
Exeter C (From trainee on 7/1/1999) FL 40+24/4 FLC 4 FAC 3+3 Others 6/1

BREVETT Rupis (Rufus) Emanuel
Born: Derby, 24 September 1969
Height: 5'8" Weight: 11.6
Club Honours: Div 2 '99
The marauding left-sided wing back was having a good season for Fulham in 1999-2000 when he incurred a severe hamstring injury at Maine Road in January. It required surgery and ended Rufus's season, but the good news is that he was back in light training by the end of April and was expected to be fully fit by the start of 2000-01. At the top of his game, Rufus is a crowd pleaser who likes to get forward at every opportunity. He is strong, quick to recover and tackles with determination.
Doncaster Rov (From trainee on 8/7/1988) FL 106+3/3 FLC 5 FAC 4 Others 10+1
Queens Park R (£250,000 on 15/2/1991) F/PL 141+11/1 FLC 9+1 FAC 8
Fulham (£375,000 on 28/1/1998) FL 78+1/1 FLC 11+1 FAC 7 Others 2

BRIDGE Wayne Michael
Born: Southampton, 5 August 1980
Height: 5'10" Weight: 11.11
International Honours: E: U21-1; Yth
First introduced into the Southampton side at the start of the 1998-99 campaign, Wayne produced some lively attacking displays on the left side of midfield, using his pace to great effect. His sudden rise was rewarded with an England U21 cap against Hungary in April 1999, when he appeared as a left wing back. But last season, with so many midfielders on the club's books, he found himself learning and adapting to a more defensive role in the reserves. His reintroduction to first-team action came in the FA Cup at Ipswich Town in December and the move proved successful. With a long career ahead of him, Wayne could well become a full international within the next few years.
Southampton (From trainee on 16/1/1998) PL 30+12/1 FLC 3 FAC 2

BRIDGES Michael
Born: North Shields, 5 August 1978
Height: 6'1" Weight: 10.11
Club Honours: Div 1 '96, '99
International Honours: E: U21-3; Yth; Sch
Leeds United beat off competition from Tottenham to sign the England U21 striker for a club record £5 million in the summer of 1999. Bought initially to partner Jimmy Floyd Hasselbaink, Michael was subsequently thrust into a main front role on the former's departure. He started as he meant to go on: after only 11 minutes of his second game, at Southampton, he scored with a delicate chip and went on to complete a hat-trick. Michael has a superb change of pace and dazzling skills and is not afraid to shoot from a distance. He scored some superb goals last season: a long-range drive at Watford after cutting inside, a flick-up-and-volley at Everton and a superb long-range volley to earn victory over Southampton at Elland Road. A constant threat with pace and guile, the only criticism of him could be that he sometimes appears to lose the ball too easily. However, he played the majority of the away legs in Europe as a lone marksman and performed superbly well. An excellent acquisition, Michael could improve further with a more experienced partner. This skilful front runner has a big future in the game.
Sunderland (From trainee on 9/11/1995) P/FL 31+48/16 FLC 8+3/5 FAC 2
Leeds U (£4,500,000 + on 29/7/1999) PL 32+2/19 FLC 2 FAC 1+1 Others 12/2

Michael Bridges

BRIGGS Keith
Born: Ashton under Lyne, 11 December 1981
Height: 5'10" Weight: 11.6
This Stockport youngster burst on to the scene with a "Man of the Match" performance in the Worthington Cup tie at Oldham last August. He signed up as a full professional a few days later and showed great promise whenever he appeared in the first team. He underlined his potential with goals against Barnsley in the Worthington Cup and in the 3-3 draw with Queens Park Rangers and will be looking to establish himself in the Hatters' first-team squad in 2000-01. Keith is a talented right wing back, who looks to have a good future in the game.
Stockport Co (From trainee on 27/8/1999) FL 4+3/1 FLC 2/1

BRIGHTWELL David John
Born: Lutterworth, 7 January 1971
Height: 6'2" Weight: 13.5
The Carlisle skipper was again an influential figure for most of the 1999-2000 campaign, even featuring as an emergency striker on a couple of occasions. Mostly, however, he was prominent at the back, using his height and power to marshal the Cumbrians' defence. David missed the last game at Brighton through injury and was one of 16 players released at the end of the season. He is the brother of Walsall's Ian Brightwell. Stop Press: David joined Hull City at the end of June.
Manchester C (From juniors on 11/4/1988) F/PL 35+8/1 FLC 2+1 FAC 5+2/1
Chester C (Loaned on 22/3/1991) FL 6
Lincoln C (Loaned on 11/8/1995) FL 5 FLC 2
Stoke C (Loaned on 11/9/1995) FL 0+1 Others 1
Bradford C (£30,000 on 22/12/1995) FL 23+1 FAC 1 Others 2
Blackpool (Loaned on 12/12/1996) FL 1+1
Northampton T (Free on 29/7/1997) FL 34+1/1 FLC 2 FAC 5 Others 2+1
Carlisle U (Free on 10/7/1998) FL 78/4 FLC 4 FAC 2 Others 3

BRIGHTWELL Ian Robert
Born: Lutterworth, 9 April 1968
Height: 5'10" Weight: 12.5
International Honours: E: U21-4; Yth
Out in the cold at Coventry, Ian joined Walsall on a free transfer last February. He made his debut for his new club against Nottingham Forest just hours after signing and quickly showed that, despite his long spell out of league football, he remains a sound and solid defender. His firm tackling was a feature of his game whether playing on the right or the left of the defence, and he was unlucky to be sent off in the game at Tranmere. Ian is the brother of David Brightwell, who played for Carlisle in 1999-2000.
Manchester C (From juniors on 7/5/1986) F/PL 285+36/18 FLC 29+2 FAC 19+4/1 Others 4+3
Coventry C (Free on 2/7/1998) FLC 1
Walsall (Free on 11/2/2000) FL 9+1

BRISCO Neil Anthony
Born: Wigan, 26 January 1978
Height: 6'0" Weight: 11.5
A strong, no-nonsense right back who can also fill in in midfield if required, Neil was mainly a reserve at Port Vale in 1999-2000. He was included in the starting line-up on the opening day at Blackburn but picked up an injury and did not surface in the first team again for three months. His own personal highlight was undoubtedly the FA Cup tie at Leeds but most of his senior appearances were towards the end of the campaign when the team was constantly chopped and changed after poor results. Neil is very keen to learn and will be looking for a more regular role in the Second Division this coming season.
Manchester C (From trainee on 4/3/1997)
Port Vale (Free on 7/8/1998) FL 12+1 FAC 2

BRISCOE Lee Stephen
Born: Pontefract, 30 September 1975
Height: 5'11" Weight: 11.12
International Honours: E: U21-5

Lee had a disappointing 1999-2000 campaign as he again failed to make the breakthrough to regular Premiership football with Sheffield Wednesday. He was in and out of the first-team squad and started only nine matches all season. He is now mostly used as a left wing back but can also take a wide-left midfield role.

Sheffield Wed (From trainee on 22/5/1994) PL 48+30/1 FLC 5+2 FAC 0+2
Manchester C (Loaned on 20/2/1998) FL 5/1

BRISSETT Jason Curtis
Born: Wanstead, 7 September 1974
Height: 5'10" Weight: 12.7

Jason played several early-season games for Walsall in 1999-2000, operating wide on the left, and scored in the narrow Worthington Cup defeat at Sunderland. After losing his place in October, he spent two months on loan at Cheltenham. He provided balance on the left side of midfield and his running and crossing added a different dimension to the team. His presence provided more than adequate cover for injuries and manager Steve Cotterill might have been tempted to try to secure him permanently had it not been for his First Division wages. Jason provided one of the season's strangest moments when he heard a whistle from within the crowd at Rochdale and caught the ball inside his penalty area. Robins goalkeeper Steve Book spared his blushes by saving the spot kick. On his return to Walsall, he was sent off in a reserve game and was later released. Stop Press: Jason was reported to have signed for Leyton Orient at the beginning of July.

Peterborough U (Free from Arsenal juniors on 14/6/1993) FL 27+8 FLC 5+1/1 FAC 2+1/1 Others 3+1/1
Bournemouth (Free on 23/12/1994) 96+28/8 FLC 5+2 FAC 4 Others 6+2/2
Walsall (Free on 31/7/1998) FL 32+10/2 FLC 4/1 FAC 1 Others 3+2
Cheltenham T (Loaned on 11/11/1999) FL 5+3 Others 1+1

BRKOVIC Ahmet
Born: Dubrovnik, Croatia, 23 September 1974
Height: 5'7" Weight: 10.8

While a free agent, Ahmet had a trial with Leyton Orient in October 1999 and soon signed a contract to the end of the season. A Croatian who had come to London to marry his Romford-born girlfriend, he is a skilful midfielder who can also play as a forward. He soon became a hit with the fans after scoring with an overhead kick at Darlington in November. Ahmet has so much time on the ball that his experience of football at a higher level seemed apparent. He played in Croatia's top division for HNK Dubrovnik (his home-town club) in 1991-92 and Varteks of Varazdin in 1997-98.

Leyton Orient (Free from HNK Dubrovnik, Croatia on 14/10/1999) FL 25+4/5 FAC 2 Others 1

BROADHURST Karl Matthew
Born: Portsmouth, 18 March 1980
Height: 6'1" Weight: 11.7

This former Bournemouth trainee made his senior debut for the Cherries in the Worthington Cup tie with Charlton last September and had a short run in the first team before damaging his ankle ligaments. He returned in mid-November as a replacement for the injured Eddie Howe and retained his place in the team until Howe was fit again. Karl is a highly promising centre back who is comfortable on the ball and shows great awareness. His potential was recognised by the club last February when he signed a two-and-a-half-year extension to his contract.

Bournemouth (From trainee on 3/7/1998) FL 16 FLC 3 FAC 1 Others 1

BROMBY Leigh
Born: Dewsbury, 2 June 1980
Height: 6'0" Weight: 11.8
International Honours: E: Sch

A teenage centre back loaned to Mansfield by Sheffield Wednesday in December 1999 when both regular central defenders were injured, Leigh made an immediate impact with his authority in the air and skilful groundwork. The original one-month loan period was extended to two and then three months but he returned to Hillsborough when injured at the end of January. It was easy to see why the then Owls manager, Danny Wilson, would not release the player on a permanent basis and offered him a new contract.

Sheffield Wed (From Liversedge on 9/7/1998)
Mansfield T (Loaned on 10/12/1999) FL 10/1 Others 1

BROOKER Paul
Born: Hammersmith, 25 November 1976
Height: 5'8" Weight: 10.0

Despite several "Man of the Match" performances for Fulham's reserve side, Paul didn't play for the Cottagers' first team in 1999-2000, although he made the substitutes' bench on a couple of occasions. Brighton manager Micky Adams, who knew all about Paul's qualities from his time at Craven Cottage, took him down to the south coast on a month's loan in February and he rapidly endeared himself to the fans. An exciting winger with electrifying pace and excellent ball control, he was used mostly on his less favoured flank, the left, during his time with Brighton. However, his arrival helped kick-start Albion's season, and he scored his first goal in the 7-1 romp at Chester City. Stop Press: Paul made a permanent switch to Brighton in the summer.

Fulham (From trainee on 1/7/1995) FL 13+43/4 FLC 1+2/1 FAC 1+3/1 Others 3+3
Brighton & Hove A (Loaned on 18/2/2000) FL 15/2

BROOKER Stephen (Steve) Michael Lord
Born: Newport, 21 May 1981
Height: 5'10" Weight: 12.4

Steve made his first-team and Premiership debut at the age of 18 as a substitute in Watford's opening game of last season, at home to Wimbledon. Although he inevitably lacked experience, Steve's poise and confidence were impressive and he continued to hone his striking skills in the reserves. He made another appearance from the bench in the third round of the FA Cup against Birmingham, but an ankle injury proved a minor set-back during December and January.

Watford (From trainee on 9/7/1999) PL 0+1 FAC 0+1

BROOMES Marlon Charles
Born: Birmingham, 28 November 1977
Height: 6'0" Weight: 12.12
International Honours: E: U21-2; Yth; Sch

The highly rated young Blackburn centre back had a curious season in 1999-2000. He was preferred to Christian Dailly at the start of the campaign and scored a classic headed goal at Huddersfield but had to leave the field in the third game with a hamstring injury. This was an old problem and it was ultimately decided that it was being caused by a misalignment of his ankle. Marlon was unable to play during the middle of the season but returned in February to help form a tight defence with Dailly. Strong and athletic, he plays with total commitment but needs to achieve greater consistency if he is to fulfil his rich potential.

Blackburn Rov (From trainee on 28/11/1994) P/FL 23+7/1 FLC 1 FAC 4
Swindon T (Loaned on 22/1/1997) FL 12/1

BROUGH John Robert
Born: Ilkeston, 8 January 1973
Height: 6'0" Weight: 13.0

John is a hard-working and versatile player who, like many of the Cheltenham squad, enjoyed a second crack at league football in 1999-2000. John was left out of the side after the opening-day defeat against Rochdale and was named as a substitute for 23 games before regaining a regular place in the starting line-up. His preferred position is centre back but John found it hard to split the Chris Banks–Mark Freeman partnership until an injury to Freeman. He filled in for three games as a makeshift striker early in the season, and was often used in the same capacity after going on as a substitute. Despite his limited opportunities, John displayed a positive attitude throughout the season and was a key player as the reserves surged to the top of their table before earning a recall. John's appetite for hard work and willingness to run and battle for everything have endeared him to the supporters at Whaddon Road.

Notts Co (From trainee on 9/7/1991)
Shrewsbury T (Free on 6/7/1992) FL 7+9/1 FLC 1+1 FAC 1 Others 1 (Free to Telford during 1994 close season)
Hereford U (Free on 4/11/1994) FL 70+9/3 FLC 5 FAC 4/1 Others 4+3
Cheltenham T (Signed on 16/7/1998) FL 15+22/2 FLC 0+1 FAC 2/1 Others 0+1

BROUGH Michael
Born: Nottingham, 1 August 1981
Height: 6'0" Weight: 11.7

After doing well with the reserves, Michael won a spot in the Notts County first team

last March during an injury crisis and then retained his place on merit until the end of the campaign. A real find for the Magpies, he is a very competitive, hard-tackling midfield player who will be looking to remain involved in the 2000-01 season.
Notts Co (From trainee on 1/7/1999) FL 11

BROUGHTON Drewe Oliver
Born: Hitchin, 25 October 1978
Height: 6'3" Weight: 12.0
For Drewe, 1999-2000 was a stop-start season. He started only five league games for Peterborough, and spent most of the second half of the campaign on loan to Nuneaton. Chances looked limited at Posh with the arrival of Jason Lee and the improved form of Andy Clarke. Drewe is a goal provider rather than poacher; he works extremely well around the penalty box and has a good first touch for such a tall man.
Norwich C (From trainee on 6/5/1997) FL 3+6/1
Wigan Ath (Loaned on 15/8/1997) FL 1+3
Brentford (£100,000 on 30/10/1998) FL 1
Peterborough U (£100,000 on 17/11/1998) FL 19+16/8 FLC 2 Others 1+1/1

BROWN Aaron Wesley
Born: Bristol, 14 March 1980
Height: 5'10" Weight: 11.12
International Honours: E: Sch
This skilful young Bristol City midfielder went to Exeter on a month's loan in January 2000. He made five appearances for the Grecians, scoring his only goal in a 2-0 win against Rochdale. Aaron's higher-league experience was evident as he helped Exeter through a difficult winter period. Back at Ashton Gate, he established himself in the Bristol City team towards the end of the season, and was in the side that lost 1-2 to Stoke City at Wembley in the Auto Windscreens Shield final. Aaron, who has been capped at U18 level for England Schools, is one of the many players from City's academy set-up who are now forcing themselves into first-team contention. When he and his younger brother Marvin appeared together against Nottingham Forest in the Worthington Cup last term they became the first pair of siblings to turn out for Bristol City since Tom and Steve Ritchie at Fulham in November 1972.
Bristol C (From trainee on 7/11/1997) FL 24+3/2 FLC 0+2 Others 3+1
Exeter C (Loaned on 6/1/2000) FL 4+1/1

BROWN Daniel (Danny)
Born: Bethnal Green, 12 September 1980
Height: 6'0" Weight: 12.0
Ironically, a few eyebrows were quizzically raised when Barnet manager John Still chose to spend £40,000 on the former Leyton Orient player in the summer of 1999 – the club's record fee for a teenager. However, this precocious midfield general produced a series of imperious displays in the opening half of the season, culminating in an emphatic brace at Southend in December. A fee that would have been an intolerable burden for most teenagers to shoulder was more than justified with some stylish displays in the middle of the park that led one national newspaper to label him the "Amber Gascoigne". Predominantly left-sided, Danny's forays out on the flank balanced Darren Currie's sorties down the right wing. Solidly built and an expert crosser of the ball, Danny was the chief architect of the famous victory at Peterborough in late November. Linked with a host of Premiership clubs, he endured a recurring back injury in the latter stages of the season, but his early showings hint that he is more than capable of performing at a higher level.
Leyton Orient (From trainee on 5/5/1998) Others 1
Barnet (Free on 25/5/1999) FL 20+4/3 FLC 0+1 FAC 1 Others 3

BROWN David Alistair
Born: Bolton, 2 October 1978
Height: 5'10" Weight: 12.6
Signed by former Hull boss Mark Hateley on Warren Joyce's recommendation (the latter having previously coached Manchester United's U16s) in the summer of 1998, David continued to hold his place as one of the most regularly employed members of the City squad in 1999-2000, even though three new forwards were added in the summer. Although his strengths would appear to be in the penalty box, his commitment and determination mean he is often seen in much deeper positions. With time on his side, his honest endeavour will gain greater reward. David pledged his future to the club last November, by signing a contract that ties him to the Tigers until August 2003.
Manchester U (From trainee on 27/10/1995)
Hull C (Free on 26/3/1998) FL 84+10/19 FLC 8/5 FAC 8/3 Others 4

BROWN Grant Ashley
Born: Sunderland, 19 November 1969
Height: 6'0" Weight: 11.12
Lincoln's longest-serving player was plagued by injuries in the first half of 1999-2000, damaging a toe in the opening game against Rotherham and then suffering a stress fracture of the foot. He eventually returned to full fitness in January and went on to make his 350th Football League appearance for the Imps when he came on as a substitute in the final home match of the campaign against Southend. This solid and dependable centre back was voted "Away Player of the Year" by the club's travelling supporters and was rewarded for ten years' service at Sincil Bank with a testimonial match against Middlesbrough in May.
Leicester C (From trainee on 1/7/1988) FL 14 FLC 2
Lincoln C (£60,000 on 20/8/1989) FL 349+2/13 FLC 20/1 FAC 13 Others 18+1/2

BROWN Gregory (Greg) Jonathan
Born: Wythenshawe, 31 July 1978
Height: 5'11" Weight: 12.6
This local lad was a stalwart defender in Macclesfield's reserve team last season, and also a regular on the first-team bench because of Town's very small senior squad. A promising left back who is quick and has a solid frame, Greg can hold off oncoming wingers, and overlap effectively with his own team's wingers coming forward. It was surprising that he did not win a regular starting place in the first team, but he overcame his frustration at his lack of regular first-team football by opting to join non-league Morecambe. He had had several previous loan spells at Christie Park.
Chester C (From trainee on 20/6/1996) FL 1+3 FAC 0+1 Others 0+1
Macclesfield T (Free on 19/12/1997) FL 9+3 FLC 0+1

BROWN John **Keith**
Born: Edinburgh, 24 December 1979
Height: 6'0" Weight: 11.0
International Honours: S: Yth
Keith joined Barnsley on loan from Blackburn Rovers last September as cover for injuries and initially filled in for Kevin Austin at left back. He eventually signed a two-and-a-half-year contract with the Oakwell club shortly before Christmas but found his first-team opportunities restricted, making only a handful more appearances in the second half of the season. He is a neat player with a calm and effective style who was also used as a left-sided central defender.
Blackburn Rov (From trainee on 16/1/1997)
Barnsley (Loaned on 10/9/1999) FL 4
Barnsley (£100,000 on 20/12/1999) FL 3+3 Others 3

Keith Brown

BROWN Marvin Robert
Born: Bristol, 6 July 1983
Height: 5'9" Weight: 11.1
International Honours: E: Yth
A very promising striker, Marvin took over the mantle of being Bristol City's youngest-ever player when coming on as a substitute at the age of 16 years 71 days in a 1-2 Worthington Cup defeat at Nottingham Forest last September. The younger brother of Aaron Brown, he is very quick, with excellent control and a good eye for goal, and much is expected of him. He was a regular member of the England U16 squad and City fans are hoping that he will go on to fulfil his obvious potential and play a big part in the club's future. Marvin played in

the City side that won the Somerset Premier Cup for only the sixth time in the club's history by beating Bath City 3-2 at the end of the season.
Bristol C (Trainee) FL 0+2 FLC 0+1 Others 0+1

BROWN Michael (Mickey) Antony
Born: Birmingham, 8 February 1968
Height: 5'9" Weight: 11.12
Club Honours: Div 3 '94

Continuing his third spell at Shrewsbury, Mickey enjoyed a fine season in 1999-2000, his haul of seven goals equalling his career best for a season. He will never score a more important goal than his 61st-minute header in the last game of the campaign at Exeter that secured Shrewsbury's league status. It has earned him a permanent place in the club's history. Strong on the ball and able to play wide on the right, Mickey can be used in midfield or as a striker. His directness on the ball excites the Gay Meadow crowd, who were delighted that Mickey was given the opportunity to renew his contract. The Shrews fans voted him their "Player of the Year".
Shrewsbury T (From apprentice on 11/2/1986) FL 174+16/9 FLC 17/2 FAC 10/1 Others 11
Bolton W (£100,000 on 15/8/1991) FL 27+6/3 FLC 0+1 FAC 3 Others 2
Shrewsbury T (£25,000 on 23/12/1992) FL 66+1/11 FLC 8/1 FAC 3 Others 2
Preston NE (£75,000 on 30/11/1994) FL 11+5/1 FLC 0+1 Others 1
Rochdale (Loaned on 13/9/1996) FL 5
Shrewsbury T (£20,000 on 12/12/1996) FL 91+36/12 FLC 3+1 FAC 4 Others 5+1

BROWN Michael Robert
Born: Hartlepool, 25 January 1977
Height: 5'9" Weight: 11.8
International Honours: E: U21-4

After he had appeared to establish himself in the Manchester City midfield in 1998-99, Michael surprisingly played no part in City's push towards the Premiership last season. His only first-team appearance was in the Worthington Cup at Burnley, when the Maine Road club had a 5-0 lead from the first leg, although he was a regular in the reserves. In November Michael joined Portsmouth on loan, linking up with his former boss Alan Ball, and he did well in the four games he played for Pompey. Ball was then sacked and Michael returned to Maine Road rather than turn out for the reserves at Fratton Park. Michael then moved to Sheffield United, initially on a month's loan, although the switch was later made permanent for a fee of around £400,000, and was an instant success at Bramall Lane. Hard working, quick and a fine passer of the ball, he immediately became a fixture in the side. He particularly enjoyed his first goal for United – a strike from the edge of the area to give the Blades a 1-0 victory over Manchester City. He produced consistent performances, chasing and chivvying in midfield for 90 minutes and creating some good chances with thoughtful passes, and looks certain to be one of Neil Warnock's key players for the coming season.
Manchester C (From trainee on 13/9/1994) F/PL 67+22/2 FLC 2+4 FAC 10+1/2 Others 4
Hartlepool U (Loaned on 27/3/1997) FL 6/1
Portsmouth (Loaned on 19/11/1999) FL 4
Sheffield U (Signed on 17/12/1999) FL 21+3/3

BROWN Simon James
Born: Chelmsford, 3 December 1976
Height: 6'2" Weight: 15.0

Simon is a young goalkeeper who was signed by Colchester after a trial during the 1999 pre-season, having been released by Tottenham after his apprenticeship and a short professional career without making the first team. As is to be expected with all young 'keepers, he had both good and bad games in 1999-2000 and he was sent off for a hand-ball after just two minutes of his home debut in the Worthington Cup, but behind United's defence last season he was at least assured of plenty of practice! Overall, it was a good first season with the club for the youngster, which has been justly rewarded with a contract for next year, when a more settled defence in front of him will surely help develop Simon's undoubted abilities still further.
Tottenham H (From trainee on 1/7/1995)
Lincoln C (Loaned on 19/12/1997) FL 1
Colchester U (Free on 20/7/1999) FL 38 FLC 1 FAC 1 Others 1

BROWN Steven (Steve) Byron
Born: Brighton, 13 May 1972
Height: 6'1" Weight: 13.10
Club Honours: Div 1 '00

One of the league's most versatile players, Steve had another great season for Charlton in 1999-2000, linking up with Richard Rufus in central defence after playing several games at right back earlier in the campaign. Strong and commanding in the air, Steve is an excellent distributor of the ball even when under pressure, and possesses a powerful right-footed shot which is often seen at set pieces. A key figure in Charlton's First Division championship triumph, this popular player scored a couple of goals, one with his head, and is also an extremely capable emergency goalkeeper, although he was not used in that capacity last season.
Charlton Ath (From trainee on 3/7/1990) P/FL 168+32/7 FLC 9+2 FAC 17/1 Others 3+2

BROWN Steven (Steve) Ferold
Born: Northampton, 6 July 1966
Height: 6'0" Weight: 11.8

This popular Wycombe midfielder enjoyed excellent form in the second half of the 1999-2000 season, impressing with his ball control and elegant attacking surges. He also scored four goals, including a spectacular 30-yard strike in the 3-0 win over Colchester in April. Steve adopts a more mature approach to his game these days, but when on form he remains one of the best performers at this level.
Northampton T (From juniors on 11/8/1983) FL 14+1/3 (Free to Irthlingborough T in December 1985)
Northampton T (Free on 21/7/1989) FL 145+13/19 FLC 10/1 FAC 12/2 Others 10+1/1
Wycombe W (£60,000 on 9/2/1994) FL 220+18/17 FLC 16+2/3 FAC 13+3/1 Others 8+2

BROWN Wayne Larry
Born: Southampton, 14 January 1977
Height: 6'1" Weight: 11.12

Wayne was an ever-present in the Chester goal last season, and the club's relegation to the Nationwide Conference did not reflect the high standard of his performances. In his fourth campaign at the Deva, he was the first-choice 'keeper ahead of Neil Cutler, despite having lost the Blues' gloves to him for most of the second half of 1998-99. Having experienced non-league football following his release by Bristol City in 1996, Wayne has already proved that he has the determination, and ability, to return to the Football League ranks.
Bristol C (From trainee on 3/7/1995) FL 1 (Free to Weston super Mare during 1996 close season)
Chester C (Free on 30/9/1996) FL 84 FLC 7 FAC 6 Others 2

BROWN Wayne Lawrence
Born: Barking, 20 August 1977
Height: 6'0" Weight: 12.6

After a year in the reserves Wayne found himself back in favour at Ipswich last season, mainly as deputy for Mark Venus on the left of a three-man central defensive unit. Being left footed, he obviously preferred this position, but towards the end of the season he was switched to the right side and coped admirably. Strong in the air and sure in the tackle, he did not let the side down and even bolstered the attack at set pieces, registering some near-misses without actually getting on the score sheet. During December his form was so good that he kept out the fit-again Venus for several games and could consider himself unlucky when he was dropped to the substitutes' bench. Wayne needs to work on his distribution, which tends to be hurried at times but does have its good moments, as was seen in the home game with Crystal Palace when his 60-yard high ball forward was perfect for David Johnson to run on to and score the only goal of the game.
Ipswich T (From trainee on 16/5/1996) FL 21+6 FLC 2 FAC 1 Others 1+1
Colchester U (Loaned on 16/10/1997) FL 0+2

BROWNING Marcus Trevor
Born: Bristol, 22 April 1971
Height: 6'0" Weight: 12.10
International Honours: W: 5

This Gillingham midfield player spent the first half of the 1999-2000 season recovering from a cruciate knee ligament injury suffered back in April 1999. He returned to action with the reserves last January and was back in the first-team squad for the home game with Blackpool, starting his only match of the season in the FA Cup fifth-round tie with Sheffield Wednesday. Further injury problems then restricted him to just a handful more appearances as a substitute. Marcus – when fully fit – is an effective ball winner in the centre of the park, strong in the tackle and with a high workrate.
Bristol Rov (From trainee on 1/7/1989) FL 152+22/13 FLC 7+3 FAC 8/1 Others 13+5/3
Hereford U (Loaned on 18/9/1992) FL 7/5
Huddersfield T (£500,000 on 17/2/1997) FL 25+8 FLC 2+2
Gillingham (Loaned on 20/11/1998) FL 1
Gillingham (£150,000 on 25/3/1999) FL 0+4 FAC 1+1 Others 0+1

BRUCE Paul Mark
Born: Lambeth, 18 February 1978
Height: 5'11" Weight: 12.0

Paul has come through from Queens Park Rangers' successful academy programme and earned a place in the first team last season following injuries to Tim Breacker, Matthew Rose and other wing backs. He normally operates on the left side of midfield and added defensive duties to his style of play in 1999-2000. After establishing himself in the team he broke a bone in his hand which kept him out for two months. However, he regained his place and held on to it until the end of the season. Paul's only other first-team experience with Queens Park Rangers was in 1997-98, when he played in just one game.

Queens Park R (From trainee on 15/7/1996) FL 12+5/1 FAC 3+1
Cambridge U (Loaned on 25/3/1999) FL 2+2

BRUMWELL Phillip (Phil)
Born: Darlington, 8 August 1975
Height: 5'8" Weight: 11.0

The only member of Darlington's 1996 Wembley play-off side still at Feethams, this versatile player fulfilled a utility role throughout the 1999-2000 season, coming in to fill various positions in defence and midfield. A local boy who relishes playing for his home-town club, Phil always produces committed displays whenever he is called upon and had completed five years' Quakers service when he was released during the summer.

Sunderland (From trainee on 30/6/1994)
Darlington (Free on 11/8/1995) FL 106+50/1 FLC 5+2 FAC 7+5/2 Others 8+3

BRYAN Derek (Del) Kirk
Born: Hammersmith, 11 November 1974
Height: 5'10" Weight: 11.5
Club Honours: Div 3 '99

Derek is a fast and exciting right-sided Brentford forward whose 1999-2000 season was badly affected by injuries. He was a regular squad member until suffering a pulled thigh muscle against Oxford that kept him out of action for a month. On his return he featured mostly as a substitute before he was injured for a second time playing against Oxford, this time in the Auto Windscreens Shield tie last January. Derek collided with the opposition 'keeper when scoring for the Bees and was carried off with a torn cruciate ligament in his right knee that required surgery. He played no further part in the campaign and is likely to be out of action for some time into the coming season.

Brentford (£50,000 from Hampton on 28/8/1997) FL 16+33/7 FLC 1+1 FAC 0+4 Others 1+2/1

BRYAN Marvin Lee
Born: Paddington, 2 August 1975
Height: 6'0" Weight: 12.2

Marvin began the 1999-2000 season as a regular at right back in the Blackpool defence, although he was only on a weekly contract. At his best he is a speedy attacking full back who defends well. He was released by Blackpool last December following an injury and on transfer deadline day he joined Bury until the end of the season. He appeared both at left back and in midfield for the Shakers during the closing weeks of the campaign, demonstrating a penchant for getting forward. After three substitute appearances, he was given a run of six successive starts and looked a useful enough acquisition to suggest that the Shakers may offer him a new contract. Stop Press: It was reported in the middle of June that Marvin had signed for Rotherham on a free transfer.

Queens Park R (From trainee on 17/8/1992)
Doncaster Rov (Loaned on 8/12/1994) FL 5/1
Blackpool (£20,000 on 10/8/1995) FL 172+10/4 FLC 10+3 FAC 8 Others 12
Bury (Free on 23/3/2000) FL 6+3

BRYANT Matthew (Matt)
Born: Bristol, 21 September 1970
Height: 6'1" Weight: 13.2

This Gillingham centre back had a frustrating time with injuries during the 1999-2000 season. He suffered back problems early on and it was not until January that he returned to first-team action in the FA Cup third round victory over Premiership club Bradford City. He then had the misfortune to aggravate his old injury in a reserve game and had just one further outing for the Gills, appearing as a substitute against Burnley in March. Matt is good in the air, very quick and can also turn out at full back if required.

Bristol C (From trainee on 1/7/1989) FL 201+2/7 FLC 9+1 FAC 11 Others 9
Walsall (Loaned on 24/8/1990) FL 13 FLC 4
Gillingham (£65,000 on 8/8/1996) FL 82+21 FLC 9+2 FAC 4+1 Others 4

BRYANT Simon Christopher
Born: Bristol, 22 November 1982
Height: 5'9" Weight: 10.7

This first-year trainee became the second-youngest player to start a league match for Bristol Rovers when, at 16 years, 9 months and 12 days, the midfielder played at Wrexham on 28 August 1999. Simon made an immediate impression with his mature performances, particularly his accurate passing and firm tackling. After featuring in 15 matches he unfortunately sustained a deep bruising of his foot on Boxing Day against Millwall at the Memorial Stadium. With his foot in plaster for six weeks, the injury sidelined him for the rest of the season, which was particularly disappointing for Simon, as he missed an opportunity to play against his older brother Matt, the Gillingham central defender. With the talented youngster having been awarded a long-term professional contract on his 17th birthday, Rovers have a fine prospect who will hopefully make a major contribution in seasons to come.

Bristol Rov (From trainee on 17/1/2000) FL 9+6 FLC 0+3

BUBB Byron James
Born: Harrow, 17 December 1981
Height: 5'7" Weight: 10.5

A fast and tricky winger who can also play in midfield, Byron spent most of the 1999-2000 season in Millwall's reserve team. Although he continued to impress, the strength of the Lions' squad was such that he remained a fringe player, and he was restricted to two substitute appearances. He showed much improvement during the campaign, and when he did play for the first team he confirmed that he will be an asset to the club.

Millwall (From trainee on 30/12/1998) FL 1+4

BUCKLE Paul John
Born: Hatfield, 16 December 1970
Height: 5'8" Weight: 11.10
Club Honours: Div 3 '92

Paul rejoined Exeter during the 1999 pre-season from Colchester. Unfortunately, he suffered an ankle injury after only 16 minutes of the opening-day win against Hull that sidelined him for several weeks. Otherwise, Paul was a virtual ever-present in City's midfield last season. He was a solid and consistent performer in the engine room throughout the campaign, and chipped in with two goals.

Brentford (From trainee on 1/7/1989) FL 42+15/1 FLC 5+1 FAC 3+1 Others 6+5
Torquay U (Free on 3/2/1994) FL 57+2/9 FLC 8 FAC 3 Others 1
Exeter C (Free on 13/10/1995) FL 22/2 FAC 1 Others 2
Northampton T (Free on 30/8/1996)
Wycombe W (Free on 18/10/1996)
Colchester U (Free on 28/11/1996) FL 96+9/7 FLC 4 FAC 2 Others 10/3
Exeter C (Free on 2/7/1999) FL 27/1 FAC 3+1 Others 5/1

BUCKLEY Adam Christian
Born: Nottingham, 2 August 1979
Height: 5'9" Weight: 11.2

This left-sided midfielder, the son of manager Alan Buckley, took his chance to play a regular role as part of the Grimsby Town senior squad in 1999-2000. Comfortable on the ball and a provider of good crosses into the box, Adam was unfortunate to occasionally be on the receiving end of some rough treatment from the fans, not because of his ability but mainly as a result of supporters' dissatisfaction with father Alan, as the Mariners struggled just above the relegation zone in the first half of the season.

Grimsby T (Signed from West Bromwich A juniors on 7/8/1997) FL 8+7 FLC 0+1 FAC 2

BUGGIE Lee David
Born: Bury, 11 February 1981
Height: 5'9" Weight: 11.0

This Bury-born youngster gained his first taste of Football League action for the Shakers as a substitute in the last 17 minutes of the final league fixture of 1999-2000 away at Notts County. A striker with a stocky build, Lee had been in impressive goalscoring form in Bury's reserve and youth teams all season and his brief call-up was reward for a season of great promise.

Bolton W (From trainee on 18/2/1998)
Bury (Free on 27/5/1999) FL 0+1

BUKRAN Gabor
Born: Hungary, 16 November 1975
Height: 5'11" Weight: 12.2
International Honours: Hungary: 1

Signed by Walsall from Spanish club Xerez just before the start of the 1999-2000 season, this skilful Hungarian midfielder made an immediate impression on his debut in the opening game of the campaign with his neat use of the ball, and three days later showed his finishing ability with a powerful volley in the Worthington Cup game at Plymouth. A member of the Hungarian international squad, Gabor was one of Walsall's most consistent players in the middle of the pitch, though he lost his place during the final vain scramble against relegation.

Walsall (Free from Xerez CD, Spain on 5/8/1999) FL 33+4/2 FLC 4/3 FAC 0+1

BULL Garry William
Born: West Bromwich, 12 June 1966
Height: 5'10" Weight: 12.2
Club Honours: GMVC '91

A prolific goalscorer throughout his career, Garry found himself out of favour at Scunthorpe after they won promotion to Division Two and started only three matches during the 1999-2000 season. He still did a good job at reserve-team level, where his experience at holding the ball up helped a young side, but he was made available for transfer before Christmas. Garry came off the substitutes' bench to score his first goal for Scunthorpe in the relegation six-pointer at Blackpool in April, but was released in the summer.

Southampton (Signed from Paget R on 15/10/1986)
Cambridge U (Signed on 29/3/1988) FL 13+6/4 FLC 0+1 Others 0+2
Barnet (£2,000 on 1/3/1989) FL 83/37 FLC 4/4 FAC 11/3 Others 8/2
Nottingham F (Free on 21/7/1993) F/PL 4+8/1 FLC 2 FAC 0+3
Birmingham C (Loaned on 12/9/1994) FL 10/6 Others 2/1
Brighton & Hove A (Loaned on 17/8/1995) FL 10/2 Others 1/2
Birmingham C (Free on 29/12/1995) FL 3+3 FLC 0+1 FAC 0+2 Others 1/1
York C (Free on 4/3/1996) FL 66+17/11 FLC 7+2/2 FAC 5+1
Scunthorpe U (Free on 24/7/1998) FL 7+23/1 FLC 0+1 FAC 0+2 Others 0+2

BULL Ronald (Ronnie) Rodney
Born: Hackney, 26 December 1980
Height: 5'8" Weight: 10.12

Ronnie, a product of the Millwall youth set-up, was given a deserved two-year contract last season after some excellent performances in the reserves in 1998-99. An adventurous left back, he loves to get forward and is very strong in the challenge considering his modest stature. Never giving any quarter, he tends to wear his heart on his sleeve, which endears him to the Millwall faithful, and he is a key figure in the club's future development.

Millwall (From trainee on 12/5/1999) FL 6+4

BULLOCK Anthony (Tony) Brian
Born: Warrington, 18 February 1972
Height: 6'1" Weight: 12.13

Tony began 1999-2000 as Barnsley's first-choice 'keeper but was dropped in favour of new signing Kevin Miller just five games into the campaign. He featured only twice more in the starting line-up, against Sheffield United in November when Miller was suspended and for the final game of the regular season when his rival was rested. He is a fine shot stopper with a commanding presence in his penalty area. Tony was released during the summer.

Barnsley (£20,000 from Leek T on 27/3/1997) FL 37+1 FLC 4 FAC 5

BULLOCK Darren John
Born: Worcester, 12 February 1969
Height: 5'9" Weight: 12.10

Bury's hard-tackling midfield man continued to demonstrate his usual mixture of enthusiasm and determination throughout the 1999-2000 season. The aggressive side of his game also unfortunately brought more of the disciplinary problems that have been a feature of his career, with a dismissal in the home game against Preston in November leading to his annual suspension. With the Shakers looking to reduce their wage bill, Darren was allowed to join Rushden & Diamonds on 27 March, signing for the Conference club on loan until the end of the season, with a view to a more permanent deal.

Huddersfield T (£55,000 from Nuneaton Borough on 19/11/1993) FL 127+1/16 FLC 11/1 FAC 8/2 Others 9/1
Swindon T (£400,000 on 24/2/1997) FL 55+11/2 FLC 2 FAC 1
Bury (£150,000 + on 15/2/1999) FL 34+5/3 FLC 2 FAC 4/1 Others 1/1

BULLOCK Lee
Born: Stockton, 22 May 1981
Height: 5'9" Weight: 11.7

This talented midfielder impressed when called upon for senior duty at York in 1999-2000, his first full season as a professional. He missed the closing weeks of the campaign owing to an ankle injury picked up in a reserve game. Lee was offered a further three-year contract in May, while his progress continues to be monitored by Newcastle and Sunderland.

York C (From trainee on 29/6/1999) FL 16+8 FLC 1 FAC 1

BULLOCK Martin John
Born: Derby, 5 March 1975
Height: 5'5" Weight: 10.7
International Honours: E: U21-1

This Barnsley wide midfield player had a frustrating time during the 1999-2000 season. He featured in the starting line-up only once in Nationwide League games, playing for 70 minutes of the home game against Nottingham Forest last October, and apart from regular appearances in the Worthington Cup matches he was rarely used – even as a substitute. In January he moved to Port Vale on loan to boost their fight against relegation. He made a very promising debut at West Bromwich and then scored against QPR, adding an extra dimension to the Vale play with his forays down the right-hand side. Unfortunately, the Vale could not afford the £400,000 asking price and the player himself declined a further month's loan, preferring to return to Oakwell. On his day Martin is a pacy, skilful winger who poses constant problems when running at opposition defences.

Barnsley (£15,000 from Eastwood T on 4/9/1993) F/PL 93+74/3 FLC 14+3 FAC 4+11/3 Others 1
Port Vale (Loaned on 14/1/2000) FL 6/1

BULLOCK Matthew
Born: Stoke, 1 November 1980
Height: 5'8" Weight: 11.0
International Honours: E: Yth

It is always a great joy for the Stoke supporters to see a local boy emerge into the team as Matthew, an England youth international, did in 1999-2000. Given a first-team chance after only a handful of reserve-team appearances by Gary Megson, he took it with both hands and made a number of starts on the right side of midfield. He lost out when Gudjon Thordarson arrived and was relegated to the reserves for further development. A shortage of true pace should be set against a high skill level, and his time will surely come again.

Stoke C (From trainee on 21/11/1997) FL 4+3 FAC 0+1

BULMAN Dannie
Born: Ashford, Surrey, 24 January 1979
Height: 5'10" Weight: 12.3

This young Wycombe midfielder found it difficult to break into the first team at the start of 1999-2000 but worked hard in the reserves and by early December he was a regular on the subs' bench. His season really took off after he scored with a brave diving header at Chesterfield, and he went on to make the starting line-up for the last seven games of the campaign. Dannie impressed with his fierce tackling, defence-splitting passes and an ability to make late runs into the box. Providing he maintains his progress and stays clear of injury, he should become an established first-team player in 2000-01.

Wycombe W (£5,000 + from Ashford T on 17/6/1998) FL 15+25/2 FLC 1+1 FAC 0+4 Others 1

BURGESS Benjamin (Ben)
Born: Buxton, 9 November 1981
Height: 6'3" Weight: 14.4

An 18-year-old from Buxton for whom Blackburn had to compensate Everton when he signed for them, Ben made his senior debut against Portsmouth last April when the rest of the Rovers strike force was out of sorts. He had a quiet game that added nothing to the good reputation he has gained with the club's U19 and reserve teams. Tall and strong, he can act as a target and likes to spread play but also has a predator's instinct for knock-in goals.

Blackburn Rov (From trainee on 25/11/1998) FL 1+1

BURGESS Daryl
Born: Birmingham, 24 January 1971
Height: 5'11" Weight: 12.4

In 1999-2000 Daryl had his leanest-ever season in terms of appearances since establishing himself in West Bromwich Albion's first team eight years ago. He had to battle for a place in the side with six other defenders all able to do the same job, but he was as resilient and determined as ever when called into action. He was unfortunately sent off early in the campaign and missed several games through suspension, making it difficult for him to reclaim his senior place. He occupied four different defensive positions during the course of the season and scored one goal – a flashing header to earn Albion a point at Bolton.

West Bromwich A (From trainee on 1/7/1989) FL 316+13/10 FLC 19+3/3 FAC 9 Others 14

Daryl Burgess

BURLEY Adam Gareth
Born: Sheffield, 27 November 1980
Height: 5'10" Weight: 12.6

A regular with the youth team the previous season, either in midfield or in attack, Adam made his Sheffield United debut, as a substitute, in the home leg of the Worthington Cup tie against Shrewsbury Town last August. Two more substitute appearances followed, in the second leg of the tie and then at home to Crystal Palace in September, his league debut. Although he was on the bench for other games, it appeared that he would otherwise be confined to the reserves, where he was a fixture. However, he made a substitute appearance in the final game of the season and scored the equalising goal against Swindon. Adam will be hoping that this will help him to establish himself as a first-team regular in 2000-01.

Sheffield U (From trainee on 5/7/1999) FL 0+2/1 FLC 0+2

BURLEY Craig William
Born: Irvine, 24 September 1971
Height: 6'1" Weight: 13.0
Club Honours: SLC '97; SPD '98
International Honours: S: 38; U21-7; Yth; Sch

Arguably Jim Smith's most effective signing of the 1999-2000 season for Derby, the Scottish international midfielder arrived at Pride Park in a £3 million transfer last December after an unhappy start to the season at Glasgow Celtic to add some steel to a team already embroiled in a relegation battle. His impact was immediate and his debut against Leeds transformed the midfield area of the side. Highly competitive, and preferring a right-sided role, he is especially effective when shooting from long distance and scored two particularly memorable goals in this fashion against Middlesbrough and Leicester. Craig struck up a partnership with Georgi Kinkladze on his arrival and their combination of skill and combativeness enabled Derby to retain their Premiership status. He is a regular in Craig Brown's Scotland side, where he can play equally effectively in a number of roles including that of wing back.

Chelsea (From trainee on 1/9/1989) P/FL 85+28/7 FLC 8 FAC 12+5/4 Others 3
Glasgow Celtic (£2,500,000 on 24/7/1997) SL 61+3/20 SLC 7 SC 6/1 Others 12/1
Derby Co (£3,000,000 on 2/12/1999) PL 18/5 FAC 1

BURNELL Joseph (Joe) Michael
Born: Bristol, 10 October 1981
Height: 5'10" Weight: 11.1

A product of Bristol City's flourishing academy set-up, Joe made significant progress in 1999-2000 to become an established member of the first-team squad and deservedly win the supporters' club "Junior Player of the Year" award. A versatile defender who is equally comfortable at full back or in midfield, he is quick, has two good feet, tackles well and is excellent in the air. He is often able to out-jump opponents taller than himself, and his first senior goal for the club was one to remember. It came on the last day of February, a brilliant header in City's 4-0 win over Exeter at Ashton Gate in the Auto Windscreens Shield area final.

Bristol C (From trainee on 24/7/1999) FL 15+2 Others 3/1

BURNETT Wayne
Born: Lambeth, 4 September 1971
Height: 5'11" Weight: 12.6
Club Honours: AMC '98
International Honours: E: Yth

After missing much of the previous campaign through injury, the creative Grimsby midfield player had another frustrating season in 1999-2000. Having picked up a groin injury on the final day of 1998-99, he returned to first-team action as a substitute in mid-September and then had a run of eight games in the starting line-up, although he was often replaced before the final whistle. Unfortunately, after two further appearances from the subs' bench, yet more groin trouble was to rule him out for the rest of the season. Wayne's midfield skills were once again sorely missed, and it is to be hoped that he will enjoy better fortune during the coming campaign.

Leyton Orient (From trainee on 13/11/1989) FL 34+6 FLC 3+1/1 FAC 3+1 Others 4
Blackburn Rov (£90,000 on 19/8/1992)
Plymouth Arg (Signed on 9/8/1993) FL 61+9/3 FLC 3 FAC 8 Others 4+1
Bolton W (£100,000 on 12/10/1995) F/PL 0+2
Huddersfield T (Signed on 6/9/1996) FL 44+6 FLC 6+1/1 FAC 1+1
Grimsby T (£100,000 on 9/1/1998) FL 42+9/3 FLC 3+2 Others 8/3

BURNS John Christopher
Born: Dublin, 4 December 1977
Height: 5'10" Weight: 11.0
International Honours: RoI: U21-2; Yth

Having had a brief taste of first-team football when he made a substitute appearance in a Worthington Cup tie in 1998-99, John finally made his league debut for Nottingham Forest last September, nearly five years after moving to the City Ground from Irish club Belvedere. A creative, tough-tackling midfielder who was once dubbed the new Roy Keane, he started four successive matches before being transferred to Bristol City in November as part of the deal that took Jim Brennan to Forest. John had to wait for his chance at Ashton Gate and his progress was hampered by injuries, but he made his full debut for his new club against Wigan in January. He shows sound technique, is strong in the tackle and looks to have the potential to develop into a good player provided he can improve his distribution.

Nottingham F (From Belvedere YC on 4/12/1994) FL 3 FLC 1+1
Bristol C (£100,000 + on 5/11/1999) FL 6+5 Others 1+1

BURNS Liam
Born: Belfast, 30 October 1978
Height: 6'0" Weight: 12.12
International Honours: NI: U21-13; Yth

This dependable no-nonsense defender finally had an extended run in the Port Vale first team in 1999-2000. A no-frills player who is not afraid to just clear his lines, Liam became a fixture in the back four following the sale of Ant Gardner to Spurs, but his own personal highlight was the FA Cup tie at Leeds in December. He looks to have a bright future in the game and should comfortably hold his own at Second Division level. Quietly spoken, he is a manager's dream off the field. He added four early-season caps to his total for Northern Ireland U21s.

Port Vale (From trainee on 2/7/1997) FL 26+3 FAC 1

BURROWS David
Born: Dudley, 25 October 1968
Height: 5'9" Weight: 11.8
Club Honours: CS '89; Div 1 '90; FAC '92
International Honours: E: B-3; U21-7

The experienced left-sided Coventry defender had a frustrating season in 1999-2000. He was sent off at both Leicester (the first dismissal of his career) and Tranmere in the early part of the campaign and missed seven games through suspension. In his first full game back he suffered a cruciate ligament injury and was out of action until February. His return coincided with a run of defeats and he lost his place to Steve Froggatt. When fit and in form, David is strong in the air and a tough tackler on the ground. When he pushes forward his crossing is excellent. His contract at Coventry ended in the summer and, though he was offered new terms at Highfield Road, rumours persisted of a move in the close season to Wolves. Stop Press: David was reported to have signed for Birmingham City at the beginning of July.

West Bromwich A (From apprentice on 8/11/1986) FL 37+9/1 FLC 3+1 FAC 2 Others 1
Liverpool (£550,000 on 20/10/1988) F/PL 135+11/3 FLC 16 FAC 16+1 Others 14
West Ham U (Signed on 17/9/1993) PL 29/1 FLC 3/1 FAC 3
Everton (Signed on 6/9/1994) PL 19 FLC 2 FAC 2
Coventry C (£1,100,000 on 2/3/1995) PL 106+5 FLC 9 FAC 9

BURTON Deon John
Born: Ashford, 25 October 1976
Height: 5'9" Weight: 11.9
International Honours: Jamaica: 24

Derby's Jamaican international striker had a frustrating campaign at Pride Park in 1999-2000 with a combination of injuries and loss of form meaning he made very few appearances in the starting line-up. It was typical of his season that when he came on as a substitute against Wimbledon in March he managed to find the net only to then suffer a knee injury. Despite his lack of domestic football, he remained a first choice for his country and was often away on international duty. A very pacy striker, Deon is at his best running at defenders and is, therefore, particularly difficult to tackle, winning free kicks with regularity around the penalty box. The season did end on a high for him, however, with his hat-trick in the reserves' final league game at West Ham confirming their league title. If he can harness his abundance of energy and steer clear of injuries, he could yet figure prominently in Jim Smith's plans for the coming season. Deon was also called up by Jamaica for the CONCACAF Gold Cup tournament last February and won further caps against Colombia and Honduras.

Portsmouth (From trainee on 15/2/1994) FL 42+20/10 FLC 3+2/2 FAC 0+2/1
Cardiff C (Loaned on 24/12/1996) FL 5/2 Others 1
Derby Co (£1,000,000 + on 9/8/1997) PL 41+28/16 FLC 3+1 FAC 7+1/3
Barnsley (Loaned on 14/12/1998) FL 3

BURTON-GODWIN Osagyefo (Sagi) Lenin Ernesto
Born: Birmingham, 25 November 1977
Height: 6'2" Weight: 13.6

The owner of possibly the longest name in English professional football, but thankfully known as Sagi, this powerfully built centre half was signed by Colchester from Crystal Palace in the 1999 close season in what was hailed as a great coup for the U's, and he enjoyed an excellent pre-season. The wheels began to come off with the mistake which led to Simon Brown's red card against his old club in the Worthington Cup, and a run of yellow cards preceded a sending-off at Bournemouth. Returning from suspension, Sagi then picked up an injury in another heavy defeat at Cambridge which effectively ended his Colchester career, as his request to be released from his contract for personal reasons was granted before he returned to fitness. He joined Sheffield United in November but was released without making a first-team appearance for the Blades. In January Sagi moved to Port Vale, earning a two-and-a-half-year contract after a promising performance in a reserve game. He would replace Ant Gardner, who was sold to Tottenham soon after his arrival, and held his place in the centre of the Vale defence for the remainder of the season. Despite a lack of great pace, his physical strength enables him to get the better of most opposing strikers. In addition to his sterling work in defence, Sagi scored two goals, both from headers, in successive home games against Charlton and Barnsley, both matches curiously ending 2-2.

Crystal Palace (From trainee on 26/1/1996) P/FL 19+6/1 FLC 1 FAC 0+1
Colchester U (Free on 26/5/1999) FL 9 FLC 2
Sheffield U (Free on 19/11/1999)
Port Vale (Free on 14/1/2000) FL 19+1/2

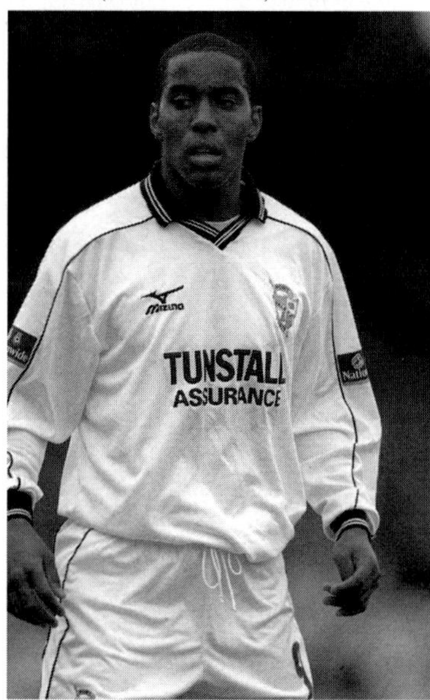

Sagi Burton-Godwin

BUSHELL Stephen (Steve) Paul
Born: Manchester, 28 December 1972
Height: 5'9" Weight: 11.6

This hard-working midfield battler missed the opening games of the 1999-2000 season as he was still recovering from a broken foot dating back to March 1999. Steve returned to the Blackpool starting line-up last October and featured regularly in the following weeks, scoring with a cracking long-distance drive against Gillingham in January. Unfortunately, he suffered a hamstring injury the following month that meant another long spell on the treatment table.

York C (From trainee on 25/2/1991) FL 156+18/10 FLC 8+1/2 FAC 5 Others 11+2/1
Blackpool (Free on 2/7/1998) FL 48+7/5 FLC 4 FAC 4 Others 3

BUTLER Philip **Anthony (Tony)**
Born: Stockport, 28 September 1972
Height: 6'2" Weight: 12.0

A dependable central defender who is good in the air and solid on the ground, Tony began the 1999-2000 season at Port Vale but niggling injuries limited his appearances in the first team. He was also ruled out by suspension after he was sent off against Nottingham Forest and, following a goal conceded at Fulham, he was substituted at half time and transferred three weeks later (on deadline day) to West Bromwich, whose manager, Gary Megson, had been his boss at Blackpool. Tony quickly slotted into the Baggies' back line, where he played alongside Matt Carbon (initially), then Frenchman Georges Santos and finally Daryl Burgess. He made an impressive debut for Albion at Maine Road and his determination, commitment and resilience went a long way in helping the Midlands club avoid relegation. Not many forwards get the better of Tony in the air and he is now looking forward to a full season with the Baggies, hopefully with a settled central defensive partner!

Gillingham (From trainee on 13/5/1991) FL 142+6/5 FLC 12 FAC 12+1 Others 5+1/1
Blackpool (£225,000 on 30/7/1996) FL 98+1 FLC 7 FAC 4 Others 4/1
Port Vale (£115,000 on 25/3/1999) FL 19
West Bromwich A (£140,000 on 23/3/2000) FL 7

BUTLER Lee Simon
Born: Sheffield, 30 May 1966
Height: 6'2" Weight: 13.6
Club Honours: Div 3 '97

The recruitment of this accomplished goalkeeper from Dunfermline was one of the shrewdest signings made by the Halifax management in 1999-2000. Quoted at £70,000 in the 1999 close season, he joined Town on a free in September. Lee was outstanding all season, pulling off a string of superb saves. His campaign was summed up at the end-of-season awards evening, when he cleaned up, winning all the "Player of the Year" trophies.

Lincoln C (Free from Haworth Colliery on 16/6/1986) FL 30 FLC 1 FAC 1
Aston Villa (£100,000 on 21/8/1987) FL 8 Others 2
Hull C (Loaned on 18/3/1991) FL 4
Barnsley (£165,000 on 22/7/1991) FL 118+2 FLC 5 FAC 9 Others 4
Scunthorpe U (Loaned on 5/2/1996) FL 2
Wigan Ath (Free on 5/7/1996) FL 63 FLC 3 FAC 2 Others 2
Dunfermline Ath (Signed on 3/7/1998) SL 35 SLC 1 SC 2
Halifax T (Signed on 24/9/1999) FL 38 FAC 3 Others 1

BUTLER Martin Neil
Born: Wordsley, 15 September 1974
Height: 5'11" Weight: 11.9

This lively and energetic striker was once again a regular on the goalscoring charts for Cambridge in 1999-2000. He is a hard-working and unselfish player, and his 14 league goals in 26 games brought him to the attention of other clubs. At the beginning of February Martin moved to Reading for a reported fee of £750,000 (to which was added a bonus of £50,000 when Reading escaped relegation), and he quickly impressed by scoring in his first two games for his new club. He then had a barren spell of nine games without a goal, and was injured for the final part of the season.

However, he had already confirmed the potential he had shown earlier in his career, and looks to be a vital part of the Royals' strike force in the coming seasons.
Walsall (From trainee on 24/5/1993) FL 43+31/8 FLC 2+1 FAC 2+5/2 Others 2+2/2
Cambridge U (£22,500 on 8/8/1997) FL 100+3/41 FLC 9/5 FAC 9+2/5 Others 3+1/1
Reading (£750,000 + on 1/2/2000) FL 17/4 Others 1

BUTLER Paul John
Born: Manchester, 2 November 1972
Height: 6'2" Weight: 13.0
Club Honours: Div 2 '97; Div 1 '99
International Honours: RoI: 1; B-1
A powerful central defender who tackles decisively, Paul endured a season of highs and lows in 1999-2000, his first term in the Premiership. Having formed a solid defensive wall with Andy Melville in Sunderland's First Division championship success, Paul now found himself alongside the experienced Steve Bould and the understanding the pair immediately struck up was vital to Sunderland's outstanding early-season form. Paul's aerial ability is useful at set pieces and he opened his goalscoring account in the Premiership in September with a thumping header against Leicester. Sunderland boss Peter Reid showed his faith in Paul by handing him the captain's armband when Bould was suspended in November. He went on to make his full international debut for the Republic of Ireland against the Czech Republic in February, becoming the first player to qualify after gaining Irish citizenship through marriage. It seemed that things couldn't get any better for the stopper. However, loss of form saw Paul briefly relinquish his place in the Sunderland side, although he was to regain his berth before the season was out.
Rochdale (From trainee on 5/7/1991) FL 151+7/10 FLC 8+1 FAC 6+2 Others 12+1
Bury (£100,000 on 22/7/1996) FL 83+1/4 FLC 8 FAC 2 Others 3/1
Sunderland (£600,000 + on 15/7/1998) P/FL 75+1/3 FLC 8+1 FAC 4

BUTLER Peter James
Born: Halifax, 27 August 1966
Height: 5'9" Weight: 11.1
The Halifax assistant manager was a vital part of the club's midfield in 1999-2000 with his tenacious qualities shining through. Peter's workrate was once again second to none, but during the home match against Swansea in March he suffered a serious knee injury that ended his season prematurely. There are fears that this may finish his playing career but the local lad has stated that he intends to continue.
Huddersfield T (From apprentice on 21/8/1984) FL 0+5
Cambridge U (Loaned on 24/1/1986) FL 14/1 Others 1
Bury (Free on 8/7/1986) FL 9+2 FLC 2/1 FAC 1
Cambridge U (Free on 10/12/1986) FL 55/9 FLC 4 FAC 2 Others 2
Southend U (£75,000 on 12/2/1988) FL 135+7/9 FLC 12/1 FAC 2 Others 11/2
Huddersfield T (Loaned on 24/3/1992) FL 7
West Ham U (£125,000 on 12/8/1992) F/PL 70/3 FLC 4 FAC 3 Others 1
Notts Co (£350,000 on 4/10/1994) FL 20 FLC 2 FAC 2 Others 3
Grimsby T (Loaned on 30/1/1996) FL 3
West Bromwich A (£175,000 on 28/3/1996) FL 52+8 FLC 2+1 FAC 1+2
Halifax T (Free on 1/8/1998) FL 63/1 FLC 4 FAC 4 Others 1

BUTLER Stephen (Steve)
Born: Birmingham, 27 January 1962
Height: 6'2" Weight: 12.12
Club Honours: GMVC '89
International Honours: E: SP-3
This experienced striker returned to Gillingham as player-coach in the summer of 1999 and continued to turn out for the club's reserve team on a regular basis in 1999-2000. He appeared several times as a substitute in the last few months of the season and scored a couple of important goals, including the crucial equaliser in extra time during the Second Division play-off final with Wigan. He set several new age-related records for the Gills during the campaign, becoming their oldest league goalscorer when he netted against Brentford last April and later on their oldest outfield player.
Brentford (Free from Windsor & Eton on 19/12/1984) FL 18+3/3 Others 2
Maidstone U (Free on 1/8/1986) FL 76/41 FLC 4/3 FAC 18/7 Others 10/4
Watford (£150,000 on 28/3/1991) FL 40+22/9 FLC 4+3 FAC 1 Others 2+1
Bournemouth (Loaned on 18/12/1992) FL 1
Cambridge U (£75,000 on 23/12/1992) FL 107+2/51 FLC 4+1 FAC 6/5 Others 3
Gillingham (£100,000 on 15/12/1995) FL 77+31/20 FLC 7+1/1 FAC 5/1 Others 1
Peterborough U (Free on 29/10/1998) FL 13+1/2 FAC 1 Others 1/1
Gillingham (Free on 2/7/1999) FL 2+8/2 FAC 2+1 Others 0+3/1

BUTLER Thomas Anthony
Born: Dublin, Ireland, 25 April 1981
Height: 5'8" Weight: 10.8
International Honours: RoI: Yth
This young Irish midfielder made his debut for Sunderland last September in a Worthington Cup tie against Walsall. Thomas showed great form last season for both the Sunderland and Republic of Ireland youth sides, despite suffering from inflamed tendons in his feet, an injury that was to sideline him for a month. However, in May, Thomas made his Premiership bow as a substitute against West Ham and he is regarded by many at Sunderland as being the most promising young player at the club. He won three caps for the Republic of Ireland at U18 level during the season.
Sunderland (From trainee on 25/6/1998) PL 0+1 FLC 0+1

BUTT Nicholas (Nicky)
Born: Manchester, 21 January 1975
Height: 5'10" Weight: 11.3
Club Honours: FAYC '92; CS '96, '97; PL '96, '97, '99, '00; FAC '96; EC '99
International Honours: E: 8; U21-7; Yth; Sch
A gritty midfielder with neat skills and a hardened edge, Nicky enjoyed a solid start to his Premiership campaign in 1999-2000, vying with Paul Scholes for a place in midfield alongside Roy Keane and filling in for the Irishman during his absence in September. Back in August he was most unfortunate to miss out on United's Super Cup clash against Lazio after getting his head in the way of a piledriver against Coventry two days earlier, which left him with double vision. Fortunately, there were no long-term effects from the injury, and he was ready to resume battle against Liverpool two games later. In October Nicky became the first United player to be red-carded in 1999-2000, during the Reds' 5-0 drubbing at Chelsea. Perhaps fortune won through adversity a little in this instance, as his three-match ban gave him an opportunity to have surgery for a long-standing hernia problem. Marking his comeback in November with his first goal of the season against Derby at Pride Park, Nicky added further strikes to his tally against Sunderland both at home and away, and scored United's solitary effort against Vasco da Gama in the World Club Championship qualifier in January. He remained an important member of the squad for the rest of the campaign and gained his fourth Premiership winners' medal. Nicky might not be one of United's most high-profile players, but Sir Alex Ferguson knows that he can depend on him. He was sent off against Watford at the end of April and missed the last game of the season through suspension. Nicky was disappointed not to be included in the England squad for Euro 2000 and will be determined to make himself part of Kevin Keegan's plans during the coming season.
Manchester U (From trainee on 29/1/1993) PL 140+38/16 FLC 5 FAC 16+2/1 Others 37+8/2

Danny Butterfield

BUTTERFIELD Daniel (Danny) Paul
Born: Boston, 21 November 1979
Height: 5'10" Weight: 11.10
Club Honours: AMC '98
International Honours: E: Yth
A graduate of John Cockerill's fruitful Grimsby youth scheme, this talented young

right back is a solid defender who is fast and tenacious when going forward. An early-season injury to first-choice right back John McDermott enabled Danny to enjoy an extended run in Division One and in the Worthington Cup, where he acquitted himself with honour and proved himself ready for football at the highest level. During this spell he was watched by several senior clubs who are no doubt still monitoring his progress. The return of McDermott to the squad, however, meant he was once again relegated to the bench, while a hand injury sidelined him for the closing weeks of the season. With McDermott as consistent as ever in his 13th season with the Mariners, one can only guess when Danny will have the chance to establish himself in the first team.

Grimsby T (From trainee on 7/8/1997) FL 34+14 FLC 6+1 FAC 1+2 Others 1+1/1

BUTTERS Guy
Born: Hillingdon, 30 October 1969
Height: 6'3" Weight: 14.2
International Honours: E: U21-3

Guy missed several games for Gillingham at the start of the 1999-2000 campaign but returned to the starting line-up once he had agreed a new contract. He went on to appear in almost every game for the Gills, producing some composed displays in the centre of the defence as the Kent club went on to win their first-ever promotion to Division One, albeit via the play-offs. He is sound in the air, a good tackler and possesses a deadly left foot that is often put to good use at set pieces.

Tottenham H (From trainee on 5/8/1988) FL 34+1/1 FLC 2+1 FAC 1
Southend U (Loaned on 13/1/1990) FL 16/3 Others 2
Portsmouth (£375,000 on 28/9/1990) FL 148+6/6 FLC 15+1/1 FAC 7 Others 7+2
Oxford U (Loaned on 4/11/1994) FL 3/1 Others 1
Gillingham (£225,000 on 18/10/1996) FL 122+2/12 FLC 4 FAC 13/1 Others 11

BYFIELD Darren
Born: Sutton Coldfield, 29 September 1976
Height: 5'11" Weight: 11.11

This tricky young Aston Villa striker was loaned to Northampton shortly before the start of the 1999-2000 campaign but, having been brought in as cover for the injured Carlo Corazzin, he missed the opening week of the season after contracting chicken pox. His quick reactions in the penalty area brought him two goals during his stay at Sixfields, but the reported £200,000 fee required by Villa for a permanent transfer was out of Town's reach and Darren was recalled by the Premiership club in mid-September. He then joined Cambridge on loan, but although he caught the eye with his speed he did not combine with United's front-line strikers, Martin Butler and Trevor Benjamin, as effectively as had been hoped and did not remain at the Abbey beyond his first month. Darren was loaned to relegation-threatened Blackpool in March but was injured in only his third game for the Seasiders, at Millwall. Clearly not figuring in Villa manager John Gregory's plans, he was allowed to join Walsall on a free transfer in June with a year of his contract remaining. It's not too long ago that he carried a £500,000 price tag, and he will be hoping to get his career back on track during the coming season.

Aston Villa (From trainee on 14/2/1994) PL 1+6 FLC 1 FAC 0+1 Others 1
Preston NE (Loaned on 6/11/1998) FL 3+2/1 Others 1
Northampton T (Loaned on 13/8/1999) FL 6/1 FLC 1/1
Cambridge U (Loaned on 17/9/1999) FL 3+1
Blackpool (Loaned on 6/3/2000) FL 3

BYRNE Christopher (Chris) Thomas
Born: Manchester, 9 February 1975
Height: 5'9" Weight: 10.4
International Honours: E: SP-1

Having been out of action since September 1998 with a cruciate ligament injury, Chris returned to the Stockport first team last August. The former hat-trick hero of Macclesfield's last Conference Championship game in 1997, he then returned to Moss Rose on loan after Macc manager Sammy McIlroy had praised his midfield abilities when he was a guest on a television programme. Chris was short of match practice but was "Man of the Match" in his first game at Hull, setting up one of the goals and causing havoc in midfield. He was less impressive thereafter but following his return to Stockport he enjoyed a decent run in the team, scoring against Huddersfield and Walsall. He appeared to have regained his lost momentum but he was then sent off against Sheffield United in November and rarely featured in manager Andy Kilner's plans for the remainder of the season.

Crewe Alex (From trainee on 21/6/1993. Free to Flixton on 1/8/1994)
Sunderland (Signed from Macclesfield T on 11/6/1997) FL 4+4 FLC 1+1
Stockport Co (£200,000 on 21/11/1997) FL 43+12/11 FLC 3/1 FAC 1+1
Macclesfield T (Loaned on 27/8/1999) FL 5

BYRNE Shaun Ryan
Born: Chesham, 21 January 1981
Height: 5'9" Weight: 11.8
International Honours: RoI: Yth (UEFA-U16 '98)

This promising young left back spent much of the 1999-2000 campaign out injured and managed only a handful of games for West Ham reserves. He made his senior debut for the Hammers when he came on as a substitute for the final ten minutes of the Premiership game at Newcastle in early January, and within days joined Second Division pace setters Bristol Rovers on a month's loan to gain further valuable experience. Showing pace and a willingness to get forward, Shaun made an impressive league debut for the Pirates at Colchester in a thrilling 4-5 defeat and three days later scored a vital last-spot-kick match-winner in a tense Auto Windscreens Shield tie penalty shoot-out at Northampton. He was a substitute against Oxford and then made a further start in another Auto Windscreens Shield tie against Reading before completing his loan spell and returning to Upton Park. He captained the Republic of Ireland U18 side, making four appearances during the season, and will be aiming to graduate to the U21s in the next couple of years.

West Ham U (From trainee on 2/7/1999) PL 0+1
Bristol Rov (Loaned on 7/1/2000) FL 1+1 Others 2

BYWATER Stephen (Steve) Michael
Born: Manchester, 7 June 1981
Height: 6'3" Weight: 13.2
Club Honours: FAYC '99
International Honours: E: Yth

Steve is one of several highly rated youngsters at West Ham and played in the team that won the FA Youth Cup in 1998-99. He was loaned to Wycombe Wanderers last September to provide cover during an injury crisis and became the club's fourth 'keeper in eight days when he made his Football League debut against Blackpool. He produced an impressive performance and then did well again in the 5-3 win over Reading the following week before being recalled to Upton Park. In November he went to Hull on loan to stand in for Steve Wilson and Lee Bracey, who were ruled out by a back injury and suspension respectively. Although conceding five goals in four City appearances, he soon displayed the certainty that persuaded West Ham to pay a record fee for a teenage 'keeper. Steve then stepped up to make his senior debut for the Hammers as a substitute for broken-leg victim Shaka Hislop in the home game with Bradford City in February. He made a shaky start, conceding four goals (although the Hammers won 5-4), but finished the campaign on a high, playing in the final three Premiership games and performing heroics for the U19s in the penalty shoot-out that ensured they won the Academy League for the second year in succession. Steve has a safe pair of hands and great confidence for one so young. Already capped by England at U16 level, he won four caps for the U18s last season.

Rochdale (Trainee) Others 1
West Ham U (£300,000 + on 7/8/1998) PL 3+1
Wycombe W (Loaned on 23/9/1999) FL 2
Hull C (Loaned on 23/11/1999) FL 4

Steve Bywater

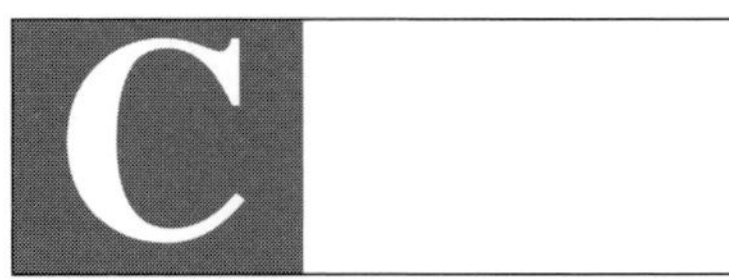

CADAMARTERI Daniel (Danny) Leon
Born: Bradford, 12 October 1979
Height: 5'7" Weight: 11.12
Club Honours: FAYC '98
International Honours: E: U21-2; Yth

In a televised match at Wimbledon last February, the young Everton forward showed all the qualities which first saw him explode on to the Premiership scene as a raw but exciting teenager two and a half years previously. Blessed with excellent natural pace and strength, Danny tormented the Dons' defence that afternoon playing as an out-and-out right winger. But a lacklustre showing just seven days later against Derby County typified the inconsistency which has dogged his career. Allowed to spend a month on loan at Fulham in November when the London club was faced by a desperate shortage of strikers due to injury, he scored in his first game (a 2-1 defeat at Stockport) but he dropped to the bench when Geoff Horsfield and Paul Peschisolido recovered. Danny has never been short of confidence, and at his best he is a handful for most defences, but his performances in an Everton jersey were restricted throughout 1999-2000 and he still has plenty to do to realise a potential which once earmarked him as a Premiership star of the future. He won a further cap for England U21s when he appeared in the European Championship play-off match with Yugoslavia in March.

Everton (From trainee on 15/10/1996) PL 29+45/9 FLC 6+3/2 FAC 4+3
Fulham (Loaned on 4/11/1999) FL 3+2/1

CADETE Santos Reis **Jorge**
Born: Mozambique, 27 August 1968
Height: 5'11" Weight: 11.11
International Honours: Portugal: 32

Jorge eventually joined Bradford City on loan last February after protracted negotiations that were delayed due to injury and illness. A former Portugal international who played for Celtic back in 1996-97, he saw the move as a way to revive his career after failing to make the starting line-up with Benfica all season. Although he showed early promise, he was mostly used as a substitute at Valley Parade and returned to Portugal at the end of the season.

Glasgow Celtic (Signed from Sporting Lisbon, Portugal on 30/3/1996) SL 32+5/30 SLC 5/1 SC 5/2 Others 3/1 (Transferred to Celta Viga, Spain on 12/9/1997)
Bradford C (Loaned from Benfica, Portugal on 25/2/2000) PL 2+5

CAHILL Timothy (Tim)
Born: Sydney, Australia, 6 December 1979
Height: 5'10" Weight: 10.11

Australian-born Tim turned in some excellent performances for Millwall in 1999-2000. A box-to-box midfielder who doesn't shirk his defensive duties, he is strong in the tackle and a good header of the ball despite his lack of height. He weighed in with his fair share of goals, scoring a total of 12 in all competitions. Due to his consistent play he has attracted interest from Premiership clubs but the Lions' fans are hoping he will stay with the club and see them into the First Division and beyond.

Millwall (Signed from Sydney U, Australia on 31/7/1997) FL 80+2/18 FLC 2+1 FAC 1 Others 8/1

CAIG Antony (Tony)
Born: Whitehaven, 11 April 1974
Height: 6'1" Weight: 13.4
Club Honours: Div 3 '95; AMC '97

Tony began 1999-2000 as second-choice 'keeper for Blackpool but quickly won back his place in the Seasiders' first team and showed some excellent form in the early part of the campaign. He retained his place until last March, when he was dropped following a disastrous 5-1 defeat at Wigan. A fine and consistent shot stopper, he will be looking to become first choice again at Bloomfield Road in the coming season.

Carlisle U (From trainee on 10/7/1992) FL 223 FLC 16 FAC 13 Others 29
Blackpool (£40,000 on 25/3/1999) FL 43 FLC 1 FAC 3 Others 2

Tony Caig

CALDERWOOD Colin
Born: Glasgow, 20 January 1965
Height: 6'0" Weight: 12.12
Club Honours: Div 4 '86; FLC '99
International Honours: S: 36

This veteran centre back began the 1999-2000 season playing alongside Gareth Southgate and Ugo Ehiogu in a three-man defence for Aston Villa. He lost his place to rising youngster Gareth Barry in mid-September but quickly returned to the first team when Ehiogu was injured. By last December he was back on the subs' bench and in March he joined Nottingham Forest, where he was needed to cover for injuries to the club's regular defenders. Colin brought experience and stability to the Reds' back four, but after making only six appearances he suffered a dislocated ankle and broken fibula against Birmingham City in April. He is expected to make a full recovery in time for the beginning of the 2000-01 season.

Mansfield T (Signed on 19/3/1982) FL 97+3/1 FLC 4 FAC 6/1 Others 7
Swindon T (£30,000 on 1/7/1985) FL 328+2/20 FLC 35 FAC 17/1 Others 32
Tottenham H (£1,250,000 on 22/7/1993) PL 152+11/6 FLC 19+1 FAC 15+1/1
Aston Villa (£225,000 on 24/3/1999) PL 23+3 FLC 3+1
Nottingham F (£70,000 on 15/3/2000) FL 6

CALVO-GARCIA Alexander (Alex)
Born: Ordizia, Spain, 1 January 1972
Height: 5'10" Weight: 11.12

Scunthorpe United's play-off hero from the previous season, Alex took a while to find his feet in Division Two in 1999-2000 as he wasn't given time and space to show off his ball skills and goalscoring ability. A midfielder with an eye for goal, he had just opened his account for the season when he sustained a broken leg in the away match at Reading at the end of November. He was ruled out for the rest of the season but signed a new two-year deal and is expected to have made a full recovery for the new campaign.

Scunthorpe U (Free from Eibar, Spain on 4/10/1996) FL 106+12/17 FLC 8/3 FAC 10/1 Others 7/2

CAMARA Aboubacar (Titi) Sidiki
Born: Guinea, 17 November 1972
Height: 6'1" Weight: 12.8
International Honours: Guinea

A £2.6 million buy from Marseille during the summer of 1999, "Titi" proved to be a sensational signing for Liverpool. He was an instant revelation, scoring on the opening day of the new season, and it was an omen for much of what was to come: spectacular goals and fluent performances from a player who gives his all in every game. A great favourite of the crowd because he wears a smile on his face and his heart on his sleeve, Titi added firepower to a Liverpool team already blessed with some world-class strikers. Even in adversity, he refuses to let his spirits drop, and he had an excellent game in the home defeat by Watford. He also played very well in the away victory over Leeds, a performance which included an equalising goal and saw him flying down the wing on numerous occasions in a fashion which had not been seen since John Barnes wore the red shirt. Titi is skilful, fast and direct, as well as being sharp in front of goal and always highly creative. The forth-coming season could see him blossom into a truly great Liverpool player, now that he has become accustomed to the demands of the Premiership.

Liverpool (£2,600,000 from Marseille, France on 14/6/1999) PL 22+11/9 FLC 0+2 FAC 2/1

CAMERON David (Dave) Anthony
Born: Bangor, 24 August 1975
Height: 6'1" Weight: 13.8

Having impressed at St Mirren, Dave bought himself out of the Army in order to join Brighton in the 1999 close season. His performances at centre forward contained plenty of effort but goals proved elusive. He made his debut when coming on as a late substitute in the 6-0 opening-day drubbing of Mansfield, and set up the last two goals. A big strong man, he soon won over the fans, but the Albion management weren't quite so appreciative. There was a very public falling-out following the February defeat at Hull, when it was made clear that he would not represent the club again. Following an unsuccessful trial at Raith, Dave rediscovered his form with a run of nine goals in nine games at Worthing in the Ryman League. He later became new Lincoln manager Phil Stant's first signing. After playing for the Imps in a testimonial against Middlesbrough in May, he agreed a two-year contract. Like Dave, Phil is a former soldier.

Falkirk (Signed from Dunipace Juniors on 17/8/1994)
East Stirling (Free on 31/8/1995) SL 0+8 (Free to Pencaitland & Ormiston during 1997 close season)
St Mirren (Signed from Whitehall Welfare on 2/2/1999) SL 3+8
Brighton & Hove A (Free on 8/7/1999) FL 6+11 FLC 0+1 Others 0+1

CAMILIERI-GIOIA Carlo
Born: Brussels, Belgium, 14 May 1975
Height: 5'11" Weight: 12.2

Having come from Belgium in the hope of making a name for himself in the English game, Carlo made two appearances for Mansfield from the subs' bench during a two-week trial period early in the 1999-2000 season. He impressed sufficiently in an attacking midfield role to be offered a short-term contract, but refused this offer, preferring to try his luck in a higher sphere when offered another trial, this time with Sheffield United.

Mansfield T (Free from Charleroi, Belgium on 10/9/1999) FL 0+2

CAMPAGNA Samuel (Sam) Patrick Philip
Born: Worcester, 19 November 1980
Height: 6'1" Weight: 11.7

This Swindon Town youngster made the step up from trainee to first-year professional in July 1999 but found his first-team opportunities limited by the presence of stalwarts such as Gareth Davies, Gareth Hall and Alan Reeves. Sam was included in the starting line-up for the home game with Crystal Palace last January and made two further appearances from the subs' bench. A hard-working central defender, he is comfortable on the ball and cool under pressure and reads the game well. He is expected to feature more regularly for the Robins in the coming season now that Reeves and Hall have both departed.

Swindon T (From trainee on 10/7/1999) FL 1+4

CAMPBELL Andrew (Andy) Paul
Born: Stockton, 18 April 1979
Height: 5'11" Weight: 11.7
International Honours: E: U21-3; Yth

Andy is a genuine "local boy makes good" story. The young striker works at his game with great application, and his efforts were rewarded with a regular place in the Middlesbrough first team in 1999-2000. It was his third season with the senior squad, and he began to receive more frequent call-ups. His manager and the backroom staff at the Riverside hold him in the highest esteem, and his future looks assured as he has signed a four-year extension to his contract. Many experienced defenders were caught unawares by Andy's electrifying pace and ball control, allied to his powerful striking on the run. He is most definitely a striker of enormous potential and is being brought along carefully – certainly one to watch out for in the future. Andy made his debut for England U21s against Yugoslavia in March, when he scored in a 3-0 victory, and he also netted one against Turkey in the European U21 Championship finals during the close season.

Middlesbrough (From trainee on 4/7/1996) F/PL 23+22/4 FLC 4+5/1 FAC 2/1
Sheffield U (Loaned on 10/12/1998) FL 5/1
Sheffield U (Loaned on 25/3/1999) FL 6/2

Andy Campbell

CAMPBELL Jamie
Born: Birmingham, 21 October 1972
Height: 6'1" Weight: 12.11

Jamie joined Brighton from Cambridge United under the Bosman ruling during the 1999 close season. He was a regular at left wing back or his less favoured position of centre half until he was sent off at Swansea City in December. Jamie scored his only goal in the home victory over Hartlepool United in November. He made a quick recovery from a triple hernia operation in January, but his involvement was restricted to being a non-playing substitute thereafter. Jamie was made available on a free transfer at the end of the season with a year of his contract to run.

Luton T (From trainee on 1/7/1991) FL 10+26/1 FLC 1+1 FAC 1+3 Others 1+2
Mansfield T (Loaned on 25/11/1994) FL 3/1 FAC 2
Cambridge U (Loaned on 10/3/1995) FL 12
Barnet (Free on 11/7/1995) FL 50+17/5 FLC 3+3/1 FAC 4+2/1 Others 1
Cambridge U (Free on 8/8/1997) FL 91/6 FLC 7 FAC 6/1 Others 4
Brighton & Hove A (Free on 7/7/1999) FL 22+1/1 FLC 2 FAC 3 Others 2

CAMPBELL Kevin Joseph
Born: Lambeth, 4 February 1970
Height: 6'1" Weight: 13.8
Club Honours: FAYC '88; FLC '93; FAC '93; ECWC '94; Div 1 '98
International Honours: E: B-1; U21-4

The rousing ovation Kevin received when he hobbled on to the Goodison Park pitch on crutches after the final home match of the 1999-2000 season showed the calibre of the season he had enjoyed for Everton. Top scorer for the second successive campaign, despite falling victim to a knee injury in early March which ended his season early, he had been hugely influential until then. Leading the forward line with pace, strength and guile, he looked a more complete striker than at any other time in his career. England coach Kevin Keegan visited Goodison Park in January to check out the form of Francis Jeffers and Nick Barmby, but left extolling the virtues of Campbell after another typical performance. His partnership with Jeffers is one of the best in the Premiership, and Evertonians will hope both players can enjoy an injury-free season in 2000-01.

Arsenal (From trainee on 11/2/1988) F/PL 124+42/46 FLC 14+10/6 FAC 13+6/2 Others 15+4/5
Leyton Orient (Loaned on 16/1/1989) FL 16/9
Leicester C (Loaned on 8/11/1989) FL 11/5 Others 1/1
Nottingham F (£3,000,000 on 1/7/1995) F/PL 79+1/32 FLC 2 FAC 11/3 Others 3 (£2,500,000 to Trabzonspor, Turkey on 7/8/1998)
Everton (£3,000,000 on 25/3/1999) PL 34/21 FLC 0+2 FAC 5

CAMPBELL Neil Andrew
Born: Middlesbrough, 26 January 1977
Height: 6'2" Weight: 13.7

Neil's chances in the Southend forward line were very limited during the 1999-2000 season under new manager Alan Little. He is built like a good old-fashioned centre forward, but faltering confidence seemed to dog him as he began to bear the brunt of the fans' anger at sub-standard team performances. He moved to Doncaster Rovers before the transfer deadline in March.

York C (From trainee on 21/6/1995) FL 6+6/1 FLC 1 FAC 0+2 Others 2
Scarborough (Free on 5/9/1997) FL 23+22/7 FLC 2 FAC 0+2 Others 3/1
Southend U (Free on 22/1/1999) FL 15+9/3 FAC 0+1 Others 1

CAMPBELL Paul Andrew
Born: Middlesbrough, 29 January 1980
Height: 6'1" Weight: 11.0

This tall, promising young player failed to establish himself in the Darlington first team in 1999-2000 and was limited to just six starts and seven appearances as a substitute, all in the first half of the campaign. He

showed that he has an eye for goal by contributing two strikes, one being the match winner against Cheltenham. Paul is a graceful midfielder who makes good use of the ball.
Darlington (From trainee on 8/7/1998) FL 13+11/4 FLC 0+2 FAC 1 Others 1+1

CAMPBELL Stuart Pearson
Born: Corby, 9 December 1977
Height: 5'10" Weight: 10.8
Club Honours: FLC '97, '00
International Honours: S: U21-14
Stuart again figured mostly from the substitutes' bench for Leicester during the 1999-2000 season, making the starting line-up only once. The right-sided midfielder remains tantalisingly promising but has not managed to force his way into regular contention yet. A deadline-day loan deal took him to Birmingham, where his opportunities were disappointingly limited. He made two appearances from the subs' bench at St Andrews before being recalled early due to an injury crisis at Filbert Street.
Leicester C (From trainee on 4/7/1996) PL 12+25 FLC 2+5 FAC 3+3
Birmingham C (Loaned on 23/3/2000) FL 0+2

CAMPBELL Sulzeer (Sol) Jeremiah
Born: Newham, 18 September 1974
Height: 6'2" Weight: 14.1
Club Honours: FLC '99
International Honours: E: 33; B-1; U21-11; Yth (UEFA-U18 '93)
The Tottenham captain had another outstanding season in the centre of the defence in 1999-2000. With his pace and great aerial ability, Sol continued to add much-needed stability to the Spurs back four, where his fabulous organisational skills proved priceless. Always one for a big occasion, Sol produced his finest performances of the season in the 3-1 home victory over Manchester United and the 2-1 win against north London rivals Arsenal. As Tottenham's form dipped in mid-season, speculation mounted as to whether Sol would be moving on from the club at the end of the campaign. Assurances came from on high, with Spurs Chairman Alan Sugar and Director of Football David Pleat announcing that the club were ready to break the bank to keep their captain, despite rumours of Manchester United and a host of Continental clubs lining up a £20 million bid to lure the defender away from London. The Spurs faithful will be hoping that negotiations come to a speedy conclusion and that Sol will be taking his place in the Tottenham team for many years to come. He was once again a key figure in the England defence, adding a further seven caps and playing in all three of his country's games in Euro 2000.
Tottenham H (From trainee on 23/9/1992) PL 225+9/8 FLC 27/4 FAC 23+2/1 Others 2

CANHAM Scott Walter
Born: Newham, 5 November 1974
Height: 5'9" Weight: 11.7
Scott was unfortunate not to play in more games for Leyton Orient in 1999-2000 as he did not let the side down when called upon. Owing to the form of the other midfielders at the club he found his appearances limited to two home games in August, against Torquay in the league and Grimsby in the Worthington Cup. He spent a month on loan at Chesham United in the Ryman League and was released in May.
West Ham U (From trainee on 2/7/1993)
Torquay U (Loaned on 3/11/1995) FL 3
Brentford (Loaned on 19/1/1996) FL 14
Brentford (£25,000 + on 29/8/1996) FL 24+11/1 FLC 4+2 FAC 1+1 Others 1+2
Leyton Orient (Free on 10/8/1998) FL 3+6 FLC 0+1 Others 1

CAPLETON Melvyn (Mel) David
Born: Hackney, 24 October 1973
Height: 5'11" Weight: 12.0
Starting the 1999-2000 season as Southend United's number one 'keeper, Mel proved himself to be an excellent shot stopper, although he was a little tentative on high crosses. The arrival of Mark Prudhoe in November seemed to have an adverse effect on him, and he was dropped for a spell. He returned all the stronger in January. A great favourite with the Roots Hall crowd, Mel will be looking to confirm his place as the Blues' first choice in the new term.
Southend U (From trainee on 1/7/1992)
Blackpool (Free on 1/8/1993) FL 9+2 FLC 1 (Free to Grays Ath on 18/10/1995)
Leyton Orient (Free on 14/9/1998) FLC 1
Southend U (Free on 23/10/1998) FL 54+2 FLC 2 FAC 1 Others 1

CARBON Matthew (Matt) Phillip
Born: Nottingham, 8 June 1975
Height: 6'2" Weight: 13.6
International Honours: E: U21-4
Matt didn't have a happy season with West Bromwich in 1999-2000: he was sent off twice, cautioned a further nine times and suspended for a total of seven matches, and also suffered his fair share of injuries (one after being involved in a car crash). But despite his problems he still put in some sterling performances at the heart of the Albion defence, and he scored a decisive equalising goal in the 1-1 draw with neighbours Wolves at Molineux. Strong in the air, Matt played his best football alongside the Icelandic international Larus Sigurdsson but next season he may well have Tony Butler as his permanent aide in the Baggies' defence.
Lincoln C (From trainee on 13/4/1993) FL 66+3/10 FLC 4/1 FAC 3 Others 4+3
Derby Co (£385,000 on 8/3/1996) P/FL 11+9 FLC 1 FAC 0+1
West Bromwich A (£800,000 on 26/1/1998) FL 87+2/5 FLC 6+1 FAC 3

CARBONARI Horacio Angel
Born: Argentina, 2 May 1973
Height: 6'3" Weight: 13.4
Nicknamed "Bazooka" for his phenomenal shooting ability, the tall Derby central defender had a competent second season in the Premiership in 1999-2000, invariably occupying a role in the centre of a three-man rearguard along the lines of a Continental sweeper. This requires him to be able to read the game astutely and pass in a more creative manner than most defenders, and this he showed himself well capable of. While liking to get forward as often as possible, Horacio is not the quickest of players and it is at set pieces where he is at his most dangerous, possessing a ferocious shot which brought him a vital goal at Tottenham towards the end of the season. Less happy in a man-marking role, he is, however, one of the cleaner tacklers in the game. He entered hospital for a hernia operation as soon as the season concluded.
Derby Co (£2,700,000 from Athletico Rosario Central, Argentina on 1/7/1998) PL 57+1/7 FLC 1 FAC 5

Horacio Carbonari

CARBONE Benito
Born: Begnara, Italy, 14 August 1971
Height: 5'6" Weight: 10.8
International Honours: Italy: U21 (UEFA-U21 '94)
This very talented Italian forward began the 1999-2000 season on the subs' bench at Sheffield Wednesday and soon afterwards became involved in a much-publicised dispute with the club. Despite prolonged negotiations the Owls were unable to persuade him to stay at Hillsborough and he joined Aston Villa last October for a nominal fee and a further sum based on appearances. Benito immediately returned to his best form and produced an outstanding display on his debut for Villa against Wimbledon. In the following months he showed that he has the ability to be as dangerous as any player in the Premiership and his goals provided a significant contribution to the club's FA Cup campaign. A thumping 25-yard drive against Darlington in the third round was followed by a magnificent hat-trick in the fifth-round tie with Leeds. All were cracking goals, with the best being a 35-yard drive that was voted as the "Match of the Day" programme's

"Goal of the Month". Sadly for Villa, he never quite turned it on for them in the Cup final against Chelsea. On his day he can be absolutely brilliant, running at defences with great pace and tight control. At the time of writing it seems he will begin the 2000-01 campaign with a new club, as Villa's efforts to agree a new contract appear to have been unsuccessful.

Sheffield Wed (£3,000,000 from Inter Milan, Italy, via Torino, Reggina, Casert, Ascoli and Napoli, on 18/10/1996) PL 86+10/25 FLC 3+1 FAC 7/1
Aston Villa (Signed on 21/10/1999) PL 22+2/3 FAC 6/5

Benito Carbone

CARDEN Paul Andrew
Born: Liverpool, 29 March 1979
Height: 5'8" Weight: 11.10

Paul was a regular substitute for Rochdale in the first three months of the 1999-2000 season, but made just three full appearances in their midfield when assistant manager Tony Ford was injured. After falling out of favour at Spotland, the combative right-footed midfielder had an unproductive trial at Hull. Paul signed for struggling Chester in March, and his wholehearted approach played a significant part in the valiant struggle to save the seemingly doomed Blues from relegation to the Conference. Relishing a physical battle, his commitment to the desperate Chester cause showed that he still has the determination to succeed at league level.

Blackpool (From trainee on 7/7/1997) FL 0+1 FAC 0+1 Others 1
Rochdale (Free on 3/3/1998) FL 30+15 FLC 0+2 FAC 3+1 Others 3
Chester C (Free on 10/3/2000) FL 9+2

CAREY Brian Patrick
Born: Cork, 31 May 1968
Height: 6'3" Weight: 14.4
International Honours: RoI: 3; U21-1

The Wrexham central defender and captain continued to act as an inspiration for his team-mates in 1999-2000. He may be lacking a bit in pace these days but Brian remains an effective organiser of the Robins' defence, while his height makes his presence effective in either penalty area. Although now into his 30s, he made a rapid recovery from any injuries and so was rarely absent from the starting line-up last season.

Manchester U (£100,000 from Cork C on 2/9/1989)
Wrexham (Loaned on 17/1/1991) FL 3
Wrexham (Loaned on 24/12/1991) FL 13/1 FAC 3 Others 3
Leicester C (£250,000 on 16/7/1993) F/PL 51+7/1 FLC 3 FAC 0+1 Others 4
Wrexham (£100,000 on 19/7/1996) FL 160/4 FLC 8 FAC 20 Others 7

CAREY Louis Anthony
Born: Bristol, 22 January 1977
Height: 5'10" Weight: 11.10
International Honours: S: U21-1

The 1999-2000 season was one of mixed fortunes for this locally born Bristol City defender. He was a regular member of the side at the outset, but a bad foot injury kept him out during the middle part of the campaign before he regained his place in time for the Auto Windscreens Shield final. Although still young himself, the refreshing decision – in the wake of manager Tony Pulis's departure – to give City's promising academy players their chance meant that Louis found himself as one of the most experienced players in the team. Although he is prone to the odd lapse, such as that which brought about Stoke's winner at Wembley, many still feel he has a valuable part to play in City's future.

Bristol C (From trainee on 3/7/1995) FL 159+7 FLC 9+1 FAC 9 Others 8+2

CAREY Shaun Peter
Born: Kettering, 13 May 1976
Height: 5'9" Weight: 10.10
International Honours: RoI: U21-2

This former Norwich City trainee once again enjoyed, or endured, a stop-start season with the Canaries in 1999-2000, gaining an extended run in the team following Phil Mulryne's serious injury before finding himself, too, on the sidelines with niggling injuries. A real team player, Shaun never stops running, working very hard at denying the opposition time and space on the ball, while always supporting his team-mates when in possession. His seemingly boundless energy levels ensure that he covers every inch of the pitch, although he is still looking for his first senior career goal. This former Republic of Ireland U21 international's contract with Norwich ends in June 2000 and at the time of writing he was awaiting a decision as to his immediate playing future.

Norwich C (From trainee on 1/7/1994) FL 50+18 FLC 5+2 FAC 1+1

CARLISLE Clarke James
Born: Preston, 14 October 1979
Height: 6'1" Weight: 12.7

Clarke is a highly promising young defender with over 100 first-team appearances for Blackpool to his name although he is still only 20. He was a regular in the Seasiders' line-up throughout 1999-2000 and was once again reported to be attracting Premiership scouts to Bloomfield Road. Strong in the air and competent on the ground, he also showed that he is more than useful in front of goal, netting five times including the opener in the 2-0 FA Cup victory over Stoke. At the end of May he was reported to have been signed by First Division Queens Park Rangers for £250,000.

Blackpool (From trainee on 13/8/1997) FL 85+8/7 FLC 4+1 FAC 3/1 Others 5

CARLISLE Wayne Thomas
Born: Lisburn, 9 September 1979
Height: 6'0" Weight: 11.6
International Honours: NI: U21-1; Yth

This speedy right-sided midfield player made excellent progress with Crystal Palace during the 1999-2000 season. Although he was troubled by injuries in the early part of the campaign, Wayne established himself as a regular in the Eagles' first-team line-up last December and remained in the squad until the end of the season. He stepped up from the Northern Ireland youth team to the U21s, making his debut as a late substitute against Finland last October.

Crystal Palace (From trainee on 18/9/1996) FL 25+7/3 FLC 0+1

CARPENTER Richard
Born: Sheerness, 30 September 1972
Height: 6'0" Weight: 13.0

A strong, tough-tackling midfielder, Richard has proved himself to be a useful player in the lower divisions, having earned promotion with Gillingham, Fulham and Cardiff. He was a key figure in the Bluebirds' successful 1998-99 campaign, and had a good spell in a midfield holding role alongside Mark Bonner last season, although his usual drive and tenacity seemed to ebb away a little towards the end of the campaign. City boss Frank Burrows left Richard out of the side early on, but after his departure the new manager, Billy Ayre, gave him a leading role. Richard was out of contract at the end of the season but was offered new terms. He is certainly a more than useful man to have around and, as his record shows, his experience could prove invaluable as Cardiff attempt to regain their Second Division place during the coming season.

Gillingham (From trainee on 13/5/1991) FL 107+15/4 FLC 2+1 FAC 9+1 Others 7/1
Fulham (£15,000 on 26/9/1996) FL 49+9/7 FLC 4/1 FAC 2/1 Others 2
Cardiff C (£35,000 on 29/7/1998) FL 69+6/2 FLC 3+1 FAC 8+1 Others 1

CARR Darren John
Born: Bristol, 4 September 1968
Height: 6'2" Weight: 13.7

Darren joined Brighton in July 1999 for £25,000 from Gillingham but suffered a number of injuries that delayed his debut until the end of October in a 0-0 draw at Cheltenham Town. He is a muscular centre half whose uncompromising style causes problems for opposition forwards. Following a tactical change that saw the Albion defence switch to a flat back four, Darren

found himself played as a makeshift centre forward during March.
Bristol Rov (From trainee on 20/8/1986) FL 26+4 FLC 2+2 FAC 3 Others 2
Newport Co (Loaned on 30/10/1987) FL 4
Newport Co (£3,000 on 28/1/1988) FL 5
Sheffield U (£8,000 on 10/3/1988) FL 12+1/1 FLC 1 FAC 3+1 Others 1
Crewe Alex (£35,000 on 18/9/1990) FL 96+8/5 FLC 8 FAC 12/2 Others 10
Chesterfield (£30,000 on 21/7/1993) FL 84+2/4 FLC 9 FAC 6+3 Others 8
Gillingham (£75,000 on 7/8/1998) FL 22+8/2 FLC 2 FAC 1 Others 3+1
Brighton & Hove A (£25,000 on 14/7/1999) FL 16+3 FAC 3 Others 2

CARR Stephen
Born: Dublin, 29 August 1976
Height: 5'9" Weight: 12.2
Club Honours: FLC '99
International Honours: RoI: 11; U21-12; Yth; Sch

Tottenham's pacy full back loves getting forward and taking on the opposition in midfield. His increased confidence on the ball going forward has seen him become a stalwart on the right flank in the Spurs back four. He also netted two superb long-range goals last season. The first, a stunning drive from 25 yards to beat Mark Bosnich in the 3-1 drubbing of Manchester United in late October, won him the coveted "Goal of the Month" award, while the second was an incredible solo effort, almost identical in conception to the first but with a looping finish, that secured a 3-1 victory over Sunderland on the final day of the season at White Hart Lane. Stephen's speed and tenacity make him a hard player to beat and his superb ability to read the game helps him create space on the right flank from which to supply the Spurs attack. He promises to be a key figure in Tottenham's future plans. A first choice for the Republic of Ireland defence, he won a further eight caps last season.
Tottenham H (From trainee on 1/9/1993) PL 133+3/3 FLC 15/1 FAC 11 Others 4

CARRAGHER James (Jamie) Lee Duncan
Born: Bootle, 28 January 1978
Height: 6'1" Weight: 13.0
Club Honours: FAYC '96
International Honours: E: 1; B-2; U21-27; Yth

Having been given a central defensive role by Liverpool in 1998-99, Jamie built upon the form he showed then with some excellent displays at the back last season. A fierce tackler, he has learned not to become too involved in the less savoury aspects of his destructive role, preferring to concentrate on the business in hand. On occasions, he found himself on the right of a three-man defensive system in 1999-2000, although Gerard Houllier favoured a 4-4-2 system in the main. "Mr Versatility", Jamie had a very good season during which he grew up a lot. Always ready to give his all for the Liverpool cause, he sometimes let his youthful exuberance and enthusiasm get the better of him on and off the pitch, but Houllier's strict training regime and sense of discipline appear to have brought Jamie into line, and his performances have improved as a result. He proved to be a very versatile player: in one game he would be doing a marking job, then he would have a holding midfield role before returning to centre half a few days later. Whatever his position, he performs without headlines or undue adulation in an efficient, no-nonsense manner. Jamie was an ever-present for England U21s during the season, winning a further eight caps to add to his already impressive total, and will be looking to make a breakthrough to the full squad in 2000-01.
Liverpool (From trainee on 9/10/1996) PL 85+7/2 FLC 6+1 FAC 4 Others 7

CARRAGHER Matthew (Matty)
Born: Liverpool, 14 January 1976
Height: 5'9" Weight: 11.4
Club Honours: Div 3 '97

A wholehearted Port Vale right back whose enthusiasm makes him popular with the supporters, Matt was a first-team regular virtually throughout the 1999-2000 season, also playing a few games at wing back, but he was disappointed when he missed his first game through suspension – a third-round FA Cup tie away to Leeds United. He scored one goal, in the home victory over Swindon Town, and the only league games he missed were in February and March when a leg injury confined him to the sidelines. Matt is now one of the Vale's more experienced players and he will be hoping to stamp his authority on the team during their forthcoming Second Division campaign.
Wigan Ath (From trainee on 25/11/1993) FL 102+17 FLC 6+1/1 FAC 10+1/2 Others 7+1
Port Vale (Free on 3/7/1997) FL 70+3/1 FLC 4

Matty Carragher

CARRICK Michael
Born: Wallsend, 28 July 1981
Height: 6'0" Weight: 11.10
Club Honours: FAYC '99
International Honours: E: Yth

Michael is one of the talented crop of youngsters developing at West Ham. He made his debut in senior football in the Inter Toto Cup against FC Jokerit in the summer of 1999 and went on to make his Premiership bow as a substitute at Bradford in August. He was then loaned to Swindon Town in November, where he enjoyed a successful spell and scored a wonder goal in the home game with Charlton, finishing off a move he had begun from inside his own half. Another loan period followed with Birmingham, but after showing initial promise he twisted his ankle joints in a reserve fixture and returned early to Upton Park. Michael has an elegant style with great passing and vision and is highly rated by the Hammers, for whom he signed a five-year contract early in the new year. He was a regular for the England U18 side in 1999-2000, winning four caps.
West Ham U (From trainee on 25/8/1998) PL 4+4/1
Swindon T (Loaned on 12/11/1999) FL 6/2
Birmingham C (Loaned on 23/2/2000) FL 1+1

CARROLL David (Dave) Francis
Born: Paisley, 20 September 1966
Height: 6'0" Weight: 12.0
Club Honours: FAT '91, '93; GMVC '93
International Honours: E: Sch

The 1999-2000 season was Dave's 12th for Wycombe and certainly one of his best. He was mostly employed as a central midfield play-maker but showed his versatility by appearing at right back and as a wide-right midfield player when called upon. Now in his mid-30s, he is still a key figure in the Chairboys' side, looking comfortable on the ball and still able to produce spectacular goals. He netted three times last season, all from outside the box, including a 30-yard rocket against West Bromwich in the Worthington Cup tie last September. Having taken his own club record total of appearances past the 275 mark, he has a further year to run on his contract and will no doubt play an important role in 2000-01.
Wycombe W (£6,000 from Ruislip Manor in 1988 close season) FL 268+10/39 FLC 21+2/1 FAC 27/5 Others 14/3

CARROLL Roy Eric
Born: Enniskillen, 30 September 1977
Height: 6'2" Weight: 12.9
Club Honours: AMC '99
International Honours: NI: 4; U21-11; Yth

Recognised by his fellow professionals with selection to the PFA award-winning Division Two side, the Wigan 'keeper once again displayed presence and maturity way beyond his years in 1999-2000. Having signed an extension to his contract at the start of the season, he played a large part in the Latics' run of 26 league games without defeat at the start of the campaign. Not only is Roy a good shot stopper, he also commands his area and is very confident coming for crosses. His performances were rewarded with two more full caps for Northern Ireland against Luxembourg and Malta in the spring. An emergency appendix operation saw him miss the last seven league games of the season but speculation continues to link him with a move to the

Premiership. He completed a century of Football League games for Wigan in the home win over Notts County in March.
Hull C (From trainee on 7/9/1995) FL 46 FLC 2 FAC 1 Others 1
Wigan Ath (£350,000 on 16/4/1997) FL 106 FLC 8 FAC 7 Others 13

CARRUTHERS Martin George
Born: Nottingham, 7 August 1972
Height: 5'11" Weight: 11.9
Martin's stay at Darlington lasted only six months. After striking up what seemed to be a promising partnership with leading scorer Marco Gabbiadini at the end of the previous season, he was limited to just seven substitute appearances in 1999-2000 before moving to Southend. Martin arrived at Roots Hall, initially on loan, in September, and never looked back. Five goals in his first six games immediately endeared him to the Southend crowd, and his willingness to chase even the most unlikely causes meant that he earned himself many unexpected goals. He fell just one short of becoming the first Shrimper to score twenty league goals in a season since Brett Angell in 1991-92. Although his partnership with Neil Tolson was broken when Neil's season finished early due to injury, Martin will be looking forward to renewing it in 2000-01.
Aston Villa (From trainee on 4/7/1990) F/PL 2+2 FAC 0+1 Others 0+1
Hull C (Loaned on 31/10/1992) FL 13/6 Others 3
Stoke C (£100,000 on 5/7/1993) FL 60+31/13 FLC 7+3/1 FAC 3+1 Others 10+4/6
Peterborough U (Signed on 18/11/1996) FL 63+4/21 FLC 5+1/2 FAC 6/4 Others 6
York C (Loaned on 29/1/1999) FL 3+3
Darlington (Signed on 25/3/1999) FL 11+6/2
Southend U (£50,000 on 17/9/1999) FL 38/19 FAC 1 Others 1

CARSLEY Lee Kevin
Born: Birmingham, 28 February 1974
Height: 5'10" Weight: 11.11
International Honours: RoI: 15; U21-1
The Ewood Park crowd was slow to respond to Lee, who joined Blackburn in March 1999, but when he was appointed captain by Tony Parkes during 1999-2000 he flourished as the club's driving force. A midfield anchor who keeps on his feet and stays mobile, he suppplied the protection the Rovers back four needed but was still able to get into forward positions. A close-season trip to Norway earned him the position of penalty taker and he proved proficient on his return, converting his first five spot kicks before failing against Wolves. Lee's season was unfortunately interrupted when he broke a bone in his foot in the FA Cup tie with Newcastle, but he still made four international appearances for the Republic of Ireland during the season.
Derby Co (From trainee on 6/7/1992) P/FL 122+16/5 FLC 10+3 FAC 12 Others 3
Blackburn Rov (£3,375,000 on 23/3/1999) P/FL 37+1/10 FAC 4/1

CARSON Daniel (Danny)
Born: Liverpool, 2 February 1981
Height: 5'6" Weight: 10.7
Danny's senior involvement for Chester in 1999-2000 totalled only four minutes, although they did come in the Worthington Cup tie at Villa Park. A product of City's youth policy who prefers a role in the middle of midfield, he gained more experience by going on loan to Winsford in the Unibond League during February along with fellow Blue Steve Malone.
Chester C (From trainee on 19/7/1999) FL 1+1 FLC 0+1

CARSS Anthony (Tony) John
Born: Alnwick, 31 March 1976
Height: 5'10" Weight: 12.0
This left-footed utility player was given another year by Chesterfield after spending most of 1998-99 on the injured list. He is comfortable on the ball, and has good vision and the ability to deliver effective crosses and corners. Tony is more suited to a left-wing-back or midfield role, but the needs of the side last time caused him to play in the middle of midfield, too. He was released in the summer.
Blackburn Rov (Free from Bradford C juniors on 29/8/1994)
Darlington (Free on 11/8/1995) FL 33+24/2 FLC 5/1 FAC 2+1 Others 4
Cardiff C (Free on 28/7/1997) FL 36+6/1 FLC 2 FAC 5+1 Others 1
Chesterfield (Free on 7/9/1998) FL 26+9/1 FLC 2 FAC 1 Others 1+1

CARTER Alfonso (Alfie) Jermaine
Born: Birmingham, 23 August 1980
Height: 5'10" Weight: 10.6
This young midfielder played consistently in Walsall's reserve side last season, with his accurate crosses a key feature of his game, but his first-team opportunities were restricted to an early-season appearance as a substitute against Sunderland in the Worthington Cup followed by his first start in the league game at Blackburn. Although Alfie was full of running, he was unable to make the impact against such strong opposition that he would have hoped for, but there is no doubt about his potential and he can be expected to be challenging for a regular place this coming season.
Walsall (From trainee on 30/4/1999) FL 1+1 FLC 0+1

CARTER Robert (Rob) Hector Andrew
Born: Stepney, 23 April 1982
Height: 6'1" Weight: 12.1
Rob was an important member of the Leyton Orient youth team that won the South East Conference Youth Alliance Championship in 1999-2000. He is a skilful attacking midfielder and was given his first-team chance in the early part of the season, making his debut against Torquay in September. He will be looking to become a regular part of the senior squad during the new campaign.
Leyton Orient (Trainee) FL 0+2 FLC 1

CARTWRIGHT Lee
Born: Rawtenstall, 19 September 1972
Height: 5'8" Weight: 11.0
Club Honours: Div 3 '96; Div 2 '00
Preston's longest-serving player signed a new contract during the summer of 1999, but a pre-season knee injury kept him out for the first five games of the new campaign. Soon after his return, he scored his first goal for seven months at Millwall, but he then became the fourth North End player to need a cartilage operation. Lee made a surprise return to the first team in January, having not trained for weeks, but he lasted only 16 minutes as a sub at Everton before being substituted himself. His speed and crossing ability from the right wing were sorely missed when he was out of the side and, although he made sufficient appearances to earn a Second Division championship medal, he will be hoping for a clear run next season after three injury-blighted campaigns.
Preston NE (From trainee on 30/7/1991) FL 234+55/21 FLC 13+2/2 FAC 17+3/1 Others 17+5/1

CARVER Joseph (Joe) Anthony
Born: Illinois, USA, 11 June 1971
Height: 5'10" Weight: 11.2
Signed from Hampton Roads Mariners of the USISL 'A'-League, Joe was introduced to the Chester set-up last October by club owner Terry Smith. The 28-year-old forward soon made his debut when coming on as a sub for Aston Villa loanee Michael Blackwood at Peterborough. Although Joe started the Blues' next Third Division game against Macclesfield, his only other City appearance – and only goal – came in the 3-2 defeat of Tranmere in the Cheshire FA Senior Cup.
Chester C (Free from Hampton Roads Mariners, USA on 24/9/1999) FL 1+1

CASEY Ryan Peter
Born: Coventry, 3 January 1979
Height: 6'1" Weight: 11.2
International Honours: RoI: Yth
A natural left-sided ball player, Ryan was tried in the left-wing-back role during 1999-2000 in Swansea's reserve-team games, and on occasions in the Swans' first team. He was regularly used in the second half of the campaign as a substitute, and a higher standard of football in the new season should bring out the best in the pacy Irish youth international.
Swansea C (From trainee on 7/5/1997) FL 10+27/1 FLC 1+1 FAC 0+1 Others 2

CASKEY Darren Mark
Born: Basildon, 21 August 1974
Height: 5'8" Weight: 11.9
International Honours: E: Yth (UEFA-U18 '93); Sch
One of the outstanding players in the lower divisions, Darren gained deserved recognition last season when he was voted Reading's "Player of the Season" by the supporters, and also selected for the PFA award-winning Division Two team. He totalled 23 goals from midfield, an incredible tally in a struggling side, and his accuracy from dead-ball situations must be the envy of many of his contemporaries. Darren captained the team towards the end of the campaign, and Reading's improvement coincided with his ability to lead by example. There were rumours of a move to a higher club, but the fans will be hoping that he continues to lead the Royals' revival.

Tottenham H (From trainee on 6/3/1992) PL 20+12/4 FLC 3+1/1 FAC 6+1
Watford (Loaned on 27/10/1995) FL 6/1
Reading (£700,000 on 28/2/1996) FL 145+14/26 FLC 9+2/4 FAC 8+1/4 Others 5/1

Darren Caskey

CASPER Christopher (Chris) Martin
Born: Burnley, 28 April 1975
Height: 6'0" Weight: 11.11
Club Honours: FAYC '92
International Honours: E: U21-1; Yth (UEFA-U18 '93)

Chris's 1999-2000 season came to an end on Boxing Day when the Reading defender sustained a broken fibula and tibia in his left leg during the game at Cardiff City. So serious was the injury that he was only able to return to light training before the end of the season. Before that incident he had shown the composed style of play at centre back that had justified the £300,000 fee Reading had paid for him the previous season. Tall, commanding and with good pace, he had held a shaky defence together during the final days of Tommy Burns's management.

Manchester U (From trainee on 3/2/1993) PL 0+2 FLC 3 FAC 1 Others 0+1
Bournemouth (Loaned on 11/1/1996) FL 16/1
Swindon T (Loaned on 5/9/1997) FL 8+1/1
Reading (£300,000 on 16/9/1998) FL 46+1 FLC 4 FAC 3 Others 1

CASSIDY Jamie
Born: Liverpool, 21 November 1977
Height: 5'9" Weight: 10.12
Club Honours: FAYC '96
International Honours: E: Yth; Sch

This young defender, previously a squad player at Liverpool, joined Cambridge shortly before the start of the 1999-2000 season hoping to shine in the Second Division. He can play on the left side of midfield as well as at left back. Unfortunately, he struggled at United and was limited to a handful of appearances. Jamie was allowed to leave the club at the end of the season.

Liverpool (From trainee on 2/3/1995)
Cambridge U (Free on 5/8/1999) FL 4+4 FLC 0+1 Others 1

CASTLE Stephen (Steve) Charles
Born: Barkingside, 17 May 1966
Height: 5'11" Weight: 12.10

The wholehearted midfielder was the Peterborough leader on the pitch as Posh forced their way back to the Second Division via the play-offs in 1999-2000. Having played under United boss Barry Fry at Birmingham, Steve also had a coaching role at London Road. Leyton Orient and Halifax had expressed an interest in his services in the 1999 close season. As his Posh contract came to an end in May, (although he was offered a two-year renewal), Hull and Plymouth reportedly joined them in the queue. Stop Press: Steve was reported to have signed for Orient at the beginning of July.

Leyton Orient (From apprentice on 18/5/1984) FL 232+11/55 FLC 15+1/5 FAC 23+1/6 Others 18+2
Plymouth Arg (£195,000 on 30/6/1992) FL 98+3/35 FLC 5/1 FAC 8/2 Others 6/1
Birmingham C (£225,000 on 21/7/1995) FL 16+7/1 FLC 11 FAC 1 Others 3/1
Gillingham (Loaned on 15/2/1996) FL 5+1/1
Leyton Orient (Loaned on 3/2/1997) FL 4/1
Peterborough U (Free on 14/5/1997) FL 96+6/17 FLC 7+1 FAC 4+1/2 Others 6+1/1

CHADWICK Luke Harry
Born: Cambridge, 18 November 1980
Height: 5'11" Weight: 11.0
International Honours: E: U21-5; Yth

A classy Manchester United winger with a penchant for scoring spectacular goals, Luke had an early run-out in the Worthington Cup against Aston Villa last September. Although United lost the game 3-0, he showed some nice touches, and he was able to add to his experience when he joined Royal Antwerp on loan until the end of the season. A regular for England at U21 level, he added five caps during the season.

Manchester U (From trainee on 8/2/1999) FL 1

CHALK Martyn Peter Glyn
Born: Swindon, 30 August 1969
Height: 5'6" Weight: 10.0

Martyn was given a brief run in Wrexham's first team last autumn but mostly featured as a substitute for the remainder of the 1999-2000 season after losing out to youngster Robin Gibson. He is a tricky wide-right midfield player who on his day can cause havoc in opposition defences but has found it difficult to achieve the consistency needed to hold down a regular first-team slot.

Derby Co (£10,000 from Louth U on 23/1/1990) FL 4+3/1 FAC 3/1 Others 0+1
Stockport Co (£40,000 on 30/6/1994) FL 29+14/6 FLC 7+1/2 FAC 2+3 Others 2+2
Wrexham (£25,000 on 19/2/1996) FL 97+39/6 FLC 3+1 FAC 11+3 Others 6

CHALLINOR David (Dave) Paul
Born: Chester, 2 October 1975
Height: 6'1" Weight: 12.6
International Honours: E: Yth; Sch

Dave had his best-ever season for Tranmere in 1999-2000, showing greater maturity and making an appearance in the Worthington Cup final. He is famous for his prodigious long throw and this again proved a valuable weapon in Rovers' attacking armoury, setting up goals for his colleagues on many occasions. However, he is also a good all-round midfield player, particularly intelligent in his distribution of the ball. He scored three goals for Rovers during the season when joining the attack for set pieces.

Tranmere Rov (Signed from Brombrough Pool on 18/7/1994) FL 100+12/6 FLC 11+1 FAC 8

CHALLINOR Paul
Born: Newcastle under Lyme, 4 April 1976
Height: 6'1" Weight: 12.2

After playing his football with Telford United in 1998-99, this central defender was given a trial by Bury in the summer of 1999 and was superb in a pre-season game against Manchester City. Paul was handed a one-year contract largely on the strength of that performance but was never really at the front of the line for a first-team place once the season commenced. He was named among the substitutes on six occasions, but it was only in the penultimate fixture of the season at Stoke that he was eventually called into use, appearing as a replacement for Danny Swailes six minutes from time. Paul was given a free transfer by the Shakers in May 2000.

Birmingham C (From trainee on 1/7/1994. Freed during 1996 close season)
Bury (Free from Telford on 6/8/1999) FL 0+1

CHALLIS Trevor Michael
Born: Paddington, 23 October 1975
Height: 5'9" Weight: 11.4
International Honours: E: U21-2; Yth

This attacking wing back continued to make an impression at Bristol Rovers during 1999-2000 with his consistent performances. The popular former England U21 defender again earned praise for his measured distribution, eager tackling and willingness to get forward but he was sent off for two bookable offences in the home match with Burnley on 30 August. Trevor temporarily lost his first-team place during November following the signing of Mark Walters, but it was not long before the hard-working Londoner regained his spot in the starting line-up. At times he was used in a central midfield role, which he relished, and he scored the first league goal of his professional career in the top-of-the-table home clash with Wigan Athletic in March.

Queens Park R (From trainee on 1/7/1994) F/PL 12+1 FAC 2
Bristol Rov (Free on 15/7/1998) FL 74+4/1 FLC 5 FAC 7 Others 2

CHAMBERLAIN Alec Francis Roy
Born: March, 20 June 1964
Height: 6'2" Weight: 13.9
Club Honours: Div 1 '96; Div 2 '98

A goalkeeper of great calmness and authority, Alec has now clocked up more than 550 league appearances for five different clubs, and over 600 senior appearances in all. By his own very high standards, he had a slightly disappointing season for Watford in 1999-2000, though as the last man in a hard-pressed defence he was always going to be under more pressure than during the club's recent promotion seasons. Things began badly when Alec dislocated a finger during pre-season training. Having been an ever-present in the league for the two previous seasons, he missed the first six Premiership matches, making his seasonal debut at West Ham in September. Despite his commitment and consistency, Alec's form began to suffer later in the season and he was dropped in February. It is a mark of the man that he came back, rested and restored, to keep goal in commanding style. He was "Man of the Match" at Newcastle and Southampton and saved a penalty to rescue a draw at home to Derby, but was replaced by Chris Day for the last three games of the season. Off the field, Alec has a burgeoning career as a radio summariser.

Ipswich T (Free from Ramsey T on 27/7/1981)
Colchester U (Free on 3/8/1982) FL 188 FLC 11 FAC 10 Others 12
Everton (£80,000 on 28/7/1987)
Tranmere Rov (Loaned on 1/11/1987) FL 15
Luton T (£150,000 on 27/7/1988) FL 138 FLC 7 FAC 7 Others 7
Sunderland (Free on 8/7/1993) FL 89+1 FLC 9 FAC 8 Others 1
Watford (£40,000 on 10/7/1996) P/FL 123 FLC 8 FAC 7 Others 3

CHAMBERS James Ashley
Born: West Bromwich, 20 November 1980
Height: 5'10" Weight: 11.8
International Honours: E: Yth

At the start of the season it was debatable which of the Chambers twins, Adam and James – both defenders – would be the first to appear in Albion's league side. It was James who got the nod and he certainly did the manager (Brian Little) justice with some dogged performances at a time when Albion were under the cosh, heading swiftly towards the relegation zone. He made his debut in the Staffordshire derby against Port Vale, partnering Matt Carbon in the back four. The game ended 0-0 and James came out with flying colours, as he did in his second outing, another 0-0 draw at Nottingham Forest. He was also used as a right back and the future certainly looks rosy for the former England youth international.

West Bromwich A (From trainee on 8/1/1999) FL 10+2

CHAPMAN Benjamin (Ben)
Born: Scunthorpe, 2 March 1979
Height: 5'7" Weight: 11.0

The 1999-2000 season was another disappointing one for this young Grimsby left back, who is noted for his determination and rugged tackling. Despite sterling performances for the reserves, the consistency of Tony Gallimore and the availability of David Smith to cover in this position seemed likely to limit his first-team chances to a single game when he played the first 75 minutes in the 0-2 fourth-round FA Cup defeat by Bolton Wanderers. However, late-season injuries gave Ben the opportunity to make his full league debut in the penultimate game of the season against Tranmere, in which he performed creditably, despite the match ending in a 2-1 home defeat.

Grimsby T (From trainee on 11/7/1997) FL 1+1 FAC 1 Others 0+1

CHAPPLE Philip (Phil) Richard
Born: Norwich, 26 November 1966
Height: 6'2" Weight: 13.1
Club Honours: Div 3 '91

Tagged as "the best defender in the Third Division" by his Peterborough boss Barry Fry, Phil has had little chance to prove the point as fitness problems have dogged his progress since arriving at London Road in July 1998. After he picked up a knee injury in November, Phil's 1999-2000 campaign finished in January with the Auto Windscreens Shield defeat by Brentford. A stylish centre half, his experience shone through when fitness allowed. With Posh promoted to the Second Division, Phil may well concentrate on his coaching duties in the new season.

Norwich C (From apprentice on 10/7/1985)
Cambridge U (Signed on 29/3/1988) FL 183+4/19 FLC 11/2 FAC 23/1 Others 17
Charlton Ath (£100,000 on 13/8/1993) FL 128+14/15 FLC 11 FAC 9 Others 5
Peterborough U (Free on 2/7/1998) FL 16+1/1 FAC 1 Others 2

CHARLERY Kenneth (Kenny) Leroy
Born: Stepney, 28 November 1964
Height: 6'1" Weight: 13.12
International Honours: St Lucia: 4

For the second successive season, Kenny finished the 1999-2000 campaign heading the Barnet scoring charts, thus proving that, despite his age, he still has the uncanny knack of finding the net. He spearheaded the attack impressively, with his guile and ability to effortlessly shield the ball from opponents before locating a team-mate to the fore. He registered braces in the home victories against both Northampton and Cheltenham, and weighed in with some important goals throughout the season that enabled the Bees to recover from a bleak slump in form and secure a play-off place. In March he was called up for St Lucia for the second leg of their World Cup qualifying tie with Surinam, but despite his experience he was unable to prevent them crashing out of the tournament in a penalty shoot-out.

Maidstone U (£35,000 from Fisher on 1/3/1989) FL 41+18/11 FLC 1+3/1 FAC 0+3 Others 5+4
Peterborough U (£20,000 on 28/3/1991) FL 45+6/19 FLC 10/5 FAC 3/1 Others 11/7
Watford (£350,000 on 16/10/1992) FL 45+3/13 FLC 3 FAC 1 Others 0+1
Peterborough U (£150,000 on 16/12/1993) FL 70/24 FLC 2 FAC 2+1/3 Others 2/1
Birmingham C (£350,000 on 4/7/1995) FL 8+9/4 FLC 3+1/2 Others 2+1
Southend U (Loaned on 12/1/1996) FL 2+1
Peterborough U (Signed on 9/2/1996) FL 55+1/12 FLC 4/1 FAC 6/6 Others 6/1
Stockport Co (£85,000 on 25/3/1997) FL 8+2
Barnet (£80,000 on 7/8/1997) FL 100+17/34 FLC 7+1 FAC 3 Others 5+2/1

CHARLES Gary Andrew
Born: Newham, 13 April 1970
Height: 5'9" Weight: 11.8
Club Honours: FMC '92; FLC '96
International Honours: E: 2; U21-4

This experienced right wing back moved to Portugal in January 1999 but spent most of his stay there on the injury list. West Ham had been tracking Gary for some time but it was only when he had recovered from a double hernia operation that manager Harry Redknapp moved in to sign him. He was then out of action due to a series of niggling injuries, and when he finally made his debut at Birmingham last November he lasted just 52 minutes before suffering a badly gashed shin. Gary featured in a handful of Premiership games later in the season but found it difficult to break Trevor Sinclair's stranglehold on his favoured position. His strengths are his speed and crossing and he will be hoping to stay free of injuries and return to his top form in 2000-01.

Nottingham F (From trainee on 7/11/1987) F/PL 54+2/1 FLC 9 FAC 8+2/1 Others 4+2
Leicester C (Loaned on 16/3/1989) FL 5+3
Derby Co (£750,000 on 29/7/1993) FL 61/3 FLC 5+1 FAC 1 Others 9
Aston Villa (Signed on 6/1/1995) PL 72+7/3 FLC 9+1 FAC 5+2 Others 6+3/1 (£1,500,000 to Benfica, Portugal on 14/1/1999)
West Ham U (£1,200,000 on 6/10/1999) PL 2+2 FLC 1

CHARLES Julian
Born: Plaistow, 5 February 1977
Height: 5'9" Weight: 11.0

This pacy young Brentford striker is very much one for the future. Julian was signed by Ron Noades in December after just a handful of games with Ryman League club Hampton and made his Football League debut as a substitute against Bristol City on Boxing Day. He spent the final months of the 1999-2000 campaign on loan to Conference outfit Woking to gain experience and will be looking to establish himself in the Bees' first-team squad in the coming season.

Brentford (£25,000 from Hampton & Richmond Borough on 23/12/1999) FL 0+2

CHARLTON Simon Thomas
Born: Huddersfield, 25 October 1971
Height: 5'8" Weight: 11.10
International Honours: E: Yth

This experienced Birmingham left back required two operations over the 1999 close season to cure a groin tendon injury and it was not until last November that he returned to first-team action. Simon remained a regular in the Blues' line-up until fracturing a bone in the top of his foot that caused him to miss the club's play-off games. A solid defender, quick in the tackle and with excellent distribution, he was released during the summer.

Huddersfield T (From trainee on 1/7/1989) FL 121+3/1 FLC 9/1 FAC 10 Others 14
Southampton (£250,000 on 8/6/1993) PL 104+10/2 FLC 9+4/1 FAC 8+1
Birmingham C (£250,000 on 5/12/1997) FL 69+3 FLC 3 FAC 3

CHARNOCK Philip (Phil) Anthony
Born: Southport, 14 February 1975
Height: 5'11" Weight: 11.2

Phil has been on the Crewe staff since 1996 and has mostly occupied a left-sided midfield role, although he can also play at full back. A pelvic injury picked up in November brought an early end to his 1999-2000 season, but he has now undergone surgery and should be back to full fitness for the start of the new campaign. A hard-

working player who uses possession intelligently, he strikes the ball well but his only goal of the season came at Walsall on 21 August.
Liverpool (From trainee on 16/3/1993) FLC 1 Others 0+1
Blackpool (Loaned on 9/2/1996) FL 0+4
Crewe Alex (Signed on 30/9/1996) FL 111+14/7 FLC 12 FAC 4 Others 6

CHARVET Laurent Jean
Born: Beziers, France, 8 May 1973
Height: 5'10" Weight: 12.3
Club Honours: ECWC '98
Laurent is a Newcastle player whose reading of the game coupled with his flexibility and heading ability equip him for a number of roles in defence or midfield. A knee injury incurred in a pre-season game in Germany disrupted his preparation for the 1999-2000 season, and after a single substitute appearance at Leeds in late September he had to wait until early November before being chosen for the starting line-up against Everton. He then picked up an ankle injury in training before the game, so his first full match came in the UEFA Cup against Roma in the Olympic Stadium, where he had a good game at right back although he was unfortunate enough to concede the doubtful penalty which decided the tie. Laurent played in three of the next four games, ending with the FA Cup tie at Tottenham, where he performed well on the right side of midfield, helping to contain the threat from David Ginola, before moving back to central defence following a substitution. However, knee ligament damage incurred in that game meant that this was his last involvement with the first-team squad for the season.
Chelsea (Loaned from Cannes, France on 22/1/1998) PL 7+4/2 FLC 0+1 Others 0+1
Newcastle U (£750,000 on 23/7/1998) PL 31+2/1 FLC 1 FAC 6 Others 4

CHENERY Benjamin (Ben) Roger
Born: Ipswich, 28 January 1977
Height: 6'0" Weight: 12.5
Comfortable in possession and positionally aware, this dependable right back was expected to do well as Cambridge stepped up to the Second Division in 1999-2000 but struggled to recapture his best form. A spell in the reserves saw an improvement in his play, and his return to first-team action was more impressive. The former Luton trainee was released by the club at the end of the season.
Luton T (From trainee on 3/3/1995) FL 2 FAC 1
Cambridge U (Free on 3/7/1997) FL 97+1/2 FLC 9 FAC 6 Others 4

CHETTLE Stephen (Steve)
Born: Nottingham, 27 September 1968
Height: 6'1" Weight: 13.3
Club Honours: FMC '89, '92; FLC '89, '90; Div 1 '98
International Honours: E: U21-12
This experienced defender began the 1999-2000 campaign as captain of Nottingham Forest but was dropped by manager David Platt following the 3-1 home defeat by Huddersfield last November. Shortly afterwards he linked up with former boss Dave Bassett in a loan move to Barnsley and the transfer was made permanent in December. He settled in quickly at Oakwell and achieved instant popularity with the supporters when scoring a great goal just two minutes into his home debut against eventual champions Charlton Athletic. Steve went on to appear regularly until the end of the season, his vast experience and cultured style proving invaluable in the Tykes' young back four.
Nottingham F (From apprentice on 28/8/1986) F/PL 398+17/11 FLC 49+3/1 FAC 36+1 Others 21+2/2
Barnsley (Free on 26/11/1999) FL 25/2 Others 3

CHILLINGWORTH Daniel Thomas
Born: Cambridge, 13 September 1981
Height: 6'0" Weight: 12.6
A local lad from Somersham, Daniel has been with Cambridge since the age of 13. A talented young centre forward, he represented the FA at schoolboy level and has attended England trials at Lilleshall. Daniel scored consistently in the youth team in 1999-2000 and was given his first-team chance at the end of the season, when he made two substitute appearances. He was voted the "Young Player of the Year" by the Cambridge fans, and was rewarded with his first professional contract in May.
Cambridge U (From trainee on 14/2/2000) FL 0+3 Others 0+1

Youssef Chippo

CHIPPO Youssef
Born: Boujaad, Morocco, 10 June 1973
Height: 5'10" Weight: 10.10
International Honours: Morocco: 43
Youssef, a Moroccan, joined Coventry from FC Porto in July. He had played for the Portuguese side in the Champions' League in 1998-99. Originally signed to play as a left-sided defender or midfield player, he started last season in the centre of midfield and quickly settled into the English game. He even outshone his more illustrious compatriot, Moustapha Hadji, during the early months of the campaign. His speed and ball skill were evident from day one but he did hit disciplinary problems with a red card against Sunderland and five bookings in the first six games of the season, mainly through over-enthusiastic tackling. While he was a regular choice, he was switched to a wide-right midfield role after the arrival of Carlton Palmer and also showed his versatility by occasionally playing on the left. He was absent on international duty in January, playing twice for his country in a rather disappointing African Nations' Cup campaign. During his first season in England he scored some outstanding goals, including 25-yarders against Leeds (voted "Goal of the Season" by Gordon Strachan), Tranmere and Burnley. His consistent performances saw him voted the Coventry players' "Player of the Season".
Coventry C (£1,200,000 from FC Porto, Portugal on 16/7/1999) PL 33/2 FLC 1/2 FAC 2/2

CHRISTIE Iyseden
Born: Coventry, 14 November 1976
Height: 6'0" Weight: 12.6
Iyseden joined Leyton Orient from Mansfield for £40,000 during the close season. A gutsy striker who has tremendous pace and a good left foot, he took time to adjust, but once settled he soon started to cause concern among Third Division defences. He scored his first goal in the vital win at Chester in December. Having finished his first season with the O's as their top league scorer, Iyseden will be looking to get among the goals again in 2000-01.
Coventry C (From trainee on 22/5/1995) PL 0+1 FLC 0+1
Bournemouth (Loaned on 18/11/1996) FL 3+1
Mansfield T (Loaned on 7/2/1997) FL 8
Mansfield T (Free on 16/6/1997) FL 44+37/18 FLC 4/5 FAC 0+4 Others 2+1
Leyton Orient (£40,000 on 2/7/1999) FL 22+14/7 FLC 2 FAC 1+1 Others 1

CHRISTIE Malcolm Neil
Born: Peterborough, 11 April 1979
Height: 5'6" Weight: 11.4
A bargain signing from Nuneaton Borough the previous season, the young striker continued to impress in the Rams' successful reserve team during 1999-2000 and began to make regular appearances from the substitutes' bench in the Premiership. His first start, at Middlesbrough in January, was a tremendous success, Malcolm finding the net twice and producing an all-round display which gave Jim Smith a real boost in the club's struggle against relegation. Further goals followed and his determination and willingness to learn were rewarded first by a new and improved four-year contract, then by Derby's "Young Player of the Year" award. Very energetic and with the priceless knack of being able to beat the offside trap with some well-timed runs, he prefers to play alongside a centre forward, so the arrival at the club of Branko Strupar should have been to his liking. He is a great favourite with the fans, who would like to see him win a regular place in the starting line-up during the coming campaign.
Derby Co (£50,000 + from Nuneaton Borough on 2/11/1998) PL 10+13/5 FLC 0+1

CLAPHAM James (Jamie) Richard
Born: Lincoln, 7 December 1975
Height: 5'9" Weight: 10.11

As he had the previous season, Jamie played in all of Ipswich's first-team games in 1999-2000 but he cannot be regarded as an ever-present as he did not start every match. He was relegated to the substitutes' bench for the home game with Manchester City so that Gary Croft could make his debut and also started the away game at Charlton on the sidelines. However, he played a part in both games. Being left footed, he operates on that side of the team either as the wing back when the manager adopts a 5-3-2 formation or as the wide midfield player if the 4-4-2 system is used. Jamie is a useful crosser of the ball and has become something of a dead-ball specialist, taking the majority of the corners and scoring some useful goals from free kicks around the edge of the box. Brentford will probably rue his ability from free kicks, as he scored in both legs of the Worthington Cup first-round tie between the sides with virtually identical dead-ball shots. The most important goal he scored, however, was in extra time in the play-off semi-final second leg against Bolton, when he took responsibility for the third penalty of the evening and gave his side the lead for the first time in the tie. Jamie is from a well-known footballing family; his father Graham Clapham played for Shrewsbury and Chester while his grandfather Bert Wilkinson played for Lincoln in the 1940s.

Tottenham H (From trainee on 1/7/1994) PL 0+1
Leyton Orient (Loaned on 29/1/1997) FL 6
Bristol Rov (Loaned on 27/3/1997) FL 4+1
Ipswich T (£300,000 on 9/1/1998) FL 111+3/5 FLC 7+1/2 FAC 3 Others 6/1

CLARE Daryl Adam
Born: Jersey, 1 August 1978
Height: 5'9" Weight: 11.12
Club Honours: AMC '98
International Honours: RoI: B-1; U21-6

A young striker with skill and pace, Daryl finally had the chance to prove his potential at Grimsby during a season of mixed fortunes in 1999-2000. Early on, he was frustrated that, despite the departure of Lee Nogan, he found himself no further up the pecking order among the Mariners' forwards. He made two early-season appearances for the Republic of Ireland at U21 level but then dropped out of the squad, an event no doubt precipitated by his lack of opportunity at First Division level. Asking to be placed on the transfer list, although this request was turned down he departed on an extended loan to Northampton in November. Daryl was the third striker Northampton took on loan last season, and Kevin Wilson's first signing as manager. He netted on his debut against Cheltenham, and scored another two in his six weeks at Sixfields. His style suggested he would fit in well with top scorer Carlo Corazzin, but the arrangement was suddenly terminated when Grimsby sold Jack Lester to Nottingham Forest. Daryl celebrated his return to Blundell Park with a spectacular 19th-minute goal against Port Vale, and little over a week later he found himself the only fit striker on the club's books as both Lee Ashcroft and Bradley Allen were sidelined with injuries. This gave him the opportunity to establish himself firmly in the side, a state of affairs that many Grimsby fans thought was long overdue.

Grimsby T (From trainee on 9/12/1995) FL 28+34/9 FLC 0+5/1 FAC 1+4 Others 4+2
Northampton T (Loaned on 12/11/1999) FL 9+1/3

CLARIDGE Stephen (Steve) Edward
Born: Portsmouth, 10 April 1966
Height: 5'11" Weight: 12.10
Club Honours: Div 3 '91, Div 2 '95; AMC '95; FLC '97

This experienced Portsmouth striker missed the start of 1999-2000 while recovering from a knee operation and it was not until October that he returned to regular first-team action. He continued to find the net with ease and finished the season as the club's leading scorer with 15 goals, including a great hat-trick against Barnsley that gave new manager Tony Pulis his first win at Fratton Park. Steve impressed once again with his exciting ball skills and never-say-die attitude, remaining as popular as ever with the supporters, who voted him "Player of the Season". He missed the final few games of the campaign after damaging medial ligaments against Charlton on Good Friday, but it is hoped he will be fit once again for the start of the 2000-01 season.

Bournemouth (Signed from Fareham on 30/11/1984) FL 3+4/1 Others 1 (£10,000 to Weymouth in October 1985)
Crystal Palace (Signed on 11/10/1988)
Aldershot (£14,000 on 13/10/1988) FL 58+4/19 FLC 2+1 FAC 6/1 Others 5/2
Cambridge U (£75,000 on 8/2/1990) FL 56+23/28 FLC 2+4/2 FAC 1 Others 6+3/1
Luton T (£160,000 on 17/7/1992) FL 15+1/2 FLC 2/3 Others 2/1
Cambridge U (£195,000 on 20/11/1992) FL 53/18 FLC 4/3 FAC 4 Others 3
Birmingham C (£350,000 on 7/1/1994) FL 86+2/35 FLC 14+1/2 FAC 7 Others 9+1/5
Leicester C (£1,200,000 on 1/3/1996) P/FL 53+10/17 FLC 8/2 FAC 4/1 Others 3+1/1
Portsmouth (Loaned on 23/1/1998) FL 10/2
Wolverhampton W (£400,000 on 26/3/1998) FL 4+1 FAC 1
Portsmouth (£200,000 on 10/8/1998) FL 70+3/23 FLC 2+2 FAC 2+1/1

CLARK Ian David
Born: Stockton, 23 October 1974
Height: 5'11" Weight: 11.7

A left-sided utility player who can play equally well in defence, midfield or attack, Ian had a good offer in September 1999 to join Leyton Orient but declined the move as he was determined to win a regular place at Hartlepool. For much of 1999-2000 he was in competition with Sam Shilton for a first-team place at left back, but in the second half of the season he made the position his own with a series of typically enthusiastic performances. Flame-haired Ian also contributed six goals as Pool reached the play-offs.

Doncaster Rov (Free from Stockton on 11/8/1995) FL 23+22/3 FLC 1+2 FAC 1+1 Others 4/1
Hartlepool U (Free on 24/10/1997) FL 89+18/15 FLC 3 FAC 3+2 Others 7+2

CLARK Lee Robert
Born: Wallsend, 27 October 1972
Height: 5'8" Weight: 11.7
Club Honours: Div 1 '93, '99
International Honours: E: U21-11; Yth; Sch

Signed by Fulham manager Paul Bracewell to bring more creativity to the side's midfield following their promotion to Division One, Lee missed only four league games in 1999-2000 but his first league goal didn't come until mid-February. He certainly made up for lost time by netting eight times in his last 12 games to finish as the club's top scorer in the league. At £3 million, Lee is Fulham's most expensive acquisition but his astute football brain, honed during his successful spells with Newcastle and Sunderland, proved to be a great asset. He was rightly named as "Man of the Match" on several occasions and, providing the rumours of a transfer come to nothing, he is likely to play a leading role as the Cottagers chase promotion once again in 2000-01.

Newcastle U (From trainee on 9/12/1989) F/PL 153+42/23 FLC 17 FAC 14+2/3 Others 7+5/1
Sunderland (£2,750,000 on 25/6/1997) FL 72+1/16 FLC 4+1 FAC 4 Others 3
Fulham (£3,000,000 on 13/7/1999) FL 42/8 FLC 6/1 FAC 4

Lee Clark

CLARK Peter James
Born: Romford, 10 December 1979
Height: 6'1" Weight: 12.7

Peter missed only three league matches in 1999-2000 and easily topped the Carlisle appearance charts. The left wing back uses his pace to good effect and can be very effective going forward, as he displayed in setting up Scott Dobie's ultimately vital added-time winning goal at Chester. He will become even more dangerous as he gains in confidence and his crossing improves. He was generally sound in his defensive duties, and youth is on his side. Peter's progress was confirmed by the reported interest of

First Division Stockport in May. Stop Press: A £250,000 move to Stockport was completed in early June.
Carlisle U (Signed from Arsenal juniors on 6/8/1998) FL 77+2/1 FLC 2 FAC 2 Others 3

CLARK Simon
Born: Boston, 12 March 1967
Height: 6'1" Weight: 12.12
Simon was one of the mainstays of the Leyton Orient defence in the first half of 1999-2000. He is dominant in the air and on the ground, and causes problems at the other end of the pitch from corners and set pieces. Simon was a first-team regular until Christmas but lost his place due to a debilitating viral infection that laid him low for the rest of the term. He was released in the summer. Stop Press: Simon was reported to have joined Colchester in early June.
Peterborough U (Free from Stevenage Borough on 25/3/1994) FL 102+5/4 FLC 5 FAC 12 Others 7+1/1
Leyton Orient (£20,000 on 16/6/1997) FL 98/9 FLC 6 FAC 9 Others 5

CLARKE Adrian James
Born: Cambridge, 28 September 1974
Height: 5'10" Weight: 11.0
Club Honours: FAYC '94
International Honours: E: Yth; Sch
Very much a bit-part player in Southend United's 1999-2000 season, Adrian never got the chance to establish himself as his wing play didn't really suit the style of football adopted by manager Alan Little. With long spells in the reserves, Adrian's chances of returning to first-team action were always limited. He joined Carlisle on loan in September and turned in some useful performances as an attacking midfielder but eventually returned to Southend. He was released in May.
Arsenal (From trainee on 6/7/1993) PL 4+3 FAC 1+1
Rotherham U (Loaned on 2/12/1996) FL 1+1 Others 1
Southend U (Free on 27/3/1997) FL 63+17/8 FLC 8+1/1 FAC 3 Others 1
Carlisle U (Loaned on 10/9/1999) FL 7

CLARKE Andrew (Andy) Weston
Born: Islington, 22 July 1967
Height: 5'10" Weight: 11.7
Club Honours: GMVC '91
International Honours: E: SP-2
After a frustrating start to his stint at Peterborough, Andy enjoyed a glorious conclusion to his first term at London Road. He missed the start of 1999-2000 due to an ankle injury picked up in a pre-season friendly against Ipswich. Although he didn't return until September, he soon found his feet and finished the season as leading scorer for Posh. He crowned the season with the winning goal in the Third Division play-off final against Darlington at Wembley. He mesmerises defenders with his footwork, and sometimes even he seems unsure which way he is going. Andy is more than capable of playing wide on the left or straight down the middle.
Wimbledon (£250,000 from Barnet on 21/2/1991) F/PL 74+96/17 FLC 13+12/4 FAC 9+8/2
Port Vale (Loaned on 28/8/1998) FL 2+4
Northampton T (Loaned on 15/1/1999) FL 2+2
Peterborough U (Free on 4/5/1999) FL 33+4/15 FAC 2/1 Others 4/2

CLARKE Christopher (Chris) Edward
Born: Leeds, 18 December 1980
Height: 6'3" Weight: 12.10
A former Wolves trainee, Chris played most of the 1999-2000 season in the Halifax reserve team after injury hampered his progress early on. On a number of occasions he was an unused substitute, but he finally made his senior bow against Shrewsbury in April. He acquitted himself well and will be looking to further his career next season. Twin brother Matthew is a fellow Shayman.
Halifax T (Free from Wolverhampton W juniors on 5/7/1999) FL 0+1

CLARKE Clive Richard
Born: Dublin, 14 January 1980
Height: 6'1" Weight: 12.3
Club Honours: AMC '00
International Honours: RoI: U21-5; Yth
One of Stoke's finds of the 1999-2000 season, Clive made the left-back or wing-back position in the first team his own, seeing off the challenge of Bryan Small. Blessed with pace and the ability to produce excellent flat crosses, Clive made his debut for the Republic of Ireland at U21 level against Macedonia last October and was a regular member of the squad. He capped a fine season with a Wembley appearance, shaking off a groin injury to play in City's Auto Windscreens Shield-winning team. Rumours have him being watched by a number of Premiership sides and Stoke will do well to keep him to his enhanced contract. A key piece in the jigsaw that Gudjon Thordarson is building to bring further success to the club, this talented left-sided player has a bright future.
Stoke C (From trainee on 25/1/1997) FL 41+3/1 FLC 3+1 FAC 1 Others 8

CLARKE Darrell James
Born: Mansfield, 16 December 1977
Height: 5'10" Weight: 11.6
Darrell missed the opening matches of 1999-2000 with ankle ligament problems but became a regular wide on the left of midfield for Mansfield after that. A local youngster who has progressed through the ranks at Field Mill, he has developed into a valuable member of the first-team squad. He likes to get forward and have a crack at goal and chipped in with some useful goals during the campaign.
Mansfield T (From trainee on 3/7/1996) FL 107+22/18 FLC 3/1 FAC 4+1/1 Others 2+2

CLARKE Matthew (Matt) John
Born: Sheffield, 3 November 1973
Height: 6'4" Weight: 13.10
Matt joined Bradford City in the summer of 1999 from Sheffield Wednesday as cover for first-choice 'keeper Gary Walsh. He began the 1999-2000 season in the reserves but was given his chance at Anfield last November and responded with a heroic performance. He then played in every game until suffering a medial knee ligament injury at Watford in January. He recovered from this two months later and, with Walsh still out, took over the goalkeeper's jersey until the end of the campaign. Matt is a capable shot stopper who is confident in the air and able to dominate his penalty box.
Rotherham U (From trainee on 28/7/1992) FL 123+1 FLC 4 FAC 3 Others 11
Sheffield Wed (£325,000 + on 10/7/1996) PL 2+2
Bradford C (Free on 5/7/1999) PL 21 FLC 1 FAC 2

CLARKE Matthew Paul
Born: Leeds, 18 December 1980
Height: 6'3" Weight: 12.7
Signed from Wolves along with his twin brother Chris during the summer of 1999, Matthew made his full senior debut for Halifax in the FA Cup first-round tie at Doncaster in October and cemented his place in the Town squad over the following couple of months. Still a youngster, Matthew has a lot to learn but his first full season of professional football will have been good grounding experience. He is eligible to play international football for St Kitts.
Halifax T (Free from Wolverhampton W juniors on 5/7/1999) FL 8+11 FAC 2+1 Others 1

CLARKE Richard James
Born: Enfield, 15 February 1980
Height: 5'11" Weight: 12.2
After being released by Luton Town in the summer of 1999, Richard started a leisure management degree course in London and played in non-league football, where he was spotted and recommended to Scunthorpe United. After a successful trial, he was signed last March on non-contract terms for the rest of the season and was given a debut at Wrexham, where he struggled to get into the game and was substituted at half time. A right back who can also play in midfield, he showed a willingness to get forward from deep. Richard was released at the end of the season.
Luton T (From trainee on 4/11/1998. Released on 1/7/1999)
Scunthorpe U (Free from Stanway Rov on 20/3/2000) FL 1

CLARKSON Ian Stewart
Born: Solihull, 4 December 1970
Height: 5'11" Weight: 12.0
Club Honours: AMC '91
A right wing back who was out for almost a year with a broken leg, Ian made a welcome comeback at the beginning of 1999-2000. Sadly, after the first two games, he had to admit defeat and retire from league football. He stated that it was too painful to play at this level, and that he did not want to spend the rest of his career on painkillers. He was released and dropped into non-league football. After a spell with Nuneaton, he signed for Kidderminster in November. He helped the Harriers to the Conference title and, due to a technicality in the insurance regulations, there was still a possibility that he would return to the Football League in 2000-01. Ian was awarded a testimonial game by Northampton at the end of last season.
Birmingham C (From trainee on 15/12/1988) FL 125+11 FLC 12 FAC 5+1 Others 17+1

Stoke C (£40,000 on 13/9/1993) FL 72+3 FLC 6 FAC 5 Others 8+2
Northampton T (Free on 2/8/1996) FL 91+3/1 FLC 7+2 FAC 6 Others 10/1

CLARKSON Philip (Phil) Ian
Born: Garstang, 13 November 1968
Height: 5'10" Weight: 12.5

This powerful midfield dynamo appeared regularly for Blackpool in 1999-2000 and took over the role of captain when Ian Hughes was out injured. He had the misfortune to suffer a stress fracture of the leg during training before the Preston match last March and this brought his season to a premature end.

Crewe Alex (£22,500 from Fleetwood T on 15/10/1991) FL 76+22/27 FLC 6+2/1 FAC 3+2/2 Others 7+4/1
Scunthorpe U (Loaned on 30/10/1995) FL 4/1
Scunthorpe U (Free on 13/2/1996) FL 45+3/18 FLC 2/1 FAC 3/2 Others 1
Blackpool (£80,000 on 6/2/1997) FL 137+4/30 FLC 9/2 FAC 6/4 Others 6/2

CLEGG Michael Jaime
Born: Ashton under Lyne, 3 July 1977
Height: 5'8" Weight: 11.8
Club Honours: FAYC '95
International Honours: E: U21-2

A very able full back who is good in the tackle and excellent on the overlap, Michael was given an early chance to shine for Manchester United last season when he lined up against Zagreb in the Champions' League in September. He also played against Aston Villa in the Worthington Cup, but that was as good as it got as he had the unenviable task of vying with the likes of the Neville brothers and Denis Irwin for a regular place in the side. Michael went to Ipswich in mid-February on a month's loan as cover for Gary Croft. He made three appearances for Town, making his debut at Crewe, where he got off to a steady start. He liked to support the attack and seemed happier when attacking than when performing his defensive duties. Croft's quick recovery meant that his loan stay was not extended. On transfer deadline day Michael joined Wigan on loan and he was asked to fill in in a variety of positions during his short spell with the Latics. He found it difficult to adjust to the pace of Second Division football and returned to Old Trafford at the end of the one-month spell.

Manchester U (From trainee on 1/7/1995) PL 4+5 FLC 5 FAC 3+1 Others 1+2
Ipswich T (Loaned on 16/2/2000) FL 3
Wigan Ath (Loaned on 23/3/2000) FL 6

CLELAND Alexander (Alex)
Born: Glasgow, 10 December 1970
Height: 5'8" Weight: 11.6
Club Honours: SPL '95, '96, '97; SC '94, '96
International Honours: S: B-2; U21-11; Sch

After making a positive impression during his first Premiership season with Everton in 1998-99, the Scottish full back had his second campaign horribly cut short by injury. Used sporadically by his old Glasgow Rangers boss, Walter Smith, during the first third of the season, he was just beginning to establish himself again in his regular right-back berth when his injury curse struck. A torn calf muscle sustained at Bradford on 28 December eventually led to surgery and wiped out the rest of the season. Tidy and versatile when fit, Alex can figure in a variety of positions, including right and left wing back and right midfield, and has even played in central defence more than competently for the Blues.

Dundee U (From juniors on 18/6/1987) SL 131+20/8 SLC 10+1 SC 7+2 Others 8+1/1
Glasgow R (Signed on 26/1/1995) SL 90+6/4 SLC 8+2 SC 13+1 Others 13+1
Everton (Free on 3/7/1998) PL 19+8 FLC 4+1 FAC 2

CLEMENCE Stephen Neal
Born: Liverpool, 31 March 1978
Height: 5'11" Weight: 11.7
Club Honours: FLC '99
International Honours: E: U21-1; Yth; Sch

Stephen appeared to mature further last season as he took his place in his favoured central midfield role for Tottenham. His growing awareness was apparent in his anticipation of where he needed to be in relation to play to really provide himself as another attacking option for his team-mates. Looking more confident on the ball and happy to organise those around him, Stephen played a key role in the games against Arsenal in November and Aston Villa in December, showing a tough edge to his skilful talents when performing the defensive side of his duties. He will undoubtedly be looking to secure a regular first-team spot during the coming season.

Tottenham H (From trainee on 3/4/1995) PL 37+18/1 FLC 4+1 FAC 3+1/1 Others 2+1

CLEMENT Neil
Born: Reading, 3 October 1978
Height: 6'0" Weight: 12.3
International Honours: E: Yth; Sch

This stylish Chelsea youngster joined Brentford on loan last November as cover for the injured Ijah Anderson. A left-sided defender, Neil made eight appearances for the Bees but the Second Division club didn't take up the option of a permanent deal. After becoming something of a forgotten man at Stamford Bridge, he had an unexpected run-out as a substitute in the Blues' FA Cup quarter-final against Gillingham in February, coming on for the last 17 minutes. This was Neil's first Chelsea appearance for almost two years as he has been overtaken for the left-sided defensive berth by contemporaries Jon Harley and Celestine Babayaro. On transfer deadline day Neil joined West Bromwich on loan for the rest of the season. Drafted into a struggling, relegation-threatened side with little league experience behind him, he faced a stern test of his character, but he battled well and gave the Baggies' back line a more secure look with his positional sense and strong kicking. Neil, the son of former Queens Park Rangers and England full back Dave Clement, is an outstanding prospect but he needs regular first-team football if he is to progress.

Chelsea (From trainee on 8/10/1995) PL 1 FLC 0+2 FAC 0+1
Reading (Loaned on 19/11/1998) FL 11/1 Others 1
Preston NE (Loaned on 25/3/1999) FL 4
Brentford (Loaned on 23/11/1999) FL 7+1
West Bromwich A (Loaned on 23/3/2000) FL 7+1

CLIST Simon James
Born: Bournemouth, 13 August 1981
Height: 5'9" Weight: 11.0

Bristol City snapped up this skilful left-sided midfield player in the summer of 1999 after he was released by Tottenham Hotspur. In City's academy set-up his good touch and eye for an opening marked him as an outstanding talent, and it was no surprise that he soon forced himself into the first team, where he created a favourable impression with the Ashton Gate fans. After two substitute appearances he made his full debut in City's 3-0 success over bottom club Chesterfield on 5 February.

Bristol C (Free from Tottenham H juniors on 24/7/1999) FL 8+1 Others 1+2

COATES Jonathan Simon
Born: Swansea, 27 June 1975
Height: 5'8" Weight: 10.4
Club Honours: Div 3 '00
International Honours: W: B-1; U21-5; Yth

Jonathan is an exciting left-sided player who is capable of operating in any position on that side of the pitch, although he generally appeared in a wide midfield role for Swansea in 1999-2000. A return to form as a goalscorer saw Jonathan score six league goals, with many efforts being from outside the penalty area. He is one of several players in the Swans camp who will benefit greatly from a higher standard of football, and he will be pushing for a place in the Wales senior squad. As well as winning a Third Division championship winners' medal, Jonathan was selected in the Opta Index "Division Three Team of the Season".

Swansea C (From trainee on 8/7/1993) FL 158+28/17 FLC 9+2/1 FAC 8 Others 10+3

COID Daniel (Danny) John
Born: Liverpool, 3 October 1981
Height: 5'11" Weight: 11.7

One of several exciting prospects among Blackpool's YTS players, Danny had a short spell in the first team last autumn and returned again towards the end of the campaign. He is a wide left-sided midfield player who showed excellent progress during 1999-2000 and scored his first-ever Football League goal against Chesterfield on the last day of the season. He has since signed a 12-month professional contract with the Seasiders.

Blackpool (Trainee) FL 13+9/1 FAC 2 Others 1

COLDICOTT Stacy
Born: Redditch, 29 April 1974
Height: 5'8" Weight: 11.8

One of a number of former West Bromwich players who have followed manager Alan Buckley from the Hawthorns to Grimsby, Stacy was a key member of the Mariners' team in 1999-2000, missing only a couple of matches. A competitive, strong-tackling midfielder, he produced some outstanding "Man of the Match" performances, notably in a pulsating victory over promotion-seeking Wolves in March, and continued to show great commitment.

West Bromwich A (From trainee on 4/3/1992) FL 64+40/3 FLC 8+1 FAC 2+2/1 Others 7+3
Cardiff C (Loaned on 30/8/1996) FL 6
Grimsby T (£125,000 on 6/8/1998) FL 77+4/2 FLC 7/1 FAC 3

COLE Andrew (Andy) Alexander
Born: Nottingham, 15 October 1971
Height: 5'11" Weight: 11.12
Club Honours: Div 1 '93; PL '96, '97, '99, '00; FAC '96, '99; CS '97; EC '99
International Honours: E: 7; B-1; U21-8; Yth, Sch

Going into 1999-2000, Andy, an elusive striker with lightning speed and good close control, was delighted to be able to start a season at Manchester United without any transfer speculation hanging over his head. Eager to renew his goalscoring partnership with Dwight Yorke, which yielded 53 goals between them during the treble-winning campaign, he opened his account against Sheffield Wednesday in United's second Premiership game, before going nap against his former club, Newcastle, with four goals (giving him eight in nine games against the Geordies) in a 5-1 win. Further strikes against Liverpool, Watford (2) and Aston Villa followed in the Premiership, while his two goals in the Champions' League against Sturm Graz and Marseille took him to within one of Denis Law's all-time European club record. Coinciding with three goals in successive games against Leicester and Derby in November, the release of his autobiography ruffled a few feathers when he launched a verbal attack on England manager Kevin Keegan for continually favouring "golden boy" Alan Shearer, while omitting him from the side. Although he was recalled by Keegan for 22 minutes against Scotland, Andy said, "I don't know whether I'm coming or going for England. But, to be honest, there is nothing more important in my eyes than Manchester United." Although international recognition was to elude him for the friendly against Argentina in March, he scored the vital winner for United against Leeds at Elland Road in February, which started an argument among statisticians as to whether it was his 100th league goal for the Reds. Some say it came against Wimbledon the following week. In March, he netted a superb strike against Fiorentina that equalled Law's 30-year-old record, and put United into the quarter-final stages of the European Cup. He was on Red-hot form as the season drew to an exciting climax, further goals against West Ham and Middlesbrough helping United to their sixth Premiership crown in eight years, while his contribution in Europe was awe inspiring. Andy's performances on both fronts earned him a place in the PFA award-winning Premiership side, but injury was to rule him out of the England squad for Euro 2000.

Arsenal (From trainee on 18/10/1989) FL 0+1 Others 0+1
Fulham (Loaned on 5/9/1991) FL 13/3 Others 2/1
Bristol C (£500,000 on 12/3/1992) FL 41/20 FLC 3/4 FAC 1 Others 4/1
Newcastle U (£1,750,000 on 12/3/1993) F/PL 69+1/55 FLC 7/8 FAC 4/1 Others 3/4
Manchester U (£6,000,000 on 12/1/1995) PL 139+26/80 FLC 2 FAC 18+2/9 Others 38+4/14

Andy Cole

COLE Ashley
Born: Stepney, 20 December 1980
Height: 5'8" Weight: 10.8
International Honours: E: Yth

A product of the Arsenal youth scheme, this exciting left back or wing back had his first taste of senior football when he came on as a substitute in the Worthington Cup tie at Middlesbrough last November. In February he was loaned to Crystal Palace to gain first-team experience and impressed with his displays at left wing back, showing excellent timing in the tackle. He then returned to Highbury to make his full Arsenal debut in the Premiership in the final game of the season at Newcastle. A strong tackler who reads the game perceptively and creates long passing movements, Ashley is quick on and off the ball, uses the overlap well and is capable of delivering an accurate cross. He is considered a player of the future at Highbury, particularly in the left-back position.

Arsenal (From trainee on 23/11/1998) PL 1 FLC 0+1
Crystal Palace (Loaned on 25/2/2000) FL 14/1

COLE Joseph (Joe) John
Born: Islington, 8 November 1981
Height: 5'9" Weight: 11.0
Club Honours: FAYC '99
International Honours: E: U21-1; Yth; Sch

Joe had an excellent season for West Ham in 1999-2000, establishing himself as a member of the first-team squad and coping admirably with the pressures of intense media attention. He began the season on the subs' bench but was soon in the starting line-up and featured regularly in the Hammers' midfield, producing some impressive displays for one so young. He scored his first goal in senior football at the end of November with a late winner in the Worthington Cup round four tie with Birmingham City, and netted for the first time in the Premiership in the 5-4 win over Bradford City last March. Unfortunately, he then suffered a broken leg at Derby in April, bringing his season to a premature close. He has a sharp footballing brain, excellent vision and possesses a repertoire of tricks to fox even the best opposition defender – and he is still only a teenager! Joe added three more caps for England U18s in the autumn and made his bow for the U21s against Argentina, but was ruled out of the European Championship in Slovakia. If he continues to make such progress and avoids serious injury, he is likely to develop into a regular with the full England team in the not too distant future.

West Ham U (From trainee on 11/12/1998) PL 19+11/1 FLC 3+1/1 FAC 1+1 Others 1+2

Joe Cole

COLEMAN Christopher (Chris)
Born: Swansea, 10 June 1970
Height: 6'2" Weight: 14.6
Club Honours: WC '89, '91; Div 1 '94; Div 2 '99
International Honours: W: 28; U21-3; Yth; Sch

In recognition of an impressive season for Fulham, during which he mostly operated on the left side of a back three, Chris was selected by his fellow professionals for the PFA First Division team in 1999-2000, having been chosen for the Second Division side during the two previous seasons. He confirmed that he is a defender of real class, always seeming to have time and rarely wasting a pass, and Fulham's poor away form, which was mainly responsible for their missing out on at least a play-off spot, could certainly not be laid at his door. A highly accomplished performer, he appeared regularly for Wales, winning a further five caps.

Swansea C (From from Manchester C juniors on 1/9/1987) FL 159+1/2 FLC 8 FAC 13/1 Others 15
Crystal Palace (£275,000 on 19/7/1991) F/PL 143+11/13 FLC 24+2/2 FAC 8/1 Others 2
Blackburn Rov (£2,800,000 on 16/12/1995) PL 27+1 FLC 2 FAC 2
Fulham (£2,100,000 on 1/12/1997) FL 111/8 FLC 12/2 FAC 11/1 Others 3

COLEMAN Simon
Born: Worksop, 13 March 1968
Height: 6'0" Weight: 11.8

Simon's performances in the heart of Southend United's defence were one of the few highlights of a generally disappointing 1999-2000 season for the club, with his command in the air and on the ground always being evident. Simon formed a better understanding with David Morley than most of his other numerous partners. Capable of keeping things simple with a high skill level, Simon also chipped in with a few useful set-piece goals, including two against Halifax Town in a 4-1 victory in September. With United looking to bring in a different type of centre half, Simon was released in May. Stop Press: It was reported at the end of June that he had signed for Rochdale.

Mansfield T (From juniors on 29/7/1985) FL 96/7 FLC 9 FAC 7 Others 7/1
Middlesbrough (£600,000 on 26/9/1989) FL 51+4/2 FAC 5 Others 10/1
Derby Co (£300,000 on 15/8/1991) FL 62+8/2 FLC 5+1 FAC 5 Others 12
Sheffield Wed (£250,000 on 20/1/1994) PL 11+5/1 FLC 3 FAC 2
Bolton W (£350,000 on 5/10/1994) P/FL 34/5 FLC 4 FAC 2
Wolverhampton W (Loaned on 2/9/1997) FL 3+1
Southend U (Free on 20/2/1998) FL 98+1/9 FLC 6 FAC 2 Others 2

COLES Daniel (Danny) Richard
Born: Bristol, 30 October 1981
Height: 6'1" Weight: 11.5

Danny is one of the many products of Bristol City's thriving academy set-up who made rapid progress in 1999-2000. Shortly after breaking his way into the reserves, this exciting central defender was given a taste of first-team action when coming on as a substitute in the 2-2 draw with Oxford United at Ashton Gate on Easter Monday.

Bristol C (Trainee) FL 0+1

COLLETER Patrick
Born: Brest, France, 6 November 1965
Height: 5'10" Weight: 10.10
International Honours: France: B

Injured towards the end of the previous season, his first at Southampton, Patrick had to wait patiently to regain the left-back spot. Restored to the side in the match at Aston Villa in November, he showed he hadn't lost any of his appetite, helping the Saints to a rare away win. Strong and determined defensively, his pace allows him to get forward either down the wings or by cutting infield.

Southampton (£300,000 from Brest, France on 23/12/1998) PL 24/1 FLC 1 FAC 2

COLLETT Andrew (Andy) Alfred
Born: Stockton, 28 October 1973
Height: 6'0" Weight: 12.10

Andy started 1999-2000 as first choice in goal at Darlington after returning to his native North-east from Bristol Rovers, but after just nine games he was sidelined with knee ligament damage and deputy Mark Samways took over. On returning to the side, Andy had to leave the field during the FA Cup tie with Southport with a torn thigh muscle. He only regained his place from his initial understudy as the Quakers closed in on a Wembley play-off place and was released during the summer.

Middlesbrough (From trainee on 6/3/1992) PL 2 Others 3
Bristol Rov (Loaned on 18/10/1994) FL 4
Bristol Rov (£10,000 on 23/3/1995) FL 103 FLC 4 FAC 7 Others 8
Darlington (Free on 6/8/1999) FL 13 FLC 2 FAC 1 Others 3

COLLINS James Ian
Born: Liverpool, 28 May 1978
Height: 5'8" Weight: 10.0

A product of Crewe's youth team, this promising young midfielder made 15 first-team appearances in 1999-2000, seven of them as a substitute, having forced his way back into the reckoning at Gresty Road after an early-season loan spell at Kidderminster. James had a run of seven successive starts beginning with the game against Charlton on 2 November, but his only taste of league action during the second half of the season was as an 89th-minute sub against Nottingham Forest in April.

Crewe Alex (From trainee on 4/7/1996) FL 13+7/1 FLC 1+2 FAC 0+1

John Collins

COLLINS John Angus Paul
Born: Galashiels, 31 January 1968
Height: 5'7" Weight: 10.10
Club Honours: SC '95
International Honours: S: 58; U21-8; Yth

After a steady start to what was his second full season in the English Premiership in 1999-2000, John began to regularly produce the form Everton fans had hoped to see from this hugely respected international star. There was no apparent reason behind the transformation – "I just started to really enjoy my football again," he said – but his midfield performances from February on were of the highest order. He won more tackles than any other Premiership player, and showed the class and style for which he became famous at Celtic and Monaco. John even showed a hitherto hidden versatility, performing soundly in a left-back role at Chelsea then even switching to right back on occasions as Everton's squad resources became stretched towards the end of the season. Despite suggestions earlier in the campaign that he had contemplated quitting English football, he indicated before it was over that he was happy to see out the two years remaining on his Everton contract. He did, however, announce his retirement from the international stage after a proud and dignified career with Scotland.

Hibernian (From Hutchison Vale BC on 9/8/1984) SL 155+8/16 SLC 7+3/1 SC 17/3 Others 4/1
Glasgow Celtic (Signed on 13/7/1990) SL 211+6/47 SLC 22/3 SC 21/3 Others 13/1 (Free to AS Monaco, France on 2/7/1996)
Everton (£2,500,000 on 7/8/1998) PL 52+3/3 FLC 3+2/1 FAC 4

COLLINS Lee
Born: Bellshill, 3 February 1974
Height: 5'8" Weight: 11.6

Having missed most of 1998-99 with a shoulder injury, Lee did not win a regular place in the Swindon line-up until last December. However, he then went on to produce a series of excellent performances, notably in the visit to Charlton and the home game with Fulham, and proved to be one of the few successes in an otherwise dismal 1999-2000 campaign for the Robins. He is a tough-tackling midfield player who is adept at hustling the opposition in the centre of the park. Lee was out of contract in the summer and has been snapped up by former boss Steve McMahon for Blackpool.

Albion Rov (Signed from Pollock on 25/11/1993) SL 43+2/1 SLC 2 SC 2 Others 2
Swindon T (£15,000 on 15/11/1995) FL 52+11/2 FAC 4 Others 1

COLLINS Samuel (Sam) Jason
Born: Pontefract, 5 June 1977
Height: 6'3" Weight: 14.0

A summer capture from Huddersfield Town, this sturdy young central defender slotted into Bury's back four with ease in the opening weeks of 1999-2000. However, just when he seemed certain to enjoy a successful season with the Shakers, Sam ruptured his medial ligaments in training on 13 September and was forced to spend the next three months recuperating. He resumed training in late November, and an injury crisis saw him rushed back a little prematurely for Bury's FA Cup replay against Cardiff, but soon afterwards he dislocated his shoulder in training and faced another disruption. His dismal season continued when, after attempting yet another comeback game in the reserves on 10 January, he strained his abductor muscle in training. A seven-week trek back to

fitness ended in March but when he returned to first-team action he was obviously struggling to regain both his fitness and his confidence. This determined and talented defender will certainly be glad to draw a line under the 1999-2000 campaign and start afresh next season – hopefully with a little more luck. He is the brother of Macclesfield's Simon Collins.
Huddersfield T (From trainee on 6/7/1994) FL 34+3 FLC 6+1 FAC 3
Bury (£75,000 on 2/7/1999) FL 19 FLC 2 FAC 0+1

COLLINS Simon Jonathan
Born: Pontefract, 16 December 1973
Height: 5'11" Weight: 13.0
Simon was one of eight 1999 close-season signings as relegated Macclesfield reshaped their squad. Other than missing matches over the Christmas and New Year period due to an attack of influenza, he was an ever-present in the team throughout the season. He is a strong central defender who is not afraid to make telling tackles, but, having played much of his early career in midfield and sometimes up front, he also has the ability to go forward to score the occasional goal. Simon is the elder brother of Huddersfield's Sam Collins.
Huddersfield T (From trainee on 1/7/1992) FL 31+21/3 FLC 6+3/2 FAC 1+4 Others 1+3
Plymouth Arg (£60,000 on 6/3/1997) FL 81+3/5 FLC 2 FAC 1 Others 1
Macclesfield T (Free on 5/7/1999) FL 37+2/3 FLC 1 FAC 2 Others 1

COLLINS Wayne Anthony
Born: Manchester, 4 March 1969
Height: 6'0" Weight: 12.0
Club Honours: Div 2 '97
The 1999-2000 season was not one to remember for Fulham's enthusiastic midfielder, who had both injuries and competition for places to contend with. He did, however, enjoy two highs in cup games. When Spurs equalised with a soft goal just before half time when the clubs met in the fourth round of the Worthington Cup, Wayne was in the right place to add the finishing touch a minute later to regain the lead and lay the foundations for a 3-1 win. A month later, in a fourth-round FA Cup tie against Wimbledon, Wayne was not only a driving force in the midfield area but also scored twice in a 3-0 win.
Crewe Alex (£10,000 from Winsford U on 29/7/1993) FL 102+15/14 FLC 5/1 FAC 8+1 Others 14+1/2
Sheffield Wed (£600,000 on 1/8/1996) PL 16+15/6 FLC 2 FAC 1
Fulham (£400,000 + on 23/1/1998) FL 34+19/4 FLC 6+1/2 FAC 6+2/2 Others 4

COLLYMORE Stanley (Stan) Victor
Born: Cannock, 22 January 1971
Height: 6'3" Weight: 13.10
International Honours: E: 3
Following his well-documented problems at Aston Villa, Stan came to Fulham on a three-month loan in July 1999. He made his debut in a friendly at Hearts and, typically, scored Fulham's second goal. An exciting, powerful striker whose great talent has not always been fully exploited, Stan started the season in the side, but a groin muscle injury at Grimsby then kept him out for a couple of weeks. With Geoff Horsfield and Paul Peschisolido scoring freely, he had to be content with substitute appearances on his return to fitness, but scored the winning goal in the Worthington Cup victory at West Bromwich before going back to Villa at the end of his loan period. Although manager John Gregory had apparently written Stan off, Leicester boss Martin O'Neill was prepared to give him a chance to prove himself and he moved to Filbert Street in February for a fee that could eventually reach £500,000 if the gamble on this talented but troubled former international works out. Early signs, despite a much-publicised case of high jinks in Spain, were promising as Stan celebrated his home debut with a cracking hat-trick to sink Sunderland: his opener, a thumping drive from the edge of the area, was later voted City's "Goal of the Season". That fixture gave a brief glimpse of what a Collymore–Heskey partnership might have achieved had Emile Heskey not signed for Liverpool shortly afterwards, but Stan soon adjusted to other partners in Tony Cottee and Darren Eadie as his undoubted class began to shine through despite an obvious lack of match fitness. Then, just as he looked to be settling in, a freak injury at Pride Park resulted in a broken leg and brought his season to a premature end. Rarely has a player made such an impact in just six outings and Stan will clearly be a key figure in the Foxes' plans for the coming season.
Wolverhampton W (From trainee on 13/7/1989)
Crystal Palace (£100,000 from Stafford R on 4/1/1991) FL 4+16/1 FLC 2+3/1
Southend U (£100,000 on 20/11/1992) FL 30/15 FAC 3/3
Nottingham F (£2,000,000 on 5/7/1993) F/PL 64+1/41 FLC 9/2 FAC 2/1 Others 2/1
Liverpool (£8,500,000 on 3/7/1995) PL 55+6/26 FLC 2+2 FAC 9/7 Others 5+2/2
Aston Villa (£7,000,000 on 16/5/1997) PL 34+11/7 FLC 1 FAC 5/3 Others 9+1/5
Fulham (Loaned on 19/7/1999) FL 1+2/1
Leicester C (£250,000 + on 11/2/2000) PL 6/4

CONLON Barry John
Born: Drogheda, 1 October 1978
Height: 6'3" Weight: 13.7
International Honours: RoI: U21-4
Barry became the second most expensive signing in York's history when he put pen to a three-year contract in July 1999 and repaid the Minstermen by finishing as top scorer in his first season at Bootham Crescent. He netted some spectacular goals: three of them came in successive games, at Shrewsbury, then at home to Carlisle United and Lincoln City, to earn vital points as York avoided the drop into the Conference. Although at times inconsistent, at his best his control and passing ability can trouble most defences. He also won three caps for the Republic of Ireland at U21 level, appearing against Yugoslavia, Croatia and Malta in the early part of the season.
Manchester C (Free from Queens Park R juniors on 14/8/1997) FL 1+6 FLC 0+1
Plymouth Arg (Loaned on 26/2/1998) FL 13/2
Southend U (£95,000 on 4/9/1998) FL 28+6/7 FAC 1 Others 1
York C (£100,000 on 20/7/1999) FL 31+9/11 FLC 2 FAC 1 Others 0+1

CONNELL Darren Stephen
Born: Liverpool, 3 February 1982
Height: 5'8" Weight: 10.8
This Blackpool YTS striker was given his league debut against Bournemouth last September and also featured as a substitute on a couple of occasions in 1999-2000. Although he finished as leading scorer for the youth team, he was not offered a professional contract at the end of the season.
Blackpool (Trainee) FL 1+2

CONNELL Lee Anthony
Born: Bury, 24 June 1981
Height: 6'0" Weight: 12.0
A former trainee at Bury, Lee began his first season as a professional in 1999-2000 and found himself given an occasional chance in the Shakers' first team during the closing fixtures, as boss Andy Preece used the opportunity to blood some of the younger players. The midfielder enjoyed a successful season in the Shakers' Pontins League team and gained a reputation at the club for his strong, confident performances and skill on the ball. Lee is just one of a number of Bury-born youth products who are threatening to make a big impression at their home-town club next season.
Bury (From trainee on 9/7/1999) FL 1+1

CONNELLY Gordon Paul John
Born: Glasgow, 1 November 1976
Height: 5'11" Weight: 12.4
International Honours: S: Yth; Sch
A Southend close-season signing from manager Alan Little's old club York City, Gordon promised much throughout the 1999-2000 season. His silky skills were originally recognised by the United boss when Gordon played against the Minstermen in a 1998 pre-season friendly for Airdrie. His swaggering, bandy-legged wing style was very effective on occasions, and there was never any doubt as to his commitment. Gordon will be hoping to produce more in the new season.
Airdrieonians (From Milngarvie W on 11/8/1995) SL 16+17/1 SC 0+1 Others 3+2/1
York C (Free on 10/8/1998) FL 28/4 FLC 2 FAC 3 Others 1
Southend U (£50,000 on 1/7/1999) FL 29+4/2 FLC 1 FAC 1 Others 1

CONNELLY Sean Patrick
Born: Sheffield, 26 June 1970
Height: 5'10" Weight: 11.10
Sean re-established himself as Stockport's regular right back last season after injury and suspension had kept him out for much of the second half of the 1998-99 campaign. He scored three times, including a spectacular flying header from the edge of the box against Tranmere and a brilliant effort in the 3-0 win over Swindon when he ran with the ball from his own half before finishing with a powerful 20-yard shot – the strike being voted "Goal of the Season" by

County fans. Calm under pressure and effective moving forward, he is now approaching 300 league games for the Hatters.

Stockport Co (Free from Hallam on 12/8/1991) FL 281+8/6 FLC 28/1 FAC 15+1 Others 15+1

CONNOLLY Karl Andrew
Born: Prescot, 9 February 1970
Height: 5'10" Weight: 11.2
Club Honours: WC '95

Karl was again the jewel in the Wrexham side in 1999-2000 with his skilful play and ability to open up defences and make things happen for the team. He was used as a wide-left midfield player and also a central striker with equal effect during the campaign, and although not as potent in front of goal as in recent seasons he still finished in double figures. He was regularly a subject of transfer rumours and may well move on in the summer under the Bosman ruling. Stop Press: Karl joined Queens Park Rangers at the end of May.

Wrexham (Free from Napoli, in local Sunday League, on 8/5/1991) FL 337+21/88 FLC 22/4 FAC 37+1/16 Others 32+1/6

CONNOR Daniel (Dan) Brian
Born: Dublin, 31 January 1981
Height: 6'2" Weight: 12.9
International Honours: RoI: Yth

Peterborough's Republic of Ireland youth international 'keeper had an early taste of senior action in February 2000. Daniel took over between the sticks for Posh when regular custodian Mark Tyler picked up a shoulder injury after only 14 minutes of the 1-2 defeat at Cheltenham. This towering figure has already had injury problems in his short career as he has suffered a broken leg and cruciate ligament damage.

Peterborough U (From trainee on 29/4/1998) FL 2+1

CONNOR Paul
Born: Bishop Auckland, 12 January 1979
Height: 6'1" Weight: 11.5
Club Honours: AMC '00

Having ended the previous season on loan at Stoke, Paul made the permanent switch to the Britannia Stadium in the summer of 1999 after being released by Middlesbrough. However, 1999-2000 was an in-and-out season for the young North-easterner, who held a striking role in the early part of the campaign but lost out to the improving Kyle Lightbourne and was denied an appearance at Wembley in the final of the Auto Windscreens Shield. He also had an injury problem mid-season, which did not help him at the crucial time when Gudjon Thordarson was rebuilding his team, but his running at the heart of opposing defences makes him popular with the fans. Still only 21, Paul will continue to develop and remains one for the future.

Middlesbrough (From trainee on 4/7/1996)
Hartlepool U (Loaned on 6/2/1998) FL 4+1
Stoke C (Free on 25/3/1999) FL 17+12/7 FLC 2+2/1 FAC 0+1 Others 2+3

COOK James (Jamie) Steven
Born: Oxford, 2 August 1979
Height: 5'10" Weight: 11.6

Jamie had a frustrating season at Oxford in 1999-2000, coming on as a substitute on 24 occasions. Although still a little lightweight, the young striker has good ball skills and should make big steps forward when he fills out a little. He did score three times during the season, with the last of those goals being a vital last-minute winner against Bury. His first league start did not come until December but he did have a few small runs as first choice after that as first Mickey Lewis and then Denis Smith took over team selection.

Oxford U (From trainee on 1/7/1997) FL 29+39/6 FLC 1+4 FAC 3+4 Others 3

COOK Paul Anthony
Born: Liverpool, 22 June 1967
Height: 5'11" Weight: 11.0

After playing a key role in Burnley's escape while on loan at Turf Moor at the end of the 1998-99 season, Paul was signed permanently in time for 1999-2000 and was an automatic choice in the side. His vision and passing ability are essential ingredients in the Burnley midfield, and his off-days tend to coincide with the team's poorer performances. He is also capable of scoring from distance, and his televised goal in the first-round FA Cup victory at Barnet was either a "Goal of the Season" contender or a cross that got lucky, depending on one's point of view!

Wigan Ath (Signed from Marine on 20/7/1984) FL 77+6/14 FLC 4 FAC 6+1 Others 5+1/1
Norwich C (£73,000 on 23/5/1988) FL 3+3 Others 1+1
Wolverhampton W (£250,000 on 1/11/1989) FL 191+2/19 FLC 7/1 FAC 5+2 Others 6+1/1
Coventry C (£600,000 on 18/8/1994) PL 35+2/3 FLC 3 FAC 3
Tranmere Rov (£250,000 on 29/2/1996) FL 54+6/4 FLC 8 FAC 1
Stockport Co (£250,000 on 24/10/1997) FL 48+1/3 FLC 1+1 FAC 2
Burnley (Free on 12/3/1999) FL 56/4 FLC 1 FAC 4/2

COOKE Andrew (Andy) Roy
Born: Shrewsbury, 20 January 1974
Height: 6'0" Weight: 12.8

Andy ended 1999-2000 as the player with the longest continuous service at Turf Moor, but the striker's fifth season with Burnley was one of mixed fortunes. A hamstring injury kept him out for over a month early in the campaign, but he returned with four goals in five games. This proved to be something of a purple patch as he then played more of a supporting role to the prolific Andy Payton, but he was always a willing chaser, using his physical advantages to good effect to set up Burnley's other Andy. The arrival of Ian Wright failed to dislodge Cooke from the front line until injury sidelined him in April.

Burnley (Signed from Newtown on 1/5/1995) FL 124+36/50 FLC 4+2/3 FAC 7+3/2 Others 9+2/2

COOKE Terence (Terry) John
Born: Birmingham, 5 August 1976
Height: 5'7" Weight: 11.4
Club Honours: FAYC '95
International Honours: E: U21-4; Yth

After earning the adulation of the Manchester City fans in 1998-99 with his scintillating performances on the right wing, Terry appeared to lose his way last season and found himself put to one side. He started the campaign in the team and played in eight of the first nine matches, although he was substituted in six of them. He was unable to produce the penetrating runs that had characterised his game in the Second Division with any consistency and didn't complement Mark Kennedy on the left flank as effectively as the supporters who had expected the two wingers to produce a stream of chances for the strikers had hoped. Terry made nine further appearances, all but one of them as a substitute, before falling out of favour after the game against Huddersfield at the end of November. After that he seemed to become a forgotten man and he asked to be placed on the transfer list in mid-February. Terry went to Wigan on loan at the beginning of March and, while he never recaptured the form that had made him a crowd favourite at Maine Road, his traditional wing play was fast and direct and was climaxed by accurate crosses. He remains dangerous at free kicks, and his only goal for the Latics came from that source in the draw at Chesterfield. There was speculation that he might well make a permanent move to the JJB Stadium during the summer.

Manchester U (From trainee on 1/7/1994) PL 1+3 FLC 1+2/1 Others 0+1
Sunderland (Loaned on 29/1/1996) FL 6
Birmingham C (Loaned on 29/11/1996) FL 1+3
Wrexham (Loaned on 30/10/1998) FL 10 Others 1
Manchester C (£1,000,000 on 13/1/1999) FL 27+7/7 FLC 3+1/1 Others 3
Wigan Ath (Loaned on 7/3/2000) FL 10/1

COOPER Colin Terence
Born: Sedgefield, 28 February 1967
Height: 5'10" Weight: 11.9
Club Honours: Div 1 '98
International Honours: E: 2; U21-8

Colin is currently enjoying his second spell at Middlesbrough and his experience is standing him and the team in good stead. Since his first sojourn on Teesside under Bruce Rioch in the heady days when the club teetered on the brink of liquidation, rapidly ascending the Football League ladder and descending it no less rapidly, Colin has matured beyond recognition. Once clear of his various injuries, "Coops" produced consistently solid displays last season, spraying accurate passes all around the pitch without venturing too far forward. He was the rock that other players depended on at the heart of the defence, and his solidity was seen to great effect in the home game against Arsenal in March. Colin's decisive tackles carry his no-nonsense trademark, and he has the uncanny knack of timing his contact perfectly, usually coming away with the ball cleanly. His 26 appearances in 1999-2000 were all highly rated and won him several "Man of the Match" awards, while highlighting how much he was missed when he was absent due to his early-season injuries.

Middlesbrough (From juniors on 17/7/1984) FL 183+5/6 FLC 18 FAC 13 Others 19+1/2

Millwall (£300,000 on 25/7/1991) FL 77/6 FLC 6 FAC 2 Others 2
Nottingham F (£1,700,000 on 21/6/1993) F/PL 179+1/20 FLC 14/2 FAC 12/1 Others 7
Middlesbrough (£2,500,000 on 22/8/1998) PL 57+1/1 FLC 5 FAC 1

COOPER Kevin Lee
Born: Derby, 8 February 1975
Height: 5'7" Weight: 10.7
Kevin was again a key figure for Stockport during 1999-2000 and he appeared in each of the club's 51 first-team games during the season. Although he scored only six goals, he was effective down both flanks and deservedly won several "Player of the Year" awards for his performances. Naturally left-footed, he is a tricky winger who complements his skilful ball-play with a phenomenal workrate and an excellent temperament.
Derby Co (From trainee on 2/7/1993) FL 0+2 FLC 0+2 Others 0+1
Stockport Co (£150,000 on 24/3/1997) FL 112+22/16 FLC 5+5/2 FAC 3 Others 1

COOPER Richard Anthony
Born: Nottingham, 27 September 1977
Height: 5'9" Weight: 10.12
International Honours: E: Yth; Sch
This hard-tackling young central defender or midfield player made his debut for Nottingham Forest on the final day of the 1999-2000 season when he came on as a substitute for the last 15 minutes at Stockport. Richard has already been capped by England at U15 schools, U18 and U20 levels and is clearly one to watch for the future.
Nottingham F (From trainee on 2/10/1996) FL 0+1

COOPER Steven (Steve) Daniel
Born: Pontypridd, 10 December 1979
Height: 5'9" Weight: 11.6
This young central defender was a regular in the Wrexham reserve team during 1999-2000 and made his bow in senior football last October in an FAW Premier Cup tie against Conwy United. His only other first-team appearance came in the Auto Windscreens Shield tie at Preston. He is another of the products of the Robins' successful youth policy and the son of the former referee, Keith Cooper. Steve was released by the Racecourse Ground club at the end of the season.
Wrexham (From trainee on 3/7/1998) Others 1

COOTE Adrian
Born: Great Yarmouth, 30 September 1978
Height: 6'2" Weight: 12.0
International Honours: NI: 6; B-1; U21-14
Despite being a regular member of the Northern Ireland squad and earning three more caps, Adrian still found it difficult to win a place in the Norwich starting line-up in 1999-2000. He did score his third senior goal in the last minute of City's early-season 2-2 draw at Walsall, but generally the consistency of Iwan Roberts kept him on the sidelines. A brave, no-nonsense centre forward, his endeavour and willingness to chase lost causes have endeared him to the City fans, whose great hopes for this Canary-supporting, Great Yarmouth-born player are as yet not totally fulfilled. Predominantly left footed, he is strong in the air and will always be a handful for any defender, because of his ceaseless foraging and physical presence.
Norwich C (From trainee on 3/7/1997) FL 17+23/3 FLC 1+2

COPPINGER James
Born: Middlesbrough, 10 January 1981
Height: 5'7" Weight: 10.6
International Honours: E: Yth
James is a highly rated forward who has been kept in the background at Newcastle. There had been reports of a possible £600,000 move to Hearts, but when this did not materialise he took the opportunity of a loan move to Hartlepool in March 2000. With the benefit of first-team football, James showed himself to be a fine opportunist in the opposition penalty area. Although he is still learning, there is no doubt that he can yet make the grade in the higher divisions. James joined Newcastle from Darlington in March 1998 for a joint £500,000 fee with Paul Robinson. Both were rated at £250,000.
Newcastle U (£250,000 + from Darlington juniors on 27/3/1998)
Hartlepool U (Loaned on 10/3/2000) FL 6+4/3 Others 1

CORAZZIN Giancarlo (Carlo) Michele
Born: Canada, 25 December 1971
Height: 5'10" Weight: 12.7
International Honours: Canada: 42 (Gold Cup 2000)
Northampton's top scorer in 1999-2000 with 15 goals, Carlo was the star of the Canada national team that won the country's first major trophy. They lifted the CONCACAF Gold Cup held in the USA during February. With four goals, he also earned the "Golden Boot" award as the competition's top scorer. Carlo's average of two goals every five games makes him one of the most prolific scorers for Northampton in recent years. His coolness in front of goal has made him a favourite with the Sixfields crowd, and it is hoped that, although his contract expired at the end of the season, he will be with Town in the Second Division.
Cambridge U (£20,000 from Vancouver 86ers, Canada on 10/12/1993) FL 104+1/39 FLC 4/2 FAC 5 Others 3/2
Plymouth Arg (£150,000 on 28/3/1996) FL 61+13/22 FLC 1+1 FAC 0+2/1 Others 2+1
Northampton T (Free on 2/7/1998) FL 63+15/30 FLC 5+2/1 FAC 3 Others 1/1

CORDEN Simon **Wayne**
Born: Leek, 1 November 1975
Height: 5'9" Weight: 11.3
A skilful left winger who crosses the ball well, Simon was not able to make the breakthrough he had hoped for at Port Vale last season. Throughout his Vale career he has produced sparkling performances for the reserves but been unable to reproduce the goods in a first-team shirt, which explains why he was again left out in the cold in 1999-2000. All in all he made just two twenty-minute appearances from the substitutes' bench, and was released on a free transfer at the end of the season. Stop Press: Wayne was reported to have joined Mansfield in early June.
Port Vale (From trainee on 20/9/1994) FL 30+36/1 FLC 4 FAC 2+1/1

CORICA Stephen (Steve) Christopher
Born: Cairns, Australia, 24 March 1973
Height: 5'8" Weight: 10.10
International Honours: Australia: 17; U23; Yth
The Wolves midfielder started ten of the club's first 14 matches last season and took a chance well at Queens Park Rangers in a more advanced role. He showed good movement but was still not quite the finished product, hitting the woodwork twice at Palace and being unable to score at home, even when playing up front. From October to Christmas he was out of the team more often than he was in it, though he did play for Australia against Brazil. He was used twice as a substitute in January, scoring in an FA Cup penalty shoot-out, but that was to be his only claim to scoring for Wolves at Molineux in competitive football in 1999-2000. He was a substitute once in February, representing Australia once more too, before his Wolves career petered out and he ultimately moved on to try his luck in Japan with Sanfrecce Hiroshima.
Leicester C (£325,000 from Marconi, Australia on 11/8/1995) FL 16/2 FAC 2
Wolverhampton W (£700,000 on 16/2/1996) FL 80+20/5 FLC 5+1 FAC 3+1

CORNFORTH John Michael
Born: Whitley Bay, 7 October 1967
Height: 6'1" Weight: 13.12
Club Honours: Div 3 '88; AMC '94
International Honours: W: 2
Released by Wycombe at the end of the previous season, John spent three months at Cardiff at the start of 1999-2000 and was reportedly keen to stay at Ninian Park. A cultured midfielder with two good feet and great passing ability, he rarely wasted the ball but the Welsh international is no longer as mobile as he once was and he was not offered a permanent deal. He moved to Scunthorpe in November on a short-term contract and scored within minutes of coming on as a substitute on his debut against Millwall. He quickly demonstrated his fine distribution and resolute tackling but his time at Glanford Park was hampered by hamstring injuries and he started only two league games. He was withdrawn after just 30 minutes of his final appearance at the start of February and was then allowed to join Third Division Exeter. His passing ability and experience helped steady the Grecians during the difficult latter part of the season and he scored two goals from the penalty spot. John was one of only two players retained by Exeter at the end of the campaign following manager Nathan Blake's colossal clear-out.
Sunderland (From apprentice on 11/10/1985) FL 21+11/2 FLC 0+1 Others 1+3
Doncaster Rov (Loaned on 6/11/1986) FL 6+1/3 Others 2

Shrewsbury T (Loaned on 23/11/1989) FL 3 Others 2
Lincoln C (Loaned on 11/1/1990) FL 9/1
Swansea C (£50,000 on 2/8/1991) FL 147+2/16 FLC 14 FAC 11/1 Others 19/1
Birmingham C (£350,000 on 26/3/1996) FL 8
Wycombe W (£50,000 on 5/12/1996) FL 35+12/6 FLC 6 FAC 2/2 Others 0+2
Peterborough U (Loaned on 13/2/1998) FL 3+1
Cardiff C (Free on 6/8/1999) FL 6+4/1 FLC 1+2
Scunthorpe U (Free on 4/11/1999) FL 2+2/1 Others 1
Exeter C (Free on 18/2/2000) FL 12/2

CORT Carl Edward Richard
Born: Southwark, 1 November 1977
Height: 6'4" Weight: 12.7
International Honours: E: U21-12

Carl played the majority of last season in a wide-right role for Wimbledon. This may not have been to his taste, but he nevertheless acquitted himself admirably, often winding himself through opposition defences like a snake in the grass. He was one of a number of players who became restless during a long and difficult season, resulting in intense transfer speculation. Carl enjoyed considerable success with the England U21 team, taking his tally to eight goals in 12 appearances, and his impressive performances can only have increased the interest shown in him by other clubs. He scored a memorable hat-trick for Wimbledon at home to Sunderland in the FA Cup and was voted "Most Improved Player of the Year" by the fans. Tall yet mobile, he is an awkward opponent in the penalty area and shows good close control on the ground. Stop Press: It was reported in early July that Carl had signed for Newcastle for a fee of £7 million.

Wimbledon (From trainee on 7/6/1996) PL 54+19/16 FLC 8+2/7 FAC 6+4/2
Lincoln C (Loaned on 3/2/1997) FL 5+1/1

COTTEE Anthony (Tony) Richard
Born: West Ham, 11 July 1965
Height: 5'9" Weight: 12.6
Club Honours: FLC '00
International Honours: E: 7; U21-8; Yth

The pint-sized livewire striker finally achieved his ambition of collecting a winners' medal at Wembley when he shared in Leicester's Worthington Cup triumph over Tranmere last season. The moment was especially sweet as he had only recently returned to action after spending nine matches on the sidelines owing to a calf injury. Tony showed he had lost none of his predatory instincts in the early part of the campaign when he helped to fire City into a top-six spot, and Leicester clearly missed the goals he regularly supplies when he was ruled out early in the new year. Still effective enough to reach his double-figure target in the goalscoring stakes, he eventually finished as the club's top marksman with 13 goals. Now nearing the end of an illustrious career, Tony will be looking towards player-management in the not too distant future as a way to stay in the game he so clearly loves.

West Ham U (From apprentice on 1/9/1982) FL 203+9/92 FLC 19/14 FAC 24/11 Others 1/1
Everton (£2,300,000 on 2/8/1988) F/PL 161+23/72 FLC 19+4/11 FAC 15+6/4 Others 11+2/12
West Ham U (Signed on 7/9/1994) PL 63+4/23 FLC 8/4 FAC 5/1 (Signed by Selangor, Malaysia on 3/3/1997)
Leicester C (£500,000 on 14/8/1997) PL 66+17/27 FLC 9/5 FAC 3+2/2 Others 0+1
Birmingham C (Loaned on 14/11/1997) FL 4+1/1

COUSINS Jason Michael
Born: Hayes, 14 October 1970
Height: 5'11" Weight: 12.4
Club Honours: GMVC '93; FAT '93

Wycombe's 1998-99 captain had to be content with a place on the subs' bench for the opening two months of last season and only came into the team when Paul McCarthy suffered a long-term injury. He makes up for a lack of speed with excellent anticipation and timing, and is particularly adept at making clean last-ditch tackles. As always, he gave total commitment in the centre of the Chairboys' defence, and he netted a single goal with a bullet-like header at Luton in October.

Brentford (From trainee on 13/7/1989) FL 20+1 Others 2+2
Wycombe W (Free on 1/7/1991) FL 231+14/6 FLC 18+1/1 FAC 25+1 Others 15

COUZENS Andrew (Andy)
Born: Shipley, 4 June 1975
Height: 5'10" Weight: 11.11
Club Honours: FAYC '93
International Honours: E: U21-3

This Blackpool midfielder began 1999-2000 as a regular in the first team but rarely featured after the defeat at Notts County last September. Andy made a brief return in March but was then injured and was released by the club in the summer.

Leeds U (From trainee on 5/3/1993) PL 17+11/1 FLC 4+1/1 Others 0+2
Carlisle U (£100,000 on 21/7/1997) FL 28+14/2 FLC 3+1/1 Others 1+3
Blackpool (Free on 5/3/1999) FL 18+3 FLC 2 Others 1

COWAN Thomas (Tom)
Born: Bellshill, 28 August 1969
Height: 5'9" Weight: 11.10

Vying with Paul Smith for the left-wing-back position at the start of the 1999-2000 season, Tom struggled to regain his Burnley first-team spot following a hamstring injury and was finally loaned to Cambridge in February. Signed to provide cover for the injured Clive Wilson, he made four first-team appearances and created a favourable impression before returning to Turf Moor in mid-March. Burnley manager Stan Ternent's preference for more attacking wing backs was sometimes called into question as Cowan remained probably the most natural left-sided defender at the club. The overall strength of Burnley's defence last season may ironically have cost Tom the regular place that many supporters assumed would be his, and he was released at the end of the season.

Clyde (From Netherdale BC on 11/7/1988) SL 16/2 SC 2
Glasgow R (Signed on 9/2/1989) SL 8+4 SC 0+1 Others 2
Sheffield U (£350,000 on 1/8/1991) F/PL 45 FLC 5 FAC 2 Others 1
Stoke C (Loaned on 1/10/1993) FL 14 FLC 1 Others 3
Huddersfield T (£150,000 on 24/3/1994) FL 137/8 FLC 13/1 FAC 9/1 Others 6
Burnley (£20,000 on 12/3/1999) FL 17+3 FLC 2 Others 0+1
Cambridge U (Loaned on 22/2/2000) FL 4

COWE Steven (Steve) Mark
Born: Gloucester, 29 September 1974
Height: 5'7" Weight: 10.10

Steve had to wait until February before appearing in the starting line-up for Swindon last season, and although he had an extended run in the team for most of the remaining games he failed to add to his goal tally. A small, busy striker, he showed some neat touches and plenty of skill. He was out of contract in the summer, but it was reported that he had been re-engaged by new boss Colin Todd.

Aston Villa (From trainee on 7/7/1993)
Swindon T (£100,000 on 22/3/1996) FL 54+34/10 FLC 3+2 FAC 1+2

COWLING Lee David
Born: Doncaster, 22 September 1977
Height: 5'9" Weight: 11.4

Signed from Nottingham Forest in the summer of 1999, Lee made his Mansfield debut at right back on the first day of the new season in the 0-6 mauling by Brighton. He ended the game with a knee injury which forced him out of action for three months until mid-November, when he returned to the second string. His first-team opportunities were limited after that but he was used as cover in a central defensive role. He seemed to lack concentration at times and consequently some errors resulted in goals being conceded. Lee was released at the end of the season.

Nottingham F (From trainee on 22/9/1994)
Mansfield T (Free on 4/8/1999) FL 3+5

COX Ian Gary
Born: Croydon, 25 March 1971
Height: 6'0" Weight: 12.2
International Honours: Trinidad & Tobago: 1

Ian started the 1999-2000 season as Bournemouth's club captain and a key figure in the centre of their defence. He performed consistently well for the Cherries, rarely missing a game until he was sold to Burnley last February. Ian had often been an outstanding performer on Bournemouth's visits to Turf Moor, and his arrival was warmly welcomed by the Clarets' fans. A defender who looks more than capable of playing at a higher level, he became part of what was surely the Second Division's most formidable back three along with Steve Davis and Mitchell Thomas. Solid in the tackle and good in the air, he uses the ball well and displays a useful turn of speed on his occasional forays forward. Ian's Burnley career began with several "Man of the Match" performances and his calm authority at the back is surely set to serve the club well. He missed the end of the season after suffering a freak wrist injury in the game at Brentford but hoped to be fit for the start of 2000-01. Ian made his international debut for Trinidad & Tobago against Morocco in January and will be hoping to win a recall to the squad for the forthcoming round of World Cup qualifiers.

Crystal Palace (£35,000 from Carshalton on 8/3/1994) F/PL 2+13 FAC 1+2/1
Bournemouth (Free on 28/3/1996) FL 172/16 FLC 14 FAC 10 Others 11/1
Burnley (£500,000 on 4/2/2000) FL 17/1

COX Neil James
Born: Scunthorpe, 8 October 1971
Height: 6'0" Weight: 13.7
Club Honours: FLC '94; Div 1 '95
International Honours: E: U21-6

A tough-tackling, uncompromising full back, Neil was one of Bolton's most popular players, due to his never-say-die attitude and never-ending commitment. Continuing where he had left off the previous season, he produced a series of excellent displays in his trademark right-back position in the early stages of the 1999-2000 campaign. Neil also has a knack of coming up with the odd goal, scoring three in five games in the autumn. His superb performances didn't go unnoticed, however, and he moved to Watford for a paltry £500,000 in early November. Neil made his debut at Sheffield Wednesday and was thereafter pretty much a fixture, although he lost his place through suspension in January after being sent off against Everton. A sound and committed defender, he understandably took a while to settle, but his influence increased towards the end of the season as he warmed to the attacking responsibilities of his wing-back role.

Scunthorpe U (From trainee on 20/3/1990) FL 17/1 FAC 4 Others 4+1
Aston Villa (£400,000 on 12/2/1991) F/PL 26+16/3 FLC 5+2 FAC 4+2/1 Others 2
Middlesbrough (£1,000,000 on 19/7/1994) P/FL 103+3/3 FLC 14+1 FAC 5/1 Others 2
Bolton W (£1,200,000 on 27/5/1997) P/FL 77+3/7 FLC 9/1 FAC 1+1 Others 3
Watford (£500,000 on 5/11/1999) PL 20+1 FAC 1

COYNE Daniel (Danny)
Born: Prestatyn, 27 August 1973
Height: 5'11" Weight: 13.0
International Honours: W: 1; B-1; U21-9; Yth; Sch

Released by Tranmere Rovers, this Welsh international goalkeeper joined Grimsby on a free transfer in the summer of 1999 to replace the departed Aidan Davison. Demonstrating lightning reactions and good positioning, he turned in some match-winning performances for the Mariners during 1999-2000. His season was almost marred in bizarre circumstances when he received a three-match ban for an alleged incident at Crystal Palace, which was reported by two police officers but went unnoticed by any of the match officials, the crowd or the Palace player concerned. Fortunately, this penalty was suspended pending an appeal and was ultimately quashed.

Tranmere Rov (From trainee on 8/5/1992) FL 110+1 FLC 13 FAC 2 Others 2
Grimsby T (Free on 12/7/1999) FL 44 FLC 1 FAC 1

CRADDOCK Jody Darryl
Born: Redditch, 25 July 1975
Height: 6'1" Weight: 12.4

An accomplished centre back, Jody began 1999-2000 as a squad player at Sunderland and joined Sheffield United early on in the season on one month's loan, which was extended to two. The tall defender produced some impressive displays during his time at Bramall Lane and there was talk of a permanent move but Sunderland did not wish to part with him. Injuries and suspensions saw him recalled to Wearside and immediately pitched into the first team for his Premiership debut against Liverpool in November. Having performed extremely well, Jody held on to his place for victories over Watford and Chelsea and, after a further spell on the sidelines, he was back in the side in February, cementing his place in the team with some solid performances. Jody's pace, heading strength and bravery in the tackle have impressed Sunderland's fans and, after he had looked to be possibly surplus to requirements at the beginning of the season, many at the Stadium of Light are now predicting a bright future for the stopper in the Premiership.

Cambridge U (Free from Christchurch on 13/8/1993) FL 142+3/4 FLC 3/1 FAC 6 Others 5
Sunderland (£300,000 + on 4/8/1997) P/FL 52+5 FLC 6+2 FAC 2+1 Others 3
Sheffield U (Loaned on 27/8/1999) FL 10

CRAMB Colin
Born: Lanark, 23 June 1974
Height: 6'0" Weight: 12.6
Club Honours: B&Q '93

Having joined Crewe from Bristol City on the eve of the 1999-2000 season for a fee of £200,000, this Scottish forward made his first appearance for his new club at Hartlepool in the Worthington Cup on 10 August and his league debut at Walsall shortly afterwards. After scoring three goals in his first six games he then had a long spell without finding the net but his powerful running and ability to link play between midfield and attack meant that he continued to make a useful contribution. Colin was relegated to the substitutes' bench on occasions in the middle of the season but retained his place in the starting line-up to the end of the campaign after scoring in successive games against Port Vale, Blackburn and Portsmouth in March.

Hamilton Ac (From juniors on 1/6/1993) SL 29+19/10 SC 0+1 Others 1+3
Southampton (£75,000 on 8/6/1993) PL 0+1
Falkirk (Signed on 30/8/1994) SL 6+2/1 SLC 0+1
Hearts (Signed on 1/3/1995) SL 3+3/1
Doncaster Rov (£25,000 on 15/12/1995) FL 60+2/25 FLC 2/1 FAC 1/1 Others 1/1
Bristol C (£250,000 on 10/7/1997) FL 38+15/9 FLC 3+1 FAC 1/1 Others 1+1
Walsall (Loaned on 27/2/1999) FL 4/4 Others 2
Crewe Alex (£200,000 on 6/8/1999) FL 33+4/6 FLC 5/1 FAC 1

CRAWFORD James (Jimmy)
Born: Chicago, USA, 1 May 1973
Height: 5'11" Weight: 11.6
Club Honours: S Div 1 '93; SLC '94
International Honours: RoI: U21-2

It was all downhill for Jimmy after Reading's first game of the 1999-2000 season, when he headed a late winner in the 2-1 victory over Bristol City. Loss of form, a sending-off at Wycombe Wanderers, and a well documented off-field incident, all combined to remove him from the first-team squad and for the remainder of the campaign he was restricted to reserve-team friendly games. A neat, steady right-sided midfield player with an eye for a penetrating crossfield pass, he was placed on the transfer list in January but attracted little interest from other clubs.

Newcastle U (£75,000 from Bohemians on 23/3/1995) PL 0+2 FLC 0+1
Rotherham U (Loaned on 27/9/1996) FL 11
Dundee U (Loaned on 20/2/1998) SL 0+2
Reading (£50,000 on 26/3/1998) FL 17+4/1 FLC 2+2 FAC 1 Others 1+1

CRESSWELL Richard Paul Wesley
Born: Bridlington, 20 September 1977
Height: 6'0" Weight: 11.8
International Honours: E: U21-4

This popular young striker had few chances to shine at Sheffield Wednesday in 1999-2000, when he was generally used as a substitute, rarely appearing in the starting line-up. He is good in the air and is always full of running but still has a few rough edges which will no doubt disappear when he gets more experience of higher-level football.

York C (From trainee on 15/11/1995) FL 72+23/21 FLC 3+3 FAC 4+2/3 Others 4
Mansfield T (Loaned on 27/3/1997) FL 5/1
Sheffield Wed (£950,000 + on 25/3/1999) PL 3+24/2 FLC 1+1/1 FAC 0+3

CRICHTON Paul Andrew
Born: Pontefract, 3 October 1968
Height: 6'1" Weight: 12.2

An automatic selection between the posts for Burnley in 1999-2000, Paul rarely let the side down and had the advantage of a solid back line to protect him in the event of occasional waywardness. He is a generally reliable shot stopper, and while his positional sense can be questionable he could rarely take personal blame for goals conceded. The security of his first-team place may be a mixed blessing for the club, who currently have no other goalkeeper with senior experience on their books.

Nottingham F (From juniors on 23/5/1986)
Notts Co (Loaned on 19/9/1986) FL 5
Darlington (Loaned on 30/1/1987) FL 5
Peterborough U (Loaned on 27/3/1987) FL 4
Darlington (Loaned on 28/9/1987) FL 3 FLC 1 Others 1
Swindon T (Loaned on 24/12/1987) FL 4
Rotherham U (Loaned on 9/3/1988) FL 6
Torquay U (Loaned on 25/8/1988) FL 13 FLC 2
Peterborough U (Signed on 3/11/1988) FL 47 FAC 5 Others 3
Doncaster Rov (Free on 25/8/1990) FL 77 FLC 5 FAC 3 Others 5
Grimsby T (Free on 9/7/1993) FL 133 FLC 7 FAC 8 Others 2
West Bromwich A (£250,000 on 9/9/1996) FL 32 FLC 1 FAC 1
Burnley (Loaned on 7/8/1998) FL 1
Burnley (£100,000 on 19/11/1998) FL 74 FLC 2 FAC 4 Others 2

CRITCHLEY Neil
Born: Crewe, 18 October 1978
Height: 5'9" Weight: 10.8

One of the many young players to have emerged from Crewe's renowned youth

scheme in recent seasons, Neil had to wait until he was within a month of his 21st birthday before making his first-team debut as an 81st-minute substitute for Kenny Lunt in the 3-0 defeat at Fulham last September. That was to be his only opportunity at senior level in 1999-2000, although he had a spell on loan at Hyde United in March. He was released in the summer.
Crewe Alex (From trainee on 4/7/1997) FL 0+1

CROFT Gary
Born: Burton on Trent, 17 February 1974
Height: 5'9" Weight: 11.8
International Honours: E: U21-4
Seemingly not in contention for a first-team place at Blackburn, Gary joined Ipswich last September for a fee of £800,000 and made his debut in the televised home game with Manchester City at the end of the month as left wing back. It proved to be a debut to remember because not only did he impress Town fans with his defensive abilities but he was also able to link up well in attack and scored what proved to be the winning goal when he picked up a loose ball on the edge of City's penalty area and shot past Nicky Weaver, with the help of a slight deflection. Things started to go sour, however, when he received a custodial sentence as a result of motoring offences and he became the first professional footballer to play in a league game while wearing a "tag". The club and the fans supported him throughout this experience and he received a tremendous reception from the crowd when he returned to action, as a substitute, in the home game against Swindon in January. Injuries and the form of other defenders meant that he did not hold down a regular place in the side but he performed well whenever he was called upon.
Grimsby T (From trainee on 7/7/1992) FL 139+10/3 FLC 7 FAC 8+2/1 Others 3
Blackburn Rov (£1,700,000 on 29/3/1996) PL 33+7/1 FLC 6 FAC 4+2
Ipswich T (£800,000 on 21/9/1999) FL 14+7/1 Others 2+1

CROOKS Lee Robert
Born: Wakefield, 14 January 1978
Height: 6'0" Weight: 12.1
International Honours: E: Yth
After appearing to have established himself in the side in 1998-99, Lee was unable to command a regular place in the Manchester City defence last season. However, although his opportunities were limited, particularly during the second half of the season, he continued to mature promisingly and always gave a good account of himself. Lee has shown that he can excel either in the middle of the defence or at right back, but he is particularly impressive when he is going forward on the overlap to produce accurate and well-flighted crosses for the stikers. In addition, he scored an early goal in the 1-1 draw at Crewe in January with a lovely low shot from outside the penalty area that was almost identical to his strike at Chesterfield the previous season.
Manchester C (From trainee on 14/1/1995) FL 52+22/2 FLC 3+2 FAC 5 Others 3

CROSBY Andrew (Andy) Keith
Born: Rotherham, 3 March 1973
Height: 6'2" Weight: 13.7
Signed from Chester for £10,000 in the 1999 close season, Andy made his Brighton debut at centre half in the 6-0 win over Mansfield on the opening day of the new campaign. He scored his first goal for the club in a memorable 2-1 victory at Leyton Orient seven days later. Andy suffered a pulled calf muscle in October but had regained his place by the end of November. He is an excellent header of the ball and makes his presence felt in both penalty areas.
Doncaster Rov (Free from Leeds U juniors on 4/7/1991) FL 41+10 FLC 1+1 FAC 2 Others 4+1/1
Darlington (Free on 10/12/1993) FL 179+2/3 FLC 10 FAC 11/1 Others 9
Chester C (Free on 8/7/1998) FL 41/4 FLC 3 FAC 1 Others 1
Brighton & Hove A (£10,000 on 28/7/1999) FL 36/3 FLC 2 FAC 1 Others 2

CROSS David Barron
Born: Bromley, 7 September 1982
Height: 5'10" Weight: 10.7
This Notts County trainee made his Football League debut when he came on as a substitute for the final 15 minutes of the Magpies' game at Chesterfield towards the end of last season. David is a tenacious ball-winning midfield player and will be looking to establish himself in the Notts first-team squad in 2000-01.
Notts Co (Trainee) FL 0+1

Garry Cross

CROSS Garry Robert
Born: Chelmsford, 7 October 1980
Height: 5'9" Weight: 12.0
Garry featured in the first-team squad at Southend United for the majority of the 1999-2000 season, but was unable to establish a regular place. A very strong and quick right back, Garry didn't let the Blues down whenever called upon, and there are high hopes at Roots Hall that their former youth-team captain will be one of the youngsters that the future of the club can be built around.
Southend U (From trainee on 2/7/1999) FL 7+1 FLC 1 Others 1

CROSS Jonathan (Jon) Neil
Born: Wallasey, 2 March 1975
Height: 5'10" Weight: 11.7
One of six Chester players offered new terms in the 1999 close season, Jonathan became one of the most experienced members of the Blues' squad. A versatile player, he can perform effectively almost anywhere but his limited appearances last season saw him mostly employed in the middle or up front. Jonathan didn't manage to break his scoring duck in the league, but prospered in the FA Cup with three goals. He has good pace and is noted as an excellent crosser of the ball but was released by the club in the summer.
Wrexham (From trainee on 15/11/1992) FL 92+27/12 FLC 4+3/1 FAC 4+1/1 Others 9+6/1
Hereford U (Loaned on 2/12/1996) FL 5/1 Others 1
Chester C (Free on 4/8/1998) FL 46+6/1 FLC 6 FAC 3+1/3 Others 2

CROSSLEY Mark Geoffrey
Born: Barnsley, 16 June 1969
Height: 6'0" Weight: 16.0
International Honours: E: U21-3. W: 3; B-1
Mark began 1999-2000 as first-choice 'keeper for Nottingham Forest but then lost his place to Dave Beasant last December and featured only twice more in the second half of the season. He is a fine shot stopper who dominates his area and possesses a powerful kick. He added to his Welsh caps with an appearance against Finland in March and finished the season with a testimonial match attended by 15,000 fans, a measure of his popularity with the Reds' supporters. Mark was out of contract in the summer and at the time of writing it appeared he was likely to move on to new pastures by the start of the 2000-01 campaign.
Nottingham F (From trainee on 2/7/1987) F/PL 301+2 FLC 39+1 FAC 32 Others 18
Millwall (Loaned on 20/2/1998) FL 13

CROUDSON Steven (Steve) David
Born: Grimsby, 14 September 1979
Height: 6'0" Weight: 12.4
The consistent form of Grimsby's first-choice goalkeeper, Danny Coyne, kept his young deputy on the bench during 1999-2000 with the exception of the away game at Fratton Park, where he replaced the senior 'keeper when he was red-carded, and two league and one FA Cup matches during Coyne's subsequent suspension. During these games Steve displayed confident handling and positioning and proved himself a more than able deputy.
Grimsby T (From trainee on 6/7/1998) FL 4+1 FLC 1 FAC 1

CROWE Dean Anthony
Born: Stockport, 6 June 1979
Height: 5'5" Weight: 11.3

A summer of work on his fitness helped Dean claim a spot in the Stoke first-team squad from the start of the 1999-2000 season but the pacy young striker was unable to capitalise on his opportunities as a substitute and had to make do with a reserve berth for much of the campaign. Gudjon Thordarson gave him another chance when he arrived as manager but Dean was unable to hold on to his position and was finally allowed to go out on loan to Northampton in February, replacing Carlo Corazzin, who was on international duty with Canada. Although he did not score in his five appearances, Dean showed enough style and skill to suggest he had something to offer. He will remember what was supposed to be his Northampton debut: having travelled all the way up to Carlisle, he was then told the game was off and had to wait another week for his first match in the Cobblers' colours. The diminutive striker then returned to Stoke before moving to Bury on loan on transfer deadline day. He made his debut in the Shakers' 2-2 draw at Burnley and impressed in each of his four appearances for the club. He scored a superb opportunist goal at home to Scunthorpe but sadly suffered a medial ligament injury during the away defeat at Cambridge United early in April and immediately returned to Stoke for treatment. He was ruled out for the rest of the season but had made such a good impression at Gigg Lane that boss Andy Preece was said to be extremely keen to make Dean a permanent signing during the summer.

Stoke C (From trainee on 5/9/1996) FL 29+31/12 FLC 2+3 Others 2/1
Northampton T (Loaned on 11/2/2000) FL 3+2
Bury (Loaned on 23/3/2000) FL 4/1

CROWE Jason William
Born: Sidcup, 30 September 1978
Height: 5'9" Weight: 10.9
International Honours: E: Yth

A right wing back who came up through the ranks at Highbury, Jason joined Portsmouth in the summer of 1999 for a £750,000 fee and went on to make a good impression in his first full season of senior football. He has the advantage of being able to kick with either foot and used his speed to good effect when making forward runs. Jason also showed his versatility by turning out in midfield when required.

Arsenal (From trainee on 13/5/1996) FLC 0+2 FAC 0+1
Crystal Palace (Loaned on 10/11/1998) FL 8
Portsmouth (£750,000 + on 7/7/1999) FL 21+4 FLC 3 FAC 0+1

CRUYFF Jordi
Born: Amsterdam, Holland, 9 February 1974
Height: 6'0" Weight: 11.0
Club Honours: PL '97; CS '96, '97
International Honours: Holland: 9

A versatile front-line player with excellent skills and a terrific shot in either foot, Jordi knew 1999-2000 was something of a make-or-break season for him at Manchester United, and Sir Alex Ferguson gave him an early chance to shine in the Charity Shield opener against Arsenal. By December, however, with only four games to his credit, and one goal, as a substitute against Wimbledon in September, there was talk of him quitting Old Trafford to try his luck in Spain. He had another opportunity to impress in the World Club Championship, and scored his second Premiership goal against Wimbledon in the return at Selhurst Park, but was unable to earn a regular place in the United starting line-up. Jordi was out of contract in the summer and West Ham were among the clubs reported to be interested in securing his services.

Manchester U (£1,400,000 from Barcelona, Spain, via Ajax, on 12/8/1996) PL 15+19/7 FLC 5 FAC 0+1 Others 6+11

CUDICINI Carlo
Born: Milan, Italy, 6 September 1973
Height: 6'1" Weight: 12.3
Club Honours: FAC '00

Yet another addition to the Italian enclave in London SW6 last season was goalkeeper Carlo Cudicini, who joined Chelsea on a year's loan in August 1999 from Serie C side Castel di Sangro. Carlo has a good goalkeeping pedigree – he is the son of famous AS Roma, AC Milan and Italy 'keeper Fabio Cudicini, who ironically played against Chelsea in a 1965 Fairs Cup tie while with Roma. He took over the deputy goalkeeper's role under Ed de Goey following Dmitri Kharine's close-season move to Celtic, relegating long-serving Kevin Hitchcock to third spot. Carlo made his first-team bow in the Champions' League qualifier in Latvia against Skonto Riga, when he replaced de Goey for the last 12 minutes; it was a measure of Chelsea's dominance that he did not touch the ball once! Carlo's first start of the season came in the Worthington Cup tie against Huddersfield Town at Stamford Bridge, when he was beaten by a wonder strike from Kenny Irons which ensured a famous giant-killing exploit. It was a very frustrating season for Carlo as de Goey maintained a remarkably high level of consistency and the Italian was stranded on the bench for 59 of the 61 first-team fixtures. However, manager Gianluca Vialli rested the big Dutchman for the last Premiership match of the season and Carlo stepped in – and kept a clean sheet – against Derby County, just a week before the FA Cup final at Wembley, where he won a winners' medal as an unused substitute. Stop Press: Chelsea were reported to have signed the Italian on a two-year contract at the beginning of July.

Chelsea (Loaned from Castel di Sangro, Italy on 6/8/1999) PL 1 FLC 1 Others 0+1

CUERVO Philippe
Born: Paris, France, 13 August 1969
Height: 5'11" Weight: 12.6

This Swindon Town midfielder spent the first half of last season recovering from a serious knee injury suffered in the early part of 1998-99. He eventually returned as a substitute against Portsmouth on Boxing Day but, despite a few more outings from the bench, he failed to make the starting line-up. When fully fit, Philippe is an attacking midfield player with considerable flair but his two-year spell in the West Country has been badly affected by injuries. He was released during the summer.

Swindon T (Free from St Etienne, France on 8/8/1997) FL 16+19 FLC 2+1

CULKIN Nicholas (Nick) James
Born: York, 6 July 1978
Height: 6'2" Weight: 13.7

A solid young Manchester United goalkeeper who has a good pair of hands and bears a passing resemblance to Peter Schmeichel, Nick enjoyed a rise to prominence in the early stages of the 1999-2000 season that is a prime example of how football's fortunes can suddenly be turned on their head. With Schmeichel seeing out his career in sunnier climes, and Mark Bosnich injured after just three games of the new campaign, he was called into the squad for the Premiership match against Arsenal at Highbury in August. Sent on for the last 12 minutes when Rai van der Gouw was stretchered off with concussion, he showed Sir Alex Ferguson he had the necessary "bottle" for the big occasion. In December, after Hull failed to agree an extended loan for Steve Bywater from West Ham, Nick became City's seventh 'keeper of the campaign – so equalling the league record – when he agreed to a loan move. He was known to Hull as their boss, Warren Joyce, had earlier coached Manchester United's U16 squad. In a particularly impressive spell Nick produced a point-winning penalty save at Leyton Orient, and the only goal he conceded came 25 minutes from the end of his fourth and final appearance, but he unfortunately missed three games with a groin strain. Although he wanted to continue his stay at Hull, with Massimo Taibi returning to Italy United needed to register Nick as cover for Mark Bosnich and Raimond van der Gouw for the second half of their Champions' League programme, which prevented him from playing for any other club.

Manchester U (£250,000 from York C juniors on 27/9/1995) PL 0+1
Hull C (Loaned on 24/12/1999) FL 4

CULLEN David **Jonathan (Jon)**
Born: Durham City, 10 January 1973
Height: 6'0" Weight: 12.0

After a loan spell with Rotherham at the start of the season when he failed to make a senior appearance, Jon joined Shrewsbury on loan from Sheffield United in September, and scored in a 4-1 victory over Carlisle. The left-sided midfielder soon fitted into the team and was part of the Shrews' best run of the season. Town could not afford to make the move permanent and he returned to United prior to another loan spell at Halifax. He moved to the Shay in January 2000 and did particularly well during his two-month stay, netting four goals. Halifax were keen to secure his services on a permanent basis after a number of quality displays but, in the end, Jon opted to accept a two-and-a-half-year contract with Peterborough. His cultured style helped Posh to secure their play-off place, and he featured in the Wembley final win against Darlington.

Doncaster Rov (From trainee on 16/9/1991) FL 8+1 FLC 2+1/1 FAC 0+1 Others 1 (Free to Spennymoor in September 1993)
Hartlepool U (Free from Morpeth on 27/3/1997) FL 33+1/12 FLC 2 FAC 1 Others 2
Sheffield U (£250,000 on 26/1/1998) FL 0+4
Shrewsbury T (Loaned on 10/9/1999) FL 10/1
Halifax T (Loaned on 17/12/1999) FL 11/5
Peterborough U (£35,000 on 3/3/2000) FL 12+1/3 Others 1

CULLIP Daniel (Danny)
Born: Bracknell, 17 September 1976
Height: 6'1" Weight: 12.7

Danny was signed by Brighton on a month's loan from Brentford in September 1999. He had served under his new boss, Micky Adams, at Griffin Park and previously at Fulham. Danny had the rare experience of scoring at both ends on his debut in the 3-2 home defeat by Chester. The loan spell led to a £50,000 permanent transfer and he became a firm favourite with the Albion fans because of his mature, no-nonsense performances in defence, his greatest assets being his heading and distribution. Widely tipped as a future Seagulls captain, Danny crowned a fine season by winning the club's "Player of the Year" award.

Oxford U (From trainee on 6/7/1995)
Fulham (Free on 5/7/1996) FL 41+9/2 FLC 8 FAC 2 Others 1
Brentford (£75,000 on 17/2/1998) FL 15 FLC 2
Brighton & Hove A (£50,000 on 17/9/1999) FL 32+1/2 FAC 4/1 Others 1

CULVERHOUSE Ian Brett
Born: Bishops Stortford, 22 September 1964
Height: 5'10" Weight: 11.2
Club Honours: UEFAC '84; Div 2 '86, '96
International Honours: E: Yth

Ian's only appearance in 1999-2000 came in Brighton's 2-0 defeat at Hull in February. He is Albion's reserve-team coach and only played because of suspensions and injuries to team-mates. His performance at centre half that day was no worse than that of his colleagues but believing he could not reach his previous high standards, Ian announced the end of his playing career shortly afterwards.

Tottenham H (From apprentice on 24/9/1982) FL 1+1
Norwich C (£50,000 on 8/10/1985) F/PL 295+1/1 FLC 23 FAC 28 Others 22/1
Swindon T (£250,000 on 9/12/1994) FL 95+2 FLC 9 FAC 10 Others 1 (Free to Kingstonian during 1998 close season)
Brighton & Hove A (Free on 18/8/1998) FL 36 FLC 1 FAC 1 Others 1

CUMMINS Michael Thomas
Born: Dublin, 1 June 1978
Height: 6'0" Weight: 11.11
International Honours: RoI: U21-2; Yth

This Republic of Ireland U21 international showed the patience of Job while waiting for a first-team chance at Middlesbrough last season. A strong-running, hard-tackling midfielder, he collected rave notices for his reserve-team performances and was occasionally called up for duty on the subs' bench, but his only appearance was in the game against Leeds in February. Although Michael gave it his best shot as usual, manager Bryan Robson was looking for results in the short term and opted to stick with his senior players. Somewhat surprisingly released by Middlesbrough, Michael joined Port Vale on a short-term contract in March to help the First Division club's ultimately unsuccessful battle against relegation. A skilful player with a languid style, he has a good shot and scored on his home debut for the Vale with a 25-yard effort. He generally impressed during his spell at Vale Park, becoming a regular in the starting line-up, and will be hoping to make the move permanent during the close season.

Middlesbrough (From trainee on 1/7/1995) PL 1+1
Port Vale (Free on 17/3/2000) FL 12/1

CUNDY Jason Victor
Born: Wimbledon, 12 November 1969
Height: 6'1" Weight: 13.13
International Honours: E: U21-3

Jason joined Portsmouth from Ipswich on a free transfer during the 1999 summer break but 1999-2000 proved to be another frustrating season as he was affected by more injury problems and only appeared in nine league games for his new club. He missed a large part of the autumn with hamstring trouble and then suffered a knee injury that required exploratory surgery in the close season and was expected to keep him out of action until around October 2000. When fully fit, he is a powerful central defender who is comfortable on the ball and shows good distribution.

Chelsea (From trainee on 1/8/1988) FL 40+1/1 FLC 6 FAC 6 Others 4
Tottenham H (£750,000 on 26/3/1992) F/PL 23+3/1 FLC 2
Crystal Palace (Loaned on 14/12/1995) FL 4
Bristol C (Loaned on 23/8/1996) FL 6/1
Ipswich T (£200,000 on 29/10/1996) FL 54+4/5 FLC 8 FAC 4 Others 2
Portsmouth (Free on 2/7/1999) FL 9 FLC 1 FAC 1

CUNNINGHAM Kenneth (Kenny) Edward
Born: Dublin, 28 June 1971
Height: 6'0" Weight: 11.8
International Honours: RoI: 31; B-2; U21-4; Yth

Kenny captained Wimbledon in the absence of Robbie Earle last season – and, like a good wine, he improves with age. He was once again outstanding at right back but, as usual, "Mr Versatile" had to fill in at centre half and left back when injuries arose during the campaign. Although he is a fine crosser of the ball, his greatest quality is his ability to read the game and close down opposing players effectively. Kenny played in every league game with the exception of the "Black Sunday" match against Southampton at the Dell in which the Dons were relegated from the Premiership. A good communicator and an extremely popular pro, he has committed himself to the club despite relegation and the harm it might do to his international prospects. Nevertheless he won a further eight caps for the Republic of Ireland during the season. He was voted "Player of the Season" by the Wimbledon fans.

Millwall (Signed from Tolka Rov on 18/9/1989) FL 132+4/1 FLC 10 FAC 1 Others 5+1/1
Wimbledon (Signed on 9/11/1994) PL 200+1 FLC 22+1 FAC 26

Kenny Cunningham

CURETON Jamie
Born: Bristol, 28 August 1975
Height: 5'8" Weight: 10.7
International Honours: E: Yth

The locally born striker continued to score consistently for Bristol Rovers throughout the 1999-2000 season, including a superb 25-yard volley at Bournemouth and a well-taken hat-trick at Oxford United in an impressive 5-0 victory. Jamie's partnership with Jason Roberts again caused problems for most Second Division defences, and his ability to take goalscoring chances, assisted by his quick feet and good positional sense, was a strong feature of Rovers' season, particularly away from home. The former Norwich City forward scored his 70th league goal for the Pirates on 1 April from the penalty spot against Stoke City.

Norwich C (From trainee on 5/2/1993) P/FL 13+16/6 FLC 0+1 FAC 0+2
Bournemouth (Loaned on 8/9/1995) FL 0+5 Others 0+1
Bristol Rov (£250,000 on 20/9/1996) FL 164+9/71 FLC 7+1/2 FAC 10/2 Others 6/2

CURLE Keith
Born: Bristol, 14 November 1963
Height: 6'1" Weight: 12.12
Club Honours: AMC '86; FMC '88
International Honours: E: 3; B-4

The 1999 close season saw the commanding central defender involved in another summer saga as to whether he would stay with Wolves, and again he did. He was excellent at his old Maine Road base in the first game of the new campaign, but a week later he was caught out by Portsmouth when chesting the ball to his 'keeper and not making a firm enough contact. Keith showed his abundant class on occasions, but seemed to be getting slightly more prone to errors. Often an excellent peacemaker, his run of misfortunes in matches with West Bromwich Albion continued when he injured team-mate Ludovic Pollet in a collision. The captain was 36 in November, and though happier in a 5-3-2 system he worked very hard in a four-man defence. The only three games he did not start all fell in January. He had a lucky day against Stockport in March when his penalty bobbled in to give Wolves their second goal of the match. Keith had a vital penalty saved at Birmingham, however, ironically by a loaned goalkeeper signed after the transfer deadline. Stop Press: He was reported to have joined Sheffield United as a player-coach at the beginning of July.

Bristol Rov (From apprentice on 20/11/1981) FL 21+11/4 FLC 3 FAC 1
Torquay U (£5,000 on 4/11/1983) FL 16/5 FAC 1/1 Others 1
Bristol C (£10,000 on 3/3/1984) FL 113+8/1 FLC 7+1 FAC 5 Others 14+1
Reading (£150,000 on 23/10/1987) FL 40 FLC 8 Others 5
Wimbledon (£500,000 on 21/10/1988) FL 91+2/3 FLC 7 FAC 5 Others 6/1
Manchester C (£2,500,000 on 14/8/1991) F/PL 171/11 FLC 18/2 FAC 14 Others 1
Wolverhampton W (£650,000 on 2/8/1996) FL 148+2/9 FLC 7/1 FAC 11/1 Others 2

CURRAN Christopher (Chris)
Born: Birmingham, 17 September 1971
Height: 5'11" Weight: 12.4

Although Chris damaged ankle ligaments and fractured an eye socket during pre-season, his consistent contributions were one of the high points for Exeter in 1999-2000. His impressive recovery from the early-term set-back was also a testament to his courage and ability. His speciality long throw-ins led to a goal on more than one occasion. With 13 players released and a further seven transfer-listed, Chris was one of only two senior professionals remaining at Exeter in the 2000 close season.

Torquay U (From trainee on 13/7/1990) FL 144+8/4 FLC 15 FAC 8 Others 10/1
Plymouth Arg (£40,000 on 22/12/1995) FL 26+4 FLC 1+1 FAC 1 Others 4
Exeter C (£20,000 on 31/7/1997) FL 75+6/5 FLC 4 FAC 7 Others 6

CURRAN Daniel (Danny) Lee James
Born: Brentwood, 14 June 1981
Height: 5'8" Weight: 9.0

Danny made his only Leyton Orient senior appearance at Grimsby in the Worthington Cup last September. He was in the third month of his intended two-year YTS stint, and was one of the many members of the club's successful South East Conference Youth Alliance title-winning side to make the first team in 1999-2000. However, Danny was then surprisingly released, and joined Purfleet of the Ryman League on a free transfer in February.

Leyton Orient (From trainee on 5/7/1999) FL 0+1 FLC 0+1 FAC 0+1 Others 0+1

CURRIE Darren Paul
Born: Hampstead, 29 November 1974
Height: 5'11" Weight: 12.7

With his unmistakable hairstyle and exquisite brand of trickery on the flank, the Barnet winger gained plenty of attention during 1999-2000, the most successful campaign of his career. He attained a place in the PFA's Division Three team following an array of captivating performances that saw him elevated to god-like status at Underhill, and was also selected in the Opta Index "Third Division Team of the Season". Despite not being endowed with blistering pace, Darren more than compensates for this with his intricate, often bewitching, foot-work, which enables him to outwit every full back in the division. In addition, his flawless crossing technique meant that the majority of Barnet's goals arrived courtesy of his dead-ball deliveries. Yet on occasion he would shun his creative responsibilities with devastating effect, and he scored some truly breathtaking goals, with his tremendous solo effort at Swansea in September eventually scooping the club's "Goal of the Season" award. Equally adept on either wing, Darren was a key figure behind the club's most successful start to a league term and his dismissal in the home defeat against Rochdale was the only blip in an otherwise impeccable year.

West Ham U (From trainee on 2/7/1993)
Shrewsbury T (Loaned on 5/9/1994) FL 10+2/2
Shrewsbury T (Loaned on 3/2/1995) FL 5
Leyton Orient (Loaned on 16/11/1995) FL 9+1
Shrewsbury T (£70,000 on 7/2/1996) FL 46+20/8 FLC 2+1/1 FAC 3
Plymouth Arg (Free on 26/3/1998) FL 5+2
Barnet (Free on 13/7/1998) FL 77+5/9 FLC 3/1 FAC 1/1 Others 5

CURTIS John Charles
Born: Nuneaton, 3 September 1978
Height: 5'10" Weight: 11.9
Club Honours: FAYC '95
International Honours: E: B-1; U21-16; Yth; Sch

This promising young Manchester United defender broke Jaap Stam's 15-game sequence when the big Dutchman was rested for the Worthington Cup tie against Aston Villa at Villa Park last October. With no other first-team opportunities forthcoming, he moved to Barnsley for an extended loan period in November and was very impressed with the experience. He did well at right back for the Tykes, making a significant contribution to their promotion campaign and scoring two goals, including one in the vital 2-1 victory over Manchester City in March. John is a very talented player with tremendous pace, strong tackling, a quick recovery and the ability to read the game well. He won a further cap for England at U21 level when he appeared against Poland last September. Stop Press: Blackburn Rovers were reported to have signed John for a £1.5 million fee at the beginning of June.

Manchester U (From trainee on 3/10/1995) PL 4+9 FLC 5 Others 0+1
Barnsley (Loaned on 19/11/1999) FL 28/2 Others 1+1

CURTIS Thomas (Tom) David
Born: Exeter, 1 March 1973
Height: 5'8" Weight: 11.7

Tom's long absence from Chesterfield's midfield due to cartilage problems was a significant factor in the club's relegation last season. His busy harrying of opponents and short, linking passes were badly missed, and he was sadly unable to make an effective return to the side while a chance of beating the drop existed. Tom will be a vital player in the Spireites' effort to get back up at the first attempt.

Derby Co (From juniors on 1/7/1991)
Chesterfield (Free on 12/8/1993) FL 235+5/12 FLC 20+1 FAC 14/1 Others 11+1

CUSACK Nicholas (Nicky) John
Born: Maltby, 24 December 1965
Height: 6'0" Weight: 12.8
Club Honours: Div 3 '00

Swansea's captain in 1999-2000, Nick continued to play to a high standard that ultimately saw him named by his fellow professionals in the PFA award-winning Third Division side. Not always appreciated by his club's supporters, he is widely respected for the exemplary manner in which he goes about his craft. On occasions last season he showed he had not forgotten his ability to lead the forward line, when he left his familiar midfield role and was pressed into service as a striker. He scored seven league goals, three of them coming in important 1-0 victories for the Swans. Earlier in the season he punctured a lung and cracked a rib against Southend at the Vetch Field but, after being sidelined for just four matches, he was back in the team, performing in his usual unobtrusive style. Nick's honest endeavour was also rewarded with a Third Division championship winners' medal.

Leicester C (Signed from Alvechurch on 18/6/1987) FL 5+11/1 FAC 0+1 Others 1+1
Peterborough U (£40,000 on 29/7/1988) FL 44/10 FLC 4/1 FAC 4/1 Others 2
Motherwell (£100,000 on 2/8/1989) SL 68+9/17 SLC 5/4 SC 3+1/2 Others 1+1/1
Darlington (£95,000 on 24/1/1992) FL 21/6
Oxford U (£95,000 on 16/7/1992) FL 48+13/10 FLC 3/2 FAC 4+2/1 Others 2+1
Wycombe W (Loaned on 24/3/1994) FL 2+2/1
Fulham (Free on 4/11/1994) FL 109+7/14 FLC 6+4/1 FAC 7+1/1 Others 5+2/3
Swansea C (£50,000 on 30/10/1997) FL 117+1/8 FLC 4/1 FAC 8/1 Others 4

CUTLER Neil Anthony
Born: Birmingham, 3 September 1976
Height: 6'1" Weight: 12.0
International Honours: E: Yth; Sch

Neil joined Aston Villa from lowly Chester City last November and spent some time on the subs' bench when regular second-choice 'keeper Peter Enckelman was out injured. He made his debut for Villa last February when he came on for the final seven minutes at Middlesbrough after David James was injured. He ended the season as third in line at Villa Park, but there is plenty of time for this former England youth international to develop into a top-class goalkeeper.

West Bromwich A (From trainee on 7/9/1993)
Chester C (Loaned on 27/3/1996) FL 1
Crewe Alex (Signed on 30/7/1996)
Chester C (Loaned on 30/8/1996) FL 5
Chester C (Free on 8/7/1998) FL 23 FLC 1 FAC 1 Others 1
Aston Villa (Signed on 30/11/1999) PL 0+1

DABIZAS Nikolaos (Nicos)
Born: Amyndaeo, Greece, 3 August 1973
Height: 6'1" Weight: 12.7
International Honours: Greece: 40

This Greek international is a strong, battling centre back who has adapted well to the English game playing for Newcastle. Powerful in the tackle, and good in the air, Nicos defends well but also enjoys joining the attack whenever possible, as he demonstrated in the late stages of the FA Cup semi-final last season when he virtually became an auxiliary striker. He believed his time at the club was coming to an end when he did not figure in the side at the start of the campaign, his first game coinciding with Ruud Gullit's last one in charge at the club. However, he then retained his place to become a regular for most of the season, apart from a suspension following his dismissal at Old Trafford for two bookings, and like so many others he was revitalised under new manager Bobby Robson, becoming a pillar of reliability at the heart of the defence. Nicos's versatility was demonstrated when he turned in a good performance when asked to undertake an unaccustomed midfield role in the home UEFA Cup tie against CSKA Sofia. His penchant for attack led to his scoring in three consecutive games (two Premiership and one FA Cup), which helped earn four points at a time when each one was vital and contributed to progress in the Cup. He thus found a place in the record books as the first defender at the club since Frank Hudspeth in 1926 to score in three consecutive games, but since Hudspeth's strikes were all penalties, and since Harry Jeffrey, who achieved the feat previously in 1894, also included a spot kick in his scores, Nicos was the first Newcastle defender to score from open play in three consecutive games. A bad injury at West Ham late in the season meant he had to be substituted, the first time in his career he had had to leave the field because of injury, although the latter turned out to be severe bruising to the calf and not as serious as at first thought, so he returned to the side after missing only one game. A regular in defence for the Greek national team, he won a total of 13 caps during the season.

Newcastle U (£1,300,000 from Olympiakos, Greece on 13/3/1998) PL 64+6/7 FLC 3 FAC 14/2 Others 8/1

DAILLY Christian Eduard
Born: Dundee, 23 October 1973
Height: 6'0" Weight: 12.10
Club Honours: SC '94
International Honours: S: 22; B-1; U21-34; Yth; Sch

Christian lost a pre-season battle for a place alongside Craig Short in the centre of the Blackburn defence at the start of the 1999-2000 campaign to Marlon Broomes but was restored to the team when Marlon pulled a hamstring after three games. After a quiet start he proved to be a revelation, strong in the air, decisive with his tackling and possessing pace and positional instinct. By half-way through the season he had become the linchpin of the defence. Christian was also probably Blackburn's most dangerous player in the other penalty area, his goal against West Bromwich being an effort a striker would have been proud of. He appeared regularly for Scotland and added a further eight caps during the season.

Dundee U (From juniors on 2/8/1990) SL 110+33/18 SLC 9/1 SC 10+2 Others 8+1/1
Derby Co (£1,000,000 on 12/8/1996) PL 62+5/4 FLC 6 FAC 4+1
Blackburn Rov (£5,300,000 on 22/8/1998) P/FL 57+3/4 FLC 3 FAC 4 Others 2

DALEY Anthony (Tony) Mark
Born: Birmingham, 18 October 1967
Height: 5'8" Weight: 11.7
Club Honours: FLC '94
International Honours: E: 7; B-1; Yth

The former Aston Villa winger joined Walsall on a free transfer from Watford during the 1999 close season and showed plenty of endeavour in the opening games of the new campaign. A direct player who, at his best, is a real crowd-pleaser, he likes to use his pace to terrorise defences but he failed to make a lasting impact at the Bescot Stadium and was released in mid-September, having started the first four games of the season and made four subsequent appearances as a substitute. Happily, Tony was able to show something of his old form after linking up with Forest Green in the Conference.

Aston Villa (From apprentice on 31/5/1985) F/PL 189+44/31 FLC 22+2/4 FAC 15+1/2 Others 15+2/1
Wolverhampton W (£1,250,000 on 6/6/1994) FL 16+5/3 FLC 4/1 FAC 0+2
Watford (Free on 7/8/1998) FL 6+6/1 FLC 1+1
Walsall (Free on 22/6/1999) FL 3+4 FLC 1

DALGLISH Paul
Born: Glasgow, 18 February 1977
Height: 5'10" Weight: 10.0
International Honours: S: U21-7

Originally on loan from Newcastle United at the end of the 1998-99 season, Paul completed his permanent move to Norwich in May 1999 for an initial fee of £300,000, a sum which could increase to £500,000 depending on future appearances. A regular member of Scotland's U21 set-up in recent seasons, this former Celtic, Liverpool, Newcastle and Bury (loan) front runner displayed only tantalising glimpses of his best form in 1999-2000 as he strove to establish an effective partnership with Iwan Roberts. Some of his best moments came when he was played wide on the right, where his strong running caused defenders real problems. He is quick and direct, with excellent close control and the ability to deliver telling crosses. Not a natural goalscorer, he likes to take his goal attempts early and this is an aspect of his game which will improve with experience. Comparisons with his father are inevitable, but Paul is a very confident individual who is more than able to stand on his own two feet.

Glasgow Celtic (From juniors on 20/7/1995)
Liverpool (Free on 14/8/1996)
Newcastle U (Free on 21/11/1997) PL 6+5/1 FLC 2/1
Bury (Loaned on 21/11/1997) FL 1+11 FAC 1
Norwich C (£300,000 on 25/3/1999) FL 25+11/2 FLC 2+1 FAC 1

DALLA BONA Samuelle (Sam)
Born: Venice, Italy, 6 February 1981
Height: 6'1" Weight: 12.0
International Honours: Italy: Yth

Chelsea almost caused a diplomatic incident when, in October 1998, they offered professional contracts to two of Italy's most promising youngsters, both of whom were with Bergamo-based Serie A club Atalanta. Gianluca Percassi, 18, and Sam Dalla Bona,

Nicos Dabizas

17, moved seamlessly into the cosmopolitan ambience of London, and Chelsea, while Italian soccer bosses threatened dire retribution, but the Blues had acted strictly within the post-Bosman guidelines. Sam was rated as the jewel in the crown of Italian youth football; the former captain of the *Azzurri* U16s and current U18s skipper, he is a powerfully built central midfielder with a tremendous goalscoring record, drawing comparisons with Chelsea colleague Gustavo Poyet. The highly rated prospect made his eagerly awaited debut as a late substitute in a Champions' League tie in November against Dutch champions Feyenoord at Stamford Bridge. In April he had consecutive substitute run-outs of 35 and 45 minutes against Coventry and Sheffield Wednesday respectively before a severe bout of chickenpox curtailed his season. The current Chelsea squad is the oldest in the Premiership, a fact readily acknowledged by manager Gianluca Vialli, who has pledged to "bring younger legs into the team", and Sam is a leading contender to force his way into a revamped Chelsea side during the coming season. With other budding talent such as Percassi, John Terry, Jon Harley, Mikael Forssell and Jody Morris ready to take up the baton from the current batch of superstars, the future looks extremely bright for the Blues.

Chelsea (Signed from Atalanta, Italy on 16/10/1998) PL 0+2 Others 0+1

DALTON Paul
Born: Middlesbrough, 25 April 1967
Height: 5'11" Weight: 13.0

Paul moved to Carlisle on loan from Huddersfield in December 1999 to cover for the injured Steve Soley. He showed some classy moments that demonstrated his Division One credentials, but doubts over his match fitness restricted his contribution to the United cause. Paul is a talented winger who is capable of scoring spectacular goals. He was released by Huddersfield in March.

Manchester U (£35,000 from Brandon U on 3/5/1988)
Hartlepool U (£20,000 on 4/3/1989) FL 140+11/37 FLC 10/2 FAC 7/1 Others 9/3
Plymouth Arg (£275,000 on 11/6/1992) FL 93+5/25 FLC 5/2 FAC 7/5 Others 6
Huddersfield T (Signed on 11/8/1995) FL 79+19/25 FLC 9+3/2 FAC 5+1
Carlisle U (Loaned on 16/12/1999) FL 3/1

DALY Jonathan (Jon) Marvin
Born: Dublin, Ireland, 8 January 1983
Height: 6'1" Weight: 12.4
International Honours: RoI: Yth

Jon became one of the youngest players to appear for Stockport in the club's history when he came on as a late substitute against Walsall last October when aged 16 years and 257 days. He made a further three appearances from the subs' bench before his season ended prematurely after he broke a bone in his leg playing in a youth international against Yugoslavia in March. A big and effective striker, he won seven caps for the Republic of Ireland U16s during 1999-2000.

Stockport Co (From trainee on 18/1/2000) FL 0+4

DANIELSSON Einer Thor
Born: Iceland, 19 January 1970
Height: 5'8" Weight: 11.3
International Honours: Iceland: 18

Signed on loan from KR Reykjavik by Stoke manager Gudjon Thordarson during their home country's close season, this Icelandic international, who plays wide on the left of midfield, arrived at the Britannia Stadium last November and made a dream start with an outstanding individual goal on his debut in the 4-0 win at Wycombe. While he appeared to lack the determination needed to win a regular berth, his skill and crossing abilities made him a real threat whenever he was called upon prior to his return to Iceland's capital.

Stoke C (Loaned from KR Reykjavik, Iceland on 22/11/1999) FL 3+5/1 Others 1

DARBY Duane Anthony
Born: Birmingham, 17 October 1973
Height: 5'11" Weight: 12.6

After missing most of 1998-99 through injury, Duane began the 1999-2000 season on top form, producing a series of inspirational performances up front for Notts County. Although troubled by a groin injury in the middle of the campaign, he returned to the starting line-up in March but was then surprisingly placed on the transfer list in the summer. A great favourite of the Notts supporters for his battling spirit and 100 per cent effort, Duane proved an effective target man and created many goals for leading scorer Mark Stallard. Stop Press: He joined Conference side Rushden & Diamonds in June.

Torquay U (From trainee on 3/7/1992) FL 60+48/26 FLC 4+3/1 FAC 1+4 Others 5+3/2
Doncaster Rov (£60,000 on 19/7/1995) FL 8+9/4 FLC 2 FAC 0+1 Others 1+1
Hull C (Signed on 27/3/1996) FL 75+3/27 FLC 5/1 FAC 4/6 Others 4/2
Notts Co (Free on 2/7/1998) FL 22+6/5 FLC 3+1/1
Hull C (Loaned on 25/3/1999) FL 4+4

Duane Darby

DARBY Julian Timothy
Born: Bolton, 3 October 1967
Height: 6'0" Weight: 11.4
Club Honours: AMC '89
International Honours: E: Sch

Preston's experienced midfielder rejected a move to Shrewsbury in the summer of 1999, and combined a coaching post at the club's School of Excellence with captaining the reserves, where his experience was passed on to North End's emerging stars. Still on the fringes of the first team, he featured in the FA Cup replay at Enfield, where he demonstrated that he has lost none of his tackling commitment or passing ability, while December finally saw Julian reach 400 league and 500 career appearances. He was out of contract in the summer and is expected to move further into coaching from now on.

Bolton W (From trainee on 22/7/1986) FL 258+12/36 FLC 25/8 FAC 19/3 Others 31+1/5
Coventry C (£150,000 on 28/10/1993) PL 52+3/5 FLC 3/1 FAC 2+2
West Bromwich A (£200,000 on 24/11/1995) FL 32+7/1 FAC 1 Others 4
Preston NE (£150,000 on 13/6/1997) FL 20+15/1 FLC 1+1 FAC 4+2/1 Others 4+2/1
Rotherham U (Loaned on 26/3/1998) FL 3

D'ARCY Ross
Born: Balbriggan, 21 March 1978
Height: 6'0" Weight: 12.2
International Honours: RoI: U21-6

Incisive in the tackle and blessed with meticulous distribution, the solidly built Dubliner showed fleeting glimpses of his outstanding pedigree after his arrival at Barnet from neighbours Tottenham last December. After spending much of his early career sidelined with a knee injury, he clearly relished the opportunity of league football. His debut was as a substitute in the home defeat against Reading in the Auto Windscreens Shield, but Ross displayed all the traits of a competent performer in his unaccustomed role of right back. His sole starting appearance was in the defeat at Macclesfield, where he was employed as a central midfielder in the absence of John Doolan. However, his favoured position is in the centre of defence and he has proved to be a revelation for the club's reserve side.

Tottenham H (From trainee on 1/7/1995)
Barnet (Free on 22/12/1999) FL 1+2 Others 0+1

DARLINGTON Jermaine Christopher
Born: Hackney, 11 April 1974
Height: 5'7" Weight: 10.10

Jermaine was one of the successes of the 1999-2000 season for Queens Park Rangers, having taken the jump from non-league football to Division One in his stride. He became a firm favourite with the crowd owing to his surging runs from defence and his strong tackling. Jermaine, a wing back, scored two goals during the campaign: both were long-range shots from outside the box after one of his runs from defence. Although preferring the right-hand side, he operates with equal effectiveness on either flank. Jermaine has earned the respect of his fellow professionals and was voted the Rangers' players' "Player of the Year" in the annual end-of-season ballot.

Charlton Ath (From trainee on 30/6/1992) FL 1+1 (Free to Dover Ath on 23/9/1993)
Queens Park R (£25,000 from Aylesbury U on 25/3/1999) FL 38/2 FLC 1 FAC 3

DARLOW Kieran Brian
Born: Bedford, 9 November 1982
Height: 6'0" Weight: 13.12

At the age of 17, and with only one reserve-team appearance under his belt, Kieran made his debut in York's last home game of the 1999-2000 season against Halifax. Coming on as a sub for Paul Talbot, he impressed with a storming performance down the left side, and made a further senior appearance in York's last outing at Leyton Orient. Kieran created a new club record by becoming the 35th player used by the Minstermen in league matches during the season.
York C (Trainee) FL 0+2

D'AURIA David Alan
Born: Swansea, 26 March 1970
Height: 5'10" Weight: 12.6
Club Honours: WC '94
International Honours: W: Yth

Praised by Hull manager Warren Joyce for the way he "[led] the side in very difficult circumstances and gave everything to the job", David continued as City's captain at the start of the 1999-2000 season. Unfortunately, illness and injury hampered his pre-season preparations and ruled him out of a number of matches during the opening weeks of the campaign. It was October before he re-established himself in the side and, although the team's fortunes then improved, he was sold to Chesterfield the following month in an attempt to control the crippling wage bill at Boothferry Park. An influential central midfielder, David came into a Chesterfield side short of creativity and immediately began to provide what had been lacking. He passed the ball with imagination and ran the midfield through presence alone, without recourse to the physical approach. Unfortunately, after just a handful of games he suffered a foot strain that refused to heal completely and ruled him out for the rest of the season. However, the Spireites' fans have seen enough to be confident that, when fit, David will be an important member of the side.
Swansea C (From trainee on 2/8/1988) FL 27+18/6 FLC 2+2 FAC 1 Others 4 (Free transfer to Merthyr Tydfil during 1991 close season)
Scarborough (Signed from Barry T on 22/8/1994) FL 49+3/8 FLC 3+2/1 FAC 4+1 Others 2
Scunthorpe U (£40,000 on 6/12/1995) FL 103+4/18 FLC 6 FAC 7/1 Others 4+1
Hull C (Free on 16/7/1998) FL 52+2/4 FLC 5+2 FAC 5 Others 2/1
Chesterfield (£50,000 on 25/11/1999) FL 4+1

DAVIDSON Callum Iain
Born: Stirling, 25 June 1976
Height: 5'10" Weight: 11.8
Club Honours: S Div 1 '97
International Honours: S: 12; U21-2

A Scottish international defender who can tackle with real power, stride forward purposefully and combine in attacking moves, Callum had a disappointing season with Blackburn in 1999-2000. At his best he is a solid and dependable performer, but he suffered from inconsistency. Dropped at times in favour of both Jeff Kenna and Steve Harkness, he regained his place but never truly played to his potential. Disappointingly, his form for Rovers rarely matched his performance at Wembley for Scotland against England. He remained a regular for Scotland, adding a further five caps.
St Johnstone (From juniors on 8/6/1994) SL 39+5/4 SLC 1 Others 3
Blackburn Rov (£1,750,000 on 12/2/1998) P/FL 63+2/1 FLC 3+1 FAC 6 Others 1+1

DAVIDSON Ross James
Born: Chertsey, 13 November 1973
Height: 5'9" Weight: 12.4

Chester's "Player of the Year" in 1998-99 made only 13 more appearances for the depleted Blues before joining Third Division promotion hopefuls Barnet on non-contract terms last November. A solid, dependable right back who likes to get forward and link up with the attack, Ross is a strong tackler and also has a tremendous shot. Barnet manager John Still had been pursuing him for more than 18 months and he made an impressive debut against Darlington, looking irresistible as he overlapped down the right flank. However, Ross was unable to establish himself as a first choice in the Bees' line-up, and Sam Stockley was able to reclaim his place. After playing against his previous club in January, Ross was reunited with former Chester manager Kevin Ratcliffe at Shrewsbury in March. Ironically, he made his debut in the vital relegation battle at Chester, producing a "Man of the Match" performance in the ultimately decisive goalless draw, and although he had some difficulty settling into a struggling side he played a leading role in Town's successful battle to retain their league status.
Sheffield U (Signed from Walton & Hersham on 5/6/1993) FL 2 Others 2
Chester C (Free on 26/1/1996) FL 132/5 FLC 11 FAC 3+1 Others 4
Barnet (Free on 5/11/1999) FL 8+1 Others 1
Shrewsbury T (Free on 9/3/2000) FL 9+1

DAVIES Gareth Melville
Born: Hereford, 11 December 1973
Height: 6'1" Weight: 11.12
International Honours: W: U21-8

The 1999-2000 campaign proved a frustrating time for Gareth as Swindon struggled unsuccessfully against relegation and he was dogged by ongoing injury problems. Having missed November with knee trouble, he then suffered a further knee injury against Nottingham Forest in March that required surgery and brought his season to a premature close. A tall, no-nonsense centre back who can marshal his defence well, Gareth is sound in the tackle and a good man marker.
Hereford U (From trainee on 10/4/1992) FL 91+4/1 FLC 5+2 FAC 4 Others 5
Crystal Palace (£120,000 on 1/7/1995) F/PL 22+5/2 FAC 2 Others 1
Cardiff C (Loaned on 21/2/1997) FL 6/2
Reading (£100,000 on 12/12/1997) FL 18+1 FLC 1 FAC 3
Swindon T (Free on 2/3/1999) FL 24 FLC 1 FAC 0+1

DAVIES Kevin Cyril
Born: Sheffield, 26 March 1977
Height: 6'0" Weight: 13.6
International Honours: E: U21-3; Yth

After a nightmare season at Blackburn in 1998-99, Kevin was desperate to prove himself at the start of the new campaign but after two disappointing matches he returned to Southampton in a deal which took Egil Ostenstad in the opposite direction. By his own admission, his rehabilitation took four months but then three goals in as many matches signalled the return to form he had hoped for. A target man, his strength in the air proved invaluable to the Saints and for someone of his powerful build he has a surprising turn of speed. Recalled to the England U21 set-up last March, he made a substitute appearance against Yugoslavia in Barcelona.
Chesterfield (From trainee on 18/4/1994) FL 113+16/22 FLC 7+2/1 FAC 10/6 Others 9+2/1
Southampton (£750,000 on 14/5/1997) PL 20+5/9 FLC 3+1/3 FAC 1
Blackburn Rov (£7,250,000 on 2/6/1998) P/FL 11+12/1 FLC 3 FAC 2/1 Others 1
Southampton (Signed on 18/8/1999) PL 9+4/6 FLC 0+1 FAC 1

DAVIES Simon
Born: Haverfordwest, 23 October 1979
Height: 5'10" Weight: 11.4
International Honours: W: B-1; U21-6; Yth

Simon entered the Peterborough record books when, amid mounting speculation, he was transferred to Tottenham for a fee of £700,000 last January. Sell-on clauses should eventually increase the fee for the highly rated Wales U21 international who, according to newspaper reports, was on the verge of a £3.6 million move to Manchester United in July 1999. Along with Matthew Etherington, who joined him in the switch to Spurs, he had an extended trial at Old Trafford in the 1999 close season and played in a private friendly game against Boca Juniors. Despite further interest from Sunderland and Aston Villa, the brilliant young midfielder signed an improved five-year contract with Peterborough in August. With Posh losing a reported £30,000 per week, his departure from the London Road ranks appeared inevitable, though. Simon made three appearances for Tottenham, featuring in the starting line-up against Manchester United at Old Trafford, and looked very sharp, with the ability to use both feet when shooting on goal. He is one of the talented young players who are likely to shape the future of the club.
Peterborough U (From trainee on 21/7/1997) FL 63+2/6 FLC 4 FAC 3 Others 3
Tottenham H (£700,000 on 10/1/2000) PL 1+2

DAVIES Simon Ithel
Born: Winsford, 23 April 1974
Height: 6'0" Weight: 11.11
Club Honours: FAYC '92
International Honours: W: 1

On his day, the Macclesfield midfielder can be as good as any in the Third Division. However, while he possesses skill and strength, the former Manchester United player is sometimes criticised for holding on to the ball too long. Subject of a bizarre sending-off during the home match with York, Simon was dismissed a full two minutes after the incident. Otherwise, he established a regular place in his first full season at Moss Rose, and will be striving for greater consistency in 2000-01.

Manchester U (From trainee on 6/7/1992) PL 4+7 FLC 4+2 Others 2+1/1
Exeter C (Loaned on 17/12/1993) FL 5+1/1 FAC 1
Huddersfield T (Loaned on 29/10/1996) FL 3
Luton T (£150,000 on 5/8/1997) FL 10+12/1 FLC 3+1 FAC 0+1 Others 3
Macclesfield T (Signed on 17/12/1998) FL 39+9/3 FLC 2 FAC 3 Others 1/1

DAVIS Sean
Born: Clapham, 20 September 1979
Height: 5'10" Weight: 12.0

Sean made his league debut for Fulham only three weeks after his 17th birthday back in October 1996 and hoped that 1999-2000 would be the season when he became a first-team regular. It was obviously going to be difficult with the experienced Lee Clark, Wayne Collins, Steve Hayward and Stephen Hughes (on loan from Arsenal) also involved in the competition for three places in midfield. He began the season well, scoring his first senior goal in the Worthington Cup win at Northampton, and kept his place for the first eight games. Sean was either in the team or on the substitutes' bench until Kevin Ball arrived in January, but after that he started only one game. He is a very talented young midfielder and must hope that he will be given more opportunities by his new manager, Jean Tigana, in 2000-01.

Fulham (From trainee on 2/7/1998) FL 16+17 FLC 3+3/2 FAC 2+1/1

DAVIS Solomon (Sol) Sebastian
Born: Cheltenham, 4 September 1979
Height: 5'8" Weight: 11.0

This young Swindon defender made sound progress in 1999-2000 despite the club's disappointing season. He established himself as a regular in the first-team line-up at left back and was rewarded in the summer when he was given a two-year contract by new boss Colin Todd. Sol has good pace, an excellent attitude to the game and shows 100 per cent commitment to the team.

Swindon T (From trainee on 29/5/1998) FL 49+10 FLC 2 FAC 1

DAVIS Stephen (Steve) Mark
Born: Hexham, 30 October 1968
Height: 6'2" Weight: 14.7
Club Honours: Div 4 '92

Burnley's record signing had another highly consistent season in 1999-2000. With solid support at the back from Mitchell Thomas and latterly Ian Cox, he was a central defender whom few Second Division forwards could expect to master, equally solid in the air and on the ground. His attacking qualities were perhaps seen less often than some supporters would have liked, but his solo runs were invariably crowd-pleasers and he still has an eye for goal. A constant danger at set pieces, Steve took over the captaincy of the side when Gordon Armstrong lost his place – a role to which he is ideally suited and in which he has plenty of experience. After a fairly quiet season on the goalscoring front by his usual standards, he found the net regularly in the run-in to promotion to end the season as Burnley's joint second-top scorer in the league. Steve's dependable performances once again earned him a place in the PFA award-winning Second Division side.

Southampton (From trainee on 6/7/1987) FL 5+1
Burnley (Loaned on 21/11/1989) FL 7+2
Notts Co (Loaned on 28/3/1991) FL 0+2
Burnley (£60,000 on 17/8/1991) FL 162/22 FLC 10/2 FAC 18/1 Others 13
Luton T (£750,000 on 13/7/1995) FL 137+1/21 FLC 19/3 FAC 5/2 Others 10/1
Burnley (£800,000 on 21/12/1998) FL 61/11 FLC 1 FAC 4 Others 1

DAVIS Steven (Steve) Peter
Born: Birmingham, 26 July 1965
Height: 6'0" Weight: 12.12
International Honours: E: Yth

A dependable centre back who is good in the air and strong in the tackle, Steve once again had an injury-interrupted season with Oxford in 1999-2000, although this time none of the injuries was long term. When he was in the team his experience helped tremendously and his return to the side for the last four games was vital, especially as the central defender knocked in a vital equaliser at Bristol City to earn a valuable point. At the veteran stage of his career now and not as quick as he used to be, Steve is still an asset to the side.

Crewe Alex (Free from Stoke C juniors on 17/8/1983) FL 140+5/1 FLC 10 FAC 3 Others 7+1
Burnley (£15,000 on 3/10/1987) FL 147/11 FLC 7 FAC 9 Others 19/1
Barnsley (£180,000 on 26/7/1991) FL 103+4/10 FLC 9 FAC 3
York C (Loaned on 12/9/1997) FL 2/1
Oxford U (£75,000 on 16/2/1998) FL 38+4/3 FLC 4 FAC 1 Others 0+1

DAVISON Aidan John
Born: Sedgefield, 11 May 1968
Height: 6'1" Weight: 13.12
Club Honours: AMC '98
International Honours: NI: 3; B-1

Signed by Sheffield United manager Adrian Heath on a free transfer from Grimsby on the eve of the 1999-2000 season after the sale of Alan Kelly, this dependable goal-keeper made his first appearance for his new club as a substitute at Manchester City after Simon Tracey was sent off and his first action for the Blades was to pick the ball out of the net following the resultant penalty. Aidan went on to concede a total of five goals – making it the worst, and probably the unluckiest, debut by a United 'keeper – as the Blades' defence collapsed. His one other outing for the club was more successful: a competent performance in the 3-1 victory over Crystal Palace. Tracey's good form kept Aidan on the bench until he moved to Bradford City in December as cover for regular 'keepers Matt Clarke and Gary Walsh. He made his debut for the Bantams at Watford in January when Clarke was injured and appeared in the next five games without letting the team down. An excellent shot stopper who has quick reflexes, Aidan eventually signed a three-and-a-half-year contract in March that will keep him at Valley Parade for the foreseeable future.

Notts Co (Signed from Billingham Synthonia on 25/3/1988) FL 1
Bury (£6,000 on 7/10/1989)
Millwall (Free on 14/8/1991) FL 34 FLC 3 FAC 3 Others 2
Bolton W (£25,000 on 26/7/1993) P/FL 35+2 FAC 8 Others 4
Hull C (Loaned on 29/11/1996) FL 9 Others 1
Bradford C (Free on 14/3/1997) FL 10
Grimsby T (Free on 16/7/1997) FL 77 FLC 10 FAC 7 Others 10
Sheffield U (Free on 6/8/1999) FL 1+1
Bradford C (Loaned on 4/1/2000) PL 5+1

Aidan Davison

DAWS Nicholas (Nick) John
Born: Manchester, 15 March 1970
Height: 5'11" Weight: 13.2
Club Honours: Div 2 '97

Bury's captain and longest-serving player, this midfield workhorse perhaps experienced one of his more disappointing seasons in recent years in 1999-2000, in terms of reproducing his best form week in, week out. The experienced campaigner nevertheless always faced each challenge head on and never hid when his form dipped or the going got tough. Indeed, Nick's record with the Shakers now sees him ranked among the very best in the club's history. With 325 league games for Bury, he lies in tenth place in the club's all-time list of appearances. He also recorded a personal milestone by recently completing a run of 218 consecutive league and cup games for the club. The run, which stretched right back to December 1995, finally ended with suspension for the home game against Oldham on 4 March.

Bury (£10,000 from Altrincham on 13/8/1992) FL 312+13/13 FLC 23+3/3 FAC 17 Others 14+2/1

Nick Daws

DAWSON Andrew (Andy)
Born: Northallerton, 20 October 1978
Height: 5'9" Weight: 10.2

A left back who loves to get forward, Andy had a solid second season with Scunthorpe in 1999-2000, although his pace and defensive skills were better tested in Division Two. He was an ever-present up to a freak accident in November when a piece of roast beef got stuck in his throat and left him briefly fighting for his life in a "critical" condition in hospital. He soon returned to action and even made a few appearances in a central midfield role, where he opened his goalscoring account for the season in the 1-1 draw at Bournemouth in January.

Nottingham F (From trainee on 31/10/1995) FLC 1
Scunthorpe U (£70,000 on 18/12/1998) FL 64+3/2 FLC 2 FAC 1 Others 5/1

DAWSON Andrew Stephen
Born: York, 8 December 1979
Height: 6'0" Weight: 11.7

In his second season as a professional for York, this promising young defender or midfielder was a regular in the senior squad for the first half of the 1999-2000 campaign. The local lad is one of the highly rated youngsters who have come up from the club's School of Excellence.

York C (From trainee on 2/7/1998) FL 18+10/1 FLC 2 FAC 1 Others 1

DAWSON Kevin Edward
Born: Northallerton, 18 June 1981
Height: 6'0" Weight: 10.10

Kevin is a product of Nottingham Forest's excellent youth scheme. He made his senior debut against Fulham last December and featured in a total of eight first-team games for the Reds. Although not particularly tall, he has a big heart and great confidence. He will be looking to appear more regularly in the first-team set-up in the coming season.

Nottingham F (From trainee on 25/6/1998) FL 4+3 FAC 1

DAY Christopher (Chris) Nicholas
Born: Walthamstow, 28 July 1975
Height: 6'3" Weight: 13.6
International Honours: E: U21-6; Yth (UEFA-U18 '93)

Chris is a promising goalkeeper who, at the age of 24, has made fewer than 50 first-team appearances for three clubs. Having spent two seasons in the reserves at Watford as understudy to the consistent Alec Chamberlain, Chris was thrown in at the deep end at the start of 1999-2000 when Chamberlain dislocated a finger during pre-season training and he found himself facing Wimbledon on the opening day of the new campaign. Understandably nervous, Chris must have been disappointed to concede three goals, including an unfortunate own goal following a misunderstanding with Richard Johnson. However, he bounced back by keeping a clean sheet at Anfield after an inspired performance. Once Chamberlain was fit, Chris returned to the reserves, but he enjoyed another brief spell in the first team during February and was recalled for the last three games of the season before being released in the summer.

Tottenham H (From trainee on 16/4/1993)
Crystal Palace (£225,000 + on 9/8/1996) FL 24 FLC 2 FAC 2
Watford (£225,000 on 18/7/1997) PL 11 FLC 1 Others 1

DAY James (Jamie) Russell
Born: Bexley, 13 September 1979
Height: 5'7" Weight: 10.12
International Honours: E: Sch

This former England schools international found his opportunities limited at Bournemouth during the 1998-99 season. After appearing in a couple of games last autumn he managed a run of six successive matches, scoring his first senior goal in the 2-1 win at Cambridge, but then rarely featured in the second half of the campaign. Although mainly used by the Cherries as a left-sided midfielder, he can also play as an orthodox full back. Jamie showed that he possesses good defensive qualities, some useful touches and a decent pass.

Arsenal (From trainee on 3/7/1997)
Bournemouth (£20,000 on 3/3/1999) FL 9+4/1 FLC 1+1 FAC 2 Others 1

DEANE Brian Christopher
Born: Leeds, 7 February 1968
Height: 6'3" Weight: 12.7
International Honours: E: 3; B-3

A combination of leg and rib injuries and suspension ensured that Brian missed a significant part of Middlesbrough's 1999-2000 season. Manager Bryan Robson knew that the gritty striker, now an integral part of the furniture at the Riverside, would give his all to help his team to victory when he got back to something like fitness, and Brian was pitched straight into the fray as soon as his injuries were almost healed. He didn't have the benefit of reserve-game action to fall back on, but he does possess an abundance of spirit and was soon leading the line with his customary aggression. A powerful striker who is good in the air, Brian is an effective target man as well as a dependable goalscorer.

Doncaster Rov (From juniors on 14/12/1985) FL 59+7/12 FLC 3 FAC 2+1/1 Others 2+2
Sheffield U (£30,000 on 19/7/1988) F/PL 197/82 FLC 16/11 FAC 23+1/11 Others 2/2
Leeds U (£2,900,000 on 14/7/1993) PL 131+7/32 FLC 8+3/2 FAC 13+3/4 Others 3
Sheffield U (£1,500,000 on 29/7/1997) FL 24/11 FLC 4/2 FAC 1 (£1,000,000 to Benfica, Portugal on 15/1/1998)
Middlesbrough (£3,000,000 on 16/10/1998) PL 53+2/15 FLC 3+1 FAC 2/1

DEARDEN Kevin Charles
Born: Luton, 8 March 1970
Height: 5'11" Weight: 13.4

This experienced lower-division goalkeeper joined Wrexham as a free agent in the summer of 1999 on a two-year contract. He proved to be a fine shot stopper for the Robins in 1999-2000 and produced an excellent performance in the FA Cup victory over Premiership giants Middlesbrough. However, perhaps his best save of the season came against Burnley last March when he denied the visitors' Andy Payton with a breathtaking point-blank save. Kevin is due to undergo minor surgery for a knee problem over the summer break.

Tottenham H (From trainee on 5/8/1988) PL 0+1 FLC 1
Cambridge U (Loaned on 9/3/1989) FL 15
Hartlepool U (Loaned on 31/8/1989) FL 10
Swindon T (Loaned on 23/3/1990) FL 1
Peterborough U (Loaned on 24/8/1990) FL 7
Hull C (Loaned on 10/1/1991) FL 3
Rochdale (Loaned on 16/8/1991) FL 2
Birmingham C (Loaned on 19/3/1992) FL 12
Brentford (Free on 30/9/1993) FL 205 FLC 17 FAC 13 Others 19
Barnet (Loaned on 5/2/1999) FL 1
Wrexham (Free on 4/6/1999) FL 45 FLC 2 FAC 5

DE BILDE Gilles Roger Gerard
Born: Zellik, Belgium, 9 June 1971
Height: 5'11" Weight: 11.6
International Honours: Belgium: 24

Sheffield Wednesday had high expectations of this Belgian international striker when he signed in the 1999 close season for a £3 million fee. He found himself playing in a team struggling at the foot of the table, and although he finished leading scorer with ten goals he failed to prevent the Owls from being relegated. He is a quality player with good pace and some neat touches but never really seemed to deliver his full potential at Hillsborough. Gilles was recalled to the Belgium team last September and won a further seven caps during the season, including an appearance as a substitute against Turkey in the Euro 2000 finals.

Sheffield Wed (£3,000,000 from PSV Eindhoven, Holland on 19/7/1999) PL 37+1/10 FLC 3/1 FAC 4

DE BLASIIS Jean Yves
Born: Bordeaux, France, 25 September 1973
Height: 5'9" Weight: 11.5
International Honours: France: Yth

A summer "Bosman" signing from Red Star Paris, this competitive midfielder quickly adjusted to the demands of the English game during his first season with Norwich in 1999-2000, holding down a regular place in the team until sustaining a cruciate ligament injury just two days into Bryan Hamilton's reign in mid-March. Primarily a defensive player, he enjoyed a stint at left wing back in mid-season, a role to which he easily adapted. Strong in the tackle, he has a good range of passing and the ability to link with his front players, although he has yet to break his English goalscoring duck. Prior to Red Star he played for Bordeaux and Caen and won French international honours at U16, '17, '18 and '20 levels.

Norwich C (Free from Paris Red Star, France on 31/7/1999) FL 26+2 FLC 1+1 FAC 1

DE FREITAS Fabian
Born: Surinam, 28 July 1972
Height: 6'0" Weight: 12.2

Fabian did not have a very successful season in 1999-2000. He was in and out of the West Bromwich Albion side throughout the campaign and in fact was named as a substitute more times than he actually started a match. Not for want of trying, he unfortunately failed to score a single league goal (in 23 outings) and as the season wore on he became more and more frustrated, although injuries didn't help matters. Unable to attain full match fitness, at times he lacked mobility when chosen, but he was a fighter and, although not at his best, he still gave all he had in the games for which he was selected.

Bolton W (£400,000 from Volendam, Holland on 19/8/1994) F/PL 24+16/7 FLC 2+4 FAC 1 Others 0+2/2 (Free to Osasuna, Spain on 6/9/1996)
West Bromwich A (Free on 21/8/1998) FL 34+27/8 FLC 5/2 FAC 1+1

DEGN Peter
Born: Aarhus, Denmark, 6 April 1977
Height: 5'10" Weight: 12.6
International Honours: Denmark: U21

A Danish U21 international, Peter made just one senior appearance for Everton last season – and even that ended after just 45 minutes. A curtailed Worthington Cup run-out against Oxford United was the only senior workout of 1999-2000 for a player comfortable anywhere down the right flank. After that his appearances were restricted exclusively to reserve-team action.

Everton (£200,000 from Aarhus, Denmark on 23/2/1999) PL 0+4 FLC 1

DE GOEY Eduard (Ed) Franciscus
Born: Gouda, Holland, 20 December 1966
Height: 6'6" Weight: 15.0
Club Honours: FLC '98; ECWC '98; ESC '98; FAC '00
International Honours: Holland: 31; U21-17

Ed had a tremendous 1999-2000 season in the Chelsea goal, setting the benchmark for consistency and breaking two 28-year-old club records in the process. His 27 clean sheets in a season took Peter Bonetti's record set in 1971-72 and his 59 first-team appearances in a season superseded John Hollins's total of 58 set in the same season. Ed was rested for the final Premiership match of the campaign and this prevented him from being ever present in the league. His calm authority and sheer physical presence were major factors in Chelsea returning the joint-best home defensive record in the Premiership – just 12 goals conceded, a total matched only by Aston Villa. A courageous 'keeper and surprisingly agile for such a big man, Ed also has a big-match temperament, as his peerless displays in Chelsea's two outstanding cup runs demonstrated. During the Champions' League exploits he defied some of Europe's top strikers, particularly against AC Milan, Lazio and Barcelona at Stamford Bridge, while in the FA Cup semi-final he kept the Blues alive with some superb saves before Gustavo Poyet's header clinched a place in the final, in which Ed kept another clean sheet, defying Aston Villa and guiding Chelsea to an FA Cup triumph. His performances over the past three seasons have established him as a crowd favourite and by common consent he is second only to the legendary Bonetti in Chelsea's list of all-time goalkeepers. Ed was recalled to the Holland squad for the Euro 2000 championship but remained third-choice behind Edwin van der Sar and Sander Westerveld and did not add to his total caps.

Chelsea (£2,250,000 from Feyenoord, Holland, via Sparta Rotterdam, on 10/7/1997) PL 100 FLC 4 FAC 13 Others 34

DELANEY Mark Anthony
Born: Fishguard, 13 May 1976
Height: 6'1" Weight: 11.7
International Honours: W: 4

Mark began the 1999-2000 campaign as first choice at right wing back for Aston Villa but then lost his place in mid-September to Steve Watson, his rival for the position. He returned to the side for a short spell in the autumn before establishing himself as a regular in the second half of the season, going on to make an appearance in the FA Cup final against Chelsea to crown a fine first full season in the Premiership. He is a busy player with good pace and is excellent when moving forward to help the midfield. Perhaps his best performance was against Arsenal last March, when he coped admirably with the threat of Marc Overmars. Mark also made his bow on the international scene last season, making his debut for Wales against Switzerland last October and adding further appearances against Qatar, Brazil and Portugal.

Cardiff C (Free from Carmarthen on 3/7/1998) FL 28 FLC 2 FAC 5/1
Aston Villa (£250,000 + on 10/3/1999) PL 25+5/1 FLC 1+2 FAC 4+1

DELAP Rory John
Born: Sutton Coldfield, 6 July 1976
Height: 6'0" Weight: 12.10
Club Honours: AMC '97
International Honours: RoI: 6; B-1; U21-4

The young Republic of Ireland international had quite a season for Derby in 1999-2000. Beginning the campaign as a right-sided defender, he also found himself being asked to play, at times, in midfield and up front. He caught the attention of the wider public after a spectacular long-distance strike against Arsenal in front of the Sky cameras, and continued to find the net throughout the season. Rory is equally adept in his defensive duties, but one of his major qualities is the pace which he brings to the right side of Derby's line-up, and he operates especially well in a right-wing-back role. He also possesses a notable long throw. Rory was capped three more times by the Republic of Ireland during the season.

Carlisle U (From trainee on 18/7/1994) FL 40+25/7 FLC 4+1 FAC 0+3 Others 12+2
Derby Co (£500,000 + on 6/2/1998) PL 65+5/8 FLC 5/1 FAC 1+1

DELORGE Laurent Jan
Born: Leuven, Belgium, 21 July 1979
Height: 5'10" Weight: 12.0

Laurent is a highly rated winger who was signed by Coventry for £1.25 million in October 1998, having only made nine appearances for Ghent in Belgium. Last season he unfortunately picked up a number of niggling injuries after recovering from the broken leg he suffered soon after arriving in England. He appeared on the bench a number of times after Christmas before coming on as a substitute in the fateful Charlton FA Cup tie, which City lost 2-3 having led 2-0 early on.

Coventry C (£1,250,000 from KAA Gent, Belgium on 12/11/1998) FAC 0+1

DE ORNELAS Fernando
Born: Caracas, Venezuela, 29 July 1976
Height: 6'0" Weight: 11.7
International Honours: Venezuela: 2

Fernando is a Venezuelan international striker who had a short spell as a non-contract player with Crystal Palace last autumn following two seasons in Hong Kong. A regular first-team squad member during his time at Selhurst Park, he moved on after suffering a hamstring injury. He later had a trial in Spain with Real Zaragoza before joining Celtic, where he made a couple of brief appearances as a substitute. His form won him a recall to the national team and he appeared as a substitute in the World Cup qualifying match with Colombia in June.

Crystal Palace (Free from Happy Valley, Hong Kong, via Deportivo Chacao, South China, on 30/9/1999) FL 5+4

DERRY Shaun Peter
Born: Nottingham, 6 December 1977
Height: 5'10" Weight: 10.13
Club Honours: Div 3 '98

Much was expected of this young Sheffield United player in 1999-2000 and he was a regular member of the side until his transfer to Portsmouth in March. He missed just two games, playing mainly on the right side of midfield, though sometimes in a more defensive role. A calm but tireless worker who can produce a telling pass, he scored his first goal for the club in the FA Cup at Rushden & Diamonds and he was also successful in the penalty shoot-out in that game. Signed by Portsmouth manager Tony Pulis to add strength to the midfield, Shaun showed himself to be an excellent acquisition over the final nine games of the season. Strong and composed, he added balance to the Pompey midfield and scored a brilliant solo goal on his home debut against West Bromwich Albion. A fine man marker, he gave 100 per cent commitment and his powerful long throws proved more than useful.

Notts Co (From trainee on 13/4/1996) FL 76+3/4 FLC 4+1 FAC 6+1/1 Others 3
Sheffield U (£700,000 on 26/1/1998) FL 62+10 FLC 4 FAC 7/1
Portsmouth (£300,000 + on 16/3/2000) FL 9/1

DERVELD Fernando

Born: Vlissingen, Holland, 22 October 1976
Height: 6'2" Weight: 12.8

Fernando arrived at Norwich on a short-term contract from FC Haarlem in Holland on transfer deadline day and impressed manager Bryan Hamilton sufficiently to earn a two-year contract. He originally came to England for a one-match trial with the reserves in February, when Bruce Rioch was in charge, before Hamilton opted to have an extended look at him. A strapping left back, Fernando appears to have all the attributes required to be effective in a more central defensive position in the future. He is very strong and more than useful in the air, and also possesses good pace for someone so physically imposing. As is so often the case with Continental imports, he has good touch and technique, and he is particularly adept at getting forward from his full-back position. Fernando made his debut in a 1-0 victory over Wolves in mid-April and featured in the starting line-up for each of Norwich's last five matches.

Norwich C (£150,000 + from Haarlem, Holland on 23/3/2000) FL 5

DESAILLY Marcel

Born: Accra, Ghana, 7 September 1968
Height: 6'1" Weight: 13.5
Club Honours: ESC '98; FAC '00
International Honours: France: 72 (WC '98, UEFA '00)

A magnificent player with a commanding presence, Marcel reaffirmed his position among the top echelon of contemporary central defenders with a string of peerless performances for Chelsea last season, particularly against Europe's leading strikers in the Champions' League. Although he sometimes seems to cruise through matches, he has the priceless ability – something he shares with team-mates Ed de Goey, Didier Deschamps, Tore Andre Flo and Gianfranco Zola – to raise his game for the big occasion. The majestic Frenchman put in two superlative performances against his old club AC Milan, shackling the dangerous strike force of Andrei Shevchenko and Oliver Bierhoff while receiving rapturous applause from the Milanese fans, who still accord him hero status. In the second phase Italian championship contenders Lazio were hot favourites to beat Chelsea in the Olympic Stadium but their fearsome forward line featuring players of the calibre of Simone Inzaghi, Roberto Mancini, Marcelo Salas and Alen Boksic was shut out by a Blues defence imperiously marshalled by Marcel. Chelsea qualified for the quarter-finals at the expense of another of his former clubs, Marseille, and fought out two titanic clashes with Barcelona, Marcel bravely leading a rearguard action at the Nou Camp as ten-man Chelsea vainly strove to reach the semi-finals. He was no less commanding on the domestic front: his athleticism and tough tackling were major factors in Chelsea's Scrooge-like defence, their total of 34 goals conceded being the third-lowest in the Premiership. As with the Champions' League, the FA Cup brought out the best in Marcel, who gave "Man of the Match" performances in the Wembley semi-final and the final itself. He lived up to his nickname of "The Rock" in the semi, when an Alan Shearer-inspired Newcastle almost wrested control of the match away from Chelsea in the second half but his resolute defending defied the Magpies before Gustavo Poyet headed a breakaway winner. In the final Aston Villa's Dion Dublin posed a different threat with his dangerous headwork, but Marcel stuck to his task superbly to nullify Villa's long-ball game and pave the way for Chelsea's FA Cup triumph. Widely recognised as one of the greatest of modern-day defenders, he has all the attributes of a world-class centre back: strength, speed, awareness, power in the air and the ability to step up into midfield and deliver probing passes. He appeared regularly for France throughout the season and was an ever-present in the team that won the Euro 2000 championship in magnificent style.

Chelsea (£4,600,000 from AC Milan, Italy, via Nantes and Marseilles, on 14/7/1998) PL 53+1/1 FAC 10 Others 24/1

DESCHAMPS Didier

Born: Bayonne, France, 15 October 1968
Height: 5'8" Weight: 11.3
Club Honours: FAC '00
International Honours: France: 101 (WC '98, UEFA '00)

Once again using their Italian connections, Chelsea swooped to clinch the signing of Didier Deschamps from Juventus in July 1999 in order to boost their Champions' League prospects. The French central midfield player has had one of the most successful careers in football history, winning French and Italian league titles and two European Cups – he skippered Marseille to victory in 1993 and was a member of the victorious Juventus side of 1996 under captain Gianluca Vialli. But all these achievements were eclipsed in Paris in July 1998, when he lifted the World Cup as captain of the triumphant French team which had destroyed Brazil. When Juventus underwent one of their periodic upheavals "Didi" jumped at the chance to join Chelsea and link up again with Vialli and fellow World Cup winners Frank Leboeuf and Marcel Desailly; Vialli is a close friend from their days in Turin and Desailly has been Didier's closest friend in football since their days as 15-year-olds at Nantes's youth academy and their time together at Marseille. As befits his reputation, Didier is a "big-match" player with the perfect temperament who always puts the needs of the team before any personal glory, and revels in the necessary, if unglamorous, aspects of a midfield player's craft: tackling, covering, supporting and generally going in where the boots are flying. He struck up a fine understanding with the feisty Dennis Wise and the pair were particularly effective in the Blues' midfield during the club's run in the Champions' League, outplaying the celebrated midfields of AC Milan, Lazio, and Barcelona along the way. His experience was also invaluable in Chelsea's run to the FA Cup final, the Frenchman playing in every match with his customary aplomb and commitment and earning a winners' medal. His deep-lying role does not allow many opportunities for strikes on goal, but the one goal he did manage during the course of the season, against Hertha Berlin, was truly memorable: he won the ball in midfield with a crunching tackle, strode forward and unleashed a swerving drive into the roof of the net from outside the box. Described in derogatory terms by a jealous Eric Cantona as "a water carrier", Didier has overcome that shallow jibe and proved himself to be the consummate professional, playing the game in an unfussy, uncomplicated fashion and giving the flair players a platform on which to perform. During the season he broke two more records: he has made the most appearances in Champions' League matches and has become the most-capped French player. He went on to become the first man to win 100 caps for France when he appeared against Portugal in the Euro 2000 semi-final and subsequently led *les Bleus* to victory in the tournament with the sensational defeat of Italy in the final. Some "water carrier"!

Chelsea (£3,000,000 from Juventus, Italy on 9/7/1999) PL 24+3 FAC 6 Others 14/1

DEVANEY Martin Thomas

Born: Cheltenham, 1 June 1980
Height: 5'10" Weight: 11.12

Martin is an exciting young striker who was born in Cheltenham of Irish parents, but joined Cheltenham Town after a three-year spell with Coventry. He began 1999-2000 on the left side of midfield but missed the middle part of the season with a broken foot sustained in a reserve-team game. He returned in March to partner Neil Grayson in attack and was a revelation, scoring four goals in his first seven games. A pacy player, Martin has the ability to bamboozle defenders with his quick feet and has already proved himself to be a cool finisher. Still only 19, he has a lot to learn but is an excellent prospect.

Coventry C (From trainee on 4/6/1997)
Cheltenham T (Free on 5/8/1999) FL 19+7/6 FLC 2

DEVINE Sean Thomas

Born: Lewisham, 6 September 1972
Height: 6'0" Weight: 13.6
Club Honours: FAYC '91
International Honours: RoI: B-1

The Wycombe striker enjoyed a magnificent season in 1999-2000, establishing a new club record by scoring 23 times in Nationwide League games. His second-half hat-trick against Reading in October was perhaps his most memorable feat, but he found the net regularly throughout the campaign. His prolific scoring rate is partly explained by a tendency to shoot at every opportunity, but he is also adept at taking on 'keepers in one-to-one situations. Sean is a crack shot with either foot, retains a cool head at all times and possesses excellent predatory instincts inside the box. His many talents extend well beyond scoring goals, for he is also an excellent deliverer of crosses from the left flank, has neat dribbling skills and holds the ball up well. If he continues to produce such a high standard of play he will soon be in contention for a place in the Republic of Ireland international squad.

Millwall (From trainee on 4/5/1991. Free to Bromley in August 1992)
Barnet (£10,000 from Famagusta, Cyprus on 5/10/1995) FL 112+14/47 FLC 9/3 FAC 5/5 Others 6
Wycombe W (£220,000 + on 18/3/1999) FL 50+1/31 FLC 4/1 FAC 5/1

Sean Devine

DEVLIN Paul John
Born: Birmingham, 14 April 1972
Height: 5'9" Weight: 11.5
Club Honours: AIC '95

Once Paul had established himself as the first-choice wide-right player at Sheffield United his 1999-2000 season blossomed, and he was a key factor in the Blades' revival after the arrival of Neil Warnock. Never a player to shirk a challenge, he succeeded, in the latter half of the season, in curbing his tendency to over-react. His speed, hard work, ability to beat a man and searching centres led to many goals and other chances. His knack of being in the right place and his hard, accurate shot meant his goal tally reached double figures. This included his memorable effort against Portsmouth in December (Warnock's first game in charge) when Paul ran half the length of the pitch before scoring with a shot from outside the penalty area. Many of the Blades' better performances were when Paul was playing well and he was chosen as the supporters' club "Player of the Year".

Notts Co (£40,000 from Stafford R on 22/2/1992) FL 132+9/25 FLC 11+1/1 FAC 8/1 Others 17+2/4
Birmingham C (Signed on 29/2/1996) FL 61+15/28 FLC 8+1/4 FAC 3+1/2
Sheffield U (£200,000 + on 13/3/1998) FL 67+20/17 FLC 3+3 FAC 6/1 Others 2
Notts Co (Loaned on 23/10/1998) FL 5

DE-VULGT Leigh Stewart
Born: Swansea, 17 March 1981
Height: 5'9" Weight: 11.2
International Honours: W: Yth

In his first year as a professional with Swansea, Leigh was capped at U18 level for Wales against Georgia at Merthyr in September 1999, then scored a spectacular equaliser in an U18 match against Italy, despite playing in an unaccustomed midfield role. Usually a full back, he made a couple of first-team appearances for the Swans in Welsh Premier Cup ties before he made his first league appearance as a substitute at Leyton Orient. Leigh's full debut followed in the Auto Windscreens Shield tie at Exeter City.

Swansea C (From trainee on 5/7/1999) FL 0+2 Others 1

DE WAARD Raymond
Born: Rotterdam, Holland, 27 March 1973
Height: 6'1" Weight: 13.6

Raymond is a tall, rangy left-winger who arrived at Norwich from Dutch top-flight outfit Cambuur Leeuwarden immediately prior to transfer deadline day last March for an initial fee of £150,000 with a further £50,000 payable dependent upon future appearances. He initially found the incessant pace of English football difficult to cope with, but his obvious quality soon enabled him to adjust his style to meet the new demands placed upon his game. He loves to isolate defenders and go past them on either side, and at full pace his elegant running style is slightly reminiscent of Keith O'Neill. He has the ability to deliver pin-point centres when running at full speed and in his first few appearances he provided the crosses for three goals. His brief eight-match run in the squad at the end of the 1999-2000 campaign has whetted the appetite of Canary fans for the forthcoming season, when they hope he will complete his acclimatisation to English football and become a constant menace to Division One defences.

Norwich C (£150,000 + from Cambuur Leeuwarden, Holland on 23/3/2000) FL 4

DEWHURST Robert (Rob) Matthew
Born: Keighley, 10 September 1971
Height: 6'3" Weight: 14.0

Having appeared in three of Hull's pre-season games, the big man lined up against the Tigers in the opening 1999-2000 league fixture for Exeter. Rob made a great start in the Grecians' defence and chipped in with two goals before he suffered a ruptured thigh muscle in October. He lost his place in the team after the management shake-up in January and was placed on the transfer list towards the end of the season. Although it won't be at Exeter, Rob will be hoping to bounce back in the new season.

Blackburn Rov (From trainee on 15/10/1990) FL 13 FLC 2 Others 1
Darlington (Loaned on 20/12/1991) FL 11/1 Others 1
Huddersfield T (Loaned on 2/10/1992) FL 7
Hull C (Free on 5/11/1993) FL 132+6/13 FLC 8 FAC 8/1 Others 7
Exeter C (Free on 9/8/1999) FL 21+2/2 FLC 2 FAC 2+1 Others 0+1

DE ZEEUW Adrianus (Arjan) Johannes
Born: Castricum, Holland, 16 April 1970
Height: 6'1" Weight: 13.11

Arjan is a commanding and influential figure who proved to be solid both on the ground and in the air at the heart of the Wigan defence in 1999-2000 following his arrival from Barnsley during the close season. His height and strength make him very dangerous at set pieces and he scored three league goals during the season. A wonderfully balanced central defender who is strong in the tackle and has great recovery ability, he also made his 200th first-team start in English football. Popular with both fans and players, Arjan collected the "Away Player of the Year" and the "Players' Player of the Year" awards, along with the runners-up spot in the fans' "Player of the Year" voting.

Barnsley (£250,000 from Telstar, Holland, via Vitesse 22, on 3/11/1995) F/PL 138/7 FLC 12 FAC 14
Wigan Ath (Free on 2/7/1999) FL 39/3 FLC 3 FAC 3 Others 3

DIAF Farid
Born: France, 19 April 1971
Height: 5'8" Weight: 10.12

Following an outstanding trial period with Preston in 1998-99, this Frenchman signed an initial three-month contract in July 1999 (later extended to the end of the season) and impressed in pre-season, but suffered a torn groin muscle two days before the start of the campaign. After a lengthy recovery, the cultured left-sided midfielder's debut from the bench against Bournemouth in November was followed by his full debut at Colchester in the next match, which saw him sustain a cheekbone fracture. Farid refused a second operation and was back on the bench within three weeks, before playing his first full match against Wrexham in the Auto Windscreens Shield. However, his Gallic flair and ball-playing talents were not sufficient to secure him a first-team place and he was released during the summer.

Preston NE (Free from Stade Rennais, France on 16/7/1999) FL 1+2 FAC 0+1 Others 2

DIBBLE Andrew (Andy) Gerald
Born: Cwmbran, 8 May 1965
Height: 6'3" Weight: 16.8
International Honours: W: 3; U21-3; Yth; Sch

The vastly experienced goalkeeper still has a commanding presence in his penalty area. He began 1999-2000 as Hartlepool's first-choice 'keeper, but was subsequently utilised as back-up to Martin Hollund. He was allowed to go to Carlisle on loan in

October to help the Cumbrians during their injury crisis. He was outstanding on his debut against Brighton, when he became United's fourth different 'keeper in as many games, and made one further appearance. He had few opportunities following his return to Victoria Park, and was one of six Hartlepool players released in May.

Cardiff C (From apprentice on 27/8/1982) FL 62 FLC 4 FAC 4
Luton T (£125,000 on 16/7/1984) FL 30 FLC 4 FAC 1 Others 1
Sunderland (Loaned on 21/2/1986) FL 12
Huddersfield T (Loaned on 26/3/1987) FL 5
Manchester C (£240,000 on 1/7/1988) P/FL 113+3 FLC 14 FAC 8+1 Others 2
Aberdeen (Loaned on 20/10/1990) SL 5
Middlesbrough (Loaned on 20/2/1991) FL 19 Others 2
Bolton W (Loaned on 6/9/1991) FL 13 Others 1
West Bromwich A (Loaned on 27/2/1992) FL 9
Glasgow R (Signed on 11/3/1997) SL 7
Luton T (Free on 15/9/1997) FL 1 FLC 2
Middlesbrough (Free on 30/1/1998) FL 2 (Free to Altrincham during 1998 close season)
Hartlepool U (Free on 25/3/1999) FL 6 FLC 2 Others 2+1
Carlisle U (Loaned on 8/10/1999) FL 2

DI CANIO Paolo

Born: Rome, Italy, 9 July 1968
Height: 5'9" Weight: 11.9

West Ham manager Harry Redknapp was thought by some to be taking a risk when he signed this hugely talented Italian in January 1999 but the gamble paid off and Paolo produced some scintillating form for the Hammers in 1999-2000. At times he displayed skills verging on the genius level in addition to scoring some magnificent goals and always working hard for the team – what more can a manager want from a striker? Two goals that will long be remembered by the Upton Park fans were a classic against Arsenal when he flicked the ball over Martin Keown before clipping a 15-yarder into the net and a superb 20-yard volley against Wimbledon. He was a constant threat to opposition defences and finished the season as the club's leading scorer with 16 goals. Paolo is rapidly becoming a cult figure with the West Ham supporters and finished the season by deservedly winning the "Hammer of the Year" award.

Glasgow Celtic (Signed from AC Milan, Italy, via AC Milan, Lazio, Ternana, Juventus and Napoli, on 3/7/1996) SL 25+1/12 SLC 2 SC 6/3 Others 2+1
Sheffield Wed (£3,000,000 on 8/8/1997) PL 39+2/15 FLC 4/2 FAC 3
West Ham U (£1,700,000 on 28/1/1999) PL 41+2/20 FLC 4/1 FAC 1 Others 6/1

DICHIO Daniele (Danny) Salvatore Ernest

Born: Hammersmith, 19 October 1974
Height: 6'3" Weight: 12.3
Club Honours: Div 1 '99
International Honours: E: U21-1; Sch

The tall Sunderland striker will no doubt look back on the 1999-2000 season with mixed feelings. Having seemingly recovered from a back injury suffered in pre-season, Danny was always going to find himself down the pecking order behind Kevin Phillips and Niall Quinn, but when Peter Reid rested the pair for the Black Cats' Worthington Cup ties Danny stepped in, bagging four goals in three games, including a spectacular effort from twenty yards against Walsall. Back in the Premiership, Danny was again confined to the bench before the aforementioned back injury flared up once more and at one stage looked to be potentially career threatening. Thankfully, such fears were to prove unfounded and the dependable target man returned to the squad, proving to be an able deputy for Quinn. Danny's aerial prowess is a particularly potent weapon and time is still on his side in terms of securing a permanent first-team slot.

Queens Park R (From trainee on 17/5/1993) P/FL 56+19/20 FLC 6/2 FAC 3+3 (Free to Sampdoria, Italy during 1997 close season)
Barnet (Loaned on 24/3/1994) FL 9/2
Sunderland (£750,000 from Lecce, Italy on 28/1/1998) P/FL 18+43/10 FLC 7+1/6 FAC 1+1 Others 1+2

DICKOV Paul

Born: Livingston, 1 November 1972
Height: 5'6" Weight: 11.9
Club Honours: ECWC '94
International Honours: S: U21-4; Yth; Sch

Paul was an ever-present for Manchester City in the league in 1999-2000 up to the game against Ipswich at the end of October. However, he then sustained a knee ligament injury that kept him sidelined until the end of the year. After regaining fitness he was unable to command a regular place in the City team, but was often used as a substitute when he was not in the starting line-up and always put a spark into the team when he came on. Despite his modest stature, Paul's workrate and tireless foraging more than made up for his relative lack of goals last season: he was always involved in the game, assisting the other forwards. Although he was disappointed not to have scored more goals, he was rightly delighted with the three he scored in the crucial home wins against Bolton and Crewe during the push for promotion, and rounded off the 4-1 win at Blackburn that clinched City's place in the Premiership with the fourth goal.

Arsenal (From trainee on 28/12/1990) PL 6+15/3 FLC 2+2/3
Luton T (Loaned on 8/10/1993) FL 8+7/1
Brighton & Hove A (Loaned on 23/3/1994) FL 8/5
Manchester C (£1,000,000 on 23/8/1996) FL 90+38/29 FLC 7+2/3 FAC 5+3/1 Others 3/2

DICKSON Mark Simon

Born: Belfast, 12 December 1981
Height: 5'7" Weight: 11.2
International Honours: NI: Yth

This Northampton youth-team striker was called up to the Northern Ireland squad for the European U18 Championship in Sweden in August 1999. After he had been given a taste of first-team action in the Cobblers' pre-season friendlies during the preparations for the 1999-2000 campaign, Mark's continuing progress at Sixfields saw him make his senior bow as an extra-time substitute for Andy Morrow in the Auto Windscreens Shield game with Bristol Rovers in January, just a month after his 18th birthday.

Northampton T (Trainee) Others 0+1

DIGBY Fraser Charles

Born: Sheffield, 23 April 1967
Height: 6'1" Weight: 13.10
Club Honours: Div 2 '96
International Honours: E: U21-5; Yth; Sch

This agile shot stopper was first-choice goalkeeper for Crystal Palace for most of the 1999-2000 campaign. His vast experience was an asset to a young team and he proved a more than competent replacement for the departed Kevin Miller. Fraser took his career total of Football League appearances past the 450 mark during the season.

Manchester U (From apprentice on 25/4/1985)
Swindon T (£32,000 on 25/9/1986) F/PL 417 FLC 33 FAC 21 Others 33+1
Crystal Palace (Free on 8/8/1998) FL 56 FLC 7 FAC 1

DI LELLA Gustavo Martin

Born: Buenos Aires, Argentine, 6 October 1973
Height: 5'8" Weight: 10.7

After looking good in the pre-season build-up, Gustavo began 1999-2000 in the Hartlepool first team. He scored a memorable goal from a free kick against Crewe Alexandra in a Worthington Cup tie, but shortly afterwards he was dropped. As he was clearly not happy at being left out of the side, he asked to be transfer-listed. Gustavo rejoined his former Pool boss Mick Tait during a loan spell at Blyth Spartans, before moving permanently to Spain with CD Mostoles.

Darlington (Free from Blyth Spartans on 2/12/1997) FL 0+5 (Free to Blyth Spartans on 3/2/1998)
Hartlepool U (Free on 20/3/1998) FL 22+9/4 FLC 2+1/1 FAC 2 Others 1

DILLON Paul William

Born: Limerick, 22 October 1978
Height: 5'9" Weight: 10.11
International Honours: RoI: U21-1; Yth

An enthusiastic left-footed centre back, Paul started off the 1999-2000 season as a Rotherham regular before losing his place following the signing of Guy Branston. He then had the misfortune to sustain an ankle injury that ruled him out for the rest of the season and he will be looking to make a fresh start in 2000-01. A very competitive Irishman with a great desire to succeed, Paul has got plenty of ability but it's his never-say-die attitude that will serve him best.

Rotherham U (From trainee on 7/3/1997) FL 65+5/2 FLC 4 FAC 6 Others 3

DI MATTEO Roberto (Robbie)

Born: Berne, Switzerland, 29 May 1970
Height: 5'10" Weight: 12.5
Club Honours: FAC '97, '00; FLC '98; ECWC '98; ESC '99
International Honours: Italy: 34

For the majority of the 1999-2000 campaign Roberto seemed a forlorn, almost forgotten figure as Chelsea created headlines with their Champions' League and FA Cup exploits, but in an extraordinary turn of events "Robbie" reaffirmed his place in the history books at the season's end. French World Cup-winning captain Didier Deschamps joined Chelsea from Juventus in

July 1999 and promptly took Roberto's favoured central midfield berth; "Didi's" formidable partnership with Dennis Wise, the growing maturity of Jody Morris and the goalscoring panache of Gustavo Poyet left the popular Italian an onlooker from the sidelines. The Fleet Street rumour mill promptly swung into action, linking Roberto with moves to the Continent's biggest clubs, and to exacerbate his problems a serious ankle injury put him out of action for most of the first three months of the season. But, having played just 90 minutes of first-team football, he came off the substitutes' bench to help turn around Chelsea's season in the most dramatic fashion. With the Blues trailing 1-0 to AC Milan in the San Siro, and their Champions' League dreams fading, he rocked his Italian compatriots with a stunning through-ball that enabled Wise to equalise and guide Chelsea to the second phase at the expense of the expensively assembled *Rossonieri*. In early December he made an emotional return to the Olympic Stadium in Rome to play against his former club Lazio, and his goal-line clearance helped the Blues to a creditable goalless draw. Four days later, at the opposite end of the footballing spectrum, at Hull City's Boothferry Park to be precise, he scored his first goal of the season in a potentially tricky third-round FA Cup tie: the ball came out to him following a goalmouth melee and from 25 yards he coolly chipped it into the net as if it were a training-ground exercise. Just as Roberto looked set for a run in the first team his injury jinx reappeared, an accidental clash against Leicester in January resulting in a fractured arm and another spell on the sidelines. However, with his season at its lowest ebb the Italian's luck began to turn. He forced his way back into the side at the expense of Dan Petrescu on the right side of midfield and produced a string of impressive performances, scoring lovely goals against Liverpool and Derby and grabbing a late place in the FA Cup final line-up against Aston Villa – making him one of only four survivors, along with Frank Leboeuf, Wise and Gianfranco Zola, from the successful 1997 team. Already the scorer of the quickest goal in a Wembley FA Cup final, Roberto created history by scoring the last FA Cup final goal under the Twin Towers. In a somewhat disappointing final, he rammed home a loose ball from close range for the only goal of the match, clinching Chelsea's third FA Cup and producing a fairy-tale ending to a topsy-turvy season.

Chelsea (£4,900,000 from Lazio, Italy, via FC Aarau, FC Zurich and Schaffhausen, on 17/7/1996) PL 101+11/15 FLC 9+1/3 FAC 15+2/5 Others 20+6/3

DINNING Tony
Born: Wallsend, 12 April 1975
Height: 6'0" Weight: 12.11

After appearing in a variety of positions for Stockport during the 1998-99 campaign, Tony settled into a central midfield role with the Hatters in 1999-2000. He proved a revelation and was a near-ever-present for the Edgeley Park club, contributing a number of spectacular goals and finishing as Stockport's leading scorer for the season. Hard working and strong in the tackle, he is popular with the supporters and was deservedly voted "Player of the Year" by the Independent Supporters' Club.

Newcastle U (From trainee on 1/10/1993)
Stockport Co (Free on 23/6/1994) FL 153+32/25 FLC 11+5/2 FAC 4+7 Others 6+1/2

Tony Dinning

DIOP Pape Seydou
Born: Dakar, Senegal, 10 January 1979
Height: 5'9" Weight: 11.0
International Honours: Senegal

Signed by Norwich on a season-long loan from Racing Club de Lens in August 1999, this totally unpredictable right back returned to France midway through his proposed stay when he joined Racing Club de Paris on a full contract. A real attacking full back, he has a tremendous turn of pace and the ability to dribble past defenders; however, it was his own lack of defensive attributes which made it difficult for him to break into the Canaries' line-up. The crowd loved his exhilarating breaks out of defence, but the coaching staff sometimes despaired of his positional play and defensive covering. He managed only three starts for the Canaries, two of which came in a more advanced role on the right flank where his defensive duties were less important. He was called up for international duty by Senegal for a friendly fixture last November while on the books at Carrow Road.

Norwich C (Loaned from RC Lens, France on 5/8/1999) FL 2+5 FLC 1+2

DISLEY Craig Edward
Born: Worksop, 24 August 1981
Height: 5'10" Weight: 11.0

A confident first-year professional with Mansfield, Craig was forced into first-team action prematurely last season by the small squad at Field Mill. The youngster played well in midfield and did not let the side down, although his inexperience did show through at times. His effort and enthusiasm could not be faulted and he could be one to watch for in the future.

Mansfield T (From trainee on 23/6/1999) FL 2+3 FAC 1

DIXON Kevin Robert
Born: Easington, 27 June 1980
Height: 5'9" Weight: 12.6
Club Honours: FAYC '97
International Honours: E: Yth

With Alan Pouton, Mark Tinkler and Steve Agnew set to leave, York's midfield ranks were beginning to look depleted as 1999-2000 approached. Kevin agreed to join City on loan from Leeds United in July, and the lively England U18 midfielder played in the opening four league and cup games before returning to Elland Road.

Leeds U (From trainee on 10/7/1997)
York C (Loaned on 5/8/1999) FL 3 FLC 1

DIXON Lee Michael
Born: Manchester, 17 March 1964
Height: 5'9" Weight: 11.8
Club Honours: Div 1 '89, '91; PL '98; FAC '93, '98; ECWC '94; CS '98, '99
International Honours: E: 22; B-4

After 13 demanding seasons with Arsenal, Lee is still the automatic choice to fill the right-wing-back position. A solid, hard-tackling defender, he has retained his exceptional speed, strength and physical fitness. He is a naturally attacking player with great distribution and crossing skills who gets forward at every opportunity. In 1999-2000 his sheer determination not only created chances for the strikers, but also rewarded him with four goals for himself. With more than 500 first-team appearances behind him, his service to the club was rewarded with a testimonial match against Real Madrid last November. The fact that more than 22,000 fans turned out on a bitterly cold evening is confirmation of the esteem in which he is held.

Burnley (From juniors on 21/7/1982) FL 4 FLC 1
Chester C (Free on 16/2/1984) FL 56+1/1 FLC 2 FAC 1 Others 3
Bury (Free on 15/7/1985) FL 45/5 FLC 4 FAC 8/1 Others 1
Stoke C (£40,000 on 18/7/1986) FL 71/5 FLC 6 FAC 7 Others 4
Arsenal (£400,000 on 29/1/1988) F/PL 410+6/24 FLC 45 FAC 44/1 Others 51/1

D'JAFFO Laurent
Born: Aquitane, France, 5 November 1970
Height: 6'0" Weight: 13.5

An exciting striker with a useful goalscoring record, Laurent proved an ideal replacement for the transfer-listed Brett Angell when he joined Stockport from Bury in a £100,000 deal at the beginning of the 1999-2000 campaign. He showed impressive form in the early-season games and contributed eight goals before being ruled out through injury. Unsettled at Edgeley Park, the big Frenchman moved on to Sheffield United last February to link up once more with his former boss Neil Warnock. Used initially as a substitute, Laurent made his first full appearance at Port Vale, where he scored with a good header. He is a strong, willing worker and can be expected to challenge for a regular place during the coming season.

Ayr U (Signed from Red Star Paris, France on 13/10/1997) SL 21+3/10 SC 2+1

Bury (Free on 28/7/1998) FL 35+2/8 FLC 4+1/1 FAC 1
Stockport Co (£100,000 on 13/8/1999) FL 20+1/7 FLC 2/1
Sheffield U (£100,000 + on 4/2/2000) FL 6+9/1

DOANE Benjamin (Ben) Nigel David
Born: Sheffield, 22 December 1979
Height: 5'10" Weight: 12.0

Ben made his first-team debut for Sheffield United as a substitute in the Worthington Cup at Shrewsbury last August, and his other appearance, also as a substitute, was in the league game at Stockport three months later. The Sheffield-born defender was a regular performer in the reserves, where he can also bolster the attack when pushed forward. In addition, he had a two-month loan spell with Conference side Kettering before returning to Bramall Lane. He will be hoping to establish himself this coming season.

Sheffield U (From trainee on 15/7/1998) FL 0+1 FLC 0+1

DOBIE Robert **Scott**
Born: Workington, 10 October 1978
Height: 6'1" Weight: 12.8

Allocated the Carlisle number seven shirt for the 1999-2000 season, Scott was often used down the right flank rather than in his accustomed central striking role. He suffered a delayed start to the campaign and did not make his first appearance until October. However, he soon notched four goals, mostly from headers. His other strikes were all against Chester. Much the most important was his injury-time winner at the Deva Stadium in April – a goal that for drama and execution almost matched that by the legendary Jimmy Glass in May 1999.

Carlisle U (From trainee on 10/5/1997) FL 60+32/14 FLC 1+5 FAC 1+1 Others 6+1
Clydebank (Loaned on 3/11/1998) SL 6

DOBSON Anthony (Tony) John
Born: Coventry, 5 February 1969
Height: 6'1" Weight: 13.2
Club Honours: FAYC '87
International Honours: E: U21-4

This left-footed central defender's career at Northampton has been hampered by injuries since his arrival in September 1998. By the end of last season, Tony had managed only 13 games. After missing the latter part of the previous campaign and the early part of 1999-2000, he made a comeback against Leyton Orient in November, only to pick up another leg injury that required another operation. His season came to an abrupt end after that single appearance and he was released in the summer.

Coventry C (From apprentice on 7/7/1986) FL 51+3/1 FLC 5+3 Others 0+1
Blackburn Rov (£300,000 on 17/1/1991) F/PL 36+5 FLC 5 FAC 2 Others 1
Portsmouth (£150,000 on 22/9/1993) FL 48+5/2 FLC 6 FAC 1+2 Others 4/1
Oxford U (Loaned on 15/12/1994) FL 5
Peterborough U (Loaned on 29/1/1996) FL 4
West Bromwich A (Free on 8/8/1997) FL 6+5 FLC 0+2 FAC 2
Gillingham (Loaned on 4/9/1998) FL 2
Northampton T (£25,000 on 11/9/1998) FL 9+3 FLC 0+1

DODD Jason Robert
Born: Bath, 2 November 1970
Height: 5'10" Weight: 12.3
International Honours: E: U21-8

Southampton's captain, and now in his 11th season at the Dell, Jason is an automatic choice for the right-back berth but he is equally effective as a central defender or midfielder. He is not the fastest of defenders, but more than makes up for it with his excellent reading of the game. Jason possesses a powerful shot and takes over the penalty duties in the absence of Matt Le Tissier – he ended last season with his 100 per cent success rate intact. He has been rewarded with a much-deserved testimonial in 2000-01.

Southampton (£50,000 from Bath C on 15/3/1989) F/PL 272+18/8 FLC 33+2/1 FAC 26/1 Others 5

DOHERTY Gary Michael Thomas
Born: Carndonagh, 31 January 1980
Height: 6'2" Weight: 13.1
International Honours: RoI: 2; U21-4; Yth

Although he is equally at home in defence or attack, Gary is an ideal target man. Prior to the start of the 1999-2000 season, he captained the Republic of Ireland's U18 team in the European Championship in Sweden, returning with a bronze medal, and he then went on to perform no less impressively for Luton's first team, both up front and at the back. Coming into the starting line-up for the third game of the season, against Blackpool, he quickly became a regular. He scored his first goal of the campaign against Bristol Rovers in the Worthington Cup and later netted a brace against Lincoln City in the FA Cup. His never-say-die approach, coupled with his strong, powerful running and accuracy in front of goal, made him virtually an ever-present in a young and talented Luton side, but after scoring five goals in successive matches in March and April he was transferred to Tottenham for a £1 million fee. Although he joined Spurs after the transfer deadline, Gary was granted special dispensation to play for his new club by the FA and made his first-team debut against Manchester United at Old Trafford in May, replacing Chris Armstrong in attack with 21 minutes to go. He also came off the bench in Tottenham's final game of the season against Sunderland. Much will be expected of him at White Hart Lane in 2000-01, when he is expected to be used in an attacking role. He made his full international debut for the Republic of Ireland when he came on as a substitute against Greece in April and was included in the starting line-up for the first time for the Nike Cup fixture with the USA at the beginning of June.

Luton T (From trainee on 2/7/1997) FL 46+24/12 FLC 0+3/1 FAC 6+2/2 Others 1+1
Tottenham H (£1,000,000 on 22/4/2000) PL 0+2

DOHERTY Thomas (Tommy) Edward
Born: Bristol, 17 March 1979
Height: 5'8" Weight: 9.13

The 1999-2000 season was bitterly frustrating for Bristol City's midfield dynamo, who had looked like being a permanent fixture just two seasons ago. After fighting his way back to fitness, following a foot injury, he sustained damage to his knee in his first outing for the reserves in a 1-0 win over Bristol Rovers in January. His tenacious spirit and ball-winning qualities were sorely missed in City's midfield, but the club's fans are hoping that he will be fully fit to feature in next season's anticipated promotion push.

Bristol C (From trainee on 8/7/1997) FL 37+17/3 FLC 3+1/1 FAC 1+1

DOIG Christopher (Chris) Ross
Born: Dumfries, 13 February 1981
Height: 6'2" Weight: 12.6
International Honours: S: U21-3; Yth; Sch

Chris is one of the many talented youngsters to emerge from Nottingham Forest's youth policy in recent seasons. A tall and commanding centre back, he featured in the Reds' starting line-up on ten occasions in 1999-2000. He played twice for Scotland at U18 level last autumn, earning promotion to the U21 squad in April when he appeared as a substitute against Holland and making the starting line-up for the President's Cup games with Northern Ireland and Wales at the end of May.

Queen of the South (Associated Schoolboy) SL 2+2
Nottingham F (From trainee on 7/3/1998) P/FL 9+4 FLC 1+1 FAC 1

DOLAN Joseph (Joe)
Born: Harrow, 27 May 1980
Height: 6'3" Weight: 12.12
International Honours: NI: U21-3; Yth

Joe is a tall, strong central defender who is very hard in the challenge, good in the air and difficult to knock off the ball. During 1999-2000 he had to compete with four other players for a place in the Millwall back line and was not a regular, but when he did start he put in some excellent performances, especially against the impressive Bristol Rovers strike force, Jason Roberts and Jamie Cureton. Displays of that standard ensure that he is watched regularly by Northern Ireland and the season saw him add to his international honours. This sometimes restricted his opportunities at club level but the experience is good for his development, which in turn will benefit Millwall.

Millwall (Free from Chelsea juniors on 15/4/1998) FL 25+1/2 FLC 1 Others 3

DOMI Didier
Born: Paris, France, 2 May 1978
Height: 5'10" Weight: 11.4
International Honours: France: U21

Didier is a cultured French defender who reads the game well and has a fine positional sense and a good turn of pace, which is an asset both in his defensive responsibilities and in the raids down the wing which have become a feature of his play. He began the 1999-2000 season in good form, alternating between full back and wing back on Newcastle's left flank. Playing for the French U21 side against Italy in November, he unfortunately hurt his left ankle, which sidelined him until the turn of the year. On his return to fitness the form of Alessandro Pistone and Aaron Hughes kept Didier out of the starting line-up and he was used primarily as a substitute, usually coming on to play wide on the left of midfield, from where he made important contributions, exemplified by the telling runs followed by pin-point centres threaded through crowded penalty areas that allowed Alan Shearer to score both the winner in the FA Cup at Blackburn and the third goal in the home victory over Manchester United. His attacking instincts enabled him to contribute a few useful goals, too, his first ever for the club coming in the home game with Wimbledon to help earn the only point won in the first seven games, another being the winner in the FA Cup quarter-final tie at Tranmere.

Newcastle U (£3,250,000 + from Paris St Germain, France on 5/1/1999) PL 33+8/3 FLC 1 FAC 5+3/1 Others 4

DOMINGUEZ Jose Manuel Martins
Born: Lisbon, Portugal, 16 February 1974
Height: 5'3" Weight: 10.0
Club Honours: Div 2 '95; FLC '99
International Honours: Portugal: 3

A utility forward, Jose started only three times and came off the bench on a further 14 occasions for Tottenham last season, once again offering manager George Graham a quick, skilful option on the wing or through the centre. As previous seasons have proved, Jose can turn a game on its head with his creativity and pace and has a powerful strike despite his small size. He will no doubt welcome the opportunity to continue as a squad player in 2000-01.

Birmingham C (£180,000 from Benfica, Portugal on 9/3/1994) FL 15+20/3 FLC 1+2 FAC 2+1 Others 2+2/1 (£1,800,000 to Sporting Lisbon, Portugal on 1/8/1995)
Tottenham H (£1,600,000 on 12/8/1997) PL 12+31/4 FLC 2+4/1 FAC 2+1 Others 0+2

DONALDSON O'Neill McKay
Born: Birmingham, 24 November 1969
Height: 6'0" Weight: 12.4

Because of a series of injuries, the Torquay fans never saw the best of this pacy striker. He was released at the end of the 1999-2000 campaign. Although past his 30th birthday, O'Neill has played little more than 100 games in his career. Yet he remains a bubbly character, and is surely due some better luck.

Shrewsbury T (Free from Hinckley T on 13/11/1991) FL 15+13/4 Others 1
Doncaster Rov (Free on 10/8/1994) FL 7+2/2 FLC 2 Others 0+1
Mansfield T (Loaned on 23/12/1994) FL 4/6 FAC 1/1
Sheffield Wed (£50,000 on 9/1/1995) PL 4+10/3
Oxford U (Loaned on 30/1/1998) FL 6/2
Stoke C (Free on 13/3/1998) FL 2
Torquay U (Free on 7/9/1998) FL 11+16/1 FAC 1+2/1 Others 2/1

DONIS Georgios (George)
Born: Greece, 22 October 1969
Height: 6'0" Weight: 12.6
International Honours: Greece: 24

Georgios became Steve Bruce's first signing for the Terriers when he joined Huddersfield from AEK Athens in June 1999 but 1999-2000 was to be a disappointing season for the flying winger, who had previously had spells with Blackburn Rovers and Sheffield United. Injury blighted his contribution and the McAlpine faithful only briefly saw his lightning pace and dribbling skills. Often used from the substitutes' bench, the Greek winger will be hoping for the chance to make a greater impact in 2000-01.

Blackburn Rov (Free from Panathanaikos, Greece on 5/7/1996) PL 11+11/2 FLC 3 FAC 0+1 (Free to AEK Athens, Greece on 20/9/1997)
Sheffield U (Free on 25/3/1999) FL 5+2/1
Huddersfield T (Free on 4/6/1999) FL 10+10 FLC 3+1 FAC 0+1

DONNELLY Paul Michael
Born: Stoke, 16 February 1981
Height: 5'7" Weight: 11.10

Paul is a promising defender who made his senior debut for Port Vale last season. A regular in the reserves, usually at right back, he made his long-awaited first-team bow against Stockport County in February at left wing back and played well. He kept his place for the next three games but unfortunately all were lost and Paul then returned to the reserves as Allen Tankard was recalled. He possesses a good shot and came close to a goal on a couple of occasions.

Port Vale (From trainee on 1/7/1999) FL 4

DONNELLY Simon Thomas
Born: Glasgow, 1 December 1974
Height: 5'9" Weight: 11.0
Club Honours: SC '95; SPD '98
International Honours: S: 10; U21-11

Simon joined Sheffield Wednesday along with Celtic colleague Phil O'Donnell during the 1999 summer break. Although he made the starting line-up for the opening game against Liverpool, he had a very frustrating 1999-2000 campaign thanks to a string of injury problems. He remained in the squad until early October and then reappeared in the new year, when he had several outings from the subs' bench, scoring one of the goals in the 3-0 victory at Derby. He can play either as an attacking midfielder or as a striker and will be hoping for an injury-free run in 2000-01 to enable him to make an impact with the Hillsborough club.

Glasgow Celtic (From Celtic BC on 27/5/1993) SL 113+33/30 SLC 11+6/4 SC 8+5/2 Others 13+7/6
Sheffield Wed (Free on 9/7/1999) PL 3+9/1 FLC 1+2 FAC 0+3

DONOVAN Kevin
Born: Halifax, 17 December 1971
Height: 5'8" Weight: 11.2
Club Honours: AMC '98

After a frustrating season for Kevin in 1998-99, when he struggled to recapture the skill and speed he showed during Grimsby's double Wembley campaign following a long lay-off due to a back injury, Mariners fans were hoping for great things from this right-sided midfielder in 1999-2000. Despite a somewhat hesitant start to the new term, as the season progressed supporters started to see more and more of the Kevin of old and the re-emergence of the ball control, speed and ability to beat defenders that had delighted the Blundell Park crowd in the past.

Huddersfield T (From trainee on 11/10/1989) FL 11+9/1 FLC 1+1 FAC 1/2 Others 4
Halifax T (Loaned on 13/2/1992) FL 6
West Bromwich A (£70,000 on 1/10/1992) FL 139+29/19 FLC 9+2/6 FAC 7+1/3 Others 15+1/4
Grimsby T (£300,000 on 29/7/1997) FL 114+1/19 FLC 11+1/2 FAC 9/1 Others 9/3

DOOLAN John
Born: Liverpool, 7 May 1974
Height: 6'1" Weight: 13.0

Arguably the most influential player in the Barnet side in 1999-2000, John excelled throughout the season and the fact that the club attained a play-off place can largely be attributed to his selfless industry in the middle of the park. John returned for pre-season training in July fully focused on fulfilling his potential and winning over the Underhill crowd. He undertook this task in his own trademark manner, combining abrasive tackling with raking crossfield passes, and underlining his outstanding ability. Barnet relied heavily on his boundless energy and infectious will to win as the season progressed, and he missed only two games throughout the season. Visibly upset following the play-off defeat at Peterborough, John had gained the adulation of the fans with his dynamic displays and his wonderful volley at Brighton on Boxing Day.

Everton (From trainee on 1/6/1992)
Mansfield T (Free on 2/9/1994) FL 128+3/10 FLC 8/1 FAC 7/2 Others 4+1/1
Barnet (£60,000 on 13/1/1998) FL 101+2/4 FLC 3+1 FAC 2 Others 5

DORIGO Anthony (Tony) Robert
Born: Australia, 31 December 1965
Height: 5'9" Weight: 10.10
Club Honours: Div 2 '89, Div 1 '92; FMC '90; CS '92
International Honours: E: 15; B-7; U21-11

When selected, the experienced former England international left wing back used his experience to shore up a sometimes creaking Derby defensive unit in 1999-2000 as well as making telling contributions to the attack, and he is still one of the best crossers of a ball in the game. He picked up a calf injury in the opening match of the season which kept him out of action for six weeks, followed by a series of small but niggling injuries as the season progressed. Tony still possesses a ferocious shot from distance and links up well with Seth Johnson on the left side of the Rams' line-up. Off the field he is involved in supplying other top players with the motor car of their choice! He was released during the summer.

Aston Villa (From apprentice on 19/7/1983) FL 106+5/1 FLC 14+1 FAC 7 Others 2
Chelsea (£475,000 on 3/7/1987) FL 146/11 FLC 14 FAC 4 Others 16/1
Leeds U (£1,300,000 on 6/6/1991) F/PL 168+3/5 FLC 12+1 FAC 16 Others 9/1 (Free to Torino, Italy during 1997 close season)
Derby Co (Free on 23/10/1998) PL 37+4/1 FLC 4 FAC 4/2

DOUGHTY Matthew (Matt) Liam
Born: Warrington, 2 November 1981
Height: 5'8" Weight: 10.4

Amid the doom and gloom of Chester's 1999-2000 campaign, one of the shining lights was the impressive progress of young Matt. A product of the club's youth policy, the Warrington-born left back made his debut in the opening-day defeat by Barnet while still only 17. Matt was involved in more than half of the Blues' games last term, with his pace sometimes used further forward. His only goal came in the Boxing Day defeat at Mansfield. The Football League has not seen the last of him.
Chester C (Trainee) FL 19+14/1 FLC 2 FAC 4

DOUGLAS Stuart Anthony
Born: Enfield, 9 April 1978
Height: 5'9" Weight: 11.5
A persistent, pacy striker who can be relied upon to show plenty of aggression, Stuart was one of several products of Luton's prolific youth policy to appear regularly in the first team during 1999-2000. Breaking something of a goal drought, he hit his first of the season in the 3-1 win at home to Gillingham in October and followed it up with another in the draw with Wycombe three days later. A bout of glandular fever briefly interrupted his run of appearances, but he scored again in the FA Cup replay at Lincoln at the end of November to give the Hatters a 1-0 win. He is a hard-working player who is always willing to chase lost causes, and remained a key member of the team for the rest of the season, although goals remained disappointingly scarce.
Luton T (From trainee on 2/5/1996) FL 87+29/14 FLC 11+2/3 FAC 7+1/1 Others 1+1

DOWE Julian Whytus Lennox
Born: Manchester, 9 September 1975
Height: 6'2" Weight: 12.5
A former Wigan trainee who had also had spells at Marbella in Spain and in Scotland, Julian worked as a fitness instructor and played for Colne Dynamos prior to signing for Rochdale early in the 1999-2000 campaign. A powerful striker, he made a string of substitute appearances, the first in the win at championship contenders Rotherham in September, before making his full debut at Swansea in October. His first senior goal was a spectacular clincher in the 3-0 FA Cup win against Burton Albion after Dale had gone seven games without a goal. Julian went to Burton on loan in December to gain further experience, before he was released at the end of the season.
Wigan Ath (From trainee on 17/9/1992. Free to Marbella, Spain on 1/7/1994)
Ayr U (Free on 25/11/1994) SL 4+3/1(Free to Woking during 1995 close season)
Rochdale (Free from Colne on 27/8/1999) FL 1+6 FAC 1+1/1

DOWIE Iain
Born: Hatfield, 9 January 1965
Height: 6'1" Weight: 13.11
International Honours: NI: 59; U23-1; U21-1
Iain was appointed assistant first-team coach at Queens Park Rangers before the 1999-2000 season started. This restricted his senior appearances to just one, as a substitute. He played in Rangers' reserves and was instrumental in developing some of the younger players who are now on the fringe of the first-team squad. Iain normally plays as a target man, but he operated in the reserves as a central defender. Earlier in the season he won three caps for Northern Ireland in their unsuccessful campaign to qualify for last summer's European Championship finals.
Luton T (£30,000 from Hendon on 14/12/1988) FL 53+13/16 FLC 3+1 FAC 1+2 Others 5/4
Fulham (Loaned on 13/9/1989) FL 5/1
West Ham U (£480,000 on 22/3/1991) FL 12/4
Southampton (£500,000 on 3/9/1991) F/PL 115+7/30 FLC 8+3/1 FAC 6/1 Others 4
Crystal Palace (£400,000 on 13/1/1995) P/FL 19/6 FAC 6/4
West Ham U (£500,000 on 8/9/1995) PL 58+10/8 FLC 10+1/2 FAC 3+1/1
Queens Park R (Signed on 30/1/1998) FL 16+14/2 FLC 0+1 FAC 0+2

DOWNER Simon
Born: Romford, 19 October 1981
Height: 5'11" Weight: 12.0
Simon made an impressive progression from the Leyton Orient youth squad to the first team in 1999-2000, and kept more experienced defenders out of the side. Simon was unfazed by facing some of the best forwards in the Third Division, and played a leading role in the O's revival in the second half of the campaign. He was watched by Premiership and First Division scouts, but signed a contract in May that ties him to Orient until 2002.
Leyton Orient (From trainee on 4/10/1999) FL 24+1 FLC 1+1 FAC 1 Others 2

DOZZELL Jason Alvin Winans
Born: Ipswich, 9 December 1967
Height: 6'1" Weight: 13.8
Club Honours: Div 2 '92
International Honours: E: U21-9; Yth
An experienced forward or midfielder with lots of top-level experience, Jason began last season with goals in the first two games – the winner at Chesterfield on the opening day being ecstatically greeted by supporters and local media as evidence that the U's were on course for the play-offs at least! Apart from one absence due to a broken arm early in the season, Jason was a regular throughout the campaign, generally appearing alongside David Gregory in midfield but occasionally playing up front as a target man. He finished an impressive season with six goals.
Ipswich T (From apprentice on 20/12/1984) F/PL 312+20/52 FLC 29+1/3 FAC 22/12 Others 22/4
Tottenham H (£1,900,000 on 1/8/1993) PL 68+16/13 FLC 8+2 FAC 4+1/1
Ipswich T (Free on 2/10/1997) FL 8/1 FLC 2/1
Northampton T (Free on 19/12/1997) FL 18+3/4 FAC 1 Others 3
Colchester U (Free on 14/10/1998) FL 61+7/9 FLC 2/1 FAC 2 Others 1+1

DRAPER Mark Andrew
Born: Long Eaton, 11 November 1970
Height: 5'10" Weight: 12.4
Club Honours: FLC '96
International Honours: E: U21-3
This experienced midfield player made just one appearance as a substitute for Aston Villa in 1999-2000, coming on as a late replacement for Steve Stone at Chelsea last August. In January he moved on loan to Spanish club Rayo Vallecano, aiming to make a return to regular first-team football, and he remained there until the end of the season.
Notts Co (From trainee on 12/12/1988) FL 206+16/40 FLC 14+1/2 FAC 10/2 Others 21+2/5
Leicester C (£1,250,000 on 22/7/1994) PL 39/5 FLC 2 FAC 2
Aston Villa (£3,250,000 on 5/7/1995) PL 108+12/7 FLC 11+1/2 FAC 10/2 Others 12+1

DREYER John Brian
Born: Alnwick, 11 June 1963
Height: 6'1" Weight: 13.2
This hard-working and versatile player started the 1999-2000 season in Bradford City's line-up but after five games he dropped out with a chest infection and then found it difficult to regain his place. He was, as ever, a great clubman, always offering 100 per cent whatever the circumstances. His first-team appearances last season were mostly in the centre of defence but he is equally at home at full back and in midfield. John has now taken his UEFA "B" coaching badge with a view to staying on in the game after he retires as a player.
Oxford U (Signed from Wallingford on 8/1/1985) FL 57+3/2 FLC 10+1 FAC 2 Others 3
Torquay U (Loaned on 13/12/1985) FL 5
Fulham (Loaned on 27/3/1988) FL 12/2
Luton T (£140,000 on 27/6/1988) FL 212+2/13 FLC 13+1/1 FAC 14 Others 8/1
Stoke C (Free on 15/7/1994) FL32+17/3 FLC 5 FAC 1 Others 4+1/1
Bolton W (Loaned on 23/3/1995) FL 1+1 Others 1+1
Bradford C (£25,000 on 6/11/1996) P/FL 72+8/2 FLC 8+2 FAC 3/3

DRURY Adam James
Born: Cambridge, 29 August 1978
Height: 5'10" Weight: 11.8
Adam is a young left back who is already well established at Peterborough. He has tremendous speed and fine timing in the tackle. He was asked to play at centre back during a 1999-2000 injury crisis, and looked a natural in that position. In a successful play-off campaign, Adam's highlight was his only goal via a magnificent 25-yard strike against Hull. Posh have already turned down large bids for him.
Peterborough U (From trainee on 3/7/1996) FL 109+10/2 FLC 6 FAC 4 Others 10

DRYDEN Richard Andrew
Born: Stroud, 14 June 1969
Height: 6'0" Weight: 13.12
Club Honours: Div 4 '90
A regular in the Southampton team under Graeme Souness, Richard has become a forgotten man at the Dell over the last two seasons, making only a handful of appearances for the club. A powerful central defender who shows great composure and poses a regular threat at set pieces, he had two spells on loan at Stoke in 1999-2000 and made clear his wish to join the club, in line with his family's desire to move nearer to his Nottingham home. Recently recovered from a serious injury, he looked the part during his first sojourn at the Britannia Stadium before another injury put

Stoke's plans to sign him on hold. Back at the Dell, he was recalled by Southampton against Newcastle in January but he hadn't trained for six weeks and not surprisingly he was not match fit and struggled. Meanwhile Stoke had kept him in mind, and prior to transfer deadline day he rejoined the club for a second loan period. With the advent of a 4-4-2 system he briefly lost his place in the starting line-up, although he contributed to City's victory in the Auto Windscreens Shield final at Wembley as a second-half substitute. He was expected to complete his switch to the Potteries during the summer.

Bristol Rov (From trainee on 14/7/1987) FL 12+1 FLC 2+1 FAC 0+2 Others 2
Exeter C (Loaned on 22/9/1988) FL 6
Exeter C (£10,000 on 8/3/1989) FL 86/13 FLC 7/2 FAC 2 Others 4
Notts Co (£250,000 on 9/8/1991) FL 30+1/1 FLC 1+1 FAC 2+1 Others 2
Plymouth Arg (Loaned on 18/11/1992) FL 5 Others 1
Birmingham C (£165,000 on 19/3/1993) FL 48 FLC 5 FAC 1
Bristol C (£140,000 on 16/12/1994) FL 32+5/2 FLC 4 FAC 1+1 Others 2
Southampton (£150,000 on 6/8/1996) PL 44+3/1 FLC 7/3
Stoke C (Loaned on 3/11/1999) FL 3
Stoke C (Loaned on 23/3/2000) FL 8+2 Others 1+1

DUBERRY Michael Wayne
Born: Enfield, 14 October 1975
Height: 6'1" Weight: 13.6
Club Honours: FLC '98; ECWC '98; ESC '99
International Honours: E: U21-5

An experienced central defender, Michael found his first-team chances at Chelsea limited after the arrival of Frank Leboeuf and Marcel Desailly, and in the summer of 1999 he joined Leeds United for £4.5 million. However, he again found that his opportunities were few and far between with Lucas Radebe and Jonathan Woodgate now barring his path, and in the second half of the season he had to contend with the re-emergence of Alfie Haaland. Nevertheless, Michael is a highly capable centre back, whose height, pace and strength make him a formidable opponent. He can only benefit from the guidance of Leeds manager David O'Leary, and will be hoping to get more games under his belt and show the United fans his undoubted talent during the coming season.

Chelsea (From trainee on 7/6/1993) PL 77+9/1 FLC 8 FAC 12/2 Others 9
Bournemouth (Loaned on 29/9/1995) FL 7 Others 1
Leeds U (£4,000,000 + on 29/7/1999) PL 12+1/1 FLC 0+1 FAC 1 Others 1

DUBLIN Dion
Born: Leicester, 22 April 1969
Height: 6'1" Weight: 12.4
Club Honours: Div 3 '91
International Honours: E: 4

This popular Aston Villa striker began 1999-2000 in impressive goalscoring form, netting in the second game of the season against Everton and adding two fine strikes in the 2-2 draw with West Ham. His tally had reached 12 by mid-December, when he had the misfortune to suffer a serious neck injury in the home game against Sheffield Wednesday. Fractured neck vertebrae were diagnosed and surgery was required to repair what could have been a life-threatening injury. Dion was not expected to return before the end of the season but he was back in action just three months later. Fittingly, he scored the vital penalty that decided the shoot-out against Bolton Wanderers in the FA Cup semi-final and went on to make the starting line-up for the final against winners Chelsea. He remains a quality centre forward, strong and determined, good in the air and with an excellent eye for goal.

Norwich C (From Oakham U on 24/3/1988)
Cambridge U (Free on 2/8/1988) FL 133+23/52 FLC 8+2/5 FAC 21/11 Others 14+1/5
Manchester U (£1,000,000 on 7/8/1992) PL 4+8/2 FLC 1+1/1 FAC 1+1 Others 0+1
Coventry C (£2,000,000 on 9/9/1994) PL 144+1/61 FLC 11+2/4 FAC 13/7
Aston Villa (£5,750,000 on 6/11/1998) PL 47+3/23 FLC 4/3 FAC 2+1/1

DUDFIELD Lawrence (Lawrie) George
Born: Southwark, 7 May 1980
Height: 6'1" Weight: 13.9

A promising young striker who joined Leicester from Kettering Town in June 1997, Lawrie was given his debut late in the 1999-2000 season as a substitute in the home fixture against Everton. He made an immediate impact when his trickery earned a free kick that almost proved decisive. He made one further appearance from the bench and also featured prominently for the reserves, where he found the net regularly. He is clearly one to watch out for in the future.

Leicester C (Signed from Kettering T on 6/6/1997) PL 0+2

DUDLEY Craig Bryan
Born: Ollerton, 12 September 1979
Height: 5'10" Weight: 11.2
Club Honours: Div 3 '98
International Honours: E: Yth

Craig had a slow start to the 1999-2000 campaign and was loaned to Chesterfield towards the end of August. He was unable to make much impact at Saltergate but returned to Boundary Park revitalised and quickly established himself as a crowd favourite, netting four times from nine starts in the autumn. Although he was in and out of the team for the remainder of the season, he proved to be the Latics striker most likely to cause problems for opposition defences, notwithstanding the fact that he added just one more goal to his early-season flourish. A right-sided forward, he has good pace, is comfortable running with the ball at his feet and cuts in dangerously from the wing.

Notts Co (From trainee on 2/4/1997) FL 11+20/3 FLC 1+2/1 FAC 1+2
Shrewsbury T (Loaned on 8/1/1998) FL 3+1
Hull C (Loaned on 10/11/1998) FL 4+3/2
Oldham Ath (Free on 25/3/1999) FL 18+7/5 FAC 2+1/1
Chesterfield (Loaned on 20/8/1999) FL 0+2

DUFF Damien Anthony
Born: Dublin, Ireland, 2 March 1979
Height: 5'10" Weight: 9.7
International Honours: RoI: 14; B-1; Yth; Sch

Apart from a spell when manager Brian Kidd puzzlingly would not pick him, Damien was the star of the Blackburn attack in 1999-2000. At his best a mesmerising dribbler, ubiquitous inspiration and brilliant crosser of a ball, he added strength to his play last season and was prepared to track back and battle. His collection of "Man of the Match" awards was simply too numerous to mention, while without him the team rarely seemed capable of any incisive movement. The Irishman made five more international appearances for his country during the season.

Blackburn Rov (Signed from Lourdes Celtic on 5/3/1996) P/FL 69+25/10 FLC 7+1/1 FAC 9+2/2 Others 1

DUFF Michael James
Born: Belfast, 11 January 1978
Height: 6'1" Weight: 11.8

A knee injury forced Michael to miss the start of the 1999-2000 season, and he made his Football League debut in the unaccustomed role of centre back in Cheltenham's 2-0 defeat against Rotherham in October. Although still only 22, Michael has already made well over 150 appearances for the Robins, having made his club debut as a 17-year-old. Michael spent much of the campaign operating on the right-hand side of midfield, having been unable to secure his favoured right-back spot due to the form of Neil Howarth. His tall frame and long legs help him to accelerate away from defenders, while his height is also a weapon at set pieces. Michael now needs to improve his crossing in order to become an even more useful player.

Cheltenham T (From trainee on 17/8/1996) FL 31/2 FAC 2 Others 1

DUFFIELD Peter
Born: Middlesbrough, 4 February 1969
Height: 5'6" Weight: 10.4

After spending most of the first half of the 1999-2000 season on Darlington's substitutes' bench, this busy little forward forced his way into the side at Lee Nogan's expense. He produced 11 goals during the latter part of the campaign. His link-up play with the other forwards was impressive, and what he lacks in stature he more than makes up for in effort. Peter scored some spectacular goals with his head, as well as finding the net with a number of opportunist strikes. Stop Press: He was reported to have signed for York at the beginning of July.

Middlesbrough (From apprentice on 4/11/1986)
Sheffield U (Free on 20/8/1987) FL 34+24/14 FLC 3+5/2 FAC 6+2/1 Others 3+2/3
Halifax T (Loaned on 7/3/1988) FL 12/6 Others 1
Rotherham U (Loaned on 7/3/1991) FL 17/4
Blackpool (Loaned on 23/7/1992) FL 3+2/1 FLC 0+1
Crewe Alex (Loaned on 15/1/1993) FL 0+2 FAC 0+1
Stockport Co (Loaned on 19/3/1993) FL 6+1/4 Others 2+1
Hamilton Ac (Signed on 24/9/1993) SL 69+3/39 SLC 2/1 SC 2 Others 3/3
Airdrie (Signed on 21/7/1995) SL 19+5/6 SLC 2+2/2 SC 3/3 Others 1
Raith Rov (Signed on 2/3/1996) SL 37+14/11 SLC 2+1/3 SC 2 Others 1+1

Morton (Signed on 8/11/1997) SL 25/9 SLC 1 SC 1
Falkirk (Signed on 27/8/1998) SL 10+7/3
Darlington (Signed on 15/1/1999) FL 31+16/14 FLC 0+2 FAC 2/1 Others 3

DUGUID Karl Anthony
Born: Letchworth, 21 March 1978
Height: 5'11" Weight: 11.7

Karl successfully built on the previous season's breakthrough to establish himself as a first choice in the Colchester starting line-up in 1999-2000. He began the season as right wing back in Mick Wadsworth's reconstructed team, but Steve Whitton soon moved him up front to utilise "Doogie's" strength, competitiveness and lightning pace as an attacking weapon. His reward was to finish the season with a career-best 12 goals despite another spell at right back to cover for Joe Dunne's injury. Most memorable of the goals was probably the late winner at Preston, which demonstrated the character of the whole team but particularly Karl's stamina, as he had spent much of the game at full back but still had the desire to get forward at the death in search of a famous victory.

Colchester U (From trainee on 16/7/1996) FL 86+45/23 FLC 2+3 FAC 4+3 Others 1+5

DUMAS Franck
Born: Bayeux, France, 9 January 1968
Height: 5'11" Weight: 12.0

Franck is a player of vast experience gained in some 370 French league games plus 35 European ties who was signed in the 1999 close season to bolster the porous Newcastle defence. Played in midfield in the opening two games of the new campaign, he looked out of place, and his form plus the problems of a groin strain kept him on the sidelines until he was restored as a sweeper, his favoured position, by new manager Bobby Robson for the visit to Highbury at the end of October. Franck revelled in the role, turning in a brilliant performance and showing why he is considered by many French critics to be the best uncapped French defender around, and looked set for a long run in the side, although he missed a further couple of matches after incurring ankle ligament damage against Watford. Assured, composed and a good reader of the game, Franck unfortunately suffered a fractured and dislocated right elbow in the home UEFA Cup match against Roma. Although Bobby Robson was keen to keep him, he never really settled on Tyneside, and while still recovering from his elbow injury he was transferred to Marseille for financial reasons, Newcastle more than doubling their money.

Newcastle U (£500,000 from AS Monaco, France on 9/7/1999) PL 6 Others 1

DUNBAVIN Ian Stuart
Born: Huyton, 27 May 1980
Height: 6'2" Weight: 13.0

Ian signed for Shrewsbury from Liverpool in December 1999 on a free transfer. The young 'keeper made his league debut as a substitute in March in the home game against Cheltenham. After deputising for regular 'keeper Paul Edwards for two more games, Ian was preferred for the final four matches. A very quick mover off his line with a really strong kick, he is gaining in confidence and is definitely one to watch for in the future.

Liverpool (From trainee on 26/11/1998)
Shrewsbury T (Free on 17/1/2000) FL 6+1

DUNCAN Andrew (Andy)
Born: Hexham, 20 October 1977
Height: 5'11" Weight: 13.0
International Honours: E: Sch

Andy started 1999-2000 where he left off at the end of the previous campaign: playing a commanding role in the centre of the Cambridge defence. However, after he had been ever present for the first 15 games, with one goal to his credit, Andy's season was cruelly cut short when he broke his leg in the home game against Burnley in mid-October. He spent the remainder of the campaign recovering, with the process slowed somewhat as he also had a heel operation. Before the end of the term he was able to play in a friendly, which should stand him in good stead for pre-season training.

Manchester U (From trainee on 10/7/1996)
Cambridge U (£20,000 on 9/1/1998) FL 76+1/2 FLC 7 FAC 2 Others 3

DUNN David John Ian
Born: Blackburn, 27 December 1979
Height: 5'10" Weight: 12.3
International Honours: E: U21-4; Yth

This locally born midfielder endured a frustrating season at Blackburn in 1999-2000 without a regular first-team place. Whenever he played he gave good value with his determined running and accomplished skills, but he was most effective during a spell in November when he was employed wide on the right. By the end of February he had had enough and submitted a transfer request, which was turned down. Under Graeme Souness, however, he gained a new momentum and contributed a cracking last-minute winner against Birmingham in March. He finished the season on a high, being selected for the England U21 squad for the European Championship in Slovakia and featuring in all three of his country's games.

Blackburn Rov (From trainee on 30/9/1997) P/FL 27+10/3 FLC 4+1/1 FAC 2+2

DUNNE Joseph (Joe) John
Born: Dublin, 25 May 1973
Height: 5'9" Weight: 11.6
International Honours: RoI: U21-1; Yth; Sch

Joe was surprisingly released by then Colchester manager Mick Wadsworth at the end of 1998-99, joining Dover in the Conference, but when Steve Whitton took over in the autumn he identified a weakness at right back and wasted no time in bringing Joe back "home", where he immediately gave the supporters a reminder of what they had been missing with a "Man of the Match" performance on his debut against Luton. A good, consistent season followed, where Joe's competitiveness and commitment were again well to the fore, and he was rewarded by taking up the captaincy on the odd occasion David Gregory was off the pitch.

Gillingham (From trainee on 9/8/1990) FL 108+7/1 FLC 7 FAC 5+1 Others 4+2
Colchester U (Free on 27/3/1996) FL 79+22/3 FLC 3+1/1 FAC 5+1 Others 7+1 (Free to Dover Ath during 1999 close season)
Colchester U (Free on 14/12/1999) FL 19+1

DUNNE Richard Patrick
Born: Dublin, 21 September 1979
Height: 6'1" Weight: 14.0
Club Honours: FAYC '98
International Honours: RoI: 3; B-1; U21-4; Yth; (UEFA-U18 '98); Sch

The young Irish defender with the build of a heavyweight boxer established himself as a regular in Everton's rearguard throughout 1999-2000. Only occasionally did Richard fill his preferred role of centre half, but it said a lot for his versatility and his willingness that he was regularly selected at right back, where he performed solidly. Deceptively quick for such a giant of a player, he is predictably powerful in the tackle and solid in the air. In full flight on the overlap he can be a formidable sight, too, and takes some stopping. The only disappointment during a progressive season for him was a disciplinary record which means he will be suspended for the first five matches of the new campaign. Richard won three more Republic of Ireland U21 caps, going on to make his debut for the full international team against Greece in April before adding caps against Scotland and Mexico, when he scored in a 2-2 draw.

Everton (From trainee on 8/10/1996) PL 50+7 FLC 3 FAC 8

DURKAN Kieran John
Born: Chester, 1 December 1973
Height: 5'11" Weight: 12.10
Club Honours: WC '95
International Honours: RoI: U21-3

Capable of playing on both wings, although usually found on Macclesfield's right flank, the former Republic of Ireland U21 international has the ability to move swiftly and make pin-point crosses. His 1999-2000 season did not really take off until the away match at Exeter at the end of September. Following the team's recent poor form, manager Sammy McIlroy decided, only some 45 minutes before kick-off, that Keiran should partner Richie Barker up front. This move proved to be an immediate success with Macc scoring three goals before the break, the third coming from Keiran. This partnership continued for many matches before he was forced out of the team by injury. Involved in all but five of Town's fixtures, on his return Keiran successfully resumed his role as a winger, scoring vital goals that earned valuable points.

Wrexham (From trainee on 16/7/1992) FL 43+7/3 FLC 3+1 FAC 4+2/2 Others 15/1
Stockport Co (£95,000 on 16/2/1996) FL 52+12/4 FLC 10+1 FAC 4/3 Others 4+2
Macclesfield T (£15,000 on 25/3/1998) FL 66+6/9 FLC 1+3 FAC 2+2 Others 1+1

DURNIN John Paul
Born: Bootle, 18 August 1965
Height: 5'10" Weight: 11.10

This hard-working, experienced striker rarely featured in Portsmouth manager Alan Ball's plans in the early part of the 1999-2000 season and moved to Blackpool on loan at the end of October. He showed he still had a good eye for goal during his spell at Bloomfield Road, scoring in the home draw with Wigan and against Ryman League club Hendon in the FA Cup before returning to Fratton Park. John had another loan spell at Carlisle in January before joining the Cumbrian club permanently on a free transfer last February. His finest moments for United came in the 2-0 victory at Peterborough in March that he secured with two long-range strikes. However, they proved to be his last goals for the club as he was released in May.

Liverpool (Free from Waterloo Dock on 29/3/1986) FLC 1+1
West Bromwich A (Loaned on 20/10/1988) FL 5/2
Oxford U (£225,000 on 10/2/1989) FL 140+21/44 FLC 7/1 FAC 7/1 Others 4+1/1
Portsmouth (£200,000 on 15/7/1993) FL 118+63/31 FLC 14+3/2 FAC 5+2 Others 4+2
Blackpool (Loaned on 1/11/1999) FL 4+1/1 FAC 1/1
Carlisle U (Free on 3/12/1999) FL 20+2/2 Others 1

DUXBURY Lee Edward
Born: Keighley, 7 October 1969
Height: 5'10" Weight: 11.13

Lee once again captained Oldham in 1999-2000, when he was mostly employed in a holding role in the centre of midfield. He remains a strong tackler, a threat when breaking forward and a quality passer of the ball. The highlight of his season was his 87th-minute goal at Wigan in January which gave Oldham a surprise 1-0 victory and ended a 24-match unbeaten run by the home team. Lee is popular with the Latics' supporters and was runner-up in last season's "Player of the Year" vote.

Bradford C (From trainee on 4/7/1988) FL 204+5/25 FLC 18+1/3 FAC 11 Others 13
Rochdale (Loaned on 18/1/1990) FL 9+1 FAC 1
Huddersfield T (£250,000 on 23/12/1994) FL 29/2 FLC 1 Others 3
Bradford C (£135,000 on 15/11/1995) FL 63/7 FLC 2 FAC 5 Others 3
Oldham Ath (£350,000 on 7/3/1997) FL 132+2/16 FLC 5 FAC 11/2 Others 3

DYCHE Sean Mark
Born: Kettering, 28 June 1971
Height: 6'0" Weight: 13.10

Sean, a 6ft central defender, joined Millwall from Bristol City in the summer of 1999. Unfortunately, he was injured in a pre-season friendly against Peterborough and was ruled out for several months, playing just a handful of reserve games. With other players suffering fitness problems, he was given his first-team chance at Luton in March only to pick up another injury which put him out for the rest of the season. His reputation as a strong, hard-tackling centre back is not in doubt but the Millwall fans have yet to see him at his best.

Nottingham F (From trainee on 20/5/1989)
Chesterfield (Free on 1/2/1990) FL 219+12/8 FLC 9 FAC 13/1 Others 16
Bristol C (£350,000 on 11/7/1997) FL 14+3 FLC 2+1
Luton T (Loaned on 4/1/1999) FL 14/1 Others 1
Millwall (£150,000 on 5/7/1999) FL 1

DYER Alexander (Alex) Constantine
Born: Forest Gate, 14 November 1965
Height: 6'0" Weight: 12.0

Alex had another outstanding season for Notts County in 1999-2000, producing a series of composed performances and scoring six valuable goals. Mostly employed as a left-sided defender, he showed skill on the ball and was rarely wasteful in his distribution. He remains a cult figure with the Magpies' supporters, who voted him "Player of the Season" at the end of the campaign.

Blackpool (Free from Watford juniors on 20/10/1983) FL 101+7/19 FLC 8+1/1 FAC 4+1 Others 7/1
Hull C (£37,000 on 13/2/1987) FL 59+1/14 FLC 2 FAC 4/1
Crystal Palace (£250,000 on 11/11/1988) FL 16+1/2 FLC 3+1 FAC 1+1 Others 3+1/3
Charlton Ath (£100,000 on 30/11/1990) FL 60+18/13 FLC 2+1 FAC 1/1 Others 3+1
Oxford U (Free on 26/7/1993) FL 62+14/6 FLC 4/1 FAC 5/1 Others 5
Lincoln C (Free on 21/8/1995) FL 1 FLC 1
Barnet (Free on 1/9/1995) FL 30+5/2 Others 1 (Freed on 9/5/1996)
Huddersfield T (Signed from FA Maia, Portugal on 13/8/1997) FL 8+4/1 FLC 3/1
Notts Co (Free on 2/3/1998) FL 50+19/6 FLC 0+2 FAC 5+1 Others 0+1

DYER Bruce Antonio
Born: Ilford, 13 April 1975
Height: 6'0" Weight: 11.3
International Honours: E: U21-11

This big and powerful Barnsley player shared duties as a striker at Oakwell with Neil Shipperley and Mike Sheron during the 1999-2000 season. Despite scoring some spectacular goals, Bruce often found himself on the subs' bench and he would undoubtedly have benefited from an extended run in the starting line-up. One of the highlights of his season was scoring two of the goals which contributed to the Tykes' 4-0 victory at Birmingham in the first leg of the play-off semi-final, a result which effectively secured the club's first-ever Wembley visit. He can be a handful for opposition defences who struggle to cope with his pace and strength.

Watford (From trainee on 19/4/1993) FL 29+2/6 FLC 4/2 FAC 1 Others 2/1
Crystal Palace (£1,100,000 on 10/3/1994) F/PL 95+40/37 FLC 9+5/1 FAC 7+3/6 Others 3+2
Barnsley (£700,000 on 23/10/1998) FL 41+19/13 FLC 3+1 FAC 2+1/1 Others 2+1/3

DYER Keiron Courtney
Born: Ipswich, 29 December 1978
Height: 5'7" Weight: 9.7
International Honours: E: 5; B-2; U21-11; Yth

The first English signing by Ruud Gullit, Kieron arrived at Newcastle from Ipswich in the summer of 1999 with a reputation as one of the game's top prospects, and his performances in his first season in the Premiership confirmed him as a footballer of exciting potential. He is a sharp, bright, inventive player with good control and an impressive engine, and he performed with distinction in a number of positions, namely right wing back, where he made an outstanding England debut against Luxembourg, right wing, a free role in midfield behind the strikers, a position which many good judges believe is where he will be most effective long-term, and even up front as in the later stages of the FA Cup semi-final. Kieron strained stomach muscles in pre-season and he therefore started the term on the bench against Villa, coming on to play the second half and immediately exciting the "Toon Army" with his drive, energy and flair. After carrying for a while a long-standing problem with circulation in the calf, he finally succumbed to the injury and underwent surgery in October, returning in the new year, when he continued to impress, never more so than at Goodison, where he ran from his own half, leaving the Everton defence trailing in his wake, before lobbing the 'keeper for an outstanding goal. Although only in his early twenties, Kieron is very mature and self-confident, as demonstrated by his performances on his England debut and in the FA Cup semi-final, where, far from being overawed, he was one of United's best players on the day. He went on to win a total of five international caps during the season and is clearly a player around whom Newcastle and England can build for the future with every hope of success.

Ipswich T (From trainee on 3/1/1997) FL 79+12/9 FLC 11/1 FAC 5 Others 5+1/2
Newcastle U (£6,000,000 on 16/7/1999) PL 27+7/3 FAC 5+1/1 Others 3

DYSON James Gareth
Born: Stourbridge, 20 April 1979
Height: 6'2" Weight: 12.0

James is a talented former Birmingham City trainee who made his bow in senior football playing on the right of midfield in the Blues' 2-1 victory at Exeter in the Worthington Cup in August 1999. He did well with the club's reserve team and made his league debut last Christmas at Molineux as a substitute striker. Unfortunately, he then suffered a broken leg in a training accident in January 2000 and this brought his season to an early close.

Birmingham C (From trainee on 1/7/1997) FL 0+2 FLC 0+1

DYSON Jonathan (Jon) Paul
Born: Mirfield, 18 December 1971
Height: 6'1" Weight: 12.12

In the year 2001, Jon will be celebrating ten years with his one and only club, Huddersfield, a feat not often seen in today's game. Nevertheless, "Mr Reliable" was regularly called upon to play in various defensive roles during 1999-2000. Always strong in the tackle, and noted for his measured distribution, the assured defender even enjoyed scoring in consecutive matches against Sheffield United and Ipswich Town, both headed goals from corners. Only suspension and a bout of shingles kept him from a first-team call-up during the Terriers' promising season.

Huddersfield T (From juniors on 29/12/1990) FL 157+26/6 FLC 16+4 FAC 9 Others 7+4

EADEN Nicholas (Nicky) Jeremy
Born: Sheffield, 12 December 1972
Height: 5'9" Weight: 12.8
Nicky was on the subs' bench for Barnsley's visit to Charlton on the opening day of the 1999-2000 season but quickly returned to the starting line-up and shortly afterwards he took over the role of club captain from Kevin Richardson. He was an important member of the Tykes' promotion campaign, and although his form occasionally dipped he helped keep the club's strikers supplied with some excellent crosses. With Dave Bassett switching formation from three centre backs to a flat back four, Nicky was initially used at right back but later moved to a wide-right midfield role, in which he linked up well with John Curtis and Craig Hignett. He is an unselfish worker who is comfortable when running forward with the ball and delivers an excellent first-time cross. Stop Press: Out of contract in the summer, Nicky was reported to have signed for Birmingham City at the beginning of July.
Barnsley (From juniors on 4/6/1991) F/PL 281+12/10 FLC 18+3/3 FAC 20 Others 4+1

EADIE Darren Malcolm
Born: Chippenham, 10 June 1975
Height: 5'8" Weight: 11.6
International Honours: E: U21-7; Yth
Darren joined Leicester City from Norwich in December 1999, having played a total of 204 games for the Canaries. Having missed much of the previous season with a knee injury, the former England U21 international was sidelined at the start of the 1999-2000 campaign with a recurrence of the problem sustained during a pre-season tour of Sweden. At his best he is one of the most effective left-sided players in the country, possessing electrifying pace and a direct style which can unsettle the very best defenders. He can operate as an orthodox winger or as a central striker, when his ability to turn and twist can create real problems for defenders. Leicester paid a club record fee of £3 million to secure his services and, despite a lack of match fitness, Darren was soon showing glimpses of the ability that Martin O'Neill had seen in him, filling in in a variety of roles during the Foxes' mid-season injury crisis. Outstanding at Highbury in the FA Cup before being harshly red-carded, he proved to be particularly threatening when employed in a free role just behind the main strikers. All he needs now is a goal to set him off and the City supporters will be looking to see the best of Darren during the coming season.
Norwich C (From trainee on 5/2/1993) P/FL 153+15/35 FLC 25+1/2 FAC 7+1/1 Others 1+1
Leicester C (£3,000,000 on 10/12/1999) PL 15+1 FAC 3

EARLE Robert (Robbie) Gerald
Born: Newcastle under Lyme, 27 January 1965
Height: 5'9" Weight: 10.10
International Honours: Jamaica: 11
A credit to the game for many years, Wimbledon's club captain was awarded the MBE in June 1999. Robbie is a true ambassador for the club and for football in general, and unselfishly promotes a host of good causes in the community as well as pursuing his own media interests. An interesting and articulate man, he is likely to succeed in anything he sets his mind to. Robbie missed the last few weeks of the 1999-2000 season after sustaining a freak injury in a reserve match at Watford. This resulted in a blood clot in his stomach and obliged him to spend six weeks in hospital. Provided that he is able to agree terms for a new contract during the summer, his leadership qualities will again be to the fore during the coming season as the Dons endeavour to return to the Premiership at the first attempt, as will his box-to-box runs, tackles and timely headed goals. He is probably a candidate to slip into a coaching role at the club in the future.
Port Vale (From juniors on 5/7/1982) FL 284+10/77 FLC 21+2/4 FAC 20+1/4 Others 18+1/5
Wimbledon (£775,000 on 19/7/1991) F/PL 280+4/59 FLC 29+1/8 FAC 35/8 Others 1/1

EARNSHAW Robert
Born: Zambia, 6 April 1981
Height: 5'8" Weight: 10.10
International Honours: W: U21-5; Yth
This speedy and exciting striker has yet to establish himself in the starting line-up at Cardiff and has had loan spells at Fulham, Middlesbrough and Greenock Morton during his short career. The Welsh U21 international made a handful of appearances towards the end of last season and, although he finished the campaign with a knee injury, City are hoping that he will break through into the first team in 2000-01. His mother was a professional footballer and professional boxer in Zambia, where Robert was born, while he has two uncles who are professional footballers. He won three more caps for Wales at U18 level in 1999-2000 and also appeared as a substitute in the end-of-season U21 friendlies against Scotland and Northern Ireland.
Cardiff C (Trainee) FL 5+11/2 FLC 0+1 FAC 0+1 Others 0+1
Greenock Morton (Loaned on 20/1/2000) SL 3/2 SC 1

EASTON Clint Jude
Born: Barking, 1 October 1977
Height: 5'11' Weight: 10.8
Club Honours: Div 2 '98
International Honours: E: Yth
A left-sided midfield player whose passing ability and vision mark him out as a potential play-maker, Clint is one of the young players who will have benefited from Watford's season in the Premiership in 1999-2000. He at last enjoyed a regular run in the first team, albeit frequently as a substitute, and has now made more than 50 league appearances for Watford, his only club. Clint started the season as an emergency left back, but was thereafter deployed wide on the left, where his enthusiasm and improved strength on the ball complemented his considerable skill. A hamstring strain sustained in November proved more serious than at first thought and lost him three months, but he was back before the end of the season.
Watford (From trainee on 5/7/1996) P/FL 45+8/1 FLC 3+2/1 FAC 3+1 Others 3

EATON Adam Paul
Born: Wigan, 2 May 1980
Height: 5'11" Weight: 11.2
Club Honours: FAYC '98
A young left back signed by Preston from Everton in the summer of 1999, Adam suffered a broken toe in pre-season but it did not hinder him too much, and he continued to make impressive progress in the reserves. A tough-tackling player who likes to get forward and support the attack, he made just one appearance for the first team in 1999-2000, coming on as a substitute in the Auto Windscreens Shield after sitting on the bench several times, but definitely looks to be one to watch for in the future.
Everton (From trainee on 2/6/1997)
Preston NE (Free on 29/6/1999) Others 0+1

EBDON Marcus
Born: Pontypool, 17 October 1970
Height: 5'10" Weight: 12.4
International Honours: W: U21-2; Yth
Chesterfield sank to the bottom of the Second Division a week after Marcus was sidelined with achilles tendon damage last November. The Spireites badly missed his fighting qualities, his creativity and his eye for the telling pass that gets the side moving forwards. Not a regular scorer himself, Marcus put away a stunning goal against Rochdale in the Worthington Cup, bringing the ball down with one foot and, on the volley, crashing it home with the other.
Everton (From trainee on 16/8/1989)
Peterborough U (Free on 15/7/1991) FL 136+11/15 FLC 14+2 FAC 12+3/1 Others 11+1
Chesterfield (£100,000 on 21/3/1997) FL 89+7/4 FLC 6+1/1 FAC 5 Others 2

ECKHARDT Jeffrey (Jeff) Edward
Born: Sheffield, 7 October 1965
Height: 6'0" Weight: 11.7
A strong, wholehearted and committed defender, Jeff was a regular in the Cardiff first team in 1999-2000 and never gave less than 100 per cent effort. He is a consistent and versatile player who can also play in midfield or up front, but he was out of contract at the end of the season and City somewhat surprisingly decided not to offer him a new deal. Jeff immediately received an offer from another Third Division club and a number of non-league outfits also showed interest. He is a qualified chiropodist and was considering his options during the summer, although he expected to continue his playing career.
Sheffield U (From juniors on 23/8/1984) FL 73+1/2 FLC 7 FAC 2 Others 5
Fulham (£50,000 on 20/11/1987) FL 245+4/25 FLC 13 FAC 5+1 Others 15/3

Stockport Co (£50,000 on 21/7/1994) FL 56+6/7 FLC 6+2/1 FAC 5/4 Others 2
Cardiff C (£30,000 on 22/8/1996) FL 123+9/14 FLC 5+2/1 FAC 11+1/1 Others 5/1

EDDS Gareth James
Born: Sydney, Australia, 3 February 1981
Height: 5'11" Weight: 10.12

This 19-year-old full back made his league debut for Nottingham Forest in the last home game of 1999-2000 against Port Vale, replacing Jim Brennan, who was absent on international duty. He did well enough to retain his first-team slot for the visit to Stockport and looks to have a good future in the game. Tall and well built, he is strong in the tackle and likes to get forward to assist the attack.

Nottingham F (From trainee on 19/2/1998) FL 2

EDGE Roland
Born: Gillingham, 25 November 1978
Height: 5'9" Weight: 11.6

This talented Gillingham youngster broke through to the first team last December and, apart from a brief spell out with a groin injury in March, he featured regularly for the Kent club for the remainder of the 1999-2000 campaign. Roland produced some excellent performances at left back and scored his first goal in senior football in the 1-0 victory over Bury in December. Neat and tidy with good ball control, he is also able to play in a midfield role if required to do so.

Gillingham (From trainee on 10/7/1997) FL 26+8/1 FAC 8+1 Others 5

EDGHILL Richard Arlon
Born: Oldham, 23 September 1974
Height: 5'9" Weight: 11.5
International Honours: E: B-1; U21-3

Richard made a promising start to the 1999-2000 season for Manchester City, filling either of the full-back positions, before a clash of heads with Mark Hughes in City's Worthington Cup defeat at Southampton put him in hospital for a night. The injury – coupled with a suspension – kept him out of the team for the next three games. Following his return to the side, Richard scored his first-ever league goal for the club, against Blackburn, coming in on the right to meet Mark Kennedy's perfect cross from the left and coolly slotting home. It was one of the most satisfyingly worked goals seen at Maine Road all season. Thereafter Richard missed only one game and he maintained his excellent form. Hard working, committed and strong in the tackle, he has the ability to play himself out of tight situations with neat flicks, close ball control and intelligent running. A reliable clubman, he was City's captain from October onwards and played a key role in their triumphant return to the Premiership.

Manchester C (From trainee on 15/7/1992) P/FL 163+1/1 FLC 17 FAC 6 Others 3

EDINBURGH Justin Charles
Born: Basildon, 18 December 1969
Height: 5'10" Weight: 12.0
Club Honours: FAC '91; FLC '99

After no fewer than ten seasons at Tottenham, the gutsy left back bade farewell to White Hart Lane with a move to Portsmouth last March, having featured in the first team only irregularly in 1999-2000. Justin will be remembered by the Spurs faithful for his committed challenges, his pace down the left and his extraordinary tenacity. Snapped up by Portsmouth manager Tony Pulis to help plug a badly leaking defence, Justin proved to be a useful signing, and his great determination made him a favourite with the Pompey fans over the final weeks of the 1999-2000 season. He enjoyed a successful testimonial match at Fratton Park in May when a crowd of 7,000 watched Portsmouth take on his former club Tottenham, and has already set himself up for a new career when he retires from playing, being the holder of a UEFA "B" coaching badge.

Southend U (From trainee on 5/8/1988) FL 36+1 FLC 2+1 FAC 2 Others 4+1/1
Tottenham H (£150,000 on 30/7/1990) F/PL 190+23/1 FLC 25+4 FAC 27+1 Others 4+2
Portsmouth (£175,000 on 6/3/2000) FL 11

EDMONDSON Darren Stephen
Born: Coniston, 4 November 1971
Height: 6'0" Weight: 12.11
Club Honours: Div 3 '95; AMC '97

A wholehearted and committed performer, Darren was again cast as a fringe player at Huddersfield last season, but when called upon would always give a solid display in the right-back position. Following a trial with Darlington in September, he made two starts for the Terriers, against Barnsley and Sheffield United in October, before joining York just before the transfer deadline in March until the end of the season. He was signed by York's new boss, Terry Dolan, who had recently vacated his post as reserve coach at the McAlpine Stadium. A strong and hard-tackling defender, Darren quickly settled in on the right-hand side of City's back line. Offered new terms in May, he will be hoping that it will be third time lucky in Yorkshire. His YT stint at Hull was terminated due to homesickness.

Carlisle U (From trainee on 17/7/1990) FL 205+9/9 FLC 15/1 FAC 15/3 Others 22/3
Huddersfield T (£200,000 + on 3/3/1997) FL 28+9 FLC 2 FAC 2+2
Plymouth Arg (Loaned on 11/9/1998) FL 4
York C (Free on 23/3/2000) FL 7

EDWARDS Andrew (Andy) David
Born: Epping, 17 September 1971
Height: 6'3" Weight: 12.10

The 1999-2000 season was yet another fine one for one of Peterborough's most consistent performers. The Posh captain missed only two games as United returned to Division Two via the play-offs. He is a commanding defender who is always a danger in the opposition's box at set pieces. Although he found the net only twice last season, his presence occupied other defenders. A good tackler and quick to recover, Andy has also served under Posh manager Barry Fry at Southend and Birmingham.

Southend U (From trainee on 14/12/1989) FL 141+6/5 FLC 5 FAC 4 Others 9/2
Birmingham C (£400,000 on 6/7/1995) FL 37+3/1 FLC 12/1 FAC 2 Others 5/1
Peterborough U (Signed on 29/11/1996) FL 156/6 FLC 8 FAC 10 Others 15/1

EDWARDS Christian (Chris) Nicholas Howells
Born: Caerphilly, 23 November 1975
Height: 6'2" Weight: 12.8
International Honours: W: 1; B-2; U21-7

Christian joined Oxford on loan from Nottingham Forest last February. A big centre back with a commanding presence who shines in aerial battles in both penalty areas, he had not played in the Forest first team all season but was brought to the Manor Ground as a stop-gap measure and made a scoring start in a 1-4 defeat by Wrexham. He made a total of five appearances for United but returned to Forest at the end of his agreed spell after Oxford's first-choice pairing had recovered from injury and returned from international duty respectively.

Swansea C (From trainee on 20/7/1994) FL 113+2/4 FLC 5 FAC 4 Others 9+1
Nottingham F (£175,000 + on 26/3/1998) PL 7+5
Bristol C (Loaned on 11/12/1998) FL 3
Oxford U (Loaned on 24/2/2000) FL 5/1

EDWARDS Jake
Born: Prestwich, 11 May 1976
Height: 6'2" Weight: 13.0

Jake failed to make the starting line-up for Wrexham in 1999-2000, the striker being restricted to two early-season outings as a substitute before joining Telford United on loan last November. He moved permanently for a £20,000 fee in January and went on to help the Conference outfit reach the semi-finals of the FA Trophy, finishing the campaign as the club's leading scorer.

Wrexham (Free from James Maddison University, USA on 13/8/1998) FL 4+7/2 Others 1+4/2

EDWARDS Michael
Born: Hessle, 25 April 1980
Height: 6'1" Weight: 12.0

His achievement in making his 100th senior appearance for Hull before his 20th birthday is a testimony to Michael's continuing progress during 1999-2000. Tagged as one of the best young prospects in the lower divisions, he previously captained Yorkshire U15s at cricket, while in schools soccer he played alongside Leeds United's Paul Robinson, Sheffield United's Curtis Woodhouse and Derby County's Lee Morris for Hull U16s. An assured defender, he added goalscoring to his CV last season with a run of three in five games. His first (in his 81st game) was against Hayes in the FA Cup. Not only was it featured on "Match of the Day", but his kit sponsor was a building company based in … Hayes! Michael signed a two-year contract in the summer of '99 but is already looking well beyond that – he is studying to become a qualified physio.

Hull C (From trainee on 16/7/1998) FL 84+7/1 FLC 5+1 FAC 8/2 Others 4+1

EDWARDS Neil Ryan
Born: Aberdare, 5 December 1970
Height: 5'9" Weight: 11.10
International Honours: W: U21-1; Yth; Sch

"Taffy" remained Rochdale's undisputed number one 'keeper throughout 1999-2000, and performed his usual heroics. He hit the national headlines early in the campaign when Dale had the best defensive record in the Football League. They started with five clean sheets in a row away from home and conceded just 17 goals in 24 games. He later suffered a groin strain, but played on until having to come off after only a couple of minutes at Exeter in January. Although he had to have a hernia operation, remarkably, he missed only six matches. Said to be too small for a 'keeper, Neil continues to defy the doubters.

Leeds U (From trainee on 10/3/1989) Others 1
Stockport Co (£5,000 on 3/9/1991) FL 163+1 FLC 11 FAC 11 Others 31
Rochdale (£25,000 on 3/11/1997) FL 112 FLC 4 FAC 7+1 Others 8

EDWARDS Paul
Born: Liverpool, 22 February 1965
Height: 5'11" Weight: 11.5
Club Honours: Div 3 '94

The regular Shrewsbury 'keeper, Paul completed his eighth season at Gay Meadow in 1999-2000. A well-respected clubman, he had one of his busiest seasons as the team generally struggled. Paul is a good shot stopper and always looks confident when handling the ball. He had a spell out with injury in March, and was not the preferred custodian for the last four games, but is likely to remain a familiar figure at Gay Meadow.

Crewe Alex (Free from Leek T on 24/2/1989) FL 29 FLC 4 FAC 3 Others 4
Shrewsbury T (Free on 6/8/1992) FL 286 FLC 16 FAC 19+1 Others 17

EDWARDS Robert (Rob)
Born: Manchester, 23 February 1970
Height: 5'9" Weight: 12.4

The tenacious Huddersfield left back-cum-midfielder made a couple of early-season starts in the first round of the Worthington Cup against Scunthorpe United but, with the exception of the game at Ipswich in February, his only league appearances in 1999-2000 were as a substitute. Always solid in defence and a handful at dead-ball situations, Rob scored a wonderful last-minute winner in the Sky-televised game against Blackburn Rovers in August, but it was a rare moment of triumph in a generally disappointing campaign. After a spell out through injury Rob will be looking to establish himself again during the coming season after showing much promise in 1998-99.

Crewe Alex (From trainee on 11/7/1988) FL 110+45/44 FLC 8/5 FAC 13+5/5 Others 9+8/4
Huddersfield T (£150,000 on 8/3/1996) FL 109+29/14 FLC 12+1/1 FAC 7+1/1

EDWARDS Robert (Rob) William
Born: Kendal, 1 July 1973
Height: 6'0" Weight: 12.2
Club Honours: Div 2 '00
International Honours: W: 4; B-2; U21-17; Yth

After Rob had rejected a new deal at Bristol City in the summer of 1999, an initial one-month contract at Preston was soon extended to three years, and he demonstrated his versatility by settling into the North End side as the regular left back in 1999-2000, having come on as a substitute in the opening game. Having scored his first goal for the club against Wrexham in the Auto Windscreens Shield, he then celebrated the 350th game of his career with his first Preston league goal 18 seconds after the restart at Cardiff. Only occasionally featuring in his more recognised midfield role as North End marched towards the Second Division championship, he gave a star performance in this position at Burnley which included a 30-yard goal. A neat, composed player wherever he plays, he likes to pass the ball around and is keen to overlap, while his height is a definite advantage at set pieces.

Carlisle U (From trainee on 10/4/1990) FL 48/5 FLC 4 FAC 1 Others 2+1
Bristol C (£135,000 on 27/3/1991) FL 188+28/5 FLC 16+3/1 FAC 13+2 Others 12+1/2
Preston NE (Free on 5/8/1999) FL 37+4/2 FLC 5 FAC 6 Others 2/1

EDWORTHY Marc
Born: Barnstaple, 24 December 1972
Height: 5'8" Weight: 11.10

Marc was the logical replacement at right back for Roland Nilsson when the Swede returned to his homeland in the summer of 1999, and for the first time since joining Coventry he was able to play in his natural position. He started last season well with some energetic displays and missed only one of the first 13 games. He showed both his speed and his excellent passing ability before it all went wrong against Newcastle when he suffered a serious ankle injury. It was later discovered to be a snapped ligament and he was in plaster for six weeks. He was back in training before the end of the season and was expected to be fit for the 2000-01 season.

Plymouth Arg (From trainee on 30/3/1991) FL 52+17/1 FLC 5+2 FAC 5+2 Others 2+2
Crystal Palace (£350,000 on 9/6/1995) F/PL 120+6 FLC 8+1/1 FAC 8 Others 6
Coventry C (£850,000 + on 28/8/1998) PL 26+6 FLC 2 FAC 1

EHIOGU Ugochuku (Ugo)
Born: Hackney, 3 November 1972
Height: 6'2" Weight: 14.10
Club Honours: FLC '96
International Honours: E: 1; B-1; U21-15

This imposing defender was once again a vital component of the Aston Villa team in 1999-2000 and sorely missed when absent. He was an ever-present until sustaining a torn calf muscle in the Worthington Cup tie against Manchester United last October, and this kept him out of action for two months. He was, as ever, rock-like in the centre of Villa's defence and made a great contribution to the club's FA Cup campaign, producing a solid display in the final when Villa lost out to Chelsea. Ugo mostly appeared in a three-man defence alongside Gareth Barry and Gareth Southgate, performing consistently well throughout the campaign and being rather unlucky not to win further international honours. Apart from his obvious physical presence, his strengths lie in his tough tackling and ability to dominate opponents in the air.

West Bromwich A (From trainee on 13/7/1989) FL 0+2
Aston Villa (£40,000 on 12/7/1991) F/PL 222+13/12 FLC 23+1/1 FAC 22+2/1 Others 16/1

EINARSSON Gunnar
Born: Reykjavik, Iceland, 7 July 1976
Height: 5'11" Weight: 11.4
International Honours: Iceland: 1; U21; Yth

This former Iceland U21 midfielder had a three-month trial at Brentford during the second half of 1999-2000 following a spell playing in the Netherlands with Roda JC. He is essentially a marker rather than a creative player but was restricted to just one start and a handful of appearances as a substitute while at Griffin Park.

Brentford (Loaned from Roda JC, Holland on 13/1/2000) FL 1+2 Others 0+1

EL KHALEJ Tahar
Born: Morocco, 16 June 1968
Height: 6'3" Weight: 13.8
International Honours: Morocco: 72

This experienced Morocco international who has represented his country in two World Cup finals and three African Nations' Cup championships joined Southampton for a bargain £300,000 fee last March. A utility man equally at home in a midfield anchor role or in the middle of defence, he made his debut as a right back at Tottenham and scored with a close-range header. Moved by manager Glenn Hoddle to partner Dean Richards in the middle of defence soon afterwards, he adapted quickly and impressed with some outstanding performances. Still a regular at international level, he appeared in all three of his country's games in the African Nations' Cup finals in the spring.

Southampton (£300,000 from Benfica, Portugal, via KAC Marrakesh, Uniao Leiria, on 10/3/2000) PL 11/1

ELLINGTON Lee Simon
Born: Bradford, 3 July 1980
Height: 5'10" Weight: 11.0

Lee was transfer-listed by Hull in the 1999 close season. After unsuccessful trials at several clubs, he joined Exeter on a non-contract basis in March. The young striker made two substitute appearances for the Grecians but was not offered a permanent contract. Manager Noel Blake had remembered Lee's two-goal salvo for Hull against Exeter in November 1997. They were his first senior goals.

Hull C (From trainee on 16/7/1998) FL 7+8/2 FLC 1+2 FAC 0+3 Others 0+3
Exeter C (Free on 13/3/2000) FL 0+1 Others 0+1

ELLINGTON Nathan Levi Fontaine
Born: Bradford, 2 July 1981
Height: 5'10" Weight: 12.10

This all-action striker remained an important member of Bristol Rovers' first-team squad in 1999-2000. "The Duke", as he was nicknamed, a former Walton and Hersham player, could always be relied upon to make an impact when being introduced from the substitutes' bench. In his three starts for Rovers Nathan scored cracking goals in the 3-0 victory at Brentford, the 1-1 draw at Wycombe Wanderers and the 5-0 rout of Oxford United. Still a teenager, he has developed his heading ability to complement his pace and close control and will certainly be a fine goalscoring prospect.

Bristol Rov (£150,000 from Walton & Hersham on 18/2/1999) FL 13+34/5 FAC 0+1 Others 1+1

ELLIOTT Matthew (Matt) Stephen
Born: Wandsworth, 1 November 1968
Height: 6'3" Weight: 14.10
Club Honours: FLC '00
International Honours: S: 9

Leicester's right-footed central defender had an outstanding season in 1999-2000. Always a rock at the heart of City's defence, Matt did not notch his first goal of the campaign until just before Christmas, when employed as an emergency striker in the FA Cup replay against non-league Hereford. He then continued to shuffle between defence and attack during the Foxes' mid-season injury crisis, often appearing in the opposition box with devastating effect. A brace against Everton got the new century off on the right note and it was his coolly placed header against Aston Villa that sent Leicester to Wembley for the seventh time in nine seasons. Leading City out beneath the Twin Towers, Matt headed a goal in each half to secure the Worthington Cup for his team and the "Man of the Match" trophy for himself. His excellent form also earned him an overdue recall to the Scotland squad and he appeared in the end-of-season friendlies with Holland and the Republic of Ireland.

Charlton Ath (£5,000 from Epsom & Ewell on 9/5/1988) FLC 1
Torquay U (£10,000 on 23/3/1989) FL 123+1/15 FLC 9/2 FAC 9/2 Others 16/1
Scunthorpe U (£50,000 on 26/3/1992) FL 61/8 FLC 6 FAC 2 Others 8
Oxford U (£150,000 on 5/11/1993) FL 148/21 FLC 16/1 FAC 11/2 Others 6
Leicester C (£1,600,000 on 18/1/1997) PL 127/20 FLC 15/3 FAC 11/2 Others 2

ELLIOTT Robert (Robbie) James
Born: Newcastle, 25 December 1973
Height: 5'10" Weight: 11.6
International Honours: E: U21-2; Yth

Robbie had an excellent season in 1999-2000, living up to the huge reputation he brought with him when he signed for Bolton from Newcastle United in 1997. His season was not completely free from injury problems, with Robbie twice missing a number of games due to abdominal trouble. It was upon recovering from these set-backs in the final third of the campaign that he really made an impression in the team. Starting off in his more familiar left-back role, Robbie was moved into midfield due to other injuries (particularly to Ricardo Gardner) and suspensions, and proved himself to be equally at home playing on the left wing or in the centre of midfield. His no-nonsense approach may have earned him a few yellow cards from some of today's stricter referees, but it is one which is favoured and enjoyed by the Reebok faithful, and one Robbie takes into every game he plays, without fail. He is a very important member of the Bolton squad.

Newcastle U (From trainee on 3/4/1991) F/PL 71+8/9 FLC 5 FAC 7+3 Others 5+1
Bolton W (£2,500,000 + on 2/7/1997) P/FL 40+13/3 FLC 4+2/2 FAC 3 Others 4+1

ELLIOTT Steven (Steve) William
Born: Swadlincote, 29 October 1978
Height: 6'1" Weight: 14.0
International Honours: E: U21-2

Having successfully recovered from a sprained ankle suffered the previous season, the locally born Derby and England U21 centre back continued to make excellent progress at the club in 1999-2000, featuring in the first team with ever-greater regularity. Very composed on the ball, and passing tidily out of defence, he is also highly effective in dealing with any aerial threat at set pieces. After Steve had played in most games from December onwards in a successful fight against relegation, Jim Smith rewarded the popular youngster with a four-year extension to his contract. He will hopefully be a feature of the Rams' defence for many years to come, having been a supporter of the club all his life.

Derby Co (From trainee on 26/3/1997) PL 28+6 FLC 6+1 FAC 2+2

ELLIOTT Stuart Thomas
Born: Willesden, 27 August 1977
Height: 5'9" Weight: 12.0

This highly rated Newcastle youngster joined Bournemouth on loan last December in search of regular first-team action. He appeared in a run of seven consecutive games as a central defender for the Cherries before returning to St James' Park. Loaned to Stockport in February, he made an uncomfortable start against Port Vale and later switched to a midfield role for the Edgeley Park club. Versatile and at his best a strong and committed player, Stuart has yet to make his senior debut for the Magpies despite several loan spells elsewhere in recent seasons.

Newcastle U (From trainee on 28/8/1995)
Hull C (Loaned on 28/2/1997) FL 3
Swindon T (Loaned on 20/2/1998) FL 1+1
Gillingham (Loaned on 23/10/1998) FL 4+1
Hartlepool U (Loaned on 29/1/1999) FL 5
Wrexham (Loaned on 22/3/1999) FL 8+1 Others 1
Bournemouth (Loaned on 3/12/1999) FL 6+2
Stockport Co (Loaned on 25/2/2000) FL 4+1

ELLIOTT Wade Patrick
Born: Eastleigh, 14 December 1978
Height: 5'9" Weight: 11.1
International Honours: E: Sch

This former England Schools international was midway through a course in communications studies and sociology at Goldsmith's College when he signed professional forms for Bournemouth from Dr Martens League club Bashley last February. He made an immediate impact for the Cherries, scoring on his full debut against Wycombe and finding the net again in the next home game with Oldham. Wade can play in the centre or on either side of midfield and impressed with his skill and commitment.

Bournemouth (£5,000 from Bashley on 4/2/2000) FL 6+6/3

ELLIS Anthony (Tony) Joseph
Born: Salford, 20 October 1964
Height: 5'11" Weight: 11.0

This experienced striker had a handful of appearances from the subs' bench for Stockport at the beginning of the 1999-2000 season and also made the starting line-up for the Worthington Cup tie at Oldham. After a couple more outings he moved to Rochdale in November, signing a contract until the end of the season. Dale were in the middle of a goal drought that saw them score just two goals in 12 games. Tony initially partnered the younger Clive Platt, helping him to fulfil some of his early promise, but when Graham Lancashire returned to fitness the two goal poachers struck up a terrific understanding that yielded 11 goals between them in as many games. Tony is a hard-working player who holds the ball up well. His unselfish running belies his years, while his finishing is as sharp as ever and he ended the season as the club's top scorer. With his career tally standing at 198 senior goals, he was offered a new deal at Spotland in May.

Oldham Ath (Free from Horwich RMI on 22/8/1986) FL 5+3 FLC 1 Others 1
Preston NE (£23,000 on 16/10/1987) FL 80+6/26 FLC 3 FAC 5 Others 11+1/5
Stoke C (£250,000 on 20/12/1989) FL 66+11/19 FLC 5+1/1 FAC 1+4 Others 3+2
Preston NE (£140,000 on 14/8/1992) FL 70+2/48 FLC 4/2 FAC 6/3 Others 6/3
Blackpool (£165,000 on 25/7/1994) FL 140+6/54 FLC 10+1/6 FAC 7/1 Others 8/3
Bury (£75,000 on 12/12/1997) FL 24+14/8 FLC 2+2
Stockport Co (£25,000 on 3/2/1999) FL 17+3/6 FLC 1+1
Rochdale (Free on 1/11/1999) FL 30+1/11 FAC 1 Others 4+1

EMBERSON Carl Wayne
Born: Epsom, 13 July 1973
Height: 6'2" Weight: 14.7
Club Honours: FAYC '91

This accomplished goalkeeper joined Walsall from Colchester during the 1999 close season, but it was always going to be difficult for him to make an impact at a level two divisions higher than he had been accustomed to. After an early-season debut in a Worthington Cup game at Plymouth, his chances were severely restricted by the fine form of Jimmy Walker, although he did make a couple of appearances as a substitute. When Jimmy was suspended near the end of the season Carl was given his chance and commanded his area in impressive fashion, but after playing his part in the win over West Bromwich he had the bad luck to break a thumb in the closing minutes.

Millwall (From trainee on 4/5/1991) Others 1
Colchester U (Loaned on 17/12/1992) FL 13
Colchester U (£25,000 on 6/7/1994) FL 178+1 FLC 9 FAC 8 Others 16
Walsall (Free on 28/6/1999) FL 3+2 FLC 1

EMBLEN Neil Robert
Born: Bromley, 19 June 1971
Height: 6'1" Weight: 13.11

Although he was used mainly as a central defender or midfield man by Wolves in 1999-2000, Neil enhanced his reputation as a utility player and was involved in all the club's competitive matches during the season. In September he made errors at home to Huddersfield that almost conceded a goal and needlessly gave away the decisive penalty. He made amends in October, however, getting the only goal in the meetings with Fulham and Sheffield United. While his 100 per cent effort made him a crowd favourite, his ball control was sometimes less impressive. At least he was selected more regularly than the previous season, even if the positional changes were not always beneficial to his career. There was one spell of three matches when he started each of them in a different position, and his role could also change during a game. When he was made a substitute against Queens Park Rangers in January, the only occasion he was not included in the starting line-up all season, he did not get the rest he needed, coming on after 21 minutes. He then scored with an emphatic header to earn a point at Walsall, before missing a good chance at Charlton on the next trip. After playing well up front against Crewe he retained his place, leaving Ade Akinbiyi on the bench, and his appearance at left back at Birmingham in April meant he had occupied every outfield role for Wolves. He is the brother of Wycombe's Paul Emblen.

Millwall (£175,000 from Sittingbourne on 8/11/1993) FL 12 Others 1
Wolverhampton W (£600,000 on 14/7/1994) FL 80+8/9 FLC 2+2/1 FAC 7+2 Others 2+1
Crystal Palace (£2,000,000 on 21/8/1997) PL 8+5 FAC 1+1/2
Wolverhampton W (£900,000 on 26/3/1998) FL 81+5/7 FLC 4+1/1 FAC 5

EMBLEN Paul David
Born: Bromley, 3 April 1976
Height: 5'11" Weight: 12.5

Having been the hero of Wycombe's 1998-99 campaign when he scored the goal that saved them from relegation, Paul had a disappointing time in 1999-2000. Mostly used by manager Lawrie Sanchez as an experimental striker, he rarely found the net himself but his high workrate meant he was a useful member of the Chairboys' strike force. Paul then had the misfortune to suffer a broken ankle after coming on as a substitute against Brentford at the end of November and this brought his season to a premature end. Paul is the brother of Neil Emblen of Wolves.

Charlton Ath (£7,500 + from Tonbridge on 16/5/1997) FL 0+4
Brighton & Hove A (Loaned on 4/11/1997) FL 15/4
Wycombe W (£60,000 on 28/8/1998) FL 40+11/2 FLC 3+3 FAC 3+4 Others 1

ENCKELMAN Peter
Born: Turku, Finland, 10 March 1977
Height: 6'2" Weight: 12.5
International Honours: Finland: 1; U21

This talented young 'keeper joined Aston Villa from TPS Turku in February 1999 but had to wait until last September before making his debut for the club when he came on for the last 39 minutes at Arsenal as a replacement for the injured David James. Peter retained his place for the next six games, keeping five clean sheets, and after being absent himself with a knee problem he returned for a further spell of Premiership action in February, when James was again ruled out. He is a fine shot stopper with a calm approach who looks to have a great future in the game. Having previously represented Finland at U21 level, he stepped up to the full international team for the first time last March when he appeared against Wales at Cardiff.

Aston Villa (£200,000 from TPS Turku, Finland on 1/2/1999) PL 9+1 FLC 3 FAC 1

ERANIO Stefano
Born: Genoa, Italy, 29 December 1966
Height: 5'11" Weight: 12.2
International Honours: Italy: 20

Derby's former Italian international had a mixed season in 1999-2000, his third at Pride Park. Initially a regular in the first team, where his precision passing and ball control on the right-hand side of midfield created numerous chances, he went into the match at Anfield in November in particularly good form only to suffer a fractured fibula in a challenge with Liverpool centre half Sami Hyypia. The injury healed slowly but Stefano was back in action three months later in the eventful relegation battle at Pride Park with Sheffield Wednesday. A hamstring injury sustained in the warm-up prior to the West Ham game in April, however, ended his season. A valuable member of the first-team squad who can also fill in at right back if asked, he has signed a new one-year contract which keeps him at the club until May 2001.

Derby Co (Free from AC Milan, Italy, via Genoa, on 15/7/1997) PL 58+9/5 FLC 4 FAC 5/1

ETHERINGTON Craig
Born: Basildon, 16 September 1979
Height: 6'0" Weight: 11.10

Craig joined Plymouth on transfer deadline day on loan from West Ham until the end of the 1999-2000 season. He is a strong and skilful midfielder, and is an excellent prospect. He made his Argyle debut in the 4-0 win at Torquay in March.

West Ham U (From trainee on 9/7/1997)
Halifax T (Loaned on 4/2/1999) FL 4 Others 1
Plymouth Arg (Loaned on 23/3/2000) FL 4+1

ETHERINGTON Matthew
Born: Truro, 14 August 1981
Height: 5'10" Weight: 11.2
International Honours: E: Yth

Having represented England at U16, U18 and U20 levels, Matthew moved to Tottenham last January along with fellow Peterborough youth product Simon Davies for a combined £1.2 million fee. He had spent a week on trial at Manchester United in the 1999 close season, and earned a glowing tribute from Sir Alex Ferguson following a private friendly match against Boca Juniors. Back at London Road, a superb winner against Northampton in the local derby was followed by "Mushy" signing an improved five-year contract with Peterborough in September. With Aston Villa, Arsenal and Celtic said to be showing an interest and Posh reported to be losing £30,000 per week, his departure seemed to be only a matter of time. An attacking left-sided midfielder, Matthew already has plenty of first-team experience as he made his Posh debut at the age of 15 years and 262 days on the last day of the 1996-97 season. He made only one start for Tottenham, against Manchester United at Old Trafford, although he was used as a substitute on four occasions. Much will be expected of this exciting prospect at White Hart Lane during the coming season.

Peterborough U (From trainee on 15/8/1998) FL 43+8/6 FLC 1+1 FAC 2+1 Others 2
Tottenham H (£500,000 on 10/1/2000) PL 1+4

EUELL Jason Joseph
Born: Lambeth, 6 February 1977
Height: 6'0" Weight: 12.7
International Honours: E: U21-6

Jason has signed a new five-year deal with Wimbledon, which should ensure that this versatile player remains with the Dons for the foreseeable future. However, there has been considerable speculation that he is looking to pastures new following the Dons' relegation to the First Division. Good in the air and often very creative with the ball at his feet, Jason was involved in all but one of Wimbledon's first-team games in 1999-2000. Now generally employed as an attacking midfield player, he has improved his all-round game compared with a couple of seasons ago, when he was used solely as a forward. He has a keen eye for goal, but sometimes gives possession away unnecessarily.

Wimbledon (From trainee on 1/6/1995) PL 85+20/22 FLC 14+2/4 FAC 8+5/1

EUSTACE John Mark
Born: Solihull, 3 November 1979
Height: 5'11" Weight: 11.12

The young midfielder made an impressive start to his career at Coventry with dominant performances during the second half of the 1999-2000 season after a series of consistent displays for the reserves. Despite making his debut in the Worthington Cup debacle at Tranmere his confidence remained intact and he scored on his FA Cup debut at Norwich. Carlton Palmer's absence gave John a chance to stake a claim on the right and his strong-running style, combined with an ability to get into the penalty box, earned him many plaudits. He scored his first Premiership goal, a penalty, against Bradford City after refusing to let any of the experienced players take the kick. He was voted the club's "Most Improved Player" and looks to have a very bright future in store.

Coventry C (From trainee on 5/11/1996) PL 12+4/1 FLC 1+1 FAC 1+2/1
Dundee U (Loaned on 17/2/1999) SL 8+3/1 SC 2

EUSTACE Scott Douglas
Born: Leicester, 13 June 1975
Height: 6'0" Weight: 14.2

The 1999-2000 season was very rewarding for the young Cambridge defender, who might have expected to be the third choice behind Andy Duncan and Marc Joseph. Following Andy's long-term injury in October, Scott was frequently a rock in the centre of defence and during the run-in to the end of the season he was at times inspirational. He also scored his first goal for the club in the win at Bury in February. After turning down new terms with Cambridge he signed for Division Three club Lincoln City in June.

Leicester C (From trainee on 9/7/1993) FL 0+1
Mansfield T (Free on 9/6/1995) FL 90+8/6 FLC 3 FAC 5/1 Others 3+1
Chesterfield (Free on 7/8/1998) FLC 0+1
Cambridge U (Free on 8/1/1999) FL 49+3/1 FLC 2 FAC 3

EVANS David **Andrew (Andy)**
Born: Aberystwyth, 25 November 1975
Height: 6'2" Weight: 12.2
International Honours: W: Yth

A tall striker, Andy was given a second chance at a career in league football when Barnsley manager Dave Bassett signed him from Welsh League club Aberystwyth Town last September. He appeared regularly for the reserves and came on as a substitute for striker Bruce Dyer in the Worthington Cup tie with Tranmere Rovers in November. Andy was then loaned to Third Division Mansfield Town in March, where he was required as a replacement for the injured Tony Lormor. He had the misfortune to make his debut in the 0-5 mauling at the Deva Stadium, and although he contributed height to the Stags' strike force he failed to make a serious impact in his spell at Field Mill.

Cardiff C (From trainee on 19/12/1994) FL 5+10 FLC 0+2 FAC 0+1 Others 0+1 (Free to Merthyr Tydfil in February 1996)
Barnsley (£15,000 from Aberystwyth on 27/9/1999) FLC 0+1
Mansfield T (Loaned on 22/3/2000) FL 4+2

EVANS Kevin
Born: Carmarthen, 16 December 1980
Height: 6'2" Weight: 12.10
International Honours: W: U21-2; Yth

Kevin was signed by Swansea on loan from Leeds in January 2000 and made his first appearance for the club against Inter Cardiff in a Welsh Premier Cup tie. Capped twice by Wales at U21 level during the 1998-99 season, he made his league debut against Lincoln City when he deputised for the injured Jason Smith. The following game at Cheltenham saw him make his first start for the Swans, the youngster impressing in a 0-0 draw. Kevin returned to Leeds a week before the end of his second month on loan.

Leeds U (From trainee on 13/1/1998)
Swansea C (Loaned on 17/1/2000) FL 1+1

EVANS Michael (Micky) James
Born: Plymouth, 1 January 1973
Height: 6'1" Weight: 13.4
International Honours: RoI: 1

The former Republic of Ireland international striker had another frustrating season for West Bromwich in 1999-2000. Mickey was again plagued by a variety of injuries, mainly muscle strains and ankle twists, and he spent as much time on the bench as he did on the pitch. At times he looked the part, playing alongside Lee Hughes, but once again he lacked a sufficiently positive approach in and around the penalty area and, in fact, scored only five goals in 38 outings for the Baggies. Competing for a place with Fabian De Freitas, he started off as first choice (alongside Lee Hughes) but after that was in and out of the side when injuries weren't affecting his daily routine.

Plymouth Arg (From trainee on 30/3/1991) FL 130+33/38 FLC 8+1 FAC 10+2/3 Others 10/2
Southampton (£500,000 on 4/3/1997) PL 14+8/4 FLC 2+1/1
West Bromwich A (£750,000 on 27/10/1997) FL 35+28/6 FLC 3+3/2 FAC 2+2/1

EVANS Paul Simon
Born: Oswestry, 1 September 1974
Height: 5'8" Weight: 11.6
Club Honours: Div 3 '94, '99
International Honours: W: U21-4; Yth

This all-action Brentford midfielder is strong in the tackle and possesses a lethal shot. Paul was the Bees' club captain in 1999-2000 and had another good season at Griffin Park, despite being hampered by recurrent hamstring trouble in the second half of the campaign. As usual he scored his quota of spectacular goals, the best against Preston last September when he lobbed the visiting 'keeper from a distance of more than 50 yards. Brentford supporters subsequently selected this sensational strike as the "Goal of the Decade" and it also featured in the "What Happened Next?" section of BBC Television's "Question of Sport" programme.

Shrewsbury T (From trainee on 2/7/1993) FL 178+20/26 FLC 12+2/4 FAC 12+1/2 Others 12/4
Brentford (£110,000 on 3/3/1999) FL 47/10 FLC 2 FAC 1 Others 2/1

EVANS Rhys Karl
Born: Swindon, 27 January 1982
Height: 6'1" Weight: 12.0
International Honours: E: Yth; Sch

This young Chelsea goalkeeper was loaned to Bristol Rovers last February and made his league debut just a month after his 18th birthday in an emphatic 4-1 victory at Oldham. A graduate of the FA School of Excellence, Rhys proved to be a confident shot stopper. He particularly impressed with his positional play and his quick distribution from defence, preferring to keep possession with his defenders. During his four-match loan spell with Rovers, he was not on the losing side and conceded just two goals. Chelsea appear to have a fine prospect on their hands for future years. Having represented England at schoolboy and U16 levels, Rhys was capped for the U17s against Luxembourg last April.

Chelsea (From trainee on 8/2/1999)
Bristol Rov (Loaned on 25/2/2000) FL 4

EVANS Stephen (Steve) James
Born: Caerphilly, 25 September 1980
Height: 6'1" Weight: 11.6
International Honours: W: Yth

A young attacking left-sided midfield player, Steve had a disappointing 1999-2000 season at Crystal Palace. He was troubled by a knee injury and added just one appearance as a substitute to his career total. Quick on the turn with good pace and skill, he will be looking to establish a more regular presence in the first-team set-up over the coming season.

Crystal Palace (From trainee on 31/10/1998) FL 0+5 FLC 0+1

EVANS Thomas (Tommy) Raymond
Born: Doncaster, 31 December 1976
Height: 6'0" Weight: 13.2

Tommy started the 1999-2000 season as Scunthorpe's first-choice goalkeeper and helped keep the score down in a number of games as the Iron struggled in Division Two. He was unlucky to be dropped in October for the on-loan Lionel Perez and didn't get a regular run again until February, keeping his place until the last match of the season. A good prospect who is an excellent shot stopper, he saved two penalties during the campaign and should progress further during 2000-01.

Sheffield U (From trainee on 3/7/1995)
Crystal Palace (Free on 14/6/1996)
Scunthorpe U (Free on 22/8/1997) FL 56+1 FLC 3 FAC 2 Others 2

EVANS Duncan **Wayne**
Born: Abermule, 25 August 1971
Height: 5'10" Weight: 12.5

Wayne proved a superb acquisition by new Rochdale boss Steve Parkin in July 1999. He was soon joined at Spotland by former Walsall team-mates Clive Platt and Richard Green. A tremendously consistent performer at right back, he showed his versatility by taking one of the three central defensive positions when Dale switched to playing 5-3-2. An ever-present, he won both of Dale's "Player of the Year" awards, and his one league goal, the winner at Macclesfield, prolonged Dale's play-off hopes until the final day of the season.

Walsall (Free from Welshpool on 13/8/1993) FL 173+10/1 FLC 14+1/1 FAC 15+1 Others 12+3
Rochdale (Free on 2/7/1999) FL 46/1 FLC 2/1 FAC 3 Others 5

EVE Angus
Born: Trinidad, 23 February 1972
Height: 5'7" Weight: 11.2
International Honours: Trinidad & Tobago

This experienced Trinidad & Tobago international brought some Caribbean flair to Chester last December. In a generally miserable season at the Deva, Angus's debut winner against Halifax was a rare highlight and an early Christmas present. The attacking midfielder signed a two-year City contract in September, but had to wait for international clearance. Angus commented: "Experts used to say that Caribbean boys couldn't make it in Europe, but we're out to prove them wrong". His Blues appearances were somewhat restricted by injuries and international calls – he won a further 11 caps during his stay with the club, scoring three goals including a double in the 5-0 victory over Netherlands Antilles in the World Cup qualifiers. Although City fans will be hoping his skills will help Chester made a quick return to Nationwide League status, they may be disappointed as he went back to Trinidad in the summer, linking up once more with Joe Public in the Trinidad Professional League.

Chester C (Signed from Joe Public, Trinidad on 16/12/1999) FL 9+5/4 Others 0+1

Tommy Evans

EVERS Sean Anthony
Born: Hitchin, 10 October 1977
Height: 5'9" Weight: 9.11

One of several of Tommy Burns's big-money buys for Reading who failed to earn a regular place in the starting line-up last season, Sean finally forced his way into the team in November but did not look strong enough to deal with the rigours of Second Division football. He showed some neat touches as a wide midfield player, but is still waiting to score his first goal for the club. He was a member of the reserve team which lost to Aylesbury United in the final of the Berks & Bucks Senior Cup.

Luton T (From trainee on 16/5/1996) FL 43+9/6 FLC 9/1 FAC 2 Others 6
Reading (£500,000 on 25/3/1999) FL 8+10 FLC 0+1 FAC 4 Others 2+1

EYJOLFSSON Sigurdur (Sigi)
Born: Iceland, 1 December 1973
Height: 6'2" Weight: 12.0

The tall Icelandic striker started the 1999-2000 season well with three goals in Walsall's two-legged Worthington Cup win over Plymouth, but he was used mainly as a substitute in the first half of the campaign. In January he joined Chester's valiant attempt to retain league status, moving to the Deva on a two-month loan. He soon became a crowd favourite, netting three goals in ten Blues appearances. A player who is very mobile and holds the ball up well, Siggi returned to the Bescot ranks in March and scored the goal that earned a point at promotion challengers Huddersfield. His cool finishing is more than useful and Walsall fans are expecting him to prosper back in Division Two next season.

Walsall (Free from IF Akranes, Iceland on 27/1/1999) FL 1+22/2 FLC 1+3/3 FAC 0+1 Others 0+1/1
Chester C (Loaned on 7/1/2000) FL 9/3 Others 1

EYRE John Robert
Born: Hull, 9 October 1974
Height: 6'0" Weight: 12.7

It was one of the worst-kept secrets in football that John, who lived in the shadow of Hull's Boothferry Park ground for twenty years and was still based in nearby Hessle, was set for his home-town team in the 1999 close season, having been an influential member of Scunthorpe United's promotion squad in 1998-99 with 17 goals. He came back to Hull some eight years after turning them down when Eddie Gray was the manager. He didn't disappoint, displaying a fine array of attacking skills, and headed the scoring list despite an injury-punctuated campaign. A back injury in August was followed by a twisted ankle in November, calf trouble in December and a groin problem in January. John also fractured and dislocated his elbow against Shrewsbury Town in February and so was unavailable for much of the run-in.

Oldham Ath (From trainee on 16/7/1993) P/FL 4+6/1 FLC 0+2
Scunthorpe U (Loaned on 15/12/1994) FL 9/8
Scunthorpe U (£40,000 on 4/7/1995) FL 151+13/43 FLC 9/2 FAC 12/3 Others 8+1/3
Hull C (Free on 5/7/1999) FL 24/8 FLC 4/2 FAC 2+1/2 Others 2

EYRE Richard Paul
Born: Poynton, 15 September 1976
Height: 5'11" Weight: 11.6

Paul is an enthusiastic right winger who was involved with the Port Vale first team, either on the pitch or on the bench, for the majority of the 1999-2000 season. A wholehearted player who will run and run for the cause, he forced his way into the starting line-up after some impressive reserve-team performances but as results went badly he was a victim of the chopping and changing. He scored his first senior goal at Sheffield United in November with a cracking shot from the edge of the box and achieved his own personal highlight with an appearance at Leeds in the FA Cup. He has a bright future in the game and will be looking to progress this coming season.

Port Vale (From trainee on 29/6/1995) FL 25+17/1 FLC 0+2 FAC 1

EYRES David
Born: Liverpool, 26 February 1964
Height: 5'11" Weight: 11.8
Club Honours: Div 2 '00

Age did nothing to dampen David's contribution to Preston's cause in 1999-2000, despite his turning 36 in February, and the wily left winger remained a first-team regular during a season that saw North End win the Second Division championship, contributing seven goals. Among the many highlights of his season were celebrating his 400th Football League game with his first goal of the campaign at Reading, and making the 500th senior appearance of his career as a sub at Millwall in October. David particularly enjoyed his double strike against former club Blackpool and playing against his boyhood heroes Everton at Goodison; the reception he received when being substituted there showed the respect in which he is held within the game.

Blackpool (£10,000 from Rhyl on 15/8/1989) FL 147+11/38 FLC 11+1/1 FAC 11/2 Others 13+2/4
Burnley (£90,000 on 29/7/1993) FL 171+4/37 FLC 17/7 FAC 14/8 Others 9/3
Preston NE (£80,000 on 29/10/1997) FL 85+18/19 FLC 3+2 FAC 10/3 Others 5/3

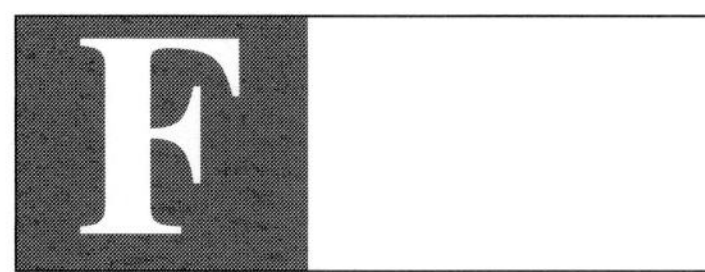

FACEY Delroy Michael
Born: Huddersfield, 22 April 1980
Height: 5'11' Weight: 13.10
Still one for the future, Delroy was not considered for a regular first-team place at Huddersfield in 1999-2000. Having signed a new four-year contract early in the season, he will be nurtured for the future. His only first-team outing was a brief appearance as a substitute in the home defeat against Portsmouth in February. With great pace and power, Delroy will be looking to make a greater impact in the new millennium.
Huddersfield T (From trainee on 13/5/1997) FL 7+21/3 FAC 0+2

FAERBER Winston
Born: Den Haag, Holland, 27 March 1971
Height: 5'11" Weight: 12.10
A right-sided wing back with a remarkable ability to beat defenders from a standing start, Winston joined Cardiff from Dutch club Den Haag under the Bosman ruling before the start of the 1999-2000 season. He is physically strong and crosses the ball well, but he found it difficult to settle into British football. This was partly due to the fact that his family were homesick (although born in Surinam, he was brought up in the Netherlands), but he went on to finish the campaign strongly. Nevertheless, Cardiff allowed him to go back to Holland after he had served only half of his two-year contract.
Cardiff C (Free from ADO Den Haag, Holland on 2/8/1999) FL 31+2/1 FLC 4 FAC 4+1 Others 1

Chris Fairclough

FAIRCLOUGH Courtney (Chris) Huw
Born: Nottingham, 12 April 1964
Height: 5'11" Weight: 11.7
Club Honours: Div 2 '90, Div 1 '92, '97; CS '92
International Honours: E: B-1; U21-7
This vastly experienced central defender was a kingpin in the heart of the York City defence in 1999-2000 until injury sidelined him at the end of December. He returned to the senior squad in the closing weeks of the campaign and is a vital member of the Bootham Crescent set-up. Captain Chris was brought to York by previous boss Neil Thompson. The duo began their careers together as Nottingham Forest juniors.
Nottingham F (From apprentice on 12/10/1981) FL 102+5/1 FLC 9+1/1 FAC 6 Others 9+2
Tottenham H (£387,000 on 3/7/1987) FL 60/5 FLC 7 FAC 3
Leeds U (£500,000 on 23/3/1989) FL 187+6/21 FLC 17+2/2 FAC 14+1 Others 14
Bolton W (£500,000 on 4/7/1995) F/PL 89+1/8 FLC 11 FAC 5
Notts Co (Free on 30/7/1998) FL 16/1 FLC 2 FAC 1
York C (Free on 17/3/1999) FL 36+1 FLC 2 FAC 1 Others 1

FARLEY Craig
Born: Oxford, 17 March 1981
Height: 6'0" Weight: 11.0
This young right back joined Colchester from Watford on a free transfer in the summer of 1999 as "one for the future". Within a matter of weeks, he was "one for the present" as defensive problems led to the youngster being brought in for an earlier-than-expected league debut against Scunthorpe. Craig then played a handful of consecutive games before more experienced players again became available, after which (apart from a few substitute appearances) he returned to continue his development in the reserves.
Colchester U (Free from Watford juniors on 5/7/1999) FL 8+6 FAC 1 Others 1

FARRELL David (Dave) William
Born: Birmingham, 11 November 1971
Height: 5'10" Weight: 11.9
Peterborough's pacy winger was often asked to fill a more conventional midfield role in 1999-2000. Comfortable on either flank, he looks at his most effective when cutting inside from the right. David was sidelined for two spells with an ankle injury and thigh strain, and he was a notable absentee. When his confidence is high, he is a match for anyone. The highlight of his season was the first hat-trick of his career. Not only were all three goals scored with shots from outside the area, but it came against Barnet to clinch Posh's place in the Third Division play-off final against Darlington at Wembley.
Aston Villa (£45,000 from Redditch U on 6/1/1992) F/PL 5+1 FLC 2
Scunthorpe U (Loaned on 25/1/1993) FL 4+1/1 Others 2
Wycombe W (£100,000 on 14/9/1995) FL 44+16/6 FLC 6 FAC 3+2 Others 2
Peterborough U (Free on 21/7/1997) FL 101+13/13 FLC 6+1/1 FAC 4 Others 8/4

FARRELL Sean Paul
Born: Watford, 28 February 1969
Height: 6'0" Weight: 13.7
Club Honours: Div 3 '98
Sean had another frustrating time with injuries in 1999-2000 and it was not until the end of February that he returned to anything like match fitness. He made several appearances from the subs' bench towards the end of the season and will be hoping to make a full return to action in 2000-01. When fit, he is a tall, strong and skilful target man who is a great leader of the front line.
Luton T (From apprentice on 5/3/1987) FL 14+11/1 FAC 2+1/1 Others 1+2/2
Colchester U (Loaned on 1/3/1988) FL 4+5/1
Northampton T (Loaned on 13/9/1991) FL 4/1
Fulham (£100,000 on 19/12/1991) FL 93+1/31 FLC 5+1/3 FAC 2/3 Others 8/1
Peterborough U (£120,000 on 5/8/1994) FL 49+17/21 FLC 4+2/1 FAC 4+1/3 Others 3+1/1
Notts Co (£80,000 on 14/10/1996) FL 49+20/19 FLC 2 FAC 6/1 Others 1

FARRELLY Gareth
Born: Dublin, 28 August 1975
Height: 6'0" Weight: 13.0
International Honours: RoI: 6; B-1; U21-11; Yth; Sch
After just one Worthington Cup appearance for Everton Gareth was loaned to Bolton last November and the deal was made permanent the following month. The former Aston Villa man made his Wanderers debut in the 2-1 win at Sheffield United, where he scored with only his second touch of the ball. Gareth was not able to build on this promising start with the club and found himself making only sporadic appearances for the Trotters in the second half of the season, as well as suffering from a few minor injury set-backs. As a player who can operate in virtually all of the midfield positions, Gareth was an important member of the Wanderers squad and his season finished on a high when he made a further appearance for the Republic of Ireland against the USA at the beginning of June.
Aston Villa (From trainee on 21/1/1992) PL 2+6 FLC 0+1
Rotherham U (Loaned on 21/3/1995) FL 9+1/2
Everton (£700,000 + on 9/7/1997) PL 18+9/1 FLC 2/1 FAC 1
Bolton W (Free on 12/11/1999) FL 8+3/1 FAC 0+1

FAULCONBRIDGE Craig Michael
Born: Nuneaton, 20 April 1978
Height: 6'1" Weight: 13.0
This tall and rangy forward joined Wrexham on a free transfer from Coventry in the summer of 1999 as manager Brian Flynn sought to beef up his strike force. He quickly made an impression at the Racecourse Ground, scoring on his debut for the club when coming on as a substitute at Blackpool on the opening day of the season and following this up with both goals in the 2-1 win over Bristol Rovers. He netted regularly in the early matches but the goals seemed to dry up as the season wore on and his partnerships with Ian Stevens and Neil Roberts became less productive. He is a player who shows keen awareness and works hard; with the right pairing up front he could become a real success in the game. He finished the season on a high, scoring both goals in the 2-0 victory over Cardiff City in the FAW Premiership Cup final and signing a new two-year contract for the Robins.
Coventry C (From trainee on 5/7/1996)
Dunfermline Ath (Loaned on 27/3/1998) SL 1+12/1 SLC 0+1
Hull C (Loaned on 18/12/1998) FL 4+6 FAC 1 Others 1+1
Wrexham (Free on 6/8/1999) FL 23+12/8 FLC 1+1 FAC 2+2/1 Others 1/1

FEAR Peter Stanley
Born: Sutton, 10 September 1973
Height: 5'10" Weight: 11.7
International Honours: E: U21-3

A player with Premiership experience signed on a free transfer from Wimbledon in the summer of 1999, Peter should have been Oxford's most significant new recruit for 1999-2000 but he was to have a frustrating season. His problems started in pre-season when he was sent off in a friendly at Ayr, causing him to miss three games, and then, as he was about to return, he damaged his ankle, which meant that his debut was delayed by many weeks. However, when he was finally able to play he started to show his class before dropping out of contention after a change of manager. A hard-working player who tackles enthusiastically but can also create openings, Peter bounced back with the appointment of Denis Smith and scored his only goal of the campaign with a great long-range shot against Chesterfield. Soon afterwards, however, his season ended with a broken ankle.

Wimbledon (From trainee on 2/7/1992) PL 51+22/4 FLC 9+2/1 FAC 4
Oxford U (Free on 13/7/1999) FL 13+6/1 FLC 3 FAC 1+1 Others 2

FENTON Anthony (Tony) Brian
Born: Preston, 23 November 1979
Height: 5'10" Weight: 10.6
International Honours: E: Yth

This young central defender joined Portsmouth from Manchester City in March 1999 and was subsequently given a one-year contract. After doing well with the reserves, he was promoted to the first-team squad, making his Football League debut as a late substitute at Ipswich last March. Keen and athletic, he needs a regular run of first-team football to develop his potential. The twin brother of City's England U18 defender Nicky Fenton, Tony was released during the close season.

Manchester C (From trainee on 26/11/1996)
Portsmouth (Free on 19/3/1999) FL 0+1

FENTON Graham Anthony
Born: Wallsend, 22 May 1974
Height: 5'10" Weight: 12.10
Club Honours: FLC '94, '96, '00
International Honours: E: U21-1

A right-sided striker and occasional midfielder, Graham was mainly used as a substitute by Leicester manager Martin O'Neill in 1999-2000, and then mostly in cup ties. Graham's only Leicester goal of the campaign was a neat header that helped to see off Crystal Palace in the early stages of the Foxes' Worthington Cup run. However, he made crucial contributions to two of City's dramatic penalty shoot-out victories, against Fulham and Arsenal. By transfer deadline day, Graham had joined Walsall on a free transfer to link up with another former Fox, Mark Robins, and scored what turned out to be the match-winner in his second game at Port Vale. During the remainder of the season he held the ball up and laid it off well and suggested that he is the sort of all-round striker that Walsall will need if they are to make a promotion challenge during the coming season.

Aston Villa (From trainee on 13/2/1992) PL 16+16/3 FLC 2+5
West Bromwich A (Loaned on 10/1/1994) FL 7/3
Blackburn Rov (£1,500,000 on 7/11/1995) PL 9+18/7 FLC 0+2 FAC 0+1
Leicester C (£1,100,000 on 8/8/1997) PL 13+21/3 FLC 3+2/1 FAC 0+4 Others 0+2
Walsall (Free on 20/3/2000) FL 8+1/1

FENTON Nicholas (Nicky) Leonard
Born: Preston, 23 November 1979
Height: 5'10" Weight: 10.4
International Honours: E: Yth

This young Manchester City centre back struggled to win a first-team place at Maine Road in the early part of 1999-2000, his only appearance coming in the second leg of the Worthington Cup tie at Southampton, where he was brought on as a substitute in extra time. A stylish player who shows impressive maturity, he moved to Notts County for an extended loan period last October. Nicky showed considerable talent at Meadow Lane, where he played an important role in the club's early-season success, but Notts failed to sign him on a permanent basis and he returned north after three months. Subsequently loaned to Bournemouth on transfer deadline day, he quickly slotted into the Cherries' back four and appeared in the final eight games of the campaign. Nicky is a composed central defender able to play a useful long ball out of defence. He is the twin brother of Tony Fenton, who played for Portsmouth in 1999-2000.

Manchester C (From trainee on 26/11/1996) FL 15 FLC 3+1 Others 1
Notts Co (Loaned on 7/10/1999) FL 13/1 Others 1
Bournemouth (Loaned on 23/3/2000) FL 8

FERDINAND Leslie (Les)
Born: Paddington, 8 December 1966
Height: 5'11" Weight: 13.5
Club Honours: FLC '99
International Honours: E: 17; B-1

Les appeared to have finally overcome the injury problems that have dogged him when he regained his place as the spearhead of the Tottenham attack at the start of the 1999-2000 campaign. Instead, he was to endure yet another injury-plagued season, punctuated by planned comebacks and reports of break-downs in training, and the fact that he scored two goals from his five starts will be no consolation to him. It is frustrating for the Tottenham faithful, who have stuck by him throughout the last three years, that such a prolific goalscorer has been prevented from producing his best form for the club and that time is now running against him. At his best, Les is strong in the air and has the ability to spread play wide before getting into position for a cross into the middle. His power and pace make him very difficult to contain and Tottenham's last three seasons could well have been much more rewarding had he been fit. With Les's contract having one year to run, manager George Graham will be monitoring his progress closely, particularly after the arrival of Ukrainian international Sergei Rebrov.

Queens Park R (£15,000 from Hayes on 12/3/1987) F/PL 152+11/80 FLC 11+2/7 FAC 6+1/3 Others 1
Brentford (Loaned on 24/3/1988) FL 3
Newcastle U (£6,000,000 on 7/6/1995) PL 67+1/41 FLC 6/3 FAC 4+1/2 Others 5/4
Tottenham H (£6,000,000 on 5/8/1997) PL 46+8/12 FLC 3+2 FAC 8+1

FERDINAND Rio Gavin
Born: Peckham, 8 November 1978
Height: 6'2" Weight: 12.1
International Honours: E: 9; U21-5; Yth

This West Ham youngster continued to impress with his mature performances in the heart of the defence in 1999-2000. He missed a few early-season games with ankle ligament trouble but was otherwise rarely absent from the starting line-up. Rio made his 100th Premiership appearance at Leicester last January at the age of 21 and has a long future in top-flight football ahead of him. He is a thoughtful and stylish player who is very comfortable on the ball and displays excellent distribution. A regular member of Kevin Keegan's England squad, he added a further cap to his total when coming on as a substitute against Argentina and also featured for the U21s in the European Championship qualifying play-off against Yugoslavia, but met with disappointment when he was omitted from the final 22 for England's Euro 2000 campaign.

West Ham U (From trainee on 27/11/1995) PL 110+5/2 FLC 10+1 FAC 9 Others 5
Bournemouth (Loaned on 8/11/1996) FL 10 Others 1

Rio Ferdinand

FERGUSON Barry
Born: Dublin, 7 September 1979
Height: 6'3" Weight: 12.10
International Honours: RoI: U21-6

A young Republic of Ireland U21 centre back who has yet to make a first-team appearance for Coventry, Barry joined Colchester on loan on transfer deadline day last season and quickly made his debut in the home draw with Blackpool. Given United's lack of central defenders at the time following Richard Wilkins's retirement and David Greene's injury, Barry proved an excellent signing and he held his place for the rest of the campaign (although he was unlucky

enough to concede an own goal against Bristol City). He is an excellent prospect who would be welcome back at Layer Road next season if a deal can be worked out. Barry won a further four U21 caps during the campaign, appearing in all three of his country's games in the Toulon Tournament at the end of May.
Coventry C (Signed from Home Farm on 4/9/1998)
Colchester U (Loaned on 23/3/2000) FL 5+1

FERGUSON Darren
Born: Glasgow, 9 February 1972
Height: 5'10" Weight: 11.10
Club Honours: PL '93
International Honours: S: U21-5; Yth
Darren linked up with Wrexham last September after a spell in Holland with Sparta Rotterdam and eventually agreed to stay after signing a two-and-a-half-year contract. He is a neat midfielder with excellent passing skills, great vision and some subtle touches. He enjoyed a fine game against Middlesbrough in the FA Cup and scored one of the goals that enabled the Robins to knock out their illustrious Premiership opponents in a famous victory. He scored four more goals during the season, including one with a fine 25-yard free kick at Cambridge last March to earn Wrexham a 4-3 win. The talented Scot was voted "Player of the Season" by the supporters and could prove a vital asset to the club over the next few years.
Manchester U (From trainee on 11/7/1990) F/PL 20+7 FLC 2+1
Wolverhampton W (£250,000 on 13/1/1994) FL 94+23/4 FLC 13+2/3 FAC 9+2/3 Others 6
Wrexham (Free on 17/9/1999) FL 37/4 FAC 5/1

FERGUSON Duncan
Born: Stirling, 27 December 1971
Height: 6'4" Weight: 14.6
Club Honours: SL '94; SLC '94; FAC '95
International Honours: S: 7; B; U21-7; Yth; Sch
Duncan is a big, powerful Newcastle striker who is rightly admired and feared because of his awesome heading ability. However, there is much more to him than just an aerial threat, as he has a good turn of speed and a touch on the ball surprisingly delicate for such a big man, abilities he uses well within a team context in that he is unselfish and seeks to create opportunities for colleagues as well as for himself. After undergoing surgery in the summer of 1999 to cure his long-standing groin problem, he suffered a leg injury in pre-season training which turned out to be two tears in the right calf muscle, delaying his first match until the fourth game, where he made a substitute appearance which he repeated in the following match, the Sunderland derby which proved to be Ruud Gullit's final game as manager. However, only a few weeks later Duncan tore a hamstring early in the UEFA Cup game at CSKA Sofia, putting him out for another month, and again on his return, after playing well against FC Zurich and his old club Everton in the space of four days, he picked up a calf strain in training which further disrupted his season. It was a month before he started another game, although he did make substitute appearances, and thereafter he enjoyed an injury-free spell during which his value to the team became clear as he began to forge a lethal partnership with Alan Shearer, creating openings for his colleagues as well as contributing his own share of goals, none more stunning than the volley for the first counter in the defeat of Manchester United. Unhappily, Duncan incurred yet another injury, this time fluid on the knee, in the FA Cup semi-final, in which he lasted little more than half an hour, his last appearance of the season. The "Toon Army" is hoping that after such an injury-ridden season the summer break will enable him to fully regain fitness, so that they can enjoy the full fruits of his all-round game and his exciting duet with Alan.
Dundee U (Signed from Carse Thistle on 1/2/1990) SL 75+2/28 SLC 2+1/2 SC 6/4
Glasgow R (£4,000,000 on 20/7/1993) SL 8+6/2 SLC 2+2/3 SC 0+3 Others 1
Everton (£4,400,000 on 4/10/1994) PL 110+6/37 FLC 8/1 FAC 8+1/4
Newcastle U (£7,000,000 + on 25/11/1998) PL 24+6/8 FAC 6+2/3 Others 2+1/1

FERRER Albert Llopes
Born: Barcelona, Spain, 6 June 1970
Height: 5'7" Weight: 10.6
Club Honours: ESC '98
International Honours: Spain: 36; U23 (OLYM '92)
After a highly successful first season in English football, Albert began his second in August 1999 in the same vein, showing the alertness, speed, composure and confidence on the ball that have made him probably the best right back in the Premiership. "Chapi" scored his first Chelsea goal in his 58th appearance for the club last November, intelligently running on to Dennis Wise's astute through-ball to drive past the Hertha Berlin goalkeeper and clinch top spot in Champions' League Group H and qualification for the second phase. Unfortunately, he suffered a treble disappointment in the early part of 2000. First, he suffered an ankle injury in January against Leicester that sidelined him for seven matches. Then, after a handful of games back in first-team action, he made an emotional return to the Nou Camp for the Champions' League quarter-final against his previous club Barcelona, but his injury flared up again and he hobbled out of a match he desperately wanted to win at half time. Missing Albert's dependability in defence, Chelsea came under increasing pressure and their 3-1 first-leg advantage was duly overturned to complete an unhappy evening for the popular Catalan. Albert now had just five matches to prove his fitness for the FA Cup final against Aston Villa; he sat out the first four in favour of Mario Melchiot but was given a run-out in the last game of the season against Derby County. Sadly, his ankle wasn't strong enough and after 31 minutes he limped out of the action once more, his dream of an FA Cup final appearance shattered, as were his hopes of a place in the Spanish squad for Euro 2000 after he had valiantly battled his way back into contention.
Chelsea (£2,200,000 from Barcelona, Spain on 15/8/1998) PL 54+1 FLC 0+1 FAC 4 Others 22/1

FESTA Gianluca
Born: Cagliari, Italy, 15 March 1969
Height: 6'0" Weight: 13.6
A tough-tackling, no-nonsense central defender with a taste for adventure, Gianluca seems to have a liking for the big occasion – especially local derbies. In Middlesbrough's game at Newcastle last October he picked up a hamstring injury which troubled him for the rest of the season and cost him a number of games as he worked hard to regain his fitness, but in the return match at the Riverside in May the Italian centre back scored a late equaliser, only his second goal of the season. The 1999-2000 campaign was the big defender's fourth at Middlesbrough. When fit he cannot resist the urge to run at the opposition on the counter-attack, although he is fortunately adept at getting back into position. In spite of all his problems, Gianluca managed 32 appearances, two of them as a substitute, and he will be hoping for an injury-free season for the Boro in 2000-01.
Middlesbrough (£2,700,000 from Inter Milan, Italy, via Cagliari, on 18/1/1997) F/PL 103+2/7 FLC 15/1 FAC 8/1

FETTIS Alan William
Born: Belfast, 1 February 1971
Height: 6'1" Weight: 12.10
International Honours: NI: 25; B-3; Yth; Sch
With the signing of Alan Kelly during the 1999 close season, it was apparent that the other Alan's days at Blackburn were numbered and in September he went to Leicester on loan to provide cover for the regular goalkeepers. His only taste of first-team action for Rovers last season was as a substitute for Kelly at Portsmouth at the end of December. Dismissed while playing for the reserves, following a disciplinary appearance he was allowed to join York in March. Teaming up again with his former Hull boss, Terry Dolan, Alan signed a contract to the end of the season. The excellent 'keeper quickly became a firm favourite with the Bootham Crescent fans. In a run of seven games he conceded just one goal, and at the end of April he was recalled to the Northern Ireland international squad. In his 13 matches for York he kept eight clean sheets and was on the losing side only twice before being offered new terms in May.
Hull C (£50,000 from Ards on 14/8/1991) FL 131+4/2 FLC 7+1 FAC 5 Others 7
West Bromwich A (Loaned on 20/11/1995) FL 3
Nottingham F (£250,000 on 13/1/1996) PL 4 FLC 1 FAC 0+1
Blackburn Rov (£300,000 on 12/9/1997) P/FL 9+2 FAC 1
York C (Free on 1/3/2000) FL 13

FEUER Anthony **Ian**
Born: Las Vegas, USA, 20 May 1971
Height: 6'7" Weight: 15.6
International Honours: USA: 1
This giant 'keeper returned to Nationwide League football after a two-year absence when he signed for Cardiff in the US close season. He then received a surprise call from one of his old clubs, West Ham, who were suffering a goalkeeping crisis with Shaka

Hislop ruled out for the season. Ian signed for the Hammers towards the end of February and went on to appear in three Premiership games before manager Harry Redknapp introduced youngster Steve Bywater for the last few matches. He performed capably for the Upton Park club and showed that he is not only extremely tall but can also make full use of his 6ft 7in frame. Stop Press: Ian was reported to have joined Wimbledon in June as a replacement for the departed Neil Sullivan.

West Ham U (£70,000 from Los Angeles Salsa, USA on 23/3/1994)
Peterborough U (Loaned on 20/2/1995) FL 16
Luton T (£580,000 on 11/9/1995) FL 97 FLC 7 FAC 5 Others 5 (Free to New England Revolution, USA on 24/3/1998)
Cardiff C (Free from Colorado Rapids, USA on 10/1/2000)
West Ham U (Free on 23/2/2000) PL 3

FICKLING Ashley Spencer
Born: Sheffield, 15 November 1972
Height: 5'10" Weight: 11.6
International Honours: E: Sch

A dependable squad player who never let Scunthorpe down when asked to play either in central defence or at right back during 1999-2000, Ashley was unlucky to find himself out of the side in the closing weeks of the season. Always in the team or on the bench during the first half of the campaign, he came back from a red card against Bristol Rovers in early September to score his first goal for the club at Chesterfield in October. A solid defender with no frills, he was out of contract in the summer but was made an offer of re-engagement.

Sheffield U (From juniors on 26/7/1991) FLC 2+1 Others 3
Darlington (Loaned on 26/11/1992) FL 14 Others 1
Darlington (Loaned on 12/8/1993) FL 1 FLC 1
Grimsby T (Free on 23/3/1995) FL 26+13/2 FLC 2+1 FAC 2+1
Darlington (Loaned on 26/3/1998) FL 8
Scunthorpe U (Free on 24/7/1998) FL 52+7/1 FLC 3 FAC 3 Others 3

FILAN John Richard
Born: Sydney, Australia, 8 February 1970
Height: 5'11" Weight: 13.2
International Honours: Australia: 1; U23

When Alan Kelly was signed by Blackburn during the 1999 close season, it appeared that John might be pushed to hold his place but Brian Kidd retained him. There were signs that the side's lack of success was causing the Australian goalkeeper some hesitancy and he was strangely indecisive when coming for crosses, which had always been his strong point. When Tony Parkes took over at Ewood Park in November he immediately dropped Filan and, confined to the reserves, John aggravated a long-standing shoulder injury. When Kelly was injured at the end of December, Filan delayed a shoulder operation to come back and looked to have held his place until, on 15 January, he had to leave the field during the game against Huddersfield after damaging his shoulder again. That was the end of his season and poses the intriguing question of whether he is the number one or number two goalkeeper at the club.

Cambridge U (£40,000 from Budapest St George, Australia on 12/3/1993) FL 68 FLC 6 FAC 3 Others 3
Coventry C (£300,000 on 2/3/1995) PL 15+1 FLC 2
Blackburn Rov (£700,000 on 10/7/1997) P/FL 49 FLC 3 FAC 5

FINCH Keith John
Born: Thorpe, 6 May 1982
Height: 6'0" Weight: 11.12

Darlington's young reserve goalkeeper was suddenly thrust into the limelight in the FA Cup tie with Southport last October. First-choice 'keeper Andy Collett was injured and Keith made his first-team debut in the second half. He produced a string of stunning stops that undoubtedly contributed to Darlington going through to the second round. He left the field to a standing ovation after his 45 minutes of glory.

Darlington (Trainee) FAC 0+1

FINNAN Stephen (Steve) John
Born: Limerick, 20 April 1976
Height: 5'10" Weight: 11.6
Club Honours: Div 3 '98; Div 2 '99
International Honours: RoI: 2; B-1; U21-8

The 1999-2000 season proved to be sound rather than spectacular for the versatile Fulham player, who was probably not helped by being switched from wing back to central midfield and back again at various times during the season. Steve never gave less than 100 per cent and, apart from a knee injury which kept him out for six weeks in October and November, he started every game. On occasions when Fulham were short of strikers through injury, Steve willingly played in that role, and he will be a very valuable asset to new manager Jean Tigana next season. He made his senior international debut in April when he played for the Republic of Ireland against Greece and also appeared in the end-of-season friendly with Scotland.

Birmingham C (£100,000 from Welling U on 12/6/1995) FL 9+6/1 FLC 2+2 Others 2+1
Notts Co (Loaned on 5/3/1996) FL 14+3/2 Others 3/1
Notts Co (£300,000 on 31/10/1996) FL 71+9/5 FLC 4 FAC 7/1 Others 1
Fulham (£600,000 on 13/11/1998) FL 54+1/4 FLC 6 FAC 8/1 Others 1

FINNEY Stephen (Steve) Kenneth
Born: Hexham, 31 October 1973
Height: 5'10" Weight: 12.8
Club Honours: Div 2 '96

The experienced forward, who was released by Leyton Orient at the end of 1998-99, had an unsuccessful summer trial with Exeter. Steve was snapped up by Barrow in the Unibond League, before returning to the league ranks with Chester in October. With the Blues slipping towards the Conference, he was largely restricted to substitute appearances.

Preston NE (From trainee on 2/5/1992) FL 1+5/1 FAC 0+1 Others 1+1
Manchester C (Free on 12/2/1993)
Swindon T (Free on 15/6/1995) FL 47+26/18 FLC 6+1/1 FAC 2+5/2 Others 2+1/1
Cambridge U (Loaned on 10/10/1997) FL 4+3/2
Carlisle U (Free on 3/7/1998) FL 22+11/6 FLC 1+1 FAC 1 Others 2
Leyton Orient (Free on 25/3/1999) FL 2+3 (Free to Barrow during 1999 close season)
Chester C (Signed on 18/10/1999) FL 4+9

FINNIGAN John Francis
Born: Wakefield, 29 March 1976
Height: 5'8" Weight: 10.11

John is a creative central midfield player for Lincoln who is equally effective as a ball winner. He rarely missed a match in the first half of 1999-2000, when he proved to be the dynamo of the Imps' engine room, but then suffered a back injury early in the new year that put him out for six weeks. He returned to first-team action at Plymouth in March but struggled to regain his early-season form.

Nottingham F (From trainee on 10/5/1993)
Lincoln C (£50,000 on 26/3/1998) FL 78+2/3 FLC 4 FAC 6/1 Others 2

FISH Mark Anthony
Born: Capetown, South Africa, 14 March 1974
Height: 6'3" Weight: 13.2
International Honours: South Africa: 59 (ANC '96)

Mark has frequently been touted as a transfer target for many big-name clubs, and it was widely expected that the Bolton defender would have moved on from the Wanderers by the beginning of last season. The fact that Mark stayed at the Reebok Stadium was a big bonus for the club, and the benefits of having a centre back of Mark's undoubted class were there for everyone to see during 1999-2000. Despite missing several fixtures due to international call-ups he produced a number of top-class displays yet again for Bolton. He played with a number of defensive partners, although the most impressive pairing had to be the one he struck up with Paul Ritchie in the latter half of the season, which coincided with Bolton's fantastic run which took them into the play-offs. Mark also seemed to cut down on his surges into the opposition's half and concentrated more on his defensive duties last season, a fact that is highlighted by the fact that he scored only one goal. There is an obvious gap in the team when he does not play (which was highlighted to such heartbreaking effect in the two Worthington Cup semi-final defeats against Tranmere last January), and Bolton will certainly be pulling out the stops to keep this highly influential player at the Reebok for at least another season. Mark made five appearances for South Africa in the African Nations' Cup finals in the spring but subsequently announced that he was to retire from international football.

Bolton W (£2,500,000 from Lazio, Italy, via Orlando Pirates, on 16/9/1997) P/FL 89 FLC 10+1/1 FAC 6 Others 5

FISHER Neil John
Born: St Helens, 7 November 1970
Height: 5'10" Weight: 11.0

Neil originally moved to Chester in June 1995. After 129 appearances for the Blues, he was released in the 1998 close season and joined Bangor. The versatile midfielder returned to City in March 1999, originally on a non-contract basis. His experience in an extremely young squad was especially valuable in 1999-2000. Although the season ended in bitter relegation disappointment, Neil can reflect on a very good campaign on a personal level.

Bolton W (From trainee on 12/7/1989) FL 17+7/1 FLC 4 FAC 1
Chester C (Free on 5/6/1995) FL 91+17/4 FLC 8 FAC 6 Others 3 (Released during 1998 close season)
Chester C (Free from Bangor C on 25/3/1999) FL 41+8/1 FLC 4 FAC 4 Others 1

FITZGERALD Scott Brian
Born: Westminster, 13 August 1969
Height: 6'0" Weight: 12.12
International Honours: RoI: B-1; U21-4

Being one of five central defenders in the Millwall squad, Scott could not be certain of a place in the starting line-up in 1999-2000. Having missed the first four games of the season, he put together a run of 21 consecutive appearances, performing with his usual reliability. He was in and out of the team during the second half of the season, but made a telling contribution to the Lions' successful campaign, relishing the additional responsibility of being made skipper. A tall Pierce Brosnan lookalike, he is good in the air with deceptive pace and reads the game well, which makes his accomplished defending appear effortless.

Wimbledon (From trainee on 13/7/1989) F/PL 95+11/1 FLC 13 FAC 5 Others 1
Sheffield U (Loaned on 23/11/1995) FL 6
Millwall (Loaned on 11/10/1996) FL 7
Millwall (£50,000 + on 28/7/1997) FL 79+2/1 FLC 4 FAC 2 Others 5

FITZPATRICK Ian Matthew
Born: Manchester, 22 September 1980
Height: 5'9" Weight: 10.6
International Honours: E: Yth; Sch

A product of Manchester United's successful youth set-up, Ian was associated with the Premiership champions from the age of nine. He signed for Halifax at the start of March 2000 and made his Town debut when he came on as a sub in the ill-tempered match at Brighton. Ian has terrific pace and the older heads at the club will help his progress.

Manchester U (From trainee on 8/7/1998)
Halifax T (Free on 2/3/2000) FL 2+6

FITZPATRICK Lee Gareth
Born: Manchester, 31 October 1978
Height: 5'10" Weight: 11.7

A promising young midfielder, Lee appeared to be making little progress in Blackburn's reserve side early in 1999-2000. He took the opportunity of a loan move to Hartlepool in November 1999, and in his first full game he scored a fine 30-yard goal against rivals Darlington. In a short first-team run he impressed Pool manager Chris Turner with his darting runs from midfield. He opted for a return to Ewood Park, but a couple of months later was back at Hartlepool on a permanent basis.

Blackburn Rov (From trainee on 2/7/1996)
Hartlepool U (Loaned on 17/9/1999) FL 6+4/1
Hartlepool U (Free on 27/1/2000) FL 10+4/1 Others 1+1

FITZPATRICK Trevor Joseph James
Born: Frimley, 19 February 1980
Height: 6'1" Weight: 12.10
International Honours: RoI: Yth

Injury played a major part in Trevor's 1999-2000 season. Inevitably, he looked a little out of sorts on his return and he will benefit from a rigorous 2000 pre-season. A youngster with a knack for knowing where the goal is, the Southend striker will be keen to recapture his 1998-99 form. A product of the club's youth policy, Trevor is a former Republic of Ireland youth international.

Southend U (From trainee on 6/7/1998) FL 9+33/5 FLC 1+2 FAC 0+1 Others 0+1

FLACK Steven (Steve) Richard
Born: Cambridge, 29 May 1971
Height: 6'2" Weight: 13.2

Steve was in and out of the Exeter starting line-up during 1999-2000. However, his aerial power and strength continued to make him difficult for the opposition to handle. The big target man was put on the transfer list in February but should have no problem finding himself a new club for 2000-01. A former professional boxer, Steve was reported to be the subject of several six-figure bids in the previous two years, while Devon neighbours Torquay were one of a number of clubs to express a more recent interest.

Cardiff C (£10,000 from Cambridge C on 13/11/1995) FL 6+5/1
Exeter C (£10,000 on 13/9/1996) FL 114+38/31 FLC 5+1 FAC 9+2/5 Others 6+2/2

FLAHAVAN Aaron Adam
Born: Southampton, 15 December 1975
Height: 6'1" Weight: 11.12

This young Portsmouth 'keeper began the 1999-2000 campaign brightly with three consecutive clean sheets but was then struck by a mystery illness and collapsed during the Worthington Cup tie against Blackburn – a repeat of a similar incident that had occurred during 1998-99. This time tests revealed a blood problem that was quickly rectified and he was back in first-team action by November. He lost his place again when a change of management brought Russell Hoult to Fratton Park and he finished the season as second choice to the newcomer. Aaron is an accomplished shot stopper who is capable of making good reflex saves, and he shows impressive command of his penalty area.

Portsmouth (From trainee on 15/2/1994) FL 73 FLC 11 FAC 1

FLANAGAN Alan
Born: Drogheda, Ireland, 9 October 1980
Height: 6'1" Weight: 13.7
International Honours: RoI: Yth

This former Swindon trainee signed a one-year contract with the club in July 1999 but had to be content with being third choice 'keeper behind Frank Talia and Steve Mildenhall in 1999-2000. He made his Football League debut on the final day of the season as a replacement for the injured Mildenhall after just 30 minutes of the game at Sheffield United and went on to distinguish himself with several fine saves. Alan is already a sound shot stopper and his physical presence enables him to dominate his penalty box. He was released during the close season.

Swindon T (From trainee on 10/7/1999) FL 0+1

FLEMING Craig
Born: Halifax, 6 October 1971
Height: 6'0" Weight: 12.10

The Norwich vice-captain enjoyed another outstandingly consistent season in 1999-2000 at the heart of a much meaner City defence. A model professional, he seldom misses a match through injury and always sets a tremendous example to the younger players at the club. Craig closely resembles an "old-fashioned" centre half with his no-nonsense approach to his defending, being prepared to throw his body in the line of shots on goal and to stand up against the most physical of centre forwards. He is also quick and deceptively strong in the air, making him a solid all-round defender. Earlier in his career, particularly while at Oldham, Craig developed a reputation for himself as a good man marker and also occasionally played at full back. He missed just a handful of matches last term with his goals, a winner at Port Vale and the first Norwich goal of the new millennium, at home to Portsmouth, being among the highlights of his third season in Canary colours.

Halifax T (From trainee on 21/3/1990) FL 56+1 FLC 4 FAC 3 Others 3+2
Oldham Ath (£80,000 on 15/8/1991) F/PL 158+6/1 FLC 12+1 FAC 11 Others 4
Norwich C (£600,000 on 30/6/1997) FL 93+5/7 FLC 10 FAC 2+1

FLEMING Curtis
Born: Manchester, 8 October 1968
Height: 5'11" Weight: 12.8
Club Honours: Div 1 '95
International Honours: RoI: 10; U23-2; U21-5; Yth

Curtis was sidelined by injury for much of the 1999-2000 season and his relatively modest total of 31 starts for Middlesbrough was as much a disappointment to him as it was to anyone else. By the end of the campaign he had regained full fitness after two knee operations and he will be hoping to redress the balance by reproducing his best form next term. He is a loyal clubman and the coming season will be his tenth with Boro. Curtis continues to play the wing-back role to perfection; he is the ideal foil for Phil Stamp and, like Christian Ziege on the other wing, he crosses the ball into the danger zone immaculately. He is still very much a part of the Republic of Ireland squad and flew back from Spain, where Middlesbrough were enjoying a training break, in response to a dramatic call to provide injury cover for the European Championship play-offs against Turkey.

Middlesbrough (£50,000 from St Patricks on 16/8/1991) F/PL 211+17/3 FLC 22+2/1 FAC 13+1 Others 7+1

FLEMING Terence (Terry) Maurice
Born: Marston Green, 5 January 1973
Height: 5'9" Weight: 10.9

Terry is a central midfield player who was used out of position for most of the 1999-2000 season when he filled in at right back to cover for Lincoln's injury problems. As captain of the team, he led by example, his combative style providing plenty of inspiration for his colleagues. He looked far more comfortable when he returned to his favoured midfield position towards the end of the campaign. Unable to agree terms for a new deal, Terry joined Plymouth on a three-year contract in June.

Coventry C (From trainee on 2/7/1991) F/PL 8+5 FLC 0+1
Northampton T (Free on 3/8/1993) FL 26+5/1 FLC 2 FAC 0+1 Others 0+1
Preston NE (Free on 18/7/1994) FL 25+7/2 FLC 4 FAC 0+1 Others 3+2
Lincoln C (Signed on 7/12/1995) FL 175+8/8 FLC 11+1/2 FAC 11/2 Others 4

FLETCHER Carl Neil
Born: Camberley, 7 April 1980
Height: 5'10" Weight: 11.7

This promising Bournemouth youngster made the breakthrough to regular first-team football in 1999-2000, rarely missing a game from mid-October through to January. Operating in the centre of midfield, he proved to have good passing skills and be willing to get forward when opportunities arose. Carl was rewarded for the progress he had made when he signed a two-and-a-half-year extension to his contract last February.

Bournemouth (From trainee on 3/7/1998) FL 20+7/3 FAC 3 Others 1

FLETCHER Steven (Steve) Mark
Born: Hartlepool, 26 June 1972
Height: 6'2" Weight: 14.9

Steve is now approaching ten years' service with Bournemouth and had another good season at Dean Court in 1999-2000, netting seven league goals and forming a successful striking partnership with Mark Stein. He missed two months with hamstring trouble at the beginning of the new year, only returning to the team in March, when he once again played an important role up front for the Cherries. A tall striker, he is adept at holding the ball up until his colleagues are able to join him in attack.

Hartlepool U (From trainee on 23/8/1990) FL 19+13/4 FLC 0+2/1 FAC 1+2 Others 2+2/1
Bournemouth (£30,000 on 28/7/1992) FL 248+18/51 FLC 24/3 FAC 14/3 Others 12/2

FLITCROFT David (Dave) John
Born: Bolton, 14 January 1974
Height: 5'11" Weight: 13.5

The younger brother of Blackburn's Garry, Dave was one of new Rochdale manager Steve Parkin's 1999 close-season signings. Although he was sent off on his home league debut, "Flicker's" bustling style in midfield made him a fixture in the engine room of the side for practically the whole season. He perfectly complemented the more stylish Jason Peake. Wanted by Second Division Chesterfield in mid-season, Dave was happy to stay with Dale.

Preston NE (From trainee on 2/5/1992) FL 4+4/2 FLC 0+1 Others 0+1
Lincoln C (Loaned on 17/9/1993) FL 2 FLC 0+1
Chester C (Free on 9/12/1993) FL 146+21/18 FLC 10+1 FAC 7 Others 8/1
Rochdale (Free on 5/7/1999) FL 40+3/2 FLC 2 FAC 1+2 Others 5

FLITCROFT Garry William
Born: Bolton, 6 November 1972
Height: 6'0" Weight: 12.2
International Honours: E: U21-10; Yth; Sch

Still recovering from an injury sustained the previous season, Garry did not reappear until Blackburn's second game of 1999-2000 at Huddersfield. Fortune did not favour the energetic midfielder. Within ten minutes he had been felled for what TV confirmed was an obvious penalty that was not given and then his header crossed the line only for the goal to be disallowed. After having to come off during the following game he needed more surgery to repair his injury and did not resume until the middle of February. He then had difficulty finding his touch, but his solid tackling stood him in good stead and he will be hoping to rediscover his best form in the coming season. Garry is the brother of Rochdale's David Flitcroft.

Manchester C (From trainee on 2/7/1991) PL 109+6/13 FLC 11+1 FAC 14/2
Bury (Loaned on 5/3/1992) FL 12
Blackburn Rov (£3,200,000 on 26/3/1996) P/FL 84+7/5 FLC 3+1/1 FAC 3+1 Others 2/1

FLO Havard
Born: Norway, 4 April 1970
Height: 6'1" Weight: 13.6
International Honours: Norway: 20

Although several Wolves players made a poor start to the 1999-2000 season, Havard seemed to suffer more criticism than most. The big striker was not 100 per cent fit and seemed unable to make his physical presence tell. After seven starts without a goal he was relegated to the bench, and then he was out injured for ten matches. He came back as a substitute to score against Swindon in November, but the signing of Michael Branch delayed his return to favour. His eighth start came in January, when he scored against leaders Charlton. Ten more games elapsed before he was back in the first eleven, and then he scored two well-taken goals against Ipswich. He generally remained on the fringes for the rest of the campaign, however, and was transfer-listed in May.

Wolverhampton W (£700,000 from Werder Bremen, Germany, via Stryn and Sogndal, on 12/1/1999) FL 27+11/9 FLC 2 FAC 1+2/1

FLO Tore Andre
Born: Strin, Norway, 15 June 1973
Height: 6'4" Weight: 13.8
Club Honours: FLC '98; ECWC '98; ESC '98; FAC '00
International Honours: Norway: 51

After a comparatively lean start to the 1999-2000 season when he went 13 matches without scoring, Tore Andre hit a purple patch in late October with outstanding performances against Galatasaray and Arsenal within four days of each other, grabbing three superb goals in the process. Surprisingly preferred to Chris Sutton at Galatasaray's intimidating "Stadium of Hell" and given a lone front-running role, he ran the Turks' defence ragged, scoring the first two goals in the Blues' crushing 5-0 victory. Then the much-vaunted Arsenal defence were made to suffer as he climbed to crash a classic far-post header past David Seaman that gave Chelsea the lead in a titanic Premiership clash at Stamford Bridge. Tore Andre's hot streak continued into November with four goals in eight days, the equaliser at Goodison Park and winner against Bradford City sandwiching two magnificent strikes against Feyenoord. The following month he again played as a lone striker over the festive period, due to injuries, and responded superbly with a match-winning brace at the Dell, a neatly taken effort against Sheffield Wednesday and two rapid-fire equalisers at Coventry – both within 30 seconds of the home side going ahead. With the resumption of the Champions' League second phase in February, Chelsea boss Gianluca Vialli decided upon Tore Andre and Gianfranco Zola as his preferred pairing for the European matches and the duo performed magnificently. The Norwegian scored a superb solo effort in Rotterdam in Chelsea's 3-1 victory over Feyenoord, then proved to be a thorn in the side of Barcelona over the two-legged quarter-final, grabbing two goals in Chelsea's exhilarating 3-1 victory at the Bridge and pouncing on goalkeeper Ruud Hesp's error with an opportunist strike to put the Blues within sight of a deserved semi-final spot at the Nou Camp. This brought his total in the Champions' League campaign to a highly creditable eight. Overall, Tore Andre finished with 19 goals and almost became the first Blues striker since Kerry Dixon in 1990 to break the 20-goal barrier. His season ended on a slightly downbeat note when on-loan superstar George Weah was preferred in the FA Cup final starting line-up, although Tore Andre replaced George for the last three minutes and collected a winners' medal. The rangy Norwegian centre forward has firmly established himself as a crowd favourite since his bargain move from Brann Bergen and it was a great relief to the Stamford Bridge faithful when, following press speculation linking him with a number of other clubs, he pledged himself to Chelsea. This was bad news for the Continental defenders who will be facing him in Chelsea's tilt at the UEFA Cup. Despite his tremendous reputation on the international scene Tore Andre scored just once in 13 internationals during the season, failing to net at all in the Norwegians' disappointing Euro 2000 campaign.

Chelsea (£300,000 from Brann Bergen, Norway, via Sogndal and Tromso, on 4/8/1997) PL 54+44/31 FLC 6+2/3 FAC 5+5/1 Others 21+9/12

FLOWERS Timothy (Tim) David
Born: Kenilworth, 3 February 1967
Height: 6'2" Weight: 14.0
Club Honours: PL '95; FLC '00
International Honours: E: 11; U21-3; Yth

Only very occasional lapses marred Tim's first season between the sticks for Leicester in 1999-2000. A £1.1 million summer signing from Blackburn, he showed a return to the form that had won him international recognition with England, particularly in making some exceptional reaction saves to deny Aston Villa in the Worthington Cup semi-final and Arsenal in the FA Cup. He helped the Foxes to victory in the Worthington Cup final and enjoyed his first Wembley success more that most, making some crucial early saves to deny Tranmere before City got a grip on the game. Tim was unlucky to suffer more than his fair share of injuries during the season, and had to be substituted three times as a result of his bravery. An excellent shot stopper, he was a most popular and worthy successor to Kasey Keller in the Leicester goal.

Wolverhampton W (From apprentice on 28/8/1984) FL 63 FLC 5 FAC 2 Others 2
Southampton (£70,000 on 13/6/1986) F/PL 192 FLC 26 FAC 16 Others 8
Swindon T (Loaned on 23/3/1987) FL 2
Swindon T (Loaned on 13/11/1987) FL 5
Blackburn Rov (£2,400,000 on 4/11/1993) PL 175+2 FLC 14 FAC 13+1 Others 12
Leicester C (£1,100,000 + on 30/7/1999) PL 29 FLC 5+1 FAC 2

FLYNN Michael (Mike) Anthony
Born: Oldham, 23 February 1969
Height: 6'0" Weight: 11.0

Mike proved once again to be an inspirational captain for Stockport in 1999-2000, making a magnificent contribution throughout the season, as he has done for several years. He appeared in the starting line-up for each of County's 51 competitive games and it is difficult to imagine the team without him. A wholehearted central defender, he is superb in the air, committed in the tackle and expert at marshalling the defence. He has now played over 300 league games for the Hatters and is approaching legendary status at Edgeley Park.

Oldham Ath (From apprentice on 7/2/1987) FL 37+3/1 FLC 1+1/1 FAC 1 Others 2
Norwich C (£100,000 on 22/12/1988)
Preston NE (£125,000 on 4/12/1989) FL 134+2/7 FLC 6 FAC 6+1/1 Others 13
Stockport Co (£125,000 on 25/3/1993) FL 316+1/14 FLC 30/2 FAC 17/1 Others 19

FLYNN Sean Michael
Born: Birmingham, 13 March 1968
Height: 5'8" Weight: 11.8

West Bromwich Albion's skipper, Sean missed several vital league games half-way through the 1999-2000 season after seriously damaging knee ligaments in his right leg during Albion's 2-2 home draw with Sheffield United in late November. The absence of the Birmingham-born midfielder, who is such an inspirational figure in the side, certainly affected the Baggies' performances. But when he came back his determination and never-say-die approach to the game, his aggressive play and total commitment were ultimately vital as relegation was avoided right at the death. Perhaps not the quickest of players in recovery, he worked overtime in centre-field, pumping up and down from penalty area to penalty area like a steam engine. He didn't score the number of goals he would have liked, but he made one or two for his colleagues nevertheless. He was released during the summer.

Coventry C (£20,000 from Halesowen T on 3/12/1991) F/PL 90+7/9 FLC 5/1 FAC 3
Derby Co (£250,000 on 11/8/1995) F/PL 39+20/3 FLC 3 FAC 3
Stoke C (Loaned on 27/3/1997) FL 5
West Bromwich A (£260,000 on 8/8/1997) FL 99+10/8 FLC 11/1 FAC 0+2

FOE Marc-Vivien
Born: Nkolo, Cameroon, 1 May 1975
Height: 6'3" Weight: 13.6
International Honours: Cameroon: 39 (ANC 2000)

This towering midfield player had an excellent season for West Ham in 1999-2000. He had a few niggling injury problems in the autumn and missed a month when he was away on international duty but was otherwise a key figure in the Hammers' team. His size gives him great presence in the centre of the field, while his talents range from precision tackling to an ability to spray passes around the park. He scored just once in Premiership games – a 15-yard strike against Sheffield Wednesday last November – and added another in the UEFA Cup win in Croatia against Osijek. He was also a regular for the Cameroon international team and was one of the stars of the side that defeated Nigeria in a penalty shoot-out to win the African Nations' Cup in February. Marc-Vivien was sold to French club Lyon in mid-May for a £6 million fee as part of the deal that brought Frederic Kanoute to Upton Park on a permanent basis.

West Ham U (£4,200,000 from RC Lens, France, via Canon Younde, on 28/1/1999) PL 38/1 FLC 3 FAC 1 Others 4+1/1

FOLAN Anthony (Tony) Stephen
Born: Lewisham, 18 September 1978
Height: 5'11" Weight: 11.8
Club Honours: Div 3 '99
International Honours: RoI: U21-6

A left-sided wide midfield player for Brentford, Tony managed just two starts for the Bees in a disappointing 1999-2000 season. He possesses the traditional winger's skills of trickery and pace and can still score spectacular goals, as he showed when he hit the equaliser against Reading last November. He then had the misfortune to break a bone in his foot during a training accident and did not return to first-team action until just before the end of the campaign. He added another Republic of Ireland U21 cap to his tally when appearing as a substitute against Yugoslavia last August.

Crystal Palace (From trainee on 22/9/1995) PL 0+1
Brentford (£100,000 on 22/9/1998) FL 20+18/5 FLC 1+2 FAC 3+1/2 Others 2

FOLEY Dominic Joseph
Born: Cork, 7 July 1976
Height: 6'1" Weight: 12.8
International Honours: RoI: 3; U21-8

A tall striker signed by Watford on a free transfer from Wolves in time for the start of the 1999-2000 season, Dominic, who had previously been on loan at Vicarage Road during the 1997-98 campaign, started only five matches and failed to make as big an impression as he would have hoped. In fairness, he was another Watford player to suffer more than his fair share of injuries, in his case a hamstring strain in November and an ankle injury sustained during training in March. Dominic scored his first-ever Premiership goal at Leeds shortly before the end of the season. He made his senior international debut against Scotland in May and made further appearances in the Nike Cup tournament in June, scoring in the 2-2 draw with Mexico and the 1-1 tie with the USA.

Wolverhampton W (£35,000 from St James' Gate on 31/8/1995) FL 4+16/3 FLC 0+3 FAC 0+1 Others 0+2
Watford (Loaned on 24/2/1998) FL 2+6/1
Notts Co (Loaned on 7/12/1998) FL 2 Others 1
Watford (Free on 11/6/1999) PL 5+7/1 FLC 0+1

FOLLAND Robert (Rob) William
Born: Swansea, 16 September 1979
Height: 5'9" Weight: 11.0
International Honours: W: U21-1; Yth

Rob's career flourished under the first two of Oxford's three managers last season before he found himself a fringe player under Denis Smith. Ironically it was Smith who had given the youngster his first-team debut two seasons ago. Mainly used as a striker or wide player in the reserves, Rob came into the side as a wing back and adapted to an unfamiliar role well, helped by his enthusiasm and energy. Although not ideally suited to his new position, Rob made 26 starts, scoring a vital goal at Reading in a local derby. He went on to make his debut for Wales U21s in June when he came on from the subs' bench in the Presidents' Cup game against Northern Ireland. It will be interesting to see how the youngster fares next time around.

Oxford U (From trainee on 3/7/1998) FL 17+8/1 FLC 4 FAC 4+1/1 Others 1

FORAN Mark James
Born: Aldershot, 30 October 1973
Height: 6'4" Weight: 14.3

Mark has been with Crewe since December 1997 but his first-team opportunities have been limited. A very tall, competitive defender, he is dominant in the air and although he has the versatility to occupy any of the positions across the back line he is naturally most effective as a centre back. He was sidelined for a while last season by a facial injury but made nine starts during the first half of the campaign. After Christmas he added only six more appearances to his tally, two as a substitute, but he remained a valuable squad member, although he was unable to add to his single goal for the club.

Millwall (From trainee on 3/11/1990)
Sheffield U (£25,000 on 28/8/1993) FL 10+1/1 FLC 1 Others 0+1
Rotherham U (Loaned on 26/8/1994) FL 3
Wycombe W (Loaned on 11/8/1995) FL 5 FLC 2
Peterborough U (£40,000 on 8/2/1996) FL 22+3/1 FAC 1 Others 2
Lincoln C (Loaned on 22/1/1997) FL 1+1
Oldham Ath (Loaned on 3/3/1997) FL 0+1
Crewe Alex (£25,000 + on 12/12/1997) FL 25+6/1 FLC 2 FAC 1

FORBES Adrian Emmanuel
Born: Ealing, 23 January 1979
Height: 5'8" Weight: 11.10
International Honours: E: Yth

This speedy and exciting right winger spent almost all of the 1999-2000 season on the Norwich transfer list but, despite some newspaper speculation, there were no firm bids for a player who made a considerable impact when he first won his way into the team under Mike Walker three seasons ago. Adrian marked his first appearance of the season, at home to Fulham in early October, with a goal, but in general his appearances were restricted by the presence of Cedric

Anselin and Paul Dalglish. He is at his best when running at defenders and committing them, having the ability to go past them on either side, often preferring to cut inside off the flank for a shot at goal. A truly wholehearted player, he never gives of less than his best, always being prepared to track back when his side are not in possession of the ball. Adrian will be hoping for better things in 2000-01, when his enthusiasm and undoubted ability should enable him to compete for a place in the starting line-up from the opening day of the season.

Norwich C (From trainee on 21/1/1997) FL 53+30/5 FLC 0+2 FAC 1+2

FORBES Steven (Steve) Dudley
Born: Stoke Newington, 24 December 1975
Height: 6'2" Weight: 13.2

Previously employed by Colchester as an industrious midfielder, Steve had an impressive 1999 pre-season, when he was played in the experimental roles of right-sided centre back in a back-three formation and right wing back. Unfortunately, he picked up an injury which kept him out of the opening games of the new campaign, and had just returned to fitness and made two substitute appearances when he then injured his ankle in an innocuous trip in training, which effectively ended his Colchester career. On his return to fitness in the spring, he was transferred to Conference side Stevenage Borough.

Millwall (£45,000 from Sittingbourne on 11/7/1994) FL 0+5 FLC 0+1 FAC 0+1
Colchester U (Signed on 14/3/1997) FL 34+19/4 FLC 1+2 FAC 3/1 Others 4+1
Peterborough U (Loaned on 3/3/1999) FL 1+2

FORBES Terrell
Born: Southwark, 17 August 1981
Height: 6'0" Weight: 12.5
Club Honours: FAYC '99

This promising West Ham youngster made the step up from trainee to first-year professional in 1999-2000 and was then loaned to Bournemouth last October to cover for injuries to defenders Eddie Howe and Karl Broadhurst. He made four appearances for the Cherries in the centre of defence before returning to Upton Park.

West Ham U (From trainee on 2/7/1999)
Bournemouth (Loaned on 18/10/1999) FL 3 FAC 1

FORD James Anthony
Born: Portsmouth, 23 October 1981
Height: 5'8" Weight: 11.0

James is one of the many talented youngsters on Bournemouth's books. He graduated from the ranks of the club's trainees to become a full professional at the beginning of last April and made his Football League debut shortly afterwards when coming on as a substitute for the final half-hour of the Cherries' home game with Chesterfield. A promising midfield player, he is expected to stake a claim for a first-team place in the 2000-01 season.

Bournemouth (From trainee on 12/4/2000) FL 0+2

FORD Michael (Mike) Paul
Born: Bristol, 9 February 1966
Height: 6'0" Weight: 12.6
Club Honours: WC '88

An exceptional organiser at the back and an inspirational leader, Cardiff's experienced club captain was once again highly influential in 1999-2000, but his season was disrupted by injuries. The worst of them was a problem with a disc in his back, which eventually forced the versatile defender to retire from the game. It was a tough decision for Mike, but he accepted medical advice not to have an operation in a bid to cure the problem. He was set to complete his UEFA "A" coaching course during the summer and is keen to become a coach or a manager. Mike managed only one goal during the season, the winner in the dying seconds of extra time in the FA Cup second-round replay against Bury.

Leicester C (From apprentice on 11/2/1984)
Cardiff C (Free from Devizes T on 19/9/1984) FL 144+1/13 FLC 6 FAC 9 Others 7
Oxford U (£150,000 on 10/6/1988) FL 273+16/18 FLC 27+1/2 FAC 12+1/1 Others 8/1
Cardiff C (Free on 29/7/1998) FL 48+3 FLC 4 FAC 10/1

FORD Robert (Bobby) John
Born: Bristol, 22 September 1974
Height: 5'9" Weight: 11.0

The hard-working midfielder started the 1999-2000 season as first choice at Sheffield United but in October he was in and out of the side. After Neil Warnock's arrival in December he re-established himself and was one of the manager's first names on the team sheet. He worked tirelessly in midfield, being prominent both in attack and in defence, and displayed the ability to produce a telling pass. On the occasions that a reshuffle of the side was needed Bobby was often moved to the right side of defence. Both he and the fans would like to see more goals – his first of the season against Tranmere in February was a fortunate sliced centre which beat the 'keeper at the near post.

Oxford U (From trainee on 6/10/1992) FL 104+12/7 FLC 14+2/1 FAC 10/2 Others 7/1
Sheffield U (£400,000 on 28/11/1997) FL 85+9/3 FLC 6/1 FAC 11+4 Others 2

FORD Ryan
Born: Worksop, 3 September 1980
Height: 5'9" Weight: 10.4

After developing as a junior with Notts County Ryan became a trainee with Manchester United, but he returned to Meadow Lane last February after failing to make a breakthrough at Old Trafford. He made his debut in senior football on the final day of the 1999-2000 season when he came on from the subs' bench for the last half-hour against Bury and will be aiming to establish himself in the first-team squad in 2000-01. A talented midfield prospect, he has signed a two-and-a-half-year contract.

Manchester U (From trainee on 11/7/1997)
Notts Co (Free on 1/2/2000) FL 0+1

FORD Tony
Born: Grimsby, 14 May 1959
Height: 5'10" Weight: 13.0
Club Honours: Div 3 '80; FLGC '82
International Honours: E: B-2

In his first term as Rochdale's player-assistant manager, Tony's extraordinary 1999-2000 season commenced with the league's most experienced player scoring against Cheltenham in their first game in the Football League. In Dale's Auto Windscreens Shield game at Carlisle in March, he became the first outfield player in the history of English football to make his 1,000th senior appearance. A regular in midfield for much of the season, Tony later rolled back the years to operate as an attacking wing back. Although he netted only a couple of times, his precise crosses set up chances for colleagues, notably in the league game against Carlisle, when all three goals were headed home from his precise corners. Off the field, he won numerous accolades for his remarkable career achievements, and was awarded the MBE in the New Year's Honours list.

Grimsby T (From apprentice on 1/5/1977) FL 321+34/55 FLC 31+3/4 FAC 15+4/2 Others 2
Sunderland (Loaned on 27/3/1986) FL 8+1/1
Stoke C (£35,000 on 8/7/1986) FL 112/13 FLC 8 FAC 9 Others 6/1
West Bromwich A (£145,000 on 24/3/1989) FL 114/14 FLC 7 FAC 4/1 Others 2+1
Grimsby T (£50,000 on 21/11/1991) FL 59+9/3 FLC 1 FAC 3
Bradford C (Loaned on 16/9/1993) FL 5 FLC 2
Scunthorpe U (Free on 2/8/1994) FL 73+3/9 FLC 4/1 FAC 7/1 Others 4 (Free to Barrow on 22/8/1996)
Mansfield T (Free on 25/10/1996) FL 97+6/7 FLC 4/1 FAC 4/1 Others 5
Rochdale (Free on 6/7/1999) FL 28+6/2 FLC 2 FAC 3 Others 3+1

FORINTON Howard Lee
Born: Boston, 18 September 1975
Height: 5'11" Weight: 11.4

Having had a £100,000 bid turned down in August 1999, Peterborough manager Barry Fry got his man a month later for a reported £300,000 fee. Confident that he would prove to be the best striker in the club's history, the Posh boss described Howard as "quick, strong and incredibly brave". A natural goalscorer, he made his United debut against Cheltenham on his 24th birthday. Although he managed to score at a rate of nearly every other game, a succession of injuries curtailed Howard's involvement in the second half of the season.

Birmingham C (Signed from Yeovil T on 14/7/1997) FL 0+4/1 FLC 1+1
Plymouth Arg (Loaned on 18/12/1998) FL 8+2/3 FLC 1+2
Peterborough U (£250,000 on 17/9/1999) FL 19+6/7 FAC 2

FORREST Craig Lorne
Born: Vancouver, Canada, 20 September 1967
Height: 6'5" Weight: 14.4
Club Honours: Div 2 '92
International Honours: Canada: 52 (Gold Cup 2000)

Craig spent most of the 1999-2000 season as second-choice 'keeper to Shaka Hislop at West Ham, but when his rival suffered a broken leg last February he stepped in for a run of seven consecutive games. Unfortunately, he then succumbed to a niggling hernia problem that forced him to miss the last few weeks of the season. He is a sound all-round goalkeeper, good on crosses and quick to clear any loose through-

balls – an ideal player to have in reserve. Craig was also very much a part of the Canada international team during the season, winning seven further caps and appearing in the side that surprised Colombia to win the CONCACAF Gold Cup in February. He was widely recognised as Canada's star performer and was voted "Most Valuable Player" of the tournament.
Ipswich T (From apprentice on 31/8/1985) F/PL 263 FLC 16 FAC 11 Others 14
Colchester U (Loaned on 1/3/1988) FL 11
Chelsea (Loaned on 26/3/1997) PL 2+1
West Ham U (£500,000 on 23/7/1997) PL 23+3 FLC 3 FAC 4

FORREST Martyn William
Born: Bury, 2 January 1979
Height: 5'10" Weight: 12.2
The reputation of this tigerish Bury midfield man really prospered during the 1999-2000 campaign, when he grasped the first-team opportunity given to him by boss Andy Preece with some style. His performances gave great cause for optimism that he is a player with a good future ahead of him at his home-town club. Stocky and small, Martyn has successfully made the transition this season to midfield after previously playing as a striker and at full back at reserve-team level under previous manager Neil Warnock. Faced with an injury crisis in December, new boss Preece gave Martyn his league debut at Gillingham and he was involved in some capacity in most games thereafter, usually as a substitute. He is rated so highly that he was offered a new two-year contract in February (which he signed), and the 21-year-old was also entrusted with the captaincy in Bury's 2-0 away win at Cardiff City in April.
Bury (From trainee on 16/7/1997) FL 9+7 FAC 0+1

FORRESTER Jamie Mark
Born: Bradford, 1 November 1974
Height: 5'6" Weight: 11.0
Club Honours: FAYC '93
International Honours: E: Yth (UEFA-U18 '93); Sch
After making only a handful of substitute appearances for Dutch club FC Utrecht, Jamie moved to Walsall on loan last January and showed some nice touches in the home wins against Bolton and Sheffield United. He was then dropped to substitute and joined Northampton on loan on transfer deadline day. A skilful, agile and competitive striker, he soon made his presence felt, scoring on his first full appearance against Southend, and went on to net a total of six goals in ten games as he helped the Cobblers to promotion. Stop Press: It was reported at the end of June that Northampton had paid a club record fee of £150,000 to sign Jamie on a permanent basis.
Leeds U (£60,000 from Auxerre, France on 20/10/1992) PL 7+2 FAC 1+1/2
Southend U (Loaned on 1/9/1994) FL 3+2
Grimsby T (Loaned on 10/3/1995) FL 7+2/1
Grimsby T (Signed on 17/10/1995) FL 27+14/6 FLC 0+2 FAC 3+1/3
Scunthorpe U (Signed on 21/3/1997) FL 99+2/37 FLC 6/2 FAC 7/4 Others 7 (Free to FC Utrecht, Holland on 1/6/1999)
Walsall (Loaned on 30/12/1999) FL 2+3
Northampton T (Loaned on 21/3/2000) FL 9+1/6

FORRESTER Mark
Born: Middlesbrough, 15 April 1981
Height: 5'9" Weight: 10.3
Mark's only 1999-2000 appearance came as a Torquay sub against Peterborough in October. He had made his full debut against the same club the previous season. The young striker was released in March, but still has enough about him to make it in league football.
Torquay U (Trainee) FL 1+5

FORSSELL Mikael
Born: Steinfurt, Germany, 15 March 1981
Height: 6'1" Weight: 12.8
International Honours: Finland: 3; U21; Yth
Following the incredible impact he made upon his arrival in English football in 1998-99, Mikael's second season was, unfortunately, somewhat of an anti-climax. The Finnish striker had started just two matches for Chelsea, against Skonto Riga and Huddersfield, when he sustained a serious knee injury in a reserve match. He was sidelined for four months and upon his recovery was loaned to Crystal Palace to allow him to regain match fitness. He produced some excellent performances for the Selhurst Park club and scored two fine goals in the 3-3 draw with Stockport last April. Having made his debut at full international level when coming on from the subs' bench against Moldova in June 1999, he won further caps in the end-of-season friendlies with Wales and Poland. Finland have been drawn in England's World Cup qualifying group and the powerful young centre forward will be desperate to impress against his adopted country. Chelsea are now in a position where they must reduce the average age of their first-team regulars and Mikael, along with a host of other young tyros, is poised to make the breakthrough that will herald a new era at Stamford Bridge.
Chelsea (Free from HJK Helsinki, Finland on 18/12/1998) PL 4+6/1FLC 1 FAC 1+2/2 Others 1
Crystal Palace (Loaned on 23/2/2000) FL 13/3

FORSTER Nicholas (Nicky) Michael
Born: Caterham, 8 September 1973
Height: 5'10" Weight: 11.5
International Honours: E: U21-4
An exciting front player with pace, good close control and the skill to beat defenders in tight situations, Nicky joined Reading from Birmingham in the summer of 1999 but reserved his best displays until near the end of the season, when he formed a superb striking partnership with Martin Butler which contributed to the Royals' best run of the campaign. He did well as a target man, too, holding the ball up and setting up scoring opportunities for other players. He is an important part of manager Alan Pardew's plans for the future.
Gillingham (Signed from Horley T on 22/5/1992) FL 54+13/24 FLC 3+2 FAC 6/2
Brentford (£100,000 on 17/6/1994) FL 108+1/39 FLC 11/3 FAC 8/1 Others 7+1/4
Birmingham C (£700,000 on 31/1/1997) FL 24+44/11 FLC 2+2/1 FAC 3+1
Reading (£650,000 on 23/6/1999) FL 31+5/10 FLC 3 FAC 2 Others 1+1

Nicky Forster

FORSYTH Richard Michael
Born: Dudley, 3 October 1970
Height: 5'11" Weight: 13.0
International Honours: E: SP-3
This experienced midfield player had a disappointing 1999-2000 season with relegated Blackpool, whom he had joined from Stoke the previous summer. He missed the first few weeks of the campaign due to a pre-season injury and was then dropped in October following a brief run of first-team action. He made several further appearances as a substitute later in the autumn but spent the final months of the season playing for the club's reserves.
Birmingham C (£50,000 from Kidderminster Hrs on 13/7/1995) FL 12+14/2 FLC 7+2 FAC 2 Others 3+1
Stoke C (£200,000 on 25/7/1996) FL 90+5/17 FLC 7/1 FAC 4 Others 1+1
Blackpool (Free on 5/7/1999) FL 10+3 FAC 0+2 Others 0+1

FORTUNE Jonathan **Jay**
Born: Islington, 23 August 1980
Height: 6'2" Weight: 11.4
Jay joined Mansfield on loan from Charlton Athletic in mid-February 2000 as a replacement for Leigh Bromby, who had returned to Sheffield Wednesday a couple of weeks before. A tall, pacy centre back who looked at home in the heart of the Stags' defence straight away, he was retained for a second month but missed a couple of matches through injury before a "swan song" in the televised game at Rotherham, where he did a good job marking his uncle, Leo Fortune-West. He returned to Charlton after that game and went straight on to the bench two days later for their match with Manchester City.
Charlton Ath (From trainee on 2/7/1998)
Mansfield T (Loaned on 18/2/2000) FL 4

FORTUNE Quinton
Born: Cape Town, South Africa, 21 May 1977
Height: 5'11" Weight: 11.11
International Honours: South Africa: 26; U23

A top-class winger with pace and dazzling ball skills, Quinton became Sir Alex Ferguson's second major signing of last season when he joined Manchester United from Atletico Madrid in August 1999, for £1.5 million. Having made his debut as a substitute in the 5-1 Premiership win over Newcastle, he scored on his first full outing against Bradford in December. Seizing his chance in the World Club Championship match against South Melbourne at the start of the new year, he netted two goals and finished the tournament as United's leading scorer. He continued in a similar vein, but minus the goals, in the Champions' League match against Valencia in March, and his performance that night certainly impressed Sir Alex, who enthused, "I think Quinton has shown he's got the temperament and attitude to go on to better things." A teenage prodigy, Quinton first came to England as a 14-year-old, when he spent several seasons on Tottenham's books as an associate schoolboy before moving on to Spain in 1995. He went on to become the youngest player to be capped by South Africa when appearing as a substitute against Keyna in September 1996 at the age of 19 years, three months and 21 days. Now a regular for the *Bafana Bafana*, he won five more caps in the African Nations' Cup finals last spring, helping South Africa to third place in the tournament.

Manchester U (£1,500,000 from Atletico Madrid, Spain on 27/8/1999) PL 4+2/2 Others 2+4/2

Quinton Fortune

FORTUNE-WEST Leopold (Leo) Paul Osborne
Born: Stratford, 9 April 1971
Height: 6'3" Weight: 13.10

After a slow start to the 1999-2000 season as far as goals were concerned, the big Rotherham striker hit a rich seam of form. Leo notched 11 goals in 11 games just after Christmas, including a hat-trick against Carlisle for the second successive season. With a total 1999-2000 goals haul of 17, he was always the Miller that opponents feared the most, literally bringing great strength to the team. He was sadly missed when an eye injury suffered at Leyton Orient towards the end of March appeared to bring his season to a premature end. Thankfully, Leo returned in time to take part in the promotion celebrations.

Gillingham (£5,000 from Stevenage Borough on 12/7/1995) FL 48+19/18 FLC 3+1/2 FAC 3+1/2
Leyton Orient (Loaned on 27/3/1997) FL 1+4
Lincoln C (Free on 6/7/1998) FL 7+2/1 FLC 2
Rotherham U (Loaned on 8/10/1998) FL 5/4
Brentford (£60,000 on 17/11/1998) FL 2+9 FAC 0+1 Others 2+1/1
Rotherham U (£35,000 on 26/2/1999) FL 54/25 FLC 2 FAC 2 Others 2

FOSTER Craig Andrew
Born: Melbourne, Australia, 15 April 1969
Height: 5'11" Weight: 12.4
International Honours: Australia: 25; Yth

Craig spent the early part of the 1999-2000 season recovering from a long-term knee injury and did not return to full fitness until last November. He is a classy midfield general who was one of the few experienced hands in a very young Crystal Palace side. He added five more appearances to his total for Australia and scored a rare goal in the 3-1 defeat by the Czech Republic. Stop Press: Craig scored the second goal for Australia in their 2-0 victory over New Zealand in the Oceania Nations' Cup final at the end of June.

Portsmouth (£320,000 from Marconi, Australia on 19/9/1997) FL 13+3/2 FAC 2/2
Crystal Palace (Free on 2/10/1998) FL 47+5/3 FAC 2

FOSTER Stephen (Steve)
Born: Mansfield, 3 December 1974
Height: 6'1" Weight: 12.0

This central defender once again proved to be one of Bristol Rovers' most consistent and reliable players in 1999-2000, and was the cornerstone of a defence which enjoyed one of the best records throughout the league. Steve, who took over as captain in the absence of Andy Tillson and led by example with some determined performances, missed just a handful of matches due to suspension and minor injuries. The former Mansfield and Woking defender scored in the 3-2 victory against Oldham at the Memorial Stadium in September but it was his role as an effective man-to-man marker who prevented opposing strikers from scoring which was his most significant contribution to Rovers' fine season.

Mansfield T (From trainee on 15/7/1993) FL 2+3 FLC 2 (Free to Telford on 22/1/1994)
Bristol Rov (£150,000 from Woking on 23/5/1997) FL 116+4/2 FLC 7 FAC 10 Others 7

FOTIADIS Panos **Andrew**
Born: Hitchin, 6 September 1977
Height: 5'11" Weight: 11.7
International Honours: E: Sch

This promising Luton forward, a former England schools international, combines pace with aggression, and if he can overcome his injury problems he has the skills and goalscoring ability to make a real impact at first-team level. Andrew stretched the back of the net in his second start of 1999-2000 in Luton's 2-1 away victory at Reading in August. In the game against Wrexham not long afterwards he was on the end of a robust tackle which saw him limping off after 46 minutes with medial knee ligament damage. He eventually made his return as a substitute at Bristol City on 28 December after missing 21 league and cup games and played some part in the next 16 matches, usually as a sub, before being sidelined for the closing weeks of the campaign.

Luton T (Free from juniors on 26/7/1996) FL 30+46/8 FLC 1+6/1 FAC 1 Others 2+2

FOWLER Jason Kenneth
Born: Bristol, 20 August 1974
Height: 6'3" Weight: 11.12

Jason was badly hampered by injuries during Cardiff's disappointing 1999-2000 season and struggled to find consistency. It was typical of his luck that, when he suffered a gashed foot during an FAW Premier Cup tie at Caernarfon, his return was delayed by an infection in the wound. An attacking midfielder with great touch, good passing skills and the ability to produce the unexpected, he was never able to find the rhythm that playing in an extended run of matches brings and even played at the heart of the defence during some games. He is naturally not the most accomplished of defenders, but his distribution from the back was a joy to watch. After a highly successful 1998-99 campaign when the Bluebirds were promoted and Jason won a place in the PFA Third Division selection, last season proved a much less rewarding experience. He was out of contract at the end of the campaign but was offered new terms by manager Billy Ayre.

Bristol C (From trainee on 8/7/1993) FL 16+9 FLC 1+2 Others 1+1
Cardiff C (Signed on 19/6/1996) FL 135+5/14 FLC 8/1 FAC 12+2/4 Others 3/1

FOWLER Robert (Robbie) Bernard
Born: Liverpool, 9 April 1975
Height: 5'11" Weight: 11.10
Club Honours: FLC '95
International Honours: E: 14; B-1; U21-8; Yth (UEFA-U18 '93)

Although it was to be a season of great disappointment due to injuries, the Liverpool striker started 1999-2000 brightly enough, and played magnificently in the home victory over Arsenal, whom he appears to relish scoring against. The eighth-minute goal against the Gunners was a brilliant 25-yard left-footed drive, and it signalled his intentions for the season after working hard in training. Sadly, Robbie was to be restricted to just 14 first-team appearances, six of them as a substitute, and scored only three goals, the last of them at the end of December. He won five more international caps for England, contributing a goal in the 2-0 victory over the Ukraine at the end of

May, but although he was selected for the final 22 for Euro 2000 he did not feature during the tournament. He will be keen to make up for lost time in 2000-01.

Liverpool (From trainee on 23/4/1992) P/FL 187+12/109 FLC 27/21 FAC 18+1/10 Others 18+2/10

FOX Christian
Born: Stonehaven, 11 April 1981
Height: 5'10" Weight: 11.5

Called up for the England U18 squad, Christian had a fine first season as a professional with York in 1999-2000. He was a near-ever-present in the senior squad, attracting the attention of a number of top clubs. He was reported to be the subject of a £500,000 bid from Newcastle in February, while Sunderland and Middlesbrough were also rumoured to be interested. His control, vision and ability to run at defences, plus his quality of passing, make the midfielder an outstanding prospect. He netted one goal in a 2-2 home draw against Torquay United. Christian won the supporters' club "Player of the Year" award and was offered a new three-year contract in May.

York C (From trainee on 29/6/1999) FL 28+6/1 FLC 1 FAC 1 Others 1

FOX Ruel Adrian
Born: Ipswich, 14 January 1968
Height: 5'6" Weight: 10.10
Club Honours: FLC '99
International Honours: E: B-2

This pacy winger made a total of just seven appearances for Tottenham last season, Ruel finding competition for midfield places really tough as Spurs manager George Graham experimented with his line-up throughout the campaign. He is an exciting player and when the ball is at his feet an air of expectation surrounds him. Ruel's speed and agility are still evident as he charges forward down the wing, and there is no doubting his enthusiasm and confidence, but, as Graham continues to bring in new midfield talent, his future at Tottenham remains uncertain. If he were to move on, there would be no shortage of interest from clubs looking to secure his services.

Norwich C (From apprentice on 20/1/1986) F/PL 148+24/22 FLC 13+3/3 FAC 11+4 Others 12+4
Newcastle U (£2,250,000 on 2/2/1994) PL 56+2/12 FLC 3/1 FAC 5 Others 4/1
Tottenham H (£4,200,000 on 6/10/1995) PL 95+11/13 FLC 7+3/1 FAC 11+1/1 Others 1

FOYLE Martin John
Born: Salisbury, 2 May 1963
Height: 5'10" Weight: 12.0
Club Honours: AMC '93

One of Port Vale's finest-ever strikers, Martin brought his career to a close at the age of 36 last February when his injured knees could take it no longer. He began the 1999-2000 season under suspension after being sent off in a friendly but then as usual gave 100 per cent whenever called upon. His six goals cemented his position as the second-highest scorer in the club's history and his final goal was typical of him, a far-post header in a 2-2 draw at champions Charlton Athletic. He has now moved on to the coaching side of things and his two-year contract takes him to ten years' service at Vale Park and a well-deserved testimonial.

Southampton (From apprentice on 13/8/1980) FL 6+6/1 FLC 0+2/2
Aldershot (£10,000 on 3/8/1984) FL 98/35 FLC 10/5 FAC 8/5 Others 6
Oxford U (£140,000 on 26/3/1987) FL 120+6/36 FLC 16/4 FAC 5/3 Others 3+1/1
Port Vale (£375,000 on 25/6/1991) FL 226+70/83 FLC 19+4/7 FAC 14+4/9 Others 13+3/9

FRADIN Karim
Born: St Martin d'Hyeres, France, 2 February 1972
Height: 5'10" Weight: 13.0

This midfield player joined Stockport last November after several years playing in the French Second Division with Nice and Niort. He had a tough debut for the Hatters against Blackburn Rovers, but as the season progressed he formed an excellent partnership with Tony Dinning in the County engine room. Neat and tidy on the ball, he showed exceptional stamina and could be found defending in his own penalty area one minute and up in the opposition box moments alter. Very much the find of the season at Edgeley Park, he contributed one goal, scoring in the 3-1 defeat by Charlton in February.

Stockport Co (Free from OGC Nice, France on 19/11/1999) FL 19+2/1

FRAIL Stephen (Steve)
Born: Glasgow, 10 August 1969
Height: 5'11" Weight: 12.3
Club Honours: S Div 1 '92; B&Q '91

This Tranmere Rovers defender again had a frustrating time with injuries during the 1999-2000 season. He made the starting line-up just once – for the visit to Huddersfield last January – and the following month he returned north of the border, signing for St Johnstone. He is best used as a right wing back or full back, which allows his solid defensive skills to be put to good use.

Dundee (Free from Possilpark YM on 10/8/1985) SL 91+10/1 SLC 2 SC 7 Others 3
Hearts (Signed on 31/3/1994) SL 45+9/4 SLC 5+1 SC 4+1 Others 1
Tranmere Rov (£90,000 on 30/1/1998) FL 10+4 FLC 1+3 FAC 0+1

FRAIN John William
Born: Birmingham, 8 October 1968
Height: 5'9" Weight: 11.9
Club Honours: AMC '91

Captain, utility player and "Mr Dependable", John was moved from wing back to midfield when Kevin Wilson took over as manager of Northampton last October. Whatever position he plays in, he always gives 100 per cent effort. His free kicks and corner kicks have brought many goals for his team-mates, and his experience makes him the ideal candidate for the captain's armband. John achieved the milestone of 150 appearances for Northampton in less than three seasons, testimony to his consistency. As the Cobblers closed in on promotion, John also played in his 500th senior game in April.

Birmingham C (From apprentice on 10/10/1986) FL 265+9/23 FLC 28/1 FAC 12 Others 22/2
Northampton T (Free on 24/1/1997) FL 138+1/3 FLC 8 FAC 7 Others 13/2

FRAMPTON Andrew (Andy) James Kerr
Born: Wimbledon, 3 September 1979
Height: 5'11" Weight: 10.10

This Crystal Palace left wing back made a good start to the 1999-2000 season but rarely featured after first Terry Phelan and then Ashley Cole were brought in on loan. Left-footed, strong in the air and a good reader of the game, Andy will be aiming to establish a regular presence in the first-team set-up in the coming season.

Crystal Palace (From trainee on 8/5/1998) FL 10+5 FLC 3 FAC 1

FRANCIS Damien Jerome
Born: Wandsworth, 27 February 1979
Height: 6'1" Weight: 11.2

Damien is a local lad whose appearances for Wimbledon in 1999-2000 were once again limited by the variety of midfield options available to the manager. Damien started on only two occasions, and made a handful of other appearances as a substitute. Although he has previously demonstrated his versatility, he had a difficult FA Cup baptism at Fulham, when he was asked to play at left back, where he looked less than comfortable. However, this resilient and elegant player has time on his side and may well find the coming season more rewarding as the Dons regroup their forces in the First Division.

Wimbledon (From trainee on 6/3/1997) PL 1+10 FLC 2+3 FAC 1

FRANCIS Kevin Michael Derek
Born: Birmingham, 6 December 1967
Height: 6'7" Weight: 16.10
Club Honours: Div 2 '95; AMC '95

Kevin had another injury-ravaged season in 1999-2000. The big striker's ruptured achilles prevented him from making a comeback for Oxford until the last few weeks of 1999, and when he returned to action it was as a substitute. He made five brief appearances before taking the opportunity to rejoin Stockport on a free transfer in March. Kevin had made his name at Edgeley Park in the early 1990s and much was expected of him but unfortunately he suffered more achilles tendon trouble against Manchester City in only his fourth game for the Hatters and missed the remainder of the season. Although rather ungainly on the ground, he is rarely beaten in the air and has scored consistently throughout his career. He was released during the summer.

Derby Co (Free from Mile Oak Rov on 2/2/1989) FL 0+10 FLC 1+2 FAC 1+2/1 Others 0+1
Stockport Co (£45,000 on 21/2/1991) FL 147+5/88 FLC 12/5 FAC 9/6 Others 25/18
Birmingham C (£800,000 on 20/1/1995) FL 32+41/13 FLC 6+5/5 FAC 3+3/2 Others 4/1
Oxford U (£100,000 + on 17/2/1998) FL 27+9/8 FAC 0+3 Others 0+1
Stockport Co (Free on 10/3/2000) FL 4

FRANDSEN Per
Born: Copenhagen, Denmark, 6 February 1970
Height: 6'1" Weight: 12.6
Club Honours: Div 1 '97
International Honours: Denmark: 19

Per started last season in his usual fine form, producing a number of "Man of the Match" displays where he was head and shoulders above every other player in the Bolton team. The busy, bustling midfielder quickly became Wanderers' top scorer, notching four goals in his first seven starts. This form was quickly noticed by other clubs and the inevitable happened when Per was sold to Blackburn in September, a move which prompted Colin Todd to resign as the club's manager. This was viewed as being a severe body-blow to the Wanderers' promotion hopes and highlighted the club's financial plight at the time but, unfortunately for Per, as the season continued his old club qualified for the play-offs while his new multi-million-pound team-mates failed to return to the Premiership at the first time of asking. Although he was supposed to be the final part of Blackburn manager Brian Kidd's jigsaw, Per proved to be merely the last signing he made. A fine prompter and thoughtful user of the ball, he found it difficult to settle into a struggling side and often went long periods without influencing the game. He was not seen at his best when required to win a fifty-fifty challenge and his famed long-range shooting appeared not to have made the short trip from the Reebok. He did score some crucial goals, with late equalisers against Crystal Palace and Norwich and a fine free kick at Barnsley, but he lost his place at times under both Tony Parkes and Graeme Souness and it seems he has some work to do to consolidate his position in the side. Per won a further international cap for Denmark when he appeared against Iran last October.

Bolton W (£1,250,000 from FC Copenhagen, Denmark, via Lille, on 7/8/1996) F/PL 129+1/22 FLC 15+1/4 FAC 4+1 Others 3/1
Blackburn Rov (£1,750,000 + on 22/9/1999) FL 26+5/5 FAC 4/1

FRASER Stuart Thomas
Born: Edinburgh, 9 January 1980
Height: 5'9" Weight: 11.4
International Honours: S: U21-3

Yet another of Luton's successful youth-policy products, this left-sided full back is equally comfortable playing on the right. Strong in the tackle, Stuart crosses the ball accurately, and in general gives his opponents a hard time. He was a regular in the Luton side during the early months of 1999-2000, scoring his first senior goal for the club in the 4-2 win against Oxford in September, but his season was disrupted when he received 11 stitches in a nasty gash after a collision with team-mate Michael McIndoe against Kingstonian in the FA Cup at the end of October. During the second half of the season he found it difficult to command a regular first-team slot because of the intense competition for places in the side, and he will be looking to make a fresh start in 2000-01. Stuart made his debut for Scotland U21s against Holland last April and added further caps in the end-of-season Presidents' Cup games against Wales and Northern Ireland.

Luton T (From trainee on 2/4/1998) FL 26+3/1 FLC 2 FAC 5 Others 2

FREDGAARD Carsten
Born: Denmark, 20 May 1976
Height: 6'0" Weight: 12.6
International Honours: Denmark: 4; U21-9; Yth

A tall, pacy left winger or central striker, Carsten, nicknamed "Lightning", joined Sunderland prior to the end of the 1998-99 season from Danish club Lyngby but remained in his home country until the end of their domestic campaign. The £1.8 million signing looked to be an important acquisition following Allan Johnston's decision not to sign a new contract and his subsequent ostracism by Peter Reid. Although Carsten began the season on the substitutes' bench, he opened his Sunderland goalscoring account with two expertly taken goals in a 5-0 Worthington Cup win at Walsall in September. However, he failed to break into the first team in the Premiership and his attacking wing play was confined to the reserves until February, when he joined West Bromwich Albion on loan until the end of the season as a short-term replacement for the transferred Kevin Kilbane. He buzzed around on the left side of midfield but never really settled in at the Hawthorns and returned to Sunderland without making much of an impact despite his pedigree. Carsten won his first full international cap for Denmark against Holland last August and went on to appear in all three of his country's Nordic Cup fixtures early in the new year.

Sunderland (£1,800,000 from Lyngby, Denmark on 5/7/1999) PL 0+1 FLC 3/2
West Bromwich A (Loaned on 9/2/2000) FL 5

Dougie Freedman

FREEDMAN Douglas (Dougie) Alan
Born: Glasgow, 21 January 1974
Height: 5'9" Weight: 11.2
International Honours: S: B-1; U21-8; Sch

Dougie began 1999-2000 as a regular in the Nottingham Forest line-up. He did well in the early part of the season, scoring eight goals by mid-October, but then suffered a loss of form and found himself in and out of the team. On his day he is an intelligent striker, good at turning defenders and with an eye for goal. He will be aiming to achieve more consistent displays in the 2000-01 campaign.

Queens Park R (From trainee on 15/5/1992)
Barnet (Free on 26/7/1994) FL 47/27 FLC 6/5 FAC 2 Others 2
Crystal Palace (£800,000 on 8/9/1995) F/PL 72+18/31 FLC 3+2/1 FAC 2+1 Others 3+2/2
Wolverhampton W (£800,000 on 17/10/1997) FL 25+4/10 FAC 5+1/2
Nottingham F (£950,000 on 12/8/1998) P/FL 48+17/18 FLC 8/4 FAC 3+1/1

FREEMAN Darren Barry Andduet
Born: Brighton, 22 August 1973
Height: 5'11" Weight: 13.0
Club Honours: Div 3 '99

Darren signed for Brighton, his home-town club, on a free transfer from Brentford in the 1999 close season. He had previously served under Seagulls manager Micky Adams at Fulham. After an operation on his knee, Darren made a sparkling start, scoring with his first touch in the pre-season friendly against Nottingham Forest, then going on to score a hat-trick on the first day of the season against Mansfield. Initially playing in his favoured position in the forward line, he returned to the right of midfield during the second half of the season. Darren had the notable distinction of scoring the first league goal of the millennium against Exeter City. A Jekyll and Hyde season saw Darren finish as top scorer with 13 goals, but also be sent off twice for off-the-ball incidents.

Gillingham (Free from Horsham on 31/1/1995) FL 4+8 FAC 0+1 Others 2/1
Fulham (£15,000 + on 4/7/1996) FL 32+14/9 FLC 2 Others 3/1
Brentford (Free on 7/7/1998) FL 16+6/6 FLC 4/1 FAC 3/2 Others 1
Brighton & Hove A (Free on 8/7/1999) FL 36+2/12 FLC 1+1 FAC 3/1 Others 1

FREEMAN David
Born: Dublin, 25 November 1979
Height: 5'10" Weight: 11.10
International Honours: RoI: U21-1; Yth

This young Irish striker graduated from Nottingham Forest's successful youth team to make three appearances as a substitute for the first team. He is a busy little player with plenty of pace and a good shot. David stepped up from the Republic of Ireland youth team to make his bow with the U21s in a friendly match with Greece last April.

Nottingham F (Signed from trainee on 9/12/1996) FL 0+3

FREEMAN Mark Wayne
Born: Walsall, 27 January 1970
Height: 6'2" Weight: 13.8

Mark is a man-mountain central defender who achieved his ambition to "play one game in the Football League" with Cheltenham in August 1999. He went on to produce a series of assured displays in the centre of defence. Mark's partnership with Chris Banks at the heart of the Robins' back line has been a feature of the club's success in recent years. Tall, strong and dominant in the air, Mark is at his best when defending crosses and long balls or close-marking opposition strikers. Not the paciest of defenders, he benefited from having quick players around him who can read the game and cover space while he attacks the ball. He briefly lost his place to John Brough in the second half of the season

but returned for the run-in. A likeable character and a very honest player who hails from Walsall, Mark replied to a question about his eligibility for international football by saying: "The only country I could play for is the Black Country."
Wolverhampton W (Signed from Bilston T on 27/10/1987. Free to Bilston T during 1988 close season)
Cheltenham T (Signed from Gloucester C on 4/3/1996) FL 36+2/2 FLC 2 FAC 2 Others 2

FREESTONE Christopher (Chris) Mark
Born: Nottingham, 4 September 1971
Height: 5'11" Weight: 11.7
Club Honours: AMC '97
Hartlepool supporters expected much of this opportunist striker in 1999-2000. He began the season with some useful goals, but then lost confidence and struggled to hold down a first-team place. He was loaned to Cheltenham in February and seemed to benefit from the change of scene. He put in particularly good performances in the home wins over Peterborough and Halifax, scoring in both games, but was less effective away from Whaddon Road. Chris chose not to take up the option of a second month with the Robins, preferring to return to Victoria Park and fight for his place there. Unfortunately, he was unable to turn things around as he had hoped, and at the time of writing a permanent move to Cheltenham seemed to be a possibility. Stop Press: Chris was reported to have signed for Shrewsbury at the beginning of July.
Middlesbrough (£10,000 from Arnold T on 2/12/1994) P/FL 2+7/1 FLC 1+1/1 FAC 0+2
Carlisle U (Loaned on 3/3/1997) FL 3+2/2 Others 2
Northampton T (£75,000 on 8/12/1997) FL 40+17/13 FLC 4/3 FAC 1+2 Others 6+1/3
Hartlepool U (£75,000 on 25/3/1999) FL 24+13/7 FLC 2 FAC 2 Others 3
Cheltenham T (Loaned on 11/2/2000) FL 5/2

Roger Freestone

FREESTONE Roger
Born: Newport, 19 August 1968
Height: 6'3" Weight: 14.6
Club Honours: Div 2 '89; Div 3 '00; AMC '94
International Honours: W: 1; U21-1; Yth; Sch
Under the supervision of Swansea goalkeeping coach Glan Letheran, Roger had his best-ever season at the Vetch Field in 1999-2000 as the club broke record after record during their Third Division championship-winning season. A slimmer, more agile 'keeper last term, Roger kept 22 clean sheets during the season to break a club record that had stood since 1924-25. It was a sign of things to come when he saved penalties against Millwall's Neil Harris in both Worthington Cup ties. His outstanding form was recognised at the end of the season when he received his first call-up to the Wales squad since 1995, and he made his belated international debut against Brazil at Cardiff's Millennium Stadium.
Newport Co (From trainee on 2/4/1986) FL 13 Others 1
Chelsea (£95,000 on 10/3/1987) FL 42 FLC 2 FAC 3 Others 6
Swansea C (Loaned on 29/9/1989) FL 14 Others 1
Hereford U (Loaned on 9/3/1990) FL 8
Swansea C (£45,000 on 5/9/1991) FL 395 FLC 24 FAC 26 Others 39

FRENCH Daniel John
Born: Peterborough, 25 November 1979
Height: 5'11" Weight: 11.4
Associated with Peterborough since the age of 13, Daniel has worked his way up through the ranks and made his senior bow with six substitute appearances in the first half of the 1999-2000 campaign. Born locally, he is a quick and intelligent right winger who showed bags of enthusiasm when coming off the Posh bench.
Peterborough U (From trainee on 6/7/1998) FL 0+6 FAC 0+1

FRENCH Jonathan (Jon) Charles
Born: Bristol, 25 September 1976
Height: 5'10" Weight: 10.10
Transfer-listed by Hull in the summer, Jon had a trial spell with Football League new boys Cheltenham Town. Returning to Humberside from his native West Country, he then settled into a regular reserve-team place. Call-ups to City's senior squad saw the former Bristol Rovers right-sided midfielder as an unused sub in two Third Division games in February, while he played in the second half of the Auto Windscreens Shield win at York City in December. He was released during the summer.
Bristol Rov (From trainee on 15/7/1995) FL 8+9/1 FLC 0+1 FAC 0+3 Others 2+1/1
Hull C (Free on 28/7/1998) FL 9+6 FLC 2+1 FAC 1 Others 0+2

FREUND Steffen
Born: Brandenburg, Germany, 19 January 1970
Height: 5'11" Weight: 11.6
Club Honours: FLC '99
International Honours: Germany: 21
Injury caused this gritty German international to miss part of the 1999-2000 campaign, which must have been particularly disappointing for Steffen as he started the season well in the midfield anchor role. It was also a blow for Tottenham as they have come to rely on his commitment and strength as the first line of defence. Steffen seemed to have settled into the English game and managed to curb his tendency to pick up too many yellow cards, having improved his timing in challenges and seemingly increased his pace. His experience shone through as he relished the challenges presented by the likes of Manchester United in a game where Steffen's performance was notable for his cool approach in keeping the midfield tight and preventing penetration from the opposition. His presence in the team adds a truly competitive edge to midfield, where he is a difficult player to beat. His renowned long throw-ins can be as effective as a well-aimed cross when deep in the opposition half, and his maturity and experience are sure to prove a great example to the younger squad members breaking through at Tottenham.
Tottenham H (£750,000 from Borussia Dortmund, Germany, via Motor Sud, Stahl Brandenburg and Schalke 04, on 29/12/1998) PL 41+3 FLC 5 FAC 7 Others 4

Steffen Freund

FRIARS Sean Martin
Born: Derry, 15 May 1979
Height: 5'8" Weight: 10.12
International Honours: NI: U21-14
It was thought that, after the departure of Bobby Petta to Celtic during the 1999 close season, Sean could be the player to take over from him at Ipswich as he plays in a similar role on the left of midfield, has a good left foot and has the ability to beat players. It did not work out that way, however, and, although he did make his first-team debut as a substitute for the last twenty minutes of the home game with Crewe, he was not given any further opportunities to show his pedigree. Sean moved on loan to Irish League club Portadown last March, where he spent the last few weeks of the campaign. A regular in the Northern Ireland U21 side, he won six more caps last season.
Liverpool (From juniors on 22/5/1996)
Ipswich T (Free on 6/7/1998) FL 0+1

FRIEDEL Bradley (Brad) Howard
Born: Lakewood, USA, 18 May 1971
Height: 6'3" Weight: 14.7
International Honours: USA: 65

Brad might well have hoped to have an extended run in the Liverpool first team last season following the departure of David James to Aston Villa, but it was not to be. Sander Westerveld became the first-choice 'keeper and the amiable American was consigned to the reserves, for whom he turned in some useful performances. He was restored to the first team for the second leg of the Worthington Cup tie against Hull at Anfield, and an injury to Westerveld meant that Brad had a run of three successive games in October, against Southampton in the Worthington Cup, and against Chelsea and Southampton in the league. Against stylish Chelsea he saved a certain goal from Tore Andre Flo, who was clean through, and stopped several genuine goalscoring opportunities. However, with Westerveld fit once more, Brad failed to make an appearance throughout the remainder of the season, and it is unlikely that his future at Anfield will be long-lasting. Despite this he continued to share goalkeeping duties for the USA with Kasey Keller and added a further five caps to an already impressive total.

Liverpool (£1,000,000 from Columbus Crew on 23/12/1997) PL 25 FLC 4 Others 1+1

FROGGATT Stephen (Steve) Junior
Born: Lincoln, 9 March 1973
Height: 5'10" Weight: 11.11
International Honours: E: U21-2

Steve's 1999-2000 season came to life in the home game with Watford at the end of October. Up until that point he had looked out of sorts and appeared to be lacking in confidence. Suddenly, though, his ability to go past his man and deliver a good cross came back, and he scored one goal and made another. A week later he was shocked to discover he was in the England squad for the European Championship play-off games with Scotland, and although he didn't appear he sat on the bench at Hampden Park. With Marcus Hall and David Burrows injured he was forced to play at left back for most of the rest of the season. He missed a handful of games after picking up an injury in a physical game with Sunderland. The England call-up seemed to give his confidence a boost and he adapted well to his full-back role.

Aston Villa (From trainee on 26/1/1991) F/PL 30+5/2 FLC 1+1 FAC 5+2/1
Wolverhampton W (£1,000,000 on 11/7/1994) FL 99+7/7 FLC 10+1/2 FAC 3 Others 2
Coventry C (£1,900,000 on 1/10/1998) PL 44+5/2 FLC 1 FAC 6/2

FUERTES Esteban Oscar
Born: Coronel Doredo, Argentina, 26 December 1972
Height: 6'1" Weight: 13.6

One of the strangest and most mysterious episodes in the history of Derby County FC began following the players' return from a training break in Portugal last winter. Passport irregularities discovered at Heathrow Airport meant that the short Pride Park career of the Rams' Argentinian striker was over as he was deported back to South America. The transfer itself had been a long-drawn-out affair involving Derby and three Argentinian parties, but Esteban showed great initial promise through August and September. Strong in the air and mobile, he netted on his home debut against Everton only for the more emotive side of his character to show through with a red card against Bradford. Derby continue to hold the player's registration but he is currently out "on loan" at Colon de Santa Fe, where he has continued to be one of the leading scorers in South American football. Stop Press: Esteban was reported to have joined French club RC Lens in the middle of June in a £4 million deal.

Derby Co (£1,900,000 from Colon de Santa Fe, Argentina on 25/8/1999) PL 8/1 FLC 2/1

FUGLESTAD Erik
Born: Randaberg, Norway, 13 August 1974
Height: 5'10" Weight: 11.4
International Honours: Norway: U21

Having completed his third season in English football in 1999-2000, Erik came to the end of his contract with Norwich City and was free to find another club. This former Norwegian international left back enjoyed an excellent second half of the season, having lost his place to Darren Kenton earlier in the campaign. He has developed his defensive qualities during his time at Carrow Road to supplement his natural attacking flair. A neat and compact player, he is a good passer of the ball, being prepared to retain possession rather than just knock it forward aimlessly. When he gets forward, he has the ability to produce quality crosses from the left flank, something which Iwan Roberts in particular has benefited from. He is still only 25, and Erik's English experiences to date can only stand him in good stead as he embarks on the next stage of his footballing career. Stop Press: He was reported to have re-joined Viking Stavanger at the end of May.

Norwich C (Free from Viking Stavanger, Norway on 8/11/1997) FL 71+3/2 FLC 2+1 FAC 3

FULLARTON James (Jamie)
Born: Glasgow, 20 July 1974
Height: 5'10" Weight: 10.6
International Honours: S: U21-17

Jamie is a hard-tackling, no-nonsense midfield player whose 1999-2000 season was interrupted by a string of injuries. He had a short spell in the Crystal Palace line-up last autumn but was then out of action with a hamstring problem, and his season came to a premature end after he suffered a calf injury at Nottingham Forest in February. He was released in the summer.

St Mirren (Free from Motherwell BC on 13/6/1991) SL 93+9/3 SLC 2 SC 4 Others 4+1 (Transferred to Bastia, France during 1996 close season)
Crystal Palace (Free on 7/8/1997) P/FL 39+6/1 FLC 2 FAC 3
Bolton W (Loaned on 25/3/1999) FL 1

[FUMACA] ANTUNES Jose Rodriguez Alves
Born: Bahia, Brazil, 15 July 1976
Height: 6'0" Weight: 11.8

A tall, slim Brazilian midfielder with an eye for goal, Jose, who prefers to be known as Fumaca, joined Crystal Palace on a non-contract basis in September 1999 and made his first appearance for the club as a substitute against Manchester City soon afterwards, but before the month was out he had moved to Newcastle, initially on trial, having been recommended by the new head coach at St James' Park, Mick Wadsworth, who had been his manager during his brief spell at Colchester the previous March. His hard work and good close control impressed sufficiently for him to be retained to the end of the season, and he made his debut against Spurs at the end of November. Although that was his only start, he became a useful squad member, appearing often on the bench, from where he made five substitute appearances. Jose is very determined to be successful in England but, although he has been with a number of English clubs, he is still registered with Brazilian side Catuense of Bahia so he would be subject to a transfer fee were he to be signed on a permanent basis.

Colchester U (Free from Catuense, Brazil on 17/3/1999) FL 1
Barnsley (Free on 25/3/1999)
Crystal Palace (Free on 7/9/1999) FL 2+1 FLC 2
Newcastle U (Free on 27/9/1999) PL 1+4 FAC 0+1

FURLONG Paul Anthony
Born: Wood Green, 1 October 1968
Height: 6'0" Weight: 13.8
Club Honours: FAT '88
International Honours: E: SP-5

The powerful Birmingham City striker made a fine start to the 1999-2000 campaign, scoring eight goals in his first 13 games. He then joined the ranks of the club's lengthy injury list when he suffered a fracture to his left kneecap during training last October. The injury required surgery and the insertion of two metal pins, and it was not until the end of March that he returned to full fitness. Paul possesses all the attributes expected of a good striker – he is strong, holds the ball up well and his shooting shows power and accuracy. He finished the season as top scorer for the club with 11 goals and it was a considerable surprise when the Blues' manager, Trevor Francis, decided to place him on the transfer list in the summer.

Coventry C (£130,000 from Enfield on 31/7/1991) FL 27+10/4 FLC 4/1 FAC 1+1 Others 1
Watford (£250,000 on 24/7/1992) FL 79/37 FLC 7/4 FAC 2 Others 4
Chelsea (£2,300,000 on 26/5/1994) PL 44+20/13 FLC 3+1 FAC 5+4/1 Others 7/3
Birmingham C (£1,500,000 on 17/7/1996) FL 102+14/49 FLC 11/3 FAC 5/3 Others 4

FUTCHER Benjamin (Ben) Paul
Born: Manchester, 20 February 1981
Height: 6'4" Weight: 12.4

Ben graduated from the ranks of Oldham's trainees to become a first-year professional in July 1999, going on to make his Football League debut as a substitute at Cardiff last October. A tall centre half who is good in the air, he was mainly used from the subs' bench or as a squad player, coming into the side against teams employing long-ball tactics. Ben is the son of former Latics favourite Paul Futcher.

Oldham Ath (From trainee on 5/7/1999) FL 1+4 FAC 0+1

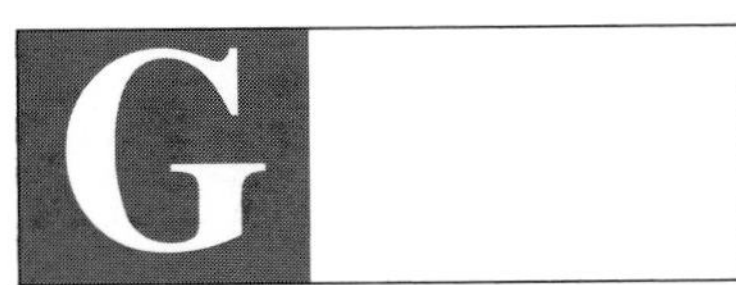

GABBIADINI Marco
Born: Nottingham, 20 January 1968
Height: 5'10" Weight: 13.4
Club Honours: Div 3 '88
International Honours: E: B-1; U21-2

Marco had another fantastic season in 1999-2000 as he topped the Third Division goalscorers' list for the second season in succession. He bagged 28 goals in total. This made him the most prolific Darlington goalscorer since the Thirties with a total of 52 goals in just two seasons. His tremendous determination and strength in holding off defenders gave the Feethams fans many thrilling moments throughout an eventful play-off campaign, producing goals of a quality not normally seen in the Third Division. Marco was selected for the PFA Third Division team and the Opta Index "Third Division Team of the Year". As Darlington turned down a £200,000 bid from Rushden, he sought a new three-year contract to finish his career with the Quakers. Stop Press: Marco was reported to have joined Northampton at the beginning of July under the Bosman ruling.

York C (From apprentice on 5/9/1985) FL 42+18/14 FLC 4+3/1 Others 4/3
Sunderland (£80,000 on 23/9/1987) FL 155+2/74 FLC 14/9 FAC 5 Others 9/4
Crystal Palace (£1,800,000 on 1/10/1991) FL 15/5 FLC 6/1 FAC 1 Others 3/1
Derby Co (£1,000,000 on 31/1/1992) F/PL 163+25/50 FLC 13/7 FAC 8+1/3 Others 16+1/8 (Free to Panionios, Greece during 1997 close season)
Birmingham C (Loaned on 14/10/1996) FL 0+2
Oxford U (Loaned on 31/1/1997) FL 5/1
Stoke C (Free on 24/12/1997) FL 2+6 FAC 1/1
York C (Free on 20/2/1998) FL 5+2/1
Darlington (Free on 8/7/1998) FL 81+1/47 FLC 4/1 FAC 4/1 Others 5+1/3

GABBIDON Daniel (Danny) Leon
Born: Cwmbran, 8 August 1979
Height: 5'10" Weight: 11.2
International Honours: W: U21-9; Yth

Danny started last season as West Bromwich Albion's first-choice right back and put in some excellent performances. But a loss of form, coupled with a niggling shin injury, upset his rhythm and he didn't figure too often during the second half of the campaign, when Andy McDermott, Daryl Burgess and then Des Lyttle were all challenging for the number two slot. He is still one for the future, though, having signed a contract which will keep him at the Hawthorns until the year 2003. He was an ever-present for Wales at U21 level, adding four more caps during the campaign.

West Bromwich A (From trainee on 3/7/1998) FL 20 FLC 4+1 FAC 2

GADSBY Matthew John
Born: Sutton Coldfield, 6 September 1979
Height: 6'1" Weight: 11.12

This up-and-coming home-grown defender played just one full game for Walsall during the 1999-2000 season. He appeared on the right flank of the defence at Crystal Palace at the end of December and gave a repeat of the excellent performances he had been producing for the Saddlers' reserve team. A battling defender who is prepared to get forward and produce the occasional teasing cross, he is a player of considerable promise and will be hoping for rather more first-team opportunities during the coming season.

Walsall (From trainee on 12/2/1998) FL 4+6 FAC 0+1 Others 0+2

GAIN Peter Thomas
Born: Hammersmith, 11 November 1976
Height: 6'1" Weight: 11.0
International Honours: RoI: U21-1; Yth

Peter is a skilful left-sided player who made good progress during the 1999-2000 season to establish himself as a regular in the Lincoln first team. He began in the left-back position but was later pushed forward into midfield with considerable success. His best performances came in the second half of the campaign, and he netted a spectacular 25-yard goal in the home win over neighbours Mansfield in March.

Tottenham H (From trainee on 1/7/1995)
Lincoln C (Loaned on 31/12/1998) FL 0+1 Others 1
Lincoln C (Signed on 26/3/1999) FL 20+15/2 FLC 2 FAC 2

GALE Shaun Michael
Born: Reading, 8 October 1969
Height: 6'1" Weight: 11.10

Shaun had a mixed season in 1999-2000, as he was in and out of the Exeter starting line-up for most of the campaign. However, the tall left-sided defender retained his tendency to get forward from defence and contribute from set pieces, while the Grecian fans also appreciated his wholehearted effort. Shaun was put on the transfer list in February along with Steve Flack, Rob Dewhurst and Warren Waugh.

Portsmouth (From trainee on 12/7/1988) FL 2+1 Others 0+1
Barnet (Free on 13/7/1994) FL 109+5/5 FLC 10 FAC 6 Others 3
Exeter C (£10,000 on 23/6/1997) FL 81+12/5 FLC 5 FAC 4/1 Others 4+2

GALLACHER Kevin William
Born: Clydebank, 23 November 1966
Height: 5'8" Weight: 11.6
International Honours: S: 49; B-2; U21-7; Yth

No Blackburn striker looked fitter or better equipped for the task than Kevin during the early weeks of 1999-2000 and his display against Walsall was probably the best produced by a Rovers forward all season. However, he did not fit into Brian Kidd's plans and was allowed to join Newcastle in October on an 18-month contract, becoming new manager Bobby Robson's first signing. Energetic and lively, he was probably seen as a relatively short-term buy, covering for injuries to the club's main strike force, but his form refuted this and he established himself in the team as of right with a string of performances which clearly impressed his new manager and which enabled him to retain his place in the Scotland side. Although his first goal was a long time in arriving, coming in the fourth-round FA Cup tie against Sheffield United, which was his 13th appearance, Kevin's very high workrate allied to his all-round game – supporting and creating space for Alan Shearer and hustling the opposition like a terrier when possession was lost – was an important factor in the side's revival, and when Duncan Ferguson returned from injury he stayed in the team, moving to play in the space behind the front men, where he proved equally effective. Kevin's flexibility was further demonstrated when he played on the right side of midfield in the FA Cup quarter-final tie at Tranmere, where he turned in a "Man of the Match" performance including excellent crosses which resulted in United's first two goals. He was disappointed to be ruled out of consideration for the FA Cup semi-final when he pulled a muscle in training, an injury which kept him idle until he made substitute appearances in the final two games of the season. Kevin appeared regularly for the Scotland international team, winning six more caps during the season.

Dundee U (Signed from Duntocher BC on 2/9/1983) SL 118+13/27 SLC 13/5 SC 20+3/5 Others 15+6/3
Coventry C (£900,000 on 29/1/1990) F/PL 99+1/28 FLC 11/7 FAC 4 Others 2
Blackburn Rov (£1,500,000 on 22/3/1993) P/FL 132+12/46 FLC 8+2/3 FAC 13/4 Others 1+1
Newcastle U (£700,000 on 1/10/1999) PL 15+5/2 FAC 4+1/1

Kevin Gallacher

GALLEN Kevin Andrew
Born: Chiswick, 21 September 1975
Height: 5'11" Weight: 12.10
International Honours: E: U21-4; Yth (UEFA-U18 '93); Sch

Kevin's appearances for Queens Park Rangers were restricted last season owing to both injury and the form of the other forwards at the club. On a number of occasions he came on as a substitute to make a telling contribution during the final stages of a match. He scored all four of his goals after coming off the bench, and his 25 appearances as a substitute are a club record

for one season. Although Kevin had an up-and-down season, it was his sixth as a professional. He has remained loyal to the club and is a popular figure with the fans.
Queens Park R (From trainee on 22/9/1992) P/FL 126+45/36 FLC 9+3/2 FAC 6+2/2

GALLIMORE Anthony (Tony) Mark
Born: Crewe, 21 February 1972
Height: 5'11" Weight: 12.6
Club Honours: Div 3 '95; AMC '98

This Grimsby Town left back again had an outstanding season in 1999-2000, performing impressively during a difficult time for the Mariners' defence when a horrendous crop of injuries made it impossible for manager Alan Buckley to field a regular back four. With central defender Peter Handyside ruled out all season and Richard Smith missing almost all the second half of the campaign, Tony supplemented his customary solid displays on the left with occasional appearances in central defence, a task in which he acquitted himself with honour.
Stoke C (From trainee on 11/7/1990) FL 6+5
Carlisle U (Loaned on 3/10/1991) FL 8
Carlisle U (Loaned on 26/2/1992) FL 8
Carlisle U (£15,000 on 25/3/1993) FL 124/9 FLC 8/1 FAC 8 Others 24/1
Grimsby T (£125,000 on 28/3/1996) FL 161+8/4 FLC 14/1 FAC 9 Others 10

Tony Gallimore

GALLOWAY Michael (Mick) Anthony
Born: Nottingham, 13 October 1974
Height: 5'11" Weight: 12.4

This left-sided midfield player made just one start for Gillingham before being loaned to Lincoln City last September. He was used out of position at left back by the Imps during his month at Sincil Bank but he contributed to a good run which saw the club win four of the five games that he played in. Mick then returned to Priestfield and was sold to Chesterfield in November. He was signed to provide the Spireites with a more combative spine to their midfield and, although he was short of match fitness when he arrived, his positive attitude and pugnacious outlook helped relieve pressure on his team-mates. However, he lost his first-team place in mid-February and was subsequently ruled out for the rest of the season by injury.
Notts Co (From trainee on 15/6/1993) FL 17+4 FLC 2 FAC 0+1 Others 4
Gillingham (£10,000 + on 27/3/1997) FL 58+17/5 FLC 3+1 FAC 1+2 Others 5
Lincoln C (Loaned on 29/9/1999) FL 5
Chesterfield (£15,000 on 5/11/1999) FL 14+1/1 Others 3

GANNON James (Jim) Paul
Born: Southwark, 7 September 1968
Height: 6'2" Weight: 13.0

Jim returned to his favoured central defensive position for Stockport in 1999-2000 and once again showed terrific form. Although troubled by a hamstring problem in the early autumn, he recovered to play an important role for the Hatters until he ruptured an anterior cruciate ligament against Manchester City in March. The injury required an operation and is likely to keep him out for the opening games of the 2000-01 campaign. With ten years' service and over 350 league appearances for County, Jim is to have a testimonial match in August, when Joe Royle is due to bring a full-strength Manchester City side to Edgeley Park.
Sheffield U (Signed from Dundalk on 27/4/1989)
Halifax T (Loaned on 22/2/1990) FL 2
Stockport Co (£40,000 on 7/3/1990) FL 350+33/52 FLC 34+4/3 FAC 19+1/1 Others 37+2/8
Notts Co (Loaned on 14/1/1994) FL 2

GARDNER Anthony
Born: Stone, 19 September 1980
Height: 6'5" Weight: 13.8

A tall centre back whose languid skills in the Port Vale defence prompted a move to Tottenham Hotspur last January for a fee that could rise to £1.5 million depending on appearances and international honours, Anthony is a talented young player who appears to have a very bright future. Excellent on the ground for such a big man, he played in the Vale's first 29 matches of 1999-2000. His natural ability and lightning pace always threatened a move to the top flight and a particularly solid performance in an FA Cup tie at Leeds left no one in any doubt that it would come sooner rather than later. Quietly spoken off the pitch, he scored three goals for the Vale last season, all away from home. He had yet to be given his Spurs debut when the season ended but seems sure to make a major impact in 2000-01.
Port Vale (From trainee on 31/7/1998) FL 40+1/4 FLC 2 FAC 1
Tottenham H (£1,000,000 on 28/1/2000)

GARDNER Ricardo Wayne
Born: Jamaica, 25 September 1978
Height: 5'9" Weight: 11.0
International Honours: Jamaica: 28

Ricardo is one of those exciting players who can light up a game with a spark of genius just when you least expect it. Colin Todd had enough faith in the Jamaican international's left-wing abilities to sell Scott Sellars to Huddersfield before the start of last season and how Ricardo repaid that faith. His performances in 1999-2000 were electrifying and he terrorised many an opposing team with his delightful skills and trickery. For a slightly built young man, Ricardo is certainly not afraid to compete with the burliest of opponents, and he is one of those special players who never seems to score an "ordinary" goal. His half-dozen goals last season were all spectacular, but the highlight was surely his phenomenal solo effort in the 1-0 victory over Huddersfield at the Reebok in October. He received the ball just inside the opposition half and proceeded to skip round three or four Huddersfield players before unleashing a twenty-yard drive that flew straight into the net. Unfortunately, Ricardo's season was cruelly cut short when he damaged knee ligaments in February, which ruled him out for the rest of the season, but for the Wanderers' fans it will be a relief and a great pleasure to see him back to his sublime best for the start of the new campaign. A member of Jamaica's team from the 1998 World Cup finals, he remained a regular in the national side until his injury, adding a further four caps.
Bolton W (£1,000,000 from Harbour View, Jamaica on 17/8/1998) FL 45+14/7 FLC 11+1/2 FAC 2+3 Others 3

GARNER Darren John
Born: Plymouth, 10 December 1971
Height: 5'9" Weight: 12.7
Club Honours: AMC '96

The first three months of the 1999-2000 season saw Rotherham's all-action midfielder hit the goal standard as never before and, at the turn of the year, he was the club's leading scorer. As his goals testify, Darren loves to get forward and he helped to form a formidable midfield with Kevin Watson and Steve Thompson. He was missed a lot towards the end of the season when first a broken hand suffered against Carlisle, and then a calf injury picked up in training kept him out of the side. Having hit ten goals in a campaign for the first time in his career, Darren was delighted to return and help the Millers clinch promotion.
Plymouth Arg (From trainee on 15/3/1989) FL 22+5/1 FLC 2+1 FAC 1 (Free to Dorchester T on 19/8/1994)
Rotherham U (£20,000 on 26/6/1995) FL 171+5/19 FLC 9+1 FAC 12/6 Others 8/1

GARNETT Shaun Maurice
Born: Wallasey, 22 November 1969
Height: 6'2" Weight: 13.4
Club Honours: AMC '90

Shaun had another steady season for Oldham in 1999-2000 and, apart from a spell out injured in the autumn, he appeared regularly in the first team. A rock-solid, no-nonsense defender, his excellence in the air more than made up for a certain lack of pace. His form appeared to dip in the last few games of the season, but with another year of his contract still to run he is expected to be a key figure for the Latics again in the 2000-01 campaign.
Tranmere Rov (From trainee on 15/6/1988) FL 110+2/5 FLC 13/1 FAC 4 Others 15+2
Chester C (Loaned on 1/10/1992) FL 9
Preston NE (Loaned on 11/12/1992) FL 10/2 Others 1
Wigan Ath (Loaned on 26/2/1993) FL 13/1
Swansea C (£200,000 on 11/3/1996) FL 15 FLC 2
Oldham Ath (£150,000 on 19/9/1996) FL 122+4/8 FLC 4 FAC 9 Others 3

GARRATT Martin Blake George
Born: York, 22 February 1980
Height: 5'8" Weight: 10.7
The 1999-2000 season was a difficult one for the highly promising left-sided defender or midfielder. Owing to injuries and off the field problems, he made only eight senior appearances for York before leaving the club in March, the remainder of his three-year contract being cancelled. It was quite a fall from the summer of 1999, when he was rumoured to be the subject of a £1 million bid from Sheffield Wednesday. Martin also had a week's trial at Leeds. Having subsequently joined Mansfield, initially on non-contract terms, Martin made his first appearance in the senior side in April, when he replaced Andy Roscoe as left wing back during the match with Barnet. After a second substitute appearance a week later he was given a contract until the end of the season but was not offered a new deal in the summer.
York C (From trainee on 2/7/1998) FL 35+10/1 FLC 2+1 FAC 3 Others 0+1
Mansfield T (Free on 23/3/2000) FL 4+2

GARVEY Stephen (Steve) Hugh
Born: Stalybridge, 22 November 1973
Height: 5'9" Weight: 11.1
Steve is a wide midfield player who delivers a good cross but he had a disappointing 1999-2000 campaign with Blackpool. He featured just once in the starting line-up (at Chesterfield last October), and apart from one further appearance from the subs' bench he spent the remainder of the season in the reserve team.
Crewe Alex (From trainee on 25/10/1991) FL 68+40/8 FLC 6+7/2 FAC 3+4/2 Others 8+3/1
Chesterfield (Loaned on 17/10/1997) FL 2+1
Blackpool (Free on 16/7/1998) FL 7+10/1

GASCOIGNE Paul John
Born: Gateshead, 27 May 1967
Height: 5'10" Weight: 11.12
Club Honours: FAYC '85; FAC '91. SPL '96, '97; SLC '97; SC '96
International Honours: E: 57; B-4; U21-13; Yth
Not for the first time, Paul's season was dominated by his activities off the field in 1999-2000, rather than those on it. He made only nine first-team starts as a result of suspension and injuries, some of them self-inflicted: a clash with Aston Villa's George Boateng in February left him with a broken forearm and ruled him out for the rest of the campaign. Thousands of youngsters adore him for everything that's good about the game; they watch and imitate his every move. Paul appears to idolise them in return and travels all over the area to schools, hospitals and the like, in response to the hundreds of requests that are made for him to make appearances and presentations. His football skills are legendary and if only one youngster acquires even a fraction of the master's ability on the pitch he will have done the game a great service. However, the "Pied Piper" must be wary of leading those who idolise him in the wrong direction. At his best, Paul is a dazzlingly inventive midfield player, whose imagination and creativity can transform matches, and the Boro fans will be hoping to see more of that form in 2000-01.
Newcastle U (From apprentice on 13/5/1985) FL 83+9/21 FLC 8/1 FAC 4/3 Others 2+1
Tottenham H (£2,000,000 on 18/7/1988) FL 91+1/19 FLC 14+1/8 FAC 6/6 (£5,500,000 to Lazio, Italy on 1/5/1992)
Glasgow R (£4,300,000 on 10/7/1995) SL 64+10/30 SLC 7/4 SC 7+1/3 Others 16/2
Middlesbrough (£3,450,000 on 27/3/1998) P/FL 39+2/4 FLC 3+2 FAC 2

Paul Gascoigne

GAUGHAN Steven (Steve) Edward
Born: Doncaster, 14 April 1970
Height: 6'0" Weight: 12.6
Having been released by Darlington at the end of 1998-99 with a year of his contract to run, the experienced midfield general played in the majority of Halifax's matches during his first season at the Shay. A good passer of the ball whose distribution is his major asset, Steve scored his first goal for the Shaymen with a close-range header against West Bromwich Albion in the Worthington Cup, but despite several near-misses he failed to find the net again during the campaign.
Doncaster Rov (Free from Hatfield Main Colliery on 21/1/1988) FL 42+25/3 FLC 2+2 FAC 4+1 Others 5+1
Sunderland (Free on 1/7/1990)
Darlington (£10,000 on 21/1/1992) FL 159+12/15 FLC 8 FAC 6/1 Others 10+1
Chesterfield (£30,000 on 16/8/1996) FL 16+4 FLC 1+1/1 FAC 0+1 Others 1
Darlington (Signed on 21/11/1997) FL 35+12/3 FLC 2 FAC 5 Others 2
Halifax T (Free on 14/7/1999) FL 29+9 FLC 2/1 FAC 2 Others 1

GAVILAN Zarate **Diego** Antonio
Born: Paraguay, 1 March 1980
Height: 5'8" Weight: 10.7
International Honours: Paraguay: 8
Considered to be one of the hottest young talents in South America, Diego became the first player from Paraguay to play in the Premiership when he joined Newcastle early in 2000. He comes from a footballing family as his father and uncle both won Paraguayan championship medals with his former club, and he was delighted to find the number eight shirt available on his arrival as it is the number he has worn all his career. He made his full international debut against Uruguay in June 1999 and starred in his country's Copa America campaign later the same year but has added just one further cap since his transfer to Newcastle. As part of the transfer deal, United negotiated an agreement with the Paraguay FA whereby the club has first call on Diego whenever there is a club v. country conflict, thus avoiding the problems caused by frequent transatlantic journeys suffered by Tino Asprilla during his spell on Tyneside and currently by Nol Solano. Although two footed, Diego is primarily a right-sided midfield player with good ball control skills and a sure touch who is very fast and lively about the field. He did not have an opportunity to show his talents to the full last season. After making two brief substitute appearances totalling some ten minutes, in the Sunderland derby and against Manchester United, shortly after his arrival, he made another for twenty minutes towards the end of the campaign in the home defeat by Leicester, followed by his first starts in the home draw with Leeds and the home victory over Coventry, in which he netted his first goal for the club, and then another outing from the bench against Derby. However, he is clearly a player with an exciting future who can expect to figure more prominently next year.
Newcastle U (£2,000,000 from Cerro Porteno, Paraguay on 4/2/2000) PL 2+4/1

GAVIN Jason Joseph
Born: Dublin, 14 March 1980
Height: 6'1" Weight: 12.7
International Honours: RoI: U21-1; Yth (UEFA-U18 '98)
Like many of his Middlesbrough colleagues, Jason missed much of the 1999-2000 campaign through injury. In his second season as a member of the first-team squad, the young central defender had to pass up a number of opportunities but he nevertheless made a total of nine first-team appearances. A committed competitor with a big heart and a good temperament, he picked up a couple of "Man of the Match" awards to add to his "Young Player of the Year" award from 1998-99. Jason made his debut for the Republic of Ireland U21s against Macedonia last October.
Middlesbrough (From trainee on 26/3/1997) PL 4+4 FLC 2 FAC 0+1

GAYLE John
Born: Bromsgrove, 30 July 1964
Height: 6'2" Weight: 15.4
Club Honours: AMC '91
A big target man with great physical presence, John began the 1999-2000 season in the starting line-up as Scunthorpe United stepped up to the Second Division. However, without a goal since January, he generally had to settle for a substitute's role

and struggled to make much impression before moving to Third Division Shrewsbury on a free transfer at the end of November. He became new manager Kevin Ratcliffe's first signing for the Shrews but a number of injuries restricted him to 18 starts, and he was disappointed by his haul of just two goals. His strength and power up front were a constant threat for opposing defences, and he did much good work outside the 18-yard box.

Wimbledon (£30,000 from Burton A on 1/3/1989) FL 17+3/2 FLC 3
Birmingham C (£175,000 on 21/11/1990) FL 39+5/10 FAC 2 Others 8+1/4
Walsall (Loaned on 20/8/1993) FL 4/1
Coventry C (£100,000 on 13/9/1993) PL 3 FLC 1+2
Burnley (£70,000 on 17/8/1994) FL 7+7/3 FLC 1+1/1 FAC 1+1/1
Stoke C (£70,000 on 23/1/1995) FL 14+12/4 FLC 2 FAC 0+1 Others 3+1
Gillingham (Loaned on 14/3/1996) FL 9/3
Northampton T (£25,000 on 10/2/1997) FL 35+13/7 FLC 1+1/2 FAC 4 Others 9+1/4
Scunthorpe U (Free on 27/7/1998) FL 38+11/4 FLC 3 FAC 1 Others 4
Shrewsbury T (Free on 25/11/1999) FL 17+1/2 Others 1

GAYLE Marcus Anthony
Born: Hammersmith, 27 September 1970
Height: 6'1" Weight: 12.9
Club Honours: Div 3 '92
International Honours: E: Yth. Jamaica: 14

Marcus has been a loyal servant to Wimbledon over the last six years, and in December 1999 he signed an extension to his contract that ties him to the club until 2003, encouraging others to make a similar commitment. The complete striker, he is rarely given due credit for his skill, and his pace and strength make him an awkward proposition for any defender to handle. Marcus is good in the air and, quite apart from the threat he poses in the opposition penalty area, he can always be counted on to get his head to the ball when defending at corners. He scored with a blistering free kick on the opening day of the season at Watford, and went on to score six other Premiership goals, enjoying a purple patch of four goals in five games in the autumn. Marcus added further caps for Jamaica in friendlies against Canada and the USA and also appeared in the CONCACAF Gold Cup games against Colombia and Honduras in February.

Brentford (From trainee on 6/7/1989) FL 118+38/22 FLC 6+3 FAC 6+2/2 Others 14+6/2
Wimbledon (£250,000 on 24/3/1994) PL 174+30/34 FLC 20+1/6 FAC 18+3/3

GAYLE Mark Samuel Roye
Born: Bromsgrove, 21 October 1969
Height: 6'2" Weight: 12.3

An experienced goalkeeper, Mark rejoined Chesterfield just before the big kick-off last August, having played on loan from Crewe a couple of years earlier. With little match practice, he was plunged straight into the first team and took a few games to settle in. He proved to have the ability to deal with ground shots and the bravery to command a busy goalmouth, but he never quite seemed to "click" with his fellow defenders – something that would not have been a problem had he had a full pre-season at Saltergate. Mark was released in the summer.

Leicester C (From trainee on 1/7/1988)
Blackpool (Free on 15/8/1989) FLC 1 (Free to Worcester C in July 1990)
Walsall (£15,000 on 8/5/1991) FL 74+1 FLC 8 FAC 1 Others 8
Crewe Alex (£35,000 on 21/12/1993) FL 82+1 FLC 6 FAC 5 Others 9 (Transferred to Rushden & Diamonds on 12/8/1998)
Chesterfield (Loaned on 20/10/1997) FL 5
Chesterfield (Free on 6/8/1999) FL 29+1 FLC 2+1 FAC 1 Others 1

GEMMILL Scot
Born: Paisley, 2 January 1971
Height: 5'11" Weight: 11.6
Club Honours: FMC '92; Div 1 '98
International Honours: S: 15; B-2; U21-4

After creating a favourable impression following his deadline week transfer the previous season, Scot started the 1999-2000 campaign in Walter Smith's first team against treble winners Manchester United. He would almost certainly have kept his place but for a succession of injuries which ultimately consigned the campaign to the "one to forget" category. A sharp and perceptive midfielder, Scot opened his goals account for the season with a strike at Sheffield Wednesday, but soon afterwards sustained a hamstring injury which was the beginning of his season's end. He received the injury in the dramatic 4-4 draw with Leeds on 24 October – and made just four substitute appearances after that as a promising season petered out on a disappointing note.

Nottingham F (From trainee on 5/1/1990) F/PL 228+17/21 FLC 29+2/3 FAC 19+2/1 Others 13+1/4
Everton (£250,000 on 25/3/1999) PL 13+8/2 FLC 2 FAC 0+1

GEORGE Liam Brendan
Born: Luton, 2 February 1979
Height: 5'9" Weight: 11.3
International Honours: RoI: U21-3; Yth (UEFA-U18 '98)

Luton's pacy young striker began the 1999-2000 campaign with a goal in the Hatters' first win of the season, against Blackpool. In a near-perfect beginning, Liam struck five times in his first eight starts but, after adding five more by mid-November, he then went through a period of only one strike in his next 13 games before finding his goal-scoring touch again. He is a tireless and gifted player who often twists and turns his opponents into mistakes, and if Luton can keep the big clubs away he will score many more goals for his side. He ended the season with 15 goals from 49 appearances, eight as a substitute, and was the club's leading scorer. Liam made his debut for the Republic of Ireland U21s against Macedonia last October and went on to win further caps against the Czech Republic and Ghana.

Luton T (From trainee on 20/1/1997) FL 42+13/13 FLC 0+5 FAC 5/2 Others 1+1

GERMAIN Steven (Steve)
Born: Cannes, France, 22 June 1981
Height: 5'10" Weight: 12.6

This young French striker was a regular in the Colchester squad at the start of the 1999-2000 season, making one full appearance and two more as a substitute without finding the net. A combination of the emergence of Tresor Lua Lua, the switching of Karl Duguid to an attacking role and the re-signing of Steve McGavin moved him well down the pecking order, and he was restricted to reserve- and youth-team football until being released and returning to France before the end of the season.

Colchester U (Free from AS Cannes, France on 25/3/1999) FL 2+7

GERRARD Paul William
Born: Heywood, 22 January 1973
Height: 6'2" Weight: 14.4
International Honours: E: U21-18

After waiting patiently in the goalkeeping shadows at Everton behind first Neville Southall and then Thomas Myhre, Paul finally announced his arrival on the Premiership stage last season with the most consistently sparkling form of his career. Taking full advantage of a summer injury to Myhre, Paul opened the season with a string of stunning saves. In Everton's opening four games of the campaign he was magnificent, and it was a surprise – and no fault of his own – that he had to wait until their fifth match before celebrating his first clean sheet. Capable of breathtaking reflex saves, Paul can still be prone to occasional lapses in concentration, but he has worked hard on ironing these out of his game and the 1999-2000 campaign was easily the best of his career. After a six-match absence with a groin strain midway through the season, Walter Smith paid him a huge compliment by instantly recalling him to his starting line-up – and he responded by recapturing some of his early-season form. He also celebrated a new, long-term contract with the club, which had hardly looked likely the previous season when he was allowed to join Oxford on loan. Still only 27, Paul can look forward to a bright future now that his career is upwardly mobile once again.

Oldham Ath (From trainee on 2/11/1991) P/FL 118+1 FLC 7 FAC 7 Others 2+1
Everton (£1,000,000 + on 1/7/1996) PL 42+1 FLC 3 FAC 3
Oxford U (Loaned on 18/12/1998) FL 16

GERRARD Steven (Steve) George
Born: Huyton, 30 May 1980
Height: 6'2" Weight: 12.4
International Honours: E: 2; U21-4; Yth

Steven had an excellent season for Liverpool in 1999-2000, bringing himself to the notice of the England manager, Kevin Keegan, who no doubt recognises in the young midfielder qualities similar to those that he himself possessed. Steven is tigerish in the tackle, and yet has all the style of a Graeme Souness and can deliver the penetrating through-ball to the front runners. He had an excellent game in the defeat at Middlesbrough in August, refusing to accept defeat and always probing for an opening. Steven is a local product, and poses a real threat to the Liverpool skipper, Jamie Redknapp. After many fine performances for the reserves, he began to establish himself in the first team last season and looks likely to have a fine career ahead of him. Against Sheffield Wednesday, he scored a brilliant goal. Having started a move deep in his own half, he picked the ball up again from Rigobert Song about 50 yards from goal. He waltzed through the Wednesday midfield and found himself confronted with the defence. A drop of his shoulder sent Des Walker the wrong way as Steven drifted out to the right, and suddenly the ball was nestling in the back of the net for a truly great goal. Steven went on to make his full international debut for England against the Ukraine in May and he later appeared as a substitute against Germany in the European Championship finals.

Liverpool (From trainee on 26/2/1998) PL 30+11/1 FAC 2 Others 1

Steve Gerrard

GHRAYIB Najwan (Naj)
Born: Israel, 30 January 1974
Height: 5'9" Weight: 11.1
International Honours: Israel: 18

Najwan joined Aston Villa from Hapoel Haifa in the summer of 1999 but found it difficult to displace Alan Wright as the club's regular left wing back. He made his debut for Villa in the Worthington Cup tie at Chester last September and had a couple of outings from the subs' bench shortly afterwards. Just as he appeared to be about to break through to the first team, he was struck down by appendicitis and it was not until well into the new year that he returned to action. He eventually started his first Premiership match against Sunderland at the end of April and will be hoping to appear more regularly for Villa in 2000-01. Najwan is a skilful left-footed player with searing pace and a good cross. Already a regular in the Israel international team, he won further caps against Slovakia and the Czech Republic during the season.

Aston Villa (£1,000,000 from Hapoel Haifa, Israel on 4/8/1999) PL 1+4 FLC 1

GIALLANZA Gaetano
Born: Dornach, Switzerland, 6 June 1974
Height: 6'0" Weight: 11.12

A Swiss-born striker with an Italian passport, Gaetano joined Norwich from Nantes on a three-month loan shortly before transfer deadline day last March. He had had a previous loan spell in England at the end of the 1998-99 season, making three substitute appearances for Bolton before returning to France. A mobile front runner whose touch, technique and awareness in front of goal make him a potential match winner in the First Division, Gaetano demonstrated his ability by scoring four goals in his first two matches for the Canaries at reserve level. His first-team debut was delayed by a groin strain, but he made three appearances before the end of the season, one of them from the bench. He was reported to have one year left on his contract with Nantes, but was expected to start the coming season elsewhere as he is out of favour with the club's coach.

Bolton W (Loaned from Nantes, France on 25/3/1998) PL 0+3
Norwich C (Loaned from Nantes, France on 23/3/2000) FL 2+1

GIBB Alistair (Ally) Stuart
Born: Salisbury, 17 February 1976
Height: 5'9" Weight: 11.7

Ally found himself out in the cold at Northampton when Ian Hendon was signed from Notts County at the end of 1998-99. Although he made the occasional first-team appearance last season, he could not command a regular place and joined Stockport in February. Snapped up for £50,000, Ally proved a bargain buy for County manager Andy Kilner. A speedy right-sided player who can perform equally well at wing back or in a wide-midfield role, Ally appeared in all but one of County's last 15 games and will be aiming to start the 2000-01 campaign in similar form.

Norwich C (From trainee on 1/7/1994)
Northampton T (Loaned on 22/9/1995) FL 9/1
Northampton T (£30,000 on 5/2/1996) FL 51+71/3 FLC 8+4 FAC 5+3 Others 6+3
Stockport Co (£50,000 on 18/2/2000) FL 13+1

GIBBENS Kevin
Born: Southampton, 4 November 1979
Height: 5'10" Weight: 12.13

This young Southampton midfielder joined Stockport on loan last September along with his Saints colleague Gary Monk. Kevin impressed as a substitute on his debut for the Hatters against Barnsley and made three further starts before returning to the Dell. He is a good box-to-box midfield player with an excellent range of passing.

Southampton (From trainee on 16/1/1998) PL 4+2 FLC 2
Stockport Co (Loaned on 9/9/1999) FL 1+1 FLC 2

GIBBS Nigel James
Born: St Albans, 20 November 1965
Height: 5'7" Weight: 11.11
Club Honours: FAYC '82; Div 2 '98
International Honours: E: U21-5; Yth

The long-serving right back has now completed his 16th season as a senior player with Watford and is fast closing in on Luther Blissett's all-time record for first-team games, having overtaken Gary Porter during the season. Nigel remains the epitome of a model professional – uncomplicated, uncomplaining and totally reliable. Following the signing of Des Lyttle, he began the season in the reserves but he was soon back, returning to play a key role in Watford's fine victory over Chelsea. The arrival of Neil Cox and the adoption of a 3-5-2 formation further limited Nigel's chances, but he remained an invaluable squad man.

Watford (From apprentice on 23/11/1983) P/FL 382+19/5 FLC 24/2 FAC 39+2 Others 17

GIBBS Paul Derek
Born: Gorleston, 26 October 1972
Height: 5'10" Weight: 11.10

Paul suffered a terrible double fracture to his left leg during the final game of the 1998-99 season. The redoubtable left full back or wing back worked tremendously hard to fight his way back and, after coming off the bench on four occasions, made the starting line-up for the first time against Swansea at Home Park in April. Mainly due to the outstanding form of Jon Beswetherick, his Pilgrim replacement, Paul was released at the end of the campaign. He was soon snapped up by Second Division Brentford.

Colchester U (Signed from Diss T on 6/3/1995) FL 39+14/3 FAC 1+1 Others 8+1
Torquay U (Free on 26/7/1997) FL 40+1/7 FLC 4/1 FAC 3/1 Others 3/1
Plymouth Arg (Free on 7/7/1998) FL 30+4/3 FLC 2

GIBSON Paul Richard
Born: Sheffield, 1 November 1976
Height: 6'3" Weight: 13.0
Club Honours: FAYC '95

Paul was again second-choice 'keeper to Darren Ward at Notts County in 1999-2000 and appeared just twice in the first team during the season, giving a good account of himself on both occasions. He was loaned to Rochdale in February to gain more senior experience. Paul had had a previous spell at Mansfield when Rochdale manager Steve Parkin was in charge there, and when Dale's Neil Edwards was injured Steve took him on loan again. Paul played five games, but wasn't kept on once Neil was in sight of a return. An impressive shot stopper, Paul was voted Notts' "Reserves' Player of the Year" last season.

Manchester U (From trainee on 1/7/1995)
Mansfield T (Loaned on 20/10/1997) FL 13
Hull C (Loaned on 6/11/1998) FL 4
Notts Co (Free on 25/3/1999) FL 2 FLC 1
Rochdale (Loaned on 4/2/2000) FL 5

GIBSON Robin John
Born: Crewe, 15 November 1979
Height: 5'6" Weight: 10.7

Robin made a full recovery from knee ligament damage suffered in March 1999 and had an excellent 1999-2000 campaign, establishing himself as a regular in the Wrexham line-up in the second half of the season. He scored the equaliser in the FA Cup tie with Middlesbrough when the Robins went on to record a shock victory, and then netted one of the fastest goals seen

at the Racecourse Ground in many years when he shot home from 12 yards after just 28 seconds of the game against Scunthorpe last March. He is developing into a hard-working winger, full of trickery and a problem for opposition defences. He was deservedly voted "Young Player of the Year" for the second season in succession.
Wrexham (From trainee on 3/7/1998) FL 21+10/2 FAC 1+2/1 Others 2+3

GIGGS Ryan Joseph
Born: Cardiff, 29 November 1973
Height: 5'11" Weight: 10.9
Club Honours: ESC '91; FAYC '92; FLC '92; PL '93, '94, '96, '97, '99, '00; CS '93, '94, '96, '97; FAC '94, '96, '99; EC '99
International Honours: W: 26; U21-1; Yth. E: Sch
A highly skilled left winger who packs a tremendous left-footed shot, Ryan endured a frustrating start to the 1999-2000 season when the curse of the hamstrings kept him out of the Manchester United side at a vital stage in September. Having embarked on a special training programme that rectified the problem without nullifying his pace, he came back to produce several electrifying performances, notably in the Champions' League against Marseille, Zagreb and Fiorentina. His most "profitable" game, however, came against Palmeiras in the Intercontinental Cup, when he picked up the keys of a brand-new car after being voted the "Man of the Match". On the goal front, Ryan scored his usual quota, starting off with a fine strike in the Premiership against Newcastle in August, while also netting against Spurs, West Ham (2) and Middlesbrough. In the Champions' League, a vital goal against Bordeaux in March helped United through the qualifying stages. He ended the season with his sixth Premiership winners' medal, creating a record he currently shares with Denis Irwin, and is now second in line to Denis as United's longest-serving pro. Ironically now the same age as George Best (the player with whom he was most often compared early in his career) when the great Reds legend retired from United in 1973, Ryan is well on his way to becoming the most honoured man in the club's history. He continued to be a key member of the Welsh squad and made a rare appearance in a friendly international in March when he scored a cracking solo goal in the 2-1 defeat by Finland.
Manchester U (From trainee on 1/12/1990) F/PL 267+23/59 FLC 17+4/6 FAC 34+3/7 Others 50+2/11

GIJSBRECHTS David (Davy)
Born: Heusden, Belgium, 20 September 1972
Height: 6'1" Weight: 13.8
Signed in the summer of 1999 by then Sheffield United manager Adrian Heath for a fee of £200,000 from the Belgian club Lokeren, Davy made his first appearance as a substitute in the Blades' 0-6 defeat at Maine Road. The central defender's full debut was not much more of a success – United lost 0-3 at Preston in the Worthington Cup. He had a run of five games in November but thereafter his opportunities were limited to appearances as a substitute or as a stand-in when Shaun Murphy or Lee Sandford were unavailable. He performed reliably, showing good heading ability and anticipation, but possibly his best performance, against Birmingham City, was brought to an early end by a wrist injury.
Sheffield U (£250,000 from KSC Lokeren, Belgium on 6/8/1999) FL 9+8 FLC 1 FAC 1

GILCHRIST Philip (Phil) Alexander
Born: Stockton on Tees, 25 August 1973
Height: 5'11" Weight: 13.12
Club Honours: FLC '00
Phil, Oxford's star defender, was sold to Leicester just one game into the 1999-2000 season. His outstanding performances over the past few seasons had not gone unnoticed and he took the opportunity to link up with his former United team-mate Matt Elliott. A left-footed centre back, Phil played a vital role in helping to shore up City's defence, either when appearing as a substitute or during an extended run in the starting line-up after Christmas. Although he did not get on to the pitch at Wembley, his contribution during earlier rounds fully justified the winners' medal he collected as a non-playing substitute. Another late run of outings saw him look more and more at home in the Premiership, and he made crucial contributions against both Everton and Newcastle. Well known for his long throw-ins, Phil is a consistently good tackler and is strong in the air. He showed plenty of composure and confidence, and is sure to be pressing for automatic selection during the coming season.
Nottingham F (From trainee on 5/12/1990)
Middlesbrough (Free on 10/1/1992)
Hartlepool U (Free on 27/11/1992) FL 77+5 FLC 4+1 FAC 4 Others 5
Oxford U (£100,000 on 17/2/1995) FL 173+4/10 FLC 16 FAC 9/1 Others 3
Leicester C (£500,000 on 10/8/1999) PL 17+10/1 FLC 5+1 FAC 3

GILKES Michael Earl Glenis McDonald
Born: Hackney, 20 July 1965
Height: 5'8" Weight: 10.10
Club Honours: FMC '88; Div 3 '86, Div 2 '94
Michael signed for Millwall in the summer of 1999 on a "Bosman" free transfer from Wolves, on a one-year contract. A left-sided midfielder, he was injured during the early part of the season and made only one first-team start prior to being recalled for the 5-0 home win against Reading in mid-November. Thereafter he missed no more than a handful of games as the Lions made sure of a play-off place. Although 34, he is still a very tricky winger with a good shot and puts defences under continuous pressure. Stop Press: Michael was called up by Barbados for their World Cup qualifying games in the middle of July.
Reading (Free from Leicester C juniors on 10/7/1984) FL 348+45/43 FLC 25+7/6 FAC 31+2/1 Others 26+2/2
Chelsea (Loaned on 28/1/1992) FL 0+1 Others 0+1
Southampton (Loaned on 4/3/1992) FL 4+2
Wolverhampton W (£155,000 on 27/3/1997) FL 33+5/1 FLC 0+1 FAC 2
Millwall (Free on 7/7/1999) FL 26+3/2 FLC 0+1

GILL Jeremy (Jerry) Morley
Born: Clevedon, 8 September 1970
Height: 5'7" Weight: 11.0
International Honours: E: SP-1
This dependable Birmingham City right back was unable to dislodge Gary Rowett from the Blues' first team during 1999-2000 but was often on the bench and showed his versatility by filling in anywhere on the right flank when required. A competitive performer who always played with passion and determination, Jerry was once again reserve-team captain last season.
Leyton Orient (Free from Trowbridge T on 16/12/1988. Free to Weston super Mare on 1/7/1990)
Birmingham C (£30,000 from Yeovil T on 14/7/1997) FL 8+9 FLC 2+1 FAC 1 Others 1

GILL Matthew James
Born: Cambridge, 8 November 1980
Height: 5'11" Weight: 12.10
Since losing his midfield place in November 1998 due to knee and ankle injury problems, Matthew has struggled to re-establish regular selection in the Peterborough senior side. Unfortunately, four of his nine starts in 1999-2000 came during Posh's worst run of the campaign, although he was included as a sub during their successful play-off games. Matthew notched his first senior goal with the 78-second opener against Swansea in United's first game of the new millennium.
Peterborough U (From trainee on 2/3/1998) FL 31+17/1 FLC 2 FAC 1 Others 1+3

GILL Wayne John
Born: Chorley, 28 November 1975
Height: 5'9" Weight: 11.0
This Chorley-born midfielder was finally given his chance to shine in the Blackburn first team last season, playing in the club's three Worthington Cup games, and was unlucky not to score with a long shot that hit the crossbar. He was loaned to Blackpool in March and created an instant impression when he found the net in the first minute of his league debut at Wigan. Quick, alert and able to find space in the penalty box, he scored in each of his first four games for the Seasiders and finished with a total of seven goals in just 12 games. Stop Press: Wayne moved to Tranmere Rovers in May in search of greater first-team opportunities.
Blackburn Rov (From trainee on 12/7/1994) FLC 3
Blackpool (Signed on 6/3/2000) FL 12/7

GILLESPIE Keith Robert
Born: Bangor, 18 February 1975
Height: 5'10" Weight: 11.3
Club Honours: FAYC '92
International Honours: NI: 32; U21-1; Yth; Sch
In his Newcastle days Keith was lauded as an exciting right winger with pace and the trickery to go past his full back before sending over telling centres. Since his move to Blackburn, however, less has been seen of

these qualities and his main value to Rovers in 1999-2000 was his defensive tracking, the Northern Irishman using his great speed and ability to spot an opponent making a run from deep to foil attacks. He was out of action for three months with an ankle injury and was not certain of a first-team place after returning to fitness. Sent on as a substitute, he inspired a comeback win against West Bromwich by bundling the ball into the net from close range on a rare excursion into the penalty area and he scored a great equaliser at Fulham with a shrewd lob. He won five more international caps during the season.

Manchester U (From trainee on 3/2/1993) PL 3+6/1 FLC 3 FAC 1+1/1
Wigan Ath (Loaned on 3/9/1993) FL 8/4 Others 2
Newcastle U (£1,000,000 on 12/1/1995) PL 94+19/11 FLC 7+1/1 FAC 9+1/2 Others 11+5
Blackburn Rov (£2,250,000 on 18/12/1998) P/FL 24+14/3 FLC 2 FAC 4+1/1

GINOLA David
Born: Gassin, France, 25 January 1967
Height: 6'0" Weight: 11.10
Club Honours: FLC '99
International Honours: France: 17

After he had such a memorable season in 1998-99, it was inevitable that the pressure would be on David to deliver the breath-taking goals and glorious skills which have become his trademark at Tottenham once more in 1999-2000. However, the talented winger turned into something of a work-horse, and a new gritty edge appeared in his game. David was happy to sit in a more central position and not hug the line, and his involvement was more "little but often" as he strove to bring other players into the game with his close one-touch skill in the heart of midfield. As manager George Graham made greater demands, David rose to the challenge and applied his skill accordingly, laying on passes deep into the line of attack and inevitably peppering his appearances with strong attacking runs down the left side. His pin-point accuracy when delivering balls into the box ensured that much of Tottenham's success in front of goal came from the Frenchman's hard work. It would be fair to say that David became a more mature player and was more alert to the opportunities which lay ahead for his team-mates, although his quick thinking occasionally ended in frustration when moves failed to pay off as Chris Armstrong and Steffen Iversen failed to match his pace when moving forward into the opposition box. Rumours of his dissatisfaction at the increased number of appearances which ended prematurely as a result of substitution were quashed as soon as they arose with David declaring his love for the club at which he has become an idol. However, although it was reported in June that Spurs had accepted a £3 million bid from Aston Villa for the Frenchman, at the time of going to press the deal had failed to materialise.

Newcastle U (£2,500,000 from Paris St Germain, France, via Toulon, Racing Paris and Brest, on 6/7/1995) PL 54+4/6 FLC 6 FAC 4 Others 7+1/1
Tottenham H (£2,000,000 on 18/7/1997) PL 100/12 FLC 13/4 FAC 11/5 Others 2+1

GISLASON Sigursteinn (Siggi)
Born: Iceland, 25 June 1968
Height: 5'9" Weight: 11.3
Club Honours: AMC '00
International Honours: Iceland: 22

This Icelandic left-sided defender/midfielder was one of Gudjon Thordarson's first signings for Stoke, joining the club on loan from KR Reykjavik last November, during the close season in his home country. Always competitive when called upon, he overcame a knock in the first half of his debut to play a handful of games for the club before returning home. Siggi won a further international cap for Iceland when he appeared in a friendly match with the Faroe Isles last August.

Stoke C (Loaned from KR Reykjavik, Iceland on 22/11/1999) FL 4+4 Others 2+2

GITTENS Jonathan (Jon) Antoni
Born: Birmingham, 22 January 1964
Height: 6'0" Weight: 12.10

This experienced campaigner was a regular in the Exeter defence in 1999-2000. Jon's composure and awareness allow him to make things look easy. One of his two goals came in the home win against his previous club, local rivals Torquay. Following manager Noel Blake's mass clear-out at the end of the term, Jon was told he will be surplus to requirements for the new season.

Southampton (£10,000 from Paget R on 16/10/1985) FL 18 FLC 4 FAC 1
Swindon T (£40,000 on 22/7/1987) FL 124+2/6 FLC 15+1 FAC 9 Others 13+1/1
Southampton (£400,000 on 28/3/1991) FL 16+3 FLC 4 Others 1
Middlesbrough (Loaned on 19/2/1992) FL 9+3/1
Middlesbrough (£200,000 on 27/7/1992) PL 13 FLC 0+1 FAC 1
Portsmouth (Free on 9/8/1993) FL 81+2/2 FLC 10 FAC 3 Others 3/1
Torquay U (Free on 5/8/1996) FL 78/9 FLC 6 FAC 4 Others 5/2
Exeter C (Free on 29/7/1998) FL 82/4 FLC 3 FAC 7/1 Others 6

GIVEN Seamus (Shay) John
Born: Lifford, 20 April 1976
Height: 6'0" Weight: 13.4
Club Honours: Div 1 '96
International Honours: RoI: 24; U21-5; Yth

While training with the Republic of Ireland team in the 1999 close season goalkeeper Shay nicked a cartilage in his right knee and he had to undergo surgery which kept him out of contention for a place in the Newcastle team until October, when he came off the bench as Steve Harper was sent off in the Worthington Cup tie at Birmingham. Then in only his second game back he broke a bone in his wrist in the home win over Derby, needing further treatment and rest, and on his return he was kept on the bench by the continuing fine form of his friendly rival Steve. Opportunity knocked again when Harper was injured just prior to the FA Cup quarter-final at Tranmere, and Shay responded with an assured display, dealing very competently with a bombardment of high balls into the box to help earn another semi-final place for the club and re-establish himself as first choice. He retained his place with a series of fine displays, sprinkled with some outstanding saves such as the two he made against Watford to seal a vital 1-0 victory, and an astonishing point-blank one from Gerald Sibon in the important foot-of-the-table clash at Hillsborough at a time when Sheffield Wednesday were threatening to come back into the match. His fast feet and lightning reflexes give him fine shot-stopping abilities, and the Tranmere game showed that he has been improving his ability to deal with high balls into the box, so helping him to develop as an all-round 'keeper of quality. Shay won a recall to the Republic of Ireland team when he appeared in the friendly match with Greece last April.

Blackburn Rov (Free from Glasgow Celtic juniors on 8/8/1994) PL 2 FLC 0+1
Swindon T (Loaned on 4/8/1995) FL 5
Sunderland (Loaned on 19/1/1996) FL 17
Newcastle U (£1,500,000 on 14/7/1997) PL 69 FLC 2+1 FAC 12 Others 8

GLASS James (Jimmy) Robert
Born: Epsom, 1 August 1973
Height: 6'1" Weight: 13.4

Jimmy is an agile 'keeper, reliable on crosses and an excellent shot stopper. Having been Carlisle's hero in 1998-99 when he saved their Nationwide League status with a sensational last-minute goal, he had a very different experience last season. He made the first team at Swindon for a run of eight consecutive games in the autumn but was then blamed for the defeat at Bolton in October despite the fact that he had kept the Robins in the game with some out-standing saves. His contract was eventually cancelled in January and he moved on to Cambridge shortly afterwards. Jimmy joined Brentford on a non-contract basis as cover for injuries on transfer deadline day. He made his debut for the Bees at Wigan when he came on as a substitute for the injured Jason Pearcey and also appeared in the final match of the 1999-2000 season against Colchester. He was released by the club in the summer.

Crystal Palace (From trainee on 4/7/1991)
Portsmouth (Loaned on 10/2/1995) FL 3
Bournemouth (Free on 8/3/1996) FL 94 FLC 4 FAC 4 Others 7
Swindon T (Free on 24/6/1998) FL 11 FLC 1
Carlisle U (Loaned on 22/4/1999) FL 3/1
Cambridge U (Free on 20/1/2000)
Brentford (Free on 23/3/2000) FL 1+1

GLASS Stephen
Born: Dundee, 23 May 1976
Height: 5'9" Weight: 11.0
Club Honours: SLC '96
International Honours: S: 1; B-2; U21-11; Sch

This left winger is a quick-footed, skilful Scottish international who had a disap-pointing season at Newcastle in 1999-2000. The knee injury which sidelined him for the latter part of the previous campaign flared up again in pre-season, causing him to miss the first eight games, by which time Nobby Solano and Kieron Dyer were established in the side ahead of him. Stephen made a substitute appearance in the rout of Sheffield Wednesday, but could not gain a regular place in the starting line-up, being restricted to two games, the Worthington Cup defeat at Birmingham and the home win over Spurs, scoring in the latter, plus a handful of substitute appearances. In February the lack of first-team opportunities led him to seek a transfer, a request which was granted. Although slightly built, Stephen has good ball control at pace and an ability to cross accurately on the run, which makes him a dangerous flank player.

Aberdeen (Free from Crombie Sports on 25/10/1994) SL 93+13/7 SLC 10/2 SC 7+2 Others 3/2
Newcastle U (£650,000 on 22/7/1998) PL 19+10/4 FLC 3 FAC 2+3 Others 2+3

GLEDHILL Lee
Born: Bury, 7 November 1980
Height: 5'10" Weight: 11.2

This rookie full back rose to prominence in the opening few months of the 1999-2000 season and quickly won over the Barnet fans with his spirit and all-round efficiency. The Bees' former youth-team captain, Lee inherited the right-back role in September and played his part in the club's meteoric rise up the table. With Sam Stockley ruled out through injury, Lee was subsequently given a lengthy run in the side and responded with a string of resourceful displays. He made his starting debut in the crucial victory at Swansea in September and made a real impact in the high-profile encounter. Quick and bursting with youthful energy, he refused to shy away from any challenges and his runs down the flank provided Barnet with an extra attacking option. In the ensuing matches Lee displayed an assured streak and maturity in his game before being loaned to Slough in January. The arrival of Ross Davidson in November signalled that he had been overhauled in the pecking order for the right-back berth, but he kept concentrating on progressing in the reserves, showing all the signs of being a future Barnet captain.

Barnet (From trainee on 2/7/1999) FL 8+3 FAC 1

GLOVER Edward Lee
Born: Kettering, 24 April 1970
Height: 5'11" Weight: 12.1
Club Honours: FLC '89; FMC '92
International Honours: S: U21-3; Yth

The Rotherham sharpshooter had to show extreme patience in battling back to fitness after suffering a severe hamstring injury in January 1999 that kept him out of first-team action until he came on as a substitute against Carlisle last February. Lee will be looking to get back to his previous high standards next season. Two weeks after his 30th birthday, the vastly experienced striker proved he's still got what it takes. In the last-day championship decider against Swansea, he "won" and scored the last-ditch penalty that kept the Millers' Division Three title hopes alive. The two events were separated by a 15-minute pitch invasion. He was released in the summer. Stop Press: Lee was reported to have signed for Macclesfield at the beginning of July.

Nottingham F (From apprentice on 2/5/1987) F/PL 61+15/9 FLC 6+5/2 FAC 8+2/1 Others 4+1/1
Leicester C (Loaned on 14/9/1989) FL 3+2/1
Barnsley (Loaned on 18/1/1990) FL 8 FAC 4
Luton T (Loaned on 2/9/1991) FL 1
Port Vale (£200,000 on 2/8/1994) FL 38+14/7 FLC 5+1/4 FAC 0+2 Others 3+2/2
Rotherham U (£150,000 on 15/8/1996) FL 70+15/29 FLC 5 FAC 9+1/3 Others 1+1
Huddersfield T (Loaned on 3/3/1997) FL 11

Shaun Goater

GOATER Leonard **Shaun**
Born: Hamilton, Bermuda, 25 February 1970
Height: 6'1" Weight: 12.0
Club Honours: AMC '96
International Honours: Bermuda: 19; Yth

Once he had got into his stride, Shaun's goalscoring and effective work as a target man were major factors in Manchester City's promotion from Division Two in 1998-99. He continued to improve his all-round game last season, winning over the remaining doubters among the club's supporters with his consistent and increasingly confident form. His workrate was also highly praised by his manager, Joe Royle, and he scored in almost every game from November onwards. Shaun topped the Division One scoring charts at the end of the season with 29 goals – four more than Charlton's Andy Hunt. His subtle lay-offs and the dexterity with which he headed the ball on for his colleagues were a delight, and he would invariably follow up and be in the right place to receive the return pass. Apart from two short periods in October and November when he was ruled out by a hamstring injury, he was virtually an ever-present as City completed their return to the Premiership. Probably his most satisfying performance was against Fulham at Maine Road in January, when he scored a hat-trick. Shaun returned to international duty with Bermuda for the first time since 1992, bagging three goals in the 5-1 win over British Virgin Islands in a World Cup qualifying match last March. This was his second hat-trick for his country and brings his tally to 18 goals from just 19 appearances.

Manchester U (From North Village, Bermuda on 8/5/1989)
Rotherham U (Free on 25/10/1989) FL 169+40/70 FLC 13+4/4 FAC 12+3/7 Others 15+5/5
Notts Co (Loaned on 12/11/1993) FL 1
Bristol C (£175,000 on 17/7/1996) FL 67+8/40 FLC 7/2 FAC 5 Others 5+1/1
Manchester C (£400,000 on 26/3/1998) FL 88+2/43 FLC 6/5 FAC 6/4 Others 3/1

GOLDBAEK Bjarne
Born: Nykobing Falster, Denmark, 6 October 1968
Height: 5'10" Weight: 12.4
International Honours: Denmark: 24; B-1

The popular Dane found his opportunities limited at Chelsea last season following the midfield acquisitions of Didier Deschamps and Gabriele Ambrosetti. A dependable, unpretentious right-sided midfielder, he started just four matches – two in the Premiership and one each in the Worthington Cup and Champions' League – in the first half of the season. Other clubs were alerted to Bjarne's possible availability and, after overtures from Birmingham City and Nottingham Forest had reportedly been rejected, the Blues allowed him to move to neighbours Fulham in December. He is a very useful utility player who, even in a star-studded squad like Chelsea's, will always do an effective job down the right flank in an aggressive, no-nonsense manner, and Blues fans were sad to see him leave. He quickly endeared himself to the Fulham crowd (not the easiest thing for an ex-Chelsea player to do) with his spectacular runs and ferocious shooting. When he was played as a wing back, Bjarne was not able to get forward often enough to cause the opposition problems, but when given a role wide on the right of a four-man midfield he was a constant danger. A seasoned international, he was a regular member of the Denmark squad during the season, winning a further eight caps and making the final 22 for Euro 2000, although he only featured in the defeat by the Czech Republic.

Chelsea (£350,000 from FC Copenhagen, Denmark, via Naestved, FC Schalke, Kaiserslautern, Tennis Borussia and FC Koln, on 10/11/1998) PL 15+14/5 FLC 3 FAC 2+4 Others 1+1
Fulham (£500,000 + on 18/1/2000) FL 16+2/3 FAC 1

GOMA Alain
Born: Sault, France, 5 October 1972
Height: 6'0" Weight: 13.0
International Honours: France: 2

Alain is a sturdy French international defender, adept at either full back or centre back, whom Ruud Gullit recruited in the summer of 1999 on a five-year contract with the aim of strengthening the Newcastle back line. He quickly settled into the centre of defence with a series of classy displays, proving to be strong in the tackle, cool on the ball and a good reader of the game, and looked to be a player around whom a solid yet constructive defence could be assembled. However, a lesion in the achilles tendon which had been troubling him for some time was aggravated in the

Worthington Cup defeat at Birmingham at the beginning of October and kept him out of the team until the end of March, when he returned for the game at Anfield. After this the competition among the clutch of centre backs at the club resulted in his being in and out of the side, which did not provide him with the chance to adjust fully to the Premiership and develop into the dominating centre back he promises to be.
Newcastle U (£4,750,000 from Paris St Germain, France on 9/7/1999) PL 14 FLC 1 Others 2

GOODEN Ty Michael
Born: Canvey Island, 23 October 1972
Height: 5'8" Weight: 12.6
Club Honours: Div 2 '96

Ty began the 1999-2000 season with Swindon but missed several weeks early on with a knee injury and then required a hernia operation later in the autumn. Once fully fit, he returned to the Robins' line-up in December but was then sold to Division Two promotion hopefuls Gillingham on New Year's Day. He quickly proved to be a useful acquisition for the Kent club, making an excellent contribution on the left side of midfield and scoring five goals. A midfield dynamo, he crosses the ball superbly, delivers fine in-swinging corners and packs a powerful shot.
Swindon T (Free from Wycombe W on 17/9/1993) P/FL 118+28/9 FLC 6+1/1 FAC 7+1/1 Others 3+1
Gillingham (£75,000 on 4/1/2000) FL 15+1/4 Others 3/1

GOODHIND Warren Ernest
Born: Johannesburg, South Africa, 16 August 1977
Height: 5'11" Weight: 11.6

It was a lengthy road to recovery for Barnet's youngest-ever captain following the severely broken leg he suffered back in November 1998. Warren eventually returned to first-team duties in February and proved that his tremendous versatility and flawless technique were still very much intact. Operating in either the right-sided central defensive berth or in the middle of the park, Warren brought a sense of calm to the team during the turbulent mid-season slump. His sensible distribution proved invaluable to the side, but his understandable lack of fitness made him susceptible to injury and he was ruled out for a further month with a groin problem. Warren returned to the squad for the play-off semi-final games against Peterborough, and is expected to assume an important role in next season's bid for promotion.
Barnet (From trainee on 3/7/1996) FL 43+19/2 FLC 5+1 FAC 1 Others 3/1

GOODING Michael (Mick) Charles
Born: Newcastle, 12 April 1959
Height: 5'8" Weight: 11.10
Club Honours: Div 3 '81, Div 2 '94

An industrious, hard-tackling midfielder, Southend's player-coach was called upon only briefly during the 1999-2000 season, sporting the squad number 40 to match his age! An incredibly fit man, Mick is now more used to passing his knowledge on to the Shrimpers on the training ground, and he will probably be more surprised than anyone if he appears in the first team during the new season.
Rotherham U (Signed from Bishop Auckland on 18/7/1979) FL 90+12/10 FLC 9/3 FAC 3
Chesterfield (Signed on 24/12/1982) FL 12
Rotherham U (£10,000 on 9/9/1983) FL 149+7/33 FLC 18/3 FAC 13/4 Others 7
Peterborough U (£18,000 on 13/8/1987) FL 47/21 FLC 8/2 FAC 1/2 Others 4/2
Wolverhampton W (£85,000 on 20/9/1988) FL 43+1/4 FLC 4 Others 5+1/1
Reading (£65,000 on 26/12/1989) FL 303+11/26 FLC 19 FAC 18+1/2 Others 16/2 (Free to Plymouth Arg as coach on 26/3/1998)
Southend U (Free on 9/7/1998) FL 19+6 FLC 2 Others 1

GOODISON Ian
Born: Jamaica, 21 November 1972
Height: 6'3" Weight: 12.10
International Honours: Jamaica

The captain in two of Jamaica's three World Cup games in France '98 swapped Kingston, Jamaica, for Kingston upon Hull in a sensational move in October 1999. Joining the Tigers with his colleague Theo Whitmore, "Pepe" brought a wealth of experience to Boothferry Park, having been a regular at international level since making his debut against Guatemala back in March 1993. Ian's transition to English football didn't run as smoothly as he would have wished. Along with the dramatic change in his surroundings and lifestyle – his first game as a contracted Tiger was for the reserves on a wet, windy night in Hartlepool – Ian was also asked to play out of his recognised position in midfield, then at right wing back. When he was restored to a more familiar central defensive role, his physical strength came to the fore as well as his coolness on the ball. Chances to impress the Hull public then became restricted by international call-ups. Appearances against Uruguay and New Zealand in the Guangzhou (China) Tournament in January were followed by the CONCACAF Gold Cup in the USA in February. Although a surprisingly early exit meant he missed only three City games, a calf injury picked up in Jamaica's last Gold Cup game against Honduras meant he had difficulty regaining his place in Hull's formidable defensive line-up.
Hull C (Free from Olympic Gardens, Jamaica on 22/10/1999) FL 17+1 FAC 3+1 Others 1

GOODLAD Mark
Born: Barnsley, 9 September 1979
Height: 6'0" Weight: 13.2

A fringe player at Nottingham Forest, this young goalkeeper joined Port Vale, initially on trial, in March 2000. After impressing in a few reserve matches, he made his Vale debut in the final game of the season against Wolves and generally handled well, keeping a clean sheet against the play-off-chasing opposition until the final four minutes. He looks to have a bright future and should feature regularly in 2000-01.
Nottingham F (From trainee on 2/10/1996)
Scarborough (Loaned on 5/2/1999) FL 3
Port Vale (Signed on 23/3/2000) FL 1

GOODMAN Jonathan (Jon)
Born: Walthamstow, 2 June 1971
Height: 6'0" Weight: 12.3
International Honours: RoI: 4

This likeable professional made only one substitute appearance for Wimbledon in 1999-2000 owing to a persistent knee injury, after a handful of appearances for the reserves which had confirmed his talent for goalscoring. A powerful forward noted for his pace and cool finishing, Jon unfortunately had to retire from the game in January following medical advice, after four operations to his knee over a two-year period.
Millwall (£50,000 from Bromley on 20/8/1990) FL 97+12/35 FLC 5+4/2 FAC 5+1 Others 3
Wimbledon (Signed on 9/11/1994) PL 28+32/11 FLC 1+2 FAC 3+4/3

GOODRIDGE Gregory (Greg) Ronald St Clair
Born: Barbados, 10 July 1971
Height: 5'6" Weight: 10.0
International Honours: Barbados

The arrival of Tony Pulis as Bristol City manager in the summer of 1999 brought a decline in the play of this exciting and skilful winger. He started off the new campaign in the first team but, after a series of disappointing displays cost him his place, he found himself mainly confined to the substitutes' bench. Greg is also the captain of the Barbados national team and led his country through preliminary ties with Grenada, Aruba and Cuba to a place in the semi-final round of the CONCACAF section of the World Cup qualifying competition for the first time ever.
Torquay U (Free from Lambada, St Vincent on 24/3/1994) FL 32+6/4 FLC 4/1 FAC 2+1 Others 3+1/1
Queens Park R (£350,000 on 9/8/1995) PL 0+7/1 FLC 0+1 FAC 0+1
Bristol C (£50,000 on 19/8/1996) FL 75+35/14 FLC 9+2/1 FAC 5+3/1 Others 1+4/1

GOODWIN Thomas (Tommy) Neil
Born: Leicester, 8 November 1979
Height: 6'0" Weight: 12.6

A product of the Leicester academy, Tommy was thrust into the limelight during the worst of City's injury problems in 1999-2000. The right-footed defender made his debut against West Ham at Filbert Street in January and did not let anyone down. He can only have benefited from the experience and will be aiming to win a more regular place in the squad during the coming season.
Leicester C (From trainee on 3/7/1998) PL 1

GORDON Dean Dwight
Born: Croydon, 10 February 1973
Height: 6'0" Weight: 13.4
Club Honours: Div 1 '94
International Honours: E: U21-13

After picking up a serious knee injury in the third game of the 1999-2000 season, Middlesbrough's left wing back was ruled out for the remainder of the campaign apart from one substitute appearance in March. When fit, Dean is a tenacious competitor who crosses the ball accurately and possesses a powerful shot. A player's value

to his team can be gauged by how much he is missed during a prolonged absence; in "Deano's" case, his contribution was shown to be immeasurable, since the defence really struggled without him.
Crystal Palace (From trainee on 4/7/1991) F/PL 181+20/20 FLC 16+3/2 FAC 14+1/1 Others 5+1
Middlesbrough (£900,000 on 17/7/1998) PL 41+1/3 FLC 2 FAC 1

GORDON Kenyatta **Gavin**
Born: Manchester, 24 June 1979
Height: 6'1" Weight: 12.0
This powerful young Lincoln striker began to show his full potential during the 1999-2000 season. His strong running and ability to win the ball in the air caused plenty of problems for opposition defences and his partnership with Lee Thorpe proved one of the most effective in the Third Division. The pair netted 29 goals between them, with Gavin hitting a career-best total of 13. He was out of contract in the summer but was reported to have agreed terms for a new deal.
Hull C (From trainee on 3/7/1996) FL 22+16/9 FLC 1+4/1 Others 1+1
Lincoln C (£30,000 on 7/11/1997) FL 69+12/19 FLC 2/1 FAC 7/1 Others 4+1

GORRE Dean
Born: Surinam, 10 September 1970
Height: 5'8" Weight: 11.7
International Honours: Holland: U21
Signed from Ajax last September, Dean was undoubtedly the bargain buy of the 1999-2000 season for Huddersfield, as the Terriers' scouting missions stretched to Holland. Once he had adjusted to the pace of the English game his outstanding midfield skills were able to flourish and he quickly established himself as one of the most skilful players on the club's books, an early glimpse of this being a spectacular long-range volley against Notts County in the Worthington Cup. Always prompting play and able to create an opening out of nothing, the Dutchman soon settled into a regular midfield role, as well as being used as an emergency striker. A hamstring injury kept him out of the side for a while before he returned with quality goals against Swindon Town, WBA and Ipswich Town. Dean was magnificent in the Sky-televised match against Manchester City, only a finger-tip save keeping out another spectacular strike. With the team pushing for promotion, however, his season turned sour with a dismissal at Swindon Town, followed by ankle ligament damage in the return against WBA. The injury was thought likely to rule him out for the rest of the campaign but he made an unexpected return in the last match of the season at Fulham.
Huddersfield T (£330,000 from Ajax, Holland on 16/9/1999) FL 26+2/4 FLC 3/1 FAC 1

GOUGH Neil
Born: Harlow, 1 September 1981
Height: 5'11" Weight: 11.8
Neil was the top scorer in the Leyton Orient team that won the South East Conference Youth Alliance in 1999-2000, and was given his first senior chance against Grimsby in the Worthington Cup in September. He made a couple of other substitute appearances before being given his full debut against Chester in April. Neil can also play as a winger, and will be looking to remain in the first-team squad in the new season.
Leyton Orient (Trainee) FL 1+3 FLC 0+1

GOUGH Richard Charles
Born: Stockholm, Sweden, 5 April 1962
Height: 6'0" Weight: 12.0
Club Honours: SPD '83, '89, '90, '91, '92, '93, '94, '95, '96, '97; SLC '89, '91, '93, '94, '97; SC '92, '93, '96
International Honours: S: 61; U21-5
Most Everton fans raised eyebrows when Walter Smith enlisted a 37-year-old centre half on a free transfer from relegated Nottingham Forest in the summer of 1999. By the end of the campaign, however, those same supporters were delighted when Richard agreed to extend his contract with the club by a further two years. One of the success stories of a much-improved Everton season, he proved an inspirational figure both on and off the pitch. "Man of the Match" on the opening day against Manchester United, he carried that form on consistently throughout the season. Dominant in the air, precise in the tackle and thoughtful in his distribution, the passing years seemed to have taken no edge off his game. He was actually installed as captain of the side until a calf injury ended his campaign five games early, but by then no one was in any doubt about the wisdom of Smith's move.
Dundee U (Free from Wits University on 21/3/1980) SL 160+8/24 SLC 33+3/9 SC 19/2 Others 30+1/3
Tottenham H (£750,000 on 17/8/1986) FL 49/2 FLC 10 FAC 6
Glasgow R (£1,500,000 on 2/10/1987) SL 318/26 SLC 35/3 SC 37/2 Others 34/4 (Free to San Jose, USA on 21/5/1998)
Nottingham F (Free on 5/3/1999) PL 7
Everton (Free on 11/6/1999) PL 29/1 FAC 3

GOULD James Robert
Born: Kettering, 15 January 1982
Height: 5'9" Weight: 11.8
A promising young midfield player who has come through the ranks at Northampton, James appeared in several pre-season friendly games during the build-up to the 1999-2000 campaign. Like fellow Northampton youth players Mark Dickson and Ryan Thompson, he made his senior debut when coming on as a substitute in the Auto Windscreens Shield game with Bristol Rovers in January, just before his 18th birthday. He was offered a professional contract the following month.
Northampton T (Trainee) Others 0+1

GOULD Ronald (Ronnie) Donald
Born: Bethnal Green, 27 September 1982
Height: 5'11" Weight: 11.5
Ronnie became the tenth Leyton Orient youth-team player to make his senior debut in 1999-2000 when he came on as a substitute at Hull in April. He is highly rated by O's manager Tommy Taylor and will be looking to be a regular squad member in 2000-01.
Leyton Orient (Trainee) FL 0+2

GRAHAM Gareth Lee
Born: Belfast, 6 December 1978
Height: 5'7" Weight: 10.2
International Honours: NI: U21-5
Gareth joined Brentford on a free transfer from Crystal Palace in September and was then loaned to Dr Martens League club Crawley Town in November. He eventually progressed to become a regular member of the Bees' first-team squad by the end of the 1999-2000 season and added four more caps for Northern Ireland at U21 level. He is combative in the tackle and a tireless worker in midfield, and will be looking to win a place in the starting line-up during the coming season.
Crystal Palace (From trainee on 19/3/1997) FL 0+1
Brentford (Free on 28/9/1999) FL 5+8

GRAHAM Mark Roland
Born: Newry, 24 October 1974
Height: 5'7" Weight: 10.12
International Honours: NI: B-4; Yth; Sch
Given a free transfer by Queens Park Rangers, for whom he started 16 league matches in 1996-97, Mark featured in Cambridge's pre-season games during the build-up to the 1999-2000 campaign. The right-sided midfielder, who is a Northern Ireland "B" international, was given a one-month contract in August but left the club after making two appearances as a substitute.
Queens Park R (From trainee on 26/5/1993) FL 16+2 FLC 2+1 FAC 2
Cambridge U (Free on 5/8/1999) FL 0+1 FLC 0+1

GRAHAM Richard Ean
Born: Dewsbury, 28 November 1974
Height: 6'2" Weight: 12.10
International Honours: RoI: U21-2
Richard was badly affected by injuries in 1999-2000 and he managed only two short runs in the Oldham first team, one last autumn and another in February. A very talented player who is comfortable on the ball, he was mostly used in a defensive central midfield role last season. Good in the air, he is particularly useful bringing the ball forward. Richard's contract at Boundary Park ended in the summer and at the time of writing it seemed he was likely to begin the 2000-01 campaign elsewhere after failing to reach agreement on a new deal.
Oldham Ath (From trainee on 16/7/1993) P/FL 139+11/14 FLC 11 FAC 13/1 Others 3

GRAINGER Martin Robert
Born: Enfield, 23 August 1972
Height: 5'11" Weight: 12.0
This reliable and competitive Birmingham City player showed his versatility by appearing in eight different positions for the club in 1999-2000. He began the season in outstanding form but was then an early victim of the Blues' injury hoodoo when he fractured a fibula in the derby match against West Bromwich Albion last September. He initially believed the injury to be a "dead

leg" and played on for 35 minutes before being substituted. He appeared mainly on the left side of defence or midfield, where his hard tackling and accurate crossing and passing were most effective. One of the highlights of his campaign was a cracking goal from a 25-yard free kick at Swindon last February, while another came in May when he was deservedly voted "Player of the Season". He missed the last few games after suffering a bad knee injury against Walsall on Easter Monday but returned to face Barnsley in the play-offs.

Colchester U (From trainee on 28/7/1992) FL 37+9/7 FLC 3 FAC 3+2 Others 3/1
Brentford (£60,000 on 21/10/1993) FL 100+1/12 FLC 6/1 FAC 9/1 Others 8/2
Birmingham C (£400,000 on 25/3/1996) FL 124+18/14 FLC 8+2/1 FAC 7+1 Others 3

GRANT Anthony (Tony) James
Born: Liverpool, 14 November 1974
Height: 5'10" Weight: 10.2
Club Honours: CS '95
International Honours: E: U21-1

An elegant midfielder with outstanding vision and the ability to deliver the ball into the openings he sees, Tony remained in the "unfulfilled potential" category at Everton in 1999-2000. He spent two months on loan at Tranmere last autumn and was so successful that the Prenton Park management would have dearly loved to make the signing permanent, lack of funds proving the obstacle. He added creativity to the centre of the Rovers team and proved to be second to none with set-piece kicks. He scored just one goal during his loan spell, netting with a 20-yard drive in the 2-0 Worthington Cup win over Oxford. Following his return to Goodison Tony had little opportunity to impress before joining Manchester City shortly before Christmas for £450,000. Two substitute appearances for his new club were followed by four league starts, but although there were signs that he would be suited to City's style of play, he was not able to command a regular place in the team and he made only one more start. Tony's manager at Maine Road is Joe Royle, his old Everton boss. Royle is a long-time admirer of his talents, and it is to be hoped that he can rekindle the career of a player with undoubted ability.

Everton (From trainee on 8/7/1993) PL 43+18/2 FLC 5+1 FAC 4+4 Others 2+2/1
Swindon T (Loaned on 18/1/1996) FL 3/1
Tranmere Rov (Loaned on 2/9/1999) FL 8+1 FLC 1/1
Manchester C (£450,000 on 24/12/1999) FL 4+4 FAC 1

GRANT Gareth Michael
Born: Leeds, 6 September 1980
Height: 5'9" Weight: 10.4

This pacy and skilful young Bradford City striker continued to make progress during 1999-2000 but has yet to make a breakthrough to regular first-team football. He made the starting line-up just once, in the Worthington Cup tie at Reading last September, and featured as a substitute only a couple of times. He scored regularly for the reserves, including a hat-trick against Bolton Wanderers, and he spent the final months of the season on loan at the Reebok Stadium after moving on transfer deadline day. Last November he received a late call-up for England U21s after injuries decimated the squad for the fixture against Yugoslavia, only to find the game cancelled for security reasons.

Bradford C (From trainee on 28/4/1998) P/FL 2+7 FLC 2+2
Halifax T (Loaned on 12/2/1999) FL 0+3 Others 0+1

GRANT John Anthony Carlton
Born: Manchester, 9 August 1981
Height: 5'11" Weight: 11.0

A promising young striker with an eye for goal, John is a product of the successful Crewe youth development programme and played regularly for the club's youth and academy U19 teams in 1999-2000. However, two days short of his 18th birthday, he was given his first-team debut on the opening day of the season when he was included in the starting line-up for the match at Crystal Palace. Although he was replaced by Paul Tait at half-time, he made five substitute appearances over the next three months and is clearly a bright prospect who can be expected to feature more regularly during the coming season.

Crewe Alex (From trainee on 7/7/1999) FL 1+3 FLC 0+2

GRANT Peter
Born: Glasgow, 30 August 1965
Height: 5'9" Weight: 11.9
Club Honours: SPL '86, '88; SC '89
International Honours: S: 2; B-2; U21-10; Yth; Sch

Although he stayed with Reading for less than a season, Peter quickly became one of the most popular players at the club. Signed on a free transfer from Norwich City in August 1999, the wiry midfield player went straight into the side and his enthusiasm and experience did much to lift those around him. He used his brain to save his legs, and passed on much of his knowledge to the youngsters he coached so conscientiously at the Reading FC Academy. Keen to further the coaching side of his game, he moved to AFC Bournemouth as player-coach just before the end of the season.

Glasgow Celtic (From juniors on 27/7/1982) SL 338+27/15 SLC 40+3/3 SC 34+4/1 Others 27/1
Norwich C (£200,000 on 22/8/1997) FL 64+4/3 FLC 4+1 FAC 2
Reading (Free on 20/8/1999) FL 27+2/1 FLC 3 FAC 0+4 Others 2

GRANT Stephen Hubert
Born: Birr, 14 April 1977
Height: 6'1" Weight: 12.0
International Honours: RoI: U21-4; Sch

Signed from Stockport on a short-term contract just before the start of the 1999-2000 season, this former Republic of Ireland U21 international striker showed some promise during his short spell at Burnley but, unable to dislodge Andy Payton and Andy Cooke, was released before making much impact. A lively forward never afraid to go for goal, Stephen never made the starting eleven but appeared as a substitute in both legs of the Worthington Cup tie against Manchester City.

Sunderland (Free from Athlone T on 10/8/1995. Free to Shamrock Rov on 17/10/1996)
Stockport Co (£30,000 on 3/9/1997) FL 10+19/4 FAC 0+1
Burnley (Free on 6/8/1999) FLC 0+2

GRANVILLE Daniel (Danny) Patrick
Born: Islington, 19 January 1975
Height: 5'11" Weight: 12.5
Club Honours: FLC '98, ECWC '98
International Honours: E: U21-3

Danny joined Manchester City on a three-month loan from Leeds at the start of the 1999-2000 season. He made his debut in the home game against Wolves on the opening day of the season but received a bad knee injury after only 15 minutes that forced him to miss the next ten league and cup games. He returned for the home win against Ipswich at the end of September and was a regular up to the game at Swindon at the start of April (missing only the match at Sheffield United due to illness). In mid-October he completed a permanent move from Elland Road for a £1 million fee. A left-sided defender who was particularly impressive when pushing forward on the overlap outside Mark Kennedy, Danny was extremely consistent and clearly revelled in the licence to attack that he enjoyed, which allowed him to score important goals in the away wins at Port Vale and West Bromwich. He is one of the fastest defenders at the club, and the speed with which he recovered denied opponents a number of scoring opportunities.

Cambridge U (From trainee on 19/5/1993) FL 89+10/7 FLC 3+2 FAC 2+2 Others 4+2
Chelsea (£300,000 + on 21/3/1997) PL 12+6 FLC 3 Others 4+1/1
Leeds U (£1,600,000 on 8/7/1998) PL 7+2 FLC 1 FAC 3 Others 0+1
Manchester C (£1,000,000 on 7/8/1999) FL 28+7/2 FAC 2

GRAVELAINE Xavier
Born: Tours, France, 5 October 1968
Height: 6'1" Weight: 12.3
International Honours: France: 4

This much-travelled French striker joined Watford, his 11th club, on a free transfer from Paris St Germain in November 1999 and left for Le Havre the following February. Despite such a fleeting stay, Xavier made an impression with his thoughtful and stylish play, most of it channelled through an educated left foot, and his departure was a matter of regret. Sent off in only his second match, against Sunderland, he had probably his best game against Southampton, when his two well-taken goals sealed a rare victory.

Watford (Free from Paris St Germain, France on 26/11/1999) PL 7/2

GRAVES Wayne Alan
Born: Scunthorpe, 18 September 1980
Height: 5'8" Weight: 12.10

Wayne made the Scunthorpe starting line-up for the first time on the opening day of the 1999-2000 season at Wigan and was a regular in the squad all campaign even though he suffered from a number of minor

injuries. Although he is versatile, and can play at either wing back, midfield, winger or striker, he is at his best running from deep, where his electric pace and determination proved a handful for opposition defences. Having played a big part in helping the club's juniors to the Wembley final of the Football League Youth Alliance Cup, Wayne can expect to feature prominently in the United first team next season.
Scunthorpe U (From trainee on 24/3/1999) FL 9+13 FLC 1+1 Others 1

GRAY Andrew (Andy) David
Born: Harrogate, 15 November 1977
Height: 6'1" Weight: 13.0
International Honours: S: Yth
Andy showed his versatility for Nottingham Forest in 1999-2000 by appearing as a right wing back as well as playing wide on the right or left of midfield. He had an extended run in the first team from November through to February, but otherwise featured only rarely as a substitute. He is a tall, right-footed player with good ball control and an excellent cross.
Leeds U (From trainee on 1/7/1995) PL 13+9 FLC 3+1 FAC 0+2
Bury (Loaned on 11/12/1997) FL 4+2/1
Nottingham F (£175,000 on 2/9/1998) P/FL 15+15 FLC 2+3 FAC 3+1
Preston NE (Loaned on 23/2/1999) FL 5
Oldham Ath (Loaned on 25/3/1999) FL 4

GRAY Ian James
Born: Manchester, 25 February 1975
Height: 6'2" Weight: 13.0
Ian continued to perform superbly for Stockport's reserves in 1999-2000, playing a significant role as the team won promotion in the Pontins League. He deputised for first-choice 'keeper Carlo Nash on a number of occasions, notably when Nash broke a finger last January, and never let the side down. An agile goalkeeper whose handling is excellent, he was transferred to Rotherham during the summer break.
Oldham Ath (From trainee on 16/7/1993)
Rochdale (Loaned on 18/11/1994) FL 12 Others 3
Rochdale (£20,000 on 17/7/1995) FL 66 FLC 4 FAC 5 Others 4
Stockport Co (£200,000 + on 30/7/1997) FL 14+2 FLC 3

GRAY Julian Raymond
Born: Lewisham, 21 September 1979
Height: 6'1" Weight: 11.0
A tall, versatile left-sided player, Julian made his first-team debut for Arsenal as a substitute in the Gunners' final Premiership game of the 1999-2000 season at Newcastle. He joined Arsenal as a trainee during the summer of 1996 and has been a regular in the U19 and reserve sides during the past two seasons. Although the left wing is his favoured position, Julian has also played at left back. He has plenty of speed, is a good crosser of the ball and is strong in the air. He is unquestionably a player for the future.
Arsenal (From trainee on 13/7/1998) PL 0+1

GRAY Kevin John
Born: Sheffield, 7 January 1972
Height: 6'0" Weight: 14.0
A gritty, robust defender, very much in the mould of Huddersfield manager Steve Bruce, Kevin started the 1999-2000 season recovering from a shoulder ligament injury. His eagerly awaited call-up didn't arrive until September, when he played in the second leg of the Worthington Cup tie against Notts County, but that was soon followed by a typically dependable and solid defensive display in a "Man of the Match" performance at Stockport County. Always dangerous at set pieces, he scored such a goal against Nottingham Forest on his 300th league appearance in November, but an injury picked up at Birmingham City in the new year unfortunately kept him on the sidelines for a while. With his never-say-die attitude the tough-tackling defender had soon reclaimed a defensive berth, hitting the back of the net against Crewe Alexandra at the McAlpine in March, but, with the team pushing for promotion, Kevin was unluckily ruled out by injury once again, an ankle problem causing him to miss the run-in.
Mansfield T (From trainee on 1/7/1990) FL 129+12/3 FLC 8/1 FAC 6+1 Others 12+2/2
Huddersfield T (Signed on 18/7/1994) FL 157+12/5 FLC 11+1 FAC 12 Others 3

GRAY Martin David
Born: Stockton on Tees, 17 August 1971
Height: 5'9" Weight: 11.4
The former Sunderland midfielder returned to his native North-east in the 1999 close season, joining Darlington from Oxford. He soon established himself in the centre of midfield with his tenacious and hard-running displays. Always a very committed competitor and great motivator, Martin missed only a handful of games all season. He is still looking for his first Darlington goal.
Sunderland (From trainee on 1/2/1990) FL 46+18/1 FLC 6+2 FAC 0+3 Others 3+1
Aldershot (Loaned on 9/1/1991) FL 3+2 Others 1
Fulham (Loaned on 20/10/1995) FL 6 Others 1
Oxford U (£100,000 on 28/3/1996) FL 115+6/4 FLC 9 FAC 4
Darlington (Free on 7/6/1999) FL 40+1 FLC 2 FAC 2 Others 4

GRAY Michael
Born: Sunderland, 3 August 1974
Height: 5'7" Weight: 10.10
Club Honours: Div 1 '96, '99
International Honours: E: 3
This talented left back became the first Sunderland player to appear for England at Wembley since Tony Towers in 1976 when he played against Sweden in June 1999. Although he certainly played his part in the Black Cats' impressive start to the 1999-2000 campaign, many fans at the Stadium of Light felt that the absence of Allan Johnston had an adverse effect on Michael as his exciting attacking forays were not as frequent as in previous seasons. Although always dependable and committed to the Sunderland cause, he even found himself ousted from his usual first-team slot for a short period, Peter Reid preferring to switch his usual right back, Chris Makin, to the opposite flank, and Michael was even used as a right winger, a position that clearly did not suit him. Speculation then began on Wearside as to whether his future lay away from the Stadium of Light but he remains a very popular figure with the Sunderland faithful and they will be hoping that the form that first brought him to the attention of Kevin Keegan will reappear next term.
Sunderland (From trainee on 1/7/1992) P/FL 238+21/14 FLC 18+4 FAC 11+1/1 Others 2

Michael Gray

GRAY Philip (Phil)
Born: Belfast, 2 October 1968
Height: 5'10" Weight: 12.5
International Honours: NI: 21; U23-1; Yth; Sch
This experienced forward has an aggressive and inventive style that is vital to Luton's game. A Northern Ireland international, he opened his account for the 1999-2000 season with the winner against Cardiff in August but his injury jinx then struck again during training, leaving him with a bad hamstring tear which was expected to keep him out until October. He then suffered two more hamstring tears before making a successful comeback as a substitute in the 1-1 draw with Chesterfield at Christmas. Back in the side, he quickly regained his scoring touch and slotted in some important goals during the second half of the season. He was out of contract at the end of the campaign, and it seemed unlikely that he would remain with the club.
Tottenham H (From apprentice on 21/8/1986) FL 4+5 FAC 0+1
Barnsley (Loaned on 17/1/1990) FL 3 FAC 1
Fulham (Loaned on 8/11/1990) FL 3 Others 2/1
Luton T (£275,000 on 16/8/1991) FL 54+5/22 FLC 4/3 FAC 2/1 Others 2
Sunderland (£800,000 on 19/7/1993) FL 108+7/34 FLC 9/4 FAC 8/3 Others 2 (Free to Nancy, France during 1996 close season)
Luton T (£400,000 from Fortuna Sittard, Holland on 19/9/1997) FL 74+7/21 FLC 9/3 FAC 3/3 Others 0+1

GRAY Stuart Edward
Born: Harrogate, 18 December 1973
Height: 5'11" Weight: 11.2
International Honours: S: U21-7

The Reading left back had a frustrating season in 1999-2000 as his first-team appearances were limited by a recurring back injury plus the arrival of new signing Matt Robinson from Portsmouth. A steady defender who is somewhat handicapped by a lack of pace but possesses a good shot, Stuart did not feature in the starting line-up for a league game after the 3-1 defeat at Luton in January and was placed on the transfer list in March. Originally a midfielder, he still has a year on his contract with Reading but has been told that he can only look forward to reserve-team football as Alan Pardew remoulds his first-team squad.

Glasgow Celtic (Free from Giffnock North AFC on 7/7/1992) SL 19+9/1 SC 1 Others 2+1
Reading (£100,000 on 27/3/1998) FL 45+5/2 FLC 8 FAC 0+1 Others 1

GRAY Wayne William
Born: Camberwell, 7 November 1980
Height: 5'10" Weight: 12.10

A free-scoring striker for the reserves, Wayne made his league and FA Cup debuts for Wimbledon last January as a substitute, although those were his only senior appearances of the season for the Dons. He subsequently moved to Swindon on loan last March and showed himself to be a quality player in the 12 games he played for the Robins. He scored two goals for the struggling First Division club, netting at Portsmouth and at home to Tranmere, and helped them to creditable victories against Huddersfield and Charlton before returning to Selhurst Park. A fine athlete, Wayne has good pace and the ability to turn defenders with ease, and 2000-01 may be the season that sees him break through into the Dons' first team.

Wimbledon (From trainee on 10/2/1999) PL 0+1 FAC 0+1
Swindon T (Loaned on 3/3/2000) FL 8+4/2

GRAYSON Neil
Born: York, 1 November 1964
Height: 5'10" Weight: 12.10
International Honours: E: SP-4

Ever-popular with the Cheltenham supporters, this super-fit player led the Robins' attack with characteristic gusto in 1999-2000 at the age of 35. Neil missed just two league games despite suffering a painful hernia in the latter part of the season. He finished top scorer at the club for the second campaign in succession, his ten league goals being supplemented by three in the cups, and his spectacular long-range volley in the 2-0 win over Plymouth Argyle will go down as one of the best goals scored at Whaddon Road for many years. Although not the tallest of forwards, Neil has the ability to time his jumps for the ball, making him a superb target man. He is willing to run all day and will chase any lost cause, using his strong frame to unsettle defenders and hold the ball up, and he shows no sign of wanting to retire despite being in his mid-thirties.

Doncaster Rov (Free from Rowntree Mackintosh on 22/3/1990) FL 21+8/6 FAC 1+1 Others 2+1/1
York C (Free on 28/3/1991) FL 0+1
Chesterfield (Free on 16/8/1991) FL 9+6 FLC 2 FAC 1 Others 1 (Free to Gateshead during 1992 close season)
Northampton T (Free from Boston U on 19/6/1994) FL 103+17/31 FLC 7+1 FAC 3 Others 10/3 (Transferred to Hereford U on 4/8/1997)
Cheltenham T (Signed on 5/3/1998) FL 39+4/10 FLC 2/1 FAC 1+1 Others 2

GRAYSON Simon Nicholas
Born: Ripon, 16 December 1969
Height: 6'0" Weight: 13.7
Club Honours: FLC '97

Simon joined Blackburn from Aston Villa during the 1999 close season and, profiting from the achilles tendon troubles of Jeff Kenna, was given first chance in the right-back position at the start of 1999-2000. First under Brian Kidd and then under Tony Parkes he appeared to be losing the contest for the position to Jeff but a bad injury suffered by Kenna at Liverpool in the FA Cup in January handed him the jersey. He was in indifferent form early on, but by March he had recovered his composure and was starting to link effectively going forward and intervene judiciously. From time to time he still made mistakes, but he was considerably sounder as the season wore on. By the end of the campaign, however, he had lost his place to Jason McAteer and he will not find it easy to regain it.

Leeds U (From trainee on 13/6/1988) FL 2 Others 1+1
Leicester C (£50,000 on 13/3/1992) F/PL 175+13/4 FLC 16+2/2 FAC 9 Others 13+1
Aston Villa (£1,350,000 on 1/7/1997) PL 32+16 FLC 1+1 FAC 4+1/2 Others 6+3
Blackburn Rov (£750,000 + on 29/7/1999) FL 31+3 FLC 0+1 FAC 2+1

GRAZIOLI Giuliano Stefano Luigi
Born: Marylebone, 23 March 1975
Height: 5'11" Weight: 12.11

Giuliano was out of contract with Peterborough at the end of the 1998-99 season and joined Swindon on a free transfer during the summer break. He made a promising start with the Robins but then missed several matches with hamstring trouble and later fractured a bone in his foot, the injury keeping him out of the team for more than four months. Returning as a substitute last March, he scored with a cracking overhead kick in the 2-1 defeat at Queens Park Rangers. Enthusiastic and always looking for the ball, he has good pace and an excellent eye for goal.

Peterborough U (Free from Wembley on 19/10/1995) FL 23+18/16 FLC 1+2 FAC 0+3/1 Others 0+2
Swindon T (Free on 15/7/1999) FL 11+8/8 FLC 2

GREAVES Mark Andrew
Born: Hull, 22 January 1975
Height: 6'1" Weight: 13.0

With the encouragement of a new two-year Hull contract, Mark began 1999-2000 – his fourth pro season – full of hope. A controversial sending-off in the opening-day defeat at Exeter and an ankle injury picked up during the Worthington Cup visit from Liverpool failed to dim his optimism. The local lad responded with a string of extremely solid performances, usually as one of three centre halves, some at right wing back. Although an ankle knock sidelined him briefly in January, the same month saw a reported £500,000 bid from Southampton. In easily coping with the Third Division's physical demands, Mark also had his best goalscoring record since hitting 11 in a season for Brigg Town in the Northern Counties East League. He capped a fine season by sweeping the board in Hull's "Player of the Year" awards.

Hull C (Free from Brigg T on 17/6/1996) FL 96+22/7 FLC 6 FAC 9/1 Others 3+1

Mark Greaves

GREEN Francis James
Born: Nottingham, 25 April 1980
Height: 5'9" Weight: 11.6

One of Peterborough's recruits from non-league football, Francis was signed from Ilkeston in March 1998. A pacy and powerful striker, he continues to fight his way ahead of more experienced and expensive Posh forwards. He usually looks dangerous when he comes off the bench, and scored his only 1999-2000 goal in the opening-day defeat of Hartlepool.

Peterborough U (£25,000 + from Ilkeston T on 2/3/1998) FL 13+18/3 FLC 0+1 FAC 1 Others 1+2

GREEN Richard Edward
Born: Wolverhampton, 22 November 1967
Height: 6'1" Weight: 13.7

With one centre back injured and two others due for suspension, Rochdale manager Steve Parkin needed an experienced replacement and signed Richard on loan from Walsall last September. He played his full part during his month with the club and might well have been signed permanently. However, a goal drought meant that a striker, rather than a defender, became Dale's main transfer priority. In January Richard was released by Walsall and signed for Northampton until the end of the season. The chances of a permanent move were increased by his immediate impact: he scored within eight minutes of his Cobblers' debut against Shrewsbury and became a more than capable replacement for the injured Lee Howey, as Northampton gained promotion to Division Two.

Shrewsbury T (From trainee on 19/7/1986) FL 120+5/5 FLC 11/1 FAC 5 Others 5/1
Swindon T (Free on 25/10/1990)
Gillingham (Free on 6/3/1992) FL 206+10/16 FLC 12+1 FAC 16+1/1 Others 6+1
Walsall (Signed on 10/8/1998) FL 22+8/1 FLC 2 FAC 2 Others 1
Rochdale (Loaned on 24/9/1999) FL 6
Northampton T (Free on 7/1/2000) FL 21/2 Others 1

GREEN Robert Paul
Born: Chertsey, 18 January 1980
Height: 6'2" Weight: 12.2
International Honours: E: Yth

Having made his debut in the local derby with Ipswich Town the previous season, Robert again found his first-team opportunities at Norwich limited by the outstanding form of Andy Marshall in 1999-2000. This former England U18 international has all the attributes necessary to go on to become a top-class goalkeeper. Athletically built, he has great agility and reflexes, making him capable of producing the very spectacular save. However, it is his temperament that sets him apart as one for the future. He is totally unflappable, as was proved when he had to make his debut in such a hothouse atmosphere, and also possesses great self-belief. Being a number two goalkeeper is always difficult and Robert will no doubt be keen to gain greater experience in 2000-01. The coaching staff at Norwich City have great faith in his potential and he is sure to press Marshall very hard for the first-choice position in the months ahead.

Norwich C (From juniors on 3/7/1997) FL 4+1

GREEN Scott Paul
Born: Walsall, 15 January 1970
Height: 5'10" Weight: 12.5
Club Honours: Div 1 '97; AMC '99

Scott is a hugely popular player among the Wigan fans, and completed a century of Football League games for the Latics during 1999-2000. He is a highly valued member of the team in the right-back position, and was given a licence to push ahead in some matches by the adoption of a three-man central defensive formation. He has plenty of confidence on the ball, and was rewarded with two league goals. A tireless worker who has a good engine, Scott was out of contract at the end of the season, and was reportedly attracting interest from Sheffield United.

Derby Co (From trainee on 20/7/1988)
Bolton W (£50,000 on 17/3/1990) P/FL 166+54/25 FLC 19+4/1 FAC 20+3/4 Others 16+4/1
Wigan Ath (£300,000 on 30/6/1997) FL 101+7/3 FLC 9 FAC 10 Others 10+1

GREENACRE Christopher (Chris) Mark
Born: Halifax, 23 December 1977
Height: 5'11" Weight: 12.8

Chris joined Mansfield on loan from Manchester City last November, a week after Lee Peacock had moved in the opposite direction, and immediately impressed with two goals for the reserves before repeating the feat on his first-team debut at home to Lincoln three days later. Much to the delight of the club's management and fans, he signed on a permanent basis after scoring six times in 11 games during his three-month loan spell. A speedy attacking player with an eye for goal, he is a real handful for opposing defenders and continued to impress during the second half of the season.

Manchester C (From trainee on 1/7/1995) FL 3+5/1 FAC 0+1
Cardiff C (Loaned on 22/8/1997) FL 11/2
Blackpool (Loaned on 5/3/1998) FL 2+2
Scarborough (Loaned on 10/12/1998) FL 10+2/2 Others 1
Mansfield T (Free on 5/11/1999) FL 31/9 Others 2

GREENE David Michael
Born: Luton, 26 October 1973
Height: 6'3" Weight: 14.4
International Honours: RoI: U21-14

A tall centre half who deservedly claimed a clean sweep of all the "Player of the Year" awards at Colchester at the end of the previous season, David had a more difficult time in 1999-2000 as the United defence in particular never had anything approaching a settled look, with David having to play with any number of partners in the middle. At the start of the season, for example, the back line included two players making their league debuts, two more with minimal experience at that level, a converted forward playing at wing back, and David! The added pressure on the defence restricted his attacking opportunities and he scored only one goal all season – but it was the winner at Oldham for Colchester's first win in 12 games, which began the revival that allowed the club to escape from relegation. David injured his knee against Bury in February and missed the rest of the season, and is expected to be leaving the U's this summer after an excellent four-year spell.

Luton T (From juniors on 3/9/1991) FL 18+1 FLC 2 FAC 1 Others 0+1
Colchester U (Loaned on 23/11/1995) FL 14/1 Others 2
Brentford (Loaned on 1/3/1996) FL 11
Colchester U (£30,000 on 21/6/1996) FL 153/15 FLC 10 FAC 7 Others 10/2

GREENING Jonathan (Jon)
Born: Scarborough, 2 January 1979
Height: 5'11" Weight: 11.7
Club Honours: EC '99
International Honours: E: U21-4; Yth

A highly talented young Manchester United forward with pace and an eye for a goal, Jonathan began last season hoping to add a few more honours to the European Cup winners' medal he gained during the treble-winning campaign. After playing in the Super Cup clash against Lazio in August, and the Worthington Cup tie against Aston Villa in October, he found that chances were few and far between. Having then played against Sturm Graz in the Champions' League in November, he remained on the fringes of first-team action. Refusing to sign a contract that had been in the offing since May 1999, he was put up for sale in February but remained at Old Trafford and was expected to agree a new deal during the summer.

York C (From trainee on 23/12/1996) FL 5+20/2 FLC 0+1 Others 1
Manchester U (£500,000 + on 25/3/1998) PL 1+6 FLC 4 FAC 0+1 Others 2+2

GREGAN Sean Matthew
Born: Guisborough, 29 March 1974
Height: 6'2" Weight: 14.7
Club Honours: Div 2'00

Sean demonstrated a growing maturity for Preston in 1999-2000, channelling his aggression in a much more constructive way than in previous seasons. He scored his first goal of the campaign at Gillingham and next found the net in his 250th Football League game at Bury, before picking up a calf injury described by the North End physio as "the worst I've ever seen". His determined tackling and developing passing skills were sorely missed while he was injured, and also made him a marked man, as demonstrated when he picked up a cracked bone in his back after a challenge made during a tumultuous performance at the JJB Stadium. Selected for the PFA award-winning Second Division team for the second consecutive season, he made a key contribution to Preston's Second Division championship triumph.

Darlington (From trainee on 20/1/1991) FL 129+7/4 FLC 8 FAC 7 Others 10+1/1
Preston NE (£350,000 on 29/11/1996) FL 127+3/9 FLC 9 FAC 13/1 Others 7

Sean Gregan

GREGG Matthew (Matt) Stephen
Born: Cheltenham, 30 November 1978
Height: 5'11" Weight: 12.0

Matthew was the Crystal Palace reserve 'keeper and second choice to Fraser Digby before breaking through to make his first-team debut at Fulham last April, some 18 months after signing for the Selhurst Park club. Alert and agile, he has plenty of promise and will be looking to appear more regularly during the coming season.

Torquay U (From trainee on 4/7/1997) FL 32 FLC 5 FAC 1 Others 1
Crystal Palace (£400,000 on 24/10/1998) FL 6
Swansea C (Loaned on 12/2/1999) FL 5

GREGORY Andrew (Andy)
Born: Barnsley, 10 October 1976
Height: 5'10" Weight: 11.6
Signed for the season on loan from Barnsley in September 1999, Andy made several early appearances in Carlisle's midfield, scoring one goal against Halifax with a stunning 30-yard effort. However, he then faded from the scene apart from one brief appearance as a substitute in April. He was not offered further terms by Carlisle.
Barnsley (From trainee on 4/7/1995)
Carlisle U (Loaned on 17/9/1999) FL 6+1/1 Others 0+1

GREGORY David Spencer
Born: Hadleigh, 23 January 1970
Height: 5'10" Weight: 12.8
Although renowned in the past as a true utility player, David completed almost the entire 1999-2000 season for Colchester in his preferred role of central midfield. Surprisingly, having been United's leading goalscorer for the previous two seasons, he ended the last campaign having missed only one game, but without a goal to his name! He captained the side whenever Richard Wilkins was out injured, and consistently gave a wholehearted and hard-working display in the middle of the park.
Ipswich T (From trainee on 31/3/1987) F/PL 16+16/2 FLC 3+2 FAC 1 Others 3+2/4
Hereford U (Loaned on 9/1/1995) FL 2 Others 1
Peterborough U (Free on 4/7/1995) FL 0+3 FLC 1 FAC 1 Others 2
Colchester U (Free on 8/12/1995) FL 169+12/17 FLC 7+1/2 FAC 7/2 Others 13/2

GRIEMINK Bart
Born: Holland, 29 March 1972
Height: 6'4" Weight: 15.4
This tall Dutch goalkeeper joined Swindon on loan last February as cover for the injured Frank Talia. He did well in the four games he played for the Robins but he was then recalled by Peterborough when first-choice 'keeper Mark Tyler was sidelined by a shoulder injury. Having waited patiently for his chance at London Road, Bart proved an able deputy, confirming that he is a fine shot stopper who gets down well for a big man. Swindon boss Jimmy Quinn had indicated that he was intending to take him to Wiltshire on a permanent basis. However, he was later relieved of his duties and since the Dutchman was out of contract at Posh at the end of the season, his future was somewhat unclear. Bart came to England in 1995, current Peterborough chief Barry Fry signing him for Birmingham.
Birmingham C (Free from WK Emmen, Holland on 9/11/1995) FL 20 FLC 3 FAC 1 Others 1+1
Peterborough U (£25,000 on 11/10/1996) FL 58 FLC 1 FAC 4 Others 4
Swindon T (Loaned on 5/2/2000) FL 4

GRIFFIN Andrew (Andy)
Born: Billinge, 7 March 1979
Height: 5'9" Weight: 10.10
International Honours: E: U21-1; Yth
Andy is a young full back who had hoped to establish himself in the Newcastle side last season. Although naturally right footed, his abilities enable him to perform equally well on either flank, while his pace and stamina mean he is just as much at home at wing back as he is at full back. Although facing a set-back when he was suspended at the start of the season because of a dismissal in a pre-season game, he then suffered a stress fracture of the lower spine which proved to be a long-term problem that would sideline him for most of the season. He finally returned to first-team action for Newcastle at the end of April when he appeared as an 88th-minute substitute against Coventry, followed by just four minutes against Middlesbrough, and he then started in the last game of the season at right back at home to Arsenal, a game in which he was delighted to notch his first-ever goal for the club. Andy is a talented player who, given freedom from injury, has the ability to become a fixture in the side for years to come. Already capped by England at U18 level, his potential was recognised by U21s manager Howard Wilkinson, who called him up to the squad towards the end of the season.
Stoke C (From trainee on 5/9/1996) FL 52+5/2 FLC 4+1 FAC 2
Newcastle U (£1,500,000 + on 30/1/1998) PL 19+2/1 FLC 1 FAC 3 Others 1

GRIFFIN Antony Richard
Born: Bournemouth, 22 March 1979
Height: 5'11" Weight: 11.2
Antony is a very quick right-sided player who joined Cheltenham on the eve of the 1999-2000 season from AFC Bournemouth for a tribunal-set £25,000 fee. He made a promising start to the campaign, catching defenders out with his speed and close control, but then suffered a series of injuries, including a fractured cheekbone, that disrupted his season. His preferred position is on the right side of midfield, but he can also play at right back or right wing back.
Bournemouth (From trainee on 7/7/1997) FL 1+5
Cheltenham T (Signed on 27/7/1999) FL 14+10 FLC 2

GRIFFIN Charles (Charlie) John
Born: Bath, 25 June 1979
Height: 6'0" Weight: 12.7
Having joined Swindon from non-league football in 1998-99, Charlie was expected to stake a claim for a regular place in the team last season. However, after several early-season outings from the subs' bench he was loaned to Conference outfit Yeovil Town in October and it was not until the last few games of the campaign that he made the starting line-up. As a striker he showed that he has the ability to be in the right place at the right time but he still needs to build up the physical side of his game.
Swindon T (£10,000 from Chippenham T on 29/1/1999) FL 7+19/2 FLC 0+1 FAC 0+1

GRIFFITHS Carl Brian
Born: Welshpool, 15 July 1971
Height: 5'11" Weight: 11.10
International Honours: W: B-1; U21-2; Yth
This striker began last season with Port Vale, but a combination of injuries and suspension limited his appearances to just a handful, all of which came from the subs' bench. He managed one goal, in the crazy 4-4 draw with Chester in the Worthington Cup, but returned to Leyton Orient for a fee of £80,000 in December. Only nine months after leaving for Vale Park, Carl made a glorious start to his third spell with the O's by hitting a hat-trick in the momentous 5-1 win at Chester. Unfortunately, he was then sidelined with a calf problem for 14 games before returning towards the end of the campaign. Carl will hope to put his injuries behind him in the new term, when he will be aiming to become the first Orient marksman to score twenty league goals in a season since Peter Kitchen in 1977-78.
Shrewsbury T (From trainee on 26/9/1988) FL 110+33/54 FLC 7+4/3 FAC 6/2 Others 7+3/3
Manchester C (£500,000 on 29/10/1993) PL 11+7/4 FLC 0+1 FAC 2
Portsmouth (£200,000 on 17/8/1995) FL 2+12/2 FLC 0+1
Peterborough U (£225,000 on 28/3/1996) FL 6+10/2 FLC 0+2/1 FAC 1+1/1 Others 0+1
Leyton Orient (Loaned on 31/10/1996) FL 5/3
Leyton Orient (£100,000 on 7/3/1997) FL 60+5/29 FLC 7+1/3 FAC 5/2 Others 2
Wrexham (Loaned on 13/1/1999) FL 4/3 Others 1/1
Port Vale (£100,000 on 25/3/1999) FL 3+5/1 FLC 0+2/1
Leyton Orient (£80,000 on 16/12/1999) FL 11/4

GRIFFITHS Gareth John
Born: Winsford, 10 April 1970
Height: 6'4" Weight: 14.0
Tremendously strong in the air and hard to pass, Gareth found his first-team opportunities at Wigan limited in 1999-2000. However, when called upon, he proved to be an invaluable squad member who can consider himself unlucky not to start more games. The tall, imposing centre half's only league goal came in the 5-1 thrashing of Blackpool in March.
Port Vale (£1,000 from Rhyl on 8/2/1993) FL 90+4/4 FLC 8 FAC 7/1 Others 7
Shrewsbury T (Loaned on 31/10/1997) FL 6
Wigan Ath (Free on 2/7/1998) FL 30+6/1 FLC 4/1 FAC 2 Others 3+1

GRIFFITHS Michael Antony
Born: Birmingham, 14 March 1970
Height: 5'11" Weight: 13.4
This former Worcester City striker was signed by Torquay last October after a couple of trials. He had caught manager Wes Saunders's eye during the clubs' FA Cup meeting in November 1998. Michael broke his leg in his first trial game, but was subsequently invited back to Devon. He has a never-say-die attitude and chases every lost cause. When introduced, Michael added strength to a rather lightweight strike force. He was the most natural target man at Plainmoor, before being released in May.
Torquay U (Signed from Worcester C on 22/10/1999) FL 8+14/3 FAC 0+3 Others 3/2

GRIMANDI Gilles
Born: Gap, France, 11 November 1970
Height: 6'0" Weight: 12.7
Club Honours: PL '98; FAC '98; CS '98, '99
Gilles is a versatile member of the Arsenal squad who is able to play either in defence or in midfield as the situation demands. He is a great team player with grit and enthusiasm, and is very much an unsung hero who rarely lets the team down. A strong tackler and fine header of the ball, he

has good distribution skills, and his commitment was rewarded with a number of well-taken goals last season. Although he was a steady performer throughout the campaign, he will be looking to improve his disciplinary record in 2000-01.

Arsenal (£1,500,000 from Monaco, France, via FC Gap, on 25/6/1997) PL 46+12/3 FLC 7 FAC 7+3/1 Others 11+3/1

GRITTON Martin
Born: Glasgow, 1 June 1978
Height: 6'1" Weight: 12.7

Martin originally joined Plymouth on a month's contract in August 1998 but his impressive performances in 1999-2000 have earned him a three-year deal. A tall, tricky centre forward, he has good pace and is comfortable on the ball. Martin started well with a goal on his full debut against Walsall in the Worthington Cup, and developed throughout the campaign. He will be pushing for a more regular first-team place next season, while combining his football with studies at Portsmouth University.

Plymouth Arg (Free from Porthleven on 7/8/1998) FL 14+18/6 FLC 1/1 FAC 0+3 Others 1

GROVES Paul
Born: Derby, 28 February 1966
Height: 5'11" Weight: 11.5
Club Honours: AMC '98

Paul's outstanding record of not having missed a game during his two spells at Grimsby came to a sad end last season after he was uncharacteristically sent off in the away game at Wolverhampton. Nevertheless, the Mariners' captain once again turned in his usual immaculate displays in midfield despite the fact that the goals were not so plentiful as in 1998-99. Paul also produced some fine displays as a central defender after a series of long-term injuries decimated the Grimsby squad in this position.

Leicester C (£12,000 from Burton A on 18/4/1988) FL 7+9/1 FLC 1/1 FAC 0+1 Others 0+1
Lincoln C (Loaned on 20/8/1989) FL 8/1 FLC 2
Blackpool (£60,000 on 25/1/1990) FL 106+1/21 FLC 6/1 FAC 9/4 Others 13/3
Grimsby T (£150,000 on 12/8/1992) FL 183+1/38 FLC 10+1/2 FAC 12/2 Others 4/1
West Bromwich A (£600,000 on 8/7/1996) FL 27+2/4 FLC 2/1 FAC 1
Grimsby T (£250,000 on 21/7/1997) FL 135/24 FLC 16/5 FAC 8/1 Others 10/2

GUDJOHNSEN Eidur Smari
Born: Reykjavik, Iceland, 15 September 1978
Height: 6'1" Weight: 13.0
International Honours: Iceland: 4; Yth

To quote last year's *Factfile*, "Eidur will definitely score goals in the future, no matter what league he is playing in." How prophetic that statement turned out to be. After he forced his way into the Bolton team at the end of the 1998-99 campaign, last season was the one when Eidur made a definite name for himself with a string of top-class performances and top-class goals. The one-time strike partner of Ronaldo proved himself to be one of the hottest properties outside the Premiership, if not the hottest of them all. Despite a relatively modest start to the season in goalscoring terms (only four goals scored in his first 13 games), Eidur still produced some excellent performances where he created a vast number of chances for himself, and it was obvious that the best was yet to come. When that best did come, he was breathtaking. A consistent scorer for the rest of the season, the Icelander produced some quite stunning goals which were a joy to behold. Perhaps the pick of a fine bunch came in the Worthington Cup quarter-final at the Reebok against Wimbledon. Picking the ball up around the half-way line, Eidur set off on a mazy run which took him past six or seven bewildered Dons players before unleashing an unstoppable drive which left Neil Sullivan stranded and produced the only goal of the game. This was quickly proclaimed as one of the goals of the season and prompted Bolton manager Sam Allardyce to immediately put a £10 million price tag on Eidur's head. While this may be a little excessive, Eidur's performances reportedly attracted the attentions of top clubs such as Liverpool, Newcastle, Sunderland, Middlesbrough and Chelsea in the closing stages of last season. Indeed, Jim Smith of Derby had a bid supposedly in the region of £3 million turned down flat by Bolton soon after his Wimbledon wonder goal. It is quite obvious that Eidur's talents are suited to a bigger stage than the Nationwide League, and it will prove to be difficult for Bolton to hold on to their prized asset for much longer. Eidur won three more caps for Iceland during the season, scoring in the 3-0 victory over Andorra last September. Stop Press: He was transferred to Chelsea in the middle of June for a fee of £4 million.

Bolton W (Free from KR Reykjavik, Iceland, via Valur and PSV Eindhoven, on 6/8/1998) FL 48+7/18 FLC 8+1/4 FAC 4+1/4 Others 4/1

Eidur Gudjohnsen

GUDJONSSON Bjarne
Born: Iceland, 26 February 1979
Height: 5'9" Weight: 11.9
Club Honours: AMC '00
International Honours: Iceland: 7

The son of the Stoke manager Gudjon Thordarson, Bjarne was signed from Genk for £250,000 last March after some initial hesitation on the part of the City board. The second of three brothers who all started the 1999-2000 season with the Belgian club, this 20-year-old is equally at home at full back or on the right side of midfield. A full international who played for Iceland under his father, he made an early favourable impression and his quick free kick in the final of the Auto Windscreens Shield at Wembley led to Peter Thorne's winning goal. He is clearly one for the future and looks capable of playing at higher levels, although he had a previous spell in England at Newcastle, where he failed to make the grade after spending 18 months at St James' Park. Bjarne added a further international cap when appearing for Iceland against Andorra last September.

Newcastle U (£500,000 from Akranes, Iceland on 14/7/1997. £125,000 to KRC Genk, Belgium on 12/11/1998)
Stoke C (£250,000 from KRC Genk, Belgium on 10/3/2000) FL 7+1/1 Others 2+3

GUDMUNDSSON Johann Birnir
Born: Reykjavik, Iceland, 5 December 1977
Height: 5'9" Weight: 13.0
International Honours: Iceland: 3; U21

The Icelandic international midfielder failed to command a first-team place at Watford in 1999-2000, though he was a regular on the bench. At his best playing wide on the right, Johann is a neat ball player who needs to impose himself more if he is to make the most of his ability.

Watford (Signed from IBK Keflavik, Iceland on 26/3/1998) P/FL 7+15/2 FLC 0+1 FAC 0+1

GUINAN Stephen (Steve) Anthony
Born: Birmingham, 24 December 1975
Height: 6'1" Weight: 13.7

A tall, powerful central striker who can hold the ball up and score goals, Steve was once again unable to command a regular place at Nottingham Forest in 1999-2000. He had been a target of Scunthorpe boss Brian Laws for a couple of years and, after making one appearance as a substitute against Grimsby in August and featuring in the starting line-up for the Worthington Cup game at Mansfield, he moved to Glanford Park on loan in September. He scored on his home debut against Bristol City but started only two games before electing to return to Forest after just one month. He then signed for Cambridge on non-contract terms in December but struggled to make an impact and was released after three months at the club. In March, this hard-working forward, moved to Plymouth, hoping to recapture the form that brought him seven goals from 11 appearances when he was on loan at Home Park the previous season. The hard-working forward quickly becoming a fixture in the Pilgrims' team, he scored twice in their final game of the season at Mansfield.

Nottingham F (From trainee on 7/1/1993) F/PL 2+5 FLC 2/1
Darlington (Loaned on 14/12/1995) FL 3/1
Burnley (Loaned on 27/3/1997) FL 0+6

Crewe Alex (Loaned on 19/3/1998) FL 3
Halifax T (Loaned on 16/10/1998) FL 12/2
Plymouth Arg (Loaned on 24/3/1999) FL 11/7
Scunthorpe U (Loaned on 10/9/1999) FL 2+1/1
Cambridge U (Free on 24/12/1999) FL 4+2 FAC 0+2 Others 1
Plymouth Arg (Free on 23/3/2000) FL 8/2

GUNNARSSON Brynjar Bjorn
Born: Iceland, 16 October 1975
Height: 6'1" Weight: 11.12
International Honours: Iceland: 21

This Icelandic international joined Stoke last January in a complicated deal with Orgryte that involved fees to two clubs; he cost Stoke around £600,000, one of the highest fees ever paid by the club. Initially seen by Gudjon Thordarson as a midfielder, he slotted into a central defensive role as the team switched to a 4-4-2 system and was outstanding in Stoke's victory in the final of the Auto Windscreens Shield at Wembley. Known for his outlandish footwear on the pitch, Brynjar will develop into a fine signing whatever his final role in the side. He won three further caps for Iceland and his splendid goal against France at the Stade de France provided testament to the fact that he is a big-occasion player.

Stoke C (£600,000 from Orgryte IS, Sweden on 4/1/2000) FL 21+1/1 Others 8/1

GUNNLAUGSSON Arnar Bergmann
Born: Akranes, Iceland, 6 March 1973
Height: 6'0" Weight: 11.10
Club Honours: FLC '00
International Honours: Iceland: 31

The left-footed midfielder or occasional striker did not really break into the Leicester first team in the way he had hoped for during 1999-2000. Nevertheless, he played a crucial role in the Foxes' success last season, getting them off to a scoring start in each of the three penalty shoot-outs during the club's two cup runs. Despite Arnar's disappointments at Filbert Street, Stoke manager Gudjon Thordarson had not forgotten him from their time together at Akranes and with the Icelandic national team, and took him to the Britannia Stadium on loan in March for the rest of the season. Blessed with a great left foot and impressive dribbling skills, Arnar was used either on the left side of midfield or in a withdrawn striking role. He finally played at Wembley in the Auto Windscreens Shield final after two previous trips to the famous old stadium when he had sat in the stand to watch. Arnar had earlier netted an important penalty against Wycombe that saved a point and put the club back on the road to a promotion push. Arnar is the twin brother of Preston's Bjarke Gunnlaugsson.

Bolton W (£100,000 from IA Akranes, Iceland, via Feyenoord, Nuremberg and Sochaux, on 7/8/1997) P/FL 24+18/13 FLC 6+3/2 FAC 1+1
Leicester C (£2,000,000 on 5/2/1999) PL 7+4 FLC 0+2 FAC 2+1
Stoke C (Loaned on 3/3/2000) FL 10+3/2 Others 5/1

GUNNLAUGSSON Bjarke Bergman
Born: Akranes, Iceland, 6 March 1973
Height: 5'9" Weight: 11.7
Club Honours: Div 2 '00
International Honours: Iceland: 27

Signed by Preston until the end of the 1999-2000 season after playing in the Icelandic Cup final in September, the twin brother of Leicester's Arnar was at first a regular substitute for his new club. His first start came against Enfield in the FA Cup, with his first goal coming in the replay, and then, in only his second start, he scored a hat-trick against Wrexham in the Auto Windscreens Shield. Called up by Iceland for the Nordic Cup matches last February, the tricky ball-playing winger won two further caps and scored the winner in a 3-2 victory over the Faroe Isles. Highly regarded by his team-mates and the North End fans, Bjarke must have despaired of ever scoring a league goal, but it finally arrived at the 23rd attempt, away to Bristol Rovers. Hard to dispossess and boasting two good feet, he ended his first season in English football with a Second Division championship medal, and his long-term future remains at Deepdale.

Preston NE (Free from KR Reykjavik, Iceland on 30/9/1999) FL 12+14/1 FLC 0+1 FAC 3+3/1 Others 2/4

Steve Guppy

GUPPY Stephen (Steve) Andrew
Born: Winchester, 29 March 1969
Height: 5'11" Weight: 11.12
Club Honours: FAT '91, '93; GMVC '93; FLC '00
International Honours: E: 1; B-1; U21-1; SP-1

Good early-season form for Leicester in 1999-2000 meant Steve was touted as a possible answer to England's problems on the left side of midfield and he was duly capped against Belgium at the Stadium of Light last October. His performance that night was steady rather than spectacular and that rather summed up his showing in a season that was blighted by a cartilage operation in December. Steve returned to action ahead of schedule to help City lift the Worthington Cup but took some time to recapture full fitness and confidence in the knee. Two of his trademark corners provided the ammunition for Matt Elliott to head the vital goals at Wembley. He showed signs of getting back to his best when he slotted home the winner against Leeds at Filbert Street in March – a goal that virtually ended the Yorkshiremen's title hopes – but was subsequently troubled further by a trapped nerve that manifested itself in back and hamstring problems.

Wycombe W (Signed from Colden Common on 1/9/1989) FL 41/8 FLC 4 FAC 8/2 Others 10
Newcastle U (£150,000 on 2/8/1994) FLC 0+1
Port Vale (£225,000 on 25/11/1994) FL 102+3/12 FLC 7 FAC 8 Others 7+1/1
Leicester C (£950,000 on 28/2/1997) PL 116+2/8 FLC 14 FAC 6/1 Others 2

GURNEY Andrew (Andy) Robert
Born: Bristol, 25 January 1974
Height: 5'10" Weight: 11.6

One of the few players to justify the transfer fee paid by Tommy Burns during his spell as Reading manager, Andy kept a regular place in the Royals' first team until near the end of the 1999-2000 season, when he gave way to Graham Murty, although he remained a reliable squad member. He was at his best playing as an attacking wing back, when he not only defended stoutly but also made assertive runs down the right flank. He has a good shot on him, too, and was unlucky not to score more than the couple of mid-season goals he did record in consecutive away games.

Bristol Rov (From trainee on 10/7/1992) FL 100+8/9 FLC 7/1 FAC 5 Others 15
Torquay U (Free on 10/7/1997) FL 64/10 FLC 6 FAC 5/1 Others 3
Reading (£100,000 on 15/1/1999) FL 40+6/2 FLC 3 FAC 5 Others 3

GUSTAFSSON Tomas
Born: Stockholm, Sweden, 7 May 1973
Height: 5'10" Weight: 12.3
International Honours: Sweden: 5

Tomas is an experienced full back who joined Coventry in December 1999 from AIK Stockholm for £250,000. After a handful of substitute appearances he made his first start at Old Trafford and kept his place before sustaining an injury at Arsenal. He was certainly not overawed against Manchester United and did a good marking job on Sunderland's Kevin Kilbane in the next game. He looked a useful acquisition with his muscular build and good close skills. His injury kept him out until the end of the season but he recovered in time to win a place in the Sweden squad for the Euro 2000 finals and he appeared in the 2-1 defeat by Italy. Tomas made his debut as a full international against Austria last August and looks set to become the successor to Roland Nilsson for both club and country.

Coventry C (£250,000 from AIK Solna, Sweden on 17/12/1999) PL 7+3 FAC 0+2

GUTTRIDGE Luke
Born: Barnstaple, 27 March 1982
Height: 5'5" Weight: 9.7

Luke is a diminutive Torquay YT midfield player with a big heart. He was used as a non-playing substitute on a number of occasions during 1999-2000, and made his first playing appearance as a substitute two minutes from the end of the 4-0 win against Mansfield in April 2000.

Torquay U (Trainee) FL 0+1

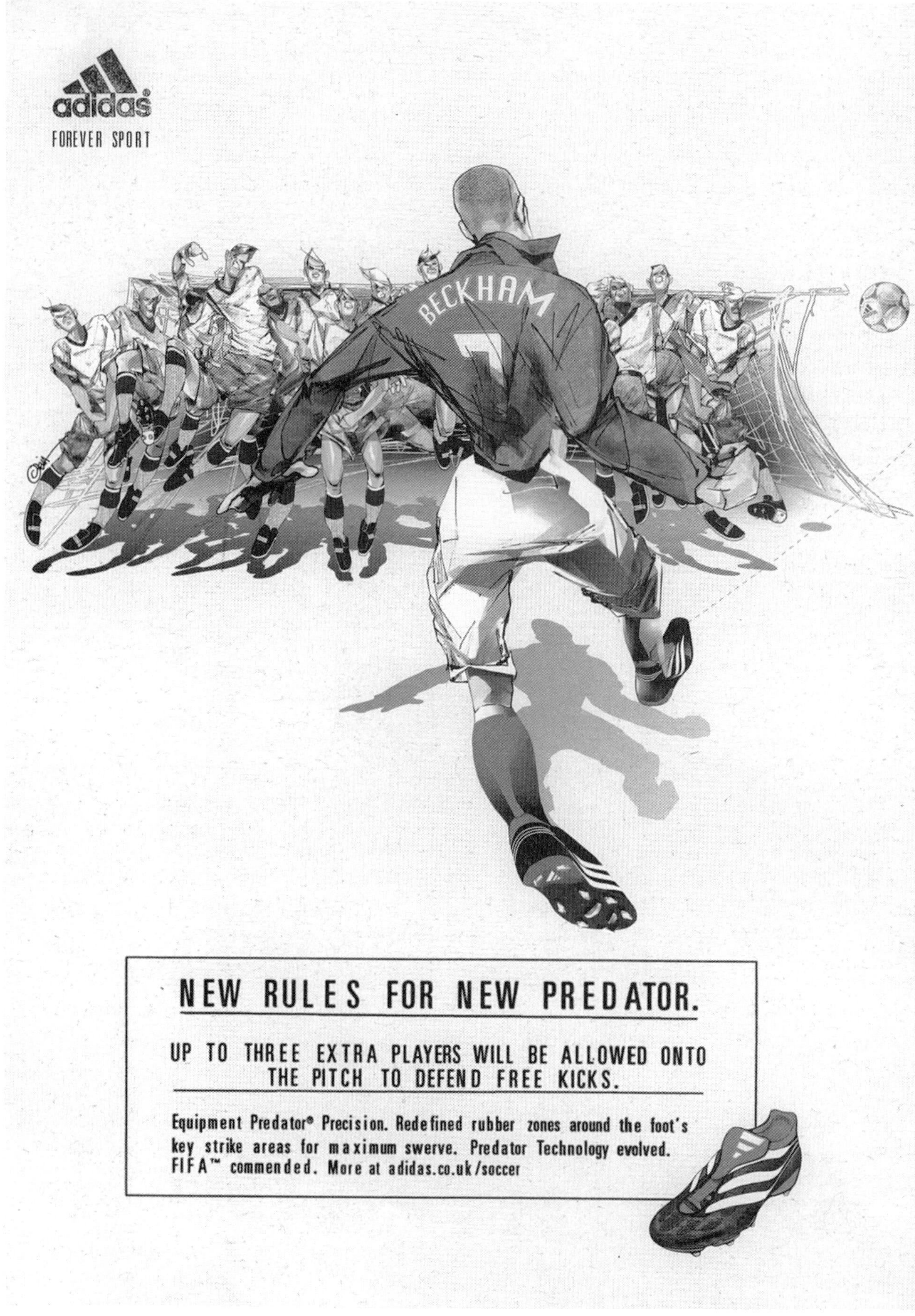

NEW RULES FOR NEW PREDATOR.

UP TO THREE EXTRA PLAYERS WILL BE ALLOWED ONTO THE PITCH TO DEFEND FREE KICKS.

Equipment Predator® Precision. Redefined rubber zones around the foot's key strike areas for maximum swerve. Predator Technology evolved. FIFA™ commended. More at adidas.co.uk/soccer

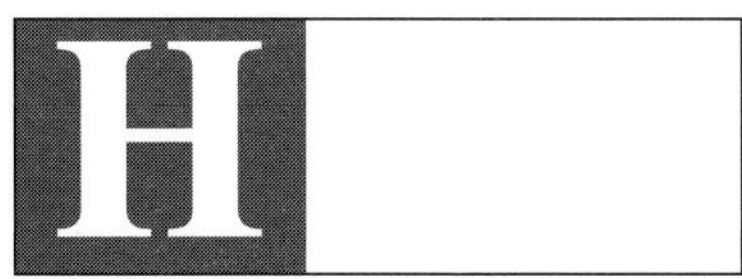

HAALAND Alf-Inge (Alfie) Rasdal
Born: Stavanger, Norway, 23 November 1972
Height: 5'10" Weight: 12.12
International Honours: Norway: 33

A versatile Norwegian, Alfie somewhat surprisingly found himself out of the Leeds first team last season until February, but after his inclusion in the side, he produced some excellent performances in central defence. He shone in the UEFA Cup matches with AS Roma and Slavia Prague, and was one of the more influential players in Rome. This came after he had been regularly linked with a number of other clubs by the media. Alfie proved what a valuable member of the Elland Road squad he is in 1999-2000, but will he be satisfied with a bit-part role? Only time will tell. Stop Press: It was reported in the middle of June that he had moved to Manchester City for a fee of £2.5 million.

Nottingham F (Signed from Bryne, Norway on 25/1/1994) F/PL 66+9/7 FLC 2+5 FAC 5+1 Others 2+3
Leeds U (£1,600,000 on 17/7/1997) PL 57+17/8 FLC 3 FAC 5+1 Others 7+2

HAARHOFF James (Jimmy) Phiri
Born: Lusaka, Zambia, 27 May 1981
Height: 5'5" Weight: 10.2

This talented young Birmingham City striker made his Football League debut last October when he came on as a late substitute for Dele Adebola against Crystal Palace. Jimmy came up through the ranks at St Andrews and appeared regularly for the club's reserve team during 1999-2000.

Birmingham C (From trainee on 12/6/1998) FL 0+1

HACKETT Christopher (Chris) James
Born: Oxford, 1 March 1983
Height: 6'0" Weight: 11.6

An Oxford United youngster, Chris came through the ranks to make a couple of substitute appearances at senior level towards the end of last season. He has tremendous pace, and is also a county-standard athlete with good times in the sprints. A striker, he looks to have a good career ahead of him and will be pushing for a regular spot next season. Chris scored his first goal for the first team in an end-of-season testimonial match against Manchester United.

Oxford U (From trainee on 20/4/2000) FL 0+2

HACKETT Warren James
Born: Plaistow, 16 December 1971
Height: 6'0" Weight: 12.5
Club Honours: FAYC '90
International Honours: St Lucia: 37

For the burly Barnet stopper, 1999-2000 proved to be a season of mixed fortunes. During the opening half of the term, Warren excelled in his role in the central defensive trio, proving to be both a thoughtful and a solid defender, with his phenomenal strength and acute positional awareness proving to be real assets to the side. His opening goal for the Bees arrived in the dramatic Worthington Cup match against Bournemouth and he was an integral part of the club's early-season success. He subsequently added to his tally in the Auto Windscreens Shield tie against Reading. But after that his luck began to change significantly. A suspension in March allowed Mike Basham to stake a claim for his place in the line-up and for the remainder of the campaign Warren was restricted to a handful of appearances. His season was ended prematurely when he suffered a knee injury in the home victory against Rotherham in April. He won a further cap for St Lucia but was unable to inspire them to victory over Surinam in the World Cup qualifying competition and they eventually went out on penalties.

Leyton Orient (Free from Tottenham H juniors on 3/7/1990) FL 74+2/3 FLC 4 FAC 8/2 Others 7
Doncaster Rov (Free on 26/7/1994) FL 46/2 FLC 4 FAC 1 Others 4
Mansfield T (£50,000 on 20/10/1995) FL 114+3/5 FLC 4 FAC 7 Others 2
Barnet (Free on 25/3/1999) FL 37+4/1 FLC 2/1 FAC 1 Others 1/1

HADDOW Alexander (Alex)
Born: Aldershot, 8 January 1982
Height: 5'8" Weight: 11.2

This talented young wide-left player graduated through Reading's centre of excellence and academy sides to make his first-team debut in a Worthington Cup tie at Peterborough last August. That was his only full appearance, although he played part of the two following games and was a non-playing substitute for four later matches. Although slightly built, he has a devastating turn of pace and likes to take defenders on. He has been rewarded with a full professional contract, and looks to have a promising future with the Royals.

Reading (From trainee on 18/3/2000) FL 1+1 FLC 1

HADJI Moustapha
Born: Ifrane, Morocco, 16 November 1971
Height: 6'0" Weight: 11.10
International Honours: Morocco: 60

It was a major coup for Coventry when they signed Moustapha from Spanish side Deportivo La Coruna in August 1999 for a then club record fee of £4 million. A star from the World Cup in 1998 and the African "Footballer of the Year" the same year, he showed his class from the start. The Moroccan with the effortless first touch played mainly in a left-sided midfield role. He reached peak fitness by the start of autumn and treated Coventry fans to some superb ball skills and dribbling displays which lit up the dark afternoons. His first goal, a header against West Ham, illustrated his deceptive ability in the air. He scored a staggering goal direct from a free kick against Newcastle and followed it up with a thunderous volley against Watford. At Christmas he scored another memorable goal in the defeat of Arsenal and his "Man of the Match" performance against Sunderland in February was stunning. Moustapha remained a regular for the Moroccan national team, winning a further nine caps during the season and appearing in his country's disappointing African Nations' Cup campaign. He will be looking to stamp his authority on the Premiership once again in 2000-01 and to turn around Coventry's dreadful record away from Highfield Road.

Coventry C (£4,000,000 from Deportivo La Coruna, Spain on 3/8/1999) PL 33/6 FLC 1 FAC 2

HAILS Julian
Born: Lincoln, 20 November 1967
Height: 5'10" Weight: 11.1

Sadly, Julian announced his retirement from the game in April 2000, finally succumbing to knee injuries that had dogged him since Christmas 1998. Julian's all-action style was greatly missed in the Southend defence during a disappointing 1999-2000 season. He accepted his fate after a ten-minute substitute outing at Mansfield in January. It was his only appearance of the campaign and the last of his league career.

Fulham (Signed from Hemel Hempstead on 29/8/1990) FL 99+10/12 FLC 5+1 FAC 2 Others 9/1
Southend U (Free on 2/12/1994) FL 143+18/7 FLC 9+2 FAC 3+1 Others 3

HALEY Grant Richard
Born: Bristol, 20 September 1979
Height: 5'8" Weight: 10.6

This young right back has been associated with Peterborough since the age of 14. Grant made good progress through the club's excellent academy to enjoy an impressive senior debut against Southend in October 1999. He was preferred to Northern Ireland U21 international Gerrard Lyttle as a replacement for the suspended Dean Hooper. Grant is a steady defender who, despite his lack of inches, is very effective in the air.

Peterborough U (From trainee on 6/7/1998) FL 1

HALFORD Stephen (Steve) Paul
Born: Bury, 21 September 1980
Height: 5'10" Weight: 12.10

One of a crop of Bury-born youngsters who were given a first-team opportunity by their home-town club in the latter stages of last season, this 19-year-old central defender appeared as a substitute in the Shakers' final home game against Reading and went on to record his full Football League debut in the final fixture of the campaign, away at Notts County. A player who has worked tremendously hard in the youth and reserve teams over the last few seasons to improve his game and earn his big chance, Steve is highly rated by the Gigg Lane hierarchy and should make an even bigger impression next season.

Bury (From trainee on 9/7/1999) FL 1+1

HALL Gareth David
Born: Croydon, 12 March 1969
Height: 5'8" Weight: 12.0
Club Honours: Div 2 '89; Div 1 '96; FMC '90
International Honours: E: Sch. W: 9; U21-1

This experienced Swindon defender showed that he is still a classy performer in 1999-2000 despite playing in a struggling team. He rarely missed a game and, although a little short of pace, he made up for it with an excellent first touch and good passing skills. Gareth is very versatile and can play at full back, as a central defender or in midfield.

Chelsea (From apprentice on 25/4/1986) F/PL 120+18/4 FLC 12+1 FAC 6 Others 10+4/1
Sunderland (£300,000 on 20/12/1995) P/FL 41+7 FLC 3 FAC 2
Brentford (Loaned on 3/10/1997) FL 6
Swindon T (Free on 22/5/1998) FL 77+3/3 FLC 4 FAC 3

HALL Marcus Thomas
Born: Coventry, 24 March 1976
Height: 6'1" Weight: 12.2
International Honours: E: B-1; U21-8

The 1999-2000 season was another frustrating one for Marcus at Coventry City. It was September before the left-sided defender was in contention for a place after recovering from his knee problems of the previous season. A player blessed with an elegant style and no shortage of skill, he was on the verge of going to Wolves on loan when Coventry's injury crisis halted the move. He then started seven successive league games during which City were unbeaten.

Coventry C (From trainee on 1/7/1994) PL 65+17/1 FLC 11+1/1 FAC 7+2

HALL Paul Anthony
Born: Manchester, 3 July 1972
Height: 5'9" Weight: 11.0
International Honours: Jamaica: 33

The right-sided attacker made only two first-team appearances for Coventry last season, both as a substitute. Neil Warnock took him to Sheffield United on loan in December but his chances were limited due to his unavailability for FA Cup matches. Paul's one full game was at Grimsby, where he played wide on the right and scored the Blades' second goal. A competent and hard-working performer, he returned to Coventry after a month but in February he joined West Bromwich on loan. Paul did well during his spell at the Hawthorns but went back to Highfield Road once more before moving to Walsall on a free transfer in March. Using his speed to his advantage, he played a substantial part in the Saddlers' brave but unsuccessful attempt to avoid relegation. He scored four goals in his first six games, including a spectacular effort on his debut against Queens Park Rangers, and ironically helped Walsall to a potentially vital end-of-season victory against West Bromwich. Paul added two further caps for Jamaica when he appeared in the two end-of-season fixtures with Morocco and Japan in the Hassan Cup tournament.

Torquay U (From trainee on 9/7/1990) FL 77+16/1 FLC 7 FAC 4+1/2 Others 5+1/1
Portsmouth (£70,000 on 25/3/1993) FL 148+40/37 FLC 10+3/1 FAC 7+1/2 Others 6+2/2
Coventry C (£300,000 on 10/8/1998) PL 2+8 FLC 2+1/1
Bury (Loaned on 18/2/1999) FL 7
Sheffield U (Loaned on 17/12/1999) FL 1+3/1
West Bromwich A (Loaned on 10/2/2000) FL 4
Walsall (Free on 17/3/2000) FL 10/4

HALL Wayne
Born: Rotherham, 25 October 1968
Height: 5'9" Weight: 10.6

During the 1999-2000 season, York City's popular left back exceeded 400 senior appearances for the club. A fine defender, "Ginner" was at his usual and consistent best before picking up a heel injury against Plymouth in November but it was not until March that the problem was finally corrected through surgery. He has now embarked on a richly deserved testimonial year, with Middlesbrough agreeing to visit Bootham Crescent in the build-up to the new season.

York C (Free from Hatfield Main Colliery on 15/3/1989) FL 337+17/9 FLC 25+1 FAC 12+1/1 Others 21/1

HALLE Gunnar
Born: Oslo, Norway, 11 August 1965
Height: 5'11" Weight: 11.2
Club Honours: Div 2 '91
International Honours: Norway: 63

This vastly experienced right back joined Bradford City from Yorkshire rivals Leeds United in the summer of 1999. He had an outstanding season in 1999-2000, starting in all but one of the club's Premiership games and making a major contribution to the Bantams' successful fight against relegation. Gunnar is strong and physical and made many fine runs down the wing, from where he was able to deliver some useful crosses for his colleagues. It was not for want of trying that he failed to score and he brought several first-class saves from opposition 'keepers. He won a further cap for Norway when appearing in the friendly with Lithuania last August.

Oldham Ath (£280,000 from Lillestrom, Norway on 15/2/1991) F/PL 185+3/17 FLC 16/2 FAC 8/2 Others 4
Leeds U (£400,000 on 13/12/1996) PL 65+5/4 FLC 3+1 FAC 8+1 Others 2
Bradford C (£200,000 on 11/6/1999) PL 37+1 FLC 1 FAC 2

Gunnar Halle

HALLIDAY Stephen (Steve) William
Born: Sunderland, 3 May 1976
Height: 5'10" Weight: 12.12

Steve signed for Carlisle in February from Motherwell and made an immediate impact at Brunton Park with six goals in his first seven appearances. A clever forward who looks very comfortable on the ball, he showed remarkable composure in the manner in which he scored some of his goals, not least his strike against league leaders Swansea in March. Steve's goals were ultimately crucial in keeping Carlisle in the Football League, but an off-the-pitch incident has sadly terminated his association with the club.

Hartlepool U (From trainee on 5/7/1994) FL 111+29/25 FLC 8+3 FAC 4+1/1 Others 5+1
Motherwell (Free on 7/7/1998) SL 3+6 SLC 3+2/2
Carlisle U (Loaned on 14/2/2000) FL 16/7 Others 2/1

HALLWORTH Jonathan (Jon) Geoffrey
Born: Stockport, 26 October 1965
Height: 6'2" Weight: 14.10
Club Honours: Div 2 '91

The 1999-2000 season was a difficult one for the Cardiff goalkeeper, who suffered a knee problem and gradually lost confidence. There was never any doubt about his shot-stopping abilities and the Bluebirds certainly missed his experience during the vital last few matches of what was to be a relegation season. A year earlier Jon had missed the last five matches as Cardiff won promotion from Division Three after damaging his ribs. This time he again missed the last five games after he injured a hand at Preston. Still a highly rated 'keeper, Jon came to the end of his three-year contract in the summer but was offered new terms for another year.

Ipswich T (From apprentice on 26/5/1983) FL 45 FLC 4 FAC 1 Others 6
Bristol Rov (Loaned on 1/1/1985) FL 2 Others 1
Oldham Ath (£75,000 on 3/2/1989) F/PL 171+3 FLC 20 FAC 20 Others 3
Cardiff C (Free on 6/8/1997) FL 123 FLC 8 FAC 15 Others 2

HAMANN Dietmar
Born: Waldsasson, Germany, 27 August 1973
Height: 6'3" Weight: 12.2
International Honours: Germany: 27

After a sometimes frustrating first season in English football with Newcastle, the German international signed for Liverpool in the summer of 1999. Useful in a central midfield role, Dietmar added an extra dimension to the Liverpool side in 1999-2000 with his penetrating runs once he had returned to fitness after damaging ankle ligaments in the first game of the season. Respected as a top-class professional, he gets stronger the longer a game goes on. He tackles effectively, passes well and scores goals, like the opener against Leeds at Anfield, but the feeling remains that we have yet to see the best of him. Dietmar won ten more caps for Germany during the season and appeared in all three of their Euro 2000 fixtures.

Newcastle U (£4,500,000 from Bayern Munich, Germany, via Wacker Munchen, on 5/8/1998) PL 22+1/4 FLC 1 FAC 7/1
Liverpool (£8,000,000 on 23/7/1999) PL 27+1/1 FAC 2

Dietmar Hamann

HAMILTON Derrick (Des) Vivian
Born: Bradford, 15 August 1976
Height: 5'11" Weight: 13.0
International Honours: E: U21-1

Des is a powerfully built former England U21 international midfield player, strong on the ball and with a liking for joining the attack. Having had a difficult 1998-99 season at Newcastle, he almost joined Southampton during the summer of 1999 for £1.5 million, but could not agree terms. He was unable to make any progress at St James' Park under either Ruud Gullit or Bobby Robson, and recorded only a single substitute appearance in the away game at CSKA Sofia. He was made available for transfer in February, and went to Norwich on loan, together with Garry Brady, just prior to transfer deadline day with a view to a permanent move during the close season. During his stint at Carrow Road Des was able to demonstrate that he had lost none of his relish for the engine-room battle, earning praise not only for his forceful tackling but also for his willingness to slow the game down and wait until a team-mate was free before making his pass, and impressing everyone with his professionalism and commitment to the Canary cause.

Bradford C (From trainee on 1/6/1994) FL 67+21/5 FLC 6/1 FAC 6 Others 4+1/2
Newcastle U (£1,500,000 + on 27/3/1997) PL 7+5 FLC 1+1/1 FAC 1 Others 2+1
Sheffield U (Loaned on 16/10/1998) FL 6
Huddersfield T (Loaned on 15/2/1999) FL 10/1
Norwich C (Loaned on 22/3/2000) FL 7

HAMILTON Ian Richard
Born: Stevenage, 14 December 1967
Height: 5'9" Weight: 11.3

After starting the 1999-2000 season as a member of the Sheffield United side the hard-working midfielder fell out of favour after five games and his few appearances thereafter were as a substitute. He went to Grimsby on loan for a month in November to help counter the Mariners' continuing injury problems and performed competently, scoring in his final game against Stockport County. The departure of Adrian Heath and the arrival of Neil Warnock as manager at Bramall Lane did not bring about a change of fortune for Ian, and after January he had to settle for a position on the bench or playing for the reserves, although he did make two more substitute appearances near the end of the season.

Southampton (From apprentice on 24/12/1985)
Cambridge U (Signed on 29/3/1988) FL 23+1/1 FLC 1 FAC 2 Others 2
Scunthorpe U (Signed on 23/12/1988) FL 139+6/18 FLC 6 FAC 6+1 Others 14+1/3
West Bromwich A (£160,000 on 19/6/1992) FL 229+11/23 FLC 13+2/1 FAC 10+1/1 Others 14+2/3
Sheffield U (Signed on 26/3/1998) FL 38+7/3 FLC 6/1 FAC 2+3 Others 2
Grimsby T (Loaned on 4/11/1999) FL 6/1

HANKIN Sean Anthony
Born: Camberley, 28 February 1981
Height: 5'11" Weight: 12.4

Sean is a young Crystal Palace central midfield player who appeared mostly in the junior and reserve teams during 1999-2000. He stepped up to make a promising Football League debut against Bolton Wanderers last March when coming on as a substitute for the injured Simon Rodger. He will be looking to gain more first-team experience in the coming season.

Crystal Palace (From trainee on 29/6/1999) FL 0+1

HANLON Richard (Richie) Kenneth
Born: Wembley, 26 May 1978
Height: 6'1" Weight: 13.7

Richie was allowed to go on a season-long loan to Welling in August 1999. Subject to a 24-hour recall, he returned to the Peterborough fold in December after notching 14 goals for the Conference outfit. A forceful midfielder with a vicious left-foot shot, he helped to steer Posh through a difficult mid-term run. He finished the season with a place on the Wembley bench for United's Third Division play-off final win against Darlington.

Southend U (Free from Chelsea juniors on 10/7/1996) FL 1+1 (Free to Welling U during 1997 close season)
Peterborough U (Signed from Rushden & Diamonds on 9/12/1998) FL 0+4/1 Others 1 (Free to Welling on 12/8/1999)
Peterborough U (Free on 17/12/1999) FL 9+7/1 Others 1+2

HANMER Gareth Craig
Born: Shrewsbury, 12 October 1973
Height: 5'6" Weight: 10.3

Shrewsbury's regular left back for most of the 1999-2000 season, Gareth passed his 100th consecutive game for the Shrews in September. Slightly built, he breaks from defence with speed and is very effective going forward. The quality of his crosses and dead-ball kicks causes opposition defences continual concern. Not a man to succumb to injury easily, he is one of the most dependable players in the Gay Meadow squad.

West Bromwich A (£20,000 from Newtown on 18/6/1996)
Shrewsbury T (£10,000 on 25/7/1997) FL 116+2/1 FLC 5 FAC 6 Others 3

HANNON Kevin Michael
Born: Prescot, 4 May 1980
Height: 5'11" Weight: 11.2

Kevin is another of the talented youngsters to emerge from Wrexham's successful youth policy in recent seasons. He signed full-time forms in July 1999 and made his Football League debut last September when he came on as a substitute at Stoke. The highly promising full back also featured in several FAW Premier Cup ties but unfortunately suffered a fractured fibula and damaged ligaments in a friendly match with Icelandic team Throttur Reykjavik, and this brought his season to a premature close.

Wrexham (From trainee on 6/5/1999) FL 0+1

HANSEN Bo
Born: Denmark, 16 June 1972
Height: 5'11" Weight: 11.10
International Honours: Denmark: 3

Bo certainly figured more for Bolton last season than in his first with the club. Because of the electric form of Eidur Gudjohnsen, it was always going to be a straight battle between Bo and Dean Holdsworth for the other striking place in the team. While Holdsworth just had the edge in terms of number of appearances, Bo was given several chances to shine in the starting eleven and took them with some relish. Bo's total of first-team starts was well into double figures and, while his goal-scoring may not have been as prolific as Gudjohnsen's, he proved himself to be a speedy and hard-working centre forward who chased every lost cause for the team. Perhaps his best performance for the Trotters came when he scored both goals in the 2-0 win over Grimsby at the Reebok in November. As a willing and capable team member, Bo will be hoping to make one of the striking positions his own in the new season.

Bolton W (£1,000,000 from Brondby, Denmark on 12/2/1999) FL 16+22/9 FLC 4+1/1 FAC 1/1 Others 0+5

HANSEN John Schnabel
Born: Mannheim, Germany, 14 September 1973
Height: 5'11" Weight: 13.1

Regarded by Cambridge fans as one of the finds of the 1999-2000 season, this attacking midfielder was signed from Esbjerg of Denmark for a small fee in February 2000. Employed mainly on the left, he struggled at first to adapt to English football but soon became a first-team regular. He attacks well and scored three excellent goals in his 16 league appearances. John had previously played for Vissenberg and Odensa.

Cambridge U (£5,000 from Esbjerg, Denmark on 16/2/2000) FL 12+4/3

HANSSON Mikael
Born: Norrkoping, Sweden, 15 March 1968
Height: 5'10" Weight: 11.2
Club Honours: AMC '00
International Honours: Sweden: 1

A Swedish international full back who joined Stoke from Norrkoping on a free transfer in December 1999, Mikael made an immediate impact and secured a regular place on the right of the defence. Blessed with great speed and outstanding crossing skills, he played a huge part in City's chase for promotion and, despite a bad knock on the eve of the Auto Windscreens Shield final at Wembley, battled through the pain to play well in the victory over Bristol City. A popular player with the fans, Mikael was a joy to behold as he terrorised Second Division defences.

Stoke C (Free from IFK Norrkoping, Sweden on 3/12/1999) FL 24+3 Others 9/1

HARDY Philip (Phil)
Born: Ellesmere Port, 9 April 1973
Height: 5'8" Weight: 11.8
Club Honours: WC '95
International Honours: RoI: U21-9

This vastly experienced left back had another fine season for Wrexham in 1999-2000 and celebrated by scoring his first-ever Football League goal in almost 350 games for the Robins. The historic strike came on Easter Monday when he finally broke his duck with a penalty kick against Colchester United at the Racecourse ground. Phil is essentially a defensive full back who is quick in the tackle and rarely gives opposition forwards much room to work in. He is now approaching the peak of his career but may face greater competition next season from the many youngsters coming through for the north Wales club.

Wrexham (From trainee on 24/11/1990) FL 333+3/1 FLC 19 FAC 36 Others 37

HAREWOOD Marlon Anderson
Born: Hampstead, 25 August 1979
Height: 6'1" Weight: 11.0

This young striker began to fulfil his earlier promise with Nottingham Forest in 1999-2000, featuring regularly in the first team squad throughout the season. He is a big player with lightning pace and he is not afraid to use his ox-like strength to leave opposition defenders sprawling in his wake. Marlon always gives 100 per cent effort for the team and is popular with the Reds' supporters.

Nottingham F (From trainee on 9/9/1996) P/FL 30+28/5 FLC 6+3/3 FAC 1+2
Ipswich T (Loaned on 28/1/1999) FL 5+1/1

HARGREAVES Christian (Chris)
Born: Cleethorpes, 12 May 1972
Height: 5'11" Weight: 12.2

Chris had an excellent 1999-2000 season for Plymouth. He is a quality midfield player with an eye for goal and has the skill to open up defences from either the left-hand side or the middle. A highly popular player at Home Park, Chris began to play a more commanding role in the side last term and scored a great goal in front of the Argyle fans at Reading in the FA Cup in December. It came as quite a surprise when he was one of eight Pilgrims who were released at the end of the season. Stop Press: It was reported at the beginning of July that Chris had signed for Northampton.

Grimsby T (From trainee on 6/12/1989) FL 15+36/5 FLC 2+2/1 FAC 1+2/1 Others 2+4
Scarborough (Loaned on 4/3/1993) FL 2+1
Hull C (Signed on 26/7/1993) FL 34+15 FLC 1 FAC 2+1/1 Others 3+1
West Bromwich A (Free on 13/7/1995) FL 0+1 Others 0+1
Hereford U (Free on 19/2/1996) FL 57+4/6 FLC 3+1 FAC 1 Others 2
Plymouth Arg (Free on 20/7/1998) FL 74+2/5 FLC 4 FAC 11/2 Others 1

HARKIN Maurice (Mo) Presley
Born: Derry, 16 August 1979
Height: 5'9" Weight: 11.11
International Honours: NI: U21-3; Yth

This Wycombe youngster missed most of the 1998-99 season after fracturing an ankle, and although he appeared as a substitute against Gillingham last August he did not make the starting line-up until the FA Cup tie with Oxford in November. This was a rarity for Maurice, for he was mostly restricted to outings from the subs' bench, only starting three more games all season. His talent was evident when he came on for the last ten minutes at Bury in February, when he laid on a goal with a quickly taken free kick and then almost scored himself with a 20-yard effort. The highlight of his season was his debut for the Northern Ireland U21s against Malta in March, when he came on as a substitute and slotted home a last-minute winner. He added two further caps at U21 level when he appeared in the end-of-season Presidents' Cup games against Wales and Scotland.

Wycombe W (From trainee on 14/2/1997) FL 16+42/2 FLC 1+2/1 FAC 2+4 Others 3/1

Steve Harkness

HARKNESS Steven (Steve)
Born: Carlisle, 27 August 1971
Height: 5'10" Weight: 11.2
International Honours: E: Yth

Brought to Ewood Park from Benfica in September 1999, Steve arrived at Blackburn short of match fitness and was not used in the first team until Tony Parkes took over as manager. For all his enthusiasm and fire in the tackle, there were occasions when the former Liverpool defender seemed to have difficulty adapting to First Division football and he found himself out of favour after a particularly difficult afternoon at Sheffield United before Christmas. However, his fortunes changed with the appointment of Graeme Souness as manager, and he was a first-team regular during the closing weeks of the season.

Carlisle U (From trainee on 23/3/1989) FL 12+1
Liverpool (£75,000 on 17/7/1989) F/PL 90+12/2 FLC 11+4/1 FAC 5+1 Others 13+3 (£750,000 to Benfica on 9/3/1999)
Huddersfield T (Loaned on 24/9/1993) FL 5 Others 1
Southend U (Loaned on 3/2/1995) FL 6
Blackburn Rov (£400,000 on 8/9/1999) FL 17 FLC 1+1 FAC 1

HARLEY Jonathan (Jon)
Born: Maidstone, 26 September 1979
Height: 5'9" Weight: 10.3
Club Honours: FAC '00
International Honours: E: U21-3; Yth

This very promising left-sided midfield player made only a handful of appearances for Chelsea during the first half of the 1999-2000 season but when injuries to Graeme Le Saux and Celestine Babayaro left Chelsea without a recognised left back for the tricky third-round FA Cup tie at Hull Jon stepped into the breach and performed superbly. His probing runs were a thorn in the side of the gallant Tigers and he supplied two beautiful crosses which were headed in by Chris Sutton and Gustavo Poyet to banish any thoughts of a cup upset as Chelsea cruised through on their way to the final. Then came a ten-match run in the first team as Babayaro was claimed by Nigeria for the African Nations' Cup and subsequently tagged on an extended holiday. Jon's performances were a revelation, culminating in a special five-day period in February when he won his first England U21 cap against Argentina on the Tuesday and the following Saturday scored his first Premiership goal: the winner against Watford. His second goal, five matches later, also clinched three points for the Blues – it was the only goal of a tight match at Elland Road to give Chelsea victory at one of their bogey grounds. His next valuable contribution came in the FA Cup semi-final at Wembley against Newcastle, when the Magpies had equalised and threatened to overrun Chelsea; Jon broke away down the left flank and floated over a pin-point cross which was headed home by Gustavo Poyet to ensure Chelsea's return to the Twin Towers and an FA Cup final clash with Aston Villa. Unfortunately, Jon suffered the disappointment of dropping to the substitutes' bench after playing in every match up to the final as Vialli opted for the greater experience of Babayaro, although he still received a winners' medal. Further consolation came with a call-up to England U21s for the European Championship finals, when he won further caps against Turkey and Slovakia. Jon's meteoric rise resulted in his being touted by the press as an outsider for England's Euro 2000 squad but, realistically, this particular tournament came too early for a player of his limited experience, particularly of the defensive side of a full back's duties. However, with Chelsea having secured his future with a renewed contract, Jon looks to be the ready-made long-term successor to Graeme Le Saux for both Chelsea and England.

Chelsea (From trainee on 20/3/1997) PL 13+7/2 FLC 0+1 FAC 5 Others 1+3

Jon Harley

HARPER Kevin Patrick
Born: Oldham, 15 January 1976
Height: 5'6" Weight: 10.10
International Honours: S: B-1; U21-7; Sch

Kevin was in and out of the Derby match-day squad during the early stages of the 1999-2000 season. The main reason that he was unable to win a place in the starting line-up was that, as an out-and-out winger, his style of play didn't fit in with the formation of the team. Kevin joined Walsall on loan in December and immediately thrilled the Saddlers' fans with his ability to go past opponents, his speed worrying even the most experienced defenders. After scoring a coolly taken goal in the 3-2 win at Crewe, he had what would have been a contender for "Goal of the Season" ruled out at Fulham. He also laid on the Walsall goal in the draw against Manchester City at Maine Road at the end of February and it was a severe blow to the Saddlers' survival hopes when he was snapped up by Portsmouth manager Tony Pulis for a £300,000 fee just over a week later. A versatile right-footed player, he can operate on the wing, in midfield or up front if required. He was in the starting line-up for Pompey's last 12 games of the season, scoring twice. He was generally impressive, adding pace and flair to the midfield, and will be hoping to help bring success back to Fratton Park in the coming season.

Hibernian (From Hutchison Vale BC on 3/8/1992) SL 73+23/15 SLC 4+5 SC 9+1/3
Derby Co (£300,000 + on 11/9/1998) PL 6+26/1 FLC 1+5 FAC 0+3/1
Walsall (Loaned on 17/12/1999) FL 8+1/1
Portsmouth (£300,000 on 6/3/2000) FL 12/2

Kevin Harper

HARPER Lee Charles Phillip
Born: Chelsea, 30 October 1971
Height: 6'1" Weight: 13.11

Lee started the 1999-2000 season as the second-choice goalkeeper at Queens Park Rangers, behind Ludo Miklosko. When Miklosko was injured, Lee took his chance and his reappearance coincided with a run of nine unbeaten games which lifted the club into the top half of the First Division. He has always been a good shot stopper but his overall game improved steadily and his performances kept him in the first team until the end of the season, even though Miklosko regained fitness. His dramatic progress earned him the runner-up spot in the supporters' "Player of the Year" awards.

Arsenal (£150,000 from Sittingbourne on 16/6/1994) PL 1
Queens Park R (£125,000 + on 11/7/1997) FL 88+1 FLC 6+1 FAC 4

HARPER Stephen (Steve) Alan
Born: Easington, 14 March 1975
Height: 6'2" Weight: 13.0

During season 1998-99 local boy Steve began to emerge as a class goalkeeper with good all-round abilities, demonstrating that he is quick and agile with a safe pair of hands, and challenge his friendly rival Shay Given for the first-team jersey at Newcastle. However, although he has been on the club's books since 1993, by the start of last season he had made more appearances on loan for both Hartlepool and Huddersfield than he had for United. A pre-season injury to Shay gave Steve an early chance to establish himself as the number one, but after only a couple of games he injured an elbow and was only fit enough for the bench. After a gap of five games he returned to the side, playing well, but he was sent off in the Worthington Cup tie at Birmingham for bringing down Andy Johnson in the box. He regained his place following the subsequent suspension and, clearly growing in confidence, produced performances that were a significant factor in the club's improved results. Steve was in particularly fine form for the FA Cup tie at Tottenham, where a superb early save from a David Ginola special was vital, and in the derby game at Sunderland, where he pulled off a series of stunning saves to help earn a valuable point. He turned his ankle on the training ground just before the FA Cup quarter-final at Tranmere, which let Shay back into the side, and the latter's fine form then kept Steve on the bench on his return to fitness. His season ended prematurely when he had to undergo an operation on a torn cartilage in late April, an injury he had been carrying for a while. He is an all-round sportsman, playing cricket for his local side, and is also a qualified referee. Steve is a distant relation of Jonathon Wilkinson, a United striker of the late 1920s.

Newcastle U (Free from Seaham Red Star on 5/7/1993) PL 25+1 FLC 1 FAC 5+1 Others 6
Bradford C (Loaned on 18/9/1995) FL 1
Hartlepool U (Loaned on 29/8/1997) FL 15
Huddersfield T (Loaned on 18/12/1997) FL 24 FAC 2

HARPER Steven (Steve) James
Born: Newcastle under Lyme, 3 February 1969
Height: 5'10" Weight: 11.12
Club Honours: Div 4 '92

Hull manager Warren Joyce made an unsuccessful attempt to sign his former Preston North End colleague midway through 1998-99 but had more joy the following summer when Steve agreed a two-year deal following his release by Mansfield. In an often difficult campaign, playing in the physically demanding wing-back role, Steve proved to be an admirably consistent performer. He was involved in all but one game, up to damaging shoulder ligaments against Southend in March. His highlight was the third hat-trick of his career, in the 4-0 December win versus Exeter. Although right footed, he prefers his usual left-sided berth.

Port Vale (From trainee on 29/6/1987) FL 16+12/2 FLC 1+2 Others 1+1
Preston NE (Signed on 23/3/1989) FL 57+20/10 FLC 1+1 FAC 1+2 Others 6+1/1
Burnley (Free on 23/7/1991) FL 64+5/8 FLC 1+2 FAC 10/3 Others 8
Doncaster Rov (Free on 7/8/1993) FL 56+9/11 FLC 2+1/1 FAC 3 Others 4
Mansfield T (£20,000 on 8/9/1995) FL 157+3/18 FLC 6 FAC 8/1 Others 7
Hull C (Free on 13/7/1999) FL 36+2/4 FLC 4 FAC 5 Others 2

HARRIES Paul Graham
Born: Sydney, Australia, 19 November 1977
Height: 6'0" Weight: 13.7

The Australian-born striker moved to Carlisle from Crystal Palace in the 1999 close season, but groin injury worries kept him on the bench early on and his full debut did not come until October. A player of undoubted skill, he struggled to impose himself and most of his appearances were as a substitute. Both his league goals were scored after he came off the bench, including a fine effort at Darlington in October.

Portsmouth (Free from NSW Soccer Academy, Australia on 8/9/1997) FL 0+1
Crystal Palace (Free on 7/9/1998)
Torquay U (Loaned on 26/2/1999) FL 5
Carlisle U (Free on 30/7/1999) FL 6+14/2 FAC 1/1 Others 0+1

HARRIS Andrew (Andy) David Douglas
Born: Springs, South Africa, 26 February 1977
Height: 5'10" Weight: 11.11

Andy joined Leyton Orient on a free transfer from Southend in the 1999 close season. He started the new term as a regular, before succumbing to a long-standing hernia injury. Andy made only brief appearances as a substitute towards the end of the season, and will be looking to shake off his injury problems in 2000-01 and become a key squad member. The former Liverpool trainee is a determined defender who is very strong in the air.

Liverpool (From trainee on 23/3/1994)
Southend U (Free on 10/7/1996) FL 70+2 FLC 5 FAC 3
Leyton Orient (Free on 5/7/1999) FL 11+4 FLC 4

HARRIS Jason Andre Sebastian
Born: Sutton, 24 November 1976
Height: 6'1" Weight: 11.7

With a year of his Preston contract to run, the young forward joined his sixth club in the summer of 1999 when former PNE midfielder Warren Joyce took him to Hull. The City boss had watched him on several occasions, seeing for himself the Londoner with the reputation of being one of the fastest players in the Football League. A groin strain in September and a more serious back injury in October affected Jason's progress and confidence. He had to wait until February for his first goal (netting a match-winning brace against Brighton), although it was his first league start since August. A player who looks at his most dangerous under pressure, Jason has the speed to trouble any Third Division defence. He is the elder brother of Richard Harris of Crystal Palace.

Crystal Palace (From trainee on 3/7/1995) FL 0+2 FLC 0+2
Bristol Rov (Loaned on 22/11/1996) FL 5+1/2 Others 1/1
Lincoln C (Loaned on 11/8/1997) FL 0+1
Leyton Orient (£20,000 on 23/9/1997) FL 22+15/7 FLC 1 FAC 2 Others 1+1
Preston NE (Signed on 28/8/1998) FL 9+25/6 FAC 2+1/1 Others 2+2
Hull C (£30,000 + on 12/7/1999) FL 18+11/4 FLC 0+3 FAC 0+1 Others 1+1

HARRIS Neil
Born: Orsett, 12 July 1977
Height: 5'11" Weight: 12.9

Neil was once again Millwall's top scorer in 1999-2000, his second season with the club, with 25 goals. "Bomber", as he is known to the Millwall faithful, is a quick-footed centre forward who is a constant threat to any defence. Opponents find it difficult to mark him as he has good pace, can shoot with either foot and is completely unpredictable. Although not tall, he is pacy and holds the ball up well, and a number of Premiership clubs have shown an interest in him. He once had a trial for Liverpool, and they must now be kicking themselves for not signing him.

Millwall (£30,000 from Cambridge C on 26/3/1998) FL 73+7/40 FLC 1+1 FAC 0+2 Others 9/3

HARRIS Richard
Born: Croydon, 23 October 1980
Height: 5'11" Weight: 10.9

Another of the promising Crystal Palace youngsters, Richard was given a brief run in the first-team squad in the early part of the 1999-2000 campaign. A defender who has a tremendous long throw, he was troubled by injury problems for much of the rest of the season. Richard is the younger brother of Hull City's Jason Harris.

Crystal Palace (From trainee on 22/12/1997) FL 1+6 FLC 1+1

HARRISON Gerald (Gerry) Randall
Born: Lambeth, 15 April 1972
Height: 5'10" Weight: 12.12
International Honours: E: Sch

Finding it impossible to break into the Sunderland team at the start of the 1999-2000 campaign, Gerry returned to Hull, where he had ended the previous season, for a second loan spell in October. However, owing to a lack of match practice, he was generally unable to reproduce the impact he had made during his previous spell at Boothferry Park. Most effective when operating as a solid, no-nonsense central defender, he made only three appearances for the Tigers this time around. The City manager, Warren Joyce (a former Burnley colleague of Gerry's) was keen to sign him permanently, but the six-figure transfer fee reportedly proved an insurmountable obstacle and Gerry returned to the Stadium of Light.

Watford (From trainee on 18/12/1989) FL 6+3 Others 1
Bristol C (Free on 23/7/1991) FL 25+13/1 FLC 2+2 FAC 1 Others 4+1
Cardiff C (Loaned on 24/1/1992) FL 10/1
Hereford U (Loaned on 19/11/1993) FL 6 FAC 1 Others 1
Huddersfield T (Free on 24/3/1994)
Burnley (Free on 5/8/1994) FL 116+8/3 FLC 5+1 FAC 6+2 Others 7+1
Sunderland (Free on 29/7/1998) FLC 1
Luton T (Loaned on 24/12/1998) FL 14 Others 1
Hull C (Loaned on 25/3/1999) FL 8
Hull C (Loaned on 1/10/1999) FL 3

HARRISON Lee David
Born: Billericay, 12 September 1971
Height: 6'2" Weight: 12.7

Lee's popularity reached even greater heights during the 1999-2000 season when the celebrated shot stopper scooped Barnet's "Player of the Year" award for the third successive year. Clearly on the threshold of his prime, Lee played a key role in the club reaching the play-offs for the second time in three campaigns. In early October, he registered three successive clean sheets and his displays at Torquay and in the home match against Darlington were, quite simply, exceptional. His distribution proved to be somewhat erratic at times, but he more than compensated for that with his breathtaking reflex saves that denied forwards from point-blank range. Having previously worked under former England great Ray Clemence at Underhill, Lee is sure to attract the interest of more highly placed clubs.

Charlton Ath (From trainee on 3/7/1990)
Fulham (Loaned on 18/11/1991) Others 1
Gillingham (Loaned on 24/3/1992) FL 2
Fulham (Free on 18/12/1992) FL 11+1 FAC 1 Others 6
Barnet (Free on 15/7/1996) FL 153 FLC 7 FAC 3 Others 9

HARSLEY Paul
Born: Scunthorpe, 29 May 1978
Height: 5'9" Weight: 11.5

One of the heroes of Scunthorpe's play-off success the previous season, Paul took time to adjust to the extra demands of Division Two football in 1999-2000 but he went through the campaign without missing a game. Often played wide on the right, he never looked comfortable and is always better suited to a central midfield role, where he can get more involved. A good passer of the ball who works hard, he chipped in with three goals during the season and can expect to develop further with another full season under his belt.

Grimsby T (From trainee on 16/7/1996)
Scunthorpe U (Free on 7/7/1997) FL 88+7/4 FLC 4 FAC 3+1/1 Others 5

HART Gary John
Born: Harlow, 21 September 1976
Height: 5'9" Weight: 12.8

The Brighton striker found his second season in league football far tougher than his first. However, Gary remained a potent attacking force in the Third Division and still scored nine goals. The 1999-2000 campaign did see his all-round team play improve, and his constant running and tireless effort up front meant he remained a firm favourite with the fans. Indeed, he was voted Albion's "Player of the Year" by the club's younger supporters. The Londoner was also appreciated by a wider audience as he won the "Nationwide Player of the Month" award for March. It was the first occasion that a Third Division player had received this prestigious award. Gary signed an extended three-and-a-half-year contract in November.

Brighton & Hove A (£1,000 from Stansted on 18/6/1998) FL 84+3/21 FLC 2+2 FAC 3 Others 3/1

HARTE Ian Patrick
Born: Drogheda, 31 August 1977
Height: 5'10" Weight: 11.8
International Honours: RoI: 22; U21-3

Ian is probably one of the most improved players at Leeds United and seems to have made the left-back spot his own. He caught the eye on a regular basis last season and is now looking the typical modern full back: good in defence, exciting going forward and

Ian Harte

possessing a lethal shot. Few Leeds fans will ever forget his explosive free kick to earn a late victory at White Hart Lane, while his willingness to cut in from the left flank and produce unerring accuracy with his right foot makes him hard to contain. He is also the side's regular penalty taker, showing consistent accuracy. Ian won three more caps for the Republic of Ireland and added another goal when scoring in the 3-2 win over the Czech Republic last February. Still only 22 and with over 100 Leeds appearances under his belt, Ian looks to have a big part to play at Elland Road in the coming seasons. His contribution to the club's success was recognised when he was named by his fellow professionals in the PFA award-winning Premiership side for last season.

Leeds U (From trainee on 15/12/1995) PL 91+7/12 FLC 4+2/1 FAC 10+2/3 Others 15/1

HARTSON John
Born: Neath, 5 April 1975
Height: 6'1" Weight: 14.6
International Honours: W: 18; U21-9; Yth

John missed most of the second half of the 1999-2000 season as a result of well-publicised injury problems. The powerful Wimbledon striker had a cartilage operation around Christmas time and a proposed transfer to Tottenham in March fell through when he failed a medical. Then, within a couple of days, he had to have a hernia operation. Despite all this John scored nine goals in 16 Premiership games – a record anyone would be proud of – including a very memorable equaliser two minutes into injury time at home to Aston Villa in the penultimate game of the season. A big, bustling centre forward who possesses both a good strike and a bullet-like header, John was a handful for every centre-back pairing he came up against. The Dons will be hoping to retain his services in the First Division in 2000-01, although his reported £10,000 goal bonus could prove very costly if he hits top goalscoring form. However, if he helps the club to promotion, it will seem like a bargain. A passionate player, John wears his heart on his sleeve. His attitude against Bradford and Villa showed what football and Wimbledon mean to him.

Luton T (From trainee on 19/12/1992) FL 32+22/11 FLC 0+1 FAC 3+3/2 Others 2
Arsenal (£2,500,000 on 13/1/1995) PL 43+10/14 FLC 2+4/1 FAC 2+1/1 Others 8+1/1
West Ham U (£3,200,000 + on 14/2/1997) PL 59+1/24 FLC 6/6 FAC 7/3
Wimbledon (£7,000,000 on 15/1/1999) PL 27+3/11 FLC 3 FAC 1

HASLAM Steven Robert
Born: Sheffield, 6 September 1979
Height: 5'11" Weight: 10.10
International Honours: E: Yth; Sch

Steven is a very promising Sheffield Wednesday youngster who made a couple of first-team appearances last August before earning a regular place in the starting line-up in the new year. Although essentially a central defender for the reserve team, he was used in a midfield role when in the senior side, where his good distribution and no-nonsense approach were found useful. He has already been capped by England at schools and youth levels and looks set for a bright future in the game.

Sheffield Wed (From trainee on 12/9/1996) PL 18+7 FLC 0+1 FAC 3

HASSELL Robert (Bobby) John Francis
Born: Derby, 4 June 1980
Height: 5'9" Weight: 12.6

During 1999-2000 this versatile Mansfield defender was again dogged by injury, which restricted his appearances. His four games in August earned him the *Match* magazine Division Three "Matchman of the Month" award, but he was in and out of the side from then on with a series of niggling hamstring injuries. When these eventually cleared up in March he trapped his hand in a car door, which further delayed his comeback for another couple of weeks! When he played, he was a valuable member of the Stags' defence. He tackles and distributes the ball well, and his pace is also useful when covering at the back.

Mansfield T (From trainee on 3/7/1998) FL 17+6/1 FLC 2 FAC 1

HAWKINS Peter Steven
Born: Maidstone, 19 September 1978
Height: 6'0" Weight: 11.6

Peter spent the closing stages of the 1999-2000 season with York. On the fringe of the Wimbledon squad, he took the chance to move up to Yorkshire in February. The left-sided defender impressed in the Minstermen's defence with his quick tackling and general ability.

Wimbledon (From trainee on 6/3/1997)
York C (Loaned on 22/2/2000) FL 14

HAWORTH Simon Owen
Born: Cardiff, 30 March 1977
Height: 6'2" Weight: 13.8
Club Honours: AMC '99
International Honours: W: 5; B-1; U21-12; Yth

Simon created a bit of history in 1999-2000 by scoring the first-ever Football League goal at Wigan's JJB Stadium. The centre forward finished the campaign as the Latics' second-top scorer with 20 goals. He is tall, strong and skilful with the ability to score superb goals, and his tremendous strike in the Wembley Second Division play-off final demonstrated his undoubted potential. He gained two more caps for Wales at U21 level and was put on stand-by for the full squad. The season also saw him complete 100 Football League games.

Cardiff C (From trainee on 7/8/1995) FL 27+10/9 FLC 4 FAC 0+1 Others 4/1
Coventry C (£500,000 on 4/6/1997) PL 5+6 FLC 2/1 FAC 0+1
Wigan Ath (£600,000 on 2/10/1998) FL 55+5/23 FLC 4/3 FAC 4/4 Others 10/4

HAY Christopher (Chris) Drummond
Born: Glasgow, 28 August 1974
Height: 5'11" Weight: 12.5

Chris was one of the stars in an otherwise disappointing Swindon team in 1999-2000 until his move to Huddersfield on transfer deadline day. He was leading scorer for the Robins with ten goals at the time of his departure but was sold for a bargain-basement fee to raise money for the cash-strapped Wiltshire club. A striker who can kick with either foot, he has plenty of skill and a lethal finish, making him an asset to any side. After a delay caused by a calf injury, Chris made his debut for the Terriers at Grimsby and played some part in all of their remaining matches.

Glasgow Celtic (Free from Giffnock North AFC on 27/5/1993) SL 9+16/4 SC 0+3 Others 0+2/1
Swindon T (£330,000 on 6/8/1997) FL 73+21/30 FLC 2+2 FAC 2+1
Huddersfield T (£70,000 on 23/3/2000) FL 2+5

HAYLES Barrington (Barry) Edward
Born: Lambeth, 17 May 1972
Height: 5'9" Weight: 13.0
Club Honours: Div 2 '99
International Honours: E: SP-2

The 1999-2000 season began badly for the Fulham striker when he was sent off in a testimonial game at Woking in August. This was followed by further dismissals at West Bromwich and Sheffield United although, to be fair, the latter was for an accidental handball on the half-way line, which could be considered a little harsh. With a three-match ban to follow, Barry had his best game in a Fulham shirt when he demolished Wimbledon almost single-handedly in a fourth-round FA Cup tie. Although he didn't score in the 3-0 victory, his crossing, close control and shooting played a part in all three goals and several other near-misses. Amazingly, although his ban was over, Barry was left on the bench for an hour in the fifth-round game against Tranmere, which Fulham lost 2-1. His game looks ideally suited to playing just behind the main strikers, where his twisting runs can cause chaos in opposing defences. Barry was one of a number of Nationwide League players called up by the Cayman Islands to play in a World Cup qualifier against Cuba early in 2000 only to have their hopes of international football dashed when FIFA ruled them ineligible at the last minute.

Bristol Rov (£250,000 from Stevenage Borough on 4/6/1997) FL 62/32 FLC 4/1 FAC 5/2 Others 3+2/2
Fulham (£2,100,000 on 17/11/1998) FL 47+18/13 FLC 3+1/2 FAC 7+1/3

HAYTER James Edward
Born: Sandown, IoW, 9 April 1979
Height: 5'9" Weight: 11.2

This talented Bournemouth youngster continued to show progress in 1999-2000 and established himself as a regular in the Cherries' line-up in the second half of the season. He scored four goals, including a brilliant effort at Wycombe on Boxing Day when he took the ball through and let fly with a 20-yard rocket shot which flew into the net. Quick and exciting, he can play as a striker or on either side of midfield.

Bournemouth (From trainee on 7/7/1997) FL 37+21/4 FLC 1+1/1 FAC 1 Others 2+1/1

HAYWARD Steven (Steve) Lee
Born: Pelsall, 8 September 1971
Height: 5'11" Weight: 12.5
Club Honours: AMC '97; Div 2 '99
International Honours: E: Yth

As always, Steve gave 100 per cent to the Fulham cause in 1999-2000 but his corners and centres were less effective than they had been in Division Two. Defences in the First Division were much tighter and opposition teams had done their homework on Fulham's set pieces. Steve lost his place in the midfield engine room when Kevin Ball arrived from Sunderland, but soon regained it at the expense of Wayne Collins or Sean Davis.

Derby Co (From juniors on 17/9/1988) FL 15+11/1 FLC 0+2 FAC 1 Others 3+4
Carlisle U (£100,000 on 13/3/1995) FL 88+2/14 FLC 6/1 FAC 4 Others 15/1
Fulham (£175,000 on 23/6/1997) FL 108+6/7 FLC 13+2 FAC 9+2/3 Others 3

HAZELL Reuben
Born: Birmingham, 24 April 1979
Height: 5'11" Weight: 12.0

Reuben made excellent progress in 1999-2000, for having begun the season without a senior appearance to his name he finished it as a regular in the Tranmere side and with a runners-up medal from the Worthington Cup final. An intelligent full back, he showed that he has considerable skill, good distribution and neat as well as economical passing abilities. A former Aston Villa trainee, he proved to be a fine recruit for Rovers, being level headed and modest off the field and a great favourite with the club's younger supporters. Reuben is the nephew of the former Queens Park Rangers player Bob Hazell.

Aston Villa (From trainee on 20/3/1997)
Tranmere Rov (Free on 5/8/1999) FL 21+2/1 FLC 5 FAC 3

Greg Heald

HEALD Gregory (Greg) James
Born: Enfield, 26 September 1971
Height: 6'1" Weight: 12.8
International Honours: E: Sch

With his awesome physique and fearless brand of tackling, Greg wore the Barnet captain's armband with distinction in 1999-2000 as he led the Bees to a play-off place. After missing the majority of the previous season with a back injury, Greg shored up the heart of a rearguard that had looked fragile in his absence. He is the club's record signing, and his commanding aerial presence in both penalty areas enabled him to net five goals during the campaign. The only blip in his season was a minute of post-millennium madness in the home clash with Southend. After scoring an emphatic own goal, Greg angrily reacted to an opponent's taunting gesture and was subsequently sent off, with Barnet sorely missing his influence during the ensuing suspension.

Peterborough U (£35,000 from Enfield on 8/7/1994) FL 101+4/6 FLC 8 FAC 8+1 Others 11/2
Barnet (Signed on 8/8/1997) FL 102/10 FLC 6/1 FAC 2 Others 5/1

HEALD Paul Andrew
Born: Wath on Dearne, 20 September 1968
Height: 6'2" Weight: 14.0

A safe and reliable goalkeeper, Paul made just one first-team appearance for Wimbledon in 1999-2000, against Leicester in March. This proved to be the last win of the season for the Dons. He put in a confident, solid performance and his long kicks certainly put the Leicester defence under extreme pressure. Paul is a very popular member of the squad, especially with the younger Dons fans, and with the departure of Neil Sullivan to Spurs he could become "top dog" this coming season.

Sheffield U (From trainee on 30/6/1987)
Leyton Orient (Signed on 2/12/1988) FL 176 FLC 13 FAC 9 Others 21
Coventry C (Loaned on 10/3/1992) PL 2
Swindon T (Loaned on 24/3/1994) PL 1+1
Wimbledon (£125,000 on 25/7/1995) PL 21 FLC 7

HEALY Brian
Born: Glasgow, 27 December 1968
Height: 6'1" Weight: 12.7
International Honours: E: SP-1

A stylish play-maker, Brian is the creative fulcrum of the Torquay midfield. Although he was not fully fit for much of the 1999-2000 season, his passing was a joy to watch. He previously served Gateshead, Spennymoor and Morecambe before belatedly breaking into the Football League ranks. Gulls manager Wes Saunders describes him as "the man who makes us tick".

Torquay U (£25,000 from Morecambe on 16/12/1998) FL 53+4/11 FLC 1 Others 3

HEALY David Jonathan
Born: Downpatrick, 5 August 1979
Height: 5'8" Weight: 11.0
International Honours: NI: 3; B-1; U21-8; Yth; Sch

A young Manchester United forward with a penchant for scoring goals, David may have had a disappointing introduction to first-team action when United were beaten by Aston Villa in the Worthington Cup last September, but he really came to the fore on his international debut for Northern Ireland. Starting off by hitting two goals on his debut against Luxembourg in February, he also scored in his next international against Malta. At club level, he went on loan to Port Vale in February until the end of the season to gain experience. The classy striker netted twice in his first four games for the Vale and later scored a particularly good goal at Tranmere with a 25-yard shot but, although he impressed, he was unable to prevent their relegation to Division Two. A nippy striker who despite being small in stature obviously has a big future in the game, he has signed a four-year contract with the Old Trafford club.

Manchester U (From trainee on 28/11/1997) FLC 0+1
Port Vale (Loaned on 25/2/2000) FL 15+1/3

HEANEY Neil Andrew
Born: Middlesbrough, 3 November 1971
Height: 5'9" Weight: 11.6
Club Honours: FAYC '88
International Honours: E: U21-6; Yth

The former Arsenal trainee returned to his native Teesside in the 1999 close season, joining Darlington from Manchester City. He immediately impressed with some classy displays, playing wide on the left and assisting in a number of goals with his accurate crosses. He also contributed some fine individual goals, mainly with spectacular shots from outside the box while his pace and skill were greatly appreciated by the fans. Neil missed a number of games towards the end of the season due to facial injuries and concussion sustained after he collided with an advertising board at Hull in March. He was one of three Quakers selected for the PFA Third Division team.

Arsenal (From trainee on 14/11/1989) F/PL 4+3 FLC 0+1
Hartlepool U (Loaned on 3/1/1991) FL 2+1
Cambridge U (Loaned on 9/1/1992) FL 9+4/2 FAC 1
Southampton (£300,000 on 22/3/1994) PL 42+19/5 FLC 4+2 FAC 6/2
Manchester C (£500,000 on 25/11/1996) FL 13+5/1 FAC 2/1 Others 1
Charlton Ath (Loaned on 26/3/1998) FL 4+2 Others 3
Bristol C (Loaned on 12/3/1999) FL 2+1
Darlington (Free on 6/8/1999) FL 33+3/5 FLC 1 FAC 3 Others 3

HEARY Thomas Mark
Born: Dublin, 14 February 1978
Height: 5'10" Weight: 11.12
International Honours: RoI: U21-4; Yth; (UEFA-U18 '98); Sch

The young Irish defender again gained a late call-up to first-team duties at Huddersfield in 1999-2000, coming into the starting line-up for the final crunch fixture at Fulham. A very confident right back who tackles with purpose, he has a good touch and passes the ball well. Thomas made his debut for the Republic of Ireland at U21 level during the season, but he was released by the Terriers during the summer.

Huddersfield T (From trainee on 17/2/1996) FL 8+4 FLC 0+1 FAC 1

HEATH Robert
Born: Newcastle under Lyme, 31 August 1978
Height: 5'8" Weight: 10.0

This popular local boy had an injury-dogged season in 1999-2000 when his many fans were expecting that it would be the campaign that would see the Stoke midfielder, who can also play at full back, emerge from the reserves. What he lacks in weight he makes up for in hard work, and it was a pity that his time in the treatment room restricted him to a mere handful of substitute appearances in a season of such importance to the club and its staff.

Stoke C (From trainee on 15/7/1996) FL 11+8 FLC 0+1 FAC 0+1 Others 2

HEATHCOTE Michael (Mick)
Born: Kelloe, 10 September 1965
Height: 6'2" Weight: 12.5

In his fourth season as captain of Plymouth, Mick continued to produce resolute and commanding displays at the heart of the Pilgrims' defence in 1999-2000. He is still dangerous at set pieces, and scored the winning goal against Reading in the FA Cup third-round replay. Mick is an example to others, which makes him one of the most valuable players at the club, and remains a firm favourite at Home Park.

Sunderland (£15,000 from Spennymoor on 19/8/1987) FL 6+3 Others 0+1
Halifax T (Loaned on 17/12/1987) FL 7/1 FAC 1
York C (Loaned on 4/1/1990) FL 3 Others 1
Shrewsbury T (£55,000 on 12/7/1990) FL 43+1/6 FLC 6 FAC 5 Others 4
Cambridge U (£150,000 on 12/9/1991) FL123+5/13 FLC 7/1 FAC 5+2/2 Others 7/2
Plymouth Arg (£70,000 on 27/7/1995) FL 191+3/13 FLC 9/1 FAC 18/3 Others 8

HECKINGBOTTOM Paul
Born: Barnsley, 17 July 1977
Height: 5'11" Weight: 12.0

Paul made the Darlington left-back spot his own after arriving from Sunderland on transfer deadline day in March 1999 and has missed only two league games since then. After loan spells at both Scarborough and Hartlepool, he grabbed the chance of regular first-team football with the Quakers and has shown maturity both as a defender and as an overlapping attacker. Paul scored his first goal for Darlington at Aston Villa last December, following up Peter Duffield's parried penalty in the 1-2 FA Cup defeat after the club had drawn the wild card to re-enter the competition in place of the absent Manchester United.

Sunderland (Free from Manchester U juniors on 14/7/1995)
Scarborough (Loaned on 17/10/1997) FL 28+1 Others 1
Hartlepool U (Loaned on 25/9/1998) FL 5/1
Darlington (Free on 25/3/1999) FL 54+1/1 FLC 2 FAC 3/1 Others 4

HEDMAN Magnus Carl
Born: Stockholm, Sweden, 19 March 1973
Height: 6'4" Weight: 13.10
International Honours: Sweden: 26; B; U21; Yth

The 1999-2000 season was a solid if unspectacular one for the big Coventry goalkeeper. His shot-stopping skills were as brilliant as ever but while he was less reluctant to come off his line at corners he was caught out on a few occasions by tricky crosses. The highlights of his campaign were the double save he made against Newcastle when he brilliantly kept out shots from Alan Shearer and Didier Domi, his three excellent saves in the game at home to West Ham and his "Man of the Match" display at Hillsborough. Magnus is now firmly established as Sweden's first-choice 'keeper and won ten more caps during the season, appearing in all three of his country's Euro 2000 fixtures. He was linked with a couple of bigger English clubs but after much speculation he decided to commit himself to Coventry for four years with a lucrative contract.

Coventry C (£500,000 from AIK Solna, Sweden on 24/7/1997) PL 85 FLC 3 FAC 9

HEFFERNAN Paul
Born: Dublin, Ireland, 29 December 1981
Height: 5'10" Weight: 10.7

This promising young striker joined Notts County from Irish junior football last October after impressing during a trial period at Meadow Lane. He scored regularly for the youth and reserve teams and was rewarded with two brief first-team outings from the subs' bench towards the end of the season. He has terrific pace and will be aiming to break through to a regular place in the first-team squad in 2000-01.

Notts Co (Signed from Newtown, Co Wicklow on 22/10/1999) FL 0+2

HEGGEM Vegard
Born: Trondheim, Norway, 13 July 1975
Height: 5'10" Weight: 11.12
International Honours: Norway: 20

The former Rosenborg right back confirmed that he is a player of some quality with his displays for Liverpool throughout the 1999-2000 season. He has pace, skill and the ability to score goals, which adds yet another dimension to a team full of goalscoring ability. Vegard can play on the right of the defence, or on the right side of midfield, a position which truly utilises his ability to produce deep, penetrating crosses and sometimes score vital goals. His versatility, however, is a double-edged sword, since his defensive responsibilities often appear to curb his natural attacking inclinations. He continued to appear regularly for Norway, winning ten further caps and appearing against Spain and Yugoslavia in the European Championship finals.

Liverpool (£3,500,000 from Rosenborg, Norway, via Orkdal, on 27/7/1998) PL 37+14/3 FLC 2+2 FAC 1 Others 4+1

HEGGS Carl Sydney
Born: Leicester, 11 October 1970
Height: 6'1" Weight: 12.10

Moving to Rushden & Diamonds in the 1999 close season, Carl briefly returned to the Football League scene last March when he joined Chester on loan, as the Blues valiantly tried to avoid relegation to the Conference. A strong, hard-working striker, he can be equally effective down either flank. He is a tremendous crosser of the ball, and City will be hoping they can retain the talented forward for their 2000-01 revival.

West Bromwich A (£25,000 from Leicester U on 22/8/1991) FL 13+27/3 FLC 2 FAC 0+1 Others 6+3/1
Bristol Rov (Loaned on 27/1/1995) FL 2+3/1

Swansea C (£60,000 on 27/7/1995) FL 33+13/7 FLC 2 FAC 2 Others 4+1/1
Northampton T (£40,000 on 31/7/1997) FL 29+17/5 FLC 3+2/2 FAC 4+1/1 Others 3+1/4 (£65,000 to Rushden & Diamonds on 23/10/1998)
Chester C (Loaned on 10/3/2000) FL 11/2

[HELDER] CHRISTOVAO Rodriguez
Born: Luanda, Angola, 21 March 1971
Height: 5'11" Weight: 13.0
International Honours: Portugal: 33

This experienced Portuguese international central defender, who prefers to go by the name of Helder, snapped a tendon at the front of his knee in an accidental collision playing for Deportivo in 1998-99, necessitating two operations and a long rehabilitation. Deportivo did not expect him to recover in time to play last season, so did not register him in their squad list. However, he recovered more quickly than anticipated and Bobby Robson, benefiting from his knowledge of the Portuguese game, took the opportunity to strengthen his Newcastle squad, which was depleted by injuries to several central defenders, by taking him on loan in November for the rest of the season, beating Tottenham to the deal. Although lacking match practice, Helder made his debut against Spurs at the end of November at very short notice when Alessandro Pistone dropped out through injury and quickly settled into the defence, demonstrating composure, confidence on the ball and an anticipation which indicated that he is a fine reader of the game. He scored his first goal in the derby at Sunderland, helping to earn a point, and his ball skills were much in evidence in the following match when he broke up a Manchester United raid delightfully and started the move which led to Newcastle's third goal. Understandably, he experienced some difficulty in adjusting to the demands and pace of the Premiership game, but he was coming to terms with them when he picked up a hamstring injury at Hillsborough in February, and on his recovery found himself in competition for a place with a by-then full complement of fit centre backs at the club, a battle which was not helped by a troublesome groin injury which ruled him out of contention for an FA Cup semi-final place, and his only other game came when injuries meant he was pressed into service as a midfielder for the home match with Leeds. Helder is rated at over £4 million by his club, who want him to return in the summer, although he has said he would consider remaining on Tyneside.
Newcastle U (Loaned from Deportivo La Coruna, Spain on 22/11/1999) PL 8/1 FAC 4

HELGUSON Heidar
Born: Iceland, 22 August 1977
Height: 6'0" Weight: 12.2
International Honours: Iceland: 9

Watford's first-ever million-pound purchase and record transfer signing, Heidar joined the club for £1.5 million from Lillestrom last January. An Icelandic international, he is an all-action centre forward with outstanding heading ability. He made a scoring debut against Liverpool, when the number of fouls against him bore testament to his nuisance value. Further goals followed, against Bradford, West Ham, Arsenal and Manchester United, and he finished with a spectacular overhead effort against Coventry that made him the club's leading scorer for the season. Only 22, Heidar seems certain to be a key man for Watford in the future. He won four more international caps, all in the early part of the season, before his move to Vicarage Road.
Watford (£1,500,000 from SK Lillestrom, Norway on 13/1/2000) PL 14+2/6

Heidar Helguson

HELMER Thomas
Born: Germany, 21 April 1965
Height: 6'1" Weight: 12.2
International Honours: Germany: 68 (UEFA '96)

A German international defender or midfielder, Thomas arrived at Sunderland during the 1999 pre-season on a free transfer from Bayern Munich and was seen by many of the Black Cats' supporters as an extremely impressive purchase. Thomas was a member of Germany's successful Euro '96 team at Wembley and came to Wearside with a reputation as an impeccable reader of the game and an excellent passer. Although Peter Reid chose to begin the campaign with a central defensive partnership of Steve Bould and Paul Butler, Thomas made an impressive debut as a substitute against Arsenal in August, steadying an overworked defence, and began the next game away at Leeds. Amazingly, at the start of September, it was revealed that his contract included a clause allowing Thomas to join a club competing in the Champions' League and he joined Hertha Berlin on loan until Christmas, helping them qualify for the group stages of the competition. An achilles tendon injury ended his spell in Germany in December and, although it was thought that he had returned to full fitness in the subsequent months, he was not to appear in a Sunderland shirt for the rest of the season. Rumours of disagreements behind the scenes began to circulate on Wearside and it will be a surprise if Thomas is still at the Stadium of Light come the next campaign. If he does move on, many Sunderland fans will be somewhat perplexed that a player of such undoubted quality and experience has been allowed to leave without showing what he can do in the Premiership.
Sunderland (Free from Bayern Munich, Germany on 16/7/1999) PL 1+1

HEMMINGS Anthony (Tony) George
Born: Burton, 21 September 1967
Height: 5'10" Weight: 12.10
International Honours: E: SP-1

Returning to the league ranks for the first time since he ended his Wycombe association in 1995, Tony added experience to the Chester attack when he signed from Ilkeston of the Dr Martens League last January. Although aged 32, he covered every blade of grass in City's desperate fight for Football League survival. He has lots of pace and a strong left-foot shot, with his effort in the 5-0 defeat of Mansfield in March probably being the Blues' "Goal of the Season".
Wycombe W (£25,000 from Northwich Vic on 8/9/1993) FL 28+21/12 FLC 1+5 FAC 2+2/1 Others 3+3/1 (Free to Macclesfield T on 31/10/1995)
Chester C (£30,000 from Ilkeston T on 21/1/2000) FL 19/2

HENCHOZ Stephane
Born: Billens, Switzerland, 7 September 1974
Height: 6'1" Weight: 12.10
International Honours: Switzerland: 40

An elegant defender with class and poise, the Swiss international joined Liverpool from Blackburn during the summer of 1999. Physically strong, he is commanding in the air, tackles ferociously and is rarely caught out of position, while his distribution from the back is superb. Stephane has formed an excellent partnership with Sami Hyypia in the middle of the Reds' back line in the Hansen–Lawrenson mould, and since he teamed up with the impressive Finn he has helped to give Liverpool greater defensive credibility. He is one of those defenders who does the right things at the right time, and is always in the right position to make a crucial interception. He was out for a long time with injury before making his debut, but his eventual presence in the side brought with it a new-found defensive assurance. Stephane performed consistently well at the highest level throughout the season and looks to be an excellent signing. He won further caps for Switzerland against Wales, the UAE and Norway during 1999-2000.
Blackburn Rov (£3,000,000 from Hamburg, Germany, via FC Bulle and Neuchatel Xamax, on 14/7/1997) PL 70 FLC 3+1 FAC 6 Others 2
Liverpool (£3,750,000 on 20/7/1999) PL 29 FLC 2 FAC 2

HENDERSON Darius Alexis
Born: Sutton, 7 September 1981
Height: 6'0" Weight: 12.8

A graduate of the Reading FC Academy,

Darius scored an amazing goal for the youth team last term when he drove the ball over the Birmingham City goalkeeper direct from Reading's kick-off. Enterprise like that earned him a late-season call-up to the first team. A big, burly, old-fashioned striker, he hit a post in the final home game of the campaign against Stoke City. Temperamentally suited to the big occasion, he has been given a professional contract for the next two years.
Reading (From trainee on 15/12/1999) FL 2+4

HENDERSON Kevin Malcolm
Born: Ashington, 8 June 1974
Height: 6'3" Weight: 13.2
Kevin joined Hartlepool in the 1999 close season, initially to provide back-up for strikers Gary Jones and Chris Freestone. A strong player who is prepared to work hard, he had to wait patiently for his chance and 2 October 1999 was an important date for him. He made his first appearance in a starting line-up after a remarkable run of 27 appearances as a substitute for Pool and his previous club, Burnley. With this breakthrough he grew in confidence, and as the season progressed he earned more success as a goalscorer than either Gary or Chris. Kevin's most memorable goal was an 18-yard overhead kick against York that won Sky TV's "Goal of the Month" award.
Burnley (Signed from Morpeth T on 17/12/1997) FL 0+14/1 FLC 0+2 Others 0+4/1
Hartlepool U (Free on 2/7/1999) FL 23+12/8 FLC 0+1 FAC 0+1 Others 1/1

Ian Hendon

HENDON Ian Michael
Born: Ilford, 5 December 1971
Height: 6'0" Weight: 12.10
Club Honours: FAYC '90; CS '91; Div 3 '98
International Honours: E: U21-7; Yth
A wing back whose telling runs down the right flank resulted in quite a few goals for his Northampton team-mates last season, Ian has an explosive free kick that added to his own tally of goals. He is a skilful player who can dribble his way out of trouble or into the opposition penalty area. Ian reads the game well and is one of those players who can turn defence into attack in one move. He scored the first goal of the Cobblers' promotion campaign from the penalty spot, yet he was only third choice, as regular penalty taker Carlo Corazzin was off the field and Roy Hunter was not playing. His overall contribution was recognised with inclusion in the PFA award-winning divisional team for the third time in his career.
Tottenham H (From trainee on 20/12/1989) FL 0+4 FLC 1 Others 0+2
Portsmouth (Loaned on 16/1/1992) FL 1+3
Leyton Orient (Loaned on 26/3/1992) FL 5+1
Barnsley (Loaned on 17/3/1993) FL 6
Leyton Orient (£50,000 on 9/8/1993) FL 130+1/5 FLC 8 FAC 7 Others 12/1
Birmingham C (Loaned on 23/3/1995) FL 4
Notts Co (£50,000 on 24/2/1997) FL 82/6 FLC 5/1 FAC 8+1
Northampton T (£30,000 on 25/3/1999) FL 51/2 FLC 2 FAC 1/1 Others 1

HENDRIE Lee Andrew
Born: Birmingham, 18 May 1977
Height: 5'10" Weight: 10.3
International Honours: E: 1; B-1; U21-13; Yth
This talented Aston Villa youngster began the 1999-2000 campaign on the subs' bench after catching a virus during the summer break but quickly returned to the starting line-up. He then featured regularly in the Villa team until suffering an ankle ligament injury against Newcastle last December that put him out of action for several weeks. Unfortunately, the injury flared up again during his comeback game against Southampton and it was not until the end of January that he returned to match fitness. He was then mostly restricted to appearances from the subs' bench in the second half of the season, including an outing in the FA Cup final when he replaced Alan Wright for the final few minutes. Lee continued to represent England at U21 level, adding six further caps to his total and joining the squad for the European Championship in Slovakia. He is a creative midfield player with good pace and the skills to unlock even the tightest of opposition defences on his day.
Aston Villa (From trainee on 18/5/1994) PL 64+21/7 FLC 4+1/3 FAC 5+8 Others 5+1

HENDRY Edward **Colin** James
Born: Keith, 7 December 1965
Height: 6'1" Weight: 12.7
Club Honours: FMC '87; PL '95; SLC '98; SPD '99; SC '99
International Honours: S: 43; B-1
The blond captain of Scotland joined Coventry from Glasgow Rangers in February 1999. The fee was not disclosed but it is believed to be on a "pay as you play" basis, i.e. the more games he plays the more money City must pay Rangers. He had endured a miserable season-and-a-half at Ibrox after suffering knee injuries and failing to convince manager Dick Advocaat that he was worth a place. Colin's swashbuckling style was evident from the start at Coventry but not even he could help the side improve its dire away record. He quickly recovered match fitness but then suffered a serious facial injury at West Ham that curtailed his season.
Dundee (Signed from Islavale on 1/7/1983) SL 17+24/2 SC 2+3/1
Blackburn Rov (£30,000 on 11/3/1987) FL 99+3/22 FLC 4 FAC 3 Others 13/1
Manchester C (£700,000 on 16/11/1989) FL 57+6/5 FLC 4+1/1 FAC 5/2 Others 4/2
Blackburn Rov (£700,000 on 8/11/1991) P/FL 229+5/12 FLC 23 FAC 17+1 Others 11
Glasgow R (£4,000,000 on 5/8/1998) SL 18+3 SLC 3+1 SC 3 Others 4+1
Coventry C (£750,000 on 3/3/2000) PL 9

Colin Hendry

HENRY Anthony Francis
Born: Stepney, 13 September 1979
Height: 6'1" Weight: 13.8
A solid central defender, Anthony initially joined Lincoln on a short-term contract after impressing while on trial during the build-up to the 1999-2000 season. He made his Football League debut in November as a substitute at Mansfield and went on to retain his place in the Imps' line-up until the middle of February. He proved particularly effective when pushed forward at free kicks and corners and scored goals in the Auto Windscreens Shield tie against Scunthorpe and in the 2-2 home draw with Northampton. His consistent performances earned him a two-year deal with the Imps, but he finished the season on the injury list after fracturing a foot playing in a reserve match.
West Ham U (From trainee on 6/6/1997)
Lincoln C (Free on 5/8/1999) FL 14+3/1 FAC 2 Others 1/1

HENRY Nicholas (Nick) Ian
Born: Liverpool, 21 February 1969
Height: 5'6" Weight: 10.12
Club Honours: Div 2 '91

Having signed for Tranmere from Walsall under the Bosman ruling in the summer of 1999, Nick proved to be one of the driving forces behind Rovers' great cup runs in 1999-2000 and won a Worthington Cup runners-up medal after appearing in the final against Leicester. He was appointed club captain and worked tirelessly in midfield, where his keen tackling and intelligent passing were of great value. He scored three times during the season, including a cracking 20-yarder that proved to be the winner in the FA Cup tie with West Ham and another superb strike which set Rovers on their way to a 3-0 victory over Bolton in the second leg of the Worthington Cup semi-final. Nick missed the last few games after being involved in a car crash but is expected to be fully fit in time for the start of the 2000-01 campaign.

Oldham Ath (From trainee on 6/7/1987) F/PL 264+9/19 FLC 30+4/3 FAC 21 Others 5
Sheffield U (£500,000 on 28/2/1997) FL 13+3 FAC 2+1 Others 2
Walsall (Free on 25/3/1999) FL 8
Tranmere Rov (Free on 5/7/1999) FL 28+2/1 FLC 6/1 FAC 4/1

HENRY Thierry
Born: Paris, France, 17 August 1977
Height: 6'1" Weight: 12.2
International Honours: France: 21 (UEFA '00); Yth (UEFA-U18 '96)

A £10.5 million signing from Juventus during the summer of 1999, Thierry has developed into the most exciting player in the Arsenal squad. A French international World Cup star, he was his country's leading goalscorer in the 1998 World Cup finals and had previously played under Gunners' manager Arsene Wenger at Monaco when he was just 17 years old. He has devastating speed, and although he can play on the flanks his strength is in the middle of the front line. A direct player with an eye for goal, Thierry got stronger and better as the season progressed. Apart from his great pace, he has wonderful dribbling skills, a dazzling ability to finish and the enthusiasm to get back and defend when the need arises. He is an unselfish player who creates chances for team-mates, and was often the difference between Arsenal and their opponents last season. His first goal for the Gunners was a wonderful strike in the away league fixture at Southampton. Just eight minutes after coming off the bench, he drove home a looping shot from outside the penalty box to secure a 1-0 victory. Although he had missed a number of chances in previous games, Thierry then went from strength to strength to become Arsenal's leading goalscorer. He recorded 15 goals in the 15 games leading up to the UEFA Cup final – a phenomenal feat. He also had a productive season at international level. Recalled to the French national team for the friendly with Scotland in March, he impressed sufficiently to win a regular place for *les Bleus*, scoring five times in ten games and playing a vital role in their sensational victory in the European Championship.

Arsenal (£8,000,000 from Juventus, Italy on 6/8/1999) PL 26+5/17 FLC 2/1 FAC 3 Others 7+5/8

Thierry Henry

HERBERT Craig Justin
Born: Coventry, 9 November 1975
Height: 5'11" Weight: 11.6

Probably the most unfortunate player at Shrewsbury in 1999-2000, Craig was competing against a number of other centre backs at the club. He was confined mainly to the reserves or the substitutes' bench and made only two appearances. He proved a solid defender both in the air and on the ground. Released at the end of the season, Craig is a player who deserves to find success elsewhere.

West Bromwich A (Free from Torquay U juniors on 18/3/1994) FL 8 FLC 2 Others 1/1
Shrewsbury T (Free on 23/7/1997) FL 30+4 FLC 3 FAC 2/1 Others 1

HERBERT Robert
Born: Durham, 29 August 1983
Height: 5'8" Weight: 11.0

Robert made Halifax history by becoming the club's youngest-ever player when he made his debut against Brighton a few days after his 16th birthday in September 1999. The record had stood for 14 years, and was set by Phil Whitehead, who has more recently kept goal for West Bromwich Albion. A back injury then ruined Robert's season. He made a couple more substitute appearances away at York and Exeter, before making his first start in the last match, at home against Macclesfield.

Halifax T (Trainee) FL 1+3 Others 0+1

HERRERA Roberto (Robbie)
Born: Torquay, 12 June 1970
Height: 5'7" Weight: 10.6

With his attacking flair and good defensive positional play, Robbie was often Torquay's best player during 1999-2000. The left wing back originally joined the Gulls on schoolboy forms before making his name at Queens Park Rangers. After over a hundred games for his home-town club, as the 2000-01 campaign dawned, Robbie still awaited his first Gulls goal.

Queens Park R (From trainee on 1/3/1988) FL 4+2 FLC 1+2 Others 1+1
Torquay U (Loaned on 17/3/1992) FL 11
Torquay U (Loaned on 24/10/1992) FL 5
Fulham (Signed on 29/10/1993) FL 143+2/1 FLC 15 FAC 13 Others 7+1
Torquay U (£30,000 on 4/8/1998) FL 73+2 FLC 4 FAC 4 Others 2

Emile Heskey

HESKEY Emile William Ivanhoe
Born: Leicester, 11 January 1978
Height: 6'2" Weight: 13.12
Club Honours: FLC '97, '00
International Honours: E: 9; B-1; U21-16; Yth

A two-footed striker with power and pace, Emile continued to pose problems for opposition defenders throughout the 1999-2000 season, first with Leicester and then with Liverpool. Some critics maintain that he doesn't score enough goals, but his overall contribution is immense, Emile regularly creating a host of goalscoring opportunities for others. He picked up a Worthington Cup winners' medal after City's defeat of Tranmere and soon afterwards earned his fifth England cap against Argentina at Wembley. It was his first international start and a rampaging performance rightly earned him a "Man of the Match" accolade. "Bruno" then departed Filbert Street for Anfield, with City receiving a club record fee of £11 million. Emile proved to be an instant hero with Kopites and his powerful physique mirrors an equally big heart. Always willing to run until he drops, he is a striker who can provide a physical presence which neither Robbie Fowler nor Michael Owen provides in quite the same way. An injury to his back just a few weeks after signing for the club hindered Emile's immediate progress, but he continued to turn in some useful performances until the end of the season. He went on to make the final 22 for England's Euro 2000 squad and made appearances from the subs' bench against Portugal and Romania.

Leicester C (From trainee on 3/10/1995) PL 143+11/40 FLC 25+2/6 FAC 11 Others 5
Liverpool (£11,000,000 on 10/3/2000) PL 12/3

HESSENTHALER Andrew (Andy)
Born: Dartford, 17 June 1965
Height: 5'7" Weight: 11.5
International Honours: E: SP-1

Gillingham's competitive midfielder was given the role of player-coach in the summer of 1999. The change did not affect his position in the side, however, and he continued to provide inspirational leadership from the centre of the park in 1999-2000. He scored eight goals during the season, including a sensational 18-yarder in the 90th minute of the Second Division play-off semi-final first leg at Stoke to ensure that the Gills went into the home leg with just a single-goal deficit. Andy was rewarded for some great performances when he was voted "Player of the Year" for the second time in three seasons. Stop Press: He was appointed Gillingham manager in the summer following the departure of Peter Taylor.

Watford (£65,000 from Redbridge Forest on 12/9/1991) FL 195/12 FLC 13/1 FAC 5/2 Others 4
Gillingham (£235,000 on 7/8/1996) FL 157+4/14 FLC 15/2 FAC 12+1/1 Others 9+1/3

Andy Hessenthaler

HEWITT James (Jamie) Robert
Born: Chesterfield, 17 May 1968
Height: 5'10" Weight: 11.9

This consistently reliable right back made his 500th league appearance for Chesterfield against Cardiff last March. Jamie has matured into a fine club servant who goes about his game with an undemonstrative effectiveness whether on the right-hand side of defence or in midfield, playing every game to the best of his ability and giving his all for his home-town club. With the advent of the Bosman ruling, few players will be content to serve one club as Jamie has done over the years.

Chesterfield (From trainee on 22/4/1986) FL 240+9/14 FLC 10/1 FAC 8+1 Others 11+2
Doncaster Rov (Free on 1/8/1992) FL 32+1 FLC 3+1/1 FAC 1 Others 3
Chesterfield (Signed on 8/10/1993) FL 247+9/12 FLC 18 FAC 15/1 Others 14/1

HEWLETT Matthew (Matt) Paul
Born: Bristol, 25 February 1976
Height: 6'2" Weight: 11.3
International Honours: E: Yth

Sidelined for much of the 1999-2000 season with injury problems, Matt was unable to show the sort of form one would expect of such a talented individual in his sporadic appearances in the Bristol City first team. The England youth international remains an enigma. A skilful midfield player who at his best can demonstrate great vision with his running off the ball, he seems to lack the confidence to really impose himself. At the end of another disappointing season for him he was released and it is to be hoped that he will be able to resurrect his career with another club.

Bristol C (From trainee on 12/8/1993) FL 111+16/9 FLC 10+2 FAC 4+1/2 Others 7+2/1
Burnley (Loaned on 27/11/1998) FL 2 Others 1

HIBBURT James Anthony
Born: Ashford, 30 October 1979
Height: 6'0" Weight: 12.8
International Honours: E: Sch

This tall and reliable Crystal Palace youngster is essentially a central defender but he has also occasionally been used in midfield for the reserves. Jamie featured three times for the Eagles in 1999-2000, making his first Football League start against Bolton last November. He will be looking to win a regular place in the first-team squad in the coming season.

Crystal Palace (From trainee on 2/11/1996) FL 1+5

HICKEY Benjamin (Ben) Joseph
Born: Sutton Coldfield, 11 November 1974
Height: 5'11" Weight: 12.0

A young midfield player, Ben returned to Darlington, his home-town club, in August 1999 after several years in the United States, where he had most recently played with Third Division club North Jersey Imperials, a minor league affiliate of the New York/New Jersey Metrostars. He was given a three-month trial period after impressing in pre-season games. However, after just one substitute appearance, against Bolton in the Worthington Cup, he failed to establish himself and was released.

Darlington (Free from North Jersey Imperials, USA, via St John's University, Connecticut Wolves, Long Island Rough Riders and Staten Island Vipers, on 9/8/1999) FLC 0+1

HICKS Graham
Born: Oldham, 17 February 1981
Height: 5'11" Weight: 13.0

The young Rochdale central defender was named as a substitute on a number of occasions during the 1999-2000 season. His only first-team appearance came in the FA Cup against Burton Albion. Replacing the suspended Keith Hill, Graham played a key role in helping Dale to keep a clean sheet. A frustrating campaign was concluded with a hernia operation.

Rochdale (From trainee on 21/1/1999) FL 1 FAC 1

HICKS Stuart Jason
Born: Peterborough, 30 May 1967
Height: 6'1" Weight: 13.0

For Stuart, 1999-2000 proved to be a season of two very difficult halves. A vastly experienced centre back with an insatiable will to win, up to the turn of the year, he was a key member of the Leyton Orient team that was surprisingly struggling at the bottom of the Third Division. After being sidelined with a virus, Stuart agreed a two-and-a-half-year deal with Chester in February. Although he is now aged 33, there'll be nobody more determined to bring the Blues back to the Football League in 2000-01.

Peterborough U (From apprentice on 10/8/1984)
Colchester U (Free from Wisbech on 24/3/1988) FL 57+7 FLC 2 FAC 5/1 Others 5
Scunthorpe U (Free on 19/8/1990) FL 67/1 FLC 4 FAC 4/1 Others 8
Doncaster Rov (Free on 10/8/1992) FL 36 FLC 2 FAC 1 Others 2
Huddersfield T (Signed on 27/8/1993) FL 20+2/1 FLC 3 FAC 3 Others 1
Preston NE (Signed on 24/3/1994) FL 11+1 FLC 2 Others 1/1
Scarborough (Signed on 22/2/1995) FL 81+4/2 FLC 5 FAC 4 Others 3
Leyton Orient (Free on 5/8/1997) FL 77+1 FLC 9 FAC 6 Others 2+1
Chester C (Free on 25/2/2000) FL 13

HIDEN Martin
Born: Stainz, Austria, 11 March 1973
Height: 6'0" Weight: 11.9
International Honours: Austria: 7

Probably the unluckiest player in the Leeds United squad, Martin, a classy Austrian defender, had just started to make his mark in 1998-99 when he sustained an injury that kept him out for nine months. He recovered and made a substitute appearance at Old Trafford in August 1999, only to suffer yet another long-term injury in the reserves that wiped out the rest of his season. Martin reads the game well, and times his tackles with precision. His ability to play right across the back four makes him an invaluable squad member and Leeds supporters can only wish him a full recovery. Stop Press: He was reported to have joined Austria Salzburg during the summer.

Leeds U (£1,300,000 from Rapid Vienna, Austria on 25/2/1998) PL 25+1 FLC 1 FAC 1 Others 4

HIGGINBOTHAM Daniel (Danny) John
Born: Manchester, 29 December 1978
Height: 6'1" Weight: 12.6

This young Manchester United defender, who is probably better known as a player with Royal Antwerp, began 1999-2000 with a life ban hanging over his head, following an alleged incident involving a referee during his time in Belgium the previous season. Despite pleading a case of mis-identity, Danny was relieved to receive a three-year suspended sentence in September. He was given several chances to shine during the course of the campaign, notably against Aston Villa in the Worthington Cup, Leicester in the Premiership and Sturm Graz in the Champions' League, and early indications suggest he's one for the future. Stop Press: Danny was reported to have joined Derby in early July.

Manchester U (From trainee on 10/7/1997) PL 2+2 FLC 1 Others 1+1

HIGNETT Craig John
Born: Prescot, 12 January 1970
Height: 5'9" Weight: 11.10
Club Honours: Div 1 '95

Craig had a magnificent season for Barnsley in 1999-2000, finishing as leading scorer with 22 goals and being voted into the PFA Division Two side by his fellow professionals. However, the campaign ended with a heartbreaking Wembley defeat by Ipswich Town in the play-off final when he finished on the losing side despite scoring twice. New manager Dave Bassett used Craig in a number of roles from midfield to out-and-out striker and he always gave of his best. His ability to make things happen in the opposition half and a knack of being in the right place at the right time to score crucial goals were of major significance to Barnsley's promotion bid. He produced one of his best performances against Walsall last December when he scored a cracking hat-trick, including a great strike from 30 yards in the closing minutes.

Crewe Alex (Free from Liverpool juniors on 11/5/1988) FL 108+13/42 FLC 9+1/4 FAC 11+1/8 Others 6+1/3
Middlesbrough (£500,000 on 27/11/1992) F/PL 126+30/33 FLC 19+3/12 FAC 9+2/3 Others 5+1
Aberdeen (Free on 1/7/1998) SL 13/2 SLC 2
Barnsley (£800,000 on 26/11/1998) FL 62+4/28 FLC 2 FAC 6/5 Others 3/2

HILEY Scott Patrick
Born: Plymouth, 27 September 1968
Height: 5'9" Weight: 11.5
Club Honours: Div 4 '90

A very good squad player, Scott was unable to secure a regular first-team place during his spell with Southampton but never let the club down when selected. Used as cover in the right-back spot, he enjoyed getting forward when given the chance and could deliver a good cross. With the arrival of Jo Tessem last November he was rather unluckily considered to be surplus to requirements at the Dell and he was allowed to join Portsmouth in a £50,000 deal in December. However, within a matter of days manager Alan Ball, who had also signed him when he was in charge at Manchester City and had previously been his boss at Exeter, was sacked. Although Scott featured in a couple of games under caretaker manager Bob McNab, he rarely played after Tony Pulis took over and, despite a fine game in the 1-0 win at Ipswich in March, he was released at the end of the season.

Exeter C (From trainee on 4/8/1986) FL 205+5/12 FLC 17 FAC 14 Others 16+2
Birmingham C (£100,000 on 12/3/1994) FL 49 FLC 7 FAC 1 Others 2
Manchester C (£250,000 on 23/2/1996) P/FL 4+5
Southampton (Free on 4/8/1998) PL 30+2 FAC 1
Portsmouth (£200,000 on 3/12/1999) FL 4+4 FAC 1

HILL Clinton (Clint) Scott
Born: Huyton, 19 October 1978
Height: 6'0" Weight: 11.6

This rugged, no-nonsense defender formed a formidable partnership with Dave Challinor at the back for Tranmere in 1999-2000. A strong and powerful player, he again achieved a certain notoriety due to his disciplinary record, receiving a red card in the Worthington Cup final against Leicester and being dismissed four times in total during the season. While this was a result more of over-enthusiasm than of malicious intent, it is an area of his game that he really must try to show improvement in over the coming season. He scored seven valuable goals, including the vital winner in the first leg of the Worthington Cup semi-final against Bolton.

Tranmere Rov (From trainee on 9/7/1997) FL 74+2/9 FLC 11/2 FAC 3+1/1

Danny Hill

HILL Daniel (Danny) Ronald
Born: Enfield, 1 October 1974
Height: 5'9" Weight: 11.10
International Honours: E: U21-4; Yth

A gifted, creative midfield player, Danny has not yet lived up to expectations at Cardiff. He started last season in the first team and looked impressive as the Bluebirds produced some delightful football. However, injury intervened and after that it was a season of fitful involvement for the Londoner. He has ability in abundance but has still not achieved real consistency over a season with any of the clubs he has played for. Danny is a joy to watch on the ball, and on his day he can be devastating. His goal at

Bristol Rovers in a 1-1 draw, helped by a superlative touch from Dai Thomas as they played a one-two, was outstanding. He was out of contract at the end of the season but Cardiff offered him new terms and will be looking for him to fulfil his undoubted potential during the coming campaign.
Tottenham H (From trainee on 9/9/1992) PL 4+6 FLC 0+2
Birmingham C (Loaned on 24/11/1995) FL 5 FLC 2
Watford (Loaned on 15/2/1996) FL 1
Cardiff C (Loaned on 19/2/1998) FL 7
Oxford U (Free on 30/7/1998) FL 1+8 FLC 0+1
Cardiff C (Free on 12/11/1998) FL 26+23/3 FLC 1 FAC 3+3 Others 2

HILL Keith John
Born: Bolton, 17 May 1969
Height: 6'0" Weight: 12.6
Keith was a tower of strength at the centre of Rochdale's defence in 1999-2000, partnering either Dave Bayliss or Mark Monington. He was consistency personified, and a tough opponent for any striker. Although he was suspended three times, he reached 150 league games for Dale near the end of the season. His only goal was important, as his winner at Carlisle earned Dale their place in the Northern Final of the Auto Windscreens Shield.
Blackburn Rov (From juniors on 9/5/1987) F/PL 89+7/3 FLC 6/1 FAC 5+1 Others 3+2
Plymouth Arg (Signed on 23/9/1992) FL 117+6/2 FLC 9 FAC 10 Others 9
Rochdale (Free on 3/7/1996) FL 149+2/6 FLC 8 FAC 7 Others 6/1

HILL Kevin
Born: Exeter, 6 March 1976
Height: 5'8" Weight: 10.3
This dynamic utility player's best games for Torquay in 1999-2000 were in a roving midfield position. Kevin's all-action style and surprising aerial ability for a relatively short player made him a firm favourite with the fans. Kevin scored some vital goals after making late runs to get into the penalty box. Signed from Torrington of the Great Mills Western League, he regularly played on the left side of a midfield trio – completed by Chris Brandon and Brian Healy – who were all recruited from non-league clubs.
Torquay U (Free from Torrington on 8/8/1997) FL 92+23/14 FLC 6+1 FAC 9/1 Others 6+1/1

HILL Matthew (Matt) Clayton
Born: Bristol, 26 March 1981
Height: 5'7" Weight: 12.6
After making his debut in Bristol City's demoralising 0-5 home defeat by Wolves in 1998-99, Matt, a graduate of the successful Ashton Gate academy set-up, came further to the fore last season. Excellent in the air, despite his lack of height, this quick-tackling full back or centre half appeared fairly regularly in the City first team in the second half of the campaign and looks to have an excellent future in the game.
Bristol C (From trainee on 22/2/1999) FL 8+9 Others 3+2

HILL Nicholas (Nicky) Damien
Born: Accrington, 26 February 1981
Height: 6'0" Weight: 12.3
A product of Bury's youth policy, this former trainee was one of a number of youngsters given their first-team chance following Andy Preece's appointment as caretaker manager last December. Able to play at centre half or left back, Nicky first appeared as a substitute for Paul Williams in a 3-2 home win against Blackpool on 22 April, and was then given his full debut two days later at Cardiff. Nicky also retained his place for the closing three games of the season as the Shakers fielded a particularly young defence in general. His strong, confident performances will have given great encouragement both to the player and to his manager.
Bury (From trainee on 9/7/1999) FL 4+1

HILLIER David
Born: Blackheath, 19 December 1969
Height: 5'10" Weight: 12.5
Club Honours: FAYC '88; Div 1 '91
International Honours: E: U21-1
The experienced former Arsenal and Portsmouth central midfielder, always comfortable in possession and an accurate dead-ball kicker, enjoyed a tremendous season with Bristol Rovers in 1999-2000. David suffered tendonitis in December followed by a neck injury in January, which broke a fine run of consecutive matches, but his presence in the Rovers midfield, where he took over the role of player-manager Ian Holloway, was one of the reasons for the significant progress made by the team. One disappointing aspect of the campaign was David's continuing inability to score for Bristol Rovers despite many near-misses and other efforts frustrated by fine saves by opposing goalkeepers. Nevertheless his promptings from midfield were much appreciated by the club's supporters.
Arsenal (From trainee on 11/2/1988) F/PL 82+22/2 FLC 13+2 FAC 13+2 Others 5+4
Portsmouth (£250,000 on 2/11/1996) FL 62+5/4 FLC 3/2 FAC 4/1
Bristol Rov (£15,000 on 24/2/1999) FL 52 FLC 4 FAC 1 Others 1

John Hills

HILLS John David
Born: Blackpool, 21 April 1978
Height: 5'9" Weight: 11.2
John is an enthusiastic young Blackpool player who featured on the left side in both defence and midfield during 1999-2000. He is quick in the tackle, delivers a decent cross and is beginning to earn a reputation as a penalty taker. He appeared regularly for Blackpool throughout the campaign apart from a couple of short spells out injured, and his consistency was rewarded when he was voted "Player of the Season" by the club's supporters.
Blackpool (From trainee on 27/10/1995)
Everton (£90,000 on 4/11/1995) PL 1+2
Swansea C (Loaned on 30/1/1997) FL 11/1
Swansea C (Loaned on 22/8/1997) FL 7
Blackpool (£75,000 on 16/1/1998) FL 78+2/4 FLC 3 FAC 4 Others 4

HIMSWORTH Gary Paul
Born: Pickering, 19 December 1969
Height: 5'8" Weight: 10.6
Now in his second spell at Darlington, this busy utility player faded out of the first-team picture after featuring in the majority of the club's games in the first four months of the 1999-2000 season. Although at his best on the left, Gary is a skilful and adroit player who can fulfil any number of roles in defence or midfield. He made only two first-team starts in the second half of the Quakers' play-off campaign.
York C (From trainee on 27/1/1988) FL 74+14/8 FLC 5 Others 5+2
Scarborough (Free on 5/12/1990) FL 83+9/6 FLC 7+2/1 FAC 1+1 Others 6+1
Darlington (Free on 16/7/1993) FL 86+8/8 FLC 5+1 FAC 6 Others 7/4
York C (£25,000 on 16/2/1996) FL 60+9/3 FLC 4 FAC 6+2/1 Others 3/1
Darlington (Signed on 5/3/1999) FL 27+6/1 FLC 2 FAC 1+1

HINCHCLIFFE Andrew (Andy) George
Born: Manchester, 5 February 1969
Height: 5'10" Weight: 13.7
Club Honours: FAC '95; CS '95
International Honours: E: 7; U21-1; Yth
This cultured left back had a consistent season for Sheffield Wednesday in 1999-2000 despite his team's relegation to Division One. He is a hard-working defender who is comfortable coming forward and is able to deliver a fine cross. Andy dropped out of the England squad during the season, the legacy of playing in a struggling team, but remains a class player at Hillsborough.
Manchester C (From apprentice on 13/2/1986) FL 107+5/8 FLC 11/1 FAC 12/1 Others 4/1
Everton (£800,000 on 17/7/1990) F/PL 170+12/7 FLC 21+2/1 FAC 12+2/1 Others 8
Sheffield Wed (£2,850,000 on 30/1/1998) PL 76/5 FLC 4 FAC 6

HINDS Richard Paul
Born: Sheffield, 22 August 1980
Height: 6'2" Weight: 11.0
This tall Yorkshireman's preferred position is in defence but he was a revelation when called upon to play in an unfamiliar midfield role after injuries decimated the Tranmere squad last April. He provided a calming

influence in the centre of the park with his neat, accurate passing and showed maturity well beyond his years. Having served an apprenticeship in the Pontins League side, this impressive youngster is expected to establish himself in the Tranmere first team in 2000-01.

Tranmere Rov (From juniors on 20/7/1998) FL 6+2

HISLOP Neil **Shaka**
Born: Hackney, 22 February 1969
Height: 6'4" Weight: 14.4
Club Honours: Div 2 '94
International Honours: E: U21-1. Trinidad & Tobago: 3

Shaka had another great season as West Ham's goalkeeper in 1999-2000, showing consistent form until he broke a leg in a freak accident in the home game with Bradford last February. Perhaps his best performance of the season came at White Hart Lane in December when he produced outstanding saves to deny Chris Perry and Chris Armstrong and earn the Hammers a 0-0 draw. He is now a good all-round 'keeper who shows full command of his box, and has improved his handling of crosses. Shaka added a couple of appearances for Trinidad & Tobago to his total, appearing against Colombia and Honduras in the autumn, but opted out of the Gold Cup tournament as the club were already losing his deputy, Craig Forrest, to the Canadian team.

Reading (Signed from Howard University, USA on 9/9/1992) FL 104 FLC 10 FAC 3 Others 9
Newcastle U (£1,575,000 on 10/8/1995) PL 53 FLC 8 FAC 6 Others 4
West Ham U (Free on 8/7/1998) PL 59 FLC 6 FAC 3 Others 6

HITCHEN Steven (Steve) James
Born: Salford, 28 November 1976
Height: 5'8" Weight: 11.8

Having enjoyed a marvellous 1998-99 campaign, when he was recognised as Macclesfield's most improved player and swept the board in their end-of-season awards, Steve endured rather different fortunes in 1999-2000. A full back who can play on either flank, he held out on his contract renewal following interest from several First Division sides and started the season on a week-to-week contract. Sadly, he was stretchered off the field after only 36 minutes of the first league game of the season against Northampton, and it was later discovered that he had severe cruciate ligament damage. Macclesfield stood by him and agreed to a full contract after the injury to save him any financial worries. Steve resumed light training at the start of February and in March successfully played in "A" team and reserve matches before returning to the first team from the bench at Leyton Orient at the beginning of April. The man who has the distinction of being Macc's first signing as a Football League club showed all the skills he had displayed before the injury.

Blackburn Rov (From trainee on 4/7/1995)
Macclesfield T (Free on 14/7/1997) FL 38+4 FLC 1+1 FAC 4

HJELDE Jon Olav
Born: Levanger, Norway, 30 April 1972
Height: 6'1" Weight: 13.7
Club Honours: Div 1 '98

This tall Norwegian centre back was again hampered by injuries in 1999-2000. He managed an unbroken run in the Nottingham Forest first team between October and early January, and went on to appear in a total of 26 Football League games during the campaign. He is strong in the air and solid in the tackle, and will be hoping to achieve a regular slot in the Forest defence next season.

Nottingham F (£600,000 from Rosenborg, Norway on 8/8/1997) P/FL 65+13/2 FLC 7/2 FAC 4

HJORTH Jesper
Born: Denmark, 3 April 1975
Height: 6'0" Weight: 12.4

Jesper is one of a number of foreign players brought to Darlington in recent seasons by manager David Hodgson. The popular Dane arrived three months into the 1999-2000 season, and after impressing on trial was signed until the end of the campaign. He figured in the majority of games after Christmas, but nearly always only as a second-half substitute. Jesper started only eight games, yet managed to contribute six crucial and spectacular goals. His strong running, close control and powerful shooting also served Odense for five seasons. Jesper was involved in their 1994-95 UEFA Cup run that saw defeats of Real Madrid and Kaiserslautern.

Darlington (Signed from OB Odense, Denmark on 11/11/1999) FL 8+14/6 FAC 0+2 Others 2+1

HOBSON Gary
Born: Hull, 12 November 1972
Height: 6'1" Weight: 13.3

The former Brighton captain found it difficult to hold down a first-team place following the influx of defenders into Micky Adams's squad. Utilised at both centre half and left back, he found himself surplus to requirements in January and went on loan to Chester, a move which later became permanent. Although the season ended in relegation to the Conference, the left-footed defender's coolness in a crisis was there for all to see. Never giving less than 100 per cent effort, Gary is excellent in possession. However, this likeable character was released at the end of the season.

Hull C (From trainee on 17/7/1991) FL 135+7 FLC 13+1 FAC 2+2/1 Others 6
Brighton & Hove A (£60,000 on 27/3/1996) FL 92+6/1 FLC 7 FAC 4+1 Others 3
Chester C (Signed on 7/1/2000) FL 20

HOCKING Matthew (Matt) James
Born: Boston, 30 January 1978
Height: 5'11" Weight: 11.12

In his first full season at York, the former Hull player figured in a number of positions. Noted for his pace and firm tackling, he was mainly used at right back, sometimes on the right of midfield and occasionally up front, where he netted winning goals at Brighton and at home to Barnet. With the change of management at Bootham Crescent in February, Matt was not so prominent as 1999-2000 drew to a close.

Sheffield U (From trainee on 16/5/1996)
Hull C (£25,000 on 19/9/1997) FL 55+2/2 FLC 6 FAC 4 Others 4
York C (£30,000 on 25/3/1999) FL 30+8/2 FLC 1+1 FAC 0+1 Others 1

HOCKTON Daniel (Danny) John
Born: Barking, 7 February 1979
Height: 5'11" Weight: 11.11

Danny joined Leyton Orient from Millwall in September 1999 in a bid to solve the Os' goalscoring problems. Unfortunately, he pulled his hamstring during his first game, against Grimsby in the Worthington Cup, and missed a number of matches. He returned briefly before rejoining Millwall in November. He did not appear in the Lions' first team in 2000-01.

Millwall (From trainee on 8/3/1997) FL 11+25/4 FLC 2+1/2 FAC 0+1 Others 0+4/1
Leyton Orient (Loaned on 13/9/1999) FL 1+4 FLC 1

HODGE John
Born: Skelmersdale, 1 April 1969
Height: 5'7" Weight: 11.12
Club Honours: AMC '94

This experienced winger again found himself on the subs' bench at Gillingham during the 1999-2000 season and five of his six starts came in cup matches. He eventually moved on loan to Northampton in March, searching for regular first-team action, and shortly afterwards the transfer was made permanent for a £25,000 fee. A ball-playing winger who is at home on either flank, John made his debut for the Cobblers as a substitute against Leyton Orient and had a hand in both goals in a 2-1 victory. He has exceptional ability and likes to take defenders on, beating them by skill and speed. John was a team-mate of Northampton manager Kevin Wilson while they were both at Walsall, and claims he laid on a lot of his goals! His new boss stated: "John is an exciting player who puts bums on seats."

Exeter C (Signed from Falmouth T on 12/9/1991) FL 57+8/10 FLC 3/1 FAC 2 Others 8+2/1
Swansea C (Signed on 14/7/1993) FL 87+25/10 FLC 6+2/3 FAC 6 Others 13+4
Walsall (Free on 23/9/1996) FL 67+9/12 FLC 5 FAC 7+1/2 Others 5+2
Gillingham (Free on 10/7/1998) FL 8+41/1 FLC 4+1 FAC 3+2/1 Others 2+4
Northampton T (£25,000 on 7/3/2000) FL 5+3

HODGES Lee Leslie
Born: Plaistow, 2 March 1978
Height: 5'5" Weight: 10.2
International Honours: E: Sch

Lee arrived at Scunthorpe in the summer of 1999 from West Ham looking for first-team football and got his wish, establishing himself as a regular on the team sheet during the 1999-2000 season. He struggled to settle up north at first but by October he was flying, running at defences and being the creative force behind all of Scunthorpe's most exciting play. Best suited to a role wide on the left rather than in a central position, he has immense skill and dribbling ability, and also scored a number of spectacular goals during the campaign. He was the runaway winner of the Scunthorpe United "Player of the Season" award.

West Ham U (From trainee on 2/3/1995) PL 0+3 FAC 0+3
Exeter C (Loaned on 13/9/1996) FL 16+1
Leyton Orient (Loaned on 28/2/1997) FL 3
Plymouth Arg (Loaned on 6/11/1997) FL 9 Others 1
Ipswich T (Loaned on 20/11/1998) FL 0+4
Southend U (Loaned on 25/3/1999) FL 10/1
Scunthorpe U (£130,000 on 8/7/1999) FL 39+1/6 FLC 2 FAC 1 Others 1/1

HODGES Lee Leslie
Born: Epping, 4 September 1973
Height: 6'0" Weight: 12.1
International Honours: E: Yth

Yet more injury problems blighted Lee's 1999-2000 season with Reading and he appeared in only half the matches. For a spell he looked as though he might fill the problem spot on the left side of midfield and he capped an inspired display at local rivals Oxford United with a goal. He has the ability to be one of the most creative players in the Second Division but needs to play more consistently to prove himself to the manager and the fans, and was given only a one-year extension to his current contract.

Tottenham H (From trainee on 29/2/1992) PL 0+4
Plymouth Arg (Loaned on 26/2/1993) FL 6+1/2
Wycombe W (Loaned on 31/12/1993) FL 2+2 FAC 1 Others 1
Barnet (Free on 31/5/1994) FL 94+11/26 FLC 6+1 FAC 6+1/4 Others 3+1
Reading (£100,000 on 29/7/1997) FL 35+15/8 FLC 6+3 FAC 4+1 Others 0+1

HODGSON Richard James
Born: Sunderland, 1 October 1979
Height: 5'10" Weight: 11.8

Out of favour at Nottingham Forest, Richard, a midfielder, had a trial at Scunthorpe in January 2000 and impressed enough in the reserves for United to sign him on non-contract terms in early March. Thrown into the first team for a relegation six-pointer against Cambridge, he struggled to get into the game and was substituted at half time. Although he is a good passer of the ball with a strong left foot, Richard was released by the Iron the following week.

Nottingham F (From trainee on 8/10/1996)
Scunthorpe U (Free on 9/3/2000) FL 1

HODOUTO Kwami
Born: Lome, Togo, 31 October 1974
Height: 5'11" Weight: 11.12

The French defender joined Huddersfield from Auxerre on a free transfer last September and made his bow in English football soon afterwards with a substitute appearance against Norwich City, quickly followed up by a start in the Worthington Cup at Notts County. He showed considerable promise, with a good touch and accurate passing, but injury and fitness problems blighted his progress after this encouraging start and he was later released, having made one more appearance.

Huddersfield T (Free from Auxerre, France on 16/9/1999) FL 1+1 FLC 1

HOGH Jes
Born: Aalborg, Denmark, 7 May 1966
Height: 6'1" Weight: 11.10
International Honours: Denmark: 57

During the 1999 close season Chelsea's complement of central defenders underwent a few changes: out went Michael Duberry and Andy Myers; in came Mario Melchiot and the vastly experienced Danish international libero, Jes Hogh. A league championship winner in both Denmark and Turkey, Jes spent four seasons with Istanbul side Fenerbahce, and his Champions' League experience with the Turkish club was crucial to Chelsea, who were looking for top-quality cover for Frank Leboeuf and Marcel Desailly. The Blues beat off stiff competition from a number of Bundesliga clubs to clinch his signature. Jes demonstrated a reliable, calm authority whenever called upon in the first half of the season to stand in for either of the French World Cup-winning duo but a nasty thigh strain sustained against Leeds in December kept him sidelined for several weeks. With Melchiot already on the long-term injury list, Chelsea were forced to bolster their defensive resources by signing Emerson Thome, thus increasing the fierce competition for places and further limiting Jes's opportunities. He appeared only a few times in the second half of the season during the Blues' runs to the Champions' League quarter-final and FA Cup final, and his season ended prematurely when he sustained a bad ankle injury while representing Denmark against Scandinavian neighbours Sweden. After appearing regularly for Denmark during the season he made the squad of 22 for the Euro 2000 finals but failed to make an appearance in the tournament.

Chelsea (£300,000 from Fenerbahce, Turkey on 15/7/1999) PL 6+3 FLC 1 FAC 2 Others 2+3

HOLDEN Dean Thomas
Born: Salford, 15 September 1979
Height: 6'0" Weight: 11.0
International Honours: E: Yth

One of the true success stories of Bolton's 1999-2000 season, Dean thrust himself into the limelight and proved himself to be a valuable asset for the Wanderers. As one of the few Bolton players to have come through the ranks, this Salford-born defender was given his first-team debut as a substitute at Fulham in November, and made his first senior start in the 3-1 defeat at Blackburn in December. Primarily a centre half but also able to operate as a right back, Dean had a good run in the starting eleven at the turn of the year when Mark Fish was on international duty, his confidence on the ball and his general awareness of the game marking him out as one for the future. He put in a string of assured performances which enabled him to retain his place in the starting line-up even when Fish returned to England. Dean's highly promising season was sadly ended when he suffered a badly broken leg in the home match against Sheffield United in March. This injury kept him out for the rest of the season but there is little doubt that he will return as confident as ever and looking to regain his place this season.

Bolton W (From trainee on 23/12/1997) FL 6+6 FLC 2 FAC 3+1

HOLDSWORTH David Gary
Born: Walthamstow, 8 November 1968
Height: 6'1" Weight: 12.10
International Honours: E: U21-1; Yth

David was a calm and assured figure in the centre of the Birmingham City defence throughout the 1999-2000 season. He performed consistently well and came up to score several crucial goals from set pieces, including a brilliant header that decided the controversial local derby with Wolves in April. He is highly regarded by manager Trevor Francis and took over the role of captain when Martin O'Connor was absent.

Watford (From apprentice on 8/11/1986) FL 249+9/11 FLC 20/2 FAC 14+1/1 Others 8+2
Sheffield U (£450,00 on 8/10/1996) FL 93/4 FLC 7 FAC 13/3 Others 5
Birmingham C (£1,200,000 on 22/3/1999) FL 51+1/6 FLC 5/1 FAC 1 Others 4

HOLDSWORTH Dean Christopher
Born: Walthamstow, 8 November 1968
Height: 5'11" Weight: 11.13
Club Honours: Div 3 '92
International Honours: E: B-1

While he has occasionally failed to live up to the expectations created by his Bolton club record fee of £3.5 million, last season was probably Dean's most fruitful yet in a Wanderers shirt. The former Wimbledon striker popped up with some vital goals and his wholehearted displays gradually won over some of the fans who had previously expressed their doubts about Dean's abilities. His confidence when taking penalties is a massive asset to the club, but unfortunately the incident from last season for which he will be best remembered was probably his glaring miss five minutes from the end of extra time in the Wembley FA Cup semi-final defeat against Aston Villa. This followed possibly Dean's best performance of the season for the Trotters in the Wembley showpiece. He went some way to making amends for this, however, by scoring the vital goal in the 1-0 win against Norwich on the last day of the season which enabled Bolton to sneak into the play-offs at the expense of Huddersfield Town. Dean maintained his fine end-of-season form in the semi-final against Ipswich and his goals and overall performance over the two legs merited a chance to return to Wembley for the final and lay the ghost of his earlier appearance there, but it was not to be.

Watford (From apprentice on 12/11/1986) FL 2+14/3 Others 0+4
Carlisle U (Loaned on 11/2/1988) FL 4/1
Port Vale (Loaned on 18/3/1988) FL 6/2
Swansea C (Loaned on 25/8/1988) FL 4+1/1
Brentford (Loaned on 13/10/1988) FL 2+5/1
Brentford (£125,000 on 29/9/1989) FL 106+4/53 FLC 7+1/6 FAC 6/7 Others 12+2/9
Wimbledon (£720,000 on 20/7/1992) PL 148+21/58 FLC 16+3/11 FAC 13+7/7
Bolton W (£3,500,000 on 3/10/1997) P/FL 61+26/26 FLC 6+3/1 FAC 3 Others 2/3

HOLLAND Christopher (Chris) James
Born: Clitheroe, 11 September 1975
Height: 5'9" Weight: 11.5
International Honours: E: U21-10; Yth

This tireless midfield player began the 1999-2000 season with Birmingham City, where he remained very much a fringe player, appearing regularly for the reserves and generally being restricted to the subs' bench for the first team. His best game for the Blues was in the home fixture with Charlton last October, when he made a rare appearance in the starting line-up. By the new year he had dropped out of the first-team squad and in February he was sold to First Division rivals Huddersfield Town. The tigerish midfielder brought a new dimension to the Terriers' midfield. Snapped up cheaply with the Bosman ruling in mind, the confident right footer never stops working and never shirks a tackle. He settled easily into Town's passing game and was soon on the score sheet with a wonderful long-range drive against Nottingham Forest which proved to be the winner. Incredibly, it was his first-ever senior goal.

Preston NE (Trainee) FL 0+1 Others 1
Newcastle U (£100,000 on 20/1/1994) PL 2+1 FLC 0+1
Birmingham C (£600,000 on 5/9/1996) FL 39+31 FLC 7+5 FAC 4 Others 1+1
Huddersfield T (£150,000 on 3/2/2000) FL 16+1/1

Matt Holland

HOLLAND Matthew (Matt) Rhys
Born: Bury, 11 April 1974
Height: 5'9" Weight: 11.12
International Honours: RoI: 3; B-1

Appointed Ipswich club captain at the start of last season when Tony Mowbray took over as first-team coach, Matt led by example in 1999-2000 and was the inspiration behind the team as they continued the success they had enjoyed in previous seasons. Incredibly, he kept up his record of not missing a game since joining the club from Bournemouth despite being called up for international duty during the season. Once again he made his presence felt in both penalty areas, supporting his forwards in attack by scoring his fair share of goals – he actually doubled his tally from 1998-99 with ten last season – and dropping back to help out the defence when it was under pressure. Matt also had a happy knack of coming up with a goal just when the team needed it, to clinch victory at Nottingham Forest, snatch a point at West Bromwich, set the side on the way to victory at Tranmere and seal a win over Port Vale. He made his full international debut for the Republic of Ireland against Macedonia last October and also appeared in the end-of-season Nike Cup games in the USA.

West Ham U (From trainee on 3/7/1992)
Bournemouth (Signed on 27/1/1995) FL 97+7/18 FLC 6 FAC 3 Others 3
Ipswich T (£800,000 on 31/7/1997) FL 138/25 FLC 15/4 FAC 7 Others 7/2

HOLLAND Paul
Born: Lincoln, 8 July 1973
Height: 5'11" Weight: 12.10
International Honours: E: U21-4; Yth; Sch

The linch-pin of Chesterfield's midfield, Paul started the 1999-2000 season in his usual creative and determined way but fell victim to a calf injury in August. He had not made a complete recovery when he was sold to Bristol City in September for £150,000 and had to overcome further injury problems before fully establishing himself in the City side. Despite a lack of pace, he brought added bite to the Robins' midfield as well as demonstrating the ability to snatch vital goals and make others, it being his headed effort that was deflected in by Damian Spencer for City's equaliser in the Auto Windscreens Shield final at Wembley. Paul was released at the end of the season.

Mansfield T (From juniors on 4/7/1991) FL 149/25 FLC 11 FAC 7/3 Others 9/1
Sheffield U (£250,000 on 20/6/1995) FL 11+7/1 FLC 2/1
Chesterfield (Signed on 5/1/1996) FL 108+6/11 FLC 11+1/2 FAC 11 Others 1
Bristol C (£200,000 on 23/9/1999) FL 22+5 FAC 3 Others 4/1

HOLLIGAN Gavin Victor
Born: Lambeth, 13 June 1980
Height: 5'10" Weight: 12.0

Gavin joined Leyton Orient on loan from West Ham in September 1999. He had scored in the FA Cup against Orient for Kingstonian during the previous campaign. O's boss Tommy Taylor remembered this goal and brought him in for a month, Gavin making a couple of appearances before returning to West Ham. A talented striker, he made his Orient debut against Torquay. He had made his Hammers bow before a crowd of over 44,000 at Liverpool seven months earlier.

West Ham U (£100,000 from Kingstonian on 5/3/1999) PL 0+1
Leyton Orient (Loaned on 17/9/1999) FL 1 FLC 1

HOLLOWAY Christopher (Chris) David
Born: Swansea, 5 February 1980
Height: 5'10" Weight: 11.7
International Honours: W: U21-2

A contract dispute and a mystery back injury kept Chris out of the Exeter side from February 2000. The latter led to a spell at the FA's national rehabilitation centre at Lilleshall in April. When fully fit, his touch and distribution on the ball made him stand out at times in midfield. One of the many promising players to come out of City's YTS ranks, Chris will be looking for a solid season in 2000-01.

Exeter C (From trainee on 9/7/1998) FL 51+13/2 FLC 2+1 FAC 1+1 Others 3

HOLLOWAY Darren
Born: Crook, 3 October 1977
Height: 5'10" Weight: 12.2
International Honours: E: U21-1

First-team opportunities appeared to be at a premium at the Stadium of Light for this attacking right back last season and, although he appeared for Sunderland in both legs of the Worthington Cup against Walsall in September, a loan spell away from Wearside was probably the best way for Darren to continue his development. This materialised in December when he moved to Bolton and he put in some convincing displays during his month-long stay at the Reebok Stadium. On his return in February he was given an opportunity in the Premiership and, although his run in the side began with a 2-5 defeat at Leicester, he held his place and performed impressively as Sunderland picked up 11 points from the next five games. Darren is an enthusiastic player and his penchant for linking up with the attack and producing quality crosses is a real asset to the side, while his height when defending set pieces can be vital. With youth still on his side, and Chris Makin's ability to play on the left of the defence possibly opening a door for him, Darren could still make the right-back berth his own.

Sunderland (From trainee on 12/10/1995) P/FL 41+12/2 FLC 2 FAC 2 Others 3
Carlisle U (Loaned on 29/8/1997) FL 5
Bolton W (Loaned on 14/12/1999) FL 3+1

HOLLUND Martin
Born: Stord, Norway, 11 August 1974
Height: 6'0" Weight: 12.9
International Honours: Norway: U21

A former Norwegian U21 international, Martin has steadily grown in confidence over the last two seasons. He was a little unlucky to begin the 1999-2000 campaign as Hartlepool's second-choice goalkeeper, but he soon regained his place and turned in some exceptional displays to silence any remaining critics. He has a particularly good record for keeping clean sheets, and had a spell of nine consecutive home games without conceding a goal in the first half of last term.

Hartlepool U (Free from SK Brann Bergen, Norway on 21/11/1997) FL 109 FLC 2 FAC 4 Others 8

HOLMES Paul
Born: Stocksbridge, 18 February 1968
Height: 5'10" Weight: 11.3

Torquay's classy right wing back returned to his old club from West Bromwich Albion in November 1999. Initially signed on loan,

Paul agreed a three-year deal in January. His pace and accurate crossing with either foot created many chances for the United attackers. A set-piece specialist, Paul played alongside Gulls boss Wes Saunders in his first spell at Plainmoor.

Doncaster Rov (From apprentice on 24/2/1986) FL 42+5/1 FAC 3+1/1 Others 1
Torquay U (£6,000 on 12/8/1988) FL 127+12/4 FLC 9 FAC 9+2 Others 13+3
Birmingham C (£40,000 on 5/6/1992) FL 12 FAC 1
Everton (£100,000 on 19/3/1993) PL 21 FLC 4 FAC 1 Others 0+2
West Bromwich A (£80,000 on 12/1/1996) FL 102+1/1 FLC 5 FAC 4 Others 3
Torquay U (Free on 11/11/1999) FL 30 FAC 3 Others 1+1

HOLMES Richard
Born: Grantham, 7 November 1980
Height: 5'10" Weight: 10.7

Richard made astonishing progress in the early part of 1999-2000 with Notts County and quickly established himself as a regular in the first-team line-up. He seemed to suffer a loss of form towards the end of the campaign but is still in his teens and surely has a great future ahead of him. He is a pacy, quick-tackling right wing back who can also play at full back if required.

Notts Co (From trainee on 23/3/1999) FL 41+8 FLC 3+1 FAC 2

HOLMES Steven (Steve) Peter
Born: Middlesbrough, 13 January 1971
Height: 6'2" Weight: 13.0

Steve made a remarkable comeback for Lincoln in the closing stages of 1999-2000 after undergoing a major operation in the summer to repair a slipped disc in his neck, a potentially life-threatening injury. He was able to return to full training in January and was back in the first team by the start of March. Steve made a fairy-tale return for the Imps against Carlisle, when he scored with his first touch of the ball just 60 seconds into the game. He took some time to get back to full fitness but finished the campaign as a first-choice centre back.

Lincoln C (From trainee on 17/7/1989)
Preston NE (£10,000 from Guisborough T, via Gainsborough Trinity, on 14/3/1994) FL 13/1 FAC 3 Others 1
Hartlepool U (Loaned on 10/3/1995) FL 5/2
Lincoln C (Loaned on 20/10/1995) FL 12/1 Others 2
Lincoln C (£30,000 on 15/3/1996) FL 130+1/17 FLC 6/2 FAC 7/1 Others 3/1

HOLSGROVE Lee
Born: Wendover, 13 December 1979
Height: 6'2" Weight: 12.5

Much was expected of this young Wycombe central midfielder in 1999-2000, and he made an excellent impression in the early-season Worthington Cup games against Wolves. However, apart from a brief spell of action in March he rarely featured in the first team, and in the summer it was announced that he would not be offered a new contract. Lee makes up for a slight lack of pace with his elegance on the ball and good passing skills, while his height and physical presence enable him to perform as a central defender if required.

Millwall (From juniors on 5/7/1996)
Wycombe W (£7,500 on 24/3/1998) FL 5+5 FLC 2

HOLSGROVE Paul
Born: Cosford, 26 August 1969
Height: 6'1" Weight: 12.11

After a spell in Scottish football, the experienced midfielder joined Darlington from Hibernian in March 2000 on transfer deadline day, and made his debut against Shrewsbury Town in early April as a substitute. However, his first appearance lasted only 18 minutes as he had to be substituted himself after sustaining a broken nose. Fortunately, Paul recovered to figure in further games towards the end of the season when his guile and accurate passing were an asset in the middle of the field.

Aldershot (From trainee on 9/2/1987) FL 0+3 Others 1 (Free to Wokingham during 1990 close season)
Luton T (£25,000 on 1/1/1991) FL 1+1 (Free to Heracles in November 1991)
Millwall (Free on 13/8/1992) FL 3+8 FLC 0+1 FAC 0+1 Others 2
Reading (Free on 10/8/1994) FL 63+7/6 FLC 8+3/1 FAC 5
Grimsby T (Loaned on 12/9/1997) FL 3+7
Crewe Alex (Free on 20/11/1997) FL 7+1/1 FAC 1
Stoke C (Free on 27/1/1998) FL 11+1/1
Brighton & Hove A (Free on 3/7/1998)
Hibernian (£150,000 on 31/7/1998) SL 9+9/1 SLC 2
Darlington (Free on 23/3/2000) FL 1+2 Others 0+1

HOLT Andrew (Andy)
Born: Stockport, 21 May 1978
Height: 6'1" Weight: 12.7

This Oldham youngster had another good season in 1999-2000 and despite playing at left back proved to be a potent attacking force for the Latics with his surges down the flank. Andy has a direct and aggressive style, crosses the ball well and is more than useful when moving up to join the attack for set pieces. Regularly watched by Premiership scouts, he is one of the best products of the Boundary Park youth system in recent years.

Oldham Ath (From trainee on 23/7/1996) FL 92+12/9 FLC 4 FAC 6+1 Others 2

HOLT Grant
Born: Carlisle, 12 April 1981
Height: 6'1" Weight: 12.7

Halifax paid £10,000 to Workington to secure this young striker's signature last September. Although he had been playing Sunday football less than a year earlier, Grant had impressed when scoring twice on his debut for the Shaymen's second string. He was restricted to just a few substitute appearances for the first team after finding the standard a little different to what he had been used to in the Unibond First Division. In March he moved on loan to Barrow to gain further experience.

Halifax T (Signed from Workington on 16/9/1999) FL 0+4 Others 1

HOLT Michael Andrew
Born: Barnoldswick, 28 July 1977
Height: 5'10" Weight: 11.12

Rochdale's new star and top scorer in 1998-99 had a much harder time in his second season at Spotland. His only run of full games came during a goal drought that saw Dale score only twice in 12 games. After a brief spell out on loan at Northwich Victoria, he came on as a substitute in the Auto Windscreens Shield Northern Final to net his only goal of the season. Michael was released in May.

Blackburn Rov (From trainee on 28/7/1995)
Preston NE (Free on 16/8/1996) FL 12+24/5 FLC 2+2/1 FAC 1+3 Others 0+1
Macclesfield T (Loaned on 25/9/1998) FL 3+1/1
Rochdale (Signed on 16/11/1998) FL 25+13/7 FLC 1+1 FAC 1+1 Others 3+2/2

HOOPER Dean Raymond
Born: Harefield, 13 April 1971
Height: 5'11" Weight: 11.6
International Honours: E: SP-1

Dean is a hard-tackling right back with good ball skills. Unfortunately, a leg injury suffered at Cheltenham in February side-lined him for the rest of the season, forcing him to miss the climax of Peterborough's play-off success. A fiery, competitive player, Dean will relish the challenge of the Second Division.

Swindon T (£15,000 from Hayes on 3/3/1995) FL 0+4 FLC 0+2 Others 2 (Free to Hayes on 4/10/1996)
Peterborough U (Loaned on 15/12/1995) FL 4
Peterborough U (Signed from Kingstonian on 6/8/1998) FL 64+3/2 FLC 4 FAC 2+1 Others 2+1

HOPE Christopher (Chris) Jonathan
Born: Sheffield, 14 November 1972
Height: 6'1" Weight: 12.7

The Scunthorpe club skipper continued to be a solid figure in the heart of the defence in 1999-2000 with strength in the air and good long-range distribution. He unfortunately picked up an ankle injury which ruled him out of the first three matches of the new millennium – ending a club-record run of 175 successive league appearances stretching back almost four years. Rumoured to have been watched by Nottingham Forest and Wolves during the season, he has now completed seven years at Glanford Park.

Nottingham F (Free from Darlington juniors on 23/8/1990)
Scunthorpe U (£50,000 on 5/7/1993) FL 278+9/19 FLC 13+1 FAC 18/1 Others 18/2

HOPE Richard Paul
Born: Stockton, 22 June 1978
Height: 6'2" Weight: 12.6

Richard is a talented young central defender in a Northampton squad blessed with a number of highly rated players in that position. When Kevin Wilson took over as manager last October, he switched from three centre backs to two and Richard found himself "the odd man out". He always proved himself capable when called upon, and even stepped into the left-back spot as a substitute. Richard will be hoping for more opportunities as the Cobblers move up into the Second Division. His father John played in goal for Sheffield United and Hartlepool.

Blackburn Rov (From trainee on 9/8/1995)
Darlington (Free on 17/1/1997) FL 62+1/1 FLC 3 FAC 1 Others 0+1
Northampton T (Signed on 18/12/1998) FL 31+5 FAC 0+1 Others 3

HOPKIN David
Born: Greenock, 21 August 1970
Height: 5'9" Weight: 11.0
International Honours: S: 7; B-1

After his success in 1998-99, David began last season where he left off by showing good form in the Leeds United first team. Indeed the midfield combination of "Hoppy", David Batty and Lee Bowyer seemed to be developing into something special, although there was always pressure from Stephen McPhail, Eirik Bakke and Matthew Jones. However, David was put on the bench against Middlesbrough in September, where he remained until the turn of the year, when injury and illness kept him out altogether. On his return to fitness, this all-action Scot was a regular for the reserves and was a major influence on the youngsters at the club. He was capped twice against Bosnia in the early part of the season.

Greenock Morton (Signed from Port Glasgow BC on 7/7/1989) SL 33+15/4 SLC 2/2 SC 2/1
Chelsea (£300,000 on 25/9/1992) PL 21+19/1 FLC 0+1 FAC 3+2
Crystal Palace (£850,000 on 29/7/1995) FL 79+4/21 FLC 6/6 FAC 3 Others 4/2
Leeds U (£3,250,000 on 23/7/1997) PL 64+9/6 FLC 7 FAC 6 Others 6+1

HOPKINS Gareth
Born: Cheltenham, 14 June 1980
Height: 6'2" Weight: 13.8

Gareth has every physical attribute needed to be a real handful as a central striker. He is tall, strong as an ox and quick across the ground, and Cheltenham manager Steve Cotterill has made it his personal mission to teach him the finer points of playing up front. Gareth's progress has been steady and he has the right attitude and willingness to learn. Top scorer for Cheltenham reserves in 1999-2000, he made just one Football League appearance, against Carlisle in October. The 2000-01 season could see him unleashed on an unsuspecting Third Division.

Cheltenham T (From trainee on 27/7/1998) FL 0+1 FAC 0+1

HOPPER Tony
Born: Carlisle, 31 May 1976
Height: 5'11" Weight: 12.8
Club Honours: AMC '97

Despite occasional injury problems, Tony had perhaps his best season to date at Carlisle in 1999-2000. As a lifelong fan of his home-town club, he can always be counted on to play for the jersey, and he turned in some battling performances on the right side of midfield. He also showed a greater willingness to get into forward positions, without unfortunately ever featuring on the score sheet. Tony was offered new terms in May.

Carlisle U (From trainee on 18/7/1994) FL 75+25/1 FLC 2+1 FAC 3+1/1 Others 7+4

HORE John
Born: Liverpool, 18 August 1982
Height: 5'11" Weight: 11.12

John was called up to make his league debut at the age of 17 in Carlisle's last match of the 1999-2000 campaign at Brighton – arguably the most important game in United's history. The big left-footed striker was promoted from the youth team as the Cumbrians' squad was depleted by injury. He performed well in very difficult circumstances and will be hoping to add to his Football League tally next term.

Carlisle U (Trainee) FL 1

HORLOCK Kevin
Born: Erith, 1 November 1972
Height: 6'0" Weight: 12.0
Club Honours: Div 2 '96
International Honours: NI: 21; B-2

Kevin continued to occupy a role in the midfield engine room for Manchester City in 1999-2000 and ended the season with ten goals to his credit. His greatest strength was his willingness to follow up his own forward passes and get into goalscoring positions to receive a lay-off from the strikers. He scored five goals by supporting the attack in this way and scored another five from the penalty spot. He grabbed both goals in the 2-1 win against Grimsby at the end of December with spectacular shots on the run from outside the penalty area. However, at the end of February he lost his place and in the next seven league games he made only one substitute appearance. Brought back into the line-up for the game against Bolton at the beginning of April, Kevin had a storming game and scored City's first goal. He went on to finish the campaign in style, having passed his personal goal tally from the previous season. His international career also remained flourishing, with Kevin appearing in three games for Northern Ireland at the start of the season and winning a further cap against Malta at the end of March.

West Ham U (From trainee on 1/7/1991)
Swindon T (Free on 27/8/1992) F/PL 151+12/22 FLC 15+2/1 FAC 12/3 Others 5+2
Manchester C (£1,250,000 on 31/1/1997) FL 115+3/28 FLC 8/2 FAC 5 Others 3/1

HORNE Barry
Born: Rhyl, 18 May 1962
Height: 5'9" Weight: 12.2
Club Honours: WC '86; FAC '95; CS '95
International Honours: W: 59

Still a controlling influence at 37, Barry played a supporting role at Huddersfield last season but continued to anchor the midfield effectively whenever called upon. Always capable of making that important tackle and creating a new opening, he rarely wasted a pass. However, it was something of a surprise when Sheffield Wednesday caretaker manager Peter Shreeves brought the veteran midfield player to Hillsborough on transfer deadline day last March. His combative and inspirational style of play proved to be of value to the Owls and his arrival in the first team heralded a brief revival with victories over Wimbledon and Chelsea. Nevertheless, Barry proved unable to stop Wednesday from dropping out of the Premiership and he became a free agent in the summer.

Wrexham (Free from Rhyl on 26/6/1984) FL 136/17 FLC 10/1 FAC 7/2 Others 15/3
Portsmouth (£60,000 on 17/7/1987) FL 66+4/7 FLC 3 FAC 6
Southampton (£700,000 on 22/3/1989) FL 111+1/6 FLC 15+2/3 FAC 15/3 Others 7/1
Everton (£675,000 on 1/7/1992) PL 118+5/3 FLC 12+1 FAC 11+1 Others 3
Birmingham C (£250,000 on 10/6/1996) FL 33 FLC 3 FAC 3
Huddersfield T (Free on 13/10/1997) FL 55+9/1 FLC 7 FAC 2
Sheffield Wed (Free on 23/3/2000) PL 7

HORSFIELD Geoffrey (Geoff) Malcolm
Born: Barnsley, 1 November 1973
Height: 5'10" Weight: 11.0
Club Honours: Div 2 '99

Geoff began last season in the same goalscoring form as he had shown the previous term, netting six times for Fulham in the first five games, but a combination of niggling injuries, the lack of a settled striking partner and poor service severely restricted his scoring opportunities thereafter. He was also the most fouled man in Division One – and that was only those decisions given in his favour! The injuries made him lose that extra yard of pace and, just as he recovered it, another injury would strike. Very hard working, he is a strong, traditional centre forward who is adept at holding the ball up and bringing his teammates into the game. Provided he stays at Craven Cottage, he will surely have more luck and provide a lot more goals for the Fulham cause in 2000-01.

Scarborough (From juniors on 10/7/1992) FL 12/1 FAC 1 Others 0+2 (Free to Halifax T on 31/3/1994)
Halifax T (Free from Witton A on 8/5/1997) FL 10/7 FLC 4/1
Fulham (£325,000 on 12/10/1998) FL 54+5/22 FLC 6/6 FAC 8+1/3

Geoff Horsfield

HOTTE Mark Stephen
Born: Bradford, 27 September 1978
Height: 5'11" Weight: 11.1

Mark spent several weeks training with

Bury during the summer of 1999 but then signed a new contract with Oldham, and after establishing himself in the Latics' first team in October he went on to produce some fine displays last season. Mostly used as a central defender by manager Andy Ritchie, he is an excellent reader of the game but his main asset is his tremendous pace.

Oldham Ath (From trainee on 1/7/1997) FL 34+3 FAC 2 Others 1

HOUGHTON Scott Aaron
Born: Hitchin, 22 October 1971
Height: 5'7" Weight: 12.4
Club Honours: FAYC '90
International Honours: E: Yth; Sch

An up-and-down 1999-2000 season for Scott saw him produce some scintillating left-wing performances. Always one for getting the Southend crowd on their feet, he scored some magnificent long-range goals, and also proved strong in getting back to help out a sometimes overworked defence. Scott will hope to produce some more consistent performances in the new season.

Tottenham H (From trainee on 24/8/1990) FL 0+10/2 FLC 0+2 Others 0+2
Ipswich T (Loaned on 26/3/1991) FL 7+1/1
Gillingham (Loaned on 17/12/1992) FL 3
Charlton Ath (Loaned on 26/2/1993) FL 6
Luton T (Free on 10/8/1993) FL 7+9/1 FLC 2+1 FAC 0+1 Others 2
Walsall (£20,000 on 2/9/1994) FL 76+2/14 FLC 0+1/1 FAC 10/3 Others 4
Peterborough U (£60,000 + on 12/7/1996) FL 57+13/13 FLC 6+2 FAC 7/1 Others 1+1/1
Southend U (Signed on 20/11/1998) FL 68+2/7 FLC 2 FAC 1 Others 1

Scott Houghton

HOULT Russell
Born: Ashby de la Zouch, 22 November 1972
Height: 6'3" Weight: 14.9

Russell began the 1999-2000 season vying with Mart Poom for a place in the Derby goal but after a series of indifferent performances he was consigned to a place on the bench. The signing of Andy Oakes from Hull meant Russell could be released to join First Division Portsmouth on loan in January, becoming Pompey manager Tony Pulis's first signing. He went straight into the team and impressed sufficiently for the switch to be made permanent shortly afterwards. Russell retained his place through to the end of the season, producing a number of magnificent saves to help keep the Fratton Park club in the First Division. He showed a good command of his area and excellent handling of crosses but would undoubtedly benefit from playing behind a settled defence. His most impressive game for Pompey was at Charlton in April, when he did much to frustrate the champions-elect.

Leicester C (From trainee on 28/3/1991) FL 10 FLC 3 Others 1
Lincoln C (Loaned on 27/8/1991) FL 2 FLC 1
Bolton W (Loaned on 3/11/1993) FL 3+1 Others 1
Lincoln C (Loaned on 12/8/1994) FL 15 Others 1
Derby Co (£300,000 on 17/2/1995) F/PL 121+2 FLC 8 FAC 7
Portsmouth (£300,000 + on 21/1/2000) FL 18

HOUSHAM Steven (Steve) James
Born: Gainsborough, 24 February 1976
Height: 5'10" Weight: 12.7

A wholehearted, fully committed player who can play as a full back or wing back or in midfield, Steve was again unlucky with niggling injuries at Scunthorpe United in 1999-2000. Available for transfer for most of the campaign, he twice left Glanford Park for loan spells with non-league outfits Gainsborough Trinity and Barrow in a bid to regain fitness. He returned from Barrow to force himself into the first team and did well in four games before he damaged his ribs at Millwall, which sidelined him for another three weeks. Always popular with the fans, he was out of contract in the summer but the club made him an offer of re-engagement.

Scunthorpe U (From trainee on 23/12/1993) FL 90+25/4 FLC 3+2 FAC 6+2/1 Others 6+4/2

HOWARD Jonathan (Jon)
Born: Sheffield, 7 October 1971
Height: 5'11" Weight: 12.6

Jon missed the start of the 1999-2000 season, a knee injury preventing him from playing for Chesterfield until the end of September. His usual reliability in scoring positions was not greatly in evidence, since a changed role led to his operating in midfield for much of the season. When he did get forward it was frequently down the right-hand side, rather than through the middle, where his knack for being in the right place at the right time has brought goals in the past.

Rotherham U (From trainee on 10/7/1990) FL 25+11/5 FLC 0+1 FAC 4/2 Others 3+1 (Free to Buxton on 11/11/94)
Chesterfield (Free on 9/12/1994) FL 126+50/29 FLC 9+1/1 FAC 12+1/2 Others 8+3/2

HOWARD Michael (Mike) Anthony
Born: Birkenhead, 2 December 1978
Height: 5'9" Weight: 11.13
Club Honours: Div 3 '00

The 1999-2000 season was another successful one for Michael as he made the Swansea left-full-back position his own. He regularly displayed the ability to defend when needed and support his midfielders on the break. An ankle injury after Christmas sidelined him for five matches, but on his return he quickly showed the consistency that has seen him miss just 14 league games over the last two seasons. Michael's contribution to Swansea's title success was rewarded by a Third Division championship winners' medal.

Tranmere Rov (From trainee on 9/7/1997)
Swansea C (Free on 6/2/1998) FL 79+3/1 FLC 5 FAC 7 Others 3

HOWARD Steven (Steve) John
Born: Durham, 10 May 1976
Height: 6'2" Weight: 14.6

Steve is a tall, strapping centre forward who is good in the air and can hold the ball up well. The fee for his transfer from Hartlepool was a Northampton club record. Not a prolific goalscorer, he is used as a target man, winning the ball to set up team-mates. After Ian Atkins left Northampton last October, Steve found himself in and out of the first team, but he declined a transfer deadline move to Carlisle. With Northampton reverting to a more attacking style playing the ball on the floor, he hopes to fit in with the pattern as they move up into the Second Division in 2000-01.

Hartlepool U (Free from Tow Law on 8/8/1995) FL 117+25/27 FLC 7+1/1 FAC 5/2 Others 7/3
Northampton T (£120,000 on 22/2/1999) FL 44+9/10 FLC 2 FAC 0+1 Others 1

HOWARTH Neil
Born: Farnworth, 15 November 1971
Height: 6'2" Weight: 13.6
Club Honours: GMVC '95, '97; FAT '96
International Honours: E: SP-1

The former Macclesfield skipper was named as a substitute for Cheltenham's first game of the 1999-2000 season but then went on to miss just one match during the remainder of the campaign. He came into the side at right back and occupied the position virtually all season (he spent a few games covering for Mark Freeman or Chris Banks in the centre of defence), holding off the challenge of previous first-choice right back Michael Duff when he returned from injury. A tall, composed player who is good in the air but also comfortable on the ball, Neil scored the winning goal in the away fixture at Hartlepool and netted with a spectacular volley in the FA Cup replay at Gillingham. He more than repaid the faith shown in him by manager Steve Cotterill when he signed him at the end of 1998-99 to play "in any position along the back four or five".

Burnley (From trainee on 2/7/1990) FL 0+1
Macclesfield T (Free on 3/9/1993) FL 49+11/3 FLC 3 FAC 2+2 Others 2
Cheltenham T (£7,000 on 24/2/1999) FL 43+1/2 FLC 2 FAC 2/1 Others 2

HOWARTH Russell Michael
Born: York, 27 March 1982
Height: 6'1" Weight: 13.10
International Honours: E: Yth

The highly rated young 'keeper made his Football League debut for York City as a

17-year-old on the opening day of the 1999-2000 season, when he starred in a 1-0 win against Swansea. Russell went on to make eight senior appearances, and also appeared as a substitute for England U17s against Luxembourg in April. His progress was further recognised with York's "Young Player of the Year" award.
York C (From trainee on 26/8/1999) FL 5+1 FLC 2

HOWE Edward (Eddie) John Frank
Born: Amersham, 29 November 1977
Height: 5'10" Weight: 11.10
International Honours: E: U21-2
Eddie is one of a number of talented youngsters who have recently progressed through the ranks at Bournemouth. He missed three months of the 1999-2000 season after damaging the medial ligaments in his knee against Stoke but returned in February and was then appointed club captain in succession to Ian Cox. Eddie is a commanding central defender who is good in the air and a fierce tackler.
Bournemouth (From trainee on 4/7/1996) FL 115+16/4 FLC 11+1/1 FAC 7/2 Others 6+2

Eddie Howe

HOWE Stephen **Robert (Bobby)**
Born: Cramlington, 6 November 1973
Height: 5'7" Weight: 10.4
International Honours: E: Yth
Bobby had an extended run in the Swindon team in the first half of 1999-2000 but failed to make any real impression, scoring just one goal. He was then mostly restricted to appearances from the subs' bench in the new year as the Robins struggled unsuccessfully against relegation. Best suited to a role as a striker or playing just behind the front two, he will be hoping to regain form in the coming season.
Nottingham F (From trainee on 5/12/1990) P/FL 6+8/2 FLC 2 Others 1+1
Ipswich T (Loaned on 17/1/1997) FL 2+1 FLC 1
Swindon T (£30,000 on 16/1/1998) FL 53+11/4 FLC 1+1 FAC 2

HOWELL Dean George
Born: Burton, 29 November 1980
Height: 6'1" Weight: 12.5
Dean was awarded a full professional contract by Notts County in July 1999 but found it hard to break through to the senior team last season. He made a single appearance as a substitute for the last 15 minutes of the game at Blackpool in March, but was considered to have made insufficient progress and was released by the club in the summer. A speedy, fast-raiding left-sided midfielder or defender, he enjoys moving down the flank to support the attack.
Notts Co (From trainee on 1/7/1999) FL 0+1

HOWELLS Lee David
Born: Perth, Australia, 14 October 1968
Height: 5'11" Weight: 11.12
International Honours: SP-2
One of several Cheltenham players who have risen with the club from the Dr Martens League to the Third Division, Lee gave up a job in a Bristol scrapyard to become a full-time footballer. It took him a while to find his feet in the Football League in 1999-2000, but by the season's end "Archie" had begun to produce his best form. A midfield all-rounder who is comfortable on the ball and a deceptively strong tackler, he will have been a little disappointed with what was a modest return of goals for a player who loves to make runs into the opposition box. Lee can also play on the right flank and spent some of his early career as a right back. He missed just one game all season and formed one third of a useful midfield alongside Mark Yates and Russell Milton.
Bristol Rov (From apprentice on 17/10/1986. Freed on 1/7/1988)
Cheltenham T (Signed from Brisbane Lions, Australia on 1/12/1991) FL 45/3 FLC 2 FAC 2 Others 2

HOWEY Lee Matthew
Born: Sunderland, 1 April 1969
Height: 6'3" Weight: 14.6
Club Honours: Div 1 '96
Lee is a strong, committed central defender who, like his partner in the Northampton back line, Ian Sampson, is capable of producing goals from set pieces. He is one of the best headers of the ball at the club, and was an important part of the Cobblers' eventually successful 1999-2000 promotion push until a knee injury ended his season on Boxing Day. The elder brother of Newcastle's Steve Howey, Lee will relish Northampton's return to Division Two in 2000-01.
Ipswich T (From trainee on 2/10/1986) (Free to Blyth Spartans in March 1988)
Sunderland (Free from Bishop Auckland on 25/3/1993) P/FL 39+30/8 FLC 1+4/2 FAC 2+4/1 Others 0+1
Burnley (£200,000 on 11/8/1997) FL 24+2 FLC 5/1 FAC 2 Others 0+1
Northampton T (£50,000 on 6/11/1998) FL 45/6 FLC 2 FAC 1 Others 2

HOWEY Stephen (Steve) Norman
Born: Sunderland, 26 October 1971
Height: 6'2" Weight: 11.12
Club Honours: Div 1 '93
International Honours: E: 4
Steve is the longest-serving player on Newcastle's books, a one-club man who started as a striker but who has become a fine centre back, accomplished enough to earn full caps for England. Tall and good in the air, he is also strong on the ground, where he is firm in the tackle and rarely exposed for pace, but he is much more than just a stopper for he reads the game well, using his anticipation to quell threats before they become too dangerous, and there is also a constructive side to his game, both through his distribution skills and his willingness to bring the ball out of defence to initiate counter-attacks. He started the season where he has spent much time in recent years, namely in the treatment room, this time recovering from a ruptured achilles tendon in the right leg, an injury incurred in the 1999 FA Cup semi-final. Fit again early in the new year, Steve was gaining match practice when he was sent off playing for the reserves against Liverpool, incurring a suspension which delayed his return to first-team duty. He finally made the bench in late February and started his first game at the beginning of March against Chelsea, and his performances quickly confirmed that his quality had been sorely missed. It is to be hoped that he can now remain injury free as he has the qualities to become a centre back around whom the club can create the solid defence it needs. Steve is the younger brother of Lee Howey of Northampton Town.
Newcastle U (From trainee on 11/12/1989) F/PL 167+24/6 FLC 14+2/1 FAC 21+2 Others 10+2

HOWIE Scott
Born: Motherwell, 4 January 1972
Height: 6'2" Weight: 13.7
Club Honours: S Div 2 '93
International Honours: S: U21-5
The tall, well-built Reading goalkeeper made a promising start to the 1999-2000 season but had a nightmare of a game at Wycombe Wanderers, where he let in two soft goals and was substituted by Peter van der Kwaak at half time. He then lost his place to new signing Phil Whitehead, but when the latter was injured Scott regained his spot between the posts. An excellent shot stopper with lightning reflexes and out-standing bravery, he showed great character by silencing the critics with a return to top form, and was reinstated as first choice with a string of consistent displays in the second half of the season.
Clyde (Signed from Ferguslie U on 7/1/1992) SL 55 SLC 3 SC 4 Others 1
Norwich C (£300,000 on 12/8/1993) PL 1+1
Motherwell (£300,000 on 13/10/1994) SL 69 SLC 4 SC 5 Others 1
Reading (£30,000 on 26/3/1998) FL 84+1 FLC 6 FAC 4 Others 5

HREIDARSSON Hermann
Born: Iceland, 11 July 1974
Height: 6'1" Weight: 13.1
Club Honours: Div 3 '99
International Honours: Iceland: 28
An Icelandic international centre back, Hermann began the 1999-2000 season in majestic form with Brentford. His perform-

ances soon attracted the attention of bigger clubs and he was sold to Wimbledon in October for a fee of £2.5 million, a new record for the Griffin Park club. One of a number of Scandinavian players brought to Selhurst Park by former Wimbledon manager Egil Olsen, Hermann is commanding both in the air and, more surprisingly for a central defender, with the ball at his feet. He possesses a good left foot which he uses with precision to find players on the other side of the pitch, and always lifts the crowd when he goes on one of his mazy forward runs. His only goal of the season for the Dons came from a corner against West Ham, but he is likely to add to this in 2000-01. Hermann won a further six caps for Iceland and scored a rare goal in their 3-0 victory over Andorra last September.

Crystal Palace (Signed from IBV, Iceland on 9/8/1997) P/FL 32+5/2 FLC 5/1 FAC 4
Brentford (£850,000 on 24/9/1998) FL 41/6 FLC 2 FAC 2/1 Others 3/1
Wimbledon (£2,500,000 on 14/10/1999) PL 24/1 FAC 2

HRISTOV Georgi
Born: Bitola, Macedonia, 30 January 1976
Height: 5'11" Weight: 12.2
International Honours: Macedonia: 30

Georgi missed most of 1998-99 with a bad knee ligament injury and was looking to re-establish himself in the Barnsley team last season. Ultimately it proved a rather disappointing campaign, for he featured mostly as a substitute despite playing well when he appeared in the starting line-up. Still only in his mid-twenties, he is a very talented player who makes scoring look easy at times. He remained a key member of the Macedonia international team and was an ever-present during 1999-2000, winning a further five caps.

Barnsley (£1,500,000 from Partizan Belgrade, Yugoslavia on 23/7/1997) P/FL 18+26/8 FLC 3+5/3 FAC 1+1 Others 0+1

HUCK William (Willie) Roger Fernend
Born: Paris, France, 17 March 1979
Height: 5'10" Weight: 11.13

After making several senior appearances for Bournemouth towards the end of 1998-99, William failed to achieve the hoped-for breakthrough last season and spent most of the campaign on the fringes of the first team. He made the starting line-up four times early on but was then relegated to the subs' bench and rarely featured at all in the new year. He is a pacy left-sided midfield player with good skills, an excellent cross and the ability to run at opposition defenders.

Arsenal (Signed from Monaco, France on 6/11/1998)
Bournemouth (£50,000 on 25/3/1999) FL 10+15 FLC 0+3/1

HUCKERBY Darren Carl
Born: Nottingham, 23 April 1976
Height: 5'10" Weight: 11.12
International Honours: E: B-1; U21-4

Darren was sold to Leeds United for £5.5 million after appearing in the first match of the season for Coventry City. In one of his early games for Leeds he returned to Highfield Road and duly scored against his former club. A striker-cum-winger of considerable speed and skill, Darren has shown erratic form throughout his career, but on his day he is a handful for any opposing defence and can score truly breathtaking goals. Used by Leeds in what was primarily a substitute role last season, he struggled to show his real worth, even though he was the reserves' top scorer. With a more regular spot in the first team, Darren is sure to add more potency to one of the brightest young squads in the country.

Lincoln C (From trainee on 14/7/1993) FL 20+8/5 FLC 2 Others 1/2
Newcastle U (£400,000 on 10/11/1995) PL 0+1 FAC 0+1
Millwall (Loaned on 6/9/1996) FL 6/3
Coventry C (£1,000,000 on 23/11/1996) PL 85+9/28 FLC 2+1 FAC 12/6
Leeds U (£4,000,000 on 12/8/1999) PL 9+24/2 FLC 0+1 FAC 1+2 Others 1+8/1

HUDSON Daniel (Danny) Robert
Born: Doncaster, 25 June 1979
Height: 5'9" Weight: 10.3

A highly promising young, home-grown midfield player, Danny had few opportunities to break into Rotherham's 1999-2000 promotion side. Yet on his first appearance of the season on Boxing Day, he scored a superb goal to set the team on the way to a magnificent 5-0 win at Peterborough. Danny is the type of player who will run all day and he loves to get forward, although lacking a little in strength.

Rotherham U (From trainee on 25/6/1997) FL 28+15/5 FLC 0+2 FAC 3+2/2 Others 3+1

HUGHES Aaron William
Born: Magherafelt, 8 November 1979
Height: 6'0" Weight: 11.2
International Honours: NI: 12; B-2; Yth

First capped by Northern Ireland at the age of 18, and now a regular in the national side, Aaron has found it rather more difficult to establish himself in the first team at Newcastle. He is a talented player, comfortable on the ball and possessing fine distribution skills, and he is blessed with an excellent temperament. His abilities enable him to perform in any of the defensive positions or in midfield but last season saw him figuring primarily at left back, where he has become a regular for his country, although many good judges expect him to gravitate towards central defence as he grows in experience. Aaron started in the first two games of the season, but although he remained in the squad his opportunities thereafter were largely limited to substitute appearances interspersed with the odd game standing in for injured colleagues. His flexibility and quality were demonstrated when in November he played at right back against Watford, then a few days later was asked to operate just in front of the back four in the UEFA Cup to do a marking job on Francesco Totti against Roma in the Olympic Stadium, when he was outstanding as he subdued the dangerous Italian playmaker, and within a few more days was standing in at left back for Alessandro Pistone against Spurs and was rated by many as the "Man of the Match". He then returned to the bench, but the unfortunate injury to Alessandro at Sunderland at the beginning of February gave Aaron a chance to establish himself at left back, and he took it eagerly to secure a regular place in the side. He had become the club's youngest Premiership player when he made his debut against Sheffield Wednesday in 1998-99, and when he scored his first-ever goal for the club to initiate the 8-0 thrashing of Wednesday last season, he also became the club's youngest-ever Premiership scorer. He also netted at Everton, and these goals demonstrate that, as he has grown more confident at Premiership level, so he has started to take opportunities to add an attacking element to his game. He looks to be a player whom Newcastle will be pleased to have as a cornerstone of their defence in years to come. Aaron won further caps for Northern Ireland against France, Turkey, Luxembourg and Hungary during last season.

Newcastle U (From trainee on 11/3/1997) PL 38+7/2 FLC 2 FAC 1+2 Others 0+2

HUGHES Andrew (Andy) John
Born: Manchester, 2 January 1978
Height: 5'11" Weight: 12.1
Club Honours: Div 3 '98

Andy had a good season in 1999-2000 with Notts County and was a key figure in the club's successful start to the campaign. He offered 100 per cent effort on the right side of midfield and his surging runs down the wing were a joy to behold for the Magpies' supporters. He also contributed seven valuable goals, including four from the penalty spot. Andy was rushed to hospital at the beginning of June for an emergency operation after rupturing his appendix but it is hoped he will be fully fit in time for the start of the 2000-01 season.

Oldham Ath (From trainee on 20/1/1996) FL 18+15/1 FLC 1+1 FAC 3+1 Others 1+2
Notts Co (£150,000 on 29/1/1998) FL 65+15/12 FLC 5 FAC 5 Others 2

HUGHES Bryan
Born: Liverpool, 19 June 1976
Height: 5'10" Weight: 11.2
Club Honours: WC '95

Bryan blossomed in Birmingham City's midfield in 1999-2000, enjoying the greater responsibilities given to him as a result of the club's never-ending injury list. He even appeared as an emergency striker over the Christmas period and not without success, for he scored four times in a run of seven games. He then bravely chose to carry on playing after breaking a toe against Swindon last February. Bryan was also involved in controversy during the fierce local derby encounter with Wolves on April Fools' Day when he was sent off for allegedly diving only for the decision to be rescinded when the referee took a second look at the evidence. He is a very talented player with good ball control, plenty of inventive ideas and the ability to escape his marker when moving forward.

Wrexham (From trainee on 7/7/1994) FL 71+23/12 FLC 2 FAC 13+3/7 Others 14+1/3
Birmingham C (£750,000 + on 12/3/1997) FL 105+19/18 FLC 8+2/1 FAC 5+1/2 Others 3

Bryan Hughes

HUGHES Ceri Morgan
Born: Pontypridd, 26 February 1971
Height: 5'10" Weight: 12.7
International Honours: W: 8; B-2; Yth

Out of favour at Wimbledon, Ceri joined Portsmouth last January, adding strength to manager Tony Pulis's middle line. He made an excellent contribution at Fratton Park during the second half of the season, helping to guide the club away from the relegation zone with a series of solid performances. He scored twice for Pompey, netting on his debut at Stockport and adding a great solo goal at Ewood Park in April. Ceri is a tenacious midfield player who works hard and has good passing skills.

Luton T (From trainee on 1/7/1989) FL 157+18/17 FLC 13/1 FAC 11/2 Others 6
Wimbledon (£400,000 + on 4/7/1997) PL 21+10/1 FLC 2+1 FAC 2+3
Portsmouth (£150,000 on 21/1/2000) FL 15/2

HUGHES Robert **David**
Born: Wrexham, 1 February 1978
Height: 6'4" Weight: 14.0
International Honours: W: B-2 ; U21-13; Yth

David signed for Shrewsbury in October 1999 on a free transfer from Aston Villa. He had made only four Premiership starts for Villa and it was clear that opportunities for the central defender there were limited, so he preferred regular first-team football at Gay Meadow. A big, commanding player, David is uncompromising in his defending, showing strong determination in everything he does. Town's long-throw man, he took his chances well when selected and scored an important first league goal in a 2-2 draw at Darlington in April. He won a further cap for Wales at U21 level when he appeared against Switzerland in the autumn.

Aston Villa (From trainee on 5/7/1996) PL 4+3
Carlisle U (Loaned on 26/3/1998) FL 1
Shrewsbury T (Free on 22/9/1999) FL 18+4/1 FAC 3 Others 1

HUGHES Garry
Born: Birmingham, 19 November 1979
Height: 6'0" Weight: 12.2

Garry became the first Northampton youth player to come through the ranks since the club moved to Sixfields when he signed a professional contract in 1998. A central defender, he put some fine performances together in the reserves in 1999-2000, and after a couple of substitute appearances made his first start for the club as a right wing back against Bristol Rovers last January. His performance suggested that he would be accomplished in either position. Garry made his first three first-team appearances in three different competitions: the FA Cup, the Auto Windscreens Shield and the Nationwide League. He will be aiming to experience the Second Division for the first time in 2000-01.

Northampton T (From trainee on 7/7/1998) FL 1+1 FAC 0+1 Others 1

HUGHES Ian
Born: Bangor, 2 August 1974
Height: 5'10" Weight: 12.8
Club Honours: Div 2 '97
International Honours: W: U21-12; Yth

Ian was Blackpool's captain for the 1999-2000 season, when he was employed as a central defender. He is a strong and competitive player who always gives 100 per cent effort for the team. He began the campaign in good form and scored with a superb 20-yard shot against Tranmere in the Worthington Cup, but was later out of action for two months around the turn of the year due to a hamstring injury.

Bury (From trainee on 19/11/1991) FL 137+24/1 FLC 13+3 FAC 6+2 Others 14+4/1
Blackpool (£200,000 on 12/12/1997) FL 82+6/1 FLC 6/1 FAC 3 Others 5

HUGHES Jamie Joseph
Born: Liverpool, 5 April 1977
Height: 6'0" Weight: 11.7

A £20,000 signing from Connah's Quay Nomads during the 1999 close season, Jamie scored on each of his first two appearances for Cardiff, both as a substitute. He netted the winner at Queens Park Rangers in the Worthington Cup in August and a late equaliser in the league against Scunthorpe less than a week later – both with overhead kicks. It was a spectacular start, but he got few further chances and spent a large part of the season on loan with League of Wales side Cwmbran Town. It was a bitterly disappointing season for the striker and even his stay at Cwmbran did not work out entirely as he might have hoped. The club reached the Welsh Cup final, but Jamie's loan spell ended in the week before the match after the permitted maximum of three months. The striker was released by Cardiff at the end of the season.

Tranmere Rov (From trainee on 9/8/1995. Free to Northwich Vic on 1/7/1996)
Cardiff C (£20,000 from Connah's Quay Nomads on 13/7/1999) FL 0+2/1 FLC 0+3/1

HUGHES Lee
Born: Smethwick, 22 May 1976
Height: 5'10" Weight: 11.6
International Honours: E: SP-4

West Bromwich Albion's leading scorer again in 1999-2000, this time with 16 goals, Lee would have certainly netted a few more if he hadn't missed ten matches through suspension and injury. In fact, the striker was sidelined for the last six vitally important relegation encounters after fracturing a kneecap while scoring in the 1-1 home draw with Ipswich Town in early April. He had not been at his best during the early part of the season. He was a lone striker most of the time and frequently found himself confronted by two, sometimes three, defenders. But he battled on and as the campaign progressed scored some very important goals for the Baggies, including a gem at Maine Road in a 2-1 defeat by Manchester City. Now he is eagerly waiting to resume his partnership up front with Bob Taylor, the player he replaced as Albion's ace marksman a year or so ago. If Lee is fully fit he will continue to score goals, and if Taylor can net a dozen or so then Albion could well be promotion contenders this season.

West Bromwich A (£250,000 + from Kidderminster Hrs on 19/5/1997) FL 96+19/57 FLC 7+2/4 FAC 5/1

HUGHES Leslie **Mark**
Born: Wrexham, 1 November 1963
Height: 5'11" Weight: 13.0
Club Honours: FAC '85, '90, '94, '97; ECWC '91, '98; ESC '91; FLC '92, '98; PL '93, '94; CS '93, '94
International Honours: W: 72; U21-5; Yth; Sch

Put in temporary charge of the Welsh national side in June 1999, Mark was finally confirmed as manager some five months later and was content to combine his new job with that of a Southampton player. He continued his midfield role with some success during the early part of last season, though this restricted his goalscoring chances. He netted just once, with a delightful chip against Newcastle in September. Although an extension to his contract was mooted, the arrival of new manager Glenn Hoddle saw him left on the subs' bench. Granted a free transfer in March, he moved north in response to an Everton injury crisis – and showed that the passing years had not dimmed his voracious appetite for a physical tussle. Signed as a direct replacement for the injured Kevin Campbell, Mark was pitched straight into his old centre-forward role. He took four games to open his goalscoring account for his fourth English club, with a near-post header against Watford, and went on to produce memorable displays in some of the club's biggest matches. Mark is no longer a regular threat in front of goal, but his ability to hold the ball up under pressure is still excellent and he was voted "Man of the Match" by Sky TV viewers following the Merseyside derby match with Liverpool. Still far from popular among Premiership referees, he was suspended for one match within a month of signing for the Toffees, but his worth during the end-of-season run-in was still huge.

Manchester U (From apprentice on 5/11/1980) FL 85+4/37 FLC 5+1/4 FAC 10/4 Others 14+2/2 (£2,500,000 to Barcelona on 1/7/86)
Manchester U (£1,500,000 on 20/7/1988) F/PL 251+5/82 FLC 32/12 FAC 34+1/13 Others 27+1/8
Chelsea (£1,500,000 on 6/7/1995) PL 88+7/25 FLC 7+3/3 FAC 13+1/9 Others 1+3/2
Southampton (£650,000 on 15/7/1998) PL 50+2/2 FLC 5 FAC 2+2
Everton (Free on 14/3/2000) PL 9/1

Mark Hughes

HUGHES Michael Eamonn
Born: Larne, 2 August 1971
Height: 5'7" Weight: 10.13
International Honours: NI: 54; U23-2; U21-1; Yth; Sch

Michael was out of favour at Wimbledon for much of the 1999-2000 season, and a move looked on the cards. However, the winger was restored to the starting line-up for the game against his former club, West Ham, at Upton Park in March and went on to play a leading role in the Dons' vain battle against relegation after marking his recall with a goal. A strong, versatile player who loves to have long-range shots at goal, Michael has excellent close control and is particularly dangerous when running at defenders. He is a firm favourite with the Wimbledon fans, and was desperately unlucky to break his leg in the penultimate game of the season at home to Aston Villa. What the Dons would have given for his creativity in the fateful final match at Southampton! An ever-present for Northern Ireland during the season, he won his 50th cap against Germany last September.

Manchester C (From trainee on 17/8/1988) FL 25+1/1 FLC 5 FAC 1 Others 1 (£450,000 to RS Strasbourg, France in 1992 close season)
West Ham U (Loaned on 29/11/1994) PL 15+2/2 FAC 2
West Ham U (Loaned on 2/10/1995) PL 28 FLC 2 FAC 3/1
West Ham U (Free on 12/8/1996) PL 33+5/3 FLC 5 FAC 2
Wimbledon (£1,600,000 on 25/9/1997) PL 70+9/8 FLC 5+1/2 FAC 6+1/2

HUGHES Richard
Born: Glasgow, 25 June 1979
Height: 5'9" Weight: 9.12
International Honours: S: U21-5; Yth

This talented Bournemouth youngster had a frustrating time with injuries during 1999-2000, missing several months with a groin problem that eventually required surgery. Richard can perform either a left or central midfield role and possesses excellent dribbling skills and a good left-foot shot. He gained a further cap for Scotland U21s when he appeared against Bosnia last September.

Arsenal (Free from Atalanta, Italy on 11/8/1997)
Bournemouth (£20,000 on 5/8/1998) FL 63+2/4 FLC 7+1 FAC 4 Others 4

Stephen Hughes

HUGHES Stephen John
Born: Reading, 18 September 1976
Height: 6'0" Weight: 12.12
Club Honours: FAYC '94; PL '98; CS '98
International Honours: E: U21-8; Yth; Sch

Stephen joined Fulham from Arsenal on loan in July 1999 with a view to a permanent transfer if things worked out. He began very well with a good display in midfield and a classy equalising goal in a pre-season friendly at St Johnstone. Having broken his arm at the end of the previous season, Stephen was lacking match fitness and he completed only one of his four appearances for the club. He then decided to return to Highbury some time before his loan period expired, determined to fight for his first-team place. However, he started only one game for the Gunners and, apart from a few substitute appearances, he was confined to the reserves. Realising that he had no future with Arsenal, Stephen eventually agreed to move to Everton in March for a bargain down payment of £500,000, although the final amount could rise to £3 million. Only the world-class nature of Arsenal's outstanding engine room prevented Stephen making a breakthrough at Highbury, but as soon as he became part of Walter Smith's rebuilding at Everton he received the regular first-team football he craved. A left-footed midfielder, he can be employed out wide or in the centre, where his clever range of passing and impressive engine are put to good use. Always willing to shoot from distance, Stephen scored his first goal in Everton colours with a typically ferocious finish to clinch a 4-2 home defeat of Watford. Already in possession of a mature outlook on the game, he seems to have a fine future ahead of him at Goodison Park.

Arsenal (From trainee on 15/7/1995) PL 22+27/4 FLC 5+3/1 FAC 7+7/1 Others 2+4/1
Fulham (Loaned on 26/7/1999) FL 3 FLC 1
Everton (£500,000 + on 10/3/2000) PL 11/1

HULBERT Robin James
Born: Plymouth, 14 March 1980
Height: 5'9" Weight: 10.5
International Honours: E: Yth; Sch

This former England youth international had a disappointing 1999-2000 season with struggling Swindon Town, for although he made the starting line-up for the opening matches he rarely featured afterwards and was eventually sold to Bristol City on transfer deadline day. After an appearance as a substitute against Oxford he made his full City debut five days later in an exciting 4-3 win at Colchester in the penultimate game of the campaign. A hard-tackling right-sided midfield player who demonstrates good ability with both feet, he has the pace and trickery to pass opposition defenders and can be expected to make a greater impact in 2000-01.

Swindon T (From trainee on 25/9/1997) FL 12+17 FLC 1+1 FAC 2
Bristol C (£25,000 on 23/3/2000) FL 1+1

HULME Kevin
Born: Farnworth, 2 December 1967
Height: 5'10" Weight: 13.2

Kevin began the 1999-2000 season on the Halifax substitutes' bench. Although he was recalled to the starting line-up for the game at Leyton Orient at the end of August, the next game, against Torquay, was to be his last for the club. The former Halifax captain followed his former team-mate, Mark Sertori, to York in September. A highly competitive central midfielder with a decisive tackle, he is a versatile player who is capable of performing effectively in just about any position. His combative style soon saw him incur the wrath of referees, leading to the inevitable suspensions, while the Minstermen also lost his services for a couple of months following a hernia operation. Kevin netted four goals for City, including a fine solo effort at Exeter.

Bury (£5,000 from Radcliffe Borough on 16/3/1989) FL 82+28/21 FLC 4+3/2 FAC 4+1/1 Others 4+8/2
Chester C (Loaned on 26/10/1989) FL 4

Doncaster Rov (£42,500 on 14/7/1993) FL 33+1/8 FLC 2/1 FAC 1 Others 2
Bury (£42,500 on 11/8/1994) FL 24+5 FLC 2 FAC 2 Others 2
Lincoln C (Signed on 28/9/1995) FL 4+1 FAC 1 Others 1+1 (Free to Macclesfield T on 15/12/1995)
Halifax T (Free on 22/11/1996) FL 32+1/4 FLC 4+1 Others 2
York C (Free on 10/9/1999) FL 23/4 FAC 1 Others 1

HULSE Robert William
Born: Crewe, 25 October 1979
Height: 6'1" Weight: 11.4

One of several promising former trainees to be given their first-team chance at Crewe in 1999-2000, Robert was sidelined by injury for more than a season earlier in his fledgling career. A tall striker, he spent three months on loan with Hyde United last season and did well, finding the net regularly. He made his senior debut for Alex as a substitute against Norwich in March and was called from the bench on three further occasions before the end of the season, scoring his first goal at Barnsley in the last match. He is highly thought of at Crewe and is expected to have a bright future in the game.

Crewe Alex (From trainee on 25/6/1998) FL 0+4/1

HUME Iain
Born: Brampton, Ontario, Canada, 31 October 1983
Height: 5'7" Weight: 11.2

This Canadian-born striker became the youngest-ever player to appear in senior football for Tranmere when he came on as a substitute for the final 15 minutes at Swindon last April aged just 16 years and 167 days, thus beating the previous record holder, the great Dixie Dean, by around six months. Iain joined Rovers from school and has steadily made his way through the youth team and reserves to the fringes of the first team. He is calm and sensible, is able to kick with both feet and has a good eye for goal. He enjoyed a steady season with the Pontins League team and will be looking for more first-team experience in 2000-01.

Tranmere Rov (Ass Schoolboy) FL 0+3

HUMPHREYS Richard (Richie) John
Born: Sheffield, 30 November 1977
Height: 5'11" Weight: 14.6
International Honours: E: U21-3; Yth

A striker with plenty of skill and quick feet, Richie joined Scunthorpe on loan from Sheffield Wednesday in August 1999 in order to build up his match fitness and improved the United attack with his close control and ability to bring others into play. He scored twice against Bournemouth and generally impressed, and it was a disappointment for the Iron fans when he decided to return to Hillsborough after just one month. Still unable to force his way into the Wednesday line-up, Richie moved to Cardiff on loan in November and started in outstanding fashion with two goals in a 3-0 win at Colchester. Unfortunately, the Yorkshireman could not find the goals Cardiff needed thereafter and went back to Sheffield without adding to his tally, but he had shown enough ability to suggest that he might have fared better with improved service.

Sheffield Wed (From trainee on 8/2/1996) PL 27+33/4 FLC 1+2 FAC 5+4/4
Scunthorpe U (Loaned on 13/8/1999) FL 6/2
Cardiff C (Loaned on 22/11/1999) FL 8+1/2 FAC 1 Others 1

HUNT Andrew (Andy)
Born: Grays, 9 June 1970
Height: 6'0" Weight: 12.0
Club Honours: Div 1 '00

Andy really hit top form for Charlton in 1999-2000 after a disappointing first season with the club in the Premiership, not only helping the Addicks to the First Division championship but also earning selection to the PFA award-winning First Division side. He finished top scorer in the division with 24 league goals, adding another in the FA Cup. Andy also scored three hat-tricks, two coming in successive games. It is surprising, however, that only seven of his goals were scored at the Valley, and three of those were in one game! Good in the air and hard working, Andy has the ability to hold the ball up where appropriate and bring other players into the game, and likes to get into the opposition penalty area whenever possible. It will be interesting to see how he fares on his return to the top flight this coming season.

Newcastle U (£150,000 from Kettering T on 29/1/1991) FL 34+9/11 FLC 3/1 FAC 2/2 Others 3
West Bromwich A (£100,000 on 25/3/1993) FL 201+11/76 FLC 12/4 FAC 7/2 Others 8+1/3
Charlton Ath (Free on 2/7/1998) P/FL 75+3/31 FLC 3 FAC 5/1

HUNT James Malcolm
Born: Derby, 17 December 1976
Height: 5'8" Weight: 10.3

The Northampton midfield dynamo came into his own last season, taking on the mantle of the injured Roy Hunter and controlling the middle of the park. James is equally at home as an attacker or breaking up opponents' attacks. His commitment, enthusiasm and all-round effort make him a great favourite with the crowd. Still in his early twenties, James was with Notts County when they were relegated to the Third Division and Northampton when they were promoted and relegated, and helped the Cobblers back up to the Second Division in 1999-2000.

Notts Co (From trainee on 15/7/1994) FL 15+4/1 FAC 0+1 Others 2+2/1
Northampton T (Free on 7/8/1997) FL 71+22/3 FLC 4+2 FAC 3+3 Others 8+1

HUNT Jonathan (Jon) Richard
Born: Camden, 2 November 1971
Height: 5'10" Weight: 11.12
Club Honours: Div 2 '95; AMC '95

Having joined Sheffield United near the end of the previous season, Jon hoped to establish himself in the first team in 1999-2000. Until January he was in and out of the side, making many of his appearances from the bench. Playing mainly on the left side of midfield, he had some good games, showing his ability to create an opening with a telling pass. However, on other occasions his contribution was disappointing and his final appearance of the campaign for United was in the FA Cup at Newcastle. On deadline day he made a loan move, until the end of the season, to Cambridge United. Jon is a quality player whose class showed in the run-in to the end of the season. In particular, he is an excellent dead-ball specialist, as he showed with a stunning goal from a free kick in the 4-0 win at Cardiff.

Barnet (From juniors in 1989-90 on) FL 12+21 FLC 1 FAC 0+1 Others 6+2
Southend U (Free on 20/7/1993) FL 41+8/6 FLC 1+3 FAC 1 Others 6+1
Birmingham C (£50,000 on 16/9/1994) FL 67+10/18 FLC 10+5/2 FAC 3+1/1 Others 8/4
Derby Co (£500,000 on 23/5/1997) PL 7+18/2 FLC 2+2 FAC 0+3
Sheffield U (Loaned on 20/8/1998) FL 4+1/1
Ipswich T (Loaned on 20/10/1998) FL 2+4
Sheffield U (Signed on 12/3/1999) FL 16+6/1 FLC 2+2 FAC 3
Cambridge U (Loaned on 23/3/2000) FL 3+4/1

HUNT Stephen (Steve)
Born: Port Laoise, Ireland, 1 August 1980
Height: 5'7" Weight: 12.6

This graduate from the Crystal Palace youth set-up was given his league debut as a substitute at Fulham last March. Steve is a midfield prospect who will be aiming to feature more regularly in the Eagles' first-team set-up in the coming season.

Crystal Palace (From trainee on 29/6/1999) FL 0+3

HUNTER Barry Victor
Born: Coleraine, 18 November 1968
Height: 6'3" Weight: 13.2
International Honours: NI: 15; B-2; Yth

A steady performer at the heart of the Reading defence, Barry is dominant in the air and shows good awareness but his future at the club was in doubt when, midway through the 1999-2000 season, he suffered a loss of form that cost him his place and the captaincy. However, he put those problems behind him to become a mainstay of the team's revival. A dour and resolute centre back who is dangerous when he moves upfield, especially from set pieces, he is still very much a part of the manager's plans for next season.

Newcastle U (Signed from Coleraine on 2/11/1987) (Freed during 1988 close season)
Wrexham (£50,000 from Crusaders on 20/8/1993) FL 88+3/4 FLC 6 FAC 7+1/1 Others 15/1
Reading (£400,000 on 12/7/1996) FL 55+6/3 FLC 4/1 FAC 3/1 Others 3
Southend U (Loaned on 12/2/1999) FL 5/2

HUNTER Roy Ian
Born: Saltburn, 29 October 1973
Height: 5'10" Weight: 12.8

Injury severely restricted Roy's involvement in Northampton's 1999-2000 promotion season. After fighting back to full fitness following his lay-off in 1998-99, the dynamic midfield player was back to his best but was then hit by another injury. This resulted in an operation in March to stitch a cartilage, and cut his appearances down to less than half his club's games. Earlier his name was being linked to Premiership sides, which was a tribute to the Cobblers' 1999 "Player of the Year". Manager Kevin Wilson has nicknamed him "Mr Northampton Town", another tribute to his commitment. Roy signed a new two-year contract in March.

West Bromwich A (From trainee on 4/3/1992) FL 3+6/1 Others 4+1
Northampton T (Free on 2/8/1995) FL 110+23/13 FLC 9 FAC 9/2 Others 12/1

HURST Paul Michael
Born: Sheffield, 25 September 1974
Height: 5'4" Weight: 9.4
Club Honours: AMC '96

After speculation that he wanted to leave Rotherham in 1999-2000, Paul battled willingly to win a regular place in the Millers' team that clinched promotion to the Second Division. With his superb spirit always very much to the fore, he is a left-sided player who can play in defence or midfield. Equally at home doing a man-to-man marking job, Paul showed his small stature means nothing when he scored with a header against Peterborough despite being marked by the 6ft 6in tall Zat Knight. The big-hearted Yorkshireman makes up for his lack of inches with a tremendous appetite for the game.

Rotherham U (From trainee on 12/8/1993) FL 143+36/8 FLC 4 FAC 12+2/2 Others 13+1

HUTCHINGS Carl Emil
Born: Hammersmith, 24 September 1974
Height: 5'11" Weight: 11.0

Early in the 1999-2000 season things looked promising for this busy midfielder, who played in Bristol City's opening seven games, notching two goals. However, after losing his place due to injury, he found it difficult to win a regular spot despite some strong displays The change of management at Ashton Gate didn't help Carl's cause, and he spent the last three months of the season on loan with his former club Brentford. He was mostly used as a right back to cover for an injury to Danny Boxall and he quickly re-established himself as a favourite of the Bees' supporters with his wholehearted performances, giving an outstanding display when he returned to Ashton Gate to play for Brentford in March.

Brentford (From trainee on 12/7/1993) FL 144+18/7 FLC 9+1 FAC 11+1 Others 11+3
Bristol C (£130,000 on 6/7/1998) FL 33+9/3 FLC 4+1/2 FAC 2+2 Others 1
Brentford (Loaned on 11/2/2000) FL 7+1

HUTCHISON Donald (Don)
Born: Gateshead, 9 May 1971
Height: 6'1" Weight: 11.8
International Honours: S: 10; B-1

Despite another impressive campaign for club and country in 1999-2000, a contract dispute makes it increasingly likely that the Everton star's long-term future will lie away from Goodison Park. Such is his versatility that Don kicked off the season at centre forward, but he was soon restored to his more favoured central midfield role – a position from which he captained the side on numerous occasions. With the ability to thread incisive and damaging passes through opposition rearguards, he can also tackle with bite and is a commanding figure in aerial tussles. The only aspect lacking from his all-round game is pace, but his quickness of thought more than makes up for that deficit. Contract talks between Hutchison and his club broke down towards the end of the season with such bitterness that he was stripped of the captaincy, axed from the first team for five matches and transfer-listed. On his return, however, he underlined his quality with an excellent headed goal at Leicester. The relationship between Everton and Hutchison may be nearing an end, but he is sure to be an influential figure for whoever signs him. He was a regular for Scotland, winning eight more caps and scoring four goals, including the winner in the second leg of the Euro 2000 play-off against England at Wembley.

Hartlepool U (From trainee on 20/3/1990) FL 19+5/2 FLC 1+1 FAC 2 Others 1
Liverpool (£175,000 on 27/11/1990) F/PL 33+12/7 FLC 7+1/2 FAC 1+2 Others 3+1/1
West Ham U (£1,500,000 on 30/8/1994) PL 30+5/11 FLC 3/2 FAC 0+1
Sheffield U (£1,200,000 on 11/1/1996) FL 70+8/5 FLC 3+2 FAC 5/1 Others 2+1
Everton (£1,000,000 + on 27/2/1998) PL 68+7/10 FLC 4+1/1 FAC 9

HYDE Graham
Born: Doncaster, 10 November 1970
Height: 5'8" Weight: 11.11

Graham worked hard in central midfield for Birmingham City during the 1999-2000 campaign and always gave 100 per cent effort. He scored his first goal for the Blues with a 25-yard rocket against Tranmere last November and generally helped knit play together while working unselfishly on behalf of the team. He was in and out of the starting line-up until succumbing to the St Andrews injury jinx in early May when he ruptured the medial ligaments in a knee and he is likely to be out of action for at least the first month of the 2000-01 season.

Sheffield Wed (From trainee on 17/5/1988) F/PL 126+46/11 FLC 17+3/2 FAC 13+5/2 Others 4/1
Birmingham C (Free on 5/2/1999) FL 33+11/1 FLC 2+1/1 FAC 2

Micah Hyde

HYDE Micah Anthony
Born: Newham, 10 November 1974
Height: 5'9" Weight: 11.5
Club Honours: Div 2 '98

This hard-working and combative midfield player had one of his best seasons for Watford in 1999-2000 and looked far from out of place in the Premiership. After missing the first two games of the season Micah resumed his familiar partnership with Richard Johnson and played with great authority and consistency. By the end of the season he had clocked up more than 250 senior appearances and added four goals to his career tally.

Cambridge U (From trainee on 19/5/1993) FL 89+18/13 FLC 3 FAC 7+2 Others 4+1
Watford (£225,000 on 21/7/1997) P/FL 116+2/9 FLC 9/2 FAC 7 Others 3

HYLDGAARD Morten Lauridsen
Born: Denmark, 27 April 1976
Height: 6'6" Weight: 13.1
International Honours: Denmark: U21

This giant goalkeeper joined Coventry from Ikast in the summer of 1999 to understudy Magnus Hedman but waited in vain for a first-team opportunity. In January he went to Division Two Scunthorpe on loan to try and provide more "presence" in goal but, arriving in a struggling side, he had an unhappy introduction to league football, looking short of confidence in the air although making a few decent saves. Morten was called back by Coventry at the start of February and released.

Coventry C (£200,000 from Ikast FS, Denmark on 9/7/1999)
Scunthorpe U (Loaned on 7/1/2000) FL 5 Others 2

HYYPIA Sami
Born: Porvoo, Finland, 7 October 1973
Height: 6'4" Weight: 13.5
International Honours: Finland: 32

Tall and powerful, Sami is straight out of the Ron Yeats mould, and he has been awarded the Liverpool captaincy, like his predecessor. A £2.6 million signing from Willem II in the summer of 1999, the Finn had a season of unqualified success in 1999-2000, marshalling the defence and appearing to stop the opposition on his own on occasions. He is elegant in the Alan Hansen mould, and not just a robust, destructive defender. "Man of the Match" in the home defeat by Manchester United, Sami was brilliant and put in a masterful display against the country's top team. He was a model of consistency in a Liverpool back four which has become more secure since his introduction into the team. His strong leadership from the back has won the adulation of Kopites the world over as well as the recognition of his fellow professionals, who selected him for the PFA award-winning Premiership side. Also a first-choice for his country, he won further caps against Germany, Northern Ireland, Wales and Latvia during the season.

Liverpool (£2,600,000 from Willem II, Holland on 7/7/1999) PL 38/2 FLC 2 FAC 2

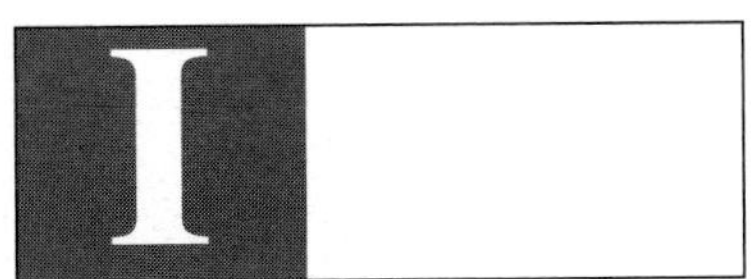

IBEHRE Jabo Oshevire
Born: Islington, 28 January 1983
Height: 6'2" Weight: 12.10
Jabo was given his Leyton Orient debut as a substitute in March 2000 at Northampton. He is a big, quick centre forward who was a vital part of the successful O's youth team. He made two more sub appearances in the Third Division, and will be looking to become a regular squad member in 2000-01.
Leyton Orient (Trainee) FL 0+3

IFILL Paul
Born: Brighton, 20 October 1979
Height: 6'0" Weight: 12.10
A tall, pacy 20-year-old who is a handful for any defender, Paul had an excellent season for Millwall in 1999-2000. After half a dozen substitute appearances during the early weeks of the season, he was brought into the starting line-up for the visit to Oxford in early October and was ever present thereafter. He was mainly employed wide on the right, although he is equally happy as an out-and-out striker. As well as being an excellent provider, he weighed in with his fair share of goals, some being match winners. His impressive performances have inevitably attracted attention from other clubs, an ongoing problem for teams like Millwall when they produce talented young players.
Millwall (From trainee on 2/6/1998) FL 50+9/12 FAC 1 Others 5+1

IGOE Samuel (Sammy) Gary
Born: Staines, 30 September 1975
Height: 5'6" Weight: 10.0
This attacking midfield player began the 1999-2000 season on the subs' bench at Portsmouth and featured in the starting line-up only intermittently before stepping down a division to join Reading in a £100,000 deal just 15 minutes before the transfer deadline. He made his debut two days later as a substitute at right wing back against Cardiff City. He was recommended by club coach Martin Allen, also ex-Portsmouth, and proved a valuable addition to the squad, although he played only one full game, away to Bury, before the end of the season. A diminutive player who makes up for his lack of height with tremendous determination and a good touch, he has signed a two-year contract, which will give him the opportunity to win a regular berth in the team.
Portsmouth (From trainee on 15/2/1994) FL 100+60/11 FLC 8+5 FAC 2+3
Reading (£100,000 on 23/3/2000) FL 3+3

ILIC Sasa
Born: Melbourne, Australia, 18 July 1972
Height: 6'4" Weight: 14.0
International Honours: Yugoslavia: 1
A tall, agile goalkeeper, Sasa made only one appearance for Charlton during the 1999-2000 season, having lost his first-team place to summer signing Dean Kiely. He was called into the side for the away game at Grimsby in November when Kiely was away on international duty, and acquitted himself well, but was back on the substitutes' bench the following week. Frustrated by his lack of senior opportunities, he was loaned to Premiership club West Ham in February to cover for a crisis caused by Shaka Hislop's broken leg and Craig Forrest's absence at the CONCACAF Gold Cup. His only appearance for the Hammers came in the disappointing 4-0 home defeat by Everton on 22 February, after which Forrest returned to claim the position and Sasa went back to the Valley.
Charlton Ath (Free from St Leonards Stamcroft on 5/10/1997) P/FL 38 FLC 2 FAC 1 Others 3
West Ham U (Loaned on 24/2/2000) PL 1

IMPEY Andrew (Andy) Rodney
Born: Hammersmith, 13 September 1971
Height: 5'8" Weight: 11.2
Club Honours: FLC '00
International Honours: E: U21-1
Leicester's right-sided winger or wing back showed outstandingly good form during the early stages of the 1999-2000 season, a period when City were particularly effective. He coolly slotted home a spot kick in the Worthington Cup penalty shoot-out against Leeds before succumbing to the club's mid-season injury jinx. He found it harder to win a regular place after recovering but appeared in the Worthington Cup final at Wembley from the substitutes' bench and was an important squad member throughout the campaign. Andy showed glimpses of his best form again in the closing weeks of the season, notably against Newcastle and Tottenham.
Queens Park R (£35,000 from Yeading on 14/6/1990) F/PL 177+10/13 FLC 15+1/3 FAC 7+3/1 Others 0+2/1
West Ham U (£1,300,000 on 26/9/1997) PL 25+2 FLC 4 FAC 3
Leicester C (£1,600,000 on 25/11/1998) PL 45+2/1 FLC 5+2 FAC 3+1

INCE Clayton
Born: Trinidad, 13 July 1972
Height: 6'3" Weight: 14.2
International Honours: Trinidad & Tobago
Having joined Crewe on trial at the start of the 1999-2000 season, Clayton was signed from Defence Force of Trinidad last September for £50,000. An international since the mid-1990s and first-choice goalkeeper for his country, he was voted "Best Goalkeeper" of the Shell Caribbean Cup competition in 1998 and 1999. International duties restricted his opportunities at club level but he won a further 12 caps for Trinidad & Tobago during the season. His only senior appearance for Alex was as a substitute for Jason Kearton at Huddersfield in March, but he will be hoping for a chance to prove himself in English football during the coming season.
Crewe Alex (£50,000 from Defence Force, Trinidad on 21/9/1999) FL 0+1

INCE Paul Emerson Carlyle
Born: Ilford, 21 October 1967
Height: 5'11" Weight: 12.2
Club Honours: CS '93, '94; FAC '90, '94; ECW '91; ESC '91; FLC '92; PL '93, '94
International Honours: E: 53; B-1; U21-2; Yth
When Paul left Liverpool in August 1999 to join Middlesbrough it looked as though he was doing so under a cloud. However, it lifted on his arrival at the Riverside and he performed impressively for Boro last season, producing many fine and battling displays that saw him control the midfield. He took over the captaincy and immediately made his presence felt with his great drive and gusto, marshalling his troops and leading by example. Recapturing his old style and flair, he performed well enough to catch England manager Kevin Keegan's eye and won back his England place for the European Championship play-off win over Scotland. Paul remains a formidable competitor who is not only a tigerish ball winner but can create openings in the opposition penalty box when he drives forward. He spent quite a while waiting for the "right" moment to have a hernia operation but didn't hesitate when the time came, and fought his way back into the side with characteristic determination. A regular for his country, he won eight more caps and played in all three of England's matches at Euro 2000.
West Ham U (From apprentice on 18/7/1985) FL 66+6/7 FLC 9/3 FAC 8+2/1 Others 4/1
Manchester U (£1,000,000 on 14/9/1989) F/PL 203+3/24 FLC 23+1/2 FAC 26+1/1 Others 24/1 (£8,000,000 to Inter Milan, Italy on 13/7/1995)
Liverpool (£4,200,000 on 22/7/1997) PL 65/14 FLC 6/1 FAC 3/1 Others 7/1
Middlesbrough (£1,000,000 on 3/8/1999) PL 32/3 FLC 3/1

Paul Ince

INGHAM Michael
Born: Preston, 9 September 1980
Height: 6'4" Weight: 13.10
International Honours: NI: Yth

Michael made seven appearances for Carlisle on loan last autumn during the club's goalkeeper crisis. Remarkably, he picked up an injury on his debut against Southend. He recovered to earn the "Star Man" accolade at Darlington, where his efforts kept the score down to a respectable level.

Sunderland (£30,000 from Cliftonville on 28/7/1999)
Carlisle U (Loaned on 1/10/1999) FL 7

INGIMARSSON Ivar
Born: Iceland, 20 August 1978
Height: 6'0" Weight: 12.7
International Honours: Iceland: 1

A calm, influential midfield player who is an accurate passer of the ball, Ivar helped IBV Vestmannaeyjar to the runner-up position in the 1999 Icelandic League before joining Torquay on a month's loan last October. The Icelandic international made four appearances for the Gulls and scored a fine goal on his debut at Barnet. He was subsequently snapped up by Ron Noades for Brentford on a permanent transfer and immediately established himself as a regular in the Bees' line-up. Ivar was also used as an occasional striker and netted the winner in a 1-0 victory at Blackpool last January.

Torquay U (Loaned from IBV Vestmannaeyjar, Iceland on 21/10/1999) FL 4/1
Brentford (£150,000 on 18/11/1999) FL 21+4/1 Others 3

INGLEDOW Jamie Graeme
Born: Barnsley, 23 August 1980
Height: 5'6" Weight: 9.7

Jamie burst on to the scene at Rotherham in 1998-99 but last season the promising young midfielder had few first-team opportunities due to the promotion-chasing form of his more experienced colleagues. However, age is very much on his side and this tough-tackling youngster still has a bright future in the game to look forward to. Jamie's 1999-2000 consolation was assisting the second-string Millers to the Division One title in the Pontins League. He was released in the summer. Stop Press: It was reported that he had joined Chesterfield during the close season.

Rotherham U (From trainee on 1/7/1998) FL 17+8/2 FLC 3 FAC 5 Others 2+1

INGLETHORPE Alexander (Alex) Matthew
Born: Epsom, 14 November 1971
Height: 5'11" Weight: 11.6

An attacking midfielder who has often played in attack, Alex started the 1999-2000 season as a first-team regular at Leyton Orient. He scored three times in his first six games and confirmed that he remains a highly effective performer with an abundance of pace and an impressive repertoire of skills. However, he lost his place due to injury problems and the form of his replacements, and after being told that his contract would not be renewed he joined Exeter on loan in February. Unfortunately, Alex broke his collarbone in the first game he started for City, the Auto Windscreens Shield southern final first leg at Bristol City, and the Exeter fans did not get to see the qualities that had made him a target for the club for some time. He had had a trial with the Grecians during the 1999 pre-season, and was offered as part of the deal that took Darren Rowbotham to Orient in November. Stop Press: Alex was reported to have made a permanent move to Exeter during the summer.

Watford (From juniors on 1/7/1990) FL 2+10/2 FLC 1+2 Others 1+1/1
Barnet (Loaned on 23/3/1995) FL 5+1/3
Leyton Orient (Signed on 19/5/1995) FL 105+18/32 FLC 6/4 FAC 3+5 Others 3+3/1
Exeter C (Loaned on 24/2/2000) FL 0+1 Others 1

INGRAM Stuart **Denevan (Denny)**
Born: Sunderland, 27 June 1976
Height: 5'10" Weight: 12.1

Hartlepool's longest-serving player and former captain, Denny looked to have settled his differences with the club as he began the 1999-2000 season in the first team. Unfortunately, after being dropped in September, he effectively became surplus to requirements. Out of the senior picture, he took on the role of reserve-team skipper and added experience to a young squad. A useful utility player, he ended the season on loan at Scarborough. A permanent move appeared likely as Denny was released in May.

Hartlepool U (From trainee on 5/7/1994) FL 192+7/10 FLC 13+2 FAC 7 Others 8

INGRAM Rae
Born: Manchester, 6 December 1974
Height: 5'11" Weight: 12.8

During the 1998-99 season Rae had to cope with the debilitating illness, ME, finishing his first full Macclesfield campaign prematurely. Throughout the 1999 close season, he followed a careful diet and took plenty of rest. The result was that he was able to resume playing in the pre-season friendlies, but not without one moment of concern on an extremely hot day when he had to be substituted. Rae began the season in dramatic fashion when he received a red card just five minutes after coming on as a substitute against Northampton on the opening day of the season. However, apart from a suspension and a short time out at the turn of the year following a hernia operation, he was ever present in the side. A skilful full back who can control the ball well, pass accurately and move round opponents with ease, he understandably showed much greater pace last season and was Macc's most improved player. Rae's return to good health was the highlight of the Moss Rose campaign, and he demonstrated his commitment to the Macc cause by turning down a trial at Norwich.

Manchester C (From trainee on 9/7/1993) P/FL 18+5 FLC 1 FAC 4
Macclesfield T (Free on 19/3/1998) FL 63+7 FLC 3 FAC 4+1 Others 1+1

INMAN Niall Edward
Born: Wakefield, 6 February 1978
Height: 5'8" Weight: 11.6
International Honours: RoI: U21-8; Yth

Following a summer knee operation, Niall struggled to regain his Peterborough place in 1999-2000. His only senior involvement of the season came with sub appearances against Chester in the league and Reading in the Worthington Cup. He had a trial with Rochdale in November, before going on loan to Doncaster for the remainder of the season in February.

Peterborough U (From trainee on 3/7/1996) FL 6+6/2 FLC 1+2 FAC 0+1

INNES Mark
Born: Glasgow, 27 September 1978
Height: 5'10" Weight: 12.1

Mark appeared regularly for Oldham in the opening games of the 1999-2000 campaign but then slipped to the fringes of the first-team squad. He was subsequently transfer-listed last March but returned towards the end of the season, when he showed good form. A left-sided midfield player, he is a quality passer of the ball and a favourite of the Boundary Park fans.

Oldham Ath (From trainee on 10/10/1995) FL 25+13/1 FLC 2 FAC 1 Others 1

IPOUA Gui (Guy)
Born: Douala, Cameroon, 14 January 1976
Height: 6'1" Weight: 12.0

Released by Bristol Rovers in the summer of 1999, Guy had trials with a number of clubs in England and Scotland before arriving at Scunthorpe in August. Thrown on as a second-half substitute against Bournemouth, the powerful forward immediately scored and two days later he netted at Cardiff following a superb 50-yard run to win a two-year contract. He continued to impress during the first half of the season, with his pace, directness and strength causing problems for all Second Division defences. But his form fell off at Christmas and he scored only once in the second half of the campaign, often having to settle for a place on the substitutes' bench. Guy is the younger brother of the Cameroon international player Samuel Ipoua.

Bristol Rov (Free from Seville, Spain on 7/8/1998) FL 15+9/3 FLC 1+1 FAC 3+1 Others 1
Scunthorpe U (Free on 27/8/1999) FL 28+12/9 FAC 1 Others 1

IRONS Kenneth (Kenny)
Born: Liverpool, 4 November 1970
Height: 5'10" Weight: 12.2

Following his move from Tranmere Rovers in the summer of 1999, the influential midfielder slotted straight into the engine room of the Huddersfield side, his long-range passing and close control ensuring that he was always at the hub of play. He is quick to support the front line and it was easy to see why he had been Tranmere's top scorer the previous season; with Kenny always keen to add to his goal tally, he was soon off the mark with goals against Crystal Palace, Notts County and Port Vale. Never a scorer of the simple goal, he netted with a screamer against Chelsea in the Worthington Cup which proved to be the winner as well as a contender for "Goal of the Season". The skilful play-maker reads the game with great perceptiveness and is always capable of that exquisite pass to release the strikers. Kenny unfortunately lost his ever-present record due to a hernia problem which inhibited his contribution during the latter stages of the season.

Tranmere Rov (From trainee on 9/11/1989) FL 313+39/54 FLC 24+7/7 FAC 14+2/3 Others 28+3/3
Huddersfield T (£450,000 on 18/6/1999) FL 39+1/3 FLC 6/2 FAC 1

IRWIN Joseph **Denis**
Born: Cork, 31 October 1965
Height: 5'8" Weight: 11.0
Club Honours: CS '93, '96, '97; ECWC '91; ESC '91; FLC '92; PL '93, '94, '96, '97, '99, '00; FAC '94, '96; EC '99
International Honours: RoI: 56; B-1; U23-1; U21-3; Yth; Sch

A highly experienced defender who is a model of consistency and a specialist goalscorer from set plays, Denis remained a key member of the Manchester United team during 1999-2000, his tenth season at Old Trafford, fighting off all pretenders to his familiar left-back slot, and passing a few milestones of his own along the way. Back in October, he became United's top man in Europe when he surpassed Peter Schmeichel's 17-match record in the Champions' League against Marseille. He added two further caps for the Republic of Ireland, appearing in the European Championship play-off matches against Turkey last November before announcing his retirement from the international game. At club level, there was no such talk of retirement as Denis emerged as one of United's most dependable performers, notching up his usual quota of goals, notably from the penalty spot against Watford, Everton and West Ham in the Premiership, and ending the season with his sixth Premiership winners' medal. Denis and team-mate Ryan Giggs now have more championship medals to their credit than any other players in the club's history. Just how much mileage he's got left in the tank it is extremely difficult to say but, with another one-year contract in the offing, he could still be renewing it when Sir Alex Ferguson's successor arrives somewhere around 2003. On current form, it's certainly worth a flutter.

Leeds U (From apprentice on 3/11/1983) FL 72/1 FLC 5 FAC 3 Others 2
Oldham Ath (Free on 22/5/1986) FL 166+1/4 FLC 19/3 FAC 13 Others 5
Manchester U (£625,000 on 20/6/1990) F/PL 326+9/22 FLC 28+3 FAC 41+1/7 Others 68/2

IVERSEN Steffen
Born: Oslo, Norway, 10 November 1976
Height: 6'1" Weight: 11.10
Club Honours: FLC '99
International Honours: Norway: 18; Yth

The Norwegian international forward had another fine season for Tottenham in 1999-2000 and continues to impress. He loves to strike from outside the 18-yard box as well as getting deep into the penalty area to dig out goals from the faintest of opportunities. Steffen produced impressive displays against Manchester United in October and Arsenal in November, and found the back of the net in both games, which helped put him up among the Premiership's top scorers. A fine hat-trick in the 7-2 trouncing of Southampton demonstrated the striker's maturity and natural awareness of the space created around him by his pace and quick thinking, and he impressed his manager, George Graham, with his consistency. With striking partner Chris Armstrong hitting a run of good form towards the end of the season, Steffen seems likely to face real competition for a place alongside new signing Sergei Rebrov in the Spurs attack in 2000-01, which is sure to provide an edge that can only benefit the team as a whole. Now established as a regular for Norway, he won 11 caps during the season, appearing in all three of their Euro 2000 games and scoring their only goal, which proved to be the winner against Spain.

Tottenham H (£2,700,000 from Rosenborg, Norway, via Nationalkam, on 7/12/1996) PL 82+10/29 FLC 7+1/3 FAC 7+2/3 Others 4/1

IWELLUMO Christopher (Chris) Robert
Born: Coatbridge, 1 August 1978
Height: 6'3" Weight: 13.8

A £25,000 signing from Aarhus in Denmark, this Scottish striker joined Stoke last March and made four substitute appearances in City's first team before the end of the season. Previously with St Mirren and a number of other Scottish league clubs, Chris is reminiscent of Dion Dublin both in appearance and in physique. His height makes him an ideal target man and with work he is capable of making his mark in the English game. He made a fleeting appearance as a substitute during City's victory in the Auto Windscreens Shield final at Wembley.

St Mirren (From juniors on 5/8/1996) SL 7+19 SLC 0+3/1 SC 1+1/1 Others 0+2 (Free to Aarhus Fremad, Denmark during 1998 close season)
Stoke C (£25,000 from AGF Aarhus, Denmark on 1/3/2000) FL 0+3 Others 0+1

IZZET Mustafa (Muzzy) Kemal
Born: Mile End, 31 October 1974
Height: 5'10" Weight: 10.12
Club Honours: FLC '97, '00
International Honours: Turkey: 1

The right-footed Leicester midfielder started the 1999-2000 season in such fine goal-scoring form that he was considered for England honours by Kevin Keegan. A calf injury interrupted his run of form and goals, but his return for the latter stages of the Worthington Cup proved a crucial factor. Indeed, only his own rustiness and the agility of the Tranmere 'keeper prevented him from getting on to the score sheet in Leicester's victory in the final at Wembley. Muzzy had taken over City's spot kick duties earlier in the campaign and duly slotted home the decisive strike in the penalty shoot-out against Leeds to keep the Foxes on the Wembley trail. Pacy and self-assured, he rounded the season off in splendid form, just as he had started it. He eventually chose to represent Turkey at international level, and after winning a place in the final 22 for Euro 2000 he made his debut in the 0-0 draw with Sweden.

Chelsea (From trainee on 19/5/1993)
Leicester C (£650,000 + on 28/3/1996) P/FL 141+2/21 FLC 19/3 FAC 9/1 Others 5

Muzzy Izzet

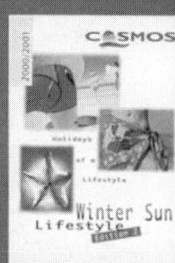

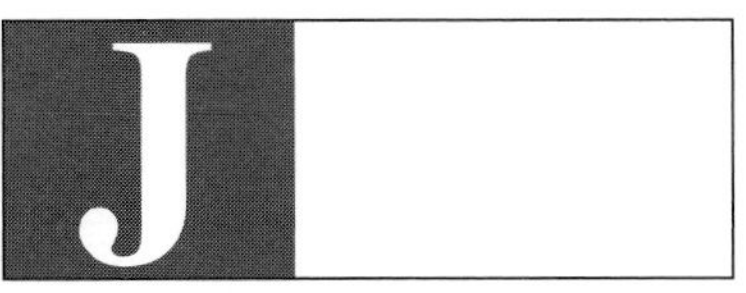

JAASKELAINEN Jussi
Born: Vaasa, Finland, 19 April 1975
Height: 6'3" Weight: 12.10
International Honours: Finland: 1

Last season was always going to be the make-or-break one for Jussi. After he had proven himself to be a capable shot stopper, his form had deserted him at the end of the 1998-99 campaign, and he lost his first-team place as a result. The new season started off in a similar fashion, with Keith Branagan establishing himself as the club's number one 'keeper at the beginning of the season. When a bad leg injury forced Branagan out of the side in October, Jussi seized his chance and never looked back. His form in 1999-2000 was that of a different player from the nervous young man with no confidence who had lost his place at the end of the previous season. While he had always been considered an excellent shot stopper, Jussi proved last season that he has worked on his all-round game. His positioning is now excellent, his kicking and distribution have improved 100 per cent, he is now supremely confident in one-on-one situations and his shot-stopping abilities are, as ever, sensational. There were simply too many occasions to describe when Jussi pulled off vital saves to keep Bolton in games last season, and he must have single-handedly saved the club an extra ten or twelve points, which ultimately enabled them to get into the play-offs at the last hurdle. There are two other quality 'keepers at Bolton in Steve Banks and Keith Branagan, but if Jussi recaptures last season's form they will not get close to claiming his number one position.

Bolton W (£100,000 + from VPS Vassa, Finland, via MPS, on 14/11/1997) FL 67+1 FLC 7 FAC 4 Others 2

Jussi Jaaskelainen

JACK Rodney (Rod) Alphonso
Born: Kingstown, St Vincent, 28 September 1972
Height: 5'7" Weight: 10.9
International Honours: St Vincent & Grenadines

Rodney's 1999-2000 season with Crewe was disrupted by injuries and international duties, with the result that he played in fewer than half the club's games. A potential match winner with a fine turn of speed and an explosive shot, the skilful striker can play either through the middle or out wide, where his pace makes him difficult to contain. Still the club's record signing, he made 25 appearances (two of them as a substitute) last season, but scored only four goals, the last of them against Manchester City on 3 January. Rodney appeared regularly for his country in their World Cup qualifying matches, netting a hat-trick in the 9-0 win over the US Virgin Islands and then scoring with a spectacular bicycle kick against St Kitts & Nevis as St Vincent moved through to the semi-final round of the CONCACAF section.

Torquay U (Free from Lambada, St Vincent on 10/10/1995) FL 82+5/24 FLC 6/1 FAC 6 Others 6/3
Crewe Alex (£650,000 on 14/8/1998) FL 58+4/13 FLC 4/2 FAC 1

JACKSON Justin Jonathan
Born: Nottingham, 10 December 1974
Height: 6'0" Weight: 11.6
Club Honours: Div 3 '98

Justin made one substitute appearance for Halifax in 1999-2000 before leaving the club early in the season. He moved to Morecambe, where he banged in over thirty goals in the Conference. It seems highly likely that this quick forward will get another chance at league level.

Notts Co (£30,000 from Woking on 26/9/1997) FL 7+18/1 FAC 3+2 Others 1
Rotherham U (Loaned on 21/1/1999) FL 2/1
Halifax T (£30,000 on 11/2/1999) FL 16+1/4

JACKSON Mark Graham
Born: Barnsley, 30 September 1977
Height: 6'0" Weight: 11.12
International Honours: E: Yth

This Leeds United reserve joined Barnsley on loan last January when the First Division club's midfield was decimated by injuries. Mark made a very successful debut with the Tykes' reserve team and was subsequently promoted to the first team for the visit to Crystal Palace, where he began the match in midfield but later switched to a back-four position, another role for which he is well equipped. This proved to be his only senior game at Oakwell and he returned to Elland Road at the end of his loan period. He is strong in the tackle, distributes the ball accurately and has good aerial skills. Mark joined Scunthorpe on a two-year contract in March after prolonged contract discussions but struggled to adjust to the pace of Second Division football. Asked to play in midfield, he was soon dropped to the substitutes' bench but should have a big role to play next season, possibly at centre half, to which his power and aerial strength seem better suited.

Leeds U (From trainee on 1/7/1995) PL 11+8 FAC 4
Huddersfield T (Loaned on 29/10/1998) FL 5
Barnsley (Loaned on 14/1/2000) FL 1
Scunthorpe U (Free on 9/3/2000) FL 6

JACKSON Matthew (Matt) Alan
Born: Leeds, 19 October 1971
Height: 6'1" Weight: 12.12
Club Honours: FAC '95
International Honours: E: U21-10; Sch

Matt signed a one-year extension to his current Norwich contract in October 1999, which was a reward for his consistency throughout the 1999-2000 campaign, in which he once again skippered the side by example. A polished central defender, he is renowned for his excellent positional play and composure when under pressure, always being prepared to pass his way out of defence rather than opting for the aimless hoof up the pitch. He is also very competitive, not only in the air, where very few strikers get the better of him, but also on the deck, where he seldom gives his opponent the time to settle on the ball. Occasionally employed at right back, he produced some of his most impressive form last season as the central player in a three-man defence, when his ability to make telling interceptions was well to the fore.

Luton T (From juniors on 4/7/1990) FL 7+2 FLC 2 Others 0+1
Preston NE (Loaned on 27/3/1991) FL 3+1 Others 1
Everton (£600,000 on 18/10/1991) F/PL 132+6/4 FLC 9 FAC 14/2 Others 4
Charlton Ath (Loaned on 26/3/1996) FL 8 Others 2
Queens Park R (Loaned on 20/8/1996) FL 7
Birmingham C (Loaned on 31/10/1996) FL 10
Norwich C (£450,000 on 24/12/1996) FL 132+3/6 FLC 5 FAC 4

JACKSON Michael Douglas
Born: Cheltenham, 26 June 1980
Height: 5'7" Weight: 10.10

Michael started out with Cheltenham's youth set-up but has had to wait patiently for his chance in the first team. A small but powerfully built midfield player who covers a lot of ground during a game, he possesses a good shot and likes to get forward whenever possible. He spent most of 1999-2000 in the reserves, and showed that he is adaptable, as he operated at right back and even in the centre of defence on occasions. He made just two substitute appearances in the Football League, his best performance of the season coming as an early replacement for the injured Mark Yates in a 2-1 Worthington Cup win over Norwich.

Cheltenham T (From trainee on 1/8/1997) FL 0+2 FLC 0+1

JACKSON Michael James
Born: Runcorn, 4 December 1973
Height: 6'0" Weight: 13.8
Club Honours: Div 2 '97, '00
International Honours: E: Yth

Preston's consistent centre half continued to attract plenty of transfer attention last season, despite signing a new contract during the summer of 1999. Rested for the Auto Windscreens Shield games, he was otherwise ever present, and played a leading role in North End's Second Division championship triumph. Good in the air and uncompromising when tackling and clearing his lines, he scored five goals during the season, the first against his former club Bury in November. He recorded a rare goal with his foot in his 150th game for the club, at Reading, and opened the scoring at Burnley – where he shackled Ian Wright all game – after only 88 seconds. His goals, which also included the winner in the table-topping clash at Wigan, were a useful addition to the defensive qualities he brings to the team, and his performances were recognised with selection for the PFA award-winning Second Division side.

Crewe Alex (From trainee on 29/7/1992) FL 5 FLC 1 FAC 1 Others 2
Bury (Free on 13/8/1993) FL 123+2/9 FLC 9/1 FAC 3 Others 12
Preston NE (£125,000 on 26/3/1997) FL 136+1/15 FLC 11 FAC 12 Others 8

JACKSON Richard
Born: Whitby, 18 April 1980
Height: 5'8" Weight: 10.12

The former Scarborough right back continued his progress at Derby in 1999-2000 by playing a major role as the reserves clinched their title. A neat and tidy player who distributes the ball sensibly, he made the first-team bench on numerous occasions but was called upon only twice, in the final games of the season against Newcastle and Chelsea.

Scarborough (From trainee on 27/3/1998) FL 21+1 FLC 2
Derby Co (£30,000 + on 25/3/1999) PL 0+2

JACOBS Wayne Graham
Born: Sheffield, 3 February 1969
Height: 5'9" Weight: 11.2

Bradford City's longest-serving player was placed on the transfer list shortly before the start of the 1999-2000 season after negotiations over a new contract broke down but he still made the starting line-up for the opening match at Middlesbrough. He impressed in the early part of the campaign but lost his place in mid-September and did not see regular first-team action again until the new year. After this he seemed to go from strength to strength and produced some excellent performances. He is strong in the tackle with good distribution and he showed a fine understanding with Peter Beagrie when attacking down the left flank.

Sheffield Wed (From apprentice on 3/1/1987) FL 5+1 FLC 3 Others 1
Hull C (£27,000 on 25/3/1988) FL 127+2/4 FLC 7 FAC 8 Others 6
Rotherham U (Free on 5/8/1993) FL 40+2/2 FLC 4 FAC 1 Others 2
Bradford C (Free on 5/8/1994) P/FL 203+6/9 FLC 15+1 FAC 10/2 Others 5

JACOBSEN Anders
Born: Norway, 18 April 1968
Height: 6'3" Weight: 13.7
Club Honours: AMC '00
International Honours: Norway: 4

The intellectual of the Stoke squad, this thoughtful Norwegian central defender joined the club at the start of the 1999-2000 season and was quickly into his stride with a whole string of "Man of the Match" performances. Outstanding in the air, he was a formidable foil to Nicky Mohan and the supporters could not believe that City had been lucky enough to secure his services without cost from Sheffield United. Injury caused him to lose his place towards the end of the season to Brynjar Gunnarsson, but whenever called upon he shone and he scored a couple of vital goals from corners. An unused substitute when Stoke won the Auto Windscreens Shield at Wembley, Anders was out of contract at the end of the season.

Sheffield U (Signed from IK Start, Norway on 24/12/1998) FL 8+4 FAC 0+1
Stoke C (Free on 11/8/1999) FL 29+4/2 FLC 3 FAC 1 Others 6+1

JAGIELKA Philip (Phil) Nikodem
Born: Manchester, 17 August 1982
Height: 5'11" Weight: 12.8
International Honours: E: Yth

This promising youngster was given a three-year contract by Sheffield United last April and shortly afterwards he was capped by England U17s when he came on as a second-half substitute against Luxembourg. A regular with the reserves and juniors at Bramall Lane, Phil was on the bench for the penultimate game of the season at Norwich but was not used and it seemed that his first taste of senior action would have to wait until the coming season. However, 24 hours after brother Steve had helped Shrewsbury stay in the league, Phil made his debut, as a substitute, in the final match, coming on for most of the second half against Swindon. He produced a lively performance in midfield and was far from overawed. He will be hoping to establish himself in the first team in 2000-01.

Sheffield U (From trainee on 8/5/2000) FL 0+1

JAGIELKA Stephen (Steve)
Born: Manchester, 10 March 1978
Height: 5'8" Weight: 11.5

The 1999-2000 season was the Shrewsbury front man's third in league football and his best yet. Although he figured infrequently early in the season, new manager Kevin Ratcliffe chose to utilise his speed on the ball in a midfield role in the latter part of the campaign. Skilful when in possession, Steve added bite to the squad and scored a vital goal at Barnet to secure a point during the run-in. Steve is the brother of Sheffield United's young star, Phil Jagielka.

Stoke C (From trainee on 15/7/1996)
Shrewsbury T (Free on 30/7/1997) FL 31+49/3 FLC 2+3 FAC 2+1/1 Others 1+1/1

JAMES Clement Junior
Born: Bracknell, 10 March 1981
Height: 5'9" Weight: 12.7

This pacy young Brentford striker was in his first year as a professional in 1999-2000. Although mostly featuring in the reserve and junior sides, Clement made his Football League debut for the Bees at Stoke in April when he was brought on for the final nine minutes of the match. He was released at the end of the season.

Brentford (From trainee on 30/6/1999) FL 0+1

JAMES David Benjamin
Born: Welwyn Garden City, 1 August 1970
Height: 6'5" Weight: 14.5
Club Honours: FAYC '89; FLC '95
International Honours: E: 1; B-1; U21-10; Yth

David joined Aston Villa for a £1.7 million fee in the summer of 1999 and went on to do much to re-establish himself as one of the country's top goalkeepers. He was first choice in the Villa goal throughout last season, missing only a handful of games due to a knee problem in September and a thigh injury sustained in February. His performance in saving Bolton's penalties in the FA Cup semi-final shoot-out was undoubtedly a high point, as was his recall to the England squad, albeit as a recognised third choice behind David Seaman and Nigel Martyn. Ultimately, however, the season ended disappointingly, with David receiving some of the blame for Chelsea's winner in the FA Cup final and then missing out on a place in Kevin Keegan's final 22 for the Euro 2000 championships. A big, powerful 'keeper who dominates his penalty area, he is quick to release the ball to set up attacks and possesses a prodigious throwing arm.

Watford (From trainee on 1/7/1988) FL 89 FLC 6 FAC 2 Others 1
Liverpool (£1,000,000 on 6/7/1992) PL 213+1 FLC 22 FAC 19 Others 22
Aston Villa (£1,800,000 on 23/6/1999) PL 29 FLC 5 FAC 5

David James

JAMES Lutel Malik
Born: Manchester, 2 June 1972
Height: 5'9" Weight: 11.0
International Honours: St Kitts & Nevis

The 1999-2000 season was a somewhat frustrating one for this pacy Bury forward. Having gained a regular place in the side in the early weeks of the campaign, he broke a bone in his leg in September in an away game at Oldham and was sidelined for the next few months. He made his comeback in November and gradually forced his way back into regular contention, scoring important goals against both Colchester United and Preston, but perhaps struggled to recapture any real consistency. Always guaranteed to give 100 per cent, Lutel jetted off to St Kitts in the spring to resume his international career, assisting their campaign in the World Cup qualifying rounds.

Scarborough (Free from Yorkshire Amateurs on 22/2/1993) FL 0+6 (Free to Guiseley during 1993 close season)
Bury (Free from Hyde U on 26/10/1998) FL 27+13/4 FLC 2+1 FAC 1+2/1

JANSEN Matthew (Matt) Brooke
Born: Carlisle, 20 October 1977
Height: 5'11" Weight: 10.13
Club Honours: AMC '97
International Honours: E: U21-6; Yth

Widely regarded as a young striker of exceptional talent when he moved to Ewood Park from Crystal Palace in January 1999, Matt did not make the progress that was expected of him at Blackburn in 1999-2000. Food poisoning and a succession of niggles kept him out of the Rovers line-up at various times during the season, but so did an inconsistency that sometimes saw him dribbling mazily but not advancing very far. Not one to look up and pass when he is in sight of goal, he disappointed with the lack of power in his shooting, but he remained popular with the Blackburn fans. His best contribution of the season was the equalising goal in the FA Cup tie against Newcastle.

Carlisle U (From trainee on 18/1/1996) FL 26+16/10 FLC 4+1/3 FAC 1+3 Others 3+3
Crystal Palace (£1,000,000 + on 12/2/1998) P/FL 23+3/10 FLC 4 FAC 0+1
Blackburn Rov (£4,100,000 on 19/1/1999) P/FL 26+15/7 FLC 1+1/2 FAC 1/1

JARMAN Lee
Born: Cardiff, 16 December 1977
Height: 6'3" Weight: 13.3
International Honours: W: U21-9; Yth

A talented right back with an outstanding right foot, Lee was once described by former Cardiff manager Kenny Hibbitt as "the best footballer at Cardiff City". However, he has tended to lack aggression for such a big player and did not develop as hoped under Hibbitt's successor, Frank Burrows. The Welsh U21 international was made captain and stayed back for extra training as Cardiff tried to bring the best out of him. Lee made only a couple of substitute appearances in 1999-2000 and was eventually released in mid-season. After trials with Carlisle, Brentford and other clubs, he had a spell with Merthyr Tydfil before joining Exeter on a weekly contract in March. Lee forced his way into the team but was released at the end of the season. He remains a player with ability, though, and league new boys Kidderminster were among those to show interest in a talented defender who has yet to achieve his potential.

Cardiff C (From trainee on 23/8/1995) FL 78+16/1 FLC 3+2 FAC 3+3/1 Others 5+2 (Free to Merthyr Tydfil 1/11/1999)
Exeter C (Free on 10/3/2000) FL 7 Others 0+1

JARRETT Jason Lee Mee
Born: Bury, 14 September 1979
Height: 6'0" Weight: 12.4

Jason signed for Wrexham last October after being released by Blackpool in the summer but featured just once in the Robins' starting line-up last season – in the 5-1 defeat at Gillingham soon after his arrival. He played three times in the FAW Premier Cup competition and then went on loan to League of Ireland club Shelbourne last January. On his return this tall young midfield player moved on for a trial period at Bury.

Blackpool (From trainee on 3/7/1998) FL 2 FAC 0+1 Others 1
Wrexham (Free on 8/10/1999) FL 1

JASZCZUN Antony (Tommy) John
Born: Kettering, 16 September 1977
Height: 5'10" Weight: 10.10

With no prospect of adding to his only first-team appearance for Aston Villa, as a substitute in the Worthington Cup in 1998-99, this young left-sided defender moved to Blackpool in a £30,000 deal last January. He scored on his home debut in the Auto Windscreens Shield against Stoke and rarely missed a game during the remainder of the season.

Aston Villa (From trainee on 5/7/1996) FLC 0+1
Blackpool (£30,000 on 20/10/2000) FL 19 Others 1/1

JEANNE Leon Charles
Born: Cardiff, 17 November 1980
Height: 5'8" Weight: 10.10
International Honours: W: U21-7; Yth

Leon did not feature in the Queens Park Rangers first team as often as expected last season after he made a promising start to his professional career in 1998-99. He is a quick forward who still has time to develop into a player of the future. A substitute against Blackburn in October, he returned to the first team for the match against Norwich at the end of March but did not manage to retain his place for the remaining games of the season. He was an ever-present for Wales at U21 level, adding a further four caps during the campaign.

Queens Park R (From trainee on 18/11/1997) FL 8+4

JEFFERS Francis
Born: Liverpool, 25 January 1981
Height: 5'10" Weight: 10.7
Club Honours: FAYC '98
International Honours: E: U21-5; Yth; Sch

Despite giving tens of thousands of Evertonians a scare on the eve of the 1999-2000 season by asking for a transfer, Francis soon settled his differences with the club and began to reproduce the form which had marked him down as a striking star of the future. The intelligence and timing of his runs across the penalty area are way in advance of his limited experience and his finishing is generally assured. He had already collected four Premiership goals by early October when a groin injury cut six weeks from his season. He scored two more on his return, before signs that he was becoming jaded by the intense demands on his young shoulders began to show. Manager Walter Smith had hinted at resting him periodically, until an ankle injury ensured an enforced rest for all but the final few weeks of the season. With the potential to become a striker of the highest calibre, Francis still has disciplinary problems to attend to. However, he made his debut for England at U21 level against Luxembourg last September and went on to play in all three games in the European Championship finals in Slovakia, where he scored from all of 35 yards in the 6-0 thrashing of Turkey. Francis's progress will need to be carefully monitored – but it could be well worth the effort.

Everton (From trainee on 20/2/1998) PL 27+10/12 FLC 0+2 FAC 6+1/1

JELLEYMAN Gareth Anthony
Born: Holywell, 14 November 1980
Height: 5'10" Weight: 10.6
International Honours: W: U21-1; Yth

Another of the youngsters to graduate from Peterborough's celebrated academy, Gareth enjoyed a remarkable first term in senior football in 1999-2000. It climaxed in a Wembley appearance as Posh beat Darlington in the Third Division play-off final in May. The Wales U21 international made his first-team bow in the FA Cup tie with Brighton in November. Although often used as an attacking left back, Gareth finished the term in a wide midfield role. He has been at the London Road club since the age of 12, having previously been associated with Norwich.

Peterborough U (From trainee on 5/8/1998) FL 14+6 FAC 0+1 Others 3+1

JEMSON Nigel Bradley
Born: Hutton, 10 October 1969
Height: 5'11" Weight: 12.10
Club Honours: FLC '90; AMC '96
International Honours: E: U21-1

Nigel returned to Oxford United last January as a free agent from Ayr United. The much-travelled striker had a successful spell at the club a few years ago but could not find that form on his return. His experience was useful and he made a good outlet, demonstrating his ability to hold the ball up and take pressure off the defence, but he failed to find the net. He had an 11-game run before moving to the bench, making just a couple more starts before being released in the summer.

Preston NE (From trainee on 6/7/1987) FL 28+4/8 FAC 2/1 Others 5+1/5
Nottingham F (£150,000 on 24/3/1988) FL 45+2/13 FLC 9/4 FAC 3+1/3 Others 1
Bolton W (Loaned on 23/12/1988) FL 4+1
Preston NE (Loaned on 15/3/1989) FL 6+3/2 Others 2/1
Sheffield Wed (£800,000 on 17/9/1991) F/PL 26+25/9 FLC 3+4 FAC 3+3/1 Others 2+2/1
Grimsby T (Loaned on 10/9/1993) FL 6/2 Others 1
Notts Co (£300,000 on 8/9/1994) FL 7+7/1 FLC 2+2/1 Others 1
Watford (Loaned on 12/1/1995) FL 3+1
Rotherham U (Loaned on 15/2/1996) FL 16/5 Others 3/4
Oxford U (£60,000 on 23/7/1996) FL 68/27 FLC 12/6 FAC 2
Bury (£100,000 on 5/2/1998) FL 17+12/1 FLC 0+2 FAC 0+1 (Free to Ayr U on 21/7/99)

Ayr U (Free on 21/7/1999) SL 9+3/5 SLC 1
Oxford U (Free on 27/1/2000) FL 13+5

JENKINS Lee David
Born: Pontypool, 28 June 1979
Height: 5'9" Weight: 11.0
Club Honours: Div 3 '00
International Honours: W: U21-5; Yth; Sch
The strong-running midfielder made just seven starts for Swansea in the league during the 1999-2000 season, finding it difficult to attain the consistency required to stake a regular claim for a midfield position. He was frequently included as one of the substitutes, and appeared regularly for Wales U21s, winning further caps against Belarus, Switzerland, Northern Ireland and Scotland. Also capable of playing at wing back, Lee won a Third Division championship winners' medal.
Swansea C (From trainee on 20/12/1996) FL 48+23/2 FLC 0+1 FAC 1+1 Others 6

JENKINS Stephen (Steve) Matthew
Born: Bristol, 2 January 1980
Height: 6'1" Weight: 13.0
Steve is a calm and composed left back who joined Brentford from Southampton in the summer of 1999 after having spent time on loan at Griffin Park during the 1998-99 season. He began 1999-2000 as a member of the first-team squad, appearing as an occasional substitute and making three starts, but dropped back into the reserve team in the second half of the campaign. He was released by the club at the end of the season.
Southampton (From trainee on 16/1/1998)
Brentford (Loaned on 25/3/1999) FL 0+1
Brentford (Free on 13/7/1999) FL 2+3 FAC 1

JENKINS Stephen (Steve) Robert
Born: Merthyr Tydfil, 16 July 1972
Height: 5'11" Weight: 12.3
Club Honours: AMC '94
International Honours: W: 12; U21-2; Yth
Huddersfield's influential Welsh international enjoyed a productive start to the 1999-2000 season, extending his contract until 2003 and earning honours against Italy and Denmark. He was missing from the Town side until October due to an ankle injury, and he then suffered damaged ribs which ruled him out after only five games. Fit again, the hard-working defender soon commanded a regular berth either at full back or in central defence, with the Terriers benefiting from his strong tackling and purposeful crossing. The competent Welshman clocked up his 150th league appearance against Norwich City at Carrow Road in February. Steve was released during the summer.
Swansea C (From trainee on 1/7/1990) FL 155+10/1 FLC 12+1 FAC 10+1 Others 26
Huddersfield T (£275,000 on 3/11/1995) FL 161+1/3 FLC 15 FAC 12

JENSEN Brian
Born: Copenhagen, Denmark, 8 June 1975
Height: 6'1" Weight: 12.4
This Danish goalkeeper was manager Brian Little's last signing before he was dismissed by West Bromwich Albion last March. In fact, he wasn't due to leave the Dutch club AZ67 Alkmaar until his contract expired at the end of the season but, with Albion in need of a 'keeper, agreement was reached for Brian to come to the Hawthorns three months prematurely, although he had been on trial with the club in January. And how Albion needed him! Secured to replace Alan Miller (sold to Blackburn Rovers), he made a winning start to his English career, helping Albion beat Tranmere Rovers 2-0, and thereafter was very impressive between the posts. An excellent shot stopper, he kicks high and long with his left foot and handles the ball well in tight situations. He is nicknamed "the Beast", and his current manager Gary Megson says: "He'll get better and better."
West Bromwich A (£100,000 from AZ Alkmaar, Holland on 3/3/2000) FL 12

JENSEN Claus William
Born: Nykobing, Denmark, 29 April 1977
Height: 5'11" Weight: 12.6
International Honours: Denmark: 1; U21
While Eidur Gudjohnsen stole the majority of the headlines for Bolton last season, it was Claus who time and again proved himself to be the true class act in the team. The skilful Danish midfielder would appear to have a talent which should eventually take him to the very top of the game and, along with Gudjohnsen, Claus is reportedly attracting the attentions of some top clubs. There can surely not have been a better player when in possession of the ball in last season's First Division. Whether he is running at players or passing the ball around the entire area of the pitch, Claus has class and quality in abundance. He is a master of the dead-ball situation, as was proven when he scored with a beauty of a free kick from 25 yards in the crucial win over fellow play-off hopefuls Wolves at the Reebok in May, and his range of passing is quite outstanding. Perhaps the only flaws to Claus's game are his reluctance to tackle hard against the more physical teams and his surprisingly modest goalscoring record relative to his talent. His return of six goals last season should have been bettered, although this will improve with time, especially when it is considered that Claus is still only 23 years of age, and there is little doubt that the Bolton faithful will overlook his apparent reluctance to "get stuck in" when this is compared to the overall quality of his game. He made his full international debut for Denmark last March when coming on from the subs' bench in the friendly fixture with Portugal.
Bolton W (£1,600,000 from Lyngby, Denmark, via Naestved, on 14/7/1998) FL 85+1/8 FLC 12/2 FAC 6 Others 5

JEPSON Ronald (Ronnie) Francis
Born: Stoke, 12 May 1963
Height: 6'1" Weight: 13.7
Club Honours: Div 2 '97
A near-permanent presence on the Burnley bench during 1999-2000, the veteran forward was always a popular sub with the Clarets' supporters. Usually tucking in behind the main strikers but always willing to go in search of a goal, he often acted as a talisman to the rest of the side when coming on late in the game, and was always prominent at goal celebrations. Ronnie contributed last-minute goals, sadly not winning ones, in both games against his and manager Stan Ternent's former club Bury.
Port Vale (Free from Nantwich T on 23/3/1989) FL 12+10 FLC 1+1 FAC 1+1
Peterborough U (Loaned on 25/1/1990) FL 18/5
Preston NE (£80,000 on 12/2/1991) FL 36+2/8 FLC 2 Others 3/4
Exeter C (£60,000 on 29/7/1992) FL 51+3/21 FLC 6/2 FAC 3/1 Others 4/1
Huddersfield T (£80,000 on 7/12/1993) FL 95+12/36 FLC 6+1/2 FAC 4/3 Others 6/1
Bury (£40,000 on 27/7/1996) FL 31+16/9 FLC 7/1 FAC 0+3 Others 1+1/2
Oldham Ath (£30,000 on 16/1/1998) FL 9/4
Burnley (Free on 29/7/1998) FL 4+42/3 FLC 2+2 FAC 0+3

JEVONS Philip (Phil)
Born: Liverpool, 1 August 1979
Height: 5'11" Weight: 11.10
Club Honours: FAYC '98
After watching youth-team colleagues like Francis Jeffers and Danny Cadamarteri get their first-team debuts and enjoy prolonged runs in the Everton side, Phil finally made his full Premiership bow against Bradford City last April. He celebrated by creating the opening goal with a deft and clever touch to Mark Pembridge, won a penalty kick for goal number two and was involved in creating a third for Nick Barmby. A strong-running striker, Phil has an exemplary attitude to the game and is prepared to chase lost causes for the good of the team. He also started the final home match of the season against Middlesbrough but was caught up in a general malaise which afflicted the entire Everton team that day and was substituted at half time. He will be hoping for more senior experience next season.
Everton (From trainee on 10/11/1997) PL 2+2 FLC 1

JOACHIM Julian Kevin
Born: Boston, 20 September 1974
Height: 5'6" Weight: 12.2
International Honours: E: U21-9; Yth; (UEFA-U18 '93)
Julian began the 1999-2000 campaign in great form, scoring the winner at Newcastle on the opening day of the season and also netting the following Wednesday in a 3-0 win over Everton. He was an automatic choice for Villa for the majority of the campaign but lost his place following an abortive attempt to play for St Vincent in the World Cup qualifying competition: he had flown out to the Caribbean only to be informed at the last minute that appearances he made for England youths and U21s some years ago ruled him out of contention. He failed to make the starting line-up for the FA Cup final and was eventually brought on for the final 15 minutes to try to retrieve a result for Villa after they had gone one down to Roberto Di Matteo's goal. Julian's main strengths are his lightning pace and a willingness to run at defenders, although his goalscoring touch seemed to desert him after the early games and he will need to work to regain this in the coming season.

Leicester C (From trainee on 15/9/1992) F/PL 77+22/25 FLC 7+2/3 FAC 4+1/1 Others 4+2/2
Aston Villa (£1,500,000 on 24/2/1996) PL 79+42/33 FLC 9+1/3 FAC 8+3/1 Others 5+1/1

JOBLING Kevin Andrew
Born: Sunderland, 1 January 1968
Height: 5'9" Weight: 12.0
Club Honours: AMC '98

Kevin played for Shrewsbury regularly during the first part of the 1999-2000 season. A skilful left-sided midfielder, he made 25 starts in the league and scored two goals. The former Shrews captain was not favoured by new manager Kevin Ratcliffe, and was released at the end of the season.

Leicester C (From apprentice on 9/1/1986) FL 4+5 FAC 0+1 Others 3/2
Grimsby T (Signed on 19/2/1988) FL 251+34/10 FLC 13+4/1 FAC 10+3/2 Others 7+7
Scunthorpe U (Loaned on 10/1/1994) Others 1
Shrewsbury T (Free on 29/7/1998) FL 66+3/3 FLC 4/1 FAC 2+1 Others 2

JOBSON Richard Ian
Born: Holderness, 9 May 1963
Height: 6'1" Weight: 13.5
Club Honours: Div 2 '91
International Honours: E: B-2

After a full season out of the game as a result of an ankle injury sustained at Easter, 1998, Richard was given a run-out in Manchester City's first reserve match of 1999-2000 which proved very successful. Manager Joe Royle then brought him on as a substitute in the third league game of the season, against Sheffield United at Maine Road, and he went on to play in every league and cup game during the remainder of the campaign. He had a marvellously consistent season as City's principal central defender, his age proving no handicap. His impressive physical presence and ability to build play up from the back using shorter passes were major factors in the club's successful promotion bid. Richard also moved forward into the opposition box regularly for corners, which resulted in two important goals, the second giving City an unexpected win at Birmingham after they had been under pressure for long periods. After the arrival at Maine Road of Spencer Prior in March, the pair formed a formidable central defensive barrier, the two players complementing each other effectively. Richard was rewarded for his efforts with a one-year extension to his contract.

Watford (£22,000 from Burton A on 5/11/1982) FL 26+2/4 FLC 2 FAC 0+1 Others 5+1
Hull C (£40,000 on 7/2/1985) FL 219+2/17 FLC 12 FAC 13/1 Others 9
Oldham Ath (£460,000 on 30/8/1990) P/FL 188+1/10 FLC 19/1 FAC 13 Others 4
Leeds U (£1,000,000 on 26/10/1995) PL 22/1 FLC 3 FAC 1
Southend U (Loaned on 23/1/1998) FL 8/1
Manchester C (Free on 12/3/1998) FL 49+1/4 FLC 3 FAC 2

JOHANSEN Michael Bro
Born: Glostrup, Denmark, 22 July 1972
Height: 5'6" Weight: 10.5
Club Honours: Div 1 '97

A firm crowd favourite at Bolton's Reebok Stadium, Michael will be sorely missed this coming season as he signed a pre-contract agreement early in 2000 to return to his native Denmark to play for FC Copenhagen. His wing wizardry will be hard to replace, and after announcing his decision early in the year he produced some of his most effective performances in his four seasons as a Bolton player. A speedy winger who also likes to run at opponents, Michael had an infectious enthusiasm for the English game and always played with a smile on his face. His workrate is phenomenal for such a diminutive player and it will prove to be very difficult for Bolton to find a replacement. Wanderers' loss is most definitely FC Copenhagen's gain.

Bolton W (£1,250,000 from FC Copenhagen, Denmark, via KB Copenhagen and B1903, on 14/8/1996) F/PL 112+25/16 FLC 16+4/4 FAC 7+1 Others 5/1

JOHN Stern
Born: Trinidad, 30 October 1976
Height: 6'1" Weight: 12.12
International Honours: Trinidad & Tobago

This exciting striker joined Nottingham Forest last November after a prolific two years with US team Columbus Crew during which he netted 52 goals in 65 games. He scored within six minutes of his debut for the Reds against Portsmouth and appeared to be settling in nicely when he suffered a cruciate knee ligament injury in January. Fortunately, he made a quicker-than-expected recovery and had returned to first-team action by the end of the season. Stern is also a regular in the Trinidad & Tobago international team and netted a hat-trick in their 4-3 victory over Colombia in Miami last September.

Nottingham F (£1,500,000 + from Columbus Crew, USA on 22/11/1999) FL 13+4/3 FAC 3

JOHNROSE Leonard (Lenny)
Born: Preston, 29 November 1969
Height: 5'10" Weight: 12.6
Club Honours: Div 2 '97

Not an automatic choice in Burnley's midfield until the second half of the 1999-2000 season, Lenny finally secured his place in the side (and the fans' affections) with a series of determined performances, filling a gap in the team. Not particularly blessed with the silky skills, he more than made up for any failings with his tigerish, never-say-die approach and was often instrumental in breaking up opposition attacks and setting up chances for the Clarets.

Blackburn Rov (From trainee on 16/6/1988) FL 20+22/11 FLC 2+1/1 FAC 0+3 Others 2
Preston NE (Loaned on 21/1/1992) FL 1+2/1
Hartlepool U (£50,000 on 28/2/1992) FL 59+7/11 FLC 5+1/4 FAC 5/1 Others 5
Bury (Signed on 7/12/1993) FL 181+7/19 FLC 16+2/2 FAC 9/1 Others 9/1
Burnley (£225,000 on 12/2/1999) FL 37+10/3 FLC 2 FAC 0+1 Others 1

JOHNSEN Jean **Ronny**
Born: Norway, 10 June 1969
Height: 6'2" Weight: 13.2
Club Honours: PL '97, '99; CS '97; FAC '99; EC '99
International Honours: Norway: 41

A classy midfielder or central defender, Ronny continued to suffer from knee injury problems when the 1999-2000 season began and was unable to take his place in the Manchester United team. After flying back to Norway to seek advice from the international team doctor, he decided his only option was to go under the surgeon's knife. He was sidelined for much of the campaign and there were certainly occasions when his authoritative presence alongside Jaap Stam was missed, but he was able to return to first-team action at Easter, coming on as a substitute at the Dell as United clinched the title against Southampton. He started the game against Chelsea at Old Trafford two days later but then sustained a groin strain against Watford. Although he was not part of the Norwegian squad for Euro 2000, Ronny is expected to be fully fit for the coming season.

Manchester U (£1,200,000 from Besiktas, Turkey, via Lyn and Lillestrom, on 26/7/1996) PL 65+13/5 FLC 2 FAC 8+2/1 Others 22+2/1

JOHNSON Andrew (Andy)
Born: Bedford, 10 February 1981
Height: 5'9" Weight: 9.7
International Honours: E: Yth

A slim, pacy striker, Andy had a fine 1999-2000 season with Birmingham City and firmly established himself as a regular in the first-team squad. He began as the first-choice partner for Paul Furlong in attack, retaining his place until last October, when he collided with the Manchester City 'keeper and suffered damage to a medial knee ligament that required surgery. He was out of action for 14 weeks and, after recovering full fitness, had to wait for loan signing Isiah Rankin to depart before winning a regular place in the starting line-up.

Birmingham C (From juniors on 11/3/1998) FL 15+11/1 FLC 3+3/1 Others 1+1

JOHNSON Andrew (Andy) James
Born: Bristol, 2 May 1974
Height: 6'0" Weight: 13.0
Club Honours: Div 1 '98
International Honours: E: Yth. W: 7

Andy missed the opening months of last season after being sidelined by injury and it was not until November that he reappeared in the Nottingham Forest first team. He featured regularly afterwards, his performances earning him further caps for Wales as a substitute against Finland and Brazil. He is a tough-tackling midfield player who always gives 100 per cent effort and is an excellent passer.

Norwich C (From trainee on 4/3/1992) F/PL 56+10/13 FLC 6+1/2 FAC 2
Nottingham F (£2,200,000 on 4/7/1997) P/FL 73+14/6 FLC 4+1/1 FAC 2

JOHNSON Damien Michael
Born: Lisburn, 18 November 1978
Height: 5'9" Weight: 11.2
International Honours: NI: 5; U21-11; Yth

Apart from a brief run in the side after Christmas, Damien made only occasional appearances in the Blackburn first team during 1999-2000. Generally employed in a role wide on the right of midfield, he is a player of great industry and a fearless tackler but he has yet to show that he can pose sufficient threat in the last third of the field to merit a regular place in the side. He tends to drift inside from the wing and sometimes wastes possession, which is a pity as other aspects of his game make him an outstanding prospect. For a player of his size he is good in the air and he scored a fine headed goal at Huddersfield, while he had a great day when Rovers met Liverpool in the FA Cup at Anfield, where he was instrumental in breaking up many attacks. He made three international appearances for Northern Ireland during the season.

Blackburn Rov (From trainee on 2/2/1996) P/FL 25+12/2 FLC 6+1 FAC 1+3 Others 0+1
Nottingham F (Loaned on 29/1/1998) FL 5+1

JOHNSON David Anthony
Born: Kingston, Jamaica, 15 August 1976
Height: 5'6" Weight: 12.3
Club Honours: FAYC '95; Div 2 '97
International Honours: E: B-1; Sch. Jamaica: 4

In 1999-2000 David had his best season, in terms of goals, since he joined Ipswich, scoring 23 times, and his prowess in front of goal kept his name in the minds of Premiership managers and their international counterparts. Rumours linking him with various clubs reared their ugly heads spasmodically throughout the season and he made the national news over his international indecision. Having played, and scored, for Jamaica against the USA at the beginning of September, he accepted an invitation to join the Welsh squad. Only injury prevented him from pulling on the red shirt but by the time the next international squads were announced he had pledged his future to Scotland, only to discover that he was ineligible after all. David's pace is still his greatest asset and he is not afraid to have a shot at goal from virtually anywhere, usually with his left foot. He started the season with a bang, scoring in six of the first seven games and notching doubles against Swindon and Barnsley. The international controversy seemed to put a brake on his goals for a while but he recovered his touch gradually and his seven goals in the last nine games helped secure third place for the second successive season. The goal he scored against Bolton in mid-August was voted "Goal of the Season" by the fans, deservedly so as it was a bit special. From a Bolton corner Jamie Clapham cleared the ball upfield to David, who was just inside the visitors' half of the field. As the ball bounced he headed it over the first defender, then he skipped around a second and planted a low left-foot shot into the corner of the net.

Manchester U (From trainee on 1/7/1994)
Bury (Free on 5/7/1995) FL 72+25/18 FLC 8+3/4 FAC 1+1 Others 3+2/1
Ipswich T (£800,000 on 14/11/1997) FL 115+2/55 FLC 8/2 FAC 7/2 Others 7

JOHNSON Gavin
Born: Stowmarket, 10 October 1970
Height: 5'11" Weight: 12.0
Club Honours: Div 2 '92; Div 3 '97

Gavin joined Colchester as a free agent after a short trial spell last autumn, having left Dunfermline the previous summer. His debut came as a substitute at Oldham in November, coinciding with United's first win in 12 attempts as they climbed off the bottom of the league, and Gavin's contribution to the rest of the season helped ensure that the upward movement continued. Despite a persistent achilles injury, he gave a consistently high level of performance, usually in midfield but also in defence when required, and was rewarded with a divisional *Match* "Man of the Month" award. Probably the best testament to Gavin's contribution is to say that very few ex-Ipswich players have been so warmly welcomed by the Layer Road faithful!

Ipswich T (From trainee on 1/3/1989) P/FL 114+18/11 FLC 10+1/2 FAC 12/2 Others 3+1/1
Luton T (Free on 4/7/1995) FL 4+1
Wigan Ath (£15,000 on 15/12/1995) FL 82+2/8 FLC 4 FAC 3 Others 1
Dunfermline Ath (Free on 1/7/1998) SL 18 SC 0+1
Colchester U (Free on 12/11/1999) FL 24+3

JOHNSON Leon Dean
Born: Shoreditch, 10 May 1981
Height: 6'0" Weight: 12.4

A first-year professional with Southend, Leon took his chance to impress last season after almost slipping the net at Roots Hall. A tall midfielder with a touch of elegance in his passing, he regularly demonstrated his skills in the reserves and was given his first taste of senior action when manager Alan Little handed him a starting place in the Blues' Auto Windscreens Shield game with Cheltenham in December. He will he hoping to earn a regular place in the squad during the coming season.

Southend U (From trainee on 17/11/1999) Others 1

JOHNSON Marvin Anthony
Born: Wembley, 29 October 1968
Height: 6'0" Weight: 13.6

A professional at Luton, his only club, since 1986, Marvin had another splendidly consistent season in 1999-2000, missing only two league games. Fittingly appointed team captain the previous season, the veteran central defender brings total commitment and wholehearted endeavour to his role in the middle of the Hatters' back line. Marvin's aerial ability, good reflexes and strength make it hard for any forward to get the better of him. An inspirational figure, his performances were up to his usual impressive standard, but he was out of contract in the summer and at the time of writing it seemed likely that he would be beginning 2000-01 elsewhere.

Luton T (From apprentice on 12/11/1986) FL 332+14/6 FLC 26+2/2 FAC 17+1/1 Others 13

JOHNSON Michael Owen
Born: Nottingham, 4 July 1973
Height: 5'11" Weight: 11.12
Club Honours: AIC '95
International Honours: Jamaica: 7

Michael is a stylish Birmingham City defender who began 1999-2000 as a regular in the centre of the Blues' defence. He is a good marker, more than capable in the air and impressive in the timing of his tackles. He lost his place in the team in the new year after being absent on international duty but was later switched to left back, where he performed admirably. Having made his full international debut for Jamaica against Sweden in May 1999, he appeared regularly again from January, taking part in the Guangzhou Tournament in China, the CONCACAF Gold Cup finals in the USA and the end-of-season Hassan Cup games in Morocco.

Notts Co (From trainee on 9/7/1991) FL 102+5 FLC 9 FAC 4 Others 15+1
Birmingham C (£225,000 on 1/9/1995) FL 153+32/10 FLC 14+6/2 FAC 5+3 Others 8

JOHNSON Richard Mark
Born: Newcastle, Australia, 27 April 1974
Height: 5'11" Weight: 12.0
Club Honours: Div 2 '98
International Honours: Australia: 1

The Australian midfield player suffered a frustrating season with Watford in 1999-2000 because of a string of injuries, which was a pity, as Richard possesses the confidence and ability to impose himself on matches and dictate play, as well as a fearsome shot from distance. His catalogue of woe began in the very first game, when he conceded an own goal at home to Wimbledon after a misunderstanding with goalkeeper Chris Day. He was carried off at Anfield with a medial ligament injury which sidelined him until October, and missed seven weeks with a hamstring strain, followed by a facial injury sustained during his reserve-team comeback. Worst of all, he injured his cruciate ligaments against Manchester United just before the end of the season and now faces the prospect of a long lay-off. On a happier note, Richard scored fine goals against Manchester United and Liverpool and received his first international honours for Australia, appearing in two friendlies against Brazil's Olympic team last November before going on to win his first full cap against the Czech Republic in March. Aged only 26, he has now made more than 250 senior appearances for Watford, his only club.

Watford (From trainee on 11/5/1992) P/FL 204+23/20 FLC 13+1/1 FAC 13+1/1 Others 5+1

JOHNSON Roger
Born: Ashford, 28 April 1983
Height: 6'3" Weight: 11.0

This talented young central defender became the youngest-ever player to appear for Wycombe in the Football League when he came on as a substitute for the second half in the final game of the 1999-2000 season at Cambridge when aged 17 years and eight days. Roger earned his chance with some impressive performances in the reserve and youth teams, and he helped the club reach the fourth round of the FA Youth Cup for the first time. He is still on a YTS contract but will be looking to gain more senior experience in 2000-01.

Wycombe W (Trainee) FL 0+1

JOHNSON Ross Yorke
Born: Brighton, 2 January 1976
Height: 6'0" Weight: 12.12

Famed for an excellent long throw which is

occasionally utilised in the opposition penalty box, the Brighton-born central defender is a product of his home-town club's youth policy. Ross was placed on the transfer list in the 1999 close season despite having a year left on his contract. Following the departure of Chris Wilder in October, he filled in at right back until losing his place to Paul Watson. Ross eventually left Albion for Colchester United in February, following a month's loan. A strong and classy player, he was virtually an ever-present through the second half of the campaign, ably picking up the mantle of senior defender following David Greene's injury, and his calm style of play helped settle United's predominantly young back division.

Brighton & Hove A (From trainee on 22/7/1994) FL 113+19/2 FLC 3+3 FAC 4 Others 4+1
Colchester U (Free on 12/1/2000) FL 17+1

JOHNSON Seth Art Maurice
Born: Birmingham, 12 March 1979
Height: 5'10" Weight: 11.0
International Honours: E: U21-11; Yth

The combative left-sided midfielder joined Derby at the end of the 1998-99 season for £3 million from Crewe. After a promising pre-season, his debut on the opening day of the new campaign at Elland Road was a great success, leading to favourable comparisons with David Batty. While he was also asked to play at left wing back, his main contribution to Derby was as a ball-winning midfielder alongside Darryl Powell. His aggressive style did not always go down well with referees and he was yellow-carded more than any other player in the Premiership, though, naturally, it made him a great favourite of the home fans. The inevitable suspension by the FA for his disciplinary record soon followed, however. With the current dearth of left-sided English talent, he will be hoping to make the jump to the full England squad sooner rather than later. Seth appeared regularly for England U21s and won a further five caps during the season.

Crewe Alex (From trainee on 12/7/1996) FL 89+4/6 FLC 5 FAC 2/1 Others 0+3
Derby Co (£3,000,000 on 21/5/1999) PL 36/1 FLC 1+1 FAC 0+1

JOHNSON Thomas (Tommy)
Born: Newcastle, 15 January 1971
Height: 5'11" Weight: 12.8
Club Honours: FLC '96
International Honours: E: U21-7

Signed on a month's loan from Glasgow Celtic last September, this busy striker found his opportunities sorely limited during his time at Everton. He made just three appearances for the club, all as a substitute, but did prove his full recovery from an appalling knee injury during that spell, which stood him in excellent stead when he returned to Scotland.

Notts Co (From trainee on 19/1/1989) FL 100+18/47 FLC 7+2/5 FAC 3+2/1 Others 14+3/4
Derby Co (£1,300,000 on 12/3/1992) FL 91+7/30 FLC 9+1/2 FAC 5/1 Others 16/8
Aston Villa (Signed on 6/1/1995) PL 38+19/13 FLC 5/2 FAC 5+2/1 Others 1+1/1
Glasgow Celtic (£2,400,000 on 27/3/1997) SL 7+2/4 SC 1+2/1 Others 2+2/2
Everton (Loaned on 24/9/1999) PL 0+3

JOHNSTON Allan
Born: Glasgow, 14 December 1973
Height: 5'9" Weight: 10.10
Club Honours: Div 1 '99
International Honours: S: 9; B-2; U21-3

It appears that in the summer of 1999 Allan was invited to sign a new contract binding him to Sunderland for the foreseeable future, declined to do so and was subsequently excluded from manager Peter Reid's plans. He is expected to move to Rangers this summer under the Bosman ruling. He spent two months on loan at Birmingham City last autumn, where he began to show impressive form in his final games after reaching full match fitness. At his best he is a tricky wide man with fine ball control, excellent crossing ability and searing pace who on his day is a difficult opponent for any defender. He was offered a third month at St Andrews but chose to return to the Stadium of Light, subsequently joining Bolton on loan at the end of January. Allan made his full debut for the Wanderers at Port Vale not long afterwards and kept his place for the rest of the season, having had his loan period extended on two occasions. He produced some quality performances on the left wing and while some cynics suggested that he was just biding his time until the summer there was no doubting his natural ability when on the ball. His first goal for Bolton came in the second game he started, a 2-1 defeat at Birmingham, and he showed on many occasions that he is as comfortable shooting with his right foot as he is with his left. Although Allan will definitely not be with Bolton in 2000-01, his contribution last season was greatly appreciated. Despite his problems at club level he won further caps for Scotland against Estonia, France and the Republic of Ireland during the season.

Heart of Midlothian (Free from Tynecastle BC on 23/6/1990) SL 46+38/12 SLC 3+2/2 SC 4+1 (Signed for Rennes, France during 1996 close season)
Sunderland (£550,000 on 27/3/1997) FL 82+4/19 FLC 8+1/1 FAC 3 Others 3
Birmingham C (Loaned on 15/10/1999) FL 7+2 FLC 1
Bolton W (Free on 21/1/2000) FL 17+2/3 FAC 2 Others 2/1

JONES Barry
Born: Prescot, 30 June 1970
Height: 5'11" Weight: 11.12
Club Honours: WC '95

Barry was once again a regular in York City's rearguard in 1999-2000, chiefly in the heart of the defence. He was placed on the transfer list early in the season, following Mark Sertori's arrival. However, he had an outstanding second half of the campaign, with his tackling and heading to the fore. New boss Terry Dolan rewarded him with a new contract, while Barry was voted "Clubman of the Year" for the second season in a row.

Liverpool (Free from Prescot Cables on 19/1/1989) Others 0+1
Wrexham (Free on 10/7/1992) FL 184+11/5 FLC 14+1/1 FAC 11+2 Others 21+1
York C (£40,000 on 17/12/1997) FL 102+3/5 FLC 4 FAC 4 Others 1

JONES Eifion Pritchard
Born: Caernarfon, 28 September 1980
Height: 6'3" Weight: 13.0
International Honours: W: Yth

Eifion is a talented defender who began the 1999-2000 campaign as a young professional on Liverpool's books. He signed for Blackpool on transfer deadline day and went on to make his Football League debut for the Seasiders in the final match of the season against Chesterfield. He will be looking to develop his first-team experience during the coming season.

Liverpool (From trainee on 6/10/1997)
Blackpool (Signed on 23/3/2000) FL 0+3

JONES Gary
Born: Huddersfield, 6 April 1969
Height: 6'1" Weight: 12.9
Club Honours: Div 3 '98

As they were signed for a combined fee of around £140,000 in March 1999, great things were expected of Gary and his Hartlepool strike partner Chris Freestone last season. Throughout the campaign Gary was a hard worker, but his efforts brought little reward in front of goal and he struggled to find any consistency as a marksman. He joined Halifax on loan in March, and scored on his debut at Lincoln. A previous "Golden Boot" winner at Notts County, his presence up front created numerous chances for his new team-mates. Gary returned to Hartlepool at the end of the season and went on to put up a good showing in the play-off games.

Doncaster Rov (Free from Rossington Main Colliery on 26/1/1989) FL 10+10/2 FLC 1 (Free to Grantham on 1/11/1989)
Southend U (£25,000 from Boston U, via Kettering T, on 3/6/1993) FL 47+23/16 FLC 3/1 FAC 2 Others 6+1/2
Lincoln C (Loaned on 17/9/1993) FL 0+4/2 Others 0+1
Notts Co (£140,000 on 1/3/1996) FL 103+14/38 FLC 5+1/1 FAC 9+1/7 Others 2+1
Scunthorpe U (Loaned on 21/2/1997) FL 9+2/5
Hartlepool U (Signed on 10/3/1999) FL 42+3/7 FLC 2 FAC 2/1 Others 2+2
Halifax T (Loaned on 23/3/2000) FL 8/1

JONES Gary Roy
Born: Birkenhead, 3 June 1977
Height: 5'10" Weight: 12.0

Gary was mainly confined to the Rochdale subs' bench until November, then grabbed the chance to re-establish his place in midfield when the regulars were rested. He started all bar two of the matches during the remainder of the 1999-2000 season. Gary also displayed a previously little-used element of his game, his right-footed shooting power. He netted twice at Hull, and took on the responsibility of being the side's penalty taker. Gary was offered new terms in May.

Swansea C (Signed from Caernarfon T on 11/7/1997) FL 3+5 FLC 0+1
Rochdale (Free on 15/1/1998) FL 59+17/9 FLC 1 FAC 3+3 Others 5+2/1

JONES Gary Steven
Born: Chester, 10 May 1975
Height: 6'3" Weight: 14.0

Gary missed most of the early part of Tranmere's 1999-2000 season through injury and it was not until mid-October that he returned to full fitness. He then became a permanent fixture in the team until the last few games of the season, winning a runners-up medal after appearing in the Worthington Cup final against Leicester. A versatile player, he can operate as a central defender or a striker or even in midfield but wherever he is employed he is always awkward for the opposition to handle. Quiet and dependable, he is a real grafter and an excellent team player. At the time of writing Gary had failed to agree a new contract with Rovers and he was expected to begin the new season elsewhere. Stop Press: It was reported at the beginning of July that he had signed for Nottingham Forest.

Tranmere Rov (From trainee on 5/7/1993) FL 117+61/28 FLC 17+2/2 FAC 9+2/3 Others 1+1

JONES Graeme Anthony
Born: Gateshead, 13 March 1970
Height: 6'0" Weight: 12.12
Club Honours: Div 3 '97; AMC '99

Graeme started just one league match for Wigan in 1999-2000 before, frustrated by his lack of first-team chances, he moved to St Johnstone in a £100,000 transfer in November. The bustling centre forward's only Wigan goal of the campaign came in the draw at Blackpool. A willing trier despite being troubled by niggling injuries, the club's former record scorer continued to pose a threat, particularly in the air.

Doncaster Rov (£10,000 from Bridlington T on 2/8/1993) FL 80+12/26 FLC 4+1/1 FAC 2+1/1 Others 5/1
Wigan Ath (£150,000 on 8/7/1996) FL 76+20/44 FLC 4+3/1 FAC 4/1 Others 6+2/6

JONES Jonathan (Jon) Berwyn
Born: Wrexham, 27 October 1978
Height: 5'10" Weight: 11.5

It was a similar story to 1998-99 for this promising youngster last season. With first-team opportunities limited at Chester, he was allowed to go out on loan and gain further experience in the League of Wales. A product of the Deva youth policy, Jon has tremendous pace and can play through the middle or on the flanks. He was released by the club during the summer but could still have a very bright future.

Chester C (From trainee on 27/3/1997) FL 11+27/2 FLC 1+3/1 FAC 0+3 Others 1+2

JONES Keith Aubrey
Born: Dulwich, 14 October 1965
Height: 5'8" Weight: 11.2
Club Honours: Div 1 '00
International Honours: E: Yth; Sch

A valuable squad member, Keith is a competitive midfield player who always gives 100 per cent, and is especially effective when asked to do a man-marking job. He was a regular in the Charlton side last season until an achilles tendon injury cost him his place at the end of 1999 and forced him to miss the remainder of the campaign, although he had made sufficient appearances to earn a First Division championship medal. Keith likes to get forward whenever possible, and scored the goal that earned Charlton a point at Barnsley at the start of their run of 14 league games without defeat. Stop Press: He was reported to have moved to Reading at the beginning of July.

Chelsea (From apprentice on 16/8/1983) FL 43+9/7 FLC 9+2/3 FAC 1 Others 4+1
Brentford (£40,000 on 3/9/1987) FL 167+2/13 FLC 15/2 FAC 13/4 Others 16/1
Southend U (£175,000 on 21/10/1991) FL 88+2/11 FLC 4 FAC 5 Others 9/1
Charlton Ath (£150,000 on 16/9/1994) P/FL 142+16/6 FLC 6+1 FAC 4+3/1 Others 3

JONES Lee
Born: Pontypridd, 9 August 1970
Height: 6'3" Weight: 14.4
Club Honours: AMC '94

After missing the final nine matches of the previous season the Welshman finally established himself as Bristol Rovers' first-choice goalkeeper in 1999-2000. Tall and commanding with a big kick, Lee had a couple of indifferent performances in October and subsequently lost his number one jersey to loan signing Stuart Taylor, the young Arsenal 'keeper, for five matches, and after sustaining a back injury in February he was replaced by teenage Chelsea 'keeper Rhys Evans for four games. A fit-again Jones worked hard and regained his place, however, producing some match-winning saves, none better than his late stop to deny Stoke's Peter Thorne during injury time in the 3-3 draw on 1 April at the Memorial Stadium.

Swansea C (£7,500 from AFC Porth on 24/3/1994) FL 6 Others 1
Bristol Rov (Signed on 7/3/1998) FL 76 FLC 6 FAC 7 Others 4

JONES Philip Lee
Born: Wrexham, 29 May 1973
Height: 5'9" Weight: 10.8
International Honours: W: 2; B-1; U21-14; Yth

After showing considerable promise in his first two seasons with Tranmere, Lee had a disappointing 1999-2000 campaign with the Prenton Park club. Injuries restricted him to just a handful of appearances in the starting line-up, with a further dozen outings from the subs' bench. At his best he is a pacy midfield player who is full of enthusiasm and imagination and capable of turning a game with one moment's brilliance. His preferred position is just behind the front men, where his imagination and eye for goal are put to good use. Lee was released on a free transfer in the summer of 1999. Stop Press: He was reported to have signed for Barnsley at the beginning of July.

Wrexham (From trainee on 5/7/1991) FL 24+15/10 FLC 2 FAC 1+2/1 Others 4+1/2
Liverpool (£300,000 on 12/3/1992) PL 0+3 FLC 0+1
Crewe Alex (Loaned on 3/9/1993) FL 4+4/1
Wrexham (Loaned on 26/1/1996) FL 20/9
Wrexham (Loaned on 31/1/1997) FL 2+4
Tranmere Rov (£100,000 on 27/3/1997) FL 58+28/16 FLC 7+3/2 FAC 0+1

JONES Mark Andrew
Born: Walsall, 7 September 1979
Height: 5'9" Weight: 11.7
International Honours: E: Yth; Sch

The young Wolves striker looked useful alongside Robbie Keane in a friendly against Liverpool during the build-up to the 1999-2000 season, heading against the bar. yet when Keane left, Mark was omitted from the 16 who were named at QPR, despite Wolves' shortage of strikers. It was believed that, if he did start a game, Wolves would have to pay his previous club, Aston Villa, £90,000. Mark came on as a substitute at Sheffield United for 25 minutes in September, before going on loan to Cheltenham in October. Quick and tenacious, he enjoyed an excellent debut against Southend, his display helping the Robins to end a run of five straight defeats with a 2-1 win. He was unlucky not to score in that game, and although his other two performances didn't live up to the first, he showed enough promise in his brief spell at the club to suggest that a good future could lie ahead for him. Back at Molineux, Mark slumped to somewhere around fifth equal in the strikers' hierarchy as injuries interrupted his progress and he needed cartilage repairs early in 2000. He was released at the end of the season.

Wolverhampton W (From trainee on 25/9/1996) FL 0+3 FLC 0+2
Cheltenham T (Loaned on 4/10/1999) FL 3

JONES Matthew Graham
Born: Llanelli, 1 September 1980
Height: 5'11" Weight: 11.5
Club Honours: FAYC '97
International Honours: W: 4; B-1; U21-7; Yth

Still only 19, Matthew made more progress with Leeds United last season. He had to be content with a substitutes' role at first, before making his first start against Aston Villa in the FA Cup in January. He looks very comfortable and capable in the centre of midfield, particularly when sitting just in front of the back four. Matthew had the honour of captaining Wales U21s against Switzerland in October and then made his full international debut when coming on from the subs' bench against the same opposition the following day. He went on to win further caps at senior level against Qatar, Brazil and Portugal and looks to have a bright future with the Elland Road club.

Leeds U (From trainee on 3/9/1997) PL 8+11 FLC 0+1 FAC 0+2 Others 3+2

JONES Nathan Jason
Born: Rhondda, 28 May 1973
Height: 5'7" Weight: 10.12

In possibly the most incredible transformation in a Southend United player ever seen, Nathan went from a fringe figure to a regular first choice and star performer during the 1999-2000 season. With the left-wing-back slot up for grabs at the start of the campaign, Nathan took the chance with both hands, producing exciting attacking play along with strong defensive performances. He is now popularly known as "Riverdance" due to his favourite step-over routine when on a run down the wing. Nathan was voted Southend's "Player of the Year". Stop Press: He was reported to have signed for Brighton during the close season after failing to agree a new contract.

Luton T (£10,000 from Merthyr Tydfil on 30/6/1995. Freed on 20/12/1995)
Southend U (Free from Nomincia, Spain on 5/8/1997) FL 82+17/2 FLC 6+2 FAC 3+1/1 Others 0+3
Scarborough (Loaned on 25/3/1999) FL 8+1

JONES Paul Neil
Born: Liverpool, 3 June 1978
Height: 6'1" Weight: 13.2

This former Tranmere trainee was working as a kitchen fitter and playing for Unibond League club Leigh RMI when he signed for Oldham last November. By February he had established himself as a regular in the first team, producing a run of excellent displays and becoming the find of the season at Boundary Park. He netted his first-ever senior goal in the 2-1 win over promotion-chasing Wigan in April and shortly afterwards signed a two-year contract with the Latics. Paul is a powerful stopper centre half who seems to have a very promising future.

Tranmere Rov (From trainee on 27/12/1995. Free to Barrow during 1997 close season)
Oldham Ath (Free from Leigh RMI on 15/11/1999) FL 16/1 Others 0+1

JONES Paul Steven
Born: Chirk, 18 April 1967
Height: 6'3" Weight: 14.8
International Honours: W: 14

The Welsh "Player of the Year" for 1999, Paul continued to give outstanding service between the sticks for Southampton last season. Without doubt one of the best shot stoppers in the Premiership, he made a save to remember at Old Trafford in September when an instinctive block drew comparisons with Gordon Banks's world-famous stop from Pele. The first part of the double save came from Teddy Sheringham's powerful header: Paul flung himself to his right to turn it away. The second was absolutely incredible: Sheringham, at almost point-blank range, smashed the loose ball and Paul hurled himself across goal to claw it out by his right-hand post. He was ever-present in the side until a serious back problem curtailed his season in April. It was an injury which required surgery and was initially thought to threaten his career. A regular for Wales in the early part of the season, he won further caps against Belarus, Switzerland and Qatar.

Wolverhampton W (£40,000 from Kidderminster Hrs on 23/7/1991) FL 33 FLC 2 FAC 5 Others 4
Stockport Co (£60,000 on 25/7/1996) FL 46 FLC 11 FAC 4 Others 4
Southampton (£900,000 on 28/7/1997) PL 100 FLC 10 FAC 5

JONES Scott
Born: Sheffield, 1 May 1975
Height: 5'10" Weight: 12.8

A versatile left-sided defender, Scott was an ever-present in the Barnsley line-up from the beginning of the 1999-2000 campaign until suffering a back injury last November that required surgery and kept him out of action for five months. He eventually recovered fitness in time to play in a few games towards the end of the season and will be hoping to have an injury-free time in 2000-01. He is strong in the tackle, good in the air for a relatively small man and a constant danger when joining the attack for set pieces.

Barnsley (From trainee on 1/2/1994) F/PL 76+7/4 FLC 7/1 FAC 4+3/2
Mansfield T (Loaned on 7/8/1997) FL 6 FLC 2

JONES Stephen (Steve) Gary
Born: Cambridge, 17 March 1970
Height: 6'1" Weight: 12.12

Big, strong and quick, this experienced striker was surprisingly transferred to Bristol City last September after starting only one league game for Charlton Athletic in 1999-2000, having been a regular squad member the previous season. Steve is capable of scoring spectacular goals, and always gives of his best, but inconsistent form had cost him his place in the Addicks' attack. Signed to replace the popular Ade Akinbiyi, he had a wretched time at Ashton Gate. Despite all his tireless efforts the goals wouldn't flow, and he was unfairly singled out by a section of City fans as the reason for many of their side's poor displays in the first half of the season. Dropped after managing only two goals in 16 games, Steve suffered a mystery stomach complaint which brought a break from the game over the Christmas period before joining Brentford for a one-month loan period that was later extended for a second month. Although he failed to find the net for the Bees, their chairman-manager, Ron Noades, was sufficiently impressed to table a £50,000 offer, but the deal fell through and Steve returned to Ashton Gate. He joined Southend on loan just before the transfer deadline. He filled the hole left by the injury to Neil Tolson. A tall, physical centre forward, Steve managed two goals during his spell with the Blues. Having started his career at Billericay, he still lives in the Southend area.

West Ham U (£22,000 from Billericay T on 16/11/1992) PL 8+8/4 FAC 2+2/1 Others 1+1
Bournemouth (£150,000 on 21/10/1994) FL 71+3/26 FLC 4/3 FAC 3/1 Others 3
West Ham U (Signed on 16/5/1996) PL 5+3 FLC 0+1 FAC 2
Charlton Ath (£400,000 on 14/2/1997) P/FL 28+24/8 FLC 3+1 FAC 1 Others 1+2
Bournemouth (Loaned on 24/12/1997) FL 5/4 Others 1/1
Bristol C (£425,000 + on 10/9/1999) FL 12+2/2 FLC 2 FAC 2+1
Brentford (Loaned on 21/1/2000) FL 6+2 Others 2
Southend U (Loaned on 17/3/2000) FL 9/2

JONES Stephen (Steve) Robert
Born: Bristol, 25 December 1970
Height: 5'10" Weight: 12.2
Club Honours: Div 3 '00

After making occasional appearances during the first half of the 1999-2000 season, Steve recaptured his right-full-back slot for the second half of the campaign to show the kind of gutsy, solid performances he has become renowned for since signing for Swansea in November 1995. Carried off against Macclesfield with a facial injury, he was back for the next game against Southend, still showing the commitment which has been a feature of his game. Long-time followers of the Swans make a comparison to the legendary Wyndham Evans, who was a fearsome competitor in the right-back position during the 1970s. Steve's season was topped with a Third Division championship winners' medal.

Swansea C (£25,000 from Cheltenham T on 14/11/1995) FL 127+6/3 FLC 2+1 FAC 8 Others 8

JONES Stuart Clive
Born: Bristol, 24 October 1977
Height: 6'1" Weight: 14.0

Stuart joined Torquay from Sheffield Wednesday, initially on loan, in February 2000 following the departure of Neville Southall. The move was made permanent after several impressive displays. A good shot stopper who has a fine kick, Stuart did not let an unhappy local-derby performance against Plymouth affect his confidence. In contrast, he made his Gulls debut in a 1-0 win against Exeter.

Sheffield Wed (£20,000 + from Weston super Mare on 26/3/1998)
Torquay U (£30,000 on 3/2/2000) FL 16

JONK Wim
Born: Volendam, Holland, 12 October 1966
Height: 6'0" Weight: 12.2
International Honours: Holland: 49

This skilful and experienced midfield player featured regularly in Sheffield Wednesday's line-up in 1999-2000 but his calm, almost laid-back, style seemed out of place amid the hurly-burly of Premiership football. His skill shone through on occasions when he would deliver a defence-splitting pass but at other times he seemed to drift in and out of the games. The midfield play-maker added another goal to his total for the Owls when he netted in the 5-1 demolition of Wimbledon last October and had chalked up two more by the end of the season.

Sheffield Wed (£2,500,000 from PSV Eindhoven, Holland, via FC Volendam, Ajax and Inter Milan, on 12/8/1998) PL 67+1/5 FLC 4 FAC 7

JORDAN Andrew Joseph
Born: Manchester, 14 December 1979
Height: 6'1" Weight: 13.1
International Honours: S: U21-4

The son of the rampaging Scottish international centre forward, Joe Jordan, Andrew has turned his talents to defending rather than scoring goals, though the strong-tackling Bristol City centre back did mark his first appearance of 1999-2000 with his side's goal in a 1-2 defeat at Nottingham Forest in the Worthington Cup. Unfortunately, it was to be nearly the end of the season before injury problems relented to allow this talented player to fully show what he is capable of. Returning to the side in March, he deservedly won "Man of the Match" accolades in his first two games, and went on to become a fixture in the City team. He made his debut for Scotland U21s against Bosnia last October and went on to gain further caps against Lithuania, France and Holland during the season.

Bristol C (From trainee on 5/12/1997) FL 9 FLC 1 FAC 1 Others 1

JORDAN Scott Douglas
Born: Newcastle, 19 July 1975
Height: 5'10" Weight: 11.8

Injuries affected the talented midfielder during 1999-2000, and at times his form for York suffered. At his best, he is one of the finest passers of the ball in the lower divisions and a very constructive player. Scott netted twice, in a 2-2 home draw against Southend United and in a victory over Halifax. Although he is still only 28 years of age, 2000-01 will be Scott's ninth senior season at Bootham Crescent.

York C (From trainee on 21/10/1992) FL 117+38/12 FLC 5+1/1 FAC 6+2/2 Others 7+4

JORGENSEN Claus Beck
Born: Denmark, 24 April 1979
Height: 5'11" Weight: 11.0

Claus joined Bournemouth from Danish Second Division outfit AC Horsens in July 1999 and once he had adapted to the speed and physical side of the English game he proved to be a tremendous success. He scored five goals from midfield and was deservedly voted "Player of the Season". He can play anywhere in the middle line and impressed with his high workrate and an ability to take on and beat opposition defenders.

Bournemouth (Free from AC Horsens, Denmark on 12/7/1999) FL 34+10/6 FLC 4 FAC 3 Others 1+1

JOSEPH Marc Ellis
Born: Leicester, 10 November 1976
Height: 6'0" Weight: 12.10

This pacy young Cambridge central defender's 1999-2000 season was interrupted by injury. Normally employed as a centre back, he spent the last part of the season out of position at left back and performed so well that he may retain his new role during the coming season. A quick and classy defender who is comfortable in possession, Marc has yet to score a first-team goal.

Cambridge U (From trainee on 23/5/1995) FL 107+16 FLC 7 FAC 3+2 Others 5+1

JOSEPH Matthew (Matt) Nathan Adolphus
Born: Bethnal Green, 30 September 1972
Height: 5'8" Weight: 10.7
International Honours: E: Yth

The 1999-2000 season was another good one for Matt, as he continued to be a vital part of the Leyton Orient defence. He is comfortable at right back or centre half, and can also be used as a man marker. Despite his size, Matt is good in the air and difficult to knock off the ball. A tenacious tackler, he followed manager Tommy Taylor from Cambridge United.

Arsenal (From trainee on 17/11/1990)
Gillingham (Free on 7/12/1992. Free to Ilves, Finland during 1993 close season)
Cambridge U (Signed on 19/11/1993) FL 157+2/6 FLC 6+1 FAC 7 Others 5
Leyton Orient (£10,000 on 22/1/1998) FL 86+3/1 FLC 4+1 FAC 6+1 Others 1+1

JOSEPH Roger Anthony
Born: Paddington, 24 December 1965
Height: 5'11" Weight: 11.10
International Honours: E: B-2

Roger had an operation on his hand during the 1999 close season, before returning briefly to captain Leyton Orient in a pre-season friendly against an Antigua XI. Unfortunately, he sustained a troublesome calf injury that kept him out until he made a brief return as a substitute against Swansea in March. It would appear to have been the experienced defender's last appearance for the O's, as he was released at the end of the season.

Brentford (Free from Southall on 4/10/1985) FL 103+1/2 FLC 7 FAC 1 Others 8
Wimbledon (£150,000 on 25/8/1988) F/PL 155+7 FLC 17+2 FAC 11+1 Others 6
Millwall (Loaned on 2/3/1995) FL 5
Leyton Orient (Free on 22/11/1996) FL 15 Others 1
West Bromwich A (Free on 28/2/1997) FL 0+2
Leyton Orient (Free on 7/8/1997) FL 26+24 FLC 3+2 FAC 0+2 Others 4

JOYCE Warren Garton
Born: Oldham, 20 January 1965
Height: 5'9" Weight: 12.0

As Hull's player-manager, Warren paid the price when the Tigers were unable to live up to huge expectations in 1999-2000, but City fans will remain grateful to the tireless boss who saved the club's Football League status the previous season. Chairman Nick Buchanan had insisted in May 1999 that Warren and John McGovern (his assistant) were an "integral and important" part of the board's plans, but they were dismissed last April. One who shuns the limelight by nature, Warren's leadership instincts come naturally. He captained England at schoolboy level in cricket and rugby union, with a neck injury suffered in an RU tour of Australia causing the change in his sporting career. Warren also has a long-standing connection with Hull – he grew up in the same village as current Hull Kingston Rovers coach Dave Harrison, and turned down the chance to play rugby league for St Helens. The City gaffer admitted that, in an ideal world, he should play no longer but suspensions and injuries dictated otherwise during what was to be his last season with the club. While his deadly free kicks remained a potent weapon in Hull's armoury, his personal highlight was the 100th goal of his senior career (in the Auto Windscreens Shield against Chester), which came two weeks before his 35th birthday and 600th league appearance. Warren's total commitment to the Hull cause both on and off the field was without question, but it was not enough.

Bolton W (From juniors on 23/6/1982) FL 180+4/17 FLC 14+1/1 FAC 11/1 Others 11/2
Preston NE (£35,000 on 16/10/1987) FL 170+7/34 FLC 8/2 FAC 6/1 Others 19/7
Plymouth Arg (£160,000 on 19/5/1992) FL 28+2/3 FLC 6/1 FAC 2 Others 2
Burnley (£140,000 on 7/7/1993) FL 65+5/9 FLC 8/1 FAC 4/1 Others 8/1
Hull C (Loaned on 20/1/1995) FL 9/3
Hull C (£30,000 on 10/7/1996) FL 137+1/12 FLC 7+1/1 FAC 8/1 Others 7/2

JULES Mark Anthony
Born: Bradford, 5 September 1971
Height: 5'8" Weight: 11.1

Released by Chesterfield in the 1999 close season, Mark enjoyed a good first term at Halifax with a number of consistent performances at left back. He is a tricky player whose mazy runs upset opposing defences, and although he did not appear on the score sheet his defensive duties more than made up for that. With an eye to the future, Mark has begun a PFA-sponsored BSc in sports fitness.

Bradford C (From trainee on 3/7/1990) FLC 0+1
Scarborough (Free on 14/8/1991) FL 57+20/16 FLC 6+2/2 FAC 1+1 Others 6/4
Chesterfield (£40,000 on 21/5/1993) FL 155+31/4 FLC 12+3/2 FAC 13+2 Others 10+1
Halifax T (Free on 5/7/1999) FL 38+4 FLC 2 FAC 2 Others 1

[JUNINHO] JUNIOR Oswaldo Giroldo
Born: Sao Paulo, Brazil, 22 February 1975
Height: 5'5" Weight: 10.0
International Honours: Brazil: 29

The samba music was turned up high when the "little fella" returned to Middlesbrough on loan from Atletico Madrid in September 1999. No one had wanted him to leave and his homecoming was as emotional and noisy as his first arrival. He inevitably found it difficult to match the expectations of his most devoted admirers while the sceptics questioned whether his individual brilliance could be integrated into the team. As they pointed out, the Brazilian's form was spasmodic, but even a spasmodic Juninho is a priceless asset, for he is capable of producing moments of magic that create a ripple of excitement around the ground and leave defenders baffled. The diminutive midfielder may not be the greatest player ever to pull on the famous old shirt but he is undeniably a brilliant one who thrills the fans and strikes fear into the opposition. A gifted artist who selflessly subordinates his talents to the team, he is the epitome of a sportsman. Boro were expected to attempt to re-sign the Brazilian on a permanent basis during the summer, although the transfer fee seemed likely to be the subject of tough negotiations.

Middlesbrough (£4,750,000 from Sao Paulo, Brazil on 3/11/1995) PL 54+2/14 FLC 9/1 FAC 6/2 Others 3 (£12,000,000 to Atletico Madrid, Spain on 25/8/1997)
Middlesbrough (Loaned on 21/9/1999) PL 24+4/4 FLC 4/1 FAC 1

JUPP Duncan Alan
Born: Guildford, 25 January 1975
Height: 6'0" Weight: 12.12
International Honours: S: U21-9

Duncan's first-team appearances for Wimbledon were once again restricted last season by the form of the ever-dependable Kenny Cunningham in the right-back role. He was more involved towards the end of the campaign, playing some part in all but one of the Dons' last eight games, and will be looking for greater opportunities in 2000-01. A pacy, confident player who likes to attack and be in the thick of the action, Duncan showed a great deal of commitment during a difficult season for the Dons as they fought to retain their Premiership status.

Fulham (From trainee on 12/7/1993) FL 101+4/2 FLC 10+2 FAC 9+1/1 Others 9+1/1
Wimbledon (£125,000 + on 27/6/1996) PL 18+6 FLC 6+1 FAC 3+2

KABBA Stephen (Steve)
Born: Lambeth, 7 March 1981
Height: 5'10" Weight: 11.12
A young striker with Crystal Palace, Steve performed well for the club's reserve team and was called up for his Football League debut at Crewe last December as a late replacement for Leon McKenzie. He was later sidelined by a hip injury and will be pushing for more regular first-team action in the coming season.
Crystal Palace (From trainee on 29/6/1999) FL 1

KACHLOUL Hassan
Born: Agadir, Morocco, 19 February 1973
Height: 6'1" Weight: 11.12
International Honours: Morocco: 5
An excellent attacking midfielder, Hassan is probably at his best on Southampton's left flank, cutting in with his close ball control and distribution. He has settled well over the last two seasons and become a firm favourite with the home crowd, who appreciate his hard work. Called into the Moroccan squad for the African Nations' Cup last season, he played just 15 minutes against Tunisia but had earlier appeared in the friendly fixtures with Belgium and Trinidad & Tobago.
Southampton (£250,000 from St Etienne, France, via Nimes, Dunkerque and Metz, on 20/10/1998) PL 47+7/10 FLC 4 FAC 2+1

Hassan Kachloul

KANDOL Tresor Osmar
Born: Zaire, 30 August 1981
Height: 6'2" Weight: 11.7
Rising up through Luton's impressive youth system, Tresor was voted the management's "Best Young Player" of 1999-2000. However, despite scoring quite frequently in the reserves, including four in one match, this talented young forward found it difficult to break into the senior team on a regular basis last season. He made only five appearances, three from the subs' bench, but undoubtedly has the ability to become an established first-team player. Time is on his side but he was out of contract in the summer and at the time of writing it seemed likely that he would start the new season elsewhere.
Luton T (From trainee on 26/9/1998) FL 3+5 FLC 1/1 Others 0+1

KANOUTE Frederic
Born: Sainte Foy Les Lyon, France, 2 September 1977
Height: 6'4" Weight: 12.10
International Honours: France: U21
Frederic joined West Ham on loan in March after spending an unhappy season at Lyon, where he was frozen out of the first-team squad. He made an immediate impact on his debut against Wimbledon, when he quickly struck up an understanding with fellow striker Paolo di Canio. Together they terrorised the Dons' defence, with Frederic heading against the bar and scoring with a cracking 15-yard strike. He produced another great display in the next home game against Coventry, finishing off with a late header to complete a 5-0 victory. He has pace, strength, good skills in the air and an excellent touch for a big man – qualities which could help him to develop into a top striker in the future. With several other clubs reported to be in pursuit of him, he chose to sign permanently for the Hammers in mid-May for a £4 million fee, Marc-Vivien Foe moving in the opposite direction for £6 million as part of the deal. Frederic appeared regularly for France U21s in the early part of the season, playing against Northern Ireland, the Ukraine and Iceland and twice against Italy.
West Ham U (Loaned from Lyon, France on 23/3/2000) PL 8/2

KANU Nwankwo
Born: Owerri, Nigeria, 1 August 1976
Height: 6'4" Weight: 13.3
Club Honours: CS '99
International Honours: Nigeria: 19; U23 (OLYM '96); Yth (World-U17 '93)
The Nigerian forward is one of the most versatile players in the Arsenal squad, and has the ability to come off the bench and turn a game around. Despite his apparently casual and relaxed style of play, he is very determined and wants nothing less than a high level of success. Although he has a slightly unorthodox style of play, Kanu has brought great skills to the Highbury squad. Whether he plays as a direct striker or just behind the front men, his all-round distribution and neat touches are first class. His reading of the game is excellent, and he frequently manoeuvres himself into space for a "tap-in" goal. Although he scored a number of crucial goals, the highlight of his 1999-2000 season was the away game at Chelsea in the Premiership. He struck an incredible hat-trick in the last 15 minutes to turn a 0-2 deficit into a 3-2 victory. His winning goal chance came from a seemingly impossible angle on the left side. It was sheer brilliance. He played in all six games for Nigeria in the African Nations' Cup tournament in the spring, when the Eagles were defeated by Cameroon on penalties in the final, and also played in two World Cup qualifying games against Eritrea during the season. Kanu has a warm personality which has endeared him greatly to the Arsenal fans, who regard him as something of a cult figure.
Arsenal (£4,500,000 from Inter Milan, Italy, via Fed Works, Iwuanyanwu National and Ajax, on 4/2/1999) PL 29+14/18 FLC 1/1 FAC 0+7/1 Others 10+6/4

KAPRIELIAN Mickael
Born: Marseille, France, 6 October 1980
Height: 5'9" Weight: 10.8
International Honours: France: Yth
This 19-year-old French striker was signed by Bolton early in 2000 and made some very promising appearances for the Wanderers' reserves, notching up some impressive goals in the latter stages of the season. He didn't get much of a chance to shine in the first team, however, as the few minutes he played against Charlton as a substitute in March were to be his only experience of league football last season. Despite this, if Mickael can sustain his excellent reserve-team performances, he may well get the first-team chance he craves in the new season.
Bolton W (Free from Martigues, France on 15/1/2000) FL 0+1

KARELSE John
Born: Zeeland, Holland, 17 May 1970
Height: 6'2" Weight: 14.11
International Honours: Holland: U21; Yth
After 13 years with NAC Breda in Holland John was brought to Newcastle on a four-year contract by Ruud Gullit in mid-August 1999 when injuries to Shay Given and Steve Harper created a goalkeeping crisis, and he went straight into the side for his debut away to Southampton. After conceding seven goals in two games, playing behind a porous defence, he suffered a knee injury in training and gave way to loan signing Tommy Wright. With first Harper and then Given returning to fitness John found it very difficult to regain the first-team spot, and his only other appearance was at Highbury at the end of October when he kept Arsenal at bay to achieve a clean sheet and help earn United's first away point of the campaign. Later in the season he asked to be allowed to move on loan to a club which could provide him with first-team playing opportunities but, although Newcastle were willing to allow this, nothing suitable emerged.
Newcastle U (£800,000 from NAC Breda, Holland on 13/8/1999) PL 3

KATCHOURO Petr
Born: Minsk, Belarus, 2 August 1972
Height: 5'11" Weight: 12.6
International Honours: Belarus: 25
Petr nearly missed the start of the 1999-2000 season when there were problems with his work permit and only the intervention of a

local MP allowed him to play in Sheffield United's opening match. Although the Belarus striker scored three times in his first eight games he was unable to recapture his best form and after mid-September most of his appearances were from the subs' bench late in the game. In February, in an attempt to restore his confidence, a loan move to Stockport County was arranged but it was prevented by work permit restrictions and in March he signed for the Chinese club Chengdu Wuniu. Petr now holds the club record for the most appearances as a substitute – in the league, the FA Cup and in total. He added two further caps against Russia and Switzerland in the early part of the season.

Sheffield U (£650,000 from Dinamo Minsk, Belarus on 19/7/1996) FL 50+45/19 FLC 8+4/3 FAC 2+9 Others 3/1

KAVANAGH Graham Anthony
Born: Dublin, 2 December 1973
Height: 5'10" Weight: 12.11
Club Honours: AMC '00
International Honours: RoI: 3; B-1; U21-9; Yth; Sch

Graham had his best season at Stoke to date in 1999-2000 with the "Man of the Match" performance when City won the Auto Windscreens Shield final at Wembley a notable highlight. While his dead-ball kicking was not as effective as in previous seasons, he turned in outstanding performances week after week alongside fellow Irishman James O'Connor in midfield. His disciplinary record was also much improved and he avoided suspension. Blessed with vision and an eye for goal, he is capable of playing at a much higher level, which would enhance his currently limited opportunities with the full Republic of Ireland squad. His name was frequently mentioned in connection with a move in the early part of the season but, to the relief of the Stoke fans, he stayed to play a full part in a successful season, earning a place in the PFA award-winning Second Division side.

Middlesbrough (Signed from Home Farm on 16/8/1991) F/PL 22+13/3 FLC 1 FAC 3+1/1 Others 7
Darlington (Loaned on 25/2/1994) FL 5
Stoke C (£250,000 + on 13/9/1996) FL 156+7/27 FLC 12+1/7 FAC 4 Others 11/3

KAVANAGH Jason Colin
Born: Meriden, 23 November 1971
Height: 5'9" Weight: 12.7
International Honours: E: Yth; Sch

Jason made just two further first-team appearances for Stoke during the early part of the 1999-2000 season before the club agreed to release him in December. An experienced right back with pace and stamina, he signed for Cambridge and was expected to bolster the United defence but, like many other U's players, he found himself in the treatment room and missing part of the season. He is a solid defender, and a prolonged run in the first team should bring greater consistency to his play. It may not happen, though, as Jason is reportedly considering a career outside the game as a financial adviser.

Derby Co (From trainee on 9/12/1988) FL 74+25/1 FLC 3+2 FAC 7 Others 8+8
Wycombe W (£25,000 on 1/11/1996) FL 84+6/1 FLC 6 FAC 3+1 Others 4
Stoke C (Free on 8/3/1999) FL 8 FLC 1
Cambridge U (Free on 3/12/1999) FL 19 FAC 3

KEANE Robert (Robbie) David
Born: Dublin, 8 July 1980
Height: 5'9" Weight: 11.10
International Honours: RoI: 17; B-1; Yth; (UEFA-U18 '98)

The brilliant forward had been close to leaving Wolves in the summer of 1999, so the club's fans were pleased to see him get a fine winner at Maine Road in the opening match of the new season. Another beauty gave Wolves a point against Portsmouth, but those were to be his last two league appearances for them, as he then moved to Coventry in a £6 million deal. Robbie made an immediate impression at Highfield Road, scoring twice on his debut against Derby. Coventry had stepped in to sign him after Aston Villa had declined to meet Wolves' asking price and Middlesbrough had failed to persuade him to join them. He fully justified his fee by showing dazzling speed and impressive dribbling and ball control, not to mention superb awareness. He scored 11 goals in his first 21 games despite playing alongside four different partners. In his first month he won the Carling "Player of the Month" and the Cisco "Young Player of the Month" awards. Robbie's goal at White Hart Lane was memorable for the way that he turned Chris Perry and was runner-up in the BBC's "Goal of the Month" competition. Then, against Villa, he scored a clinical winner that brought the house down. The peak of his season was probably scoring the winner in the Christmas game against Arsenal with a cheeky flick past the bemused pair of Tony Adams and David Seaman. He scored three times in eight appearances for the Republic of Ireland during the season but was sorely missed in the second leg of the European Championship play-off with Turkey when suspension kept him out. His form tailed off in the latter weeks of the campaign after an injury forced him to miss a handful of games. He was voted runner-up in the PFA's "Young Player of the Year" award.

Wolverhampton W (From trainee on 26/7/1997) FL 66+7/24 FLC 7+2/3 FAC 3+2/2
Coventry C (£6,000,000 on 20/8/1999) PL 30+1/12 FAC 3

KEANE Roy Maurice
Born: Cork, 10 August 1971
Height: 5'10" Weight: 12.10
Club Honours: FMC '92; CS '93, '96, '97; PL '94, '96, '97, '99, '00; FAC '94, '96, '99
International Honours: RoI: 46; U21-4; Yth; Sch

An inspirational midfielder with excellent skills and a hardened edge, Roy started the 1999-2000 season with a huge question mark hanging over his future as the Manchester United board considered whether they should break their rigid wage structure in order to keep him at Old Trafford on a new improved contract. Despite the uncertainty about his future, Roy continued to play his heart out for the Reds while waiting to see what transpired in December, the effective deadline. With the Italian giants, Juventus, waiting patiently in the wings for any breakdown in the talks, Roy's brace against Arsenal at Highbury in August was a classic example of his true value to the side. Having then kick-started United's Champions' League campaign with a sensational strike against Sturm Graz, he was a key figure as the Reds made impressive progress in both the Champions' League and the Premiership. Despite a troublesome knee injury keeping him out of the side for a lengthy spell in October, he came back to notch the winner against Palmeiras in the Intercontinental Cup in Japan, which momentarily crowned United "Champions of the World". With the speculation surrounding his future reaching fever pitch as "D-Day" approached, United fans breathed a huge sigh of relief as Roy signed a new contract, reportedly worth £55,000 a week, in December. Emphasising his value to the club with a goal against Valencia in the Champions' League on the day the new deal was announced, he then notched two in successive games against Bradford and Sunderland. Despite the disappointment of missing out on the World Club Championship in Brazil at the turn of the year, he came back from a three-match suspension to score important goals against Bordeaux and Fiorentina that took United through to the quarter-finals of the European Cup. Unfortunately, in the second leg against Real Madrid at Old Trafford, Roy's own goal was the prelude to United's dethronement as European Champions, but he had the considerable consolation of leading the side to another Premiership title three days later and fittingly won both the PFA and the football writers' "Player of the Year" awards, as well as earning selection for the PFA award-winning Premiership team. Roy is also a crucial figure for the Republic of Ireland, for whom he won a further four caps last season.

Nottingham F (£10,000 from Cobh Ramblers on 12/6/1990) F/PL 114/22 FLC 17/6 FAC 18/3 Others 5/2
Manchester U (£3,750,000 on 22/7/1993) PL 177+8/24 FLC 9+2 FAC 29+1/1 Others 48/14

Roy Keane

KEARTON Jason Brett
Born: Ipswich, Australia, 9 July 1969
Height: 6'1" Weight: 11.10
Club Honours: FAC '95

Crewe's dependable Australian goalkeeper has missed only seven games since making his debut for the club in October 1996. In 1999-2000 Jason was an ever-present for the second successive season (although he was forced to leave the field in the closing stages of the game against Huddersfield in March), bringing his unbroken run of appearances to 104. An excellent shot stopper who is good in one-on-one situations and comes out confidently for crosses, Jason instils confidence in his defenders. Voted the supporters' "Player of the Year", he is very consistent, but his performance at Blackburn last season was, in his own words, the best of his career.

Everton (Free from Brisbane Lions, Australia on 31/10/1988) PL 3+3 FLC 1 FAC 1
Stoke C (Loaned on 13/8/1991) FL 16 Others 1
Blackpool (Loaned on 9/1/1992) FL 14
Notts Co (Loaned on 19/1/1995) FL 10 Others 2
Crewe Alex (Free on 16/10/1996) FL 165 FLC 11 FAC 7 Others 6

KEATES Dean Scott
Born: Walsall, 30 June 1978
Height: 5'6" Weight: 10.10

This energetic little midfielder once again battled away bravely all over the pitch for Walsall in 1999-2000, making important contributions in defence, setting up attacks and occasionally getting on the end of balls into opponents' danger areas. Despite his lack of inches, Dean headed an early-season goal at Plymouth and another at Barnsley in December. A wholehearted, tenacious player, he has become a key member of the Walsall squad.

Walsall (From trainee on 14/8/1996) FL 98+15/4 FLC 11+1/1 FAC 8 Others 11/2

KEEBLE Christopher (Chris) Mark
Born: Colchester, 17 September 1978
Height: 5'9" Weight: 11.5

Chris is the son of 1950s Colchester legend Vic Keeble. Having been told he would not be retained by Ipswich, Chris came to Layer Road for a trial and was signed permanently on transfer deadline day last March, having impressed in a couple of reserve games. He was seen as a player for next season, but made his debut as a substitute against Cambridge at Easter, and within minutes had scored the goal which made the U's safe from relegation – and what a goal it was, a flying bullet header in the great tradition of his father! Chris was then involved in all the remaining games, and the United fans look forward to seeing more of him in 2000-01.

Ipswich T (From trainee on 2/6/1997) FL 0+1
Colchester U (Free on 23/3/2000) FL 2+3/1

KEEGAN John Kevin Paul
Born: Liverpool, 5 August 1981
Height: 5'11" Weight: 11.9

One of the several promising York teenagers who have graduated through the youth ranks, this left-sided defender was thrust into senior action in 1999-2000 owing to injury problems. John made an impressive Football League debut in December at home to Southend United. The Liverpool-born lad is one for the future.

York C (Trainee) FL 2+1

KEEGAN Michael Jerard
Born: Wallasey, 12 May 1981
Height: 5'10" Weight: 11.0

A first-year professional with Swansea in 1999-2000, Michael was labelled as one of the best passers of the ball at the club. During the 1998-99 season he had been selected in the England U18 squad for training at Lilleshall, a considerable achievement for a player with a club in the lower divisions. After first-team appearances in the Welsh Premier Cup competition, he made his league debut as a substitute against Rochdale in October, supplying the cross for the only goal of the game. His full debut came in the next match against Second Division Colchester United in the FA Cup. The young midfielder made further starts against Leyton Orient, Plymouth and Peterborough, as well as in the Auto Windscreens Shield tie at Exeter.

Swansea C (From trainee on 5/7/1999) FL 3+1 FAC 1 Others 2

KEELER Justin Jack
Born: Hillingdon, 17 April 1978
Height: 5'11" Weight: 11.6

Justin was playing for Wessex League club Christchurch and working at his local Tesco's store when he joined Bournemouth on a short-term contract last January. He made his senior debut when coming on from the subs' bench in the Auto Windscreens Shield tie with Bristol City and also appeared as a substitute in the end-of-season games. A promising attacking midfield player, he was given a one-year contract in the summer.

Bournemouth (Free from Christchurch on 10/1/2000) FL 0+3 Others 0+1

KEEN Kevin Ian
Born: Amersham, 25 February 1967
Height: 5'7" Weight: 10.10
International Honours: E: Yth; Sch

Kevin became Gary Megson's first signing for Stoke when he agreed a new contract in the summer of 1999, having been given a free transfer by previous manager Brian Little. The industrious midfielder was a regular during Megson's reign, his best performance being when he came off the bench in the home leg of the Worthington Cup tie against Macclesfield Town and turned the game with his direct running. A great team man, he lost his place when he broke an arm in training and struggled to regain it when he had returned to fitness. He was released at the end of the season.

West Ham U (From apprentice on 8/3/1984) FL 187+32/21 FLC 21+1/5 FAC 15+7/1 Others 14+2/3
Wolverhampton W (£600,000 on 7/7/1993) FL 37+5/7 FLC 2+1 FAC 5/1 Others 4/1
Stoke C (£300,000 on 19/10/1994) FL 147+30/10 FLC 13+3/2 FAC 6 Others 3+1

KEEN Peter Alan
Born: Middlesbrough, 16 November 1976
Height: 6'0" Weight: 12.0

A capable young goalkeeper, Peter made a difficult start to his Carlisle career after moving to Brunton Park from Newcastle shortly before the start of the 1999-2000 season, conceding five goals at Halifax on his debut and a total of 13 in his first three appearances. Luke Weaver's injury gave him a further chance in the last three games of the season, however. This time he showed a lot more promise: he pulled off some fine saves against Darlington and was Carlisle's star performer in the vital final fixture at Brighton. Peter was offered new terms in May after departing boss Martin Wilkinson had stated he would not be required.

Newcastle U (From trainee on 25/3/1996)
Carlisle U (Free on 4/8/1999) FL 6

Peter Keen

KEISTER John Edward Samuel
Born: Manchester, 11 November 1970
Height: 5'8" Weight: 11.0
International Honours: Sierra Leone: 3

A determined midfield player, John made a brave comeback for Walsall at the start of the 1999-2000 season after a serious knee injury in August 1998, but after just two substitute appearances (one of them in the fine win over Birmingham) he moved to Chester in January to help in their valiant but vain battle against relegation. John made a sensational debut for City, as he was sent off against Darlington after only 44 minutes. At least his dismissal gave an indication that the Blues had recruited a much-needed tough-tackling ball winner in the middle of the park. On the constructive side, John is a good passer who likes to get forward into dangerous positions. He proved to be a valuable addition to the Chester squad, but was released in the summer.

Walsall (Free from Faweh FC on 18/9/1993) FL 78+28/2 FLC 4+1 FAC 10+2 Others 2+2
Chester C (Free on 7/1/2000) FL 8+2 Others 1

KEITH Joseph (Joe) Richard
Born: Plaistow, 1 October 1978
Height: 5'7" Weight: 10.6

Joe was signed by Colchester on a free transfer from West Ham in the summer of 1999, having been a member of the youth and academy set-up at Upton Park for three years. He had an impressive pre-season at either left back or left wing back, and went straight into the first team for the win at Chesterfield on the opening day, keeping his place thereafter for all but one game when he was injured. All in all, he had an excellent debut season, capped with two goals – one coming in the televised Worthington Cup game at Crystal Palace and the other being the first in United's shock win at Preston. Joe deservedly won the "Away Supporters' Player of the Year" award.

West Ham U (From trainee on 9/7/1997)
Colchester U (Free on 5/7/1999) FL 45/1 FLC 2/1 FAC 1 Others 1

KELLER Marc
Born: Colmar, France, 14 January 1968
Height: 5'11" Weight: 12.4
International Honours: France: 5

Although on the subs' bench for West Ham's opening game of the 1999-2000 season against Tottenham, Marc returned to the starting line-up for the second leg of the Inter Toto final against Metz and enjoyed a good run in the team in the autumn. He scored just once – an 18-yard strike against Bournemouth in the Worthington Cup – and as the season progressed found himself in and out of the side. Marc was used both as a wide midfield player and as a wing back, but looked happier in the former role, where his attacking qualities were put to better use. He was particularly effective when moving forward down the left flank, from where he was able to deliver a string of inviting crosses. Nevertheless, one of his best games all season came in the wing-back role, where he was outstanding in the derby game at Highbury in May.

West Ham U (Free from Karlsruhe, Germany, via Colmer, Mulhouse and Strasbourg, on 27/7/1998) PL 36+8/5 FLC 4+1/1 Others 4

KELLY Alan Thomas
Born: Preston, 11 August 1968
Height: 6'2" Weight: 14.3
International Honours: RoI: 30; U23-1; Yth

Alan was brought to Blackburn by Brian Kidd during the summer of 1999 and it was ironic that the Irish goalkeeper should have to wait until Kidd was dismissed to gain a first-team position. Earlier he had been fielded only in the Worthington Cup with John Filan being immediately restored for league duty. On coming in, he confirmed the form that had made him the Republic of Ireland's "Player of the Year", being a great shot stopper and organiser. However, he sometimes looked a little uncertain when coming for crosses and is not so relaxed with his kicking as Filan. His best display was probably on his return to Bramall Lane, where he produced some amazing reflex saves, and he also kept out a penalty against Fulham. His ability to recover from injury appears to be limitless. A groin strain suffered playing for Ireland did not sideline him and a bad leg injury at Portsmouth kept him out for barely a fortnight. He won eight further international caps during the season.

Preston NE (From apprentice on 25/9/1985) FL 142 FLC 1 FAC 8 Others 13
Sheffield U (£200,000 on 24/7/1992) P/FL 213+3 FLC 15 FAC 22 Others 2
Blackburn Rov (£675,000 on 30/7/1999) FL 29+1 FLC 2 FAC 3

David Kelly

KELLY David Thomas
Born: Birmingham, 25 November 1965
Height: 5'11" Weight: 12.1
Club Honours: Div 1 '93
International Honours: RoI: 26; B-3; U23-1; U21-3

Despite his advancing years David showed that he had lost none of his ability as a predatory striker in 1999-2000, when he finished as Tranmere's second-top scorer after hitting the net a total of 15 times in league and cup games. Fittingly, he bagged Tranmere's only goal in the Worthington Cup final at Wembley to raise the hopes of the club's supporters at a time when the team were down to ten men – unfortunately, there was to be no equaliser and Leicester eventually ran out 2-1 winners. He also scored the first hat-trick of his Rovers career in the Worthington Cup thrashing of Coventry. Although admitting to having "dodgy" knees, David never stops running and proved to be as sharp as ever in front of goal. He is a great crowd favourite at Prenton Park and was rewarded for his fine performances with a further one-year contract.

Walsall (Signed from Alvechurch on 21/12/1983) FL 115+32/63 FLC 11+1/4 FAC 12+2/3 Others 14+3/10
West Ham U (£600,000 on 1/8/1988) FL 29+12/7 FLC 11+3/5 FAC 6 Others 2+1/2
Leicester C (£300,000 on 22/3/1990) FL 63+3/22 FLC 6/2 FAC 1 Others 2/1
Newcastle U (£250,000 on 4/12/1991) FL 70/35 FLC 4/2 FAC 5/1 Others 4/1
Wolverhampton W (£750,000 on 23/6/1993) FL 76+7/26 FLC 5/2 FAC 11/6 Others 4/2
Sunderland (£1,000,000 on 19/9/1995) P/FL 32+2/2 FLC 2+1 FAC 3
Tranmere Rov (£350,000 on 5/8/1997) FL 69+19/21 FLC 16+1/13 FAC 11+1/3

KELLY Garry
Born: Drogheda, 9 July 1974
Height: 5'8" Weight: 11.8
International Honours: RoI: 31; U21-5; Yth; Sch

After he was sidelined for the whole of the 1998-99 season with a shin injury and Leeds then signed Danny Mills for £4 million in the summer, it appeared that Garry had a huge mountain to climb to regain his first-team place. But after just six games of the 1999-2000 campaign the Garry Kelly of old returned to the right-back slot like he had never been away. Very quick and eager to get forward, he is also very assured in the defensive aspect of his game and his speed of thought, tackling and will to win all serve to make him a very consistent performer. Garry has now made over 250 appearances for Leeds and has committed himself to the club by signing a new contract which should enable him to see out his career at Elland Road. He deservedly won his place back in the Republic of Ireland set-up last season, and also received the honour of being selected by his fellow professionals to appear in the PFA award-winning Premiership side.

Leeds U (Signed from Home Farm on 24/9/1991) PL 214+7/2 FLC 20+1 FAC 22+1 Others 15

KELLY Gary Alexander
Born: Preston, 3 August 1966
Height: 5'11" Weight: 13.6
Club Honours: FAYC '85
International Honours: RoI: B-1; U23-1; U21-8

Although Gary had a slow start to 1999-2000, he remained first-choice 'keeper for Oldham and rarely missed a game throughout the season despite competition from Northern Ireland U21 cap David Miskelly. A superbly agile shot-stopping 'keeper, he was called up to the Republic of Ireland full international squad as a replacement for his injured brother Alan for the Euro 2000 play-off second leg fixture against Turkey last November.

Newcastle U (From apprentice on 20/6/1984) FL 53 FLC 4 FAC 3 Others 2
Blackpool (Loaned on 7/10/1988) FL 5
Bury (£60,000 on 5/10/1989) FL 236 FLC 14 FAC 13 Others 29
Oldham Ath (£10,000 on 27/8/1996) FL 157 FLC 7 FAC 12 Others 3

KELLY Seamus
Born: Tullamore, Eire, 6 May 1974
Height: 6'1" Weight: 13.0

The Irish goalkeeper was called into action as Cardiff's 1999-2000 season neared its tense climax, just as he had been 12 months earlier. During City's 1998-99 promotion campaign he replaced Jon Hallworth for the last five matches and helped steer the Bluebirds to promotion. This time Jon was injured six matches from the end of the season, and Seamus was plunged into the fray once again. Unfortunately, the outcome was rather different, as Cardiff were relegated. The 'keeper was released at the end of the season and was reported to have returned home to Ireland.

Cardiff C (Free from UCD Dublin on 3/8/1998) FL 12+1

KENNA Jeffrey (Jeff) Jude
Born: Dublin, 27 August 1970
Height: 5'11" Weight: 12.2
International Honours: RoI: 27; B-1; U21-8; Yth; Sch

The Blackburn defender's 1999-2000 season was curtailed first by his slow recovery from an achilles tendon injury and then by a recurrence of the injury at Liverpool in January. In his few appearances he was steady and reliable, and while not reaching great heights he appeared to have the right-back position to himself by virtue of his consistency and his ability to cover across the defence. Unfortunately, he broke down in March attempting a comeback and has had to have another operation on his achilles tendon. He won a further cap for the Republic of Ireland last November when he came on as a substitute in the second leg of the European Championship play-off tie with Turkey.

Southampton (From trainee on 25/4/1989) F/PL 110+4/4 FLC 4 FAC 10+1 Others 3
Blackburn Rov (£1,500,000 on 15/3/1995) P/FL 148+1/1 FLC 14 FAC 13 Others 7

KENNEDY Mark
Born: Dublin, 15 May 1976
Height: 5'11" Weight: 11.9
International Honours: RoI: 29; U21-7; Yth; Sch

Mark joined Manchester City from Wimbledon during the 1999 close season for a fee of £1 million, rising to £1.5 million after a certain number of appearances. He is an enterprising left winger who crosses the ball accurately and, with Terry Cooke already in the squad, his arrival held out the prospect of a feast of traditional wing play from the Maine Road club. Mark made an exciting start to the season, revitalising the team's attack, and scored four spectacular goals in his first six games with fierce, dipping left-foot shots from outside the area after he had cut inside from the wing. When he returned to action after missing three games in late November he seemed less effective, and the goals dried up. He did not score again until he bagged a late brace at home to Norwich in mid-February, but he steadily returned to form and it was noticeable that opposing teams were multiple-marking him as soon as he set off on his fast runs down the flank. He formed a close understanding with left back Danny Granville and played a key role as City secured the second automatic promotion spot, lifting the team with three match-winning long-range shots towards the end of the season. He was recognised by his fellow professionals with selection to the PFA award-winning First Division side. On the international front, Mark consolidated his place in the Republic of Ireland national team, winning seven more caps and contributing goals against Yugoslavia and Scotland. He scored an excellent goal from 30 yards out to clinch a 2-1 win against Yugoslavia.

Millwall (From trainee on 6/5/1992) FL 37+6/9 FLC 6+1/2 FAC 3+1/1
Liverpool (£1,500,000 on 21/3/1995) PL 5+11 FLC 0+2 FAC 0+1 Others 0+2
Queens Park R (Loaned on 27/1/1998) FL 8/2
Wimbledon (£1,750,000 on 27/3/1998) PL 11+10 FLC 4+1/1 FAC 2
Manchester C (£1,000,000 + on 15/7/1999) FL 41/8 FLC 4/2 FAC 2

Mark Kennedy

KENNEDY Peter Henry James
Born: Lurgan, 10 September 1973
Height: 5'9" Weight: 11.11
Club Honours: Div 2 '98
International Honours: NI: 6; B-1

The left-sided midfielder was one of several Watford players to suffer a frustrating season with injuries in 1999-2000. Having undergone a cartilage operation during the summer, Peter started the campaign confidently and had the distinction of scoring Watford's first goal in the Premiership – a penalty against Wimbledon on the opening day of the season. But a mysterious back injury ruled him out for four months from October, and a knee injury sustained against Tottenham in March further disrupted his season. Watford particularly missed the balance he brings to the left side of the team, and his prowess at set pieces. Nevertheless, Peter has now played more than 100 league games for the Hornets. Now a regular member of the Northern Ireland international squad, he added four caps last season.

Notts Co (£100,000 from Portadown on 28/8/1996) FL 20+2 FLC 1 FAC 2+1/1 Others 0+1
Watford (£130,000 on 10/7/1997) P/FL 97+1/18 FLC 9/2 FAC 6/2 Others 3

KENNEDY Richard Joseph
Born: Waterford, 28 August 1978
Height: 5'10" Weight: 10.12

An enthusiastic ball-winning midfield player who joined Brentford from Wycombe in the summer of 1999, Richard made his Football League debut as a substitute against Cardiff at the end of September. He then had the misfortune to be sent off for two bookable offences in his first start, ironically against Wycombe. Richard featured in a few more games in 1999-2000 and he will be looking to establish a regular presence in the Bees' first-team squad during the coming season.

Crystal Palace (From trainee on 29/3/1997)
Wycombe W (Free on 15/10/1998)
Brentford (Free on 14/7/1999) FL 4+5 Others 1

KENNY Patrick (Paddy) Joseph
Born: Halifax, 17 May 1978
Height: 6'1" Weight: 14.6

Following the departure of Dean Kiely to Charlton during the summer of 1999, Bury found themselves with 21-year-old Paddy, fresh from non-league football, as the only senior goalkeeper on their books. He was handed the number 13 shirt and expected to take a back seat as manager Neil Warnock looked to sign an experienced 'keeper. Such a signing never materialised, though; Paddy started the season in the first team and ended up being the Shakers' only ever-present player. He enjoyed a highly consistent first season in the Football League, pulled off a number of incredible saves and visibly matured as the season progressed. The supporters voted him "Player of the Season" and his form has reportedly been monitored by several other clubs.

Bury (£10,000 + from Bradford PA on 28/8/1998) FL 46 FLC 2 FAC 4 Others 1

KENTON Darren Edward
Born: Wandsworth, 13 September 1978
Height: 5'10" Weight: 11.11

A very versatile player who combines solid defensive techniques with great ability on the ball, especially when running at defenders, Darren made great strides at Norwich in 1999-2000 after a period when he was transfer-listed and his Carrow Road future looked uncertain. Having graduated through the Norwich youth system, he has always had great potential and after signing a new contract in December 1999 he seemed to become increasingly consistent. Darren can play anywhere across the defensive line and has, on occasion, also played in wide midfield roles. A very solid tackler, he possesses great pace to enable him to make challenges which would be beyond most defenders. His strength in the air enables him to play more centrally when required, while his natural attacking instincts were often demonstrated on some mazy runs down the flank. A very laid-back individual, he scored his second senior goal in the televised match at Grimsby.

Norwich C (From trainee on 3/7/1997) FL 52+7/2 FLC 5+1 FAC 0+1

KEOWN Martin Raymond
Born: Oxford, 24 July 1966
Height: 6'1" Weight: 12.4
Club Honours: PL '98; FAC '98; CS '98, '99
International Honours: E: 33; B-1; U21-8; Yth

A central defender of the highest quality, Martin is a crucial member of the Arsenal back four. When both are fully fit, he and Tony Adams are arguably the best pair of

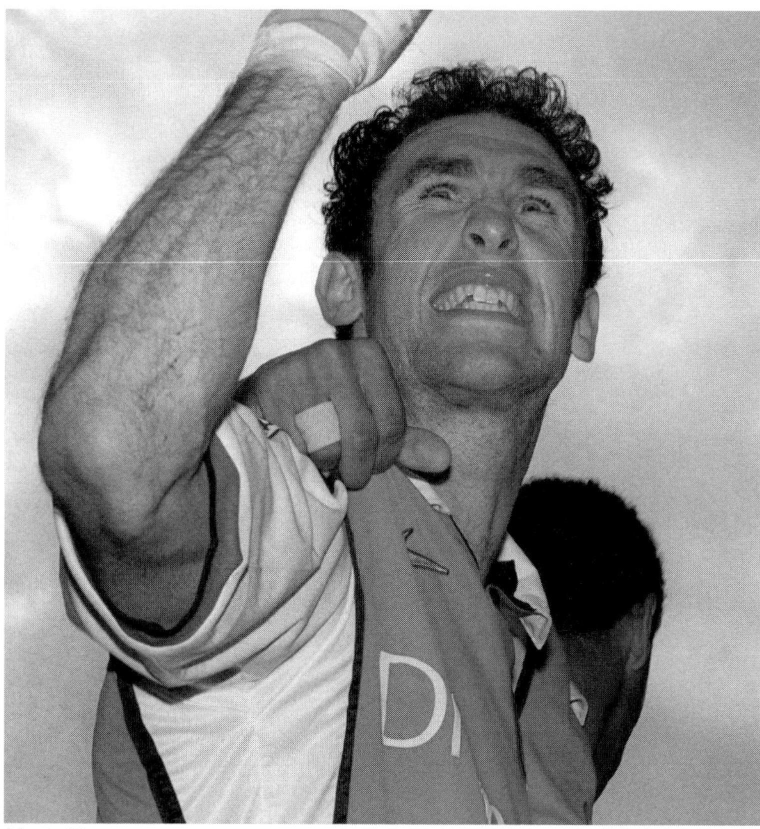
Martin Keown

central defenders in the country. Strong in the air and on the ground, Martin possesses exceptional speed for a big man. An aggressive tackler with good distribution skills, he is dangerous at set pieces, where his height and strength are always liable to create difficulties in the opposition goal-mouth. A calf injury caused him to miss a number of games during the middle of the 1999-2000 season, and shortly after returning to full fitness he broke a bone in his hand which sidelined him again. An automatic selection for the England international squad, he won a further ten caps and appeared in all three of his country's matches in Euro 2000.

Arsenal (From apprentice on 2/2/1984) FL 22 FAC 5
Brighton & Hove A (Loaned on 15/2/1985) FL 21+2/1 FLC 2/1 Others 2/1
Aston Villa (£200,000 on 9/6/1986) FL 109+3/3 FLC 12+1 FAC 6 Others 2
Everton (£750,000 on 7/8/1989) F/PL 92+4 FLC 11 FAC 12+1 Others 6
Arsenal (£2,000,000 on 4/2/1993) PL 208+18/4 FLC 16+2/1 FAC 21+2 Others 27+5/1

KERR David William
Born: Dumfries, 6 September 1974
Height: 5'11" Weight: 12.7

Although David was re-engaged by Mansfield last summer, his appearances were limited in 1999-2000 as he was used mainly as a squad player, never having a run in the side. He can play either in midfield or defence, where his strong running and tackling are an asset, and stayed relatively injury free after a double leg fracture nearly ended his career three seasons ago. In December he made what must have been one of the shortest substitute appearances in history when he walked on to the pitch against Bury in the Auto Windscreens Shield only to walk off again seconds later after Andy Roscoe scored the "golden goal". David was made available on a free transfer at the end of the season, although his contract still had a year to run.

Manchester C (From trainee on 10/9/1991) PL 4+2
Mansfield T (Loaned on 22/9/1995) FL 4+1 Others 1
Mansfield T (£20,000 on 31/7/1996) FL 56+24/4 FLC 2+1 FAC 0+1 Others 3+1

KERRIGAN Daniel (Danny) Anthony
Born: Basildon, 4 July 1982
Height: 5'7" Weight: 10.4

This young midfielder forced himself into the first-team reckoning at Southend during 1999-2000 with some excellent performances in the reserves, culminating in a call-up to the England U17 squad. Similar in style to Leeds's David Batty, Danny includes hard tackling and accurate passing in his armoury. He will be looking to establish a regular place in the Blues' line-up next season.

Southend U (Trainee) FL 0+4 FAC 0+1 Others 1

KERRIGAN Steven (Steve) John
Born: Baillieston, 9 October 1972
Height: 6'1" Weight: 12.4
Club Honours: S Div 2 '97

Strong in the air and possessing a good turn of pace, Steve was Shrewsbury's target man during the early stages of the 1999-2000 season. A knee ligament injury in November saw the popular striker miss 12 games. He has never been the most prolific of goalscorers and his 20 league starts brought only three goals, all by mid-October, although he bagged three more in the FA Cup. As he returned to fitness, he was transferred to Halifax just before deadline day, earning Shrewsbury a £20,000 fee. Steve made an immediate impression for the Shaymen with three quality goals, including a last-gasp winner against his previous club on Easter Monday. A worrying head injury sidelined him towards the end of the term. Thankfully, it was not as serious as at first feared. With a good pre-season behind him, Steve could be the answer to Halifax's goalscoring problems.

Albion Rov (Free from Newmains Juveniles on 22/7/1992) SL 46+7/14 SLC 2/1 SC 1 Others 1
Clydebank (Signed on 11/2/1994) SL 17+13 SLC 1+1 Others 2+1/2
Stranraer (Signed on 4/11/1995) SL 19+2/5 SC 1
Ayr U (Signed on 25/6/1996) SL 26+7/17 SLC 2/2 SC 1 Others 2/2
Shrewsbury T (£25,000 on 21/1/1998) FL 63+13/15 FLC 2+1 FAC 3/3
Halifax T (Signed on 23/3/2000) FL 7/3

KETSBAIA Temuri
Born: Georgia, 18 March 1968
Height: 6'0" Weight: 13.0
International Honours: Georgia: 34

This Georgian international is an exciting if unpredictable Newcastle striker who enjoys running at opposition defences from deep before unleashing his explosive finishing. Thus his preferred role is to play just behind the main strike force, but being a good professional he can be depended upon to always give wholehearted commitment whatever position he finds himself in, and last season he was used occasionally as a front-line striker, but more often as an additional front man brought on as a substitute. Temuri started in the first four games of the season, but then gave way to the returning Duncan Ferguson. He was recalled to the side on the latter's further injury, but damaged medial ligaments in the away game at Leeds which led to a month's lay-off. After a short run of four games, Duncan's return saw Temuri drop to the bench again for most of the remainder of the season, although frequently he was brought on in the later stages of matches to supplement the attack against tiring defences, and he did start in the season's last three games. He has now become the most used substitute in the club's history. It was reported that a firm transfer offer was made for him by an unnamed club just before the transfer deadline, but that Newcastle had turned this down. Temuri was capped three more times for Georgia, scoring goals in the friendly tournament games with Slovakia and Romania last February.

Newcastle U (Free from AEK Athens, Greece, via Dynamo Sukhumi, Dynamo Tbilisi and Anorthosis Famagusta, on 10/7/1997) PL 41+37/8 FLC 1+1 FAC 8+8/4 Others 7+6/2

KEWELL Harold (Harry)
Born: Sydney, Australia, 22 September 1978
Height: 6'0" Weight: 11.10
Club Honours: FAYC '97
International Honours: Australia: 9; Yth

Harry is the "Jewel in the Crown" at Leeds and was very unlucky not to have been named "Footballer of the Year" for last season. His performances playing as a left-sided midfielder or central striker were dazzling. Harry's got the full repertoire in his locker: he has wonderful balance and ball control and a left foot that is as powerful as it is nimble. He is always a potent threat. In 1999-2000 Harry began to convert his mesmeric ability into goals. Few who saw it will ever forget his long-range effort to defeat Roma in the UEFA Cup. The way he left Sol Campbell on his backside to swipe the ball into an empty net at Elland Road in February was equally memorable. Harry was a consistent thorn in the side of opposing defences, and as early as August he produced a marvellous performance at Old Trafford to run Manchester United ragged. This 21-year-old is already one of the most exciting players in the Premiership, combining pace, sublime control, heading ability and a ferocious shot. He has the ability to go on and become a world star, and received the honour of being named by his fellow professionals in last season's PFA award-winning side as well as winning the PFA "Young Player of the Year" award. Harry added another cap for Australia when he appeared in the friendly match with Hungary last February.

Leeds U (Signed from the Australian Academy of Sport on 23/12/1995) PL 100+6/21 FLC 6/3 FAC 12/5 Others 16/5

KIDD Ryan Andrew
Born: Radcliffe, 6 October 1971
Height: 6'0" Weight: 12.10
Club Honours: Div 3 '96, Div 2 '00

A summer operation to relieve a breathing problem was a precursor to Ryan's early season at Preston in 1999-2000, which saw him miss games through yet another ankle injury, illness and a broken hand at Christmas. All this meant that the versatile, long-serving left-sided defender was in and out of the starting line-up throughout the campaign before returning at left back at Burnley in March. Finally enjoying an injury-free spell, he showed his continuing development into a reliable, top-class player, confirming that he is strong in the air and a superb recovery defender, as demonstrated by his last-gasp tackle on ex-North Ender Kurt Nogan to preserve a point against Cardiff. He ended the campaign with a Second Division championship medal but will be hoping to avoid any repetition of the fitness problems that dogged him last season in 2000-01.

Port Vale (From trainee on 12/7/1990) FL 1 FLC 0+2 Others 0+1
Preston NE (Free on 15/7/1992) FL 223+15/9 FLC 16+2/1 FAC 17 Others 16+1/1

KIELY Dean Laurence
Born: Salford, 10 October 1970
Height: 6'1" Weight: 13.5
Club Honours: Div 2 '97; Div 1 '00
International Honours: E: Yth; Sch. RoI: 4; B-1

Signed by Charlton Athletic for £1 million in the close season from Bury, Dean was given the number one shirt for 1999-2000 and put in some fine performances early in the new campaign, cementing his place as first-choice 'keeper. A good shot stopper, he commands his area well and is generally comfortable with crosses. He kept 19 clean sheets, equalling a Charlton record and matching his achievement with Bury the previous season, and ended the season with a First Division championship medal. He also made his international debut for the Republic of Ireland against Turkey in November and went on to win three more caps before the end of the season.

Coventry C (From trainee on 30/10/1987)
York C (Signed on 9/3/1990) FL 210 FLC 9 FAC 4 Others 16
Bury (£125,000 on 15/8/1996) FL 137 FLC 13 FAC 4 Others 3
Charlton Ath (£1,000,000 on 26/5/1999) FL 45 FLC 2 FAC 4

KILBANE Kevin Daniel
Born: Preston, 1 February 1977
Height: 6'0" Weight: 12.10
International Honours: RoI: 15; U21-11

A tall, rangy left winger, the Republic of Ireland international was one of West Bromwich Albion's most impressive performers during the first half of the 1999-2000 season, scoring and making important goals. He was then signed by Sunderland in December for £2.5 million to fill the void left by contract rebel Allan Johnston, in turn leaving an enormous hole on Albion's left-hand side that was to remain gaping for the rest of the campaign. He made an immediate impact, too, appearing as a substitute at the Stadium of Light a week later against Southampton, instantly beating his full back and crossing for Kevin Phillips to score and secure a Sunderland victory. However, Kevin was not to taste victory again until March as the team embarked upon its most barren period of games without a win for 17 years, a run that saw the Irishman endure some totally unfair abuse from the stands. Although it is true that Kevin took time to settle and adapt to his new surroundings and the step up into the Premiership, he constantly showed a willingness to take defenders on and tackle back when necessary, never hiding when things were not going his or the team's way. A regular for his country, Kevin won a further ten caps during the season.

Preston NE (From trainee on 6/7/1995) FL 39+8/3 FLC 4 FAC 1 Others 1+1
West Bromwich A (£1,000,000 on 13/6/1997) FL 105+1/15 FLC 12/2 FAC 4/1
Sunderland (£2,500,000 on 16/12/1999) PL 17+3/1

KILFORD Ian Anthony
Born: Bristol, 6 October 1973
Height: 5'10" Weight: 11.0
Club Honours: Div 3 '97; AMC '99

Wigan's longest-serving player, Ian made his 150th start in Football League games in the Second Division play-off final against Gillingham at Wembley last May. A central midfielder, he was again asked to play in a variety of positions during 1999-2000. While he continued to demonstrate that he is a willing servant of the club, he found it hard to hold down a regular place, and a hernia operation forced him to miss a crucial part of the campaign. Ian was out of contract at the end of the season, but was offered a new deal.

Nottingham F (From trainee on 3/4/1991) FL 0+1
Wigan Ath (Loaned on 23/12/1993) FL 2+1/2 FAC 0+1
Wigan Ath (Free on 13/7/1994) FL 145+29/28 FLC 11+1 FAC 12+2/1 Others 13+2/2

KILGANNON Sean
Born: Stirling, 8 March 1981
Height: 5'11" Weight: 11.8

Sean beavered away in the Middlesbrough reserve and junior teams in 1999-2000, busily turning out good, solid performances and preparing himself for the regular first-team squad place which seems sure to be his in the near future. A strong-tackling, hard-running midfielder, he made his debut as a late substitute in the game against Newcastle in May, helping Boro hang on to a hard-earned point. The likeable young Scot is likely to figure more often during the coming season.

Middlesbrough (From trainee on 5/7/1999) PL 0+1

KILTY Mark Thomas
Born: Sunderland, 24 June 1981
Height: 5'11" Weight: 12.5

After making his debut in 1998-99, this promising Darlington trainee was limited to one substitute appearance against Torquay and one start against Brighton last season. However, his constant good form in midfield in the very successful reserve team marks him out as one destined to break through in the not-too-distant future.

Darlington (From trainee on 17/7/1999) FL 1+3

KIMBLE Alan Frank
Born: Dagenham, 6 August 1966
Height: 5'9" Weight: 12.4
Club Honours: Div 3 '91

Alan had another consistent season for Wimbledon in 1999-2000. One of the Dons' main set-piece specialists, he has a marvellous left foot and scored a cracking goal at Huddersfield in the Worthington Cup from 25 yards from a free kick, his first goal for the club. An experienced left back who uses the ball well and has a useful turn of speed, he is particularly effective when he is pushing forward, and featured regularly in the first team up until the beginning of April. Alan has a lively character, and is always ready with a cheeky grin or a wave for the camera. He plays in a similar fashion, with a smile on his face, but is wholehearted in his commitment to the cause.

Charlton Ath (From juniors on 8/8/1984) FL 6
Exeter C (Loaned on 23/8/1985) FL 1 FLC 1
Cambridge U (Free on 22/8/1986) FL 295+4/24 FLC 23+1 FAC 29/1 Others 22
Wimbledon (£175,000 on 27/7/1993) PL 168+13 FLC 20+3/1 FAC 23

KINET Christophe
Born: Huy, Belgium, 31 December 1972
Height: 5'8" Weight: 10.12
Christophe joined Millwall last February from French side Racing Strasbourg in a £75,000 deal and made his debut as a substitute against Bournemouth. A winger by trade, he is clever, very tricky and, although small of stature, surprisingly strong. As well as being brought off the bench in two more matches he made several reserve appearances before suffering an injury which sidelined him for the rest of the season. He will be anxious for an early opportunity to prove his worth in 2000-01.
Millwall (£75,000 from Racing Strasbourg, France on 9/2/2000) FL 0+3 Others 0+2

KING Ledley Brenton
Born: Stepney, 12 October 1980
Height: 6'2" Weight: 13.6
International Honours: E: U21-4; Yth
This athletic youngster made his first-team debut for Tottenham in October 1999 against Derby County and followed it up with an appearance in the 3-1 defeat at Manchester United in May, showing a calmness and poise similar to that of Tottenham captain Sol Campbell. Terrific aerial ability coupled with a no-nonsense commitment in the challenge made Ledley an instant hit at White Hart Lane and he promises to develop into a strong defender as his experience grows. Having made his debut for England U21s against Luxembourg last September, he went on to appear in all three of his country's games in the European Championship finals in Slovakia.
Tottenham H (From trainee on 22/7/1998) PL 2+2

KING Marlon Francis
Born: Dulwich, 26 April 1980
Height: 6'1" Weight: 11.12
With his prodigious pace, undoubted skill and razor-sharp finishing, Marlon was expected to make a major contribution to the Barnet team in 1999-2000 and, on occasion, he provided the Bees' fans with doses of pure adrenalin. The season heralded further glory for Marlon but he found his first-team outings somewhat sporadic because of the fruitful partnership of Ken Charlery and Scott McGleish in the opening months of the campaign. Marlon is consumed by a raw desire to reach the upper echelons of the league as soon as possible, and it was a frustrating time for the youngster, but when his opportunity arrived he took it gratefully. When an injury ruled McGleish out of contention in late November, Marlon responded gloriously, netting four goals in five days as Barnet swept aside both Carlisle and Peterborough. The consensus was that he was set to re-establish his first-team niche, but that proved not to be the case. In the latter stages of the season, he weighed in with some important goals to boost Barnet's flagging bid for promotion, with a brace at Halifax, but his only contribution in the play-offs was as a second-half substitute at Peterborough. Stop Press: Marlon was reported to have joined Gillingham during the summer for a £250,000 fee.
Barnet (From trainee on 9/9/1998) FL 36+17/14 FLC 0+2 FAC 0+1 Others 2+2

KING Stuart Samuel David
Born: Derry, 20 March 1981
Height: 5'10" Weight: 10.4
International Honours: NI: Yth
A young left-footed winger able to play on either flank, relying on pace and trickery to beat his man, Stuart failed to make as much progress as he would have liked with Preston in 1999-2000, making just one appearance in the first team, as a late substitute in the Auto Windscreens Shield game against Wrexham in December. The coming season will be an important one in the Northern Ireland youth international's development.
Preston NE (From trainee on 18/5/1998) Others 0+2

Georgi Kinkladze

KINKLADZE Georgiou (Georgi)
Born: Tbilisi, Georgia, 6 November 1973
Height: 5'8" Weight: 11.2
International Honours: Georgia: 35
Georgi was initially brought to Derby last November on loan from Ajax, where he had found himself out of favour, and Jim Smith's gamble on the unpredictable dribbling skills of the Georgian international in a bid to salvage a disappointing season undoubtedly paid off. The Pride Park fans immediately took to the player who, after regaining his match fitness, became a regular in the first team, playing a roving role behind the two strikers. He got off the mark with a splendid goal against Wimbledon, and all at Derby were delighted when, in April, he signed a three-year contract, an undisclosed transfer fee being paid to Ajax. He was deservedly recalled to the Georgian national team last March and responded with a goal in the 1-1 draw with Israel.
Manchester C (£2,000,000 from Dinamo Tbilisi, Georgia on 17/8/1995) P/FL 105+1/20 FLC 6 FAC 9/2 (£5,000,000 to Ajax, Holland on 15/5/1998)
Derby Co (Signed on 26/11/1999) PL 12+5/1 FAC 1

KINSELLA Mark Anthony
Born: Dublin, 12 August 1972
Height: 5'9" Weight: 11.8
Club Honours: GMVC '92; FAT '92; Div 1 '00
International Honours: RoI: 16; B-1; U21-8; Yth
An inspirational captain and immensely talented right-sided midfield player, Mark led Charlton to the First Division championship in 1999-2000 and also earned a place in the PFA award-winning First Division side. He controls the Charlton midfield and, along with Graham Stuart, generates the majority of the team's attacking moves from the middle of the pitch. Extremely comfortable on the ball, he is prepared to hit a 40-yard pass to change the direction of play when appropriate. Mark is also capable of scoring spectacular goals from long range, and is the club's free-kick specialist. He found the net on three occasions during the season, scoring twice in the televised 4-2 win at Walsall. A regular member of the Republic of Ireland team, he won seven more caps last season.
Colchester U (Free from Home Farm on 18/8/1989) FL 174+6/27 FLC 11/3 FAC 11/1 Others 9+1/5
Charlton Ath (£150,000 on 23/9/1996) P/FL 159/17 FLC 3+2 FAC 8+1/3 Others 3

KIPPE Frode
Born: Oslo, Norway, 17 January 1978
Height: 6'4" Weight: 13.10
Club Honours: AMC '00
International Honours: Norway: U21
A talented young Norwegian defender signed from Lillestrom in January 1999 for a substantial fee, Frode made his belated debut for Liverpool as a substitute in the second leg of the Worthington Cup tie against Hull at Anfield last September. He replaced Vladimir Smicer on the right side of midfield, and acquitted himself well in the 25 minutes he was on the pitch. It was to be his only appearance of the season for the Reds but in December he joined Stoke on a three-month loan. Originally brought to the club to replace the suspended Anders Jacobsen, he played consistently well and held his place throughout the period. Frode scored a wonder goal against Preston in a Sky-televised game and there was great disappointment that he returned to Anfield and missed the Wembley appearance in the final of the Auto Windscreens Shield he had played such a part in earning. He became a real favourite at the Britannia Stadium and the Stoke fans would love to see more of him.
Liverpool (£700,000 from Lillestrom, Norway on 7/1/1999) FLC 0+1
Stoke C (Loaned on 24/12/1999) FL 15/1 Others 5

KIRKLAND Christopher (Chris)
Born: Leicester, 2 May 1981
Height: 6'3" Weight: 11.7
International Honours: E: Yth

A young goalkeeper who starred for Coventry's successful youth side in 1998-99, Chris received an unexpected call-up to first-team duty last September when injuries to Magnus Hedman and Steve Ogrizovic meant he started the home leg of the Worthington Cup tie against Tranmere. He performed well and was also on the bench on a number of occasions during the season. Already capped by England at U16 level, he won his first U18 cap against France last March.

Coventry C (From trainee on 6/5/1998) FLC 1

KITSON Paul
Born: Murton, 9 January 1971
Height: 5'11" Weight: 10.12
International Honours: E: U21-7

This experienced West Ham striker had a frustrating time in 1999-2000 due to the form of the club's two main front men, Paulo Wanchope and Paolo di Canio. After appearing regularly in the pre-season Inter Toto games, he made just a handful of appearances in the first half of the season, coming on from the subs' bench or covering for short-term injuries. He then damaged his back, which put him out of action for some six weeks, and on returning to fitness he moved to runaway First Division leaders Charlton on loan just before the transfer deadline in March, the Addicks aiming to bolster their attack and find a goalscoring partner for Andy Hunt. Paul scored in his second game as a substitute when he hit the winner at Selhurst Park against Crystal Palace. He holds the ball up well, has good pace and an excellent workrate, but he featured in only six games due to persistent injuries, starting just twice. He will be looking for regular first-team football in 2000-01.

Leicester C (From trainee on 15/12/1988) FL 39+11/6 FLC 5/3 FAC 1+1/1 Others 5/1
Derby Co (£1,300,000 on 11/3/1992) FL 105/36 FLC 7/3 FAC 5/1 Others 13+1/9
Newcastle U (£2,250,000 on 24/9/1994) PL 26+10/10 FLC 3+2/1 FAC 6+1/3 Others 0+1
West Ham U (£2,300,000 on 10/2/1997) PL 43+11/15 FLC 2+3/1 FAC 2+1/1 Others 1+3/1
Charlton Ath (Loaned on 21/3/2000) FL 2+4/1

KIWOMYA Christopher (Chris) Mark
Born: Huddersfield, 2 December 1969
Height: 5'9" Weight: 11.2
Club Honours: Div 2 '92

Chris was a regular in the Queens Park Rangers first team last season, missing only one league game in the entire campaign, and ended the season as the club's joint top scorer with 14 goals. He formed a good understanding with striking partner Rob Steiner in the first half of the season, and following Steiner's injury he found success with a number of different partners up front. Chris played mostly on the left side of the front line, but was just as effective operating in a more central role when required.

Ipswich T (From trainee on 31/3/1987) F/PL 197+28/51 FLC 14+1/8 FAC 14/2 Others 5+1/3
Arsenal (£1,500,000 on 13/1/1995) PL 5+9/3 Others 1+2 (Free to Selangar, Malaysia on 21/8/1997)
Queens Park R (Free on 28/8/1998) FL 54+6/19 FLC 2+1 FAC 2+1/1

Chris Kiwomya

KNIGHT Alan Edward
Born: Balham, 3 July 1961
Height: 6'1" Weight: 13.11
Club Honours: Div 3 '83
International Honours: E: U21-2; Yth

Although he was employed by Portsmouth primarily as a goalkeeping coach, the club retained Alan's registration in 1999-2000 and he added three more appearances to his total during the season, twice being called upon as a substitute and making the starting line-up at Norwich in January. When he came on from the subs' bench at Blackburn in the Worthington Cup tie last September, he reached the landmark total of 800 senior games for Pompey. Alan is a legendary figure at Fratton Park and even though he is now in his late thirties he remains an excellent shot stopper and capable of fine reflex saves. His record of more than 20 years' service with the club is almost unique in modern times and his is the highest total of appearances by a goalkeeper for a single club in the domestic game.

Portsmouth (From apprentice on 12/3/1979) FL 683 FLC 51+3 FAC 43 Others 21

KNIGHT Richard
Born: Burton, 3 August 1979
Height: 6'1" Weight: 14.0
International Honours: E: Yth

This talented young Derby County goalkeeper spent the first two months of the 1999-2000 season on loan at Birmingham City, where he was covering for an injury to Ian Bennett. Although mostly sitting on the bench or playing for the reserves during his spell at St Andrews, he had one senior outing when he came on as a substitute for the final 16 minutes of the Worthington Cup game at Exeter. In October he was loaned to Hull to help out while Lee Bracey was suspended and Steve Wilson was injured but the goalkeeping jinx that afflicted the Tigers in 1999-2000 struck again and he became a one-game wonder, Derby recalling him when Mart Poom and Andy Oakes were sidelined. A couple of months later he joined Macclesfield on loan at deadline time on a Friday evening when Lee Martin was unable to play because of a back injury, a situation which presented the club with a sudden crisis since their other 'keeper, Ryan Price, had just moved to non-league Telford United. Richard was included in the side for the game at Northampton the next day and was only introduced to his team-mates at the pre-match meal. Although he conceded a couple of goals, he acquitted himself well, as he did in his other two matches for the club. He then had the first of two highly impressive spells at Oxford. During the first Richard made only two appearances, one of them as a substitute, but he returned shortly afterwards to play the last 11 games of the season, keeping out both regular 'keepers. He made many marvellous saves, showing the maturity of a much older player, and created a very favourable impression. He was out of contract at Derby in the summer and was not expected to remain at Pride Park. Stop Press: It was reported in June that Richard had signed a three-year contract with Oxford.

Derby Co (Signed from Burton A on 25/6/1997)
Carlisle U (Loaned on 26/3/1999) FL 6
Birmingham C (Loaned on 4/8/1999) FLC 0+1
Hull C (Loaned on 7/10/1999) FL 1
Macclesfield T (Loaned on 3/12/1999) FL 3
Oxford U (Loaned on 19/1/2000) FL 1+1
Oxford U (Loaned on 13/3/2000) FL 11

KNIGHT Zatyiah (Zat)
Born: Solihull, 2 May 1980
Height: 6'6" Weight: 13.8

The tall full back or midfielder joined Peterborough on loan from Fulham last February, only a week after playing on behalf of the Cottagers against the Posh reserve team. An extremely skilful player with good close control, Zat made a valuable contribution as United qualified for a Third Division play-off place.

Fulham (Signed from Evesham U on 19/2/1999)
Peterborough U (Loaned on 25/2/2000) FL 8

KNOWLES Darren Thomas
Born: Sheffield, 8 October 1970
Height: 5'6" Weight: 11.6

Darren began the 1999-2000 season on a high by making his 100th consecutive league appearance for Hartlepool. He was soon brought back down to earth when he was dropped from the side for the first time at the end of August. A great battler, the popular right back was soon back, and it was typical of him that later in the season he turned out more than once when not fully recovered from injury. At the end of the season, he was the first Pool player to be re-signed for 2000-01.

Sheffield U (From trainee on 1/7/1989)
Stockport Co (£3,000 on 14/9/1989) FL 51+12 FLC 2+4 Others 14+1

Scarborough (Free on 4/8/1993) FL 139+5/2 FLC 11+1 FAC 9 Others 7
Hartlepool U (Free on 27/3/1997) FL 142+1/1 FLC 6 FAC 5 Others 8

KOEJOE Samuel (Sammy)
Born: Paramaribo, Surinam, 17 August 1974
Height: 6'1" Weight: 12.2

Sammy, a Dutch national, joined Queens Park Rangers in a £250,000 transfer from Salzburg of Austria in November 1999. Signed as cover for the strikers, he made only six starts, scoring his first goal for the club in the Easter win over Ipswich. Sammy has a bustling style of play and his pace makes him one to watch for in the future when he has adapted to the English game.
Queens Park R (£250,000 from Salzburg, Austria on 29/11/1999) FL 5+6/1 FAC 1+1

KONCHESKY Paul Martyn
Born: Barking, 15 May 1981
Height: 5'10" Weight: 10.12
International Honours: E: Yth

A very exciting prospect, Charlton Athletic's youngest-ever debutant is extremely self-assured and comfortable on the ball, which he uses well when moving out of defence, often linking with John Robinson on the left side of midfield. He possesses a powerful shot but has yet to score a goal at senior level. Paul, who can also play in midfield, started only six league games, all at left back, last season due to the consistency of Chris Powell but, when called upon, slotted into the side with ease. A regular in the England youth set-up, he won five caps at U18 level last season.
Charlton Ath (From trainee on 25/5/1998) P/FL 9+4 FLC 3 FAC 0+1

KONJIC Muhamed
Born: Bosnia, 14 May 1970
Height: 6'4" Weight: 13.7
International Honours: Bosnia-Herzegovina: 19

Muhamed is the captain of Bosnia, and was the first Bosnian to play in the Premiership, but he had a miserable time at Coventry last season. The former Monaco defender won a first-team place after the debacle in the Worthington Cup at Tranmere and played four successive games before he suffered a knee injury. When he was fit he was unable to break into the first team because of the form of Gary Breen and Paul Williams, and then in December he fractured a cheekbone in a training ground collision with Noel Whelan. Muhamed – or "Big Mo", as he is known – sat on the bench for 14 games but was called upon only twice. The purchase of Colin Hendry will have left this tough and uncompromising defender wondering what he has to do to get a game. When fit, he remained a first choice for Bosnia-Herzegovina.
Coventry C (£2,000,000 from AS Monaco, France, via Slobada Tuzla, Croatia Belisce, Croatia Zagreb and FC Zurich, on 5/2/1999) PL 6+2 FLC 1+1

KOOGI Anders Bo
Born: Denmark, 8 September 1979
Height: 5'10" Weight: 11.1
International Honours: Denmark: Yth

The Danish youth international enhanced his cosmopolitan tag when he was subject to a bid from a Sicilian-based Italian Third Division side in July 1999. Although he opted to stay at Peterborough, Andre's only 1999-2000 Posh appearance came as a sub at Plymouth in August before he went on loan to Cambridge City in February. The classy midfielder had trials at Ipswich and Southend before being released by Peterborough in May.
Peterborough U (From trainee on 21/7/1997) FL 0+2

KORSTEN Willem
Born: Boxtell, Holland, 21 January 1975
Height: 6'3" Weight: 12.10
International Honours: Holland: U21

A tall left-sided midfielder who can also be used in attack, Willem joined Tottenham from Vitesse Arnhem during the 1999 close season, having turned down a permanent move to Leeds, where he had spent three months on loan in 1998-99. He did not make his Spurs debut until the home game against Sheffield Wednesday in January because of persistent injury problems, and there were suggestions even then that he was not fully match fit after he struggled to impress. Willem made sporadic appearances during the remainder of the season and sometimes found the frustration of the Tottenham fans directed at him. There is no doubting the abilities of this strong and skilful Dutchman, who has great pace for one so tall and is also surprisingly agile. Willem will be hoping for an injury-free season in 2000-01 to allow him to stake his claim for a regular first-team spot.
Leeds U (Loaned from Vitesse Arnhem, Holland, via NEC Nijmegen, on 11/1/1999) PL 4+3/2 FAC 2+1
Tottenham H (£1,500,000 on 9/7/1999) PL 4+5

KOUMAS Jason
Born: Wrexham, 25 September 1979
Height: 5'10" Weight: 11.0

This confident Tranmere youngster appeared to be fitter and stronger in 1999-2000. He made the Rovers starting line-up for the first few games of the campaign but then missed several matches through injury, and when he recovered fitness he was generally used from the subs' bench. He scored two goals during the season, including one from a great 20-yard free kick in the 2-1 victory over Birmingham last March. A hard-running creative midfield player, he demonstrates good all-round skills in dribbling, passing and shooting. He continues to attract an array of scouts from Premiership clubs to Prenton Park, but for the moment seems content to develop his career with Rovers.
Tranmere Rov (From trainee on 27/11/1997) FL 20+26/5 FLC 5+4/1 FAC 1

KOZLUK Robert (Rob)
Born: Mansfield, 5 August 1977
Height: 5'8" Weight: 11.7
International Honours: E: U21-2

The fair-haired right wing back generally had a good first full season with Sheffield United in 1999-2000 but there were ups and downs. After a few indifferent displays early in the campaign he suffered a loss of confidence, missing a few games as a result, but after Neil Warnock's arrival his performances improved. He is quick, generally showing good anticipation and at times some real skill, while his attacking play and crosses regularly set up chances for the forwards and his long throw into the penalty area was frequently used as an attacking ploy. However, he is susceptible to occasional lapses of concentration or judgement. A troubled performance against Birmingham City in March, including an own goal, resulted in his temporary replacement by new signing Andy Woodward, but he regained his place and produced some confident displays in the final five games of the season.
Derby Co (From trainee on 10/2/1996) PL 9+7 FLC 3 FAC 2+1
Sheffield U (Signed on 12/3/1999) FL 46+3 FLC 2 FAC 2

KRIZAN Ales
Born: Slovenia, 25 July 1971
Height: 5'9" Weight: 12.12
International Honours: Slovenia: 25

Ales had a disappointing time at Barnsley in 1999-2000, featuring in the first team on only one occasion, for the Worthington Cup tie at Tranmere at the end of November. He is a talented left-sided defender who reads the game well and has a powerful long throw. His contract was eventually cancelled by mutual agreement in February.
Barnsley (£400,000 from Maribor Branik, Slovenia on 30/7/1997) P/FL 13 FLC 5 FAC 1

KULCSAR George
Born: Budapest, Hungary, 12 August 1967
Height: 6'2" Weight: 13.4
International Honours: Australia: 3

George was at the centre of a meningitis scare at Queens Park Rangers last September. Happily, he made a complete recovery and was able to regain a first-team spot two months later, although he was unable to command a regular place in the side due to the number of other central midfield players at the club. Not noted for his goalscoring, George is a strong ball winner who never stops running.
Bradford C (£100,000 from Royal Antwerp, Belgium on 7/3/1997) FL 23+3/1
Queens Park R (£250,000 on 17/12/1997) FL 33+9/1 FLC 0+2 FAC 1

KYD Michael Robert
Born: Hackney, 21 May 1977
Height: 5'8" Weight: 12.10

With two injury-blighted seasons behind him, 1999-2000 was always going to be a difficult season for this lightning-quick Cambridge forward. Sadly, Michael suffered another knee injury in the latter part of the campaign which may force him to retire from the game. When he did play, there were glimpses of the skill that he showed in his early days at United and, with three goals during the season, he showed that he had not lost his scoring touch. He was released at the end of the season.
Cambridge U (From trainee on 18/5/1995) FL 88+36/23 FLC 7+2/1 FAC 7+2/1 Others 4+2

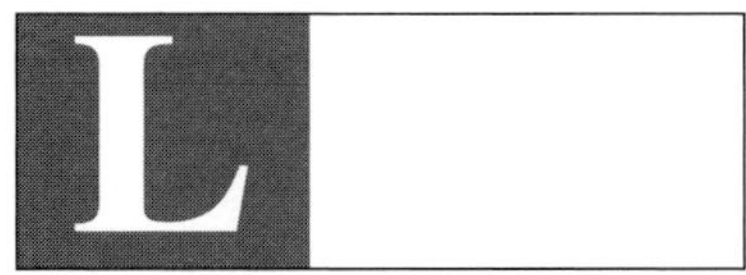

LACEY Damian James
Born: Bridgend, 3 August 1977
Height: 5'9" Weight: 11.3
Club Honours: Div 3 '00

Damian re-established himself in the Swansea side in 1999-2000, having his longest run in the first team since making his debut for the Swans at the start of the 1996-97 season. While he is renowned for his tackling ability and workrate in midfield, an improvement in his passing also caught the eye last season. Unfortunately, a stress fracture in his foot in February saw him sidelined and, following swelling in his ankle, he was ruled out for the rest of the season. Happily, Damian had done enough to earn a Third Division championship winners' medal.

Swansea C (From trainee on 1/7/1996) FL 46+14/1 FLC 3 FAC 2+1 Others 2

LAIRD Kamu
Born: Port of Spain, Trinidad, 23 December 1975
Height: 5'8" Weight: 11.6

Kamu began the 1999-2000 campaign playing for Ryman League club Dulwich Hamlet and joined Chester last December along with his fellow countryman Angus Eve. A neat player with some skilful touches, he scored on his City debut against Halifax but after only a handful more first-team outings he returned to Dulwich in February. A former student at Augusta State University, he has a degree in fine arts.

Chester C (Signed from Dulwich Hamlet on 17/12/1999) FL 2+1/1

LAMBERT Christopher **James (Jamie)**
Born: Henley, 14 September 1973
Height: 5'7" Weight: 11.2

A player who, at his best, shows exciting dribbling skills, creative flair and an ability to score goals, Jamie came to Oxford as a free agent in August 1999 after his release by Reading the previous season and spent some time trying to gain a permanent deal after being signed on non-contract forms. Although not match fit, he impressed, making ten starts, some as a striker and some wide in midfield, with another six appearances as a substitute, scoring twice, but despite this he was not taken on. With money at the Manor Ground very tight, Jamie moved on and later had a trial with Port Vale.

Reading (From juniors on 3/7/1992) FL 77+48/16 FLC 8+3/2 FAC 9+2/1 Others 2+3/1
Walsall (Loaned on 16/10/1998) FL 4+2
Oxford U (Free on 27/8/1999) FL 8+5/2 FAC 2+1

LAMBERT Rickie Lee
Born: Liverpool, 16 February 1982
Height: 6'2" Weight: 12.1

Rickie is a promising young Blackpool YTS player who featured in the club's pre-season games and was given a surprise league debut as a late substitute at Wrexham on the opening day of the 1999-2000 campaign. A central midfield player who featured mostly in the reserve and junior teams, he made two further appearances from the subs' bench during the season.

Blackpool (Trainee) FL 0+3

LAMBOURDE Bernard
Born: Guadaloupe, 11 May 1971
Height: 6'1" Weight: 12.4
Club Honours: FLC '98

A very underrated member of Chelsea's star-studded squad, Bernard demonstrated his value to the Blues in his first start of the 1999-2000 season at Middlesbrough in September. Replacing the injured Albert Ferrer in the unfamiliar right-back position, he stole upfield to score his first Premiership goal and Chelsea's first-ever at the Riverside Stadium. This clinched victory in one of the Blues' hoodoo fixtures, for it was their first away win at Middlesbrough for 68 years! In complete contrast, Bernard's only other goal of the season came at Chelsea's happy hunting ground, Tottenham. He reacted intelligently to Dennis Wise's quickly taken free kick to notch the only goal of the game and extend the Blues' unbeaten record at White Hart Lane to ten years. An enormously versatile defender, Bernard looks most comfortable in central defence, but always performed reliably when asked to deputise for the regular incumbents on either flank at full back. The competition for places in the middle of the Chelsea back four is particularly fierce with recent acquisitions Emerson Thome, Jes Hogh and Mario Melchiot plus the rapidly maturing John Terry all hoping to grab a regular first-team spot and interrupt the Frank Leboeuf–Marcel Desailly partnership, and Bernard certainly has a tough battle on his hands to jump the queue and play week in, week out.

Chelsea (£1,600,000 from Bordeaux, France, via Cannes, on 10/7/1997) PL 29+10/2 FLC 6+1 FAC 5 Others 3+5/1

LAMEY Nathan James
Born: Leeds, 14 October 1980
Height: 5'8" Weight: 13.0

This young forward joined Cambridge from Wolverhampton Wanderers at the start of the 1999-2000 season, but when he made his first-team debut in March he appeared to have difficulty adjusting to the pace of the Second Division. An extended run in the reserves should help him build up the fitness levels required for senior football. A pacy and exciting striker, Nathan also turned out for the youth team.

Wolverhampton W (From trainee on 25/10/1997)
Cambridge U (Free on 10/8/1999) FL 2+1

LAMPARD Frank James
Born: Romford, 20 June 1978
Height: 6'0" Weight: 12.6
International Honours: E: 1; B-1; U21-18; Yth

Frank had another good season at West Ham in 1999-2000, when he again showed that he seems destined for a lengthy career in top-flight football. This hard-working midfield player never shirks a challenge, has good vision, great passing skills and an eye for goal. He netted 14 times in all games during the season, including a cracking 25-yarder against Heerenveen in a pre-season Inter Toto match and a great header at Wimbledon on Boxing Day. He captained England U21s in the European Championship finals in Slovakia, adding a further six caps during the season, and made his full international debut against Belgium last October.

West Ham U (From trainee on 1/7/1995) PL 102+16/16 FLC 12+1/8 FAC 9/1 Others 6/2
Swansea C (Loaned on 6/10/1995) FL 8+1/1 Others 1+1

Frank Lampard

LANCASHIRE Graham
Born: Blackpool, 19 October 1972
Height: 5'10" Weight: 11.12
Club Honours: Div 4 '92, Div 3 '97

Graham had another stop-start season in 1999-2000. He began with two goals in the first four games as Rochdale went to the top of Division Three. The potent striker was injured in the game against Halifax in September, which prompted a Dale goal drought. He eventually returned in January and netted in his first full game back. "Lanky" added seven more in eight games in tandem with Tony Ellis to shoot Dale back into the play-off picture. A training injury ruled him out for another six games at a vital stage, though. Out of contract in May, Graham was offered new terms.

Burnley (From trainee on 1/7/1991) FL 11+20/8 FLC 1+1 FAC 2+2/1 Others 2+4
Halifax T (Loaned on 20/11/1992) FL 2 Others 1+1
Chester C (Loaned on 21/1/1994) FL 10+1/7
Preston NE (£55,000 on 23/12/1994) FL 11+12/2 Others 1+1
Wigan Ath (£35,000 on 12/1/1996) FL 20+10/12 FLC 2+1/4
Rochdale (£40,000 on 2/10/1997) FL 48+19/20 FLC 3+1/1 Others 3+2/1

LANCASTER Martyn Neil
Born: Wigan, 10 November 1980
Height: 6'0" Weight: 12.7

The young Chester defender continued to make good progress, despite the traumatic events at the Deva in 1999-2000. A product of the club's youth system, Martyn is a hard-working player who looks comfortable on the ball. He has already caught the attention of a number of scouts, so it seems likely that he will make a return to the league ranks.

Chester C (From trainee on 23/1/1999) FL 22+6 FLC 3 FAC 1+2 Others 1+1

LANGLEY Richard Barrington Michael
Born: Harlesden, 27 December 1979
Height: 5'10" Weight: 11.4
International Honours: E: Yth

A central midfielder, Richard has been one of the recent successes of the Queens Park Rangers youth academy. After making a full recovery from a serious leg injury that kept him out for four months in 1998-99, he established himself as a regular last season, missing only a handful of games. Though not a prolific goalscorer, he did manage four goals in 1999-2000 and was voted "Young Player of the Year" by members of the supporters' club.

Queens Park R (From trainee on 31/12/1996) FL 43+6/4 FLC 2/1 FAC 3

LARKIN Colin
Born: Dundalk, Ireland, 27 April 1982
Height: 5'9" Weight: 10.4
International Honours: RoI: Yth

Although this pacy Wolves striker was not yet 17 and a half, a shortage of players in his position meant he was given an unexpectedly early first-team chance last season. He came on as a substitute at home to Wycombe in the Worthington Cup, and within four minutes had scored with a well-struck volley. However, a few days later at home to Walsall he was in from the start and his inexperience was clearly seen. He spent much of the season continuing his development in the youth team, with occasional reserve appearances. Colin made three appearances for the Republic of Ireland U17s in a tournament in Slovakia last May, scoring in a 1-1 draw with Turkey.

Wolverhampton W (From trainee on 19/5/1999) FL 1 FLC 0+1/1

LARUSSON Bjarnolfur (Bjarne)
Born: Iceland, 11 March 1976
Height: 5'11" Weight: 12.8

This skilful midfielder did not make the same impact with Walsall in Division One in 1999-2000 as he had in his first season with the club in Division Two, and after being in and out of the side during the first half of the campaign he made only occasional substitute appearances in the second half. He did, however, score a stunning 30-yard goal at Gillingham in December to take the third-round FA Cup replay into extra time. Bjarne was released on a free transfer at the end of the season.

Hibernian (Signed from IB Vestmannaeyar, Iceland on 17/10/1997) SL 3+4/1
Walsall (Free on 25/9/1998) FL 45+14/3 FLC 0+1 FAC 4/1 Others 6/1

LAUNDERS Brian Terence
Born: Dublin, 8 January 1976
Height: 5'10" Weight: 11.12
International Honours: RoI: U21-9; Yth

Signed by Colchester manager Mick Wadsworth in the summer of 1999 after a period on loan the previous season, this attacking midfielder played in the first eight games of the new campaign but then dropped out with injury. Mystery surrounds subsequent events as the player was sacked for alleged "serious misconduct" and he left the club in less than ideal circumstances, although both a tribunal and subsequent appeal upheld United's decision. Brian returned briefly to his first club, Crystal Palace, in October and featured in two games for the Eagles before moving on to Sheffield United. Signed by Adrian Heath, initially on a temporary basis to allow his immediate availability, he came on as a half-time substitute at Stockport County. An injury after 11 minutes resulted in his substitution, and Heath's resignation three days later meant that Brian's possible permanent signing never materialised. Thus ended one of the shortest-ever Sheffield United careers.

Crystal Palace (Signed from Cherry Orchard on 2/9/1993) P/FL 1+3 FLC 0+2
Crewe Alex (Free on 8/8/1996) FL 6+3 FLC 1+1 (Free to BV Veendam, Holland during 1997 close season)
Derby Co (Loaned on 11/9/1998) PL 0+1
Colchester U (Loaned on 25/3/1999) FL 1
Colchester U (Free on 19/7/1999) FL 6 FLC 2
Crystal Palace (Free on 29/10/1999) FL 1+1
Sheffield U (Free on 19/11/1999) FL 0+1

Jacob Laursen

LAURSEN Jacob
Born: Vejle, Denmark, 6 October 1971
Height: 5'11" Weight: 12.0
International Honours: Denmark: 25

Derby's Danish international central defender had yet another impressive season at Pride Park in 1999-2000, when he was an automatic selection on the right side of a three-man centre-back formation, though he can also play in a wider position when required. His is an underrated role and he excels when asked to do a man-to-man marking job. Jacob has a tendency to play the ball long out of defence, bypassing midfield. He was replaced last season as team captain by Darryl Powell, and announced his retirement from international football towards the end of the campaign.

Derby Co (£500,000 from Silkeborg, Denmark on 17/7/1996) PL 135+2/3 FLC 9 FAC 7

LAVIN Gerard
Born: Corby, 5 February 1974
Height: 5'10" Weight: 11.0
International Honours: S: U21-7

Released by Millwall during the summer of 1999, Gerard signed for Bristol City but his career with the club could not have got off to a worse start, as he was given a red card in the opening game of the new season at Reading. On his return from suspension he produced some excellent displays at right back, showing good positional sense and the ability to go past defenders. It was somewhat of a surprise, therefore, that he was unable to retain his place in the City side after the turn of the year.

Watford (From trainee on 11/5/1992) FL 121+5/2 FLC 11/1 FAC 6 Others 2+1
Millwall (£500,000 on 23/11/1995) FL 67+7 FLC 2 FAC 3+1 Others 8/1
Bristol C (Free on 6/8/1999) FL 18+1 FLC 1 FAC 2 Others 1

LAWRENCE James (Jamie) Hubert
Born: Balham, 8 March 1970
Height: 5'11" Weight: 12.11
Club Honours: FLC '97

Jamie spent the early part of 1999-2000 on the injury list at Bradford City with a thigh problem and he then had to undergo a double hernia operation. He was back playing for the reserves within five weeks of surgery and showed some of the best form of his career over the next few months. Although easily recognised by his liking for different hair colourings, he is also a quality footballer who operated both as a full back and in midfield. Always consistent, he has the ability to run at the opposition at speed and is ferocious in the tackle. His season ended early after he fractured his jaw in a training accident last March and he had to have an operation.

Sunderland (Signed from Cowes on 15/10/1993) FL 2+2 FLC 0+1
Doncaster Rov (£20,000 on 17/3/1994) FL 16+9/3 FLC 2 FAC 1 Others 3
Leicester C (£125,000 on 6/1/1995) P/FL 21+26/1 FLC 3+4/2 FAC 1+1
Bradford C (£50,000 on 17/6/1997) P/FL 90+11/8 FLC 4+1 FAC 4+1/1

LAWRENCE Liam
Born: Retford, 14 December 1981
Height: 5'10" Weight: 11.3

One of the stars of the Mansfield youth team which advanced to the fourth round of the FA Youth Cup last season, Liam was also given his chance to impress at senior level, initially as a substitute in the Auto Windscreens Shield match at home to Blackpool in January, when he replaced Tony Lormor. A keen and enthusiastic forward with good close control and passing ability which should ensure his future in the game, he was a regular on the subs' bench after the turn of the year.

Mansfield T (Trainee) FL 0+2 Others 0+1

LAWRENCE Matthew (Matt) James
Born: Northampton, 19 June 1974
Height: 6'1" Weight: 12.12
International Honours: E: Sch

Matt continued to be one of the key figures in Wycombe's line-up in 1999-2000, rarely missing a match before his surprise transfer to Millwall last March. The Millwall management had been watching him for quite some time and, with patience, finally got their man. He quickly made an impact in the team, giving a number of excellent performances. Matt is a very reliable right back who is adept at nullifying the threat posed by opposing wingers. He reads the game well, which enables him to get into position while making what he does look effortless, and is a good header of the ball who gives no quarter in the tackle. However, it is his attacking skills which make him so valued, his surging runs down the right flank and useful inswinging crosses making him a potent attacking force.

Wycombe W (£20,000 from Grays Ath on 19/1/1996) FL 13+3/1 FLC 4 FAC 1 Others 0+1
Fulham (Free on 7/2/1997) FL 57+2 FLC 4+1 FAC 2 Others 5
Wycombe W (£86,000 + on 2/10/1998) FL 63/4 FLC 4 FAC 7 Others 3
Millwall (£200,000 on 21/3/2000) FL 9 Others 2

LAWSON Ian James
Born: Huddersfield, 4 November 1977
Height: 5'11" Weight: 11.5

Ian was nicknamed "Sniffer" by Bury boss Neil Warnock when he arrived at Gigg Lane on a free transfer from Huddersfield in the summer of 1999. The livewire striker certainly lived up to his manager's tag, too, as he hit the goal trail with consistency in the early weeks of the season, including his first-ever hat-trick in a 5-2 home win against Colchester. His ability to carve out a chance marked him as one of the Second Division's rising stars and he clocked up 12 league and cup goals, averaging almost a goal every two games. Ian missed much of December due to a hamstring injury and just as he was nearing full fitness once again he was transferred to Stockport for £150,000 – purely due to Bury's poor financial situation. He went on to score four times in 13 starts for County. Although not the tallest of strikers, his timing makes him a formidable opponent in the air, and with excellent pace and an eye for goal he is expected to make a big impact with the First Division club in 2000-01.

Huddersfield T (From trainee on 26/1/1995) FL 13+29/5 FLC 1+4 FAC 1+1
Blackpool (Loaned on 6/11/1998) FL 5/3
Blackpool (Loaned on 8/1/1999) FL 4
Bury (£75,000 on 16/7/1999) FL 20+5/11 FLC 2 FAC 3+1 Others 1
Stockport Co (£150,000 on 17/2/2000) FL 13+2/4

LAZARIDIS Stanley (Stan)
Born: Perth, Australia, 16 August 1972
Height: 5'9" Weight: 11.12
International Honours: Australia: 28; Yth

Stan joined Birmingham City in the summer of 1999 and made an immediate impression by scoring with a stunning free kick on his debut for the club against Fulham. He was an influential force playing in a wide position in midfield, where his mazy dribbling and accurate crosses proved to be of great value in pulling opposition defences apart. He was yet another player affected by the Blues' injury hoodoo, suffering knee ligament damage against Tranmere last November which required surgery. He returned to the first-team squad in the new year and appeared regularly after that as the team pushed on into a play-off slot. He also added three more caps for Australia to his tally, appearing against Hungary, the Czech Republic and Paraguay. Stop Press: Stan appeared for Australia in the Oceania Nations' Cup final at the end of June when they defeated New Zealand 2-0 to win the trophy.

West Ham U (£300,000 from West Adelaide, Australia on 8/9/1995) PL 53+16/3 FLC 6+1 FAC 9+1
Birmingham C (£1,600,000 on 29/7/1999) FL 26+5/2 FLC 3 FAC 0+1 Others 1+1

LEABURN Carl Winston
Born: Lewisham, 30 March 1969
Height: 6'3" Weight: 13.0

A likeable and considerate man, Carl enjoys cult status at Wimbledon. Though often under-valued, the powerful striker always gives his all. Used predominantly as a substitute in 1999-2000, he did manage to help Carl Cort to a hat-trick against Sunderland in the Worthington Cup in one of the few games he started. His heading ability makes him an awkward opponent for any defender, and he has the ability to hold the ball up and bring others into the game.

Charlton Ath (From apprentice on 22/4/1987) FL 276+46/53 FLC 19/5 FAC 19+2/4 Others 9+5/4
Northampton T (Loaned on 22/3/1990) FL 9
Wimbledon (£300,000 on 9/1/1998) PL 34+22/4 FLC 5+6/1 FAC 4

LEADBITTER Christopher (Chris) Jonathan
Born: Middlesbrough, 17 October 1967
Height: 5'9" Weight: 10.6
Club Honours: Div 3 '91

Chris returned to Plymouth from Torquay in the 1999 close season, and proved to be a shrewd signing. He was strong and influential in midfield, and his experience helped many of the younger players at Home Park. A good talker and full of running, Chris is noted for his hard tackling, which was often at the heart of Plymouth's performances.

Grimsby T (From apprentice on 4/9/1985)
Hereford U (Free on 21/8/1986) FL 32+4/1 FLC 2 FAC 2 Others 3
Cambridge U (Free on 2/8/1988) FL 144+32/18 FLC 12/3 FAC 16+2/3 Others 11+2/1
Bournemouth (£25,000 on 16/8/1993) FL 45+9/3 FLC 6+1 FAC 5 Others 2
Plymouth Arg (Free on 27/7/1995) FL 46+6/1 FLC 2 FAC 6/1 Others 5+1/1 (Free to Dorchester T during 1997 close season)
Torquay U (Free on 27/11/1997) FL 58+5/2 FLC 1 FAC 1+2 Others 5+1
Plymouth Arg (Free on 6/7/1999) FL 28+3/2 FLC 1 FAC 6 Others 1

LEANING Andrew (Andy) John
Born: Goole, 18 May 1963
Height: 6'1" Weight: 14.7

Prior to the 1999-2000 season, Andy had played second fiddle to Billy Mercer in the Chesterfield goal for some years, fulfilling the function of goalkeeper coach at the same time. With Mercer injured and out of the team at the start of the new season, Andy got his longest run in the side – six games – but suffered a ruptured muscle in his leg and was forced to retire from football in January 2000.

York C (Free from Rowntree Mackintosh on 1/7/1985) FL 69 FLC 4 FAC 8 Others 5
Sheffield U (Free on 28/5/1987) FL 21 FLC 2 FAC 2
Bristol C (£12,000 on 27/9/1988) FL 75 FLC 5 FAC 7 Others 2
Lincoln C (Free on 24/3/1994) FL 36 FLC 6 FAC 3 Others 6 (Freed during 1996 season)
Dundee (Free on 19/7/1996)
Chesterfield (Free on 1/10/1996) FL 22 FLC 4 FAC 2 Others 1

LEBOEUF Frank
Born: Marseille, France, 22 January 1968
Height: 6'0" Weight: 12.6
Club Honours: FAC '97, '00; FLC '98; ECWC '98
International Honours: France: 30 (WC '98, UEFA '00)

Following a season of trials and tribulations in which Frank suffered a welter of criticism both from the media and within the game itself, he finally emerged with his pride intact: he was a member of the Chelsea team which won the FA Cup at Wembley last May thanks in no small measure to his decisive intervention. The French centre back ran into disciplinary problems during the first half of the season and an extended ban saw him miss vital fixtures in both the Premiership and the FA Cup. With Marcel Desailly and Jes Hogh injured, Chelsea could ill afford his enforced absence and decided to buy Emerson Thome from Sheffield Wednesday. The big Brazilian's impressive form gave him a strong claim to one of the centre-back positions, prompting press speculation over Frank's future, but manager Gianluca Vialli reunited the French World Cup-winning pair for the big European and FA Cup ties as the Blues chased a cup double. The Champions' League defeat at Barcelona was seized on by the media as an indication that Chelsea should revamp their defence, and stories linking Frank with a return to his native France or a move to Italy continued to appear into the close season. At his best, he is a solid defender whose majestic long passes from the back can switch play in an instant. He reads the game superbly and competes courageously, but always relishes the opportunity to move forward with the ball. The FA Cup final was a chance for Frank to exorcise the ghosts of his previous Wembley appearance, when he was given a torrid time by Newcastle's Alan Shearer in the semi-final. Chelsea narrowly led Aston Villa in the final thanks to a Roberto Di Matteo goal when, with just a few minutes remaining, Frank kicked a goalbound Benito

Carbone shot off the line to secure Chelsea's second FA Cup triumph in the last four seasons. It was a fitting climax to a traumatic campaign for a player who is adored by the Chelsea faithful. Although not a first choice for France, he still won eight more caps during the season and played his part as a member of the squad which gloriously won the Euro 2000 championship in the summer.

Chelsea (£2,500,000 from Strasbourg, France via Hyeres, Meaux and Laval, on 12/7/1996) PL 119/17 FLC 8/1 FAC 16/3 Others 30+1/3

LEE Alan Desmond
Born: Galway, 21 August 1978
Height: 6'2" Weight: 13.9
International Honours: RoI: U21-5

Alan joined Burnley from Aston Villa in a £150,000 deal shortly before the start of the 1999-2000 season. However, he had little chance to make a mark in his first season at Turf Moor, initially because of the consistency of the regular front two, and then due to a knee injury which was expected to rule him out for the second half of the season, although he recovered more quickly and was back on the bench by March. A tall, skilful striker, he has yet to show Burnley fans that he possesses the killer instinct in front of goal but will surely get more chance to do so next time around. He was capped by the Republic of Ireland at U21 level against Yugoslavia and Malta in the early part of the season.

Aston Villa (From trainee on 21/8/1995)
Torquay U (Loaned on 27/11/1998) FL 6+1/2 Others 2/1
Port Vale (Loaned on 2/3/1999) FL 7+4/2
Burnley (£150,000 on 8/7/1999) FL 2+13 FLC 1+1 FAC 0+2 Others 1/1

LEE Christian (Chris) Earl
Born: Aylesbury, 8 October 1976
Height: 6'2" Weight: 11.7

This young striker joined Gillingham from Northampton in the summer of 1999 for a tribunal fee of £35,000 and showed considerable promise in the early games of the 1999-2000 campaign. He scored against Brighton in the Worthington Cup and also in the 1-1 draw at Stoke but then suffered a knee injury that required complex surgery and did not begin training again until the new year. Tall and quick, he will be hoping for an injury-free run in 2000-01 to allow him to stake a case for regular first-team action at Priestfield Stadium.

Northampton T (Free from Doncaster Rov juniors on 13/7/1995) FL 25+34/8 FLC 2/2 FAC 3+3 Others 6+2
Gillingham (£35,000 + on 3/8/1999) FL 1+2 FLC 1+1

LEE David John
Born: Bristol, 26 November 1969
Height: 6'3" Weight: 14.7
Club Honours: Div 2 '89; FLC '98
International Honours: E: U21-10; Yth

The former Chelsea defender left Bristol Rovers at the end of 1998-99 and spent two months at Crystal Palace without making a senior appearance. After a spell at Colchester, he joined Exeter on a short-term basis in February 2000 but made an inauspicious start to his City career when he was sent off after 12 minutes of his debut at York. He played only six times before being released.

Chelsea (From trainee on 1/7/1988) F/PL 119+32/11 FLC 13+7/1 FAC 10+4 Others 6+2/1
Reading (Loaned on 30/1/1992) FL 5/5
Plymouth Arg (Loaned on 26/3/1992) FL 9/1
Portsmouth (Loaned on 12/8/1994) FL 4+1
Sheffield U (Loaned on 19/12/1997) FL 5
Bristol Rov (Free on 23/12/1998) FL 10+1/1 FAC 3/1 (Freed during 1999 close season)
Crystal Palace (Free on 28/10/1999)
Colchester U (Free on 10/1/2000)
Exeter C (Free on 24/2/2000) FL 3+1 Others 2

LEE David Mark
Born: Whitefield, 5 November 1967
Height: 5'7" Weight: 11.0
Club Honours: Div 1 '97; AMC '99

David's first-team football for Wigan in 1999-2000 was limited to just four substitute appearances, and it was apparent that there was no place for him in the plans of manager John Benson. On his day one of the most exciting wingers in the Second Division with the ability to take on his markers before delivering an excellent cross, David showed what he is capable of during a two-month loan spell at Blackpool in the autumn. He appeared regularly in the Seasiders' line-up and scored once with a fine 18-yard drive in the 2-0 victory at Wycombe. He was also top scorer for the Wigan reserve side that won the Pontins League Division Two title. He was released at the end of the season, and a permanent switch to Bloomfield Road seemed likely.

Bury (From juniors on 8/8/1986) FL 203+5/35 FLC 15/1 FAC 6 Others 19+1/4
Southampton (£350,000 on 27/8/1991) F/PL 11+9 FAC 0+1 Others 1+1
Bolton W (£300,000 on 2/11/1992) P/FL 124+31/17 FLC 19+1/2 FAC 13+2 Others 8+1/1
Wigan Ath (£250,000 on 16/7/1997) FL 61+22/11 FLC 6+3/2 FAC 4+2/2 Others 5+4/1
Blackpool (Loaned on 18/10/1999) FL 9/1 FAC 1 Others 1

LEE Graeme Barry
Born: Middlesbrough, 31 May 1978
Height: 6'2" Weight: 13.7

The 1999-2000 season was another good one for Hartlepool's young central defender. It culminated in his winning recognition by earning a place in the Opta Index Division Three "Team of the Season". Graeme rarely has a bad game, and is a player who always seems to make a quick recovery from injury. Already a regular goalscorer from set pieces, late in the season he acquitted himself particularly well when he played in a handful of games as a striker. With a total of eight goals, Graeme was Pool's third-top scorer.

Hartlepool U (From trainee on 2/7/1996) FL 122+7/13 FLC 5+2/1 FAC 6 Others 9+1/2

LEE Jason Benedict
Born: Forest Gate, 9 May 1971
Height: 6'3" Weight: 13.8
Club Honours: Div 2 '98

Although the team was ultimately relegated for want of a goalscorer, Jason hardly got a look-in at Chesterfield before resurrecting his career with a move to Peterborough, initially on loan, in the first week of the new millennium. Posh boss Barry Fry, who took him to Southend in 1993, had tried to sign the big forward in August to cover for the injured Andy Clarke. Jason reportedly displayed his determination to make the move to London Road permanent by agreeing to take a reduction in the money owed to him by Chesterfield. The switch was confirmed in March, when he also turned down the chance to represent the Cayman Islands in a World Cup qualifier. Having played such a vital role in their improvement, he missed Posh's Wembley Third Division play-off win against Darlington due to a knee injury.

Charlton Ath (From trainee on 2/6/1989) FL 0+1 Others 0+2
Stockport Co (Loaned on 6/2/1991) FL 2
Lincoln C (£35,000 on 1/3/1991) FL 86+7/21 FLC 6 FAC 2+1/1 Others 4
Southend U (Signed on 6/8/1993) FL 18+6/3 FLC 1 FAC 1 Others 5+3/3
Nottingham F (£200,000 on 4/3/1994) F/PL 41+35/14 FLC 4+3/1 FAC 0+5 Others 4+2
Charlton Ath (Loaned on 5/2/1997) FL 7+1/3
Grimsby T (Loaned on 27/3/1997) FL 2+5/1 FAC 1
Watford (£200,000 on 16/6/1997) FL 36+1/11 FLC 4 FAC 4 Others 1
Chesterfield (£250,000 on 28/8/1998) FL 17+11/1 FAC 0+2 Others 0+2
Peterborough U (£50,000 on 3/1/2000) FL 23/6 Others 2/1

Jason Lee

LEE Martyn James
Born: Guildford, 10 September 1980
Height: 5'6" Weight: 9.0

Martyn spent much of 1999-2000 struggling to win a place in the Wycombe squad, but after some sparkling displays for the reserves he eventually made the subs' bench last April and went on to appear in the starting line-up for the last three games of the season. A young and talented midfielder, he has an excellent left foot and can deliver a useful, teasing cross into the box. Although lacking in inches, he is very determined and will be looking to feature more regularly in the senior team in 2000-01.

Wycombe W (From trainee on 30/1/1999) FL 5+2

Rob Lee

LEE Robert (Rob) Martin
Born: West Ham, 1 February 1966
Height: 5'11" Weight: 11.13
Club Honours: Div 1 '93
International Honours: E: 21; B-1; U21-2

Over the years this long-serving player had become a popular and vital cog in the Newcastle midfield, often contributing important goals via his box-to-box surges. Therefore there was much astonishment when Ruud Gullit did not even allocate him a squad number at the start of the 1999-2000 season, but sent him to train with the reserves and juniors instead with a clear message that he had no future at the club. On Ruud's departure Rob was immediately recalled to the team, and the quality of his performances quickly demonstrated that he still had much to offer, as he made light of his years and again became a fixture in the side for the rest of the season. Playing in a more withdrawn role than previously, he became the hub of the team, operating in midfield just in front of the defence, from where his good control, his vision and his passing ability enabled him to be a highly influential play-maker while his anticipation and tackling allowed him to provide a shield for the defence. Although absent from the FA Cup quarter-final at Tranmere through suspension, he returned in time for the semi-final, where he scored Newcastle's equaliser with a powerful header. This was United's first goal in four visits to the Twin Towers, and Rob's first since scoring, also against Chelsea, in May 1998. He has amassed by far the most appearances for the club in the Premiership, and his performances in a difficult season showed that he still has a contribution to make at the top level. His popularity was demonstrated when, on being substituted in the final minutes of the last game of the season, at home to Arsenal, he left the field to a standing ovation.

Charlton Ath (Free from Hornchurch on 12/7/1983) FL 274+24/59 FLC 16+3/1 FAC 14/2 Others 10+2/3
Newcastle U (£700,00 on 22/9/1992) F/PL 256+9/43 FLC 16/3 FAC 27/5 Others 25/4

LEGG Andrew (Andy)
Born: Neath, 28 July 1966
Height: 5'8" Weight: 10.7
Club Honours: WC '89, '91; AIC '95
International Honours: W: 5

Wholehearted and committed, Andy is a Welshman and he is proud to play for Cardiff. He took every "Player of the Year" award on offer at the club last season and won them all by a considerable margin. A hard-working midfielder who can also perform effectively at full back, he continued to produce good form on the left and his long throw remained a threat. He reportedly took a big pay cut when he joined Cardiff the previous season to escape isolation at Reading, where he was one of a number of players excluded from the first-team squad. New Reading boss Alan Pardew praised Andy when Cardiff played at the Madejski Stadium last March, and said he wished the Welshman was in his team.

Swansea C (Signed from Britton Ferry on 12/8/1988) FL 155+8/29 FLC 9+1 FAC 16/4 Others 15+3/5
Notts Co (£275,000 on 23/7/1993) FL 85+4/9 FLC 11 FAC 7+1 Others 13+2/6
Birmingham C (Signed on 29/2/1996) FL 31+14/5 FLC 3+1 FAC 2+1
Ipswich T (Loaned on 3/11/1997) FL 6/1 FLC 1
Reading (£75,000 on 20/2/1998) FL 12 FLC 1
Peterborough U (Loaned on 15/10/1998) FL 5
Cardiff C (Free on 16/12/1998) FL 60+6/4 FLC 4 FAC 5+3

LEITCH Donald **Scott**
Born: Motherwell, 6 October 1969
Height: 5'9" Weight: 12.2

Swindon's captain produced some fine performances in what was a mainly disappointing 1999-2000 season for the club. Although he missed several weeks with hamstring trouble in the early part of the campaign, he returned to action in November and rarely missed another game. Scott linked up well with Lee Collins in the centre of the park for the Robins, where they worked hard to close down the opposition. An excellent midfield anchor man, he is strong in the tackle and has the ability to spread play out to the flanks. He was released during the summer.

Dunfermline Ath (Free from Shettleston Juniors on 4/4/1990) SL 72+17/16 SLC 6+1/3 SC 3 Others 1
Hearts (Signed on 6/8/1993) SL 46+9/2 SLC 1+2/1 SC 3 Others 2
Swindon T (£15,000 on 29/3/1996) FL 119+3/1 FLC 8/2 FAC 3

LENNON Neil Francis
Born: Lurgan, 25 June 1971
Height: 5'9" Weight: 13.2
Club Honours: FLC '97, '00
International Honours: NI: 33; B-1; U23-1; U21-2; Yth

Leicester's fiery right-footed midfield dynamo may have scored only one goal during City's triumphant Worthington Cup run last season, a neatly taken effort against Crystal Palace in the opening game, but his overall contribution was immense. Returning from injury and clearly not match fit, Neil played a vital role in both legs of the semi-final against Aston Villa, then must have run Matt Elliott close for the "Man of the Match" award against Tranmere in the final at Wembley, where the classy play-maker ran the show during the first half and was desperately unlucky to see a well-worked free kick fly narrowly over the crossbar. He scored his single league goal with a top-corner effort against Aston Villa. A regular in the Northern Ireland squad, he won six more caps last season.

Manchester C (From trainee on 26/8/1989) FL 1
Crewe Alex (Free on 9/8/1990) FL 142+5/15 FLC 8+1/1 FAC 16/1 Others 15+1
Leicester C (£750,000 on 23/2/1996) P/FL 154+1/6 FLC 22/3 FAC 8 Others 5

Oyvind Leonhardsen

LEONHARDSEN Oyvind
Born: Kristiansund, Norway, 17 August 1970
Height: 5'10" Weight: 11.2
International Honours: Norway: 67

A tremendously underrated attacking midfielder, Oyvind joined Tottenham in the 1999 close season after being frozen out at Liverpool under Gerard Houllier. He made an immediate impact in the Spurs first team, combining well with Tim Sherwood in getting forward and penetrating through the centre. Oyvind netted five goals in his first dozen appearances at Tottenham and became an immediate hit with the White Hart Lane crowd. His stamina and workrate are among his finest attributes and he is always looking to carve out a chance from nothing. He showed the ability to gain possession and quickly switch defence into attack while bringing the wide players into the game. His never-say-die attitude typified by a late winner at Southampton that gave Spurs all three points when the game looked destined for a draw has certainly impressed his new manager, George Graham. Injury hampered his progress later in the season, and despite returning in March Oyvind aggravated an ankle injury on the final day of the season, which sadly ruled him out of Norway's Euro 2000 campaign. A regular at international level before his injury problems, he added a further five caps last season, scoring against both Greece and Slovenia in September.

Wimbledon (£660,000 from Rosenborg, Norway, via Clausenengen and Molde, on 8/11/1994) PL 73+3/13 FLC 7+2/1 FAC 17/2
Liverpool (£3,500,000 on 3/6/1997) PL 34+3/7 FLC 4+2 FAC 1 Others 3+2
Tottenham H (£3,000,000 on 6/8/1999) PL 21+1/4 FLC 2/1 Others 4/1

LEONI Stephane
Born: Metz, France, 1 September 1976
Height: 5'11" Weight: 11.8
International Honours: France: U21

This former French U21 international full back, who had been a regular in Bristol Rovers' starting line-up the previous season, had to be patient for further first-team opportunities in 1999-2000. Having had a short trial at Oxford United in September, two months later Stephane suffered serious cuts to his body in an accident at home and was sidelined for six weeks. Usually seen on the right, he made his first full start of the season in the 1-0 victory over Wycombe Wanderers in March in the unfamiliar left-full-back position and also appeared in a midfield role in the 2-0 defeat by top-of-the-table Preston North End. He was released at the end of the season.
Bristol Rov (Free from Metz, France on 17/8/1998) FL 27+11 FLC 1+1 FAC 4/1 Others 1

LE SAUX Graeme Pierre
Born: Jersey, 17 October 1968
Height: 5'10" Weight: 12.2
Club Honours: PL '95; FLC '98; ESC '98
International Honours: E: 35; B-2; U21-4

The most glaring, palpable weakness in the England national side is the lack of a top-quality left-sided wing back who can attack down that flank, reach the byline and whip in decent left-foot crosses. The only player who fits the bill is Graeme Le Saux of Chelsea but, unfortunately for England, Graeme suffered a serious ankle injury last October which limited his 1999-2000 season to just ten starts. Euro 2000 was the second successive European Championship which the unlucky Graeme has been forced to miss – a broken leg sustained while he was a Blackburn player kept him out of the 1996 tournament. Although Chelsea were well served by Celestine Babayaro and Jon Harley in his absence, the Blues, like England, missed his aggression and high-powered energy. With Graeme fully fit, Chelsea look particularly strong on the left flank and boss Gianluca Vialli will have a real conundrum to solve when all three players are available for selection.
Chelsea (Free from St Paul's, Jersey, on 9/12/1987) F/PL 77+13/8 FLC 7+6/1 FAC 7+1 Others 8+1
Blackburn Rov (£750,000 on 25/3/1993) PL 127+2/7 FLC 10 FAC 8 Others 6+1
Chelsea (£5,000,000 on 8/8/1997) PL 62+3/1 FLC 5/1 FAC 7/1 Others 15+1

LESCOTT Aaron Anthony
Born: Birmingham, 2 December 1978
Height: 5'8" Weight: 10.9

Unable to win a first-team place at Aston Villa, this youngster joined Lincoln on loan last March to gain experience of first-team football. Although his preferred position is in the centre of midfield, he was used in a wide-left or wide-right role at Sincil Bank and returned to Villa Park without completing a full 90 minutes with the Third Division club.
Aston Villa (From trainee on 5/7/1996) FAC 0+1
Lincoln C (Loaned on 14/3/2000) FL 3+2

LESTER Jack William
Born: Sheffield, 8 October 1975
Height: 5'10" Weight: 11.8
Club Honours: AMC '98
International Honours: E: Sch

During the first half of 1999-2000 this stylish striker built up a first-class strike partnership with Lee Ashcroft for Grimsby which by mid-season was beginning to reap its reward with some fine goals. His increasing skills, speed in the box and continuing ability to cause consternation among opposition defences drew increasing attention from bigger clubs. With his contract up in June and Grimsby unable to entice him to re-sign with improved terms, the club decided to cash in on what was left of his contract, and after speculative links with several clubs he moved down the A46 to Nottingham Forest in a £300,000 deal, marking his farewell appearance with the winning goal at Fulham. He scored just twice in 12 starts for the Reds but netted the fastest goal ever scored at the City Ground when he shot home from the edge of the area after just 14 seconds against Norwich City in March. A small central striker, with good pace and skill and an excellent workrate, he will be expected to make a greater impact during the coming season.
Grimsby T (From juniors on 8/7/1994) FL 93+40/17 FLC 13+4/6 FAC 7+2/2 Others 4+4
Doncaster Rov (Loaned on 20/9/1996) FL 5+6/1
Nottingham F (£300,000 on 28/1/2000) FL 12+3/2

LE TISSIER Matthew (Matt) Paul
Born: Guernsey, 14 October 1968
Height: 6'1" Weight: 13.8
International Honours: E: 8; B-6; Yth

A huge favourite with the Southampton faithful, Matthew suffered a season of frustration in 1999-2000, a whole series of niggling injuries restricting his appearances. Just three goals short of achieving membership of the Premiership 100 club at the start of the season, he soon knocked two off the target at Old Trafford, coming off the bench to score the softest goal of his career – a harmless effort which squirmed between the 'keeper's legs – followed by a side-footed effort from 12 yards. His creative qualities and deadly shots were sorely missed as the club battled to avoid another relegation dogfight. After nearly four months out with hamstring and then achilles problems, he returned to the team and a new manager in the form of his former England boss, Glenn Hoddle. His 100th Premiership goal came against Sunderland at the Dell in April when he converted a penalty – his 49th successful spot kick in 50 attempts.
Southampton (From apprentice on 17/10/1986) F/PL 375+56/161 FLC 42+8/26 FAC 30+2/12 Others 11+1/9

LEVER Mark
Born: Beverley, 29 March 1970
Height: 6'3" Weight: 13.5
Club Honours: AMC '98

In contrast to the previous season, when he had to fight for his place at the centre of the Grimsby defence, Mark found himself the kingpin in this position in 1999-2000, playing alongside various partners as both Peter Handyside and Richard Smith were missing for long spells with injuries. A powerful header of the ball and a forceful tackler, he played a vital role in holding together the defence during a season in which the Mariners struggled in this department, mainly due to manager Alan Buckley's difficulties in being able to name a regular back four, Mark himself being sidelined for a short spell early in the season. Out of contract in the summer and unable to agree new terms, he was expected to leave Blundell Park under the Bosman ruling during the close season.
Grimsby T (From trainee on 9/8/1988) FL 343+18/8 FLC 22+2 FAC 17+3 Others 18

LEWIS Edward (Eddie) James
Born: Cerritos, California, USA, 17 May 1974
Height: 5'9" Weight: 11.12
International Honours: USA: 22

Spotted by Fulham scouts while playing for the USA in the CONCACAF Gold Cup, Eddie was signed just before the transfer deadline in March for £1.3 million from San Jose Clash. An attacking left-sided midfielder, Eddie had an excellent debut game at Barnsley, although being described as the "American David Beckham" (despite having modelled his game on Ryan Giggs) makes it almost impossible for him to match the expectations that have been created. The loss of form of the team as a whole after losing out on the play-offs meant that Eddie didn't make quite the hoped-for impact in the last few games, but 2000-01 should see him terrorise Division One defences with his pace, accurate crosses and corners. A regular for the USA in the last two seasons, he was a member of the team that won a bronze medal in the Confederation Cup in August 1999 and has been capped against Russia and South Africa since his arrival at Craven Cottage.
Fulham (£1,300,000 from San Jose Clash, USA on 17/3/2000) FL 6+2

LEWIS Graham
Born: Reading, 15 February 1982
Height: 5'10" Weight: 11.12

Graham is a talented young Lincoln striker who made his Football League debut at Torquay last September while still a second-year trainee. He was then out injured before being recalled to the Imps' first team for the last few games of the 1999-2000 season. He put in some useful performances partnering Lee Thorpe in the City attack and is also capable of playing on the left side of midfield.
Lincoln C (Trainee) FL 3+2

LEWIS Karl **Junior**
Born: Wembley, 9 October 1973
Height: 6'5" Weight: 12.4

This former Fulham trainee joined Gillingham in the summer of 1999 after a successful season with Ryman League club Hendon, where he had scored 28 goals. He took full advantage of his second opportunity to build a professional career and won rave reviews for his performances during the 1999-2000 campaign. Having established himself in the team early on, he was rarely absent for the remainder of the season and contributed six goals from midfield.

Fulham (From trainee on 3/7/1992) FL 4+1 FAC 1 (Free to Dover Ath during 1993 close season)
Gillingham (Free from Hendon on 3/8/1999) FL 37+5/6 FLC 2 FAC 5+2 Others 4

LEWIS Michael (Mickey)
Born: Birmingham, 15 February 1965
Height: 5'8" Weight: 12.4
International Honours: E: Yth

Having retired as a player a couple of years ago, Mickey began 1999-2000 at Oxford as first-team sponge man and team-bus driver for the club's reserves. However, he made a return to league football following a series of injuries to the club's regular central defenders and showed he had lost none of his never-say-die spirit and unwavering commitment, especially in United's win at Everton in the Worthington Cup. Mickey was appointed first-team coach with the manager's responsibilities following the resignation of Malcolm Shotton and looked after the team for several months before handing over to Denis Smith. Even after this he made a single further appearance from the subs' bench.

West Bromwich A (From apprentice on 18/2/1982) FL 22+2 FLC 4+1 FAC 4
Derby Co (£25,000 on 16/11/1984) FL 37+6/1 FLC 2 FAC 0+1 Others 4
Oxford U (Signed on 25/8/1988) FL 279+26/7 FLC 17+3 FAC 12+1 Others 11+1

LIBURD Richard John
Born: Nottingham, 26 September 1973
Height: 5'9" Weight: 11.1

This experienced Notts County player did not feature regularly in the first team until the second half of 1999-2000 and then suffered through being played out of position as a right-footed left back. His best role for the Magpies has been as an orthodox right back, where his strong tackling and ability to get down the wing to help out the attack are most useful. Richard always worked hard for the team and scored his only goal of the season in the 2-2 draw with Bristol City in February.

Middlesbrough (£20,000 from Eastwood T on 25/3/1993) FL 41/1 FLC 4 FAC 2 Others 5
Bradford C (£200,000 on 21/7/1994) FL 75+3/3 FLC 6+2 FAC 2+2 Others 2
Carlisle U (Free on 26/2/1998) FL 9
Notts Co (Free on 4/8/1998) FL 51+15/2 FLC 1+1 FAC 4+3

LIDDELL Andrew (Andy) Mark
Born: Leeds, 28 June 1973
Height: 5'7" Weight: 11.6
Club Honours: AMC '99
International Honours: S: U21-12

Andy was an integral member of Wigan's promotion push in 1999-2000 and his efforts received their proper reward when he collected the "Player of the Year" award. He is a hard-working player who never gave less than 100 per cent effort, and his unselfish running regularly unlocked defences for his fellow forwards. At his best playing behind the two strikers, he showed his quality with nine goals, his 50th in the Football League coming in the draw at Bristol Rovers in March. Andy has been linked with moves to Dundee United and Huddersfield.

Barnsley (From trainee on 6/7/1991) F/PL 142+56/34 FLC 11+2/3 FAC 5+7/1 Others 2+1
Wigan Ath (£350,000 on 15/10/1998) FL 69/18 FLC 3 FAC 3/1 Others 11

Andy Liddell

LIDDLE Craig George
Born: Chester le Street, 21 October 1971
Height: 5'11" Weight: 12.7

Craig's second full season at Darlington was a continuation of his first, with consistent quality performances in the centre of defence or at right back. He missed only two games in league and cup throughout the 1999-2000 campaign, and his reading of the game was of a standard usually seen only at a higher level. He was an inspiration to those around him with his professional approach and dependability at all times, and proved extremely popular with the fans. Out of contract at the end of the season, Craig made it clear that he wanted to stay at Feethams. A fine campaign was recognised with selection in the PFA Third Division team.

Aston Villa (From trainee on 4/7/1990. Free to Blyth Spartans in August 1991)
Middlesbrough (Free on 12/7/1994) P/FL 20+5 FLC 3+2 FAC 2 Others 2
Darlington (Free on 20/2/1998) FL 104/4 FLC 4 FAC 6 Others 6/1

LIGHTBOURNE Kyle Lavince
Born: Bermuda, 29 September 1968
Height: 6'2" Weight: 12.4
Club Honours: AMC '00
International Honours: Bermuda: 22; Yth

If ever a player went from zero to hero with the Stoke supporters it was Kyle in 1999-2000. The Bermudian striker terrorised Division Two defences throughout the season and he blossomed first under Gary Megson and then under Gudjon Thordarson. His hard work deserved more than his modest tally of nine goals, but his pairing with Peter Thorne was fundamental to Stoke's push for promotion. A pacy player who poses a threat to defences both in the air and on the ground, he had more than most to celebrate after the Auto Windscreens Shield victory at Wembley as the team were in great danger of losing their place in the competition in the first-round game at home to Darlington when Kyle came off the bench to score two (the second a "golden goal") and see them through to the ultimate prize. He won another cap when he played and scored in Bermuda's 5-1 victory over the US Virgin Islands in a World Cup qualifying match last March. Kyle is one of the few current players to have represented his country at two sports, having appeared for Bermuda at cricket in an ICC qualifying tournament before he came to England.

Scarborough (Signed from Pembroke Hamilton, Bermuda on 11/12/1992) FL 11+8/3 FLC 1 Others 0+1
Walsall (Free on 17/9/1993) FL 158+7/65 FLC 8/3 FAC 16+2/12 Others 7/5
Coventry C (£500,000 + on 18/7/1997) PL 1+6 FLC 3
Fulham (Loaned on 13/1/1998) FL 4/2 Others 1/1
Stoke C (£500,000 on 16/2/1998) FL 72+17/16 FLC 4 FAC 2/1 Others 7+2/3

LIGHTFOOT Christopher (Chris) Ian
Born: Warrington, 1 April 1970
Height: 6'2" Weight: 13.6

Chris was again used as a utility player by Crewe in 1999-2000, occupying a variety of defensive roles as injuries to other players dictated. A reliable, consistent performer, he made 16 starts with five further appearances as a substitute and maintained his record of scoring at least once every season with a goal at home to Stockport in April. A wholehearted performer, he is aggressive and strong in possession with good passing technique, and has repaid his transfer fee many times over.

Chester C (From trainee on 11/7/1988) FL 263+14/32 FLC 15+2/1 FAC 16+2/1 Others 14+2/5
Wigan Ath (£87,500 on 13/7/1995) FL 11+3/1 FLC 2 FAC 2 Others 3
Crewe Alex (£50,000 on 22/3/1996) FL 63+24/4 FLC 3+2 FAC 1+1/1 Others 3+2

LILLEY Derek Symon
Born: Paisley, 9 February 1974
Height: 5'11" Weight: 12.7
Club Honours: S Div 2 '95
International Honours: S: Yth

Derek joined Oxford just prior to the start of the 1999-2000 campaign for a reported fee of £75,000 from Leeds United. Although he is a quick striker, it took him some time to win over the fans as he struggled for goals early on. However, as the season went on he became a vital member of the squad and he ended it on a high, by now playing in a wide-right position. He scored eight times in all, but his four goals late in the season contributed ten points which were a tremendous help to the club's efforts to avoid relegation. Ironically, one of those was against Bury, with whom he had been on loan the season before when his only goal for the Shakers had played a big part in United's relegation.

Greenock Morton (Free from Everton BC on 13/8/1991) SL 157+23/57 SLC 5+1/4 SC 9+4/4 Others 6+4/5
Leeds U (£500,000 + on 27/3/1997) PL 4+17/1 FLC 0+3 FAC 0+1 Others 0+1
Heart of Midlothian (Loaned on 30/12/1998) SL 3+1/1 SC 1
Bury (Loaned on 25/3/1999) FL 5/1
Oxford U (£75,000 on 6/8/1999) FL 36+8/7 FLC 3+2 FAC 5/1 Others 1

LINDLEY James (Jim) Edward
Born: Sutton in Ashfield, 23 July 1981
Height: 6'2" Weight: 13.0

This talented young Notts County goal-keeper became a first-year professional in July 1999 after coming up through the ranks at Meadow Lane. He appeared on the subs' bench several times during 1999-2000 and made his Football League debut when he came on as a substitute for the injured Darren Ward at Cardiff in September.

Notts Co (From trainee on 1/7/1999) FL 0+1

LING Martin
Born: West Ham, 15 July 1966
Height: 5'8" Weight: 10.8
Club Honours: Div 2 '96

Martin remained a vital part of Leyton Orient's midfield at the start of the 1999-2000 campaign, but shortly after scoring the winning goal at Rotherham in November he dropped out of the first-team reckoning. He was advised that his contract wouldn't be renewed at the end of the season, and after a move to Swindon had fallen through he joined Brighton on a non-contract basis on transfer deadline day. The experienced midfielder or forward is a stylish player who is always looking for the ball, and his early performances for Albion suggested that his composure and assurance would prove useful assets. However, he was released in May and returned to Orient to coach the London club's immensely impressive youth team, although he will remain registered as a player.

Exeter C (From apprentice on 13/1/1984) FL 109+8/14 FLC 8 FAC 4 Others 5
Swindon T (£25,000 on 14/7/1986) FL 2 FLC 1+1
Southend U (£15,000 on 16/10/1986) FL 126+12/31 FLC 8/2 FAC 7/1 Others 11+1/3
Mansfield T (Loaned on 24/1/1991) FL 3
Swindon T (£15,000 on 28/3/1991) F/PL 132+18/10 FLC 11+1/1 FAC 10+1/1 Others 12+1/1
Leyton Orient (Free on 23/7/1996) FL 143+5/8 FLC 13 FAC 9+1 Others 5/1
Brighton & Hove A (Free on 23/3/2000) FL 2+6/1

LINIGHAN Andrew (Andy)
Born: Hartlepool, 18 June 1962
Height: 6'3" Weight: 13.10
Club Honours: Div 1 '91; FLC '93; FAC '93; ECWC '94
International Honours: E: B-4

The veteran Crystal Palace central defender had a marvellous 1999-2000 campaign and was voted "Player of the Season" by the supporters. Consistent, hard tackling and good in the air, he was as dependable as ever and his experience was invaluable to the Eagles' youngsters. Andy missed only the last game of the season and used his commanding presence to score a couple of goals when coming up for corners. He was released in the close season. From a footballing family, Andy is the brother of Brian (Bury) and David (Mansfield) and the son of former Lincoln and Darlington player Brian Linighan.

Hartlepool U (Free from Henry Smiths BC on 19/9/1980) FL 110/4 FLC 7+1/1 FAC 8 Others 1/1
Leeds U (£20,000 on 15/5/1984) FL 66/3 FLC 6/1 FAC 2 Others 2
Oldham Ath (£65,000 on 17/1/1986) FL 87/6 FLC 8/2 FAC 3 Others 4
Norwich C (£350,000 on 4/3/1988) FL 86/8 FLC 6 FAC 10 Others 4
Arsenal (£1,250,000 on 4/7/1990) F/PL 101+17/5 FLC 13+1/1 FAC 12+2/1 Others 9+1/1
Crystal Palace (£150,000 on 27/1/1997) F/PL 108+2/4 FLC 5+2 FAC 3+2 Others 3
Queens Park R (Loaned on 25/3/1999) FL 4+3

LINIGHAN Brian
Born: Hartlepool, 2 November 1973
Height: 6'4" Weight: 12.0

After almost three frustrating years performing exclusively in Bury's Pontins League team, this giant central defender finally gained his first-team chance, albeit a fleeting one, last March. Brian made his Football League debut for the Shakers appearing as a second-half substitute for Sam Collins at Millwall and took his chance well, being decisive in defence and causing problems with his height at set pieces in attack. He retained his place for the next two games against Chesterfield and Blackpool, but after that it was back to Pontins League football – and he was eventually handed a free transfer in May.

Sheffield Wed (From trainee on 16/7/1992) PL 1 FLC 1 FAC 1
Bury (Free on 2/7/1997) FL 2+1 FLC 0+2

LINIGHAN David
Born: Hartlepool, 9 January 1965
Height: 6'2" Weight: 13.0
Club Honours: Div 2 '92

In the opening weeks of 1999-2000 David continued where he had left off the previous season, the veteran centre back performing resolutely in the middle of the Mansfield back four. Demonstrating that he remains an accomplished defender both in the air and on the ground, he formed an effective part-nership with new recruit Neil Richardson and was an ever-present in the side until the end of November, when a broken wrist at Halifax forced him out of the side for two months. David was released at the end of the season.

Hartlepool U (From juniors on 3/3/1982) FL 84+7/5 FLC 3+1/1 FAC 4 Others 2
Derby Co (£25,000 on 11/8/1986)
Shrewsbury T (£30,000 on 4/12/1986) FL 65/1 FLC 5 FAC 3 Others 1
Ipswich T (£300,000 on 23/6/1988) F/PL 275+2/12 FLC 21 FAC 18/1 Others 11
Blackpool (£80,000 on 17/11/1995) FL 97+3/5 FLC 6/2 FAC 2/1 Others 8
Dunfermline Ath (Free on 1/7/1998) SL 1 SLC 1
Mansfield T (Free on 25/3/1999) FL 38 FLC 2 FAC 1 Others 1

LISBIE Kevin Anthony
Born: Hackney, 17 October 1978
Height: 5'8' Weight: 10.12
International Honours: E: Yth

Finding it impossible to force his way into the Charlton team, Kevin joined Reading on loan last November, but his spell with the Royals was far from successful as he was hardly match-fit when he arrived, and he played only one full game, against Scunthorpe. Although his previous loan spell at Gillingham had improved his reputation as an up-and-coming striker, he failed to impress at the Madejski, and was sent back to the Valley before his month's loan was completed. During a disappointing season, Kevin made only one appearance for Charlton, as a substitute in the FA Cup tie against Queens Park Rangers in January. An extremely quick forward who possesses a hard and accurate shot, he can play either in a central striking role or wide on the right, and is able to hold the ball up or put in an accurate cross from the byline. Kevin will be looking for greater opportunities to demonstrate his talents in 2000-01.

Charlton Ath (From trainee on 24/5/1996) P/FL 5+38/2 FLC 0+5 FAC 0+2
Gillingham (Loaned on 5/3/1999) FL 4+3/4
Reading (Loaned on 26/11/1999) FL 1+1

LITTLE Colin Campbell
Born: Wythenshawe, 4 November 1972
Height: 5'10" Weight: 11.0

The lively Crewe forward, still the only player to have recorded a hat-trick for the club in the First Division, has to work hard to retain his place in Dario Gradi's side but was an ever-present last season until the turn of the year. Thereafter he was occasionally relegated to the subs' bench although he returned to the starting line-up for the last five matches of the season. Colin is a player who enjoys scoring goals, but his league tally of four from 36 appearances (three as a substitute) was down on previous seasons; however, he continues to pose a threat when running at defenders in the box and can always be relied upon to give everything he has.

Crewe Alex (£50,000 from Hyde U on 7/2/1996) FL 100+43/28 FLC 10+2/6 FAC 5/1 Others 5/3

LITTLE Glen Matthew
Born: Wimbledon, 15 October 1975
Height: 6'3" Weight: 13.0

One of Stan Ternent's more mystifying decisions of 1999-2000 was to play Glen on the left side of Burnley's midfield, for, although he is a capable performer in that position, on the right he is a tormentor of defences and at his best a player who looks wasted at Second Division level. Thankfully, the left-sided experiment was short lived. Glen is in his element going down the right, beating defenders, as much by sheer unorthodoxy as by speed, and providing pinpoint crosses, usually for Andy Payton. He scored Burnley's "Goal of the Season", a superb solo effort when he took on the entire Bristol Rovers defence to secure three vital points for the Clarets, and also came up with the winning goal in the final match at Scunthorpe to secure Burnley's promotion. Glen gained recognition from his fellow professionals when he was selected for the PFA award-winning Second Division side.

Crystal Palace (From trainee on 1/7/1994. Free to Glentoran on 11/11/1994)
Burnley (£100,000 on 29/11/1996) FL 92+16/12 FLC 4+2 FAC 6+1 Others 4+1/1

LITTLEJOHN Adrian Sylvester
Born: Wolverhampton, 26 September 1970
Height: 5'9" Weight: 11.0
International Honours: E: Yth

Undoubtedly one of the most skilful players on Bury's books, Adrian is a forward whose tremendous pace allows him to run at defenders with great effect, and he can attack through the middle, or down either flank. His raids brought him a highly respectable total of ten goals during the 1999-2000 season, with many of them being spectacular long-range finishes. However, Adrian remains a highly frustrating player, as he could achieve even more if he applied himself better. Perhaps the coming season will see him fulfil his abundant potential.

Walsall (Free from West Bromwich A juniors on 24/5/1989) FL 26+18/1 FLC 2+1 FAC 1+1 Others 4+1
Sheffield U (Free on 6/8/1991) F/PL 44+25/12 FLC 5+1 FAC 3+2/1 Others 2/1
Plymouth Arg (£100,000 on 22/9/1995) FL 100+10/29 FLC 6 FAC 6+2/3 Others 6
Oldham Ath (Signed on 20/3/1998) FL 16+5/5 FLC 2/1
Bury (£75,000 on 13/11/1998) FL 45+17/10 FLC 2/1 FAC 4/1 Others 1

LIVERMORE David
Born: Edmonton, 20 May 1980
Height: 5'11" Weight: 12.1

David joined Millwall from Arsenal on loan at the beginning of 1999-2000 and made his debut on the opening day of the season at Cardiff. His performance after coming on as a substitute confirmed his potential and the Lions signed him. Although he started his career as a central defender, he was employed by his new club on the left of midfield. He is good in the air and strong in the challenge, a quality that is not always appreciated by the officials. David certainly gives no quarter, which has naturally made him popular with the Millwall fans. Although he was out of the side for a couple of months before Christmas, the unfortunate injury to Marc Bircham allowed him to enjoy an extended run in the team during the second half of the season which saw him develop into one of the best midfielders in the Second Division.

Arsenal (From trainee on 13/7/1998)
Millwall (£30,000 on 30/7/1999) FL 29+3/2 FLC 2 Others 3

LIVINGSTONE Stephen (Steve) Carl
Born: Middlesbrough, 8 September 1968
Height: 6'1" Weight: 13.6
Club Honours: AMC '98

Formerly a striker in the old "centre forward" mould, Steve found himself converted almost permanently to his secondary role as a central defender in 1999-2000 as injuries once again decimated the Grimsby squad in this department, putting in his usual solid and reliable performances. On several occasions, however, he was moved forward during late adjustments to the formation as the side fought to rescue a match. This ploy achieved notable success in the third-round FA Cup tie against Stockport County, when he shared two last-minute goals with Bradley Allen to snatch the tie at the death.

Coventry C (From trainee on 16/7/1986) FL 17+14/5 FLC 8+2/10 Others 0+1
Blackburn Rov (£450,000 on 17/1/1991) F/PL 25+5/10 FLC 2 FAC 1/1
Chelsea (£350,000 on 23/3/1993) PL 0+1
Port Vale (Loaned on 3/9/1993) FL 4+1
Grimsby T (£140,000 on 29/10/1993) FL 178+46/33 FLC 13+6/4 FAC 9+5/4 Others 4+3

LJUNGBERG Fredrik
Born: Sweden, 16 April 1977
Height: 5'9" Weight: 11.6
Club Honours: CS '99
International Honours: Sweden: 17; U21-12

A quick and skilful Swedish international, Fredrik has developed into a solid, attacking member of the Arsenal midfield. An aggressive tackler with good stamina, he got stronger as the 1999-2000 season developed, adopting a never-say-die attitude to the game. He has good distribution skills, using both long and short balls to good effect. He reads the game well, and his pace and strength led to him scoring a number of

Fredrik Ljungberg

crucial goals last season. He netted both at home and away in the Premiership against Manchester United, the latter effort earning the Gunners a 1-1 draw. His goal against Werder Bremen in the home leg of the quarter-final of the UEFA Cup set up a 2-0 victory. Now established as a regular for Sweden, he won seven more caps last season, appearing in all three of his country's games in Euro 2000.

Arsenal (£3,000,000 from BK Halmstad, Sweden on 17/9/1998) PL 32+10/7 FLC 2 FAC 4+1 Others 12+3/2

LLEWELLYN Christopher (Chris) Mark
Born: Swansea, 29 August 1979
Height: 5'11" Weight: 11.6
International Honours: W: 2; B-1; U21-10; Yth

Chris continued his footballing education in 1999-2000, enhancing his reputation with a series of hard-working displays for Norwich in a number of positions. By his own admission a central striker, Chris was given the unenviable task of filling Darren Eadie's boots on the left flank when the former Carrow Road favourite left for Leicester in December 1999. To his eternal credit, he did exactly that, winning over some of the more critical City fans with a number of excellent performances. A very direct player, he likes nothing better than getting his head down and heading straight for goal, running at defenders; he is also a good crosser of the ball and, last season, added a touch more aggression and willingness to run for the whole 90 minutes to his game. Chris continued to catch the eye of the Welsh selectors and won further U21 caps against Belarus, Switzerland, Northern Ireland and Scotland.

Norwich C (From trainee on 21/1/1997) FL 55+27/9 FLC 4+2 FAC 2+1/1

LOCK Anthony (Tony) Charles
Born: Harlow, 3 September 1976
Height: 5'11" Weight: 13.0

Tony is a strong, left-sided attacker who was somewhat surprisingly released by then Colchester manager Mick Wadsworth at the end of the 1998-99 season. When Steve Whitton took over last August he invited Tony back for a trial spell, following which he was re-signed on a month-to-month deal. He has worked hard at both his fitness and his game, and enjoyed a good spell towards the end of the season, including goals against Gillingham and Luton. He has now been offered a contract for the coming season, and all Colchester fans are pleased to see him back.

Colchester U (From trainee on 18/4/1995) FL 41+47/11 FLC 0+2 FAC 1+4 Others 1+6

LOCKE Adam Spencer
Born: Croydon, 20 August 1970
Height: 5'11" Weight: 12.7

A hard-working midfielder with a taste for moving forward in support of his front line, Adam signed for Luton in August 1999 after declining Bristol City's offer of a new contract. Having featured in Luton's pre-season programme and worked hard on his fitness after collecting some niggling injuries, he made his league debut for Town against Brentford in September and found the net a week later in the 4-2 win over Oxford. By December he had established himself in the team and, injuries permitting, he remained a key member of the squad for the rest of the season, bringing some much-needed experience to the Luton line-up. He was out of contract during the summer, and the club will be looking to renew his deal for at least another term.

Crystal Palace (From trainee on 21/6/1988)
Southend U (Free on 6/8/1990) FL 56+17/4 FLC 5 FAC 2+1 Others 6+1
Colchester U (Loaned on 8/10/1993) FL 4 Others 1
Colchester U (Free on 23/9/1994) FL 64+15/8 FLC 5+1 FAC 5 Others 8+5
Bristol C (Free on 23/7/1997) FL 61+4/4 FLC 6 FAC 3 Others 2/1
Luton T (Free on 24/8/1999) FL 27+7/3 FAC 3+1 Others 1

LOCKWOOD Matthew (Matt) Dominic
Born: Southend, 17 October 1976
Height: 5'9" Weight: 10.12

Matt is an excellent left wing back, and is Leyton Orient's free-kick specialist and penalty taker. He has been watched by Premiership and First Division scouts, as he is recognised as having one of the best left feet in the Third Division. Matt can also play in central midfield. Orient will be looking to retain his services, not least because he finished 1999-2000 as their joint top scorer on seven goals with Iyseden Christie and Steve Watts. He is rated in the £1 million bracket, and Tottenham's reported interest was vindicated when Matt was deservedly included in the PFA divisional team.

Queens Park R (Free from Southend U juniors on 2/5/1995)
Bristol Rov (Free on 24/7/1996) FL 58+5/1 FLC 2+1 FAC 6 Others 4+2
Leyton Orient (Free on 7/8/1998) FL 77+1/9 FLC 6/2 FAC 6 Others 3

LOGAN Richard Anthony
Born: Barnsley, 24 May 1969
Height: 6'1" Weight: 13.3

The Scunthorpe "Player of the Year" in 1999, Richard found life tougher in Division Two during the 1999-2000 season and struggled to shake off a back problem for most of the first half of the campaign. Still played regularly at centre half, where he showed physical strength in the air and on the ground, he is also the club's long-throw expert and remained an attacking threat at set pieces. He was released at the end of the season and signed for local rivals Lincoln in the summer.

Huddersfield T (Free from Gainsborough Trinity on 15/11/1993) FL 35+10/1 FLC 3 FAC 1 Others 9
Plymouth Arg (£20,000 on 26/10/1995) FL 67+19/12 FLC 4/1 FAC 2+2 Others 8
Scunthorpe U (Free on 2/7/1998) FL 77+3/7 FLC 1 FAC 4 Others 3

LOGAN Richard James
Born: Bury St Edmunds, 4 January 1982
Height: 6'0" Weight: 12.5
International Honours: E: Yth; Sch

Richard was not able to break into the Ipswich first team last season, although he was on the bench a few times. He came on as a substitute for the last five minutes at Huddersfield in November but that was to prove his only taste of first-team football. A predominantly right-footed striker with a good turn of pace, he scored regularly for the reserves. Richard was called up by England youths during the season, appearing for the U18s against France in March and for the U17s in Luxembourg the following month.

Ipswich T (From trainee on 6/1/1999) FL 0+3

LOMAS James (Jamie) Duncan
Born: Chesterfield, 18 October 1977
Height: 5'11" Weight: 12.0

James came close to breaking through to a regular first-team place at Chesterfield last term, despite being sidelined by a debilitating virus as the season started. As cover for injured players, he was used in several midfield or defensive roles, but is at his most impressive getting forward down the right flank, where he can deliver an effective cross. He was released at the end of the season.

Chesterfield (From trainee on 16/9/1996) FL 17+13 FLC 2+1 FAC 1/1 Others 2+3

LOMAS Stephen (Steve) Martin
Born: Hanover, Germany, 18 January 1974
Height: 6'0" Weight: 12.8
International Honours: NI: 35; B-1; Yth; Sch

This all-action midfielder had another fine season in 1999-2000 as West Ham's captain. Steve rarely missed a game until breaking a toe playing for Northern Ireland against Malta at the end of March – and then he actually played on for the Hammers against Manchester United the following Saturday before the injury was diagnosed. He is a good ball winner, passes accurately and has a long throw that often causes problems for opposition defences. Steve featured regularly for the Northern Ireland international team during the season, adding a further five caps to his total.

Manchester C (From trainee on 22/1/1991) P/FL 102+9/8 FLC 15/2 FAC 10+1/1
West Ham U (£1,600,000 on 26/3/1997) PL 95/4 FLC 7/1 FAC 8/1 Others 6

LORMOR Anthony (Tony)
Born: Ashington, 29 October 1970
Height: 6'0" Weight: 13.6

Tony was an ever-present at centre forward for Mansfield in 1999-2000 until an injury at the end of February forced him out of the side. By that time he was the leading scorer and had formed a good understanding with new forward partner Chris Greenacre, the replacement for Lee Peacock. He led the line well, and although not the fastest of players makes up for this with wholehearted effort.

Newcastle U (From trainee on 25/2/1988) FL 6+2/3
Lincoln C (£25,000 on 29/1/1990) FL 90+10/30 FLC 1+2/3 FAC 4/2 Others 6
Peterborough U (Free on 4/7/1994) FL 2+3 FAC 1 Others 1+1
Chesterfield (Free on 23/12/1994) FL 97+16/35 FLC 8/4 FAC 5/3 Others 7+1/3
Preston NE (£130,000 + on 5/11/1997) FL 9+3/3 FAC 3 Others 3

Notts Co (Loaned on 20/2/1998) FL 2+5
Mansfield T (£20,000 on 16/7/1998) FL 68+6/20 FLC 2+1 FAC 3/3 Others 4/1

LOUIS-JEAN Matthieu
Born: Mont St Aignan, France, 22 February 1976
Height: 5'9" Weight: 10.12
International Honours: France: U21

Matthieu began last season as a first choice in the Nottingham Forest defence, appearing as a right-sided wing back. He lost his place in November when Riccardo Scimeca was switched to right back but later returned in the new year. He is a defender who is comfortable on the ball, reads the game well and enjoys getting forward to help out the attack.

Nottingham F (Signed from Le Havre, France on 14/9/1998) P/FL 41+2 FLC 5+2 FAC 2

LOVELL Stephen (Steve) William Henry
Born: Amersham, 6 December 1980
Height: 6'1" Weight: 12.7

This tall young striker began the 1999-2000 season with Bournemouth but after appearing as a substitute in the opening game against Cambridge he moved down the south coast to join Portsmouth for a £250,000 fee. Still very inexperienced, he made the starting line-up for Pompey in the two Worthington Cup matches against Torquay, scoring from 12 yards in the 3-0 second-leg victory, but otherwise featured only a couple of times from the subs' bench. He was subsequently loaned to Exeter last March to provide him with regular first-team action. Quick and with an eye for goal, Steve made a terrific start by scoring the only goal on his debut against Halifax, and helped to fix City's goalscoring problems during his spell with the club.

Bournemouth (From trainee on 15/7/1999) FL 1+7
Portsmouth (£250,000 on 13/8/1999) FL 0+3 FLC 2+1/1
Exeter C (Loaned on 20/3/2000) FL 4+1/1

LOW Joshua (Josh) David
Born: Bristol, 15 February, 1979
Height: 6'1" Weight: 12.0
International Honours: W: U21-1; Yth

Josh moved to Leyton Orient from Bristol Rovers on a free transfer in the summer of 1999. An attacking right winger, he scored against Hartlepool in September but was reportedly unable to settle in London. He returned to the West in October, joining Cardiff on loan before agreeing a permanent deal with the Welsh club. Josh has the ability to go past defenders with ease, using his pace to leave opponents standing. However, while his free-running style delights the fans and throws opposition defenders into a panic, it could not secure him a regular first-team place at Ninian Park. Too often, once he had beaten his man, he failed to deliver a quality cross. Reading were certainly impressed by him when the two clubs met on Boxing Day and eventually had three defenders lining up to stop him, while Bolton made an enquiry about signing the youngster after the Bluebirds played at the Reebok Stadium in the FA Cup. He remained at Cardiff and the club's coaching staff will be keen to ensure that he develops the mental discipline to turn all that exciting approach play into consistent service for his strikers.

Bristol Rov (From trainee on 19/8/1996) FL 11+11 FLC 0+2 FAC 2+2 Others 2
Leyton Orient (Free on 27/5/1999) FL 2+3/1 FLC 1
Cardiff C (Free on 20/11/1999) FL 12+5/2 FAC 1 Others 0+1

LOWE David Anthony
Born: Liverpool, 30 August 1965
Height: 5'10" Weight: 11.9
Club Honours: AMC '85; Div 2 '92, Div 3 '97
International Honours: E: U21-2; Yth

This experienced striker joined Wrexham from Wigan in the 1999 close season as manager Brian Flynn took measures to strengthen his attack. However, although he began the season as a first choice, he soon lost his place and after a spell on the subs' bench he dropped out of the first-team set-up. He joined progressive Conference club Rushden & Diamonds on loan last January to assist in their bid for promotion to Football League status but after a successful two months with the Northamptonshire club he failed a medical when all set to move permanently and returned to North Wales. He was made available on a free transfer in the summer of 2000.

Wigan Ath (From apprentice on 1/6/1983) FL 179+9/40 FLC 8 FAC 16+1/4 Others 18/9
Ipswich T (£80,000 on 26/6/1987) FL 121+13/37 FLC 10/2 FAC 3 Others 10+2/6
Port Vale (Loaned on 19/3/1992) FL 8+1/2
Leicester C (£250,000 on 13/7/1992) F/PL 68+26/22 FLC 4+3/1 FAC 2+2 Others 3
Port Vale (Loaned on 18/2/1994) FL 18+1/5
Wigan Ath (£125,000 on 28/3/1996) FL 85+23/26 FLC 7 FAC 4+2/3 Others 5+1/1
Wrexham (Free on 5/7/1999) FL 4+6/1 FLC 1

Tresor Lua Lua

LUA LUA Lomano **Tresor**
Born: Zaire, 28 December 1980
Height: 5'8" Weight: 12.2

A sublimely talented attacker, Colchester's young star was probably one of the most talked-about players in the lower divisions last season, when he fulfilled the immense promise he had shown in 1998-99. He is an unpredictable player with natural pace and balance and the ability to beat opponents any number of ways, with his only apparent weaknesses being that he doesn't know when it is better to pass the ball, and that he doesn't score any easy goals! His total of 14 goals in his first full season is impressive, especially as he was used as a substitute half the time, and each and every one of them was memorable. Expect more of the same next year!

Colchester U (Signed from Leyton College on 25/9/1998) FL 30+24/13 FLC 2/1 FAC 1/1 Others 1

LUCAS David Anthony
Born: Preston, 23 November 1977
Height: 6'2" Weight: 13.10
International Honours: E: Yth

David started last season as Preston's number one 'keeper, but following a controversial sending-off in the home defeat by Wigan he lost his place to Tepi Moilanen and thereafter featured only when Tepi was rested. The FA Cup match against Enfield was his first game for 11 weeks, and it was to be another 12 weeks before he featured again, subsequently returning to the bench for the rest of the season. Already capped by England U20s, David is highly thought of at Deepdale and has proved himself to be an excellent shot stopper, although he is not as strong on crosses as he might like, and still has a bright future in the game ahead of him.

Preston NE (From trainee on 12/12/1994) FL 46 FLC 2 FAC 5 Others 8
Darlington (Loaned on 14/12/1995) FL 6
Darlington (Loaned on 3/10/1996) FL 7
Scunthorpe U (Loaned on 23/12/1996) FL 6 Others 2

LUCAS Richard
Born: Chapeltown, 22 September 1970
Height: 5'10" Weight: 12.6

Richard did not enjoy the best of seasons in 1999-2000, with a series of niggling injuries hampering his efforts and places in the Halifax first team at a premium. He is generally a left-sided defender, but his versatility and professional attitude shone through whenever he was called upon, and he never let the team down. Richard was released in the summer.

Sheffield U (From trainee on 1/7/1989) FL 8+2 FAC 1 Others 0+1
Preston NE (£40,000 on 24/12/1992) FL 47+3 FAC 4 Others 4+1
Lincoln C (Loaned on 14/10/1994) FL 4 Others 2
Scarborough (Free on 5/7/1995) FL 63+9 FLC 6 FAC 3+1 Others 2
Hartlepool U (Free on 27/3/1997) FL 49/2 FLC 2 FAC 1 Others 1
Halifax T (Free on 7/8/1998) FL 39+9 FLC 3+1 FAC 2+1 Others 2+1/1

LUCKETTI Christopher (Chris) James
Born: Rochdale, 28 September 1971
Height: 6'0" Weight: 13.6
Club Honours: Div 2 '97

Signed from Bury in the summer of 1999, Chris slotted into the Huddersfield defence as if he had been there for years. An accomplished centre back, he had previously been chased by Town's last manager, Peter Jackson, and following Bury's relegation it seemed Chris was certain to move on. The Terriers' new team captain, he produced "Man of the Match" performances in the club's first two fixtures of 1999-2000, capped by a headed goal against Scunthorpe United in the Worthington Cup. Rarely beaten in the air and tremendous in the tackle, he turned in a series of dominant displays which were a major factor in Town's rise up the table. Unfortunately, an innocuous challenge at Bolton Wanderers in October left him with a broken leg which kept him on the sidelines until February. His assured performances on his return left no doubt that he is vital to Town's future development.

Rochdale (Trainee) FL 1
Stockport Co (Free on 23/8/1990)
Halifax T (Free on 12/7/1991) FL 73+5/2 FLC 2/1 FAC 2 Others 4
Bury (£50,000 on 1/10/1993) FL 235/8 FLC 16 FAC 11/1 Others 15/1
Huddersfield T (£750,000 + on 14/6/1999) FL 26 FLC 5/1

LUDDEN Dominic James

Born: Basildon, 30 March 1974
Height: 5'8" Weight: 11.0
International Honours: E: Sch

Dominic suffered a groin strain in Preston's opening game of 1999-2000, and a niggling stomach injury meant that he failed to make much impression on the first team thereafter, playing in only five matches. Lightning fast from left back and a provider of telling crosses and free kicks, he also possesses a fearsome shot when cutting inside, and many North End fans hope he still has a future at the club, as his contract was due to expire in the summer.

Leyton Orient (Signed from Billericay T on 6/7/1992) FL 50+8/1 FLC 1 FAC 0+1 Others 6/1
Watford (£100,000 on 7/8/1994) FL 28+5 FLC 3 FAC 2+1 Others 2
Preston NE (Free on 31/7/1998) FL 29+6 FLC 2 FAC 2 Others 3

LUMSDON Christopher (Chris)

Born: Newcastle, 15 December 1979
Height: 5'7" Weight: 10.6

A right-sided midfielder, Chris's impressive form in Sunderland's pre-season saw him elevated to the first-team squad for the club's return to the Premiership in the campaign's curtain raiser at Stamford Bridge against Chelsea. However, he found himself stuck out on the left wing and, after the Black Cats had crashed heavily, he was replaced by Stefan Schwarz for the next game. The youngster did, however, appear in his "natural" position of central midfield against Walsall in the Worthington Cup the following month, where his passing ability shone and he turned in an excellent performance. With a Premiership place looking unlikely, though, Peter Reid allowed Chris to spend a month on loan at Blackpool last February. During his spell at Bloomfield Road he showed good pace and accuracy in his passing and crossing. He scored with a 20-yard drive in his final match for the Seasiders against Notts County and will be aiming to establish himself in the North-east club's first-team squad in the coming season.

Sunderland (From trainee on 3/7/1997) P/FL 2 FLC 1+1
Blackpool (Loaned on 3/2/2000) FL 6/1

LUND Andreas

Born: Norway, 7 May 1975
Height: 6'3" Weight: 12.12
International Honours: Norway: 8

Andreas joined Wimbledon from Norwegian club Molde in a £2.5 million deal last February. He arrived with a good goal-scoring pedigree and was an instant success with a goal on his debut at Chelsea. A big, strong lad who is good in the air, he seemed well suited to the Dons' direct style but didn't quite make the hoped-for impact. He managed only one more goal and ended the season on the substitutes' bench. Andreas's physical presence was expected to be a real asset for the Dons as they strove to regain their Premiership place in 2000-01, and it was something of a surprise when he was loaned back to Molde, causing him to miss the first three months of the English season. Having made his debut for Norway against Jamaica in May 1999, he has done well when called up for international duty, scoring four times in seven appearances, but he remains on the fringe of the squad and was disappointed to miss out on a place in the final 22 for Euro 2000.

Wimbledon (£2,500,000 from Molde, Norway on 11/2/2000) PL 10+2/2

LUNDEKVAM Claus

Born: Norway, 22 February 1973
Height: 6'3" Weight: 12.10
International Honours: Norway: 7

A Norwegian international central defender with a maternal grandmother from Liverpool, Claus has now spent four seasons at the Dell and he continues to develop into a strong, commanding figure. A leggy, unflappable defender who loves to surge upfield with the ball rather than kick and run, he forged a good understanding with new-boy Dean Richards in 1999-2000. Recalled to the Norwegian national team in January 2000, he produced a solid performance in a goalless draw against Iceland in a Nordic Cup fixture.

Southampton (£400,000 from SK Brann, Norway on 3/9/1996) PL 114+6 FLC 16+2 FAC 5

LUNDIN Pal Michael

Born: Osby, Sweden, 21 November 1964
Height: 6'5" Weight: 14.0

Pal was unable to secure the number one jersey at Oxford United in 1999-2000 but still managed to be the 'keeper with the most starts for the club during the season. The Swedish shot stopper, and former wrestler, got great length on his clearances, and although he often punched the ball instead of catching it he did make a number of good saves and also helped his team to win an Auto Windscreens Shield tie with Wycombe when he saved a penalty and then slotted home the clinching kick. He was not retained, however, and returned to Sweden at the end of April.

Oxford U (Free from Osters IFV, Sweden on 2/3/1999) FL 28+1 FLC 1 FAC 4 Others 3

LUNT Kenneth (Kenny) Vincent

Born: Runcorn, 20 November 1979
Height: 5'10" Weight: 10.0
International Honours: E: Yth; Sch

A graduate of the FA School at Lilleshall who represented England at schoolboy and youth level, Kenny has developed into a very accomplished midfield player since making his senior debut for Crewe in 1997-98. He reads the game well, uses the ball intelligently and also contributed goals against Walsall in August, Grimsby in January and Port Vale in March. A consistent, versatile player, he missed only three matches and seems set to play a big part in Alex's future.

Crewe Alex (From trainee on 12/6/1997) FL 74+28/6 FLC 7+3/1 FAC 1+1

LUZHNY Oleg

Born: Ukraine, 5 August 1968
Height: 6'1" Weight: 12.3
Club Honours: CS '99
International Honours: USSR: 8. Ukraine: 35

Signed by Arsenal from Dynamo Kiev, where he had been club captain, in June 1999, Oleg has been an international for over a decade, having made his debut for the USSR back in the late 1980s. Renowned for his galloping runs upfield for club and country, he is a strong-tackling right wing back who can play equally well in the centre of defence. During the 1999-2000 season, Oleg provided good cover when either Tony Adams or Martin Keown was ruled out through injury. He is strong in the air with a powerful kick and can also contribute effectively in midfield. His versatility makes him an essential squad player. A regular for the Ukraine national side, he has added six caps to his tally since arriving at Highbury.

Arsenal (£1,800,000 from Dinamo Kiev, Ukraine on 9/7/1999) PL 16+5 FLC 2 FAC 1 Others 6+1

LYTTLE Desmond (Des)

Born: Wolverhampton, 24 September 1971
Height: 5'9" Weight: 12.13
Club Honours: Div 1 '98

The accomplished right back joined Watford on a free transfer from Nottingham Forest at the start of the 1999-2000 season to replace the departed Darren Bazeley. As a seasoned Premiership player with more than 300 senior appearances to his credit, Des seemed an ideal addition to the comparatively inexperienced Watford squad. His defensive qualities were not in doubt but, despite his best efforts, he found it difficult to add sufficient creative flair, and he went on loan to West Bromwich Albion just before the transfer deadline. At the Hawthorns, Des's attacking play added a new dimension to Albion's midfield area. He became part of a new four-man defence at a crucial time in the season – when Albion were battling against relegation – and proved a vital acquisition. His surging runs enabled his midfielders to gain a lot more space, and his crosses produced three crucial goals when it mattered most. Stop Press: It was reported at the beginning of June that Des had joined West Bromwich on a permanent basis.

Leicester C (From trainee on 1/9/1990)
Swansea C (£12,500 from Worcester C on 9/7/1992) FL 46/1 FLC 2 FAC 5 Others 5
Nottingham F (£375,000 on 27/7/1993) F/PL 177+8/3 FLC 19+1 FAC 16 Others 8
Port Vale (Loaned on 20/11/1998) FL 7
Watford (Free on 28/7/1999) PL 11 FLC 1
West Bromwich A (Loaned on 21/3/2000) FL 8+1

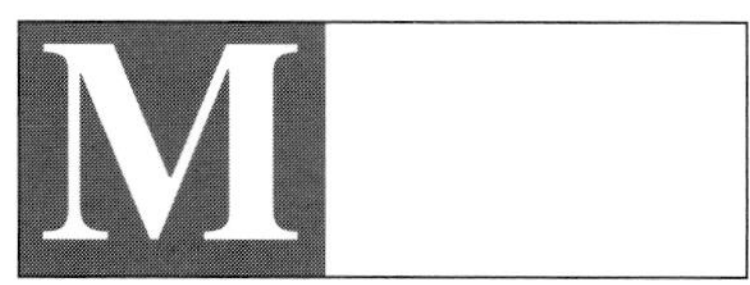

McALLISTER Gary
Born: Motherwell, 25 December 1964
Height: 6'1" Weight: 11.12
Club Honours: S Div 1 '85; Div 1 '92; CS '92
International Honours: S: 57; B-2; U21-1

Gary's retirement from international football and his subsequent long rest in the summer of 1999 seemed to rejuvenate his club form, and the 1999-2000 season was his best in a Coventry City shirt. An ever-present, he also hit the goalscoring heights with 13 goals, including four penalties, which made him the club's leading scorer. He has never missed a penalty for the Sky Blues, scoring 11 since taking over the duties from Dion Dublin. He scored City's first goal of the season, a high-pressure last-minute penalty at Wimbledon to earn a point. His form blossomed after the arrival at Highfield Road of Carlton Palmer in September, which allowed him to leave the defensive midfield duties to Palmer and concentrate not only on play-making but also on getting into the opposition box more. The partnership proved to be very successful as the side lost only two of the next 16 games. After Palmer's injury Gary's rich vein of form continued while the side as a whole struggled, and he deservedly won the club's "Player of the Year" award. He scored a crucial late goal to clinch a 1-0 home win over Everton and his performance in the final home game with Sheffield Wednesday was almost perfect with two well-taken goals and two other thunderous shots rattling the crossbar. Gary's contract ended in the summer and he accepted an offer to join Liverpool with the aim of going out at the top.

Motherwell (Signed from Fir Park BC on 5/9/1981) SL 52+7/6 SLC 3+1 SC 7/2
Leicester C (£125,000 on 15/8/1985) FL 199+2/47 FLC 14+1/3 FAC 5/2 Others 4
Leeds U (£1,000,000 on 2/7/1990) F/PL 230+1/31 FLC 26/5 FAC 24/6 Others 14/4
Coventry C (£3,000,000 on 26/7/1996) PL 119/20 FLC 11/5 FAC 10/1

McATEER Jason Wynn
Born: Birkenhead, 18 June 1971
Height: 5'10" Weight: 11.12
International Honours: RoI: 34; B-1

It is well known that Jason prefers to play in the centre of midfield but he was disappointing in this role for Blackburn in 1999-2000 and looked far more comfortable playing wide on the right. He started the season with a hangover from the previous campaign in the form of nerve damage to his leg which was slow to heal. It was not until late October that he returned to the team but his switching from inside to outside did not encourage consistency. Disciplinary problems and then a hamstring injury in March sidelined him for a while. Not known for his sharpness in front of goal, Jason earned three points for his side with the winner at Stockport. Towards the end of the season, under Graeme Souness, he played at right back, but still appears to be happier further forward. Despite his injury problems he added four more caps for the Republic of Ireland during the season.

Bolton W (Signed from Marine on 22/1/1992) P/FL 109+5/8 FLC 11/2 FAC 11/3 Others 8+1/2
Liverpool (£4,500,000 on 6/9/1995) PL 84+16/3 FLC 12+1 FAC 11+1/3 Others 12+2
Blackburn Rov (£4,000,000 on 28/1/1999) P/FL 37+4/3 FAC 3

McAULEY Hugh Francis
Born: Plymouth, 13 May 1976
Height: 5'10" Weight: 11.4

One of the leading scorers in the Nationwide Conference during 1998-99, Hugh was signed by Cheltenham from Leek Town in the summer of 1999 and went straight into the first team. He spent the first half of the new season partnering Neil Grayson in attack but then lost his place, first to loan signing Chris Freestone and then to Martin Devaney. Hugh scored his first Football League goal from the penalty spot against Hull but a miss against Barnet seemed to affect his confidence. An intelligent player who is good at linking others with the attack, often dropping a little deeper to this end, Hugh also made a number of reserve-team appearances in midfield. Although used mostly as a substitute in the second half of the campaign, Hugh is certainly one for the future, especially if some increased body strength and, more significantly, self-belief can be allied to his natural ability.

Cheltenham T (Signed from Leek T on 15/7/1999) FL 22+17/4 FLC 2 FAC 1 Others 2/1

McAULEY Sean
Born: Sheffield, 23 June 1972
Height: 5'11" Weight: 11.12
International Honours: S: U21-1; Yth

Sean found himself out of favour at Scunthorpe as the start of the 1999-2000 season approached, but a move to York fell through when he picked up an ankle injury that ruled him out of the first month of the campaign. He was eventually given another chance at Glanford Park, where he filled in capably at left back, showing defensive experience and good set-piece ability. A target of the terrace boo-boys, Sean needed a move to kick-start his career and, with Rochdale looking for an experienced left back, he signed a two-and-a-half-year contract with the club in February. Unfortunately, he arrived during a down-turn in Dale's form that prompted a switch to a 5-3-2 formation. It left Sean slightly out in the cold after just five games, but he was recalled towards the end of the campaign.

Manchester U (From trainee on 1/7/1990)
St Johnstone (Signed on 22/4/1992) SL 59+3 SLC 3/1 SC 3 Others 1
Chesterfield (Loaned on 4/11/1994) FL 1/1 FAC 1+1 Others 2
Hartlepool U (Free on 21/7/1995) FL 84/1 FLC 6 FAC 3 Others 3
Scunthorpe U (Signed on 26/3/1997) FL 63+6/1 FLC 5 FAC 5 Others 2
Scarborough (Loaned on 25/3/1999) FL 6+1
Rochdale (Free on 11/2/2000) FL 10+3

MACAULEY Stephen (Steve) Roy
Born: Lytham, 4 March 1969
Height: 6'1" Weight: 12.0
Club Honours: FAYC '86

One of the longest-serving members of the Crewe squad, having been with the club since March 1992, Steve was once again a regular in the heart of the Alex defence last season. A very popular member of the club's staff, he is a powerful header of the ball, and as well as being a commanding figure at the back he poses a considerable threat in opposition penalty areas at set pieces. He scored four goals in 1999-2000, one of them a penalty against Walsall, two others coming in the 2-3 defeat by Birmingham in February.

Manchester C (From trainee on 5/11/1987. Released during 1988 close season)
Crewe Alex (£25,000 from Fleetwood T on 24/3/1992) FL 208+14/25 FLC 16 FAC 13/1 Others 20/3

McAVOY Andrew (Andy) David
Born: Middlesbrough, 28 August 1979
Height: 6'0" Weight: 12.0

Andy is an attacking right-sided midfielder who had attracted Hartlepool's attention for several months before they signed him from Blackburn in November 1999. An extremely competitive player, in his early games he showed signs that he had the right qualities to succeed and win a regular place. Unfortunately, as the season wore on he faded a little, and he was limited to appearances made when coming on from the substitutes' bench.

Blackburn Rov (From trainee on 14/7/1997)
Hartlepool U (Free on 24/11/1999) FL 5+11 Others 1+3

McCALL Stephen (Steve) Harold
Born: Carlisle, 15 October 1960
Height: 5'11" Weight: 12.6
Club Honours: UEFAC '81
International Honours: E: B-1; U21-6; Yth

A vastly experienced player and now Plymouth's assistant manager, Steve still puts on his boots when the need arises. As he made his league debut for Ipswich in September 1979, Steve was playing top-grade football before a number of his Pilgrims colleagues were born. Although his appearances reduced as the 1999-2000 campaign wore on, his ball skills are still a delight to watch, and his experience both on and off the field has become crucial to Argyle's success. Steve scored his only goal of the season with a tremendous volley at Chester in November. In May, he was linked to the vacant manager's post at Carlisle, his home-town club.

Ipswich T (From apprentice on 5/10/1978) FL 249+8/7 FLC 29 FAC 23+1/1 Others 18+1/3
Sheffield Wed (£300,000 on 3/6/1987) FL 21+8/2 FLC 2+3 FAC 1 Others 0+1
Carlisle U (Loaned on 8/2/1990) FL 6
Plymouth Arg (£25,000 on 26/3/1992) FL 97+3/5 FLC 5 FAC 6 Others 6
Torquay U (Free on 12/7/1996) FL 43+8/2 FLC 3+1 Others 4/1
Plymouth Arg (Free on 7/8/1998) FL 28+5/1 FLC 3+1 FAC 4+2

McCALL Andrew **Stuart** Murray
Born: Leeds, 10 June 1964
Height: 5'7" Weight: 12.0
Club Honours: Div 3 '85; SPL '92, '93, '94, '95, '96; SLC '92, '93; SC '92, '93, '96
International Honours: S: 40; U21-2

Stuart captained Bradford City in 1999-2000 and led the team by example as the driving force in midfield. He belied his age, running around like a teenager, tackling ferociously and powering in free kicks with a venomous right foot. He missed the first four games while recovering from surgery to solve groin and achilles problems but was rarely absent for the rest of a season which saw the Bantams escape relegation with a last-day victory over Liverpool.

Bradford C (From apprentice on 1/6/1982) FL 235+3/37 FLC 16/3 FAC 12/3 Others 12+1/3
Everton (£850,000 on 1/6/1988) FL 99+4/6 FLC 11/1 FAC 16+2/3 Others 8+1
Glasgow R (£1,200,000 on 15/8/1991) SL 186+8/14 SLC 15/3 SC 25+2 Others 28/2
Bradford C (Free on 4/6/1998) P/FL 76+1/4 FLC 5 FAC 3+1

Stuart McCall

McCAMMON Mark Jason
Born: Barnet, 7 August 1978
Height: 6'5" Weight: 14.5

A tall and commanding figure, Mark is surprisingly quick for a big man, but the striker had limited opportunities in the Charlton side in 1999-2000. He made his debut early in the season as a substitute against Bolton at the Valley and was given his full debut at Tranmere shortly afterwards. Only two further appearances, both as a substitute, were to follow, and he joined First Division strugglers Swindon on loan in January. He is highly rated at the Valley and proved to be quick and hard working for the Robins, although he failed to find the net in his four appearances for them. He returned to Charlton after picking up an injury.

Cambridge U (Free from Cambridge C on 31/12/1996) FL 1+3 FAC 0+1 Others 1
Charlton Ath (Free on 17/3/1999) FL 1+3 FLC 0+1
Swindon T (Loaned on 3/1/2000) FL 4

McCANN Gavin Peter
Born: Blackpool, 10 January 1978
Height: 5'11" Weight: 11.0

The tall midfielder had been something of a bit-part player in Sunderland's march to the First Division championship in 1998-99 but by the conclusion of last season many of the club's fans were rueing the fact that Gavin, having established himself in the first team, had had his season cut short by a cruciate knee ligament injury in February. Peter Reid has stated that he believes that Gavin can go on to gain England recognition and his form last term certainly backed this up. A combative player, Gavin is also adept on the ball, as shown by his FA Cup goal against Portsmouth in December, a solo effort that saw him beat three men before slotting the ball home. Gavin also found the net against Manchester United, Derby, Leicester and Watford, and looked to be the answer to Sunderland's lack of a goalscoring midfielder before injury struck. On a darker note, Gavin's over-exuberance found him in referees' note-books too often last season but, with experience, this will no doubt be eradicated. Gavin was also honoured by the Sunderland fans, who voted him their "Young Player of the Year".

Everton (From trainee on 1/7/1995) PL 5+6
Sunderland (£500,000 on 27/11/1998) P/FL 26+9/4 FLC 1+1/1 FAC 3+1/2

McCARTHY Jonathan (Jon) David
Born: Middlesbrough, 18 August 1970
Height: 5'9" Weight: 11.5
International Honours: NI: 16; B-2

Jon enjoyed outstanding form in the early part of the 1999-2000 season appearing as a wide midfield player for Birmingham City. His pace, trickery and crossing skills were all assets to the team and he scored a fine individual goal at Barnsley last November. He then had the misfortune to receive a broken right leg in the next game against Tranmere that kept him out until April. He returned to first-team action ahead of schedule with the leg fully mended only to suffer a second fracture in the same place while playing against Manchester City, just four games into his comeback. Jon also added four more caps for Northern Ireland to his tally last autumn.

Hartlepool U (From juniors on 7/11/1987) FL 0+1 (Free to Shepshed Charterhouse in March 1989)
York C (Free on 22/3/1990) FL 198+1/31 FLC 8/1 FAC 11/3 Others 15/3
Port Vale (£450,000 on 1/8/1995) FL 93+1/12 FLC 10/2 FAC 7/1 Others 8/2
Birmingham C (£1,500,000 on 11/9/1997) FL 97+8/8 FLC 8+1 FAC 4 Others 2

McCARTHY Paul Jason
Born: Cork, 4 August 1971
Height: 5'10" Weight: 13.12
International Honours: RoI: U21-10; Yth; Sch

This powerful Wycombe central defender formed an impressive partnership with Jamie Bates in the early games of the 1999-2000 season. He then succumbed to a bad ankle injury at the end of September, and it was not until the new year that he returned to first-team action. Paul spent further time on the injury list during what was a frustrating second half of the campaign and will be hoping to avoid such problems in the coming season. He scored two goals, including a spectacular overhead kick in the 1-1 Worthington Cup draw at West Bromwich. Strong in the air and solid on the ground, he is a constant threat when coming up to join the attack for corners.

Brighton & Hove A (From trainee on 26/4/1989) FL 180+1/6 FLC 11/1 FAC 13 Others 12/1
Wycombe W (£100,000 on 5/7/1996) FL 111+11/3 FLC 10+1/2 FAC 8 Others 4

McCARTHY Sean Casey
Born: Bridgend, 12 September 1967
Height: 6'1" Weight: 12.12
International Honours: W: B-1

A strong, powerful and experienced Plymouth forward, Sean is extremely difficult to handle because of his physical presence, and strength in aerial challenges. Although he had a few injuries during 1999-2000, he often scored important goals, including the winner against arch-rivals Exeter in November, while a terrific effort at York in February was the 200th goal of his career. Sean also contributed to the development of Argyle's younger strikers.

Swansea C (Signed from Bridgend T on 22/10/1985) FL 76+15/25 FLC 4+1/3 FAC 5+2/4 Others 9+1/6
Plymouth Arg (£50,000 on 18/8/1988) FL 67+3/19 FLC 7/5 FAC 3/1 Others 0+1/1
Bradford C (£250,000 on 4/7/1990) FL 127+4/60 FLC 10+2/10 FAC 8/2 Others 8+1/7
Oldham Ath (£500,000 on 3/12/1993) P/FL 117+23/42 FLC 10/1 FAC 6+1/1 Others 4/1
Bristol C (Loaned on 26/3/1998) FL 7/1
Plymouth Arg (Signed on 7/8/1998) FL 35+10/9 FLC 2+1/2 FAC 8

McCLARE Sean Patrick
Born: Rotherham, 12 January 1978
Height: 5'10" Weight: 11.12
International Honours: RoI: U21-3

The 1999-2000 campaign was a big disappointment for this young Barnsley player after it seemed that he had established himself as a first-team squad member in 1998-99. An energetic, hard-working midfielder, Sean featured mostly as a substitute and, although he scored twice in early-season games, he made the starting line-up on only one occasion under new manager Dave Bassett. He was then sent on loan to Third Division Rochdale on transfer deadline day and was in the Dale squad for all their remaining matches, although he spent some time on the bench while he regained match fitness.

Barnsley (From trainee on 3/7/1996) FL 24+16/5 FLC 7+3 FAC 5/1
Rochdale (Loaned on 22/3/2000) FL 5+4

McCLEN James (Jamie) David
Born: Newcastle, 13 May 1979
Height: 5'9" Weight: 10.12

Jamie is a local lad who has progressed to Newcastle's first-team squad via the club's School of Excellence. He is a hard worker with good control at pace and enjoys breaking forward from his midfield position

to strike at goal, while his shooting carries a surprising threat for someone of his size. In 1999-2000 he started in both Ruud Gullit's last two games, at home to Wimbledon and Sunderland, but thereafter dropped to the bench until the turn of the year, making only one further start, at Leeds, although he was brought off the bench a number of times. Jamie was not chosen for most of the second half of the season, although clearly he is a player who is being nurtured for the future and he remained part of the first-team squad so that he could continue to learn his trade through involvement with the senior players, and made brief substitute appearances in the final three games of the season.
Newcastle U (From trainee on 4/7/1997) PL 4+6 Others 0+3

McCONNELL Barry
Born: Exeter, 1 January 1977
Height: 5'10" Weight: 10.3
After starting the 1999-2000 campaign in Exeter's attack, Barry was slightly out of sorts and lost his place. However, he was a revelation when switched to right back against Rochdale in January, and retained his place in the new role. His awareness of team-mates and superb first touch were in firm evidence. Manager Noel Blake praised him as being the best all-round technical player at the club, but he was released during the close season.
Exeter C (From trainee on 4/8/1995) FL 62+43/12 FLC 3+2/1 FAC 2+5 Others 3+1

McDERMOTT Andrew (Andy)
Born: Sydney, Australia, 24 March 1977
Height: 5'9" Weight: 11.3
International Honours: Australia: U23
The Australian-born defender contested the West Bromwich right-back spot with Danny Gabbidon and Daryl Burgess during the first half of the 1999-2000 season but was never really a regular in the Albion side. He was used as a wing back at times, but his crossing let him down on occasions. Andy did have the pleasure of scoring his only goal of the season in the local derby against Wolverhampton Wanderers – a stunning low drive from the edge of the penalty area. From March onwards he was out of favour again following the signing of Des Lyttle, and he was released during the summer.
Queens Park R (Signed from Australian Institute of Sport on 4/8/1995) FL 6/2
West Bromwich A (£400,000 on 27/3/1997) FL 49+3/1 FLC 4/1 FAC 0+1

McDERMOTT John
Born: Middlesbrough, 3 February 1969
Height: 5'7" Weight: 11.0
Club Honours: AMC '98
"Macca" missed most of the pre-season preparation for 1999-2000, his 14th season with Grimsby, due to an achilles tendon injury. Starting the campaign on the bench, he made only two substitute and three full appearances before once again being forced out of the squad with a knee injury, followed by a hamstring problem which kept him out of the game until mid-December when, despite some admirable performances by his young deputy, Danny Butterfield, he regained his place. He quickly proved that this long absence had not diminished his game, with his customary strong tackling and forward running much in evidence.
Grimsby T (From trainee on 1/6/1987) FL 419+18/7 FLC 30+2 FAC 28+2/2 Others 21

MacDONALD Charles (Charlie) Lea
Born: Southwark, 13 February 1981
Height: 5'9" Weight: 11.10
A young striker who has been a prolific goalscorer for Charlton's youth team and reserves, Charlie was brought on as a substitute against Nottingham Forest in January before making his full debut a week later in the FA Cup fourth-round tie against Queens Park Rangers at the Valley, when he scored the only goal of the game. Despite an impressive performance he was dropped for the next game and made only two more appearances, both as a substitute. Although short for a striker, Charlie has great strength for his age and is difficult to dispossess. He holds the ball up well and is a good finisher. Given the chance he should have a great future in the game.
Charlton Ath (From trainee on 10/11/1998) FL 0+3 FAC 1/1

McDONALD Thomas (Tom)
Born: Walthamstow, 15 September 1980
Height: 6'2" Weight: 12.4
This young defender made his senior debut for Southend as a substitute at Halifax in February 2000. A right back by trade, Tom will now be looking to follow Gary Cross into the team on a more regular basis in the new season.
Southend U (From trainee on 4/8/1999) FL 1+2

McELHOLM Brendan (Benny) Anthony
Born: Omagh, 7 July 1982
Height: 5'11" Weight: 12.2
International Honours: NI: Yth
Benny is the Northern Ireland U18 captain, and made the transition from youth team to first team at Leyton Orient last season without looking out of place. Like Simon Downer, he marked some of the best strikers in the Third Division and confidently took the challenge in his stride. Benny will be looking to become a first-team regular in 2000-01, and also make further progress with the Northern Ireland squad.
Leyton Orient (Trainee) FL 3

McEWEN David (Dave)
Born: Westminster, 2 November 1977
Height: 6'0" Weight: 11.0
Signed by Tottenham from non-league side Dulwich Hamlet last January, David made his first-team debut for Spurs as a second-half substitute at home to Derby in April. Having initially joined Tottenham on a part-time basis while studying for a business studies degree at the University of London, he must have been more than a little surprised at his rapid elevation into the first team. A lively young forward, David will be hoping for further opportunities to impress during the coming season.
Tottenham H (Free from Dulwich Hamlet on 6/1/2000) PL 0+1

McGAVIN Steven (Steve) James
Born: North Walsham, 24 January 1969
Height: 5'9" Weight: 12.8
Club Honours: GMVC '92; FAT '92; Div 2 '95
One of the goalscoring heroes of Colchester's non-league double season in 1992, Steve was brought back to his spiritual home from Northampton by Steve Whitton in October 1999. It is fair to say that there were some who doubted the wisdom of the move, but the manager himself had no doubts, and the player responded in style. Steve finished the season with 16 goals from 32 starts – an average of a goal every other game – and deservedly won the main "Player of the Year" award at the end of the season. While Steve was a success in his first spell at Layer Road, in 1999-2000 the fans saw a fitter, more experienced and fully developed professional.
Ipswich T (From trainee on 29/1/1987. Free to Thetford T in August 1987)
Colchester U (£10,000 from Sudbury T on 28/7/1992) FL 55+3/17 FLC 2 FAC 6/2 Others 4
Birmingham C (£150,000 on 7/1/1994) FL 16+7/2 FLC 1+1/1 FAC 3+1/2 Others 1+3
Wycombe W (£140,000 on 20/3/1995) FL 103+17/14 FLC 5+2 FAC 6+1/3 Others 4+2
Southend U (Free on 2/2/1999) FL 4+7
Colchester U (Free on 11/10/1999) FL 30+4/16 FAC 1 Others 1

McGHEE David Christopher
Born: Worthing, 19 June 1976
Height: 5'11" Weight: 12.4
Leyton Orient saved David from the soccer scrap heap after he was released by Brentford. He missed the entire 1998-99 season through injury, and was playing non-league football before being given a trial in the Orient reserve team. Manager Tommy Taylor was impressed with his attitude and, after being signed on non-contract forms, David was rewarded with a full contract in February. A wholehearted midfielder, he will be determined to make the most of his second chance.
Brentford (From trainee on 15/7/1994) FL 95+22/8 FLC 5+2/1 FAC 9/1 Others 8+1 (Freed on 22/1/1999)
Leyton Orient (Free from Stevenage Borough on 11/11/1999) FL 17+6/1 Others 1

McGIBBON Patrick (Pat) Colm
Born: Lurgan, 6 September 1973
Height: 6'2" Weight: 13.12
Club Honours: AMC '99
International Honours: NI: 7; B-5; U21-1; Sch
Pat is a strong and reliable Wigan central defender who is dominant in the air and quick in the tackle. He celebrated his 100th Football League start in the match at Bristol Rovers last March. His poised performances at the heart of a three-man central defensive partnership in 1999-2000 led to a recall to the Northern Ireland squad. Pat scored his only league goal of the campaign in the 1-1 draw against Cambridge in August. He was offered new terms at the end of the season.
Manchester U (£100,000 from Portadown on 1/8/1992) FLC 1
Swansea C (Loaned on 20/9/1996) FL 1
Wigan Ath (£250,000 on 3/3/1997) FL 107+8/8 FLC 6+1 FAC 8 Others 15

McGLEISH Scott
Born: Barnet, 10 February 1974
Height: 5'9" Weight: 11.3
A favourite with the Barnet fans, Scott experienced something of a roller-coaster ride during the 1999-2000 season. He enjoyed a whirlwind start to the campaign, plundering seven goals in the opening eight games, but then he endured every striker's worst nightmare – the dreaded lean spell in front of the target. In fact, it took him two months before he scored again in the important home clash against Darlington. After the dawning of the new year, Scott found himself competing for a place in the forward line with Marlon King and he scored a vital equaliser in the home draw with struggling Shrewsbury to keep Barnet's bid for promotion alive. His phenomenal level of fitness enables him to forage tirelessly in attack and force defensive errors. Also, despite his modest stature, he is able to out-jump much taller opponents with devastating effect.
Charlton Ath (Free from Edgware T on 24/5/1994) FL 0+6
Leyton Orient (Loaned on 10/3/1995) FL 4+2/1 Others 1/1
Peterborough U (Free on 4/7/1995) FL 3+10 FLC 0+1 FAC 0+1 Others 3+1/2
Colchester U (Loaned on 23/2/1996) FL 10+5/6 Others 2
Cambridge U (Loaned on 2/9/1996) FL 10/7 FLC 1
Leyton Orient (£50,000 on 22/11/1996) FL 36/7 FLC 3/1 FAC 1 Others 1
Barnet (£70,000 on 1/10/1997) FL 92+23/31 FLC 4/3 FAC 3 Others 6+2

McGLINCHEY Brian Kevin
Born: Derry, 26 October 1977
Height: 5'7" Weight: 10.2
International Honours: NI: B-1; U21-14
Signed by Gillingham from Port Vale before the start of the 1999-2000 season, this young left wing back made several appearances in the first half of the campaign but rarely featured in the Gills' promotion run-in, particularly after the more experienced Ty Gooden was signed early in the new year. He is predominantly left-footed with good pace and crossing ability. Brian added a further four caps to his already impressive total for Northern Ireland at U21 level during the season.
Manchester C (From trainee on 4/12/1995)
Port Vale (Free on 1/7/1998) FL 10+5/1 FLC 0+1 FAC 1
Gillingham (Free on 3/8/1999) FL 6+7/1 FLC 3+1 FAC 4/1 Others 1

McGOVERN Brian
Born: Dublin, 28 April 1980
Height: 6'3" Weight: 12.7
International Honours: RoI: U21-2; Yth
This young central defender joined Arsenal as a trainee during the summer of 1997 after being spotted playing for Dublin youth team Cherry Orchard. He is a strong tackler, and uses the ball well. Good in the air, especially at set pieces, he is a player for whom the club have high hopes. To allow him to add to his experience, Brian was loaned to Queens Park Rangers last December. Unfortunately, he suffered an injury which meant that he stayed for only one month of his three-month loan period. Fit again, he made his Arsenal debut when he came on as a substitute at Newcastle in the final Premiership game of the 1999-2000 season. He finished the season on a high, winning his first U21 caps against Greece and Colombia.
Arsenal (Signed from Cherry Orchard on 5/9/1997) PL 0+1
Queens Park R (Loaned on 24/12/1999) FL 3+2

McGOWAN Gavin Gregory
Born: Blackheath, 16 January 1976
Height: 5'8" Weight: 11.10
Club Honours: FAYC '94
International Honours: E: Yth; Sch
A hard-running, strong-tackling full back who can operate on either flank, with a preference for the right, Gavin did not make the expected progress during 1999-2000, his second full season as a Luton player. He badly bruised knee ligaments in pre-season, and had a set-back after he resumed training. Fast and skilful, he has plenty of ability but he did not make his first senior appearance of the campaign until January and his opportunities thereafter were limited, although his committed tackles continued to attract the attention of referees. If he can steer clear of injuries, next season should see him competing again for a regular first-team place.
Arsenal (From trainee on 1/7/1994) PL 3+3 FAC 1
Luton T (Loaned on 27/3/1997) FL 2
Luton T (Loaned on 11/7/1997) FL 6+2
Luton T (Free on 29/7/1998) FL 37+7 FLC 7 FAC 2

McGOWAN Neil William
Born: Glasgow, 15 April 1977
Height: 5'10" Weight: 10.12
Neil joined Oxford from Albion Rovers for a £20,000 fee in August 1999. The defender, who was mainly used at left back, took a while to adjust to the Second Division from part-time football in Scotland but soon showed why he was signed. After a string of substitute appearances he broke into the side as a regular in November and, apart from a suspension, he was a regular for three months before breaking his leg at Oldham. He had expected to be ruled out for the season but did return for the last four matches, which allowed Paul Powell to move upfield.
Stranraer (Signed from Bonnyton Thistle on 1/8/1995) SL 1+3 SLC 0+1
Albion Rov (Free on 9/8/1996) SL 60+2 SLC 2 SC 4 Others 1
Oxford U (£20,000 on 19/8/1999) FL 15+5 FLC 0+2 FAC 2+1 Others 2

McGREAL John
Born: Liverpool, 2 June 1972
Height: 5'11" Weight: 12.8
Signed from Tranmere Rovers just prior to the start of the 1999-2000 season, John immediately settled into the Ipswich side in the middle of the back three between Manu Thetis and Mark Venus and demonstrated why the club had invested £650,000 in him. Considered unlucky to have been shown a red card at Portsmouth, he was cool under pressure and confident in the tackle and immediately endeared himself to the crowd. However, it wasn't until Tony Mowbray was reintroduced to the side following the home debacle against Queens Park Rangers that John's attacking abilities came to the fore. With Mowbray restored to the centre, John moved to the right side of the back line, which gave him more space to join his attack, and his accurate crosses to the far post created a number of scoring opportunities for his forwards, although he wasn't able to score himself. He missed the latter part of the season because of a recurring ankle injury.
Tranmere Rov (From trainee on 3/7/1990) FL 193+2/1 FLC 20+1 FAC 8 Others 7+2
Ipswich T (£650,000 on 4/8/1999) FL 34 FLC 4 FAC 1 Others 1

McGREGOR Mark Dale Thomas
Born: Chester, 16 February 1977
Height: 5'11" Weight: 11.5
Mark has been a near-ever-present for Wrexham in the last two seasons and now sees the right-back position as his own. He likes to get forward as often as possible to help out in attack and his height enables him to be used as a central defender when the need arises. He is still only 23 and with more than 200 Football League appearances to his name already he would appear to have a long and successful career ahead of him. He scored his only goal of 1999-2000 on the last day of the season with a cracking 35-yard drive to deny Gillingham automatic promotion.
Wrexham (From trainee on 4/7/1995) FL 194+7/6 FLC 7 FAC 23+1 Others 10

Mark McGregor

McGREGOR Paul Anthony
Born: Liverpool, 17 December 1974
Height: 5'10" Weight: 11.6
Released by Preston in the close season, Paul signed for Plymouth in time for the start of the 1999-2000 campaign. He is a skilful player who can play either on the right-hand side of midfield or in attack, and his pace often caused opposing defences difficulty. Paul has an eye for goal, and

scored hat-tricks against Barnet in November and local rivals Torquay in March. He finished as the Pilgrims' top scorer with 16 goals, and has an important role to play in manager Kevin Hodges's plans for the future.

Nottingham F (From trainee on 13/12/1991) F/PL 7+23/3 FAC 0+3 Others 0+4/1
Carlisle U (Loaned on 25/9/1998) FL 3/2
Carlisle U (Loaned on 20/11/1998) FL 6+1/1 Others 1
Preston NE (Free on 24/3/1999) FL 1+3
Plymouth Arg (Free on 6/7/1999) FL 44/13 FLC 2 FAC 7/3

Paul McGregor

McHUGH Frazer
Born: Nottingham, 14 July 1981
Height: 5'9" Weight: 12.5
This Swindon youngster found it difficult to break into a struggling side in 1999-2000. He had a brief spell in the first-team squad at the beginning of the season but then dropped out of the reckoning and rarely featured again apart from a couple of games early in the new year. Frazer is a creative midfield player with good vision and neat ball control who will be looking to establish himself in the Robins' line-up during the coming season.

Swindon T (From trainee on 5/8/1999) FL 10+5 FLC 0+2

McINDOE Michael
Born: Edinburgh, 2 December 1979
Height: 5'8" Weight: 11.0
After he had appeared to establish himself in the Luton first team the previous season, much was expected of Michael in 1999-2000 but, although his talent was never in question, his abundant promise was sadly to remain unfulfilled. Most of his senior appearances last term were from the substitutes' bench and he dropped out of the first-team reckoning altogether after Christmas. A constructive left-sided midfielder who uses the ball with care and imagination, he endeavoured to regain his lost momentum in the reserves but was to leave the club before the end of the season. It is to be hoped that he will be able to make a fresh start elsewhere in 2000-01. Stop Press: Michael was reported to have signed for Hereford at the beginning of July.

Luton T (From trainee on 2/4/1998) FL 19+20 FLC 4+1 FAC 0+4 Others 1

McINTOSH Martin Wyllie
Born: East Kilbride, 19 March 1971
Height: 6'2" Weight: 12.0
International Honours: S: B-2; Sch
This cultured left-sided central defender was a regular in the Stockport County line-up for the first half of the 1999-2000 season, but then dropped out of the team and eventually returned to Scotland, joining Hibernian in a £250,000 deal last February. Rock solid during his time in the centre of the County defence, he was dominant in the air and very comfortable on the ball.

St Mirren (Free from Tottenham H juniors on 30/11/1988) SL 2+2
Clydebank (Signed on 17/8/1991) SL 59+6/10 SLC 2 SC 4+1/1 Others 3/1
Hamilton Ac (Signed on 1/2/1994) SL 99/12 SLC 5 SC 5 Others 5/1
Stockport Co (£80,000 on 15/8/1997) FL 96+3/5 FLC 5+1 FAC 4

McINTYRE James (Jimmy)
Born: Dumbarton, 24 May 1972
Height: 5'11" Weight: 12.2
Club Honours: SC '97
International Honours: S: B
The 1999-2000 season was another disappointing one for the former Scottish "B" international, one of a number of Tommy Burns's signings for Reading who failed to impress new manager Alan Pardew. Jimmy was unable to win over the crowd because of his failure to score regularly, and his best displays came in an unfamiliar role wide on the left. He did manage a handful of goals but not enough to prevent him from being transfer-listed before the end of the season. Never certain of a regular place in the starting line-up, he now finds himself well down the pecking order.

Bristol C (Free from Duntochter BC on 10/10/1991) FL 1 Others 0+1
Exeter C (Loaned on 11/2/1993) FL 12+3/3 Others 4/1
Airdrie (Signed on 23/9/1993) SL 32+22/10 SLC 3+3/1 SC 1+4 Others 2+2/2
Kilmarnock (Signed on 22/3/1996) SL 42+4/9 SLC 2+1 SC 5+1/2 Others 2/1
Reading (£420,000 on 26/3/1998) FL 43+21/10 FLC 2+1 FAC 2+2/1 Others 2+1

MACKAY Malcolm (Malky) George
Born: Bellshill, 19 February 1972
Height: 6'1" Weight: 11.7
This big former Celtic central defender found it difficult to dislodge the consistent Craig Fleming/Matt Jackson partnership at the heart of the Norwich rearguard last season. A strong and resolute performer, he is at his best when facing an aerial bombardment, seemingly relishing the prospect of competing for each and every high ball and throwing himself into challenges when all seems lost. He is surprisingly quick when in full stride, and his wholehearted approach to the game is an excellent example to others. A natural leader on the pitch, he is always encouraging his team-mates, willing them on to greater efforts. Malky is also a real threat when he goes forward at set-piece situations, and it is amazing that he has not added to his single goal in Canary colours, scored on only his second appearance back in September 1998.

Queens Park (From juniors on 8/12/1989) SL 68+2/6 SLC 3/2 SC 2 Others 2
Glasgow Celtic (Signed on 6/8/1993) SL 32+5/4 SLC 5+1 SC 4/1 Others 4+1
Norwich C (£350,000 on 18/9/1998) FL 40+8/1 FLC 4+1 FAC 1

McKEEVER Mark Anthony
Born: Derry, 16 November 1978
Height: 5'9" Weight: 11.8
International Honours: NI: Yth. RoI: U21-4
This promising left-sided wide midfield player managed to break into the Sheffield Wednesday first-team squad last December but then sustained an injury to his foot which brought his season to a premature close. He is a talented youngster with the pace and skills of an old-fashioned left winger and looks to have a good future in the game.

Peterborough U (Trainee) FL 2+1 FLC 1
Sheffield Wed (£500,000 + on 15/4/1997) PL 2+3 FLC 0+1 FAC 0+1
Bristol Rov (Loaned on 10/12/1998) FL 5+2
Reading (Loaned on 8/3/1999) FL 6+1/2

MACKEN Jonathan Paul
Born: Manchester, 7 September 1977
Height: 5'10" Weight: 12.8
Club Honours: Div 2 '00
International Honours: E: Yth
The 1999-2000 season saw Jonathan's emergence as a striker of some quality as he ended Preston's Second Division championship-winning campaign as the club's top scorer. After scoring on the opening day, he continued to hit the net consistently all season. The highlights of this intelligent forward's year included six in six during September and October, scoring in his 100th game for North End, the equaliser at Arsenal and the first FA Cup goal of his career. His strength on the ball and growing self-confidence allowed him to reach 16 goals by the turn of the year, before tiredness gradually began to tell for a player who featured in all but two of Preston's 59 games. He came back strongly from two barren spells, first by netting twice against Wycombe and then by scoring his 25th goal at Bristol Rovers after six games without a goal. Not surprisingly, he joined three team-mates in the PFA's Second Division select side.

Manchester U (From trainee on 10/7/1996)
Preston NE (£250,000 on 31/7/1997) FL 90+25/36 FLC 9+2/4 FAC 8+3/1 Others 6+3/1

McKENNA Paul Stephen
Born: Chorley, 20 October 1977
Height: 5'7" Weight: 11.12
Club Honours: Div 2 '00
Local boy Paul continued to progress well at Preston last season, featuring regularly in the first-team squad when fit. He scored his

first goal of the season with a 25-yard screamer at Brentford, and claimed the winner in the FA Cup tie at Bristol Rovers at the end of October after being rebuked for not scoring enough goals. Injured the following week, the busy young midfielder required a hernia operation which kept him out of action for three months, but after a few more niggles he was able to contribute his combative ball-winning and incisive running to the North End cause as the club closed in on the Second Division championship.

Preston NE (From trainee on 2/2/1996) FL 56+14/3 FLC 6 FAC 2+2/2 Others 4+1

McKENZIE Leon Mark
Born: Croydon, 17 May 1978
Height: 5'11" Weight: 11.2

Leon is yet another of the talented Crystal Palace youngsters who appeared regularly in 1999-2000. Although out of action at the beginning of the season after suffering a knee injury at the end of 1998-99, the young striker made an explosive return to first-team duty against Queens Park Rangers last November, heading home Andy Martin's cross in the first minute of the game. He rarely missed a match thereafter and finally appears to have established himself as a regular in the Eagles' starting line-up.

Crystal Palace (From trainee on 7/10/1995) F/PL 42+35/7 FLC 4/1 FAC 2+4
Fulham (Loaned on 3/10/1997) FL 1+2
Peterborough U (Loaned on 13/8/1998) FL 4/3
Peterborough U (Loaned on 30/11/1998) FL 10/5 Others 1/1

Leon McKenzie

MacKENZIE Neil David
Born: Birmingham, 15 April 1976
Height: 6'2" Weight: 12.5

Two substitute appearances at the start of the campaign were the only first-team opportunities for this tall, skilful midfielder at Stoke in 1999-2000, a season that had promised so much. Successive managers had been unwilling to give Neil the run in the side that would have boosted his confidence and in October he joined Cambridge, this time on a permanent basis, having had a spell on loan at the Abbey the previous season. Unfortunately, he suffered a knee injury that caused him to miss part of the season, but he confirmed that he has the potential to do well for United next term.

Stoke C (Free from West Bromwich A juniors on 9/11/1995) FL 15+27/1 FLC 1+1 FAC 0+1 Others 0+1
Cambridge U (Loaned on 24/3/1999) FL 3+1/1
Cambridge U (£45,000 on 14/10/1999) FL 19+3 FAC 5 Others 0+1

McKINNON Raymond (Ray)
Born: Dundee, 5 August 1970
Height: 5'8" Weight: 9.11
International Honours: S: U21-6; Sch

A skilful Scottish midfielder noted for his measured style and ability to use both feet equally well, Ray made a considerable impression during his first season with Luton, 1998-99. However, last season he was unable to show his earlier form and after making one start and three substitute appearances during the early weeks of the campaign he left the club, subsequently playing for Livingston in his native Scotland.

Dundee U (From juniors on 12/8/1986) SL 46+7/6 SLC 2 SC 5+1/1 Others 1
Nottingham F (£750,000 on 31/7/1992) PL 5+1/1 FLC 1
Aberdeen (£300,000 on 8/2/1994) SL 22+4 SLC 4+1 SC 3 Others 2
Dundee U (Signed on 3/11/1995) SL 29+15/6 SLC 1+2 SC 6+3
Luton T (Free on 6/8/1998) FL 29+4/2 FLC 5+1 FAC 2

McKINNON Robert (Rob)
Born: Glasgow, 31 July 1966
Height: 5'10" Weight: 11.12
International Honours: S: 3; B-2

Rob was one of a number of experienced performers who were recruited by Carlisle in the last three months of the 1999-2000 season. Injuries limited the veteran defender's effectiveness but he scored a stunning goal against Hartlepool, one of his former clubs, in the Auto Windscreens Shield and he always impressed with his distribution and dead-ball kicking. Although his loan from Hearts ended in May, it was thought that Rob would return to Brunton Park for the new season.

Newcastle U (Signed from Rutherglen Glencairn on 6/11/1984) FL 1
Hartlepool U (Free on 5/8/1986) FL 246+1/7 FLC 15 FAC 15 Others 15
Motherwell (Signed on 8/1/1992) SL 152/8 SLC 4 SC 4 (Free to FC Twente, Holland on 9/8/1996)
Heart of Midlothian (Free on 14/7/1998) SL 14+2 SLC 1+1 Others 1
Hartlepool U (Loaned on 11/2/1999) FL 7
Carlisle U (Loaned on 14/2/2000) FL 8 Others 2/1

McLAREN Andrew (Andy)
Born: Glasgow, 5 June 1973
Height: 5'10" Weight: 11.8
Club Honours: SC '94
International Honours: S: U21-4; Sch

Although his contract was due to run until 2001, Andy parted company with Reading midway through the 1999-2000 season. A midfielder who plays wide on the right and has the ability to take defenders on, he had played in four early-season matches, lost form, joined Scottish Division One club Livingston for a three-month loan spell beginning in October, failed to make his mark there and returned to Reading. His season then ran into serious trouble after he reportedly failed a drug test and was subsequently sacked by the club, apparently for being absent from training.

Dundee U (Free from Rangers BC on 20/6/1989) SL 115+50/12 SLC 9+5/1 SC 12+5/3 Others 8+2/2
Reading (£100,000 on 25/3/1999) FL 9/1 FLC 1+1

McLAREN Paul Andrew
Born: High Wycombe, 17 November 1976
Height: 6'0" Weight: 13.4

Bad luck with injuries prevented this promising Luton midfielder from doing justice to his rich talent in 1998-99, but much was expected of him last season. He started the campaign well, featuring regularly in the first team and producing some solid displays. His robust tackling, strong running and ability to produce well-struck crosses make him difficult to contain and are important to Luton's expansive style. Unfortunately, a tight hamstring followed by a dislocated toe sidelined him again for a while, but he was able to reclaim his place before the end of the season in preparation for an uninterrupted campaign in 2000-01.

Luton T (From trainee on 5/1/1994) FL 102+30/2 FLC 6+4/1 FAC 8/1 Others 8

Paul McLaren

McLAUGHLIN Brian
Born: Bellshill, 14 May 1974
Height: 5'4" Weight: 8.10
Club Honours: SC '95
International Honours: S: U21-8

Following a spell with Dundee United in 1998-99, this speedy left winger joined Second Division Wigan in the 1999 close season. His first-team involvement for the

Latics last term was limited to a substitute appearance against York in the Worthington Cup and a start against Burnley in the Auto Windscreens Shield. However, he was top scorer in the reserve side that collected the Pontins League Division Two title. At the end of the season he had a trial in France with Niort, although he failed to make a senior appearance with them.
Glasgow Celtic (Free from Giffnock North AFC on 7/7/1992) SL 38+37/5 SLC 1+4 SC 3+4/1 Others 2+3
Dundee U (Free on 27/3/1999) SL 1+2
Wigan Ath (Free on 2/7/1999) FLC 0+1

McLEAN Aaron
Born: Hammersmith, 25 May 1983
Height: 5'6" Weight: 10.2
In his first year as a trainee at Leyton Orient, Aaron was handed his senior debut in the Os' Auto Windscreens Shield game at Reading in December 1999, coming on as a substitute. A member of Orient's very successful youth team, he also made three appearances from the bench in the Third Division in April. Despite his small size the young striker is a terrier-like player who unsettles bigger and more experienced centre halves. Aaron will be looking to become a regular first-team squad member during the coming season.
Leyton Orient (Trainee) FL 0+3 Others 0+1

McLEAN Ian James
Born: Leeds, 13 September 1978
Height: 5'10" Weight: 11.4
Ian made just one appearance for Oldham in 1999-2000, making the starting line-up for the home game with Burnley in August. A strong-tackling left back, he found it impossible to dislodge Andy Holt in the Latics' team and was eventually made available on a free transfer last December.
Bradford C (From trainee on 1/1/1997)
Oldham Ath (Free on 13/10/1998) FL 6

McLOUGHLIN Alan Francis
Born: Manchester, 20 April 1967
Height: 5'8" Weight: 10.10
International Honours: RoI: 42; B-3
This popular midfield player was a regular in the Portsmouth line-up in the first half of the 1999-2000 season and was then surprisingly sold to Wigan in December after the club received an offer of £250,000 they felt unable to refuse. Alan is very much a creator in the middle of the park with neat skills and the ability to get forward into good attacking positions, but he struggled to reproduce the form that saw him gain international honours following the move. His only goal for his new club came against Gillingham in the Latics' last game of the old year. Alan unfortunately sustained a slipped disc in the match at Bristol Rovers in March, which was his 450th in the Football League. He will be hoping for better fortune during the coming season. Alan was capped for the Republic of Ireland against Croatia and Malta at the beginning of the season.
Manchester U (From apprentice on 25/4/1985)
Swindon T (Free on 15/8/1986) FL 101+5/19 FLC 11+3/5 FAC 4+2 Others 10/1
Torquay U (Loaned on 13/3/1987) FL 21+3/4
Southampton (£1,000,000 on 13/12/1990) FL 22+2/1 FLC 0+1 FAC 4 Others 1
Aston Villa (Loaned on 30/9/1991) Others 1
Portsmouth (£400,000 on 17/2/1992) FL 297+12/54 FLC 27/7 FAC 15+1/7 Others 9/1
Wigan Ath (£250,000 on 9/12/1999) FL 11+4/1 Others 2

McNEIL Martin James
Born: Rutherglen, 28 September 1980
Height: 6'1" Weight: 12.7
A second-year professional at Cambridge, Martin had to wait until November for his first-team opportunity. However, he then became a regular in the United line-up, his commanding and composed performances belying the fact that he was still a teenager. The big Scot continues to make good progress, and looks like a centre half of considerable potential.
Cambridge U (From trainee on 15/12/1998) FL 33+2 FLC 1 FAC 6

McNIVEN David Jonathan
Born: Leeds, 27 May 1978
Height: 5'11" Weight: 12.0
David again failed to make the breakthrough to regular first-team football with Oldham in 1999-2000, and although he scored in the 2-1 victory over Luton last October he was transfer-listed shortly afterwards. He eventually moved to Scarborough on loan in February before signing permanently for Conference club Southport the following month. A small striker with good pace, he had the misfortune to be dogged by a series of injuries. He is the twin brother of Oldham's Scott McNiven and the son of former Bradford City star David McNiven.
Oldham Ath (From trainee on 25/10/1995) FL 8+18/2 FLC 1+2

McNIVEN Scott Andrew
Born: Leeds, 27 May 1978
Height: 5'10" Weight: 12.1
International Honours: S: U21-1; Yth
Scott made the switch from right back to a role on the right side of a three-man defence at the start of 1999-2000 and went on to show some of the best form of his career in the early part of the season. A near-ever-present for Oldham, he showed great stamina and contributed a goal in the 2-1 defeat at Gillingham last September. At the time of writing his future at Boundary Park remains unclear, for with his contract due to end in the summer he has yet to agree a new one. He is the twin brother of David McNiven and the son of former Bradford City favourite David senior.
Oldham Ath (From trainee on 25/10/1995) FL 129+13/3 FLC 8+1 FAC 12+1/1 Others 7

McPHAIL Stephen
Born: Westminster, 9 December 1979
Height: 5'10" Weight: 12.0
Club Honours: FAYC '97
International Honours: RoI: 2; U21-6; Yth; (UEFA-U18 '98)
Stephen is one of the current crop of exciting youngsters at Leeds United. He made his first full appearance of 1999-2000 in the victory over Sheffield Wednesday in October, and remained in the first-team picture for the rest of the season. A mercurial midfielder with a sweet left foot, superb vision and the ability to unlock the meanest of defences, he covers his fair share of ground and makes many important tackles. Stephen scored his first goals for the club at Chelsea in December but will be looking to increase his tally in the coming season. Stephen made his full international debut for the Republic of Ireland against Scotland in May and also appeared in the Nike Cup matches in the United States. Stop Press: He scored his first international goal in the 2-1 victory over South Africa on 11 June.
Leeds U (From trainee on 23/12/1996) PL 34+11/2 FLC 2+1 FAC 3 Others 11

Stephen McPhail

McPHEE Christopher (Chris) Simon
Born: Eastbourne, 20 March 1983
Height: 5'11" Weight: 11.9
As a first-year scholarship youngster, Chris was a member of Brighton's Southern Premier Merit Division-winning youth team in 1999-2000. His consistent performances up front led to his first-team debut when he came on as a substitute in the defeat at Swansea in December after the Albion squad had been ravaged by flu. Chris went on to make several more appearances as a sub. He is widely regarded as an excellent prospect for the future.
Brighton & Hove A (Trainee) FL 0+4

McPHERSON Keith Anthony
Born: Greenwich, 11 September 1963
Height: 5'10" Weight: 12.0
Club Honours: FAYC '81; Div 4 '87, Div 2 '94
The veteran central defender's appearances were limited in 1999-2000 due to the size of the Brighton squad. Keith was a reliable performer whenever called upon and scored his first Albion goal in the 7-1 away win at Chester in February. He reached the milestone of 500 league appearances in the game against Shrewsbury in April, shortly before being released.

West Ham U (From apprentice on 12/9/1981) FL 1
Cambridge U (Loaned on 30/9/1985) FL 11/1
Northampton T (£15,000 on 23/1/1986) FL 182/8 FLC 9/1 FAC 12 Others 13
Reading (Signed on 24/8/1990) FL 264+7/8 FLC 21+1/1 FAC 12+1 Others 9+1
Brighton & Hove A (Free on 19/3/1999) FL 33+2/1 FLC 1 FAC 3

McSHEFFREY Gary
Born: Coventry, 13 August 1982
Height: 5'7" Weight: 10.4
International Honours: E: Yth

The Coventry-born striker set the FA Youth Cup and the youth league alight with his goalscoring feats in 1998-99. Last season he struggled with injuries and as a result got few opportunities to display his ability in a Coventry shirt. He made two starts, both against Tranmere in the Worthington Cup, and three substitute appearances in the league, and looked a little overawed. He won five caps for England U18s and played a crucial role for the Sky Blues' youth team as they reached a second successive FA Youth Cup final, scoring several goals including a hat-trick at Huddersfield and one in the first leg of the final.

Coventry C (From trainee on 27/8/1999) PL 0+4 FLC 2

McSPORRAN Jermaine
Born: Manchester, 1 January 1977
Height: 5'8" Weight: 10.10

This lightning-quick Wycombe striker enjoyed a highly successful 1999-2000 campaign, his first full season in the professional game. He produced a run of sparkling form in the opening matches, winning widespread praise for his performance in the 4-2 Worthington Cup victory at Molineux, when he scored twice as the Wolves' defence failed to cope with his pace. He then dropped off a little in mid-season, missing most of January after undergoing an appendix operation, but bounced back in the spring to finish with a goal tally in double figures. Jermaine rarely scores ordinary goals and his efforts last season included an outrageous 25-yard chip against Wolves and a magnificent solo effort in the home game with Cardiff when he took the ball from midway in his own half, sprinted down the touchline and cut in before unleashing a 20-yard rocket into the net. Jermaine mostly featured up front partnering Sean Devine, but he is equally at home on the right flank, where he can beat defenders with ease and deliver a fine cross.

Wycombe W (Signed from Oxford C on 5/11/1998) FL 43+21/13 FLC 4/2 FAC 4+1 Others 2+1/2

McVEIGH Paul
Born: Belfast, 6 December 1977
Height: 5'6" Weight: 10.5
International Honours: NI: 1; U21-11; Yth; Sch

Norwich manager Bryan Hamilton moved swiftly to snap up this Northern Irish international striker from Tottenham on a free transfer on transfer deadline day last March. Paul's contract at White Hart Lane was due to expire in the summer and the Premiership club allowed him to further his career with the Canaries. A quick-witted front runner, he was the leading scorer for Spurs reserves for two successive seasons. Sharp and lively around the penalty area, he is an instinctive player who likes to take his goal attempts early and can also spot his team-mates who may be better placed. Paul made his City debut as a substitute in the final game of the season, at Bolton, and will be looking to make a real impact at Carrow Road in 2000-01. A regular for Northern Ireland U21s, he won further caps against France, Turkey, Germany and Finland during the season.

Tottenham H (From trainee on 10/7/1996) PL 2+1/1
Norwich C (Free on 23/3/2000) FL 0+1

MADDISON Neil Stanley
Born: Darlington, 2 October 1969
Height: 5'10" Weight: 12.0

Neil is devoted to the Middlesbrough cause and was delighted with his move back to the North from Southampton in October 1997. Unfortunately, despite his versatility (he has already played in seven positions) and a sequence of injuries to experienced colleagues, he has not been able to secure a regular first-team place and he made only 15 senior appearances last season, almost half of them as a substitute. Neil appears to be content to wait for his chance but, while he rightly remains optimistic, his career at the Riverside has probably reached its peak.

Southampton (From trainee on 14/4/1988) F/PL 149+20/19 FLC 9+5 FAC 8+5 Others 1
Middlesbrough (£250,000 on 31/10/1997) P/FL 32+24/4 FLC 7 FAC 4

MADDIX Daniel (Danny) Shawn
Born: Ashford, 11 October 1967
Height: 5'11" Weight: 12.2
International Honours: Jamaica: 2

Danny has been with Queens Park Rangers for over ten years and has made more than 300 first-team starts. He is one of the most popular figures at the club, both with the supporters and with his fellow players. A central defender who has pace and a strong tackle, his presence was sorely missed after he incurred a serious knee injury last November. Despite hopes of a speedy return to fitness, Danny suffered a set-back in his recovery and missed the rest of the season. Before the injury he was one of a number of team captains employed by the club owing to the large number of injuries suffered by wearers of what came to be seen as the "dreaded armband".

Tottenham H (From apprentice on 25/7/1985)
Southend U (Loaned on 1/11/1986) FL 2
Queens Park R (Free on 23/7/1987) F/PL 258+34/13 FLC 25/3 FAC 21+2/2 Others 2+3

MAGILTON James (Jim)
Born: Belfast, 6 May 1969
Height: 6'0" Weight: 14.2
International Honours: NI: 40; U23-2; U21-1; Yth; Sch

An injury picked up in a pre-season friendly meant that Jim was not available to play for Ipswich at the start of the 1999-2000 season and once he reached match fitness, because the side were playing so well, he found it difficult to claim a regular first-team place. However, he made his presence felt when he did get an opportunity, coming on as a substitute for the last nine minutes of the Barnsley game and scoring the final goal in a 6-1 thrashing. Once he had established himself in the team he took over the main play-maker role, providing numerous goalscoring opportunities for his forwards and orchestrating the team's overall play. Jim became the club's penalty taker midway through the season but really came into form when it mattered, at the end of the season. He had a superb game at Charlton, when a win was needed to keep alive Ipswich's chances of automatic promotion. Jim opened the scoring with a superb free kick from the edge of the box, and went on to control the game, laying on further goals for David Johnson and Martijn Reuser to secure a comprehensive victory. However, he saved his best performance for the second leg of the play-off semi-final against Bolton, when he scored his first-ever professional hat-trick. First of all he converted a penalty, then he played a one-two with Johnson on the edge of the penalty area before he jinked round three defenders and smashed the ball into the roof of the net and finally, in the last minute, he latched on to Tony Mowbray's knock-down and drilled a low shot into the corner of the net. He also had a second penalty attempt brilliantly saved by the 'keeper! To cap a fine season Jim was recalled to the Northern Ireland side by new manager Danny McIlroy for the friendly with Luxembourg last February.

Liverpool (From apprentice on 14/5/1986)
Oxford U (£100,000 on 3/10/1990) FL 150/34 FLC 9/1 FAC 8/4 Others 6/3
Southampton (£600,000 on 11/2/1994) PL 124+6/13 FLC 12+2/2 FAC 12/3
Sheffield Wed (£1,600,000 on 10/9/1997) PL 14+13/1 FLC 2 FAC 1
Ipswich T (£682,500 on 15/1/1999) FL 52+5/7 FLC 3 FAC 1 Others 5/3

MAHER Kevin Andrew
Born: Ilford, 17 October 1976
Height: 6'0" Weight: 12.5
International Honours: RoI: U21-4

Kevin turned his 1998-99 disappointments around last season, eventually winning back a regular place in the Southend team and the hearts of the Roots Hall faithful. A tenacious midfielder who is strong in the tackle, Kevin also possesses excellent passing ability, something that was missing from the Blues' midfield for a large part of the 1999-2000 season. With his confidence restored by boss Alan Little, Kevin was offered new terms in May.

Tottenham H (From trainee on 1/7/1995)
Southend U (Free on 23/1/1998) FL 70+6/5 FLC 5 FAC 1 Others 1/1

MAHON Alan Joseph
Born: Dublin, 4 April 1978
Height: 5'10" Weight: 11.5
International Honours: RoI: 1; U21-18; Yth; Sch

Alan was probably the most skilful player on Tranmere's books in 1999-2000, performing with energy, determination and imagination in the centre of the park. When his constructive distribution and a classy first touch are also taken into account, it is not surprising that he is rumoured to be on the verge of a big-money move to the Premiership now that his contract is up. He had an excellent season for Rovers, winning a runners-up medal as a member of the side that was defeated by Leicester City in the Worthington Cup final, and continued to represent the Republic of Ireland. He added three caps at U21 level to his already impressive total and made his debut for the full international team in the friendly with Greece last April.

Tranmere Rov (From trainee on 7/4/1995) FL 84+36/13 FLC 12+6/2 FAC 3+2

MAHON Gavin Andrew
Born: Birmingham, 2 January 1977
Height: 6'0" Weight: 13.2
Club Honours: Div 3 '99

Gavin is a skilful Brentford midfield player, comfortable with either foot, an accurate passer and in possession of a useful shot. He was a regular in the Bees' line-up for most of the 1999-2000 season until sidelined by a foot ligament injury. He captained the team occasionally in the absence of Paul Evans and Scott Marshall and scored spectacularly with a 25-yard drive in the 4-3 win over Scunthorpe last November.

Wolverhampton W (From trainee on 3/7/1995)
Hereford U (Free on 12/7/1996) FL 10+1/1 FLC 4
Brentford (£50,000 + on 17/11/1998) FL 66/7 FLC 2 FAC 2 Others 6

MAKIN Christopher (Chris) Gregory
Born: Manchester, 8 May 1973
Height: 5'10" Weight: 11.2
Club Honours: Div 1 '99
International Honours: E: U21-5; Yth; Sch

The Sunderland full back had an eventful season in 1999-2000, immediately adapting to the step-up from the First Division to the Premiership. Chris is one of the most popular players at the Stadium of Light thanks to his all-action style and commitment, and finally opened his goalscoring account for the Black Cats last term. In the derby with Newcastle in February, only two brilliant Steve Harper saves denied him his elusive first goal, but on the final day of the season he found the net against Spurs at White Hart Lane, much to the delight of the travelling Sunderland fans. Chris also had the honour of leading the side in the absence of Steve Bould and proved himself to be a competent skipper. One black spot was the strong-tackling defender's tendency to find his way into referees' notebooks too often and he picked up a red card away at Middlesbrough in November. However, Chris's tenacity is perhaps his strongest asset so, in today's climate, disciplinary points are perhaps an occupational hazard.

Oldham Ath (From trainee on 2/11/1991) F/PL 93+1/4 FLC 7 FAC 11 Others 1+1 (Transferred to Marseille during 1996 close season)
Wigan Ath (Loaned on 28/8/1992) FL 14+1/2
Sunderland (£500,000 on 5/8/1997) P/FL 94+3/1 FLC 11 FAC 5 Others 1+1

MALEY Mark
Born: Newcastle, 26 January 1981
Height: 5'9" Weight: 12.3
International Honours: E: Yth; Sch

The young Sunderland full back continued to make progress in the reserves last season, making one first-team appearance in the Worthington Cup at home to Walsall in September in a 3-2 win. Small but pacy, Mark has great potential and, although his chances of a first-team slot appear limited at present, with Chris Makin, Michael Gray and Darren Holloway barring his path, he can take comfort in the fact that Peter Reid is always willing to give young players at Sunderland an opportunity to stake a claim for a place in his side.

Sunderland (From trainee on 30/1/1998) FLC 2

MALONE Stephen (Steve)
Born: Glasgow, 28 April 1978
Height: 5'7" Weight: 10.6

This young defender joined Chester City last September after playing in minor Scottish football. He appeared in the starting line-up for the FA Cup replay against Whyteleafe at the beginning of November but was substituted after just 15 minutes and his only other game for the Blues came in a Cheshire Senior Cup tie. He was later reported to have moved on loan to Unibond League club Winsford in February along with colleague Danny Carson.

Chester C (Signed from Knightswood on 13/9/1999) FAC 1

MALZ Stefan
Born: Ludwigshafen, Germany, 15 June 1972
Height: 6'0" Weight: 12.3

A left-sided midfield player bought by Arsenal in June 1999 for £610,000 from TSV 1860 Munich, Stefan scored a goal on his debut in the 2-1 victory over Preston in the Worthington Cup. It was a dream start for the 27-year-old, but it was to be another four months before he made his full league debut. He is a hard tackler and good passer of the ball but, although he is regarded as an important squad member at Highbury, he found it difficult to break into the first team last season.

Arsenal (£610,000 from TSV 1860 Munich, Germany on 14/7/1999) PL 2+3/1 FLC 2/1 FAC 2 Others 0+2

MANN Neil
Born: Nottingham, 19 November 1972
Height: 5'10" Weight: 12.1

A remarkable recovery saw Neil return for Hull's last game of 1998-99, having damaged the lateral ligament in his left knee at Scunthorpe the previous November. Further heartache was not far away, though, in only his third game of the new season. A very skilful left-sided operator, Neil re-opened the same injury and damaged the cruciate ligament in the home Worthington Cup tie with Liverpool. He broke down again in training in November, and underwent a third career-saving operation in March to reconstruct the cruciate. One of Hull's most popular players, he will probably be out of action until the new year. It is to be hoped there will be a happy ending to a two-year injury nightmare.

Grimsby T (Free from Notts Co juniors on 6/9/1990)
Hull C (Free from Grantham T, via Spalding, on 30/7/1993) FL 127+35/9 FLC 12+4 FAC 6+2/1 Others 8+2/1

MANNINGER Alexander (Alex)
Born: Salzburg, Austria, 4 June 1977
Height: 6'2" Weight: 13.3
Club Honours: FAC '98; CS '99
International Honours: Austria: 4; U21

Alex provides first-class cover for David Seaman in the Arsenal goal and will be the natural replacement when the England number one decides to move on. He recovered well from a serious wrist injury which he sustained in training at the end of the 1998-99 season, and played the first dozen games of the 1999-2000 season when Seaman was injured. A great shot stopper with exceptionally sharp reflexes, he is equally strong in the air and on the ground. He is very fast when coming off his line, and possesses good distribution skills with both hand and foot. He has progressed to such an extent that, when Seaman is fit, Gunners manager Arsene Wenger has a difficult choice to make. Alex made his senior international debut for Austria against Sweden in August 1999 and won three more caps before being dropped from the squad in the spring because he was not a regular first choice at Highbury, although it is surely only a matter of time before he is.

Arsenal (£500,000 from Graz, Austria, via Vorwaerts and Salzburg, on 17/6/1997) PL 27+1 FLC 7 FAC 8 Others 7

MANNINI Moreno
Born: Imola, Italy, 15 August 1962
Height: 6'0" Weight: 12.0
International Honours: Italy: 10

This veteran former Italian international defender joined Nottingham Forest in the summer of 1999 after 15 years and over 350 Serie A games with Italian giants Sampdoria. He made the starting line-up for the opening game of last season at Ipswich but struggled to get to grips with the requirements of First Division football and featured in only a handful more games for the Reds. In January it was announced that he was retiring from the game and would return to Italy.

Nottingham F (Free from Sampdoria, Italy on 6/8/1999) FL 7+1 FLC 1

MARCELINO Elena Sierra
Born: Santander, Spain, 26 September 1971
Height: 6'2" Weight: 13.0
International Honours: Spain: 5

After playing in the European Cup-Winners' Cup final Spanish international centre back Marcelino, who prefers to be referred to by that single name, joined Newcastle in the summer of 1999 as part of Ruud Gullit's intended revitalisation of his defence. Tall and strong, he is very composed yet determined on the field, but he suffered a series of injuries in 1999-2000 which proved very disruptive, destroying any continuity for him and preventing him from fully adapting to the pace and style of the English game, while also costing him his place in the Spanish international side. Thus he started the season in the Newcastle team against Villa but suffered a groin injury, compounded by a problem with his hip. Marcelino played in only one of the next eight fixtures, before starting a short run from the end of September to mid-November when he played six times. He was beginning to settle to life in the Premiership when the hip problem, diagnosed as a torn muscle on the joint, resurfaced and consigned him to the treatment room again. He returned at the year's end to begin another short run of games, but the hip injury persisted and he also suffered hamstring and groin strain problems towards the end of January. Marcelino's misfortune continued with an ankle injury incurred in training in early February, and doubtless he was pleased to see the end of the season in the hope that in 2000-01 he will be less afflicted by injury, and thus able to show the Premiership the full range of his undoubted abilities.

Newcastle U (£5,800,000 from Real Mallorca, Spain on 16/7/1999) PL 10+1 FAC 1+1 Others 2

MARCELLE Clinton (Clint) Sherwin
Born: Trinidad, 9 November 1968
Height: 5'4" Weight: 10.0
International Honours: Trinidad & Tobago

Still out in the cold at Barnsley, Clint joined Scunthorpe on loan in October 1999 and made an impressive debut up front, where his pace, skill and movement added much to the Iron's attack. A permanent move fell through when the player couldn't agree personal terms and his form suffered as he failed to score in any of his nine starts. After two months he returned to Oakwell, but he parted company with the club at the end of February.

Barnsley (Free from Felgueiras, Portugal on 8/8/1996) F/PL 37+32/8 FLC 3+5 FAC 6+1/1
Scunthorpe U (Loaned on 10/10/1999) FL 8+2 FAC 1

[MARCELO] CIPRIANO Dos Santos
Born: Niteroi, Brazil, 11 October 1969
Height: 6'0" Weight: 13.8

A back injury kept Sheffield United's leading scorer of the previous season on the sidelines for the Blades' first two matches of 1999-2000. He made his first start in the Worthington Cup at Shrewsbury in late August, playing with his usual effort and enthusiasm and scoring twice. Difficulties arose over United's wish to extend his contract, which finished at the end of the season. He was reported to want a move either to Portugal or to a Premiership side, but he eventually switched to Birmingham City in October. Marcelo made a great start to his Birmingham career when he scored both goals in a 2-2 draw with Queens Park Rangers, including one from a superb 25-yard shot. He was out for a month with ankle ligament trouble after being injured against Tranmere in November, and then found he was mostly used as a substitute in the second half of the season when Isiah Rankin arrived on loan from Bradford City. A hard-working striker who is good in the air and has the ability to find space in the box at will, he will be expecting to make a greater impact in 2000-01.

Sheffield U (£400,000 from Deportivo Alaves, Spain, via Benfica on 6/10/1997) FL 47+19/24 FLC 3+1/2 FAC 10+1/5 Others 1+1/1
Birmingham C (£500,000 on 25/10/1999) FL 14+11/5 FAC 1+1 Others 1+1/1

MARESCA Enzo
Born: Salerno, Italy, 10 February 1980
Height: 5'11" Weight: 12.0
International Honours: Italy: Yth

It came as a body blow to all West Bromwich supporters when the Italian midfielder was transferred to Juventus for £4.5 million on the last weekend of January 2000. Enzo had been in splendid form during the first half of the season, when his driving power from centre-field had given the team a purposeful look about it. Early on in the proceedings he did suffer a few injury worries (a back strain being the worst) but he quickly overcame those set-backs to produce some sparkling displays. He linked up well with wide-man Kevin Kilbane and fellow midfielder Richard Sneekes and he scored two cracking goals, both from distance.

West Bromwich A (Free from Cagliari, Italy on 25/8/1998) FL 28+19/5 FLC 1+3 FAC 2

MARGAS Javier
Born: Chile, 10 May 1969
Height: 6'1" Weight: 13.8
International Honours: Chile: 56

Javier returned to West Ham at the beginning of last season after spending some time at home in Chile recovering from a knee injury suffered back in December 1998. Now fully fit, he showed himself to be a classy defender who is hard tackling and good in the air; he also became an instant favourite with the supporters when he dyed his hair claret and blue. He was a regular in the Hammers' starting line-up from October through to February and scored his first-ever goal in the Premiership when he headed home a corner in the 5-0 victory over Coventry last April. An experienced international for Chile, he made the squad for the Copa America tournament in the summer of 1999 and featured against Argentina and Peru in the opening rounds of their World Cup qualifying group for 2002.

West Ham U (£2,000,000 from Catolica University, Chile on 3/8/1998) PL 18+3/1 FLC 2 Others 2+1

MARIC Silvio
Born: Zagreb, Croatia, 20 March 1975
Height: 5'10" Weight: 12.2
International Honours: Croatia: 16

Silvio came to Newcastle from Croatia with a big reputation as a skilful player with an eye for goal who prefers to play just behind the main strike force, although he can also play up front if required. After a settling-in period during 1998-99 he was expected to make a big impression in his first full season, but things did not go his way. He was on the bench for much of the first half of the campaign, only making the starting line-up on half a dozen occasions. Although he was in the Croatia squad for the European Championship qualifier against Yugoslavia in August, Silvio did not make the team, which led him to request a transfer, believing that his lack of match practice at the top level was damaging his international prospects. He scored his first-ever Newcastle goal in the UEFA Cup match away to FC Zurich, his twentieth appearance for the club, and he scored again in the home leg, leaving the field to a standing ovation when substituted. However, he still failed to establish himself in the side, and he was given permission before Christmas to try to negotiate a return to his former club, but found they could not afford the fee. The latter half of the season saw Silvio make only a handful of substitute appearances, although he scored a stunning hat-trick in the final 11 minutes to rescue a Northumberland Senior Cup semi-final for the reserves, and it is thought there will be problems with his work permit for the coming season as he hasn't played enough games for it to be renewed.

Newcastle U (£3,650,000 from Zagreb, Croatia on 26/2/1999) PL 12+11 FLC 1 FAC 1+3 Others 3/2

MARINELLI Carlos Ariel
Born: Buenos Aires, Argentina, 14 March 1982
Height: 5'8" Weight: 11.6

Carlos is one of a group of young South Americans that Middlesbrough manager Bryan Robson invited to the Riverside for training and assessment last season. Signed from Boca Juniors in October, the tall Argentinian midfielder made a couple of appearances in the Premiership as a substitute and gave a good account of himself in training – his trickery reportedly left even Paul Gascoigne and Juninho bemused. Robson would be the first to concede that Carlos still has a lot to learn, but he clearly has exceptional talent and it is to be hoped that, in the long term, he will be able to fulfil his obvious potential.

Middlesbrough (£1,500,000 from Boca Juniors, Argentina on 27/10/1999) PL 0+2

MARRIOTT Alan
Born: Bedford, 3 September 1978
Height: 6'1" Weight: 12.5

This young goalkeeper signed a short-term contract for Lincoln in the summer of 1999 after impressing in pre-season trials. Previously with Tottenham, he performed competently in the reserve team and received his Football League debut against Torquay last February. Alan then retained his place in the Imps' line-up until the end of the campaign, growing in confidence with every game and developing into an effective shot stopper. One of his best performances came at Shrewsbury, where he made several excellent saves including one from the penalty spot to help Lincoln to a 2-1 victory. He was selected as "Young Player of the Season" in May.

Tottenham H (From trainee on 3/7/1997)
Lincoln C (Free on 5/8/1999) FL 18

MARRIOTT Andrew (Andy)
Born: Sutton in Ashfield, 11 October 1970
Height: 6'1" Weight: 12.6
Club Honours: Div 4 '92; FMC '92; WC '95
International Honours: E: U21-1; Yth; Sch. W: 5

The Sunderland goalkeeper again proved himself a dependable deputy for first choice Thomas Sorensen, appearing in Worthington Cup matches against Walsall (twice) and Wimbledon. His only Premiership appearance was also against the Dons in January, and although Sunderland went down by the only goal of the game Andy's excellent handling and speed off his line prevented a bigger defeat.

Arsenal (From trainee on 22/10/1988)
Nottingham F (£50,000 on 20/6/1989) F/PL 11 FLC 1 Others 1
West Bromwich A (Loaned on 6/9/1989) FL 3
Blackburn Rov (Loaned on 29/12/1989) FL 2
Colchester U (Loaned on 21/3/1990) FL 10
Burnley (Loaned on 29/8/1991) FL 15 Others 2
Wrexham (£200,000 on 8/10/1993) FL 213 FLC 10 FAC 22 Others 21
Sunderland (£200,000 + on 17/8/1998) P/FL 2 FLC 3

MARSDEN Christopher (Chris)
Born: Sheffield, 3 January 1969
Height: 5'11" Weight: 10.12

Demonstrating a rugged, uncompromising and enthusiastic style of play, Chris was one of the unsung heroes at Southampton during the 1999-2000 season. His ability to motivate his team-mates and his coolness under pressure made him a valuable member of the team, qualities which were sorely missed when injury sidelined him for two months up to Christmas. A busy midfielder whose crisp passing should be well suited to new manager Glenn Hoddle's preferred style of play, Chris likes to push forward at every opportunity but didn't manage to score in his 20 appearances (four as a substitute) last season.

Sheffield U (From apprentice on 6/1/1987) FL 13+3/1 FLC 1 Others 1
Huddersfield T (Signed on 15/7/1988) FL 113+8/9 FLC 15+1 FAC 6+2 Others 10
Coventry C (Loaned on 2/11/1993) PL 5+2
Wolverhampton W (£250,000 on 11/1/1994) FL 8 FAC 3
Notts Co (£250,000 on 15/11/1994) FL 10 FLC 1 Others 1/1
Stockport Co (£70,000 on 12/1/1996) FL 63+2/3 FLC 13 FAC 4 Others 4/1
Birmingham C (£500,000 on 9/10/1997) FL 51+1/3 FLC 5/3 FAC 2
Southampton (£800,000 on 2/2/1999) PL 33+2/2 FLC 0+2 FAC 1

MARSH Christopher (Chris) Jonathan
Born: Sedgley, 14 January 1970
Height: 5'11" Weight: 13.2

Walsall's longest-serving player took the move into the First Division in his stride last season and was an ever-present until February, when an injury sustained at Norwich caused him to miss six games. He returned as good as ever with his stout-hearted defending and enterprising overlapping from right back playing a prominent part in the Saddlers' valiant struggle against relegation. Never one to duck a challenge, he also played bravely in goal against Barnsley on 1 April after Jimmy Walker had been sent off in the tenth minute.

Walsall (From trainee on 11/7/1988) FL 351+34/23 FLC 23+2/1 FAC 33+1/3 Others 24+1/3

MARSHALL Andrew (Andy) John
Born: Bury St Edmunds, 14 April 1975
Height: 6'2" Weight: 13.7
International Honours: E: U21-4; Yth (UEFA-U18 '93)

The 1999-2000 season was an excellent one for this former England U21 international, who once again proved himself to be one of the top goalkeepers outside the Premiership with his impressive displays for Norwich. In goalkeeping terms, at the age of 25, Andy is still serving his apprenticeship, but with nearly 200 senior appearances to his credit he now has an added maturity about his performances. Always a great shot stopper, he showed last season that his all-round game has developed immeasurably. He is decisive in dealing with crosses and communicates well with the defenders in front of him, and although his kicking is still sometimes erratic he has worked very hard at improving this aspect of his game. The future looks very bright for this confident and spectacular goalkeeper, and if he can maintain his rate of improvement he will surely be pressing for senior international recognition.

Norwich C (From trainee on 6/7/1993) P/FL 153+1 FLC 13 FAC 4+1
Bournemouth (Loaned on 9/9/1996) FL 11
Gillingham (Loaned on 21/11/1996) FL 5 FLC 1 Others 1

MARSHALL Ian Paul
Born: Liverpool, 20 March 1966
Height: 6'1" Weight: 13.10
Club Honours: Div 2 '91; FLC '00

The left-footed Leicester striker was plagued with injuries throughout the 1999-2000 season but still managed to play a crucial role in City's Worthington Cup triumph. Ian laid on a goal in the first game against Crystal Palace and netted himself in the return leg to set the Foxes on their way. Thrust back into action for the quarter-final against Fulham, Ian gave a perfect demonstration of his never-say-die attitude and unstinting effort as he scored twice and laid on a third goal as City clawed back a two-goal deficit with six minutes remaining before snatching an unlikely victory on penalties. A popular figure at Filbert Street, Ian recovered from another injury to make a Wembley appearance from the bench and earn a richly deserved winners' medal. He was released in the summer.

Everton (From apprentice on 23/3/1984) FL 9+6/1 FLC 1+1/1 Others 7
Oldham Ath (£100,000 on 24/3/1988) F/PL 165+5/36 FLC 17 FAC 14/3 Others 2+1/1
Ipswich T (£750,000 on 9/8/1993) P/FL 79+5/32 FLC 4/3 FAC 9/3
Leicester C (£875,000 on 31/8/1996) PL 49+34/18 FLC 4+2/4 FAC 6+2/3 Others 2/1

MARSHALL Lee Alan
Born: Nottingham, 1 August 1975
Height: 5'10" Weight: 10.8
International Honours: E: U21-1

After two seasons during which he was a fringe player at Scunthorpe, 1999-2000 was another frustrating season for Lee, whose performances for the reserves deserved more first-team opportunities. A tidy midfielder who is good on the ball and likes to get forward, he did well in his one start of the season at Stoke City in October but incredibly made only one substitute appearance during the rest of the campaign. Put on the transfer list in November, he had a trial with Conference outfit Scarborough in February but they did not take their interest further. He was released at the end of the season.

Nottingham F (From trainee on 3/8/1992)
Stockport Co (Free on 20/3/1995) FL 1 (Free to Eastwood T on 24/8/1996)
Scunthorpe U (£5,000 on 6/6/1997) FL 18+27/2 FLC 0+3 FAC 2+2 Others 1

Lee Marshall (Norwich City)

MARSHALL Lee Keith
Born: Islington, 21 January 1979
Height: 6'0" Weight: 11.11
International Honours: E: U21-1

After he won England U21 honours the previous season, the 1999-2000 campaign proved to be a difficult one for this former Enfield player, as he struggled to find the consistency which was a hallmark of his first in senior football. Lee started the season as a regular member of the Norwich squad, scoring in successive away matches at Cheltenham and Walsall before falling out of favour and finding himself in and out of the team. The tall, hard-running midfielder then seemed to find a new lease of life following the appointment of Bryan Hamilton as the Canaries' boss, rediscovering his best form with a series of excellent performances, capped by a fine spell of four goals in three games in early April. Three of those goals came from headers as he proved to be an aerial threat

both in open play and at set pieces. Full of energy, Lee has the capacity to cover every blade of grass in the course of 90 minutes and his long forward runs in anticipation of receiving the ball make him very difficult to mark. Originally signed as an attacking right back, he seems to have settled firmly into a midfield role, although his adaptability remains a big plus point for any manager.
Norwich C (Signed from Enfield on 27/3/1997) FL 61+20/8 FLC 7+1/1 FAC 1

MARSHALL Scott Roderick
Born: Edinburgh, 1 May 1973
Height: 6'1" Weight: 12.5
International Honours: S: U21-5; Yth
A tall centre back who reads the game well, Scott had the difficult task of replacing the classy Hermann Hreidarsson after moving to Brentford from Southampton last October but coped admirably. He retained his place in the Bees' back four until suffering a hamstring injury against Stoke in January that kept him out of action for three months. Scott eventually returned to first-team action shortly before the end of the 1999-2000 season.
Arsenal (From trainee on 18/3/1991) PL 19+5/1 FLC 1+1
Rotherham U (Loaned on 3/12/1993) FL 10/1 Others 1
Sheffield U (Loaned on 25/8/1994) FL 17
Southampton (Free on 3/8/1998) PL 2
Brentford (£250,000 on 15/10/1999) FL 22/2 FAC 2/1

MARSHALL Shaun Andrew
Born: Fakenham, 3 October 1978
Height: 6'1" Weight: 12.12
A graduate of Cambridge's youth team, Shaun started the 1999-2000 season as United's second-choice goalkeeper. He grabbed his first-team chance in October, and a series of assured displays and vital saves ensured that he remained between the posts until a thigh muscle injury ended his season in March. Commanding in the box, Shaun should start next season as United's regular 'keeper.
Cambridge U (From trainee on 21/2/1997) FL 45+1 FLC 1 FAC 6

MARTIN Andrew (Andy) Peter
Born: Cardiff, 28 February 1980
Height: 6'0" Weight: 10.12
International Honours: W: U21-1; Yth
This young Crystal Palace striker made good progress during the 1999-2000 campaign. He was given an extended run in the first-team squad between October and February, and proved to be good in the air with some neat touches on the ground. Andy scored his first-ever league goal with a header in the opening minute of the Boxing Day visit to Charlton.
Crystal Palace (From trainee on 28/2/1997) FL 12+10/2

MARTIN Jae Andrew
Born: Hampstead, 5 February 1976
Height: 5'11" Weight: 11.10
A revelation in Peterborough's pre-season games, Jae struggled to live up to expectations when the 1999-2000 league campaign began. Although he was selected by his former Southend and Birmingham boss Barry Fry in the early weeks of the term, the left-sided midfielder went on loan to Welling in February. Jae was released in May. Stop Press: He was reported to have joined Woking during the summer.
Southend U (From trainee on 7/5/1993) FL 1+7 FLC 1+1 Others 0+1
Leyton Orient (Loaned on 9/9/1994) FL 1+3 Others 1
Birmingham C (Free on 1/7/1995) FL 1+6 Others 0+2
Lincoln C (Signed on 21/8/1996) FL 29+12/5 FLC 5/1 FAC 1 Others 0+1
Peterborough U (Free on 2/7/1998) FL 7+12/1 FLC 1+1 Others 1

MARTIN John (Johnny)
Born: Bethnal Green, 15 July 1981
Height: 5'6" Weight: 9.12
After five outings during the previous term, Johnny played most of the 1999-2000 season in Leyton Orient's youth and reserve teams, before making his return to the first-team fold in February at home to Southend. He is a skilful left-sided midfielder who, although only small in size, is not fazed by his more powerful opponents. A former trainee at Brisbane Road, Johnny will be looking to strengthen his senior claim in the new season.
Leyton Orient (From trainee on 6/8/1998) FL 9+1 FLC 2 Others 2

MARTIN Lee Brendan
Born: Huddersfield, 9 September 1968
Height: 6'0" Weight: 13.0
International Honours: E: Sch
Lee was signed in the 1999 close season by Macclesfield as cover for goalkeeper Ryan Price. He spent the early part of the 1999-2000 campaign on the first-team bench and

Andy Martin

playing for the reserves. With Price suffering a dip in form, Lee's chance came in the middle of October against Chester. He made an immediate impact, helping the team to achieve only one defeat in his first ten games, which included keeping four clean sheets. Unfortunately, a rib injury then ruled him out for three matches. On his return Lee continued to command his area, position himself well and make some spectacular saves but this excellent run came to an end seven matches later when he injured his back. During the season he reached the milestone of 200 league appearances. When fully recovered, he was unable to reclaim his place due to the consistent performances of on-loan 'keeper Tony Williams. Lee went back between the posts for Macc when Tony was recalled to Blackburn at the end of March. He is also studying at Salford University to become a physiotherapist.

Huddersfield T (From trainee on 1/7/1987) FL 54 FAC 4 Others 5
Blackpool (Free on 31/7/1992) FL 98 FLC 8 FAC 4 Others 7
Rochdale (Free on 8/11/1996)
Halifax T (Free on 12/8/1997) FL 37 FLC 4 FAC 1 Others 1
Macclesfield T (Free on 19/7/1999) FL 21 FAC 2 Others 1

MARTINDALE Gary
Born: Liverpool, 24 June 1971
Height: 6'0" Weight: 12.1
Club Honours: Div 3 '98

Dogged by injuries throughout his Rotherham career, Gary was showing signs of getting back to his best at the start of last season before bad luck cost him his place again. A striker with an eye for a half-chance, he scored three goals in his 13 appearances, although they all came from the penalty spot. With his opportunities at Millmoor limited, Gary went on loan to Telford in transfer deadline week to the end of 1999-2000. He was released by Rotherham in the summer.

Bolton W (Signed from Burscough on 24/3/1994)
Peterborough U (Signed on 4/7/1995) FL 26+5/15 FLC 4/1 FAC 4 Others 4/2
Notts Co (£175,000 on 6/3/1996) FL 34+32/13 FLC 3+1 FAC 3+1 Others 5+1/3
Mansfield T (Loaned on 7/2/1997) FL 5/2
Rotherham U (Signed on 12/3/1998) FL 17+10/6 FLC 1+2 FAC 0+2/1 Others 0+1

MARTINEZ Roberto
Born: Balaguer Lerida, Spain, 13 July 1973
Height: 5'10" Weight: 12.2
Club Honours: Div 3 '97

The last of Wigan's "Three Amigos" found his first-team opportunities limited in 1999-2000 and was restricted to just 14 league starts. A skilful right-footed midfielder who has the ability to deliver a defence-splitting pass, Roberto made his 150th Football League start for the club during the season. He is a clinical finisher, and his three league goals were all strikes from outside the penalty box.

Wigan Ath (Free from CFS Vipla Balaguer, Spain on 25/7/1995) FL 123+30/17 FLC 8/1 FAC 10+2/4 Others 5+5/2

Nigel Martyn

MARTYN Antony **Nigel**
Born: St Austell, 11 August 1966
Height: 6'2" Weight: 14.7
Club Honours: Div 3 '90; FMC '91; Div 1 '94
International Honours: E: 14; B-6; U21-11

There is no doubting the quality of Leeds United's last line of defence: recognised for many years as being one of the most consistent goalkeepers in the Premiership, the England international would surely benefit any side in world football. In a successful 1999-2000 season at Elland Road, Nigel's contribution was again second to none, as he proved time and again what an excellent shot stopper he is. Outstanding saves that spring to mind include the fingertip effort at Spurs from David Ginola's shot and a diving swoop to deny Kevin Phillips at the Stadium of Light, while no one who saw it could ever forget his heroics at Roma in the UEFA Cup – well, Totti, Delvecchio and Co. won't after a string of astonishing saves. Always working hard at his game, Nigel gets better and better and will surely be a key figure if David O'Leary's young side are to improve on last season's success in the coming campaign. Nigel is deservedly an integral part of the England international set-up, and was again selected by his fellow professionals to take his place in the PFA award-winning Premiership side. He added four more caps during the season, making a surprise appearance for the injured David Seaman in the Euro 2000 game against Romania.

Bristol Rov (Free from St Blazey on 6/8/1987) FL 101 FLC 6 FAC 6 Others 11
Crystal Palace (£1,000,000 on 21/11/1989) F/PL 272 FLC 36 FAC 22 Others 19
Leeds U (£2,250,000 on 26/7/1996) PL 146 FLC 10 FAC 16 Others 16

MASON Gary Ronald
Born: Edinburgh, 15 October 1979
Height: 5'8" Weight: 10.6
International Honours: S: U21-1; Sch

Although the highly rated Manchester City midfielder had made considerable progress the previous season, he was restricted to reserve football in 1999-2000. Realising he needed a new challenge, Gary joined Hartlepool on loan in November. Unfortunately, he did not settle particularly well at Victoria Park in a two-month spell. He is extremely fit, and is a skilful player best suited to a passing game. With City back in the Premiership, he may need to bide his time before Joe Royle believes he is ready to do a job for their first team.

Manchester C (From trainee on 21/10/1996) FL 18+1 FLC 3/1 FAC 2
Hartlepool U (Loaned on 12/11/1999) FL 5+1 FAC 1 Others 1

MATHIE Alexander (Alex)
Born: Bathgate, 20 December 1968
Height: 5'10" Weight: 11.7
Club Honours: Div 2 '00
International Honours: S: Yth

An experienced forward loaned from Dundee United by Preston last September as cover for injured strikers Steve Basham and Kurt Nogan, Alex made his debut the following day in the win at Gillingham. Two goals on his home debut against Sheffield United in the Worthington Cup endeared him to the home fans, and his goal against Bristol City was the 100th of his senior career, in his 300th senior game. From mid-October, he made regular appearances from the bench, before returning to Scotland in December, having added nine substitute appearances to nine starts, which in total produced four goals and earned him a Second Division championship medal.

Glasgow Celtic (From juniors on 15/5/1987) SL 7+4 SC 1 Others 0+1
Morton (£100,000 on 1/8/1991) SL 73+1/31 SLC 2/1 SC 5/3 Others 7/9
Port Vale (Loaned on 30/3/1993) FL 0+3
Newcastle U (£285,000 on 30/7/1993) PL 3+22/4 FLC 2+2
Ipswich T (£500,000 on 24/2/1995) P/FL 90+19/38 FLC 10+3/8 FAC 2+2 Others 6/1
Dundee U (£700,000 on 16/10/1998) SL 13+10/1 SLC 0+1 SC 4+2
Preston NE (Loaned on 17/9/1999) FL 5+7/2 FLC 2/2 FAC 1+2 Others 1

MATIAS Pedro Manuel Miguel
Born: Madrid, Spain, 11 October 1973
Height: 6'0" Weight: 12.0
International Honours: Spain: U21

This Spanish left-sided midfielder joined Tranmere Rovers for a three-month trial period at the start of the 1999-2000 season. He made his debut for the club at Stockport at the end of August but subsequently featured only a handful more times as a substitute before moving on to Walsall in October. The one-time Real Madrid player made his first-team debut for the Saddlers in a thrilling Friday evening win over Birmingham. Useful in the air and skilful on the ground, Pedro quickly showed the ability to go past opponents and, although he saw his main role as providing made-to-measure crosses, he scored several spectacular goals, notably a chip shot against Fulham that left Sky viewers breathless.

Macclesfield T (Free from Logrones, Spain, via Real Madrid and Almeria, on 3/12/1998) FL 21+1/2 FAC 1
Tranmere Rov (Free on 5/8/1999) FL 1+3
Walsall (Free on 7/10/1999) FL 30+3/6 FAC 2

MATRECANO Salvatore
Born: Napoli, Italy, 5 October 1970
Height: 5'11" Weight: 12.6
International Honours: Italy: U21 (UEFA-U21 '92)

Salvatore joined Nottingham Forest in the summer of 1999 after three seasons with Italian club Perugia. He is an experienced centre back who adapted well to the rigours of First Division football but unfortunately he suffered a cruciate knee ligament injury at Port Vale last October that led to a long lay-off. He is a tall and commanding defender with plenty of confidence. Salvatore returned to action for the Reds' reserves at the very end of last season and is expected to be fully fit for the start of 2000-01.

Nottingham F (£1,200,000 from Perugia, Italy on 6/8/1999) FL 11 FLC 2

MATTEO Dominic
Born: Dumfries, 24 April 1974
Height: 6'1" Weight: 11.12
International Honours: E: B-1; U21-4; Yth

Like a good wine, Dominic has improved with age and grown with his increasing experience in a variety of defensive roles. Before the 1999-2000 season, he lacked the consistency necessary to perform at the highest level in the Premiership, but as the campaign unfolded he learned to adjust to the mental demands of his role. Despite rumours that he would be sold to Celtic, Gerard Houllier kept faith with the 25-year-old, who repaid his manager's faith in him by turning in some fine performances, mainly at left back. A player with skill, pace, athleticism and an intelligent footballing brain, Dominic has only played in that position for a year, and is still learning his trade there, though his performances in the latter part of the season seemed to indicate that he was learning fast.

Liverpool (From trainee on 27/5/1992) PL 112+15/1 FLC 9 FAC 6+2/1 Others 10+1
Sunderland (Loaned on 28/3/1995) FL 1

MATTHEW Damian
Born: Islington, 23 September 1970
Height: 5'11" Weight: 10.10
Club Honours: Div 1 '94
International Honours: E: U21-9

The luckless midfielder's Northampton career totalled just 70 minutes in two seasons. Damian made his bow for the club against Stoke at the start of the 1998-99 season, but was sacrificed for a defender when Colin Hill was sent off. The next game, against Brighton in the Worthington Cup saw him replaced at half time with a back injury that eventually led to an operation. Last season he made a comeback as an 81st-minute substitute against Peterborough in August. It was to be his last appearance in a Northampton shirt as his injuries then got the better of him, and he was advised to quit the game.

Chelsea (From trainee on 13/6/1989) F/PL 13+8 FLC 5 Others 1
Luton T (Loaned on 25/9/1992) FL 3+2 Others 1
Crystal Palace (£150,000 on 11/2/1994) F/PL 17+7/1 FLC 2+1 FAC 1
Bristol Rov (Loaned on 12/1/1996) FL 8 Others 2/1
Burnley (£65,000 on 23/7/1996) FL 50+9/7 FLC 6+1/1 FAC 2/1 Others 3
Northampton T (Free on 7/7/1998) FL 1+1 FLC 1

MATTHEWS Jason Lee
Born: Paulton, 13 March 1975
Height: 6'0" Weight: 12.4

Jason joined Exeter after impressing against them for Taunton Town during a 1999 pre-season friendly. Manager Peter Fox admired his goalkeeping skills from the other end of the pitch, as the veteran custodian took the gloves for the last time due to the Grecians' 'keeping injury crisis. Jason's heroics were seen by millions of "Match of the Day" TV viewers as he came on at half time for the injured Stuart Naylor during the FA Cup tie versus Everton in December. He kept out everything that Everton threw at him, making a superb dive at the feet of Nick Barmby and an excellent save from Francis Jeffers as Exeter gained a creditable scoreless draw. Jason broke into the first team towards the end of the season, but was just one of 13 Grecians who were subsequently released.

Exeter C (Free from Taunton T on 9/8/1999) FL 11+1 FLC 0+1 FAC 0+1 Others 4

MATTHEWS Lee Joseph
Born: Middlesbrough, 16 January 1979
Height: 6'3" Weight: 12.6
Club Honours: FAYC '97
International Honours: E: Yth

This young Leeds United striker was loaned to Gillingham last March after the Kent club found their regular strike force reduced by injuries. Lee started just two games for the Gills before returning to Elland Road. Tall and quick, he has a good touch but needs to develop his strength to make the break-through to regular senior football.

Leeds U (From trainee on 15/2/1996) PL 0+3 FLC 0+1
Notts Co (Loaned on 24/9/1998) FL 4+1
Gillingham (Loaned on 23/3/2000) FL 2+3

MATTHEWS Robert (Rob) David
Born: Slough, 14 October 1970
Height: 6'0" Weight: 13.0
Club Honours: Div 2 '97
International Honours: E: Sch

This experienced Stockport winger missed the first four months of the 1999-2000 season while recovering from an operation on a troublesome knee and, once fit, moved to Blackpool on loan at the end of December. He showed dazzling form in the month he spent at Bloomfield Road, scoring three times from seven starts before returning to Edgeley Park. Although he then had a brief run in the County first team, netting in the 1-1 draw at Queens Park Rangers, Rob dropped out of the starting line-up once Ally Gibb arrived from Northampton and will be looking for regular first-team football in 2000-01.

Notts Co (Free from Loughborough University on 26/3/1992) FL 23+20/11 FLC 0+2 FAC 3+2/2 Others 4+3
Luton T (£80,000 on 17/3/1995) FL 6+5 FLC 0+1
York C (£90,000 on 8/9/1995) FL 14+3/1 FAC 1 Others 3
Bury (£100,000 on 12/1/1996) FL 54+20/11 FLC 4+5/3 FAC 1 Others 3
Stockport Co (£120,000 on 12/11/1998) FL 22+5/3 FAC 1+1
Blackpool (Loaned on 28/12/1999) FL 5+1/2 Others 2/1

MAUGE Ronald (Ronnie) Carlton
Born: Islington, 10 March 1969
Height: 5'10" Weight: 11.10
International Honours: Trinidad & Tobago: 3

An experienced tough-tackling midfielder who joined Bristol Rovers from Plymouth in the summer of 1999, Ronnie proved a very popular signing. Despite being sent off in his second league match at Gillingham in August, he always gave 100 per cent. His physical presence and ability to create good openings for team-mates were features of his early-season form, which brought him to the attention of Trinidad & Tobago. Ronnie made his full international debut for them at the age of 30 against Canada on 9 January and added further caps against Morocco and Mexico. However, he then suffered a broken left leg in February playing in his country's opening match of the CONCACAF Gold Cup tournament against Mexico and was sidelined for the rest of the season. He was certainly missed during Rovers' final run-in.

Charlton Ath (From trainee on 22/7/1987)
Fulham (Free on 21/9/1988) FL 47+3/2 FLC 4 FAC 1 Others 2
Bury (£40,000 on 30/7/1990) FL 92+16/10 FLC 8+2/2 FAC 8/2 Others 10+2
Manchester C (Loaned on 26/9/1991) Others 0+1
Plymouth Arg (£40,000 on 22/7/1995) FL 119+16/14 FLC 6 FAC 11/3 Others 5+1/1
Bristol Rov (Free on 5/7/1999) FL 22 FLC 4 FAC 1 Others 2

MAUTONE Stefano (Steve)
Born: Myrtleford, Australia, 10 August 1970
Height: 6'1" Weight: 13.2
International Honours: Australia: U23

This tall and brave Australian goalkeeper signed for Wolves on the eve of the 1999-2000 season but didn't play for the first team during his brief spell at Molineux. In November he joined Crystal Palace on a weekly contract and he appeared twice as cover for first-choice 'keeper Fraser Digby before moving on to Second Division promotion candidates Gillingham in March. He provided experienced cover for the Priestfield Stadium club and made his only appearance in the vital 2-1 victory over Wigan in April after Vince Bartram found himself delayed by a traffic accident on the M25. He was released during the close season.

West Ham U (£30,000 from Canberra Cosmos, Australia on 29/3/1996) PL 1 FLC 2
Crewe Alex (Loaned on 6/9/1996) FL 3
Reading (Signed on 17/2/1997) FL 29 FLC 5
Wolverhampton W (Free on 6/8/1999)
Crystal Palace (Free on 26/11/1999) FL 2
Gillingham (Free on 16/3/2000) FL 1

MAVRAK Darko
Born: Mostar, Croatia, 19 January 1969
Height: 6'0" Weight: 12.11

After making four early-season substitute appearances for Walsall in 1999-2000, Darko played in the home defeats by Manchester City and Sunderland in mid-September but was replaced in both games. He was a substitute once more in the next game, against Blackburn, and then spent the rest of the season in the reserves. A cool finisher when he is employed as a striker, he was one of several players who failed to hold down the key role on the left-hand side of midfield for the Saddlers last season.

Walsall (Free from Falkenberg FF, Sweden on 27/1/1999) FL 13+4/2 FLC 1+2 Others 3

MAXWELL Layton Jonathan
Born: Rhyl, 3 October 1979
Height: 5'8" Weight: 11.6
International Honours: W: U21-5; Yth

A product of the Liverpool Academy, Layton is an orthodox winger and is capable of beating players and getting crosses into the box. A Welsh youth international, he made his first-team debut for Liverpool in the Worthington Cup against Hull City last September, scoring with a brilliant right-footed shot at the Kop end in a 4-2 win. He is possibly one to watch for in the future if he can produce his best form at senior level on a consistent basis. Capped three more times for Wales at U21 level, he scored in the 2-2 draw with Northern Ireland during the close season. Stop Press: It was reported in June that Layton would be starting 2000-01 on loan at Stockport.

Liverpool (From trainee on 17/7/1997) FLC 1/1

MAY David
Born: Oldham, 24 June 1970
Height: 6'0" Weight: 13.5
Club Honours: CS '94, '96; PL '96, '97, '99; FAC '96, '99; EC '99

A very able central defender with good recovery skills and excellent heading ability, David had a wretched time with injuries in 1999-2000 and made only one full appearance for Manchester United – in the Champions' League against Sturm Graz in November, followed by an outing as a substitute against Leicester in the very next game. He went to Huddersfield on loan in December and showed his great defensive qualities during his debut at Crewe, looking very assured, but a back-related injury cut short his spell with the Yorkshire club after a mere 76 minutes' action. Then, just when it seemed that he was on his way back to fitness, he broke down again in training in April. It was not David's season, unfortunately.

Blackburn Rov (From trainee on 16/6/1988) F/PL 123/3 FLC 12+1/2 FAC 10/1 Others 5
Manchester U (£1,400,000 on 1/7/1994) PL 65+15/6 FLC 7/1 FAC 6 Others 14+2/1
Huddersfield T (Loaned on 24/12/1999) FL 1

MAYO Kerry
Born: Haywards Heath, 21 September 1977
Height: 5'10" Weight: 13.4

When all hope seemed lost for the locally born flame-haired midfielder last season, he re-established himself in the Brighton team. Kerry's 1999-2000 revival followed a couple of super-sub performances when he came off the bench late on to score vital goals. He went on to play at left back, keeping out the more experienced Jamie Campbell. Out of contract at the end of the season, Kerry was offered new terms.

Brighton & Hove A (From trainee on 3/7/1996) FL 111+13/8 FLC 4 FAC 1+6/2 Others 1+3

MAYO Paul
Born: Lincoln, 13 October 1981
Height: 5'11" Weight: 11.9

Paul was released by Nottingham Forest early in the 1999-2000 campaign and joined Lincoln as a scholarship lad in October. He progressed through the Imps' junior and reserve sides and made his senior debut at Swansea in February. He was an ever-present for the rest of the campaign, mostly appearing in his preferred left-back position but also being used as a left wing back. Paul is a fearless defender who always looks to push forward. His long throws caused havoc in opposition defences, while his inswinging corners set up many chances for the Imps in the closing stages of the season. He signed a new three-year contract in April.

Lincoln C (From trainee on 6/4/2000) FL 19

MEAKER Michael John
Born: Greenford, 18 August 1971
Height: 5'11" Weight: 12.0
International Honours: W: B-1; U21-2

This versatile forward found it very difficult to break into the Bristol Rovers team in 1999-2000 and had to be content with opportunities from the substitutes' bench when they arose. Michael was transfer-listed in November and, after making only his third appearance of the campaign in the 3-1 victory over Chesterfield, he moved to Swindon on loan on transfer deadline day for the remainder of the season, linking up again with his former QPR team-mate Jimmy Quinn, the County Ground manager, who used him as a wide-right player. He showed considerable ability in his six appearances for the Robins and proved to be a useful addition to the squad, confirming that he remains a tricky performer with exciting attacking skills.

Queens Park R (From trainee on 7/2/1990) F/PL 21+13/1 FLC 2/1 FAC 3/1 Others 0+1
Plymouth Arg (Loaned on 20/11/1991) FL 4 Others 1
Reading (£550,000 on 19/7/1995) FL 46+21/2 FLC 3/1 FAC 0+3
Bristol Rov (Free on 7/8/1998) FL 17+5/2 FLC 2+1 FAC 4+1
Swindon T (Loaned on 23/3/2000) FL 6

MEAN Scott James
Born: Crawley, 13 December 1973
Height: 5'11" Weight: 13.8

Scott rejoined Bournemouth under the Bosman ruling in July 1999 after an unhappy few seasons when he had been badly affected by injuries. He scored in the 2-1 win over Cambridge United on the opening day of the season and appeared regularly for the Cherries during 1999-2000 apart from a spell out with groin trouble in the autumn. Unfortunately, he failed to show the sort of form that was expected of him and he was released in the summer. On his day he is a stylish central midfield player with good passing ability and fine vision.

Bournemouth (From trainee on 10/8/1992) FL 52+22/8 FLC 7+1 FAC 2+1 Others 4
West Ham U (£100,000 on 18/7/1996) PL 0+3
Port Vale (Loaned on 21/8/1998) FL 1
Bournemouth (Free on 5/7/1999) FL 26+6/4 FLC 5 FAC 0+1 Others 2

MEECHAN Alexander (Alex) Thomas
Born: Plymouth, 29 January 1980
Height: 5'10" Weight: 10.10

A promising young striker who has impressed with his goalscoring ability in the Bristol City team after being released by Swindon during the 1998 close season, Alex greatly increased his first-team experience in 1999-2000 with a total of 15 appearances, eight as a substitute. Quick, with good control, he looks an ideal poacher, and after he notched his first league goal in a 1-4 defeat at Millwall in early March Ashton Gate fans predict many more from this bright prospect.

Swindon T (Trainee) FL 0+1
Bristol C (Signed on 6/7/1998) FL 5+8/4 FLC 1 FAC 0+1 Others 1

MEIJER Erik
Born: Holland, 2 August 1969
Height: 6'2" Weight: 13.10
International Honours: Holland: 1

A first-class signing from the Bundesliga during the summer of 1999, the giant Dutch striker showed during his first season with Liverpool that he is excellent on the floor, but even better with his head. He is a menace to even the biggest and strongest defenders, as Hull City found to their cost in the first leg of the clubs' Worthington Cup tie when big Erik scored twice to earn the "Man of the Match" accolades. He has an excellent professional attitude and commands respect with his demeanour. A real trier, he never shirks a challenge and excites the crowd with his wholehearted attitude, and he has proved to be a valuable addition to the Anfield squad.

Liverpool (Free from Bayer Leverkusen, Germany on 13/7/1999) PL 7+14 FLC 3/2

MELCHIOT Mario
Born: Amsterdam, Holland, 4 November 1976
Height: 6'1" Weight: 11.8
Club Honours: FAC '00
International Honours: Holland: U21-13

When Ajax announced that Mario Melchiot would be allowed to leave the club in the summer of 1999 as part of a shake-up by manager Jan Wouters, a host of European clubs, including Liverpool, West Ham, Aston Villa and Benefica, were alerted but Chelsea, displaying their customary stealth in the transfer market, moved in quickly to clinch the signature of this rugged player on a Bosman free transfer. A league and cup winner in Holland with the Amsterdam giants, Mario is a powerfully built player with an aggressive style, able to win the ball with a crunching tackle and use it constructively, and his imposing physical presence makes him a formidable opponent in the air. Mario is also a versatile player, at home anywhere in the back four or as a midfield anchorman. These attributes were an obvious attraction for Chelsea, but an added bonus for the Blues was Mario's Champions' League experience – an invaluable asset as the club undertook its first foray into Europe's premier club competition. But disaster struck for the big Dutchman before the season began: a broken bone in his foot required two operations which sidelined him until the Blues' Premiership encounter with Middlesbrough on Easter Saturday, which meant that he had missed a total of 55 first-team fixtures. Upon his long-awaited debut Mario replaced the injury-stricken Albert Ferrer at right back and he looked perfectly at ease in the top flight, particularly in the two difficult matches against Manchester United and Liverpool that followed. In an incredible twist of fate Mario then became an FA Cup final hero in only his sixth first-team appearance. Standing in for the luckless Ferrer at right back at Wembley, he materialised on the left wing and, in a manoeuvre straight out of the Ajax coaching manual, bamboozled an Aston Villa defender with a "Cruyff" turn. The free kick he gained resulted in Roberto Di Matteo's winning goal. Together with Emerson Thome, Jes Hogh, Bernard Lambourde and John Terry, Mario gives Chelsea ample cover in central defence for French World Cup winners Frank Leboeuf and Marcel Desailly, but he may prove to be most effective as a foraging midfield player.

Chelsea (Free from Ajax, Holland on 5/7/1999) PL 4+1 FAC 1

MELLON Michael (Micky) Joseph
Born: Paisley, 18 March 1972
Height: 5'10" Weight: 12.11

A midfield man always at his happiest when instigating attacks, Micky began the season as an automatic choice in Burnley's line-up but later had to vie with John Mullin for his place in the side. He never gave less than 100 per cent for the cause but was occasionally guilty of going into blind alleys. Nevertheless, he was always a potential danger man, as he showed to some effect when scoring a spectacular and well-celebrated winner against his old club Blackpool.

Bristol C (From trainee on 6/12/1989) FL 26+9/1 FLC 3 FAC 1+1 Others 5+3
West Bromwich A (£75,000 on 11/2/1993) FL 38+7/6 FLC 3+2 FAC 0+1 Others 6/1
Blackpool (£50,000 on 23/11/1994) FL 123+1/14 FLC 9/1 FAC 4 Others 7/2
Tranmere Rov (£285,000 on 31/10/1997) FL 45+12/3 FLC 4 FAC 3+1
Burnley (£350,000 on 8/1/1999) FL 53+9/5 FLC 2 FAC 4

MELTON Stephen (Steve)
Born: Lincoln, 3 October 1978
Height: 5'11" Weight: 12.2

Steve featured just three times for Nottingham Forest in the early part of last season before languishing in the reserves for several months and eventually moving on to Stoke at the end of February on a free transfer. A hard-working midfield player, quick in the tackle and accurate in his passing, he is highly regarded by Stoke's John Rudge, who had tracked him for some time, and was regularly used as a substitute following his move to the Britannia Stadium. He was released during the summer.

Nottingham F (From trainee on 9/10/1995) P/FL 2+1 FLC 1
Stoke C (Free on 28/2/2000) FL 0+5 Others 0+2

MELVILLE Andrew (Andy) Roger
Born: Swansea, 29 November 1968
Height: 6'0" Weight: 13.10
Club Honours: WC '89; Div 1 '96
International Honours: W: 39; B-1; U21-2

Released by Sunderland in the summer of 1999, Andy was quickly recruited by Fulham's new manager, Paul Bracewell, to further strengthen a defence which had conceded only 32 league goals in 1998-99. Playing on the right side of a back three if Simon Morgan was playing, and in the centre if Kit Symons was in, Andy showed great consistency, and his distribution from the back was again excellent. It took him a while to win over the crowd but he did so eventually. Andy remained a regular in the Wales international team, winning five further caps during the season.

Swansea C (From trainee on 25/7/1986) FL 165+10/22 FLC 10 FAC 14+1/5 Others 13/2
Oxford U (£275,000 on 23/7/1990) FL 135/13 FLC 12/1 FAC 6 Others 6/1
Sunderland (£750,000 + on 9/8/1993) P/FL 204/14 FLC 18+1 FAC 11 Others 2
Bradford C (Loaned on 13/2/1998) FL 6/1
Fulham (Free on 1/7/1999) FL 40/3 FLC 6 FAC 4

Andy Melville

MENDONCA Clive Paul
Born: Islington, 9 September 1968
Height: 5'10" Weight: 12.6
Club Honours: Div 1 '00

Clive had another frustrating season in 1999-2000 after a superb start. The Charlton striker scored a hat-trick on the opening day of the season, but played only 19 league games in total due to persistent injury problems. He still managed to finish second-top scorer, however, and won a First Division championship medal. Clive is very comfortable on the ball and, despite not being particularly quick, has the ability to turn a defender and gain a yard of space. He is deadly in front of goal, and one wonders how many times he would have scored if he had been fit all season.

Sheffield U (From apprentice on 10/9/1986) FL 8+5/4 FLC 0+1 Others 1
Doncaster Rov (Loaned on 26/2/1988) FL 2
Rotherham U (£35,000 on 25/3/1988) FL 71+13/27 FLC 5+2/1 FAC 4+1/2 Others 4+2/1
Sheffield U (£110,000 on 1/8/1991) FL 4+6/1 FLC 0+2 Others 0+1

Grimsby T (Loaned on 9/1/1992) FL 10/3
Grimsby T (£85,000 on 13/8/1992) FL 151+5/57 FLC 10+1/3 FAC 8/2 Others 2/1
Charlton Ath (£700,000 on 23/5/1997) P/FL 78+6/40 FLC 6+1/1 FAC 3/1 Others 2/3

MERCER William (Billy)
Born: Liverpool, 22 May 1969
Height: 6'2" Weight: 13.5

Billy was prevented by injury from taking his regular place in the Chesterfield goal at the start of the 1999-2000 season and in October he was transferred to Bristol City. With Keith Welch having moved to Northampton, the Liverpudlian proved to be the quality 'keeper that City had been seeking. Despite playing for much of the remainder of the season while not fully fit, he maintained a high standard throughout, and his frequently brilliant displays helped the club recover from a poor start. Billy is considered by many to be Tony Pulis's shrewdest signing for City during his short tenure of the Ashton Gate hot seat, and the fans are hoping that next season a fully fit Mercer will help bring promotion. He was voted City's "Player of the Season" by both the supporters' club and the Junior Reds, and his vast experience will be put to good use next season as he is to assist ex-City great Mike Gibson as goalkeeper coach.

Liverpool (From trainee on 21/8/1987)
Rotherham U (£50,000 on 16/2/1989) FL 104 FLC 12 FAC 12 Others 10
Sheffield U (£75,000 on 12/10/1994) FL 4
Chesterfield (£93,000 on 5/9/1995) FL 149 FLC 8 FAC 10 Others 7
Bristol C (£300,000 on 28/10/1999) FL 25 FAC 2 Others 5

MERINO Carlos Alberto
Born: Bilbao, Spain, 15 March 1980
Height: 5'8" Weight: 10'6"

This young midfield prospect joined Nottingham Forest from Spanish junior club Urdaneta after an impressive display against them in a youth tournament. He made his senior debut as a substitute in the Worthington Cup game at Mansfield last August and started a Football League game for the first time against Bolton at the end of October. He is a busy little player with lots of skill but turned down a new contract in the spring and opted to return to Spain and sign for Athletic Bilbao.

Nottingham F (Free from Urdaneta, Spain on 15/9/1997) FL 3+6 FLC 1+2

MERSON Paul Charles
Born: Harlesden, 20 March 1968
Height: 6'0" Weight: 13.2
Club Honours: Div 1 '89, '91; FLC '93; FAC '93; ECWC '94
International Honours: E: 21; B-4; U21-4; Yth

Although now approaching the veteran stage of his career, Paul had an excellent season in 1999-2000 for Aston Villa, culminating in a fine performance in the FA Cup final against eventual winners Chelsea. He began slowly and was mostly used as a substitute before winning a regular place in the starting line-up last December. However, he then returned to top form and was one of the main inspirations behind Villa's remarkable revival in the new year. He literally had to be forced off the field after suffering a badly cut head and concussion in the fifth-round tie against Leeds in January and his magnificent performances won him the "Carling Player of the Month" award in February. There was even talk of a return to the England squad but this was ruled out when he announced his retirement from international football in the spring. A very talented player, he performed best when operating just behind the two strikers, a position that allowed him to find space and pose problems for opposition defences. Paul capped a fine year at Villa Park when he was deservedly voted "Player of the Season" by the club's supporters.

Arsenal (From apprentice on 1/12/1985) F/PL 289+38/78 FLC 38+2/9 FAC 28+3/4 Others 27+2/7
Brentford (Loaned on 22/1/1987) FL 6+1 Others 1+1
Middlesbrough (£4,500,000 + on 15/7/1997) P/FL 48/11 FLC 7/3 FAC 3/1
Aston Villa (£6,750,000 on 10/9/1998) PL 45+13/10 FLC 5+2 FAC 7

Craig Middleton

MIDDLETON Craig Dean
Born: Nuneaton, 10 September 1970
Height: 5'10" Weight: 11.12

This committed, combative player was in and out of the Cardiff team in 1999-2000 and eventually signed for Halifax in March. He is at his best as an attacking midfield player and has shown that he can score goals in that role, although he can also operate effectively at right back, in central defence or just behind the front two. Craig joined Plymouth at the end of January on a month's loan and went straight into the squad for the game at Peterborough. He soon showed his eye for goal, scoring twice in his six appearances. Pilgrims boss Kevin Hodges wanted to retain his services but following a change of manager at Cardiff Craig was recalled to Ninian Park. When Halifax saw off competition from Plymouth and Exeter to sign him, many Bluebirds fans were disappointed to see him leave. During his ten games for the Shaymen he showed that he is a player who will create chances, and he capped a fine performance at Northampton with one of the goals in a thrilling 4-3 victory. Craig teams up with Graham Mitchell at the Shay; they were key figures in Cardiff's promotion from Division Three in 1998-99.

Coventry C (From trainee on 30/5/1989) F/PL 2+1 FLC 1
Cambridge U (Free on 20/7/1993) FL 55+4/10 FLC 3 FAC 1 Others 1
Cardiff C (Free on 30/8/1996) FL 95+24/8 FLC 3+1 FAC 13+1/3 Others 4+2
Plymouth Arg (Loaned on 27/1/2000) FL 6/2
Halifax T (£25,000 on 16/3/2000) FL 10/1

MIDGLEY Craig Steven
Born: Bradford, 24 May 1976
Height: 5'8" Weight: 11.7

The 1999-2000 campaign was a disappointing one for Hartlepool's diminutive but hard-working striker or attacking midfielder. He started the season as a reserve, and had to wait patiently for the right opportunity. Early in 2000 he looked to have got back to his best form, but he was then unlucky to receive a serious collarbone injury in training which kept him out for two months. A useful squad player, his 15 appearances as a substitute in league games is the highest-ever total by a Pool player in one season.

Bradford C (From trainee on 4/7/1995) FL 0+11/1 FAC 0+4 Others 1
Scarborough (Loaned on 7/12/1995) FL 14+2/1
Scarborough (Loaned on 14/3/1997) FL 6/2
Darlington (Loaned on 1/12/1997) FL 1 Others 0+1/1
Hartlepool U (£10,000 on 13/3/1998) FL 37+18/10 FLC 2+1 FAC 2/1 Others 5+1/1

MIDGLEY Neil Alan
Born: Cambridge, 21 October 1978
Height: 5'11" Weight: 11.10

Neil joined Luton on two months' loan in September 1999 from Ipswich Town, and made his league debut as a Luton player, scoring three goals in ten games. A busy worker in attack, he made his Ipswich debut in December against West Bromwich Albion as a substitute and scored with a fine far-post header. After another couple of substitute outings he made his first full appearance at Port Vale but found his opportunities limited when Marcus Stewart joined the club and Neil finished the season on loan at Kidderminster, scoring some vital goals which helped them clinch the Conference title.

Ipswich T (From trainee on 2/6/1997) FL 1+3/1
Luton T (Loaned on 24/9/1999) FL 8+2/3

MIGLIORANZI Stefan
Born: Pocos de Caldas, Brazil, 20 September 1977
Height: 6'0" Weight: 11.12

Stefan began last season as a regular in the Portsmouth line-up. He gave an impressive performance in the opening game against

Sheffield United, when he scored with a neat chip, and added a second goal in the 2-0 win over Stockport. However, his progress was interrupted when he damaged a knee against Charlton in October, and although he featured again briefly at the turn of the year he suffered a recurrence of the injury and remained out of action until the summer. He is a useful midfield prospect who will be looking to recover full fitness for the start of the 2000-01 season. Stefan was a member of the St John's University team that won the NCAA Division One soccer title in 1996 when one of his team-mates was Darlington's Ben Hickey.

Portsmouth (Free from St John's University, NY, USA on 8/3/1999) FL 16+4/2 FLC 2+1 FAC 1

MIKLOSKO Ludek (Ludo)
Born: Ostrava, Czechoslovakia, 9 December 1961
Height: 6'5" Weight: 14.0
International Honours: Czechoslovakia: 40

Ludo started the 1999-2000 season as the first-choice goalkeeper at Queens Park Rangers and kept his place until he was injured in the away game at Birmingham at the end of September. Despite regaining his match fitness after two months he was unable to displace Lee Harper from between the sticks; Ludo's opportunities were limited to two outings as a substitute in the FA Cup tie against Torquay. These appearances could be unique in that Harper was injured in both the original game and the replay, and had to be replaced twice in the same tie.

West Ham U (£300,000 from Banik Ostrava, Czechoslovakia on 19/2/1990) F/PL 315 FLC 25 FAC 25 Others 8
Queens Park R (£50,000 on 2/10/1998) FL 40 FLC 2 FAC 1+2

MILDENHALL Stephen (Steve) James
Born: Swindon, 13 May 1978
Height: 6'4" Weight: 14.0

Steve was again second-choice 'keeper at Swindon in 1999-2000 and played just a handful of games deputising for Frank Talia. His height and quickness off the line are an advantage to him but he really needs an extended run in the starting line-up to gain confidence. With the Robins announcing that they would not be renewing Talia's contract at the end of the season, Steve will be hoping that he finally gets the opportunity to play regular first-team football.

Swindon T (From trainee on 19/7/1996) FL 7+3 FLC 2 FAC 1

MILLEN Keith Derek
Born: Croydon, 26 September 1966
Height: 6'2" Weight: 12.4
Club Honours: Div 3 '92; Div 2 '98

After injuries had blighted his 1998-99 season Keith was unable to claim a first-team place at Watford as the new campaign took shape and in November he was transferred to Bristol City. Signed for a modest £35,000, the veteran central defender did much to add stability to City's defence after the club's disappointing start to the season. His sound positional sense and strong defensive play helped to turn the season around, and his experience was vital when he took over as captain, following Shaun Taylor's injury. Keith did well to play on for some weeks with an achilles tendon injury, but by the time he stood down he had fully convinced the fans that Tony Pulis had pulled off an outstanding signing at such a low cost.

Brentford (From apprentice on 7/8/1984) FL 301+4/17 FLC 26/2 FAC 18/1 Others 30+1
Watford (Signed on 22/3/1994) FL 163+2/5 FLC 10+1 FAC 14 Others 1
Bristol C (£35,000 on 12/11/1999) FL 28/2 FAC 2 Others 6

MILLER Alan John
Born: Epping, 29 March 1970
Height: 6'3" Weight: 14.6
Club Honours: FAYC '88; ECWC '94; Div 1 '95
International Honours: E: U21-4; Yth; Sch

Alan was West Bromwich Albion's first-choice 'keeper for the first half of the 1999-2000 season before a back injury knocked him down a peg. He struggled to regain full fitness, allowing young Chris Adamson an extended run in the first team. When he was ready for a recall, however, Albion changed managers and it was no surprise, following the arrival of Brian Jensen, when Alan was transferred to Blackburn Rovers. He again produced some fine performances for the Baggies, especially in three goalless encounters against Fulham, Charlton and Crystal Palace when he was voted "Man of the Match". He made only one appearance for Rovers before the end of the season, against Sheffield United, and will not find it easy to overcome the competition he faces from John Filan and Alan Kelly.

Arsenal (From trainee on 5/5/1988) PL 6+2
Plymouth Arg (Loaned on 24/11/1988) FL 13 FAC 2
West Bromwich A (Loaned on 15/8/1991) FL 3
Birmingham C (Loaned on 19/12/1991) FL 15 Others 1
Middlesbrough (£500,000 on 12/8/1994) P/FL 57 FLC 3 FAC 2 Others 2
Grimsby T (Loaned on 28/1/1997) FL 3
West Bromwich A (£400,000 on 28/2/1997) FL 98 FLC 9 FAC 3
Blackburn Rov (£50,000 + on 15/2/2000) FL 1

MILLER Barry Steven
Born: Ealing, 29 March 1976
Height: 6'0" Weight: 11.7

This former Brentford apprentice joined Gillingham from Farnborough in the summer of 1999 and made his debut against Brighton in an early-season Worthington Cup match. He featured as a substitute on a number of occasions in September but then suffered a knee injury. He was subsequently loaned to Woking from March to the end of the season to gain further experience. Barry is a right-sided or central defender with good passing skills.

Gillingham (Free from Farnborough T on 3/8/1999) FL 1+3 FLC 1+2

MILLER Charles (Charlie)
Born: Glasgow, 18 March 1976
Height: 5'9" Weight: 10.8
Club Honours: SPD '95, '96, '97; SLC '97
International Honours: S: U21-8; Sch

A maverick Scottish midfield player who joined Watford for £350,000 last September after impressing while on trial, Charlie had made his name as a midfield prodigy at Rangers, but rather lost his way after being replaced by Paul Gascoigne. Still only 24, he soon demonstrated his talent for the telling pass in a promising debut against Leeds, but his lack of match fitness cost him a regular place in the starting line-up after a handful of games and his influence on the team was at best peripheral.

Glasgow R (From juniors on 2/7/1992) SL 54+30/10 SLC 9+2/1 SC 5+1/2 Others 7+9/2
Leicester C (Loaned on 26/3/1999) PL 1+3
Watford (£350,000 + on 1/10/1999) PL 9+5 FLC 1 FAC 1

MILLER Kevin
Born: Falmouth, 15 March 1969
Height: 6'1" Weight: 13.0
Club Honours: Div 4 '90

Kevin began the 1999-2000 season in dispute with his club, Crystal Palace, and then signed a three-year contract with Barnsley at the end of August. He immediately installed himself as the Tykes' first-choice goalkeeper and remained so throughout the campaign. He performed consistently well, although perhaps his best game was against his former colleagues at Selhurst Park in January, when he capped a fine performance with a penalty save. He is an excellent shot stopper who is very sound on crosses.

Exeter C (Free from Newquay on 9/3/1989) FL 163 FLC 7 FAC 12 Others 18
Birmingham C (£250,000 on 14/5/1993) FL 24 FLC 4 Others 2
Watford (£250,000 on 7/8/1994) FL128 FLC 10 FAC 10 Others 3
Crystal Palace (£1,000,000 + on 21/7/1997) P/FL 66 FLC 3 FAC 5
Barnsley (£250,000 on 27/8/1999) FL 41 FLC 4 FAC 1 Others 3

MILLER Paul Anthony
Born: Woking, 31 January 1968
Height: 6'0" Weight: 11.7

This unsung player was one of Lincoln's most consistent performers during the 1999-2000 season. Paul worked hard in the centre of midfield and he created a host of chances with his penetrating runs into the opposition penalty area. His final tally of seven league and cup goals was his best yet for the Imps. Nearing 300 league appearances by the end of the term, Paul is one of the most experienced members of the City squad.

Wimbledon (From Yeovil T on 12/8/1987) F/PL 65+15/10 FLC 3+3 FAC 3 Others 1
Newport Co (Loaned on 20/10/1987) FL 6/2
Bristol C (Loaned on 11/1/1990) FL 0+3 Others 2
Bristol Rov (£100,000 on 16/8/1994) FL 100+5/22 FLC 7/1 FAC 5/4 Others 11/2
Lincoln C (Free on 8/8/1997) FL 83+13/11 FLC 3 FAC 5 Others 3/1

MILLER Robert (Rob)
Born: Bedford, 28 March 1980
Height: 5'8" Weight: 11.6

Released by Coventry in the summer of 1999, the former West Ham trainee featured in Cambridge's pre-season games during the build-up to 1999-2000 and signed a one-month contract in August 1999. A right back or midfielder, Rob made only one senior

Kevin Miller

appearance for the U's, as an early substitute at Millwall in September, before joining Stevenage in December.
Coventry C (Free from West Ham juniors on 18/8/1998)
Cambridge U (Free on 5/8/1999) FL 0+1

MILLER Thomas (Tommy) William
Born: Easington, 8 January 1979
Height: 6'1" Weight: 11.12
The attacking midfielder increased his workrate in 1999-2000 to become one of the best in the lower divisions. Almost certainly Hartlepool's most valuable asset since Don Hutchison ten years ago, he attracted the attention of several big clubs but Pool manager Chris Turner was determined to hold on to him. Early in the campaign he proved himself a more than useful goal-scorer, bagging a hat-trick against Barnet, and he finished the season as Hartlepool's top scorer with 16 goals. Tommy still lacks some consistency, but on his day is a real match winner. He was recognised by his fellow professionals with a place in the PFA Division Three team.
Hartlepool U (From trainee on 8/7/1997) FL 84+7/19 FLC 4/1 FAC 4/1 Others 7/3

MILLIGAN Jamie
Born: Blackpool, 3 January 1980
Height: 5'6" Weight: 9.12
Club Honours: FAYC '98
International Honours: E: Yth
A product of Everton's successful youth academy, Jamie is that rarest of breeds, a naturally left-sided Englishman. An U18 international, he made his breakthrough into Everton's Premiership side in the final match of last season. Given a handful of all-too-brief substitute appearances the previous campaign, he came on for the whole second half against Middlesbrough and acquitted himself well. Still small and slight, his delivery – especially of dead balls – is excellent.
Everton (From trainee on 13/6/1997) PL 0+4

MILLIGAN Michael (Mike) Joseph
Born: Manchester, 20 February 1967
Height: 5'8" Weight: 11.0
International Honours: RoI: 1; B-2; U23-1; U21-1
This highly experienced Norwich midfielder played the 500th game of his club career against Crystal Palace last March, but his overall contribution to the Canaries' 1999-2000 campaign was limited by the form of Darel Russell, Shaun Carey and Jean-Yves de Blasiis in the Norwich engine room. An extremely competitive player, he thrives on the hustle and bustle of the midfield areas, where his ability to win the ball and then use it effectively makes him an asset for any team. Mike always watches the ball when making challenges, often enabling him to steal it when he seems to have been beaten. His distribution is uncomplicated, but very effective, keeping the ball moving at all times. His Carrow Road contract was due to expire in June 2000 and there were no early indications as to his future, although he was reported to have turned down the opportunity of joining Shrewsbury Town as player-coach earlier in the season. Stop Press: Mike is understood to have joined Blackpool during the summer.
Oldham Ath (From apprentice on 2/3/1985) FL 161+1/17 FLC 19+1/1 FAC 12/1 Others 4
Everton (£1,000,000 on 24/8/1990) FL 16+1/1 FLC 0+1 FAC 1 Others 4+1/1
Oldham Ath (£600,000 on 17/7/1991) F/PL 117/6 FLC 11/1 FAC 9 Others 1/1
Norwich C (£800,000 on 27/6/1994) P/FL 113+11/5 FLC 11+1 FAC 6

MILLS Daniel (Danny) John
Born: Norwich, 18 May 1977
Height: 5'11" Weight: 11.9
International Honours: E: U21-14; Yth
A series of outstanding performances in a struggling Charlton side earned the full back a £4 million transfer to Leeds in the summer of 1999. Danny began the new season as the first-choice right back and scored his first goal against Sunderland in United's fourth game. But in the face of fierce competition after the return from injury of Gary Kelly he was forced out of the side after the victory at Watford in October, and played only a bit-part role thereafter. A strong right back with pace and a good shot, Danny can also play in central defence or as a wing back. Despite his lack of opportunities at Elland Road he remained part of the England U21 set-up.
Norwich C (From trainee on 1/11/1994) FL 46+20 FLC 3+2/1 FAC 2

Charlton Ath (£350,000 on 19/3/1998) P/FL 45/3 FLC 3 FAC 1 Others 2
Leeds U (£4,370,000 on 1/7/1999) PL 16+1/1 FLC 1/1 FAC 0+1 Others 2

MILLS Rowan **Lee**
Born: Mexborough, 10 July 1970
Height: 6'1" Weight: 13.9

A hard-working target man who packs a good shot in either foot, Lee found it difficult going with Bradford in 1999-2000, his first season of Premiership football, and often had to battle against the odds as a lone striker. He had a good spell in October, when he scored four goals in a run of five games, but generally struggled to find the net. He lost his first-team place after the shock FA Cup defeat at Gillingham in January and eventually moved to Manchester City in March on loan until the end of the season. Lee made his debut at Barnsley the day after signing but made little impact, partly because he was asked to play wide on the wing. He came on as a substitute against Bolton four weeks later and was more involved, foraging down the middle and contributing to Paul Dickov's late goal that sealed an important win, but he made only one more appearance for the Maine Road club, again from the bench.

Wolverhampton W (Signed from Stocksbridge PS on 9/12/1992) FL 12+13/2 FLC 1 FAC 3+1/1 Others 3/1
Derby Co (£400,000 on 24/2/1995) FL 16/7
Port Vale (£200,000 on 1/8/1995) FL 81+28/35 FLC 7+3/5 FAC 0+3 Others 6/4
Bradford C (£1,000,000 on 7/8/1998) P/FL 63+2/28 FLC 5+1/1 FAC 4/1
Manchester C (Loaned on 10/3/2000) FL 1+2

MILOSAVLJEVIC Goran
Born: Kraljevo, Yugoslavia, 11 April 1967
Height: 6'3" Weight: 12.2

A Yugoslavian defender, Goran came to Chester from the lower levels of French football in September 1999 and made his debut in the prestigious Worthington Cup tie against Aston Villa. Understandably finding it difficult to settle in his new surroundings, the 32-year-old was also tried in midfield and up front and appeared to improve as he played more games. Subsequently falling out of favour, Goran considered furthering his playing career in China and left the Deva in the summer.

Chester C (Signed from US Montelimar, France on 10/9/1999) FL 11+1 FLC 2 FAC 3 Others 1

MILTON Russell Maurice
Born: Folkestone, 12 January 1969
Height: 5'8" Weight: 12.1
International Honours: E: SP-2

Cheltenham's "Player of the Year" in 1999-2000, Russell must rank as one of the best ball players in the Third Division. He is a left-footed midfielder with wonderful touch, balance and the vision to make his passes count, and his lack of real pace was probably the only thing that prevented him from playing at this level earlier in his career. Russell missed the start of last season with a knee injury but made his Football League debut at Brighton at the age of 30 in September 1999. He went on to become a fixture in the centre or on the left of the Cheltenham midfield, playing a key role as the team climbed to the threshold of the play-offs. Russell had never scored for Cheltenham before the start of the campaign but ended it as second-top scorer with 11 in all competitions.

Arsenal (From apprentice on 26/2/1987. Free to Double Flower during 1988 close season)
Cheltenham T (Signed from Dover Ath on 12/8/1997) FL 38/9 FAC 2/1 Others 2/1

MIMMS Robert (Bobby) Andrew
Born: York, 12 October 1963
Height: 6'3" Weight: 14.4
Club Honours: Div 1 '87; CS '87
International Honours: E: U21-3

A player-coach at York, the experienced 'keeper was a first-team regular for most of the 1999-2000 season and showed consistent form between the sticks. New boss Terry Dolan, however, was looking to the future and released him in March. After turning down St Johnstone, Bobby followed another recent Minsterman, Martin Garratt, to Mansfield. Signed after two very competent performances against the Stags in the league, Bobby joined Mansfield as cover and also to undertake some coaching duties. He was kept on the sidelines until a string of unfavourable results forced his inclusion for the game with Hull City at Field Mill. In a dire match he did not have much work but could do nothing about the 20-yard screamer that won the game for the visitors. He signed a new one-year contract in the summer.

Halifax T (From apprentice on 5/8/1981)
Rotherham U (£15,000 on 6/11/1981) FL 83 FLC 7 FAC 3 Others 1
Everton (£150,000 on 30/5/1985) FL 29 FLC 2 FAC 2 Others 4
Notts Co (Loaned on 13/3/1986) FL 2 Others 1
Sunderland (Loaned on 11/12/1986) FL 4
Blackburn Rov (Loaned on 23/1/1987) FL 6
Manchester C (Loaned on 24/9/1987) FL 3
Tottenham H (£325,000 on 25/2/1988) FL 37 FLC 5 FAC 2
Aberdeen (Loaned on 16/2/1990) SL 6 SC 2
Blackburn Rov (£250,000 on 22/12/1990) F/PL 126+2 FLC 15 FAC 9 Others 4
Crystal Palace (Free on 30/8/1996) FL 1
Preston NE (Free on 5/9/1996) FL 27 FLC 2 FAC 2
Rotherham U (Free on 8/8/1997) FL 43 FAC 4
York C (Signed on 14/8/1998) FL 63 FLC 1 FAC 2 Others 2
Mansfield T (Free on 22/3/2000) FL 5

MINTO Scott Christopher
Born: Heswall, 6 August 1971
Height: 5'9" Weight: 12.7
Club Honours: FAC '97
International Honours: E: U21-6; Yth

This talented left-sided player appeared for West Ham in the first three games of the 1999-2000 season but then went down with achilles trouble and was sidelined for several months. He returned to first-team action shortly before Christmas and again showed consistent form for the Hammers until tearing a cartilage in his knee against Coventry last April. Scott is a versatile player who can perform equally well as a full back or in a wing-back role. He has good pace, excellent passing skills and loves to move forward to help out the attack.

Charlton Ath (From trainee on 2/2/1989) FL 171+9/7 FLC 8/2 FAC 8+2 Others 7/1
Chelsea (£775,000 on 28/5/1994) PL 53+1/4 FLC 3/1 FAC 9 Others 5+1 (Free to Benfica, Portugal on 30/6/1997)
West Ham U (£1,000,000 on 15/1/1999) PL 29+4 FLC 1 FAC 1 Others 1

MINTON Jeffrey (Jeff) Simon Thompson
Born: Hackney, 28 December 1973
Height: 5'6" Weight: 11.10

The central midfielder joined Port Vale from Brighton in the summer of 1999 under the Bosman ruling but at times struggled to adapt to football at a level two divisions higher than he had previously experienced. He scored three penalties to continue his 100 per cent professional record from the spot in the first seven games but was left out a month later amidst claims that he could not settle in the area, being out of London for the first time. After scoring his only goal from open play at Barnsley, Jeff was only used sparingly in the new year due to first a loss of form and then sinus trouble. He was transfer-listed at the end of the season.

Tottenham H (From trainee on 11/1/1992) FL 2/1 FLC 0+1
Brighton & Hove A (Free on 25/7/1994) FL 167+7/31 FLC 12/1 FAC 7 Others 5
Port Vale (Free on 1/7/1999) FL 23/3 FLC 2/1 FAC 1

MISKELLY David Thomas
Born: Newtonards, 3 September 1979
Height: 6'0" Weight: 12.9
International Honours: NI: U21-4; Yth

Oldham's second-choice 'keeper again found it difficult to dislodge Gary Kelly and made just three senior appearances in the 1999-2000 season. A talented goalkeeper, he has a safe pair of hands but really needs to gain more regular first-team experience to progress. David was a regular in the Northern Ireland U21 squad and won further caps against France, Malta, Scotland and Wales.

Oldham Ath (From trainee on 1/7/1997) FL 3 FLC 1

MITCHELL Graham Lee
Born: Shipley, 16 February 1968
Height: 6'1" Weight: 12.13

Halifax's club captain missed only one game in 1999-2000 and excelled at the heart of Town's defence. Graham is a consistent performer whose reading of the game is exceptional and can soon turn defence into attack. An experienced player who is an inspiration to others at the Shay, he also scored three goals. Having played in Scotland and Wales, Graham now appears extremely settled in his native Yorkshire.

Huddersfield T (From trainee on 16/6/1986) FL 235+9/2 FLC 13+2/1 FAC 27/1 Others 24/1
Bournemouth (Loaned on 24/12/1993) FL 4
Bradford C (Signed on 23/12/1994) FL 64+1/1 FLC 8 FAC 2 Others 4
Raith Rov (Signed on 10/10/1996) SL 22+1 SLC 0+1 SC 1 Others 0+1
Cardiff C (Free on 4/8/1998) FL 46 FLC 2 FAC 5 Others 1
Halifax T (£45,000 on 20/7/1999) FL 45/2 FLC 2 FAC 3/1

MITCHELL Paul Alexander
Born: Stalybridge, 26 August 1981
Height: 5'11" Weight: 12.3

A product of the youth system at Wigan, Paul was a second-year YTS player when he made his debut as a substitute in the Auto Windscreens Shield tie against Burnley last December. An old-style centre back, hard tackling and enthusiastic, he was a regular in the reserve side that clinched the Pontins League Division Two title. Paul was rewarded with a professional contract at the end of the season.

Wigan Ath (Trainee) FLC 0+1

MITTEN Charles (Charlie) Henry
Born: Plumstead, 9 October 1974
Height: 6'2" Weight: 12.7

Charlie joined Gillingham from Conference outfit Dover on a three-year contract last October as second choice to regular 'keeper Vince Bartram. He made one first-team appearance for the Gills in the Auto Windscreens Shield tie with Torquay United in December but was considered too inexperienced for further senior action at present, and manager Peter Taylor turned to Steve Mautone when he required cover for Bartram later in the season. Tall and slim, Charlie kicks well from his right foot.

Gillingham (Signed from Dover Ath on 8/10/1999) Others 1

MOHAN Nicholas (Nicky)
Born: Middlesbrough, 6 October 1970
Height: 6'1" Weight: 14.0
Club Honours: AMC '00

Nicky was a rock at the heart of the Stoke defence throughout the 1999-2000 season with just occasional breaks because of injury and suspension depriving the team of his strength and commanding presence. He took over as team captain early in the campaign, a move which seemed to boost not only his confidence but the form and spirit of the whole side, and lifted the Auto Windscreens Shield after an excellent performance against Bristol City at Wembley in April. Although he had a variety of central defensive partners, his form never wavered and his dominance in the air was a cornerstone of the club's push for promotion.

Middlesbrough (From juniors on 18/11/1987) F/PL 93+6/4 FLC 11 FAC 9+1 Others 11
Hull C (Loaned on 26/9/1992) FL 5/1
Leicester C (£330,000 on 7/7/1994) PL 23 FLC 2 FAC 1
Bradford C (£225,000 on 13/7/1995) FL 83/4 FLC 8 FAC 5 Others 5
Wycombe W (Loaned on 14/8/1997) FL 6
Wycombe W (£75,000 on 10/10/1997) FL 52/2 FLC 3 FAC 4 Others 3
Stoke C (Free on 2/3/1999) FL 55/5 FLC 3 Others 8

MOILANEN Teuvo (Tepi) Johannes
Born: Oulu, Finland, 12 December 1973
Height: 6'5" Weight: 13.12
Club Honours: Div 2 '00
International Honours: Finland: 3

A 1999-2000 season which saw Tepi reclaim a place in Finland's international squad in March, earn a Second Division championship medal and set new seasonal club records for clean sheets in the league (24) and in all matches (28) did not start too auspiciously; following David Lucas's first-half injury-time dismissal against Wigan, Tepi's first action was to face a penalty, and he then conceded an early second-half goal following an unfortunate mistake. Settling in well after a year out of the first team, he reached 100 Football League and club appearances and despite being lobbed from the half-way line straight from the restart after a North End goal at Brentford (as seen on BBC TV's "A Question of Sport"), he became a model of consistency, showing superb shot-stopping abilities and dominating his box on crosses, as would be expected of such a big man. Tepi won another cap for Finland when he came on from the subs' bench during the friendly with Wales last March.

Preston NE (£120,000 from FF Jaro, Finland, via Ilves, on 12/12/1995) FL 101+1 FLC 11 FAC 8 Others 2
Scarborough (Loaned on 12/12/1996) FL 4
Darlington (Loaned on 17/1/1997) FL 16

MONCUR John Frederick
Born: Stepney, 22 September 1966
Height: 5'7" Weight: 9.10

This reliable West Ham midfield player is now nearing the end of his career but still played an important role for the club in 1999-2000. John featured regularly in the autumn before suffering a hip injury that sidelined him from November through to February. He returned to the starting line-up against Bradford in spectacular fashion with a cracking goal from 25 yards and then missed only a handful of the remaining matches. His tremendous workrate and combative approach to the game were complemented by excellent passing skills, and although in his mid-thirties he showed he still has a lot to offer.

Tottenham H (From apprentice on 22/8/1984) FL 10+11/1 FLC 1+2
Doncaster Rov (Loaned on 25/9/1986) FL 4
Cambridge U (Loaned on 27/3/1987) FL 3+1
Portsmouth (Loaned on 22/3/1989) FL 7
Brentford (Loaned on 19/10/1989) FL 5/1 Others 1
Ipswich T (Loaned on 24/10/1991) FL 5+1
Swindon T (£80,000 on 30/3/1992) F/PL 53+5/5 FLC 4 FAC 1 Others 4/1
West Ham U (£900,000 on 24/6/1994) PL 118+15/6 FLC 12/2 FAC 6+1/1 Others 4

Mark Monington

MONINGTON Mark David
Born: Bilsthorpe, 21 October 1970
Height: 6'1" Weight: 14.0
Club Honours: AMC '96

Rochdale's uncompromising centre back had a rather injury-hit 1999-2000 season. Mark missed the first few weeks and then suffered three further spells out of action. On the bright side, he netted two braces when going up for set pieces. He nearly hit a hat-trick against Carlisle in March when his third effort was cleared off the line. Mark was offered new terms in May.

Burnley (From juniors on 23/3/1989) FL 65+19/5 FLC 5 FAC 4+1/1 Others 4+2
Rotherham U (Signed on 28/11/1994) FL 75+4/3 FLC 3 FAC 1 Others 4
Rochdale (Free on 6/7/1998) FL 59+2/5 FAC 7/1 Others 7/3

MONK Garry Alan
Born: Bedford, 6 March 1979
Height: 6'0" Weight: 13.0

Garry is a powerfully built central defender who, although still young, has been a regular for the Southampton second team for the past three seasons, having arrived as a trainee from Torquay in 1997. In September he joined Stockport on loan with his colleague Kevin Gibbens but had a difficult debut against Barnsley and was replaced at half time. To his credit, he returned to the team four days later and gave an accomplished display, but he went back to the Dell when his month's loan period was up. Garry's only first-team appearances for Southampton in 1999-2000 were in January, when he came on as a substitute in the defeat at Newcastle before playing a full game at home against Everton the following week. Against the Toffees he replaced Jason Dodd at right back and shaped up well. Tall, strong and quick, he is well thought of at the Dell and is most definitely one for the future.

Torquay U (Trainee) FL 4+1
Southampton (From trainee on 23/5/1997) PL 5+1 FAC 0+1
Torquay U (Loaned on 25/9/1998) FL 6
Stockport Co (Loaned on 9/9/1999) FL 2 FLC 2

MONKOU Kenneth (Ken) John
Born: Surinam, 29 November 1964
Height: 6'3" Weight: 14.4
Club Honours: FMC '90
International Honours: Holland: U21

The capture of Ken from Southampton in August 1999 was a major coup for Huddersfield. A classy centre back who is strong in the air and confident when in possession, he made his debut in the home game against Scunthorpe United in the Worthington Cup and looked every bit a Premiership player. Showing outstanding awareness, the Dutchman quickly formed an impressive partnership with Chris Lucketti that boded well for the rest of the season. Dangerous at set pieces, he scored a headed goal against local rivals Barnsley before making a happy return to Stamford Bridge for the Worthington Cup tie against Chelsea, in which it looked as though he could have played all night and not lost a tackle. Town steadily climbed the league table with Ken playing a leading role in their success, only for niggling injuries to keep him on the sidelines for long periods. Had he remained fit, Huddersfield might well have been contenders for an automatic promotion place until the end of the season.

Chelsea (£100,000 from Feyenoord, Holland on 2/3/1989) FL 92+2/2 FLC 12 FAC 3 Others 10
Southampton (£750,000 on 21/8/1992) PL 190+8/10 FLC 18+1/2 FAC 16/1
Huddersfield T (Free on 23/8/1999) FL 19/1 FLC 4

MOODY Paul
Born: Portsmouth, 13 June 1967
Height: 6'3" Weight: 14.9

Paul was signed by Millwall in the summer of 1999 from Fulham for £150,000. A big, bustling striker, he weighed in with his fair share of goals last season, netting five in two matches in November after a lay-off due to injuries to his knee and back. A threat to any defence, he is excellent in the air and able to hold the ball up well. He has the strength to trouble defenders, just brushing them aside and usually finishing with a good shot that is equally hard with either foot.

Southampton (£50,000 from Waterlooville on 15/7/1991) F/PL 7+5 FLC 1 FAC 0+1
Reading (Loaned on 9/12/1992) FL 5/1 Others 1
Oxford U (£60,000 on 19/2/1994) FL 98+38/49 FLC 10+4/4 FAC 7+1/5 Others 3/3
Fulham (£200,000 on 4/7/1997) FL 29+11/19 FLC 2+2 FAC 1+1 Others 2/1
Millwall (£150,000 on 5/7/1999) FL 24+8/11 FLC 1+1 Others 3

Tommy Mooney

MOONEY Thomas (Tommy) John
Born: Billingham, 11 August 1971
Height: 5'10" Weight: 12.6
Club Honours: Div 2 '98

This striker or utility player endured a desperately frustrating season through injury in 1999-2000. One of Watford's most popular players, whose wholehearted approach is much appreciated by the fans, Tommy started the season proudly wearing the number nine shirt, although he can play anywhere on the left side of the field. A scrambled goal at Anfield to clinch a famous victory made him an instant folk hero, and he followed up with a headed winner against Bradford the following week. But a month later he fell awkwardly during the home win over Chelsea, sustaining a knee injury that required two operations and ruled him out for all but the last few weeks of the season.

Aston Villa (From trainee on 23/11/1989)
Scarborough (Free on 1/8/1990) FL 96+11/30 FLC 11+2/8 FAC 3 Others 6/2
Southend U (£100,000 on 12/7/1993) FL 9+5/5 FLC 1+1 Others 2+3
Watford (Signed on 17/3/1994) P/FL 183+28/41 FLC 17/1 FAC 10+1/1 Others 4

MOORE Darren Mark
Born: Birmingham, 22 April 1974
Height: 6'2" Weight: 15.6
International Honours: Jamaica: 3

This powerful central defender began the 1999-2000 season on the transfer list at Bradford after failing to agree a new contract and started just once for the Premiership new boys in a Worthington Cup tie against Reading, before being sold to Portsmouth last November. He proved an asset to the south coast club, producing a number of solid performances in their successful struggle to avoid relegation. Darren is impressive in the air, very strong in the tackle and has a no-nonsense approach to the game. He made his international debut for Jamaica against Saudi Arabia in July 1999 and has since added further caps against Canada and Panama.

Torquay U (From trainee on 18/11/1992) FL 102+1/8 FLC 6 FAC 7/2 Others 8/2
Doncaster Rov (£62,500 on 19/7/1995) FL 76/7 FLC 4 FAC 1 Others 3/1
Bradford C (£310,000 + on 18/6/1997) FL 62/3 FLC 6/1 FAC 2
Portsmouth (£500,000 + on 15/11/1999) FL 25/1 FAC 1

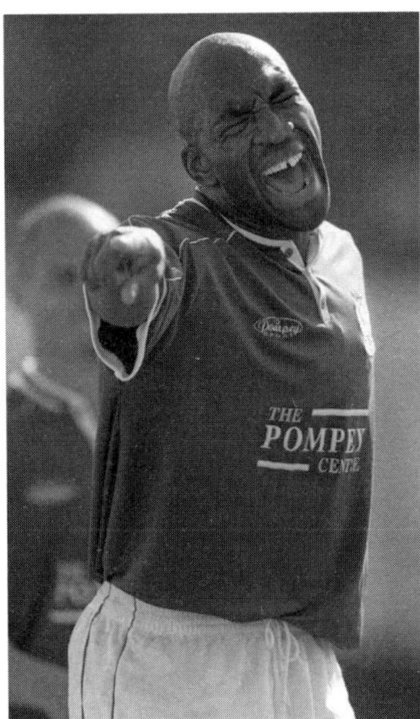

Darren Moore

MOORE Ian Ronald
Born: Birkenhead, 26 August 1976
Height: 5'11" Weight: 12.0
International Honours: E: U21-7; Yth

Stockport's record signing had a fine season in 1999-2000 and finished the campaign with a haul of ten league goals. His talents include a high workrate, a strong shot and excellent skills on the ball, and now he has started scoring regularly he would appear to be the complete striker. A great favourite with the County fans, Ian is expected to lead the attack once again in the 2000-01 campaign.

Tranmere Rov (From trainee on 6/7/1994) FL 41+17/12 FLC 3+2/1 FAC 1+1 Others 0+1
Bradford C (Loaned on 13/9/1996) FL 6
Nottingham F (£1,000,000 on 15/3/1997) F/PL 3+12/1 FLC 0+2 FAC 1
West Ham U (Loaned on 26/9/1997) PL 0+1
Stockport Co (£800,000 on 31/7/1998) FL 66+10/13 FLC 6/1 FAC 3/1

MOORE Joe-Max
Born: Tulsa, USA, 23 February 1971
Height: 5'9" Weight: 10.10
International Honours: USA: 79

Richard Gough's influence at Everton last season did not extend just to his commanding defensive displays. He also recommended New England Revolution striker Joe-Max Moore to Walter Smith, having been impressed with him during his time playing in the USA. The Everton manager was similarly impressed during a trial spell and signed the international striker on a free transfer. The little forward did not disappoint. After scoring twice in late substitute appearances against Tottenham and against Preston North End in the FA Cup he was handed a run of first-team starts and scored in every one! He struck in five successive games and showed his enthusiastic workrate and vitality about the box were perfectly suited to the English Premiership. Despite being small for a striker, he climbed magnificently to head another goal against Watford and ended the season with a total of eight. A clinical finisher, Joe-Max looks likely to enjoy an even more successful season next term with a full pre-season under his belt.

Everton (Free from New England Revolution, USA on 7/12/1999) PL 11+4/6 FAC 1+2/2

MOORE Neil
Born: Liverpool, 21 September 1972
Height: 6'1" Weight: 12.9

Having recovered from a serious back injury, Neil was released by Burnley in the 1999 close season and subsequently joined Macclesfield, his eighth league club. He initially played for the reserves before signing on a non-contract basis during December. Immediately taking his place in the first team, this tall centre back instilled confidence in his fellow defenders, and put in some solid performances. He is good in the air and useful up front for set pieces, and these qualities were well illustrated by his 94th-minute goal at home against Peterborough United to earn Macc an unlikely draw. Unfortunately for Town, Neil, who has Premiership experience with

Everton, accepted the offer of a contract with non-league Telford United in March 2000.

Everton (From trainee on 4/6/1991) PL 4+1 FLC 0+1
Blackpool (Loaned on 9/9/1994) FL 7 Others 1
Oldham Ath (Loaned on 16/2/1995) FL 5
Carlisle U (Loaned on 25/8/1995) FL 13 Others 2
Rotherham U (Loaned on 20/3/1996) FL 10+1
Norwich C (Free on 8/1/1997) FL 2
Burnley (Free on 29/8/1997) FL 48+4/3 FLC 3+1 FAC 2/1 Others 4
Macclesfield T (Free on 10/12/1999) FL 12+3/2 Others 1

MORALEE Jamie David
Born: Wandsworth, 2 December 1971
Height: 5'11" Weight: 11.0

An experienced forward, Jamie joined Colchester in the 1999 close season on a free transfer, following an injury-ravaged spell at Brighton, and after a promising pre-season sadly missed the big kick-off through injury. On returning to fitness, he had spells in and out of the team, being a regular on the bench when not in the starting eleven. He found goals hard to come by, managing only one in the Auto Windscreens Shield and one in the league, and the recruitment of Steve McGavin and reversion of Karl Duguid to striking duties moved him down the pecking order of forwards. Jamie was eventually released at the end of the season.

Crystal Palace (From trainee on 3/7/1990) FL 2+4
Millwall (Free on 3/9/1992) FL 56+11/19 FLC 3+1/1 FAC 1 Others 3+1
Watford (£450,000 on 13/7/1994) FL 40+9/7 FLC 6+1 FAC 5
Crewe Alex (Free on 8/8/1996) FL 10+6 FLC 1+1 FAC 2 (Free to Royal Antwerp, Belgium on 9/3/1998)
Brighton & Hove A (Free on 10/8/1998) FL 22+9/3 FLC 2 FAC 0+1 Others 1/1
Colchester U (Free on 5/7/1999) FL 20+7/1 FLC 0+1 Others 1/1

MORGAN Alan Meredith
Born: Aberystwyth, 2 November 1973
Height: 5'10" Weight: 11.4
International Honours: W: U21-2; Yth; Sch

After a disappointing 1998-99 campaign when he was affected by injury problems Alan bounced back in 1999-2000 to enjoy considerable success. He appeared regularly in the Tranmere line-up and produced what was probably the performance of his life against Coventry in the Worthington Cup last September. His preferred slot is in midfield, where he was an impressive anchorman, but he showed he could take any position that was asked of him. He is a very gutsy player who never shirks a challenge despite being relatively small in stature.

Tranmere Rov (From trainee on 8/5/1992) FL 38+18/1 FLC 6+2/1 FAC 3+2

MORGAN David **Bari** Rees
Born: Carmarthen, 13 August 1980
Height: 5'6" Weight: 10.8

A first-year professional in 1999-2000, Bari was one of Swansea's non-playing substitutes for the Christmas game at Leyton Orient when influenza ravaged the club's playing squad. Two weeks later the young striker or midfielder made his first-team debut as a substitute in the Auto Windscreens Shield tie at Exeter City.

Swansea C (From trainee on 5/7/1999) Others 0+1

MORGAN Christopher (Chris) Paul
Born: Barnsley, 9 November 1977
Height: 5'10" Weight: 12.9

Chris began 1999-2000 in Barnsley's reserves and it was only because of injuries that he was promoted to first-team duty at the end of September. He took full advantage of the opportunity to finally establish himself as a regular in the starting line-up and was rarely absent for the rest of the season. He showed greater maturity in his play, learning to control the aggression that has let him down in the past, and developed into a key figure in a relatively young defence. Strong both in the air and on the ground, he is a player who gives 100 per cent every time he steps on to the field. Chris scored his first-ever senior goal in the Worthington Cup tie with Bradford City and the great progress he made was recognised when he was voted the club's "Player of the Season".

Barnsley (From trainee on 3/7/1996) P/FL 64+3 FLC 7/1 FAC 5 Others 3

MORGAN Simon Charles
Born: Birmingham, 5 September 1966
Height: 5'10" Weight: 12.5
Club Honours: Div 2 '99
International Honours: E: U21-2

Simon again performed impressively for Fulham in 1999-2000 whenever he was called upon. With four top-class central defenders in the first-team squad (the other three all being current Welsh internationals), it was greatly to Simon's credit that he started 26 league games. A wholehearted competitor with a crunching tackle, he acquitted himself well in the First Division, and his only disappointment was that he failed to add to his 57 goals for the club. The coming season is Simon's testimonial year, the highlight of which will be a match against Tottenham in early August. Simon has always been the perfect pro, and he deserves to have a highly successful and lucrative night.

Leicester C (From apprentice on 15/11/1984) FL 147+13/3 FLC 14/1 FAC 4+1 Others 3
Fulham (£100,000 on 12/10/1990) FL 343+9/48 FLC 33/2 FAC 19/3 Others 17/4

MORGAN Stephen (Steve) Alphonso
Born: Oldham, 19 September 1968
Height: 5'11" Weight: 11.8
Club Honours: Div 3 '97
International Honours: E: Yth

The last of Hull's seven summer signings, Steve was well known to City boss Warren Joyce as they spent many long hours travelling together between Lancashire and Devon during their days at Plymouth. The burly left-sided defender or midfielder earned a one-year contract after an impressive performance in a pre-season friendly against Bradford City. The Tigers had to wait to use his strength and experience as an achilles tendon troubled him and, after breaking into the first team, he then suffered a hamstring injury and a calf strain. As well as proving an excellent addition to the defensive ranks, Steve developed the happy knack of scoring crucial goals in Auto Windscreens Shield games, finding the net against York and Chester. He was released during the summer.

Blackpool (From apprentice on 12/8/1986) FL 135+9/10 FLC 13/2 FAC 16/1 Others 10+1/1
Plymouth Arg (£115,000 on 16/7/1990) FL 120+1/6 FLC 7 FAC 6 Others 5
Coventry C (£110,000 on 14/7/1993) PL 65+3/2 FLC 5/3 FAC 5
Bristol Rov (Loaned on 1/3/1996) FL 5 Others 2
Wigan Ath (Free on 10/7/1996) FL 31+5/2 FLC 2 FAC 1 Others 4
Bury (Loaned on 26/9/1997) FL 5
Burnley (Free on 7/8/1998) FL 17 FLC 2 FAC 1
Hull C (Free on 29/7/1999) FL 17+2/1 FAC 3+1 Others 2/1

MORLEY Benjamin (Ben)
Born: Hull, 22 December 1980
Height: 5'9" Weight: 10.1

Having hit the national headlines in 1998-99, Ben experienced the other side of football fortunes last season with a succession of injuries. The versatile Hull right wing back pulled a hamstring in training just before the start of the campaign, and then his preparations were further hindered by illness. He also damaged his calf in a youth-team fixture against Scarborough, and his only first-team activity came as an added-time substitute for David Brown in the February win against Brighton.

Hull C (From trainee on 10/12/1998) FL 6+15 FLC 1+1 FAC 2/1 Others 1+1

MORLEY David Thomas
Born: St Helens, 25 September 1977
Height: 6'2" Weight: 12.7

A skilful and composed centre half, David eventually forced himself into the Southend first team in 1999-2000, striking up a very good partnership with Simon Coleman. Excellent in the air and with a midfielder's touch on the ground, David also filled in at centre forward at times of need. He proved himself to be essential to the Blues' defence, and is likely to be a cornerstone of the team in the new season.

Manchester C (From trainee on 3/1/1996) FL 1+2/1
Ayr U (Loaned on 14/3/1998) SL 4
Southend U (Signed on 28/8/1998) FL 55+4 FLC 4 FAC 0+2 Others 1

MORRELL Andrew (Andy) Jonathan
Born: Doncaster, 28 September 1974
Height: 5'11" Weight: 12.0

Andy featured in a handful of Football League games at Wrexham in 1999-2000, his first full season as a professional, scoring just once, in his first appearance as a substitute at Colchester last October. However, he created a massive impression in the BBC Wales-sponsored FAW Premier Cup, scoring four times in a 5-0 win over TNS Llansantffraid and then netting seven in the 8-0 demolition of Merthyr Tydfil. He thus equalled Archie Livingstone's all-time record tally achieved in September 1943 when Wrexham defeated Tranmere 9-0 and also earned himself a £10,000 bonus as top

goalscorer in the competition. Andy came into the full-time game late but he is a striker who certainly knows where the goal is and deserves the chance to finally make it at the Racecourse Ground.
Wrexham (Free from Newcastle Blue Star on 18/12/1998) FL 8+12/1 FAC 0+1 Others 1+1

MORRIS Andrew (Andy)
Born: Prescot, 18 March 1982
Height: 5'10" Weight: 11.1
A product of Wigan's youth policy, this promising midfielder made a Roy of the Rovers-style dream debut last season, coming off the substitutes' bench to grab a last-minute winner against Burnley in the Auto Windscreens Shield in December. A forceful, competitive player with an eye for goal, the second-year trainee was offered a professional contract. He was also voted the "Young Player of the Year" for the second consecutive season.
Wigan Ath (Trainee) Others 0+2/1

MORRIS Andrew (Andy) Dean
Born: Sheffield, 17 November 1967
Height: 6'4" Weight: 15.12
Rochdale's big centre forward started in the first two games of the 1999-2000 season. The second was against his former club Chesterfield, whose fans gave him a great reception. However, his only other appearance came as a substitute, either side of a three-month loan spell at Conference side Scarborough. As he clearly did not figure in Dale's plans, Andy was released in May.
Rotherham U (From juniors on 29/7/1985) FL 0+7 FLC 0+1
Chesterfield (£500 on 12/1/1988) FL 225+41/55 FLC 15+2/8 FAC 15+2/4 Others 18+4/3
Exeter C (Loaned on 4/3/1992) FL 4+3/2
Rochdale (Free on 23/12/1998) FL 26+6/7 FLC 1+1 Others 3/1

MORRIS Jody Steven
Born: Hammersmith, 22 December 1978
Height: 5'5" Weight: 10.12
Club Honours: ECWC '98; FAC '00
International Honours: E: U21-7; Yth; Sch
Although Chelsea's acquisition of another world-class midfield maestro in the form of Didier Deschamps inevitably presented him with a formidable challenge, the career of Jody Morris progressed in leaps and bounds last season. Given far more responsibility by boss Gianluca Vialli, he looked at ease at the very highest level, be it in the Premiership or against the giants of the Champions' League. Jody scored his first goal of the season by slamming a crisp shot under goalkeeper Massimo Taibi to round off Chelsea's five-goal rout of Manchester United. His second, a close-range chested effort against Sheffield Wednesday, went into the record books as the last Premiership goal of the old millennium. If any proof was required of the influence of Chelsea's star foreigners on Jody, it came in the FA Cup fourth round when he produced a mazy "Zola-esque" dribble and chip to create a headed goal for Dennis Wise that finished off Nottingham Forest's brave resistance. With intense competition from top-class internationals for a regular place in Chelsea's midfield, Jody understandably suffered his share of disappointments. One such came with his omission from the Blues' FA Cup semi-final line-up at Wembley against Newcastle but any lingering unhappiness was clearly assuaged three days later against Coventry when he was given the captain's armband in an appreciative gesture by Vialli. Fortunately for Jody, Chelsea's semi-final victory gave him another chance to play on the famous hallowed turf, albeit only for one minute as a substitute for Gianfranco Zola, and he ended the day with an FA Cup winners' medal. Jody added a further cap for England U21s against Poland last September. Vialli has declared his intention to lower the age of the team and to utilise homegrown talent. Fulfilling both these criteria, Jody is certain to be in the vanguard of Chelsea's new era.
Chelsea (From trainee on 8/1/1996) PL 48+25/5 FLC 6/2 FAC 6+3/1 Others 9+7

MORRIS Lee
Born: Blackpool, 30 April 1980
Height: 5'10" Weight: 11.2
International Honours: E: U21-1; Yth
A foot injury sustained in a pre-season friendly kept Lee out of the Sheffield United side for two months at the start of 1999-2000. During that time rumours circulated about a move to Derby County once he was fit, and they proved to be correct following his one, lively 12-minute substitute appearance for the Blades at Crewe in October. The fee, initially £1.8 million, could double depending on appearances.

Jody Morris

Having signed a four-year contract, Lee made a very promising debut for his new club in the home game with Tottenham the next day. He is a talented and very quick forward who, although preferring to play in a central role, is used mostly on the left side of the attack. A broken toe suffered in early November followed by a bone graft operation on the foot he had injured previously effectively ended his season but it is hoped he will be fit for the coming campaign. Lee is the son of the former Sheffield United player Colin Morris.
Sheffield U (From trainee on 24/12/1997) FL 14+12/6 FAC 2+5/2 Others 0+1
Derby Co (£1,800,000 + on 7/6/1999) PL 2+1

MORRISON Andrew (Andy) Charles
Born: Inverness, 30 July 1970
Height: 6'0" Weight: 14.8
Aiming to continue the form he showed during his excellent season in Division Two, Andy started 1999-2000 as Manchester City captain. A powerful, resolute centre back who is particularly good in the air, he encountered disciplinary problems early on in the campaign. He then missed another three games after picking up a mystery knee injury at Southampton in the Worthington Cup, but he played in the next seven before he broke down again at the end of October. Andy was out of action for the remainder of the season, and it seemed that each report that he was on schedule for a return to full fitness was followed by news of another set-back. When fit, he is an inspirational figure and can be relied upon to urge his team-mates to keep battling, and City certainly missed his strong, commanding presence in the middle of the defence.
Plymouth Arg (From trainee on 6/7/1988) FL 105+8/6 FLC 10+1/1 FAC 6 Others 2+1
Blackburn Rov (£500,000 on 5/8/1993) PL 1+4 FAC 1
Blackpool (£245,000 on 9/12/1994) FL 47/3 FAC 2 Others 4
Huddersfield T (£500,000 on 4/7/1996) FL 43+2/2 FLC 8 FAC 2
Manchester C (£80,000 on 29/10/1998) FL 33+1/4 FLC 2 FAC 4 Others 1

MORRISON Clinton (Clint) Hubert
Born: Wandsworth, 14 May 1979
Height: 6'1" Weight: 11.2
Another exciting Crystal Palace youngster, Clint has all the makings of a top striker – he is quick off the mark, has a good first touch, is able to hold the ball up well and, most importantly, is a constant danger in the penalty box. His form in 1999-2000 provided a bright spot for the financially troubled club and attracted the attention of a number of Premiership outfits. He finished leading scorer for the Eagles for the second season in a row, hitting the net 12 times.
Crystal Palace (From trainee on 29/3/1997) P/FL 55+12/26 FLC 5+2/3 FAC 1

MORRISON David (Dave) Ellis
Born: Walthamstow, 30 November 1974
Height: 5'11" Weight: 12.10
Dave made 16 appearances for Leyton Orient in 1999-2000, but his season was interrupted by injury, and by manager Tommy Taylor's decision to play a formation without wingers. Dave was advised that his contract wouldn't be renewed, and took the option of loan stints at Stevenage and Dover.
Peterborough U (£30,000 from Chelmsford C on 12/5/1994) FL 59+18/12 FLC 4+1/1 FAC 5+3 Others 6+2
Leyton Orient (£25,000 on 21/3/1997) FL 21+25/3 FLC 2+5 FAC 1 Others 1+1

MORRISON-HILL Jamie Steven
Born: Plymouth, 8 June 1981
Height: 5'8" Weight: 10.4
A former YTS trainee, Jamie continued his football education in 1999-2000, his first season as a professional at Plymouth. He has pace and skill and is looking to build up his strength to push for a regular first-team place. A bright prospect, Jamie made his full debut against Torquay in the Auto Windscreens Shield in January. He has been offered month-to-month terms for the new season.
Plymouth Arg (From trainee on 6/7/1999) FL 0+1 Others 1

MORROW Andrew (Andy) Gareth
Born: Bangor, NI, 5 October 1980
Height: 5'8" Weight: 9.10
International Honours: NI: Yth; Sch
A young striker who has risen through the ranks at Northampton, Andy was given his first taste of league football when Kevin Wilson took over as manager last October. He brought the youngster on as a substitute against Torquay, and Andy almost marked his debut with a goal when his shot was inches wide of the target. He has won U18 caps for Northern Ireland and, although first-team places for strikers at Northampton are currently at a premium, his is certainly a name for the future.
Northampton T (From trainee on 16/12/1998) FL 0+4 Others 2

MORROW Stephen (Steve) Joseph
Born: Bangor, NI, 2 July 1970
Height: 6'0" Weight: 11.6
Club Honours: FAYC '88; FLC '93; ECEC '94
International Honours: NI: 39; B-1; U23-2; Yth; Sch
Steve was one of several Queens Park Rangers players whose appearances in 1999-2000 were severely restricted owing to injury. At the start of the season he made a successful move from his normal defensive position into a midfield role. He played in the first three games and was able to regain his place in November after returning to fitness. In the home game against Sheffield United at the end of the month he fell awkwardly on his shoulder. The injury turned out to be more serious than was first thought as it was discovered that he had ruptured ligaments in the shoulder. This required a number of operations, which kept Steve out of the first team for the rest of the season.
Arsenal (From trainee on 5/5/1988) F/PL 39+23/1 FLC 7+4/2 FAC 5+2 Others 1+4
Reading (Loaned on 16/1/1991) FL 10
Watford (Loaned on 14/8/1991) FL 7+1 Others 1
Reading (Loaned on 30/10/1991) FL 3
Barnet (Loaned on 4/3/1992) FL 1
Queens Park R (£1,000,000 on 27/3/1997) FL 66+1/2 FLC 4 FAC 2

MORTIMER Paul Henry
Born: Kensington, 8 May 1968
Height: 5'11" Weight: 12.7
International Honours: E: U21-2
A free-transfer close-season signing from Charlton Athletic, this cultured midfield player really looked the part for Bristol City early in the 1999-2000 season before hamstring problems curtailed his effectiveness. Throughout his career Paul has shown that he is a very skilful player with good vision who is comfortable on the ball and can pass with real accuracy. With a year still remaining on his contract, the Ashton Gate fans are hopeful that he will regain full fitness for the forthcoming campaign.
Charlton Ath (Free from Farnborough T on 22/9/1987) FL 108+5/17 FLC 4+1 FAC 8 Others 3+1
Aston Villa (£350,000 on 24/7/1991) FL 10+2/1 FLC 2
Crystal Palace (£500,000 on 18/10/1991) F/PL 18+4/2 FLC 1 FAC 1 Others 3
Brentford (Loaned on 22/1/1993) FL 6 Others 2
Charlton Ath (£200,000 on 5/7/1994) P/FL 67+19/15 FLC 4+1/1 FAC 3/1 Others 0+1
Bristol C (Free on 5/8/1999) FL 22+1 FLC 3/1 FAC 2

MOSES Adrian (Ade) Paul
Born: Doncaster, 4 May 1975
Height: 5'10" Weight: 12.8
International Honours: E: U21-2
Ade began the 1999-2000 season at centre back for Barnsley but new manager Dave Bassett switched him to the right-full-back position early on. He was just beginning to settle into his new role when he succumbed to a niggling groin injury that required an operation last November. It was only in late March that he returned to action with the reserves and it is hoped that he will be fully fit in time for the start of the 2000-01 season. He is a versatile defender whose pace and tackling skills make him an ideal man marker.
Barnsley (From juniors on 2/7/1993) F/PL 126+11/3 FLC 13 FAC 15

MOSS Darren Michael
Born: Wrexham, 24 May 1981
Height: 5'10" Weight: 11.0
International Honours: W: Yth
Despite Chester's relegation in 1999-2000, this successful graduate from the club's youth policy and former Wales youth international has a tremendous future ahead of him. A possible move to Aston Villa fell through last season, but Darren continues to attract the attention of leading clubs. A fast and skilful midfielder, he was also used in wider positions last term to notable effect.
Chester C (From trainee on 14/7/1999) FL 33+9 FLC 1+1 FAC 4 Others 1

MOSS Neil Graham
Born: New Milton, 10 May 1975
Height: 6'2" Weight: 13.10
A highly promising young goalkeeper, Neil has had few opportunities to prove himself since joining Southampton in 1995 but when he came off the bench at Sunderland last

December to replace a concussed Paul Jones he proceeded to distinguish himself, saving a penalty from prolific ex-Southampton trainee Kevin Phillips. However, a quick return by Jones left his capable understudy still waiting for an extended run between the sticks. Following speculation that he was to leave the club on a Bosman free transfer at the end of the season, Neil agreed a new two-year deal in March. Soon afterwards, an injury to Jones gave him a prolonged run in the first team, and he saw out the season as the Saints' regular 'keeper.

Bournemouth (From trainee on 29/1/1993) FL 21+1 FLC 1 FAC 3+1 Others 2
Southampton (£250,000 on 20/12/1995) PL 17+2 FLC 2
Gillingham (Loaned on 8/8/1997) FL 10 FLC 2

MOWBRAY Anthony (Tony) Mark
Born: Saltburn, 22 November 1963
Height: 6'1" Weight: 13.2
International Honours: E: B-2

Appointed Ipswich first-team coach during the summer of 1999, after John Gorman decided not to stay with the club, Tony retained his registration as a player although he had no real intention of playing first-team football. However, he was recalled to the side in mid-October following a defensive disaster in the home game with Queens Park Rangers that produced Town's heaviest defeat of the season, 1-4. He immediately brought stability to the defence, Charlton were despatched 4-2 in the next game and Tony kept his place in the team for the rest of the campaign. He is still commanding in the air and has a great ability to organise the defence around him, and although he is reaching the stage where he could be classed as a "veteran" his reading of the game allows him to be in the right place at the right time. He managed only one goal during the season, at Blackburn, but what a cracker it was. Following a corner, Tony scored with a right-foot volley from the edge of the penalty area which screamed into the top corner of the net. He featured strongly in the play-off final at Wembley and doubled his goal tally for the season when he equalised with a powerful header from Jim Magilton's cross.

Middlesbrough (From apprentice on 27/11/1981) FL 345+3/25 FLC 28+2/2 FAC 23/1 Others 23+1/1
Glasgow Celtic (£1,000,000 on 8/11/1991) SL 75+3/6 SLC 7 SC 5 Others 6
Ipswich T (£300,000 on 6/10/1995) FL 125+3/5 FLC 7/1 FAC 9 Others 8/2

MUGGLETON Carl David
Born: Leicester, 13 September 1968
Height: 6'2" Weight: 13.4
International Honours: E: U21-1

The experienced Stoke goalkeeper was loaned to Mansfield in September when, with regular 'keeper Ian Bowling still unavailable through injury, Barry Richardson returned to Lincoln at the end of his loan period. Carl produced some terrific performances during his two-month stay at Field Mill, impressing the fans with his outstanding shot-stopping and exemplary positioning. In December he moved to Chesterfield on loan, rejoining the club some 12 years after he had made his league debut for them while on loan from Leicester. The Spireites' defence immediately benefited from Carl's authoritative, confident presence, and his sure groundwork was instrumental in securing a rare away point at Brentford. He returned to Stoke for the remainder of the season, and was on the substitutes' bench when City won the Auto Windscreens Shield at Wembley.

Leicester C (From apprentice on 17/9/1986) FL 46 FAC 3 Others 5
Chesterfield (Loaned on 10/9/1987) FL 17 Others 2
Blackpool (Loaned on 1/2/1988) FL 2
Hartlepool U (Loaned on 28/10/1988) FL 8 Others 2
Stockport Co (Loaned on 1/3/1990) FL 4
Stoke C (Loaned on 13/8/1993) FL 6 FLC 1 Others 2
Glasgow Celtic (£150,000 on 11/1/1994) SL 12 SC 1
Stoke C (£150,000 on 21/7/1994) FL 137 FLC 14 FAC 3 Others 6
Rotherham U (Loaned on 1/11/1995) FL 6 Others 1
Sheffield U (Loaned on 28/3/1996) FL 0+1
Mansfield T (Loaned on 9/9/1999) FL 9
Chesterfield (Loaned on 9/12/1999) FL 5

MULLIN John Michael
Born: Bury, 11 August 1975
Height: 6'0" Weight: 11.10

Often linked with a return to Turf Moor during his four years at Sunderland, John finally came back to his home-town club Burnley just before the start of the 1999-2000 season. Now playing in a deeper role than in his first spell at the club, and looking a much more complete player for his higher-level experience, he is at his best running at defences and creating space for the main strikers. Injured at the beginning of the season, once he established himself in the side John was a regular, although the improvement in Lenny Johnrose's form later in the campaign meant that John sometimes had to compete with Micky Mellon for one of the midfield places in Stan Ternent's preferred 5-3-2 formation.

Burnley (From trainee on 18/8/1992) FL 7+11/2 FAC 2
Sunderland (£40,000 + on 12/8/1995) P/FL 23+12/4 FLC 5+1 FAC 2+1
Preston NE (Loaned on 13/2/1998) FL 4+3 Others 1
Burnley (Loaned on 26/3/1998) FL 6
Burnley (Free on 20/7/1999) FL 27+10/5 FAC 4/1 Others 1

MULLINS Hayden Ian
Born: Reading, 27 March 1979
Height: 6'0" Weight: 11.12
International Honours: E: U21-3

Hayden had an excellent 1999-2000 campaign in the Crystal Palace midfield and his performances attracted the scouts from Premiership clubs. He was a favourite to depart by the transfer deadline in view of the club's precarious financial position, and it was a surprise (and a relief) to the Eagles' supporters that he remained at Selhurst Park. Mostly used in midfield, where his ball control and passing skills are put to good use, he is also developing an eye for goal and scored ten times last season.

Crystal Palace (From trainee on 28/2/1997) FL 83+2/15 FLC 7/1 FAC 2

Hayden Mullins

MULRYNE Phillip (Phil) Patrick
Born: Belfast, 1 January 1978
Height: 5'8" Weight: 10.11
Club Honours: FAYC '95
International Honours: NI: 5; B-1; U21-3; Yth

Expectations at Norwich for this former Manchester United midfielder were high at the outset of the 1999-2000 campaign, and his early-season form only enhanced his reputation. Then, on 28 August, in the home fixture with Blackburn Rovers, he had the misfortune to suffer a double compound fracture of his right leg, which resulted in over seven months on the sidelines. A tremendous attitude towards this set-back allied to his real determination to fight his way back to fitness led to his return to competitive action on 8 April, at Portsmouth, and Canary fans were soon given a glimpse of what they had been missing. Phil is one of the dying breed of creative midfielders whose game is based on inventive passing rather than sheer pace and power. He combines the vision to see the incisive pass with the ability and range of passing to actually deliver it. His natural attacking inclinations also take him into goalscoring positions on a regular basis, and that potential goals contribution from midfield was sorely missed by City as they strove to reach the play-off race. A regular member of the full Northern Ireland squad prior to his injury, Phil will be hoping to add to his tally of caps in the 2002 World Cup qualifying campaign.

Manchester U (From trainee on 17/3/1995) PL 1 FLC 3 FAC 0+1
Norwich C (£500,000 on 25/3/1999) FL 13+3/2 FLC 2

MUNROE Karl Augustus
Born: Manchester, 23 September 1979
Height: 6'0" Weight: 11.0

Phil Mulryne

After signing for Macclesfield in October 1999, Karl spent the majority of the season playing for Town's reserve team. He made the first of four substitute appearances when Hull visited Moss Rose in January but had to wait until April, and the long trip to Torquay, before making his full league debut. Karl is a strong centre back, but was also used in midfield, providing a real physical presence and often making challenging tackles. Prior to joining the Macc ranks, his only senior experience came in the last half-hour of Swansea's final game of the 1997-98 season.
Swansea C (From trainee on 9/7/1998) FL 0+1
Macclesfield T (Free on 14/10/1999) FL 1+4

MURDOCK Colin James
Born: Ballymena, 2 July 1975
Height: 6'2" Weight: 13.0
Club Honours: Div 2 '00
International Honours: NI: 3; B-3; Yth; Sch
A regular place in the Northern Ireland squad was fitting reward for a consistent 1999-2000 season for Preston's tall left-sided centre back. Often vying with Ryan Kidd for the spot alongside Michael Jackson, he was magnificent against Kevin Campbell in the FA Cup tie at Everton, and made his 100th North End appearance at Oxford. Colin made his debut in senior international football for Northern Ireland when he came on from the subs' bench against Luxembourg in February and won further caps against Malta and Hungary. A new contract was just reward for his contribution to Preston's ultimately successful Second Division championship challenge, where his dominance in the air and timely tackles were seen to good effect.
Manchester U (From juniors on 21/7/1992)
Preston NE (£100,000 on 23/5/1997) FL 84+9/4 FLC 6 FAC 6+2 Others 7

MURPHY Daniel (Danny) Benjamin
Born: Chester, 18 March 1977
Height: 5'9" Weight: 10.8
International Honours: E: U21-5; Yth; Sch
An indefatigable midfield dynamo, Danny was again restricted to just a few appearances for Liverpool in 1999-2000. A central midfield player, he can beat players, works hard, scores goals and is committed to the Liverpool cause, but rarely gets an opportunity to prove himself in the first team with a long run, although he continues to shine regularly in the reserves. Danny is a fine passer of the ball, is intelligent and can finish from midfield, and his absences from the team have been due in the main to Gerard Houllier trying either to accommodate a specialist defensive midfielder or to play with a lone striker. The consequences of Houllier's tactical awareness should not be seen as a reflection on Danny's genuine ability. He signed a new two-year extension to his contract in February and will be hoping for greater opportunities during the coming season.
Crewe Alex (From trainee on 21/3/1994) FL 110+24/27 FLC 7 FAC 7/4 Others 15+3/3
Liverpool (£1,500,000 + on 17/7/1997) PL 15+25/3 FLC 3+1/3 FAC 2+1 Others 0+1
Crewe Alex (Loaned on 12/2/1999) FL 16/1

MURPHY John James
Born: Whiston, 18 October 1976
Height: 6'2" Weight: 14.0
John is a tall central striker who joined Blackpool over the 1999 close season from Chester City. He proved an asset to the Seasiders' attack with his bustling style and aerial strength, and finished 1999-2000 as the club's leading scorer with ten goals.
Chester C (From trainee on 6/7/1995) FL 65+38/20 FLC 6+3/1 FAC 1+2 Others 3+1
Blackpool (Signed on 6/8/1999) FL 34+5/10 FLC 1 FAC 3 Others 1+1

MURPHY Joseph (Joe)
Born: Dublin, Ireland, 21 August 1981
Height: 6'2" Weight: 13.6
International Honours: RoI: U21-2; Yth; (UEFA-U16 '98)
A product of Tranmere's Irish nursery outfit Stella Maris, this young goalkeeper made a dream debut against Oxford in the Worthington Cup tie last October when he saved a penalty. He had a lengthy spell of first-team action in the autumn before losing his place after suffering a broken collarbone in the Worthington Cup quarter-final against Middlesbrough last December. He made a surprise return for the FA Cup tie with Newcastle in February and was then preferred to John Achterberg, his rival for the position, in the Worthington Cup final against Leicester. Tall and athletic, he has all the makings of a top-class 'keeper with excellent handling, good distribution skills and total command of his own penalty area. Already a youth international for the Republic of Ireland, Joe added four further caps at U18 level and went on to make his bow for the U21s during the Toulon Tournament in May with appearances against Colombia and Portugal. He is already attracting considerable interest from Premiership clubs, although he would probably benefit from a further season in Division One before stepping up.
Tranmere Rov (From trainee on 5/7/1999) FL 21 FLC 4 FAC 2

MURPHY Matthew (Matt) Simon
Born: Northampton, 20 August 1971
Height: 6'0" Weight: 12.2
Matt was top scorer for Oxford with 17 goals in 1999-2000, having at last made himself a regular in the side. Having been offered a new contract in the summer of 1999, he eventually agreed to new terms from United and went on to miss just one game, and that an Auto Windscreens Shield tie. Matt started the season on fire with six goals in the opening six games and carried this good form through until the turn of the year. He scored just four times after Boxing

Day but still ended with his best-ever return. At home just behind the strikers or pushing through from midfield, he also spent time as a striker, acquitting himself well.

Oxford U (£20,000 from Corby T on 12/2/1993) FL 131+75/32 FLC 9+8/7 FAC 10+3/5 Others 5+3/3
Scunthorpe U (Loaned on 12/12/1997) FL 1+2 Others 1

Matt Murphy

MURPHY Shaun Peter
Born: Sydney, Australia, 5 November 1970
Height: 6'1" Weight: 12.0
Club Honours: AIC '95
International Honours: Australia: 5; U23; Yth

Shaun was signed by then Sheffield United manager Adrian Heath from West Bromwich Albion in the 1999 close season and immediately became a fixture in the United defence. Never shirking a challenge, he showed himself to have good defensive anticipation, both on the floor and particularly in the air. His distribution sometimes left room for improvement and his clearances did not always go where intended but, as his performances improved, he won round the initially sceptical fans. His height and heading ability were used in the opposition penalty area at set pieces and he was unfortunate not to have scored more goals. Shaun made his full international debut for Australia against Chile in February and went on to win a further four caps. Stop Press: He played and scored for Australia in their 2-0 victory over New Zealand in the Oceania Nations' Cup final at the end of June.

Notts Co (Signed from Perth Italia, Australia on 4/9/1992) FL 100+9/5 FLC 5+2 FAC 6/1 Others 12+1/1
West Bromwich A (£500,000 on 31/12/1996) FL 60+11/7 FLC 3 FAC 4
Sheffield U (Free on 22/7/1999) FL 42/3 FLC 4 FAC 2

MURPHY Stephen
Born: Dublin, 5 April 1978
Height: 5'11" Weight: 11.6
International Honours: RoI: Yth

The Irish-born left-sided midfield player failed to command a regular place in the Halifax team in 1999-2000, although he was a useful squad member. Stephen scored with a stunning left-footed strike at Hartlepool in August to cap Town's first away win of the campaign. He was released at the end of the season.

Huddersfield T (Free from Belvedere YC on 16/5/1995)
Halifax T (Free on 8/8/1998) FL 20+7/1 FLC 4 FAC 0+1 Others 0+1

MURRAY Adam David
Born: Birmingham, 30 September 1981
Height: 5'8" Weight: 10.10
International Honours: E: Yth

The former "Young Player of the Year" at Derby reinforced the high opinion in which he is held in 1999-2000, his second year as a professional, with a consistent season in the reserves, for whom he was a key figure throughout the campaign. Used as a combative ball winner on the right side of midfield, Adam is also a creative passer of the ball, but he found it difficult to break through into the first team and had to be content, mostly, with the occasional appearance from the substitutes' bench.

Derby Co (From trainee on 7/10/1998) PL 1+11

MURRAY Daniel (Dan)
Born: Cambridge, 16 May 1982
Height: 6'2" Weight: 12.7

Dan is another of the youngsters from the Peterborough Academy who were given a first-team opportunity in 1999-2000. The confident centre half featured in the March draw at Macclesfield and the 3-1 win against Exeter in April as late-season injuries sidelined his more senior colleagues. Dan looked very assured and seems set to progress and become another Posh youth success.

Peterborough U (From trainee on 7/3/2000) FL 2

MURRAY Jade (Jay) Alan
Born: Islington, 23 September 1981
Height: 5'9" Weight: 11.5

Jay was rewarded with his Leyton Orient debut as a substitute against Rotherham last March, after being second-top scorer for the Os' youth team. He is a player who, despite his size, is not afraid to get stuck in. Jay also causes problems with his pace, and does not hesitate to shoot on sight. He will be looking forward to more first-team opportunities in the new season.

Leyton Orient (Trainee) FL 0+2

MURRAY Karl Anthony
Born: Islington, 24 June 1982
Height: 5'11" Weight: 12.6

A product of Shrewsbury's youth policy, Karl made his first-team debut at Sheffield United in August 1999 in the Worthington Cup. His impressive performance earned him a trial with the Blades. He went on to play a part in 16 league and cup games for the Shrews, scoring his first goal in a 1-2 defeat in December at Rochdale. He quickly endeared himself to Gay Meadow followers with his impressive workrate and all-action displays in his midfield role. He is happy to take responsibility and keen to get forward. With continued development, Karl could well feature more frequently in the future.

Shrewsbury T (From trainee on 7/2/2000) FL 6+6/1 FLC 2 FAC 2

MURRAY Paul
Born: Carlisle, 31 August 1976
Height: 5'9" Weight: 10.5
International Honours: E: B-1; U21-4; Yth

This left-footed Queens Park Rangers player did not feature in the early games of the 1999-2000 season. However, his return to first-team action in October coincided with an improvement in the club's results. Although not always a regular selection, Paul made over 20 starts, mostly on the right side of midfield and occasionally as the right wing back.

Carlisle U (From trainee on 14/6/1994) FL 27+14/1 FLC 2 FAC 1 Others 6+1
Queens Park R (£300,000 on 8/3/1996) P/FL 111+23/7 FLC 8/1 FAC 9

MURRAY Scott George
Born: Aberdeen, 26 May 1974
Height: 5'10" Weight: 11.0

Signed by Bristol City from Aston Villa at the end of 1997, Scott proved to be a revelation in 1999-2000. Despite being troubled by a hernia problem he used his blistering pace to good effect in a role wide on the right of midfield. Rarely out of the starting line-up, he demonstrated much-improved shooting ability, which resulted in many fine goals, and the consensus is that, with a bit more composure and control, City's flying Scotsman could be on the way to becoming an Ashton Gate folk hero.

Aston Villa (£35,000 from Fraserburgh on 16/3/1994) PL 4
Bristol C (£150,000 on 12/12/1997) FL 68+28/9 FLC 6+2 FAC 3+1/3 Others 7+1/2

MURRAY Shaun
Born: Newcastle, 7 December 1970
Height: 5'8" Weight: 11.2
International Honours: E: Yth; Sch

Shaun struggled to win a place in the Notts County team during 1999-2000 and after battling his way back at the turn of the year he was then injured and missed the rest of the season. Although short in height, he is a very skilful left-footed midfield player who can turn a match with his passing ability. He can take a wide left-sided role or operate as a play-maker from the centre of midfield.

Tottenham H (From trainee on 10/12/1987)
Portsmouth (£100,000 on 12/6/1989) FL 21+13/1 FLC 2+1/1 FAC 1+3 Others 2+2
Scarborough (Signed on 1/11/1993) FL 29/5 FAC 2 Others 2
Bradford C (£200,000 on 11/8/1994) FL 105+25/8 FLC 7+2/1 FAC 4+2 Others 4/2
Notts Co (Free on 4/8/1998) FL 36+8/3 FLC 3 FAC 7/1

MURTY Graeme Stuart
Born: Saltburn, 13 November 1974
Height: 5'10" Weight: 11.10

After recovering from a series of drawn-out injuries, Graham returned to the Reading first team last October. He played intermittently to begin with, then won a regular place at right wing back for the last three months of the season and was able to show just what a good player he is. He became an excellent crosser of the ball, and his pace and covering got Reading out of many difficult situations when the team were forced on the defensive. With his confidence regained and the crowd on his side, Graham looks set to be a valuable first choice in the team again during the coming season.

York C (From trainee on 23/3/1993) FL 106+11/7 FLC 10/2 FAC 5+1 Others 6+2
Reading (£700,000 on 10/7/1998) FL 22+4 FAC 4+1 Others 0+2

MUSCAT Kevin Vincent
Born: Crawley, 7 August 1973
Height: 5'11" Weight: 12.2
International Honours: Australia: 17; U23; Yth

The Wolves full back's rugged style has earned him something of a reputation, but he is very popular at Molineux. He played in all but two of Wolves' games last season but, as in the past, he was obliged to operate in the left-back role at times, although he prefers the right side. A strong tackler who enjoys pushing forward, Kevin celebrated his return to right back with a goal against Manchester City at the start of December and a good run of form followed. In January he almost scored from the half-way line at Walsall, underlining the fact that he has more skill than he is sometimes given credit for. Kevin was sometimes used by Wolves in midfield, where many fans felt he should be given a run. However, an injury to left back Lee Naylor in March meant he reverted to that role. He became the club's penalty taker in April, scoring twice before the season was out. A regular in the Australian national side, he won further caps against Hungary, the Czech Republic and Paraguay. Stop Press: Kevin was one of several English-based players who appeared for Australia in their 2-0 victory over New Zealand in the Oceania Nations' Cup at the end of June.

Crystal Palace (£35,000 from South Melbourne on 16/8/1996) FL 51+2/2 FLC 4/1 FAC 2 Others 2
Wolverhampton W (£200,000 on 22/10/1997) FL 104+2/11 FLC 6 FAC 9

MUSSELWHITE Paul Stephen
Born: Portsmouth, 22 December 1968
Height: 6'2" Weight: 14.2
Club Honours: AMC '93

The experienced Port Vale goalkeeper held the number one spot for the majority of the 1999-2000 campaign. After beginning the season on the subs' bench, he was recalled after just three games and held his place until February, when he was sent off at Grimsby for handling outside the area. During this enforced break he had a hernia operation but he arguably then returned too early, producing a couple of below-par performances. Paul then bruised his ribs in training and missed the remainder of the season, being unable to regain a first-team spot even when fit. He was released on a free transfer at the end of the campaign.

Portsmouth (From apprentice on 1/12/1986)
Scunthorpe U (Free on 21/3/1988) FL 132 FLC 11 FAC 7 Others 13
Port Vale (£20,000 on 30/7/1992) FL 312 FLC 15 FAC 21 Others 19

MUSTOE Neil John
Born: Gloucester, 5 November 1976
Height: 5'9" Weight: 12.10
Club Honours: FAYC '95

Strong and quick, Neil is a vital cog in Cambridge's midfield, although his determination sometimes gets the better of him. A tenacious tackler who can always be relied upon for excellent non-stop performances, he was a regular on United's left flank in 1999-2000 but his season was interrupted by an ankle injury. Once a "Fergie Fledgling" at Manchester United, he will be looking to add to his goal tally during the coming season after failing to score last term.

Manchester U (From trainee on 1/7/1995)
Wigan Ath (Signed on 7/1/1998) Others 0+1
Cambridge U (Free on 9/7/1998) FL 56+11/3 FLC 5 FAC 4+1 Others 2

MUSTOE Robin (Robbie)
Born: Witney, 28 August 1968
Height: 5'11" Weight: 11.12
Club Honours: Div 1 '95

Robbie enjoyed a well-earned testimonial season at Middlesbrough in 1999-2000, having joined the club ten years ago from Oxford. He has been a great servant to Boro and has always shown total commitment to the cause. A real powerhouse, he excels in midfield, always pushing forward and never frightened of having a shot himself if the opportunity arises. Injuries and the arrival of Juninho made it difficult for him to win a regular first-team place last season, but Robbie made 18 Premiership starts and displayed his old consistency whenever he had the chance. An inspirational figure, he always shows the same unquenchable enthusiasm for the game, and collected a number of well-deserved "Man of the Match" awards.

Oxford U (From juniors on 2/7/1986) FL 78+13/10 FLC 2 FAC 2 Others 3
Middlesbrough (£375,000 on 5/7/1990) F/PL 283+21/23 FLC 43+2/7 FAC 22/2 Others 12+1/1

MUTTON Thomas (Tommy) James
Born: Huddersfield, 17 January 1978
Height: 5'8" Weight: 10.2

A £20,000 signing from League of Wales side Bangor City in September 1999, Tommy completed his move to Swansea following an impressive trial period that saw him score on his reserve-team debut against Plymouth. Formerly an apprentice with Burnley, he made his Swans debut as a substitute at Hull. Raw but with electric pace, Tommy was injured within a few minutes of the start of his full debut against Mansfield. His return to the first team two months later saw the striker score his first Swansea goal in a win over Colchester United in the Auto Windscreens Shield.

Swansea C (£20,000 from Bangor C on 16/9/1999) FL 1+1 FLC 0+1 Others 2/1

MYERS Andrew (Andy) John
Born: Hounslow, 3 November 1973
Height: 5'10" Weight: 13.11
Club Honours: FAC '97; ECWC '98
International Honours: E: U21-4; Yth

This versatile left-sided player joined Bradford from Chelsea on a four-year contract in the summer of 1999 but missed the start of the new season with a thigh injury. He made his debut for the Bantams in mid-September when he came on from the subs' bench against Tottenham but failed to win a regular place at Valley Parade. He was mostly used at full back by City but eventually lost his place to the in-form Wayne Jacobs and didn't feature in the team at all after January. He moved to Portsmouth on loan on transfer deadline day and played some part in Pompey's last eight games of the season. He is very quick off the mark and his pace is a great asset both when attacking and when covering back in defence.

Chelsea (From trainee on 25/7/1991) F/PL 74+10/2 FLC 2+1 FAC 9+3 Others 4+3
Bradford C (£800,000 on 16/7/1999) PL 10+3 FLC 2 FAC 1
Portsmouth (Loaned on 23/3/2000) FL 4+4

MYHRE Thomas
Born: Sarpsborg, Norway, 16 October 1973
Height: 6'4" Weight: 13.12
International Honours: Norway: 13

Having ended the 1998-99 campaign as Everton's first-choice goalkeeper, Thomas saw last season blighted by a series of unfortunate injuries. After sustaining a broken ankle at an international training camp with Norway in the summer of 1999, he slipped soon afterwards and damaged a bone in his other ankle! Paul Gerrard took full advantage of his absence to establish himself as number one at Goodison – and it was only when Gerrard himself was injured that Thomas returned in January. For five of his six appearances, the Norwegian showed all his old qualities: confident cross taking, athleticism and presence. A shaky display in an FA Cup quarter-final against Aston Villa, however, accelerated Gerrard's return and, anxious to gain match sharpness ahead of the Euro 2000 finals, Thomas accepted an invitation to join Birmingham City on loan after the transfer deadline when the St Andrews club were decimated by injuries and left with two 16-year-olds as the only fit goalkeepers on the club's books. He had a memorable debut for the Blues in the ferocious local derby against Wolves in April when he saved a first-half penalty and helped his team to a 1-0 victory. Thomas established himself as first choice in the Norway line-up at the beginning of the year and went on to win a further seven caps, appearing in all three of his country's games in Euro 2000.

Everton (£800,000 from Viking Stavanger, Norway on 28/11/1997) PL 64 FLC 3 FAC 7
Glasgow R (Loaned on 24/11/1999) SL 3 SLC 1 Others 2
Birmingham C (Loaned on 31/3/2000) FL 7 Others 2

Phil Neville

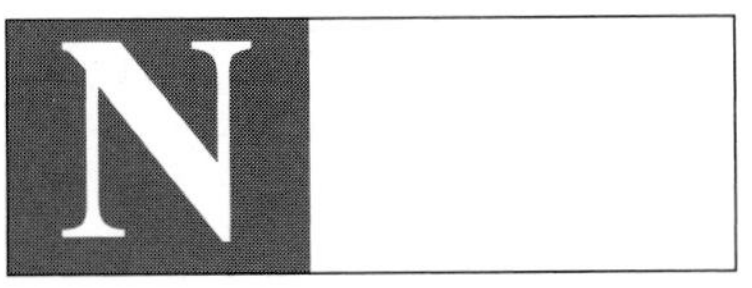

NAISBITT Daniel (Danny) John
Born: Bishop Auckland, 25 November 1978
Height: 6'1" Weight: 11.12

Acquired as an understudy for Lee Harrison during the 1999 close season, Danny impressed in the opening stages of the new campaign with some competent displays in the Barnet goal. The self-styled "Spennymoor Cat" assumed responsibilities between the posts on five occasions during the season and showed that he is both an able deputy for and a suitable successor to Harrison. He capped off a wonderful performance at Cheltenham with a miraculous penalty save and impressed the fans with his impeccable distribution. His progress was clearly illustrated when he registered his first clean sheet in the crucial home victory against Plymouth in March, but his season was curtailed when, just three days later, he suffered a severe knee injury.

Walsall (From Middlesbrough juniors on 7/7/1997)
Barnet (Free on 3/8/1999) FL 3+1 FLC 1

NASH Carlo James
Born: Bolton, 13 September 1973
Height: 6'5" Weight: 14.1

This giant goalkeeper had an excellent season with Stockport in 1999-2000, producing a series of outstanding performances that had Premiership scouts flocking to Edgeley Park. He then broke a finger against Tranmere in January and when he returned five weeks later he struggled to recover his best form. Carlo is a good all-round 'keeper who, at 26, is still young enough to make the move to top-grade football.

Crystal Palace (£35,000 from Clitheroe on 16/7/1996) FL 21 FLC 1 Others 3
Stockport Co (Free on 7/6/1998) FL 81 FLC 5 FAC 3

NASH Martin John
Born: Regina, Canada, 27 December 1975
Height: 5'11" Weight: 12.5
International Honours: Canada: 16 (Gold Cup 2000); U23-11

For Martin, an attacking midfielder who joined Chester from the Vancouver 86ers last September, 1999-2000 turned out to be quite a season. Although he was restricted to a handful of appearances with the Third Division strugglers, he hit the international headlines with his performances for Canada in their sensational success in the CONCACAF Gold Cup in February. He came on as a substitute and provided two goals in a shock defeat of favourites Mexico. Martin was rewarded with a starting place in the final against Colombia, ahead of Fulham's Paul Peschisolido. He supplied the corner kick that Dundee United's Jason De Vos headed home to set the Canadians on the road to their most unlikely victory. Martin's skills came to the notice of a wider audience and he earned a trial with St Johnstone in March. He returned to North America in April and joined Rochester Raging Rhinos. He is part of a sporting family: brother Steve is a basketball star with Dallas Mavericks in the NBA.

Stockport Co (Free from Regina, Canada on 27/11/1996) FL 0+11 FLC 0+1 Others 2+1/1 (Freed during 1998 close season)
Chester C (Free from Vancouver 86ers, Canada on 24/9/1999) FL 12+4 FAC 3+1

Carlo Nash

NAYLOR Anthony (Tony) Joseph
Born: Manchester, 29 March 1967
Height: 5'7" Weight: 10.8

The experienced Port Vale striker will admit that last season turned out to be a stop-start affair for him. It began promisingly enough with a spell when he scored five goals in five games early on but as the team struggled Tony's form suffered, not helped by the continual changing of his strike partners. He scored the 100th league goal of his career against Ipswich but only managed one more before spending most of the second half of the campaign on the subs' bench. Recalled against Huddersfield three games from the end, he responded with a superb goal which proved that he still has the talent.

Crewe Alex (£20,000 from Droylsden on 22/3/1990) FL 104+18/45 FLC 7+2/5 FAC 9/7 Others 12/9
Port Vale (£150,000 on 18/7/1994) FL 166+45/57 FLC 13+1/8 FAC 10+1/1 Others 5+1/3

NAYLOR Glenn
Born: Goole, 11 August 1972
Height: 5'10" Weight: 11.10

Glenn found himself confined to the substitutes' bench virtually throughout 1999-2000, his fourth season with Darlington, and made only a handful of starts at the very end of the campaign. The skilful forward provided excellent cover for the regular strike force. He managed to find the net on three occasions and could always be relied upon to inject some pace into proceedings when brought off the bench. Glenn was released in the summer.

York C (From trainee on 5/3/1990) FL 78+33/30 FLC 2+4 FAC 4+1/2 Others 3+4
Darlington (Loaned on 13/10/1995) FL 3+1/1 Others 1+1
Darlington (Signed on 26/9/1996) FL 108+38/31 FLC 3+1/1 FAC 9+2/2 Others 5+3

NAYLOR Lee Martyn
Born: Walsall, 19 March 1980
Height: 5'9" Weight: 11.8
International Honours: E: U21-1; Yth

The only genuine left back at Wolves, Lee was very impressive at times in 1999-2000 but found it difficult to achieve consistency. He was involved in the club's first nine games of the season, producing some good crosses, before losing his confidence. Little was then seen of him until December, when he began to look the part once more, giving the team a better balance. In February he scored a lovely goal from a free kick against Tranmere, which he followed with a competent England U21 debut against Argentina. His form then dipped slightly, and when on as a substitute at Swindon he sustained a fractured eye socket which ruled him out until the last three matches of the season.

Wolverhampton W (From trainee on 10/10/1997) FL 55+14/3 FLC 7 FAC 7/1

NAYLOR Richard Alan
Born: Leeds, 28 February 1977
Height: 6'1" Weight: 13.7

Richard started the 1999-2000 season well, being included in the Ipswich team from the first game against Nottingham Forest and, indeed, scoring Town's first goal of the season in that game when he headed home a free kick from Mark Venus. He also made the second goal for David Johnson when he nodded a long ball into his path. Richard's inclusion in the team was part of a tactical change by Ipswich manager George Burley, who decided to use Johnson and Naylor as the main strikers with James Scowcroft playing in midfield, just behind them. This system seemed to work well but there was a change of tactics after 11 games and Richard found himself back on the substitutes' bench. Thereafter he switched between the bench and the starting line-up, often being brought on very late in matches when he had little opportunity to influence the outcome. The arrival of Marcus Stewart put Richard further back in the pecking order, although when his name was mentioned in connection with a possible part-exchange deal Burley reportedly said that he still figured in his plans. Richard saved his best performance to the very last, coming on in the play-off final at Wembley for the injured Johnson and playing a starring role. He put Ipswich into the lead when he ran on to Stewart's flick and beat the goalkeeper with a right-foot shot. He was also involved in the build-up to Stewart's goal, holding the ball up on the edge of the box before playing in Jamie Clapham, and he put the ball through for Martijn Reuser to score the goal that sealed the win.

Ipswich T (From trainee on 10/7/1995) FL 48+50/19 FLC 5+5/1 FAC 1+3 Others 0+4/1

NAYLOR Stuart William
Born: Wetherby, 6 December 1962
Height: 6'4" Weight: 12.10
International Honours: E: B-3; Yth

Stuart was plucked from retirement at the start of 1999-2000 to solve Exeter's goalkeeping shortage at the age of 36. His shot stopping, organisational ability and experience shone through. In front of a national TV audience, he was knocked unconscious during a memorable FA Cup tie after a brave challenge on Everton's Kevin Campbell. It was a testament to his fitness and professionalism that he made a total of 37 appearances for City in all competitions. Out of contract in the summer, Stuart joined Rushden & Diamonds on loan in March, with a view to a permanent move.

Lincoln C (Free from Yorkshire Amateurs on 19/6/1980) FL 49 FLC 4 FAC 2 Others 6
Peterborough U (Loaned on 23/2/1983) FL 8
Crewe Alex (Loaned on 6/10/1983) FL 38
West Bromwich A (£100,000 on 18/2/1986) FL 354+1 FLC 22 FAC 13 Others 20
Crewe Alex (Loaned on 23/8/1994) FL 17 FLC 2 FAC 2 Others 3
Bristol C (Free on 13/8/1996) FL 37 FLC 4 FAC 4 Others 1
Mansfield T (Loaned on 11/12/1998) FL 6
Walsall (Free on 8/3/1999)
Exeter C (Free on 6/8/1999) FL 31 FLC 2 FAC 4 Others 1

NDAH George Ehialimolisa
Born: Dulwich, 23 December 1974
Height: 6'1" Weight: 11.4
International Honours: E: Yth

George began the 1999-2000 season with First Division strugglers Swindon but was then transferred to Wolves for a £1 million fee last October. He was again outstanding for the Robins in the early matches and scored one goal – a header from a corner in the 2-1 defeat at Crewe. He can play either as a striker or on the left side of midfield and his talents include an electrifying turn of speed, high workrate and a good eye for goal. George made a lively debut for Wolves against Port Vale and continued to show enthusiasm but midway through his third appearance he had the misfortune to suffer a broken leg playing against local rivals West Bromwich Albion. Wolves' injury jinx had struck again. He was hopeful of a March return but the crack in the tibia took a long time to heal. George was a substitute at Birmingham in April but was clearly not ready for the first team, and missed the remainder of the season.

Crystal Palace (From trainee on 10/8/1992) F/PL 33+45/8 FLC 7+6/2 FAC 3+1/1 Others 4+1
Bournemouth (Loaned on 13/10/1995) FL 12/2 Others 1
Gillingham (Loaned on 29/8/1997) FL 4
Swindon T (£500,000 on 21/11/1997) FL 66+1/14 FLC 4/1 FAC 3
Wolverhampton W (£1,000,000 on 21/10/1999) FL 3+1

NDLOVU Peter
Born: Bulawayo, Zimbabwe, 25 February 1973
Height: 5'8" Weight: 10.2
International Honours: Zimbabwe: 22

Peter maintained his reputation as a tricky performer on Birmingham City's flanks last season with his searing pace, fine close control and unpredictable movement on and off the ball. He suffered an ankle ligament injury in the surprise Worthington Cup victory over Newcastle last October that required surgery and kept him out until the end of February. He scored two fine goals for the reserves on his comeback but saw very little first-team action in the final weeks of the season. He added three further international appearances for Zimbabwe to his total, appearing in an African Nations' Cup qualifier against Senegal in July 1999 and twice against the Central African Republic in World Cup qualifying games last April.

Coventry C (£10,000 from Highlanders, Zimbabwe on 16/8/1991) F/PL 141+36/37 FLC 10/2 FAC 5+4/2 Others 0+1
Birmingham C (£1,600,000 on 15/7/1997) FL 68+27/20 FLC 12+1/3 FAC 2+1/1 Others 2+2

NEIL Gary Derek Campbell
Born: Glasgow, 16 August 1978
Height: 6'0" Weight: 12.10

Gary's 1999-2000 season was ruined by a series of niggling injuries, and he was not able to lay claim to a regular place in the centre of defence. He had a superb game at Plymouth in January in the Auto Windscreens Shield, and the Gulls' faith in the powerfully built defender was shown by the offer of new terms in May.

Leicester C (From trainee on 3/7/1997)
Torquay U (Free on 25/3/1999) FL 10+4 Others 3

NEILL Lucas Edward
Born: Sydney, Australia, 9 March 1978
Height: 6'1" Weight: 12.0
International Honours: Australia: 2; U23-8; Yth

Lucas is a tall, elegant player who returned to the Millwall line-up in 1999-2000 with renewed vigour after struggling with injury at the end of the previous season. He started the new campaign in the side and remained a first-team regular, except when away on international duty. An excellent full back who is equally at home on either side of midfield, he makes good penetrating runs, has a tremendous shot with either foot and has superb defensive skills. Lucas is seen as an integral part of Millwall's future although, because of his consistently impressive performances, he has been watched by several big clubs. A regular for Australia's "Olyroos" (U23s), he won seven caps during the season and will be hoping to be selected for the final squad for the Olympic Games tournament in the autumn.

Millwall (Free from Australia Academy of Sport on 13/11/1995) FL 103+21/11 FLC 5+1 FAC 4 Others 10+1

NEILSON Alan Bruce
Born: Wegburg, Germany, 26 September 1972
Height: 5'11" Weight: 12.10
International Honours: W: 5; B-2; U21-7

After enduring a season when he was dogged by injury in 1998-99, the Fulham defender must have thought that last season could only be better, and heading a goal in his first game of the season, against Charlton at the end of August, probably reinforced his hopes. However, a hamstring injury in the next match sidelined him for a while and, although he was included in the match-day squad of 16 on several occasions, he had to wait until Steve Finnan was injured before he returned to the starting line-up against Wolves in mid-October. Unfortunately, another hamstring pull meant that he had to come off at half time, and he made only two further appearances. Alan was a consistent starter in the reserves in the second half of the season, either at right back or in central defence, and must surely have better luck in 2000-01, the last year of his current Fulham contract.

Newcastle U (From trainee on 11/2/1991) F/PL 35+7/1 FLC 4 Others 4
Southampton (£500,000 on 1/6/1995) PL 42+13 FLC 7 FAC 1+1
Fulham (£250,000 on 28/11/1997) FL 24+2/2 FLC 0+2 FAC 4 Others 2

NETHERCOTT Stuart David
Born: Ilford, 21 March 1973
Height: 6'1" Weight: 13.8
International Honours: E: U21-8

Stuart, who signed for Millwall from Spurs in 1998, had an excellent season in 1999-2000, being ever present in the side until late on in the campaign when a head injury and then an ankle problem kept him sidelined. At 6 ft he is a strong-tackling defender who is excellent in the air, hardly ever losing a header, and an inspirational presence at the heart of the defence. Stuart is also a great skipper who leads by example, always encouraging his men to give more, even when it might seem that there isn't anything left! His performances last season made him the main contender for the club's "Player of the Season" award.

Tottenham H (From trainee on 17/8/1991) PL 31+23 FAC 5+3/1
Maidstone U (Loaned on 5/9/1991) FL 13/1 Others 1
Barnet (Loaned on 13/2/1992) FL 3
Millwall (Signed on 22/1/1998) FL 82 FLC 2 FAC 2 Others 10

NEVILLE Gary Alexander
Born: Bury, 18 February 1975
Height: 5'11" Weight: 12.8
Club Honours: FAYC '92; PL '96, '97, '99, '00; FAC '96, '99; CS '96; EC '99
International Honours: E: 39; Yth (UEFA-U18 '93)

The hard-tackling Manchester United full back, who is equally effective in the centre of defence, discovered in 1999-2000 that the quest for glory can have certain drawbacks, particularly when he was sidelined at the start of the season with a troublesome groin strain that had initially flared up during United's treble-winning campaign. Having come through a specially organised match against Steve Bruce's youth team at Huddersfield in August, Gary made his first full appearance of the season against Lazio in the Super Cup final in Monaco. Although he played in United's resounding 5-1 Premiership win against Newcastle at Old Trafford in the very next game, more problems resurfaced in the same area, which kept him out until the start of December. In that time, he also missed out on England's vital Euro 2000 play-off matches against Scotland at Hampden and Wembley. Fit once again, Gary became a growing influence in defence, though two crucial errors in the World Club Championship match against Vasco da Gama in January put paid to United's chances of progressing further in the tournament. On his return home he was soon back in the groove, and his consistency was instrumental in helping United to their sixth Premiership title in eight years. A regular in the England set-up, he won a further seven caps during the season, appearing in all his country's Euro 2000 games over the summer.

Manchester U (From trainee on 29/1/1993) PL 167+4/2 FLC 4+1 FAC 21+2 Others 46+4

NEVILLE Philip (Phil) John
Born: Bury, 21 January 1977
Height: 5'11" Weight: 12.0
Club Honours: FAYC '95; PL '96, '97, '99, '00; FAC '96, '99: CS '96, '97; EC '99
International Honours: E: 29; U21-7; Yth; Sch

A superb right back who is equally effective on the left, Phil may have lost out to Sunderland's Kevin Phillips as the "hottest shot" in the country in August 1999 but his versatility kept him at the top of the charts for Manchester United during another action-packed campaign. Although his achievements are often overshadowed by the exploits of his brother Gary, every manager in the country would dearly love to have a player of his undoubted talent included in their squad. Certainly, Sir Alex Ferguson knew how lucky he was, particularly at the start of the season when Phil assumed the right-back mantle when Gary was kept out of the side with a groin strain. With Phil combining well with Denis Irwin on the other flank, the back four ticked over nicely until Gary was fit to resume in early December. Although his role was then generally confined to filling in for Irwin, as and when required, or taking an active role from the subs' bench, Phil also showed his worth on the left side of midfield in one game, while the central defensive role has always been within his capabilities, and he ended the season with his fourth Premiership winners' medal. Perhaps the only downside to such adaptability is its effect on his chances of winning a regular place in the England team. However, it did not prevent him appearing in all 12 England matches during the season. An automatic choice, most recently on the left side of the defence, he had the great misfortune to concede a last-minute penalty in the vital match against Romania which saw England eliminated from the competition. However, as a truly committed professional, he will no doubt put this disappointment to one side and start the new season in excellent form for his club once again.

Manchester U (From trainee on 1/6/1994) PL 105+26/1 FLC 5+1 FAC 14+4 Others 24+11/1

NEWBY Jonathan (Jon) Philip Robert
Born: Warrington, 28 November 1978
Height: 6'0" Weight: 12.4
Club Honours: FAYC '96

A product of the Anfield Academy, Jon has been a prolific goalscorer for Liverpool at youth level. He made his debut in the first team against Hull in the Worthington Cup at Anfield last September, coming on as a late substitute. He looked sharp and used his considerable pace to set up Karl-Heinz Riedle's farewell goal. A very skilful player who causes defences problems, Jon joined Crewe on loan early in March, making his debut for the club against Norwich. Playing either wide on the right or in the middle, he made a total of six appearances, one as a substitute, before returning to Anfield at the end of his second month at Gresty Road. He started training full-time with the Reds' first team a year ago, in an effort to help him build up his physical strength and presence on the park. If he maintains this regime, he may well have a bright future.

Liverpool (From juniors on 23/5/1997) PL 0+1 FLC 0+1 FAC 0+2
Crewe Alex (Loaned on 3/3/2000) FL 5+1

NEWELL Michael (Mike) Colin
Born: Liverpool, 27 January 1965
Height: 6'2" Weight: 12.0
Club Honours: AMC '85; PL '95
International Honours: E: B-2; U21-4

This vastly experienced striker joined

Blackpool last February on a free transfer from Conference club Doncaster Rovers. Mike did well at Bloomfield Road, showing good skills in the air and the ability to hold the ball up well. He scored just once for the Seasiders with a cracking header at Cambridge that sealed a rare 2-0 victory for the club.

Crewe Alex (Free from Liverpool juniors on 28/9/1983) FL 3
Wigan Ath (Free on 31/10/1983) FL 64+8/25 FLC 6/1 FAC 8/6 Others 5+1/3
Luton T (£100,000 on 9/1/1986) FL 62+1/18 FAC 5/1
Leicester C (£350,000 on 16/9/1987) FL 81/21 FLC 9/5 FAC 2 Others 4
Everton (£850,000 on 27/7/1989) FL 48+20/15 FLC 7+3/4 FAC 6+4 Others 6/2
Blackburn Rov (£1,100,000 on 15/11/1991) F/PL 113+17/28 FLC 14+2/8 FAC 9+2/6 Others 9+1/6
Birmingham C (£775,000 on 26/7/1996) FL 11+4/1 FLC 4/2 FAC 0+1
West Ham U (Loaned on 21/12/1996) PL 6+1
Bradford C (Loaned on 17/3/1997) FL 7
Aberdeen (£160,000 on 21/7/1997) SL 32+12/6 SLC 4/4 SC 1+1
Crewe Alex (Free on 25/3/1999) FL 1+3 (Free to Doncaster Rov on 3/6/1999)
Blackpool (Free on 10/2/2000) FL 12+1/2

NEWHOUSE Aidan Robert
Born: Wallasey, 23 May 1972
Height: 6'2" Weight: 13.10
International Honours: E: Yth

There can't be many footballers who have scored two goals on their home debut and then virtually disappeared from the scene. However, Aidan did jut that in 1999-2000, having joined Brighton from Swansea during the summer. After the opening-day rout of Mansfield he made 11 further appearances, although his only other start was at Gillingham in the Worthington Cup. Aidan left Albion in November, and subsequently signed for Conference club Sutton United.

Chester C (From trainee on 1/7/1989) FL 29+15/6 FLC 5+1 FAC 0+2 Others 2+3/1
Wimbledon (£100,000 on 22/2/1990) F/PL 7+16/2 FLC 1+1 FAC 2 Others 0+1
Port Vale (Loaned on 21/1/1994) FL 0+2 FAC 0+1
Portsmouth (Loaned on 2/12/1994) FL 6/1
Torquay U (Loaned on 7/12/1995) FL 4/2
Fulham (Free on 20/6/1997) FL 7+1/1 FLC 3+1/3
Swansea C (£30,000 on 31/10/1997) FL 8+6 FAC 2 Others 0+1
Brighton & Hove A (Free on 2/8/1999) FL 1+11/2 FLC 1 FAC 0+1

NEWMAN Richard (Ricky) Adrian
Born: Guildford, 5 August 1970
Height: 5'10" Weight: 12.6

Ricky featured in the Millwall team less regularly than he would have hoped in 1999-2000. Although he usually plays in a holding role in midfield, he is equally adept at full back. Last season, however, he faced strong competition in both positions and he spent much of the campaign on the subs' bench before going on loan to Reading until the end of the season on transfer deadline day. Although his early opportunities were limited, he strengthened his bid for a permanent contract with an outstanding display at Notts County, where he scored the winning goal in a 2-1 victory with a stunning 30-yard volley. His confidence lifted, Ricky continued to impress as an aggressive central midfielder who can get forward quickly to support the attack and shoot with either foot while waiting for a decision on his future.

Crystal Palace (From juniors on 22/1/1988) F/PL 43+5/3 FLC 5 FAC 5+2 Others 2
Maidstone U (Loaned on 28/2/1992) FL 9+1/1
Millwall (£500,000 on 19/7/1995) FL 144+6/5 FLC 11 FAC 5 Others 7
Reading (Loaned on 17/3/2000) FL 4+3/1

NEWMAN Robert (Rob) Nigel
Born: Bradford on Avon, 13 December 1963
Height: 6'2" Weight: 13.4
Club Honours: AMC '86

Although not making his first appearance of the 1999-2000 season until December due to injury, Rob was just as popular with the Southend United fans as he had ever been. A towering centre half with superb distribution skills, "Buzz" made one of the Blues' defensive spots his own in the new year. In a first step towards management, he was offered a coaching position in May while the club retained his playing registration.

Bristol C (From apprentice on 5/10/1981) FL 382+12/52 FLC 29+1/2 FAC 27/2 Others 33/5
Norwich C (£600,000 on 15/7/1991) F/PL 181+24/14 FLC 22+2/2 FAC 13/1 Others 7
Motherwell (Loaned on 12/12/1997) SL 11 SC 3
Wigan Ath (Loaned on 26/3/1998) FL 8
Southend U (Free on 28/7/1998) FL 50+5/7 FLC 4/1 FAC 1 Others 1

NEWSOME Jonathan (Jon)
Born: Sheffield, 6 September 1970
Height: 6'2" Weight: 13.11
Club Honours: Div 1 '92; CS '92

This experienced Sheffield Wednesday central defender struggled to find his best form at the start of the 1999-2000 campaign and then had the misfortune to suffer a serious ankle injury. He subsequently had to undergo a cartilage operation and failed to recover full fitness before the summer break. Jon eventually announced his retirement from the game last May.

Sheffield Wed (From trainee on 1/7/1989) FL 6+1 FLC 3
Leeds U (£150,000 on 11/6/1991) F/PL 62+14/3 FLC 3 FAC 3+1 Others 5
Norwich C (£1,000,000 on 30/6/1994) P/FL 61+1/7 FLC 9 FAC 5/1
Sheffield Wed (£1,600,000 on 16/3/1996) PL 50+4/4 FLC 3 FAC 6+1
Bolton W (Loaned on 18/11/1998) FL 6

NEWTON Adam Lee
Born: Grays, 4 December 1980
Height: 5'10" Weight: 11.6
Club Honours: FAYC '99

This talented young wing back began the season with a somewhat frustrating loan spell at Portsmouth and on returning to West Ham he made his debut in Premiership football when he came on for the final 15 minutes at Coventry last September. He made further appearances from the subs' bench against Osijek in a UEFA Cup tie and in the return game with Coventry in April. Adam was one of the stars of West Ham's FA Youth Cup-winning team of 1998-99 and, like Michael Carrick and Stephen Bywater, he is being slowly eased into first-team football by manager Harry Redknapp. His strengths are his lightning pace and good ball control, and he can play either as a wing back or as a full back. Adam has already attracted the attention of England U21s boss Howard Wilkinson, and was called up to the squad for the friendly against Denmark last October.

West Ham U (From trainee on 1/7/1999) PL 0+2 Others 0+1
Portsmouth (Loaned on 2/7/1999) FL 1+2 FLC 2

NEWTON Christopher (Chris) John
Born: Leeds, 5 November 1979
Height: 6'0" Weight: 11.8

Chris is the first player to graduate into the Football League from Halifax's Northern Youth Academy ranks. He didn't fulfil his potential in 1999-2000, though, and was only called upon on a few occasions. Chris spent a month on loan at Barrow in the Unibond League around the turn of the year. On his return, he did not figure in manager Mark Lillis's plans and he was released at the end of the season.

Halifax T (From trainee on 17/7/1998) FL 12+10/1 FAC 0+1 Others 0+1

NEWTON Edward (Eddie) John Ikem
Born: Hammersmith, 13 December 1971
Height: 5'11" Weight: 12.8
Club Honours: FAC '97; FLC '98; ECWC '98
International Honours: E: U21-2

Eddie had a very disappointing time after joining Birmingham City from Chelsea on a free transfer in the 1999 close season. Although he is undoubtedly still a skilful player, his style was considered unsuitable for the Blues' rigorous midfield and he also suffered from a nagging shin injury. He made just four starts, two of which were in Worthington Cup games, and was otherwise restricted to reserve football. Despite this he showed an excellent attitude at St Andrews before eventually being allowed to move to Oxford United on a short-term contract on transfer deadline day. A steadying influence in midfield, Eddie took over from the injured Peter Fear and his ability to clear up and help the defence was important as United battled successfully to stay up. He showed his undoubted class in his seven games at the Manor but was released in the summer and he was reported to have gone to play in China.

Chelsea (From trainee on 17/5/1990) F/PL 139+26/8 FLC 15+2/1 FAC 15+3/1 Others 11+2
Cardiff C (Loaned on 23/1/1992) FL 18/4
Birmingham C (Free on 13/7/1999) FL 2+2 FLC 2+2 FAC 0+1
Oxford U (Free on 23/3/2000) FL 7

NEWTON Shaun O'Neill
Born: Camberwell, 20 August 1975
Height: 5'8" Weight: 11.7
Club Honours: Div 1 '00
International Honours: E: U21-3

Shaun had a much better season for Charlton in 1999-2000, recapturing his old form and playing a leading role as the Addicks romped to the First Division championship. The right-sided winger has lightning pace and loves to go past defenders and cut back to deliver balls into the penalty area or get to the byeline and put in accurate crosses. Shaun found the net himself on five occasions, his goals including a spectacular 30-yard screamer against Queens Park Rangers at the Valley. He is also able to play in the right-wing-back position, which is useful when the formation is changed during games, as is not unusual at Charlton.

Charlton Ath (From trainee on 1/7/1993) P/FL 188+42/20 FLC 17+1/3 FAC 10+4/1 Others 7+1/2

NGONGE Felix **Michel**
Born: Huy, Belgium, 10 January 1967
Height: 6'0" Weight: 12.8
International Honours: DR Congo: 6

A well-built striker with a deceptive turn of pace, Michel was a regular in the Watford first team last season before going on loan to Huddersfield in March. A consistent goal-scorer, he got off the mark in the first game of the season against Wimbledon, and scored in three consecutive matches – against Sheffield Wednesday, Newcastle and Sunderland – during November, though his close control was sometimes found wanting by Premiership standards. Michel made his Huddersfield debut from the substitutes' bench against West Bromwich. Very quick and exciting on the ball, he proved to be a valuable asset during the Terriers' ill-fated promotion push, but a troublesome late-season calf injury unfortunately interrupted his contribution. Called up by the Democratic Republic of Congo in January for the African Nations' Cup finals, he won a further two caps against Algeria and South Africa.

Watford (Free from Samsunspor, Turkey, via KRC Harelbeks, on 17/7/1998) P/FL 29+16/9 FLC 3+1/1 FAC 1 Others 3/1
Huddersfield T (Loaned on 17/3/2000) FL 0+4

NICHOLLS Kevin John Richard
Born: Newham, 2 January 1979
Height: 6'0" Weight: 11.0
International Honours: E: Yth

An aggressive, tough-tackling midfielder who is good on the ball, Kevin joined Wigan from Charlton in the summer of 1999, but his first season with the Latics was unfortunately spoilt by injuries. A knee problem that required surgery delayed his debut, and when it came it found him short of match practice. Kevin returned later in the promotion push to show glimpses of the form that saw him gain international recognition, and will benefit from the opportunity to regain full fitness during the summer.

Charlton Ath (From trainee on 29/1/1996) FL 4+8/1 FLC 2+2
Brighton & Hove A (Loaned on 26/2/1999) FL 4/1
Wigan Ath (£250,000 + on 22/6/1999) FL 6+2

NICHOLLS Mark
Born: Hillingdon, 30 May 1977
Height: 5'10" Weight: 10.4
Club Honours: FLC '98

This very talented young striker had a particularly frustrating season at Chelsea in 1999-2000, finding himself pushed even further down the pecking order with the acquisition of Chris Sutton and George Weah. Mark made just two fleeting substitute appearances, against Skonto Riga and Huddersfield, before joining Reading on loan at the end of December. He scored a late equaliser on his debut at Gillingham with a superb volley on the turn, becoming the Royals' first goalscorer of the new millennium, but failed to find the target again during his five league appearances. He did, however, score twice in the club's shock 2-1 defeat of Bristol Rovers in the Auto Windscreens Shield, though this was not enough to persuade Reading to make the move permanent. Mark joined Grimsby on an extended loan in February following the departure of Jack Lester and injuries to Lee Ashcroft and Bradley Allen. However, he appeared to have difficulty in adjusting to the pace of First Division football, often being substituted late in the game. Following the return to fitness of Ashcroft and Allen, he was largely restricted to the bench, and ended the season in the reserves. Perhaps a move away from Stamford Bridge is needed to kick-start a very promising career that has become becalmed since the departure of previous Chelsea manager Ruud Gullit.

Chelsea (From trainee on 1/7/1995) PL 11+25/3 FLC 4+3 FAC 1+3 Others 0+5
Reading (Loaned on 30/12/1999) FL 4+1/1 Others 2/2
Grimsby T (Loaned on 24/2/2000) FL 6

NICHOLS Jonathan (Jon) Anthony
Born: Plymouth, 10 September 1980
Height: 6'0" Weight: 11.12

This first-year professional had very few opportunities to shine at Torquay during the 1999-2000 season, being kept out of the team by the consistent form of regular full backs Paul Holmes and Robbie Herrera. He made just three appearances and was eventually released in the summer.

Torquay U (From trainee on 1/7/1999) FL 6+1 FAC 1 Others 1

NICHOLSON Shane Michael
Born: Newark, 3 June 1970
Height: 5'10" Weight: 12.2
Club Honours: GMVC '88

Shane had an excellent season at Stockport in 1999-2000 after moving from Chesterfield under the Bosman ruling the previous summer. He made the left-back position his own and produced a series of consistent performances throughout the season. A calm and collected defender who is able to push forward and deliver an accurate cross, he has sufficient experience to know his limitations and play to his strengths. Shane contributed one goal during the campaign, netting with a simple tap-in to give the Hatters a 1-0 win over Port Vale last September.

Lincoln C (From trainee on 19/7/1988) FL 122+11/6 FLC 8+3 FAC 6/1 Others 7+1
Derby Co (£100,000 on 22/4/1992) FL 73+1/1 FLC 4 FAC 4/1 Others 5
West Bromwich A (£150,000 on 9/2/1996) FL 50+2 FLC 2 FAC 2 Others 4
Chesterfield (Free on 21/8/1998) FL 23+1 Others 1
Stockport Co (Free on 4/6/1999) FL 42/1 FLC 3 FAC 1

NIELSEN Allan
Born: Esbjerg, Denmark, 13 March 1971
Height: 5'8" Weight: 11.2
Club Honours: FLC '99
International Honours: Denmark: 35

This versatile attacking midfielder became increasingly frustrated at Tottenham after making only three first-team starts and a further four appearances from the subs' bench last autumn. The reported rift between Allan and Spurs manager George Graham had allegedly been resolved, but the Dane's hopes of regaining a regular place in the starting line-up were to remain unfulfilled. He made another ten appearances between December and February, five of them as a substitute, but then dropped out of contention once more. With the club openly searching for new young talent, Allan lost his prized international place and agreement was reached for him to join First Division Wolves on loan on transfer deadline day in order to get some first-team football. Although Allan lacked match fitness when he arrived at Molineux, he quickly adapted to the First Division and scored twice in his seven games for Wolves, becoming very popular with the club's fans. Allan's return to fitness ensured he had a place in Denmark's squad of 22 for the European Championship finals and he featured in the games in what proved to be a very disappointing tournament for the Danes. His future at Tottenham appears to be in doubt, although many of the club's supporters would be very pleased to see him restored to the starting line-up.

Tottenham H (£1,650,000 from Brondby, Denmark, via Esbjerg, Bayern Munich, Sion, Odense and FC Copenhagen, on 3/9/1996) PL 78+18/12 FLC 10+1/3 FAC 5+2/3 Others 1
Wolverhampton W (Loaned on 23/3/2000) FL 7/2

NIESTROJ Robert Waldemar
Born: Poland, 2 December 1974
Height: 5'10" Weight: 11.3

The quiet German midfielder, who joined Wolves from Fortuna Dusseldorf in November 1998, never really settled in England and only made the first team for 12 minutes in 1999-2000, at Sheffield United in September. There was a brief loan to German club Bochum in October but he surprisingly rejected the chance of a permanent move. Prior to Christmas, however, he was loaned to Nurnberg for the rest of the season.

Wolverhampton W (£300,000 + from Fortuna Dusseldorf, Germany on 13/11/1998) FL 2+4 FAC 1

NIGHTINGALE Luke Raymond
Born: Portsmouth, 22 December 1980
Height: 5'10" Weight: 12.5

This promising young Portsmouth striker had a few first-team opportunities in the early part of the 1999-2000 season and scored twice in the 3-0 victory over Torquay in the Worthington Cup. He later suffered a broken nose in a reserve fixture and when he had recovered fitness he was unable to find his way back into the senior team despite scoring regularly with the second string. Luke is strong and skilful with good pace and will be aiming to feature more regularly in the first-team squad in 2000-01.

Portsmouth (From trainee on 23/11/1998) FL 7+19/3 FLC 2/2 FAC 1+1/1

NIMNI Avi
Born: Israel, 26 April 1972
Height: 6'0" Weight: 12.7
International Honours: Israel: 47

In an attempt to instil a bit more creativity into the Derby midfield area, Jim Smith obtained the services of this former Atletico Madrid player and experienced Israeli international from Tel Aviv on a three-month loan period last November. He took the field for the reserves just hours after flying into the country but showed no fatigue as he scored the winning goal. Avi made his debut at Arsenal three days later and impressed in his preferred position on the left side of the midfield quartet. A bout of influenza restricted his subsequent appearances but he scored Derby's consolation goal in a 2-1 defeat at Everton in February in what proved to be his final appearance for the club before returning home due to what were described as "contractual problems" with the player's management company. Avi was recalled to the Israel national team shortly after leaving Pride Park, scoring in a 4-1 victory over Russia on his return to the side, and added two further caps against the Czech Republic and Hungary.

Derby Co (Signed from Maccabi Tel Aviv, Israel on 26/11/1999) PL 2+2/1 FAC 1

NIXON Eric Walter
Born: Manchester, 4 October 1962
Height: 6'4" Weight: 14.6
Club Honours: AMC '90

This veteran 'keeper returned to Tranmere Rovers in the summer of 1999 primarily as a goalkeeping coach, but he was registered as a player too and was called on three times last season to cover for emergencies. Although advancing in years, he did not let the team down and kept a clean sheet in the Worthington Cup fourth-round tie with Barnsley at the end of November. Eric remains as vociferous as ever and is always quick to take command of his penalty box, as well as being the worst practical joker on the Prenton Park staff.

Manchester C (£1,000 from Curzon Ashton on 10/12/1983) FL 58 FLC 8 FAC 10 Others 8
Wolverhampton W (Loaned on 29/8/1986) FL 16
Bradford C (Loaned on 28/11/1986) FL 3
Southampton (Loaned on 23/12/1986) FL 4
Carlisle U (Loaned on 23/1/1987) FL 16
Tranmere Rov (£60,000 on 24/3/1988) FL 341 FLC 34 FAC 19 Others 45+1
Reading (Loaned on 9/1/1996) FLC 1
Blackpool (Loaned on 5/2/1996) FL 20 Others 2
Bradford C (Loaned on 13/9/1996) FL 12
Stockport Co (£100,000 on 28/8/1997) FL 43 FLC 2 FAC 2
Wigan Ath (Loaned on 28/8/1998) FL 1
Wigan Ath (Free on 24/3/1999) FL 2
Tranmere Rov (Free on 20/7/1999) FL 1+1 FLC 0+1

NOEL-WILLIAMS Gifton Ruben Elisha
Born: Islington, 21 January 1980
Height: 6'1" Weight: 14.6
Club Honours: Div 2 '98
International Honours: E: Yth

The 1999-2000 season was one of bitter frustration for Watford's big centre forward, who had finished the previous campaign as the club's leading scorer despite missing three months with a broken leg. Gifton began the Premiership campaign still trying to regain full fitness and did not return to first-team action until the game at Sheffield Wednesday in November. However, his leg continued to be troublesome and by Christmas he was back in the treatment room, having played only one full game. In March he flew to the United States for further specialist advice. Gifton has been scoring goals for Watford since he was 16 years old – he is the club's youngest-ever scorer – and everyone hopes that he can put his injury worries behind him and begin to fulfil his rich potential.

Watford (From trainee on 13/2/1997) P/FL 56+36/19 FLC 3+1/1 FAC 7/4

NOGAN Kurt
Born: Cardiff, 9 September 1970
Height: 5'11" Weight: 12.7
Club Honours: Div 2 '00
International Honours: W: B-1; U21-2

This lively striker started the first four games of the 1999-2000 season for Preston, scoring twice, but was then relegated to the bench for two games after the return of Steve Basham. After two further starts, Kurt was replaced by Alex Mathie for five games before reclaiming his place. A possible move to Hull fell through in December, before he scored his first goal for two months at Cardiff amid rumours of a transfer there. After losing his place through a hamstring injury in January, Kurt failed to feature again until he moved to Ninian Park in transfer deadline week, although he had made sufficient appearances to earn a Second Division championship medal. The Bluebirds' fans helped pay the £100,000 fee to bring the Cardiff-born striker back to South Wales but the expectations aroused by his arrival were always unrealistic. He scored against Burnley, one of his former clubs, but he had injury problems from the outset and never looked fully fit. He is, though, a proven goalscorer and will be a key figure in City's plans as they bid to escape from the Third Division during the coming season.

Luton T (From trainee on 11/7/1989) FL 17+16/3 FLC 1+3/1 Others 1+1
Peterborough U (Free on 30/9/1992) Others 1
Brighton & Hove A (Free on 17/10/1992) FL 97/49 FLC 10/7 FAC 5+1 Others 7/4
Burnley (£250,000 on 24/4/1995) FL 87+5/33 FLC 8/5 FAC 3 Others 5/4
Preston NE (£150,000 + on 13/3/1997) FL 74+19/27 FLC 4+3 FAC 6+3/3 Others 4+3/1
Cardiff C (£50,000 + on 23/3/2000) FL 4+2

NOGAN Lee Martin
Born: Cardiff, 21 May 1969
Height: 5'9" Weight: 11.0
Club Honours: AMC '98
International Honours: W: 2; B-1; U21-1

The much-travelled striker made Darlington his ninth league club when he signed from Grimsby in the 1999 close season. He soon struck up a good understanding with leading scorer Marco Gabbiadini, with his darting runs and intelligent flicks catching the eye, and scored three goals in the early part of the season. Their partnership struggled to live up to its early promise, however, and Lee lost his place to Peter Duffield just before Christmas and managed only six starts during the second half of the season. Nevertheless, manager David Hodgson appreciated his contribution to the cause, and publicly praised Lee's tremendous attitude.

Oxford U (From trainee on 25/3/1987) FL 57+7/10 FLC 4+1 FAC 2+1/1 Others 4+1/1
Brentford (Loaned on 25/3/1987) FL 10+1/2
Southend U (Loaned on 17/9/1987) FL 6/1 FLC 2 Others 1/1
Watford (£350,000 on 12/12/1991) FL 97+8/26 FLC 5+2/3 FAC 2/1 Others 1+2
Southend U (Loaned on 17/3/1994) FL 4+1
Reading (£250,000 on 12/1/1995) FL 71+20/26 FLC 5+1/1 FAC 2 Others 3/2
Notts Co (Loaned on 14/2/1997) FL 6
Grimsby T (£170,000 on 24/7/1997) FL 63+11/10 FLC 9+1/2 FAC 4/2 Others 8/2
Darlington (Free on 21/7/1999) FL 19+12/2 FLC 2/2 FAC 3 Others 1+2/1

NOLAN Ian Robert
Born: Liverpool, 9 July 1970
Height: 6'0" Weight: 12.1
International Honours: NI: 12

Ian returned to first-team action with Sheffield Wednesday last August following a badly broken leg suffered in February 1998. He is a steady but unspectacular full back with stamina and excellent crossing ability who can play on either side but is stronger in the right-back position. He remained a regular for the Owls until the end of the season and also won back his place in the Northern Ireland international team, winning five more caps. Stop Press: It was reported at the beginning of July that Ian had signed for Bradford City.

Tranmere Rov (£10,000 from Marine on 2/8/1991) FL 87+1/1 FLC 10/1 FAC 7 Others 9
Sheffield Wed (£1,500,000 on 17/8/1994) PL 164+1/4 FLC 15+1 FAC 15

NOLAN Kevin Anthony Jance
Born: Liverpool, 24 June 1982
Height: 6'1" Weight: 13.5

Outstanding displays in the Bolton reserve and youth teams earned Kevin a four-year deal last February and it is hoped that he will be the first of many fine Bolton Academy youngsters to make the grade. A former Liverpool schools player, Kevin is capable of fulfilling a defensive role in the heart of the back four, but it is in the midfield area where he made his impact when he was given his first-team chance in the latter stages of 1999-2000. Making his senior debut as a second-half substitute in the home game against Charlton in March, Kevin made an immediate impact in the 20 or so minutes he was on the pitch. His tough tackling is something Bolton have lacked since the departure of Per Frandsen and Jamie Pollock and he came very close to marking his debut with a fine goal when an audacious 30-yard effort clipped the woodwork and went out of play. Kevin made a total of four substitute appearances, but he did not figure too much in the final run-in, mainly due to some niggling injuries. Despite this, he has shown enough promise in his handful of outings to date to suggest that he is definitely a name to watch for in the future.

Bolton W (From trainee on 22/1/2000) FL 0+4

NORMANN Runar
Born: Harstad, Norway, 1 March 1978
Height: 6'3" Weight: 12.11
International Honours: Norway: U21

Runar is a Norwegian midfield player who joined Coventry for £1 million in July 1999 from Lillestrom after a recommendation from City's European scout, Ray Clarke. He impressed during the club's pre-season tour in Germany but picked up an ankle injury which kept him on the sidelines until November. After a number of reserve-team outings he made two substitute appearances before his first full start against Charlton in the FA Cup. He impressed in the first half, having a hand in both goals, but faded in the second. After several more substitute appearances he got his next start near the end of the season against West Ham, when he didn't find life on the left flank too easy.

Coventry C (£1,000,000 from Lillestrom, Norway on 3/8/1999) PL 1+7 FAC 1

NORTHMORE Ryan
Born: Plymouth, 5 September 1980
Height: 6'1" Weight: 13.0

A promising young goalkeeper in his first year as a pro at Torquay, Ryan was given his chance in 1999-2000 in the Auto Windscreens Shield games, and did not put a foot wrong. He also played two league games following Neville Southall's departure, but a shoulder injury let in Stuart Jones. Ryan was unable to force his way back into the side, although he did have the consolation of a new contract at the end of the season.

Torquay U (From trainee on 1/7/1999) FL 2+1 Others 3

NOSWORTHY Nayron
Born: Brixton, 11 October 1980
Height: 6'0" Weight: 12.0

This versatile Gillingham youngster was mostly used in midfield or at full back by Gillingham during 1999-2000, although he was also employed as a striker when required. A tough-tackling player of considerable potential, he established himself as a regular in the first-team squad during the season. Nayron scored his first-ever goal in senior football in the 4-1 win at Scunthorpe last November.

Gillingham (From trainee on 30/12/1998) FL 15+17/1 FLC 1+2 FAC 2+6 Others 0+3

NOTMAN Alexander (Alex) McKeachie
Born: Edinburgh, 10 December 1979
Height: 5'7" Weight: 10.11
International Honours: S: U21-8; Yth; Sch

Signed by Sheffield United on loan from Manchester United last January, initially for one month with the loan subsequently being extended for a second month, Alex immediately came into the side as a partner for Marcus Bent in attack. The diminutive striker quickly showed an ability to hold the ball and make a telling pass. As he adjusted to the pace of first-team football his performances improved and he showed that he had an eye for goal, being in the right place to score on three occasions. Alex won five more caps for Scotland U21s, scoring in the 1-1 draw with Northern Ireland at the end of May.

Manchester U (From trainee on 17/12/1996) FLC 0+1
Sheffield U (Loaned on 20/1/2000) FL 7+3/3
Aberdeen (Loaned on 11/2/2000) SL 0+2

NOWLAND Adam Christopher
Born: Preston, 6 July 1981
Height: 5'11" Weight: 11.6

Adam is a young Blackpool striker who was appearing in his third season of league football in 1999-2000, although he is still a teenager. He featured regularly in the first-team squad up until last Christmas, although he was mostly used as a substitute, making the starting line-up on only eight occasions. He still has a long way to go to fulfil the promise he showed as a 16-year-old, but will be looking to establish himself as a first-team regular in the coming season.

Blackpool (From trainee on 15/1/1999) FL 18+41/6 FLC 1+2 FAC 2+1/1 Others 0+2

NUGENT Kevin Patrick
Born: Edmonton, 10 April 1969
Height: 6'1" Weight: 13.3
International Honours: RoI: Yth

Kevin finished 1999-2000 as Cardiff captain and was also joint-top goalscorer with Jason Bowen on 17. Though he is not the quickest of strikers, he is an effective target man and strong in the air. He can also hold the ball up and bring others into the game. Kevin is one of the Cardiff players who, with the right support, can be expected to shine in Division Three during the coming season, having been City's top scorer during their promotion season in 1998-99.

Leyton Orient (From trainee on 8/7/1987) FL 86+8/20 FLC 9+3/6 FAC 9/3 Others 9+1/1
Plymouth Arg (£200,000 on 23/3/1992) FL 124+7/32 FLC 11/2 FAC 10/3 Others 5+3
Bristol C (Signed on 29/9/1995) FL 48+22/14 FLC 2+2 FAC 3+2/1 Others 2+1
Cardiff C (£65,000 on 4/8/1997) FL 79+5/25 FLC 6+1/1 FAC 9/6

NUNEZ Garcia **Milton** Omar
Born: Honduras, 30 October 1972
Height: 5'5" Weight: 10.8
International Honours: Honduras: 31

A diminutive Honduran international striker who joined Sunderland last March from Greek side PAOK Salonika for an initial £1.6 million, "Tyson", as he prefers to be called, due to his powerful physique resembling that of the heavyweight boxer, made his name with Uruguayan club Nacional and came to the North-east with the reputation of being a forward with blistering pace and a powerful shot in either foot. This seemed to be the case when he had his first outing for the reserves shortly after signing, and he received a tremendous welcome at the Stadium of Light when making his first-team debut against Wimbledon as a substitute in April. This was to be his only Premiership appearance last term, and Sunderland fans hope that next season he will be available on enough occasions to establish himself fully at the club. Already an experienced international, "Tyson" has won three more caps for Honduras since joining Sunderland, scoring in a 3-1 win over Panama at the beginning of May. Stop Press: He helped Honduras to a second leg victory over Haiti in the World Cup qualifiers in the middle of June to earn his country a place in the semi-final round of the CONCACAF group, where they will now meet El Salvador, Jamaica and St Vincent.

Sunderland (£1,600,000 from PAOK Salonika, Greece, via Comunicaciones, Nacional, on 23/3/2000) PL 0+1

NUZZO Raffaele
Born: Monza, Italy, 21 February 1973
Height: 6'2" Weight: 10.7

This experienced goalkeeper came to Coventry on a 12-month loan deal during the 1999 close season after failing to break through into Inter's Serie A line-up, being restricted to the odd first-team game in the Italian Cup. He appeared in a number of reserve games and was in goal in City's 5-1 drubbing at Tranmere in the Worthington Cup. Raffaele was not considered to be at fault for the defeat but was subsequently not given a further first-team chance and his loan was cut short in November after Steve Ogrizovic returned from injury.

Coventry C (Loaned from Inter Milan, Italy on 13/7/1999) FLC 1

NYAMAH Kofi
Born: Islington, 20 June 1975
Height: 5'9" Weight: 11.10

A speedy left-sided player, Kofi played in both the full-back and his preferred wing-back positions for Exeter during the 1999-2000 campaign. In either role, he loved to take on players and whip in crosses. Perhaps as a result of not knowing his best position, and not being able to hold down a regular place, Kofi made a transfer request in February, which was granted. He was out of contract in the summer and it would seem unlikely that his future lies at St James Park.

Cambridge U (From trainee on 19/5/1993) FL 9+14/2 FLC 0+2 FAC 3+1/1 Others 4) Free to Kettering T during 1995 close season
Stoke C (£25,000 on 24/12/1996) FL 9+8 FLC 1+1
Luton T (Free on 20/8/1998) FLC 0+1 FAC 1 (Free to Kingstonian on 20/12/1998)
Exeter C (Free on 6/8/1999) FL 23+12/1 FLC 1 FAC 1 Others 3+1

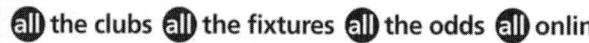

OAKES Michael Christian
Born: Northwich, 30 October 1973
Height: 6'2" Weight: 14.6
Club Honours: FLC '96
International Honours: E: U21-6

The third-choice goalkeeper at Aston Villa behind David James and Peter Enckelman, Michael was signed by Wolves for a bargain fee in October 1999 and immediately made a fine impression for the reserves. He had to wait a few weeks for his first-team chance but took it well, emerging from the 1-0 defeat at Tranmere with credit. He followed this with a competent home debut against Manchester City. Michael is a fine shot stopper, as he showed when making a number of excellent diving saves at Wigan and then performing well at Charlton early in the new year. He was superb in the 2-1 win over Ipswich, who forced 23 corners, and by the end of the campaign he was fast establishing himself as one of the best 'keepers in the First Division.

Aston Villa (From juniors on 16/7/1991) PL 49+2 FLC 3 FAC 2 Others 5
Scarborough (Loaned on 26/11/1993) FL 1 Others 1
Wolverhampton W (£400,000 + on 29/10/1999) FL 28 FAC 3

Stefan Oakes

OAKES Stefan Trevor
Born: Leicester, 6 September 1978
Height: 5'11" Weight: 12.4
Club Honours: FLC '00

After starting the 1999-2000 season as a promising young squad member, Stefan soon took advantage of Leicester's injury crisis to win a regular place in the starting line-up. The right-footed midfielder netted his first goals for the club to see off Crystal Palace in the Worthington Cup, where only a rushed penalty miss denied him a hat-trick, and later demonstrated his cultured left foot to good effect with his first Premiership strike from a free kick against Sunderland. Another missed spot kick, during the penalty shoot-out against Arsenal in the FA Cup, ultimately proved of no consequence. Such was his impact during the post-Christmas spell that he won a place in the starting line-up for the Worthington Cup final at Wembley, even though Martin O'Neill had a full squad to choose from. The younger brother of Sheffield Wednesday's Scott Oakes, Stefan was named as the Foxes' "Young Player of the Season".

Leicester C (From trainee on 3/7/1997) PL 17+8/1 FLC 7/2 FAC 3

OAKLEY Matthew (Matt)
Born: Peterborough, 17 August 1977
Height: 5'10" Weight: 12.1
International Honours: E: U21-4

Last season saw a new, mature Matt Oakley stamping his authority on the Southampton midfield. With much stronger competition for places, Matt was forced to develop much more quickly to make progress at the Dell. Playing in the middle of midfield, he likes to push forward, and a combination of his surging runs and his excellent passing produced a number of stunning goals. His self-confidence and positive approach to the game were reflected in his own willingness to have a dig last season: two goals at the Dell against Manchester City in the Worthington Cup were scored on the run from 20 yards out.

Southampton (From trainee on 1/7/1995) PL 107+18/9 FLC 14+1/2 FAC 6+2/1

OATWAY Anthony (Charlie) Philip David Terry Frank Donald Stanley Gerry Gordon Stephen James
Born: Hammersmith, 28 November 1973
Height: 5'7" Weight: 10.10
Club Honours: Div 3 '99

Introduced to the Brighton ranks during the 1999 close season by Micky Adams, his former boss at Brentford, this no-nonsense performer added bite to the Albion midfield. Charlie weighed in with important goals, including a brace in the 3-3 draw at Plymouth in September. He proved to be a valuable asset and looked more settled after the Seagulls' formation changed to the more balanced 4-4-2. The reason for his plethora of Christian names is that he was named after the Queens Park Rangers players of the early '70s.

Cardiff C (Free from Yeading on 4/8/1994) FL 29+3 FLC 2/1 FAC 1+1 Others 3+1
Torquay U (Free on 28/12/1995) FL 65+2/1 FLC 3 FAC 1
Brentford (£10,000 on 21/8/1997) FL 37+20 FLC 1+2/1 FAC 4 Others 0+1
Lincoln C (Loaned on 21/10/1998) FL 3
Brighton & Hove A (£10,000 on 9/7/1999) FL 42/4 FLC 2 FAC 4 Others 2

O'BRIEN Andrew (Andy) James
Born: Harrogate, 29 June 1979
Height: 6'3" Weight: 12.4
International Honours: E: U21-1; Yth. RoI: U21-6

Andy formed a solid partnership with David Wetherall in the centre of Bradford City's defence during 1999-2000, his first season of Premiership football. Always cool under pressure, he was rarely in disciplinary trouble and showed maturity beyond his years in the club's successful struggle against relegation. Andy was voted the players' "Player of the Year" and the supporters' "Young Player of the Year". He also appeared regularly for the Republic of Ireland U21s and won a further five caps.

Bradford C (From trainee on 28/10/1996) P/FL 96+19/3 FLC 5 FAC 7

O'BRIEN Michael (Mick) George
Born: Liverpool, 25 September 1979
Height: 5'5" Weight: 10.6
Club Honours: FAYC '98
International Honours: E: Sch

Mick is a left-sided midfielder with bags of skill. He is especially dangerous at set pieces, with the ability to curl the ball round the defensive wall. He lost his way a little at Torquay in 1999-2000 from mid-season onwards but definitely has an exciting future. Mick missed the closing stages of the campaign owing to the effects of a car accident. Although offered new terms in May, he was also attracting the attention of Bury. Mick captained Everton's 1998 FA Youth Cup-winning team.

Everton (From trainee on 7/10/1997)
Torquay U (Free on 29/7/1999) FL 25+5/4 FLC 2 FAC 4/2 Others 1

O'CALLAGHAN George
Born: Cork, 5 September 1979
Height: 6'1" Weight: 10.10
International Honours: RoI: Yth

George is a slightly built midfielder of real promise who made the breakthrough at Port Vale towards the end of last season, earning a regular place wide on the right. The campaign began badly for George when he was sent off twice in the reserves and, since the subsequent suspensions covered first-team games, was unavailable far too often to be considered. His first start wasn't until March in a defeat at Crewe but his enthusiasm and never-say-die attitude meant that he remained in the side, making a total of eight starts before the end of the season. He has signed a new two-year contract and will be looking to be more of a first-team regular in 2000-01.

Port Vale (From trainee on 10/7/1998) FL 12+3 FAC 0+1

O'CONNOR James Kevin
Born: Dublin, 1 September 1979
Height: 5'8" Weight: 11.6
Club Honours: AMC '00
International Honours: RoI: U21-3; Yth

The 1999-2000 season could scarcely have gone better for this fiery and competitive midfielder, who must have been one of the first names on the Stoke team sheet for every game. He established an excellent midfield partnership with Graham Kavanagh and capped a fine season by winning an Auto Windscreens Shield winners' medal and the club's "Player of the Season" award. James won a long-overdue call-up to the

Republic of Ireland U21 squad for the end-of-season Toulon Tournament, when he appeared in all three games against Colombia, Ghana and Portugal.
Stoke C (From trainee on 5/9/1996) FL 46/6 FLC 3/1 FAC 1 Others 9+1/2

O'CONNOR Kevin Patrick
Born: Blackburn, 24 February 1982
Height: 5'11" Weight: 12.0
This promising Brentford striker was one of several youngsters introduced to league football by chairman-manager Ron Noades towards the end of the 1999-2000 season. Kevin made his debut as a substitute in the Auto Windscreens Shield tie at Exeter and went on to sign professional forms for the Bees a couple of days later. He subsequently appeared in a few more first-team games and will be looking to feature more prominently in the coming season.
Brentford (From trainee on 4/3/2000) FL 6 Others 0+1

O'CONNOR Martyn John
Born: Walsall, 10 December 1967
Height: 5'9" Weight: 11.8
International Honours: Cayman Isles: 1
Martyn is an enthusiastic and intelligent central midfield player who was Birmingham City's captain in 1999-2000. He had another reliable campaign, driving the team on towards the play-offs and rarely letting his colleagues down. He made his debut on the international scene last February when appearing for the Cayman Isles in a friendly with Jamaica but was one of a number of English-based players who were prevented from appearing for the tiny nation against Cuba in the World Cup qualifiers by a late FIFA intervention. He immediately put the disappointment behind him and showed himself to be a true professional by returning home earlier than planned and turning out for the Blues against Portsmouth just 24 hours later.
Crystal Palace (£25,000 from Bromsgrove Rov on 26/6/1992) FL 2 Others 1+1
Walsall (Loaned on 24/3/1993) FL 10/1 Others 2/1
Walsall (£40,000 on 14/2/1994) FL 94/21 FLC 6/2 FAC 10/2 Others 3/1
Peterborough U (£350,000 on 12/7/1996) FL 18/3 FLC 4 FAC 2
Birmingham C (£500,000 + on 29/11/1996) FL 129+4/11 FLC 13/3 FAC 5 Others 4

ODEJAYI Olukayode (Kayo)
Born: Nigeria, 21 February 1982
Height: 6'2" Weight: 12.2
A cousin of former Bristol City favourite Ade Akinbiyi, this young striker has been learning his trade in the club's flourishing academy. A tall, pacy lad, he had a taste of first-team action when coming on from the bench in the 3-0 home success over Chesterfield last February, and made two more substitute appearances in the last two games of the season. He seems likely to feature more prominently in 2000-01.
Bristol C (Trainee) FL 0+3

Martyn O'Connor

O'DONNELL Philip (Phil)
Born: Bellshill, 25 March 1972
Height: 5'10" Weight: 10.10
Club Honours: SC '91, '95; SPD '98
International Honours: S: 1; U21-8
This hard-working left-sided midfield player joined Sheffield Wednesday in the summer of 1999 along with his Celtic team-mate Simon Donnelly. Unfortunately, Phil had a most frustrating time at Hillsborough through injuries and made just one appearance as a substitute, replacing Petter Rudi for the second half against Everton last September. His 1999-2000 season was eventually finished prematurely by surgery on his troublesome knee in January and he will be hoping to return to full fitness in time for the start of 2000-01.
Motherwell (From juniors on 30/6/1990) SL 123+1/15 SLC 6 SC 11+1/2 Others 3
Glasgow Celtic (£1,750,000 on 9/9/1994) SL 77+13/15 SLC 6+1 SC 12+4/4 Others 7+1/1
Sheffield Wed (Free on 9/7/1999) PL 0+1

ODUNSI Saheed **Adeleke (Leke)**
Born: Lambeth, 5 December 1980
Height: 5'9" Weight: 11.8
A product of Millwall's youth scheme, Leke is a very strong midfield player who competes for the ball effectively and is capable of playing an incisive pass. Although he was in the starting line-up for the opening game of the 1999-2000 season at Cardiff, thereafter he had to be satisfied with three substitute appearances due to the impressive form of Millwall's other midfielders. He is developing well and will no doubt figure prominently in Millwall's future plans.
Millwall (From trainee on 24/2/1999) FL 3+4 Others 0+1

OGRIZOVIC Steven (Steve)
Born: Mansfield, 12 September 1957
Height: 6'4" Weight: 15.0
Club Honours: FAC '87
"Oggy" recovered from surgery on a severe neck injury in 1999 and was back playing last October with a one-year extension to his Coventry contract. He was a regular in goal for the reserves and was praised by the club's management for passing on some of his vast experience to the youngsters. When Magnus Hedman picked up a back injury in March the 42-year-old stepped in to give brilliant displays against Arsenal at Highbury and at home to Liverpool. The latter was his 600th appearance for Coventry. A month later he announced his retirement from football with the club asking him to take up a coaching role within the youth academy. His final game was against Sheffield Wednesday on the last day of the season, when he received a wonderful reception before, during and after the match.
Chesterfield (Signed from ONRYC on 28/7/1977) FL 16 FLC 2

Liverpool (£70,000 on 18/11/1977) FL 4 Others 1
Shrewsbury T (£70,000 on 11/8/1982) FL 84 FLC 7 FAC 5
Coventry C (£72,000 on 22/6/1984) F/PL 507/1 FLC 49 FAC 34 Others 11

O'KANE John Andrew
Born: Nottingham, 15 November 1974
Height: 5'10" Weight: 12.2
Club Honours: FAYC '92; Div 2 '97

John was originally signed by Bolton on loan from Everton last November, primarily to act as a stop-gap for the recently departed Neil Cox, who had moved to Watford. John made an immediate impact in the right-back role and he was quickly snapped up on a free transfer at the same time that Bolton signed Gareth Farrelly from Everton. John drifted in and out of the first team for the remainder of the 1999-2000 season, although the performances of the ex-Manchester United man suggested that he has all the right qualities to make a successful career for himself with the Wanderers. A versatile and dependable player, John will be certain to figure for the Trotters in some capacity during the new season.

Manchester U (From trainee on 29/1/1993) PL 1+1 FLC 2+1 FAC 1 Others 1
Bury (Loaned on 25/10/1996) FL 2+2/2
Bury (Loaned on 16/1/1997) FL 9/1 Others 1
Bradford C (Loaned on 31/10/1997) FL 7
Everton (£250,000 + on 30/1/1998) PL 14 FAC 1+2
Burnley (Loaned on 31/10/1998) FL 8
Bolton W (Signed on 19/11/1999) FL 7+4/1 FLC 2 FAC 1+1

John O'Kane

OLDFIELD David Charles
Born: Perth, Australia, 30 May 1968
Height: 5'11" Weight: 13.4
International Honours: E: U21-1

A box-to-box midfielder, David was a regular in the Stoke squad in 1999-2000 until the arrival of the new Icelandic owners. He rarely featured in the side under Gudjon Thordarson but was never found wanting when called on either in his favoured midfield role or on occasions up front. The Australian's experience was used to maximum effect after he joined Peterborough on transfer deadline day, his calming influence in midfield guiding Posh into the Third Division play-offs. His value was highlighted in the Wembley final win against Darlington when, due to an injury to Jason Lee, David played as a striker alongside the speedy Andy Clarke.

Luton T (From apprentice on 16/5/1986) FL 21+8/4 FLC 4+2/2 FAC 0+1 Others 2+1/2
Manchester C (£600,000 on 14/3/1989) FL 18+8/6 FLC 2+1/2 Others 0+1/1
Leicester C (£150,000 on 12/1/1990) F/PL 163+25/26 FLC 10+1/1 FAC 6/3 Others 11+3/2
Millwall (Loaned on 24/2/1995) FL 16+1/6
Luton T (£150,000 on 21/7/1995) FL 99+18/18 FLC 11/2 FAC 2 Others 7+2/4
Stoke C (Free on 2/7/1998) FL 50+15/7 FLC 4+1 FAC 2 Others 1+1
Peterborough U (Free on 23/3/2000) FL 9 Others 3

O'LEARY Kristian (Kris) Denis
Born: Port Talbot, 30 August 1977
Height: 6'0" Weight: 13.4
Club Honours: Div 3 '00
International Honours: W: Yth

Kris started the 1999-2000 season in the Swansea first team, but an ankle injury in November followed by a hamstring problem in December saw him miss many matches during the campaign. Apart from one start as a central defender in February against Chester Kris's role during the last three months of the season was that of a substitute. He showed his versatility by regularly being brought on in the second half to strengthen the midfield, and was rewarded with a Third Division championship winners' medal.

Swansea C (From trainee on 1/7/1996) FL 61+20/3 FLC 4 FAC 4+1 Others 2+2

OLIVER Adam
Born: West Bromwich, 25 October 1980
Height: 5'9" Weight: 11.2
International Honours: E: Yth

Adam is a determined, hard-working midfielder who was given little opportunity to show his worth at West Bromwich during 1999-2000, appearing in only 16 first-team matches, all but two as a substitute. He went on to score his first senior goal two minutes from the end of Albion's thrilling 4-4 draw with Bolton in April. With another season under his belt, he is now looking ahead to the future and hopefully an extended run in Albion's midfield engine room, although he will have to battle for a place with several other players.

West Bromwich A (From trainee on 15/8/1998) FL 1+15/1 FLC 0+1 FAC 1

OLIVER Michael
Born: Middlesbrough, 2 August 1975
Height: 5'10" Weight: 12.4

After being made available for transfer at the end of the 1998-99 season, Michael was determined to remain at Darlington and fight for a first-team place. This determination certainly paid off as he established himself in the side last term and played in all but eight matches in league and cup. Michael's game is characterised by hard running and non-stop effort. Although not renowned for his marksmanship, he scored two crucial goals: one against Bolton in the Worthington Cup and a last-minute winner over Southend in the league. He was released in the summer.

Middlesbrough (From trainee on 19/8/1992) Others 0+1
Stockport Co (£15,000 on 7/7/1994) FL 17+5/1 FLC 0+2 FAC 2 Others 1
Darlington (Free on 30/7/1996) FL 135+16/14 FLC 7+1/1 FAC 10+1 Others 6+3

OMOYINMI Emmanuel (Manny)
Born: Nigeria, 28 December 1977
Height: 5'6" Weight: 10.7
International Honours: E: Sch

This West Ham youngster was relatively unknown at the beginning of 1999-2000 but by Christmas his name was on the lips of every Hammers fan and for all the wrong reasons. A pacy player with plenty of skill who can perform on either flank or as a striker, Manny went on loan to Gillingham in the early part of the season, creating an instant impression when he scored after just six minutes of his debut against Oldham and also playing in the Worthington Cup matches against Bolton. He then made a brief appearance for the last few minutes of extra time in West Ham's fourth-round tie with Aston Villa in the same competition. The tie had to be replayed and the Upton Park club eventually went out to a team they had originally beaten. Manny was to some extent exonerated from blame for the error when two members of the club's administrative staff resigned over the issue. However, he was then sent out on loan to Scunthorpe and Barnet and his West Ham career was effectively at an end. Manny made a bright start to his spell with Scunthorpe with a goal on his home debut against Blackpool. But after he reportedly received death threats from disgruntled Hammers fans his form suffered and he began to lose confidence in a struggling side. He returned to Upton Park after two months and then joined Barnet in February. Unfortunately, Manny did not make the hoped-for impact during his spell at Underhill. His best performance for the club came as a substitute in the home draw against Shrewsbury. His close control enabled him to embark on a series of purposeful runs down the right flank and he subsequently created the equaliser for Scott McGleish. Manny showed glimpses of devastating skill that hinted he could have been a revelation during his stint with the Bees, but he was used only sparingly and, when he did appear, he seemed unable to produce his best form. He was released by West Ham in the summer. Stop Press: It was reported in mid-June that Manny had signed for Oxford.

West Ham U (From trainee on 17/5/1995) PL 1+8/2 FLC 0+2 FAC 1+1

Bournemouth (Loaned on 30/9/1996) FL 5+2
Dundee U (Loaned on 20/2/1998) SL 1+3 SC 0+1
Leyton Orient (Loaned on 19/3/1999) FL 3+1/1
Gillingham (Loaned on 3/9/1999) FL 7+2/3 FLC 2
Scunthorpe U (Loaned on 21/12/1999) FL 6/1 Others 1
Barnet (Loaned on 25/2/2000) FL 1+5

O'NEIL Gary Paul
Born: Bromley, 18 May 1983
Height: 5'10" Weight: 11.0
Gary became the youngest player ever to appear for Portsmouth when he came on as a substitute in the home game with Barnsley last January when aged 16 years and 256 days, beating the previous record by just three days. An exciting midfield player with good vision, great composure and the ability to create space, he looks to have a sound future in the game. Gary developed through the ranks at Fratton Park and has signed a contract that will tie him to the south coast club until 2004.
Portsmouth (Trainee) FL 0+1

O'NEILL John Joseph
Born: Glasgow, 2 January 1974
Height: 5'11" Weight: 12.0
John was restricted to appearances from the subs' bench and in the reserves at Bournemouth in the first half of the 1999-2000 season before winning a regular place in the starting line-up from December. He scored three goals, including a brilliant effort at Bristol City last August which was perhaps the highlight of his campaign. A versatile player, he can perform in any of the midfield roles or as a striker and shows good vision and the confidence to run with the ball. His contract was up in the summer of 2000, and after failing to agree a new one with the Cherries it looks as though he may begin the 2000-01 season elsewhere.
Queens Park (From school on 25/7/1991) SL 70+21/30 SLC 2+1 SC 2 Others 0+1
Glasgow Celtic (Signed on 16/5/1994) SL 0+2
Bournemouth (Free on 29/3/1996) FL 79+42/10 FLC 4+6 FAC 4+4/2 Others 6+4

O'NEILL Keith Padre Gerard
Born: Dublin, 16 February 1976
Height: 6'1" Weight: 12.7
International Honours: RoI: 13; U21-1; Yth; Sch
Keith has settled well at Middlesbrough since his arrival in March 1999. He suffered a number of injuries last season that restricted his appearances but he remained in great heart. Although he has spent most of his career as an orthodox left winger, he was mainly employed as a left wing back, taking the position in his stride whenever Christian Ziege was either unavailable or required elsewhere. Always razor sharp, Keith has great pace and never shirks a tackle, while his pin-point crosses from the left side are a joy to watch. He added a further appearance for the Republic of Ireland when coming on from the subs' bench against Macedonia last October.
Norwich C (From trainee on 1/7/1994) P/FL 54+19/9 FLC 8+3/1 FAC 3
Middlesbrough (£700,000 + on 19/3/1999) PL 18+4 FLC 3

O'NEILL Michael Andrew Martin
Born: Portadown, 5 July 1969
Height: 5'11" Weight: 11.10
Club Honours: AMC '99
International Honours: NI: 31; B-2; U23-1; U21-1; Yth; Sch
A hard-working midfielder with the ability to deliver a crisp pass, Michael enjoyed an excellent season for Wigan in 1999-2000 until injuries forced him to miss the final third of the campaign. He scored his first league goal for the Latics in the win at Notts County at Christmas, while his other goal of the campaign was a late equaliser against Millwall a month later. Michael collected a hamstring injury in the game at Bristol Rovers in March, while a groin strain sustained on his return for the reserves ruled him out of the play-offs. He was made available for transfer in May.
Newcastle U (Signed from Coleraine on 23/10/1987) FL 36+12/15 FLC 2 FAC 3+2/1 Others 1
Dundee U (Signed on 15/8/1989) SL 49+15/11 SLC 3+2/1 SC 2 Others 3+2/1
Hibernian (Signed on 20/8/1993) SL 96+2/19 SLC 9/3 SC 6/2
Coventry C (£500.000 on 26/7/1996) PL 3+2 FLC 1
Aberdeen (Loaned on 22/1/1998) SL 4+1 SC 0+1
Reading (Loaned on 2/3/1998) FL 9/1
Wigan Ath (Free on 18/9/1998) FL 65+1/2 FLC 5 FAC 7 Others 8/3

O'NEILL Paul Dennis
Born: Farnworth, 17 May 1982
Height: 5'11" Weight: 11.2
A second-year trainee at Macclesfield, this central defender spent the vast majority of last season playing for the club's "A" and reserve teams. He made his Football League debut when he came on for the final 15 minutes of the 2-5 defeat at Brighton last March and will be looking to gain more experience in the coming season.
Macclesfield T (Trainee) FL 0+1

ONUORA Ifem (Iffy)
Born: Glasgow, 28 July 1967
Height: 6'1" Weight: 13.10
Iffy seemed to struggle to find his best form in a disappointing Swindon team in the first half of the 1999-2000 season before moving back to Gillingham, the club he had left some 21 months earlier. Initially on loan, he signed a two-and-a-half-year contract shortly afterwards. He proved a useful asset up front for the Gills, scoring six goals, including one in the second leg of the play-off semi-final against Stoke. Iffy is a big, strong target man who is effective at holding the play up and has a good eye for goal.
Huddersfield T (Signed from Bradford University on 28/7/1989) FL 115+50/30 FLC 10+6/4 FAC 11+3/3 Others 13+3/3
Mansfield T (£30,000 on 20/7/1994) FL 17+11/8 FAC 0+1 Others 1
Gillingham (£25,000 on 16/8/1996) FL 53+9/23 FLC 6/1 FAC 4/2 Others 1
Swindon T (£120,000 on 13/3/1998) FL 64+9/25 FLC 4 FAC 2+1
Gillingham (£125,000 on 3/1/2000) FL 21+1/6 Others 3/1

OPARA Kelechi Chrysantus
Born: Oweri, Nigeria, 21 December 1981
Height: 6'0" Weight: 12.6
Another Colchester youth-team regular, Kelechi built on his first-team debut at the end of the previous season with a series of substitute appearances and two starts in 1999-2000. A lively forward, he has yet to score his first goal, but had a major influence on the away win at Notts County in January, when he won the penalty for the opening goal, then produced a strong run along the right wing to set up Steve McGavin's second of the game. Overall, it was a season of some considerable promise for the young star which bodes well for the future.
Colchester U (Trainee) FL 2+15 Others 0+1

O'REILLY Alexander (Alex)
Born: Laughton, 15 September 1979
Height: 6'2" Weight: 12.4
International Honours: RoI: U21-11; Yth; (UEFA-U18 '98)
This talented young goalkeeper stepped up from West Ham's fourth team into Northampton's first when he joined the Cobblers at the beginning of 1999-2000 on a season-long loan. Alex went straight into the first team when first choice Keith Welch was injured in pre-season training. In the nine games he played for Northampton last term, Alex gave a good account of himself. A regular for the Republic of Ireland at U21 level, he won five more caps during the season.
West Ham U (From trainee on 13/8/1998)
Northampton T (Loaned on 6/8/1999) FL 7 FLC 1 Others 1

ORMEROD Anthony
Born: Middlesbrough, 31 March 1979
Height: 5'10" Weight: 11.8
International Honours: E: Yth
A gifted young winger who is now an established member of the Middlesbrough squad, Anthony had a quiet season at the Riverside in 1999-2000. His only call-up was for the Manchester United game when he came off the subs' bench for a while. Anthony has lost none of his confidence or maturity in the presence of the galaxy of stars with whom he now rubs shoulders daily, and the brightly burning young talent will surely explode on to the scene at the highest level in the near future. Anthony had an extended loan period with York in the first half of the season. Making his debut in the Yorkshire derby at Hull, the talented left winger found it difficult at times to come to terms with the hurly-burly of Third Division football.
Middlesbrough (From trainee on 16/5/1996) FL 8+10/3 FLC 2+2 FAC 2
Carlisle U (Loaned on 18/1/1999) FL 5+1 Others 1+1
York C (Loaned on 24/9/1999) FL 9+3 Others 1

ORMEROD Brett Ryan
Born: Blackburn, 18 October 1976
Height: 5'11" Weight: 11.4
Brett had a great start to 1999-2000 when he scored twice for Blackpool against Wrexham on the opening day of the season. A hard-working young striker, he appeared in all but one of the Seasiders' games up to the end of October before suffering a broken

leg at Wycombe. This brought his season to a premature close and he had yet to recover full fitness by the beginning of the summer.
Blackpool (£50,000 from Accrington Stanley on 21/3/1997) FL 48+18/15 FLC 4 FAC 1+1/1 Others 3

ORMEROD Mark Ian
Born: Bournemouth, 5 February 1976
Height: 6'0" Weight: 12.11
Mark started the 1999-2000 season in Brighton's goal, before losing his place after five games to Mark Walton. His subsequent sporadic appearances were mainly due to illness or injury to Walton. He handed in a transfer request in January. Mark has been a popular player over the years since coming through the youth ranks at Albion, but was released in May.
Brighton & Hove A (From trainee on 21/7/1994) FL 85 FLC 4 FAC 1 Others 3

OSBORN Mark
Born: Bletchley, 18 June 1981
Height: 6'2" Weight: 14.1
Wycombe's 19-year-old youth 'keeper made a surprise entrance into senior football when he came on as a substitute for the injured Mark Westhead in the Worthington Cup tie agains West Bromwich Albion last September. He then went on to make his full debut against Cambridge at the beginning of October, producing a good performance and keeping a clean sheet as the Chairboys recorded a 1-0 victory. Having been third choice at Adams Park for most of last season, Mark will be aiming to become the club's number two in 2000-01.
Wycombe W (From trainee on 13/3/1999) FL 1 FLC 0+1

OSBORN Simon Edward
Born: Croydon, 19 January 1972
Height: 5'9" Weight: 11.4
The steady, composed Wolves midfield man played in the 1999-2000 season-opener, only for a knee injury to rule him out of the next four matches. Simon missed only one of the following 21 games, yet failed to score. He made an invaluable contribution, continually harrying opponents, but his industry was not always appreciated by the crowd. A hamstring injury put him out for five games and he came back as a substitute, but when he started a match a few days later he lasted only 20 minutes. An operation was needed on his knee, due to a flaky cartilage. Simon missed 13 games, returning as a substitute at Norwich.
Crystal Palace (From trainee on 3/1/1990) F/PL 47+8/5 FLC 11/1 FAC 2 Others 1+3
Reading (£90,000 on 17/8/1994) FL 31+1/5 FLC 4 Others 3
Queens Park R (£1,100,000 on 7/7/1995) PL 6+3/1 FLC 2
Wolverhampton W (£1,000,000 on 22/12/1995) FL 135+7/11 FLC 5/2 FAC 9+1 Others 2

O'SHEA John Francis
Born: Waterford, 30 April 1981
Height: 6'3" Weight: 11.12
International Honours: RoI: U21-2; Yth; (UEFA-U16 '98)
A talented young Manchester United central defender, John made his first-team debut in the Worthington Cup against Aston Villa last September. He joined Bournemouth on loan in January and showed himself to be an accomplished performer in the 11 games he played for the Cherries. He scored with a header at Millwall when joining the attack for a corner but eventually chose to return to Old Trafford. Although he knows he faces an uphill struggle competing for a first-team place against the likes of Jaap Stam, Mikael Silvestre and Henning Berg, John is quite prepared to give it his best shot. He was capped five times by the Republic of Ireland at U18 level last season before stepping up to make a couple of appearances for the U21s in the Toulon Tournament in May.
Manchester U (Signed from Waterford U on 2/9/1998) FLC 1
Bournemouth (Loaned on 18/1/2000) FL 10/1 Others 1

OSTENSTAD Egil
Born: Haugesun, Norway, 2 January 1972
Height: 6'0" Weight: 13.0
International Honours: Norway: 17
Offered a new four-year contract by Southampton in August 1999, Egil turned down the deal and agreed to join Blackburn Rovers in a swap transfer which saw Kevin Davies move the other way. Since he had played well in the opening matches and scored in the 1-0 win at Coventry (the club's first opening-day victory since 1991), it came as something of a surprise to many Saints' supporters that Egil was dropping down to the First Division. Arriving at Blackburn with an enviable reputation, the Norwegian striker made a flying start to his Ewood career with two goals in his second game, at Norwich. Thereafter Egil struggled to live up to expectations, although there is no doubt that, as his goal against Wolves demonstrated, he is a natural finisher. Difficult to contain when he is at his best, he is good in the air and a powerful runner but his tally of just eight goals during a stop-start season for Rovers was a disappointment and he will be looking for a better return in 2000-01.
Southampton (£800,000 from Viking Stavanger, Norway on 3/10/1996) PL 80+16/28 FLC 9/3 FAC 3+1/2
Blackburn Rov (Signed on 18/8/1999) FL 21+7/8 FLC 1 FAC 1+1

OSTER John Morgan
Born: Boston, 8 December 1978
Height: 5'9" Weight: 10.8
International Honours: W: 4; B-1; U21-9; Yth
The young Welsh international winger joined Sunderland from Everton in August 1999 for £1 million, and began the new season in the first team, making his debut at the Stadium of Light against Watford, before losing his place to Gavin McCann. Although right-sided, John was mainly used down the left flank during his sporadic first-team appearances and showed himself to be a ball-playing winger who is prepared to beat a full back and put in telling crosses. Sunderland fans are hoping that next season he will be pushing Nicky Summerbee hard for a place in the side. John won a further cap for Wales when he appeared against Switzerland at Wrexham last October.
Grimsby T (From trainee on 11/7/1996) FL 21+3/3 FAC 0+1/1
Everton (£1,500,000 on 21/7/1997) PL 22+18/1 FLC 4+1/1 FAC 2+3/1
Sunderland (£1,000,000 on 6/8/1999) PL 4+6 FLC 3

O'SULLIVAN Wayne St John
Born: Akrotiri, Cyprus, 25 February 1974
Height: 5'9" Weight: 11.2
Club Honours: Div 2 '96
International Honours: RoI: U21-2
Although offered new terms by promoted Cardiff, Wayne joined Plymouth in the 1999 close season. He is a versatile player who proved to be a vital member of the Pilgrims' squad last season. He operated mainly at right wing back, his strong defending and attacking forward runs making him an automatic choice. A firm favourite with the Home Park crowd, Wayne is a consistent and reliable player who always gives 100 per cent. He scored his first goal for Argyle in the win against Mansfield in October.
Swindon T (From trainee on 1/5/1993) FL 65+24/3 FLC 11/1 FAC 1+3 Others 3+2
Cardiff C (£75,000 on 22/8/1997) FL 78+7/4 FLC 1+2 FAC 10/1 Others 2
Plymouth Arg (Free on 30/7/1999) FL 45/2 FLC 2 FAC 7 Others 1

Wayne O'Sullivan

OVENDALE Mark John
Born: Leicester, 22 November 1973
Height: 6'2" Weight: 13.2
Mark had another excellent season as Bournemouth's 'keeper in 1999-2000, rarely missing a game and picking up the "Players' Player of the Season" award. He has matured into one of the best goalkeepers in the lower divisions, proving to be a fine shot stopper who has full command of his penalty area and gathers crosses and corners with ease.

Mark Ovendale

Northampton T (Free from Wisbech on 15/8/1994) FL 6 Others 2 (Free to Barry T during 1995 close season)
Bournemouth (£30,000 on 14/5/1998) FL 89 FLC 10 FAC 7 Others 5

OVERMARS Marc
Born: Ernst, Holland, 29 March 1973
Height: 5'8" Weight: 11.4
Club Honours: PL '98; FAC '98; CS '98
International Honours: Holland: 60

A groin injury caused Marc to miss Arsenal's opening game of the 1999-2000 season but once he had regained full fitness he again showed tremendous pace and skill. On his day, he is one of the most exciting left-sided wingers in the Premiership and is a threat to any defence. He was exceptional in the away match at AIK Solna in the Champions' League last November, scoring twice. Two weeks later, he tore the Middlesbrough defence apart, scoring a hat-trick and creating a host of other chances. Marc is a great crosser of the ball from either flank, and his accuracy creates many chances for the strikers. A regular for Holland when fit, he featured in all five of their games in Euro 2000, scoring twice in the 6-1 thrashing of Yugoslavia in the quarter-finals of the competition.
Arsenal (£7,000,000 from Ajax, Holland on 10/7/1997) PL 91+9/25 FLC 3+1/2 FAC 15+2/7 Others 18+3/7

OWEN Gareth
Born: Chester, 21 October 1971
Height: 5'8" Weight: 12.0
Club Honours: WC '95
International Honours: W: B-1; U21-8

Gareth, like his Wrexham colleague Phil Hardy, seems to be a permanent fixture at the Racecourse Ground. He has proved to be a vital cog in the Robins' engine room over the years, being a powerful forager with a fine long pass and a cracking shot. Although still only 28 and with plenty of football left in him, he recently completed ten years' service with the club and he is due to be rewarded with a well-deserved testimonial against Manchester United.
Wrexham (From trainee on 6/7/1990) FL 280+48/34 FLC 11+1 FAC 25+7 Others 36+2/1

OWEN Michael James
Born: Chester, 14 December 1979
Height: 5'9" Weight: 11.2
Club Honours: FAYC '96
International Honours: E: 22; U21-1; Yth; Sch

Michael had a season of mixed fortunes in 1999-2000, mainly due to injuries – particularly that hamstring – though when he was in the Liverpool team, he made a significant contribution, and maintained a respectable goals-per-game ratio. He is a natural goalscorer, but doubts have begun to emerge about his level of fitness or his tendency to break down and sustain injuries. It does not help Liverpool's cause for him to be out of the reckoning for long periods, though it may well assist Michael from a psychological point of view, since his absences provide recovery time from the physical and mental rigours of the Premiership. Recovering in time for Euro 2000 last summer, he featured in all three of England's matches, scoring in the final game against Romania.
Liverpool (From juniors on 18/12/1996) PL 87+8/48 FLC 8/6 FAC 3/2 Others 8+2/3

OWERS Gary
Born: Newcastle, 3 October 1968
Height: 5'11" Weight: 12.7
Club Honours: Div 3 '88

This Notts County midfielder took several matches to settle down in 1999-2000 before returning to form as a ball winner in the centre of the park. Very much an unsung hero for the Magpies, Gary worked quietly and effectively as a midfield anchor man, thus releasing others to play a more creative role. He maintained his record of scoring in every season of his professional career, finding the net four times during the campaign.
Sunderland (From apprentice on 8/10/1986) FL 259+9/25 FLC 25+1/1 FAC 10+2 Others 11+1/1
Bristol C (£250,000 on 23/12/1994) FL 121+5/9 FLC 9/1 FAC 9 Others 9/2
Notts Co (£15,000 on 30/7/1998) FL 81+3/7 FLC 5+1 FAC 7/1 Others 1

OWUSU Lloyd Magnus
Born: Slough, 12 December 1976
Height: 6'1" Weight: 14.0
Club Honours: Div 3 '99

This tall, strong and speedy Brentford striker continued to hit the net regularly in the first half of the 1999-2000 season, although his goalscoring touch seemed to disappear in the second half of the campaign. Lloyd still finished as leading scorer for the Bees for the second year in succession and will be looking to improve on his total of 12 goals in the coming season, only his third as a full-time professional.
Brentford (£25,000 from Slough T on 29/7/1998) FL 81+6/34 FLC 1+4/2 FAC 5/2 Others 3+2/1

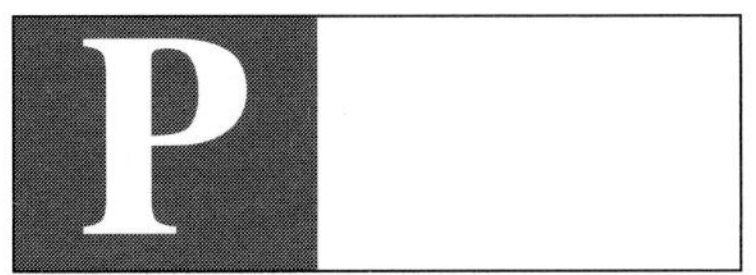

PADULA Diego **Gino** Mauro
Born: Buenos Aires, Argentina, 11 July 1976
Height: 5'9" Weight: 12.1
After spells with River Plate, Huracan and Xerez, where he played in the same side as current Walsall team-mate Gabby Bukran, "Gino" had trials with Bristol Rovers, Dundee United and Derby County before linking up with the Saddlers last November. Initially signed on trial, he impressed in his first full game, a 2-0 win over Huddersfield, and made a total of 21 successive appearances before injury kept him out of four late-season matches. A quick, skilful left back, he won several "Man of the Match" awards with his determined tackling, ability in the air and readiness to move forward.
Bristol Rov (Free from Xerez, Spain on 15/10/1999)
Walsall (Free on 11/11/1999) FL 23+2 FAC 2

PAGE Robert John
Born: Llwynpia, 3 September 1974
Height: 6'0" Weight: 12.5
Club Honours: Div 2 '98
International Honours: W: 13; B-1; U21-6; Yth; Sch
A resolute central defender, Robert was one of the players to emerge with most credit from Watford's Premiership season in 1999-2000 and was a worthy winner of the club's "Player of the Year" award. At times the team's defensive frailties were all too evident, but Robert stood firm and repelled all boarders, particularly in the air. As captain, his determination and pride in his performance set a fine example to the other players and ensured the team maintained its spirit in the face of much adversity. Robert missed only two matches, both through suspension, and has now made over 200 appearances for Watford, his only club. After several seasons of trying, he at last scored his first league goal – a far-post header at Hillsborough. For a player who has worked hard to add an attacking dimension to his game, it was a fitting reward. A regular member of the Welsh international team, he was an ever-present last season, adding a further six caps.
Watford (From trainee on 19/4/1993) P/FL 173+7/1 FLC 12 FAC 11+1 Others 6/1

PAHARS Marians
Born: Latvia, 5 August 1976
Height: 5'9" Weight: 10.9
International Honours: Latvia: 38
A powerful, pocket-sized forward, Marians possesses electrifying pace and a sharp eye for goal. A regular in the Southampton team and considered to be one of the finest players ever to have come out of Latvian football, he scored some outstanding goals last term. At Old Trafford in September he nutmegged a bemused Jaap Stam to score after an outstanding run, while a long-range effort against Derby County, witnessed by the Sky cameras, was measured at 29.1 yards and travelled at 63.5 miles per hour. Glenn Hoddle's arrival as Southampton's new manager saw Marians pushed into a slightly withdrawn role which enabled him to run at defenders face on, either from the right or the left flank, rather than start with his back to goal. The tactic certainly proved effective. Another wonder goal, scored against Middlesbrough, began with an electrifying run starting deep on the right. He cut inside and, with a precise low shot, sent the ball into the far corner of the net. Marians won four more caps for Latvia during the season, featuring against Georgia, Norway, Romania and Finland.
Southampton (£800,000 from Skonto Riga, Latvia on 25/3/1999) PL 35+4/16 FLC 3 FAC 2

Marians Pahars

PAINTER Peter **Robert (Robbie)**
Born: Wigan, 26 January 1971
Height: 5'11" Weight: 12.2
An admirable and experienced lower-division pro, Robbie always gives 100 per cent effort and has got a good footballing brain. Although predominantly a centre forward, he spent much of the 1999-2000 season occupying a wide-right position. To his credit, Robbie emerged with eight league goals to top Halifax's goalscoring charts.
Chester C (From trainee on 1/7/1988) FL 58+26/8 FLC 2+2 FAC 7+1/3 Others 3+3
Maidstone U (£30,000 on 16/8/1991) FL 27+3/5 FLC 2 FAC 1+1 Others 0+2
Burnley (£25,000 on 27/3/1992) FL 16+10/2 FLC 2 FAC 1
Darlington (Signed on 16/9/1993) FL 104+11/28 FLC 2+4/1 FAC 5+1/2 Others 9/3
Rochdale (Signed on 10/10/1996) FL 101+11/30 FLC 3/1 FAC 7 Others 4+2
Halifax T (Free on 31/7/1999) FL 38+4/8 FLC 2 FAC 3 Others 1

PALLISTER Gary Andrew
Born: Ramsgate, 30 June 1965
Height: 6'4" Weight: 14.13
Club Honours: FAC '90, '94, '96; CS '93, '94, '96, '97; ECWC '91; ESC '91; FLC '92; PL '93, '94, '96, '97
International Honours: E: 22; B-9
Gary returned to Middlesbrough for his second spell with the club in the 1998 close season and fitted in so well that it was hard to imagine that he had ever been away. Boro manager Bryan Robson was well aware of his recurring back injury but the consensus at the Riverside was that he would respond well to treatment and play in more matches than he missed. Unfortunately, the reverse has probably been nearer the mark, although his performances when fit have more than made up for his absences. A commanding centre back who is always in the thick of the defensive action, Gary is vastly experienced and totally dependable. He is a powerful and skilful header of the ball at both ends of the pitch, and his forays upfield for set pieces cause mayhem in the opposition goalmouth. Gary was involved in an alarming incident in the derby game with Newcastle at St James' Park in October, when he got in the way of one of Mark Schwarzer's punches as he went to head the ball clear. He was laid out cold but he fortunately suffered nothing worse than concussion. Gary is also a wizard at bringing the youngsters on and teaching them the disciplines of team work and so on. Every one of them speaks highly of the benefit they have derived from his attention.
Middlesbrough (Free from Billingham T on 7/11/1984) FL 156/5 FLC 10 FAC 10/1 Others 13
Darlington (Loaned on 18/10/1985) FL 7
Manchester U (£2,300,000 on 29/8/1989) F/PL 314+3/12 FLC 36 FAC 38/1 Others 45+1/1
Middlesbrough (£2,500,000 on 24/7/1998) PL 47/1 FLC 3 FAC 2

PALMER Carlton Lloyd
Born: Rowley Regis, 5 December 1965
Height: 6'2" Weight: 13.3
International Honours: E: 18; B-5; U21-4
Carlton featured three times for Nottingham Forest last August, scoring a superb late winner against Grimsby, before he returned to the Premiership with Coventry. He joined City on a three-month loan in September and had an immediate impact as the midfield anchor man. His vast experience and awkward style make him an asset to the midfield of any top-flight club, and the Sky Blues paid £500,000 for him before the end of his loan. His arrival gave Gary McAllister just what he needed: someone who could sit in front of the back four and win the ball, leaving him to be the play-maker with less defensive responsibility. Carlton also demonstrated his aerial ability in the box with an excellent headed goal against Newcastle. The team lost only two of his first 16 games and time and again his telescopic legs would emerge from tackles with the ball. He was also a big inspiration in the dressing room, with his personality, motivational ability and professionalism making a telling contribution. Coventry's downturn in form in the spring coincided with Carlton's absence through a hamstring injury which required surgery.
West Bromwich A (From apprentice on 21/12/1984) FL 114+7/4 FLC 7+1/1 FAC 4 Others 6
Sheffield Wed (£750,000 on 23/2/1989) F/PL 204+1/14 FLC 31/1 FAC 18/2 Others 8+1/1
Leeds U (£2,600,000 on 30/6/1994) PL 100+2/5 FLC 12 FAC 12/1 Others 4/1

Southampton (£1,000,000 on 26/9/1997) PL 44+1/3 FLC 5 FAC 2
Nottingham F (£1,100,000 on 21/1/1999) P/FL 14+2/1
Coventry C (£500,000 on 17/9/1999) PL 15/1 FLC 1 FAC 3

PALMER Ryan Warren John
Born: Camberwell, 2 February 1980
Height: 6'1" Weight: 11.8

Ryan was signed by Brighton on a free transfer from Fulham in June 1999. New Brighton boss Micky Adams was his first manager at Craven Cottage, and regarded Ryan as one for the future. A defender or midfielder, his only start came in midfield in the defeat at Swansea City in December when the Albion squad was ravaged by flu. Ryan was released at the end of the season.

Fulham (From trainee on 2/7/1998)
Brighton & Hove A (Free on 8/7/1999) FL 1

PALMER Stephen (Steve) Leonard
Born: Brighton, 31 March 1968
Height: 6'1" Weight: 12.13
Club Honours: Div 2 '92, '98
International Honours: E: Sch

Watford's man for all seasons and all positions, Steve was an ever-present last season – a tribute to his fitness and consistency. He has now made more than 300 league appearances and is an object lesson in how to play hard but fair. Steve started the season in what is perhaps his best position – just in front of the back four – but later moved back into defence, where he renewed his successful partnership with Robert Page. As one of the senior players in the team, Steve is a constant source of advice and encouragement to his team-mates.

Ipswich T (Free from Cambridge University on 1/8/1989) F/PL 87+24/2 FLC 3 FAC 8+3/1 Others 4+2
Watford (£135,000 on 28/9/1995) P/FL 185+11/7 FLC 13+1 FAC 9+1 Others 7

PAMAROT Noe
Born: Paris, France, 14 April 1979
Height: 6'2" Weight: 13.0

This tough-tackling, no-nonsense central defender came to Portsmouth on loan from OGC Nice last September after impressing in a couple of pre-season games. He featured as a substitute on two occasions and made the starting line-up for the trip to the Hawthorns in November but dropped back into the reserves after manager Alan Ball was sacked. Pompey eventually declined the opportunity to buy him at the end of the season and he returned to France.

Portsmouth (Loaned from OGC Nice, France on 7/9/1999) FL 1+1 FLC 0+1

PANAYI Sofroni **James (Jimmy)**
Born: Hammersmith, 24 January 1980
Height: 6'1" Weight: 14.0

This young Watford defender was pressed into first-team action at Coventry last October when the club were without several senior players. It was a difficult debut, but James came through it well and will surely benefit from the experience. Having undergone a shoulder operation during the summer of 1999, James suffered further problems and unfortunately had to have another later in the season.

Watford (From trainee on 3/7/1998) PL 2

PANOPOULOS Mikael (Mike)
Born: Greece, 9 October 1976
Height: 6'1" Weight: 11.7

Mike was playing in Greece for Aris Solonika at the start of 1999-2000 when he was spotted by Alan Ball, who signed him for Portsmouth. He had a decent run in the starting line-up on arriving at Fratton Park but suffered a string of niggling injuries and missed the last six weeks of the season after damaging back muscles. Mike is a talented midfield player who can produce exciting football on his day but needs to produce his best form more consistently.

Portsmouth (£500,000 from Aris Salonika, Greece on 8/9/1999) FL 18+4/1 FLC 2 FAC 1

PARKER Scott Matthew
Born: Lambeth, 13 October 1980
Height: 5'7" Weight: 10.7
Club Honours: Div 1 '00
International Honours: E: Yth; Sch

This very talented young midfield player was unable to break into the Charlton side on a regular basis last season but looked impressive when he did play and made sufficient appearances to earn a First Division championship medal. Scott has an excellent touch and reads the game well, while his distribution is also impressive. Very self-assured, he likes to take players on and is not afraid to hit a long crossfield pass if appropriate. He possesses a powerful shot and likes to shoot from long range when the opportunity arises. He scored his first senior goal against Queens Park Rangers at the Valley in March when his close-range tap-in won the game for the Addicks.

Charlton Ath (From trainee on 22/10/1997) P/FL 5+17/1 FLC 1+2 FAC 1+2

PARKIN Brian
Born: Birkenhead, 12 October 1965
Height: 6'3" Weight: 14.7
Club Honours: Div 3 '90

This experienced goalkeeper returned for a second spell at Bristol Rovers last October, initially as goalkeeping coach, almost a decade after winning a Third Division championship medal with the club. In his long career, Brian has always been very dependable. Following an injury to first-choice 'keeper Lee Jones, the 35-year-old took over at half time in the 1-0 home win over Cambridge on New Year's Day, his first appearance for Rovers since January 1996. In his next match, an Auto Windscreens Shield tie at Northampton, Brian pulled off a vital save in a penalty shoot-out to ensure Rovers' progress in the competition. He showed his ability again in the following league game against Gillingham and was recalled for the final "must-win" match of the season at Cardiff. However, despite a "Man of the Match" performance from Brian the Welsh side beat Rovers and denied them a place in the play-offs.

Oldham Ath (From juniors on 31/3/1983) FL 6 FLC 2
Crewe Alex (Free on 30/11/1984) FL 98 FLC 7 FAC 2 Others 6
Crystal Palace (Free on 1/7/1988) FL 20 FLC 3 Others 2
Bristol Rov (Free on 11/11/1989) FL 241 FLC 15 FAC 12 Others 23
Wycombe W (Free on 24/7/1996) FL 25 FLC 4
Shrewsbury T (Free on 14/9/1998)
Notts Co (Free on 2/10/1998) FL 1
Wimbledon (Free on 26/3/1999) (Free to Yeovil during 1999 close season)
Bristol Rov (Free on 22/10/1999) FL 2+1 Others 1

PARKIN Jonathan (Jon)
Born: Barnsley, 30 December 1981
Height: 6'4" Weight: 13.7

This promising young Barnsley striker recorded two further senior appearances as a substitute in 1999-2000 but spent most of the season with the reserve and academy teams, for whom he scored regularly. He was interrupted by a series of minor injuries but now that he is fully fit he is expected to spend the summer in Finland to gain experience. Jonathan is a robust player with a powerful shot and is definitely one to look out for in the future.

Barnsley (From trainee on 5/1/1999) FL 0+2 FLC 0+1 FAC 0+1

PARKINSON Andrew (Andy) John
Born: Liverpool, 27 May 1979
Height: 5'8" Weight: 10.12

This young Tranmere forward had another excellent season in 1999-2000, chipping in with nine goals and making the line-up for the Worthington Cup final with Leicester last February. He was best used wide on the right, where his blistering pace and old-fashioned wing skills were prominent. Although there is a temptation to see Andy as a lightweight due to his lack of physical presence, he always shows great commitment and has the ability to score sensational goals, as he demonstrated in the Worthington Cup tie with Middlesbrough last December. Quiet and modest off the field, Andy is developing into a thoughtful and cultured player often compared to his former Anfield team-mate Michael Owen.

Tranmere Rov (From Liverpool juniors on 12/4/1997) FL 58+26/10 FLC 11+4/3 FAC 6+2/1

PARKINSON Gary Anthony
Born: Thornaby, 10 January 1968
Height: 5'11" Weight: 13.5

Absent since January 1999 following a serious knee injury, Gary made an emotional return to first-team action for Preston as a late substitute in the last game of the 1999-2000 season at Bristol City. At his best, the experienced, tough-tackling right back combines sterling defensive qualities with explosive free kicks from distance and consistently successful penalty taking. Having battled back well, he still has several good years ahead of him in the game.

Middlesbrough (Free from Everton juniors on 17/1/1986) FL 194+8/5 FLC 20/1 FAC 17/1 Others 19
Southend U (Loaned on 10/10/1992) FL 6
Bolton W (Free on 2/3/1993) FL 1+2 Others 4
Burnley (Signed on 27/1/1994) FL 134+1/4 FLC 12 FAC 10 Others 6/1
Preston NE (£50,000 on 30/5/1997) FL 71+2/6 FLC 6 FAC 7/1 Others 6/1

PARKINSON Philip (Phil) John
Born: Chorley, 1 December 1967
Height: 6'0" Weight: 12.8
Club Honours: Div 2 '94

Reading's longest-serving player and club captain, Phil missed the beginning and the end of last season with injuries, but showed enough in between to prove that his leadership and spirit are still vital to the Royals' cause. A tough-tackling midfielder, he is now approaching the veteran stage, but can be relied on to win far more than his fair share of tackles. Greatly admired by the supporters for his rapport with them, he is the club's PFA delegate and also finds time to coach the academy U14 squad.

Southampton (From apprentice on 7/12/1985)
Bury (£12,000 on 8/3/1988) FL 133+12/5 FLC 6+1 FAC 4/1 Others 13/1
Reading (£37,500 on 10/7/1992) FL 256+23/14 FLC 23+1/2 FAC 18/1 Others 7+2

PARKS Anthony (Tony)
Born: Hackney, 28 January 1963
Height: 5'10" Weight: 11.5
Club Honours: UEFAC '84; S Div 1 '94; B&Q '94

Tony joined Halifax as goalkeeping coach but also acted as Lee Butler's understudy during 1999-2000. He made his only league appearance at Leyton Orient in August, and played in both legs of the Worthington Cup clash with West Bromwich Albion. A natural leader, Tony was offered a new contract for the coming season.

Tottenham H (From apprentice on 22/9/1980) FL 37 FLC 1 FAC 5 Others 5
Oxford U (Loaned on 1/10/1986) FL 5
Gillingham (Loaned on 1/9/1987) FL 2
Brentford (£60,000 on 24/8/1988) FL 71 FLC 7 FAC 8 Others 5
Fulham (Free on 27/2/1991) FL 2
West Ham U (Free on 15/8/1991) FL 6 FAC 3
Stoke C (Free on 21/8/1992) FL 2 FLC 1
Falkirk (Free on 14/10/1992) SL 112 SLC 8 SC 4 Others 4
Blackpool (Free on 6/9/1996)
Burnley (Free on 13/8/1997) FLC 2 (Free to Barrow on 14/10/1998)
Doncaster Rov (Loaned on 13/2/1998) FL 6
Scarborough (Free on 26/2/1999) FL 15
Halifax T (Free on 5/7/1999) FL 1 FLC 2

PARLOUR Raymond (Ray)
Born: Romford, 7 March 1973
Height: 5'10" Weight: 11.12
Club Honours: FLC '93; ECWC '94; PL '98; FAC '93, '98; CS '98, '99
International Honours: E: 7; B-1; U21-12

A strong-tackling right-sided midfielder, Ray is a regular in the Arsenal line-up. He is always looking to get forward into scoring positions, and his excellent stamina enables him to get back quickly to defend when required. Although he missed a number of games in mid-season due to an ankle injury, he came back refreshed and fitter. His finest performance of the season was undoubtedly in the away leg of the UEFA Cup quarter-final at Werder Bremen. He scored the first hat-trick of his career to help seal the Gunners' fine 4-2 victory on the night. Consistently impressive form earned him a place in England's starting line-up for the first time against Luxembourg last September but, although he added three more caps, he failed to win a place in the squad for the European Championship finals in the summer.

Arsenal (From trainee on 6/3/1991) F/PL 199+36/18 FLC 19+3 FAC 27/2 Others 25+5/4

PARRISH Sean
Born: Wrexham, 14 March 1972
Height: 5'10" Weight: 11.8

This dynamic Welsh midfield player showed in 1999-2000 that he had recovered well from the spate of injuries he had received over the previous two seasons. Sean put in some fine performances on the left side of Northampton's midfield during the campaign, and rediscovered his scoring boots. Before his injuries Sean was being watched by the Welsh selectors; he is still in his twenties and with a successful promotion campaign behind him, it is to be hoped that Wales will look at his talents again. However, he was released by Northampton during the summer. Stop Press: It was reported at the end of June that Sean had signed for Chesterfield.

Shrewsbury T (From trainee on 12/7/1990) FL 1+2 FLC 1 Others 3 (Free to Telford during 1992 close season)
Doncaster Rov (£20,000 on 28/5/1994) FL 64+2/8 FLC 3+1 FAC 2/1 Others 3
Northampton T (£35,000 + on 2/8/1996) FL 103+6/13 FLC 8+1/1 FAC 2 Others 5/2

PARSONS David
Born: Greenwich, 25 February 1982
Height: 6'1" Weight: 12.7

David was a stalwart member of Leyton Orient's South East Conference Youth Alliance-winning side in 1999-2000. Like many of his young colleagues, he was rewarded with a first-team call-up, although he had to wait until the last game of the season against York for his chance. He is an excellent attacking midfielder who is a pin-point passer of the ball and uses his size to good effect. David will be aiming to be a regular member of the first-team squad during the coming season.

Leyton Orient (Trainee) FL 1

PARTRIDGE Scott Malcolm
Born: Leicester, 13 October 1974
Height: 5'9" Weight: 11.2
Club Honours: Div 3 '99

This speedy Brentford striker showed great form in the early part of the 1999-2000 campaign when the Bees were riding high near the top of Division Two. Scott has excellent ball control with the skills to mesmerise opposition defences, and even when not scoring goals his hard work and passing ability make him an asset to the team. He will be looking to re-establish his goalscoring touch in the coming season.

Scott Partridge

Bradford C (From trainee on 10/7/1992) FL 0+5 FLC 1+1
Bristol C (Free on 18/2/1994) FL 24+33/7 FLC 2+3/1 FAC 1+3
Torquay U (Loaned on 13/10/1995) FL 5/2
Plymouth Arg (Loaned on 22/1/1996) FL 6+1/2
Scarborough (Loaned on 8/3/1996) FL 5+2
Cardiff C (£50,000 on 14/2/1997) FL 29+8/2 FLC 2 FAC 2 Others 1
Torquay U (Signed on 26/3/1998) FL 33+1/12 FLC 2 FAC 2/1 Others 2/1
Brentford (£100,000 on 19/2/1999) FL 50+5/13 FLC 2 FAC 1+1 Others 1+1

PASSI Franck
Born: Bergerac, France, 28 March 1966
Height: 5'9" Weight: 11.9
Franck originally joined Bolton on a month's contract from Compestella of Spain in December 1999, and Sam Allardyce did not need much prompting to extend that loan period to the end of the season after the Frenchman produced some fine performances in the centre of midfield. A veteran of two Champions' League semi-finals with Monaco, Franck has played with some exceptional players during his time, including Laurent Blanc, Alain Giresse, Eric Cantona and Jean-Pierre Papin. He added some much-needed bite to the Bolton midfield and his non-stop displays were a welcome boost to a sometimes tired-looking central unit. It is not known at the time of writing if Franck's stay at the Reebok will be made permanent, but it would certainly be a distinct advantage for Bolton if they could keep this vastly experienced player on their books into the new season.
Bolton W (Free from Compostela, Spain on 25/11/1999) FL 7+8 FLC 2 FAC 2+1 Others 0+1

PATERSON Jamie Ryan
Born: Dumfries, 26 April 1973
Height: 5'5" Weight: 10.6
A reported £150,000 bid from Rushden & Diamonds early last season seemed to unsettle the diminutive Halifax midfielder. Jamie had scored a hat-trick against Carlisle in September, and his apparent availability attracted interest from a number of other clubs. However, he netted only one goal in the second half of the season and the anticipated transfer failed to materialise. A new contract has been on the table for some time as Jamie considers his future.
Halifax T (From trainee on 5/7/1991) FL 34+10/5 FLC 0+1 FAC 1 Others 3
Falkirk (Signed on 11/12/1994) SL 1+3
Scunthorpe U (£18,000 on 12/10/1995) FL 34+21/2 FAC 4+1/1 Others 3
Halifax T (Free on 30/7/1997) FL 56+8/17 FLC 3+1/1 FAC 4/1

PATERSON Scott
Born: Aberdeen, 13 May 1972
Height: 5'11" Weight: 12.10
Signed on non-contract terms from Carlisle in September 1999, Scott made seven appearances for Cambridge before being released the following March. It was felt that he had been hampered by a lack of pre-season training and a series of niggling injuries. He subsequently joined Plymouth on non-contract terms, having produced some impressive performances for Argyle's reserves while on trial. Scott can play in the centre of defence or in midfield and shows a good touch on the ball. He made his full debut at Exeter in the Devon derby, but was released at the end of the season.
Liverpool (£15,000 from Cove R on 19/3/1992)
Bristol C (Free on 4/7/1994) FL 40+10/1 FLC 6 FAC 2 Others 3
Cardiff C (Loaned on 7/11/1997) FL 5
Carlisle U (Free on 23/7/1998) FL 18+1/1 FLC 2 Others 0+1
Cambridge U (Free on 24/9/1999) FL 6
Plymouth Arg (Free on 3/3/2000) FL 5

PATTERSON Jamie
Born: Paignton, 11 February 1981
Height: 5'8" Weight: 10.2
Jamie's two-minute substitute appearance at Gillingham in the Auto Windscreens Shield was his only first-team action for Torquay in 1999-2000. He is an energetic attacking midfielder who has time on his side to make it in the professional game. However, his future progress may be hampered as Torquay have withdrawn their reserve team from the Avon Insurance Combination League.
Torquay U (From trainee on 1/7/1999) Others 0+1

PATTERSON Mark
Born: Leeds, 13 September 1968
Height: 5'10" Weight: 12.4
Mark appeared regularly at right back for Gillingham in the opening games of the 1999-2000 campaign but then had the misfortune to suffer a double fracture of the left leg at Millwall last October. The injury put him out of action for several months and it was not until March that he recovered sufficiently to appear in a couple of reserve games. It is hoped that he will make a return to full fitness in time for the start of the 2000-01 season.
Carlisle U (From trainee on 30/8/1986) FL 19+3 FLC 4 Others 1
Derby Co (£60,000 on 10/11/1987) FL 41+10/3 FLC 5+2 FAC 4 Others 5+1/2
Plymouth Arg (£85,000 on 23/7/1993) FL 131+3/3 FLC 3 FAC 8 Others 9
Gillingham (£45,000 on 30/10/1997) FL 74/2 FLC 3 FAC 3 Others 4

PAYNE Stephen (Steve) John
Born: Pontefract, 1 August 1975
Height: 5'11" Weight: 12.5
Club Honours: GMVC '95, '97; FAT '96
International Honours: E: SP-1
This versatile defender joined Chesterfield from Macclesfield in the summer of 1999 but soon fell victim to damaged ankle ligaments, causing him to miss much of the side's struggle against relegation. He returned to make several appearances as a forward in March, with some success, his good all-round awareness and speed off the mark enabling him to poach a couple of important goals.
Huddersfield T (From trainee on 12/7/1993)
Macclesfield T (Free on 23/12/1994) FL 71+6/2 FLC 6 FAC 5 Others 2
Chesterfield (Signed on 8/7/1999) FL 15+3/3 FLC 1 Others 0+1

PAYTON Andrew (Andy) Paul
Born: Whalley, 23 October 1967
Height: 5'9" Weight: 11.13
The Burnley striker was at the peak of his goalscoring prowess for much of 1999-2000. Hat-tricks against Colchester and Oxford were just the tip of the iceberg for a player for whom scoring goals is really the only reason to be on the pitch. Partnered normally by Andy Cooke but occasionally by Graham Branch, Andy had much better service than during the previous campaign and took full advantage. Never selfish, the local hero was always Burnley's man most likely to find the back of the net and the side's attacks were usually geared to that fact. The arrival of Ian Wright, coinciding with a three-game suspension for Payton, looked as if it might threaten his place, but he returned to score his 200th career goal at Wrexham and never looked back. His total of 27 league goals was the best by a Burnley player since 1965-66, and the joint-second best of the post-war era. His signing of a three-year contract should ensure that his career ends with the club he supported as a boy.
Hull C (From apprentice on 29/7/1985) FL 116+28/55 FLC 9+2/1 FAC 8 Others 3/1
Middlesbrough (£750,000 on 22/11/1991) FL 8+11/3 FAC 1+3
Glasgow Celtic (Signed on 14/8/1992) SL 20+16/15 SLC 3+2/5 SC 1+1 Others 3
Barnsley (Signed on 25/11/1993) FL 100+8/41 FLC 7/3 FAC 6+1/1
Huddersfield T (£350,000 on 4/7/1996) FL 42+1/17 FLC 7/3 FAC 2
Burnley (Signed on 16/1/1998) FL 97+3/55 FLC 2/1 FAC 5/2 Others 6/3

PEACOCK Darren
Born: Bristol, 3 February 1968
Height: 6'2" Weight: 12.12
Club Honours: WC '90
Darren was sent home from Blackburn's pre-season tour with a leg injury and it was the middle of September before the former Newcastle centre back featured in the first team in 1999-2000. He remains a doughty competitor and his experience was a considerable asset to the Rovers defence but there were signs that he was having difficulties with the pace of the game. Heavy defeats at Barnsley and Bolton early in the new year contributed to his demotion in favour of Marlon Broomes and, although he was restored to the starting line-up in March by new manager Graeme Souness, he was overlooked for the rest of the campaign.
Newport Co (From apprentice on 11/2/1986) FL 24+4 FLC 2 FAC 1 Others 1+1
Hereford U (Free on 23/3/1989) FL 56+3/4 FLC 6 FAC 6/1 Others 6
Queens Park R (£200,000 on 22/12/1990) F/PL 123+3/6 FLC 12/1 FAC 3 Others 2
Newcastle U (£2,700,000 on 24/3/1994) PL 131+2/2 FLC 13+1/2 FAC 11 Others 17+1
Blackburn Rov (Free on 2/7/1998) P/FL 42+5/1 FLC 4 FAC 6 Others 2

PEACOCK Gavin Keith
Born: Eltham, 18 November 1967
Height: 5'8" Weight: 11.8
Club Honours: Div 1 '93
International Honours: E: Yth; Sch
Gavin is the Queens Park Rangers captain as well as the club's most experienced player. When fit, he is an automatic choice for the central midfield position, his ability to make strong runs forward making him a potent

attacking threat. However, his appearances last season were limited after he suffered a number of injuries, the most serious being a pulled hamstring which he sustained in the away game at West Bromwich in October. This kept him out of action until the new year, apart from a three-game spell in November during which the injury recurred. He had started the season by scoring in five successive matches. Despite missing half of the campaign, his tally of ten goals was still an improvement on 1999-2000.

Queens Park R (From apprentice on 19/11/1984) FL 7+10/1 FAC 0+1
Gillingham (Loaned on 5/10/1987) FL 6 Others 2
Gillingham (£40,000 on 16/12/1987) FL 63+1/11 FLC 4 FAC 2 Others 3/1
Bournemouth (£250,000 on 16/8/1989) FL 56/8 FLC 6 FAC 2 Others 2
Newcastle U (£275,000 on 30/11/1990) FL 102+3/35 FLC 6/5 FAC 6/2 Others 3/4
Chelsea (£1,250,000 on 12/8/1993) PL 92+11/17 FLC 6/1 FAC 14+4/9 Others 7
Queens Park R (£1,000,000 on 22/11/1996) FL 132+6/30 FLC 8/3 FAC 7/2

PEACOCK Lee Anthony
Born: Paisley, 9 October 1976
Height: 6'0" Weight: 12.8
Club Honours: AMC '97
International Honours: S: U21-1; Yth

This strong and powerful marksman started the 1999-2000 season for Mansfield where he had left off at the end of the previous campaign, by scoring goals. He scored a hat-trick against Peterborough and would have had another against Shrewsbury a few weeks later but for a missed penalty. Lee was the Stags' leading goalscorer with eight in all competitions when Manchester City stepped in with a favourable offer in November and he moved to Maine Road. He made his debut for City as a substitute at Queens Park Rangers, where he showed promise and laid on an accurate through-ball for Kevin Horlock to score the equalising goal. His first full game came in the FA Cup win at Chester but, like most of the side that day, he struggled to make much impact. Lee was used only sporadically thereafter, but he linked up well with the midfield players on occasion, relishing the service provided by Ian Bishop in particular. He will be looking to make his mark in the Premiership next season.

Carlisle U (From trainee on 10/3/1995) FL 52+24/11 FLC 2+3 FAC 4+1/1 Others 6+4
Mansfield T (£90,000 on 17/10/1997) FL 79+10/29 FLC 4/1 FAC 4 Others 4/2
Manchester C (£500,000 on 5/11/1999) FL 4+4 FAC 1+1

PEACOCK Richard John
Born: Sheffield, 29 October 1972
Height: 5'10" Weight: 11.5

A right-sided midfield player, Richard missed long periods of Lincoln's 1999-2000 season after suffering a string of injuries. He began as first choice but lost his place after suffering a gashed shin at Northampton in August and then injured a knee ligament at Darlington in October. An attempted come-back against Peterborough in November lasted just 23 minutes, and it was not until the new year that he recovered full fitness. Richard regularly featured in the first-team squad for the rest of the campaign and was occasionally switched to the left side of midfield as the Imps attempted to find a balanced formation.

Hull C (Signed from Sheffield FC on 14/10/1993) FL 144+30/21 FLC 12+3/2 FAC 7+1/1 Others 5+1
Lincoln C (Free on 21/1/1999) FL 19+15/3 FLC 1+1/1

PEAKE Jason William
Born: Leicester, 29 September 1971
Height: 5'11" Weight: 12.10
International Honours: E: Yth; Sch

Rochdale's play-maker, Jason had an outstanding 1999-2000 season, showing why he is rated as one of the best passers in the lower divisions. This was confirmed by Opta Index, as he was selected in their "Division Three Team of the Season". They logged a divisional best of 1,323 successful passes. A near-ever-present, he passed 200 appearances for the club in his two spells at Spotland, and also weighed in with his share of goals. His overhead kick at Halifax in February was a "Goal of the Season" contender. Stop Press: Jason was reported to have signed for Plymouth at the beginning of July.

Leicester C (From trainee on 9/1/1990) FL 4+4/1 Others 1+1
Hartlepool U (Loaned on 13/2/1992) FL 5+1/1
Halifax T (Free on 26/8/1992) FL 32+1/1 FAC 1 Others 2
Rochdale (Signed on 23/3/1994) FL 91+4/6 FLC 3 FAC 5/2 Others 7/1
Brighton & Hove A (Signed on 30/7/1996) FL 27+3/1 FLC 2 FAC 2 Others 1
Bury (Free on 8/10/1997) FL 3+3
Rochdale (Free on 2/7/1998) FL 74+7/11 FLC 4 FAC 7/1 Others 6

PEARCE Dennis Anthony
Born: Wolverhampton, 10 September 1974
Height: 5'10" Weight: 11.0
Club Honours: Div 3 '98

Dennis had a frustrating time for Notts County in 1999-2000, being constantly affected by injuries and rarely getting a decent run in the starting line-up. Although very successful as a left back, he has found it difficult to adapt to the wing-back role despite the fact that he can overlap well down the left flank.

Aston Villa (From trainee on 7/6/1993)
Wolverhampton W (Free on 3/7/1995) FL 7+2 FLC 1 FAC 1
Notts Co (Free on 21/7/1997) FL 82+9/3 FLC 5+1 FAC 9+1 Others 3

PEARCE Alexander **Gregory (Greg)**
Born: Bolton, 26 May 1980
Height: 5'10" Weight: 11.7

The 1999-2000 season saw Greg rewarded for patient development in Chesterfield's reserves by a six-game run in the side before Christmas. Despite the fact that that was a difficult time for the team, he showed great composure at centre half, being both combative in the air and comfortable with the ball at his feet. Although he lost his place to the fit-again Ian Breckin, Greg did enough to promise much for the future. He has something of the young Paul Futcher about him, and would make an excellent eventual successor to Breckin at Saltergate.

Chesterfield (From trainee on 24/3/1998) FL 8+3 Others 0+1

PEARCE Ian Anthony
Born: Bury St Edmunds, 7 May 1974
Height: 6'3" Weight: 14.4
Club Honours: PL '95
International Honours: E: U21-3; Yth

Ian had the misfortune to tear a knee ligament playing for West Ham against Tottenham on the opening day of the 1999-2000 campaign. The injury required an operation and he missed the whole of the remainder of the season as a result. A tall and powerful central defender, he is good in the air and skilful on the ground. It is hoped he will be fit to resume a promising career by the start of the 2000-01 season.

Chelsea (From juniors on 1/8/1991) F/PL 0+4 Others 0+1
Blackburn Rov (£300,000 on 4/10/1993) PL 43+19/2 FLC 4+4/1 FAC 1+2 Others 6+1
West Ham U (£1,600,000 + on 19/9/1997) PL 64/3 FLC 5 FAC 7/1

PEARCE Stuart
Born: Hammersmith, 24 April 1962
Height: 5'10" Weight: 13.0
Club Honours: FLC '89, '90; FMC '89, '92
International Honours: E: 78; U21-1

This experienced defender joined West Ham on a free transfer in the summer of 1999 and was immediately appointed captain for the opening match of the new season. He impressed with his committed attitude in early games but then suffered a fractured leg playing against Watford at the beginning of September. After being sidelined for several months he eventually returned to first-team action last February, but after only three games back he fractured the same leg in the same place during the home game with Southampton on 8 March and was ruled out for the remainder of the campaign. Stuart remains a tough-tackling defender with hugely inspirational leadership qualities and a great enthusiasm for the game. He added to his impressive total of England caps when he received a surprise call-up for the European Championship qualifying game against Luxembourg last September – at the age of 37. It is hoped that he will make a full recovery from his injury and return to match fitness in time for the start of the 2000-01 campaign.

Coventry C (£25,000 from Wealdstone on 20/10/1983) FL 52/4 FAC 2
Nottingham F (£200,000 on 3/6/1985) F/PL 401/63 FLC 60/10 FAC 37/9 Others 24/6
Newcastle U (Free on 21/7/1997) PL 37 FLC 2 FAC 7 Others 5+1/1
West Ham U (Free on 5/8/1999) PL 8

PEARCEY Jason Kevin
Born: Leamington, 23 July 1971
Height: 6'1" Weight: 13.12
Club Honours: Div 3 '99

This competent shot-stopping 'keeper was second choice to Andy Woodman in the Brentford line-up until recalled to the first team early last March. However, after a run of just five games he suffered what appeared to be an innocuous "dead leg" at Wigan that caused him to be substituted. Muscle bleeding developed and Jason needed a series of operations to correct a problem that could potentially have cost him the leg. It is hoped he will make a full recovery and be back in action in the coming season.

Mansfield T (From trainee on 18/7/1989) FL 77 FLC 5 FAC 2 Others 7
Grimsby T (£10,000 on 15/11/1994) FL 49 FLC 3 FAC 1
Brentford (Free on 9/7/1998) FL 23 FLC 4 FAC 2 Others 1

PEDERSEN Tore
Born: Fredrikstad, Norway, 29 September 1969
Height: 6'0" Weight: 12.6
International Honours: Norway: 46

Tore joined Wimbledon on a free transfer from Eintracht Frankfurt under the Bosman ruling in the 1999 close season. He was to be the first of many Scandinavian signings made by Egil Olsen during his brief spell as the Dons' manager. A vastly experienced international defender, he lost no time at all in settling into the middle of the Wimbledon back line, instantly striking up an effective partnership with his new team-mates. However, he was cruelly struck down by a knee injury after looking very impressive in his first six games and didn't feature in the first team again during the remainder of the campaign.

Oldham Ath (£500,000 from SK Brann Bergen, Norway on 30/11/1993) PL 7+3 FAC 2+1 (£500,000 to SK Brann Bergen, Norway on 19/4/1994)
Blackburn Rov (£500,000 from St Pauli, Germany on 15/9/1997) PL 3+2 FLC 3 (£225,000 to Eintracht Frankfurt, Germany on 29/10/1998)
Wimbledon (Free on 1/7/1999) PL 6

PEER Dean
Born: Stourbridge, 8 August 1969
Height: 6'2" Weight: 12.4
Club Honours: AMC '91

This reliable midfield player was released by Northampton at the end of 1998-99, but was taken on again when the Cobblers suffered an injury crisis at the start of the new season. Dean was mainly used as cover, but always gave a good account of himself and never let the side down. When his short-term contract expired in January, he chose the security of an 18-month deal with Shrewsbury and was an ever-present in his midfield utility role for the remainder of the season. Although he has still to score his first Shrewsbury goal, Dean was regularly looking to get the team going with his defence-splitting passes. He joined the Shrews in difficult circumstances, and his ability on the ball should provide greater results in 2000-01.

Birmingham C (From trainee on 9/7/1987) FL 106+14/8 FLC 14+1/3 FAC 2+1 Others 11+1/1
Mansfield T (Loaned on 18/12/1992) FL 10 Others 1
Walsall (Free on 16/11/1993) FL 41+4/8 FLC 2 FAC 4+2 Others 3
Northampton T (Free on 22/8/1995) FL 97+31/6 FLC 6+2/1 FAC 7 Others 9+5
Shrewsbury T (Free on 26/1/2000) FL 19

PEMBRIDGE Mark Anthony
Born: Merthyr Tydfil, 29 November 1970
Height: 5'8" Weight: 12.0
International Honours: W: 36; B-2; U21-1; Sch

After a dream move to European giants Benfica turned sour due to political in-fighting at the Portuguese club, Mark was delighted when a move to Everton on the eve of the 1999-2000 season gave him the chance to return to the English Premiership, where his down-to-earth qualities of hard work and determination are fully appreciated. After only four appearances in Royal Blue a knee injury forced him out of action for a month, but on his return he enjoyed an unbroken run of 30 successive matches. Usually employed either in central midfield or wide on the left, Mark also showed his versatility on occasions at left wing back. He even weighed in with a couple of goals, at home to Sunderland and Bradford City. Joined at Everton by his national team manager, Mark Hughes, towards the end of the season, he was desperately disappointed that a hamstring injury ruled him out of Wales's high-profile friendly match against Brazil, but that was one of the few disappointments of a solid season for Mark.

Luton T (From trainee on 1/7/1989) FL 60/6 FLC 2 FAC 4 Others 4
Derby Co (£1,250,000 on 2/6/1992) FL 108+2/28 FLC 9/1 FAC 6/3 Others 15/5
Sheffield Wed (£900,000 on 19/7/1995) PL 88+5/12 FLC 6/1 FAC 7/1 (Free to Benfica, Portugal on 1/7/1998)
Everton (£800,000 on 6/8/1999) PL 29+2/2 FAC 5

PENNANT Jermaine
Born: Nottingham, 15 January 1983
Height: 5'6" Weight: 10.0
Club Honours: FAYC '00
International Honours: E: Yth

Jermaine became the youngest-ever Arsenal first-team player (at 16 years and 319 days) when he came on as a substitute in the Worthington Cup tie at Middlesbrough last November. One of the most exciting prospects at Highbury, he is a regular member of the U19 and reserve teams despite his age. A quick, attacking right-sided midfield player who possesses an abundance of natural talent, he is always looking to get forward. He has great dribbling skills, and is usually prepared to take on a number of opponents. He is a good crosser of the ball and has a powerful shot, which helps him score his fair share of goals. Currently progressing under the youth scheme at Arsenal, he is an intelligent player with good vision, for whom a bright future is predicted. Having previously been capped for England U15s, Jermaine appeared regularly for the U16 team last season.

Notts Co (Associated Schoolboy) FAC 0+1 Others 0+1
Arsenal (From trainee on 16/3/2000) FLC 0+1

PENNOCK Adrian Barry
Born: Ipswich, 27 March 1971
Height: 6'1" Weight: 13.5

Adrian had another good season for Gillingham in 1999-2000 and was a key member of the team that won promotion to the First Division via the play-offs. Apart from a brief spell out with hamstring trouble in December he was rarely absent from the Gills' defence during the campaign and he contributed a single goal, in the FA Cup first-round replay against Cheltenham. He is a steady and reliable player who is always looking to pass the ball. Adrian agreed a new two-and-a-half year contract with the Kent club last November.

Norwich C (From trainee on 4/7/1989) FL 1
Bournemouth (£30,000 on 14/8/1992) FL 130+1/9 FLC 9 FAC 12/1 Others 8
Gillingham (£30,000 on 4/10/1996) FL 119+1/2 FLC 6 FAC 9/1 Others 11/1

PENRICE Gary Kenneth
Born: Bristol, 23 March 1964
Height: 5'8" Weight: 11.7

The experienced midfielder, who also played a prominent role as assistant manager, made a limited number of appearances for Bristol Rovers, all as a substitute, in the early part of the 1999-2000 season. Coming on for Jamie Cureton at Wigan's JJB Stadium on 11 September, Gary was unfortunate not to score a hat-trick with some late goalscoring chances in the top-of-the-table clash.

Bristol Rov (Free from Mangotsfield on 6/11/1984) FL 186+2/54 FLC 11/3 FAC 11/7 Others 13+2/2
Watford (£500,000 on 14/11/1989) FL 41+2/17 FAC 4/1 Others 1/1
Aston Villa (£1,000,000 on 8/3/1991) FL 14+6/1
Queens Park R (£625,000 on 29/10/1991) F/PL 55+27/20 FLC 5+2/2 FAC 2+2/1 Others 1
Watford (£300,000 on 15/11/1995) FL 26+13/2 FLC 2+1 FAC 1 Others 1+1
Bristol Rov (Free on 18/7/1997) FL 48+21/6 FLC 2+1 FAC 7+4/2 Others 3

PEPPER Colin **Nigel**
Born: Rotherham, 25 April 1968
Height: 5'10" Weight: 12.4

Signed on extended loan from Aberdeen in December 1999, Nigel played just three games for Southend before a serious injury forced him to return to Scotland for rehabilitation. On his return, his midfield presence was more than useful to the Blues, with his stamina proving a great asset. One of four Shrimpers who had played under manager Alan Little at York, Nigel has stated that he is keen to return to Roots Hall in the new season.

Rotherham U (From apprentice on 26/4/1986) FL 35+10/1 FLC 1/1 FAC 1+1 Others 3+3
York C (Free on 18/7/1990) FL 223+12/39 FLC 16+2/3 FAC 12/2 Others 15+1
Bradford C (£100,000 on 28/2/1997) FL 47+5/11 FLC 4/1 FAC 1
Aberdeen (£300,000 on 26/11/1998) SL 11+3 SLC 1
Southend U (Loaned on 24/12/1999) FL 9+3/2

PERCASSI Gianluca (Luca)
Born: Milan, Italy, 25 August 1980
Height: 5'9" Weight: 11.0
International Honours: Italy: Yth

Gianluca joined Chelsea from Atalanta with Sam Dalla Bona in October 1998 in a double deal that rocked Italian football. A right back who was capped by Italy at youth international level, Luca faces a stiff battle to claim a first-team place as he is currently languishing behind Albert Ferrer, Bernard Lambourde and Mario Melchiot in the queue. He is a contender for the dubious distinction of having spent the least time on the pitch of any player to appear in first-team football during the 1999-2000 season, his only outing coming as a last-minute substitute in the FA Cup fourth-round tie against Nottingham Forest in January. Although his involvement last term was minimal, Gianluca is very highly regarded at Stamford Bridge and will certainly play a major role in the future.

Chelsea (Free from Atalanta, Italy on 5/8/1998) FLC 0+1 FAC 0+1

PEREZ Lionel
Born: Ardeche, France, 24 April 1967
Height: 5'11" Weight: 13.4

Having joined Scunthorpe on loan from Newcastle in October 1999, this flamboyant goalkeeper starred on his debut in the televised win at Burnley and went on to become a cult figure during what amounted to nearly three months at Glanford Park. Lionel left at the end of October to answer a goalkeeping crisis back at Newcastle but returned three days later for a second loan spell. He is a brilliant shot stopper, and his displays coincided with Iron's best spell of the season, so it was a disappointment when he elected to return to St James' Park at the end of December. The experienced former Sunderland 'keeper signed for Cambridge on loan on transfer deadline day. Once again becoming a firm favourite with the fans, he was a steadying influence on a young defence and played a vital role in helping Cambridge avoid relegation in the run-in to the end of the season.

Sunderland (£200,000 from Bordeaux, France on 21/8/1996) P/FL 74+1 FLC 2 FAC 4 Others 3
Newcastle U (Free on 2/7/1998)
Scunthorpe U (Loaned on 8/10/1999) FL 13
Cambridge U (Loaned on 23/3/2000) FL 9

PERKINS Christopher (Chris) Peter
Born: Nottingham, 9 January 1974
Height: 5'11" Weight: 11.0

Chris joined Hartlepool from Chesterfield in the 1999 close season on a Bosman free transfer. He is a useful left-sided full back or wing back who looked to be a quality signing for Pool manager Chris Turner. He had wanted a fresh start, but he soon became unsettled in the North-east and struggled to find his best form. Chris was loaned back to Chesterfield in December, where his fortunes dramatically improved and a permanent move was soon agreed. His return to Saltergate came with the club struggling against the drop, and Chris worked hard to turn things round from a left-sided midfield berth. His pace enabled him to cover a lot of ground and link well with forwards and defenders.

Mansfield T (From trainee on 19/11/1992) FL 3+5 Others 0+1
Chesterfield (Free on 15/7/1994) FL 136+11/3 FLC 9+1/1 FAC 13 Others 9+3/1
Hartlepool U (Free on 14/7/1999) FL 7+1 FLC 1
Chesterfield (Free on 7/10/1999) FL 29+2 Others 2+1

PERON Jean (Jeff) Francois
Born: St Omer, France, 11 October 1965
Height: 5'9" Weight: 11.0

This talented midfield player appeared regularly for Portsmouth at the beginning of the 1999-2000 season but then suffered damage to his calf muscle in mid-October that put him out of action for a month. Once fully fit, he moved to Second Division high-fliers Wigan on a short-term contract and the little Frenchman soon became popular with the fans. A left-footed player with pace, a lovely touch and a great ability to run with the ball, Jeff impressed with his vision and distribution and never let the side down when called into action. He was released at the end of the season.

Walsall (Free from Caen, France, via Lens and RC Strasbourg, on 22/8/1997) FL 38/1 FLC 5 FAC 4 Others 5
Portsmouth (£125,000 on 3/9/1998) FL 46+2/3 FLC 4 FAC 2
Wigan Ath (Free on 30/11/1999) FL 19+4 FAC 1 Others 1+1

PERPETUINI David Peter
Born: Hitchin, 26 September 1979
Height: 5'8" Weight: 10.8

This young left-sided defender or midfielder was one of the plus points of Watford's 1999-2000 season. An exciting player, David is a tough tackler and is always eager to get involved. Drafted in for his Premiership debut against Tottenham on Boxing Day, he responded by scoring a fine goal against Southampton two days later and demonstrated enough poise and confidence to ensure further appearances. A competitive, pacy player who likes to push forward down the wing and cross the ball, he seems ideally suited to the wing-back role.

Watford (From trainee on 3/7/1997) P/FL 13+1/1

PERRETT Russell
Born: Barton on Sea, 18 June 1973
Height: 6'3" Weight: 13.2

A centre back who is strong in the air and has considerable ability on the ground, Russell was never able to enjoy a good run in the Cardiff team in 1999-2000 following his move from Portsmouth during the 1999 close season. He was hit by a series of relatively minor knocks that nevertheless took time to heal, but a good pre-season and an injury-free run will surely see him installed at the heart of City's defence as they look to return to Division Two at the first attempt. Much to his frustration, Russell ended the season injured, having failed to recover from a kick to the knee. He nevertheless offered to play in the Bluebirds' vital end-of-season matches, but was ordered to rest by the club's medical staff. He made the transition from non-league Lymington to First Division football with Portsmouth earlier in his career and must now adapt to life in Division Three.

Portsmouth (Signed from Lymington on 30/9/1995) FL 66+6/2 FLC 5 FAC 4
Cardiff C (£10,000 on 21/7/1999) FL 26+1/1 FAC 5/1 Others 1

PERRY Christopher (Chris) John
Born: Carshalton, 26 April 1973
Height: 5'8" Weight: 11.1

An athletic central defender renowned for his surprising aerial ability, Chris joined Tottenham from Wimbledon in the 1999 close season to partner Sol Campbell at the centre of defence. Looking lean and pacy, he impressed from the outset with his confidence on the ball, forging a partnership with skipper Campbell in which one clearly understood what the other needed. Chris also proved his worth at set pieces and is a regular in the opposition 18-yard box at corners and free kicks. His efforts were rewarded with a fine headed goal at Bradford to earn Tottenham a draw and another in the UEFA Cup first round first leg against FC Zimbru. Chris appears to have secured his spot in the back four and will be looking forward to using his place at Tottenham to catch the eye of Kevin Keegan as the 2002 World Cup qualifying campaign gets under way.

Wimbledon (From trainee on 2/7/1991) PL 158+9/2 FLC 21 FAC 24/1
Tottenham H (£4,000,000 on 7/7/1999) PL 36+1/1 FLC 2 FAC 2 Others 4/1

PERRY Jason
Born: Caerphilly, 2 April 1970
Height: 6'0" Weight: 11.12
Club Honours: WC '92, '93; Div 3 '93
International Honours: W: 1; B-2; U21-3; Yth; Sch

The tough defender has been haunted by injury since moving to Hull in December 1998. Jason fought with typical tenacity during the 1999 pre-season to earn the number four squad number and a starting place for the opening-day trip to Exeter. His involvement lasted only 72 minutes as he damaged ankle ligaments. His only other 1999-2000 start came in the Auto Windscreens Shield at York in December. Jason is a real character in the dressing room and an excellent talker, whose experience has been put to good use when captaining the reserves. He turned down a £25,000 move to Chester City in January.

Cardiff C (From trainee on 21/8/1987) FL 278+3/5 FLC 22 FAC 14+1 Others 25+1
Bristol Rov (Free on 4/7/1997) FL 24+1 FLC 2 FAC 2+1 Others 2
Lincoln C (Free on 14/7/1998) FL 10+2 FLC 2 FAC 1
Hull C (Free on 18/12/1998) FL 8+1 Others 3+1

PERRY Mark James
Born: Ealing, 19 October 1978
Height: 5'11" Weight: 12.10
International Honours: E: Yth; Sch

Mark is one of a number of recent successes for the Queens Park Rangers youth policy. Although a regular in the reserves, he did not make a first-team appearance last season until March, when he came in as cover for the established defenders, who were ruled out by injury. Mark's performances were so impressive that he was able to hold on to his place for the remainder of the season. An excellent reader of the game, he is comfortable on the ball and tackles and passes effectively. His normal position is on the right side of the defence, but he can play in a more forward midfield role when needed.

Queens Park R (From trainee on 26/10/1995) FL 18+3/1 FLC 2

PESCHISOLIDO Paolo (Paul) Pasquale
Born: Scarborough, Canada, 25 May 1971
Height: 5'7" Weight: 10.12
Club Honours: Div 2 '99
International Honours: Canada: 35; U23-11

The 1999-2000 season was another disappointing one for Fulham's clever striker. Four league goals in 30 appearances (12 of them as a substitute) was a poor return for such a skilful forward, but it must be remembered that the majority of his goals in previous seasons have been solo efforts and First Division defences proved to be more difficult to penetrate. More creativity in the Fulham midfield might yet allow Paul the chance to show his true worth again. Paul played in four of Canada's games in the CONCACAF Gold Cup in the spring but missed the final with a groin injury. He has since added a further three caps and scored in the 2-1 victory over Honduras at the end of May, his first goal for his country since October 1996.

Birmingham C (£25,000 from Toronto Blizzards, Canada on 11/11/1992) FL 37+6/16 FLC 2/1 FAC 0+1 Others 1+1
Stoke C (£400,000 on 1/8/1994) FL 59+7/19 FLC 6/3 FAC 3 Others 5+1/2
Birmingham C (£400,000 on 29/3/1996) FL 7+2/1
West Bromwich A (£600,000 on 24/7/1996) FL 36+9/18 FLC 4+1/3 FAC 1
Fulham (£1,100,000 on 24/10/1997) FL 69+26/24 FLC 5+1/4 FAC 9+1/2 Others 2

PETHICK Robert (Robbie) John
Born: Tavistock, 8 September 1970
Height: 5'10" Weight: 11.12

An experienced attacking full back, Robbie enjoyed a good season in 1999-2000, providing many accurate crosses which led to goals for the Bristol Rovers strikers. The tough-tackling defender scored his first goal for the club on 22 January in an emphatic 5-0 victory at Oxford United, and was also on the score sheet on 1 April, notching Rovers' first goal in the thrilling 3-3 home draw with Stoke City with a powerful drive from just inside the penalty area.

Portsmouth (£30,000 from Weymouth on 1/10/1993) FL 157+32/3 FLC 13+3 FAC 9 Others 3+1
Bristol Rov (£15,000 on 19/2/1999) FL 49+1/2 FLC 4 FAC 1 Others 2

PETIT Emmanuel (Manu)
Born: Dieppe, France, 22 September 1970
Height: 6'1" Weight: 12.7
Club Honours: PL '98; FAC '98; CS '98, '99
International Honours: France: 41 (WC '98, UEFA '00)

Emmanuel has established himself as one of the finest midfield players in the Premiership, and his partnership with fellow French international Patrick Vieira is crucial to Arsenal's continued success. He is a strong, creative player with the ability to deliver passes and crosses with pin-point accuracy. Many goals have been scored as a result of his reading of the game. A great favourite with the Arsenal fans, Emmanuel is a strong tackler and an excellent striker of the dead ball. He is always liable to score and in the second game of the 1999-2000 season, at Derby, he netted with a superb strike from 30 yards out. Unfortunately, his season was again curtailed by injury. His left knee, injured at Sunderland in only the third game of the campaign, kept him out for ten weeks. When he returned it continued to give him problems, and he often played with the leg heavily strapped. Emmanuel added a further nine caps for France during the season, appearing three times in the Euro 2000 games including in the semi-final against Holland. He received a winners' medal for the tournament, although he was only an unused substitute for the final when *les Bleus* sensationally defeated Italy 2-1 with a "golden goal" strike from David Trezeguet.

Arsenal (£3,500,000 from AS Monaco, France, via ES Argues, on 25/6/1997) PL 82+3/9 FLC 3 FAC 13/2 Others 16+1

PETRACHI Gianluca
Born: Lecce, Italy, 14 January 1969
Height: 5'10" Weight: 11.9

This experienced Italian arrived at Nottingham Forest in the summer of 1999 with his colleague Salvatore Matrecano after spending the previous season in Serie A with Perugia. He was a regular in the Reds' side until losing his place through injury in mid-September but rarely featured after that. He is a right-sided midfield player with good pace and a combative approach to the game.

Nottingham F (£1,200,000 from Perugia, Italy on 6/8/1999) FL 10+3 FLC 2

PETRESCU Daniel (Dan) Vasile
Born: Bucharest, Romania, 22 December 1967
Height: 5'9" Weight: 11.9
Club Honours: FAC '97; FLC '98; ECWC '98
International Honours: Romania: 92

One of the last survivors of the Glenn Hoddle era at Chelsea, "Super Dan" maintained his reputation for snatching vital, match-winning goals in 1999-2000. He smashed the only goal of the game at Wimbledon – his sixth in total against his favourite opposition – and, perhaps more crucially, settled the tense Champions' League match against Galatasaray at Stamford Bridge with a coolly taken effort. This secured three valuable points which played a major role in Chelsea's progress to the second phase of the competition. Dan played on the right side of midfield in manager Gianluca Vialli's preferred 4-4-2 system; he has developed a great understanding with right back Albert Ferrer and the pair instigated many incisive attacks down that flank. The most-capped international while in Chelsea colours, Dan created another club record by becoming the first overseas player to make 200 first-team appearances for the Blues. A great favourite with the crowd, he signed a new two-year contract which, he hopes, will allow him to finish his career with his beloved Chelsea. Despite scoring a smartly taken goal at Old Trafford a month before the FA Cup final, a sub-standard performance saw him substituted by Vialli, and consequently cost him his place at Wembley to a rejuvenated Roberto Di Matteo. Dan has the priceless ability to ghost into space and punish unsuspecting defences. This was perfectly demonstrated at the France '98 World Cup when he materialised to score Romania's winner against England. Kevin Keegan's team ran into their nemesis again in a Euro 2000 Group A match in Charleroi, and he helped his country to a victory that ended England's hopes of reaching the quarter-finals. Although he missed the quarter-final through suspension, Dan was a regular for his country last season, winning a further nine caps during the campaign to take his total ever-closer to a century.

Sheffield Wed (£1,250,000 from Genoa, Italy, via Steava and Foggia, on 6/8/1994) PL 28+9/3 FLC 2 FAC 0+2
Chelsea (£2,300,000 on 18/11/1995) PL 134+16/18 FLC 8/2 FAC 20+1/1 Others 24+5/3

PETTERSON Andrew (Andy) Keith
Born: Freemantle, Australia, 29 September 1969
Height: 6'2" Weight: 14.7

The former Charlton goalkeeper signed permanent forms for Portsmouth last July after spending time on loan with the Fratton Park club during the 1998-99 season. Although second choice to Aaron Flahaven in the early games of 1999-2000, Andy was soon back in the starting line-up but found it difficult to keep a clean sheet playing behind a constantly changing defence. He lost his first-team place in mid-November and when new manager Tony Pulis arrived in the new year Andy went out on loan to Wolves until the end of the season. He is a good shot-stopping 'keeper, quick to leave his line when required and with a powerful kick.

Luton T (Signed on 30/12/1988) FL 16+3 FLC 2 Others 2
Ipswich T (Loaned on 26/3/1993) PL 1
Charlton Ath (£85,000 on 15/7/1994) P/FL 68+4 FLC 6 FAC 1 Others 4
Bradford C (Loaned on 8/12/1994) FL 3
Ipswich T (Loaned on 26/9/1995) FL 1
Plymouth Arg (Loaned on 19/1/1996) FL 6
Colchester U (Loaned on 8/3/1996) FL 5
Portsmouth (Loaned on 13/11/1998) FL 13
Portsmouth (Free on 5/7/1999) FL 17 FLC 1+1

PETTY Benjamin (Ben) James
Born: Solihull, 22 March 1977
Height: 6'0" Weight: 12.5
Club Honours: AMC '00

This promising young centre back, who is comfortable in any defensive role, continued to make steady progress with Stoke during 1999-2000. He was able to sustain one decent run in the first team and the rest of the time he was a regular on the bench. Ben coped well with his spell in the starting line-up and his confidence would undoubtedly grow further with additional opportunities. Gudjon Thordarson is an admirer but it seems the City manager would like to see him develop the ruthless streak that he appreciates in his central defenders. Ben certainly has the talent to maintain his development in 1999-2000.

Aston Villa (From trainee on 10/5/1995)
Stoke C (Free on 27/11/1998) FL 16+8 FLC 1 FAC 1 Others 3+3

PEYTON Warren
Born: Manchester, 13 December 1979
Height: 5'10" Weight: 10.9

Warren joined Rochdale last October and was immediately selected as a substitute for the FA Cup tie against Burton. However, he didn't come on and had to wait until the new year before rejoining the senior squad. Warren eventually made his debut in midfield against York in January, when three regulars were missing. It remained his only first-team action, and he was released in the summer.

Rochdale (Signed from Morecambe on 25/10/1999) FL 1

PHELAN Terence (Terry) Michael
Born: Manchester, 16 March 1967
Height: 5'8" Weight: 10.6
Club Honours: FAC '88
International Honours: RoI: 41: B-1; U23-1; U21-1; Yth

After finally shaking off a series of dreadful injury problems, the Republic of Ireland left back looked fit and sharp during an impressive pre-season for Everton and came on as a substitute on the opening day against treble winners Manchester United. Any hopes Terry may have harboured of this heralding a revival of his Everton career, however, were dashed when he was stretchered off in agony during a Worthington Cup tie at Oxford. Fortunately, the injury to his knee was not as severe as it had originally seemed, but he faced a lengthy spell on the sidelines and never received another chance in an Everton shirt. In October he went to Crystal Palace on loan and he remained at Selhurst Park for three months, the maximum permitted under Football League regulations. Sharp in the tackle and very quick, Terry filled the Eagles' troublesome left-back position and impressed with his obvious class. When Palace were unable to offer him a contract due to the financial restrictions affecting the club, Fulham quickly stepped in to sign him from Everton and he was to be one of the success stories of the season at Craven Cottage. The injury to Rufus Brevett at Manchester City in January meant that a left-sided defender was a top priority and Terry fitted the bill to perfection. His pace in an attacking role enabled him to make numerous overlaps to help out the midfielders, and his ability to get back to defend equally fast was a great tribute to his fitness. In addition, Terry scored the important first goal in the victories against Walsall and Sheffield United, giving him two goals in 17 games, a decent tally bearing in mind that he had previously scored only three times in 360 league matches during his long career. Recalled to the Republic of Ireland team for the end-of-season friendly with Scotland, he added further caps in the US Nike Cup matches in June.

Leeds U (From apprentice on 3/8/1984) FL 12+2 FLC 3 Others 2
Swansea C (Free on 30/7/1986) FL 45 FLC 4 FAC 5 Others 3
Wimbledon (£100,000 on 29/7/1987) FL 155+4/1 FLC 13+2 FAC 16/2 Others 8
Manchester C (£2,500,000 on 25/8/1992) PL 102+1/2 FLC 11 FAC 8/1
Chelsea (£900,000 on 15/11/1995) PL 13+2 FLC 0+1 FAC 8
Everton (£850,000 on 1/1/1997) PL 23+2 FLC 1+1 FAC 1
Crystal Palace (Loaned on 23/10/1999) FL 14
Fulham (Free on 3/2/2000) FL 17/2

PHILLIPS David Owen
Born: Wegburg, Germany, 29 July 1963
Height: 5'10" Weight: 12.5
Club Honours: FAC '87
International Honours: W: 62; U21-4; Yth

The former Welsh international missed the start of the 1999-2000 campaign at Lincoln with an ankle injury and then found his comeback delayed due to knee problems. When he recovered full fitness, David was used in a variety of positions including both right and left back and the right side of midfield but he was given few opportunities in the first team. He was released in the summer.

Plymouth Arg (From apprentice on 3/8/1981) FL 65+8/15 FLC 2+1 FAC 12+1 Others 4/1
Manchester C (£65,000 on 23/8/1984) FL 81/13 FLC 8 FAC 5 Others 5/3
Coventry C (£150,000 on 5/6/1986) FL 93+7/8 FLC 8 FAC 9/1 Others 5+1/2
Norwich C (£525,000 on 31/7/1989) F/PL 152/18 FLC 12 FAC 14/1 Others 8/1
Nottingham F (Signed on 20/8/1993) F/PL 116+10/5 FLC 16+1 FAC 10+2 Others 4
Huddersfield T (Free on 14/11/1997) FL 44+8/3 FAC 7
Lincoln C (Free on 25/3/1999) FL 15+2 FAC 1+1

PHILLIPS Gareth Russell
Born: Pontypridd, 19 August 1979
Height: 5'8" Weight: 9.8
International Honours: W: Yth; Sch

Gareth appeared regularly on the subs' bench for Swansea in the first half of 1999-2000. He appeared in the FA of Wales Premier Cup and went on to make the starting line-up for the Auto Windscreens Shield tie at Exeter. Having previously made his debut in midfield at Cambridge back in November 1996, he was used in the wing-back role at Exeter, a position he regularly occupied for the Swans' reserve team last season. He was offered a new one-year contract in May.

Swansea C (From trainee on 9/7/1998) FL 2+9 FLC 0+1 Others 1

PHILLIPS James (Jimmy) Neil
Born: Bolton, 8 February 1966
Height: 6'0" Weight: 12.7
Club Honours: Div 1 '97

The ever-dependable Bolton left back remains one of the most popular players at the Reebok, despite the fact that he now figures in the first team only sporadically. A skilful player with a cultured left foot who links up well with the attack, he had a good run in the side in the first half of last season, but the form of Robbie Elliott and Mike Whitlow meant that Jimmy spent much of the latter half of the season on the sidelines. The remainder of his appearances were mostly as a substitute, although the highlight of his season surely came in the 4-4 draw with Walsall, when he took possession on the wing and delicately lobbed the ball over the Walsall 'keeper. Jimmy may well say that his effort was actually intended as a cross, but the 12,000 Bolton fans who went wild at the time would probably disagree! A fine servant to the club, Jimmy was out of contract in the summer but was offered terms of re-engagement.

Bolton W (From apprentice on 1/8/1983) FL 103+5/2 FLC 8 FAC 7 Others 14
Glasgow R (£95,000 on 27/3/1987) SL 19+6 SLC 4 Others 4
Oxford U (£110,000 on 26/8/1988) FL 79/8 FLC 3 FAC 4 Others 2/1
Middlesbrough (£250,000 on 15/3/1990) F/PL 139/6 FLC 16 FAC 10 Others 5/2
Bolton W (£250,000 on 20/7/1993) P/FL 210+11/3 FLC 29+3/1 FAC 10 Others 9+2/2

Kevin Phillips

PHILLIPS Kevin Mark
Born: Hitchin, 25 July 1973
Height: 5'7" Weight: 11.0
Club Honours: Div 1 '99
International Honours: E: 5; B-1

The headlines continue to come thick and fast for the Sunderland striker who last season became the first player at the club since Dickie Davis in 1949-50 to top the goalscoring charts in English football's top division. After one particular TV pundit predicted that Kevin would struggle to get into double figures having made the step-up from Division One, the striker hit the net on 30 occasions, becoming only the third forward to reach this target since the Premiership's inception. His haul contained a variety of strikes: thirty-yarders with either foot, powerful headers, tap-ins and curling top-corner drives, proving that Kevin is one of the most complete strikers in English football. He is pacy, strong and good in the air for a man of his height, while his tremendous partnership with Niall Quinn continued to reap rich dividends for Sunderland and he wrote himself into Wearside folklore with three goals in two games against derby rivals Newcastle, including the winner at St James' Park in August and a late equaliser that rescued a point at the Stadium of Light in February. Kevin rounded off a great first season in the Premiership by finishing runner-up to Manchester United skipper Roy Keane in both the PFA and Football Writers' "Player of the Year" awards as well as being included in the PFA award-winning Premiership side. Naturally, he picked up the Sunderland supporters' and club "Player of the Year" awards. His excellent form won him further caps for England against Belgium, Argentina, Brazil and Malta, but although selected for the final 22 for Euro 2000 he did not feature in any of his country's games.

Watford (£10,000 from Baldock on 19/12/1994) FL 54+5/23 FLC 2/1 FAC 2 Others 0+2
Sunderland (£325,000 + on 17/7/1997) P/FL 104+1/82 FLC 5/2 FAC 5/4 Others 3/2

PHILLIPS Lee
Born: Aberdare, 18 March 1979
Height: 6'1" Weight: 12.2
International Honours: W: Yth

This young right back was given only a handful of chances at Cardiff last season and was released by the club in the summer. Ironically, he came on as a substitute during City's last game of the season when Jeff Eckhardt limped off and produced one of his best displays for the Bluebirds in a 1-0 victory. Lee is a product of Cardiff's youth development programme and earned a call-up to the Wales U21 squad, although he has yet to win his first cap at this level. However, he was not quite able to secure a regular first-team spot at Cardiff.

Cardiff C (From trainee on 14/7/1997) FL 11+5 FLC 2+1 Others 0+1

PHILLIPS Lee Paul
Born: Penzance, 16 September 1980
Height: 5'11" Weight: 12.0

With a series of injuries behind him, 1999-2000 was a season of development for the locally born Plymouth youngster, who made most of his Argyle appearances from the substitutes' bench. Lee is a promising attacker who has good pace, and will be looking for a more prominent role in the first team in the new season.

Plymouth Arg (From trainee on 9/7/1998) FL 14+30/1 FAC 3+3 Others 2+1

PHILLIPS Martin John
Born: Exeter, 13 March 1976
Height: 5'10" Weight: 11.10

Martin again failed to make the breakthrough to a regular first-team slot at Portsmouth in 1999-2000, only appearing in the starting line-up for the two Worthington Cup ties with Torquay under Alan Ball's management. Caretaker boss Bob McNab then gave him a couple of run-outs around the turn of the year before he returned to his first club Exeter City on loan. Martin is a skilful winger with the ability to beat defenders and deliver an accurate cross, and will be looking for regular first-team action in the 2000-01 season.

Exeter C (From trainee on 4/7/1994) FL 36+16/5 FLC 1+2 FAC 2+2 Others 1+5
Manchester C (£500,000 on 25/11/1995) P/FL 3+12 FLC 0+1
Scunthorpe U (Loaned on 5/1/1998) FL 2+1 Others 1
Exeter C (Loaned on 19/3/1998) FL 7+1
Portsmouth (£50,000 + on 27/8/1998) FL 4+20/1 FLC 2+2 FAC 0+1
Bristol Rov (Loaned on 24/2/1999) FL 2

PHILLIPS Steven (Steve) John
Born: Bath, 6 May 1978
Height: 6'1" Weight: 11.10

With Keith Welch's departure to Northampton Town in the close season, Steve began 1999-2000 as Bristol City's first choice between the sticks. He managed to retain his form and enthusiasm despite manager Tony Pulis continually stating that he was seeking another 'keeper, and was perhaps unfortunate to be eventually replaced when Billy Mercer was signed from Chesterfield. Though sometimes let down by poor distribution and a marked reluctance to come off his line, Steve gave a number of sound performances when coming in for the injured Mercer towards the end of the season.

Bristol C (Signed from Paulton Rov on 21/11/1996) FL 36 FLC 4 FAC 2 Others 1

PHILLIPS Wayne
Born: Bangor, 15 December 1970
Height: 5'10" Weight: 11.2
International Honours: W: B-1

This central midfield player returned to Wrexham from Stockport County in the summer of 1999 with great expectations but 1999-2000 proved an extremely frustrating season for him. He featured in the first four games but then suffered what appeared to be a minor ankle injury at Cardiff last August. The injury failed to clear up and eventually required an operation which in turn led to further problems including a build-up of calcium at the front of the ankle. He was ruled out for the rest of the campaign and will be hoping for better fortune in 2000-01.

Wrexham (From trainee on 23/8/1989) FL 184+23/16 FLC 17+1 FAC 12+2/1 Others 18+6/1
Stockport Co (£200,000 on 13/2/1998) FL 14+8 FLC 1 FAC 1
Wrexham (£50,000 on 23/7/1999) FL 3 FLC 1

PHILPOTT Lee
Born: Barnet, 21 February 1970
Height: 5'10" Weight: 12.9
Club Honours: Div 3 '91

Lee is a skilful left winger who can beat defenders almost at will when on form. He was a regular in Lincoln's line-up for the first part of the 1999-2000 season until being dropped after the 5-2 defeat at Mansfield in November. He then fell out of favour when the team switched from his preferred 4-4-2 formation and he made the starting line-up only three more times. Lee was released in the summer.

Peterborough U (From trainee on 17/7/1986) FL 1+3 FAC 0+1 Others 0+2
Cambridge U (Free on 31/5/1989) FL 118+16/17 FLC 10/1 FAC 19/3 Others 15/2
Leicester C (£350,000 on 24/11/1992) F/PL 57+18/3 FLC 2+1 FAC 6+2 Others 4+1
Blackpool (£75,000 on 22/3/1996) FL 51+20/5 FLC 5/1 FAC 4 Others 0+2
Lincoln C (Free on 21/7/1998) FL 33+14/3 FLC 1+2 FAC 1+2 Others 1+3

PICKERING Albert (Ally) Gary
Born: Manchester, 22 June 1967
Height: 5'10" Weight: 11.8

Having been released by Burnley at the end of 1998-99, the experienced right back had an unsuccessful pre-season trial with Hull in the summer of 1999. Having dropped down into non-league football at the beginning of the season, he joined Cambridge on a short-term contract last December but moved on to Third Division strugglers Chester in January without making a senior appearance for the U's. With his assured manner adding confidence to the Blues' rearguard, his seven-game Deva stay coincided with their best spell of a desperate season.

Rotherham U (£18,500 from Buxton on 2/2/1990) FL 87+1/2 FLC 6 FAC 9 Others 7
Coventry C (£80,000 on 27/10/1993) PL 54+11 FLC 5+1 FAC 4/1
Stoke C (£280,000 on 15/8/1996) FL 81+2/1 FLC 10 FAC 2
Burnley (Free on 17/12/1998) FL 21/1 (Free to Radcliffe Borough during 1999 close season)
Cambridge U (Free on 3/12/1999)
Chester C (Free on 14/1/2000) FL 7/1

PIERCY John William
Born: Forest Gate, 18 September 1979
Height: 5'11" Weight: 12.4
International Honours: E: Yth

A versatile midfielder, John made his first-team debut for Tottenham in the third-round Worthington Cup tie against Crewe last October. He looked sharp and confident despite his lack of experience and made an intelligent contribution. John then made three Premiership appearances over the next few weeks before continuing his development in the reserves. He will be looking to establish himself as a regular first-team squad member during the coming season.

Tottenham H (From trainee on 2/7/1998) PL 1+2 FLC 1

PIERRE Nigel Nigus
Born: Trinidad, 2 June 1979
Height: 5'11" Weight: 11.11
International Honours: Trinidad & Tobago: 4; U23

A young striker who had been highly recommended to Bristol Rovers by Manchester United manager Sir Alex Ferguson and Trinidad & Tobago team-mate Dwight Yorke, Nigel made his league debut when he came on as a substitute against Oldham Athletic in Rovers' emphatic 4-1 victory at Boundary Park last February. He made a good impression on Rovers' supporters on his home debut when replacing Mark Walters in the defeat of Wycombe Wanderers, but after an appeal for a work permit to the Department of Employment proved unsuccessful, he had to return to his former club Joe Public. Having made his international debut for Trinidad & Tobago against Morocco in January, Nigel won three more caps while with the Pirates, scoring the winner in the away leg of the World Cup qualifying tie against the Dominican Republic. Stop Press: Nigel won four more international caps in the warm-up games for Trinidad & Tobago's CONCACAF Group semi-final qualifying-

round matches for the 2002 World Cup, scoring in a 4-1 victory over Cuba and opening the possibility of a return to the UK in the coming season.
Bristol Rov (£50,000 from Joe Public, Trinidad on 24/2/2000) FL 1+2

PILKINGTON Kevin William
Born: Hitchin, 8 March 1974
Height: 6'1" Weight: 13.0
Club Honours: FAYC '92
International Honours: E: Sch
Kevin was mainly the number two goalkeeper at Port Vale in 1999-2000, but he featured in the starting line-up during the closing weeks of the season after Paul Musselwhite had suffered bruised ribs. Kevin had begun the campaign as first choice in the Vale goal, but after just three games he broke his leg in training and he did not return to first-team action until February. Unfortunately, he gave a goal away on his comeback against Stockport County and after one more game he was left out again, only for the injury to Musselwhite to bring an early recall. A tall 'keeper who is a good shot stopper, he was released on a free transfer at the end of the season.
Manchester U (From trainee on 6/7/1992) PL 4+2 FLC 1 FAC 1
Rochdale (Loaned on 2/2/1996) FL 6
Rotherham U (Loaned on 22/1/1997) FL 17
Port Vale (Free on 1/7/1998) FL 23 FLC 1 FAC 1

PINAMONTE Lorenzo
Born: Foggia, Italy, 9 May 1978
Height: 6'3" Weight: 13.4
Many Bristol City fans were incensed that the club allowed this promising striker to leave last February for a paltry £75,000. Having received limited first-team opportunities at Ashton Gate, Lorenzo had joined Brighton on loan in December 1999. The big centre forward from Foggia certainly worried Third Division defences, and he was rewarded with two goals in the home win over Exeter. Unusually for someone so tall, he was more at home when the ball was played to feet. Albion lost out in a protracted bidding battle, and Lorenzo eventually signed for Brentford. He was mostly restricted to outings from the subs' bench for the Bees but showed good potential as a target man and will be looking to win a place in the starting line-up for the coming season. He scored just one goal for Brentford, netting with a rasping left-foot shot from 20 yards against Millwall in April.
Bristol C (Free from Foggia, Italy on 18/9/1998) FL 3+4/1 FLC 1+2
Brighton & Hove A (Loaned on 17/12/1999) FL 8+1/2
Brentford (£75,000 on 4/2/2000) FL 5+10/1 Others 0+1

PINAULT Thomas
Born: Grasse, France, 4 December 1981
Height: 5'10" Weight: 11.1
A young French midfielder brought to Colchester by Mick Wadsworth in the summer of 1999 as a player for the future, Thomas looked impressive in pre-season and began the new campaign on the bench, making a handful of late substitute appearances in the early weeks before the upheaval following Wadsworth's resignation and the realities of life at the bottom of the league meant more experienced players were the order of the day. Once survival was assured, Thomas was given his first start at Wrexham on Easter Monday and looks a good prospect for the next few seasons.
Colchester U (Free from AS Cannes, France on 5/7/1999) FL 1+3 FLC 0+1

PINNOCK James Edward
Born: Dartford, 1 August 1978
Height: 5'9" Weight: 11.11
This young Gillingham striker again struggled to make the first-team squad in 1999-2000, featuring as a substitute in a couple of early-season games and making the starting line-up for the Auto Windscreens Shield tie with Torquay in early December. He had a loan spell with Dr Martens League club Margate in October but was otherwise restricted to reserve-team football. Although a proven scorer at junior level, he has yet to make the breakthrough at senior level at Priestfield and will be looking to do so in 2000-01.
Gillingham (From trainee on 2/7/1997) FL 0+9 FLC 1+2 Others 1+3

PISTONE Alessandro
Born: Milan, Italy, 27 July 1975
Height: 5'11" Weight: 12.1
International Honours: Italy: U21 (UEFA-U21 '96)
Alessandro had a difficult time during 1998-99 with only two full and one substitute appearances for Newcastle plus a loan spell at Venezia, and in the summer of 1999 he was informed by United manager Ruud Gullit that he did not have a future at the club. He was given a run-out in the pre-season friendly at Hartlepool, but collected an injury which sidelined him for a couple of months. During this time Bobby Robson took over the reins at St James' Park and declared that everyone would be given a fair chance, which encouraged Alessandro. He was recalled to the bench for the home UEFA Cup match against CSKA Sofia, although he did not come on, returning to senior football in England in October when he played for the Rest of the World in Sir Alex Ferguson's testimonial and then making a substitute appearance the following evening in the Worthington Cup tie at Birmingham, where he was booked for shirt tugging before he had even touched the ball! He was chosen to play against Derby at the end of October following an injury to Didier Domi, his first start for the club in over a year. Alessandro determinedly set about taking the opportunity to re-establish himself, and achieved just that with a series of fine displays at left back, switching occasionally to left wing back as the defensive formation was adjusted. He is sound defensively with impressive pace and a strong tackle, exhibits good control over the ball, and is always on the look-out for the chance to break down the wing and cross dangerous balls into the box. Although he is naturally right footed, he prefers to play on the left flank, but he can also perform well on the right, as he demonstrated in the 0-0 draw at Highbury at the end of October which brought United their first away point of the season. Alessandro was playing well, his form so impressive that he retained his place even when Domi returned to fitness, and missed out only on the Premiership and FA Cup games at home to Spurs with a calf strain and a hamstring problem respectively. Having established himself in the side, rebuilding his career, he was unlucky to suffer a broken fibula in his right leg in the derby at Sunderland, which was expected to end his season. However, he made a very rapid recovery, and returned to the side at the end of April for the final run-in. He scored his first-ever goal for the club in the derby at Middlesbrough, although a hamstring injury caused him to miss the final match at home to Arsenal. Stop Press: Alessandro was reported to have been transferred to Everton for a fee of £3 million at the beginning of July.
Newcastle U (£4,300,000 from Inter Milan, Italy, via Vicenza, Solbiatese and Crevalcore, on 31/7/1997) PL 45+1/1 FLC 1+1 FAC 8 Others 7

PITTS Matthew
Born: Middlesbrough, 25 December 1979
Height: 5'11" Weight: 12.8
Signed from Sunderland in the 1999 close season, Matthew featured at right back and on the right side of midfield for Carlisle last term. Still only 20, he produced some gutsy performances for the Cumbrians and will especially recall the two encounters with Leyton Orient. Matthew made his league debut against them in August, then scored his first goal in the return fixture in December.
Sunderland (From trainee on 25/6/1998)
Carlisle U (Free on 1/7/1999) FL 20+9/1 FLC 2 Others 2/1

PLATT Clive Linton
Born: Wolverhampton, 27 October 1977
Height: 6'4" Weight: 13.0
A big, tall striker, Clive joined Rochdale on loan from Walsall at the start of the 1999-2000 season. His athletic and skilful leading of the front line soon had the fans clamouring for him to be signed up and in September the move was made permanent. Clive was the star of Dale's remarkable comeback to win 4-3 at Brighton in December, when he scored twice in the last ten minutes. He also suffered a couple of lean spells, when his confidence deserted him. However, he ended the season as he had begun it and is a great prospect for the future.
Walsall (From trainee on 25/7/1996) FL 18+14/4 FLC 1+2/1 FAC 0+1 Others 1+6
Rochdale (£70,000 + on 5/8/1999) FL 31+10/9 FAC 3/1 Others 4

PLATT David Andrew
Born: Chadderton, 10 June 1966
Height: 5'10" Weight: 11.12
Club Honours: PL '98; FAC '98
International Honours: E: 62; B-3; U21-3
The former England captain was appointed player-manager of Nottingham Forest in

July 1999. He made a couple of early-season appearances as a substitute and started his first game at Sheffield United last October, when he was sent off in injury time. Following this he wisely decided to focus on management and did not pick himself again during 1999-2000.

Manchester U (Signed from Chadderton on 24/7/1984)
Crewe Alex (Free on 25/1/1985) FL 134/55 FLC 8/4 FAC 3/1 Others 7
Aston Villa (£200,000 on 2/2/1988) FL 121/50 FLC 14/10 FAC 4/2 Others 6/6 (£5,500,000 to Bari, Italy on 20/7/1991)
Arsenal (£4,750,000 from Sampdoria, Italy on 14/7/1995) PL 65+23/13 FLC 7+3/2 FAC 3+3 Others 2+2 (Retired on 23/7/1998)
Nottingham F (Free on 3/8/1999) FL 1+2

PLATTS Mark Anthony
Born: Sheffield, 23 May 1979
Height: 5'8" Weight: 11.13
International Honours: E: Yth; Sch

For this talented Torquay left-sided midfielder, 1999-2000 was a season bedevilled by a series of niggling injuries. He showed that he has an astute footballing brain, and in the future he should score many more goals with his powerful left foot. Mark became Sheffield Wednesday's youngest-ever outfield player when he made his Premiership debut in February 1996.

Sheffield Wed (From trainee on 16/10/1996) PL 0+2
Torquay U (Free on 9/3/1999) FL 14+16/1 FLC 1+1 FAC 0+2 Others 2

PLUMMER Christopher (Chris) Scott
Born: Isleworth, 12 October 1976
Height: 6'3" Weight: 12.9
International Honours: E: U21-5; Yth

A tall central defender, Chris has been with Queens Park Rangers for a number of years, having progressed through the club's youth set-up. His first-team appearances have been limited due to the regular central defenders holding their places. However, last season he had an extended run in the side between November and January due to the non-availability of Karl Ready, Matthew Rose and Danny Maddix. He regained his place in March and had played in over 20 games by the end of the campaign – his highest tally in one season for the club. Chris is assured on the ball and his height can cause problems for opposing teams at corner and free kicks, though he is still waiting to score his first goal.

Queens Park R (From trainee on 1/7/1994) F/PL 29+5 FLC 2 FAC 3

POINTON Neil Geoffrey
Born: Warsop, 28 November 1964
Height: 5'10" Weight: 12.10
Club Honours: Div 1 '87; CS '87

After skippering Walsall to promotion in 1998-99 Neil began to feel the pace as the Saddlers fought to stay afloat in the First Division last season but never shirked a challenge and held on to his spot on the left flank of the defence until replaced by Diego Padula in November. He then moved on to Chesterfield for a vain battle against relegation, making his debut in the 1-0 win over Brentford that ended the club's record 21-match winless streak. He slotted straight in at left back, looking classy and composed, with a conclusive tackle and sound positional awareness. His experience was undoubtedly vital to any chance of avoiding the drop but injury caused his absence during the crucial run-in to the season's end. Neil was released in the summer.

Scunthorpe U (From apprentice on 10/8/1982) FL 159/2 FLC 9/1 FAC 13 Others 4
Everton (£75,000 on 8/11/1985) FL 95+7/5 FLC 6+2 FAC 16+2 Others 9+3
Manchester C (£600,000 on 17/7/1990) FL 74/2 FLC 8 FAC 4 Others 4
Oldham Ath (£600,000 on 10/7/1992) F/PL 92+3/3 FLC 5 FAC 7+1/2
Heart of Midlothian (£50,000 on 6/10/1995) SL 64+3/3 SLC 7 SC 5 Others 2
Walsall (Free on 22/7/1998) FL 61 FLC 5+1 FAC 2 Others 6
Chesterfield (Free on 7/1/2000) FL 9+1 Others 2

POLLET Ludovic
Born: Vieux-Conde, France, 18 June 1970
Height: 6'1" Weight: 12.11

This French central defender joined Wolves from Le Havre on an extended loan in September 1999 and made his debut as a substitute at home to Huddersfield. Ludovic did not seem at ease in the 4-4-2 formation, but got his chance to impress when the system was changed shortly afterwards. He soon looked a class import: his tackles were well timed, his distribution was good and he was strong in the air. The only blemish was a sending-off for two bookable offences at Fulham. Wolves manager Colin Lee's plan to borrow him to the end of the season was revised as he feared another club might come in, and the Wolves board were happy to make the deal permanent. Ludovic was outstanding in the 4-1 eclipse of Manchester City, and even scored in two successive games later in December. By now it did not matter which system Wolves played, they could rely on the Frenchman. It was a shock when a moment of slackness by him cost a goal at Norwich in April. Nevertheless, he was voted the club's "Player of the Season" by the fans.

Wolverhampton W (Free from Le Havre, France on 10/9/1999) FL 38+1/5 FAC 3

POLLITT Michael (Mike) Francis
Born: Farnworth, 29 February 1972
Height: 6'4" Weight: 14.0

Rated by many as the best goalkeeper in Division Three and the only Miller selected in the 1999-2000 PFA award-winning divisional team, Mike played a major role in Rotherham's promotion success and was voted the club's "Player of the Year". He pulled off many vital saves at crucial times, while his handling was always immaculate. The confident custodian topped the century mark for successive United appearances, no mean feat for a 'keeper. Always brave, he commands his area superbly and, at times, is as good as a sweeper. Stop Press: Mike was reported to have signed for Chesterfield during the summer.

Manchester U (From trainee on 1/7/1990)
Bury (Free on 10/7/1991)
Lincoln C (Free on 1/12/1992) FL 57 FLC 5 FAC 2 Others 4
Darlington (Free on 11/8/1994) FL 55 FLC 4 FAC 3 Others 5
Notts Co (£75,000 on 14/11/1995) FL 10 Others 2
Oldham Ath (Loaned on 29/8/1997) FL 16
Gillingham (Loaned on 12/12/1997) FL 6
Brentford (Loaned on 22/1/1998) FL 5
Sunderland (£75,000 on 23/2/1998)
Rotherham U (Free on 14/7/1998) FL 92 FLC 4 FAC 7 Others 5

POLLOCK Jamie
Born: Stockton, 16 February 1974
Height: 5'11" Weight: 14.0
Club Honours: Div 1 '95, '97
International Honours: E: U21-3; Yth

Jamie did not start the 1999-2000 season in the Manchester City side owing to strong competition from the wealth of midfield players at the club. His first full game was at Burnley in the second leg of the Worthington Cup tie between the clubs after City had won the first 5-0. After a run of consistently good form in the reserves, Jamie forced his way into the first team for the away win at Port Vale at the end of October. For the next game, against Portsmouth at Maine Road, he was back on the subs' bench, but he came on in the 60th minute and scored City's fourth goal right at the death. His next appearance was at Charlton, where he produced an excellent performance which earned him a run of ten games. Out of contention during January and February, he was then recalled at Crystal Palace in March and held his place for another six matches. His goal at Stockport County was well worked: he ran on to a through pass and confidently placed the ball wide of the 'keeper. Jamie is a terrier-like player, who has a talent for finding space to receive the ball and enjoys running at defences head on. He will always give 100 per cent effort, and his all-action style is guaranteed to please the crowd.

Middlesbrough (From trainee on 18/12/1991) F/PL 144+11/17 FLC 17+2/1 FAC 13+1/1 Others 4+1 (Free to Osasuna, Spain on 6/9/96)
Bolton W (£1,500,000 on 22/11/1996) F/PL 43+3/5 FLC 4+1/1 FAC 4/2
Manchester C (£1,000,000 on 19/3/1998) FL 49+9/5 FLC 5 FAC 4+1 Others 1+1

POLSTON John David
Born: Walthamstow, 10 June 1968
Height: 5'11" Weight: 11.12
International Honours: E: Yth

A series of niggling injuries restricted John's first-team appearances for Reading last season, but when he did play the central defender showed touches of real class. Whether lining up alongside Barry Hunter or Linvoy Primus he excelled as a covering centre back and could win the ball reliably, either on the ground or in the air. He scored his only goal of the season with an injury-time equaliser in the 1-1 draw with Oldham, and also collected a Berks & Bucks Senior Cup runners-up medal with the reserve team.

Tottenham H (From apprentice on 16/7/1985) FL 17+7/1 FLC 3+1
Norwich C (£250,000 on 24/7/1990) F/PL 200+15/8 FLC 20+1/2 FAC 17+1/1 Others 9/1
Reading (Free on 6/7/1998) FL 16+2/1 FLC 1 FAC 4 Others 1

POOLE Kevin
Born: Bromsgrove, 21 July 1963
Height: 5'10" Weight: 12.11
Club Honours: FLC '97

Kevin began 1999-2000 as the first-choice 'keeper for Birmingham City but then lost his place for the Worthington Cup tie against Newcastle United. He returned to the first team the following month when Ian Bennett was out of favour but was again replaced by his rival following a 1-0 defeat at Nottingham Forest last December. Kevin then had the misfortune to fall victim to a groin problem just as Bennett broke his thumb. The injury required a hernia operation and kept him out until the summer. He is an excellent shot stopper who performed consistently whenever given his chance.

Aston Villa (From apprentice on 26/6/1981) FL 28 FLC 2 FAC 1 Others 1
Northampton T (Loaned on 8/11/1984) FL 3
Middlesbrough (Signed on 27/8/1987) FL 34 FLC 4 FAC 2 Others 2
Hartlepool U (Loaned on 27/3/1991) FL 12
Leicester C (£40,000 on 30/7/1991) F/PL 163 FLC 10 FAC 8 Others 12
Birmingham C (Free on 4/8/1997) FL 55 FLC 6 FAC 2 Others 2

POOM Mart
Born: Tallin, Estonia, 3 February 1972
Height: 6'4" Weight: 13.6
International Honours: Estonia: 71

The Estonian international goalkeeper had his most successful season in English football to date in 1999-2000, having established himself as an automatic selection in the Derby side once a niggling wrist injury had cleared up. His height makes him a commanding presence in the penalty area and his reach enabled him to produce some outstanding saves, particularly towards the close of the season, Mart often single-handedly keeping his team in the game. An injury-time save in the vital drawn match at Bradford over Easter further endeared him to the Derby supporters, who went on to select him as the club's "Player of the Year" by an overwhelming margin. He remained a first choice for the Estonian national team, winning further caps against the Faroe Isles, Scotland, Luxembourg and Belarus.

Portsmouth (£200,000 from FC Wil, Switzerland on 4/8/1994) FL 4 FLC 3 (Signed by Tallin SC, Estonia on 9/5/1996)
Derby Co (£500,000 on 26/3/1997) PL 83+2 FLC 6 FAC 5

Mart Poom

POPPLETON David John
Born: Doncaster, 19 December 1979
Height: 5'6" Weight: 10.7
Club Honours: FAYC '98

This young central midfield player signed a short-term contract for Lincoln in the summer of 1999 after being released by Everton. He made his first-team debut at Barnsley in a Worthington Cup tie, but after showing some neat touches he suffered a back injury that put him out of contention. David returned to the first team at Brighton in November but was released the following month and later dropped into non-league football, first with Bradford Park Avenue and later at Ilkeston Town.

Everton (From trainee on 4/7/1997)
Lincoln C (Free on 9/8/1999) FL 4+1 FLC 1+1

PORTER Andrew (Andy) Michael
Born: Holmes Chapel, 17 September 1968
Height: 5'9" Weight: 12.0
Club Honours: AMC '93, '99

Andy made a handful of appearances for Wigan during the early stages of the 1999-2000 season. Displaying his usual aggression in the middle of the park, he never let the side down when called upon but, finding his first-team opportunities increasingly limited, he went to Mansfield on loan in October to cover for injuries and stiffen up the midfield. However, having played in half a dozen matches he returned to Wigan after injury prematurely brought the loan spell to an end. Known as "the footballing farmer", as he has an interest in the family farming business, the vastly experienced midfielder agreed to a further two-month loan spell at struggling Chester in February. His strong tackling added some steel to the Blues' engine room, but he was unable to halt City's slide towards relegation.

Port Vale (From trainee on 29/6/1987) FL 313+44/22 FLC 22+1 FAC 20+4/3 Others 26+2/1
Wigan Ath (Free on 28/7/1998) FL 8+13/1 FLC 0+3 FAC 1 Others 3+3
Mansfield T (Loaned on 22/10/1999) FL 5 FAC 1
Chester C (Loaned on 5/2/2000) FL 16

POTTER Daniel (Danny) Raymond John
Born: Ipswich, 18 March 1979
Height: 6'0" Weight: 13.4

An accomplished goalkeeper, Danny suffered

a serious knee injury in Exeter's pre-season game against Charlton that kept him out of action for the majority of the 1999-2000 season. Having Stuart Naylor and Jason Matthews in such fine form made it hard for him to break back into the side, so he went on loan to Weymouth and Salisbury. Danny was one of 13 Grecians released at the end of the season.

Colchester U (Free from Chelsea juniors on 3/10/1997)
Exeter C (Free on 8/8/1998) FL 9

POTTER Graham Stephen
Born: Solihull, 20 May 1975
Height: 6'1" Weight: 11.12
International Honours: E: U21-1; Yth

Mainly a squad player at West Bromwich in 1999-2000, Graham was brought into the first team when injuries intervened to play as a left wing back or wide down the left by both Brian Little and Gary Megson. A willing competitor when called into action, he was never a regular in the side but nevertheless always gave 100 per cent effort out on the park. Injuries reduced his opportunities but towards the end of the season he was down to third choice following the arrival of five new faces at the Hawthorns, four of them capable of occupying the same positions as Graham. A dearth of left-sided players prompted Reading to bring Graham to the Madejski Stadium on loan in mid-season. He did reasonably well in a team which was struggling at the time of his arrival, but was ineligible to play in FA Cup matches so his value to the Royals was diminished. He made five appearances and was anxious to secure a contract with the club but returned to West Bromwich after a month when his loan period was up. He was released by Albion during the summer. Stop Press: Graham was reported to have signed for York at the beginning of July.

Birmingham C (From trainee on 1/7/1992) FL 23+2/2 FAC 1 Others 6
Wycombe W (Loaned on 17/9/1993) FL 2+1 FLC 1 Others 1
Stoke C (£75,000 on 20/12/1993) FL 41+4/1 FLC 3+1 FAC 4 Others 5
Southampton (£250,000 + on 23/7/1996) FL 2+6 FLC 1+1
West Bromwich A (£300,000 + on 14/2/1997) FL 31+12 FLC 0+3 FAC 1
Northampton T (Loaned on 24/10/1997) FL 4 Others 1
Reading (Loaned on 2/12/1999) FL 4 Others 1

POTTER Lee
Born: Salford, 3 September 1978
Height: 5'11" Weight: 12.10

Lee continued at the start of 1999-2000 where he had left off previously, as a regular goalscorer for Bolton reserves. His only first-team appearance for the Wanderers came as a substitute in the Worthington Cup tie against Gillingham, and it was no surprise when he was loaned to Halifax Town in December. Halifax later made the deal permanent for £300,000. Lee scored on his debut at Chester, and a superbly taken diving header followed away at Rotherham, but then the goals dried up as he spent a spell on the substitutes' bench. The experience of Third Division football will have done him a power of good, and he can be expected to make a greater impact during the coming season.

Bolton W (From trainee on 3/7/1997) FLC 0+1
Halifax T (£30,000 on 17/12/1999) FL 13+6/2

POTTS Steven (Steve) John
Born: Hartford, USA, 7 May 1967
Height: 5'8" Weight: 10.11
International Honours: E: Yth

Although Steve is coming towards the end of his career he showed that he could still be relied upon to do a competent job for West Ham in 1999-2000. He appeared in the first eight Premiership games without letting the team down but then dropped out of the starting line-up. Returning to regular action in the new year, he suffered an achilles injury in the replayed Worthington Cup tie against Aston Villa and did not feature again until the final few games of the season. Steve is a dependable defender who reads the game well, has good pace and is quick in the tackle.

West Ham U (From apprentice on 11/5/1984) F/PL 360+31/1 FLC 37+2 FAC 41+1 Others 19+1

POUNEWATCHY Stephane Zeusnagapa
Born: Paris, France, 10 February 1968
Height: 6'1" Weight: 15.2
Club Honours: AMC '97

Brought over from France on trial by Scunthorpe in January 2000, this experienced centre back made his debut in the Auto Windscreens Shield game against Chesterfield, where his defensive experience, strength and tackling were immediately shown off. Suffering from flu, he went back to France for three weeks before returning to Glanford Park. His second spell with the club ended early, however, when he failed to report for training for two days and was released.

Carlisle U (Free from Gueugnon, France on 6/8/1996) FL 81/3 FLC 7 FAC 5 Others 9/2
Dundee (Free on 1/7/1998) SL 2+1 SLC 1
Port Vale (Free on 28/8/1998) FL 2
Colchester U (Free on 17/2/1999) FL 15/1 (Freed during 1999 close season)
Scunthorpe U (Free on 24/1/2000) Others 1

POUTON Alan
Born: Newcastle, 1 February 1977
Height: 6'0" Weight: 12.8

This highly promising young midfielder joined Grimsby from York City for £150,000 in August 1999 after impressing during a short loan spell. Although he was employed mainly as a substitute, some fine performances established him firmly as an integral part of the senior squad. Hard running, strong tackling and capable of some devastating runs into the box, he gave a particularly outstanding performance in the goalless home draw against Huddersfield in April as the Mariners fought to keep clear of the relegation zone.

Oxford U (Free from Newcastle U juniors on 7/11/1995)
York C (Free on 8/12/1995) FL 79+11/7 FLC 5+1 FAC 5/1 Others 2
Grimsby T (£150,000 on 5/8/1999) FL 19+16/1 FLC 3+2 FAC 1+1

POWELL Christopher (Chris) George Robin
Born: Lambeth, 8 September 1969
Height: 5'10" Weight: 11.7
Club Honours: Div 1 '00

Charlton's first-choice left back, Chris played a leading role as Charlton raced to the First Division championship in 1999-2000 and was also selected by his fellow professionals for the PFA award-winning First Division side. A player who always looks comfortable on the ball, is calm under pressure and has good control, he likes to push forward down the left wing and cross the ball from the byline, or cut inside, and was also used as a wing back on occasions. Chris is still looking for his first goal for the club, but came close in a couple of games. He shows good awareness, distributes the ball well out of defence and rarely has a poor game, and seems likely to have little difficulty in readjusting to Premiership football.

Crystal Palace (From trainee on 24/12/1987) FL 2+1 FLC 0+1 Others 0+1
Aldershot (Loaned on 11/1/1990) FL 11
Southend U (Free on 30/8/1990) FL 246+2/3 FLC 13 FAC 8 Others 21
Derby Co (£750,000 on 31/1/1996) F/PL 89+2/1 FLC 5 FAC 5/1
Charlton Ath (£825,000 on 1/7/1998) P/FL 78 FLC 3 FAC 5

POWELL Darren David
Born: Hammersmith, 10 March 1976
Height: 6'3" Weight: 13.2
Club Honours: Div 3 '99

This huge, hard-working Brentford central defender formed an excellent partnership with Hermann Hreidarsson in the centre of the Bees' back four in the early part of the 1999-2000 campaign. However, he suffered a groin injury last November that kept him out of action for two months and never quite returned to his early-season form. Darren is still learning in the professional game but has a growing reputation and there has already been speculation about a transfer to a bigger club.

Brentford (£15,000 from Hampton on 27/7/1998) FL 69/4 FLC 5 FAC 2 Others 3+1/1

POWELL Darryl Anthony
Born: Lambeth, 15 November 1971
Height: 6'0" Weight: 12.10
International Honours: Jamaica: 6

The underrated Derby County captain, who plays the anchor role in midfield, allowing the more naturally creative elements of the team to perform, had another consistent season in 1999-2000. An almost automatic first-team selection, his enthusiasm for the game would be difficult to match but his is the sort of role where a great deal of hard work is taken for granted by many fans. Darryl does not find the net too often but scored what he admitted was "a fluke" to win the local derby at Filbert Street in December. He also shows a refreshing aptitude for dealing with the media in his role as team spokesman. He added a further cap for Jamaica when appearing in a friendly against Canada last September.

Portsmouth (From trainee on 22/12/1988) FL 83+49/16 FLC 11+3/3 FAC 10 Others 9+5/4
Derby Co (£750,000 on 27/7/1995) F/PL 137+20/8 FLC 7+1 FAC 7+1

POWELL Paul
Born: Wallingford, 30 June 1978
Height: 5'8" Weight: 11.6

As predicted when Oxford were relegated the previous season, Paul became one of the best left-sided players in the Second Division and caused havoc virtually every time he got the ball on his left foot in a wide position. Most of the season Paul was used as a left back but he did have spells on the left side of midfield, and late in the season as a left winger. A pacy player with silky dribbling skills, he ended the season as the club's second-highest scorer with 12 goals, and while some of them were from the penalty spot he did score a number of spectacular efforts, as seen against Nottingham Forest in the FA Cup, as well as a vital goal at Bristol City at the end of the campaign to help keep Oxford up. Many supporters are already resigned to losing their star asset before too long as the scouts were queueing up to watch him by the end of the season. Paul deservedly won the club's "Player of the Year" award, finishing well ahead of his nearest challengers.
Oxford U (From trainee on 2/7/1996) FL 91+17/10 FLC 5+2 FAC 7+1/3 Others 2+2/3

Paul Powell

POWER Graeme Richard
Born: Harrow, 7 March 1977
Height: 5'10" Weight: 10.10
International Honours: E: Yth; Sch

Used both in the centre of the defence and at left back by Exeter, this hard-working and dependable player had another consistent season in 1999-2000. Although he has yet to score a senior goal, Graeme was once again a valued member of the team.
Queens Park R (From trainee on 11/4/1995)
Bristol Rov (Free on 15/7/1996) FL 25+1 FAC 1 Others 1+2
Exeter C (Free on 6/8/1998) FL 68+1 FLC 3 FAC 7 Others 4

POWER Lee Michael
Born: Lewisham, 30 June 1972
Height: 6'0" Weight: 11.10
International Honours: RoI: B-1; U21-13; Yth

Lee scored his only Halifax goal of 1999-2000 against Torquay at the end of August, and his appearances were to be very limited. He left the full-time game in November to go into business and joined Dr Martens League club Boston United, helping them to the championship and a long-awaited return to the Conference.
Norwich C (From trainee on 6/7/1990) F/PL 28+16/10 FLC 1 FAC 0+1 Others 0+2
Charlton Ath (Loaned on 4/12/1992) FL 5
Sunderland (Loaned on 13/8/1993) FL 1+2 FLC 2/1
Portsmouth (Loaned on 15/10/1993) FL 1+1 Others 1
Bradford C (£200,000 on 8/3/1994) FL 14+16/5 FLC 0+2 FAC 0+2/1 Others 1+1/1
Peterborough U (£80,000 on 26/7/1995) FL 25+13/6 FLC 2+2 FAC 1+2 Others 1/1
Dundee (Free on 14/12/1996) SL 9+1/4 SC 3/2
Hibernian (Free on 20/3/1997) SL 9+2/2 SLC 1
Plymouth Arg (Free on 4/8/1998) FL 7+9 FLC 1+1 Others 0+1
Halifax T (Signed on 11/12/1998) FL 17+8/5 FLC 0+2

POYET Gustavo (Gus) Augusto
Born: Montevideo, Uruguay, 15 November 1967
Height: 6'2" Weight: 13.0
Club Honours: ECWC '98; ESC '98; FAC '00
International Honours: Uruguay: 31

Whenever Gustavo takes a knock, no matter how slight, a collective intake of breath is felt around the crowd at Chelsea's Stamford Bridge ground. He had catastrophic luck with injuries during his first two seasons with the club and Blues fans know how important this influential midfielder is to Chelsea's quest for silverware. He started the 1999-2000 season with a bang: in the opening Premiership match against Sunderland he notched Chelsea's first goal of the campaign with a header from a corner and later, even though the season was just 78 minutes old, he scored possibly the "Goal of the Season" with a mid-air, bicycle-kick volley. Three days later he scored another, only fractionally less spectacular, goal: a left-footed curling drive from the edge of the box against Skonto Riga in the Blues' initial Champions' League game. In October he produced a "Man of the Match" performance in Chelsea's televised 5-0 demolition of Manchester United. Gustavo's two goals – the first after just 29 seconds – were the catalyst for a sensational result and Chelsea's record victory over United. Following some unconvincing away Premiership performances, Chelsea boss Gianluca Vialli moved Gustavo into a more attacking role, just behind the front two, for the third-round FA Cup tie at Hull. He responded by scoring his first hat-trick for ten years in the classic manner, with his right foot, his head and his left foot, to ease the Blues through a potentially tricky tie. Appointed acting captain for the Christmas fixtures, he played a prominent role in Chelsea's resurgence, creating four of the Blues' five goals over the festive period, including all three against Sheffield Wednesday. This kick-started Chelsea's season again as they embarked on a 20-match unbeaten run in domestic competitions which ultimately led to another FA Cup final appearance. Again, the Blues were grateful for the Uruguayan's opportunism: a sweet half-volley put them ahead against Newcastle in the Wembley semi-final before the Magpies equalised and took the match by the scruff of the neck, but Gustavo ghosted in to bury a superb header that booked a return trip to Wembley for the last final before the famous old stadium's redevelopment. A winners' medal was to be his reward. The rigours of the season, and long-distance trips to represent Uruguay, seemed to take their toll and Gustavo was omitted from the glamorous Champions' League clashes against Barcelona in favour of the hard-working Jody Morris, but he finished the season on a high note with goals in each of the last two Premiership matches. Thankfully, for the first time, the Blues got a full season from the genial Uruguayan, and his total of 18 goals in all competitions is an amazing return for a midfield player and an indication of his ability to find space and quick thinking. A powerful figure who is particularly good in the air, he uses the ball imaginatively and his performances last season were a reminder of how much he was missed when he was injured during the previous two campaigns. Recalled to the Uruguay national team, he featured in the opening two rounds of their World Cup qualifying games against Bolivia and Paraguay.
Chelsea (Free from Real Zaragoza, Spain, via Bella Vista, on 15/7/1997) PL 57+18/25 FLC 3/2 FAC 6/6 Others 19+7/4

PREECE Andrew (Andy) Paul
Born: Evesham, 27 March 1967
Height: 6'1" Weight: 12.0

The Bury striker may have turned 33 years old recently, but he can never in his long career have experienced such an eventful season as the one just passed. Andy went on trial to Portuguese club Santa Clara in pre-season and his Gigg Lane future looked bleak. He returned, however, to claim a regular place in Neil Warnock's forward line – playing much of the time only with the aid of painkilling injections to numb the effects of a back problem. When Warnock departed in December, it was Andy, as one of the senior players, who was chosen to take over as caretaker manager. He greatly impressed everyone with the way that he went about the task of guiding the Shakers to safety, blooding a number of youngsters and yet also remaining fair to the senior players. Throughout he continued to play his part on the field as well as off – scoring 12 goals to end the season as leading scorer, his height and ability to hold the ball up being crucial. He was widely expected to be given the job on a full-time basis in the summer.
Northampton T (Free from Evesham on 31/8/1988) FL 0+1 FLC 0+1 Others 0+1 (Free to Worcester C during 1989 close season)
Wrexham (Free on 22/3/1990) FL 44+7/7 FLC 5+1/1 FAC 1/2 Others 5/1
Stockport Co (£10,000 on 18/12/1991) FL 89+8/42 FLC 2+1 FAC 7/3 Others 12+2/9
Crystal Palace (£350,000 on 23/6/1994) PL 17+3/4 FLC 4+2/1 FAC 2+3

Blackpool (£200,000 on 5/7/1995) FL 114+12/35 FLC 8+2/1 FAC 2+3/2 Others 12/2
Bury (Free on 6/7/1998) FL 49+33/15 FLC 6+1 FAC 2+1

PREECE David William
Born: Bridgnorth, 28 May, 1963
Height: 5'6" Weight: 11.6
Club Honours: FLC '88
International Honours: E: B-3

Cambridge's assistant manager was mainly used as a substitute in 1999-2000. Time might be catching up with David, but in those rare appearances he showed that he is still an excellent passer of the ball. He also displayed the touches of quality that made him such a respected midfielder in his days at Luton.

Walsall (From apprentice on 22/7/1980) FL 107+4/5 FLC 18/5 FAC 6/1 Others 1
Luton T (£150,000 on 6/12/1984) FL 328+8/21 FLC 23/3 FAC 27/2 Others 8+1/1
Derby Co (Free on 11/8/1995) FL 10+3/1 FLC 2
Birmingham C (Loaned on 24/11/1995) FL 6 Others 1
Swindon T (Loaned on 21/3/1996) FL 7/1
Cambridge U (Free on 6/9/1996) FL 40+33/2 FLC 3+2 Others 2+1

PREECE Roger
Born: Much Wenlock, 9 June 1968
Height: 5'8" Weight: 10.11

In the twilight of his league career, Roger played just five games for Shrewsbury in 1999-2000 before being released. An uncompromising midfield player who always gives his all, Roger had probably regarded his role at Gay Meadow more as that of a youth-team coach than as that of a player. He rejoined former Shrews' boss Jake King at Telford in March.

Wrexham (Free from Coventry C juniors on 15/8/1986) FL 89+21/12 FLC 2+1 FAC 5 Others 8+1/1
Chester C (Free on 14/8/1990) FL 165+5/4 FLC 10 FAC 8/1 Others 11 (Free to Southport on 18/10/1996)
Shrewsbury T (Free from Telford on 4/7/1997) FL 46+6/3 FLC 1 FAC 2

PRESSMAN Kevin Paul
Born: Fareham, 6 November 1967
Height: 6'1" Weight: 15.5
International Honours: E: B-3; U21-1; Yth; Sch

This experienced Sheffield Wednesday goalkeeper spent much of the 1999-2000 season as deputy to Pavel Srnicek but when his rival injured a shoulder last March Kevin seized his chance and went on to retain his place until the end of the campaign. He is an excellent shot stopper with good kicking ability who will be aiming to retain his position as first-choice 'keeper for the 2000-01 campaign.

Sheffield Wed (From apprentice on 7/11/1985) F/PL 264+2 FLC 33 FAC 16 Others 4
Stoke C (Loaned on 10/3/1992) FL 4 Others 2

PRICE Jason Jeffrey
Born: Pontypridd, 12 April 1977
Height: 6'2" Weight: 11.5
Club Honours: Div 3 '00
International Honours: W: U21-7

A danger to the opposition when using his pace to break from midfield, Jason is capable of scoring at least a dozen goals a season, considering the promising positions he finds himself in. He is regularly used as a right back by Swansea, but the return to form of Steve Jones during the second half of 1999-2000 saw Jason employed mainly in a wide attacking role in midfield, from where he scored seven goals. He won further caps for Wales at U21 level against Belarus and Switzerland and went on to cap a fine season by winning a Third Division championship winners' medal.

Swansea C (Free from Aberaman on 17/7/1995) FL 92+11/13 FLC 8/1 FAC 4/1 Others 2+1

PRICE Ryan
Born: Wolverhampton, 13 March 1970
Height: 6'5" Weight: 14.0
Club Honours: AMC '95; GMVC '97; FAT '96
International Honours: E: SP-6

The giant 'keeper did not fare well on Macclesfield's return to Division Three in 1999-2000. With the back four having been totally rearranged and initially looking unsettled, Ryan was called upon to work a lot harder between the posts than he had done during the previous two seasons. After 11 league games and only three wins, he was rested in mid-October for the more experienced Lee Martin. In mid-November he was loaned to Conference club Telford United but ironically he was then recalled after just a week and came on from the bench to replace Martin, thus making his 100th Football League appearance for Macclesfield. However, he then signed permanently for Telford shortly afterwards.

Birmingham C (£40,000 from Stafford R on 9/8/1994) Others 1
Macclesfield T (£15,000 on 3/11/1995) FL 99+1 FLC 8 FAC 6 Others 2

PRIEST Christopher (Chris)
Born: Leigh, 18 October 1973
Height: 5'9" Weight: 10.10

A 1999 close-season signing from Chester, Chris took time to settle into his midfield role at Macclesfield, but then turned in some very good performances. Operating from box to box, he is a good passer of the ball and can get forward to score goals. Chris's two late goals in the home match against Carlisle secured victory. The second, scored in the 90th minute, can be claimed as the last goal to be scored in the 20th century by a Nationwide League player. In the latter part of the season he appeared to suffer a lack of form, but this was due to a hernia problem which led to an operation during March.

Everton (From trainee on 1/6/1992)
Chester C (Loaned on 9/9/1994) FL 11/1 Others 2
Chester C (Free on 11/1/1995) FL 151+5/25 FLC 6 FAC 6/1 Others 6
Macclesfield T (Free on 5/7/1999) FL 34+2/4 FLC 2/1 FAC 2

PRIESTLEY Philip (Phil) Alan
Born: Wigan, 30 March 1976
Height: 6'3" Weight: 13.5

Rochdale's long-standing deputy to Neil Edwards, Phil was the club's substitute goalkeeper throughout the 1999-2000 season. He eventually came on when Neil limped off after just two minutes at Exeter in December. He then had the disappointment of seeing a more experienced 'keeper brought in on loan. Nevertheless, he did make two full appearances before Dale's regular 'keeper returned to the fray in mid-March.

Rochdale (Free from Atherton LR on 23/9/1998) FL 2+1 Others 1

PRIMUS Linvoy Stephen
Born: Forest Gate, 14 September 1973
Height: 6'0" Weight: 14.0

One of the most classy and consistent Reading players during a generally drab 1999-2000 season, Linvoy attracted the attention of several higher-division clubs. At the end of the campaign it looked as though the Royals would find difficulty in meeting the central defender's wage demands and holding on to him. His power both in the air and on the ground did much to stabilise the defence when it was going through a torrid mid-season period and, besides playing well himself, he did much to encourage the less experienced players around him.

Charlton Ath (From trainee on 14/8/1992) FL 4 FLC 0+1 Others 0+1
Barnet (Free on 18/7/1994) FL 127/7 FLC 9+1 FAC 8/1 Others 4
Reading (£400,000 on 29/7/1997) FL 94+1/1 FLC 9 FAC 6 Others 4

PRINGLE Ulf **Martin**
Born: Sweden, 18 November 1970
Height: 6'2" Weight: 12.3
Club Honours: Div 1 '00
International Honours: Sweden: 1

A tall and quick striker, Martin works very hard and uses his considerable pace to get behind defenders and slip into scoring positions. Unfortunately, his goalscoring touch was missing during his 1999-2000 season with Charlton and he managed only four goals throughout the season, although he set up several goals for his team-mates. It didn't help that he was carrying a shin injury for part of the season but he still made a valuable contribution to the Addicks' successful pursuit of the First Division championship. Martin can shoot with both feet, although he favours his right, and is good in the air, but needs to try and develop greater confidence in his undoubted ability in front of goal.

Charlton Ath (Signed from Benfica, Portugal on 8/1/1999) P/FL 27+23/7 FLC 2 FAC 2

PRIOR Spencer Justin
Born: Southend, 22 April 1971
Height: 6'3" Weight: 13.4
Club Honours: FLC '97

This brave and rugged centre back lost his place in the Derby line-up to Steve Elliott last season after expressing his discontent over tactics and training methods. Though he always gave 100 per cent and was a great favourite with the home crowd, his days at the club were inevitably numbered after that and when, after an aborted move to Hearts, Manchester City manager Joe Royle offered terms just before the transfer deadline the deal was agreed by all sides for a fee of £500,000. A powerfully built player with a deceptive turn of speed, Spencer came into the City team for the home game against West Bromwich Albion and made a relatively inconspicuous start. After that, he quickly settled into the side, showing total command at the back and impressive agility for such a large man. Good in the air, he is dangerous in the opposition penalty area at set pieces and scored his first goal for the club in his fourth game, against Crewe Alexandra, with a close-range header following a corner, adding another early on in the following game away at Grimsby. City now have two strong central defenders of similar style and physique, and it will be interesting to see if they play together in the Premiership in 2000-01.

Southend U (From trainee on 22/5/1989) FL 135/3 FLC 9 FAC 5 Others 7/1
Norwich C (£200,000 on 24/6/1993) P/FL 67+7/1 FLC 10+1/1 FAC 0+2 Others 2
Leicester C (£600,000 on 17/8/1996) PL 61+3 FLC 7 FAC 5 Others 2
Derby Co (£700,000 on 22/8/1998) PL 48+6/1 FLC 5 FAC 4
Manchester C (£500,000 + on 23/3/2000) FL 9/3

PRITCHARD David (Dave) Michael
Born: Wolverhampton, 27 May 1972
Height: 5'8" Weight: 11.5
International Honours: W: B-1

An enthusiastic, competitive player, Dave made the switch from his accustomed right-full-back berth at Bristol Rovers to a ball-winning midfield role in 1999-2000 and thoroughly enjoyed it. After five years in league football he opened his goal account with the winner at Chesterfield in November, but a deep bruise to his knee sustained at Colchester United on 8 January kept him out of action for three months. He made one reserve-team comeback before having to undergo another scan on his injured knee, which unfortunately required further surgery.

West Bromwich A (From trainee on 5/7/1990) FL 1+4 (Free to Telford during 1992 close season)
Bristol Rov (£15,000 on 25/2/1994) FL 156+2/1 FLC 11 FAC 12+1 Others 10+1

PROKAS Richard
Born: Penrith, 22 January 1976
Height: 5'9" Weight: 11.4
Club Honours: Div 3 '95; AMC '97

Richard once again performed an anchor man role in the centre of Carlisle's midfield in 1999-2000. However, he showed a more creative side to his game on occasions, and a tally of just one goal (a last-minute header against Chester in January) was a poor reward for his enterprising efforts during the campaign. Richard remains a player who wears his heart on his sleeve, but his dismissal in the last match at Brighton was a disappointing conclusion to a season which had seen him put in some sterling performances. He was offered new terms in May, and was also linked with a move to Halifax.

Carlisle U (From trainee on 18/7/1994) FL 158+17/3 FLC 10+1 FAC 7 Others 18+5/1

Martin Pringle

PRUDHOE Mark
Born: Washington, 8 November 1963
Height: 6'0" Weight: 14.0
Club Honours: GMVC '90; Div 4 '91

Mark was signed from Premiership Bradford City in November 1999 as Southend's goalkeeping coach and cover for Mel Capleton. He was immediately thrown into the first team but, unfortunately, a couple of errors along with an injury eventually allowed Capleton to reclaim the 'keeper's jersey. Mark's experience will be put to good use as Southend look to improve their poor goals conceded record from 1999-2000.

Sunderland (From apprentice on 11/9/1981) FL 7
Hartlepool U (Loaned on 4/11/1983) FL 3
Birmingham C (£22,000 on 24/9/1984) FL 1 FLC 4
Walsall (£22,000 on 27/2/1986) FL 26 FLC 4 FAC 1
Doncaster Rov (Loaned on 11/12/1986) FL 5
Grimsby T (Loaned on 26/3/1987) FL 8
Hartlepool U (Loaned on 29/8/1987) FL 13
Bristol C (Loaned on 6/11/1987) FL 3 Others 2
Carlisle U (£10,000 on 11/12/1987) FL 34 FLC 2
Darlington (£10,000 on 16/3/1989) FL 146 FLC 8 FAC 9 Others 6
Stoke C (£120,000 on 24/6/1993) FL 82 FLC 6+1 FAC 5 Others 7
Peterborough U (Loaned on 30/9/1994) FL 6
York C (Loaned on 14/2/1997) FL 2
Bradford C (£70,000 on 17/7/1997) FL 8 FLC 1
Southend U (Free on 9/11/1999) FL 6

PRUTTON David Thomas
Born: Hull, 12 September 1981
Height: 6'1" Weight: 11.10
International Honours: E: Yth

The emergence of this talented young right-sided midfield player was the high point of an otherwise dismal 1999-2000 season for Nottingham Forest. David made his debut in senior football for the Reds in the Worthington Cup tie at Bristol City last September and never looked back. Despite his youth and inexperience he looked impressive in a team that underachieved last season and he showed little weakness in his game apart from a lack of goals. Capped four times by England at U18 level last season, he appears to have a great future ahead of him.

Nottingham F (From trainee on 1/10/1998) FL 33+1/2 FLC 2 FAC 3

PURSE Darren John
Born: Stepney, 14 February 1977
Height: 6'2" Weight: 12.8
International Honours: E: U21-2

Darren made good progress at Birmingham City during 1999-2000 when he took advantage of Michael Johnson's absence on international duties to establish himself as the regular partner of David Holdsworth in the centre of the defence. Dominating in the air and fierce in the tackle, he was used as an emergency striker over the Christmas period when the club had an injury crisis. He scored with a bullet-like header in the Worthington Cup victory over Newcastle and was voted "Young Player of the Season" as a reward for his consistent performances.

Leyton Orient (From trainee on 22/2/1994) FL 48+7/3 FLC 2 FAC 1 Others 7+1/2
Oxford U (£100,000 on 23/7/1996) FL 52+7/5 FLC 10+1/2 FAC 2
Birmingham C (£800,000 on 17/2/1998) FL 46+20/2 FLC 7+1/1 FAC 1 Others 2+1

Professional Footballers Association
20 Oxford Court
Bishopsgate
Manchester
M2 3WQ

Tel: 0161 236 0575
Fax: 0161 228 7229
www.givemefootball.com

PFA Enterprises Ltd (London)
4th Floor
10 Bow Lane
London
EC4M 9AL

Tel: 0207 329 9966
Fax: 0207 329 3355
email: garry.nelson@ukonline.co.uk

* * * * *

F.F.E. & V.T.S. Ltd
2 Oxford Court
Bishopsgate
Manchester
M2 3WQ

Tel: 0161 236 0637
Fax: 0161 228 7229

* * * * *

PFA Financial Management
91 Broad Street
Birmingham
B15 1AU

Tel: 0121 644 5277
Fax: 0121 644 5288

PFA Enterprises Ltd (Manchester)
2 Oxford Court
Bishopsgate
Manchester
M2 3WQ

Tel: 0161 228 2733
Fax: 0161 236 4496
email: gberry@thepfa.co.uk

* * * * *

PFA Coaching Department
2 Oxford Court
Bishopsgate
Manchester
M2 3WQ

Tel: 0161 236 08O8
Fax: 0161 236 4496

* * * * *

Football in the Community
11 Oxford Court
Bishopsgate
Manchester
M2 3WQ

Tel: 0161 236 0583
Fax: 0161 236 4459

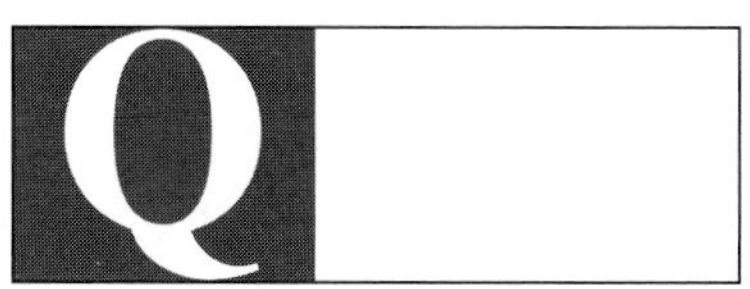

QUAILEY Brian Sullivan
Born: Leicester, 21 March 1978
Height: 6'1" Weight: 13.11
International Honours: St Kitts & Nevis: U23

Confined to an understudy role at West Bromwich Albion, this tall and well-built striker joined Blackpool on loan last December. He made a bright start in his first game for the Seasiders at Wrexham but was then injured in the Auto Windscreens Shield tie against Notts County and returned to the Hawthorns. Scunthorpe took his contract over at the start of February and he immediately won a regular place in the starting line-up, showing a great workrate, strength and an eye for goal. Brian scored five times in nine games – including two spectacular long-range efforts – prior to the end of March, when he picked up an ankle injury which kept him out for a couple of weeks. He made his debut in international football for the St Kitts U23 team against Jamaica in an Olympic qualifying game last September, scoring his side's only goal in a 2-1 defeat.

West Bromwich A (Signed from Nuneaton Borough on 22/9/1997) FL 1+6 FLC 0+1
Exeter C (Loaned on 23/12/1998) FL 8+4/2 Others 2/1
Blackpool (Loaned on 3/12/1999) FL 1 Others 1
Scunthorpe U (Free on 3/2/2000) FL 13+1/5

QUASHIE Nigel Francis
Born: Peckham, 20 July 1978
Height: 6'0" Weight: 12.4
International Honours: E: B-1; U21-4; Yth

Nigel had a disappointing 1999-2000 season with Nottingham Forest and never really seemed to settle in the East Midlands. He appeared regularly in the Reds' line-up until the end of October but was then in and out of the side. On his day he is a talented midfield player with good passing ability and a powerful shot. He spent some time on the transfer list and may well prefer a move back to London.

Queens Park R (From trainee on 1/8/1995) P/FL 50+7/3 FLC 0+1 FAC 4/2
Nottingham F (£2,500,000 on 24/8/1998) P/FL 37+7/2 FLC 7/1 FAC 1+1

QUIGLEY Michael Anthony
Born: Manchester, 2 October 1970
Height: 5'7" Weight: 11.4

Discarded by previous Hull manager Mark Hateley in the summer of 1998, Michael was invited back by new boss Warren Joyce after a spell at Altrincham. This has been mainly for his assistance behind the scenes: on the scouting front, he recommended Andy Oakes prior to his signing from Winsford, and his contacts instigated the audacious recruitment of Jamaicans Ian Goodison and Theo Whitmore. Michael was more involved on the playing side last season, although the diminutive midfielder chiefly played for the reserves with infrequent substitute appearances in the first team. He was out of contract in the summer and at the time of writing it seemed likely that he would be starting the new season elsewhere.

Manchester C (From trainee on 1/7/1989) P/FL 3+9 Others 1
Wrexham (Loaned on 17/2/1995) FL 4
Hull C (Free on 5/7/1995) FL 36+18/3 FLC 3+4/1 FAC 3 Others 3

QUINN Alan
Born: Dublin, 13 June 1979
Height: 5'9" Weight: 11.7
International Honours: RoI: U21-4; Yth (UEFA-U18 '98)

Alan provided one of the few promising features of Sheffield Wednesday's disappointing 1999-2000 campaign. Although he was sent off for an over-zealous challenge in only his second game of the season against Bristol City in the FA Cup, he came back from suspension to win a regular place in the Owls' line-up in the new year. He is a hard-working, tough-tackling midfield player with plenty of skill and looks to be a bright prospect for the future. He won his first cap at U21 level for the Republic of Ireland against the Czech Republic and added three more appearances in the Toulon Tournament in May.

Sheffield Wed (Signed from Cherry Orchard on 6/12/1997) PL 19+2/3 FAC 2+1

QUINN Barry Scott
Born: Dublin, 9 May 1979
Height: 6'0" Weight: 12.2
International Honours: RoI: 3; U21-11; Yth (UEFA-U18 '98)

A young Irish midfield player who had made a handful of appearances for Coventry the previous season, Barry failed to make much of an impact in the first half of 1999-2000, appearing only once, out of position at right back in a home defeat against Leeds. After Christmas he got further opportunities at full back, once again facing the prodigious Harry Kewell, but never looked wholly confident. He played in midfield at Chelsea and had an excellent game with some strong tackling and sensible distribution but within a fortnight he suffered a badly bruised ankle on his full international debut for the Republic of Ireland against Greece. A fixture for the U21s, for whom he won eight caps last season, Barry also won further honours for the senior team in the US Nike Cup games in the summer.

Coventry C (From trainee on 28/11/1996) PL 11+7 FLC 1

QUINN James (Jimmy) Martin
Born: Belfast, 18 November 1959
Height: 6'0" Weight: 13.10
Club Honours: Div 2 '94
International Honours: NI: 48; B-1

Although he had been the manager of Swindon Town since October 1998, Jimmy was also registered as a player to cover for emergencies and he turned out in a handful of games last season, notably during the autumn when the Robins had three strikers out injured. Now into his forties, he was mostly used as a late substitute to come on and hustle defenders and to seek openings with his aerial ability. His pace may have gone but he made up for it with a high workrate. However, the club were relegated to Division Two and Jimmy was sacked as manager shortly before the end of the season.

Swindon T (£10,000 from Oswestry on 31/12/1981) FL 34+15/10 FLC 1+1 FAC 5+3/6 Others 1/2
Blackburn Rov (£32,000 on 15/8/1984) FL 58+13/17 FLC 6+1/2 FAC 4/3 Others 2/1
Swindon T (£50,000 on 19/12/1986) FL 61+3/30 FLC 6/8 FAC 5 Others 10+1/5
Leicester C (£210,000 on 20/6/1988) FL 13+18/6 FLC 2+1 FAC 0+1 Others 0+1
Bradford C (Signed on 17/3/1989) FL 35/14 FLC 2/1 Others 1
West Ham U (£320,000 on 30/12/1989) FL 34+13/18 FLC 3/1 FAC 4+2/2 Others 1
Bournemouth (£40,000 on 5/8/1991) FL 43/19 FLC 4/2 FAC 5/2 Others 2/1
Reading (£55,000 on 27/7/1992) FL 149+33/71 FLC 12+4/12 FAC 9/5 Others 6+3/6
Peterborough U (Free on 15/7/1997) FL 47+2/25 FLC 6/1 FAC 3/3 Others 3+1/1
Swindon T (Free on 5/11/1998) FL 1+6 FAC 1

QUINN Stephen **James (Jimmy)**
Born: Coventry, 15 December 1974
Height: 6'1" Weight: 12.10
International Honours: NI: 21; B-2; U21-1; Yth

By his own admission, Jimmy did not have a good season with West Bromwich in 1999-2000. He struggled at times when asked to play up front alongside Lee Hughes, preferring to occupy a withdrawn midfield role where he could run at defenders. Nevertheless, he competed well, but one feels that he should have scored more goals than he did. He was in and out of the Albion side in the latter part of the season and will be hoping for a return to regular first-team football in 2000-01. He appeared regularly for Northern Ireland, winning six more caps and scoring in the friendly games against Luxembourg and Malta in the spring.

Birmingham C (Trainee) FL 1+3
Blackpool (£25,000 on 5/7/1993) FL 128+23/37 FLC 10+4/5 FAC 5+1/4 Others 7+4/2
Stockport Co (Loaned on 4/3/1994) FL 0+1
West Bromwich A (£500,000 on 20/2/1998) FL 81+12/8 FLC 3+2/1 FAC 2

QUINN Niall John
Born: Dublin, 6 October 1966
Height: 6'4" Weight: 15.10
Club Honours: FLC '87; Div 1 '99
International Honours: RoI: 77; B-1; U23-1; U21-6; Yth; Sch

The giant Sunderland striker seems to get better with age and last season his partnership with goal machine Kevin Phillips made the transformation from the First Division quite easily, the pair grabbing 44 goals between them, 14 of which belonged to Niall. Almost unbeatable in the air, his first touch and awareness of the position of his team-mates are pivotal to Sunderland's attacking options, and when he is not creating chances for others he is usually scoring them himself, notching a vital strike away at Newcastle in Sunderland's 2-1 derby victory in August, and scoring spectacular efforts at home to Chelsea and Wimbledon, both stunning volleys, and a twenty-yard precision lob against Southampton at the Dell. Niall signed an extension to his contract during the season and at the time of writing it had been reported that Sunderland were preparing an improved deal for the Irishman, who was made club captain following the departure of Kevin Ball, that will, it was hoped, keep him at the Stadium of Light for the rest of his career. Niall continued to appear regularly for the Republic of Ireland, winning eight more caps during the season and scoring in the 1-1 draw with Macedonia last October.

Arsenal (From juniors on 30/11/1983) FL 59+8/14 FLC 14+2/4 FAC 8+2/2 Others 0+1
Manchester C (£800,000 on 21/3/1990) F/PL 183+20/66 FLC 20+2/7 FAC 13+3/4 Others 3/1
Sunderland (£1,300,000 on 17/8/1996) F/PL 112+11/48 FLC 5+1/4 FAC 5/1 Others 2/2

Niall Quinn

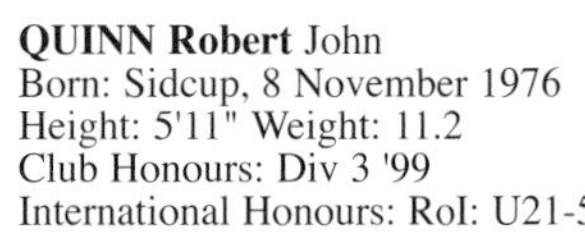

QUINN Robert John
Born: Sidcup, 8 November 1976
Height: 5'11" Weight: 11.2
Club Honours: Div 3 '99
International Honours: RoI: U21-5

This strong-tackling Brentford player showed his value to the club in the 1999-2000 campaign by appearing in a variety of midfield and defensive positions. He is a reliable and consistent performer with good distribution and never let the side down even when the team's form dipped in the second half of the season.

Crystal Palace (From trainee on 11/3/1995) F/PL 18+5/1 FLC 2+1/1 Others 2+1
Brentford (£40,000 on 9/7/1998) FL 76+11/2 FLC 5+1 FAC 5/2 Others 6/1

QUINN Wayne Richard
Born: Truro, 19 November 1976
Height: 5'10" Weight: 11.12
International Honours: E: B-1; U21-2; Yth

After an uncertain start to the 1999-2000 season when he was not selected by Sheffield United on some occasions, Wayne's performances as a left-sided wing back improved after the arrival of new manager Neil Warnock. His defensive play was better and he was a much greater threat coming forward, regaining something of the form of two seasons ago. He has the ability to beat a man and his searching centres produced many penalty area incidents, ensuring that he was high on the "goal assists" list. Despite his hard shot, his only goal was in the penalty shoot-out at Rushden. He was initially given credit for the goal against Stockport in March, but it was later awarded to Curtis Woodhouse when video evidence clearly showed he had deflected the shot.

Sheffield U (From trainee on 6/12/1994) FL 110+5/3 FLC 11+1 FAC 12+1 Others 2

Wayne Quinn

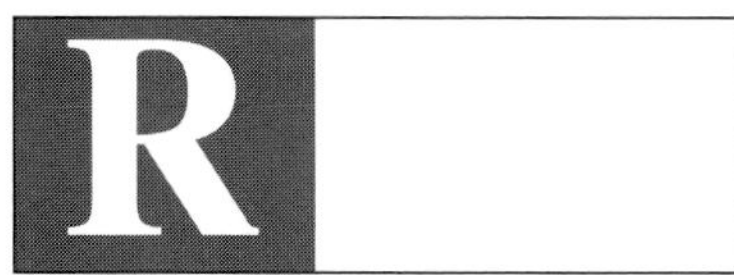

RACHEL Adam
Born: Birmingham, 10 December 1976
Height: 5'11" Weight: 12.8

Adam is an agile shot stopper who began the 1999-2000 season as third in line for the goalkeeper's position at Aston Villa before signing a two-year contract with Blackpool last September. He was quickly called up for first-team action, making his debut for his new club at Bristol Rovers in October. He subsequently returned to the reserves and was unable to break through into the first team again due to the intense competition from Tony Caig and Phil Barnes.

Aston Villa (From trainee on 10/5/1995) PL 0+1
Blackpool (Free on 28/9/1999) FL 1

RACHUBKA Paul Stephen
Born: California, USA, 21 May 1981
Height: 6'1" Weight: 13.5
International Honours: E: Yth

Paul is a young Manchester United goal-keeper who made his first-team debut in the World Club Championship match against South Melbourne in January. He certainly gave a good account of himself that day, keeping a cool head while playing in front of 60,000 Brazilians in the Maracana. His assured display will not have gone unnoticed by Sir Alex Ferguson, which bodes well for his future prospects at Old Trafford. Previously capped by England at U16 and U20 levels, he made his debut for the U18s in the crushing 9-0 victory over minnows San Marino last October.

Manchester U (From trainee on 7/7/1999) Others 0+1

RADEBE Lucas
Born: Johannesburg, South Africa, 12 April 1969
Height: 6'1" Weight: 11.8
International Honours: South Africa: 61 (ANC '96)

"The Chief" is now acknowledged as one of the more accomplished defenders in the Premiership, and rightly so. Signed by Leeds from Kaizer Chiefs for £250,000 in 1994, he must be one of the bargains of the decade. Captain of both club and country, he led South Africa in their first-ever World Cup finals in France in 1998. Lucas had a fine season for Leeds in 1999-2000, and his influence on the team was crucial. He reads the game superbly, which enables him to produce many last-ditch saving tackles, and he can also be used as a fine man marker to smother top-class opposition, while his distribution is also very good. The Leeds defence looked a different unit without him when he missed several games in January while away on international duty. Even so, Lucas shrugged off thousands of exhausting air miles to fulfil his commitments to club and country. Although still waiting for his first Premiership goal, he scored twice in Leeds's UEFA Cup campaign. They were very different goals: a last-ditch header to defeat Spartak Moscow and a candidate for "Goal of the Season" while sitting on the ground at Partizan Belgrade. Lucas is a player of immense stature and will surely be a cornerstone of Leeds's future successes. He was also a key figure for South Africa in the African Nations' Cup finals in the spring, appearing in all six of the *Bafana Bafana*'s games as they went on to finish in third place in the tournament.

Leeds U (£250,000 from Kaizer Chiefs, South Africa on 5/9/1994) PL 133+11 FLC 9+3 FAC 14+2/1 Others 14/2

RAE Alexander (Alex) Scott
Born: Glasgow, 30 September 1969
Height: 5'9" Weight: 11.12
Club Honours: Div 1 '99
International Honours: S: B-4; U21-8

The combative Sunderland midfielder believes that 1999-2000 was the best season of his career so far and few Sunderland supporters would disagree. When injuries sidelined Gavin McCann and Stefan Schwarz, Alex took his chance to firmly establish himself in the heart of Sunderland's midfield, turning in some excellent performances. The Scotsman is small in stature but big in heart and commitment, but his tackling strengths and willingness to get stuck in often belie his undoubted ability on the ball, while he can also weigh in with important goals such as his crucial equaliser against Derby in February, which rescued his side from a home defeat. However, while his contributions with the ball were impressive, Alex ran into several disciplinary problems during the second half of the season and this is an area of his game that he needs to improve upon.

Falkirk (Free from Bishopbriggs on 15/6/1987) SL 71+12/20 SLC 5/1 SC 2+1
Millwall (£100,000 on 20/8/1990) FL 205+13/63 FLC 13+2/1 FAC 13/6 Others 10/1
Sunderland (£750,000 on 14/6/1996) F/PL 71+22/10 FLC 8+1/2 FAC 4 Others 0+2

RAMAGE Craig Darren
Born: Derby, 30 March 1970
Height: 5'9" Weight: 11.8
International Honours: E: U21-3

After having a horrific time with injuries in 1998-99 Craig returned to full fitness and joined Notts County on a free transfer last August following an impressive pre-season trial at Meadow Lane. He proved to be a quality signing, bringing skill and experience to the middle line and orchestrating the team in his role as play-maker. He scored six goals, all in the early part of the season when the Magpies were doing well at the top of the table, but his form seemed to dip towards the end of the campaign when the team's performances also fell away somewhat.

Derby Co (From trainee on 20/7/1988) FL 33+9/4 FLC 6+1/2 FAC 3+1/1 Others 0+3
Wigan Ath (Loaned on 16/2/1989) FL 10/2 Others 0+1
Watford (£90,000 on 21/2/1994) FL 99+5/27 FLC 8+1/2 FAC 7
Peterborough U (Loaned on 10/2/1997) FL 7 Others 1
Bradford C (Free on 24/6/1997) FL 24+11/1 FLC 0+2
Notts Co (Free on 5/8/1999) FL 36+4/4 FLC 4/2 FAC 2

Craig Ramage

RAMMELL Andrew (Andy) Victor
Born: Nuneaton, 10 February 1967
Height: 6'1" Weight: 13.12

This wholehearted Walsall striker scored early-season match-winners in local derbies against Wolves, Birmingham and West Bromwich in 1999-2000 but a niggling calf injury meant that he missed a number of games and then had to battle for his place when fit again. He took part in the gallant but vain battle against relegation at the end of the season, the high spot for Andy being another goal in the win that completed a double over West Bromwich.

Manchester U (£40,000 from Atherstone U on 26/9/1989)
Barnsley (£100,000 on 14/9/1990) FL 149+36/44 FLC 11+3/1 FAC 12+1/4 Others 8/1
Southend U (Signed on 22/2/1996) FL 50+19/13 FLC 3+3/1 FAC 2+1 Others 1
Walsall (Free on 15/7/1998) FL 60+9/23 FLC 3/1 FAC 3+1 Others 5/1

RAMSAY Scott Alan
Born: Hastings, 16 October 1980
Height: 6'0" Weight: 13.0

This locally born teenage striker made his Brighton debut when coming on as a substitute in the home defeat by York in October 1999. Despite his high workrate, Scott was unfortunate in front of goal until the 5-2 home victory against Macclesfield in March, when he scored twice. His appearances were restricted to those as a late substitute until the departure of Bobby Zamora towards the end of the season, when

he was given his chance of a regular run in the starting eleven.
Brighton & Hove A (From trainee on 29/6/1999) FL 8+16/2 FAC 0+2 Others 1

RANKIN Isaiah (Izzy)
Born: Edmonton, 22 May 1978
Height: 5'10" Weight: 11.6
Isaiah is a young Bradford City striker with electric pace and an eye for goal. He began the 1999-2000 campaign on the injury list with hamstring trouble and then suffered a further reaction in his comeback game for the reserves at Newcastle in early September. He returned to first-team action at Anfield last November but by January he had yet to start a game and was loaned to Birmingham City. At St Andrews he immediately struck up an effective partnership with Dele Adebola and he scored four times in 13 games for the Blues, including a double in the crucial 3-1 victory at Barnsley. Isaiah was eventually recalled to Valley Parade to cover for an injury crisis but, although he made several appearances from the subs' bench, he failed to make the starting line-up.
Arsenal (From trainee on 12/9/1995) PL 0+1
Colchester U (Loaned on 25/9/1997) FL 10+1/5 Others 1
Bradford C (£1,300,000 on 14/8/1998) P/FL 15+21/4 FLC 2/1 FAC 0+2
Birmingham C (Loaned on 19/1/2000) FL 11+2/4

RANKINE Simon **Mark**
Born: Doncaster, 30 September 1969
Height: 5'9" Weight: 12.11
Club Honours: Div 2 '00
An unsteady start to the 1999-2000 season by the highly experienced Preston player included his 400th Football League game in the home defeat by Wigan, but he recovered his form to forge a strong central midfield partnership with Sean Gregan where his terrier-like tackling and strong runs in support of the attack often took the eye. He played the 500th senior game of his career at Bristol Rovers in the FA Cup, and although he picked up a groin strain which hampered him for several weeks he still managed to miss hardly a game all season. The only blot on a successful campaign which brought him a Second Division championship medal would be his failure to convert at least one of the many chances his 100 per cent effort created into a goal.
Doncaster Rov (From trainee on 4/7/1988) FL 160+4/20 FLC 8+1/1 FAC 8/2 Others 14/2
Wolverhampton W (£70,000 on 31/1/1992) FL 112+20/1 FLC 9+1 FAC 14+2 Others 7+2
Preston NE (£100,000 on 17/9/1996) FL 139+5/4 FLC 12 FAC 12/1 Others 4

RAPLEY Kevin John
Born: Reading, 21 September 1977
Height: 5'9" Weight: 10.8
Club Honours: Div 3 '99
This busy and inventive striker struggled to break into the first team at Notts County in 1999-2000 due to the success of the partnership of Mark Stallard and Duane Darby. He spent much of the time on the subs' bench and consequently managed only three goals all season. Kevin is a pacy right-footed striker capable of darting runs and quick turns and has an excellent eye for goal.
Brentford (From trainee on 8/7/1996) FL 27+24/12 FLC 3+5/3 FAC 0+2 Others 1
Southend U (Loaned on 20/11/1998) FL 9/4
Notts Co (£50,000 on 23/2/1999) FL 21+24/5 FAC 1+1/1 Others 1

RAVEN Paul Duncan
Born: Salisbury, 28 July 1970
Height: 6'1" Weight: 12.12
International Honours: E: Sch
This dependable centre back started the 1999-2000 season on the transfer list at West Bromwich – shortly after his testimonial year had ended. Obviously disappointed, having spent more than ten years at the Hawthorns, he quickly made his point with some excellent performances in pre-season friendlies and was named as a substitute for the opening league game against Norwich. A wholehearted competitor, he came off the bench to score a dramatic equaliser (his first goal for the Baggies since March 1997) and played in the next seven games before suffering a hamstring injury. He overcame that set-back and regained his place in the first eleven but was then delivered a cruel blow when he suffered a serious mouth injury in a training ground accident. This knocked him back considerably but, such is the man, he battled on, trained as normal (spending a lot of time working on his own) and is now looking ahead to starting his 11th season with the club – although he will have to fight for his place along with six more defenders of similar style. On 26 February 2000 (away at Blackburn) Paul reached a personal milestone – his 300th senior appearance for the Baggies.
Doncaster Rov (From juniors on 6/6/1988) FL 52/4 FLC 2 FAC 5 Others 2
West Bromwich A (£100,000 on 23/3/1989) FL 249+10/15 FLC 20/2 FAC 10/3 Others 15/1
Doncaster Rov (Loaned on 27/11/1991) FL 7
Rotherham U (Loaned on 29/10/1998) FL 11/2

RAWLINSON Mark David
Born: Bolton, 9 June 1975
Height: 5'10" Weight: 11.4
Mark again failed to win regular first-team football at Bournemouth in 1999-2000, when he was restricted to just four starts and a single outing from the subs' bench before being released by the Cherries at the end of the season. Although essentially a central midfield player, he can also take the right-back role if required. Mark has good passing skills and is not afraid to tackle.
Manchester U (From trainee on 5/7/1993)
Bournemouth (Free on 1/7/1995) FL 48+31/2 FLC 3+1 FAC 2+1 Others 4

REA Simon
Born: Kenilworth, 20 September 1976
Height: 6'1" Weight: 13.2
Simon joined Peterborough on a three-year contract after originally being recruited on a three-month loan from Birmingham in August 1999. He had been the captain of the Blues' youth team when Posh boss Barry Fry was in charge at St Andrews. As his only senior action dated back to the 1995-96 season, Simon wasn't given an extended run until March. The left-sided central defender responded in magnificent fashion, and finished the term with a Wembley appearance as Posh beat Darlington in the Third Division play-off final.
Birmingham C (From trainee on 27/1/1995) FL 0+1 Others 1+1
Peterborough U (Free on 24/8/1999) FL 11+3/1 FLC 0+1 Others 2/1

READ Paul Colin
Born: Harlow, 25 September 1973
Height: 5'10" Weight: 12.11
International Honours: E: Sch
A former Arsenal trainee, Paul moved on to Wycombe in January 1997 after failing to make the grade at Highbury. Although it was apparent that he was a sharp striker with a goalscorer's instincts, he did not make a major impact during his two and a half seasons with the club and in the summer of 1999 he went to Sweden to try his luck with Ostersunds. In early December Paul returned to the UK looking for a club. He made one fairly unimpressive substitute appearance for Luton as a non-contract player in the Auto Windscreens Shield at Oxford and that was to be his only first-team opportunity in senior football in 1999-2000. He subsequently had a brief trial at Sheffield United in the new year.
Arsenal (From trainee on 11/10/1991)
Leyton Orient (Loaned on 10/3/1995) FL 11 Others 1
Southend U (Loaned on 6/10/1995) FL 3+1/1 Others 1
Wycombe W (£130,000 on 17/1/1997) FL 32+25/9 FLC 4/2 FAC 1+2/1 Others 1 (Freed during 1999 close season)
Luton T (Free from Ostersunds FK, Sweden on 6/12/1999) Others 0+1

READY Karl
Born: Neath, 14 August 1972
Height: 6'1" Weight: 13.3
International Honours: W: 5; B-2; U21-5; Sch
A regular central defender for seven seasons, Karl has made over 200 first-team appearances for Queens Park Rangers. He was one of the many players to wear the captain's armband last term, though he missed 12 games in the middle of the season owing to a back injury. Otherwise he was a first choice for one of the two or three – depending on formation – central defensive positions. He is comfortable both on the ball and in the air and is a former Welsh international, although he has not been able to regain a place in his country's side in recent years. Although not a regular goalscorer, he scored twice in 1999-2000 to take his club tally into double figures.
Queens Park R (From trainee on 13/8/1990) F/PL 187+16/10 FLC 9+2/1 FAC 8

REDDY Michael
Born: Kilkenny City, Ireland, 24 March 1980
Height: 6'1" Weight: 11.7
International Honours: RoI: U21-3; Yth
This young striker joined Sunderland from League of Ireland club Kilkenny City in August 1999. He made his first-team debut in October when he replaced John Oster in the Worthington Cup tie at Wimbledon and

immediately set about causing the Dons' defence untold problems with his pace and willingness to run with the ball. Tall and bearing a striking resemblance to the recently departed Michael Bridges, Michael immediately found a place in the affections of the Sunderland fans when, in only his third first-team appearance, he came off the bench at Middlesbrough to score his first Sunderland goal, a crucial equaliser, firing home the rebound after Mark Schwarzer had saved Kevin Phillips's penalty. Michael made his debut for the Republic of Ireland U21s against Greece in April and won further caps in the end-of-season games with Ghana and Portugal.

Sunderland (£50,000 from Kilkenny City on 30/8/1999) PL 0+8/1 FLC 0+1 FAC 0+1

REDFEARN Neil David
Born: Dewsbury, 20 June 1965
Height: 5'9" Weight: 13.0
Club Honours: Div 2 '91

Neil is a hard-tackling midfield battler who joined Bradford City in the 1999 close season on a two-year contract. He began the 1999-2000 campaign as a regular in the starting line-up, forming a strong partnership with Stuart McCall and Dean Windass in the centre of the park for City. However, he lost his place last January after the Bantams altered their formation and rather surprisingly moved on to Second Division Wigan Athletic shortly before the transfer deadline. Strong and determined, Neil led by example and became the Latics' penalty taker, claiming a 100 per cent success rate with five strikes. He scored both boals in the 2-0 victory over Notts County in April, adding a late spot kick to his opening goal which came directly from a free kick.

Bolton W (Free from Nottingham F juniors on 23/6/1982) FL 35/1 FLC 2 FAC 4
Lincoln C (£8,250 on 23/3/1984) FL 96+4/13 FLC 4 FAC 3/1 Others 7
Doncaster Rov (£17,500 on 22/8/1986) FL 46/14 FLC 2 FAC 3/1 Others 2
Crystal Palace (£100,000 on 31/7/1987) FL 57/10 FLC 6 FAC 1 Others 1
Watford (£150,000 on 21/11/1988) FL 22+2/3 FLC 1 FAC 6/3 Others 5/1
Oldham Ath (£150,000 on 12/1/1990) FL 56+6/16 FLC 3/1 FAC 7+1/3 Others 1
Barnsley (£150,000 on 5/9/1991) F/PL 289+3/71 FLC 21/6 FAC 20/6 Others 5
Charlton Ath (£1,000,000 on 1/7/1998) PL 29+1/3 FLC 2/1 FAC 1
Bradford C (£250,000 on 3/8/1999) PL 14+3/1 FLC 1+1 FAC 2
Wigan Ath (£112,500 on 17/3/2000) FL 12/6 Others 3

REDKNAPP Jamie Frank
Born: Barton on Sea, 25 June 1973
Height: 6'0" Weight: 12.10
Club Honours: FLC '95
International Honours: E: 17; B-1; U21-19; Yth; Sch

An injury to his knee and subsequent operation robbed Liverpool of Jamie's services for long periods during the 1999-2000 season and, with rumours of his impending sale to a London club circulating, Pool did not have the best of this fine player. However, when he was in the team, he made a valuable contribution. Liverpool's skipper at the start of the season, he sustained a cartilage injury and was ruled out of the side for almost four months. Whether Jamie can remain a regular in the midfield is largely dependent on Stephen Gerrard, who has been in brilliant form, and also the attitude of Gerard Houllier, who may decide that Jamie's Anfield days are coming to an end and that he should resurrect his career in pastures new. Capped three more times by England in the early part of the season, he scored in the 2-1 victory over Belgium last October.

Bournemouth (From trainee on 27/6/1990) FL 6+7 FLC 3 FAC 3 Others 2
Liverpool (£350,000 on 15/1/1991) F/PL 205+28/29 FLC 26/5 FAC 17+1/2 Others 19+4/3

REDMILE Matthew (Matt) Ian
Born: Nottingham, 12 November 1976
Height: 6'3" Weight: 14.10
Club Honours: Div 3 '98

This young Notts County central defender made real progress in 1999-2000. Rarely absent all season, he showed excellent form on a consistent basis and contributed goals in the FA Cup replay with Bournemouth and in the 1-0 home win over Preston. Matt shows considerable skill for such a huge man and is beginning to attract the attention of Premiership scouts once again.

Notts Co (From trainee on 4/7/1995) FL 133+6/7 FLC 10 FAC 13/1 Others 4

REDMOND Stephen (Steve)
Born: Liverpool, 2 November 1967
Height: 5'11" Weight: 11.7
Club Honours: FAYC '86
International Honours: E: U21-14; Yth

Bury's evergreen defender continued to use his vast experience to the greatest advantage throughout the 1999-2000 season and was a regular choice at centre back until February, when he finally made way for younger blood, in the shape of Danny Swailes. Steve also undertook a coaching role while continuing to play, being named as assistant manager on a caretaker basis in December following Neil Warnock's departure. It was a role that he tackled with great enthusiasm and Steve looks certain to continue in the position on a permanent basis for the new season.

Manchester C (From apprentice on 3/12/1984) FL 231+4/7 FLC 24 FAC 17 Others 11
Oldham Ath (£300,000 on 10/7/1992) P/FL 195+10/4 FLC 20 FAC 10+2 Others 1+1
Bury (Free on 3/7/1998) FL 54+5/1 FLC 4 FAC 4 Others 1

REED Adam Maurice
Born: Bishop Auckland, 18 February 1975
Height: 6'1" Weight: 12.0

Adam was unable to command a regular place in the Darlington side in 1999-2000 due to the presence of the experienced pairing of Neil Aspin and Steve Tutill in the centre of defence. However, because of injuries to these two at various times during the season, he did make a considerable number of starts. He is now an increasingly experienced defender, having made over a hundred league appearances for Darlington, and can always be relied upon to stand in very capably, with his adept reading of the game and aerial strength his main assets.

Darlington (From trainee on 16/7/1993) FL 45+7/1 FLC 1+1 FAC 1 Others 3
Blackburn Rov (£200,000 on 9/8/1995)
Darlington (Loaned on 21/2/1997) FL 14
Rochdale (Loaned on 5/12/1997) FL 10 Others 2/1
Darlington (Free on 17/7/1998) FL 45+7/2 FLC 2 FAC 2+1 Others 1+3

REED Martin John
Born: Scarborough, 10 January 1978
Height: 6'0" Weight: 11.6

Having started the campaign with a trial at Lincoln, the hard-tackling central defender was chiefly on the fringe of first-team action at York during 1999-2000. When called up for senior duty, Martin always showed 100 per cent commitment, and gave a particularly fine display in a draw at Darlington in January at left back.

York C (From trainee on 4/7/1996) FL 38+6 FLC 2 FAC 3+1 Others 1

REES Jason Mark
Born: Aberdare, 22 December 1969
Height: 5'5" Weight: 10.2
International Honours: W: 1; B-1; U21-3; B-1; Yth; Sch

A popular ball winner in the middle of the pitch, Jason was again a firm favourite with the Exeter fans last season, his tenacity and never-say-die attitude winning him a regular place in the first-team line-up. Always willing to go over and applaud the supporters for their encouragement after the final whistle, Jason chipped in with four goals, only to be surprisingly released at the end of the season.

Luton T (From trainee on 1/7/1988) FL 59+23 FLC 3+2 FAC 2+1 Others 5+1/2
Mansfield T (Loaned on 23/12/1993) FL 15/1 Others 1
Portsmouth (Free on 18/7/1994) FL 30+13/3 FLC 2+1 FAC 0+1
Exeter C (Loaned on 31/1/1997) FL 7
Cambridge U (Free on 8/8/1997) FL 17+3 FLC 2 Others 1
Exeter C (Free on 29/7/1998) FL 86+1/5 FLC 4 FAC 8 Others 6

REEVES Alan
Born: Birkenhead, 19 November 1967
Height: 6'0" Weight: 12.0

Alan provided a wealth of experience at the back for Swindon in the 1999-2000 season but proved unable to prevent the club from being relegated to the Second Division. He was rarely absent from the starting line-up and scored a single goal with a header in the 4-2 defeat by Crystal Palace last January. He is a tall central defender who is excellent in the air and always a threat when joining the attack for free kicks and corners.

Norwich C (Free from Heswall on 20/9/1988)
Gillingham (Loaned on 9/2/1989) FL 18
Chester C (£10,000 on 18/8/1989) FL 31+9/2 FLC 1+1 FAC 3 Others 3
Rochdale (Free on 2/7/1991) FL 119+2/9 FLC 12/1 FAC 6 Others 5
Wimbledon (£300,000 on 6/9/1994) PL 52+5/4 FLC 2+2 FAC 8
Swindon T (Free on 23/6/1998) FL 66+1/3 FLC 3/1

Alan Reeves

REEVES David Edward
Born: Birkenhead, 19 November 1967
Height: 6'0" Weight: 12.6
Club Honours: Div 3 '95
When David scored four against Cambridge last August, Chesterfield supporters hoped for much from him and the season. He didn't let the fans down: although the campaign ended in relegation, David's consistent, hard-working displays were the most enjoyable feature of it. Throughout 1999-2000 he played under the weight of speculation about a transfer to a host of other clubs, without it once affecting his commitment to Chesterfield. He has proved to be an excellent servant to the Spireites. David ended the season as Chesterfield's top scorer with 14 goals, and was voted the supporters' club "Player of the Year".
Sheffield Wed (Free from Heswall on 6/8/1986) FL 8+9/2 FLC 1+1/1 FAC 1+1 Others 0+1
Scunthorpe U (Loaned on 17/12/1986) FL 3+1/2
Scunthorpe U (Loaned on 1/10/1987) FL 6/4
Burnley (Loaned on 20/11/1987) FL 16/8 Others 2/1
Bolton W (£80,000 on 17/8/1989) FL 111+23/29 FLC 14+1/1 FAC 8+5/5 Others 9+2/7
Notts Co (£80,000 on 25/3/1993) FL 9+4/2 FLC 1+1
Carlisle U (£121,000 on 1/10/1993) FL 127/48 FLC 9/5 FAC 9/4 Others 23/7
Preston NE (Signed on 9/10/1996) FL 45+2/12 FLC 3+1/3 FAC 2/3 Others 1
Chesterfield (Signed on 6/11/1997) FL 106+3/29 FLC 7/3 FAC 3+1/1 Others 5/2

REID Paul Mark
Born: Carlisle, 18 February 1982
Height: 6'2" Weight: 11.8
One of the latest highly rated products to emerge from the youth ranks at Carlisle, Paul established himself as a first-choice defender in the early weeks of 2000. Blessed with pace and a positive attitude, he looks to have a bright future in the game. Paul was invited to join Leeds United for a seven-a-side tournament in Singapore in June. Stop Press: It was reported at the end of June that Paul had joined Glasgow Rangers.
Carlisle U (From trainee on 19/2/1999) FL 17+2 Others 3

REID Paul Robert
Born: Oldbury, 19 January 1968
Height: 5'9" Weight: 11.8
It took a little time for the midfielder to win over the Bury supporters following his arrival at Gigg Lane from Oldham Athletic in the summer of 1999. Gradually, though, the Shakers' supporters began to warm to Paul's committed style and tackling ability as he gained an extended run in the side. A back injury kept him sidelined for most of November and then he was forced to serve a three-match ban following a dismissal on 4 April at Cambridge United. Paul is one of those players who perhaps sometimes go unnoticed but get through a tremendous amount of work.
Leicester C (From apprentice on 9/1/1986) FL 140+22/21 FLC 13/4 FAC 5+1 Others 6+2
Bradford C (Loaned on 19/3/1992) FL 7
Bradford C (£25,000 on 27/7/1992) FL 80+2/15 FLC 3/2 FAC 3 Others 5/1
Huddersfield T (£70,000 on 20/5/1994) FL 70+7/6 FLC 9/1 FAC 5+1 Others 1
Oldham Ath (£100,000 on 27/3/1997) FL 93/6 FLC 4/1 FAC 8 Others 1
Bury (Free on 2/7/1999) FL 37+2/2 FLC 2 FAC 2

REID Shaun
Born: Huyton, 13 October 1965
Height: 5'8" Weight: 12.2
The brother of Sunderland manager Peter Reid, Shaun was again an inspiration to those around him in 1999-2000 but his fourth season at Chester ended in demotion to the Conference. His campaign came to an abrupt halt when he suffered a horrific facial injury in a Worthington Cup game with Port Vale. A hard-tackling, no-nonsense midfielder, Shaun returned in November for the FA Cup tie at Stalybridge. The veteran never gave anything less that 100 per cent when called upon, although many of his energies are now channelled into coaching. He was released at the end of the season.
Rochdale (From apprentice on 20/9/1983) FL 126+7/4 FLC 10/2 FAC 5/1 Others 12
Preston NE (Loaned on 12/12/1985) FL 3
York C (£32,500 on 23/12/1988) FL 104+2/7 FLC 7 FAC 4 Others 5/1
Rochdale (Free on 16/8/1992) FL 106+1/10 FLC 8 FAC 5/1 Others 8+1/2
Bury (£25,000 on 5/7/1995) FL 20+1/1 FLC 5 FAC 1 Others 2
Chester C (£30,000 on 25/11/1996) FL 53+9/2 FLC 4 FAC 3 Others 4

REID Steven John
Born: Kingston, 10 March 1981
Height: 6'1" Weight: 12.4
International Honours: E: Yth
Tall for a winger, Steven is good in the air, tackles enthusiastically and loves running at defences with the ball but he had difficulty forcing his way into Millwall's starting line-up in 1999-2000 due to the form of Paul Ifill and Michael Gilkes. Apart from a brief spell in the side in the autumn, he had few first-team opportunities but when he does get a chance this 19-year-old can be relied upon to give 100 per cent, performing with total commitment, an attribute the Millwall fans love about their young players. Always enthusiastic, there is no doubt that he will play a big part in the club's future success.
Millwall (From trainee on 18/5/1998) FL 36+11 FLC 1+1 FAC 1 Others 7

REILLY Alan
Born: Dublin, 22 August 1980
Height: 5'11" Weight: 12.6
Alan is a talented winger whom Halifax signed from Manchester City in December 1999. He was plunged straight into the first team at Hartlepool United in the Auto Windscreens Shield. An Irishman with a cultured left foot, he regularly showed his crossing ability during the second half of the league campaign and great things are expected of him in the new season.
Manchester C (From trainee on 23/9/1998)
Halifax T (Free on 3/12/1999) FL 15+5 Others 1

REUSER Martijn Franciscus
Born: Amsterdam, Holland, 1 February 1975
Height: 5'9" Weight: 11.7
International Honours: Holland: 1; U21-12
Martijn joined Ipswich on loan from Vitesse Arnhem just before transfer deadline day last March and took his place on the substitutes' bench for the home game with Fulham. With the match heading for a stalemate, he came on for the last 15 minutes and became a hero with the fans when, in the last minute, he ran on to Jim Magilton's through-ball and fired under the 'keeper to secure the three points. He featured in most games thereafter and appears to be adjusting well to the English game. He has a good turn of pace, can beat players in one-to-one situations and can pass well with either foot. His best performance was in the home game with Port Vale when he came on for the last 20 minutes and stole the show, creating the third goal for Matt Holland with a perfectly weighted through-ball. Ipswich tended to use him as a substitute, bringing him on for the last twenty minutes or so, and, although he would have preferred to be on the pitch from the start, he showed he has the right attitude by scoring vital goals once he had got a taste of the action. This was clearly demonstrated in the play-offs, when he got the clinching goal against Bolton and then, in the final at Wembley, showed tremendous composure and confidence to run on to Richard Naylor's ball, shrug off a defender and power a shot past the 'keeper. Stop Press: It was reported in the middle of June that Martijn had completed a permanent transfer to Ipswich for an initial fee of £1 million.
Ipswich T (Loaned from Vitesse Arnhem, Holland on 23/3/2000) FL 2+6/2 Others 0+3/2

RIBEIRO Bruno
Born: Setubal, Portugal, 22 October 1975
Height: 5'8" Weight: 12.2
Signed from Leeds by then Sheffield United manager Adrian Heath for around £500,000 in October 1999, the Portuguese midfielder made an impressive start at Swindon, showing skill and determination, but then injured a knee at Wolverhampton in his second game, which kept him out of the team for a month. Returning perhaps before he was fully fit, he completed only two full games – scoring a fine goal at West Bromwich – before another month on the sidelines. Despite regular appearances from the bench, usually late in the game, manager

Neil Warnock put Bruno on the transfer list, feeling that, given the club's limited resources, he was not the most suitable player for the Blades' quest for promotion. Many fans were surprised that he was not given more of a chance to show his potential, particularly when he was still with the club after the transfer deadline, and they were pleased when he made the starting line-up for the final four games of the season.

Leeds U (£500,000 from Vittoria Setubal, Portugal on 18/7/1997) PL 35+7/4 FLC 3+1/1 FAC 4/1 Others 1+1
Sheffield U (£500,000 on 25/10/1999) FL 9+11/1 FAC 1+1

Bruno Ribeiro

RICARD Cuesta **Hamilton**
Born: Colombia, 12 January 1974
Height: 6'2" Weight: 14.5
International Honours: Colombia: 29

After emerging as Middlesbrough's top goalscorer in 1998-99, his first full season at the Riverside, Hamilton went through a barren patch in 1999-2000 but started banging the goals in again in the last quarter of the season as his confidence came back in abundance. The fans had quickly caught on to the idea that Boro nearly always win when "Ham the Man" scores and they were delighted with his return to form. Watching him score from the penalty spot was a particular pleasure: he would run up almost nonchalantly and slot the ball home with aplomb. Big and strong, he really is a grafter and he may have benefited from a lay-off during the long and arduous Premiership season. Hamilton was a member of the Colombia squad that took part in the Copa America tournament in July 1999 and won further caps last season against Brazil and Bolivia in the opening rounds of their World Cup qualifying group.

Middlesbrough (£2,000,000 + from Deportivo Cali, Colombia on 13/3/1998) P/FL 64+15/29 FLC 8+1/5 FAC 2

RICHARD Fabrice
Born: Saintes, France, 16 August 1973
Height: 6'1" Weight: 12.4

Fabrice started the 1999-2000 season on the Colchester bench before winning a starting place in the defence after Warren Aspinall's departure. A natural centre half who looks somewhat uncomfortable when asked to play at full back, he was never really established in the team and couldn't quite convince the supporters that he would make the grade in a struggling back division. In the spring it was decided that Fabrice would be allowed to return to his native France and attempt to find himself another club there.

Colchester U (Signed from AS Cannes, France on 22/3/1999) FL 23+1 FLC 0+1 FAC 1

RICHARDS Dean Ivor
Born: Bradford, 9 June 1974
Height: 6'2" Weight: 13.5
International Honours: E: U21-4

An England U21 international while at Wolves, Dean's ambition to play Premiership football was realised during the summer of 1999 when he joined Southampton on a Bosman free transfer. A tall, commanding central defender, he proved a more than worthy replacement for Ken Monkou and a capable goalscorer to boot – he scored several crucial goals, including match winners against Ipswich Town in the FA Cup and Aston Villa. An automatic choice in the Saints' defence, he can only get better against stronger opposition. Dean was named the club's "Player of the Season" by supporters.

Bradford C (From trainee on 10/7/1992) FL 82+4/4 FLC 7/1 FAC 4/1 Others 3+2
Wolverhampton W (£1,850,000 on 25/3/1995) FL 118+4/7 FLC 11 FAC 10/1 Others 2
Southampton (Free on 28/7/1999) PL 35/2 FLC 4/2 FAC 1/1

RICHARDS Ian
Born: Barnsley, 5 October 1979
Height: 5'8" Weight: 11.5

Ian bided his time in the Halifax reserve team for most of the 1999-2000 season before seizing his opportunity in the closing months. He made an impressive full debut in the 1-1 draw at Lincoln in March. His potential was confirmed when he won the supporters' "Rising Star" award. Ian will be competing for a regular midfield berth in the new season.

Blackburn Rov (From trainee on 11/7/1997)
Halifax T (Free on 5/7/1999) FL 5+1

RICHARDS Justin
Born: West Bromwich, 16 October 1980
Height: 5'10" Weight: 11.0

A reserve-team striker with West Bromwich, Justin was called into senior action just once during the 1999-2000 season, coming off the bench for the last six minutes of extra time when the Baggies were defeated 2-0 by Blackburn Rovers in an FA Cup replay at Ewood Park in late

Dean Richards

December. He did well at second-team level, however, scoring four goals in helping Albion finish in mid-table in the Pontins League.

West Bromwich A (From trainee on 8/1/1999) FL 0+1 FAC 0+1

RICHARDS Tony Spencer
Born: Newham, 17 September 1973
Height: 5'11" Weight: 13.1

Tony was unable to command a regular place in the Leyton Orient line-up last season because of injury problems. Having previously successfully switched from right wing to centre forward, he is adept at holding the ball up. He will be looking to regain full fitness and return to the first team in the new season. Tony is also a long throw expert.

West Ham U (From trainee on 14/8/1992. Free to Hong Kong R during 1993 close season)
Cambridge U (Signed from Sudbury T on 10/8/1995) FL 29+13/5 FLC 1 Others 3
Leyton Orient (£10,000 on 21/7/1997) FL 47+16/11 FLC 3+3/1 FAC 2/3 Others 5

RICHARDSON Barry
Born: Wallsend, 5 August 1969
Height: 6'1" Weight: 12.1

Barry was a big favourite with the Lincoln fans during 1999-2000 but not always so popular with the management at the club. He was loaned to Mansfield at the beginning of the season to cover for injured regular goalkeeper Ian Bowling but went back to Sincil Bank in September. He was immediately restored as the Imps' first-choice 'keeper and returned to Field Mill in December with Lincoln, conceding five goals as the Stags won the home leg of the local derby. Barry remained an ever-present until being dropped in favour of young Alan Marriott in February. He made a surprise loan move to Premiership club Sheffield Wednesday on transfer deadline day, where he was required as cover for injuries. He made no senior appearances for the Hillsborough club and was released by Lincoln at the end of the season.

Sunderland (From trainee on 20/5/1988)
Scunthorpe U (Free on 21/3/1989)
Scarborough (Free on 3/8/1989) FL 30 FLC 1 Others 1
Stockport Co (Free on 6/8/1991)
Northampton T (Free on 10/9/1991) FL 96 FLC 4 FAC 5 Others 8
Preston NE (£20,000 on 25/7/1994) FL 20 FLC 2 FAC 3 Others 2
Lincoln C (£20,000 on 20/10/1995) FL 131 FLC 5 FAC 11 Others 3
Mansfield T (Loaned on 5/8/1999) FL 6 FLC 2

RICHARDSON Ian George
Born: Barking, 22 October 1970
Height: 5'10" Weight: 11.1
Club Honours: Div 3 '98
International Honours: E: SP-1

Ian had another good season for Notts County in 1999-2000, providing a touch of class in midfield and occasionally in the centre of the defence. He was an inspirational figure in either role, impressing with his last-ditch tackles and ability to outjump much taller players when coming up at set pieces. Very popular with the Magpies' supporters, he contributed four goals during the season.

Birmingham C (£60,000 from Dagenham & Redbridge on 23/8/1995) FL 3+4 FLC 3+1 FAC 2 Others 1+2
Notts Co (£200,000 on 19/1/1996) FL 112+8/14 FLC 8 FAC 9/1 Others 6

RICHARDSON Jonathan (Jon) Derek
Born: Nottingham, 29 August 1975
Height: 6'0" Weight: 12.6

Jon had another consistent season in 1999-2000 and missed only a handful of games. The Exeter captain, he led by example by always remaining calm and poised on the right side of defence. Only one booking was a credit to his fair play and professionalism. Arguably the most surprising victim of the Grecians' mass end-of-term clear-out, Jon was transfer-listed with a year of his contract to run.

Exeter C (From trainee on 7/7/1994) FL 242+5/8 FLC 11/3 FAC 15/1 Others 13

RICHARDSON Kevin
Born: Newcastle, 4 December 1962
Height: 5'9" Weight: 12.0
Club Honours: FAC '84; CS '84; Div 1 '85, '89; ECWC '85; FLC '94
International Honours: E: 1

This veteran midfield player began 1999-2000 as Barnsley captain but was very quickly dropped by new manager Dave Bassett and eventually moved on loan to Blackpool last January, signing permanently two months later. He appeared regularly for the Seasiders for the rest of the season but was unable to prevent them from being relegated to the Third Division. Despite his

Barry Richardson

years he is still a great organiser and more than capable with set-piece kicks.
Everton (From apprentice on 8/12/1980) FL 95+14/16 FLC 10+3/3 FAC 13/1 Others 7+2
Watford (£225,000 on 4/9/1986) FL 39/2 FLC 3 FAC 7 Others 1
Arsenal (£200,000 on 26/8/1987) FL 88+8/5 FLC 13+3/2 FAC 9/1 Others 3 (£750,000 to Real Sociedad on 1/7/1990)
Aston Villa (£450,000 on 6/8/1991) P/FL 142+1/13 FLC 15/3 FAC 12 Others 10
Coventry C (£300,000 on 16/2/1995) PL 75+3 FLC 8/1 FAC 7
Southampton (£150,000 on 10/9/1997) PL 25+3 FLC 4 FAC 1
Barnsley (£300,000 on 17/7/1998) FL 28+2 FLC 4 FAC 2+1
Blackpool (Loaned on 10/1/1999) FL 20/1 Others 2

RICHARDSON Leam Nathan
Born: Leeds, 19 November 1979
Height: 5'7" Weight: 11.4
This young Blackburn defender hails from Leeds so it was fitting that he should be given his chance last season in the Worthington Cup tie in his home city. A determined character who tackles with relish, he had a fine debut and displayed dash and enthusiasm coming forward. It remains a mystery that he was not added to the first-team squad on more occasions and he will be hoping for greater opportunities in 2000-01.
Blackburn Rov (From trainee on 31/12/1997) FLC 1

RICHARDSON Lee James
Born: Halifax, 12 March 1969
Height: 5'11" Weight: 11.0
Signed by Bury on loan from Huddersfield Town towards the end of August 1999, the skilful midfield play-maker immediately took Darren Bullock's position in midfield. Although Lee went on to start five games for the Shakers and scored Bury's goal in a 1-1 draw at Luton Town on 4 September, he was obviously nowhere near full fitness and was allowed to return to the McAlpine Stadium at the end of his month's loan. He subsequently left Huddersfield and joined Livingston.
Halifax T (From trainee on 6/7/1987) FL 43+13/2 FLC 4 FAC 4+2 Others 6
Watford (£175,000 on 9/2/1989) FL 40+1/1 FLC 1+1 FAC 1
Blackburn Rov (£250,000 on 15/8/1990) FL 50+12/3 FLC 1 Others 2+2
Aberdeen (£152,000 on 16/9/1992) SL 59+5/6 SLC 2/1 SC 8/2 Others 3/1
Oldham Ath (£300,000 on 12/8/1994) FL 82+6/21 FLC 6/2 FAC 3 Others 4
Stockport Co (Loaned on 15/8/1997) FL 4+2
Huddersfield T (£65,000 on 24/10/1997) FL 29+7/3 FAC 0+2
Bury (Loaned on 27/8/1999) FL 5/1

RICHARDSON Neil Thomas
Born: Sunderland, 3 March 1968
Height: 6'0" Weight: 13.9
Club Honours: AMC '96
This experienced central defender joined Mansfield from near neighbours Rotherham United during the 1999 close season. He is not the paciest of defenders but his accurate distribution and aerial capabilities made him a mainstay at the heart of the defence until a knee injury sustained at Cheltenham in January which required surgery forced him out of the side for a lengthy spell. He was released during the summer.
Rotherham U (Signed from Brandon U on 18/8/1989) FL 168+16/9 FLC 14+1/1 FAC 12+1/1 Others 11+2/1
Exeter C (Loaned on 8/11/1996) FL 14 Others 2
Mansfield T (Free on 5/8/1999) FL 31 FLC 2 FAC 1 Others 1

RICHARDSON Nicholas (Nick) John
Born: Halifax, 11 April 1967
Height: 6'1" Weight: 12.6
Club Honours: Div 3 '93; WC '93
This Chester stalwart's influence in the centre of midfield almost saved the Blues from their seemingly inevitable relegation to the Conference last season. A good creative player who can perform with credit at right back if required, he also weighed in with spectacular goals at Hull and Shrewsbury. Nick now has over 150 Chester appearances to his name and will be hoping to lead City's climb back to the Football League.
Halifax T (Free from Emley on 15/11/1988) FL 89+12/17 FLC 6+4/2 FAC 2+1/1 Others 6/1
Cardiff C (£35,000 on 13/8/1992) FL 106+5/13 FLC 4 FAC 6 Others 12+2/2
Wrexham (Loaned on 21/10/1994) FL 4/2
Chester C (Loaned on 16/12/1994) FL 6/1
Bury (£22,500 on 8/8/1995) FL 3+2 FLC 1
Chester C (£40,000 on 7/9/1995) FL 158+11/11 FLC 11/1 FAC 8/2 Others 5/1

RICKERS Paul Steven
Born: Pontefract, 9 May 1975
Height: 5'10" Weight: 11.0
Paul was once again a near-ever-present for Oldham in 1999-2000 and showed his versatility by appearing as a right wing back and on the right side of midfield in addition to his favoured central midfield role. He contributed three goals, including a great 20-yard drive in the 2-1 win at Scunthorpe last March. Solid but unspectacular, he works hard for the team and always gives 100 per cent effort wherever he plays.
Oldham Ath (From trainee on 16/7/1993) FL 191+8/16 FLC 9 FAC 13+1 Others 3+1

RICKETTS Michael Barrington
Born: Birmingham, 4 December 1978
Height: 6'2" Weight: 11.12
This well-built young striker with a penchant for getting into goalscoring positions netted some excellent goals for Walsall during the 1999-2000 season, the pick of them coming in the 3-2 win at Crewe in January when he held off several challenges before finding the net. Although apparently unsettled at the Bescot Stadium, he ended the season as the club's leading scorer with 11 goals.
Walsall (From trainee on 13/9/1996) FL 31+45/14 FLC 2+4 FAC 2+2 Others 3+1/1

RIDLER David (Dave) George
Born: Liverpool, 12 March 1976
Height: 6'1" Weight: 12.2
David competed with young Steve Roberts for a place alongside skipper Brian Carey in the centre of Wrexham's defence last season. He is a player who always seems to have time and impressed many at the Racecourse with his no-nonsense displays. Although troubled by a back injury, he remained a member of the first-team squad throughout the 1999-2000 season and occasionally filled in at left back.
Wrexham (Free from Rockys on 3/7/1996) FL 82+10/1 FLC 3 FAC 9+2 Others 8+1/1

RIEDLE Karl-Heinz
Born: Weiler, Germany, 16 September 1965
Height: 5'10" Weight: 11.6
International Honours: Germany: 42
The German striker made only one league appearance for Liverpool in 1999-2000, coming off the bench in the second game of the season against Watford, although he also featured in the starting line-up for the second leg of the Worthington Cup tie against Hull, scoring twice. Karl-Heinz showed a hunger for success which he was unable to fulfil in his time at Anfield. A wonderful player, he was, perhaps, just past his best, and with the arrival of Titi Camara and Erik Meijer at the club his days were clearly numbered. He was sold to Fulham at the end of September and it certainly showed how far the London club had come from the depths of Division Three only four years earlier that they were able to attract such a high-profile import to the Cottage. Karl-Heinz was recruited after it had been decided not to sign Stan Collymore on a permanent contract, and showed his class on his debut by netting a close-range equaliser en route to a 2-1 win at Norwich. His total of five league goals for his new club should ensure that Karl-Heinz, who took over as caretaker manager when Paul Bracewell was dismissed, will be a serious contender for a starting place in attack next season.
Liverpool (£1,600,000 from Borussia Dortmund, Germany, via Augsburg, Blau-Weiss 90, Werder Bremen and Lazio, on 4/8/1997) PL 34+26/11 FLC 3+4/2 FAC 2 Others 3+4/2
Fulham (£250,000 on 28/9/1999) FL 15+6/5 FAC 1

RIGBY Anthony (Tony) Angelo
Born: Ormskirk, 10 August 1972
Height: 5'10" Weight: 12.12
Club Honours: Div 2 '97
Shrewsbury tried to sign Tony in 1998-99 but had to wait until last September to capture the midfielder. He made his debut as a substitute in a 1-0 win at Cheltenham. Out of first-team action for some while, he needed time to gain match fitness and did not make his full debut until the end of October. Tony is essentially a creative player and his strength is his ability to pass the ball. However, he did not fit into new manager Kevin Ratcliffe's plans and was released in January.
Crewe Alex (From trainee on 16/5/1990)
Bury (Free from Barrow, via Lancaster C and Runcorn & Burscough, on 6/1/1993) FL 120+46/19 FLC 5+3/2 FAC 5+3/1 Others 13+3/2 (Free to Altrincham during 1999 close season)
Scarborough (Loaned on 14/2/1997) FL 5/1
Shrewsbury T (Free on 6/10/1999) FL 4+4/1 FAC 2

RIGGOTT Christopher (Chris)
Born: Derby, 1 September 1980
Height: 6'3" Weight: 12.2
International Honours: E: Yth
This highly promising young centre back

produced consistent form in Derby County's reserve team and was rewarded with a substitute appearance in the final Premiership game of the 1999-2000 season at Chelsea. Contracted to the club until 2003, he is one of the many bright young prospects at Pride Park and will be expecting to feature more often in 2000-01.

Derby Co (From trainee on 5/10/1998) PL 0+1

RIMMER Stephen (Steve) Anthony
Born: Liverpool, 23 May 1979
Height: 6'3" Weight: 13.2

Having been released by Manchester City, Paul joined Port Vale in the summer of 1999, but the tall central defender spent the majority of last season in Vale's reserves. His big chance came in the Christmas game at Barnsley, when he was called off the subs' bench at half time to replace the injured Mark Snijders. It proved to be a memorable first league appearance of his career for the youngster, as he was unfortunately sent off, and he only made it off the bench once more in the remainder of the campaign. Steve was released on a free transfer at the end of the season.

Manchester C (From trainee on 29/5/1996) Others 1
Port Vale (Free on 8/7/1999) FL 0+2

RIOCH Gregor (Greg) James
Born: Sutton Coldfield, 24 June 1975
Height: 5'11" Weight: 12.10

A totally committed and extremely enthusiastic left back, Gregor gives his all in every match, although he has a tendency to over-commit himself. Signed from Hull in the 1999 close season, he was handed the Macclesfield captaincy at the beginning of the new campaign, but manager Sammy McIlroy relieved him of this responsibility during October because he felt that he was asking too much of him. However, he retained the role of penalty taker, with one of his three converted spot kicks included in a brace on his victorious 3-2 return to Hull in August. The son of Bruce Rioch, Gregor missed only four games during the season, and his impressive first term at Moss Rose led to a rumoured £150,000 bid from Norwich in February – while his father was still in charge of the Canaries.

Luton T (From trainee on 19/7/1993)
Barnet (Loaned on 17/9/1993) FL 3 FLC 2 Others 1
Peterborough U (Free on 11/8/1995) FL 13+5 FLC 2 FAC 2+1 Others 2+1
Hull C (Free on 10/7/1996) FL 86+5/6 FLC 7/3 FAC 5/1 Others 3
Macclesfield T (Free on 5/7/1999) FL 42/5 FLC 2 FAC 2 Others 1

RIPLEY Stuart Edward
Born: Middlesbrough, 20 November 1967
Height: 5'11" Weight: 13.0
Club Honours: PL '95
International Honours: E: 2; U21-8; Yth

The 1999-2000 season was one of mixed fortunes for the former England winger. Stuart's form with Southampton returned spectacularly after an indifferent 1998-99 campaign. His tireless tracking up and down the right flank, coupled with his delivery of quality crosses, won over the fans, who had initially been slow to take to him. His willingness to get stuck in naturally made them warm to him as well. Although he was a first-team regular, troublesome injuries returned to jinx him. Forced out early on by a hamstring injury, Stuart then developed a painful achilles problem which was to sideline him for over two months towards the end of the season.

Middlesbrough (From apprentice on 23/12/1985) FL 210+39/26 FLC 21+2/3 FAC 17+1/1 Others 20+1/1
Bolton W (Loaned on 18/2/1986) FL 5/1 Others 0+1
Blackburn Rov (£1,300,000 on 20/7/1992) PL 172+15/13 FLC 18 FAC 14/3 Others 8+1
Southampton (£1,500,000 on 10/7/1998) PL 34+11/1 FLC 3 FAC 2+1

Stuart Ripley

RITCHIE Paul Simon
Born: Kirkcaldy, 21 August 1975
Height: 5'11" Weight: 12.0
Club Honours: SC '98
International Honours: S: 6; B; U21-7; Sch

A hugely influential centre half, Paul was signed by Bolton on loan for three months from Hearts at the end of December 1999, primarily to cover for Mark Fish's absence on international duty. His performances at the heart of the defence suggested that Bolton had acquired a player of genuine quality and, with rumours flying around that he would be signing for Rangers in the summer, he was signed on a short-term contract until the end of the season. Paul did a fine job of deputising for the absent Fish, although his greatest contributions to the team came when Fish returned to action in the final third of the season. The pair struck up an immediate understanding and formed a formidable partnership at the heart of the Bolton defence, making a crucial contribution to Wanderers' fine late run which took them into the play-offs. He is an assured and confident player with excellent passing and distribution, and it was a disappointment for the Bolton fans when he completed his expected move to Rangers in the summer. Paul added a further four caps for Scotland in the 1999-2000 season.

Heart of Midlothian (From Links U on 31/7/1992) SL 132+1/5 SLC 10+1 SC 11/3 Others 6
Bolton W (Free on 22/12/1999) FL 13+1 FLC 1 FAC 3+1 Others 2

RIVERS Mark Alan
Born: Crewe, 26 November 1975
Height: 5'11" Weight: 11.2

Mark has been a regular member of Crewe's first team since graduating through the club's youth programme in the mid-1990s. He has occupied most of the forward positions at one time or another but is probably most effective in a wide role, while

Mark Rivers

his height makes him dangerous at corners and free kicks. Although he was a substitute for the opening game of last season at Crystal Palace, he came on for Phil Charnock and scored a late equaliser, earning himself a place in the starting line-up for the next league match, when he scored again. He was briefly absent through injury in the middle of the season but finished the campaign strongly with four goals in his last four matches, taking his total for the season to nine. He is now approaching 50 goals for the club, and is the leading scorer among Alex's current players.

Crewe Alex (From trainee on 6/5/1994) FL 145+25/36 FLC 12+1/6 FAC 9/3 Others 6+3/3

RIZZO Nicholas (Nicky) Anthony
Born: Sydney, Australia, 9 June 1979
Height: 5'10" Weight: 12.0
International Honours: Australia: 1; U23-8

Nicky is an attacking midfield player with neat ball control and a good turn of speed. The 1999-2000 season was a relatively disappointing one for him as he made the starting line-up for Crystal Palace on just three occasions. Regularly used as a substitute in the campaign's early games, he had a month out with an ankle injury and was also absent on international duties. He added four more caps for Australia's U23 team and will be hoping to win a place in their squad for the Olympic Games tournament in the coming autumn.

Liverpool (Signed from Sydney Olympic, Australia on 26/9/1996)
Crystal Palace (£300,000 on 31/7/1998) FL 15+21/1 FLC 1+3/1 FAC 1

ROACH Neville
Born: Reading, 29 September 1978
Height: 5'10" Weight: 11.1

Neville was a fringe squad player at Southend during 1999-2000. His speed and trickery up front never quite commanded a place in the starting line-up. Neville was loaned to Chester City, but returned after only one reserve game, and finished the campaign in the Southend second team. He was released at the end of the season.

Reading (From trainee on 10/5/1997) FL 5+11/1 FLC 1+4/1 FAC 0+1 Others 0+1
Southend U (£30,000 on 26/2/1999) FL 13+3/2 FLC 1+1 Others 0+1

ROBERTS Andrew (Andy) James
Born: Dartford, 20 March 1974
Height: 5'10" Weight: 13.0
Club Honours: FAYC '91
International Honours: E: U21-5

Andy enjoyed an extended run in the Wimbledon first team at the start of the 1999-2000 season, but injury and competition for places limited his opportunities in the second half of the campaign. A strong, tough-tackling midfielder who goes about his work in a professional manner, Andy will be a good bet for a starting position during the coming season as the Dons attempt to gain promotion from Division One. Commitment and honesty will be essential if they are to succeed and Andy excels in both departments.

Millwall (From trainee on 29/10/1991) FL 132+6/5 FLC 12/2 FAC 7 Others 4/1
Crystal Palace (£2,520,000 on 29/7/1995) F/PL 106+2/2 FLC 7+1 FAC 8 Others 6/1
Wimbledon (£1,200,000 + on 10/3/1998) PL 49+7/3 FLC 8+1 FAC 3+1

Andy Roberts

ROBERTS Benjamin (Ben) James
Born: Bishop Auckland, 22 June 1975
Height: 6'1" Weight: 12.11
International Honours: E: U21-1

Out in the cold at Middlesbrough, where he was the third-choice goalkeeper behind Mark Schwarzer and Marlon Beresford, Ben joined Luton on loan in February 1999. He made his debut shortly afterwards against Brentford, replacing Nathan Abbey, and retained his place for the rest of the season. Brave and agile, he is an excellent shot stopper and, although he looked a little uncertain at first, as his confidence returned he began to show signs of his Premiership pedigree.

Middlesbrough (From trainee on 24/3/1993) F/PL 15+1 FLC 2+1 FAC 6 Others 1
Hartlepool U (Loaned on 19/10/1995) FL 4 Others 1
Wycombe W (Loaned on 8/12/1995) FL 15
Bradford C (Loaned on 27/8/1996) FL 2
Millwall (Loaned on 12/2/1999) FL 11 Others 4
Luton T (Loaned on 24/2/2000) FL 14

ROBERTS Christian (Chris) John
Born: Cardiff, 22 October 1979
Height: 5'10" Weight: 12.8
International Honours: W: U21-1; Yth

This promising striker was released by Cardiff at the end of the 1999-2000 season. He has pace and a fierce shot, but it wasn't quite enough. Chris spent a short spell on loan with Drogheda in Ireland during the campaign and was a regular goalscorer for City's reserves. However, his chances at first-team level were restricted and the Welsh U21 international was unable to persuade manager Billy Ayre that he was worth a new contract.

Cardiff C (From trainee on 8/10/1997) FL 6+17/3 FLC 2 FAC 2+3 Others 0+2

ROBERTS Gareth Wyn
Born: Wrexham, 6 February 1978
Height: 5'7" Weight: 12.6
Club Honours: FAYC '96
International Honours: W: 3; B-1; U21-10

Gareth joined Tranmere on loan at the beginning of August 1999 after a disappointing spell in Greece and quickly signed permanent forms for Rovers after a number of impressive displays. He was a regular in the first team from mid-September and appeared in the starting line-up for the Worthington Cup final with Leicester, making a miraculous recovery after suffering what was initially believed to be a broken leg against Newcastle the week before. He proved to be steady, solid and tenacious at full back for Rovers, performing consistently well yet remaining very much an unsung hero. Already capped by Wales at U21 level, he gained his first full cap when coming on as a substitute against Finland in March and also appeared in the end-of-season fixtures against Brazil and Portugal.

Liverpool (From trainee on 22/5/1996. £50,000 to Panionios, Greece on 15/1/1999)
Tranmere Rov (Free on 5/8/1999) FL 36+1/1 FLC 7 FAC 3

ROBERTS Iwan Wyn
Born: Bangor, 26 June 1968
Height: 6'3" Weight: 14.2
International Honours: W: 10; B-1; Yth; Sch

Iwan led the Norwich goalscoring charts for the second successive season in 1999-2000, proving himself to be a real threat to Division One defences in a campaign when he reached the milestones of 450 career league games and 150 career league goals. A robust front runner who excels with his back to goal, being able to receive the ball when under the severest of pressure, Iwan also has the poacher's knack of being in the right place at the right time to convert chances in and around the six-yard box. A virtual ever-present in the City line-up last season, he signed a new contract in January 2000, tying him to the Carrow Road club until June 2002. His popularity with the Canary fans is immense, something which was enhanced by his two goals in the 2-0 local derby success at Ipswich last March. His overall strength, enthusiasm and goal-scoring abilities have also been noted by new Wales boss Mark Hughes, who awarded him further caps against Finland, Brazil and Portugal.

Watford (From trainee on 4/7/1988) FL 40+23/9 FLC 6+2/3 FAC 1+6 Others 5
Huddersfield T (£275,000 on 2/8/1990) FL 141+1/50 FLC 13+1/6 FAC 12/4 Others 14/8
Leicester C (£100,000 on 25/11/1993) P/FL 92+8/41 FLC 5/1 FAC 5/2 Others 1
Wolverhampton W (£1,300,000 + on 15/7/1996) FL 24+9/12 FLC 2 FAC 0+1 Others 2
Norwich C (£900,000 on 9/7/1997) FL 113+7/41 FLC 9+2/7 FAC 2/1

ROBERTS Jason Andre Davis
Born: Park Royal, 25 January 1978
Height: 5'11" Weight: 12.7
International Honours: Grenada: 5

This powerful, well-built striker's contribution to the Bristol Rovers team during the 1999-2000 season was remarkable. His first touch had improved and his understanding with strike partner Jamie Cureton once again realised over 50 league goals between them. Always a threat to defenders, particularly when he is allowed to run with the ball, Jason remains one of the best strikers outside the Premiership. His goal at Cambridge in April when he received the ball in his own half and set off on a powerful run, going past five defenders before beating the goalkeeper from just inside the penalty area, was described by manager Ian Holloway as the best goal he had ever seen. Few Rovers fans would argue with that. Jason continued to represent Grenada, appearing against Barbados in the qualifying round for the 2002 World Cup.

Wolverhampton W (£250,000 from Hayes on 12/9/1997)
Torquay U (Loaned on 19/12/1997) FL 13+1/6 Others 1
Bristol C (Loaned on 26/3/1998) FL 1+2/1
Bristol Rov (£250,000 on 7/8/1998) FL 73+5/38 FLC 6/3 FAC 6/7 Others 3

ROBERTS Neil Wyn
Born: Wrexham, 7 April 1978
Height: 5'10" Weight: 11.0
International Honours: W: 1; B-1; U21-2; Yth

The 1999-2000 season was one to remember for this young Welsh striker. Having recovered from a bad leg injury, he then suffered a broken wrist during the summer of 1999 and missed the opening games of the new campaign for Wrexham. He was back in action in October, when he appeared as a substitute for Wales U21s against Switzerland and then made his full international debut in the senior match against the Swiss when he came on for the final 12 minutes as a replacement for Nathan Blake. Neil then crowned a glorious week by scoring with a superb 18-yard volley the following Saturday against Chesterfield. He impressed with his high workrate and willingness to probe hard for openings, but it was still a surprise to some when he was sold to Wigan Athletic for a £450,000 fee last February. The Welshman took time to settle into his new environment, but his ability to use his body to hold the ball up was soon apparent. His first goal for the Latics came in the 2-2 draw at Bournemouth, but he missed the play-offs following an operation on his ankle. Neil is the older brother of Wrexham central defender Steve Roberts.

Wrexham (From trainee on 3/7/1996) FL 58+17/17 FLC 1/1 FAC 11+1/4 Others 2+2/2
Wigan Ath (£450,000 on 18/2/2000) FL 8+1/1

ROBERTS Stephen (Steve) Wyn
Born: Wrexham, 24 February 1980
Height: 6'0" Weight: 12.7
International Honours: W: U21-2; Yth

Steve continued to make steady progress as a central defender for Wrexham in 1999-2000, wisely nursed along by manager Brian Flynn. He shared centre-back duties with David Ridler in the slot alongside club captain Brian Carey for most of the season and made a good impression with his unhurried style of play – invariably the hallmark of a talented player. His assured performances attracted the attention of Premiership scouts and in the close season he won his first caps for Wales at U21 level, appearing in the Presidents' Cup games with Northern Ireland and Scotland. Steve is the younger brother of Wigan striker Neil.

Wrexham (From trainee on 16/1/1998) FL 16+3 FAC 3/1 Others 0+1

ROBERTS Stuart Ian
Born: Carmarthen, 22 July 1980
Height: 5'7" Weight: 9.8
International Honours: W: U21-3

A member of the Swansea squad for the first two months of the 1999-2000 season, Stuart was sidelined with what was initially diagnosed as a virus. It later turned out to be exhaustion as a consequence of having insufficient rest in the close season. An ankle problem midway through the term also delayed his return to fitness, resulting in his being confined to occasional substitute appearances during the second half of the Swans' Third Division championship campaign. Despite his enforced absence, the plucky striker still played a part as he made a good impression on a local radio station with his informed comments during match reports.

Swansea C (From trainee on 9/7/1998) FL 24+19/4 FLC 3+2 FAC 3 Others 4+2

ROBERTSON Mark William
Born: Sydney, Australia, 6 April 1977
Height: 5'9" Weight: 11.4
International Honours: Australia: U23-5; Yth

There was little opportunity for Mark's career to progress at Burnley this season, as the increased strength of Stan Ternent's squad left him as a fringe player. He was eventually loaned to Wollongong Wolves in his homeland, with a view to increasing his chances of selection for the "Olyroos" in the Sydney Olympics. His skills either at full back or in midfield should give him a future in the Football League, but his chances at Turf Moor may now be limited. Mark added a further U23 cap when he appeared as a late substitute against Tunisia in November.

Burnley (Free from Marconi Stallions, Australia on 3/10/1997) FL 27+9/1 FLC 1+1 Others 3+2

ROBINS Mark Gordon
Born: Ashton under Lyne, 22 December 1969
Height: 5'8" Weight: 11.11
Club Honours: FAC '90; ECWC '91; ESC '91; FLC '97
International Honours: E: U21-6

A much-travelled striker who has seen service with both Manchester clubs, Mark came to Walsall in time for the pre-season tour of France in 1999 and made certain of a place in the first team for the opening league and cup games. A floated cross that fortuitously found the net in the Worthington Cup tie at Plymouth set him off on a purposeful season in which he played with a variety of striking partners and scored eight goals in addition to providing unselfish support for his team-mates with his lay-offs and ability to create space. Stop Press: Mark was reported to have moved to Rotherham in mid-June.

Manchester U (From apprentice on 23/12/1986) FL 19+29/11 FLC 0+7/2 FAC 4+4/3 Others 4+3/1
Norwich C (£800,000 on 14/8/1992) PL 57+10/20 FLC 6+3/1 Others 1+1
Leicester C (£1,000,000 on 16/1/1995) P/FL 40+16/12 FLC 5+4/5 FAC 4+2 Others 1+1
Reading (Loaned on 29/8/1997) FL 5 (Signed by Deportivo Orense, Spain on 15/1/1998)
Manchester C (Free from Panionios, Greece on 25/3/1999) FL 0+2
Walsall (Free on 5/8/1999) FL 30+10/6 FLC 4/1 FAC 2/1

ROBINSON Carl Phillip
Born: Llandrindod Wells, 13 October 1976
Height: 5'10" Weight: 12.10
International Honours: W: 2; B-2; U21-6; Yth

The right-sided midfielder did not make as much progress as expected with Wolves in 1999-2000, despite starting the first nine games of the season. Thereafter, Carl was in and out of the Wolves team, but he made a perfectly timed run in the FA Cup tie at Wigan to head a late winner, which made him popular, as a replay would have caused the cancellation of the players' Christmas party! He was involved in all the January fixtures but was still dropped on occasions later in the season and Wolves' fans continued to see only glimpses of his best form, such as his superb volleyed winner at Swindon in March. Mark made his debut in senior international football for Wales when he came on from the subs' bench against Belarus in September and added a further cap in the end-of-season friendly with Portugal.

Wolverhampton W (From trainee on 3/7/1995) FL 78+23/14 FLC 7 FAC 12/2
Shrewsbury T (Loaned on 28/3/1996) FL 2+2 Others 1

Carl Robinson

ROBINSON Jamie
Born: Liverpool, 26 February 1972
Height: 6'1" Weight: 12.8
Club Honours: Div 3 '95

The big central defender signed a short-term contract with Exeter last October. Jamie had been released by Torquay in the 1999 close season and, although several clubs had shown an interest, he was keen to stay in Devon, and had been training with Plymouth. Nevertheless, with his chances becoming restricted with the Grecians, he answered Chester's call in January when he joined them on a free transfer. As well as performing dependably in his recognised position, Jamie also impressed in a new midfield role. Despite City's relegation, the Liverpudlian could still have a bright future at the Deva.

Liverpool (From trainee on 4/6/1990)
Barnsley (Free on 17/7/1992) FL 8+1 Others 3
Carlisle U (Signed on 28/1/1994) FL 46+11/4 FLC 1+2 FAC 3 Others 7+6/1
Torquay U (Free on 2/7/1997) FL 75/1 FLC 6 FAC 5 Others 4
Exeter C (Free on 30/9/1999) FL 11+1 FAC 3 Others 0+1
Chester C (Free on 21/1/2000) FL 9

John Robinson

ROBINSON John Robert Campbell
Born: Bulawayo, Rhodesia, 29 August 1971
Height: 5'10" Weight: 11.7
Club Honours: Div 1 '00
International Honours: W: 22; U21-5

John broke the record for international appearances by a Charlton Athletic player that had stood for 40 years when he earned his 20th Welsh cap in March 2000, just one highlight of a 1999-2000 season which also brought him a First Division championship medal and selection for the PFA award-winning First Division side. A tricky winger who, although right footed, can play on either wing or at wing back, he loves to take players on and is a good crosser of the ball with either foot, often cutting inside to have a shot. He scored a spectacular goal at Huddersfield when he hit the ball on the run at an angle from fully 25 yards, and scored a total of seven league goals during the campaign, which made him joint third-top scorer. John appeared regularly for Wales, adding six more caps during the season.

Brighton & Hove A (From trainee on 21/4/1989) FL 57+5/6 FLC 5/1 FAC 2+1 Others 1+2/2
Charlton Ath (£75,000 on 15/9/1992) P/FL 249+13/32 FLC 16+2/4 FAC 14+2/3 Others 5+1

ROBINSON Leslie (Les)
Born: Shirebrook, 1 March 1967
Height: 5'9" Weight: 12.4

Les was once again ultra-reliable in 1999-2000 and was one of only two Oxford players to appear in every league match – and indeed the only one to play in all 59 of the club's games. As with every other season that Les has played at the Manor Ground, he was totally dependable and he provided inspirational leadership with his never-say-die attitude. Used mainly as a right back, Les also appeared as a centre back and in a holding role in midfield, performing in each position with typical spirit. He did not manage a goal last season but took his overall tally of games for Oxford to over 450. Stop Press: It was reported in mid-June that he had moved to Mansfield.

Mansfield T (Free from Nottingham F juniors on 6/10/1984) FL 11+4 Others 1
Stockport Co (£10,000 on 27/11/1986) FL 67/3 FLC 2 FAC 4 Others 4
Doncaster Rov (£20,000 on 24/3/1988) FL 82/12 FLC 4 FAC 5 Others 5/1
Oxford U (£150,000 on 19/3/1990) FL 379+5/3 FLC 38/8 FAC 22+1 Others 13

ROBINSON Mark James
Born: Rochdale, 21 November 1968
Height: 5'9" Weight: 12.4
Club Honours: Div 2 '96

Mark has been Swindon's regular right back for six years and had another good season for the club in 1999-2000 despite the disappointment of the team's relegation to Division Two. He played a further 40 league games during the season and has now made more then 250 senior appearances for the Robins in all competitions. He remains a reliable defender who is able to bring the ball confidently out of defence and deliver quality crosses into the opposition penalty area.

West Bromwich A (From apprentice on 10/1/1987) FL 2 FLC 0+1
Barnsley (Free on 23/6/1987) FL 117+20/6 FLC 7+2 FAC 7+1 Others 3+2/1
Newcastle U (£450,000 on 9/3/1993) F/PL 14+11 FAC 1
Swindon T (£600,000 on 22/7/1994) FL 220+7/3 FLC 19 FAC 12 Others 6+1

ROBINSON Marvin Leon St
Born: Crewe, 11 April 1980
Height: 6'0" Weight: 12.9

This powerfully built young forward scored regularly for Derby's reserves but despite producing a number of committed displays when given an opportunity, usually as a substitute, he found it difficult to break through to the first-team squad in 1999-2000. He made his full debut for the club in the most difficult of games, against Manchester United, and showed a lot of promise. This was followed by the signing of a contract tying him to the club until June 2003, but his season was then blighted when he received a custodial sentence, although Derby have stated they will welcome him back to the club when he is released.

Derby Co (From trainee on 8/7/1998) PL 3+6

ROBINSON Matthew Richard
Born: Exeter, 23 December 1974
Height: 5'11" Weight: 11.8

This experienced wing back began the 1999-2000 season at Portsmouth, where he enjoyed regular first-team football under Alan Ball and caretaker manager Bob McNab before being sold to Reading last January when new boss Tony Pulis began to prune Pompey's extensive playing staff. Matt can play equally well on either side of the defence, from where he makes useful forward runs, taking on and beating opponents with ease. Signed for just £150,000, he looked like one of the bargains of the season following his move to the Madejski Stadium, producing some classy performances at left wing back. His distribution was excellent, he tackled and headed ferociously, and also brought off some point-saving goal-line clearances when the 'keeper was beaten. At the other end of the pitch he was unlucky not to score on several occasions, and looks to be well worth the two-and-a-half-year contract he has been given.

Southampton (From trainee on 1/7/1993) PL 3+11 FAC 1+2
Portsmouth (£50,000 on 20/2/1998) FL 65+4/1 FLC 3+2 FAC 3
Reading (£150,000 on 28/1/2000) FL 19 Others 1

ROBINSON Paul Derrick
Born: Sunderland, 20 November 1978
Height: 5'11" Weight: 11.12

Paul is a quick and lively Newcastle striker who leads the line with poise and ambition, has the control to take on and beat defenders, and packs a useful shot. Seen as a young talent for the future, he was expected to start the 1999-2000 season learning his trade as understudy to Alan Shearer and Duncan Ferguson. However, with the latter injured an opportunity for early promotion presented itself and Paul responded well, impressing during Newcastle's pre-season when he scored three times in five games to earn a place on the bench for the season's opener at home to Villa, coming on for his debut late in the game, and after further substitute appearances in the next two matches he made the starting line-up for the visit of Wimbledon. He then found himself the centre of attention when he was chosen for the following game, the home derby with Sunderland, ahead of England and club captain Alan Shearer, who was consigned to the bench, but he acquitted himself well and made the defence-splitting pass from which Kieron Dyer scored the Newcastle goal. With Shearer reinstated in the team Paul was back on the bench himself for the next match, a situation which continued for two months, during which time he was frequently brought on, although he failed to regain the starting position despite netting his first goal for the club in the home draw with CSKA Sofia in the UEFA Cup. With the return to fitness of Duncan Ferguson and the arrival at the club of Kevin Gallacher Paul's prospects of selection were much diminished, and on Christmas Eve he requested a transfer, but he withdrew it in February when he decided to use the opportunity to learn from the club's senior strikers and develop his abilities so that he could challenge for a first-team spot again. He returned to contention late in the season when, following a spate of injuries to the club's senior strikers, he made a substitute appearance in the home game against Leicester.

Darlington (From trainee on 14/7/1997) FL 7+19/3 FLC 0+1 FAC 2+4/1 Others 0+1
Newcastle U (£250,000 + on 27/3/1998) PL 2+9 FLC 0+1 Others 0+4/1

ROBINSON Paul Peter
Born: Watford, 14 December 1978
Height: 5'9" Weight: 11.12
Club Honours: Div 2 '98
International Honours: E: U21-3

This Watford-born left back has now made more than 100 first-team appearances for his home-town club despite being only 21. After overcoming a thigh problem at the start of last season, Paul was a regular for the rest of the campaign, apart from a brief spell in November, when he was sidelined by an ankle injury. A lively character on and off the pitch, he is still subject to occasional rash moments, but is a strong tackler and a fine passer of the ball when he ventures upfield. He remained part of the England U21 squad and won a further cap against Poland in September.

Watford (From trainee on 13/2/1997) P/FL 77+18/2 FLC 4+1 FAC 5+2 Others 5

ROBINSON Philip (Phil) Daniel
Born: Manchester, 28 September 1980
Height: 5'9" Weight: 11.0

Phil is a young Blackpool defender who was given a brief run in the first team last October. He spent most of the remainder of the 1999-2000 season playing for the club's reserves and featured just once more when he came on as a substitute in the Auto Windscreens Shield tie against Mansfield. He was released in the summer.

Blackpool (From trainee on 15/1/1999) FL 6+5 FLC 0+1 FAC 2 Others 6+5

ROBINSON Phillip (Phil) John
Born: Stafford, 6 January 1967
Height: 5'10" Weight: 11.7
Club Honours: Div 4 '88, Div 3 '89, '98; AMC '88, '91, '00

Phil started the 1999-2000 season as Stoke's club captain but drifted out of the first-team squad at the turn of the year as new boss Gudjon Thordarson rebuilt the side with Scandinavian imports. Whether in midfield or defence, this hard-tackling professional never gave less than 100 per cent. With Phil now aged 33, the club indicated their willingness to release him on a free transfer and he may decide to secure his future in the game using his physiotherapy qualifications.

Aston Villa (From apprentice on 8/1/1985) FL 2+1/1
Wolverhampton W (£5,000 on 3/7/1987) FL 63+8/8 FLC 6 FAC 3/1 Others 8+2
Notts Co (£67,500 on 18/8/1989) FL 65+1/5 FLC 6/1 FAC 1+1 Others 9+1
Birmingham C (Loaned on 18/3/1991) FL 9 Others 2+1
Huddersfield T (£50,000 on 1/9/1992) FL 74+1/5 FLC 4 FAC 8/1 Others 8
Northampton T (Loaned on 2/9/1994) FL 14 FLC 1 FAC 1 Others 2
Chesterfield (£15,000 on 9/12/1994) FL 60+1/17 FLC 1 FAC 2 Others 8/4
Notts Co (£80,000 on 16/8/1996) FL 63+14/5 FLC 4 FAC 6+1/1 Others 1
Stoke C (Free on 23/6/1998) FL 53+9/2 FLC 4 FAC 3 Others 1+1

ROBINSON Stephen (Steve)
Born: Lisburn, 10 December 1974
Height: 5'9" Weight: 11.3
International Honours: NI: 5; B-4; U21-1; Yth; Sch

Steve had another excellent campaign for Bournemouth in 1999-2000 despite one or two minor problems with injuries. Essentially an attacking midfield player, he showed a high workrate and scored his fair share of goals – he reached double figures again last season. Already a full Northern Ireland international, he won further caps when coming on from the subs' bench against Luxembourg and Hungary. Steve signed for newly promoted Preston North End in a £375,000 deal at the end of May.

Tottenham H (From trainee on 27/1/1993) PL 1+1
Bournemouth (Free on 20/10/1994) FL 227+13/51 FLC 14/1 FAC 15+1/5 Others 16/3

ROBINSON Steven (Steve) Eli
Born: Nottingham, 17 January 1975
Height: 5'9" Weight: 11.3

Steve was out of action at the beginning of the 1999-2000 campaign following knee surgery and did not make his first senior appearance for Birmingham City until the FA Cup tie at Watford last December, when he replaced Jerry Gill for the last half hour. He remained in the first-team squad until the end of January but then suffered further knee problems that required another operation and kept him out until the end of the season. He is a popular midfield player full of running and with good distribution.

Birmingham C (From trainee on 9/6/1993) FL 53+24 FLC 6/1 FAC 2+2/1 Others 2
Peterborough U (Loaned on 15/3/1996) FL 5

ROBSON Mark Andrew
Born: Newham, 22 May 1969
Height: 5'7" Weight: 10.2
Club Honours: Div 3 '98

After missing a large part of the 1998-99 campaign through injury, Mark began last season on the subs' bench for Notts County. However, he very quickly decided that his knee problems had not been fully overcome and he announced his retirement from the full-time game at the end of September. He subsequently linked up with Ryman League club Boreham Wood, where he spent the remainder of the season. When fully fit, Mark is a small, speedy wing man who has the ability to create openings with his excellent passing skills.

Exeter C (From apprentice on 17/12/1986) FL 26/7 FAC 2 Others 2
Tottenham H (£50,000 on 17/7/1987) FL 3+5 FLC 1
Reading (Loaned on 24/3/1988) FL 5+2
Watford (Loaned on 5/10/1989) FL 1
Plymouth Arg (Loaned on 22/12/1989) FL 7
Exeter C (Loaned on 3/1/1992) FL 7+1/1 Others 3/1
West Ham U (Free on 14/8/1992) F/PL 42+5/8 FLC 2 FAC 2/1 Others 4+1
Charlton Ath (£125,000 on 17/11/1993) FL 79+26/9 FLC 4+2 FAC 10/2 Others 2
Notts Co (Free on 23/6/1997) FL 26+6/4 FLC 2+1 FAC 3 Others 1
Wycombe W (Loaned on 17/10/1999) FL 1+3

ROCHA Carlos
Born: Lisbon, Portugal, 4 December 1974
Height: 6'1" Weight: 12.7

Bury boss Neil Warnock brought this striker across the Atlantic for a trial in July 1999. After playing in the club's pre-season friendly matches, the former New England Revolution man was rewarded with a three-month contract at Gigg Lane and given a further chance to impress in Bury's Pontins League team. Carlos was also named as a substitute for the first team on five occasions, though, being called into action in the matches against Colchester, Oldham and Bournemouth. Released in November, he had a brief period at Lincoln on non-contract terms, appearing as an unused substitute against Rochdale at the end of the same month. A brief spell in Portugal followed but by February he had returned to the USA and was playing indoor soccer with the Philadelphia Kixx.

Bury (Free from Boston Bulldogs, USA, via Rhode Island Stingrays, New England Revolution, on 6/8/1999) FL 0+3

RODDIE Andrew (Andy) Robert
Born: Glasgow, 4 December 1971
Height: 5'10" Weight: 11.6
International Honours: S: U21-5; Yth; Sch

A non-contract signing from St Mirren in August 1999, Andy played two games for Carlisle at the start of the new campaign. Despite a "Man of the Match" rating in his only full appearance against Hartlepool, he was not retained and a few weeks later was playing for Clydebank. Andy then went on to join Stranraer.

Aberdeen (Free from Glasgow U on 16/4/1988) SL 5+22/5 SC 0+1
Motherwell (Free on 20/8/1994) SL 24+31 SLC 2+2 SC 0+1 Others 1
Notts Co (Free on 27/1/1997) Others 1 (Freed in February 1997)
St Mirren (Free from Ljungskile SK, Sweden on 11/10/1997) SL 19/1 SC 1 (Freed during 1998 close season)
Carlisle U (Free from Happy Valley, Hong Kong on 12/8/1999) FL 1+1

RODGER Simon Lee
Born: Shoreham, 3 October 1971
Height: 5'9" Weight: 11.9
Club Honours: Div 1 '94

Crystal Palace's club captain showed excellent form throughout 1999-2000 until his campaign ended prematurely after he ruptured his ankle ligaments against Bolton last March. Simon is a hard-working and combative left-sided midfield player who leads by example. Although only an occasional scorer, he managed to find the net in each of the Eagles' three opening matches.

Crystal Palace (£1,000 from Bognor Regis T on 2/7/1990) F/PL 185+22/10 FLC 21+1/1 FAC 7+3 Others 5+2
Manchester C (Loaned on 28/10/1996) FL 8/1
Stoke C (Loaned on 14/2/1997) FL 5

RODGERS Luke John
Born: Birmingham, 1 January 1982
Height: 5'7" Weight: 11.2

A product of Shrewsbury's youth policy, Luke made his debut when he came on as a substitute in the opening game of the 1999-2000 season against Torquay and he went on to make substitute appearances on a total of eight occasions. A very speedy striker who shows no hesitation in running with the ball, he was rewarded with his first goal in the 1-2 defeat by Brighton in the penultimate league game of the term.

Shrewsbury T (Trainee) FL 0+6/1 FAC 0+1 Others 0+1

RODRIGUEZ Bruno
Born: Corsica, 25 November 1972
Height: 6'0" Weight: 12.5

This experienced French striker joined Bradford City in the summer of 1999 from Paris St Germain with the intention of spending the whole of last season on loan at Valley Parade. Bruno made his debut for the Bantams as a late substitute against Tottenham but made the starting line-up on only one occasion, for the Worthington Cup tie against Reading. He struggled to settle in Yorkshire and eventually returned to France towards the end of last October. He was subsequently sold to Lens for a £1.6 million fee in December and later featured in their UEFA Cup campaign that ended when they were eliminated by Arsenal in the semi-finals.

Bradford C (Loaned from Paris St Germain, France on 10/9/1999) PL 0+2 FLC 1+2

RODRIGUEZ Daniel (Dani) Ferreira
Born: Madeira, Portugal, 3 March 1980
Height: 6'0" Weight: 11.8
International Honours: Portugal: U21

Signed from Portuguese side Farense in March 1999 after a promising loan spell at Bournemouth, this quick and very skilful striker settled in well at Southampton last season and made solid progress. He was the top scorer for the reserves and represented Portugal at U21 level. Dani was given his first taste of Premiership football when he came on as a substitute against Leicester at the end of April and had another outing from the bench in the final game of the season against Wimbledon.

Bournemouth (Loaned from CS Farense, Portugal on 1/10/1998) FL 0+5 Others 0+2
Southampton (£170,000 on 3/3/1999) PL 0+2

ROGERS Alan
Born: Liverpool, 3 January 1977
Height: 5'9" Weight: 12.6
Club Honours: Div 1 '98
International Honours: E: U21-3

Alan was in great form for Nottingham Forest in 1999-2000 and had his best season yet with the City Ground club. He was used both as a left wing back and a wide left-sided midfield player and it was to the latter role that he appeared best suited. He is quick to join the attack and gets himself into excellent goalscoring positions. He finished the campaign as joint top scorer with Doug Freedman on 11 goals, thus more than doubling his previous career total achieved in over 150 games.

Tranmere Rov (From trainee on 1/7/1995) FL 53+4/2 FLC 1 FAC 1
Nottingham F (£2,000,000 on 10/7/1997) P/FL 116+1/14 FLC 13/1 FAC 2+1/1

ROGERS Kristian Raleigh John
Born: Chester, 2 October 1980
Height: 6'3" Weight: 12.6
International Honours: E: Sch

This highly talented young goalkeeper made his first-team bow for Wrexham in the FAW Premier Cup tie against TNS Llansantffraid last January and went on to make his Football League debut in the home game with Colchester United on Easter Monday, when he produced a super performance and was deservedly voted "Man of the Match". Kristian has all-round talents as a sportsman for, having represented England U18 schools at soccer, he also played cricket for Cheshire Second XI and turned down the offer of a contract with Durham and the MCC in favour of the Racecourse Ground club.

Wrexham (Free from Chester C juniors on 14/8/1998) FL 1

ROGERS Mark Alvin
Born: Guelph, Ontario, Canada, 3 November 1975
Height: 6'1" Weight: 12.12

Mark followed a rather unique path to a professional career, having originally come to Europe to watch the 1998 World Cup finals before setting up a number of trials with British clubs to keep fit. He impressed Wycombe in a 1998-99 pre-season game but then had to go back to Canada to obtain a work permit and only returned to the Adams Park club at the end of 1998. He eventually made his senior debut as a substitute against Notts County last October, but soon after his breakthrough he was sidelined with a pulled calf muscle. On recovering full fitness he featured regularly for the Chairboys in the second half of last season and will be looking to retain his place in the 2000-01 campaign. Mark is a versatile player: having begun as a central defender he has turned out as a stand-in right back and can also play a central midfield role. He is comfortable on the ball, strong in the tackle and has a good turn of speed.

Wycombe W (Free from Burnaby Canadians, Canada on 23/12/1998) FL 19+6 FAC 4 Others 1

ROGERS Paul Anthony
Born: Portsmouth, 21 March 1965
Height: 6'0" Weight: 12.0
Club Honours: Div 3 '97; AMC '99
International Honours: E: SP-6

Signed on a free transfer from Wigan in July 1999, Paul was immediately installed as Brighton's captain. Somewhat of an enigma, he had the habit of popping up with some important high-quality goals from central midfield. Paul made more appearances than any other Seagull last season, and he especially benefited from the switch to 4-4-2.

Sheffield U (£35,000 from Sutton U on 29/1/1992) F/PL 120+5/10 FLC 8+1/1 FAC 4 Others 1
Notts Co (Signed on 29/12/1995) FL 21+1/2 FAC 1 Others 6/1
Wigan Ath (Loaned on 13/12/1996) FL 7+2/3
Wigan Ath (£50,000 on 7/3/1997) FL 85+6/2 FLC 6 FAC 3 Others 8/1
Brighton & Hove A (Free on 8/7/1999) FL 44+1/8 FLC 2 FAC 4/1 Others 2

ROGET Leo Thomas Earl
Born: Ilford, 1 August 1977
Height: 6'1" Weight: 12.2

Leo had another mixed season for Southend in 1999-2000. He held down a regular first-team centre-half slot until Christmas, when David Morley, Simon Coleman and Rob Newman took control. Consistently good in the air, Leo ran into one or two disciplinary problems and this is an area of his game where he needs to tighten up. Described by manager Alan Little as "an enigma who leaves a lot on the training field", Leo was offered new terms for the 2000-01 campaign.

Southend U (From trainee on 5/7/1995) FL 79+15/3 FLC 6 FAC 2 Others 1

ROPER Ian Robert
Born: Nuneaton, 20 June 1977
Height: 6'3" Weight: 13.4

After a highly successful 1998-99 campaign for Walsall in which he made the one central defensive position his own, Ian had to battle for a place last season, with Adrian Viveash and Tony Barras starting off as the men in possession at the heart of the defence. He regained his place, however, in time to give two tremendous displays in the local derby wins in successive weeks against Birmingham and West Bromwich in October. His command in the air was a feature of Walsall's season and in the vital last few games in which they just failed to stave off relegation he was one of their outstanding players.

Walsall (From trainee on 15/5/1995) FL 87+16/2 FLC 2+4 FAC 5+1/1 Others 11+1

ROSCOE Andrew (Andy) Ronald
Born: Liverpool, 4 June 1973
Height: 5'11" Weight: 12.0
Club Honours: AMC '96

Signed with Neil Richardson from Rotherham in the summer of 1999, Andy started his Mansfield career in the left-wing-back berth. He did not seem best suited to the defensive side of that position, but when played in a more attacking role supplied some great crosses from the left wing. He also scored a couple of spectacular goals from free kicks, including the "golden goal" which beat Bury in the Auto Windscreens Shield. Andy was released in the summer. Stop Press: He was reported to have joined Exeter at the end of June.

Bolton W (Free from Liverpool juniors on 17/7/1991) FL 2+1 Others 1+1

Rotherham U (£70,000 on 27/10/1994) FL 184+18/18 FLC 10 FAC 10/2 Others 11/2
Mansfield T (Free on 5/8/1999) FL 29+10/2 FLC 2 FAC 1 Others 0+1/1

ROSE Matthew David
Born: Dartford, 24 September 1975
Height: 5'11" Weight: 11.1
Club Honours: FAYC '94
International Honours: E: U21-2
Matthew started the 1999-2000 season in Queens Park Rangers' defence playing either as a right back or a central defender. He made a smooth transition to a midfield role following an injury to Gavin Peacock and managed to hold on to that position until he himself sustained a calf injury in December. A successful operation to relieve blocked arteries enabled him to return to the defence in late January. Unfortunately, he suffered another injury in early spring which kept him out of the side until the end of the season. Matthew's tackling is sound and he finally broke his goalscoring duck for the club in the away game at Barnsley in February.
Arsenal (From trainee on 19/7/1994) PL 2+3
Queens Park R (£500,000 on 20/5/1997) FL 67+7/1 FLC 5 FAC 1

ROSS Neil James
Born: Birmingham, 10 August 1982
Height: 6'0" Weight: 12.2
This former Leeds trainee was snapped up by Stockport manager Andy Kilner last January and made a great impact at Edgeley Park by scoring five goals in seven starts for the club's reserve team. He was duly promoted to the first-team squad, making his debut from the subs' bench against Ipswich in April, and also coming on briefly at Huddersfield. A talented young striker, he will be looking to establish himself in the team in the 2000-01 season.
Leeds U (From trainee on 12/8/1999)
Stockport Co (Free on 28/1/2000) FL 0+2

ROUGIER Anthony (Tony) Leo
Born: Tobago, 17 July 1971
Height: 6'0" Weight: 14.1
International Honours: Trinidad & Tobago
A striker who can also play wide, Tony became Port Vale's most capped player in 1999-2000. On his day he is an excellent dribbler who is difficult to shake off the ball and he ended the season as the Vale's leading scorer. He showed greater consistency in the first half of the season but his form dipped a little in the new year when he had several absences due to international duties. A practising Christian, he can never be ignored and was an automatic choice for the Vale team when available. A regular for Trinidad & Tobago, for whom he often featured at right back, Tony captained his country for most of the season, winning a further 12 caps and leading the Soca Warriors to a semi-final spot in the CONCACAF Gold Cup.
Raith Rov (Free from Trinity Prospect, Trinidad on 9/3/1995) SL 47+10/2 SLC 3/3 SC 4+1/1 Others 4+1/1
Hibernian (Signed on 10/7/1997) SL 34+11/4 SLC 4
Port Vale (£175,000 on 4/1/1999) FL 41+10/8 FLC 2/1 FAC 1

ROUSSEL Cedric
Born: Mons, Belgium, 6 January 1978
Height: 6'2" Weight: 12.5
International Honours: Belgium: U21
Cedric was a surprise loan signing from Ghent in October 1999 who originally expected to get the occasional game for Coventry before returning to Belgium at the end of the season. The young striker made an inauspicious debut as a substitute in City's home game against Newcastle and got his first start a few weeks later against Watford. In his second full game he scored a good goal in the 2-1 victory over Aston Villa and won over the fans with his wholehearted approach. Cedric played a major part in the club's good form of December and January and ended the season with nine goals in 25 appearances. His good form prompted Coventry to enter into negotiations for his transfer from Ghent and despite strong rumours of other Premiership clubs being interested he demonstrated tremendous loyalty by signing for City for £1.2 million. The highlight of his season was undoubtedly scoring twice at Old Trafford despite the side losing 3-2. Cedric seemed to be pushing for a place in Belgium's Euro 2000 squad until he was forced to withdraw from the country's "B" squad after suffering from concussion at Middlesbrough. After sustaining a knee injury in training in April he had keyhole surgery and was ruled out of the last few games. It was a very creditable first season and the good understanding he developed with Robbie Keane augurs well for the future.
Coventry C (£1,200,000 from KAA Ghent, Belgium on 19/10/1999) PL 18+4/6 FAC 2+1/3

Cedric Roussel

ROWBOTHAM Darren
Born: Cardiff, 22 October 1966
Height: 5'10" Weight: 12.13
Club Honours: Div 4 '90
International Honours: W: Yth
Sidelined for a spell by a broken foot but also out of favour at times when fit, Darren was restricted to only a few appearances for Exeter in 1999-2000. A vastly experienced forward with vision, awareness and the ability to bring others into the game, he is worshipped by the City fans and still made a valuable contribution when called upon. He was allowed to go to Leyton Orient on a two-month loan in November as the O's looked for a solution to their goalscoring problems. Unfortunately, Darren didn't manage to open his account in his seven appearances and he returned to St James Park following the appointment of Noel Blake as Exeter manager only to be released at the end of the season.
Plymouth Arg (From juniors on 7/11/1984) FL 22+24/2 FLC 1 FAC 0+3/1 Others 1+1
Exeter C (Signed on 31/10/1987) FL 110+8/47 FLC 11/6 FAC 8/5 Others 5/1
Torquay U (£25,000 on 13/9/1991) FL 14/3 FAC 3/1 Others 2
Birmingham C (£20,000 on 2/1/1992) FL 31+5/6 FLC 0+1 Others 3+1
Mansfield T (Loaned on 18/12/1992) FL 4
Hereford U (Loaned on 25/3/1993) FL 8/2
Crewe Alex (Free on 6/7/1993) FL 59+2/21 FLC 3/1 FAC 4/3 Others 6+2/1
Shrewsbury T (Free on 28/7/1995) FL 31+9/9 FLC 3+2/2 FAC 4/1 Others 1+3
Exeter C (Free on 24/10/1996) FL 108+10/37 FLC 4 FAC 8/4 Others 2/1
Leyton Orient (Loaned on 11/11/1999) FL 4+2 Others 0+1

ROWBOTHAM Jason
Born: Cardiff, 3 January 1969
Height: 5'9" Weight: 11.12
Club Honours: S Div 1 '95; SLC '95
Jason is a highly experienced Plymouth defender who has been plagued by injuries over the past three years or so. He started the 1999-2000 season confidently but, once again, injury halted his progress. He made a comeback towards the end of the campaign, scoring a spectacular winning goal from 35 yards against Northampton in April. Probably most effective in the sweeper role, Jason is in his second spell at Home Park. He was one of eight Pilgrims released in May.
Plymouth Arg (From trainee on 20/7/1987) FL 8+1 FLC 0+1
Shrewsbury T (Free on 26/3/1992)
Hereford U (Free on 17/10/1992) FL 3+2/1 FAC 1
Raith Rov (Free on 31/7/1993) SL 47+9/1 SLC 3+2 SC 2+1 Others 1
Wycombe W (£40,000 on 14/9/1995) FL 27 FLC 2 FAC 2 Others 2
Plymouth Arg (Free on 11/10/1996) FL 42+9/1 FLC 3 FAC 1+1 Others 2+1

ROWE Rodney Carl
Born: Huddersfield, 30 July 1975
Height: 5'8" Weight: 12.8
Starting his third season at York, Rodney figured in the opening games of 1999-2000 and scored at Wigan in the Worthington Cup. A lively striker who is always a danger in the box with his pace and control, he was not able to gain a regular first-team slot, however, and was loaned to Halifax in September. He scored two quality goals at Macclesfield and Carlisle during his two-month stay at the Shay but the offer of a

contract with Gillingham was too good to turn down and he joined the Second Division club in November for a bargain £30,000 fee, making his debut for the Gills as a substitute at Cardiff. He went on to score his first goal for Gillingham in the Boxing Day victory over Colchester and added three more before the end of the season.

Huddersfield T (From trainee on 12/7/1993) FL 14+20/2 FLC 0+2 FAC 6+1/2 Others 3/1
Scarborough (Loaned on 11/8/1994) FL 10+4/1 FLC 4/1
Bury (Loaned on 20/3/1995) FL 1+2
York C (£80,000 on 19/2/1997) FL 74+23/20 FLC 5+1/2 FAC 2+3/3 Others 2/2
Halifax T (Loaned on 24/9/1999) FL 7+2/2 FAC 1
Gillingham (£45,000 on 25/11/1999) FL 8+14/4 Others 1

ROWETT Gary
Born: Bromsgrove, 6 March 1974
Height: 6'0" Weight: 12.10

Gary had another marvellous campaign at right back for Birmingham City in 1999-2000. He is a strong and athletic defender who makes it difficult for wingers to get past him and is a potent attacking force with his surging runs and superb crosses. One highlight of his season was his near-post header which earned the Blues a 1-0 victory at Premiership Watford in the third-round FA Cup tie while another came last May when he was voted into the PFA's First Division team for the second year in succession. Stop Press: Gary was reported to have signed for Leicester at the beginning of July.

Cambridge U (From trainee on 10/9/1991) FL 51+12/9 FLC 7/1 FAC 5+2 Others 5/3
Everton (£200,000 on 21/5/1994) PL 2+2
Blackpool (Loaned on 23/1/1995) FL 17
Derby Co (£300,000 on 20/7/1995) P/FL 101+4/2 FLC 8/2 FAC 5+2
Birmingham C (£1,000,000 on 17/8/1998) FL 87/6 FLC 9/3 FAC 3/1 Others 4/1

ROWLAND Keith
Born: Portadown, 1 September 1971
Height: 5'10" Weight: 10.0
International Honours: NI: 18; B-3; Yth

A left-sided player with Queens Park Rangers, Keith can operate either as a wing back or in a more traditional midfield role. He is a former Northern Ireland international but was not a regular starter for Rangers in 1999-2000. His appearances were limited to acting as cover for injured players, although he was used as a substitute on a number of occasions.

Bournemouth (From trainee on 2/10/1989) FL 65+7/2 FLC 5 FAC 8 Others 3
Coventry C (Loaned on 8/1/1993) PL 0+2
West Ham U (£110,000 on 6/8/1993) PL 63+17/1 FLC 3+2 FAC 5+1
Queens Park R (Signed on 30/1/1998) FL 28+24/3 FLC 1+1 FAC 1+1

ROWLANDS Martin Charles
Born: Hammersmith, 8 February 1979
Height: 5'9" Weight: 10.10
Club Honours: Div 3 '99
International Honours: RoI: U21-8

This creative right-sided midfield player really blossomed for Brentford in the 1999-2000 season. His mazy runs and teasing crosses caused havoc in opposition defences while his long-range passing and positional sense both showed improvement. Martin was the supporters' "Player of the Year" and also earned another six caps for the Republic of Ireland U21 side. He has an extremely promising future in the game.

Brentford (£45,000 from Farnborough T on 6/8/1998) FL 70+6/10 FLC 5+1 FAC 4+1 Others 6/1

ROY Eric
Born: Nice, France, 26 September 1967
Height: 5'9" Weight: 10.10

A French schemer who joined Sunderland for £200,000 from Olympique Marseille in August 1999, having put in a very impressive performance as a trialist during Kevin Ball's testimonial against Sampdoria, Eric is a tall, stylish midfielder who uses the ball inventively, playing seemingly effortless passes. He made his first-team debut as a substitute against Leicester in September and scored his first Sunderland goal in a 5-0 Worthington Cup victory at Walsall two weeks later, a game in which he showed his versatility by turning in a solid performance at centre half. Injuries to Gavin McCann and Stefan Schwarz allowed Eric an extended run in the team in the new year and he formed a fine partnership with Alex Rae as Sunderland recovered from a mid-season slump to finish the campaign strongly.

Sunderland (£200,000 from Marseille, France on 25/8/1999) PL 19+5 FLC 3/1 FAC 2

Neil Ruddock

RUDDOCK Neil
Born: Wandsworth, 9 May 1968
Height: 6'2" Weight: 12.12
Club Honours: FLC '95
International Honours: E: 1; B-1; U21-4; Yth

Neil missed the opening matches of West Ham's 1999-2000 campaign after aggravating an old hamstring injury in a pre-season Inter Toto Cup game with FC Jokerit. He eventually returned as a substitute for the UEFA Cup game in Croatia against Osijek and then showed excellent form over the next few months, being particularly prominent in the victories over Arsenal and Liverpool. The second half of the season proved frustrating for Neil as he was ruled out by a damaged eye socket suffered on Boxing Day at Wimbledon and then injured a knee, which restricted him to just a handful more first-team appearances. Although now in his thirties, he is still a very effective defender, his imposing physical presence being supported by powerful tackling, strength in the air and a great left foot.

Millwall (From apprentice on 3/3/1986) Others 3+1/1
Tottenham H (£50,000 on 14/4/1986) FL 7+2 FAC 1+1/1
Millwall (£300,000 on 29/6/1988) FL 0+2/1 FLC 2/3 Others 1+1
Southampton (£250,000 on 13/2/1989) FL 100+7/9 FLC 14+1/1 FAC 10/3 Others 6
Tottenham H (£750,000 on 29/7/1992) PL 38/3 FLC 4 FAC 5
Liverpool (£2,500,000 on 22/7/1993) PL 111+4/11 FLC 19+1/1 FAC 11 Others 5+1
Queens Park R (Loaned on 26/3/1998) FL 7
West Ham U (£100,000 + on 31/7/1998) PL 39+3/2 FLC 4+1 FAC 3 Others 2+1/1

RUDI Petter
Born: Kristiansund, Norway, 17 September 1973
Height: 6'2" Weight: 12.0
International Honours: Norway: 27

This tall left-sided attacking midfield player was an ever-present with Sheffield Wednesday in 1999-2000 until suffering a leg injury last December. When he recovered he was unable to find his best form and rarely featured for the Owls. On his day Petter is a skilful and effective performer who is comfortable on the ball and capable of exciting the crowd with his penetrating runs. He won another cap for Norway against Greece last September but was ruled out of contention for the Euro 2000 squad after suffering an achilles injury at the end of the season.

Sheffield Wed (£800,000 from Molde, Norway on 17/10/1997) PL 70+6/8 FLC 5/1 FAC 6+1/1

RUFUS Richard Raymond
Born: Lewisham, 12 January 1975
Height: 6'1" Weight: 11.10
Club Honours: Div 1 '00
International Honours: E: U21-6

Richard was voted "Player of the Year" by the Charlton Athletic supporters' club in 1999-2000, and he certainly had a great season, missing only two league games as the Addicks romped to the First Division championship and earning a place in the PFA award-winning First Division side. A tall and very quick central defender, Richard is commanding in the air and has greatly improved his distribution. He is a strong and determined tackler, is very calm under pressure and reads the game well. He loves to get forward for corners and set pieces and scored six times during the campaign, including two goals in one game at Grimsby in November.

Charlton Ath (From trainee on 1/7/1993) P/FL 213+3/7 FLC 13 FAC 11 Others 5/1

RUSSELL Alexander (Alex) John
Born: Crosby, 17 March 1973
Height: 5'9" Weight: 11.7

The influential midfielder's skill was sadly missed by Cambridge when a thigh injury ruled him out after the first few matches of the 1999-2000 season. Alex returned for a handful of games in the new year before requiring another operation. The news that he would be able to come back for the last two matches of the season lifted the club and everyone at the Abbey will be hoping that he enjoys better fortune during the coming season.

Rochdale (£4,000 from Burscough on 11/7/1994) FL 83+19/14 FLC 5/1 FAC 1+1 Others 2+3
Cambridge U (Free on 4/8/1998) FL 50+2/6 FLC 6 FAC 5 Others 2

RUSSELL Craig Stewart
Born: Jarrow, 4 February 1974
Height: 5'10" Weight: 12.6
Club Honours: Div 1 '96

Loaned to Darlington by Manchester City, Craig became an instant hero at Feethams when he scored the only goal of the game against Exeter after coming on as a substitute for his debut last September. His pace down the left flank added some zest to the attack, but in 11 league starts he was able to find the net only once more. He returned to Maine Road after two months with the Quakers. Craig later joined Oxford on loan for a month just prior to the transfer deadline. The nippy striker failed to score and returned to City after his spell ended. Oxford manager Denis Smith had been hoping his former Sunderland striker would rediscover his Roker Park form, but sadly this was not to be the case.

Sunderland (From trainee on 1/7/1992) P/FL 103+47/31 FLC 7+6/1 FAC 6+3/2 Others 2
Manchester C (£1,000,000 on 14/11/1997) FL 22+9/2 FAC 5+1/2
Tranmere Rov (Loaned on 7/8/1998) FL 3+1
Port Vale (Loaned on 29/1/1999) FL 8/1
Darlington (Loaned on 3/9/1999) FL 11+1/2
Oxford U (Loaned on 11/2/2000) FL 5+1
St Johnstone (Loaned on 29/3/2000) SL 1/1

RUSSELL Darel Francis Roy
Born: Stepney, 22 October 1980
Height: 5'11" Weight: 11.9
International Honours: E: Yth

The 1999-2000 season was an exciting one for this former England Youth international as he won a regular place in the Norwich midfield and enhanced his glowing reputation with a series of stirring displays. Darel is a strong, forceful midfielder who thrives on getting forward into goalscoring positions, a trait highlighted by his match-winning two goals in the live televised clash with Bolton at Carrow Road in October. An incredibly mature individual, he more than holds his own in the fierce Division One midfield areas, winning more than his fair share of tackles and displaying great stamina with non-stop running. Still only 19, Darel will be hoping to continue his footballing education this coming season, and add England U21 recognition to his collection of honours.

Norwich C (From trainee on 29/11/1997) FL 36+11/5 FLC 2 FAC 1

RUSSELL Kevin John
Born: Portsmouth, 6 December 1966
Height: 5'9" Weight: 10.12
Club Honours: Div 2 '93
International Honours: E: Yth

"Rooster" again proved to be an important member of the Wrexham squad in 1999-2000. His high workrate and enthusiasm for the cause were always in evidence and when on the subs' bench he offered manager Brian Flynn a variety of options. Extremely versatile, Kevin returned to his former role as a striker at relegation-threatened Cambridge last March and obliged with two well-taken goals in a vital 4-3 win. He subsequently showed his value to the team with further strikes against Scunthorpe and Bournemouth as the Robins came out of a bad patch to pull well clear of relegation worries by the end of the season. He is due to undergo minor surgery for a knee injury during the summer break.

Portsmouth (Free from Brighton & Hove A juniors on 9/10/1984) FL 3+1/1 FLC 0+1 FAC 0+1 Others 1+1
Wrexham (£10,000 on 17/7/1987) FL 84/43 FLC 4/1 FAC 4 Others 8/3
Leicester C (£175,000 on 20/6/1989) FL 24+19/10 FLC 0+1 FAC 1 Others 5/2
Peterborough U (Loaned on 6/9/1990) FL 7/3
Cardiff C (Loaned on 17/1/1991) FL 3
Hereford U (Loaned on 7/11/1991) FL 3/1 Others 1/1
Stoke C (Loaned on 2/1/1992) FL 5/1
Stoke C (£95,000 on 16/7/1992) FL 30+10/5 FLC 3 FAC 2 Others 4+1/1
Burnley (£150,000 on 28/6/1993) FL 26+2/6 FLC 4/1 FAC 4 Others 1/1
Bournemouth (£125,000 on 3/3/1994) FL 30/1 FLC 3/1 FAC 2/1
Notts Co (£60,000 on 24/2/1995) FL 9+2
Wrexham (£60,000 on 21/7/1995) FL 139+22/13 FLC 6+1/1 FAC 18+4/4 Others 9

RUSSELL Lee Edward
Born: Southampton, 3 September 1969
Height: 5'11" Weight: 12.0

Undoubtedly one of the star players of Torquay's 1999-2000 campaign, this composed central defender goes about his job with the minimum of fuss, and his distribution is first class. After less than 150 appearances in 11 years at Portsmouth, Lee is revelling in the opportunity of regular first-team football with the Gulls. Should the need arise, he can also operate at left wing back or in midfield.

Portsmouth (From trainee on 12/7/1988) FL 103+20/3 FLC 8+2 FAC 4+2 Others 5+2
Bournemouth (Loaned on 9/9/1994) FL 3
Torquay U (Free on 25/3/1999) FL 44 FLC 2 FAC 4 Others 1

RUSSELL Matthew Lee
Born: Dewsbury, 17 January 1978
Height: 5'11" Weight: 11.5

Matthew was one of three Halifax signings from Scarborough during the 1999 close season. However, he didn't seem to settle at the Shay, and accepted the opportunity to return to Scarborough in October. A bright future still lies ahead for the right-sided midfielder or wing back.

Scarborough (From trainee on 3/7/1996) FL 21+23/3 FLC 0+2 FAC 1+1 Others 1
Doncaster Rov (Loaned on 26/3/1998) FL 4+1
Halifax T (£50,000 + on 5/7/1999) FL 3+4 FLC 0+1

RYAN Keith James
Born: Northampton, 25 June 1970
Height: 5'11" Weight: 12.8
Club Honours: FAT '91, '93; GMVC '93

Wycombe's popular club captain completed ten seasons for the club in 1999-2000, taking his total of Football League appearances close to the 200 mark. After his frustrating time in 1998-99, Keith managed to stay clear of injuries and returned to his favoured midfield anchor role to become a key influence for the Chairboys. He provided inspiration from the centre of the park, always giving 100 per cent effort, and impressed once again with his speed, workrate and strong tackling. He was used as a central striker towards the end of the season, showing himself to be a more than useful target man and netting twice in the 3-0 victory over Colchester in April. He is to have a well-deserved testimonial match this August when Leicester City are due to visit Adams Park.

Wycombe W (Signed from Berkhamstead T during 1990 close season) FL 188+7/19 FLC 13/3 FAC 12+3/4 Others 13+1/1

RYAN Michael Stuart
Born: Stockport, 3 October 1979
Height: 5'9" Weight: 11.4

This young full back joined Wrexham as a non-contract player in the summer of 1999 after impressing during a trial period at the Racecourse Ground. He made his league debut as a substitute at Blackpool on the opening day of the season, and after a couple more appearances from the subs' bench he won a place in the starting line-up against Bristol Rovers at the end of August. He looked a decent prospect but after three further first-team outings he was released by the club.

Manchester U (From trainee on 8/7/1998)
Wrexham (Free on 25/3/1999) FL 4+3

RYAN Robert (Robbie) Paul
Born: Dublin, 16 May 1977
Height: 5'10" Weight: 12.0
International Honours: RoI: U21-12; Yth; Sch

This strong-tackling left back had an excellent season for Millwall in 1999-2000. Although facing competition from Jamie Stuart for this position he made it his own with some excellent performances. A pacy player who likes to get forward at every opportunity, he produced a stream of good crosses that resulted in many goalscoring opportunities. Well liked and respected by all the Millwall faithful, Robbie has yet to score for the club but the way he links with the attack it can only be a matter of time before he gets on the score sheet.

Huddersfield T (Free from Belvedere on 26/7/1994) FL 12+3 FLC 2
Millwall (£10,000 on 30/1/1998) FL 71+5 FLC 2 FAC 2 Others 5

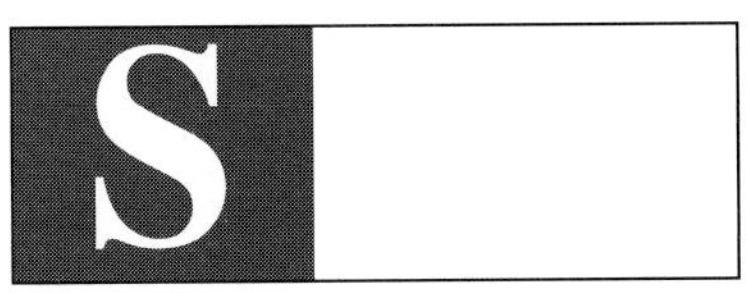

SADLIER Richard Thomas
Born: Dublin, 14 January 1979
Height: 6'2" Weight: 12.10
International Honours: RoI: U21-1; Yth

A tall, gangly centre forward, Richard made great progress at Millwall during 1999-2000. As well as being a dangerous striker, he works diligently to recover possession and is now also one of the key figures when the Lions are defending at set pieces around their own penalty box. His pace has greatly improved as has his heading. A forward who can hold the ball up well, he has developed into an excellent all-round player. However, an injury towards the end of the season unfortunately sidelined him during the run-in as the club chased a play-off place. His excellent form earlier in the season earned him his first cap for the Republic of Ireland U21s in October, when he came on as a substitute for the final 15 minutes against Macedonia.

Millwall (Signed from Belvedere on 14/8/1996) FL 49+23/13 FLC 4/1 FAC 2 Others 5+2/2

SALAKO John Akin
Born: Nigeria, 11 February 1969
Height: 5'10" Weight: 12.8
Club Honours: FMC '91; Div 1 '94, '00
International Honours: E: 5

Signed early in the season from Fulham after a period on loan, John was used mainly as a substitute by Charlton in 1999-2000, starting only four league games. He is not as fast as he once was, but is still an excellent crosser of the ball and particularly effective at free kicks and corners. He reads the game well and proved a useful addition to the Charlton squad. John scored a couple of valuable goals, including the winner against his former club Crystal Palace at the Valley, and his contribution to the Addicks' successful season was rewarded with a First Division championship medal.

Crystal Palace (From apprentice on 3/11/1986) F/PL 172+43/22 FLC 19+5/5 FAC 20/4 Others 11+3/2
Swansea C (Loaned on 14/8/1989) FL 13/3 Others 2/1
Coventry C (£1,500,000 on 7/8/1995) PL 68+4/4 FLC 9/3 FAC 4/1
Bolton W (Free on 26/3/1998) PL 0+7
Fulham (Free on 22/7/1998) FL 7+3/1 FLC 2/1 FAC 2+2 Others 1
Charlton Ath (£150,000 + on 20/8/1999) FL 4+23/2 FAC 2+2

SALT Phillip (Phil) Thomas
Born: Oldham, 2 March 1979
Height: 5'11" Weight: 11.9

Phil made the Oldham starting line-up a couple of times last August but spent a significant part of 1999-2000 out of action with an ankle injury, the problem being caused by tendons rubbing against the bone, and only returned to the first team for the last few games of the campaign. The only local lad in the Latics' squad, he has yet to fulfil his early promise and establish himself as a regular member of the team. A tireless grafter in the centre of midfield with good passing skills, he will be hoping to achieve a breakthrough in the coming season.

Oldham Ath (From trainee on 1/7/1997) FL 8+8 FLC 1+1 FAC 1/1 Others 2

SAMPSON Ian
Born: Wakefield, 14 November 1968
Height: 6'2" Weight: 13.3

Ian is a dependable centre back, who at one stage last season was Northampton's second-highest scorer and none of the goals were from the penalty spot. The club's vice-captain, he is one of the best headers of the ball in the lower divisions, a clean, crisp tackler and a no-frills defender who works on a safety-first basis. He is also Northampton's longest-serving player, and is now under his third manager at the club. Ian celebrated the Cobblers' promotion to Division Two by signing a new two-year contract.

Sunderland (Signed from Goole T on 13/11/1990) FL 13+4/1 FLC 1 FAC 0+2 Others 0+1
Northampton T (Loaned on 8/12/1993) FL 8
Northampton T (Free on 5/8/1994) FL 241+3/21 FLC 15 FAC 7/1 Others 16/2

SAMUEL JLloyd
Born: Trinidad, 29 March 1981
Height: 5'11" Weight: 11.4
International Honours: E: Yth

This talented Aston Villa youngster made his debut in senior football last September when he came on as a substitute in a Worthington Cup tie with Chester and went on to start his first Premiership game against Derby at the end of March. He then featured several times for Villa in the last few games of the season, replacing Gareth Southgate, who was struggling with an ankle injury. JLloyd capped a fine season by appearing on the subs' bench, although not used, for the FA Cup final against Chelsea and will be seeking to establish himself as a regular in the Villa first-team squad in 2000-01. He also won England U18 honours, winning four caps and captaining the team against France in March.

Aston Villa (From trainee on 2/2/1999) PL 5+4 FLC 0+1

SAMWAYS Mark
Born: Doncaster, 11 November 1968
Height: 6'2" Weight: 14.0

After being told he could leave Darlington in the summer of 1999, having made just one first-team appearance the previous season, Mark elected to stay. He finally made his league debut for the club when coming on as a substitute for the injured Andy Collett against Rochdale last September. He then kept his place and became first choice for the majority of the season. Mark made a total of 37 appearances in league and cup, and kept 12 clean sheets. The experienced shot stopper has now topped over 400 appearances for his four Football League clubs. He was released by Darlington in the summer.

Doncaster Rov (From trainee on 20/8/1987) FL 121 FLC 3 FAC 4 Others 10
Scunthorpe U (Signed on 26/3/1992) FL 180 FLC 10 FAC 16 Others 16
York C (Free on 18/7/1997) FL 29 FLC 4 FAC 1
Darlington (Free on 22/7/1998) FL 33+1 FAC 2 Others 2

SANDFORD Lee Robert
Born: Basingstoke, 22 April 1968
Height: 6'1" Weight: 13.4
Club Honours: AMC '92; Div 2 '93
International Honours: E: Yth

Lee, the Sheffield United captain, signed a new two-year contract at the start of the 1999-2000 season. He made an uncertain start to the campaign, particularly when he was played on the left-hand side of the defence, and was not too comfortable with aspects of his attacking duties. Once he returned to the centre of the back line he produced the consistent and reliable performances that had been his hallmark the previous season. Not the fastest of defenders, he showed good anticipation, often being in the right place to make crucial interventions. He did the simple things well, playing within his limitations, and was always a threat in the opposition penalty area at corners and free kicks, although his goal tally was a little disappointing.

Portsmouth (From apprentice on 4/12/1985) FL 66+6/1 FLC 11 FAC 4 Others 2+1
Stoke C (£140,000 on 22/12/1989) FL 255+3/8 FLC 19 FAC 16/2 Others 31/4
Sheffield U (£500,000 on 22/7/1996) FL 117+6/3 FLC 9+1 FAC 14/1 Others 3+1
Reading (Loaned on 5/9/1997) FL 5

SANTOS Georges
Born: Marseille, France, 15 August 1970
Height: 6'3" Weight: 14.0

This tall, slightly awkward-looking midfield player began the 1999-2000 season as a regular in the Tranmere starting line-up but after an early-season dismissal he rarely featured at all in manager John Aldridge's team and on transfer deadline day he was transferred to West Bromwich. Georges had become a cult hero at Prenton Park with his wholehearted approach to the game and high workrate. One of Gary Megson's first signings as manager, Georges became the first Frenchman to appear for West Bromwich when he moved to the Hawthorns. Although he prefers to play in midfield, where he is very effective as a ball winner, he can also operate dependably at centre back. He occupied both positions for the Baggies and was a key performer in the side during the last few weeks of the season when relegation threatened the club. Strong in the tackle, the 30-year-old former Olympic Marseille player performed with great commitment in the eight games in which he started and made a valuable contribution. Stop Press: It was reported at the beginning of July that Georges had signed for Sheffield United.

Tranmere Rov (Free from Toulon, France on 29/7/1998) FL 46+1/2 FLC 6 FAC 1
West Bromwich A (£25,000 on 23/3/2000) FL 8

SAROYA Nevin
Born: Hillingdon, 15 September 1980
Height: 6'1" Weight: 13.0

Nevin was one of several youngsters

introduced to first-team action by Brentford chairman-manager Ron Noades towards the end of the 1999-2000 season. This tall midfielder developed through the Bees' junior ranks and made his Football League debut as a second-half substitute at Oxford last April, becoming the first player of Asian origin to appear in the club's first team. He will be looking to feature more regularly in the senior squad over the coming season.
Brentford (From trainee on 30/6/1999) FL 0+1

SARR Mass
Born: Unification Town, Liberia, 6 February 1973
Height: 5'11" Weight: 13.0
International Honours: Liberia
Just six appearances, each time as a second-half substitute, was Mass's contribution to Reading's 1999-2000 season, and although the experienced Liberian international undoubtedly has great talent he was unable to produce his best form for the Royals. One of a number of Tommy Burns's big-money signings who disappointed, he was placed on the transfer list by incoming manager Alan Pardew in January. With little interest shown by English clubs, a move abroad seemed likely.
Reading (£158,000 from Hadjuk Split, Croatia, via Olimpique Ales, on 17/7/1998) FL 18+13/3 FLC 2 FAC 0+1 Others 0+3

SAUNDERS Dean Nicholas
Born: Swansea, 21 June 1964
Height: 5'8" Weight: 10.6
Club Honours: FAC '92; FLC '94
International Honours: W: 73
Dean is now almost at the veteran stage of his career but still provided a useful contribution to Bradford City's first season of Premiership football. He got off to a great start with his new club when he scored the last-minute winner at Middlesbrough in the opening match and was a regular in the Bantams' line-up throughout the campaign. He formed an effective strike partnership with Dean Windass when the two were paired together last February and netted a fine goal in the memorable home victory over Arsenal. He continued to be nippy and alert up front and always came back to help his defence out. Dean also won four more caps for Wales, scoring once in the 2-1 win over Belarus last September.
Swansea C (From apprentice on 24/6/1982) FL 42+7/12 FLC 2+1 FAC 1 Others 1+1
Cardiff C (Loaned on 29/3/1985) FL 3+1
Brighton & Hove A (Free on 7/8/1985) FL 66+6/21 FLC 4 FAC 7/5 Others 3
Oxford U (£60,000 on 12/3/1987) FL 57+2/22 FLC 9+1/8 FAC 2/2 Others 2/1
Derby Co (£1,000,000 on 28/10/1988) FL 106/42 FLC 12/10 FAC 6 Others 7/5
Liverpool (£2,900,000 on 19/7/1991) F/PL 42/11 FLC 5/2 FAC 8/2 Others 6/10
Aston Villa (£2,300,000 on 10/9/1992) F/PL 111+1/37 FLC 15/7 FAC 9/4 Others 8/1 (£2,350,000 to Galatasaray, Turkey on 1/7/1995)
Nottingham F (£1,500,000 on 16/7/1996) F/PL 39+4/5 FLC 5+1/2 FAC 2/2
Sheffield U (Free on 5/12/1997) FL 42+1/17 FLC 4/3 FAC 6/2 Others 2 (£500,000 to Benfica, Portugal on 10/12/1998)
Bradford C (Free on 6/8/1999) PL 28+6/3 FLC 1+1/1 FAC 1+1/2

SAUNDERS Mark Philip
Born: Reading, 23 July 1971
Height: 5'11" Weight: 11.12
This experienced Gillingham player was pressed into service as a stand-in central defender at the start of 1999-2000 before reverting to a more familiar midfield role. Mark scored a crucial goal to end Brentford's unbeaten record last October and netted an equally vital goal to bring the Gills level and ultimately set them on the path to victory against Premiership club Sheffield Wednesday in the FA Cup fifth-round tie. A hard-working box-to-box player, his season ended prematurely in March due to an ankle injury.
Plymouth Arg (Signed from Tiverton T on 22/8/1995) FL 60+12/11 FLC 1+1 FAC 2+3 Others 2
Gillingham (Free on 1/6/1998) FL 48+12/5 FLC 3 FAC 6+1/1 Others 3+3

SAVAGE David (Dave) Thomas Patrick
Born: Dublin, 30 July 1973
Height: 6'1" Weight: 12.7
International Honours: RoI: 5; U21-5
A former Republic of Ireland international, Dave moved to Northampton midway through 1998-99, and settled into a midfield role that saw him net five goals in as many games in the club's last-ditch attempt to avoid relegation. Following the change of manager at Sixfields last season, Dave played in a wider role, a position he was accustomed to at Millwall. His jinking runs, where he likes to take on several players, often brought the Cobblers' supporters to their feet. Hopefully, a return to Division Two will lead to more international honours.
Brighton & Hove A (Signed from Kilkenny on 5/3/1991. Free to Longford T in May 1992)
Millwall (£15,000 on 27/5/1994) FL 104+28/6 FLC 11/2 FAC 6+2/2 Others 2/1
Northampton T (£100,000 on 7/10/1998) FL 61+9/10 FLC 2 FAC 3 Others 2

Dave Savage

SAVAGE Robert (Robbie) William
Born: Wrexham, 18 October 1974
Height: 6'1" Weight: 11.11
Club Honours: FAYC '92; FLC '00
International Honours: W: 16; U21-5; Yth; Sch
This right-footed midfielder or wing back produced some of his best-ever form for Leicester during the 1999-2000 season. He was particularly influential during the middle months of the campaign, when everyone around him seemed to become injured, and contributed the vital pin-point cross for Matt Elliott to head the winner against Aston Villa in the Worthington Cup semi-final. He also slotted home vital penalties in two shoot-outs during the season and was an important contributor to the victory in the final at Wembley, where he exorcised the ghost of 12 months previously. He netted a single spectacular goal at Newcastle during the campaign, and regained his place in the Wales national team after a season of consistent club performances in which he continued to show his energy, self-belief and willingness to fight for the Leicester cause. Robbie won three further caps, featuring against Switzerland, Finland and Brazil.
Manchester U (From trainee on 5/7/1993)
Crewe Alex (Free on 22/7/1994) FL 74+3/10 FLC 5 FAC 5 Others 8/1
Leicester C (£400,000 on 23/7/1997) PL 92+12/4 FLC 13+2 FAC 7/1 Others 0+1

Robbie Savage

SAWYERS Robert (Rob)
Born: Dudley, 20 November 1978
Height: 5'10" Weight: 11.7
His progress throughout the 1999-2000 campaign led many to believe that Rob rightfully deserved to land Barnet's "Most Improved Player" award, but he narrowly missed out on that particular accolade. Operating as a left-sided defensive midfielder, he matured into an outstanding prospect, showing confidence when surging

forward but never shirking his responsibilities at the back. His purposeful, snaking runs down the left flank delighted the Bees' fans and he weighed in with three goals, including a brace against Lincoln. Often a victim of tactical switches, his contribution to the club's play-off bid was sometimes overlooked; however, the slightly built full back could develop into an outstanding prospect if he maintains last season's form.
Barnet (Free from Wolverhampton W juniors on 22/10/1997) FL 53+2/2 FLC 3 Others 4

SCALES John Robert
Born: Harrogate, 4 July 1966
Height: 6'2" Weight: 13.5
Club Honours: FAC '88; FLC '95, '99
International Honours: E: 3; B-2
Injury and a lack of match fitness wrecked the 1999-2000 season for John, who, having made a promising start in the home victories over Newcastle and Everton in August, was then out of action for six months before reappearing on the bench for the game against Chelsea in February. There is no doubting the ability of this strong, versatile defender but, with competition for places in a strong back four hotting up, he was allowed to leave the club on a free transfer in the summer. John will be anxious to have an injury-free season in 2000-01 as he tries to relaunch his career in fresh surroundings. Stop Press: It was reported in early July that he had signed for Premiership newcomers Ipswich.
Bristol Rov (Free from Leeds U juniors on 11/7/1985) FL 68+4/2 FLC 3 FAC 6 Others 3+1
Wimbledon (£70,000 on 16/7/1987) F/PL 235+5/11 FLC 18+1 FAC 20+1 Others 7+1/4
Liverpool (£3,500,000 on 2/9/1994) PL 65/2 FLC 10/2 FAC 14 Others 4+1
Tottenham H (£2,600,000 on 11/12/1996) PL 29+4 FLC 4/1

SCARLETT Andre Pierre
Born: Wembley, 11 January 1980
Height: 5'4" Weight: 9.6
A diminutive right-sided midfielder with boundless energy, Andre is yet another of the bright prospects who have emerged from the prolific Luton youth system in recent years. Unfortunately, this "mighty atom" had few opportunities in the 1999-2000 campaign to develop the promise he had previously shown. The wealth of talent the club possesses restricted him to four senior appearances, two of them as a substitute, although his two starts, against Reading and Cardiff in January, both ended in 3-1 victories. A skilful and tenacious player who gives his all whenever he is called upon and has never let his manager down, he will be aiming for an extended run in the first team in 2000-01.
Luton T (From trainee on 8/7/1998) FL 4+5/1 FAC 0+1 Others 0+2

SCHNOOR Stefan
Born: Neumunster, Germany, 24 April 1971
Height: 5'10" Weight: 11.10
While the stylish German defender possibly made less of an impact in 1999-2000, his second season at Derby, than he had during the previous campaign, there was again no doubt about his versatility or his popularity with the home crowd. Naturally left-sided, he alternated in the second half of the season between left wing back, where he showed a willingness to join in with the attack whenever possible, and a more central position in which he was arguably more effective. The latter role was something of a revelation to the crowd and this may prove to be a permanent switch for the coming season. Stefan is one of the growing number of players to operate their own website.
Derby Co (Free from Hamburg, Germany, via Neumunster FC, on 13/7/1998) PL 42+10/2 FLC 2+1 FAC 3

SCHOFIELD Daniel (Danny) James
Born: Doncaster, 10 April 1980
Height: 5'10" Weight: 11.3
The teenage striker made several early-season appearances for Huddersfield from the substitutes' bench in 1999-2000. Danny shows a good touch and, with his eagerness to chase every cause another asset, the astute striker will be looking to make a future impact. Still only 19 and having recently signed a new contract, he looks to have a bright future in the game.
Huddersfield T (£2,000 from Brodsworth on 8/2/1999) FL 1+2 FLC 0+2 FAC 0+1

SCHOFIELD John David
Born: Barnsley, 16 May 1965
Height: 5'11" Weight: 11.8
John's sound reputation as a hard worker in defence and midfield made him a welcome addition to the Tigers' squad when he left Mansfield for Hull, with Steve Harper, in the summer of 1999. Penalties played a major part in his first City season. With Lee Bracey sent off against Macclesfield, John briefly took the goalkeeping gloves for the third time in his career but couldn't stop ex-Tiger Gregor Rioch's spot kick. Unfortunately, he missed the vital kick when Rochdale knocked City out of the Auto Windscreens Shield in a penalty shoot-out. John's versatility was used to the full over the first part of the season, but he was largely restricted to the bench after the FA Cup visit of Chelsea in December. He was appointed youth-team coach at Lincoln City during the summer.
Lincoln C (Free from Gainsborough Trinity on 10/11/1988) FL 221+10/11 FLC 15/2 FAC 5+2 Others 13+1
Doncaster Rov (Free on 18/11/1994) FL 107+3/12 FLC 4 FAC 2 Others 3
Mansfield T (£10,000 on 8/8/1997) FL 81+5 FLC 4 FAC 4 Others 4
Hull C (Free on 28/7/1999) FL 13+12 FLC 4 FAC 2+2 Others 1+1

SCHOLES Paul
Born: Salford, 16 November 1974
Height: 5'7" Weight: 11.10
Club Honours: PL '96, '97, '99, '00; FAC '96, '99; CS '96, '97
International Honours: E: 27; Yth (UEFA-U18 '93)
A prolific goalscorer who can play as an out-and-out striker or in central midfield, Paul might still be something of an unsung hero as far as the Old Trafford press pack are concerned, but he continued to lead from the front with some outstanding performances for Manchester United and England during the course of another glittering campaign in 1999-2000. Vying for a midfield berth with Nicky Butt at the start of the season, Paul took only two games to open his account with a goal against Sheffield Wednesday at Old Trafford in August. Although he was playing with a long-standing hernia from the outset, it certainly didn't affect his predatory instincts in front of goal, with notable strikes against Coventry and Aston Villa in the Premiership, and Marseille and Valencia in the Champions' League, and an important brace for England in the Euro 2000 qualifier against Scotland. Sacrificing a trip to the sunnier climes of Brazil for the inaugural World Club Championship at the turn of the year, he underwent surgery on his troublesome hernia that proved instantly beneficial when United returned home. Notching his sixth goal of the campaign against Coventry at Highfield Road in February, Paul rounded off that month with a prestigious honour in being named England's "Player of the Year" for 1999-2000. As the season entered its exciting climax, his fabulous strike against Bradford kept United in line for another Premiership success, while a hat-trick against West Ham on 1 April proved there's no fooling with Paul once he's inside the box. Despite scoring a last-minute penalty against Real Madrid in the European Cup quarter-final at Old Trafford, he will have to wait another year to see if he can make up for the winners' medal so cruelly denied him the season before. A regular for England under Kevin Keegan, he added ten caps during the season, appearing in all three of his country's games in Euro 2000 and scoring with a great header against Portugal.
Manchester U (From trainee on 29/1/1993) PL 117+43/41 FLC 6+2/5 FAC 8+6/4 Others 34+10/10

SCHWARZ Stefan Hans
Born: Malmo, Sweden, 18 April 1969
Height: 5'10" Weight: 12.6
International Honours: Sweden: 66
This experienced Swedish international became Sunderland's record signing when he arrived at the Stadium of Light from Spanish giants Valencia on the eve of the 1999-2000 season for £4 million. Having spent a season in the Premiership with Arsenal in the mid-'90s, Stefan re-adapted immediately to the English game and made his debut against Watford at home in a 2-0 win as Sunderland began the season impressively. Although essentially a central midfielder renowned for his tigerish tackling and sensible distribution, Stefan filled the vacant role on the left side of midfield impeccably, striking up a good understanding with full back Michael Gray. Even though he found the net only once last term, his goal was one of the best scored by Sunderland all season: a sweet left-foot volley from a right-wing cross that won all three points against Sheffield Wednesday in September. A fine season was to end

terribly, however, as Stefan, having been voted Swedish "Player of the Year" in November after playing a starring role as Sweden qualified for the Euro 2000 finals, sustained a freak injury while playing for his country against Austria in April. A ruptured achilles tendon was the diagnosis, one which ruled Stefan out of the rest of Sunderland's Premiership campaign and the aforementioned international summer tournament.

Arsenal (£1,750,000 from Benfica, Portugal on 31/5/1994) PL 34/2 FLC 4 FAC 1 Others 10/2 (£2,500,000 to Fiorentina, Italy on 27/7/1995)
Sunderland (£3,500,000 from Valencia, Spain on 9/8/1999) PL 27/1 FAC 2

SCHWARZER Mark
Born: Sydney, Australia, 6 October 1972
Height: 6'5" Weight: 13.6
International Honours: Australia: 9; Yth

The big Australian goalkeeper has proved to be an inspired choice to fill the gap left by Stephen Pears since moving to Middlesbrough from Bradford in February 1997. Mark is now firmly established in the Boro team and is a very popular member of the squad. With his great height, he dominates the goalmouth, and his commanding presence gives his team-mates great confidence. He did not have a spectacular season in 1999-2000, something he puts down to the lack of continuity in the rest of the team caused by injuries, although he missed only one match himself. Mark declined an offer from his national coach to travel with the squad at the beginning of the season because he was informed that he wouldn't get a game, preferring to concentrate on his efforts to help Middlesbrough achieve greater consistency. One particular highlight of the campaign was his two penalty saves in the Worthington Cup penalty shoot-out against Arsenal, which took Boro through to the quarter-finals. Shortly after his arrival at the Riverside Mark was given a four-year extension to his contract which ensures that he will be a Middlesbrough player until 2004, and his many admirers are in no doubt that he will develop into one of the top 'keepers in the Premiership. He won three more caps for his country, appearing against Chile, Slovakia and Bulgaria in February.

Bradford C (£350,000 from Kaiserslautern, Germany, via Blacktown, Marconi and Dynamo Dresden, on 22/11/1996) FL 13 FAC 3
Middlesbrough (£1,500,000 on 26/2/1997) F/PL 113 FLC 15 FAC 5

Mark Schwarzer

SCHWINKENDORF Jorn
Born: Germany, 27 January 1971
Height: 6'5" Weight: 14.4

Many Cardiff supporters were confused following the arrival of this tall German at Ninian Park last November. He was thought to be a centre half, but made little use of his height and rarely won the ball in the air. He was paraded as a holding midfield player and did a fair job during the first half of the home game against Preston before being injured. Jorn clearly has ability, but he never looked comfortable with the physical, competitive style of football played in the Second Division. Jorn arrived with a wealth of experience, having made several appearances for SC Freiburg in the Budesliga top division in 1998-99, but clearly found it difficult to settle in South Wales and he was made available for transfer at the end of the season.

Cardiff C (£110,000 from SV Waldhof Mannheim, Germany, via SC Freiburg, on 22/11/1999) FL 5 FAC 1

SCIMECA Riccardo
Born: Leamington Spa, 13 June 1975
Height: 6'1" Weight: 12.9
Club Honours: FLC '96
International Honours: E: B-1; U21-9

Riccardo became one of David Platt's first signings as player-manager of Nottingham Forest and was one of the few successes in a dismal 1999-2000 season for the Reds. He appeared in a variety of roles, beginning at centre back before switching to central midfield and finally settling at right back, and was appointed club captain after Steve Chettle moved to Barnsley. He led the team by example, showing great confidence as well as excellent skills and good control in tight situations.

Aston Villa (From trainee on 7/7/1993) PL 50+23/2 FLC 4+3 FAC 9+1 Others 5+2
Nottingham F (£3,000,000 on 23/7/1999) FL 38 FLC 4 FAC 3

SCOTT Andrew (Andy)
Born: Epsom, 2 August 1972
Height: 6'1" Weight: 11.5
Club Honours: Div 3 '99

A left-sided Brentford forward, Andy has good pace and control and delivers a fine cross. He began the 1999-2000 season in excellent form on the left wing but suffered an injury in November which kept him out of action for two months. On his return he took on a utility role within the squad, appearing at left back and in central midfield, and even took over the goalkeeper's jersey for the last 15 minutes at Oldham after Andy Woodman was sent off. Andy is the brother of Rob Scott, who plays for Rotherham United.

Sheffield U (£50,000 from Sutton U on 1/12/1992) P/FL 39+36/6 FLC 5/2 FAC 2+1 Others 3+1/3
Chesterfield (Loaned on 18/10/1996) FL 4+1/3
Bury (Loaned on 21/3/1997) FL 2+6
Brentford (£75,000 on 21/11/1997) FL 87+9/15 FLC 5+1/2 FAC 2 Others 5/3

Andy Scott

SCOTT Keith James
Born: Westminster, 9 June 1967
Height: 6'3" Weight: 14.3
Club Honours: GMVC '93; FAT '93

The big, bustling striker was in and out of the Reading team for most of the 1999-2000 season, and the signing of Martin Butler restricted his opportunities even further. Keith made 34 first-team appearances but played the full 90 minutes on only eight occasions, although he did become the first Reading player to score a "golden goal" winner, in the 2-1 win at Barnet in the Auto Windscreens Shield. He was told at the end of the season that he was surplus to requirements despite having a year still to run on his contract.

Lincoln C (Free from Leicester U on 22/3/1990) FL 7+9/2 FLC 0+1 Others 1+1
Wycombe W (£30,000 in March 1991 on 1/3/1991) FL 15/10 FLC 4/2 FAC 6/1 Others 2/2
Swindon T (£375,000 on 18/11/1993) P/FL 43+8/12 FLC 5/3 Others 3/1
Stoke C (£300,000 on 30/12/1994) FL 22+3/3 FAC 2/1 Others 0+1
Norwich C (Signed on 11/11/1995) FL 10+15/5 FLC 0+2 FAC 0+2
Bournemouth (Loaned on 16/2/1996) FL 8/1
Watford (Loaned on 7/2/1997) FL 6/2 Others 2
Wycombe W (£55,000 on 27/3/1997) FL 60+3/20 FLC 1+1/1 FAC 5/1 Others 1+1
Reading (£250,000 on 24/3/1999) FL 19+15/5 FLC 2+1/2 FAC 2+1 Others 1+2/1

SCOTT Philip (Phil) Campbell
Born: Perth, 14 November 1974
Height: 5'9" Weight: 11.2
Club Honours: S Div 1 '97
International Honours: S: U21-4

This attacking midfield player had another frustrating season for Sheffield Wednesday in 1999-2000 as he was again plagued by injury problems. He made his first start for the Owls at Southampton at the end of last August and also featured briefly in the line-up in the new year before again succumbing to injury. Phil will be hoping to recover full fitness to allow him to show his undoubted talents in the coming season.

St Johnstone (Signed from Scone Thistle on 30/7/1991) SL 115+19/27 SLC 6+2/2 SC 9+1/4 Others 5/2
Sheffield Wed (£75,000 on 26/3/1999) PL 2+7/1 FAC 1+1

SCOTT Richard Paul
Born: Dudley, 29 September 1974
Height: 5'9" Weight: 12.8

Equally at home in midfield or at right back, Richard benefited from an extended run in the Peterborough team. He managed only three goals last season but could have had his own "Goal of the Season" contest as they were all terrific strikes. Remarkably, two of them were superb last-ditch long-range efforts that clinched victories at home and away against Hull. An industrious player and a fine distributor of the ball, Richard served under Posh boss Barry Fry at Birmingham.

Birmingham C (From trainee on 17/5/1993) FL 11+1 FLC 3+1 Others 3
Shrewsbury T (Signed on 22/3/1995) FL 91+14/18 FLC 6 FAC 8+1/3 Others 8+1/1
Peterborough U (Signed on 20/7/1998) FL 47+14/7 FLC 1+1 FAC 1 Others 5+1

SCOTT Robert (Rob)
Born: Epsom, 15 August 1973
Height: 6'1" Weight: 11.10

Originally signed by Rotherham as a striker, Rob was converted first into a right wing back and then into a central defender with enormous success. His intelligent reading of the game makes him a natural for a place at the back. Rob is good in the air, while he also has a great turn of speed. Despite his having had a shoulder pinned in 1998, another major asset is his long throw, which created several goals for the Millers during their promotion-winning campaign. Rob is the younger brother of Brentford's Andy Scott.

Sheffield U (£20,000 from Sutton U on 1/8/1993) FL 2+4/1 FLC 0+1 Others 2+1
Scarborough (Loaned on 22/3/1995) FL 8/3
Northampton T (Loaned on 24/11/1995) FL 5 Others 1
Fulham (£30,000 on 10/1/1996) FL 65+19/17 FLC 3+5 FAC 3/1 Others 2+2/1
Carlisle U (Loaned on 18/8/1998) FL 7/3
Rotherham U (£50,000 on 17/11/1998) FL 38+2/2 FLC 1+1 FAC 4/1 Others 5

SCOWCROFT James (Jamie) Benjamin
Born: Bury St Edmunds, 15 November 1975
Height: 6'1" Weight: 12.2
International Honours: E: U21-5

James had his best season yet in Ipswich colours in 1999-2000, finally matching his undoubted skills with a consistency of performance which saw him collect numerous "Man of the Match" awards during the campaign. For much of the season he played on the right side of midfield rather than as an out-and-out striker and he seemed to thrive on the experience. He was happy to revert to playing his usual role of target man when required, sometimes in the middle of a game, and his ability in the air means that he is able to create chances for his colleagues with his knock-downs. However, the success of his midfield role was based on his ability to arrive late in the box undetected and make an attempt on goal. In the home game with Huddersfield he was first on the scene after the 'keeper had parried Jim Magilton's shot and was able to poke the ball into the net. He linked up well with Marcus Stewart, particularly in the play-off game at Bolton after David Johnson was injured. He was deservedly voted the club's "Player of the Year" by the supporters, winning more than double the number of votes cast for the second-placed player.

Ipswich T (From trainee on 1/7/1994) FL 141+27/43 FLC 16+2/5 FAC 8 Others 7+4/1

SCULLY Anthony (Tony) Derek Thomas
Born: Dublin, 12 June 1976
Height: 5'7" Weight: 11.12
International Honours: RoI: B-1; U21-10; Yth; Sch

Tony normally operates on the right wing for Queens Park Rangers, but has also played on the left side in attack or as a wing back. Although he is a skilful ball winner, he was unable to command a first-team place last season and started only two games. In an attempt to get more first-team action he spent a short period on loan at Walsall in March, but was not seen in the Saddlers' first team. On his return from the loan period he made a further appearance for Rangers as a substitute.

Crystal Palace (From trainee on 2/12/1993) FL 0+3
Bournemouth (Loaned on 14/10/1994) FL 6+4 Others 2
Cardiff C (Loaned on 5/1/1996) FL 13+1
Manchester C (£80,000 on 12/8/1997) FL 1+8
Stoke C (Loaned on 27/1/1998) FL 7
Queens Park R (£155,000 on 17/3/1998) FL 19+19/2 FLC 4+1 FAC 0+1

SEABURY Kevin
Born: Shrewsbury, 24 November 1973
Height: 5'10" Weight: 11.11

Showing a loyalty rare in modern times, Kevin has now completed eight seasons as a pro at Shrewsbury, and has made over 200 starts. A very dependable right-sided wing back who can also play in midfield, he was ever present in 1999-2000 until the end of January when a knee cartilage injury forced him to sit out 14 games. His ability to make vital goal-line clearances is incredible. A very popular club man, strong in the tackle and speedy going forward, Kevin failed to find the net last season, but still has plenty to offer.

Shrewsbury T (From trainee on 6/7/1992) FL 197+21/7 FLC 10+2/1 FAC 12 Others 9+2

SEAMAN David Andrew
Born: Rotherham, 19 September 1963
Height: 6'4" Weight: 14.10
Club Honours: Div 1 '91; PL '98; FAC '93, '98; FLC '93; ECWC '94; CS '98
International Honours: E: 59; B-6; U21-10

A calf injury sustained during pre-season preparations caused David to miss Arsenal's opening dozen games of the 1999-2000 season. Once he was fully fit, however, he again proved to be the number one goalkeeper in England. Relaxed and composed both on and off the field, he makes a massive contribution to the continued success achieved by the Highbury club. A strong, brave 'keeper who is fast off his line, he has safe hands and a strong kick. His distribution is excellent, varying between long and short throws to the wing backs and long kicks to the strikers. Many attacking moves originate from his foresight. A great shot stopper, he is exceptionally agile for a big man. His breathtaking save diving low to his left in the away leg of Arsenal's UEFA Cup tie against Deportivo La Coruna was his save of the season and a fine demonstration of his agility. David won a further seven caps for England, appearing in the opening two games of Euro 2000 before a late injury forced him out of the crucial match against Romania.

Leeds U (From apprentice on 22/9/1981)
Peterborough U (£4,000 on 13/8/1982) FL 91 FLC 10 FAC 5
Birmingham C (£100,000 on 5/10/1984) FL 75 FLC 4 FAC 5
Queens Park R (£225,000 on 7/8/1986) FL 141 FLC 13 FAC 17 Others 4
Arsenal (£1,300,000 on 18/5/1990) F/PL 336 FLC 32 FAC 43 Others 46+1

SEARLE Damon Peter
Born: Cardiff, 26 October 1971
Height: 5'11" Weight: 10.4
Club Honours: WC '92, '93; Div 3 '93
International Honours: W: B-1; U21-6; Yth; Sch

Damon began the 1999-2000 campaign in the Carlisle first team, but lost his place early in the season before going to Rochdale on loan in September. He spent three months at Spotland, taking over as Dale's regular left back. Showing excellent form going forward, he was expected to sign permanently, but the deal eventually fell through, and he returned to Brunton Park early in the new year. A seasoned campaigner with a good left foot, Damon turned in some sterling performances in the closing weeks of the campaign and may yet be staying at United. After being told by former boss Martin Wilkinson that he would not be retained, Damon was offered new terms in May.

Cardiff C (From trainee on 20/8/1990) FL 232+2/3 FLC 9/1 FAC 13 Others 29
Stockport Co (Free on 28/5/1996) FL 34+7 FLC 2+1 FAC 2 Others 1
Carlisle U (Free on 6/7/1998) FL 57+9/3 FLC 4 FAC 1 Others 4+1/1
Rochdale (Loaned on 17/9/1999) FL 13+1

SEARLE Stephen (Stevie)
Born: Lambeth, 7 March 1977
Height: 5'10" Weight: 11.13

With his flawless distribution and impeccable temperament, Stevie was expected to feature prominently for Barnet during 1999-2000, but he was afflicted by a series of injuries and ill fortune. In the opening-day victory at Chester, he received a severe laceration to the leg that ruled him out for three weeks. When he was fit enough to return to first-team duties, he fruitlessly tried to dislodge the established midfield partnership of John Dooland and Frazer Toms. Predominantly right sided, Stevie was forced to compete with virtual ever-present Doolan for the vacant berth in the side with minimal success. However, when he did appear, his displays could not be faulted and he rarely squandered possession, always using the ball constructively. After impressing in the victory against Plymouth in March, he was selected to appear in the subsequent match against Brighton, only to sustain a serious ankle injury that ended his campaign prematurely.

Barnet (Free from Sittingbourne on 1/8/1997) FL 67+17/5 FAC 2 Others 5+1

SEBOK Vilmos
Born: Budapest, Hungary, 13 June 1973
Height: 6'3" Weight: 13.1
International Honours: Hungary: 33

After Vilmos had appeared in most of Bristol City's games during the first three months of the 1999-2000 season, the club's manager, Tony Pulis, decided that this Hungarian international defender was not the type of player that City needed in their defence. Many fans disagreed, though perhaps it would be true to state that his cultured play was out of place in the hurly-burly of Second Division action. Vilmos eventually moved on loan to German club Waldhof Mannheim and was released by City in the summer. A regular for his country, he won seven more caps last season.

Bristol C (£200,000 from Upjest Dosza, Hungary, via Tatabanya and REAC, on 15/1/1999) FL 18+5 FLC 4

SEDGEMORE Benjamin (Ben) Redwood
Born: Wolverhampton, 5 August 1975
Height: 5'11" Weight: 12.10
International Honours: E: Sch

Ben again found it difficult to establish a regular place in Macclesfield's midfield in the early weeks of the 1999-2000 campaign. He was given his chance at the beginning of October, initially coming on from the bench, and then starting regularly, and he forged a useful partnership with Chris Priest, notably making good use of his turn of pace. Towards the end of the season, his form dipped and he was often either on the bench or substituted. His natural enthusiasm ensures that Ben will bounce back in the new season, and give of his best. Like his younger brother Jake of Conference club Hednesford he is a former England schools international.

Birmingham C (From trainee on 17/5/1993)
Northampton T (Loaned on 22/12/1994) FL 1
Mansfield T (Loaned on 25/8/1995) FL 4+5 Others 1
Peterborough U (Free on 10/1/1996) FL 13+4 FAC 1
Mansfield T (Free on 6/9/1996) FL 58+9/6 FLC 1 FAC 2+1 Others 2
Macclesfield T (£25,000 on 19/3/1998) FL 61+14/3 FLC 4 FAC 6/1 Others 2

SEDGLEY Stephen (Steve) Philip
Born: Enfield, 26 May 1968
Height: 6'1" Weight: 13.13
Club Honours: FAC '87, '91
International Honours: E: U21-11

This Wolves midfielder-cum-central defender was a regular in the starting line-up for the first half of the 1999-2000 season before falling from favour and losing his place in December. Despite his apparent unhappiness, Steve reportedly refused at least one chance of leaving. In the early part of 2000 he re-established himself in the first team, scoring in five games out of seven – and this does not include one in a penalty shoot-out! A seasoned campaigner who remains an accomplished dead-ball exponent, Steve continued to play well and retained his place until the end of the season. However, he was released during the summer.

Coventry C (From apprentice on 2/6/1986) FL 81+3/3 FLC 9/2 FAC 2+2 Others 5+1
Tottenham H (£750,000 on 28/7/1989) F/PL 147+17/9 FLC 24+3/1 FAC 22+1/1 Others 5+3
Ipswich T (£1,000,000 on 15/6/1994) P/FL 105/15 FLC 10/2 FAC 5 Others 5/1
Wolverhampton W (£700,000 on 29/7/1997) FL 91+10/8 FLC 7 FAC 8+1/1

SEDGWICK Christopher (Chris) Edward
Born: Sheffield, 28 April 1980
Height: 5'11" Weight: 10.10

A young midfielder who plays wide on Rotherham's right, Chris improved enormously during the 1999-2000 season and has a big future in front of him. He is an exciting dribbler, can cross a good ball and has a great turn of speed. As his confidence built during the Millers' promotion campaign, Chris was the one the team looked for to make things happen against defensive-minded opponents. He popped up with some vital goals, including a spectacular individual effort in front of a live television audience against Mansfield.

Rotherham U (From trainee on 16/8/1997) FL 53+22/9 FLC 1+2 FAC 3+4 Others 2+2/1

SELLARS Scott
Born: Sheffield, 27 November 1965
Height: 5'8" Weight: 10.0
Club Honours: FMC '87; Div 1 '93, '97
International Honours: E: U21-3

Signed from Bolton Wanderers in the

summer of 1999, Scott started the new season as a regular in the Huddersfield midfield and showed his undoubted Premiership pedigree. Predominantly left sided and always comfortable in possession, Scott invariably gave a busy display of quality passing and crossing, coupled with the vision to unlock any defence with a well-timed through-ball. He was proudly made captain against his old club at the Reebok Stadium in October, and opened his goalscoring account three days later with a sweet right-foot volley against Stockport County. With the season growing in momentum, Scott was often brought on from the substitutes' bench to contribute his silky skills to the Terriers' cause, an important squad member at the age of 34.

Leeds U (From apprentice on 25/7/1983) FL 72+4/12 FLC 4/1 FAC 4 Others 2/1
Blackburn Rov (£20,000 on 28/7/1986) FL 194+8/35 FLC 12/3 FAC 11/1 Others 20/2
Leeds U (£800,000 on 1/7/1992) PL 6+1 FLC 1+1 Others 1
Newcastle U (£700,000 on 9/3/1993) F/PL 56+5/5 FLC 6+1/2 FAC 3 Others 4/1
Bolton W (£750,000 on 7/12/1995) P/FL 106+5/15 FLC 8+1 FAC 5/1 Others 0+1
Huddersfield T (Free on 30/7/1999) FL 23+11/1 FLC 1+1/1 FAC 1

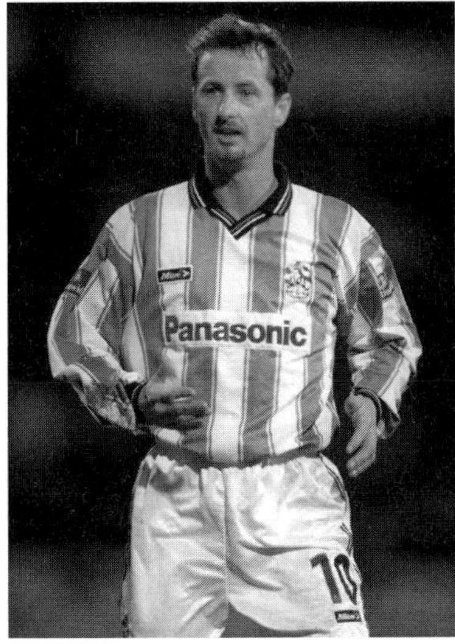

Scott Sellars

SENDA Daniel (Danny) Luke
Born: Harrow, 17 April 1981
Height: 5'10" Weight: 10.0
International Honours: E: Yth

This former England youth international was mostly used as a substitute by Wycombe in 1999-2000, although he made the starting line-up on three occasions. Danny performed promisingly in early-season outings from the bench but it was not until the Boxing Day game with Bournemouth that he finally looked a first-team player, causing havoc on the right wing and coming close to scoring. He netted his first goal in senior football with a thunderous volley from the edge of the area at Wrexham last February, and will be aiming to gain a regular place in the Chairboys' line-up in 2000-01. Danny is a wide-right midfielder with good pace and attacking skills, but he still needs to develop the physical aspect of his game.

Wycombe W (Signed from Southampton juniors on 26/1/1999) FL 5+28/1 Others 0+1

SENIOR Michael Graham
Born: Huddersfield, 3 March 1981
Height: 5'9" Weight: 11.6

This Huddersfield-born youngster made his one and only 1999-2000 appearance for his home-town club against Notts County in the Worthington Cup when he came on from the subs' bench for the final 15 minutes. The central midfielder showed some nice touches and almost marked his debut with a snap-shot effort which crashed against a post. He will be hoping for more opportunities during the forthcoming season.

Huddersfield T (From trainee on 8/7/1999) FLC 0+1

SERRANT Carl
Born: Bradford, 12 September 1975
Height: 6'0" Weight: 11.2
International Honours: E: B-1; U21-2; Yth

Carl is a strong, solid player who is very quick and able to play in any of the back-line positions, or as a defensive midfielder. After a disappointing first season at Newcastle, he was encouraged to find himself beginning the 1999-2000 campaign in the first team against Villa. Dropped to the bench for the second fixture, he was recalled for the next game at Southampton, but was stretchered off after only 13 minutes. Carl made only one further appearance, as a substitute in the UEFA Cup game at FC Zurich, before a loan transfer to Sheffield United was arranged for him in December, but the move was frustrated by the need for a cartilage operation which sidelined him for over six weeks, during which time he was made available for transfer.

Oldham Ath (From trainee on 22/7/1994) FL 84+6/1 FLC 7 FAC 6/1 Others 3
Newcastle U (£500,000 + on 9/7/1998) PL 5+1 Others 0+1
Bury (Loaned on 18/2/1999) FL 15

SERTORI Mark Anthony
Born: Manchester, 1 September 1967
Height: 6'2" Weight: 14.2
Club Honours: GMVC '88

The tough-tackling centre back made a surprise move from Halifax to York last September after playing in Town's first seven matches. He quickly settled in at Bootham Crescent, performing very effectively in his customary no-nonsense style. In March Mark was switched to centre forward by new manager Terry Dolan, and his ability to hold the ball up helped City put together an unbeaten run of nine games. He scored just once, but his effort at Cheltenham was sufficient to earn three valuable points.

Stockport Co (Signed from East Manchester on 7/2/1987) FL 3+1 FLC 1
Lincoln C (Free on 1/7/1988) FL 43+7/9 FLC 6 FAC 4/1 Others 5/2
Wrexham (£30,000 on 9/2/1990) FL 106+4/3 FLC 8+1 FAC 6 Others 9+1
Bury (Free on 22/7/1994) FL 4+9/1 FLC 1 FAC 2+1 Others 1+2/1
Scunthorpe U (Free on 22/7/1996) FL 82+1/2 FLC 6 FAC 7 Others 4+1
Halifax T (Free on 7/7/1998) FL 44+1 FLC 6 FAC 1 Others 2
York C (£25,000 on 3/9/1999) FL 37+3/1 FAC 1 Others 1

SHAIL Mark Edward David
Born: Sandviken, Sweden, 15 October 1966
Height: 6'1" Weight: 13.3
International Honours: E: SP-1

Apart from a substitute appearance at Reading in the opening game of the season, Mark became a forgotten man at Bristol City in 1999-2000. A long-serving centre back who defends solidly both in the air and on the ground, Mark can always be relied upon to give 100 per cent. He spent most of the season with City's young reserve team before being released at the end of the campaign. Stop Press: Mark was reported to have signed for league newcomers Kidderminster in June.

Bristol C (£45,000 from Yeovil on 25/3/1993) FL 117+11/4 FLC 5+1 FAC 11/1 Others 4

SHARP Kevin Phillip
Born: Ontario, Canada, 19 September 1974
Height: 5'9" Weight: 11.11
Club Honours: FAYC '93; Div 3 '97; AMC '99
International Honours: E: Yth (UEFA-U18 '93); Sch

Kevin is a confident and reliable left back with Wigan whose 1999-2000 campaign was interrupted by both injuries and suspensions. Solid defensively, he has a good turn of pace and enjoys the wing-back role. He also made his 150th Football League appearance during the season.

Leeds U (£60,000 from Auxerre, France on 20/10/1992) PL 11+6 Others 0+1
Wigan Ath (£100,000 on 30/11/1995) FL 126+19/10 FLC 3+2 FAC 6+3 Others 15+1/1

SHARPE Lee Stuart
Born: Halesowen, 27 May 1971
Height: 6'0" Weight: 12.12
Club Honours: ECWC '91; FLC '92; PL '93, '94, '96; CS '94
International Honours: E: 8; B-1; U21-8

Lee signed permanent forms for Bradford City in the summer of 1999 following a successful loan spell at the end of the previous season. He missed the first two months of 1999-2000 after damaging ankle ligaments in a pre-season friendly and did not return to first-team action until the middle of October. He then remained in the first-team squad until early in the new year before suffering further injury problems. Used as a left wing back and also in a wide midfield role, he showed that he can still weave his magic on the wing with his close control and ability to pass defenders.

Torquay U (From trainee on 31/5/1988) FL 9+5/3 Others 2+3
Manchester U (£185,000 on 10/6/1988) F/PL 160+33/21 FLC 15+8/9 FAC 22+7/3 Others 18+2/3

Leeds U (£4,500,000 on 14/8/1996) PL 28+2/5 FLC 3/1 FAC 0+1 Others 1+2
Bradford C (£200,000 on 25/3/1999) P/FL 19+8/2 FLC 0+1 FAC 1+1

SHARPLING Christopher (Chris) Barry
Born: Bromley, 21 April 1981
Height: 5'11" Weight: 11.10

This former Crystal Palace junior made his first appearances in league football in 1999-2000, his second season as a professional at Selhurst Park. A tall left-sided defender, he did well in the reserves and will be aiming to feature more regularly in the first-team set-up in the 2000-01 campaign.
Crystal Palace (From juniors on 20/8/1998) FL 1+5

SHAW Paul
Born: Burnham, 4 September 1973
Height: 5'11" Weight: 12.4
International Honours: E: Yth

Paul had to compete with three other players for the centre-forward role at Millwall in 1999-2000 and, due to the form of Neil Harris and Richard Sadlier, he did not start as many games as he might have expected, given that he was the club's second-highest scorer the previous season. He is still very quick, hard to mark and turns his defender well. He also has a good shot with either foot and when given a first-team chance never let the side down. He is a firm favourite with the Millwall faithful.
Arsenal (From trainee on 18/9/1991) PL 1+11/2 FAC 0+1
Burnley (Loaned on 23/3/1995) FL 8+1/4
Cardiff C (Loaned on 11/8/1995) FL 6
Peterborough U (Loaned on 20/10/1995) FL 12/5 Others 2
Millwall (£250,000 on 15/9/1997) FL 88+21/26 FLC 6/2 FAC 2 Others 5+6

Richard Shaw

SHAW Richard Edward
Born: Brentford, 11 September 1968
Height: 5'9" Weight: 12.8
Club Honours: FMC '91; Div 1 '94

A dependable central defender, Richard enjoyed another solid season with Coventry in 1999-2000. He is a player with no frills but who always gives 100 per cent. In October his form earned him a two-year extension to his contract. After almost 200 games for City all that is missing is a goal! He caught the club's injury bug in November, requiring keyhole surgery on his knee, and he was perhaps rushed back into action too soon. With stiff competitiion from the likes of Colin Hendry, Paul Williams and Gary Breen, it seems that Richard will have to fight to win a regular place in the first team in the coming season.
Crystal Palace (From apprentice on 4/9/1986) F/PL 193+14/3 FLC 28+2 FAC 18 Others 12+1
Hull C (Loaned on 14/12/1989) FL 4
Coventry C (£1,000,000 on 17/11/1995) PL 152+3 FLC 12 FAC 13+1

SHEARER Alan
Born: Newcastle, 13 August 1970
Height: 6'0" Weight: 12.6
Club Honours: PL '95
International Honours: E: 63; B-1; U21-11; Yth

During 1999-2000 Alan once again spent the season in the spotlight, and once again answered his critics in the best way possible – with an impressive tally of goals for both Newcastle and England, his total of 30 for the club being a season's best for him since his return to Tyneside. A series of serious injuries in recent years was suggested by his detractors to have reduced his effectiveness, but under the guidance of his new manager, Bobby Robson, he adapted his game, adopting a more sideways stance when receiving the ball which enables him to turn and attack opposing defences more readily. He may have lost a little of his pace, but he remains a formidable striker with a good all-round game, strong on the ball and difficult to dispossess, very dangerous in the air, and adept at moving to the wing to create space for his colleagues, for whom he then supplies excellent crosses. But first and foremost Alan is a goalscorer, blessed with a poacher's instinct, able to take chances with his head or with either foot from close in or through his powerful shooting from a distance. Captain of his club and his country, he readily accepts responsibility, leads by example and is highly influential both on and off the field. Alan committed himself to his home-town club of Newcastle by signing a new five-year contract before the start of the season but was then sent off for the first time in his career in the opening game of the campaign against Aston Villa for two bookable offences, the second of which was highly debatable and provoked an outburst by manager Ruud Gullit. Following the subsequent suspension he only made the bench for the derby game against Sunderland, a decision which attracted much media attention and concern among the "Toon Army". Defeat in the match precipitated Gullit's resignation, following which Alan was immediately recalled to the side. He was rejuvenated by the arrival of Robson, and replied to his critics with a hat-trick for England against Luxembourg. In the next home Premiership match against Sheffield Wednesday he equalled the Premiership individual scoring record with five goals, the first time he had scored more than three in a single senior match, and he followed this with another two at Leeds and three in the next two games plus one for England against Belgium. Alan's developing partnership with Duncan Ferguson, with both finding the net regularly, was a key factor in the side's steady improvement as the season progressed. Desperately keen for success for Newcastle, he was bitterly disappointed by the defeat in the FA Cup semi-final, although he delivered a fine display in the match himself, giving Frank Leboeuf a torrid time and contributing to the Newcastle goal with an excellent cross. He continued to find the net regularly in both Premiership and cups, and remains the all-time Premiership leading scorer, while his goal in the season's finale against Arsenal was the 300th of his career. Alan is a fixture in the England team, although in February he announced that he will retire from international football after Euro 2000 to enable him to focus all his attention on his efforts for his club, and to allow him to spend more time with his young family. The scorer of six goals in 12 international games last season, including the header that defeated Germany in Euro 2000, he will be sorely missed by his country in the future.
Southampton (From trainee on 14/4/1988) FL 105+13/23 FLC 16+2/11 FAC 11+3/4 Others 8/5
Blackburn Rov (£3,600,000 on 24/7/1992) PL 132+6/112 FLC 16/14 FAC 8/2 Others 9/2
Newcastle U (£15,000,000 on 30/7/1996) PL 111+4/64 FLC 4/2 FAC 21/16 Others 13/4

SHEERIN Joseph (Joe) Earnan
Born: Hammersmith, 1 February 1979
Height: 6'1" Weight: 13.9

This tall striker joined Bournemouth from Chelsea last February but then aggravated an old hamstring injury and it was not until early April that he made his debut for the Cherries at Oxford. Joe showed promise in six end-of-season appearances and netted a fine goal with an overhead strike in the 3-0 victory over Oldham. He has signed an 18-month contract and will be hoping to establish himself as a regular member of the club's strike force in the 2000-01 season.
Chelsea (From trainee on 9/7/1997) PL 0+1
Bournemouth (Signed on 28/2/2000) FL 3+3/1

SHEFFIELD Jonathan (Jon)
Born: Bedworth, 1 February 1969
Height: 5'11" Weight: 12.10

Already established as Plymouth's first-choice 'keeper, Jon continued to impress with his confident displays throughout 1999-2000. His ability as a shot stopper together with his confidence in the air helped save many important points for Argyle. Although hailing from the Midlands, Jon has close family links with the Plymouth area which have been a factor in enabling him to settle in well. Offered new terms, he faces competition for the 'keeper's jersey in 2000-01 from former Leicester custodian John Hodges.
Norwich C (From apprentice on 16/2/1987) FL 1
Aldershot (Loaned on 22/9/1989) FL 11 Others 1
Aldershot (Loaned on 21/8/1990) FL 15 Others 1

Cambridge U (Free on 18/3/1991) FL 56 FLC 3 FAC 4 Others 6
Colchester U (Loaned on 23/12/1993) FL 6
Swindon T (Loaned on 28/1/1994) PL 2
Hereford U (Loaned on 15/9/1994) FL 8 FLC 2
Peterborough U (£150,000 on 20/7/1995) FL 62 FLC 8 FAC 6 Others 5
Plymouth Arg (£100,000 on 28/7/1997) FL 126 FLC 5 FAC 11 Others 2

SHELDON Gareth Richard
Born: Birmingham, 31 January 1980
Height: 5'11" Weight: 12.0

Scunthorpe United's Wembley hero from the previous May failed to make the progress expected during 1999-2000. An ankle injury saw him miss the start of the campaign and he struggled to win a place even on the substitutes' bench for long spells. Gareth scored twice in two starts in January but was again left out soon afterwards. A right-sided striker, who can also play down the middle or at wing back, he has blistering pace and a talent which the club will be hoping to harness more effectively next season.

Scunthorpe U (From trainee on 4/2/1999) FL 13+21/3 FLC 1 FAC 0+1 Others 2+3/3

SHELTON Andrew (Andy) Marc
Born: Sutton Coldfield, 19 June 1980
Height: 5'11" Weight: 12.0

A product of Chester's youth policy, Andy was mainly used on the right wing during 1999-2000. He is a player with lots of pace who likes to get forward, and the highlight of his season was his goal in the 4-4 Worthington Cup draw with First Division Port Vale last August. Andy is the son of Gary Shelton, whose former clubs include Sheffield Wednesday and Chester, where he is now the assistant manager.

Chester C (From trainee on 7/7/1998) FL 14+22/1 FLC 5/1 FAC 1+2 Others 1+1/1

SHEPHEARD Jonathan (Jon) Thomas
Born: Oxford, 31 March 1981
Height: 6'3" Weight: 12.4

This young centre back broke into the Oxford side during their defensive problems last January. He made a couple of appearances in the Auto Windscreens Shield before making his Football League debut as a substitute at Oldham in January. A tall, lanky player, he was included in the starting line-up for the home game against Preston the following Tuesday but did not play for the first team thereafter, although he was on the bench on a few occasions.

Oxford U (From trainee on 28/6/1999) FL 1+1 Others 2

SHERIDAN Darren Stephen
Born: Manchester, 8 December 1967
Height: 5'5" Weight: 11.5

Following a close-season move from Oakwell, Darren was reunited with John Benson, the coach who introduced him to league football at Barnsley, and appeared in a variety of roles on the left side for Wigan in 1999-2000. A combative midfield player with a great range of passing, Darren got on the score sheet on four occasions and it was his goal against Millwall that took the Latics through to the Second Division play-off final. He is the younger brother of Oldham's John Sheridan.

Barnsley (£10,000 from Winsford U on 12/8/1993) F/PL 149+22/5 FLC 9+4/1 FAC 9+2/1 Others 1+1
Wigan Ath (Free on 2/7/1999) FL 25+6/3 FLC 4 FAC 1+1 Others 5/1

SHERIDAN John Joseph
Born: Stretford, 1 October 1964
Height: 5'10" Weight: 12.0
Club Honours: FLC '91; Div 1 '97
International Honours: RoI: 34; B-1; U23-2; U21-2; Yth

John had another excellent campaign for Oldham in 1999-2000 and was again voted "Player of the Season" by the supporters. Although now in the twilight of his career, he was still the key man for the Latics to such an extent that on the occasions when he was absent the team clearly missed him and looked a different side. Capable of an exceptional range of passing, he remained a quality play-maker in the centre of the pitch, with the highlight of his season coming last September when he scored with a brilliant 45-yard free kick at Bristol Rovers. John signed an extension to his contract in January that should keep him at Boundary Park until 2002, and the possibility of his taking up a coaching role at the club has already been mentioned. He is the older brother of Wigan's Darren Sheridan.

Leeds U (Free from Manchester C juniors on 2/3/1982) FL 225+5/47 FLC 14/3 FAC 11+1/1 Others 11/1
Nottingham F (£650,000 on 3/8/1989) FLC 1
Sheffield Wed (£500,000 on 3/11/1989) F/PL 187+10/25 FLC 24/3 FAC 17+1/3 Others 4/2
Birmingham C (Loaned on 9/2/1996) FL 1+1 FLC 2
Bolton W (£180,000 on 13/11/1996) F/PL 24+8/2 FLC 2 FAC 2 (Free to Doncaster Rov in 1998 close season)
Oldham Ath (Free on 20/10/1998) FL 64+2/3 FLC 1+1 FAC 7/1 Others 1

SHERINGHAM Edward (Teddy) Paul
Born: Liam, 2 April 1966
Height: 5'11" Weight: 12.5
Club Honours: Div 2 '88; FMC '92; CS '97; PL '99, '00; FAC '99; EC '99
International Honours: E: 38; U21-1; Yth

A natural goalscorer who is widely acclaimed as one of the most intelligent strikers in the Premiership, Teddy made a pivotal contribution to Manchester United's triumph in the FA Cup and the Champions' League in the final week of the 1998-99 campaign after coming on as a substitute, but his seat on the bench had hardly cooled when he was back on it again at the start of last season. Despite that, he was still determined to show there was more mileage in the tank, as his 19 full starts and six goals during the season so ably testified, and his loyalty was rewarded with a second Premiership winners' medal. Rumours suggested that he was the target of numerous clubs ranging from Fulham and Charlton to Real Mallorca and Sporting Lisbon. The speculation was ended when he signed a new contract with United in the summer. The extent of his first-team involvement during the coming season remains to be seen but, whatever the future may hold, few United fans will forget that night in Barcelona in May 1999 when he really did help to make their dreams come true.

Millwall (From apprentice on 19/1/1984) FL 205+15/93 FLC 16+1/8 FAC 12/5 Others 11+2/5
Aldershot (Loaned on 1/2/1985) FL 4+1 Others 1
Nottingham F (£2,000,000 on 23/7/1991) FL 42/14 FLC 10/5 FAC 4/2 Others 6/2
Tottenham H (£2,100,000 on 28/8/1992) PL 163+3/75 FLC 14/10 FAC 17/13
Manchester U (£3,500,000 on 1/7/1997) PL 50+25/16 FLC 1/1 FAC 3+4/4 Others 14+13/4

SHERON Michael (Mike) Nigel
Born: St Helens, 11 January 1972
Height: 5'10" Weight: 11.13
International Honours: E: U21-16

This gifted striker began the 1999-2000 season in superb form for Barnsley and scored regularly in the period up to the end of October. His scoring touch then seemed to disappear and his form dipped, although he retained the confidence of manager Dave Bassett and eventually broke his run with a two-goal strike in the 4-1 win at Walsall in April. Even when not scoring, he worked hard and showed some intelligent running off the ball. He is a very skilful player who links up well with his colleagues and is able to beat opponents with ease.

Manchester C (From trainee on 5/7/1990) F/PL 82+18/24 FLC 9+1/1 FAC 5+3/3 Others 1
Bury (Loaned on 28/3/1991) FL 1+4/1 Others 2
Norwich C (£1,000,000 on 26/8/1994) P/FL 19+9/2 FLC 6/3 FAC 4/2
Stoke C (£450,000 on 13/11/1995) FL 64+5/34 FLC 4/5 FAC 1 Others 2
Queens Park R (£2,750,000 on 2/7/1997) FL 57+6/19 FLC 2+2/1 FAC 2
Barnsley (£1,000,000 on 27/1/1999) FL 42+9/11 FLC 4/2 FAC 1+2

SHERWOOD Timothy (Tim) Alan
Born: St Albans, 6 February 1969
Height: 6'0" Weight: 12.9
Club Honours: PL '95
International Honours: E: 3; B-1; U21-4

One of Tottenham manager George Graham's early signings for the club, Tim again proved highly influential in 1999-2000 despite missing much of the final quarter of the season through injury. It was no coincidence that his absence came at the same time as a dip in form for Tottenham, who clearly missed his strong organisational skills and experience in the heart of midfield. Tim's stature and breadth of ability were particularly evident when he took the captain's armband in the absence of Sol Campbell, and with four fine goals in his first seven outings of the season he provided a much-needed additional source of goals. Tim's tenacity and full-bloooded commitment meant that he was as happy scrapping in his own 18-yard box for loose balls as he was picking up possession in the final third of the field and unleashing cracking right-foot drives. He will have been disappointed not to have featured in Kevin Keegan's Euro 2000 squad, but promises to be a key figure for Tottenham during the coming season. An injury-free campaign could provide the platform for him to bid for a recall.

Regardless of international aspirations, Tottenham fans can be assured that Tim will be giving his usual high level of commitment in the hope of pushing the club into the top six in 2000-01.

Watford (From trainee on 7/2/1987) FL 23+9/2 FLC 4+1 FAC 9 Others 4+1
Norwich C (£175,000 on 18/7/1989) FL 66+5/10 FLC 7/1 FAC 4 Others 5+1/2
Blackburn Rov (£500,000 on 12/2/1992) F/PL 239+7/25 FLC 24+1/2 FAC 15+2/4 Others 12
Tottenham H (£3,800,000 on 5/2/1999) PL 35+6/10 FLC 2/1 FAC 5/1 Others 3/1

SHIELDS Anthony (Tony) Gerald
Born: Derry, 4 June 1980
Height: 5'7" Weight: 10.10

A product of Peterborough's impressive youth policy, the diminutive midfielder was promoted to the attack in 1999-2000. He had filled the role in his youth-team days, and responded with two headed goals. Tony then rarely featured in the new year after Posh suffered a mid-term slump. A tenacious player who is not afraid to get stuck in, he looks to have a bright future in the game.

Peterborough U (From trainee on 6/7/1998) FL 21+13/1 FLC 2/1 FAC 1 Others 0+1

SHIELDS Gregory (Greg)
Born: Falkirk, 21 August 1976
Height: 5'9" Weight: 11.2
Club Honours: Div 1 '00
International Honours: S: U21-2; Yth; Sch

Having joined Charlton Athletic from Dunfermline on trial not long after the start of the 1999-2000 season, Greg quickly broke into the side and made the right-back spot his own with some good performances, earning himself a full contract in the process. A good tackler, he has the ability to push forward down the right wing and get balls into the penalty area for the front men. He also found the net himself on two occasions, one goal coming after a run from defence and the other from a 25-yard blaster. He suffered a knee injury in January 2000, damaging his cartilage, and took no further part in the season, but he had already made a significant contribution to the Addicks' First Division championship challenge and was rewarded with a winners' medal.

Glasgow R (From Rangers BC on 1/7/1993) SL 7 SLC 1+1 Others 2
Dunfermline Ath (Signed on 30/6/1997) SL 75 SLC 6 SC 4 Others 1
Charlton Ath (£580,000 on 26/8/1999) FL 21/2 FLC 2 FAC 3

SHILTON Samuel (Sam) Roger
Born: Nottingham, 21 July 1978
Height: 5'10" Weight: 11.6

Sam joined Hartlepool on a month-to-month contract last September but, after he had turned in several impressive displays as an attacking left back, he was soon secured on a permanent deal. On his day an exciting player, he unfortunately failed to maintain his early momentum and in the second half of the season he was often left out of the side. Saddled with always being identified as the son of a famous father, Sam can be satisfied with his progress during the season.

Plymouth Arg (Trainee) FL 1+2 FAC 0+1
Coventry C (£12,500 on 31/10/1995) PL 3+4 FLC 1+1 FAC 0+1
Hartlepool U (Free on 9/7/1999) FL 16+5/3 FAC 2 Others 2

SHIPPERLEY Neil Jason
Born: Chatham, 30 October 1974
Height: 6'1" Weight: 13.12
International Honours: E: U21-7

This big and powerful striker joined Barnsley on a three-year contract in the summer of 1999, thus linking up once again with his former manager Dave Bassett. Neil tore a hamstring in a Worthington Cup tie with Lincoln last August and spent most of the first half of the season struggling to overcome a series of niggling injuries. He featured more regularly in the new year when he hit a great run of form, scoring eight times in 13 games to boost the Oakwell club's promotion campaign. He has some neat touches for such a big man and is both good in the air and at holding the ball up. He finished the season in double figures, netting one of his most crucial goals with a superb strike in the play-off semi-final first leg, thus setting the Tykes on their way to a stunning 4-0 win at Birmingham City and a first-ever Wembley appearance.

Chelsea (From trainee on 24/9/1992) PL 26+11/7 FLC 4+2/1 FAC 3/1 Others 2
Watford (Loaned on 7/12/1994) FL 5+1/1
Southampton (£1,250,000 on 6/1/1995) PL 65+1/12 FLC 5+1/2 FAC 10/5
Crystal Palace (£1,000,000 on 25/10/1996) F/PL 49+12/20 FLC 3 FAC 2 Others 3/1
Nottingham F (£1,500,000 on 22/9/1998) PL 12+8/1 FAC 1
Barnsley (£700,000 on 7/7/1999) FL 32+7/13 FLC 2+1/1 FAC 1 Others 3/1

SHOREY Nicholas (Nicky)
Born: Romford, 19 February 1981
Height: 5'9" Weight: 10.10

Nicky is a young left back or left midfielder who followed the familiar 1999-2000 Leyton Orient path of graduating from youth team to first team with little fuss. He is a good crosser of the ball, notably setting up Dean Smith's goal at Rochdale in March with an inswinging corner. The son of a club scout, Nicky has made a total of seven senior appearances although still in his first year as a trainee.

Leyton Orient (From trainee on 5/7/1999) FL 4+3

SHORT Christian (Chris) Mark
Born: Munster, Germany, 9 May 1970
Height: 5'10" Weight: 12.2
Club Honours: AIC '95

The 1999-2000 season proved disastrous for this ever-popular right back. A mystery illness again dogged his season and just as he was recapturing his form he was knocked back again. Towards the end of the season he paid himself for a trip to Canada to see a world-renowned doctor, who has given him hope for the future. On his day, this solid, pacy defender, who can also be used in a central role if required, is one of the best attacking full backs in the Second Division and it is to be hoped that those days will return next term. He is the brother of Blackburn's Craig Short.

Scarborough (Free from Pickering T on 11/7/1988) FL 42+1/1 FLC 5 FAC 1 Others 3+1
Notts Co (£100,000 on 5/9/1990) FL 77+17/2 FLC 7 FAC 4+1 Others 8+1/1
Huddersfield T (Loaned on 23/12/1994) FL 6 Others 1
Sheffield U ((Signed on 29/12/1995) FL 40+4 FLC 3+1 FAC 7 Others 1+1
Stoke C (Free on 2/7/1998) FL 33+2 FLC 4+1 FAC 1

SHORT Craig Jonathan
Born: Bridlington, 25 June 1968
Height: 6'1" Weight: 13.8

Signed from Everton just before the start of the 1999-2000 season, Craig arrived at Blackburn looking short of match fitness. A tall, commanding centre back with the ability to bring the ball out of defence, he is at his best in bruising personal duels with a traditional centre forward and his experience ensures that few opponents are able to get the better of him. A hernia operation kept him out in mid-season but he returned to the side at Fulham in March and was a regular under Graeme Souness in the closing weeks of the season, producing an outstanding performance at Portsmouth. He did not score during the campaign but was unlucky to have a headed goal disallowed at Walsall in October. Craig is the older brother of Stoke City's Chris Short.

Scarborough (Free from Pickering T on 15/10/1987) FL 61+2/7 FLC 6 FAC 2 Others 7/1
Notts Co (£100,000 on 27/7/1989) FL 128/6 FLC 6/1 FAC 8/1 Others 16/2
Derby Co (£2,500,000 on 18/9/1992) FL 118/9 FLC 11 FAC 7/4 Others 7
Everton (£2,700,000 on 18/7/1995) PL 90+9/4 FLC 7 FAC 4 Others 3
Blackburn Rov (£1,700,000 + on 3/8/1999) FL 17 FLC 1

SHUTTLEWORTH Barry
Born: Accrington, 9 July 1977
Height: 5'8" Weight: 11.0

Barry is a left-sided defender who received very limited first-team chances at Blackpool during the 1999-2000 campaign. He played a couple of games early in the season and featured again in December but spent the rest of the time in the reserves. He was released in the summer.

Bury (From trainee on 5/7/1995)
Rotherham U (Free on 1/8/1997) FAC 0+1 Others 1
Blackpool (Free on 7/8/1998) FL 16+3/1 FLC 3 FAC 1

SIBON Gerald
Born: Dalen, Holland, 19 April 1974
Height: 6'5" Weight: 13.5

Sheffield Wednesday had high hopes of this tall striker, who was signed from Ajax during the 1999 close season. However, he had a disappointing campaign in a struggling side and failed to make a significant impact in the Premiership. Although he appeared in the starting line-up for the first few games, he soon found himself replaced by Andy Booth and it was only when Booth was injured at the turn of the year that he had a decent run in the team. Gerald showed great skill on the ball at times but managed just five goals all season as the Owls were relegated to the First Division. At the time of writing it remains to

be seen whether he will stay at Hillsborough or seek a move elsewhere.
Sheffield Wed (£2,000,000 from Ajax, Holland on 16/7/1999) PL 12+16/5 FLC 1+1 FAC 3+1/1

Gerald Sibon

SIGURDSSON Larus Orri
Born: Akureyri, Iceland, 4 June 1973
Height: 6'0" Weight: 13.11
International Honours: Iceland: 31

Larus left Stoke after a handful of games at the start of the 1999-2000 season, moving on to West Bromwich Albion, where he partnered Matt Carbon in the centre of defence. After running into disciplinary problems he came back strongly only to severely damage his right knee during the game at Edgeley Park against Stockport, an injury that forced him to miss the last ten league games of Albion's relegation dog-fight. Playing on the right-hand side of Albion's back four (occasionally occupying a more central position depending on circumstances), he looked solid and composed in his early appearances for his new club. He was hoping to be fully fit for the start of the 2000-01 campaign. An Icelandic international, Larus won further caps against the Faroe Isles, Andorra, the Ukraine and France before his injury.
Stoke C (£150,000 from Thor, Iceland on 21/10/1994) FL 199+1/7 FLC 15 FAC 6+1 Others 6
West Bromwich A (£325,000 on 17/9/1999) FL 27 FAC 1

SILVESTRE Mikael Samy
Born: Tours, France, 9 August 1977
Height: 6'0" Weight: 13.1
Club Honours: PL '00
International Honours: France: U21; Yth (UEFA-U18 '96)

A stylish defender who keeps a cool head under pressure, Mikael became Sir Alex Ferguson's second major signing of the new season for Manchester United when he joined the Reds from Inter Milan for £4.5 million last September. Useful as either a central defender or a full back, he made his debut in the 5-0 reverse at Chelsea in October, before replacing Henning Berg as United's key central defender alongside Jaap Stam in December. Despite periods of inconsistency, probably brought about by his interchanging role with Berg throughout October and November, his name was rarely off the team sheet throughout the rest of the campaign and he ended it with a Premiership winners' medal. Once Ronny Johnsen and David May are fit again it will be a four-horse race for that fiercely contested slot alongside Stam. With Mikael having already held his own against Henning Berg while graduating with full honours during his first season at the club, who's to say that he won't be first past the post – by a short head. He was a regular for France U21s in the early part of the season, adding a further six caps.
Manchester U (£4,000,000 from Inter Milan, Italy on 10/9/1999) PL 30+1 Others 5+2

[SILVINHO] SILVIO DE CAMPOS
Junior
Born: Sao Paulo, Brazil, 30 June 1974
Height: 5'9" Weight: 10.9
Club Honours: CS '99
International Honours: Brazil: 2

Silvinho is an exciting, predominantly left-sided defender bought by Arsenal from Brazilian side Corinthians in June 1999. He quickly established himself in the Gunners' line-up at the start of the new season at the expense of Nigel Winterburn, for whom he was intended as an eventual replacement. He is a strong tackler who also played on the left side of midfield during the campaign. He has good speed to overlap, get forward and deliver telling crosses to the front men. Silvinho demonstrates great accuracy from dead-ball situations, and also shows intelligent movement off the ball. His consistently good performances have made him popular with the Arsenal fans, and resulted in his being selected for Brazil

Silvinho

against England and Wales in the end-of-season friendlies.

Arsenal (£4,000,000 from Corinthians, Brazil on 20/7/1999) PL 23+8/1 FLC 2 FAC 3 Others 8+2

SIMB Jean-Pierre
Born: Paris, France, 4 September 1974
Height: 6'0" Weight: 12.0

A totally unorthodox French midfielder or striker, Jean-Pierre was a great crowd pleaser at Torquay last season. However, he was mostly used from the subs' bench, making the starting line-up only once, and in February he was released by the club.

Torquay U (Free from Paris Red Star, France on 19/3/1999) FL 4+16/1 FLC 0+2 FAC 0+2 Others 0+2

SIMBA Amara Sylla
Born: Paris, France, 23 December 1961
Height: 6'1" Weight: 11.8
International Honours: France: 3

By his standards, Amara had a quiet season at Leyton Orient in 1999-2000. He made only 17 appearances and scored three goals, but this former French international still showed his class, even though he is in the veteran stage of his career. Amara was told his contract would not be renewed and joined Conference club Kingstonian on loan on transfer deadline day. Unexpectedly, it led to a glorious end to his season when he scored the winner in Kings' FA Trophy final victory against Kettering at Wembley.

Leyton Orient (Free from Leon, Mexico on 7/10/1998) FL 27+10/13 FLC 0+2 FAC 5+2/1 Others 3

SIMONSEN Steven (Steve) Preben
Born: South Shields, 3 April 1979
Height: 6'3" Weight: 13.2
International Honours: E: U21-4; Yth

One of the most promising young goal-keepers in Britain, Steven is courageous and athletic and his positioning and distribution are excellent but he has yet to make the impact that was expected when he joined Everton from Tranmere in September 1998. He added to his limited experience at the top level with a handful of senior run-outs in 1999-2000. He made his debut in a Worthington Cup match at Oxford in September, and also played in the Goodison return a fortnight later. His only Premiership appearance came at Southampton as a sixth-minute substitute for the injured Paul Gerrard.

Tranmere Rov (From trainee on 9/10/1996) FL 35 FLC 4 FAC 3
Everton (£3,300,000 on 23/9/1998) PL 0+1 FLC 2

SIMPKINS Michael (Mike) James
Born: Sheffield, 28 November 1978
Height: 6'1" Weight: 12.0

Michael started 1999-2000 in Chesterfield's midfield, performing reliably, with good positional awareness. As the season developed into one of struggle, he was laid up with a hernia between November and February, and subsequent appearances were restricted to the reserves.

Sheffield Wed (From trainee on 4/7/1997)
Chesterfield (Free on 26/3/1998) FL 8+2 FLC 2+1

SIMPSON Fitzroy
Born: Trowbridge, 26 February 1970
Height: 5'8" Weight: 12.0
International Honours: Jamaica: 29

This combative midfield player provided plenty of entertainment for Portsmouth fans in the first half of the 1999-2000 season but was then sold to Scottish club Hearts as Pompey sought to raise money for a major restructuring of the team. Fitzroy's assets are his pace, stamina and strength in the tackle, and he can also play in a defensive role if required. A member of the Jamaica international squad, he earned a further cap against Canada last September and also featured against Romania "B" in May.

Swindon T (From trainee on 6/7/1988) FL 78+27/9 FLC 15+2/1 FAC 2+1 Others 3+2
Manchester C (£500,000 on 6/3/1992) P/FL 58+13/4 FLC 5+1 FAC 4+1
Bristol C (Loaned on 16/9/1994) FL 4
Portsmouth (£200,000 on 17/8/1995) FL 139+9/10 FLC 12+1 FAC 8

SIMPSON Michael
Born: Nottingham, 28 February 1974
Height: 5'9" Weight: 10.8
Club Honours: AIC '95

Michael was very much an unsung hero of the Wycombe midfield in 1999-2000, usually operating in a deep role from where he was able to take the ball from the defence and feed it to the strike force. Many of his better displays were away from Adams Park, when the team was under greater pressure, and he produced a particularly effective performance at Burnley last January. A hard worker who is strong in the tackle, he shows fine ball control in tight situations. He scored just one goal last season, netting in the FA Cup tie with Oxford City, although he also scored in the abandoned replay against the same opponents.

Notts Co (From trainee on 1/7/1992) FL 39+10/3 FLC 4+1 FAC 2+1 Others 7+3
Plymouth Arg (Loaned on 4/10/1996) FL 10+2
Wycombe W (£50,000 on 5/12/1996) FL 99+18/5 FLC 5+1 FAC 8+2/2 Others 5

SIMPSON Paul David
Born: Carlisle, 26 July 1966
Height: 5'6" Weight: 11.10
International Honours: E: U21-5; Yth

The left-sided attacker came close to signing for Tranmere in the summer of 1999, but ultimately remained with Wolves after accepting a late contract offer. However, the club signed Andy Sinton soon afterwards, and Paul knew his first-team chances would be restricted. Still capable of producing telling centres and hitting powerful long-range shots, he started the second match of the season, in the Worthington Cup at Wycombe, but was then used only as a substitute. This was a shame, because early in the season he looked good when he came on, hitting the bar with a 30-yard chip at Nottingham Forest. His perfectly placed corner created a winner at Wigan in the FA Cup third round in December, and he had the misfortune to hit the bar at Charlton. His first league start of the season came in March, and that was to be his final first-team appearance of the campaign. Paul was given a free transfer at the end of the season.

Manchester C (From apprentice on 4/8/1983) FL 99+22/18 FLC 10+1/2 FAC 10+2/4 Others 8+3
Oxford U (£200,000 on 31/10/1988) FL 138+6/43 FLC 10/3 FAC 9/2 Others 5/2
Derby Co (£500,000 on 20/2/1992) P/FL 134+52/48 FLC 12+3/6 FAC 4+4/1 Others 14+2/2
Sheffield U (Loaned on 6/12/1996) FL 2+4
Wolverhampton W (£75,000 on 10/10/1997) FL 32+20/6 FLC 2+1 FAC 2+5
Walsall (Loaned on 17/9/1998) FL 4/1
Walsall (Loaned on 11/12/1998) FL 6

SINCLAIR Frank Mohammed
Born: Lambeth, 3 December 1971
Height: 5'9" Weight: 12.9
Club Honours: FAC '97; FLC '98, '00
International Honours: Jamaica: 15

A right-footed wing back or central defender, Frank performed solidly for Leicester throughout the 1999-2000 campaign. Again demonstrating his pace, power and commitment, he hit a good run of form to help hold the team together during the deepest of the mid-season injury crisis. He did not allow two injury-time own goals during the first week of the season to upset him unduly and his luck soon improved. After being dropped for the 1998-99 Worthington Cup final against Tottenham, Frank took particular pleasure in helping the Foxes earn their return trip last season and fully enjoyed the glory of victory this time around. He is still a regular with the Jamaica team when commitments allow and added a further five caps during the season.

Chelsea (From trainee on 17/5/1990) F/PL 163+6/7 FLC 17+1/1 FAC 18/1 Others 13/3
West Bromwich A (Loaned on 12/12/1991) FL 6/1
Leicester C (£2,000,000 on 14/8/1998) PL 64+1/1 FLC 13 FAC 5/1

SINCLAIR Trevor Lloyd
Born: Dulwich, 2 March 1973
Height: 5'10" Weight: 12.10
International Honours: E: B-1; U21-14; Yth

This exciting and versatile West Ham player was mostly used as a wing back in 1999-2000 but also appeared in a wide midfield position and occasionally as an out-and-out striker when injuries robbed the club of front men Paulo Wanchope and Paolo di Canio. Trevor was a near-ever-present and his excellent performances won him a call-up to the England squad for the friendly with Belgium last October. He has great pace and the skill to match, making him an effective performer both in defensive and attacking situations. Trevor capped a fine season at Upton Park when he was voted runner-up in the "Hammer of the Year" award.

Blackpool (From trainee on 21/8/1990) FL 84+28/15 FLC 8 FAC 6+1 Others 8+5/1
Queens Park R (£750,000 on 12/8/1993) P/FL 162+5/16 FLC 13/3 FAC 10/2
West Ham U (£2,300,000 + on 30/1/1998) PL 86/21 FLC 5+1 FAC 3 Others 6/1

SINTON Andrew (Andy)
Born: Cramlington, 19 March 1966
Height: 5'8" Weight: 11.5
Club Honours: FLC '99
International Honours: E: 12; B-3; Sch

Andy joined Wolves on a "Bosman free" from Tottenham in the summer of 1999. An experienced player who can perform well on the left wing or on that side of midfield, or even at full back, he first caught the eye for his new club, strangely enough, in a 4-2 defeat by Wycombe in the Worthington Cup. At home to Huddersfield, he was the major factor in Wolves' putting in a staggering 42 crosses. The departures of Steve Bull and Robbie Keane meant that the club needed an exciting player to lift the crowd, and Andy seemed to be the man. However, a string of poor results led to a change in formation and Andy was dropped. He was then injured playing for the reserves but after an absence of five games he came off the bench to create goals in three successive matches. The team reverted to 4-4-2 and Andy continued to excel, making him a target for some rough treatment as he loved taking players on. When Keith Curle missed the odd game in January, Andy was made captain. He was 34 in March but shrugged off knocks very quickly and, while not as effective as earlier in the season, continued to do a sound job for the rest of the campaign.

Cambridge U (From apprentice on 13/4/1983) FL 90+3/13 FLC 6/1 FAC 3 Others 2/1
Brentford (£25,000 on 13/12/1985) FL 149/28 FLC 8/3 FAC 11/1 Others 14/2
Queens Park R (£350,000 on 23/3/1989) F/PL 160/22 FLC 14 FAC 13/2 Others 3/1
Sheffield Wed (£2,750,000 on 19/8/1993) PL 54+6/3 FLC 13 FAC 5
Tottenham H (£1,500,000 on 23/1/1996) PL 66+17/6 FLC 6+3 FAC 4+4/1
Wolverhampton W (Free on 13/7/1999) FL 31+4 FLC 1 FAC 3

SISSON Michael Anthony
Born: Sutton in Ashfield, 24 November 1978
Height: 5'9" Weight: 10.10

A former YTS lad who was rewarded with a full Mansfield contract in the summer of 1999, Michael put in some excellent performances in the heart of the Stags' midfield last season, and his workrate, passing and tackling were sorely missed when he was out of the side. A medial ligament strain early on, then an ankle injury in February and a dislocated elbow in March restricted his appearances, but he is definitely one to watch for in the future.

Mansfield T (From trainee on 27/1/1998) FL 24+3/2 FLC 2 Others 2

SKELTON Aaron Matthew
Born: Welwyn Garden City, 22 November 1974
Height: 5'11" Weight: 12.6

Aaron is a versatile Colchester midfielder or defender who possesses a powerful shot from distance. He missed the start of the 1999-2000 season while continuing his recovery from the broken leg he suffered at Wycombe the previous March, and the team missed his contribution. He returned to action in October, and due to defensive injuries was used as a centre back for much of the campaign. In all, he featured in over half of Colchester's games last season, and he also scored four goals. Aaron is hoping that his injury problems are now firmly behind him.

Luton T (From trainee on 16/12/1992) FL 5+3 FLC 0+1 FAC 2 Others 2
Colchester U (Free on 3/7/1997) FL 71+10/11 FLC 1 FAC 4+1 Others 4+1

SKELTON Gavin Richard
Born: Penrith, 27 March 1981
Height: 5'9" Weight: 11.0

Gavin is a locally born left-footed midfielder who made several effective appearances for Carlisle in the early months of the 1999-2000 campaign, usually coming off the bench. Although he later faded from contention, Gavin should have a future at the club as time is still on his side.

Carlisle U (From trainee on 19/5/1999) FL 1+6 FLC 1+1

SKINNER Craig Richard
Born: Heywood, 21 October 1970
Height: 5'9" Weight: 11.6

The 1999-2000 season was an unlucky and disappointing one for the hard-working right-sided York midfielder. Craig suffered knee ligament damage in a pre-season game at Gainsborough and then broke down during a training session in November before having a spell at the FA's National Rehabilitation Centre at Lilleshall. He figured in only a handful of senior games in the second half of the campaign, and was put on the transfer list by new boss Terry Dolan.

Blackburn Rov (From trainee on 13/6/1989) FL 11+5 FLC 0+1 FAC 1 Others 3/1
Plymouth Arg (Signed on 21/8/1992) FL 42+11/4 FLC 4 FAC 5+2/1 Others 3+1
Wrexham (£50,000 on 21/7/1995) FL 70+17/10 FLC 3+3/1 FAC 8+1 Others 3+1
York C (£20,000 on 25/3/1999) FL 4+6

SKINNER Stephen (Steve) Karl
Born: Whitehaven, 25 November 1981
Height: 6'0" Weight: 12.3

This teenage striker joined Carlisle United from Northern Alliance club Northbank Carlisle. Steven enjoyed a couple of substitute appearances last November against Barnet and Rotherham, and will be hoping for further opportunities during the coming season.

Carlisle U (Trainee) FL 0+2

SLADE Steven (Steve) Anthony
Born: Hackney, 6 October 1975
Height: 6'0" Weight: 11.2
International Honours: E: U21-4

Although Steve has been at Queens Park Rangers for four seasons he has yet to command a regular first-team place. Essentially a right-sided attacker, he can also play as a central striker. His good off-the-ball movement helps create chances and his height makes him a threat in the air. He made a number of appearances last season, coming into the side as one of the replacements for Rob Steiner during January and February and scoring in his first game, at Wolverhampton Wanderers. He was released during the summer.

Tottenham H (From trainee on 1/7/1994) PL 1+4 FLC 0+1 FAC 0+2
Queens Park R (£350,000 on 12/7/1996) FL 27+41/6 FLC 3+4/1 FAC 1+2
Brentford (Loaned on 13/2/1997) FL 4

SMALL Bryan
Born: Birmingham, 15 November 1971
Height: 5'9" Weight: 11.9
International Honours: E: U21-12; Yth

After starting Stoke's first two matches of 1999-2000, this strong, tenacious left-sided wing back lost his first-team place to the emerging Clive Clarke, for whom he covered for most of the first half of the season. His cause was not helped by a series

Michael Sisson

of leg injuries, and he rarely found favour in the Gudjon Thordarson era. Although, on his day, he is still a fine overlapping wing back who crosses the ball accurately, the club indicated in the spring that they would release him at the end of his current contract.

Aston Villa (From trainee on 9/7/1990) F/PL 31+5 FLC 2 FAC 2+1 Others 4
Birmingham C (Loaned on 9/9/1994) FL 3
Bolton W (Free on 20/3/1996) F/PL 11+1 FLC 1 FAC 3
Luton T (Loaned on 8/9/1997) FL 15
Bradford C (Loaned on 19/12/1997) FL 5
Bury (Free on 30/1/1998) FL 18/1
Stoke C (Free on 14/7/1998) FL 40+5 FLC 3 FAC 2 Others 2

SMART Allan Andrew Colin
Born: Perth, 8 July 1974
Height: 6'2" Weight: 12.10
Club Honours: AMC '97

This honest and hard-working Watford striker finished the 1999-2000 season strongly after enduring a frustrating six months because of various injuries. Allan had finished the previous campaign on a high, having scored a memorable goal in Watford's play-off victory, and was entitled to approach the new term with confidence. He missed the start of the season with an ankle injury, but came back to score the winner against Chelsea – a goal very reminiscent of his Wembley strike. A week later, he suffered a torn cartilage at Arsenal which kept him out until February. Fortunately, he soon recovered his scoring knack, getting Watford's only goal in the return at Chelsea and scoring in three consecutive matches against Sheffield Wednesday, Tottenham and Everton. During this run, he perfected his goal celebration – mimicking the shot putter on the Scott's Porridge Oats packet – and was rewarded with a year's supply of breakfast cereal. On the fringe of the Scottish international squad, he will be hoping for an injury-free season in 2000-01.

St Johnstone (From juniors on 24/1/1991)
Brechin C (Free on 30/12/1991)
Inverness Caledonian Thistle (Free on 28/7/1993) SL 2+2 SLC 1+1
Preston NE (£15,000 on 22/11/1994) FL 17+4/6 FAC 2/1 Others 1+1
Carlisle U (Loaned on 24/11/1995) FL 3+1
Northampton T (Loaned on 13/9/1996) FL 1
Carlisle U (Signed on 9/10/1996) FL 41+3/16 FLC 1/1 FAC 4 Others 4+1
Watford (£75,000 + on 2/7/1998) P/FL 47+2/12 FLC 1+2 FAC 1 Others 0+3/1

SMEETS Axel
Born: Karawa, DR Congo, 12 April 1974
Height: 5'10" Weight: 12.1
International Honours: Belgium: U21

Axel became one of Adrian Heath's first signings when he joined Sheffield United in the summer of 1999. He made his debut, playing as a right-sided attacking midfielder, in the opening game of the season at Portsmouth and had the misfortune to be sent off for two yellow cards. He found the transition to English football difficult, and after playing in the first three games he made only one other start, in the Worthington Cup against Preston in September. After Neil Warnock's arrival he made just one substitute appearance before being placed on the transfer list. He was released on a free transfer in the summer.

Sheffield U (Free from AA Ghent, Belgium on 30/7/1999) FL 2+3 FLC 2 FAC 0+1

SMICER Vladimir (Vlad)
Born: Czechoslovakia, 24 May 1973
Height: 5'11" Weight: 11.3
International Honours: Czech Republic: 43; U21-7. Czechoslovakia: 1

A summer signing from Lens, the Czech got his Liverpool career off to a flying start with a great performance on the opening day of the 1999-2000 campaign against Sheffield Wednesday. From then on, however, his season was one of mixed fortunes, and generally he failed to live up to expectations, unable to bring his international form to his club football. Vladimir took a long time to become used to the pace and physical nature of the English game, and picked up rather too many injuries. Filling the gap left by the departure of Steve McManaman, he showed that he is a fine dribbler of the ball, though he also has the ability to find the back of the net. A number of niggling injuries prevented Vladimir from showing his true ability, but if he regains full fitness he could just be a star of the Premiership next season. He won five more caps for the Czech Republic, appearing in all three of their games in Euro 2000, where he scored both goals in the 2-0 victory over Denmark.

Liverpool (£3,750,000 from RC Lens, France on 14/7/1999) PL 13+8/1 FLC 2 FAC 2

SMITH Alan
Born: Wakefield, 28 October 1980
Height: 5'9" Weight: 11.10
International Honours: E: U21-2; Yth

After bursting on to the scene so excitingly in 1998-99, Alan had a quieter time with Leeds United last term. He had to undertake a different role in the side after the departure of Jimmy Floyd Hasselbaink, and the goals didn't come quite so easily. But there is no doubting his talent and, although he is sometimes portrayed by the media as being over-aggressive, the point is that in his role as a target man he gives as good as he gets. The majority of his goals last season came from within the six-yard box. He scored with a superb first touch, turn and shot at Tottenham to typify his excellent movement, control and vision. Alan won further caps for England U21s against Denmark and Argentina and remains in line for a successful career in the game.

Leeds U (From trainee on 26/3/1998) PL 35+13/11 FLC 1 FAC 4+3/3 Others 2+6/1

SMITH Alexander (Alex) Philip
Born: Liverpool, 15 February 1976
Height: 5'7" Weight: 11.10

The tricky left winger's 1999-2000 season with Port Vale was blighted by injury. After starting both games against his old club Chester in the Worthington Cup, he injured his ankle in the next league game against Tranmere Rovers and did not reappear in the first team for another six months. Alex managed six starts after his return to fitness but the team lost five of those games and he was substituted against Sheffield United after being blamed by the manager for a goal that was conceded. He was not selected for the run-in until the final game against Wolves and was transfer-listed at the end of the season.

Everton (From trainee on 1/7/1994)
Swindon T (Free on 12/1/1996) FL 17+14/1
Huddersfield T (Free on 6/2/1998) FL 4+2
Chester C (Free on 8/7/1998) FL 32/2 FLC 4/1 Others 1
Port Vale (£75,000 on 25/3/1999) FL 16+5 FLC 2

SMITH Bryan James
Born: Swindon, 26 August 1983
Height: 6'1" Weight: 12.0

This very promising Swindon trainee made his Football League debut in the final home game of the 1999-2000 campaign when he came on as a substitute for the last 15 minutes against Barnsley. Bryan impressed in his brief entry to senior football, showing he is an effective tackler and can distribute the ball accurately. A central defender, he will be looking to win a full professional contract and gain more first-team experience in the 2000-01 season.

Swindon T (Trainee) FL 0+1

SMITH Daniel (Danny) Lee
Born: Southampton, 17 August 1982
Height: 5'11" Weight: 11.4

Danny captained Bournemouth's youth team during the 1999-2000 season and made his Football League debut at Stoke in April, when he came on from the subs' bench for the final few minutes. An exciting midfield prospect, he is expected to receive further opportunities with the Cherries' first team in 2000-01.

Bournemouth (From trainee on 12/4/2000) FL 0+1

SMITH David
Born: Stonehouse, 29 March 1968
Height: 5'8" Weight: 10.7
Club Honours: AMC '98
International Honours: E: U21-10

A hard and effective worker who is able to operate on the left flank or in defence, David once again faced competition from both Kingsley Black and Adam Buckley for his favoured position on the left of Grimsby's midfield in 1999-2000, but by late mid-season his consistency had enabled him to establish himself as automatic first choice in this position. He is adept at taking on defenders and putting in telling crosses.

Coventry C (From apprentice on 7/7/1986) P/FL 144+10/19 FLC 17 FAC 6 Others 4+1
Bournemouth (Loaned on 8/1/1993) FL 1
Birmingham C (Signed on 12/3/1993) FL 35+3/3 FLC 4 FAC 0+1 Others 1
West Bromwich A (£90,000 on 31/1/1994) FL 82+20/2 FLC 4+2 FAC 1+3 Others 4+1
Grimsby T (£200,000 on 16/1/1998) FL 81+3/7 FLC 6+3/1 FAC 2 Others 7/1

SMITH David (Dave) Christopher
Born: Liverpool, 26 December 1970
Height: 5'9" Weight: 12.9

David made a bright start to the 1999-2000 campaign for Stockport, scoring the opening-day winner at Grimsby to give Andy Kilner the perfect start to his managerial career. However, he lost his place following the defeat by Barnsley at the beginning of September and rarely featured in the squad for the rest of the season. A hard-working left-sided midfield player who is able to play the ball accurately over both short and long distances, he looks set to resume his career away from Edgeley Park.

Norwich C (From trainee on 4/7/1989) F/PL 13+5 FAC 2+1 Others 1+1
Oxford U (£100,000 on 5/7/1994) FL 193+5/2 FLC 23+1/1 FAC 9+1 Others 7
Stockport Co (Free on 4/2/1999) FL 24+2/2 FLC 1

SMITH Dean
Born: West Bromwich, 19 March 1971
Height: 6'1" Weight: 12.10

Leading by example throughout a hard 1999-2000 season, Dean showed why he is Leyton Orient's captain. He had several different partners at centre half, but never complained and just got on with his job. Dean again added some important goals to his contribution, and missed only three games. However, the Os' former penalty taker has lost that responsibility to Matt Lockwood.

Walsall (From trainee on 1/7/1989) FL 137+5/2 FLC 10 FAC 4 Others 10
Hereford U (£75,000 on 17/6/1994) FL 116+1/19 FLC 10/3 FAC 7 Others 11+1/4
Leyton Orient (£42,500 on 16/6/1997) FL 124/22 FLC 12 FAC 9/3 Others 5

SMITH James (Jamie) Jade Anthony
Born: Birmingham, 17 September 1974
Height: 5'7" Weight: 11.4

Jamie began the 1999-2000 campaign in good form but then suffered an achilles tendon injury which required surgery and kept him out of action for a six-week spell. He had been back only a short while when he was injured again at Nottingham Forest last February and did not return until the last few games of the season. An attacking right wing back, he scored two goals, both of them coming in the Worthington Cup ties against Colchester United.

Wolverhampton W (From trainee on 7/6/1993) FL 81+6 FLC 10+1 FAC 2 Others 4/1
Crystal Palace (Signed on 22/10/1997) P/FL 68+3 FLC 7/2 FAC 5+1
Fulham (Loaned on 25/3/1999) FL 9/1

SMITH Jason Leslie
Born: Bromsgrove, 6 September 1974
Height: 6'3" Weight: 13.7
Club Honours: Div 3 '00
International Honours: E: Sch

In only his second full season in the Football League, Jason consolidated his position in the centre of the Swansea defence with consistent displays alongside Matthew Bound in 1999-2000. He is a strong competitor in aerial challenges, and his commitment is not questioned. He is as solid as a rock in defence, and his speed across the field is also surprising for a big man. With his ability in the air, his single goal return was disappointing compared with his four during the previous campaign. Jason used to work for a pharmaceutical company, and he certainly got the formula right last season as he claimed his Third Division championship winners' medal.

Coventry C (Signed from Tiverton T on 5/7/1993. Free to Tiverton T on 15/7/1995)
Swansea C (£10,000 on 1/7/1998) FL 85/5 FLC 6 FAC 6/1 Others 5/1

SMITH Martin Geoffrey
Born: Sunderland, 13 November 1974
Height: 5'11" Weight: 12.6
Club Honours: Div 1 '96
International Honours: E: U21-1; Yth; Sch

After declining the new deal offered by Sunderland and turning down a move to Ipswich, Martin signed a one-year contract with Sheffield United during the summer of 1999 and was an immediate hit with two goals in his first full appearance, in the Worthington Cup against Shrewsbury Town. Although having a tendency to "disappear" from a game, he certainly proved he has an eye for goal and, despite playing behind the front two for most of his time at Bramall Lane, showed he could score from a range of distances and angles. He scored 12 goals in his first 17 games for the Blades but was not happy with the new contract offered for the following season and, after nearly joining Nottingham Forest, he moved to Huddersfield Town in February. Martin was brought to the McAlpine as a replacement for the Ipswich-bound Marcus Stewart and was immediately thrust into first-team action. The left-sided striker showed great promise, impressing his new club's fans with some very skilful displays, and soon boosted his confidence with a double strike against Wolverhampton Wanderers, showing great close control on the run and smooth shooting ability. This was quickly followed by goals against Walsall and WBA, only for a hamstring injury to cruelly put him on the sidelines.

Sunderland (From trainee on 9/9/1992) P/FL 90+29/25 FLC 10+6/2 FAC 7+3/1
Sheffield U (Free on 6/8/1999) FL 24+2/10 FLC 3+1/4 FAC 3/1
Huddersfield T (£300,000 on 3/2/2000) FL 10+2/4

SMITH Neil James
Born: Lambeth, 30 September 1971
Height: 5'9" Weight: 12.12
Club Honours: FAYC '90; Div 2 '99

Signed from Fulham in August 1999 for £100,000, Neil made his Reading debut in midfield against Luton alongside other new signings Peter Grant and Nicky Forster. He scored his only goal of the season with a header in the 2-2 draw versus Preston North End, but impressed throughout the campaign with his aggression and enthusiasm. His ability to defend and cover perceptively enables Darren Caskey to make runs forward, so the pair make a good combination at the heart of the Royals' line-up. Neil was one of the undoubted successes of the season, and his transfer fee now looks to be a bargain.

Tottenham H (From trainee on 24/7/1990)
Gillingham (£40,000 on 17/10/1991) FL 204+9/10 FLC 14+1/1 FAC 18/2 Others 7+1/2
Fulham (Signed on 4/7/1997) FL 62+11/1 FLC 3+1 FAC 6+3/1 Others 1+1
Reading (£100,000 on 20/8/1999) FL 26+10/1 FLC 3 FAC 1 Others 2+1

SMITH Paul Antony
Born: Hastings, 25 January 1976
Height: 5'11" Weight: 11.7

Paul is a right-sided player who was mainly used as a wing back by Lincoln during 1999-2000. He showed good defensive qualities, the ability to push forward and an eye for goal, netting six times during the season. He missed the final two months of the campaign after damaging a knee ligament at Plymouth in March.

Nottingham F (£50,000 from Hastings T on 13/1/1995)
Lincoln C (£30,000 on 17/10/1997) FL 60+12/10 FLC 3+1 FAC 6/1 Others 3

SMITH Ian **Paul**
Born: Easington, 22 January 1976
Height: 6'0" Weight: 13.3

Paul had much better luck with injuries in 1999-2000, although a shin problem did rule him out for a spell in the winter months. He surprisingly started the season as Burnley's first-choice left back, and was usually employed in that position, with Stan Ternent preferring a formation of three central defenders and two wing backs. Paul is certainly a better player going forward than defending and is still capable of beating men and putting in telling crosses, although some speed seems to have gone since 1996-97, when he showed his best form to date.

Burnley (From trainee on 10/7/1994) FL 69+29/4 FLC 3+1 FAC 5+1 Others 5

SMITH Paul William
Born: East Ham, 18 September 1971
Height: 5'11" Weight: 13.0

Paul replaced Andy Hessenthaler as Gillingham's captain for the 1999-2000 season and again impressed as a consistent performer in the centre of midfield. A near-ever-present, he led the Gills to their best-ever performance in the FA Cup and promotion to Division One for the first time in the club's history. He remains a crowd favourite for his never-say-die attitude and once again contributed the odd vital goal, including a last-minute strike that clinched the 5-3 aggregate victory over Stoke in the play-off semi-final.

Southend U (From trainee on 16/3/1990) FL 18+2/1 Others 0+1
Brentford (Free on 6/8/1993) FL 159/11 FLC 12/1 FAC 12/3 Others 15/2
Gillingham (Signed on 25/7/1997) FL 134+1/10 FLC 7 FAC 10 Others 9+2/2

SMITH Peter (Pete) Edward
Born: Skelmersdale, 31 October 1980
Height: 6'0" Weight: 11.0

The 1999-2000 season was a mixed one for young Peter. Although he was restricted to four starts, his performances led to rave reviews about his ability, passing and workrate. His skills would be better suited to a team higher on confidence than Exeter. Like his YT colleagues Robert Speakman and John Wilkinson, Peter was offered a contract for the 2000-01 campaign.

Exeter C (From trainee on 2/7/1999) FL 3+5 FLC 0+1 FAC 1

SMITH Peter Lee
Born: Rhyl, 15 September 1978
Height: 5'10" Weight: 10.8
International Honours: E: Yth; Sch

A graduate of the FA School at Lilleshall who made his senior debut for Crewe as a 19-year-old in May 1998, Peter has subsequently found it difficult to secure a regular place in the first team. The skilful young striker certainly has talent but his only appearances last season were as a substitute and he has yet to score for the club in senior football. He will be hoping ro receive further opportunities to unlock his potential during the coming season.

Crewe Alex (From trainee on 12/7/1996) FL 1+16 FLC 3 FAC 0+1
Macclesfield T (Loaned on 25/9/1998) FL 12/3 Others 1

SMITH Richard Geoffrey
Born: Lutterworth, 3 October 1970
Height: 6'0" Weight: 13.12

Following the pre-season injury to Peter Handyside, Richard formed a dependable partnership with Mark Lever at the centre of Grimsby's defence during the opening weeks of 1999-2000. However, after running into disciplinary problems in November he then suffered a serious back injury that put him out of action for the rest of the season. He has had more than his fair share of bad luck in terms of injuries, and there is no doubt that, despite some fine performances by Lever, the absence of both Richard and Handyside caused severe problems for the Mariners' usually solid defence.

Leicester C (From trainee on 15/12/1988) F/PL 82+16/1 FLC 4 FAC 6/1 Others 12
Cambridge U (Loaned on 6/9/1989) FL 4 FLC 1
Grimsby T (Loaned on 8/9/1995) FL 8
Grimsby T (£50,000 on 11/3/1996) FL 70+3 FLC 10 FAC 2

SMITH Gareth **Shaun**
Born: Leeds, 9 April 1971
Height: 5'10" Weight: 11.0

The long-serving Crewe defender joined the club from non-league Emley back in 1991 and has now made well over 350 first-team appearances for the club. Although his regular position is left back, Shaun can also perform effectively in a central defensive role and is the club's regular penalty taker. He scored from the spot three times in 1999-2000 but, although he proved of nuisance value at set pieces in the opposition penalty area, those were his only goals of the season. A great competitor who is strong in the tackle, gets forward well and has a good recovery rate, he missed a number of games through injury in the middle of the season but was back to his best form before the end of the campaign.

Halifax T (From trainee on 1/7/1989) FL 6+1 Others 1 (Free to Emley in May 1991)
Crewe Alex (Free on 31/12/1991) FL 295+20/36 FLC 17+1/3 FAC 14+2/3 Others 19+2/3

SMITH Thomas (Tommy) William
Born: Hemel Hempstead, 22 May 1980
Height: 5'8" Weight: 11.4
International Honours: E: Yth

The young Watford striker emerged with great credit from only his second full season in 1999-2000 and will certainly benefit from his Premiership experience. Tommy is only slightly built, but shows good control, and an excellent turn of pace. He scored a fine individual goal in his first full game of the season, at home to Middlesbrough, and, though he failed to add to his tally until Manchester United visited Vicarage Road at the end of April, when he gave an outstanding display, he demonstrated an impressive ability to lay on chances for team-mates, notably Allan Smart. Tommy is following in the footsteps of his father Dave, who was also on Watford's books, while brother Jack plays for the club's academy teams.

Watford (From trainee on 21/10/1997) P/FL 16+15/4 FLC 0+1 FAC 0+1

SNEEKES Richard
Born: Amsterdam, Holland, 30 October 1968
Height: 5'11" Weight: 12.2

Although Richard had previously scored his fair share of goals for West Bromwich Albion, it was not until his 44th game of the season that he found the net in 1999-2000. On that occasion he converted a spot kick in the 2-2 draw at Barnsley, following up with another penalty in the amazing 4-4 draw with Bolton a week later. He finally scored in open play when he gave the Baggies a vital lead against Charlton on the final day of the season when Albion desperately needed to win to preserve their First Division status. The pony-tailed central midfielder still played confidently, though, and he was a very consistent performer in the engine room, where he looked international class early on alongside the Italian, Enzo Maresca. He did, however, blot his copybook when he got himself sent off in Albion's 5-0 hammering at Sheffield United. He acted as play-maker in the majority of matches, capitalising on his ability to spray passes to the flanks; he was negotiating a new deal in readiness for the start of the 2000-01 campaign and Albion's fans were hoping manager Gary Megson would be able to sort it out for him.

Bolton W (£200,000 from Fortuna Sittard, Holland, via Ajax and Volendam, on 12/8/1994) P/FL 51+4/7 FLC 11+1/3 FAC 2/1
West Bromwich A (£385,000 on 11/3/1996) FL 169+13/28 FLC 14/1 FAC 6/2

SNIJDERS Mark Werner
Born: Alkmaar, Holland, 12 March 1972
Height: 6'2" Weight: 13.12

This classy Port Vale central defender began the 1999-2000 season in the reserves before being called up for a game at Wolves in October. He then played as one of three centre backs as Vale changed formation to 5-3-2 and he held his place until the new year, even when the team reverted to a flat back four. An excellent passer of the ball who has had to adjust to the demands of English football, Mark played at Leeds in the FA Cup but a Christmas groin strain and the arrival of Sagi Burton led to a spell on the sidelines. He returned at Crewe in March only to be sent off in the last minute, and a month later illness forced him out again, but he was recalled for the final two games. Mark was released on a free transfer at the end of the season.

Port Vale (Free from AZ Alkmaar, Holland on 8/9/1997) FL 46+9/2 FLC 2 FAC 3

SODJE Efetobore (Efe)
Born: Greenwich, 5 October 1972
Height: 6'1" Weight: 12.0
Club Honours: GMVC '96
International Honours: Nigeria: 2

A big defender who possesses a great turn of pace and is strong and biting in the tackle, Efe joined Luton on a free transfer from Macclesfield at the start of the 1999-2000 season and was an instant hit with the fans. He was then called up by Nigeria for the African Nations' Cup finals, missing several games and incurring the wrath of his manager by failing to remain in touch. Luton subsequently released him and he signed a short-term contract with Colchester on transfer deadline day, instantly winning the "Man of the Match" award for a stunning centre-back display against Gillingham on his debut. (Ironically, Efe had already made his mark at Layer Road earlier in the season when he was sent off during Luton's 3-0 defeat in December). He then missed the next game while making club history as the first U's player to gain full international honours when he played for Nigeria against Eritrea in a World Cup qualifier on 9 April. He appeared in the return leg as the Eagles raced to a 4-0 aggregate victory and added a further two league appearances for Colchester before being released at the end of the season.

Macclesfield T (£30,000 from Stevenage Borough on 11/7/1997) FL 83/6 FLC 6 FAC 6/1 Others 1
Luton T (Free on 12/8/1999) FL 5+4 FLC 2 FAC 2+1 Others 1
Colchester U (Free on 23/3/2000) FL 3

SOLANO Nolberto (Nol) Albino
Born: Lima, Peru, 12 December 1974
Height: 5'8" Weight: 10.8
International Honours: Peru: 45

With the Peruvian having become fully acclimatised to England and the demands of the Premiership, the 1999-2000 season saw Nol mature into a very influential player for Newcastle, operating on the right of midfield, where his good close control and his pace enable him to develop incisive raids down the wing, creating the space for accurately delivered centres for his strikers. He is also something of a dead-ball specialist and his delivery from open play on the wing and from free kicks was a feature of the side's play, leading to numerous goals. Nol quickly developed a good understanding with Kieron Dyer and the interchangeability of the two players during a game gave an extra dimension to Newcastle's attacking style. He was a regular in the side until he picked up a bad groin injury in January, and before he had recovered from this he was called up by Peru for the Gold Cup in February, hardly a surprise as he has achieved superstar status in his home country, for whom he has played since the age of 19. Having played three times for his country in the Copa America tournament in July 1999, Nol won a further three caps last season, scoring for Peru in their 2-0 victory over Paraguay in a World Cup qualifying group match in March. During the latter stages of the season he was subject to strong rumours about an impending transfer to Real Madrid for a sum reputed to be £10 million.

Newcastle U (£2,763,958 from Boca Juniors, Argentina, via Cristal Alianza Lima, Sporting and Deportivo Municipal, on 17/8/1998) PL 53+6/9 FLC 2 FAC 10 Others 7+1/1

Nol Solano

SOLEY Stephen (Steve)
Born: Widnes, 22 April 1971
Height: 5'11" Weight: 12.8
International Honours: E: SP-1

Signed from Portsmouth 24 hours earlier, Steve scored on his Carlisle debut on the opening day of the 1999-2000 season against Leyton Orient. Although he arrived on loan, the attacking midfielder soon earned a contract with his forward running and eagerness to recapture the goalscoring performances he had shown in the Conference. By the end of the campaign, he was the club's top scorer with nine goals, and he will be looking to develop his midfield role in the new season.

Portsmouth (£30,000 from Leek T on 22/7/1998) FL 1+7 FLC 0+4
Macclesfield T (Loaned on 19/3/1999) FL 5+5
Carlisle U (Signed on 6/8/1999) FL 35+2/8 FAC 1 Others 3/1

SOLSKJAER Ole Gunnar
Born: Kristiansund, Norway, 26 February 1973
Height: 5'10" Weight: 11.10
Club Honours: PL '97, '99, '00; FAC '99; EC '99
International Honours: Norway: 34

A well-balanced striker with a powerful shot in either foot, Ole showed with his performances for Manchester United in 1999-2000 that his appetite for goals hadn't diminished one jot after scoring that last-gasp winner against Bayern Munich that brought the European Cup back to Old Trafford after an absence of 31 years. Having pledged his future to the Reds when Leeds expressed an interest in signing him in the wake of Jimmy Floyd Hasselbaink's departure from Elland Road in August, he staked his claim for a regular place in Sir Alex Ferguson's "team of all the talents" with a goal as a substitute in their second Premiership game of the season at home to Sheffield Wednesday. Confined mostly to the subs' bench throughout September and October, Ole opened his European account with a goal against Sturm Graz at Old Trafford in November, before plundering four goals against Everton at the beginning of December. Rounding that month off with a goal in United's Champions' League game against Valencia, he then proved to be the scourge of Merseyside again in March, when he netted the all-important equaliser against Liverpool at Old Trafford. With further goals against West Ham and Sunderland (2) as the season reached its exciting climax, Ole seems quite content to await his chance on the bench, while scoring at vital times. Although he would walk into any other Premiership side, he made a telling contribution to the Reds' championship triumph and seems more than happy to remain in his role as United's "Super Sub". In contrast he is a regular in the starting line-up for Norway, for whom he won 12 caps last season, appearing in all three games in what proved to be a disappointing Euro 2000 for the Scandinavians.

Manchester U (£1,500,000 from Molde, Norway on 29/7/1996) PL 64+38/47 FLC 4/3 FAC 5+8/3 Others 20+20/7

SOLTVEDT Trond Egil
Born: Voss, Norway, 15 February 1967
Height: 6'1" Weight: 12.8
International Honours: Norway: 4

Surprisingly allowed to leave Coventry City in August 1999, Trond opted to move to Southampton in a £300,000 deal after turning down his former club Rosenborg. A useful addition to the Saints' midfield, he immediately won over the supporters with an outstanding display against Newcastle on his debut. A willing and tireless worker who loves to get forward at every opportunity, he found himself in the right place at the right time when he netted an opportunist goal against Liverpool in October. Despite losing his place in January, Trond continued to figure regularly on the bench and is a valuable squad member.

Coventry C (£500,000 from Rosenborg, Norway, via Viking Stavanger and Brann, on 24/7/1997) PL 47+10/3 FLC 1+4/1 FAC 5+2
Southampton (£300,000 on 13/8/1999) PL 17+7/1 FLC 4/1 FAC 1+1

SONG Bahanag **Rigobert**
Born: Nkanglicock, Cameroon, 1 July 1976
Height: 5'9" Weight: 11.10
International Honours: Cameroon: 39 (ANC 2000)

Unfortunately for Liverpool fans, Rigobert's finest moment of the 1999-2000 season came in scoring the winning penalty in the final of the African Nations' Cup for Cameroon. It had been hoped that he would be winning silverware with Liverpool, but that was not to be, although he performed well whenever he was in the side. A versatile defender who can play either at right back or in the centre, he is powerful in the air and confident on the ball, has a little bit of pace, tackles aggressively and relishes the challenge of a physical encounter. The new season will bring with it the usual plethora of high expectations, not least for fans of this fine player, who will hope that he has a long, sustained run in the first team to allow him to showcase his undoubted skills. An ever-present for his country in their African Nations' Cup triumph in February, he will now turn his attention to ensuring they qualify for the 2002 World Cup finals.

Liverpool (£2,720,000 from Salernitana, Italy, via Tonnerre Yaoundi and Metz, on 29/1/1999) PL 24+7 FLC 2 FAC 0+1

Danny Sonner

SONNER Daniel (Danny) James
Born: Wigan, 9 January 1972
Height: 5'11" Weight: 12.8
International Honours: NI: 6; B-4

Danny had a disappointing 1999-2000 campaign with Sheffield Wednesday after beginning the season in the starting line-up. He was dropped after the 4-0 defeat at Old Trafford last August, and although he was recalled to the team for a lengthy spell of action he found it difficult to achieve his best form. He is a hard-working central midfield player with good passing skills and a strong right-foot shot. Danny was recalled to the Northern Ireland squad by new manager Sammy McIlroy and earned further caps against Luxembourg, Malta and Hungary.

Burnley (Free from Wigan Ath juniors on 6/8/1990) FL 1+5 FLC 0+1/1 Others 0+2 (Free to Preussen Koln, Germany during 1993 close season)
Bury (Loaned on 21/11/1992) FL 5/3 FAC 3 Others 1/1
Ipswich T (Free from FC Erzgebirge Aue, Germany on 12/6/1996) FL 28+28/3 FLC 6+4/1 FAC 1+1 Others 0+1
Sheffield Wed (£75,000 on 15/10/1998) PL 42+11/3 FLC 3+1/1 FAC 4+2

SORENSEN Thomas
Born: Denmark, 12 June 1976
Height: 6'4" Weight: 13.10
Club Honours: Div 1 '99
International Honours: Denmark: 1; B-1; U21

An impressive first season in the Premiership saw the Sunderland goalkeeper establish himself as one of the most promising custodians in the country in 1999-2000. The tall shot stopper, whose razor-sharp reflexes and safe hands were crucial to Sunderland's excellent season, also made his debut for Denmark against Israel in November and travelled to the Euro 2000 finals as understudy to Peter Schmeichel. Thomas has obviously picked up some of the ex-Manchester United legend's traits as several times last term he could be seen giving his back four a verbal dressing-down, leaving them in no doubt as to who was in charge in the penalty area. Thomas appears to have an excellent future and has the potential to become one of the world's top goalkeepers.

Sunderland (£500,000 + from Odense BK, Denmark on 6/8/1998) P/FL 82 FLC 9 FAC 4

SORVEL Neil Simon
Born: Whiston, 2 March 1973
Height: 6'0" Weight: 12.9
Club Honours: GMVC '95, '97; FAT '96

Neil returned to Crewe, his first club, on a free transfer from Macclesfield in the summer of 1999 and immediately secured a place in midfield. A busy player who tackles enthusiastically, uses the ball with care and enjoys running at opposition defences, he was an ever-present during his first season as a First Division player. He also possesses a powerful shot, and ended the campaign with six goals to his credit.

Crewe Alex (From trainee on 31/7/1991) FL 5+4 FAC 1+1 Others 4
Macclesfield T (Free on 21/8/1992) FL 79+7/7 FLC 4+1 FAC 5 Others 0+1
Crewe Alex (Free on 9/6/1999) FL 46/6 FLC 5 FAC 1

SOUTER Ryan John
Born: Bradford, 5 February 1978
Height: 5'10" Weight: 12.0

Ryan had to be content with reserve-team football once more for the majority of the 1999-2000 season but the Bury defender enjoyed a brief taste of first-team action when, as a substitute, he replaced Andy Woodward in the December away game at Gillingham. He played at centre half that day but, having made another substitute appearance against Bristol Rovers in March, he was given his full Football League debut at left back in an away game at Cambridge on 4 April. Injuries to Paul Williams and Dean Barrick gave him his chance but, unfortunately for Ryan, the Shakers had two players sent off in the first half and it proved to be something of a baptism of fire for the defender as Bury went down 3-0. He also retained his place for the away game at Millwall four days later.

Bury (£6,000 from Weston super Mare on 8/1/1999) FL 2+3

SOUTHALL Neville
Born: Llandudno, 16 September 1958
Height: 6'1" Weight: 14.0
Club Honours: FAC '84, '95; CS '84, '85, '95; Div 1 '85, '87; ECW '85
International Honours: W: 92

Torquay's 1998-99 "Player of the Year", Neville started last season where he had left off with a series of brilliant performances. However, his high standards dropped a little in December and January, and United boss Wes Saunders took what he described as "the hardest decision of my managerial career so far" by releasing the legendary 'keeper. This should not detract from the wonderful contribution he made to Torquay both on and off the field, and all Gulls supporters feel privileged that he became part of their club. The veteran former Welsh international 'keeper subsequently made a surprise return to Premiership football when he appeared for Bradford City against local rivals Leeds United last March. He thus became the oldest player ever to appear in the league for City at the age of 41 years and 178 days. Neville spent part of his time working as a goalkeeping coach at Valley Parade, Huddersfield and York throughout the season, but signed a week-to-week contract for the Bantams as cover for Gary Walsh and Matt Clarke after leaving Torquay. Although believed to be in line for the vacant manager's post at Cardiff, Neville has since become coach to the Wales U16 squad.

Bury (£6,000 from Winsford U on 14/6/1980) FL 39 FAC 5
Everton (£150,000 on 13/7/1981) F/PL 578 FLC 65 FAC 70 Others 37
Port Vale (Loaned on 27/1/1983) FL 9
Southend U (Loaned on 24/12/1997) FL 9
Stoke C (Free on 27/2/1998) FL 12 (Free to Doncaster Rov on 23/7/98)
Torquay U (Free on 10/12/1998) FL 53 FLC 2 FAC 4 Others 2
Bradford C (Free on 3/2/2000) PL 1

SOUTHALL Leslie **Nicholas (Nicky)**
Born: Stockton, 28 January 1972
Height: 5'10" Weight: 12.12

Nicky switched from a role as an attacking midfielder to the wing-back position during the 1999-2000 season and impressed onlookers with the way he adapted to the change. He was a key member of the Gills' team that reached the sixth round of the FA Cup and won promotion to the First Division via the play-offs, scoring a number of crucial goals including a brilliant 25-yard volley that knocked Sheffield Wednesday out of the Cup. Nicky is a tireless worker with good pace and an excellent cross who can operate on either flank.

Hartlepool U (Free from Darlington juniors on 21/2/1991) FL118+20/24 FLC 6+1/3 FAC 4+4 Others 6+2
Grimsby T (£40,000 on 12/7/1995) FL 55+17/5 FLC 3+3/1 FAC 4+3/2
Gillingham (Free on 9/12/1997) FL 101+9/15 FLC 3+1/1 FAC 8/3 Others 12

Nicky Southall

SOUTHGATE Gareth
Born: Watford, 3 September 1970
Height: 6'0" Weight: 12.8
Club Honours: Div 1 '94; FLC '96
International Honours: E: 37

The classy Aston Villa defender had another fine season in 1999-2000. As ever, he was a model of consistency, leading the team through their dismal early-season performances to recovery in the new year and an eventual Cup final appearance at Wembley against Chelsea. Gareth had the unfortunate experience of scoring an own goal and then being sent off for two yellow-card offences at Leicester last September but bounced back in his own unflappable style, and in January he was awarded the "Carling Player of the Month" award. In the final weeks of the season he was hampered by ongoing ankle and achilles problems and missed several games in the run-in to Villa's first FA Cup final appearance in 43 years, but otherwise he was a near-ever-present. Gareth is an accomplished and intelligent centre back, comfortable on the ball and an excellent man marker. He remained a part of the England set-up throughout the season and earned six further caps, making Kevin Keegan's final 22 for Euro 2000, where he featured as a substitute in the 2-3 defeat by Romania.

Crystal Palace (From trainee on 17/1/1989) F/PL 148+4/15 FLC 23+1/7 FAC 9 Others 6
Aston Villa (£2,500,000 on 1/7/1995) PL 160/5 FLC 16/1 FAC 18/1 Others 13

SPARROW Matthew
Born: Scunthorpe, 3 October 1981
Height: 5'11" Weight: 10.6

A member of Scunthorpe United's successful junior side, Matthew broke into the first team at the age of 17 last August and was a regular substitute during the season. A versatile player who can play either at wing back, winger or central midfield, he is good on the ball and has the ability to go past players. Still a trainee at Glanford Park, he is confidently expected to make more good progress during 2000-01.

Scunthorpe U (Trainee) FL 2+9 FLC 0+1 Others 0+1

SPEAKMAN Robert (Rob)
Born: Swansea, 5 December 1980
Height: 5'11" Weight: 11.6

Robert was mainly used from the bench by Exeter in 1999-2000, and four of his five goals came as a substitute. He has a natural goalscorer's instinct, with great alertness around the box. His highlight was a superb volleyed equaliser at Peterborough. Robert will be looking to establish himself as one of City's first-choice strikers in the new season. He has already earned the Grecian tag of "the new Darren Rowbotham".

Exeter C (From trainee on 2/7/1999) FL 4+14/3 FLC 0+2 FAC 0+1 Others 1+3/2

SPEDDING Duncan
Born: Camberley, 7 September 1977
Height: 6'1" Weight: 11.1

The Northampton left wing back settled into that position last season after injury robbed him of part of 1998-99. New manager Kevin Wilson then moved him to the left-back spot in an effort to release John Frain into a midfield role. Duncan's runs along the wing resulted in many quality crosses that created plenty of chances as Town gained promotion from Division Three.

Southampton (From trainee on 24/5/1996) PL 4+3 FLC 0+1
Northampton T (£60,000 on 14/7/1998) FL 59+9/2 FLC 4+2 FAC 1 Others 3

Gareth Southgate

SPEED Gary Andrew
Born: Deeside, 8 September 1969
Height: 5'10" Weight: 12.10
Club Honours: Div 2 '90, Div 1 '92; CS '92
International Honours: W: 58; U21-3; Yth

During a difficult 1999-2000 season for Newcastle, Gary responded by regularly turning in wholehearted and influential performances operating as an important cog in the centre of the side's midfield, where he formed a useful partnership with Rob Lee following the latter's re-instatement. He is an energetic player who enjoys breaking forward to join the attack, but he does not neglect his defensive responsibilities and is always ready to track back when the opposition have possession. Although not especially tall, Gary is a fine header of the ball, and his threat in the box often created space for his colleagues, while his attacking flair enabled him to amass 12 goals during the season, a fine tally from midfield, none more important than the late headed equaliser in the FA Cup third round away at Tottenham, which he followed with the opening goal in the replay. Gary's long run of games in the Premiership (he appeared in all the club's matches in 1998-99) was broken when he was suspended for the home game against Tottenham at the end of November for collecting five bookings, only the second suspension of his career, following which he was ever present for most of the rest of the season, missing out on the game against his former club Leeds due to gastro-enteritis. Proud to be captain of Wales, he won six further caps during the season. Gary is a great competitor who never gives less than 100 per cent for club or country.

Leeds U (From trainee on 13/6/1988) F/PL 231+17/39 FLC 25+1/11 FAC 21/5 Others 14+3/2
Everton (£3,500,000 on 1/7/1996) PL 58/16 FLC 5/1 FAC 2/1
Newcastle U (£5,500,000 on 6/2/1998) PL 83+4/14 FLC 2+1 FAC 16/5 Others 8/1

SPENCER Damian Michael
Born: Ascot, 19 September 1981
Height: 6'1" Weight: 14.5

This exciting young striker made his first-team debut for Bristol City last season, having profited from the football education provided by the club's successful academy. A strong, hard-working forward, he has the pace, control on the ground and power in the air to really make his mark in the game. Damian had his first taste of action at senior level when coming on as a substitute in City's 3-0 home win over Chesterfield in early February, and made his full debut in the 0-1 home defeat by Gillingham in mid-March. Many felt he should have been on from the start in the Auto Windscreens Shield final at Wembley, but after coming off the bench he made his presence felt when deflecting in Paul Holland's goal-bound header. Most City fans are convinced that with continued hard work and application he has the ability to become a fully established first-teamer.

Bristol C (Trainee) FL 6+3/1 Others 1+2/1

SPINK Dean Peter
Born: Birmingham, 22 January 1967
Height: 6'0" Weight: 14.8
Club Honours: Div 3 '94

Dean had a disappointing 1999-2000 campaign with Wrexham. He found it difficult to break into the Robins' first team in the early part of the season and was loaned to his previous club, Shrewsbury, last November. He made one start and three appearances as a substitute during his spell at Gay Meadow, all as a forward. Expectations were understandably high, but Dean needed more opportunity to settle to his task, especially as he had spent much of his time at Wrexham in central defence. On his return to the Racecourse Ground he featured more regularly but he then had the misfortune to suffer a bad knee injury at Scunthorpe in March. The initial diagnosis was that he had snapped the cruciate ligaments but following surgery doctors discovered it was not quite so serious and he is now expected to be fit in time for the coming season. Dean can play both as a striker and as a central defender and with his strength and courage is always a handful for the opposition. He was released during the close season.

Aston Villa (£30,000 from Halesowen T on 1/7/1989)
Scarborough (Loaned on 20/11/1989) FL 3/2 Others 1
Bury (Loaned on 1/2/1990) FL 6/1
Shrewsbury T (£75,000 on 15/3/1990) FL 244+29/52 FLC 22+2/1 FAC 18+2/6 Others 19+2/3
Wrexham (£65,000 on 15/7/1997) FL 72+13/9 FLC 2+1/1 FAC 6+3 Others 7+1
Shrewsbury T (Loaned on 1/11/1999) FL 1+3

SPINK Nigel Philip
Born: Chelmsford, 8 August 1958
Height: 6'2" Weight: 14.6
Club Honours: EC '82; ESC '82; FLC '94
International Honours: E: 1; B-2

The veteran former Aston Villa goalkeeper spent most of his time on the Millwall bench in 1999-2000 due to the form of Tony Warner, and made only one first-team appearance, at Wigan in January. Twenty years after his debut, he is still an excellent shot stopper who commands the penalty area. He has also given a lot of help to Warner, working with his younger rival in training, while the knowledge that an experienced and highly regarded goalkeeper like Nigel was ready to come in at any time helped keep Tony on his toes. Nigel was released during the summer.

Aston Villa (£4,000 from Chelmsford C on 1/1/1977) F/PL 357+4 FLC 45 FAC 28 Others 25+1
West Bromwich A (Free on 31/1/1996) FL 19 FLC 3 Others 2
Millwall (£50,000 on 26/9/1997) FL 44 FLC 2 FAC 2 Others 5

SPOONER Nicholas (Nicky) Michael
Born: Manchester, 5 June 1971
Height: 5'10" Weight: 11.9

Having completed his first season with US-'A' League club Charleston Battery, Nicky returned to England in November 1999 to join Chester on a short-term contract. With nearly ten years' experience at Bolton behind him, the gutsy centre back brought some much-needed stability to the struggling Blues defence. Looking calm and assured on the ball, he was a real asset but, unfortunately for City, he managed only nine appearances before heading back to America for their new season in March.

Bolton W (From trainee on 12/7/1989) FL 22+1/2 FLC 2 FAC 3 Others 0+1 (Free to Charleston Battery, USA on 23/3/1999)
Oldham Ath (Loaned on 30/10/1998) FL 2
Chester C (Free on 5/11/1999) FL 9 FAC 2

SPRING Matthew John
Born: Harlow, 17 November 1979
Height: 5'11" Weight: 11.5

Matthew was again a regular in the Luton side in 1999-2000, starting all but three of the club's matches. A tenacious midfielder with a biting tackle, he has impressive vision and reads the game well, while his surging runs into the opposition's half are the springboard of many of Town's attacks. He also has a powerful shot and, given a sight of goal, is prepared to try his luck from any angle. The powerful midfield raider scored a spectacular goal in the FA Cup against Kingstonian at the end of October when one of these missiles screamed into the roof of the net from 30 yards. Shortly afterwards, he became one of the youngest players to captain the club, in the match against Preston. He is likely to be a central figure in Luton's future plans.

Luton T (From trainee on 2/7/1997) FL 95+7/9 FLC 8 FAC 7+1/2 Others 1

SRNICEK Pavel (Pav)
Born: Ostrava, Czechoslovakia, 10 March 1968
Height: 6'2" Weight: 14.9
Club Honours: Div 1 '94
International Honours: Czech Republic: 34

Pavel had another competent season as Sheffield Wednesday's 'keeper in 1999-2000 despite the fact that the club were struggling near the foot of the Premiership table. He was first choice for most of the campaign until losing his place last March following a shoulder injury. He is an excellent shot stopper with quick reflexes who is good in one-to-one situations but he still needs to work hard on his handling of crosses. He remains first choice for the Czech Republic, for whom he won a further nine caps during the season, appearing in all three of their games in Euro 2000.

Newcastle U (£350,000 from Banik Ostrava, Czechoslovakia on 5/2/1991) F/PL 148+1 FLC 10+1 FAC 11 Others 17 (Free to Banik Ostrava, Czechoslovakia during 1998 close season)
Sheffield Wed (Free on 12/11/1998) PL 44 FLC 2 FAC 6

STALLARD Mark
Born: Derby, 24 October 1974
Height: 6'0" Weight: 13.6

Mark proved to be one of Notts County's most impressive players in 1999-2000 and finished the season as the club's leading scorer with 13 goals. He formed a very productive partnership with Duane Darby in the early matches when Notts were riding high in the table, but the goal supply dried up when Darby was injured and, although several partners were tried, he found the net only occasionally during the remainder of the campaign. Mark is a skilful striker who can turn his marker and deliver useful shots with either foot, and is very effective at finding goalscoring positions.

Derby Co (From trainee on 6/11/1991) FL 19+8/2 FLC 2+1/2 FAC 2+1 Others 3/2
Fulham (Loaned on 23/9/1994) FL 4/3
Bradford C (£110,000 on 12/1/1996) FL 33+10/10 FLC 2/1 FAC 0+1 Others 3/2
Preston NE (Loaned on 14/2/1997) FL 4/1
Wycombe W (£100,000 on 7/3/1997) FL 67+3/23 FLC 5+1/1 Others 2/1
Notts Co (£10,000 on 3/3/1999) FL 44+6/17 FLC 4 FAC 1 Others 1

STAM Jakob (Jaap)
Born: Kampen, Holland, 17 July 1972
Height: 6'3" Weight: 14.0
Club Honours: EC '99; FAC '99; PL '99, '00
International Honours: Holland: 36

This wonderfully balanced central defender is supreme in the air and strong in the tackle with great recovery skills. How he missed out on some kind of award in England during Manchester United's treble-winning campaign was a mystery, all the more so when UEFA voted him the best defender in Europe. The big plus for him as the 1999-2000 season began was being an automatic choice on Sir Alex Ferguson's team sheet, an honour reserved for only one other United player – Roy Keane. Certainly, for consistency, he stood head and shoulders above any of his team-mates, and completed a run of 27 consecutive Premiership games from August until March. To pick out one outstanding performance is always going to be difficult in Jaap's case because he is so consistent, but his stature, particularly in Europe, where he helped United all the way to the quarter-final stages, is immense. Although some might argue that he's not quite in the Steve Bruce–Gary Pallister bracket when it comes to scoring goals, he remains the rock upon which the Reds' defence is built. It was interesting to note that Sir Alex had no hesitation in naming him captain in Roy Keane's absence from the side in February and, in true Jaap style, he took it all in his stride. Despite missing a couple of Premiership games in March, he returned for the key moments in guiding United to a second successive title success. Having mastered some of the best attacks that English and Continental opponents could throw at him last season, he must have been in the equation when the football writers named their "Footballer of the Year". Although Jaap didn't win it, few United fans will shed any tears. They know his true value, as do his fellow professionals, who included him in the PFA award-winning Premiership side. A regular for his country, he won 11 more caps during the season and was a valued member of the Holland team that reached the semi-finals of Euro 2000 only to make a disappointing exit in a penalty shoot-out.

Manchester U (£10,750,000 from PSV Eindhoven, Holland, via Zwolle, Cambuur and Willem II, on 17/7/1998) PL 63/1 FAC 6+1 Others 32

STAMP Darryn Michael
Born: Beverley, 21 September 1978
Height: 6'2" Weight: 12.0

A bad knee ligament injury suffered in August hampered Darryn's progress last season, forcing him out of action until the end of November. A tall striker, he established himself in the Scunthorpe side towards the end of January before being loaned to Third Division Halifax in February. The month's loan did not prove particularly successful and he returned to Glanford Park after five games. Available for transfer, he has good ball skills but must add more consistency to his play if he is to make the breakthrough at league level.

Scunthorpe U (Signed from Hessle on 7/7/1997) FL 14+31/5 FLC 1+3 FAC 2 Others 2+1/1
Halifax T (Loaned on 18/2/2000) FL 5

STAMP Philip (Phil) Lawrence
Born: Middlesbrough, 12 December 1975
Height: 5'10" Weight: 13.5
International Honours: E: Yth

Phil was one of the many players to catch the Middlesbrough injury bug last season, and his contribution was restricted to a mere dozen games or so, playing as a wing back, as decreed by the manager's chosen formation. He performed sterling service, even though his early days were either spent on the wing or in midfield. Manager Bryan Robson has described him as the perfect "play anywhere" squad member, but Phil loves the complete involvement of the wing-back role and says it keeps him fully in the game for 90 minutes. His robust tackling leaves him prone to injury, just as Robson's did in his playing days, and his absences may have caused him to suffer a slight loss of confidence since he broke through into the first team, but that will soon disappear when he gets fully back on song.

Middlesbrough (From trainee on 4/2/1993) P/FL 61+30/5 FLC 13+3/1 FAC 6+4/1 Others 5+1

Jaap Stam

STANSFIELD James Edward
Born: Dewsbury, 18 September 1978
Height: 6'2" Weight: 13.0

A previous winner of Halifax's "Rising Star" award, James found it difficult to break into the first team in 1999-2000, and usually appeared only to cover for injuries and suspensions to centre back Paul Stoneman. The reserve-team skipper for most of the season, he struggled to show his ability on the senior stage. This could be explained by a niggling ankle injury that kept him out for several weeks.

Huddersfield T (From trainee on 21/7/1997)
Halifax T (Free on 7/7/1998) FL 22+2/1 FAC 1 Others 3

STANT Phillip (Phil) Richard
Born: Bolton, 13 October 1962
Height: 6'0" Weight: 13.4
Club Honours: Div 3 '93; WC '93

This veteran striker celebrated his 37th birthday during 1999-2000 but he still featured regularly in Lincoln's first-team squad while carrying out his main role as the club's assistant manager. Phil was mostly employed as a late substitute, coming on to unsettle opposition defences; he started just three times but still added a further three goals to his already impressive career tally. He stepped up to become manager of the Imps in the summer of 2000.

Reading (Free from Camberley on 19/8/1982) FL 3+1/2
Hereford U (Free from Army on 25/11/1986) FL 83+6/38 FLC 3/2 FAC 3/2 Others 11/7
Notts Co (£175,000 on 18/7/1989) FL 14+8/6 FLC 2/1 FAC 0+1 Others 3+2
Blackpool (Loaned on 5/9/1990) FL 12/5
Lincoln C (Loaned on 22/11/1990) FL 4
Huddersfield T (Loaned on 3/1/1991) FL 5/1
Fulham (£60,000 on 8/2/1991) FL 19/5 Others 1
Mansfield T (£50,000 on 1/8/1991) FL 56+1/32 FLC 4/1 FAC 2 Others 2
Cardiff C (£100,000 on 4/12/1992) FL 77+2/34 FLC 2/2 FAC 6+1/4 Others 10/3
Mansfield T (Loaned on 12/8/1993) FL 4/1 FLC 1/1
Bury (£90,000 on 27/1/1995) FL 49+13/23 FLC 5+1/4 FAC 1 Others 5
Northampton T (Loaned on 22/11/1996) FL 4+1/2
Lincoln C (£30,000 on 26/12/1996) FL 42+22/20 FLC 2+1/1 FAC 2+6 Others 1+1

STANTON Nathan
Born: Nottingham, 6 May 1981
Height: 5'9" Weight: 11.3
International Honours: E: Yth

A former England U16 international who had made a handful of appearances for Scunthorpe over the previous two seasons, Nathan came bursting through the ranks to become a first-team regular during the second half of 1999-2000 and immediately established himself as arguably the club's best defender. He is equally at home at right back or at centre half, his strength and electric pace proving valuable assets to an overworked defence, and also showed attacking instincts when playing a couple of matches as a right winger! Nathan ended the season with a "Player of the Year" award. Highly promising, he has all the attributes to go right to the top.

Scunthorpe U (From trainee on 19/3/1999) FL 30+9 FLC 1 FAC 0+1 Others 2

STATON Luke Roy
Born: Doncaster, 10 March 1979
Height: 5'7" Weight: 11.2
International Honours: E: Yth; Sch

Local youngster Luke made only one appearance for Bolton last season, that being as a second-half substitute for Ricardo Gardner in the Worthington Cup win over Gillingham. Able to play anywhere in the midfield area, he was released during the summer and will be hoping to find greater first-team opportunities elsewhere.

Blackburn Rov (From trainee on 14/3/1996)
Bolton W (Signed on 4/1/1999) FLC 0+1

STAUNTON Stephen (Steve)
Born: Drogheda, Ireland, 19 January 1969
Height: 6'1" Weight: 12.12
Club Honours: FAC '89; Div 1 '90; FLC '94, '96
International Honours: RoI: 84; U21-4; Yth

Steve had only one good run in the Liverpool team last season and he was not seen in the first team at all after mid-January due to injury, but his proven defensive qualities added strength to the Liverpool squad. Steve invariably gave his all for the Liverpool cause but is now behind Dominic Matteo in the pecking order for the left-back role at Anfield. He continued to appear regularly for the Republic of Ireland, winning six more caps and scoring in the 3-2 victory over Malta last September.

Liverpool (£20,000 from Dundalk on 2/9/1986) FL 55+10 FLC 6+2/4 FAC 14+2/1 Others 1/1
Bradford C (Loaned on 13/11/1987) FL 7+1 FLC 2 Others 1
Aston Villa (£1,100,000 on 7/8/1991) F/PL 205+3/16 FLC 17+2/1 FAC 19+1/1 Others 15+1
Liverpool (Free on 3/7/1998) PL 38+5 FLC 5/1 FAC 2 Others 5+1

STEELE Lee Anthony
Born: Liverpool, 7 December 1973
Height: 5'8" Weight: 12.7

The diminutive striker has scored 40 goals in three years at Shrewsbury. Injury interrupted his 1999-2000 season, but his skill was still very apparent. Difficult to dispossess, Lee is at his best with the ball at his feet in the box. A sight of goal will bring a well-struck effort. It was a lean year at Shrewsbury and often service to the front men was sadly lacking. He was unable to agree a new contract at the end of the season, and at the time of writing it appears he will begin the 2000-01 campaign elsewhere.

Shrewsbury T (£30,000 + from Northwich Vic on 23/7/1997) FL 104+9/37 FLC 5/3 FAC 4+1 Others 3

STEIN Earl **Mark** Sean
Born: Capetown, South Africa, 29 January 1966
Height: 5'6" Weight: 11.10
Club Honours: FLC '88; AMC '92; Div 2 '93
International Honours: E: Yth

Mark had another fine campaign with Bournemouth in 1999-2000 and finished top scorer for the second season in a row despite missing the last few games after suffering an injury to his left knee. Although now in his mid-thirties, he is still quick, extremely sharp in the box and an excellent finisher. In addition to his qualities as a striker, he is also a tireless runner who will drop back to help out in midfield if required. At the time of writing it appears that Mark will be playing elsewhere in the 2000-01 season as he is out of contract and has failed to agree new terms at Dean Court.

Luton T (From juniors on 31/1/1984) FL 41+13/19 FLC 4+1 FAC 9/3 Others 3/1
Aldershot (Loaned on 29/1/1986) FL 2/1
Queens Park R (£300,000 on 26/8/1988) FL 20+13/4 FLC 4/2 FAC 2+1/1 Others 4
Oxford U (Signed on 15/9/1989) FL 72+10/18 FLC 4 FAC 2+1 Others 3
Stoke C (£100,000 on 15/9/1991) FL 94/50 FLC 8/8 FAC 4 Others 17/10
Chelsea (£1,400,000 on 28/10/1993) PL 46+4/21 FLC 0+1 FAC 9/2 Others 2+1/2
Stoke C (Loaned on 22/11/1996) FL 11/4
Ipswich T (Loaned on 22/8/1997) FL 6+1/2 FLC 3+1/1
Bournemouth (Signed on 4/3/1998) FL 90/30 FLC 10/7 FAC 7/2 Others 8/5

Rob Steiner

STEINER Robert (Rob) Herman
Born: Finsprong, Sweden, 20 June 1973
Height: 6'2" Weight: 13.5
International Honours: Sweden: 3

Rob returned to Queens Park Rangers on a permanent basis during the summer of 1999, having enjoyed two successful loan periods at Loftus Road the previous season. He is a central striker and was the first choice in that position from the start of the 1999-2000 season – he missed only three games before becoming yet another of the club's injury victims. He suffered a serious back injury, which required surgery, and was unable to recover in time to make a comeback before the end of the season.

Bradford C (Loaned from Norrkoping, Sweden on 31/10/1996) FL 14+1/4 FAC 1/1
Bradford C (£500,000 on 31/7/1997) FL 26+11/10 FLC 3/1 FAC 1
Queens Park R (Loaned on 6/11/1998) FL 1+7/1
Queens Park R (Loaned on 2/3/1999) FL 4/2
Walsall (Loaned on 25/3/1999) FL 10/3
Queens Park R (£215,000 on 29/7/1999) FL 24/6 FLC 1 FAC 2

STEPHENSON Paul
Born: Wallsend, 2 January 1968
Height: 5'10" Weight: 12.12
International Honours: E: Yth

Following a disappointing 1998-99 season with Hartlepool, Paul looked to be reaching the end of his playing career at Nationwide League level. However, a switch from right wing to central midfield in 1999-2000 provided the spark he needed. He began the season as a revitalised player, and went on to become Hartlepool's only ever-present. Throughout the season Paul played a major role in the club's rise to a play-off position, and he fully deserved the Pool "Player of the Year" award.

Newcastle U (From apprentice on 2/1/1986) FL 58+3/1 FLC 3+1 FAC 2 Others 2
Millwall (£300,000 on 10/11/1988) FL 81+17/6 FLC 3/1 FAC 9/2 Others 8/1
Gillingham (Loaned on 21/11/1992) FL 12/2 Others 2
Brentford (£30,000 on 4/3/1993) FL 70/2 FLC 6/1 FAC 1+1 Others 5
York C (£35,000 on 7/8/1995) FL 91+6/8 FLC 9+2 FAC 5 Others 2+2/1
Hartlepool U (Free on 20/3/1998) FL 73+3/7 FLC 2+1/1 FAC 3+1 Others 7

Paul Stephenson

STEVENS Ian David
Born: Malta, 21 October 1966
Height: 5'10" Weight: 12.6
Club Honours: AMC '89

This hard-working Wrexham striker forged an excellent partnership with young Craig Faulconbridge at the start of the 1999-2000 campaign, the pair finding the net nine times in the opening ten matches. Unfortunately, Ian then suffered a groin injury and also contracted a viral infection, and together they put a brake on what had promised to be an exciting season. He rarely featured at all after early November and was loaned to Cheltenham last March, but played just one game for the Third Division new boys – a 2-1 home win over Northampton. He returned to the Racecourse Ground early, reportedly having decided that the travelling from his Lancashire home was too much. Wrexham released him in the summer.

Preston NE (From apprentice on 22/11/1984) FL 9+2/2 Others 1
Stockport Co (Free on 27/10/1986) FL 1+1 FAC 0+1 Others 0+1 (Free to Lancaster C on 27/11/1986)
Bolton W (Free on 25/3/1987) FL 26+21/7 FLC 1+2 FAC 4/2 Others 3+1
Bury (Free on 3/7/1991) FL 100+10/38 FLC 3+1 FAC 2+2 Others 7+1/2
Shrewsbury T (£20,000 on 11/8/1994) FL 94+17/37 FLC 2+1 FAC 4+2/2 Others 10+2/12
Carlisle U (£100,000 on 13/5/1997) FL 64+14/26 FLC 2 FAC 2/1 Others 3/2
Wrexham (Free on 5/7/1999) FL 14+2/4 FLC 2 FAC 1+1
Cheltenham T (Loaned on 21/3/2000) FL 1

STEWART Gareth John
Born: Preston, 3 February 1980
Height: 6'0" Weight: 12.8
International Honours: E: Yth; Sch

Gareth joined Bournemouth on a free transfer from Blackburn in July 1999 and spent the 1999-2000 season as second-choice 'keeper to Mark Ovendale. He made his Football League debut at Wigan last November when Ovendale was injured in the pre-match warm-up but featured in the first team on only two further occasions. He produced some impressive performances for the Cherries' reserve team and will be looking for more regular senior action in the coming season.

Blackburn Rov (From trainee on 11/2/1997)
Bournemouth (Free on 2/7/1999) FL 3

STEWART Jordan Barrington
Born: Birmingham, 3 March 1982
Height: 5'11" Weight: 11.12

A promising product of the Leicester Academy, Jordan was given an early taste of first-team action during the worst of the Foxes' injury troubles last season. A right-footed midfielder, he showed both composure and promise in coming off the bench against West Ham and in the televised FA Cup tie at Chelsea. Jordan joined Second Division Bristol Rovers on transfer deadline day for a one-month loan spell to broaden his football education and made his Rovers debut in a top-of-the-table clash at the New Den in which Millwall came out on top despite the debutant producing a "Man of the Match" performance. A former Aston Villa trainee, Jordan made three further brief substitute appearances for the Pirates.

Leicester C (From trainee on 22/3/2000) PL 0+1 FAC 0+1
Bristol Rov (Loaned on 23/3/2000) FL 1+3

STEWART William Paul **Marcus**
Born: Bristol, 7 November 1972
Height: 5'10" Weight: 11.0
International Honours: E: Sch

Marcus started last season with a new regular striking partner at Huddersfield in the form of Clyde Wijnhard and the pairing was soon to become the most potent in the First Division. Marcus leads the line magnificently with his close control and clinical finishing, and the fans' favourite was finding the net with regularity. Even when the goals dried up for a spell he was still creating chances for others, and his eye for finding space in front of goal and telling runs always set him apart from the others. However, speculation about a move away from the club was mounting, and Marcus's double strike at Crystal Palace was to be his swansong in the blue and white stripes. Town's record signing became the club's record sale when he joined Ipswich in February for £2.5 million, the highest fee the Suffolk club had ever paid. Marcus made an immediate impact with goals in his first two games, dribbling round the 'keeper at Barnsley and scoring with a left-foot shot from the edge of the penalty area in his home debut against his old club. From then on he was dogged by injuries and only regained full fitness towards the end of the campaign. Marcus led the fight-back in the play-off semi-final at Bolton, scoring both Ipswich goals in a 2-2 draw. He notched a spectacular volley from well outside the box in the first half and then equalised when he ran on to Martijn Reuser's pass, rounded the 'keeper and calmly curled the ball round the defenders on the goal line. Marcus had a fine match in the play-off final at Wembley, scoring the crucial third goal when he headed Jamie Clapham's cross into the corner of the net. His talents were acknowledged by his fellow professionals, who included him in the PFA award-winning First Division select.

Bristol Rov (From trainee on 18/7/1991) FL 137+34/57 FLC 11/5 FAC 7+1/3 Others 16+1/14
Huddersfield T (£1,200,000 + on 2/7/1996) FL 129+4/58 FLC 18/7 FAC 9/3
Ipswich T (£2,500,000 on 1/2/2000) FL 9+1/2 Others 3/3

STILLIE Derek Daniel
Born: Irvine, 3 December 1973
Height: 6'0" Weight: 12.0
International Honours: S: U21-14

The understudy to Roy Carroll at Wigan for the majority of the 1999-2000 season, this Scottish goalkeeper proved to be a more than suitable replacement when called into action. A close-season capture, Derek gave some impressive displays as a shot stopper, and also showed good kicking ability. He played in the last seven matches and collected the "Man of the Match" award in the play-off win over Millwall, retaining the goalkeeper's shirt for the Wembley final.

Aberdeen (From juniors on 3/5/1991) SL 22+1 SLC 2 SC 3
Wigan Ath (Free on 5/8/1999) FL 12+1 FLC 1 FAC 2 Others 3

STIMAC Igor
Born: Metkovic, Croatia, 6 September 1967
Height: 6'2" Weight: 13.0
International Honours: Croatia: 48

This giant Croatian central defender began last season with Derby County before moving to West Ham in September. He settled in quickly at Upton Park, giving a series of assured performances before falling victim to a calf injury that kept him out of the team for a couple of months. He marked his return to fitness by scoring with a late header to snatch a point for the Hammers at Newcastle in early January, his only goal of the season. He is good in the tackle, uses the ball well and shows excellent distribution. Igor is an experienced international and a regular in the Croatia team, winning eight further caps during 1999-2000.

Derby Co (£1,570,000 from Hadjuk Split, Croatia, via Cibalia Vinkovic, on 31/10/1995) F/PL 84/3 FLC 2 FAC 7
West Ham U (£600,000 on 10/9/1999) PL 24/1 FLC 2 Others 2

STOCCO Thomas (Tom) Luca
Born: London, 4 January 1983
Height: 6'2" Weight: 12.5

This lanky YTS striker became an instant hit with Torquay fans when he came on as a substitute for his home debut against Third Division leaders Rotherham in March 2000 and headed the winning goal. He followed this up with another against Mansfield and shows a deft touch for one so young.

Torquay U (Trainee) FL 2+6/2

STOCK Brian Benjamin
Born: Winchester, 24 December 1981
Height: 5'11" Weight: 11.2

Brian is one of the several promising youngsters who made the grade with Bournemouth in 1999-2000. He had his first taste of Football League action when he came on as a substitute against Colchester last January and then made the starting line-up for four games towards the end of the season. He proved to be a quick midfield player who is not afraid to run at defenders and will be aiming to consolidate his place in the first-team squad in 2000-01.

Bournemouth (From trainee on 25/1/2000) FL 4+1

STOCKDALE Robert (Robbie) Keith
Born: Redcar, 30 November 1979
Height: 5'11" Weight: 11.3

Robbie is one of a number of youngsters at Middlesbrough who look set for great things in the future. A talented young midfielder, he made 11 Premiership appearances last season, scoring one goal, and is growing in stature by the week. He came through the junior ranks and is a credit to the backroom staff at the Riverside. His tackles are strong and decisive and his pace on the ball is breathtaking. His goal, against Watford in May, was a product of his dogged perseverance.

Middlesbrough (From trainee on 2/7/1998) P/FL 24+7/1 FLC 5 FAC 1

STOCKLEY Samuel (Sam) Joshua
Born: Tiverton, 5 September 1977
Height: 6'0" Weight: 12.0

Quick, eager and capable of prodigious amounts of running throughout the duration of a match, Sam can look back with fond memories on his 1999-2000 season with Barnet. However, at the start of the term his prospects were somewhat uncertain when, after a groin injury, he found himself consigned to the reserves. With initially Lee Gledhill and latterly Ross Davidson occupying his favoured right-sided defensive role, Sam found himself out of contention for the first time since his arrival at Underhill at the end of 1996. However, the wiry, agile defender earned lavish praise for his spirit, mobility and skill and, when he returned, he produced some of the best displays of his career. This upsurge in form culminated with his stunning strike at Hull in April – his first senior goal after over 150 appearances.

Southampton (From trainee on 1/7/1996)
Barnet (Free on 31/12/1996) FL 132+5/1 FLC 8 FAC 2 Others 8

STOCKWELL Michael (Micky) Thomas
Born: Chelmsford, 14 February 1965
Height: 5'9" Weight: 11.4
Club Honours: Div 2 '92

The Ipswich stalwart is the epitome of the ideal squad player – always available when required and always ready to give his all for the cause. His first-team appearances were limited last season but he maintained his high standards whenever he was asked to play, whether at wing back or in midfield, showing his customary enthusiasm and appetite. Although he started just under half Town's games he was a useful player to have in waiting on the substitutes' bench because of his versatility. He scored twice last season, against Charlton in October and Swindon in January. The best of the two was against Charlton, when he cut in from the right-hand edge of the penalty box and fired a low shot past the 'keeper. Micky was given a free transfer at the end of the season.

Ipswich T (From apprentice on 17/12/1982) F/PL 464+42/35 FLC 43+5/5 FAC 28+3/2 Others 22+4/2

STOKES Dean Anthony
Born: Birmingham, 23 May 1970
Height: 5'9" Weight: 11.2

Dean started the 1999-2000 season as Rochdale's regular left back, and played in the first eight games, from which Dale picked up 16 points. However, he was replaced when Damon Searle came in on loan in September. He regained his place in mid-season for a spell, then must have been disappointed to be displaced by another newcomer when Sean McAuley was signed. A strong, pacy defender, Dean was released in May.

Port Vale (£5,000 from Halesowen T on 15/1/1993) FL 53+7 FLC 1+1 FAC 4 Others 5+3
Rochdale (Free on 15/7/1998) FL 28+2 FLC 4 FAC 3 Others 3

Dean Stokes

STONE Steven (Steve) Brian
Born: Gateshead, 20 August 1971
Height: 5'8" Weight: 12.7
Club Honours: Div 1 '98
International Honours: E: 9

The 1999-2000 campaign was a disappointing one for this Aston Villa midfielder, who failed to fully establish himself as a regular in the starting line-up. He began the season on the subs' bench but then suffered a back injury at Chelsea last August that put him out of action for a month. On recovering he was again used mostly as a substitute, but he worked extremely hard at his game and eventually made the breakthrough back to regular first-team football in January. He then lost his place again in the final weeks of the season and made just a brief appearance for the last 15 minutes of the FA Cup final against Chelsea. Steve is a pacy wide-right midfield player with a good cross and the ability to run with the ball at opposition defenders. He will be aiming to make the right-wing position at Villa Park his own in 2000-01.

Nottingham F (From trainee on 20/5/1989) F/PL 189+4/23 FLC 14+1/2 FAC 9 Others 12/2
Aston Villa (£5,500,000 on 12/3/1999) PL 19+15/1 FLC 3+3/1 FAC 2+4/1

STONEBRIDGE Ian Robert
Born: Lewisham, 30 August 1981
Height: 6'0" Weight: 11.4
International Honours: E: Yth

A former trainee at Tottenham, Ian impressed during 1999-2000, his first season as a professional at Plymouth. He showed a lot of strength for a youngster, and an eye for goal. He possesses an ability way beyond his years, which was recognised with an international call-up to the England U18 squad within a month of his first senior game. He won his first cap against Switzerland, and was capped three more times, scoring two goals during the qualifying rounds of the U18 European Championship. Ian scored his first Plymouth goal in only his second appearance and, before an injury in January, he was Argyle's top scorer. If he continues to work hard at his game, he is sure to go far. He was arguably "the find of the season" in the Third Division, and several bigger clubs are already rumoured to have enquired about buying him.

Plymouth Arg (Free from Tottenham H juniors on 13/7/1999) FL 27+4/9 FLC 2/1 FAC 7/1 Others 0+1

STONEMAN Paul
Born: Tynemouth, 26 February 1973
Height: 6'1" Weight: 13.6

Paul was Halifax Town's "Mr Dependable" once again in 1999-2000. Week in, week out, he is a highly consistent performer whose defensive skills make him a crowd favourite. He carried on at times when suffering from injuries, and was voted runner-up to Lee Butler in the "Player of the Season" awards. Currently the longest-serving player at the Shay, Paul has signed a contract that ties him to Town to the end of the 2001-02 season.

Blackpool (From trainee on 26/7/1991) FL 38+5 FLC 5 FAC 3 Others 3
Colchester U (Loaned on 23/12/1994) FL 3/1
Halifax T (Free on 12/7/1995) FL 76+1/8 FLC 6 FAC 3 Others 2

STONES Craig
Born: Scunthorpe, 31 May 1980
Height: 5'11" Weight: 11.2

Craig is a neat young midfielder who can operate either on the right flank or in the centre of the park. He mostly played in the Lincoln reserves during 1999-2000 with his first-team opportunities limited to three brief appearances as a second-half substitute. He was loaned to Dr Martens League club Grantham Town in March and was then released at the end of the season.

Lincoln C (From trainee on 1/7/1997) FL 10+11 FAC 1+2 Others 2

STOWELL Michael (Mike)
Born: Portsmouth, 19 April 1965
Height: 6'2" Weight: 14.2

This long-serving Wolves goalkeeper began the 1999-2000 season in fine form, appearing in the first 20 games to extend his run of consecutive matches to 74. He crowned an excellent display at Fulham with a brilliant reflex save but then lost his place at the end of November. He was boosted by a further year's extension to his contract in February and shortly afterwards underwent surgery on his ankle to correct a long-standing problem. Having completed ten years' service at Molineux, Mike has been rewarded with a testimonial match in July, when Aston Villa are due to provide the opposition.

Preston NE (Free from Leyland Motors on 14/2/1985)
Everton (Free on 12/12/1985) Others 1

Chester C (Loaned on 3/9/1987) FL 14 Others 2
York C (Loaned on 24/12/1987) FL 6
Manchester C (Loaned on 2/2/1988) FL 14 FAC 1
Port Vale (Loaned on 21/10/1988) FL 7 Others 1
Wolverhampton W (Loaned on 17/3/1989) FL 7
Preston NE (Loaned on 8/2/1990) FL 2
Wolverhampton W (£250,000 on 28/6/1990) FL 377 FLC 29 FAC 21 Others 11

STRACHAN Gavin David
Born: Aberdeen, 23 December 1978
Height: 5'11" Weight: 11.7
International Honours: S: U21-8; Yth

Although Gavin broke into Coventry's first-team squad in 1997-98, he has yet to establish himself as a regular in the senior team. The midfielder made only two starts last season, at Tranmere in the Worthington Cup and at Derby when City were hit by injuries and Carlton Palmer's suspension. A total of just two other substitute appearances will hardly have excited the manager's son and there is possibly a question mark over his future at Highfield Road, after John Eustace and Barry Quinn leap-frogged him in the midfield pecking order. Gavin continued to represent Scotland at U21 level, winning further caps against Estonia and Lithuania in the autumn.

Coventry C (From trainee on 28/11/1996) PL 3+9 FLC 1+1 FAC 2+2
Dundee (Loaned on 27/1/1999) SL 4+2

STREET Kevin
Born: Crewe, 25 November 1977
Height: 5'10" Weight: 10.8

A locally born player who has emerged from Crewe's remarkably successful youth development programme, Kevin has had to wait patiently to establish himself in the first team since making his debut in November 1997. A hard-working midfielder who can play anywhere across the pitch but enjoys being involved in the thick of the action, he made his first appearance of 1999-2000 as a substitute in the first leg of the Worthington Cup tie against Ipswich and was included in the starting line-up for the next game against Swindon, opening the scoring with 13 minutes played. Thereafter he was usually a member of the match-day squad, making a total of 31 appearances during the season (ten of them as a substitute), mostly on the right flank. There were to be no more goals, but the prospects for 2000-01 are encouraging.

Crewe Alex (From trainee on 4/7/1996) FL 39+44/7 FLC 1+3 FAC 1+1

STREVENS Benjamin (Ben) John
Born: Edgware, 24 May 1980
Height: 6'1" Weight: 11.0

Ben is a cultured front runner with every chance of developing into an outstanding asset for Barnet following a productive debut season in the professional ranks in 1999-2000. Signed from non-league Wingate & Finchley in January 1999, he effortlessly made the transition to Division Three football. Early on in the campaign, he made a handful of substitute appearances before returning to the club's second string. However, after going to Slough on loan in January, the young striker displayed an intelligence, vision and willingness to work that indicated that he will evolve into a key figure next season. He showed his outstanding ability in the final league match at Rochdale, when he replaced Ken Charlery early in the second half.

Barnet (Free from Wingate & Finchley on 13/1/1999) FL 0+6 FLC 0+1 Others 0+1

STRODDER Gary John
Born: Cleckheaton, 1 April 1965
Height: 6'1" Weight: 13.3
Club Honours: Div 3 '98

Gary is Hartlepool's most experienced professional, and a player who can always be counted upon to give 100 per cent effort in every game. Early in 1999-2000, he was out for three months with an achilles injury. However, on his return in December, he was soon back to his best as he added bite to the heart of Pool's three-man central defence. Despite his reputation as a tough-tackling, no-nonsense player Gary stayed out of trouble apart from a couple of disciplinary problems in the latter stages of the campaign.

Lincoln C (From apprentice on 8/4/1983) FL 122+10/6 FLC 7+1 FAC 2+1 Others 5+1
West Ham U (£150,000 on 20/3/1987) FL 59+6/2 FLC 8 FAC 4+2 Others 2
West Bromwich A (£190,000 on 22/8/1990) FL 123+17/8 FLC 8+1 FAC 7/1 Others 10
Notts Co (£145,000 on 14/7/1995) FL 116+5/10 FLC 9 FAC 10+1 Others 7
Rotherham U (Loaned on 29/1/1999) FL 3
Hartlepool U (£25,000 on 25/2/1999) FL 41+1 FLC 1 Others 3

STRONG Gregory (Greg)
Born: Bolton, 5 September 1975
Height: 6'2" Weight: 11.12
International Honours: E: Yth; Sch

This big, powerful centre half figured in the Bolton side quite often at the start of the 1999-2000 season due to the absence of Mark Fish. The Bolton-born player enjoyed a good run of form during this time, producing some solid performances against the likes of Ipswich, Birmingham and Manchester City. Despite this good work it was apparent that Greg would probably lose his place in the starting line-up when Fish returned, and this proved to be the case. He subsequently found his first-team chances were few and far between and, limited to a handful of substitute appearances, he eventually went on loan to Motherwell for the remainder of the season.

Wigan Ath (From trainee on 1/10/1992) FL 28+7/3 FLC 5 FAC 1 Others 3+1
Bolton W (Signed on 10/9/1995) P/FL 10+2/1 FLC 8+2
Blackpool (Loaned on 21/11/1997) FL 11/1 Others 1
Stoke C (Loaned on 24/3/1999) FL 5/1
Motherwell (Loaned on 17/3/2000) SL 11

STRUPAR Branko
Born: Croatia, 9 February 1970
Height: 6'3" Weight: 13.7
International Honours: Belgium: 11

The unexpected departure of Esteban Fuertes last winter left Derby short of a forward in a particularly important and difficult season, so it was with great relief that Jim Smith signed Branko, a striker of international class. Though born in Croatia, he is a naturalised Belgian and his cult status at Genk was such that Pride Park welcomed hundreds of Genk fans to watch their hero at various times towards the close of the season. Two goals on his debut against Watford were the best possible start but he seemed to take some time to settle into life in this country and, though a regular in the team, goals proved hard to come by. Branko is very much the old-fashioned bustling kind of centre forward, his physical presence making up for a lack of pace. He showed how effective he can be at set pieces with a tremendous free kick in the vital game at Bradford in April. Derby fans are hoping that he will forge a long-term striking partnership with Malcolm Christie, who plays so effectively alongside the big striker. Branko made his international debut for his adopted country against Finland in August 1999 and hit a purple patch in the autumn, when he scored six times in a run of five games. However, although he featured in all three of Belgium's matches in Euro 2000, he failed to add to his goal tally.

Derby Co (£3,000,000 from KRC Genk, Belgium on 17/12/1999) PL 13+2/5

STUART Graham Charles
Born: Tooting, 24 October 1970
Height: 5'9" Weight: 11.10
Club Honours: FAC '95; Div 1 '00
International Honours: E: U21-5; Yth

Graham built up a strong partnership with Mark Kinsella in the heart of the Charlton Athletic midfield last season, and most of the team's attacking moves were started either by the former Chelsea and Everton man or by his midfield partner. Hard working and a strong tackler, Graham is an intelligent player and an excellent distributor of the ball. Playing slightly in front of Kinsella, he likes to get forward and scored seven goals from midfield during the season, making him the club's joint third-top scorer. A key figure in Charlton's First Division championship-winning team, he also turned out as a forward when required.

Chelsea (From trainee on 15/6/1989) F/PL 70+17/14 FLC 11/2 FAC 5+2/1 Others 3+2/1
Everton (£850,000 on 19/8/1993) PL 116+20/22 FLC 9/3 FAC 10+3/5 Others 2+1/1
Sheffield U (£850,000 on 28/11/1997) FL 52+1/11 FLC 4 FAC 10+1/1 Others 0+1
Charlton Ath (£1,100,000 on 25/3/1999) P/FL 42+4/11 FLC 2 FAC 3

STUART Jamie Christopher
Born: Southwark, 15 October 1976
Height: 5'10" Weight: 11.0
International Honours: E: U21-4; Yth

The 1999-2000 season proved very frustrating for the versatile Millwall defender. Apart from a run of seven games in the autumn and two further appearances in January he was restricted to the subs' bench due to the excellent form of Robbie Ryan and the ever-improving Ronnie Bull. Jamie is a strong tackler who likes to get forward and is equally at home in the sweeper position and at left back. He will be hoping for greater involvement this coming season.

Charlton Ath (From trainee on 18/1/1995) FL 49+1/3 FLC 8+1 FAC 3 Others 0+1
Millwall (Free on 25/9/1998) FL 42+2 FLC 2 FAC 1 Others 6

STURRIDGE Dean Constantine
Born: Birmingham, 27 July 1973
Height: 5'8" Weight: 12.1

Derby's longest-serving player, Dean had a somewhat disappointing campaign in 1999-2000, being in and out of Jim Smith's line-up for the first half of the season then dropping down the pecking order following the arrival of Branko Strupar and the emergence of Malcolm Christie. He regained his place in February only for a hamstring injury to rule him out for a while. A predominantly right-sided striker, Dean prefers to play off a central target man. Still one of the quickest players at the club, he remains a player who can bring a game to life with a spectacular strike at goal or a fast and mazy run. Early-season transfer rumours – yet again – amounted to nothing and a proposed loan move to Birmingham was also cancelled at the last minute. Dean is the younger brother of Simon Sturridge, who played for Northampton last season.

Derby Co (From trainee on 1/7/1991) P/FL 141+37/52 FLC 9+2/4 FAC 8/2 Others 2+1
Torquay U (Loaned on 16/12/1994) FL 10/5

STURRIDGE Simon Andrew
Born: Birmingham, 9 December 1969
Height: 5'6" Weight: 11.8
Club Honours: AMC '91

A diminutive, all-action striker, Simon came to Northampton at the start of last season but his first-team appearances became limited after November. Although lightweight, he is speedy and tricky and can be a handful for any defender. Unable to command a regular place, he decided on a transfer deadline move to Shrewsbury on loan, with a view to a permanent transfer. His only Shrews goal earned a vital point at champions Swansea, but there could be better to come from Simon as he has suffered terrible luck with injuries in recent years. The older brother of Derby's Dean Sturridge, he was released by Northampton in the summer.

Birmingham C (From trainee on 8/7/1988) FL 129+21/30 FLC 10+4/1 FAC 8/2 Others 14/5
Stoke C (£75,000 on 24/9/1993) FL 43+28/14 FLC 2+2 FAC 3+4/1 Others 8+3
Blackpool (Loaned on 9/3/1999) FL 5/1
Northampton T (Free on 2/8/1999) FL 10+8/1 FAC 1
Shrewsbury T (Loaned on 2/3/2000) FL 10+1/1

SUGDEN Ryan Stephen
Born: Bradford, 26 December 1980
Height: 6'1" Weight: 11.10

This highly rated Oldham youngster was mostly used as a substitute by the Latics during 1999-2000, making the starting line-up on only four occasions. Having scored regularly for the reserves in recent seasons, he netted his first goal at senior level against Blackpool in April when he equalised in the final minute to condemn the Seasiders to relegation to the Third Division. Ryan is a tall striker with a good eye for goal, but still needs to work hard to increase his pace and strength.

Oldham Ath (From trainee on 25/11/1998) FL 3+16/1 FLC 1+1

SUKER Davor
Born: Osijek, Croatia, 1 January 1968
Height: 6'1" Weight: 12.5
International Honours: Croatia: 57. Yugoslavia: 2; Yth (World Yth-U20 '87)

This Croatian international striker was signed by Arsenal from Real Madrid in the summer of 1999 for £3.5 million. He won the "Golden Boot" award at the 1998 World Cup in France, and more recently was voted "Croatian Player of the Century". A proven goalscorer, Davor settled quickly at Highbury and scored twice in the first game he started for the Gunners, at home against Aston Villa. Although he scored six goals in as many weeks during September and October, he spent much of the season on the substitutes' bench. Davor has a great instinct for goal and the ability to make a chance out of nothing. He has a great left foot with the skill to put power and bend into his shots, and is very threatening when he gets into the opposition's penalty box. He was given a free transfer in the summer. A regular for Croatia, he added eight caps during the season, scoring the winner against the Republic of Ireland at the beginning of September. Stop Press: Davor was reported to have signed for West Ham at the end of June.

Arsenal (Free from Real Madrid, Spain on 20/8/1999) PL 8+14/8 FLC 1/1 FAC 3 Others 3+10/2

Neil Sullivan

SULLIVAN Neil
Born: Sutton, 24 February 1970
Height: 6'0" Weight: 12.1
International Honours: S: 16

The Wimbledon goalkeeper had another outstanding season in 1999-2000. He missed just one Premiership match, and although only Watford conceded more goals than the Dons this certainly wasn't a reflection on his solid performances. Although it was never a secret that Neil would be leaving Wimbledon, his only club, when his contract expired at the end of the season, his commitment and effort during a tough campaign could never be questioned. He also performed well for Scotland in two memorable European Championship qualification play-off matches against England, and his place as his country's first-choice 'keeper seems secure. An outstanding shot stopper who commands his penalty area and organises his defence impressively, Neil has served the Dons well over many years. He was out of contract in the summer and signed for Tottenham, a move that allows him to remain in the top flight and link up again with his former team-mate Chris Perry.

Wimbledon (From trainee on 26/7/1988) F/PL 180+1 FLC 18 FAC 25
Crystal Palace (Loaned on 1/5/1992) FL 1

Nicky Summerbee

SUMMERBEE Nicholas (Nicky) John
Born: Altrincham, 26 August 1971
Height: 5'11" Weight: 12.8
Club Honours: Div 1 '99
International Honours: E: B-1; U21-3

Right winger Nicky was probably Sunderland's main supply line for goalscoring opportunities last term and firmly established himself as one of the best crossers of the ball in the English game. He has the skill and pace to beat a full back, but even if he does not get past the defender he has the knack of still managing to whip in the dangerous centres which led to many chances last season for Niall Quinn and Kevin Phillips. An alleged bust-up with manager Peter Reid saw Nicky out of favour for a short period but his return to the side reaped instant dividends when he opened the scoring at the Stadium of Light against Everton in March with a free kick, which led to Sunderland securing their first win of 2000. Another spell on the sidelines followed but once again he was back against West Ham in May, producing a scintillating cross for Phillips to head the only goal of the game. A popular figure with the Sunderland fans, Nicky is proof that players who can regularly deliver a good ball into the opposition penalty area are worth their weight in gold in the Premiership.

Swindon T (From trainee on 20/7/1989) F/PL 89+23/6 FLC 9+1/3 FAC 2+4 Others 7/1
Manchester C (£1,500,000 on 24/6/1994) P/FL 119+12/6 FLC 11+2/2 FAC 12/2
Sunderland (£1,000,000 on 14/11/1997) P/FL 87+6/7 FLC 6+1 FAC 4+1 Others 3/1

SUMMERBELL Mark
Born: Durham, 30 October 1976
Height: 5'9" Weight: 11.9

Mark is one of a number of youngsters who have come through the ranks at Middlesbrough, and is tagged with a "hands off" warning to other clubs. A cultured young midfielder who is hard working and strong in the tackle, he made nearly 20 Premiership appearances last season and proved that he can hold his own in the highest company. He improved with every outing and will soon make a midfield position his own.

Middlesbrough (From trainee on 1/7/1995) F/PL 30+14 FLC 1+3/2

Daryl Sutch

SUTCH Daryl
Born: Beccles, 11 September 1971
Height: 6'0" Weight: 12.0
International Honours: E: U21-4; Yth

Daryl enjoyed a well-deserved testimonial season at Norwich in 1999-2000, highlighted by a well-attended match against top Dutch side AZ Alkmaar in July 1999. An unsung hero of the Canaries' line-up, his value to the side can be measured by the fact that he hardly ever misses a game, either through injury or by being out of favour. He has developed into a technically excellent right back, having, earlier in his career, been a bit of a utility man. Daryl is an excellent athlete, being both quick over the ground and well balanced in the tackle. His heading has improved in recent seasons and the good passing habits he developed as part of City's Premiership days remain, as he always tries to use the ball constructively. With approaching 300 senior appearances for Norwich already to his credit, he is by far and away the club's longest-serving player and at the age of just 29 he has scope to add to that already impressive tally.

Norwich C (From trainee on 6/7/1990) F/PL 210+36/9 FLC 19+3 FAC 8+3 Others 2+3

SUTTON Christopher (Chris) Roy
Born: Nottingham, 10 March 1973
Height: 6'3" Weight: 13.5
Club Honours: PL '95
International Honours: E: 1; B-2; U21-13

After losing three top-class centre forwards, Mark Hughes, Pierluigi Casiraghi and Gianluca Vialli, through a variety of causes, Chelsea broke their transfer record – smashing through the eight-figure barrier – during the 1999 close season to secure the physical presence of the England striker from relegated Blackburn Rovers. It was felt in many quarters that the lack of a front man who could hold the ball up was all that prevented the Blues clinching the Premiership title that their cavalier football so deserved in 1998-99. Chris initially settled well into the Chelsea routine, with the rotation policy wisely favoured by Vialli (now the Blues' manager, of course) keeping the strikers fit and sharp. It took Chris eight Premiership matches to break his goalscoring duck but his first league goal for the club was certainly worth waiting for: a classic soaring header which helped Chelsea smash Manchester United's 29-match unbeaten record. The Blues' 5-0 victory came on 3 October and, unbelievably, that was his one and only league goal of the season – a disappointing return from 28 Premiership appearances. Chris certainly

Chris Sutton

couldn't be faulted for effort but the harder he tried the tougher things seemed to get and his frustration became obvious when he was sent off against Hertha Berlin following an outburst of dissent. Possibly his best performance of the season came at Everton in November when, following Frank Leboeuf's sending-off, he was pressed into service as an emergency centre half and played superbly as ten-man Chelsea plundered a draw. Tore Andre Flo and Gianfranco Zola had struck up a wonderful Champions' League partnership and the on-loan signing of George Weah restricted Chris's opportunities still further. Another disappointment came with his omission from the Blues' victorious FA Cup final squad, Chris being a mere spectator. His two other goals during the season came against Skonto Riga and Hull in the Champions' League and FA Cup respectively. In fairness to Chris, Chelsea's patient, probing, chess-like approach probably doesn't suit his robust style; his halcyon days at Blackburn resulted from the service provided by direct wingers like Stuart Ripley and Jason Wilcox. At the season's end Chelsea were linked to a myriad of top-class forwards, and following the arrival of Jimmy Floyd Hasselbaink and Eidur Gudjohnsen it seemed certain that Chris would be allowed to move on.

Norwich C (From trainee on 2/7/1991) F/PL 89+13/35 FLC 8+1/3 FAC 10/5 Others 6
Blackburn Rov (£5,000,000 on 13/7/1994) PL 125+5/47 FLC 11+1/7 FAC 9/4 Others 7+3/1
Chelsea (£10,000,000 on 16/7/1999) PL 21+7/1 FAC 3+1/1 Others 3+4/1

SVENSSON Mathias (Matt)
Born: Boras, Sweden, 24 September 1974
Height: 6'0" Weight: 12.4
Club Honours: Div 1 '00
International Honours: Sweden: 2

Matt had a great 1999-2000 campaign after suffering so badly from injuries in the previous season. He appeared regularly in the Crystal Palace starting line-up and was top scorer for the Eagles with nine goals when he was sold to eventual First Division champions Charlton Athletic last January. A hard-running, bustling striker who leads the line well, Matt works very hard and is unselfish, often setting up goalscoring chances for his team-mates. He only managed to score twice for the Addicks, which was disappointing after his early-season form for Palace, but he ended the campaign with a championship medal as a reward for his efforts and better things are expected of him next season in the Premiership.

Portsmouth (£200,000 from Elfsborg, Sweden on 6/12/1996) FL 34+11/10 FLC 1/1 FAC 3+2/1 (£100,000 to Tirol Innsbruck, Austria on 15/7/1998)
Crystal Palace (£100,000 on 29/9/1998) FL 26+6/10 FLC 2 FAC 1
Charlton Ath (£600,000 on 28/1/2000) FL 13+5/2

SWAILES Christopher (Chris) William
Born: Gateshead, 19 October 1970
Height: 6'2" Weight: 12.11

The Bury central defender was ever present and enjoying another commanding and consistent season for the Shakers in 1999-2000 as the Boxing Day fixture against Burnley approached. However, Chris was sent off against the Clarets to mark the start of a nightmare introduction to the year 2000. Having served his three-match ban, he picked up a stomach strain almost immediately afterwards. This was followed in March by a hernia problem that brought a further two-month lay-off. He was finally able to begin another comeback in the home game against Blackpool – with just five matches remaining.

Ipswich T (From trainee on 23/5/1989)
Peterborough U (£10,000 on 28/3/1991. Free to Boston U in August 1991)
Doncaster Rov (Free from Bridlington T on 27/10/1993) FL 49 FLC 2/1 FAC 1 Others 2
Ipswich T (£225,000 on 23/3/1995) P/FL 34+3/1 FLC 3 Others 2
Bury (£200,000 on 14/11/1997) FL 82+1/6 FLC 7 FAC 6 Others 1

SWAILES Daniel (Danny)
Born: Bolton, 1 April 1979
Height: 6'3" Weight: 13.0

This former Bury trainee looked to have an uncertain future at Gigg Lane at the start of the 1999-2000 season when he found himself played out of position in midfield and attack for the Shakers' reserve team. The departure of Neil Warnock in December 1999, however, brought new opportunities for Danny, with new boss Andy Preece giving the youngster his first-team chance. Injuries to both Andy Woodward and Sam Collins in January saw Danny drafted in at centre half for his full league debut in the away game at Brentford, and he did so well that he retained his place for the majority of the remaining games. With impressive positional sense, Danny is good in the air and is also useful in attack from set pieces, scoring three important goals for the Shakers last term. His progress was rewarded with an extended two-year contract in February.

Bury (From trainee on 9/7/1997) FL 18+6/3 FLC 0+2 FAC 2+1

SWALES Stephen (Steve) Colin
Born: Whitby, 26 December 1973
Height: 5'8" Weight: 10.6

With Hull being so strong in their defensive ranks, Steve had the misfortune of suffering a series of injuries last season. A regular starter in the opening weeks of the campaign, his problems began with a back injury at Brighton. He then picked up a rib injury and flu in October before damaging an achilles tendon in training. Often used at right wing back, although chiefly left footed, Steve created an interesting partnership with Steve Harper – a right-footed left wing back.

Scarborough (From trainee on 3/8/1992) FL 51+3/1 FAC 5 Others 3
Reading (£70,000 on 13/7/1995) FL 33+10/1 FLC 6+1 FAC 6
Hull C (Free on 7/12/1998) FL 37+5 FLC 2+1 Others 2

SWAN Iain
Born: Glasgow, 16 October 1979
Height: 6'3" Weight: 12.6

This Oldham youngster made the starting line-up just once during 1999-2000, appearing in the team for the Worthington Cup tie at home to Stockport back in August. He was subsequently loaned to Unibond League outfit Leigh RMI in February before finishing the campaign back in Scotland with Partick Thistle. A giant centre back of the old-fashioned stopper type, he has a no-nonsense style and good aerial skills. He was released at the end of the season.

Oldham Ath (From trainee on 12/11/1996) FL 1 FLC 1 FAC 0+1
Partick Thistle (Loaned on 17/3/2000) SL 0+2

SWAN Peter Harold
Born: Leeds, 28 September 1966
Height: 6'2" Weight: 15.9
Club Honours: AMC '93

The big defender and occasional striker spent much of the 1999-2000 season on the sidelines with a cruciate ligament injury from the previous campaign. He saw little first-team action for Burnley, where he found it impossible to break into the side on a regular basis, and he was released in February, subsequently joining York, where he teamed up with his former Hull boss, Terry Dolan. Peter's imposing physical presence at the heart of the defence, along with his coolness and experience, led to the Minstermen giving him a contract for the 2000-01 season.

Leeds U (From trainee on 6/8/1984) FL 43+6/11 FLC 3/2 FAC 3 Others 1+2
Hull C (£200,000 on 23/3/1989) FL 76+4/24 FLC 2+3/1 FAC 2 Others 1
Port Vale (£300,000 on 16/8/1991) FL 105+6/5 FLC 6 FAC 9/1 Others 12/1
Plymouth Arg (£300,000 on 22/7/1994) FL 24+3/2 FLC 2/1 FAC 2
Burnley (£200,000 on 4/8/1995) FL 47+2/7 FLC 2 FAC 3 Others 6
Bury (£50,000 on 8/8/1997) FL 26+11/6 FLC 1+1 FAC 1
Burnley (Free on 28/8/1998) FL 11+8
York C (Free on 14/3/2000) FL 9

SYMONS Christopher (Kit) Jeremiah
Born: Basingstoke, 8 March 1971
Height: 6'2" Weight: 13.7
Club Honours: Div 2 '99
International Honours: W: 32; B-1; U21-2; Yth

With four top-class central defenders vying for three places at the back for Fulham in 1999-2000, and Chris Coleman and Andy Melville playing in every game for which they were available, Kit, who had missed only one match the previous season, shared the third spot with Simon Morgan. Kit was as reliable as ever, and his reading of the game and distribution were excellent; however, just one below-par performance (in a 1-0 win!) in early February was sufficient to keep him out of the starting line-up until the penultimate game of the season.

Portsmouth (From trainee on 30/12/1988) FL 161/10 FLC 19 FAC 10 Others 13+1/1
Manchester C (£1,600,000 on 17/8/1995) P/FL 124/4 FLC 6 FAC 9
Fulham (Free on 30/7/1998) FL 72+2/13 FLC 9+1 FAC 11

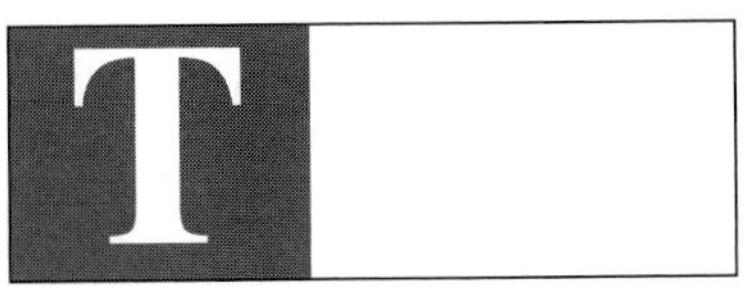

TAAFFE Steven (Steve) Lee
Born: Stoke, 10 September 1979
Height: 5'6" Weight: 9.0
Steven is an exciting winger who, despite his small stature, forced his way into the Stoke first team at the start of 1999-2000 after a series of excellent pre-season performances. When his form faltered slightly he continued to develop in the reserves, having few opportunities under Gary Megson and none under Gudjon Thordarson. Time is on Steven's side, however, and there is little doubt his pace and enthusiasm will ultimately be rewarded.
Stoke C (From trainee on 8/8/1996) FL 3+5 FLC 1

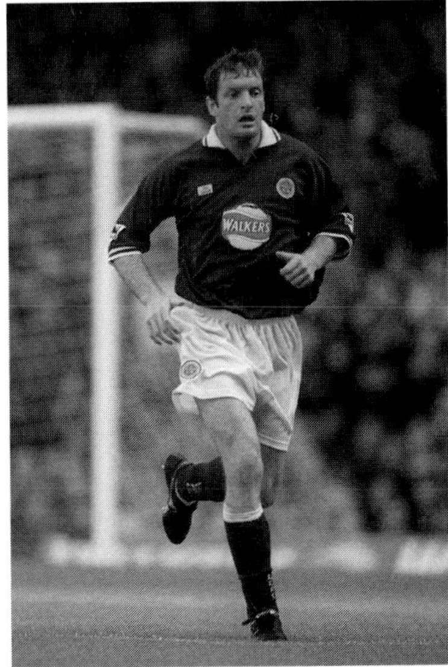

Gerry Taggart

TAGGART Gerald (Gerry) Paul
Born: Belfast, 18 October 1970
Height: 6'1" Weight: 13.12
Club Honours: Div 1 '97; FLC '00
International Honours: NI: 46; U23-2; Yth; Sch
Leicester's left-footed central defender enjoyed an outstanding season in 1999-2000, winning a regular place at the heart of City's defence and earning a cult following among the fans with his knack of popping up with vital strikes. Gerry scored a total of seven goals, including a cracking effort against Tottenham and a fine brace against Sheffield Wednesday. He won a long-overdue recall to the Northern Ireland international squad under new manager Sammy McIlroy in April, and was made captain against Hungary. His solidarity and willingness to get stuck in when the chips were down were key factors in Leicester's Worthington Cup success and he was deservedly voted the Foxes' "Player of the Season".
Manchester C (From trainee on 1/7/1989) FL 10+2/1 Others 1
Barnsley (£75,000 on 10/1/1990) FL 209+3/16 FLC 15/1 FAC 14/2 Others 6/1
Bolton W (£1,500,000 on 1/8/1995) F/PL 68+1/4 FLC 8/1 FAC 4
Leicester C (Free on 23/7/1998) PL 39+7/6 FLC 12+2/2 FAC 6+1

TAIBI Massimo
Born: Palermo, Italy, 18 February 1970
Height: 6'3" Weight: 12.13
This experienced Italian goalkeeper joined Manchester United from Venezia last September, following an injury to Mark Bosnich in United's third Premiership game of the campaign. Although his registration was initially held up due to red tape, he was given a real baptism of fire when he was pitched into the side for the Premiership match against Liverpool at Anfield. With barely a touch of the ball in the opening exchanges, his first job was to pick it out of the net after 23 minutes. After ninety, however, he'd done enough to earn himself the Sky "Man of the Match" award, and was warmly congratulated by his team-mates. After Massimo had held his place for the next four games, the return of Mark Bosnich and the excellent form of Rai van der Gouw meant a swift return to the reserves, and he left to join the Italian side Reggina on loan soon afterwards, declaring that Old Trafford hadn't seen the last of him. However, following the signing of Fabien Barthez from Monaco during the close season, it seemed likely that his future lay away from Old Trafford.
Manchester U (£4,500,000 from Venezia, Italy, via Como, Piacenza and AC Milan on 2/9/1999) PL 4

TAIT Jordan Alexander
Born: Berwick, 27 September 1979
Height: 5'10" Weight: 11.5
This young left back joined Oldham on a free transfer in August 1999 and made his debut in senior football when he came on from the subs' bench for the last 20 minutes of the Worthington Cup tie with Stockport a couple of days later. He made one further appearance as a substitute but found his way blocked by the in-form Andy Holt. Jordan will be aiming to break through into the Latics' first-team squad on a regular basis during the coming season.
Newcastle U (From trainee on 2/7/1998)
Oldham Ath (Free on 19/8/1999) FL 0+1 FLC 0+1

TAIT Paul
Born: Newcastle, 24 October 1974
Height: 6'1" Weight: 11.10
A lively forward signed by Crewe from Conference side Northwich during the summer of 1999, Paul was given his full debut against Portsmouth last November after five substitute appearances and marked the occasion with the second goal in a 2-0 win. Thereafter he missed only two matches, although he was sometimes used as a sub, and he ended the season with 34 appearances (14 as a substitute) and six goals to his credit. He will be looking to build on this promising start in 2000-01.
Everton (From trainee on 8/7/1993)
Wigan Ath (Free on 22/7/1994) FL 1+4 (Free to Runcorn on 16/2/1996)
Crewe Alex (Signed from Northwich Vic on 9/6/1999) FL 19+14/6 FAC 1

TAIT Paul Ronald
Born: Sutton Coldfield, 31 July 1971
Height: 6'1" Weight: 10.10
Club Honours: Div 2 '95; AMC '95
A consistent, competitive midfielder, Paul started the majority of Oxford's games in 1999-2000, winning the ball regularly and passing it with care. He was always willing to start an attack, but with the United forward line drawing blanks on a large number of occasions his work often came to nothing. He did not manage a goal but gave a good account of himself as he enjoyed regular first-team football once again.
Birmingham C (From trainee on 2/8/1988) FL 135+35/14 FLC 13+2 FAC 6+2 Others 13+5/4
Northampton T (Loaned on 24/12/1997) FL 2+1
Oxford U (Free on 15/1/1999) FL 51 FLC 5 FAC 4 Others 2

TALBOT Paul Michael
Born: Gateshead, 11 August 1979
Height: 5'10" Weight: 10.12
Paul moved to York from Newcastle United in March 2000, and made his Football League debut at Peterborough. The left-sided full back or midfielder had been with the Magpies since he was 14, and was snapped up by City after being released by Bobby Robson. His York contract was not renewed in May.
Newcastle U (From trainee on 4/7/1997)
York C (Free on 3/3/2000) FL 5+1

TALBOT Stewart Dean
Born: Birmingham, 14 June 1973
Height: 5'11" Weight: 13.7
Stewart spent the first half of the 1999-2000 season recovering from a double fracture of the right leg sustained towards the end of the previous campaign. He eventually recovered fitness, returning to the Port Vale line-up against QPR in February in an unfamiliar right-back role. Soon afterwards he suffered another injury but he returned for a run of three games towards the end of the season, when he featured in midfield, his regular position. A wholehearted player who covers a lot of ground, Stewart was released on a free transfer at the end of the season.
Port Vale (Signed from Moor Green on 10/8/1994) FL 112+25/10 FLC 4+3 FAC 4+1 Others 2+3/1

TALIA Francesco (Frank)
Born: Melbourne, Australia, 20 July 1972
Height: 6'1" Weight: 13.6
Club Honours: Div 2 '96
Frank continued to be Swindon's first-choice 'keeper in 1999-2000, comfortably seeing off challenges to his position from Steve Mildenhall and Jimmy Glass. However, last season was a disappointing time for him as the Robins were relegated

from the First Division and Frank was informed that his contract would not be renewed when it expired in the summer. Frank is a good shot stopper who shows an excellent command of his area.

Blackburn Rov (Free from Sunshine George Cross, Australia on 28/8/1992)
Hartlepool U (Loaned on 29/12/1992) FL 14 Others 1
Swindon T (£150,000 on 8/9/1995) FL 107 FLC 9 FAC 2

TALLON Gerrit (Gary) Thomas
Born: Drogheda, 5 September 1973
Height: 5'9" Weight: 12.1

Having been one of the mainstays of the Mansfield team in 1998-99, Gary was hampered by injuries last season, suffering a groin strain in mid-September and later picking up a knee injury while attempting a comeback with the reserves. Once fit again, he was used as a squad player for the rest of the season. A good crosser of the ball, he plays on the left side either in midfield or in defence, and likes to get stuck in, which makes him a favourite with those on the terraces.

Blackburn Rov (£30,000 from Drogheda on 27/11/1991)
Kilmarnock (Free on 20/6/1996) SL 4 SLC 1 SC 1
Chester C (Loaned on 26/3/1997) FL 1
Mansfield T (Free on 1/12/1997) FL 68+7/2 FLC 3 FAC 2 Others 5

TANKARD Allen John
Born: Fleet, 21 May 1969
Height: 5'10" Weight: 12.10
International Honours: E: Yth

Port Vale's regular left back proved to be as dependable as ever last season, also filling in in midfield on occasion. Strong in the tackle and never one to give less than 100 per cent, he was rarely out of the team when fit. As one of the Vale's "elder statesmen" (approaching his 450th league appearance), Allen will be looking to help bring some of the youngsters through in 2000-01. He scored just one goal in 1999-2000, a crashing header in the 3-1 victory at Sheffield United in November.

Southampton (From apprentice on 27/5/1987) FL 5 Others 2
Wigan Ath (Free on 4/7/1988) FL 205+4/4 FLC 15/1 FAC 13 Others 20
Port Vale (£87,500 on 26/7/1993) FL 233+9/7 FLC 19 FAC 15/1 Others 8+1

TANN Adam John
Born: Kings Lynn, 12 May 1982
Height: 6'0" Weight: 11.5
International Honours: E: Yth

A product of the Cambridge youth team, this versatile young defender has been with the club since the age of 13. He continued his development with the youth team in 1999-2000 and also played for the reserves. Adam's progress was rewarded with his first-team debut against Barnet in the Auto Windscreens Shield in January and he showed enough promise to suggest that he will become a regular in years to come. He was a regular in the England youth set-up during the season, winning one cap for the U17s and appearing four times for the U18s.

Cambridge U (From trainee on 7/9/1999) Others 1

TARICCO Mauricio Ricardo
Born: Buenos Aires, Argentine, 10 March 1973
Height: 5'9" Weight: 11.7

A versatile full back who favours the right flank, Mauricio had a consistent season for Tottenham in 1999-2000, picking up where he had left off at the end of the previous campaign. He loves to get forward and act as a provider, and he is exceptionally talented for a defender at keeping the ball close to his feet when running at pace. Being able to anticipate the forward pass well, Mauricio favours dropping a yard or two behind the receiving opponent and taking him on with the ball on the ground. He is strong in the challenge and quick to move forward after gaining possession. He supplies the midfield with well-timed passes into the heart of the action and is able to create space around him as he does so. Mauricio will be aiming to continue to provide consistency and creativity for Tottenham in the middle of the park in the coming season.

Ipswich T (£175,000 from Argentinos Juniors, Argentina on 9/9/1994) FL 134+3/4 FLC 18/3 FAC 8 Others 7
Tottenham H (£1,800,000 on 4/12/1998) PL 41+1 FLC 2 FAC 3+1 Others 3

TATE Christopher (Chris) Douglas
Born: York, 27 December 1977
Height: 6'0" Weight: 11.10

Having finished the 1998-99 season as joint top scorer for relegated Scarborough, Chris made a quick return to the Nationwide League when he joined Halifax Town for a club record fee in July 1999. Big and strong, he never seemed out of his depth but he returned to Scarborough in November, the Shaymen recuperating most of their outlay as the original fee was structured in staged payments. Chris is sufficiently talented and young enough to return to the league ranks in the future.

Sunderland (Free from York C juniors on 17/7/1996)
Scarborough (Free on 5/8/1997) FL 21+28/13 FLC 0+1 FAC 0+1 Others 2+1
Halifax T (£150,000 on 5/7/1999) FL 18/4 FLC 2 FAC 2/1

TAYLOR Craig
Born: Plymouth, 24 January 1974
Height: 6'1" Weight: 13.2

Craig appeared as a substitute for Swindon in the opening two games of 1999-2000 and then made the starting line-up for the following match before being sold to Plymouth Argyle – where he had had a spell on loan in October 1998 – with the season only a couple of weeks old. A useful central defender, he is good in the air and a strong tackler, and uses the ball well. Craig went on to become a first-team regular for Argyle, and the supporters were quick to appreciate his value to the team. Craig's contribution included vital strikes against Devon rivals Exeter and Torquay, and he also captained the side on a couple of occasions. Craig is the younger brother of Bristol City's Shaun Taylor.

Exeter C (From trainee on 13/6/1992) FL 2+3 FLC 1 Others 2+2 (Free to Bath C on 18/3/1994)
Swindon T (£25,000 from Dorchester T on 15/4/1997) FL 47+8/2 FLC 0+1 FAC 3
Plymouth Arg (Loaned on 16/10/1998) FL 6/1
Plymouth Arg (£30,000 on 20/8/1999) FL 41/3 FAC 5

TAYLOR Daniel (Danny) John
Born: Oldham, 28 July 1982
Height: 6'0" Weight: 11.10

A second-year trainee at Rochdale, Danny figured in both the youth team and the reserves during the 1999-2000 season, playing on the left-hand side of either attack or defence. With several senior players missing, he was drafted in to the first-team squad for the final match of the season against Barnet and enjoyed a 13-minute run-out as a substitute.

Rochdale (Trainee) FL 0+1

TAYLOR Gareth Keith
Born: Weston super Mare, 25 February 1973
Height: 6'2" Weight: 13.8
International Honours: W: 8; U21-7

Gareth was included in the Manchester City first-team squad at the start of the 1999-2000 season, making two starts in the Worthington Cup, against Burnley and Southampton, and six substitute appearances in the league, scoring three goals. His role as a complementary striker to Shaun Goater was a difficult one in which to achieve consistency, but he stuck at his task and was rewarded with a good run of ten games (two as a substitute), during which he scored three goals. His best match of the season for City was at home against Portsmouth, where he scored two goals in a 4-2 win. The arrival of his namesake Robert from Gillingham pushed Gareth down the strikers' pecking order, and he did not play for City again after coming on as a substitute against Stockport in December. He then went on loan to Port Vale the following month but although he played well on his debut against Birmingham City he failed to produce his best form in subsequent outings. After returning briefly to Maine Road he was loaned to Queens Park Rangers and scored once in six games for the west London club before being injured. On his return to Manchester he was placed on the transfer list.

Bristol Rov (Free from Southampton juniors on 29/7/1991) FL 31+16/16 FLC 3+1 FAC 1+1 Others 5
Crystal Palace (£750,000 on 27/9/1995) FL 18+2/1 FAC 2/1
Sheffield U (Signed on 8/3/1996) FL 56+28/25 FLC 8+3/2 FAC 5+2 Others 1+2
Manchester C (£400,000 on 26/11/1998) FL 28+15/9 FLC 2+1/1 FAC 3 Others 1+3
Port Vale (Loaned on 21/1/2000) FL 4
Queens Park R (Loaned on 14/3/2000) FL 2+4/1

TAYLOR Ian Kenneth
Born: Birmingham, 4 June 1968
Height: 6'1" Weight: 12.4
Club Honours: AMC '93; FLC '96

This versatile Aston Villa player was a near-ever-present in the team for the first half of the 1999-2000 campaign until suffering an ankle injury at the end of January. He then tore a hamstring in the FA Cup semi-final against Bolton Wanderers and only returned to first-team action for the final Premiership game against champions Manchester Untied. He did remarkably well to make the starting line-up for the FA Cup final against Chelsea but failed to inspire his home-town team to victory over the cosmopolitan London side. Ian began the season in a defensive midfield position, but once new signing George Boateng had settled in he was released to play a more attacking role and responded with a spell of six goals in six games around the turn of the year. His strengths include a high workrate, tenacity in the tackle and a commitment to the cause, but above all he is a Villa man through and through, having supported the club from the terraces in his youth.

Port Vale (£15,000 from Moor Green on 13/7/1992) FL 83/28 FLC 4/2 FAC 6/1 Others 13/4
Sheffield Wed (£1,000,000 on 12/7/1994) PL 9+5/1 FLC 2+2/1
Aston Villa (£1,000,000 on 21/12/1994) PL 161+14/21 FLC 16+2/7 FAC 12+2/1 Others 11+1/3

TAYLOR John Patrick
Born: Norwich, 24 October 1964
Height: 6'2" Weight: 13.12
Club Honours: Div 3 '91

Known as the "King of the Abbey", John turned out in three-quarters of Cambridge's games in 1999-2000 while also acting as player-coach and reserve-team manager. He is the most experienced player in the team, and the hat-trick that he scored at Cardiff in April not only ensured United's survival in the Second Division but also saw him become the first player to score a century of goals for the club. John is an excellent example for the club's young strikers, and there is every chance of his name appearing on the score sheet again during the coming season.

Colchester U (From juniors on 17/12/1982)
Cambridge U (Signed from Sudbury T on 24/8/1988) FL 139+21/46 FLC 9+2/2 FAC 21/10 Others 12+2/2
Bristol Rov (Signed on 28/3/1992) FL 91+4/44 FLC 4/1 FAC 3 Others 5
Bradford C (£300,000 on 5/7/1994) FL 35+1/11 FLC 4/2 FAC 2 Others 3
Luton T (£200,000 on 23/3/1995) FL 27+10/3 FLC 2 Others 1/1
Lincoln C (Loaned on 27/9/1996) FL 5/2
Colchester U (Loaned on 8/11/1996) FL 8/5 Others 1
Cambridge U (Free on 10/1/1997) FL 85+50/37 FLC 3+5/2 FAC 5+5/1 Others 1+1/1

TAYLOR Maik Stefan
Born: Hildeshein, Germany, 4 September 1971
Height: 6'4" Weight: 14.2
Club Honours: Div 2 '99
International Honours: NI: 11; B-1; U21-1

Maik had another superb season in the Fulham goal in 1999-2000. An ever-present, he kept 24 clean sheets in all matches. His catching of corners and crosses was quite outstanding and he made many magnificent saves. Only Manchester City conceded fewer goals than Fulham in Division One, and in the entire Football League only Swansea conceded fewer than the Cottagers' 13 at home. Despite the challenge of Wigan's Roy Carroll, Maik remains the regular 'keeper for Northern Ireland, for whom he won a further seven caps last season.

Barnet (Free from Farnborough on 7/6/1995) FL 70 FLC 6 FAC 6 Others 2
Southampton (£500,000 on 1/1/1997) PL 18
Fulham (£800,000 + on 17/11/1997) FL 120 FLC 12 FAC 13 Others 3

TAYLOR Martin
Born: Ashington, 9 November 1979
Height: 6'4" Weight: 15.0
International Honours: E: Yth

This young central defender made a number of appearances for Blackburn during the first half of the 1999-2000 season, including a run of four games in December. Tall and powerfully built, he produced some sound performances before losing out to the more experienced Darren Peacock. Martin then joined Darlington on loan in January to provide cover when both regular centre backs, Neil Aspin and Steve Tutill, were out injured. Although he played only four games, he was never on the losing side and impressed with his neat control and passing ability as well as with his obvious aerial power. He linked up with Adam Reed in the centre of the defence, with whom he had played during his time at Blackburn. He was later loaned to First Division Stockport on transfer deadline day to cover the gap in the centre of the defence left by Jim Gannon's injury. He did well in seven appearances at Edgeley Park and boss Andy Kilner expressed an interest in making the move permanent, although the size of the transfer fee required by Rovers is likely to be an obstacle. Comfortable on the ball and amazingly quick footed for such a big man, Martin has also appeared as a striker when called upon.

Blackburn Rov (From trainee on 13/8/1997) P/FL 4+2 FLC 2 FAC 1 Others 0+1
Darlington (Loaned on 18/1/2000) FL 4
Stockport Co (Loaned on 23/3/2000) FL 7

TAYLOR Martin James
Born: Tamworth, 9 December 1966
Height: 6'0" Weight: 14.6

Martin had an excellent season as Wycombe's goalkeeper in 1999-2000 and proved to be the team's best player on many occasions with several high-quality performances, notably in the two fixtures with Millwall and in the visits to Brentford and Preston. He kicks confidently with both feet and has the ability to make great reflex saves – even when the ball appears to have passed him. Martin signed a new two-year contract in the spring and was deservedly voted "Player of the Year" at the end of the season.

Derby Co (Signed from Mile Oak Rov on 2/7/1986) F/PL 97 FLC 7 FAC 5 Others 11
Carlisle U (Loaned on 23/9/1987) FL 10 FLC 1 FAC 1 Others 2
Scunthorpe U (Loaned on 17/12/1987) FL 8
Crewe Alex (Loaned on 20/9/1996) FL 6
Wycombe W (Free on 27/3/1997) FL 135 FLC 8 FAC 10 Others 4

TAYLOR Matthew Simon
Born: Oxford, 27 November 1981
Height: 5'10" Weight: 11.10

Graduating directly from Luton's youth team to the senior side, Matthew made his league debut on the opening day of the 1999-2000 season and retained his place for the rest of the campaign, starting all but a handful of Town's matches. A fast-raiding midfielder or wing back, he is deadly with either foot and can terrorise defenders with a series of well-delivered crosses and corners. After notching up a couple of goals in pre-season games, he opened his league account with a stunner, which could have been a contender for "Goal of the Season" in the win against Wrexham in September. A constant attacking menace, he hit the woodwork twice with powerful strikes in the match against Oxford United. He has signed a new three-year contract with the club, and looks set for a very bright future in the game.

Luton T (From trainee on 9/2/1999) FL 39+2/4 FLC 1 FAC 5/1

TAYLOR Robert (Bob)
Born: Horden, 3 February 1967
Height: 5'10" Weight: 12.12

An eternal crowd favourite, Bob found himself competing with Dean Holdsworth and Bo Hansen for the right to partner the talented Eidur Gudjohnsen up front for Bolton in 1999-2000. Despite a poor goal return his wholehearted performances ensured he retained the fans' affections at the Reebok Stadium, but new manager Sam Allardyce allowed him to leave for his former club West Bromwich Albion on transfer deadline day. Returning to the Hawthorns on a three-year contract, he immediately lifted spirits at the club and, more importantly, was quickly back in business netting some vital goals, including his 100th league goal for the Albion. His tally of five included both in the crucial 2-1 home win over Grimsby Town and the clincher against Charlton on the final day of the campaign which earned Albion a 2-0 victory to ensure their First Division status. Powerful in the air and no mean player on the ground, he unfortunately managed just a couple of games playing alongside Lee Hughes, but this coming season, acting as the main target man, he should be just as effective as a goal-maker as he was as a goalscorer in the mid-1990s. The Albion will certainly be hoping so … and they will be looking for him to continue to find the net like always.

Leeds U (Free from Horden Colliery on 27/3/1986) FL 33+9/9 FLC 5+1/3 FAC 1 Others 4+1/1
Bristol C (£175,000 on 23/3/1989) FL 96+10/50 FLC 6+1/2 FAC 9+1/5 Others 3/1
West Bromwich A (£300,000 on 31/1/1992) FL 211+27/96 FLC 16/6 FAC 6+2/3 Others 16+3/8
Bolton W (Free on 8/1/1998) P/FL 57+20/21 FLC 6+5/2 FAC 4+1/2 Others 3/2
West Bromwich A (£90,000 on 23/3/2000) FL 8/5

TAYLOR Robert Anthony
Born: Norwich, 30 April 1971
Height: 6'1" Weight: 13.8

This classy striker began the 1999-2000 season on the bench for Gillingham but soon hit top form, netting hat-tricks in the home games with Wrexham and Bristol City. He had been tracked for some time by Premiership hopefuls Manchester City and after hitting a particularly hot streak with ten goals from six games he was sold to the Maine Road club for a £1.5 million fee last November. Apart from an obvious eye for goal, Robert has some neat touches, good passing ability and a useful right-foot shot. The big-framed forward also shields the ball well and has a deceptive turn. Robert made his City debut at Wolverhampton, where he performed well considering he had only arrived at Maine Road two days before. He was troubled by injuries during the remainder of the campaign and his appearances were somewhat spasmodic. However, he scored important goals at Nottingham Forest and Crystal Palace, and started in the last three games of the campaign, scoring twice as City clinched the second automatic promotion place.

Norwich C (From trainee on 26/3/1990)
Leyton Orient (Loaned on 28/3/1991) FL 0+3/1
Birmingham C (Signed on 31/8/1991)
Leyton Orient (Free on 21/10/1991) FL 54+19/20 FLC 1+1 FAC 2+1 Others 2+1
Brentford (£100,000 on 24/3/1994) FL 172+1/56 FLC 16/6 FAC 10/8 Others 14/4
Gillingham (£500,000 on 6/8/1998) FL 56+2/31 FLC 2+1/1 FAC 3/2 Others 7/5
Manchester C (£1,500,000 on 30/11/1999) FL 14+2/5

TAYLOR Scott Dean
Born: Portsmouth, 28 November 1970
Height: 5'9" Weight: 11.8
Club Honours: Div 2 '94; FLC '97

After two seasons out of action with a serious knee injury Scott was released by Leicester City in the summer of 1999 and accepted an invitation to join Wolves for a pre-season tour of Sweden. He had the misfortune to suffer yet more injury problems, but they happily proved less serious and in September he returned to senior football for the first time since April 1997. He scored one and made the other in the 2-1 win at Barnsley the following month but then found himself relegated to the subs' bench. He had another injury scare when he damaged lateral knee ligaments at Blackburn in January but he was fit again by the middle of February when he featured in the starting line-up against Tranmere. His positive attitude endeared him to the club's supporters, who also appreciated the fact that he got stuck into the tackle. Scott was out of contract in the summer but signed a new deal that will keep him at Molineux for a further 12 months.

Reading (From trainee on 22/6/1989) FL 164+43/24 FLC 7+5/1 FAC 11+2/3 Others 12+4/1
Leicester C (£250,000 on 12/7/1995) P/FL 59+5/6 FLC 7+3 FAC 2+1 Others 3
Wolverhampton W (Free on 23/9/1999) FL 18+10/3

TAYLOR Scott James
Born: Chertsey, 5 May 1976
Height: 5'10" Weight: 11.4

Scott enjoyed a consistent 1999-2000 season with Tranmere, scoring some useful goals and winning a Worthington Cup runners-up medal after making the starting line-up for the final against Leicester. Operating as a striker, he showed himself to be a cool finisher with excellent control and the ability to confuse opposition defenders by producing the unexpected. His build-up play was again impressive, as was his willingness to work hard for the team.

Millwall (£15,000 from Staines on 8/2/1995) FL 13+15 FLC 0+2/2 FAC 1+1
Bolton W (£150,000 on 29/3/1996) P/FL 2+10/1 FLC 0+4/1 FAC 1/1
Rotherham U (Loaned on 12/12/1997) FL 10/3 Others 1
Blackpool (Loaned on 26/3/1998) FL 3+2/1
Tranmere Rov (£50,000 on 9/10/1998) FL 54+17/12 FLC 10/4 FAC 2+3

TAYLOR Shaun
Born: Plymouth, 26 February 1963
Height: 6'1" Weight: 13.0
Club Honours: Div 4 '90; Div 2 '96

Shaun has proved an inspirational figure in the centre of defence for Bristol City ever since he arrived at the club in 1996. However, having only returned to fitness from a previous long-term injury in April 1999, he had the misfortune to miss a large part of the 1999-2000 campaign after suffering another cruciate injury. He is a model professional who has endeared himself to the Ashton Gate fans, and his never-say-die attitude will not be lost despite doubts over his fitness. Shaun is one of a number of senior players at the club whose experience is being put to good use as he has been appointed as senior coach in tandem with ex-City player Leroy Rosenior, although he is still intending to play at first-team level in the new campaign. Shaun is the older brother of Plymouth's Craig Taylor.

Exeter C (Free from Bideford T on 10/12/1986) FL 200/16 FLC 12 FAC 9 Others 12
Swindon T (£200,000 on 26/7/1991) F/PL 212/30 FLC 22+1/2 FAC 14 Others 10/1
Bristol C (£50,000 + on 6/9/1996) FL 105/7 FLC 8/2 FAC 8/1 Others 5

TAYLOR Stuart James
Born: Romford, 28 November 1980
Height: 6'4" Weight: 13.4
International Honours: E: Yth

This young Arsenal goalkeeper had a spell on loan at Bristol Rovers last autumn and looked confident in his four league games for the Pirates, which included a Bristol derby in which he kept a clean sheet. He appears to have a bright future ahead of him, but may have to seek further experience on loan with other clubs before making his mark at Highbury. Previously capped by England at U16 and U18 levels, he will be looking to win a place in the U21 squad in the near future.

Arsenal (From trainee on 8/7/1998)
Bristol Rov (Loaned on 24/9/1999) FL 4

TEALE Shaun
Born: Southport, 10 March 1964
Height: 6'0" Weight: 13.8
Club Honours: FLC '94
International Honours: E: SP-1

Recruited by Carlisle from Motherwell last February to bolster the Cumbrians' defence, Shaun brought a wealth of top-flight experience with him to Brunton Park. Once he had adjusted to life in Division Three, he gave some commanding performances, not least in the vital relegation battles in April against Chester and Exeter, where he looked in a different class to most others on the pitch. Shaun was especially dominant in the air, while his distribution skills were an object lesson to anybody who saw them. After he had been overlooked for the vacant manager's post in May, it seemed unlikely that he would return for the new campaign.

Bournemouth (£50,000 from Weymouth on 22/1/1989) FL 99+1/4 FLC 8 FAC 5/1 Others 3
Aston Villa (£300,000 on 25/7/1991) P/FL 146+1/2 FLC 15/3 FAC 13 Others 6
Tranmere Rov (£450,000 on 14/8/1995) FL 54 FLC 8 (Free to Happy Valley, Hong Kong on 15/8/1997)
Preston NE (Loaned on 6/2/1997) FL 5
Motherwell (Free on 7/8/1998) SL 47/4 SLC 4/1 SC 3
Carlisle U (Loaned on 4/2/2000) FL 18 Others 2

TELFER Paul Norman
Born: Edinburgh, 21 October 1971
Height: 5'9" Weight: 11.6
International Honours: S: 1; B-2; U21-3

This solid and dependable Scot had another good season at Coventry in 1999-2000. After a sluggish start to the campaign on the right of midfield he lost his place, only to be called in at right back after Marc Edworthy's injury. Despite criticism from a section of the fans Paul performed well in an unaccustomed role and always gave 100 per cent. He twisted a knee at Old Trafford in February and was out for six weeks before returning to first-team action when Tomas Gustafsson was injured. His consistent form was rewarded with a full Scottish cap in March against World Champions France when manager Craig Brown was full of praise.

Luton T (From trainee on 7/11/1988) FL 136+8/19 FLC 5 FAC 14/2 Others 2/1
Coventry C (£1,500,000 on 11/7/1995) PL 151+9/6 FLC 13/2 FAC 14+3/4

TENNEBO Thomas
Born: Bergen, Norway, 19 March 1975
Height: 6'2" Weight: 12.2

A trialist from Norwegian Second Division club Fana, Thomas impressed Hartlepool manager Chris Turner so much that he was given a two-year contract at the beginning of the 1999-2000 season. In a short first-team run, he showed some good touches with his bursts from midfield. It was decided that he needed to build up his fitness if he was to adapt to the English game, and he had further success in the reserves. Thomas was unable to win back a regular senior place, and made only occasional first-team appearances during the remainder of his first season.

Hartlepool U (Free from Fana, Norway on 13/8/1999) FL 6+5 FLC 1 Others 1

TERRY John George
Born: Barking, 7 December 1980
Height: 6'0" Weight: 12.4
Club Honours: FAC '00

This highly promising young centre back made enormous strides at Chelsea during the 1999-2000 season and always looked comfortable whenever pitched into first-team action. He scored his first senior goal with a bullet header against Gillingham in the FA Cup quarter-final before joining First Division Nottingham Forest on loan shortly before transfer deadline day to gain further experience. Although he was initially hampered by a broken toe, John started five games for the Reds and added a further appearance as a substitute before returning to Stamford Bridge. His season finished on a high note when he was selected as one of Chelsea's substitutes for the FA Cup final at Wembley, where he collected a winners' medal. A precocious talent, John has the benefit of learning his trade from Chelsea's wealth of top-class international central defenders and is being groomed to play a major role in the Blues' pursuit of honours during the coming decade.
Chelsea (From trainee on 18/3/1998) PL 2+4 FLC 1+1 FAC 4+3/1 Others 1
Nottingham F (Loaned on 23/3/2000) FL 5+1

TESSEM Jo
Born: Orlandet, Norway, 28 February 1972
Height: 6'3" Weight: 12.10
A police officer in Norway before his transfer to Southampton in November 1999, Jo was first spotted by the Saints when he played against them in a pre-season tour match at Molde. He made the move to England after the Norwegians' exit from the Champions' League. Having played as a striker in his homeland, he proved his versatility on his debut against Tottenham by operating in an unaccustomed right-back position. However, it was in an attacking midfield role that Jo was to shine – his winning goals against Everton and Sheffield Wednesday went a long way towards repaying the £600,000 fee. At the time of writing he had yet to make his Norwegian international debut, but without doubt he will take the step up soon.
Southampton (£600,000 from Molde, Norway on 19/11/1999) PL 23+2/4 FLC 1 FAC 2

TESTIMITANU Ivan
Born: Moldova, 27 April 1974
Height: 5'10" Weight: 11.2
International Honours: Moldova: 30
Although he recovered from the serious knee injury he sustained at the Hawthorns the previous season, the 1999-2000 campaign proved a big disappointment for Bristol City's Moldovan international. He fought his way back into the City side and scored some vital goals, but was unable to recapture the outstanding form he had displayed prior to his injury, when he had been a vital member of the team as a midfield ball winner and provider, his total commitment endearing him to the Robins' fans. A £225,000 signing from FC Zimbru, where he had been a member of a team which regularly won the Moldovan league championship, Ivan lost his place at Ashton Gate towards the end of the season. He remained a regular in his country's national team, winning further caps against Armenia, Slovakia, San Marino and Russia last season.
Bristol C (£225,000 from FC Zimbru Chisinau, Moldova on 24/12/1998) FL 19+5/2 FAC 3+1 Others 3

THATCHER Benjamin (Ben) David
Born: Swindon, 30 November 1975
Height: 5'10" Weight: 12.7
International Honours: E: U21-4; Yth
A natural leader, Ben is an old-fashioned, tough, no-nonsense left back who invariably gives his all. He seemed well qualified to fill the problem position on England's left flank last season, and was perhaps a little unfortunate to miss out on a call-up to the squad in the autumn. He was again hampered by injuries, and the Dons will be hoping he has a clear run during the coming season as they attempt to make an immediate return to the Premiership. Ben has consistently improved year on year at Wimbledon and, all things being equal, should be pressing for an England place this season. He possesses a fine left foot and has the determination, vision and ability to make overlapping runs from defence against even the strongest opposition.
Millwall (From trainee on 8/6/1992) FL 87+3/1 FLC 6 FAC 7 Others 1
Wimbledon (£1,840,00 on 5/7/1996) PL 82+4 FLC 12 FAC 5

THEOBALD David John
Born: Cambridge, 15 December 1978
Height: 6'3" Weight: 12.0
This tall centre half signed for Brentford during the 1999 close season after spending three years as a professional at Ipswich Town without seeing first-team action. David made his league debut as a substitute against Cardiff City last September and had a brief run in the first team playing in the right-back position. He will be looking to extend his experience over the coming season and to win a regular place in the Bees' first-team squad.
Ipswich T (From trainee on 2/6/1997)
Brentford (Free on 8/7/1999) FL 6+4 Others 1

THETIS Jean-Manuel (Manu)
Born: Dijon, France, 5 November 1971
Height: 6'3" Weight: 14.12
Manu started last season on the right of a three-man central defensive unit at Ipswich and was a key figure in the club's successful start to the campaign. He appeared to carry the can for the poor defensive display in the home game with Queens Park Rangers, however, and this together with a bad achilles injury meant that he made only four further appearances. He retains his popularity with the fans, who love it when he makes one of his surges upfield and links up with the attack.
Ipswich T (£50,000 from Seville, Spain on 11/9/1998) FL 44+3/2 FLC 5/1 FAC 2 Others 2+1

THIRLWELL Paul
Born: Washington, 13 February 1979
Height: 5'11" Weight: 11.4
This young midfielder has made good progress at Sunderland since making his debut in the club's First Division championship season in 1998-99. Paul spent two months on loan at Swindon at the beginning of last season; he impressed in the 12 games he played for the Robins, but was recalled to the North-east when the Premiership club faced an injury crisis among their midfield players. He went on to become something of a lucky mascot for the Black Cats, making eight appearances and not finishing on the losing side until the final day of the season when Sunderland lost 1-3 at Spurs. Indeed, one of his best displays was in the 4-1 demolition of Chelsea at the Stadium of Light in December when he gave a commanding performance against such illustrious opponents. Paul's main attributes are his sensible use of the ball and his self-confidence, which is reflected in his willingness to shoot for goal at any opportunity. A regular first-team place looks to be a real possibility for Paul in the near future.
Sunderland (From trainee on 14/4/1997) P/FL 8+2 FLC 2+1 FAC 0+1
Swindon T (Loaned on 8/9/1999) FL 12

THOGERSEN Thomas
Born: Copenhagen, Denmark, 2 April 1968
Height: 6'2" Weight: 12.10
This experienced Dane switched from a right-wing-back role to midfield for Portsmouth in 1999-2000 with considerable success. He showed some useful skills and contributed five goals, including a double in the 5-1 victory over Walsall last October. Hamstring trouble kept him out for two months but he returned to the Pompey line-up in the new year and remained a regular until the end of the season. Thomas is strong and physical in his approach to the game and possesses a tremendous right foot.
Portsmouth (£100,000 from Brondby, Denmark, via Frem, on 5/8/1998) FL 61+8/5 FLC 5 FAC 0+1

THOM Stuart Paul
Born: Dewsbury, 27 December 1976
Height: 6'2" Weight: 11.12
Stuart had the misfortune to suffer a broken collarbone playing for Oldham at Luton last October and this caused him to miss a large part of the 1999-2000 campaign. It was not until April that he returned to the first team and then he was employed as an experimental target man, where his height proved effective. He was previously known as a strong central defender who kicks well with either foot, and it will be interesting to see whether Latics boss Andy Ritchie switches him permanently to a striker's role during the coming season.
Nottingham F (From trainee on 11/1/1994)
Mansfield T (Loaned on 24/12/1997) FL 5 Others 2
Oldham Ath (£45,000 on 21/10/1998) FL 28+6/3 FLC 1 FAC 1 Others 1

THOMAS Daniel (Danny) Justin
Born: Leamington, 1 May 1981
Height: 5'7" Weight: 10.10
Danny was thrust into Leicester's first-team squad to cover for a long injury list in the middle of the 1999-2000 season and acquitted himself well during his three

substitute appearances. A left-sided wing back, the youngster shows plenty of promise and will be looking to win a regular squad place next season.

Leicester C (Free from Nottingham F juniors on 13/5/1998) PL 0+3

THOMAS David (Dai) John
Born: Caerphilly, 26 September 1975
Height: 5'10" Weight: 12.7
Club Honours: Div 2 '98
International Honours: W: U21-2

After scoring a number of crucial goals to help Cardiff City earn promotion in 1998-99 Dai struggled to make an impact last season. One reason for this appeared to be that he was generally paired up front with Kevin Nugent, a player of very similar style in that both are strong, aggressive target men who need to play alongside a contrasting striker to get the best out of them. Dai started the season at centre forward against Millwall, but was taken off at half time in the 1-1 draw and never really got back into the groove after that. He was given a free transfer at the end of the season, even though he had two years of his contract to run. However, he seemed determined to train hard through the summer and battle his way back into contention at Ninian Park.

Swansea C (From trainee on 25/7/1994) FL 36+20/10 FLC 2 FAC 0+1 Others 5+3/3
Watford (£100,000 on 17/7/1997) FL 8+8/3 FAC 1+3
Cardiff C (£50,000 on 20/8/1998) FL 21+10/5 FAC 0+3 Others 1

THOMAS Geoffrey (Geoff) Robert
Born: Manchester, 5 August 1964
Height: 6'1" Weight: 13.2
Club Honours: FMC '91; Div 1 '98
International Honours: E: 9; B-3

Geoff joined up with former boss Dave Bassett at Barnsley in the summer of 1999 but was still recovering from an injury at the start of 1999-2000. He made his debut for his new club in the Worthington Cup tie at Stockport in mid-September but again spent much of his season struggling to overcome a series of niggling injuries. When fit, he showed that he remains a powerful midfield player with a good left foot and is still capable of scoring the odd goal or two. He will be hoping to finally get a break from the injuries that have plagued his career in the coming season.

Rochdale (Free from Littleborough on 13/8/1982) FL 10+1/1 Others 0+1
Crewe Alex (Free on 22/3/1984) FL 120+5/20 FLC 8 FAC 2 Others 2+1
Crystal Palace (£50,000 on 8/6/1987) F/PL 192+3/26 FLC 24/3 FAC 13+1/2 Others 15+1/4
Wolverhampton W (£800,000 on 18/6/1993) FL 36+10/8 FLC 1 FAC 1 Others 6
Nottingham F (Free on 18/7/1997) P/FL 18+7/4 FLC 2/1
Barnsley (Free on 1/7/1999) FL 13+14/4 FLC 2 FAC 1 Others 0+2

THOMAS James Alan
Born: Swansea, 16 January 1979
Height: 6'0" Weight: 13.0
International Honours: W: U21-10

James is a highly rated young Blackburn Rovers striker who was loaned to Blackpool last March to gain experience. He is pacy and showed good ability both in the air and on the ground. He scored his first-ever league goal for the Seasiders with a brave diving header at Colchester.

Blackburn Rov (From trainee on 2/7/1996)
Blackpool (Loaned on 21/3/2000) FL 9/2

THOMAS Martin Russell
Born: Lymington, 12 September 1973
Height: 5'8" Weight: 12.6
Club Honours: Div 3 '00

A very popular player with the Swansea supporters due to his commitment and drive from midfield, Martin suffered a head injury early in the 1999-2000 season at Millwall in the Worthington Cup that kept him out of action for a couple of games. Limited to a substitute role midway through the term, Martin came off the bench at Peterborough to score the first Swans goal, starting a memorable comeback that earned them a 3-2 win. A tireless worker around the field, Martin is always looking to score goals from midfield, and his shooting ability from the edge of the penalty area is a feature of his game. His efforts were rewarded with a Third Division championship winners' medal.

Southampton (From trainee on 19/6/1992)
Leyton Orient (Free on 24/3/1994) FL 5/2
Fulham (Free on 21/7/1994) FL 59+31/8 FLC 6+1 FAC 4/1 Others 7+1/2
Swansea C (Free on 30/7/1998) FL 58+12/7 FLC 6 FAC 4/2 Others 4/1

THOMAS Mitchell Anthony
Born: Luton, 2 October 1964
Height: 6'2" Weight: 13.0
International Honours: E: B-1; U21-3; Yth

Widely considered a standby signing when he joined Burnley in the summer of 1999, Mitchell proved to be not only an automatic choice for the Clarets but a leading contender for the club's "Player of the Year" award. He was a commanding figure in the back line, where his experience proved an asset as he resumed his partnership with Steve Davis that had first been forged at Luton. Although he was a danger man going forward and a threat at set pieces, Mitchell's value to the side was undoubtedly as part of the three-man central defence favoured by Stan Ternent, and his authority, positional sense and coolness were major factors in the improvement in Burnley's goals-against tally during 1999-2000.

Luton T (From apprentice on 27/8/1982) FL 106+1/1 FLC 5 FAC 18
Tottenham H (£233,000 on 7/7/1986) FL 136+21/6 FLC 28+1/1 FAC 12/1
West Ham U (£525,000 on 7/8/1991) FL 37+1/3 FLC 5 FAC 4 Others 2
Luton T (Free on 12/11/1993) FL 170+15/5 FLC 12+1 FAC 6 Others 5+1
Burnley (Free on 2/7/1999) FL 44 FLC 2 FAC 4 Others 1

THOMAS Roderick (Rod) Clive
Born: Harlesden, 10 October 1970
Height: 5'5" Weight: 11.0
Club Honours: FAYC '89; Div 3 '95; AMC '97
International Honours: E: U21-1; Yth; Sch

The lively winger struggled to regain his form after recovering from an ankle injury suffered in 1998-99. Rod began last season in the Brighton starting eleven, and scored in the opening-day 6-0 victory over Mansfield. He soon lost his place, though, and subsequently suffered a stop-start campaign. Rod was put on the transfer list in May, although Albion will demand a fee.

Watford (From trainee on 3/5/1988) FL 63+21/9 FLC 3+2 FAC 0+1 Others 3+1
Gillingham (Loaned on 27/3/1992) FL 8/1 Others 1
Carlisle U (Free on 12/7/1993) FL 124+22/16 FLC 11+1/3 FAC 9+4 Others 22+4/9
Chester C (Free on 4/7/1997) FL 28+16/7 FLC 3+2 FAC 2
Brighton & Hove A (£25,000 on 8/10/1998) FL 25+21/4 FLC 2 FAC 2+1

THOMAS Stephen (Steve)
Born: Hartlepool, 23 June 1979
Height: 5'10" Weight: 12.0
International Honours: W: Yth

This highly thought of Wrexham youngster was again dogged by injuries in 1999-2000 and, although he appeared as a substitute in the Worthington Cup tie against Preston last August, his next first-team action was not until January, when he played in an FAW Premier Cup tie. He was a regular on the subs' bench in the final matches of the season and came on twice, against Bristol City and Colchester. Stephen is a strong and combative midfield player who looks to have a great future in the game.

Wrexham (From trainee on 4/7/1997) FL 1+6 FLC 0+1

THOMAS Wayne
Born: Walsall, 28 August 1978
Height: 5'9" Weight: 12.10

A midfielder who is noted for his perceptive long passes and is comfortable in possession, Wayne started the 1999-2000 season on loan at Mansfield but was allowed to return to Walsall in September as the Stags' injury problems eased. His steadying influence and experience were very valuable in some of the early matches, but he became surplus to requirements with the arrival of Mark Blake. Although he made only one appearance from the subs' bench at Bescot, he was praised by manager Ray Graydon for his positive attitude. Wayne joined Shrewsbury in January on a free transfer after a spell on loan. A skilful midfielder who battles well for the ball, he is confident going forward and took responsibility for converting a vital point-winning penalty at Carlisle. Wayne is seen as a good investment for the future.

Walsall (From trainee on 25/7/1996) FL 18+20 FLC 0+1 FAC 2 Others 1+4/1
Mansfield T (Loaned on 6/8/1999) FL 4+1
Shrewsbury T (Free on 20/1/2000) FL 11+2/1

THOMAS Wayne Junior Robert
Born: Gloucester, 17 May 1979
Height: 5'11" Weight: 11.12

This young Torquay central defender enjoyed another fine season in 1999-2000 and continues to attract the attention of bigger clubs. Wayne kept many an experienced centre forward quiet during the Gulls' Third Division campaign. Although now settled on the right side of United's three-man central defensive unit, he has played in a variety of positions. Stop Press: Wayne was reported to have been transferred to Stoke at the beginning of June.

Torquay U (From trainee on 4/7/1997) FL 89+34/5 FLC 2+1/1 FAC 7/1 Others 6+4

THOME Emerson August
Born: Porto Alegre, Brazil, 30 March 1972
Height: 6'1" Weight: 13.4

This impressive Brazilian centre back was the subject of transfer speculation at Sheffield Wednesday during the 1999 close season and this seemed to have an unsettling effect on him in the opening games of 1999-2000. He remained a cult figure with the Owls' supporters but just as he began to hit a run of good form he was sold to Premiership rivals Chelsea last December. Emerson is a traditional "stopper" central defender who is good in the tackle and very comfortable on the ball. His presence was badly missed by the Hillsborough club in the second half of the campaign. Chelsea's boss Gianluca Vialli made his move in the wake of the central defensive crisis that struck the Blues when they lost Marcel Desailly, Jes Hogh and Frank Leboeuf through various causes following the home defeat by Leeds, and signed the Brazilian for a bargain £2.5 million – half the price quoted by Wednesday five months previously. Nicknamed "The Wall", he certainly proved to be a lucky omen for the Blues and did not taste defeat until his 17th first-team outing, which came, ironically, at Hillsborough against his old club. He made just one Champions' League appearance, replacing the suspended Leboeuf for the home quarter-final tie against Barcelona, where he gave a masterly performance against Patrick Kluivert, Rivaldo et al. Unfortunately for "Emmo", he appeared for Wednesday in a third-round FA Cup tie against Bristol City and so missed out on a place in Chelsea's victorious Wembley side. More Continental than Brazilian in style, Emerson is physically strong, quick and comfortable on the ball. He faces a tough challenge to gain a regular spot at Stamford Bridge with the French World Cup-winning pair barring his way, but he showed enough ability in his first half-season at Chelsea to give Vialli pleasant selection problems. The Blues' qualification for the UEFA Cup will ensure that the famed rotation policy comes into force, and Emerson is certain to figure prominently as Chelsea chase more silverware.

Sheffield Wed (Free from Benfica, Portugal on 23/3/1998) PL 60+1/1 FLC 5+1 FAC 4/1
Chelsea (£2,700,000 on 23/12/1999) PL 18+2 Others 1

THOMPSON Alan
Born: Newcastle, 22 December 1973
Height: 6'0" Weight: 12.8
Club Honours: Div 1 '97
International Honours: E: U21-2; Yth

Alan began 1999-2000 as a regular in the Aston Villa line-up but then lost his place at the beginning of November. He returned to the first team only in the last weeks of the season but failed to make even the subs' bench for the FA Cup final. He scored two goals – a crucial last-minute winner in his comeback game at Sheffield Wednesday and another in the 2-2 draw with Leicester. Villa mostly employed him on the left side of midfield, where his strength in delivering quality crosses was put to good use. Alan is also a dead-ball expert of some repute and will be looking to finally win a regular first-team place at Villa Park in 2000-01.

Newcastle U (From trainee on 11/3/1991) FL 13+3 FAC 1 Others 3
Bolton W (£250,000 on 22/7/1993) P/FL 143+14/33 FLC 24+1/5 FAC 6+2/2 Others 7+1/1
Aston Villa (£4,500,000 on 12/6/1998) PL 36+10/4 FLC 3+3/1 FAC 1 Others 3

THOMPSON Andrew (Andy) Richard
Born: Cannock, 9 November 1967
Height: 5'5" Weight: 10.1
Club Honours: Div 4 '88, Div 3 '89; AMC '88

This experienced Tranmere left back had a disappointing time in 1999-2000; he was sent off for a second yellow-card offence in the third game of the season against Huddersfield and found his first-team oppurtunities restricted by a series of injuries. He then missed the last few months of the campaign with ligament trouble and was released on a free transfer in the summer. At his best he is a diligent, consistent defender who is more effective as an organiser than as a creative force.

West Bromwich A (From apprentice on 16/11/1985) FL 18+6/1 FLC 0+1 FAC 2 Others 1+1
Wolverhampton W (£35,000 on 21/11/1986) FL 356+20/43 FLC 22 FAC 20/1 Others 33/1
Tranmere Rov (Free on 21/7/1997) FL 91+5/4 FLC 13+1 FAC 5+1

THOMPSON Barry Crawford
Born: Glasgow, 12 July 1975
Height: 6'1" Weight: 12.12

Barry joined Carlisle from Icelandic football on non-contract terms last October. He became United's fifth goalkeeper in eight matches when he appeared in the FA Cup tie against Dr Martens League club Ilkeston Town last October. Despite his efforts the Cumbrians lost the match 1-2 and Barry eventually moved back to Scotland, where he made three appearances for Ross County later in the season.

Dundee (Signed from Aviemore Thistle on 13/8/1993)
East Fife (Free on 13/10/1997) SL 1
Montrose (Free on 5/2/1998) SL 0+1 (Free to Carnustie Panmuir on 22/10/1998)
East Stirling (Free on 12/12/1998) SL 19 SC 1 (Free to Thor A on 17/5/1999)
Carlisle U (Free on 1/10/1999) FAC 1

THOMPSON David Anthony
Born: Birkenhead, 12 September 1977
Height: 5'7" Weight: 10.0
Club Honours: FAYC '96
International Honours: E: U21-8; Yth

David first emerged as a possible star of the future towards the end of the 1997-98 season, but last season he really began to show that he deserves all the praise that has come his way as he became a regular in the Liverpool first team. Unfortunately, he then ran into disciplinary problems but after a spell with the academy team he returned to show greater maturity and commitment in his game. A regular in the England U21 set-up, he added a further five caps during the season.

Liverpool (From trainee on 8/11/1994) PL 24+24/5 FLC 5 FAC 0+1 Others 2
Swindon T (Loaned on 21/11/1997) FL 10

David Thompson

THOMPSON Glyn William
Born: Telford, 24 February 1981
Height: 6'1" Weight: 12.4

This young goalkeeper added just one senior game for Shrewsbury last season, in a Worthington Cup tie at home to Sheffield United, before the club decided to cash in on his huge potential and he was sold to Fulham for a substantial fee in October. The Cottagers then allowed Glyn to go to Mansfield on a three-month loan starting in January after another injury to Ian Bowling. He was thrown in at the deep end, arriving in Mansfield for the first time on the morning of his debut against Southend United. Not surprisingly, he showed some nerves at first, but he settled in well and did not let the club down with some confident handling of the ball and neat shot stopping. Glyn has a fine stature for a goalkeeper and the determination to succeed. Shrewsbury supporters will be looking out for his progress.

Shrewsbury T (From trainee on 14/12/1998) FL 1 FLC 1
Fulham (£50,000 on 20/11/1999)
Mansfield T (Loaned on 21/1/2000) FL 16

THOMPSON Marc
Born: York, 15 January 1982
Height: 5'10" Weight: 12.3

A locally born lad who has come through the youth ranks at York, Marc was handed his senior debut in Terry Dolan's first game in charge, at Plymouth, in February 2000.

Equally at home on the right side of defence or midfield, the hard-tackling youngster created an immediate impression and should have a bright future. Marc was rewarded with a new contract at the end of the campaign.

York C (Trainee) FL 9+1

THOMPSON Neil
Born: Beverley, 2 October 1963
Height: 5'10" Weight: 13.8
Club Honours: GMVC '87; Div 2 '92
International Honours: E: SP-4

Neil had a nightmare first season as player-manager of York in 1999-2000. As he and his team struggled to come to terms with Third Division football, he was under pressure from September. He was dismissed in February with the club languishing in 21st place. Neil made only a handful of first-team appearances because of a troublesome calf injury, but always led by example. He eventually moved to one of his former clubs, Scarborough, in the closing weeks of the season on a non-contract basis.

Hull C (Free from Nottingham F juniors on 28/11/1981) FL 29+2
Scarborough (Free on 1/8/1983) FL 87/15 FLC 8/1 FAC 4 Others 9/1
Ipswich T (£100,000 on 9/6/1989) F/PL 199+7/19 FLC 14+1/1 FAC 17/1 Others 8/2
Barnsley (Free on 14/6/1996) F/PL 27/5 FLC 4 FAC 1
Oldham Ath (Loaned on 24/12/1997) FL 8
York C (Free on 2/3/1998) FL 42/8 FLC 2/1

THOMPSON Philip (Phil) Paul
Born: Blackpool, 1 April 1981
Height: 5'11" Weight: 12.0

This young Blackpool central defender had a disappointing 1999-2000 season after failing to build on the promise he showed during the previous campaign. He made just three starts for the Seasiders, all in the opening matches of the season, and was otherwise restricted to reserve-team football. Phil will be aiming to win a regular place in the first-team squad for the coming season.

Blackpool (From trainee on 4/9/1998) FL 21+5/2 FLC 3

THOMPSON Richard Omar
Born: Lambeth, 2 May 1974
Height: 5'7" Weight: 12.5

This nippy striker joined Wycombe from Dr Martens League club Crawley Town towards the end of the 1998-99 season and eventually made his senior debut last January when he came on as a substitute in the Auto Windscreens Shield tie against Oxford. After a few more outings from the subs' bench he made the starting line-up for the home game with Oldham in March and worked so hard that he was admitted to hospital afterwards suffering from dehydration. Richard was released by manager Lawrie Sanchez at the end of last season.

Wycombe W (Free from Crawley T on 16/3/1999) FL 1+5 Others 0+1

THOMPSON Ryan James Daley
Born: Lambeth, 24 June 1982
Height: 5'11" Weight: 11.11

A prolific goalscorer for Northampton's youth and reserve teams, Ryan is a product of the Third Division club's Centre of Excellence. He created a stir with his performances in some of the Cobblers' pre-season games prior to the start of the 1999-2000 campaign, and also impressed when making his senior debut as a substitute for Ally Gibb in January's Auto Windscreens Shield encounter with Bristol Rovers. He was offered a one-year contract in April and a bright future is predicted for a youngster who has come on in leaps and bounds since Kevin Wilson took over as manager at Sixfields.

Northampton T (Trainee) Others 0+1

THOMPSON Steven (Steve) James
Born: Oldham, 2 November 1964
Height: 5'10" Weight: 13.5
Club Honours: AMC '89

This vastly experienced Rotherham midfielder had yet another successful season in 1999-2000. Due to his excellent passing ability it was generally felt that whenever Steve played well then so did the team. An expert from the penalty spot, he has yet to miss for the Millers. He is also a superb striker of free kicks from just outside the penalty area. Steve contributed six goals to United's promotion campaign but was released in the summer. Stop Press: He was reported to have signed for Halifax in early June.

Bolton W (From apprentice on 4/11/1982) FL 329+6/49 FLC 27/2 FAC 21/4 Others 39/2
Luton T (£180,000 on 13/8/1991) FL 5 FLC 2
Leicester C (Signed on 22/10/1991) P/FL 121+6/18 FLC 6/2 FAC 8/1 Others 11+3/4
Burnley (£200,000 on 24/2/1995) FL 44+5/1 FLC 2 Others 1+1
Rotherham U (Free on 24/7/1997) FL 87+16/14 FLC 3 FAC 6+2/1 Others 4+1

THOMSON Andrew (Andy)
Born: Motherwell, 1 April 1971
Height: 5'10" Weight: 10.13

Andy linked up again with his former boss Peter Taylor at Gillingham shortly before the start of the 1999-2000 season. He scored in his first game for the Gills at Bury on the opening day of the season and went on to net several crucial goals, notably in the FA Cup victories over Premiership clubs Bradford City and Sheffield Wednesday. He was sidelined by an ankle injury at the end of March but returned to the first-team squad in time for the Second Division play-offs. Andy then wrote his name into the Gills' record books when he scored a last-minute diving header in the play-off final against Wigan to clinch promotion to Division One for the first time in the club's history. A tireless, hard-working striker, he finished as second-top scorer for the Kent club with nine goals.

Queen of the South (Free from Jerviston BC on 28/7/1989) SL 163+12/93 SLC 8/3 SC 7+2/5 Others 9/8
Southend U (£250,000 on 4/7/1994) FL 87+35/28 FLC 4+1 FAC 3+2 Others 1+2
Oxford U (Free on 21/7/1998) FL 25+13/7 FLC 1 FAC 0+1
Gillingham (Signed on 5/8/1999) FL 20+8/9 FLC 3 FAC 5/4 Others 0+1/1

THOMSON Andrew (Andy) John
Born: Swindon, 28 March 1974
Height: 6'3" Weight: 14.12

The Bristol Rovers central defender enjoyed an excellent season in 1999-2000, showing great strength and determination. Andy also provided good attacking play down the right flank and was responsible for several pin-point crosses which produced goals for Rovers' strikers. He scored himself against Cardiff, Luton and Oldham and was highly regarded by the supporters in his first full season at the Memorial Stadium.

Swindon T (From trainee on 1/5/1993) P/FL 21+1 FLC 5/1 Others 3
Portsmouth (£75,000 on 29/12/1995) FL 85+8/3 FLC 4 FAC 6+1
Bristol Rov (£60,000 on 15/1/1999) FL 64/4 FLC 4 FAC 1 Others 1

THOMSON Steven (Steve)
Born: Glasgow, 23 January 1978
Height: 5'8" Weight: 10.4
International Honours: S: Yth

This strong and hard-tackling midfield player began 1999-2000 as a regular in the Crystal Palace line-up and was beginning to fulfil some of the promise he had previously shown. Unfortunately, he then suffered a bad knee injury last October and he did not return to first-team action until the middle of March. Steve will be looking to regain a regular slot in the Eagles' line-up during the coming season.

Crystal Palace (From trainee on 9/12/1995) FL 28+9 FLC 2+1/1

THORNE Peter Lee
Born: Manchester, 21 June 1973
Height: 6'0" Weight: 13.6
Club Honours: Div 2 '96; AMC '00

The popular Mancunian had an outstanding season in 1999-2000, when he became the first City player for some time to net more than 20 goals in a season. His performances, particularly in the second half of the campaign, were a revelation: he netted four in the home game against Chesterfield and less than a month later a hat-trick at Bristol Rovers, followed by another hat-trick against Bury in May. His winning goal in the Auto Windscreens Shield final at Wembley typified his sharpness and answered any possible doubts that had previously been expressed about his goalscoring abilities.

Blackburn Rov (From trainee on 20/6/1991) Others 0+1
Wigan Ath (Loaned on 11/3/1994) FL 10+1
Swindon T (£225,000 on 18/1/1995) FL 66+11/27 FLC 5+1/4 FAC 4+2 Others 1+1/1
Stoke C (£350,000 + on 25/7/1997) FL 107+8/24 FLC 9/6 FAC 3+1 Others 6+1/6

THORNLEY Benjamin (Ben) Lindsay
Born: Bury, 21 April 1975
Height: 5'9" Weight: 11.12
Club Honours: FAYC '92
International Honours: E: U21-3; Sch

The lively winger spent much of the early part of the 1999-2000 season on the Huddersfield substitutes' bench, although he was often brought on to tease opposing defences with his pace and accurate crossing. A regular place was gained as the campaign gathered momentum, with Ben giving some solid wing and defensive displays which were rewarded with a goal against Swindon Town at the McAlpine. However, a lack of form and consistency saw him return to the bench towards the end of the season.

Manchester U (From trainee on 29/1/1993) PL 1+8 FLC 3 FAC 2
Stockport Co (Loaned on 6/11/1995) FL 8+2/1 Others 1
Huddersfield T (Loaned on 22/2/1996) FL 12/2
Huddersfield T (£175,000 + on 3/7/1998) FL 48+15/5 FLC 8 FAC 4/1

THORPE Anthony (Tony) Lee
Born: Leicester, 10 April 1974
Height: 5'9" Weight: 12.6

After he had been unable to win a regular place at Bristol City more than a year after he arrived at Ashton Gate it was perhaps no surprise that Tony moved back to his former club Luton Town on loan last November. However, a permanent move failed to materialise and shortly after his return to Bristol manager Tony Pulis moved on to Portsmouth. Tony was then given his first decent run in the City line-up by caretaker boss Tony Fawthrop and seized the opportunity to impress. His quick reflexes and speed of movement gave him time and space in the box and he demonstrated a lethal ability to find the net. Tony's season had turned full circle and he finished off as the club's leading scorer with a respectable haul of 17 goals.

Luton T (Free from Leicester C juniors on 18/8/1992) FL 93+27/50 FLC 5+4/5 FAC 4+3/2 Others 4+3/3
Fulham (£800,000 on 26/2/1998) FL 5+8/3 Others 1+1
Bristol C (£1,000,000 on 23/6/1998) FL 33+14/15 FLC 2+2/2 Others 5/3
Reading (Loaned on 5/2/1999) FL 6/1
Luton T (Loaned on 25/3/1999) FL 7+1/4
Luton T (Loaned on 26/11/1999) FL 3+1/1

THORPE Jeffrey (Jeff) Roger
Born: Whitehaven, 17 November 1972
Height: 5'10" Weight: 12.8
Club Honours: Div 3 '95

The longest-serving player at Carlisle, Jeff was dogged by continuing injury and health problems in 1999-2000 that limited his contribution to the cause. Once again, most of his appearances were from the substitutes' bench and this versatile left-sided performer was eventually forced to retire from the game in April. Jeff is now hoping to remain in the game in a coaching role.

Carlisle U (From trainee on 2/7/1991) FL 104+72/6 FLC 8+5 FAC 4+3 Others 8+8/1

THORPE Lee Anthony
Born: Wolverhampton, 14 December 1975
Height: 6'1" Weight: 12.4

This hard-working striker hit 16 league and cup goals in 1999-2000 to finish as Lincoln's leading scorer for the third consecutive season. His pace and strength made him a handful for opposition defences and he forged a useful partnership with Gavin Gordon up front for the Imps. After recovering from a hernia operation, he was in excellent form early in the new year when he scored ten times in a run of 13 matches. Lee was deservedly named "Player of the Season" by the club's supporters.

Blackpool (From trainee on 18/7/1994) FL 2+10 FLC 0+1 FAC 1 Others 1
Lincoln C (Free on 4/8/1997) FL 117+7/38 FLC 4+1/1 FAC 10/1 Others 2+1/1

TIATTO Daniele (Danny) Amadio
Born: Melbourne, Australia, 22 May 1973
Height: 5'7" Weight: 12.0
International Honours: Australia: 10; U23

Although he was not an automatic choice for Manchester City in 1999-2000, Danny remained a valued member of the Maine Road squad. He is equally comfortable either at left back or on the left wing, switching between the two roles to suit the manager's tactical requirements. His greatest asset is that, despite being short in stature, he is very quick, his neat ball control enabling him to nip through defences. His total commitment makes him a crowd pleaser and he was one of the best dribblers in the First Division last season. Danny's game strengthened during the run-in to the end of the campaign, and he made a vital contribution to the club's late push for the second automatic promotion place. He won a further three full caps during the season, appearing for the Socceroos against Chile, Bulgaria and Hungary. Stop Press: Danny was one of several English-based players who appeared for Australia in the final of the Oceania Nations' Cup in June when they won the trophy, defeating New Zealand 2-0.

Stoke C (Loaned from FC Baden, Switzerland on 25/11/1997) FL 11+4/1
Manchester C (£300,000 on 15/7/1998) FL 34+18 FLC 4/1 FAC 0+1 Others 1

TIERNEY Francis (Fran)
Born: Liverpool, 10 September 1975
Height: 5'10" Weight: 11.0
International Honours: E: Yth

Francis struggled to make an impact with Notts County in the 1999-2000 campaign and rarely featured in the first team apart from a brief spell last February. He has plenty of ability, particularly his passing and dead-ball skills, but was unable to produce it consistently in the Magpies' first team. He was released by the club at the end of the season.

Crewe Alex (From trainee on 22/3/1993) FL 57+30/10 FLC 6 FAC 1+4 Others 5+6/3
Notts Co (Free on 2/7/1998) FL 19+14/4 FLC 0+1 FAC 1+4/1 Others 2

TILER Carl
Born: Sheffield, 11 February 1970
Height: 6'3" Weight: 13.10
International Honours: E: U21-13

A strong, tall and dominant central defender, Carl missed most of Charlton Athletic's First Division championship-winning season in 1999-2000 due to injury. He didn't make his first appearance as a substitute until late February and started only four games due to the superb form of Richard Rufus and Steve Brown in the Addicks' defence, but he nevertheless made a useful contribution to Charlton's successful season. Carl is dominant in the air and likes to get forward for corners, scoring one of the goals in the home win over Grimsby Town with a thundering header.

Barnsley (From trainee on 2/8/1988) FL 67+4/3 FLC 4 FAC 4+1 Others 3+1
Nottingham F (£1,400,000 on 30/5/1991) F/PL 67+2/1 FLC 10+1 FAC 6 Others 1
Swindon T (Loaned on 18/11/1994) FL 2
Aston Villa (£750,000 on 28/10/1995) PL 10+2/1 FLC 1 FAC 2
Sheffield U (£650,000 on 26/3/1997) FL 23/2 FLC 5 Others 3
Everton (£500,000 on 28/11/1997) PL 21/1 FLC 1 FAC 1
Charlton Ath (£700,000 on 30/9/1998) P/FL 31+7/2 FAC 1+1

TILLSON Andrew (Andy)
Born: Huntingdon, 30 June 1966
Height: 6'2" Weight: 12.10

Bristol Rovers' long-serving central defender and captain, Andy enjoyed another successful season at the heart of the Pirates' defence in 1999-2000, remaining injury free throughout, which was one of the reasons Rovers enjoyed such a sound defensive record. A good organiser, he invariably showed excellent composure under pressure and always posed a threat at set pieces, scoring his only goal of the season at Notts County in a 2-0 victory.

Grimsby T (Free from Kettering T on 14/7/1988) FL 104+1/5 FLC 8 FAC 10 Others 5
Queens Park R (£400,000 on 21/12/1990) FL 27+2/2 FLC 2 Others 1
Grimsby T (Loaned on 15/9/1992) FL 4 Others 1
Bristol Rov (£370,000 on 7/11/1992) FL 250+3/11 FLC 16/1 FAC 11 Others 19+1/2

Andy Tillson

TINDALL Jason
Born: Mile End, 15 November 1977
Height: 6'1" Weight: 11.10
This versatile Bournemouth player spent the 1999-2000 season on the fringes of the first team, appearing in just a handful of games. He missed several weeks in the autumn with an ankle injury, but even when fit he rarely threatened to win a regular place in the team. His main role is in the centre of midfield but he can also play as a central defender and at left back. He will be pushing for more regular first-team action in the coming season.
Charlton Ath (From trainee on 18/7/1996)
Bournemouth (Free on 3/7/1998) FL 10+15/1 FLC 1+2 Others 1

TINKLER Eric
Born: Capetown, South Africa, 30 July 1970
Height: 6'2" Weight: 12.8
International Honours: South Africa: 38 (ANC '96)
This big and powerful midfield player had a great season with Barnsley in 1999-2000 and produced his best football since joining the Oakwell club. He appeared regularly from mid-October and he was most useful when employed just in front of the back four, where his strength in the tackle was effective in breaking up opposition attacks. His height proved useful at set pieces in either penalty area and he contributed the occasional goal. Eric also won a recall to the South Africa international team for the African Nations' Cup finals in the spring, earning five more caps as the *Bafana Bafana* went on to finish in third place.
Barnsley (£650,000 from Cagliari, Italy on 23/7/1997) P/FL 70+13/9 FLC 8+1 FAC 6 Others 3

TINKLER Mark Roland
Born: Bishop Auckland, 24 October 1974
Height: 5'11" Weight: 13.3
Club Honours: FAYC '93
International Honours: E: Yth (UEFA-U18 '93); Sch
Mark joined Southend from York City in August 1999 and immediately showed signs of being a class player. His first-time control and passing abilities had not been seen at Roots Hall since the time of Mike Marsh, and he soon became a favourite. However, as the team's form dipped so did his own performances and he struggled to control games in the way he had previously done. Mark will be hoping to return to his best form again in the 2000-01 campaign.
Leeds U (From trainee on 29/11/1991) PL 14+11 FLC 1 Others 0+1
York C (£85,000 on 25/3/1997) FL 88+2/8 FLC 6 FAC 5 Others 2
Southend U (£40,000 on 13/8/1999) FL 41 FLC 1 FAC 1 Others 1

TINNION Brian
Born: Stanley, 23 February 1968
Height: 6'0" Weight: 13.0
Bristol City had cause to be thankful for this long-serving midfielder's contribution during a difficult 1999-2000 season. It was one of his best-ever campaigns, during which he demonstrated a high level of consistency and produced many outstanding performances. His passing, both long and short, is exceptional and most onlookers could not fail to appreciate that they were watching a talent unique in Second Division football, even if it is only his left foot that possesses such wizardry. His performance in the 2-2 home draw with Stoke was the best by one of the club's players in many a long day. He came off the bench early in the second half to turn in an immaculate display, with many scintillating passes from midfield. Brian's talented left foot combined with his knowledge of the game has been a contributory factor in the progress of many players who have teamed up with him on the left flank, including Martin Scott, Darren Barnard, Jim Brennan and his present partner, Mickey Bell. Following City's managerial merry-go-round of recent years, Brian is one of the senior players who have been appointed to a coaching position as the club attempts to form a "boot room" on the old Liverpool model.
Newcastle U (From apprentice on 26/2/1986) FL 30+2/2 FLC 5 Others 1+1
Bradford C (£150,000 on 9/3/1989) FL 137+8/22 FLC 12/1 FAC 9/4 Others 7+1/2
Bristol C (£180,000 on 23/3/1993) FL 259+12/20 FLC 20 FAC 16+2/5 Others 10+2

TINSON Darren Lee
Born: Birmingham, 15 November 1969
Height: 6'0" Weight: 13.12
Club Honours: GMVC '97

Darren Tinson

A powerfully built central defender, Darren was the only member of the Macclesfield back four at the start of the 1999-2000 season who had been on the club's books at the end of the previous campaign and, not surprisingly, it took some time for the new unit to gel together. Nevertheless he continued to show a strong presence and a good turn of speed, and was by far the best of the defenders in the air. In October, he was handed the responsibility of captaining the team and during the season was the first of the ex-Conference Macclesfield players to reach 100 league appearances. That was recognised with a special presentation by Silk FM, the local radio station. In the last match of the season Darren scored his first-ever league goal, his last goal having been recorded in the Conference in 1997.

Macclesfield T (£10,000 from Northwich Vic on 14/2/1996) FL 127/1 FLC 8 FAC 6 Others 2

TIPTON Matthew John
Born: Conway, 29 June 1980
Height: 5'10" Weight: 11.7
International Honours: W: U21-4; Yth

This young Oldham striker made regular appearances from the subs' bench in 1999-2000, the highlight of his season coming when he scored in the 2-1 victory over Wigan in April. A pacy forward with good skills on the ground, he did well with the Latics' reserves but only rarely featured in the first-team starting line-up. Matthew continued to represent Wales at U21 level and won a further cap against Northern Ireland at the beginning of June.

Oldham Ath (From trainee on 1/7/1997) FL 25+35/5 FLC 1 FAC 2+4 Others 0+3

Matthew Tipton

TODD Andrew (Andy) John James
Born: Derby, 21 September 1974
Height: 5'10" Weight: 11.10
Club Honours: Div 1 '97, '00

After he had been Bolton's most improved player in the previous two seasons, much was expected of Andy at the start of 1999-2000. A regular in the team in the first two months of the campaign, he again produced some consistently high-quality performances in the heart of the Wanderers defence, and it looked as though he was going to build on the solid work of previous years. Things fell apart, however, soon after the resignation of his father Colin in September 1999 and shortly afterwards Andy moved on to Charlton Athletic. He failed to gain a regular place in the Addicks team but his ability to play both in central defence and in midfield meant that he was brought into the side as a stand-in on various occasions, mostly in a midfield role, and he ended the season with a First Division championship medal. Andy is a strong, commanding type of player and is confident on the ball whatever his position. He likes to get forward for set pieces but has yet to score for his new club.

Middlesbrough (From trainee on 6/3/1992) FL 7+1 FLC 1+1 Others 5
Swindon T (Loaned on 27/2/1995) FL 13
Bolton W (£250,000 on 1/8/1995) P/FL 66+18/2 FLC 14+5/1 FAC 1 Others 3
Charlton Ath (£750,000 on 18/11/1999) FL 5+7 FAC 3+1

TODD Lee
Born: Hartlepool, 7 March 1972
Height: 5'6" Weight: 11.2

This experienced Bradford defender did not feature in the first team during the Bantams' epic fight for Premiership survival in 1999-2000. He was loaned to Walsall in September but experienced mixed fortunes during his two matches for the First Division club. He pulled off more than one spectacular goal-line clearance in the home game against Manchester City but when Sunderland visited the Bescot Stadium in the Worthington Cup he was withdrawn at half time after getting something of a run-around from the Premiership club's forwards. An adaptable player, Lee is most comfortable at right back but can be relied upon to give 100 per cent effort whatever his position, making up for his lack of height with a big heart. He will be looking to return to regular first-team football in 2000-01.

Stockport Co (Free from Hartlepool U juniors on 23/7/1990) FL 214+11/2 FLC 24+2 FAC 17/2 Others 33+1
Southampton (£500,000 on 28/7/1997) PL 9+1 FLC 1
Bradford C (£250,000 + on 6/8/1998) FL 14+1 FLC 2
Walsall (Loaned on 17/9/1999) FL 1 FLC 1

TOLLEY Jamie Christopher
Born: Ludlow, 12 May 1983
Height: 6'0" Weight: 11.3

Jamie stepped up from Shrewsbury's youth ranks for his first taste of senior action in 1999-2000. The midfielder made his debut as a substitute in the FA Cup against Northampton, and his league debut at Rochdale in the Shrews' last game of the century. Still to make his first appearance in the starting line-up, Jamie will be hoping to feature regularly in the first-team squad in the coming season.

Shrewsbury T (Trainee) FL 0+2 FAC 0+2

TOLSON Neil
Born: Stourbridge, 25 October 1973
Height: 6'2" Weight: 12.4

A 1999 close-season signing from York, Neil immediately looked like the centre forward Southend had been seeking for many years. Good in the air and with a nose for goal, he scored on his debut to make him an immediate favourite at Roots Hall. However, just as his partnership with Martin Carruthers was beginning to bear fruit he suffered a groin injury that required a hernia operation and brought his season to a premature close. He is likely to resume his goalscoring exploits in the Third Division next term.

Walsall (From trainee on 17/12/1991) FL 3+6/1 FAC 0+1/1 Others 1+2
Oldham Ath (£150,000 on 24/3/1992) PL 0+3
Bradford C (£50,000 on 2/12/1993) FL 32+31/12 FLC 1+4/1 FAC 3+1/1 Others 2+2/3
Chester C (Loaned on 6/1/1995) FL 3+1
York C (£50,000 on 15/7/1996) FL 66+18/18 FLC 7+2/3 FAC 6+1/2 Others 0+2/1
Southend U (Free on 2/7/1999) FL 29+2/10 FLC 2 FAC 1

TOMLINSON Graeme Murdoch
Born: Watford, 10 December 1975
Height: 5'10" Weight: 12.7

The 1999-2000 season proved a frustrating time for Graeme as he struggled to win a regular place in the Macclesfield Town starting line-up, mostly being used as a substitute. However, when he was given opportunities he demonstrated good awareness in the box and an ability to round defenders with ease. Eventually given a decent run in the team towards the end of the campaign when the forward line was decimated by injuries, he responded with some fine displays, providing the opening from which Damian Whitehead scored at Brighton and then finding the net himself in the following match against Shrewsbury.

Bradford C (Trainee) FL 12+5/6 FAC 0+1
Manchester U (£100,000 on 12/7/1994) FLC 0+2
Luton T (Loaned on 22/3/1996) FL 1+6
Bournemouth (Loaned on 8/8/1997) FL 6+1/1
Millwall (Loaned on 26/3/1998) FL 2+1/1
Macclesfield T (Free on 9/7/1998) FL 22+24/6 FLC 2+2 FAC 4+2/4 Others 1

TOMS Frazer Peter
Born: Ealing, 13 September 1979
Height: 6'1" Weight: 11.0

With his sumptuous skills and scintillating pace, Frazer made a stunning impact in the opening few months of his league career following his move to Barnet in the summer of 1999, crowned by his exquisite volley against York in late August. During the Bees' pre-season campaign he established a first-team berth with some telling displays on the left side of midfield and many

predicted that it would not be long before he would leave Underhill for more exalted surroundings. However, in hindsight, it was a season of education for this enthralling entertainer after he had been thrown into the ultra-competitive ranks of Division Three. The slightly built youngster proved that there was enough courage and industry in his game to complement his total mastery of the ball. The crowning moment for this predominantly left-sided performer arrived in the Auto Windscreens Shield at Cambridge when, as a substitute, he stole the show with a piece of sublime individualism. He swept past a trio of U's defenders before sliding the ball into the net to give the Bees their first-ever "golden goal" victory.
Charlton Ath (From trainee on 2/7/1998)
Barnet (Free on 2/7/1999) FL 27+12/1 FLC 2 FAC 1 Others 1+2/1

TORPEY Stephen (Steve) David James
Born: Islington, 8 December 1970
Height: 6'3" Weight: 14.6
Club Honours: AMC '94
This tall striker began the 1999-2000 campaign at Bristol City, where he demonstrated that he could hold the ball up well despite the fact that goals were a scarce commodity. He retained his place in the team for the first half of the season, the highlight of which was his wonderful strike against Reading in December. It was somewhat of a surprise when he was sold to Scunthorpe Untied, who paid out a new club record fee for his services at the start of February. Continuing to show a good work-rate, aerial strength and the ability to link with his team-mates, Steve opened his United scoring account against Reading two weeks later and remained a key member of the attack even when he wasn't scoring.
Millwall (From trainee on 14/2/1989) FL 3+4 FLC 0+1
Bradford C (£70,000 on 21/11/1990) FL 86+10/22 FLC 6 FAC 2+1 Others 8/6
Swansea C (£80,000 on 3/8/1993) FL 151+11/44 FLC 9+2/2 FAC 10/5 Others 18+3/6
Bristol C (£400,000 on 8/8/1997) FL 53+17/13 FLC 4+1/1 FAC 3 Others 3+1
Notts Co (Loaned on 7/8/1998) FL 4+2/1 FLC 1+1/1
Scunthorpe U (£200,000 on 3/2/2000) FL 15/1

TOWNSEND Andrew (Andy) David
Born: Maidstone, 27 July 1963
Height: 5'11" Weight: 13.6
Club Honours: FLC '94, '96
International Honours: RoI: 70; B-1
After appearing in five of Middlesbrough's first six matches at the beginning of last season this inspirational midfield player signed for West Bromwich Albion. Unfortunately, a string of niggling injuries to his knee and hamstring disrupted his early outings at the Hawthorns and after this he never really got going. At his best a driving, competititve force in the centre of the park, Andy was not as effective as the Baggies' fans had hoped and after more injury problems early in the new year he eventually took over from Cyrille Regis as player-manager of Albion's reserve team.
Southampton (£35,000 from Weymouth on 15/1/1985) FL 77+6/5 FLC 7+1 FAC 2+3 Others 3+2
Norwich C (£300,000 on 31/8/1988) FL 66+5/8 FLC 3+1 FAC 10/2 Others 3
Chelsea (£1,200,000 on 5/7/1990) P/FL 110/12 FLC 17/7 FAC 7 Others 4
Aston Villa (£2,100,000 on 26/7/1993) PL 133+1/8 FLC 20/2 FAC 12 Others 10/1
Middlesbrough (£500,000 on 29/8/1997) P/FL 73+4/3 FLC 7 FAC 4/1
West Bromwich A (£50,000 on 17/9/1999) FL 15+3 FLC 2

TOWNSEND Benjamin (Ben)
Born: Reading, 8 October 1981
Height: 5'10" Weight: 11.3
This young Wycombe trainee received a surprise Football League debut on the final day of the 1999-2000 season when he was included in the starting line-up for the visit to Cambridge. He produced a confident display and has since been rewarded with a one-year contract at Adams Park. Ben captained the Chairboys' youth team, leading them to the fourth round of the FA Youth Cup for the first time ever, and as the only specialist right back on the club's books he will be aiming to gain more senior experience in 2000-01.
Wycombe W (Trainee) FL 1

TRACEY Richard Shaun
Born: Dewsbury, 9 July 1979
Height: 5'11" Weight: 11.0
The speedy Carlisle striker netted with a fine header against Leyton Orient on the opening day of 1999-2000 and produced some hard-working performances during the first half of the campaign when he netted seven goals. He was then mostly restricted to outings from the subs' bench, failing to add to his total in the new year. Although he demonstrated his potential on occasions, especially in the air, he was released during the summer. However, the feeling persists that greater confidence in his own ability could pay real dividends.
Sheffield U (From trainee on 4/6/1997)
Rotherham U (Free on 24/2/1998) FL 0+3 FAC 1+1
Carlisle U (Free on 12/3/1999) FL 35+12/10 FLC 2 FAC 1 Others 1+1

TRACEY Simon Peter
Born: Woolwich, 9 December 1967
Height: 6'0" Weight: 13.12
Following the pre-season departure of Alan Kelly, Simon made the Sheffield United number one spot his own in 1999-2000 with a series of excellent performances. In the club's poor start to the season he kept the scoreline respectable on several occasions with good shot stopping and the confident way he dealt with centres. One of the highlights of the season came in the penalty shoot-out which decided the FA Cup tie against Conference outfit Rushden & Diamonds. Simon brought off a fine save to clinch the match and was chaired off the field by the overjoyed supporters. He managed to steer clear of injury, the only game he missed being due to suspension, and the forthcoming season could well see the club's longest-serving player make his 300th appearance.
Wimbledon (From apprentice on 3/2/1986) FL 1 Others 1
Sheffield U (£7,500 on 19/10/1988) F/PL 248+3 FLC 15 FAC 17 Others 10
Manchester C (Loaned on 27/10/1994) PL 3
Norwich C (Loaned on 31/12/1994) PL 1 FAC 2
Wimbledon (Loaned on 2/11/1995) PL 1

TRAORE Djimi
Born: Paris, France, 1 March 1980
Height: 6'3" Weight: 13.10
International Honours: France: Yth
Ostensibly a centre half, this young Frenchman has done well in Liverpool's reserve team, particularly at left back. He tackles well, but his strength is his distribution, Djimi specialising in playing long, accurate passes out of defence. He made his first-team debut in the first leg of the Worthington Cup tie against Hull last September, where he acquitted himself well, and also played in the second leg at Anfield. He is expected to enjoy a long run at left back next season, with a move into central defence after two or three years. Djimi represented France U18s in the UEFA championship finals held in Sweden in July 1999 and looks to have a great future in the game.
Liverpool (£550,000 from Laval, France on 18/2/1999) FLC 2

TREES Robert (Rob) Victor
Born: Manchester, 18 December 1977
Height: 5'11" Weight: 12.2
After being a regular for Bristol Rovers in 1998-99 this versatile player had to wait patiently for his opportunities in the first team last season. He spent September on loan at Conference club Altrincham and on his return received a rare call-up in the Auto Windscreens Shield tie against Northampton Town, when he came on as a replacement for the injured David Hillier. An attacking midfielder who can also play at full back or on the flanks, Rob produced a "Man of the Match" performance in the 3-1 defeat of Wrexham in January, during which he scored his first-ever league goal with an excellent right-foot shot, but it was not enough to secure his place in the team.
Manchester U (From trainee on 5/7/1996. Free to Stalybridge Celtic during 1997 close season)
Bristol Rov (Free from Witton A on 22/6/1998) FL 38+8/1 FLC 1+2 FAC 6 Others 1+1

TRETTON Andrew (Andy) David
Born: Derby, 9 October 1976
Height: 6'0" Weight: 12.9
The Shrewsbury central defender was injured for the start of the 1999-2000 season and although he came back for three games early on it was decided that he needed more time to recover. He returned in November and was then ever-present until the season's end, apart from a one-game suspension. He played a captain's role and formed a very useful partnership with Spencer Whelan, and then David Hughes. Strong in the air and on the ground, Andy looks to use the ball sensibly, and is a constant danger at set pieces.
Derby Co (From trainee on 18/10/1993)
Shrewsbury T (Free on 12/12/1997) FL 69+1/4 FLC 1 FAC 3 Others 2

Andy Tretton

Steve Tully

TROLLOPE Paul Jonathan
Born: Swindon, 3 June 1972
Height: 6'0" Weight: 12.6
Club Honours: Div 2 '99
International Honours: W: 5; B-1
The number and quality of the midfielders at Fulham manager Paul Bracewell's disposal meant that Paul was again on the fringes of the first team in 1999-2000 apart from a run of 14 consecutive starts between September and November on the left side of a midfield trio with Lee Clark and Steve Hayward. He appeared to be the only candidate to take over the left-back berth when Rufus Brevett was sidelined for the rest of the season, but Terry Phelan was signed and Paul had to be satisfied with the occasional place on the bench. Paul is the son of John Trollope, who holds the Swindon Town appearance record.
Swindon T (From trainee on 23/12/1989)
Torquay U (Free on 26/3/1992) FL 103+3/16 FLC 9+1/1 FAC 7 Others 8+1
Derby Co (£100,000 on 16/12/1994) F/PL 47+18/5 FLC 3+2/1 FAC 3+1
Grimsby T (Loaned on 30/8/1996) FL 6+1/1
Crystal Palace (Loaned on 11/10/1996) FL 0+9
Fulham (£600,000 on 28/11/1997) FL 49+17/5 FLC 6+2 FAC 3+5 Others 4/1

TROUGHT Michael (Mike) John
Born: Bristol, 19 October 1980
Height: 6'2" Weight: 13.0
This young central defender found it very difficult to break into a Bristol Rovers team which had a settled back five for most of the 1999-2000 season. Mike was transfer-listed in November after his fitness and performances were evaluated, but returned to first-team action in the new year, when he featured in the league games against Colchester and Oxford and the Auto Windscreens Shield tie with Northampton. Noted for his coolness when in possession, he spent much of the season on the bench as an unused substitute but remains an important squad member.
Bristol Rov (From trainee on 18/3/1999) FL 8+5 FAC 3+1 Others 2

TULLY Stephen (Steve) Richard
Born: Paignton, 10 February 1980
Height: 5'9" Weight: 11.0
Torquay's young right wing back had limited opportunities following the signing of Paul Holmes in November 1999, but his all-action commitment marks him out as a valuable squad player. Although slight of build, Steve is strong and aggressive. He is also rated as the best crosser at the Devon club. His sponsor in 1999-2000 was Sky Sports' Helen Chamberlain.
Torquay U (From trainee on 18/5/1998) FL 45+14/2 FLC 2+1 FAC 2+1 Others 6

TURLEY James
Born: Manchester, 24 June 1981
Height: 5'6" Weight: 10.6
James graduated from the ranks of York's trainees in the summer of 1999 to become a first-year professional at Bootham Crescent. A very lively and enthusiastic striker, he made a number of senior appearances in the second half of the campaign and netted an excellent goal in a 2-2 home draw against Torquay. The reserves' top scorer, James scored his second league goal in the last game of the season, a victory against Halifax at Bootham Crescent, and was offered a new contract for 2000-01.
York C (From trainee on 29/6/1999) FL 9+2/2

TURNER Andrew (Andy) Peter
Born: Woolwich, 23 March 1975
Height: 5'10" Weight: 11.12
International Honours: RoI: U21-7. E: Yth; Sch
Given the chance to resurrect his career at Rotherham last season after losing his way somewhat, Andy showed glimpses of the form that made Terry Venables sign him at Spurs, Portsmouth and Crystal Palace. He is a left-footed player in the old-fashioned winger mode. An excellent crosser of the ball, he helped to provide many openings for the strikers. When in a confident mood, Andy can turn defences inside out and, having gained promotion at the first attempt at Millmoor, he will be looking to continue his climb back up the league ladder.
Tottenham H (From trainee on 8/4/1992) PL 8+12/3 FLC 0+2/1 FAC 0+1
Wycombe W (Loaned on 26/8/1994) FL 3+1
Doncaster Rov (Loaned on 10/10/1994) FL 4/1 Others 1/1
Huddersfield T (Loaned on 28/11/1995) FL 2+3/1
Southend U (Loaned on 28/3/1996) FL 4+2
Portsmouth (£250,000 on 4/9/1996) FL 34+6/3 FLC 2+2 FAC 1
Crystal Palace (Free on 27/10/1998) FL 0+2
Wolverhampton W (Free on 25/3/1999)
Rotherham U (Free on 1/7/1999) FL 26+6/1 FLC 2 Others 1

TURNER Ross Keith
Born: Sheffield, 17 June 1979
Height: 5'11" Weight: 12.0

Ross was working as an electrician and playing in the Northern Counties East League with Worsborough Bridge when he joined Scunthorpe United on trial last March. An accomplished young goalkeeper, he showed promise in his appearances for the club's reserve team and went on to make his Football League debut against Burnley on the final day of the 1999-2000 season. He was released in the summer.

Scunthorpe U (Free from Worsbrough Bridge on 6/3/2000) FL 1

TUTILL Stephen (Steve) Alan
Born: York, 1 October 1969
Height: 5'10" Weight: 12.6
International Honours: E: Sch

Steve missed the first two months of the 1999-2000 season for Darlington due to an injury sustained in a pre-season friendly at Doncaster. On his return to fitness he formed a formidable partnership in the centre of the defence with the equally experienced Neil Aspin. Between them, they boasted well over a thousand first-team games for their previous clubs. Steve's strong tackling and aerial power were sorely missed in the new year when he was sidelined by a fractured cheekbone but he returned to action towards the end of the season. He scored his first goal for Darlington in the FA Cup tie against Southport with a typically powerful header.

York C (From trainee on 27/1/1988) FL 293+8/6 FLC 21 FAC 18+1 Others 22+3/1
Darlington (Free on 20/2/1998) FL 65+5 FLC 1 FAC 6/1 Others 5

TUTTLE David (Dave) Philip
Born: Reading, 6 February 1972
Height: 6'1" Weight: 12.10
Club Honours: FAYC '90
International Honours: E: Yth

This strong-tackling central defender featured in the first two games of the 1999-2000 campaign for Crystal Palace before moving north to join former boss Dave Bassett at Barnsley. He had a brief spell of first-team action on joining the Oakwell club but then struggled to keep his place. His opportunities after this were very limited and he eventually returned to London, signing for Second Division Millwall last March, to bolster a defence weakened by long-term injuries to the regular central defenders. Dave made a great impact on his arrival at the New Den and although he picked up an injury in only his second game he had returned to action by the end of the season.

Tottenham H (From trainee on 8/2/1990) F/PL 10+3 FLC 3+1 Others 1/1
Peterborough U (Loaned on 21/1/1993) FL 7
Sheffield U (£350,000 on 1/8/1993) P/FL 63/1 FLC 2 FAC 3
Crystal Palace (Signed on 8/3/1996) F/PL 73+8/5 FLC 7 FAC 2 Others 5
Barnsley (£150,000 on 18/8/1999) FL 11+1 FAC 1
Millwall (£200,000 on 2/3/2000) FL 7+1 Others 2

TWISS Michael John
Born: Salford, 18 December 1977
Height: 5'11" Weight: 12.8

An exciting young forward with an eye for goal, Michael showed some nice touches when making his first start for Manchester United in the Worthington Cup tie against Aston Villa last September. Later in the season he had a brief trial with Norwich City, featuring in two reserve games and scoring in a 2-0 victory over Wycombe before returning to Old Trafford at the beginning of March. He was released in the summer.

Manchester U (From trainee on 5/7/1996) FLC 1 FAC 0+1
Sheffield U (Loaned on 6/8/1998) FL 2+10/1 FAC 2+3

TYLER Mark Richard
Born: Norwich, 2 April 1977
Height: 6'0" Weight: 12.9
International Honours: E: Yth

Mark enjoyed another superb season in 1999-2000, as he helped Peterborough towards success in the Third Division play-offs. A broken shoulder suffered at Cheltenham in February kept him out for two months but he returned in time for the play-off games. Very agile and a fine shot stopper, he is a goalkeeper who is capable of playing at a higher level.

Peterborough U (From trainee on 7/12/1994) FL 112 FLC 7 FAC 6 Others 13

TYSON Nathan
Born: Reading, 4 May 1982
Height: 5'10" Weight: 11.5

A product of the Reading Academy, Nathan made his first-team debut for the club as a late substitute in the penultimate game of the 1999-2000 season, a 1-1 draw at Bury. He also sat on the bench twice without being used, but his outstanding pace and determination mark him out as a great prospect for the future. In youth-team games he has often been employed as a lone striker, although his favoured first-team position appears to be as a wide player.

Reading (From trainee on 18/3/2000) FL 0+1

Dave Tuttle

UV

UHLENBEEK Gustav (Gus) Reinier
Born: Paramaribo, Surinam, 20 August 1970
Height: 5'10" Weight: 12.6
Club Honours: Div 2 '99

A right wing back with tremendous pace, Gus impressed at times for Fulham in 1999-2000 with his rampaging forays down the right flank and 100 per cent effort. He had a good run in the side while Steve Finnan was out injured, but when Bjarne Goldbaek was signed from Chelsea his first-team prospects were always going to be pretty bleak, and he was released during the summer.

Ipswich T (£100,000 from Tops SV, Holland, via Ajax and Cambuur, on 11/8/1995) FL 77+12/4 FLC 5+3 FAC 4+3 Others 7+1
Fulham (Free on 22/7/1998) FL 22+17/1 FLC 4+1 FAC 3+2 Others 1

David Unsworth

UNSWORTH David Gerald
Born: Chorley, 16 October 1973
Height: 6'1" Weight: 14.2
Club Honours: FAC '95; CS '95
International Honours: E: 1; U21-6; Yth

Already boasting a reputation as a solid and reliable defender, David showed an unerring eye from the penalty spot for Everton last season and ended the campaign with a total of nine goals, only three short of top scorer Kevin Campbell. One of those strikes was a stunning free kick from 20 yards in an FA Cup tie against Preston North End, as David displayed his all-round footballing talents. Most naturally employed on the left of a three-man defence, he spent much of the campaign at left back, a role he applied himself to diligently and enthusiastically. He also had occasions in midfield, and was handed the captaincy of the side at White Hart Lane in August. His consistency of performance also applied to fitness. He missed just four games through injury during a season when he was impressive throughout.

Everton (From trainee on 25/6/1992) F/PL 108+8/11 FLC 5+2 FAC 7 Others 4/1
West Ham U (£1,000,000 + on 18/8/1997) PL 32/2 FLC 5 FAC 4
Aston Villa (£3,000,000 on 28/7/1998)
Everton (£3,000,000 on 22/8/1998) PL 65+2/7 FLC 4 FAC 8/4

UNSWORTH Lee Peter
Born: Eccles, 25 February 1973
Height: 5'11" Weight: 11.8

Although he is an extremely versatile defender who can play in a number of positions, Lee was restricted to a handful of first-team appearances for Crewe in 1999-2000. He was in the starting line-up for the first three matches of the season but after that he started only two more games, the last of them against Nottingham Forest in April, also having five outings as a substitute. After more than a hundred league appearances for the club, he is still waiting for his first goal. He was released during the close season.

Crewe Alex (Signed from Ashton U on 20/2/1995) FL 93+33 FLC 10+1/1 FAC 5+1/1 Others 8+2

UPSON Matthew James
Born: Stowmarket, 18 April 1979
Height: 6'1" Weight: 11.4
International Honours: E: U21-6; Yth

Matthew is an intelligent young Arsenal central defender whose excellent distribution skills see him mixing play up between long and short balls. A good tackler and strong in the air, he reads the game well. During the summer of 1999 he spent a lot of time in the gym working on weights to improve his strength. In the absence of Tony Adams through injury, Matthew played with great maturity alongside Martin Keown in the games against Derby, Sunderland and Manchester United at the beginning of the 1999-2000 season. A series of injuries limited his appearances thereafter, and his season came to an abrupt end in December when he ruptured a cruciate ligament during the game at Leicester. Prior to his injury he had been a regular in the England U21 set-up, winning further caps against Luxembourg, Poland and Denmark.

Luton T (From trainee on 24/4/1996) FL 0+1 Others 1
Arsenal (£1,000,000 on 14/5/1997) PL 10+8 FLC 6 FAC 2 Others 2+1

VAESEN Nico Jos-Theodor
Born: Ghent, Belgium, 28 September 1969
Height: 6'3" Weight: 12.8

Huddersfield's Belgian import was ever present during the 1999-2000 season, his second with the Terriers, and he celebrated his 50th league appearance against Norwich City in September. Most successful teams have a strong last line of defence, and Huddersfield's rise in the last two years owes much to the classy shot stopper. Nico is confident, shows great handling and agility, and is always quick to turn defence into attack. With Huddersfield pushing for a play-off berth, he clocked up his 100th senior appearance for the club along with his fourth clean sheet in a row, a feat not achieved by a Town goalkeeper since 1994-95. The only thing missing was a call-up to the Belgium squad for Euro 2000.

Huddersfield T (£80,000 from SC Eendracht Aalst, Belgium on 10/7/1998) FL 89 FLC 10 FAC 6

VAN BLERK Jason
Born: Sydney, Australia, 16 March 1968
Height: 6'1" Weight: 13.0
International Honours: Australia: 26; Yth

Jason's versatility was put to the test during the course of the 1999-2000 season when he was asked to occupy four different positions for West Bromwich Albion – right and left back, central midfield and wide left. Wherever he was asked to play he never shirked a tackle, showing total commitment to the cause as the Baggies battled against relegation. He scored his first goal of the season (and his first for Albion) in a crucial 3-2 win over Portsmouth in November, ending a nine-match home run without a victory. He remained a member of Australia's national squad, winning further caps against Chile, Bulgaria and the Czech Republic last season.

Millwall (£300,000 from Go Ahead Eagles, Holland on 8/9/1994) FL 68+5/2 FLC 5 FAC 6+1 Others 1+1
Manchester C (Free on 9/8/1997) FL 10+9 FLC 0+1 FAC 0+1
West Bromwich A (£250,000 on 13/3/1998) FL 71+2/1 FLC 5+1 FAC 1

VAN DER GOUW Raimond (Rai)
Born: Oldenzaal, Holland, 24 March 1963
Height: 6'3" Weight: 13.10
Club Honours: EC '99; FAC '99; PL '00

A highly experienced goalkeeper with a safe pair of hands, Rai enjoyed a new lease of life last season after being confined to the shadows during Peter Schmeichel's long reign between the posts for Manchester United. Although he must have expected more of the same when Mark Bosnich joined the club during the summer, that all changed in August when Bosnich was forced out first by hamstring problems, then by a run of patchy form. While the signing of Massimo Taibi intensified competition for places among the goalkeeping fraternity at Old Trafford, especially during September, when Rai alternated with Taibi, the Dutchman more than held his own, particularly in Europe, where Sir Alex Ferguson preferred his experience, and ended the season with another Premiership winners' medal. Interestingly enough, Rai became the oldest post-war goalkeeper at Old Trafford in September, and the club's fourth-oldest post-war player behind Jack Warner, Bill Foulkes and Bryan Robson. If he continues to maintain the same kind of form over the next few seasons, he could well have something in common with Methuselah!

Manchester U (Signed from Vitesse Arnhem, Holland, via Go Ahead Eagles, on 12/7/1996) PL 21+5 FLC 6 Others 11

VAN DER KWAAK Peter
Born: Haarlem, Holland, 12 October 1968
Height: 6'4" Weight: 13.13

Peter's only taste of first-team action for Reading in 1999-2000 came in the embarrassing 5-3 defeat at Wycombe Wanderers. Number one 'keeper Scott Howie let in two soft first-half goals, and the tall Dutchman replaced him at half time before letting in three more. Reading promptly signed Phil Whitehead from West Bromwich and Peter found himself third choice. He was on the bench for the Royals 29 times last term without being brought into action. He went to Carlisle on loan for a month in February and became United's sixth 'keeper of the campaign and their ninth in under a year when he made his debut at Hartlepool in February. Apart from the 5-0 defeat at Lincoln, Peter conceded just three goals in three games before the end of his loan spell at Brunton Park. He then returned to Holland after agreeing a two-year deal with Go Ahead Eagles.

Reading (Free from Ajax, Holland on 7/8/1998) FL 3+1 FLC 1
Carlisle U (Loaned on 22/2/2000) FL 2 Others 2

VAN DER LAAN Robertus (Robin) Petrus
Born: Schiedam, Holland, 5 September 1968
Height: 6'0" Weight: 13.8
Club Honours: AMC '93

Having missed most of the 1998-99 campaign through injury, Robin returned to full fitness and was an important member of Dave Bassett's promotion-seeking squad last season. He was mostly used in an attacking midfield role but also occasionally appeared up front as a target man. Key features of his play were his strength in the tackle and a willingness to drive forward from the centre of the park. Robin missed several games though injury in the second third of the season, and although he returned in the spring he played only a bit part in the play-offs after twisting a knee in the opening minutes of the semi-final first leg against Birmingham City.

Port Vale (£80,000 from Wageningen, Holland on 21/2/1991) FL 154+22/24 FLC 11+1/1 FAC 9+1/1 Others 11+1/1
Derby Co (£675,000 on 2/8/1995) F/PL 61+4/8 FLC 6+2 FAC 3+1/3
Wolverhampton W (Loaned on 11/10/1996) FL 7
Barnsley (£325,000 + on 17/7/1998) FL 36+13/4 FLC 5+1/3 FAC 0+1 Others 1

VAN HEUSDEN Arjan
Born: Alphen, Holland, 11 December 1972
Height: 6'3" Weight: 14.7

Arjan started the 1999-2000 season as Cambridge's first-choice 'keeper and produced some excellent performances as United came to terms with higher-league football. Injured against Gillingham in October, he was unable to reclaim his first-team place, except for two outings, and was allowed to leave the Abbey at the end of the season. Exeter were the first club to express an interest.

Port Vale (£4,500 from VV Noordwijk, Holland on 15/8/1994) FL 27 FLC 4 Others 2
Oxford U (Loaned on 26/9/1997) FL 11 FLC 2
Cambridge U (Free on 4/8/1998) FL 41+1 FLC 6 FAC 1 Others 4

VANNINEN Jukka
Born: Riihimaki, Finland, 31 January 1977
Height: 5'7" Weight: 12.1

Hailing from Finland, Jukka was offered a contract at Exeter last December after impressing during a trial. He made six appearances in midfield and displayed admirable composure. Jukka will be looking to start from the off in 2000-01 in order to make his breakthrough in England.

Exeter C (£5,000 from Rovaniemi Rops, Finland on 2/12/1999) FL 3+2 Others 1

VARTY John **William (Will)**
Born: Workington,, 1 October 1976
Height: 6'0" Weight: 12.4
Club Honours: AMC '97

Having initially moved to Millmoor on loan in March 1999, Will proved a superb summer signing as Rotherham bolstered their defence to launch a successful promotion bid. An ever-present until he suffered a broken nose at his former club Carlisle United at the end of November, Will won his place back again in mid-March to play a vital part in the exciting end-of-term run-in. He is an unflappable central defender who is very much at ease in the sweeper's role. Will can also play at right wing back with just as much comfort. Nothing seems to ruffle him.

Carlisle U (From trainee on 10/7/1995) FL 79+3/1 FLC 8+1 FAC 3 Others 9+1
Rotherham U (Free on 12/3/1999) FL 40+1 FLC 2 FAC 2 Others 2+1

VASSELL Darius
Born: Birmingham, 13 June 1980
Height: 5'7" Weight: 12.0
International Honours: E: U21-2; Yth

This promising Aston Villa youngster had a frustrating season in 1999-2000, when he was hit by a string of injuries and failed to establish himself as a regular in the first-team squad. Having made several appearances as a substitute, he made the starting line-up for the first time for the Worthington Cup tie against Chester City only to sustain a hamstring injury. He made a quick return to the first team at Sunderland in October but had to be substituted shortly after half time, again suffering with hamstring trouble. When fit, he was once again back on the subs' bench but had the misfortune to break an ankle at Chelsea last January, which kept him out of action for some time. Darius is a fast, skilful striker with excellent close control and the ability to upset opposition defences – definitely one to watch for in the future. He added to his England U21 experience with a further appearance as a substitute against Poland last September.

Aston Villa (From trainee on 14/4/1998) PL 1+16 FLC 1+5 FAC 0+2 Others 0+3/2

VAUGHAN Anthony (Tony) John
Born: Manchester, 11 October 1975
Height: 6'1" Weight: 11.2
International Honours: E: Yth; Sch

Despite making a satisfying contribution to Manchester City's promotion to Division One in 1998-99, Tony was a fringe player at Maine Road last season. The powerful defender had only two first-team outings, both as a substitute, at Fulham in the league and at Burnley in the Worthington Cup. In September he joined Cardiff on loan for three months and he performed well during his spell at Ninian Park. The Welsh club were keen to sign him and agreed a fee with Manchester City, but the deal fell through and he returned to Maine Road, where he was placed on the transfer list. A spell on loan at Nottingham Forest followed in February, and after he had appeared in six games for the Reds manager David Platt signed him permanently on transfer deadline day for a £350,000 fee. Tony was used both as a centre back and a left full back and appeared regularly for Forest until the end of the season.

Ipswich T (From trainee on 1/7/1994) P/FL 56+11/3 FLC 4+2 FAC 2 Others 4
Manchester C (£1,350,000 on 9/7/1997) FL 54+4/2 FLC 6+1 FAC 3 Others 3+1
Cardiff C (Loaned on 15/9/1999) FL 14 Others 1
Nottingham F (£350,000 on 8/2/2000) FL 10

VAUGHAN John
Born: Isleworth, 26 June 1964
Height: 5'10" Weight: 13.1
Club Honours: Div 3 '91, '96

This experienced goalkeeper began the 1999-2000 season as Lincoln's first choice but was dropped in mid-September following a heavy defeat at Torquay. He was unable to regain his place and in November he returned to Colchester, where he had had a previous spell in 1997, on loan to provide cover following an injury to Simon Brown. He made his debut at Oldham, where his display helped ensure United's first win in 12 games. He appeared in a total of six matches for the U's before returning to Lincoln, and then moved on loan again in January, this time to Chesterfield. He showed composure and confidence in his performances for the Spireites before returning to Sincil Bank for the final few weeks of the campaign. He was released in the summer.

West Ham U (From apprentice on 30/6/1982)
Charlton Ath (Loaned on 11/3/1985) FL 6
Bristol Rov (Loaned on 5/9/1985) FL 6
Wrexham (Loaned on 3/10/1985) FL 4
Bristol C (Loaned on 4/3/1986) FL 2
Fulham (£12,500 on 21/8/1986) FL 44 FLC 4 FAC 4 Others 3
Bristol C (Loaned on 21/1/1988) FL 3
Cambridge U (Free on 6/6/1988) FL 178 FLC 13 FAC 24 Others 16
Charlton Ath (Free on 5/8/1993) FL 5+1 FAC 2 Others 1+1
Preston NE (Free on 26/7/1994) FL 65+1 FLC 2 FAC 2 Others 5
Lincoln C (Free on 14/8/1996) FL 62 FLC 7 FAC 1 Others 3
Colchester U (Loaned on 3/2/1997) FL 5 Others 1
Colchester U (Loaned on 12/11/1999) FL 6
Chesterfield (Loaned on 22/1/2000) FL 3 Others 1

VEGA Ramon
Born: Zurich, Switzerland, 14 June 1971
Height: 6'3" Weight: 13.0
Club Honours: FLC '99
International Honours: Switzerland: 19

Despite his credentials, the Swiss international defender has been a fringe player at Tottenham since George Graham took over as manager in October 1998. The arrival of Chris Perry from Wimbledon signalled that the 1999-2000 season would be a tough one for Ramon, who, it is fair to say, rose to the challenge well on those rare occasions when he was given an opportunity. Restricted to a handful of first-team outings, he hit the back of the net in the 2-1 defeat at Middlesbrough in December and sent out a timely reminder to Graham not to eliminate him from his future plans. When he is fit, Ramon is strong in the air and quick on the ball, but injury and a lack of match fitness meant that he had few further chances to impress and he will approach the new season seeking assurances that he has a future with the club.

Tottenham H (£3,750,000 from Cagliari, Italy, via Trimbach and Grasshoppers, on 11/1/1997) PL 45+9/7 FLC 7+1/1 FAC 8+1

Mark Venus

VENUS Mark
Born: Hartlepool, 6 April 1967
Height: 6'0" Weight: 13.11
Club Honours: Div 3 '89

Mark again featured prominently on the left side of a central defensive three for Ipswich last season, using his favoured left foot to set up some memorable goalscoring opportunities for his attacking colleagues. Although he is a recognised expert from dead-ball situations, he had few opportunities last season and after relinquishing his post as the club's penalty taker it was not surprising that his goal tally was much reduced. Mark missed several matches in the second half of the campaign with ankle trouble and was due to have an operation during the summer break.

Hartlepool U (From juniors on 22/3/1985) FL 4 Others 0+1
Leicester C (Free on 6/9/1985) FL 58+3/1 FLC 3 FAC 2 Others 2+1
Wolverhampton W (£40,000 on 23/3/1988) FL 271+16/7 FLC 17+1/1 FAC 15+1 Others 17/2
Ipswich T (£150,000 on 29/7/1997) FL 84+2/12 FLC 12/2 FAC 3 Others 7

VERNAZZA Paolo Andrea Pietro
Born: Islington, 1 November 1979
Height: 6'0" Weight: 11.10
International Honours: E: Yth

A very talented young Arsenal midfield player, Paolo is a product of the club's successful youth policy. Strong and powerful with good natural skill, he always produces a high workrate from box to box. He is a good header of the ball, and shows fine judgement with both long and short passes. Paolo moved to Portsmouth on loan in January and showed considerable talent in his two months at Fratton Park, adding strength and class to the Pompey midfield. He was originally due to spend three moths with the south coast club but the loan was terminated early when manager Tony Pulis needed to reduce the wage bill to enable him to bring in new signings. Already capped by England at U18 and U20 levels, he will be aiming to break through into the Gunners' first-team squad in the coming season.

Arsenal (From trainee on 18/11/1997) PL 2+1 FLC 3 Others 1+1
Ipswich T (Loaned on 2/10/1998) FL 2
Portsmouth (Loaned on 14/1/2000) FL 7

VEYSEY Kenneth (Ken) James
Born: Hackney, 8 June 1967
Height: 5'11" Weight: 12.7

Ken signed for Plymouth on the eve of the 1999-2000 season from Torquay, and deputised for first-choice 'keeper Jon Sheffield during the campaign. A good shot stopper, he helped Argyle through two rounds of the FA Cup with capable performances against Brentford and Reading. He was released at the end of the season.

Torquay U (Signed from Dawlish T on 19/11/1987) FL 72 FLC 2 FAC 10 Others 9
Oxford U (£110,000 on 29/10/1990) FL 57 FLC 2 FAC 4 Others 4
Reading (Free on 17/8/1993)
Exeter C (Free on 14/10/1993) FL 11+1 Others 3 (Free to Dorchester T on 17/9/1994)
Torquay U (Free on 11/8/1997) FL 37 FLC 1 FAC 4 Others 3
Plymouth Arg (Free on 6/8/1999) FL 5+1 FLC 1 FAC 2

VICKERS Stephen (Steve)
Born: Bishop Auckland, 13 October 1967
Height: 6'1" Weight: 12.12
Club Honours: AMC '90; Div 1 '95

Steve has been with Middlesbrough since 1993 and has seen many changes during his time with the club. The big defender has always given his best and has offered a great example to the youngsters coming through the ranks. A dependable stopper, he is a strong tackler with a no-nonsense attitude towards clearing the ball from the danger area. His application gradually won over the initially sceptical Boro fans and his solid performances at the back are now much appreciated. Steve made 30 Premiership starts in 1999-2000. He continued to venture forward for set pieces and scored a single goal, against Chesterfield in the Worthington Cup in September.

Tranmere Rov (Signed from Spennymoor U on 11/9/1985) FL 310+1/11 FLC 20+1/5 FAC 19/3 Others 36/1
Middlesbrough (£700,000 on 3/12/1993) P/FL 217+10/8 FLC 26+2/3 FAC 16+1 Others 2

VICTORY Jamie Charles
Born: Hackney, 14 November 1975
Height: 5'10" Weight: 12.0
International Honours: E: SP-1

After taking time to adjust to the Third Division, Jamie enjoyed yet another exemplary season for Cheltenham in 1999-2000. Incredibly, he has missed just one league match since joining the club in 1996 and had clocked up well over 150 consecutive games by the end of the campaign. He is a left-sided defender with a languid style whose strengths are pace, tackling technique and the ability to get forward and score goals. His only real weakness is an over-reliance on his left foot, although he has shown in the past that he can use his right as well. Ever present in all 53 of Cheltenham's first-team matches last season, Jamie has a fine disciplinary record for a defender. He operated mostly as a left back but also made a handful of appearances in midfield. He was reported to have attracted the attention of higher-division clubs during the season.

West Ham U (From trainee on 1/7/1994)
Bournemouth (Free on 1/7/1995) FL 5+11/1 FLC 1+1 Others 1+1
Cheltenham T (Free on 1/7/1996) FL 46/4 FLC 2/1 FAC 2 Others 2

VIEIRA Patrick
Born: Dakar, Senegal, 23 June 1976
Height: 6'4" Weight: 13.0
Club Honours: PL '98; FAC '98; CS '98, '99
International Honours: France: 30 (WC '98, UEFA '00)

A tall, strong, dominating player at the heart of Arsenal's midfield, Patrick has forged a partnership with fellow French international Emmanuel Petit which is one of the strongest in the Premiership. He possesses good attacking and defensive skills and is a strong, aggressive tackler who wins many 50-50 balls. With an extremely powerful shot, he can score exciting goals from long range. His distribution, whether on the ground or over the top, is first class, and he sets up many scoring opportunities for his team-mates. He matured greatly last season, and consequently his poor disciplinary record showed improvement. He is regarded by his manager, Arsene Wenger, as being a world-class player and was selected by his fellow professionals for the PFA award-winning side for the second year running. Now established as a regular in the French national team, he added 16 caps during the season and featured in all six Euro 2000 games, proving a key figure for *les Bleus* as they defeated Italy in a sensational final to take the trophy.

Arsenal (£3,500,000 from AC Milan, Italy, via AS Cannes, on 14/8/1996) PL 124+4/9 FLC 5 FAC 18+1/1 Others 22

VILJANEN Ville
Born: Finland, 2 February 1971
Height: 6'2" Weight: 13.5
International Honours: Finland: 1

A big, solid central striker who joined Port Vale, originally on trial, last February, having been released from a similar spell with Portsmouth, Ville scored on his full debut at Crewe and extended his burst of

scoring to four in six games, including a particularly good 25-yard shot against Charlton Athletic, to earn a contract until the end of the season. He could not keep up that rate of scoring but overall he did well enough on his first acquaintance with English football to alert other clubs to his potential.
Port Vale (Free from Vastra Frolunda, Sweden on 25/2/1999) FL 11+4/4

VINCENT Jamie Roy
Born: Wimbledon, 18 June 1975
Height: 5'10" Weight: 11.8
Huddersfield's most improved player during the 1999-2000 season, Jamie slotted easily into his left-full-back or wing-back role and added a new dimension to Town's play. Always strong in the tackle and an excellent header of the ball, he seldom wasted possession and became a constant threat to opposing defences when going forward. The Terriers regularly benefited from his dead-ball accuracy and excellent crossing ability, and he was finally rewarded with his first goal for the club in an away draw at Norwich in February. It was easy to see why the previous season had brought him selection for the PFA award-winning Second Division side.
Crystal Palace (From trainee on 13/7/1993) FL 19+6 FLC 2+1/1 FAC 1
Bournemouth (Loaned on 18/11/1994) FL 8
Bournemouth (£25,000 + on 30/8/1996) FL 102+3/5 FLC 7+1 FAC 8 Others 9/1
Huddersfield T (£440,000 + on 25/3/1999) FL 40+3/2 FLC 1+2 FAC 1

VINDHEIM Rune
Born: Hoyanguer, Norway, 15 May 1972
Height: 5'11" Weight: 12.4
Rune became the third Norwegian on the staff at Hartlepool when he was signed on a short-term contract in September 1999 to help solve a temporary injury crisis. A central defender who can also play in midfield, he fitted in well and looked set to become a permanent member of the playing staff. Unfortunately, a dispute over terms saw the offer of a contract withdrawn, and he left the club under something of a cloud.
Burnley (Free from SK Brann, Norway on 2/10/1998) FL 8/2 FAC 1 Others 1
Hartlepool U (Free on 17/9/1999) FL 7 FAC 1

VINNICOMBE Christopher (Chris)
Born: Exeter, 20 October 1970
Height: 5'9" Weight: 10.12
Club Honours: SPD '91
International Honours: E: U21-12
Chris played the first two games of the 1999-2000 campaign for Wycombe and then had the misfortune to suffer an injury in training that kept him out of action until October. On returning to the side he produced a series of consistent displays at left back, rarely missing a game for the rest of the season. A much-underrated member of the team, he rarely put a foot wrong in defence and showed some fine attacking skills when taking the ball down the wing and delivering quality crosses.
Exeter C (From trainee on 1/7/1989) FL 35+4/1 FLC 5/1 Others 2

Chris Vinnicombe

Glasgow R (£150,000 on 3/11/1989) SL 14+9/1 SLC 1+2 Others 1
Burnley (£200,000 on 30/6/1994) FL 90+5/3 FLC 9 FAC 2 Others 7+1/1
Wycombe W (Free on 6/8/1998) FL 72+4 FLC 5 FAC 4 Others 2

VIVAS Nelson David
Born: Buenos Aires, Argentina, 18 October 1969
Height: 5'6" Weight: 10.6
International Honours: Argentina: 26
Predominantly a defender, Nelson can also play in midfield but he was unable to command a regular first-team place at Arsenal in 1999-2000, making just three starts. He was eventually allowed to join Spanish club Celta Vigo until the end of the campaign. He appeared for Argentina in the Copa America tournament in July 1999 and also won further caps against Brazil (twice), Colombia and Spain in the early part of the season.
Arsenal (£1,600,000 from Lugano, Switzerland on 5/8/1998) PL 11+17 FLC 3/1 FAC 4+2 Others 3+6

VIVEASH Adrian Lee
Born: Swindon, 30 September 1969
Height: 6'2" Weight: 12.13
In what was his fifth season at Walsall Adrian took over the captain's armband from Neil Pointon last November and gave his all in a vain endeavour to keep the Saddlers in Division One. It was typical of his spirit that in the game against Ipswich in October he played on with his head heavily bandaged. His main assets are his power in the air, strength in the tackle and a determination to win at all times. Stop Press: Adrian was reported to have signed for Reading during the summer.
Swindon T (From trainee on 14/7/1988) FL 51+3/2 FLC 6+1 FAC 0+1 Others 2
Reading (Loaned on 4/1/1993) FL 5 Others 1/1
Reading (Loaned on 20/1/1995) FL 6
Barnsley (Loaned on 10/8/1995) FL 2/1
Walsall (Free on 16/10/1995) FL 200+2/13 FLC 12 FAC 15/2 Others 13/1

VLACHOS Michail
Born: Athens, Greece, 20 September 1967
Height: 5'11" Weight: 12.10
International Honours: Greece: 6
Michail struggled to hold down a regular place in the Portsmouth team during 1999-2000 and failed to feature after Tony Pulis took over as manager, eventually moving on to Walsall in February in search of regular first-team action. Michail is a reliable player who is good in the air, strong in the tackle and an excellent man marker. He was mostly used by Pompey on the left side of midfield but can also play as a left wing back. Following his move to Walsall, the Greek international (who had played against the Saddlers earlier in the season) immediately showed his ability and came close to getting a match-winner in his opening game at Manchester City. Soon afterwards, he scored with a powerful header against Charlton but after 11 successive games he lost a little of his edge and he was replaced in midfield by Dean Keates for the last four games. He was released during the close season.
Portsmouth (Signed from AEK Athens, Greece on 30/1/1998) FL 55+2 FLC 4/1 FAC 3
Walsall (Free on 25/2/2000) FL 11/1

WAINWRIGHT Neil
Born: Warrington, 4 November 1977
Height: 6'0" Weight: 11.5

This tall young outside right found his opportunities for regular first-team football restricted at Sunderland last season and, having made two Worthington Cup appearances for the Black Cats against Walsall in September, he was allowed to join Darlington on loan in February for three months. Neil made his debut at Feethams in the live Sky TV game against Peterborough, in which he scored. He then went on to score three more in the next four games with his direct, orthodox wing play, cutting in and shooting from the edge of the box. Although he did not find the net again, his speed on the right flank and accurate crossing produced a number of goals for the central strikers, and it was thrilling to see Darlington operate with two pacy wingers, with Neil Heaney on the left.

Wrexham (From trainee on 3/7/1996) FL 7+4/3 FAC 1 Others 1
Sunderland (£100,000 + on 9/7/1998) FL 0+2 FLC 4+1
Darlington (Loaned on 4/2/2000) FL 16+1/4

WALKER Andrew (Andy) Francis
Born: Glasgow, 6 April 1965
Height: 5'8" Weight: 11.6
Club Honours: S Div 1 '85; SPD '88; SC '88
International Honours: S: 3; U21-1

The experienced former Celtic forward signed for Carlisle at the start of the 1999-2000 season on a short-term contract. Although he displayed some neat touches in his five appearances, he returned to Scotland at the beginning of September, signing for Partick Thistle before moving on to Alloa Athletic in the new year.

Motherwell (Free from Baillieston Juniors on 31/7/1984) SL 65+12/7 SLC 2+4/1 SC 9+2/2
Glasgow Celtic (£350,000 on 1/7/1987) SL 86+22/40 SLC 9+6/8 SC 8+3/6 Others 5+2/3
Newcastle U (Loaned on 1/9/1991) FL 2 FLC 1
Bolton W (£160,000 on 9/1/1992) FL 61+6/44 FLC 3/1 FAC 9+3/8 Others 5/2
Glasgow Celtic (£550,000 on 1/7/1994) SL 26+16/9 SLC 6+1/2 SC 3+2 Others 2+1/1
Sheffield U (£500,000 on 23/2/1996) FL 32+20/20 FLC 2/2 FAC 1 Others 0+2/1
Hibernian (Loaned on 12/12/1997) SL 6+2/2 SC 1
Raith Rov (Loaned on 13/3/1998) SL 8+1/3
Ayr U (Free on 15/7/1998) SL 31+2/15 SLC 3/1 SC 4/3
Carlisle U (Free on 4/8/1999) FL 3 FLC 2

WALKER Andrew (Andy) William
Born: Bexley, 30 September 1981
Height: 6'0" Weight: 11.10

This young Colchester goalkeeper gained further senior experience in 1999-2000 when he was called on after only two minutes of the first leg of the Worthington Cup tie against Crystal Palace following Simon Brown's dismissal. He also appeared in the second leg and in two Nationwide League fixtures during the campaign. He generally impressed and after making steady progress once again at Layer Road he looks to have a bright future in the game.

Colchester U (Trainee) FL 3 FLC 1+1

WALKER Desmond (Des) Sinclair
Born: Hackney, 26 November 1965
Height: 5'11" Weight: 11.13
Club Honours: FLC '89, '90; FMC '89, '92
International Honours: E: 59; U21-7

Des had another excellent season in central defence for Sheffield Wednesday in 1999-2000 despite the club's relegation problems. He may not be as pacy as he was in younger days but he remains a class player, with his decisive tackling, timely interceptions and ability to read the game making him a formidable opponent. Des is regarded as one of the Owls' best-ever signings and certainly a disappointing campaign would have been much worse without his presence.

Nottingham F (From apprentice on 2/12/1983) FL 259+5/1 FLC 40 FAC 27 Others 14 (£1,500,000 to Sampodoria on 1/8/92)
Sheffield Wed (£2,700,000 on 22/7/1993) PL 264 FLC 23 FAC 22

Ian Walker

WALKER Ian Michael
Born: Watford, 31 October 1971
Height: 6'2" Weight: 13.1
Club Honours: FAYC '90; FLC '99
International Honours: E: 3; B-1; U21-9; Yth

Ian had a disappointing 1999-2000 season by his own very high standards, for although he was the first-choice 'keeper for Tottenham throughout the campaign he struggled to remain in the England squad and was not selected for the final 22 for Euro 2000. As agile as ever, he sometimes found it difficult to exert his usual authority playing behind a somewhat shaky defence. At his best, Ian kept impressive clean sheets against the likes of Liverpool and Kaiserslautern in the UEFA Cup. Undoubtedly, the talent that saw him establish himself as one of the top 'keepers in the Premiership is still very much there but Tottenham's acquisition of Neil Sullivan from relegated Wimbledon means he will have to fight for his place in the coming season.

Tottenham H (From trainee on 4/12/1989) F/PL 254+1 FLC 22 FAC 25 Others 6
Oxford U (Loaned on 31/8/1990) FL 2 FLC 1

WALKER James (Jimmy) Barry
Born: Sutton in Ashfield, 9 July 1973
Height: 5'11" Weight: 13.5

This brave and agile 'keeper kept Walsall in with a shout on numerous occasions during the 1999-2000 season. His long run of consecutive first-team matches stretched to 157 before it was broken when he missed the Worthington Cup tie against Plymouth but he remained the club's first choice throughout the campaign. With a career total approaching 250 games for the Bescot club, he is currently third in the Saddlers' all-time list of appearances for a goalkeeper behind current coach Mick Kearns and 1950s star Jackie Lewis.

Notts Co (From trainee on 9/7/1991)
Walsall (Free on 4/8/1993) FL 231+1 FLC 15 FAC 19 Others 16

WALKER Justin Matthew
Born: Nottingham, 6 September 1975
Height: 5'11" Weight: 12.12
International Honours: E: Yth; Sch

Justin was another Scunthorpe player who took a while to adjust to life in Division Two in 1999-2000, finding that he didn't have as much space and time when in possession. A hard-working midfielder who can pass the ball well, he was nevertheless virtually always a first choice in the club's midfield. He failed to score during the season and was unsuccessful from the penalty spot in the away match at Gillingham in March. Justin was surprisingly released at the end of the season. Stop Press: He was reported to have signed for local rivals Lincoln City during the summer break.

Nottingham F (From juniors on 10/9/1992)
Scunthorpe U (Signed on 26/3/1997) FL 126+6/2 FLC 8 FAC 6 Others 7/1

WALKER Richard Martin
Born: Birmingham, 8 November 1977
Height: 6'0" Weight: 12.0

Richard made excellent progress at Aston Villa in 1999-2000, taking advantage of injuries to Dion Dublin and Darius Vassell to force his way into the first-team squad in the second half of the campaign. He scored his first-ever Premiership goal when he netted in the 4-0 victory over Watford in February and then added a superb header in the 1-1 draw with Arsenal the following month, his performances earning him the offer of a new contract. He is a pacy striker with a good first touch and fine aerial skills and looks to have a great future in the game.

Aston Villa (From trainee on 13/12/1995) PL 2+4/2 FLC 1+1
Cambridge U (Loaned on 31/12/1998) FL 7+14/3 Others 1+2/1

WALKER Richard Neil
Born: Derby, 9 November 1971
Height: 6'0" Weight: 12.0

Richard is one of several Cheltenham players who spent much of the club's first season in the Football League watching from the sidelines. He began 1999-2000 with a thigh injury that kept him out of action and he was then unable to break into a remarkably settled back four. He remained patient and turned in some committed performances in the Robins' successful reserve team before earning a recall for the crucial fixture with Darlington at Easter. He did well in that game and held down a place in the final weeks of the season as Cheltenham narrowly missed out on the play-offs. A left-sided defender who can operate at either full back or centre half, Richard is hoping to become more involved in the new season provided he can stay clear of the injury problems that have blighted his Cheltenham career to date.

Notts Co (From trainee on 3/7/1990) FL 63+4/4 FLC 10 FAC 1+2 Others 8+1 (Free to Hereford U on 24/7/1997)
Mansfield T (Loaned on 23/3/1995) FL 4
Cheltenham T (Signed on 23/10/1998) FL 6+1

WALLWORK Ronald (Ronnie)
Born: Manchester, 10 September 1977
Height: 5'10" Weight: 12.9
Club Honours: FAYC '95
International Honours: E: Yth

A highly talented Manchester United forward who is a brilliant striker of the ball, especially with his left foot, Ronnie started last season with a life ban hanging over his head, following an alleged incident with a referee during a loan spell with Belgian club Royal Antwerp in the 1998-99 season. He maintained his innocence throughout, claiming it was a case of mistaken identity, and the threatened ban certainly didn't stop Sir Alex Ferguson from including him in the squad for the Premiership battle against Liverpool in September. After celebrating that win at Anfield, Ronnie was celebrating again the following week when the ban was lifted pending an appeal, and he was issued with a three-year suspended sentence instead. Despite making only fleeting appearances in the side for the rest of the season, his future at Old Trafford continued to look promising.

Manchester U (From trainee on 17/3/1995) PL 0+6 FLC 0+2 Others 1
Carlisle U (Loaned on 22/12/1997) FL 10/1 Others 2
Stockport Co (Loaned on 18/3/1998) FL 7

WALSCHAERTS Wim
Born: Antwerp, Belgium, 5 November 1972
Height: 5'10" Weight: 12.4

A consistent performer, Wim continued to display his admirable qualities on the right side of Leyton Orient's midfield throughout a mixed 1999-2000 campaign. He is a tireless box-to-box runner and, although not bought with a goalscoring pedigree, he still added to his tally. Wim can also play on the left of midfield or at right back if required. His presence was sorely missed when he was absent for several matches after breaking his arm in a training accident last September.

Leyton Orient (Free from KFC Tielen, Belgium on 30/7/1998) FL 76+4/6 FLC 6+1 FAC 6/2 Others 1

Gary Walsh

WALSH Daniel (Danny) Gareth
Born: Pontefract, 23 September 1979
Height: 5'11" Weight: 12.1

Danny made just one appearance for Oldham in 1999-2000, coming on as a late substitute for Mark Innes at Bristol City in November. A young central midfield player with a good range of passing, he reads the game well but needs to gain more first-team experience to make further progress.

Oldham Ath (From trainee on 7/7/1998) FL 0+2

WALSH David (Dave)
Born: Wrexham, 29 April 1979
Height: 6'1" Weight: 12.8
International Honours: W: U21-2

This young Wrexham goalkeeper found himself competing with the talented Kristian Rogers for a place in the club's reserve team after the signing of Kevin Dearden in the 1999 close season. He had previously appeared for the Robins in the FAW Premier Cup and he did so again in 1999-2000 while also turning out in the Auto Windscreens Shield tie against Preston North End. David was a regular member of the Wales U21 squad and won his first caps in the end-of-season Presidents' Cup games against Northern Ireland and Scotland.

Wrexham (From trainee on 4/7/1997) Others 1

WALSH Gary
Born: Wigan, 21 March 1968
Height: 6'3" Weight: 15.10
Club Honours: ECWC '91; ESC '91; FAC '94
International Honours: E: U21-2

Gary began the 1999-2000 season as first-choice 'keeper for Bradford City and showed some sparkling form in the opening matches. He has excellent reflexes, is agile and alert and seems to be improving as he gets older. He then had the misfortune to suffer a torn cartilage in his knee in a reserve match last November. Surgery was required but he failed to make a full recovery and he underwent a second operation on the knee in February that kept him out of action until the end of the campaign.

Manchester U (From juniors on 25/4/1985) F/PL 49+1 FLC 7 Others 6
Airdrie (Loaned on 11/8/1988) SL 3 SLC 1
Oldham Ath (Loaned on 19/11/1993) PL 6
Middlesbrough (£500,000 on 11/8/1995) PL 44 FLC 9 FAC 4
Bradford C (£500,000 + on 26/9/1997) P/FL 92 FLC 7 FAC 3

WALSH Michael Shane
Born: Rotherham, 5 August 1977
Height: 6'0" Weight: 13.2

A highly rated defender with Port Vale, Michael was just running into his best form last season when he suffered a cruciate ligament injury in a game at Swindon in October, ending his season early. Strong in the tackle, he can play at right back or in the centre of the back four, and his absence for much of the campaign can be cited as one of the reasons for the Vale's failure to stay in the First Division. Also a long-throw expert, he scored one goal at Wolves, heading in a far-post free-kick. He will be hoping for an injury-free season in 2000-01.

Scunthorpe U (From trainee on 3/7/1995) FL 94+9/1 FLC 4 FAC 9 Others 5
Port Vale (£100,000 on 30/7/1998) FL 28+3/2 FLC 3+1 FAC 1

WALSH Steven (Steve)
Born: Preston, 3 November 1964
Height: 6'3" Weight: 14.9
Club Honours: AMC '85; FLC '97, '00

This left-footed central defender has become "Mr Leicester City" over the years. A bad injury on the opening day of the 1999-2000 season was just the first of a number of such set-backs that again dogged Steve's campaign. Nevertheless, he continued to battle his way into contention and his whole ethic was encapsulated in the drama of the Worthington Cup quarter-final against Fulham. There, an unfortunate error presented the visitors with a two-goal lead late in the game; undaunted, Steve led the charge to the other end, laid on one goal, then blasted home the equaliser as the Foxes snatched victory from the jaws of defeat. However, suspension cost him the chance of another Wembley appearance in the final against Tranmere. Despite all his injury problems, he continued to close in on a top-three spot in the club's all-time appearance chart, finishing the season just 12 games short of that mark.

Wigan Ath (From juniors on 11/9/1982) FL 123+3/4 FLC 7 FAC 6 Others 10+2
Leicester C (£100,000 on 24/6/1986) P/FL 352+16/53 FLC 39+1/4 FAC 16+1/1 Others 23/4

WALTERS Mark Everton
Born: Birmingham, 2 June 1964
Height: 5'10" Weight: 12.8
Club Honours: FAYC '80; ESC '82; SPD '89, '90, '91; SLC '89, '91; FAC '92; FLC '95
International Honours: E: 1; B-1; U21-9; Yth; Sch

Mark appeared regularly in midfield for Swindon in the early part of the 1999-2000 season before he was allowed to move to Bristol Rovers on a free transfer to help cut the huge wage bill at the County Ground. The experienced former England winger made an immediate impression both with the Rovers supporters and with his new team-mates. Used as a left wing back or in central midfield, Mark scored spectacularly with a 25-yard free kick on his home debut against Luton in a 3-0 victory. He added a number of other goals including another superb effort from a free kick in the thrilling 3-3 home draw with Stoke. Now into his late thirties, he is still able to turn a game with his skill and this more than compensates for a decline in his pace.

Aston Villa (From apprentice on 18/5/1982) FL 168+13/39 FLC 20+1/6 FAC 11+1/1 Others 7+3/2
Glasgow R (£500,000 on 31/12/1987) SL 101+5/32 SLC 13/11 SC 14/6 Others 10/2
Liverpool (£1,250,000 on 13/8/1991) F/PL 58+36/14 FLC 10+2/4 FAC 6+3 Others 8+1/1
Stoke C (Loaned on 24/3/1994) FL 9/2
Wolverhampton W (Loaned on 9/9/1994) FL 11/3
Southampton (Free on 18/1/1996) PL 4+1 FAC 4
Swindon T (Free on 31/7/1996) FL 91+21/25 FLC 9+1/2 FAC 3+1/2
Bristol Rov (Free on 17/11/1999) FL 28+2/9 Others 0+2

WALTON David (Dave) Lee
Born: Bedlington, 10 April 1973
Height: 6'2" Weight: 14.8
Club Honours: Div 3 '94

The commanding centre back has been a regular member of the Crewe side since signing from Shrewsbury in 1997 but he missed much of the 1999-2000 campaign after suffering a back injury before the start of the season. Surgery was required, but Dave returned to the fray as a substitute against Swindon in February and was soon back in his rightful place at the heart of the Alex defence. An inspirational player, he will be hoping to avoid any further fitness problems next season.

Sheffield U (Free from Ashington on 13/3/1992)
Shrewsbury T (Signed on 5/11/1993) FL 127+1/10 FLC 7 FAC 10/1 Others 11/1
Crewe Alex (£500,000 + on 20/10/1997) FL 73+3/1 FLC 4 FAC 1

WALTON Mark Andrew
Born: Merthyr Tydfil, 1 June 1969
Height: 6'4" Weight: 15.8
International Honours: W: U21-1

Despite starting the 1999-2000 season as Brighton's second-choice 'keeper, Mark quickly regained his place. However, he was then dropped for the home game against Cheltenham and immediately handed in a transfer request only to be recalled to the team at Peterborough the following week. Injury and illness permitting, he then appeared regularly for Albion for the rest of the campaign. Mark is the son of Ron Walton, who is currently youth coach at Swansea.

Luton T (From juniors on 21/2/1987)
Colchester U (£15,000 on 5/11/1987) FL 40 FLC 3 FAC 8 Others 5
Norwich C (£75,000 on 15/8/1989) FL 22 FLC 1 FAC 5

Dave Walton

Wrexham (Loaned on 27/8/1993) FL 6
Dundee (Free on 27/1/1994)
Bolton W (Free on 2/3/1994) FL 3 (Free to Wroxham on 9/9/1994)
Fulham (Free from Fakenham T on 12/8/1996) FL 40 FLC 5 Others 3
Gillingham (Loaned on 6/2/1998) FL 1
Brighton & Hove A (£20,000 on 15/7/1998) FL 58 FLC 2 FAC 4 Others 2

WANCHOPE Pablo (Paulo) Cesar
Born: Costa Rica, 31 July 1976
Height: 6'4" Weight: 12.6
International Honours: Costa Rica: 23

This exciting Costa Rican striker joined West Ham from Derby during the 1999 summer break and quickly established an effective if unorthodox partnership with Paolo di Canio. He showed great pace and again proved a handful for opposition defences with his strength and ability to retain the ball under pressure. He was in great scoring form in early April, netting five times in three games including a superb chip over Newcastle 'keeper Shay Given to earn the Hammers a sensational victory in the last minute of the game. Paulo never seemed to fully win over the Upton Park fans despite a dozen goals and the support of his manager Harry Redknapp. He played three times for Costa Rica in the CONCACAF Gold Cup finals in the spring, scoring once in the 2-2 draw with South Korea.

Derby Co (£600,000 from CS Heridiano, Costa Rica on 27/3/1997) PL 65+7/23 FLC 6+1/5 FAC 4
West Ham U (£3,250,000 on 28/7/1999) PL 33+2/12 FLC 3 FAC 0+1 Others 5+1/2

WANLESS Paul Steven
Born: Banbury, 14 December 1973
Height: 6'1" Weight: 13.12

Cambridge's "Captain Courageous", Paul is a man whose blood is rumoured to be black and amber. The tough-tackling midfielder was always in the thick of the action in 1999-2000 as he led from the front. He was United's "Player of the Year" for the second season in a row, and it would be difficult to imagine a Cambridge line-up without him. Paul is due to make his 200th senior appearance for the club in the opening weeks of the new term.

Oxford U (From trainee on 3/12/1991) FL 12+20 FLC 0+3/1 Others 2+2
Lincoln C (Free on 7/7/1995) FL 7+1 Others 2
Cambridge U (Free on 8/3/1996) FL 167+6/23 FLC 9 FAC 11+1/1 Others 4

WARD Ashley Stuart
Born: Manchester, 24 November 1970
Height: 6'2" Weight: 13.10

Ashley had the thankless task of leading the Blackburn attack in 1999-2000 as the club searched in vain for an escape route from the First Division. Ever willing, he offers boundless supplies of effort and enthusiasm which ensure that, while he may lack the silky skills and extra pace required to prosper at the highest level, defenders facing him can be sure of a testing 90 minutes. Strong in the air, he is an effective target man but he had a disappointing season in front of goal. He was ruled out for a while after Christmas with a dislocated shoulder but was soon back in the fray, and retained his place to the end of what had been a turbulent season at Ewood Park.

Manchester C (From trainee on 5/8/1989) FL 0+1 FAC 0+2
Wrexham (Loaned on 10/1/1991) FL 4/2 Others 1
Leicester C (£80,000 on 30/7/1991) FL 2+8 FLC 2+1 FAC 0+1 Others 0+1
Blackpool (Loaned on 21/11/1992) FL 2/1
Crewe Alex (£80,000 on 1/12/1992) FL 58+3/25 FLC 4/2 FAC 2/4 Others 7/5
Norwich C (£500,000 on 8/12/1994) P/FL 53/18 FLC 6/3 FAC 1
Derby Co (£1,000,000 on 19/3/1996) F/PL 32+8/9 FLC 1+1 FAC 2/1
Barnsley (£1,300,000 + on 5/9/1997) P/FL 45+1/20 FLC 9/4 FAC 6/1
Blackburn Rov (£4,250,000 + on 31/12/1998) P/FL 52+2/13 FLC 2 FAC 4+1

Ashley Ward

WARD Darren
Born: Worksop, 11 May 1974
Height: 6'2" Weight: 14.2
Club Honours: Div 3 '98
International Honours: W: 1; B-1; U21-2

This very accomplished goalkeeper had another excellent season with Notts County in 1999-2000, when he was the team captain. He missed just a couple of games through injury and once again produced a number of top-class displays. Darren was also a regular member of the Wales squad and made his full international debut in the end-of-season friendly with Portugal. His form is such that it now seems only a matter of time before he moves on to a higher grade of football.

Mansfield T (From trainee on 27/7/1992) FL 81 FLC 5 FAC 5 Others 6
Notts Co (£160,000 on 11/7/1995) FL 216 FLC 15 FAC 18 Others 10

WARD Darren Philip
Born: Harrow, 13 September 1978
Height: 6'0" Weight: 12.6

Having successfully returned from long-term injury towards the end of the 1998-99 campaign, Darren had an operation to remove a metal plate from his leg at the start of last season. With no immediate prospect of a first-team place at Watford, he went on loan to Queens Park Rangers for three months, and it proved to be the making of him. He played in 14 matches, regained his sharpness and appetite for the game and soon became very popular with the Rangers fans. Darren eventually returned to Vicarage Road in March ready to challenge for a first-team place. He got his chance at Everton, coming on as a second-half substitute to subdue the experienced Mark Hughes, and finished the season as part of a back three as Graham Taylor experimented with different formations; he also scored his first senior goal, at Middlesbrough. Only 21, Darren seems back on course to fulfil his considerable potential.

Watford (From trainee on 13/2/1997) P/FL 16+2/1 FAC 1 Others 0+1
Queens Park R (Loaned on 17/12/1999) FL 14 FAC 1

WARD Gavin John
Born: Sutton Coldfield, 30 June 1970
Height: 6'3" Weight: 14.12
Club Honours: Div 3 '93; WC '93; AMC '00

This popular 'keeper had a truly outstanding season for Stoke in 1999-2000. A good shot stopper and very capable on crosses, he held on to his first-team place despite competition from the reliable Carl Muggleton. There was no recurrence of the niggling injuries which had interrupted his season in the past, and he is truly the best signing Brian Little made during his time at the helm of the club. There are so many highlights, including City's victory in the Auto Windscreens Shield final at Wembley, but the fact that on two separate occasions he saw off attacks by opposing fans who breached security and entered on to the field of play will secure his place in City supporters' folklore for years to come and strengthened his hard-man image.

Shrewsbury T (Free from Aston Villa juniors on 26/9/1988)
West Bromwich A (Free on 18/9/1989)
Cardiff C (Free on 5/10/1989) FL 58+1 FAC 1 Others 7
Leicester C (£175,000 on 16/7/1993) F/PL 38 FLC 3 FAC 0+1 Others 4
Bradford C (£175,000 on 13/7/1995) FL 36 FLC 6 FAC 3 Others 2
Bolton W (£300,000 on 29/3/1996) F/PL 19+3 FLC 2 FAC 4
Burnley (Loaned on 14/8/1998) FL 17
Stoke C (Free on 25/2/1999) FL 52 FLC 4 FAC 1 Others 9

WARD Mitchum (Mitch) David
Born: Sheffield, 19 June 1971
Height: 5'8" Weight: 11.7

A willing and versatile utility man, Mitch found his opportunities severely restricted at Everton during what was for him a frustrating 1999-2000 campaign. After kicking off the season in the starting line-up against the treble winners, Manchester United, Mitch was handed the captaincy of a weakened team against Oxford in the Worthington Cup, then did not figure again until a substitute appearance at West Ham – five months later! A valuable squad player, he is capable of operating at full back, on either flank or in midfield, and his attitude is unquestioned. Frustrated by a lack of opportunity, however, he may well conclude that to get regular first team football he may have to seek opportunities elsewhere.

Sheffield U (From trainee on 1/7/1989) F/PL 135+19/11 FLC 8+3/2 FAC 7+2/2 Others 5+1/1
Crewe Alex (Loaned on 1/11/1990) FL 4/1 FAC 1/1 Others 2
Everton (£850,000 on 25/11/1997) PL 18+6 FLC 2+1 FAC 2

WARDLEY Stuart James
Born: Cambridge, 10 September 1975
Height: 5'11" Weight: 12.7

Without doubt, Stuart was one of the finds of the 1999-2000 season. He was signed by Queens Park Rangers during the summer of 1999 from Essex Senior League club Saffron Walden Town. A tireless midfielder, he supports the front line with great effect. He made his full debut in the sixth game of the campaign and missed only one match from then to the end of the season. He proved to be a regular goalscorer, and was the first Rangers player to hit a tally in double figures for two seasons. In total he scored 14 goals, making him joint top scorer with Chris Kiwomya. The fans recognised his contribution to the improvement in results by voting him the supporters' club "Player of the Year".

Queens Park R (£15,000 from Saffron Walden T on 22/7/1999) FL 41+2/11 FAC 3/3

WARE Paul David
Born: Congleton, 7 November 1970
Height: 5'9" Weight: 11.8

Paul struggled to win a regular place in the Macclesfield line-up at the start of the 1999-2000 campaign despite scoring the winning goal at Hull with a spectacular bicycle kick. However, after a successful loan spell with Conference outfit Nuneaton Borough he returned to the first-team squad, mostly featuring as a substitute to come off the bench and vary Macc's options in the centre of the park. A competitive player, he will be looking for greater first-team involvement during the coming season. Stop Press: It was reported at the end of June that Paul had signed for Rochdale.

Stoke C (From trainee on 15/11/1988) FL 92+23/10 FLC 7+1 FAC 4+1 Others 12+2/4
Stockport Co (Signed on 8/9/1994) FL 42+12/4 FLC 6+1/1 FAC 2 Others 3/1 (Free to Hednesford T on 15/7/1997)
Cardiff C (Loaned on 29/1/1997) FL 5
Macclesfield T (Free on 14/7/1999) FL 9+9/2 FLC 1

WARHURST Paul
Born: Stockport,, 26 September 1969
Height: 6'1" Weight: 13.6
Club Honours: PL '95
International Honours: E: U21-8

Still a hugely talented footballer, Paul's 1999-2000 season with Bolton was blighted by numerous injuries throughout the year. The fact that his longest run was six consecutive games tells its own story, and sadly every time he seemed to be making a successful comeback another injury would halt his progress. His calf was the main area for concern, as it caused Paul to pull up in a few games and meant that he was constantly in the treatment room. When he did play, however, he stamped his authority on every game with a touch of class as an added bonus. A big, powerful and versatile player, Paul performed in the centre of midfield for Bolton with considerable success. His main assets are his vision and an ability to deliver the perfectly weighted pass to split the opposition defence wide open. Paul's importance to the team was such that he was rushed back from yet another injury set-back to play in the final game of the season against Norwich, when he produced a "Man of the Match" performance as Bolton confirmed their place in the play-offs. He will be hoping to remain clear of injuries in the coming season, and providing he does so he should remain a key figure at the Reebok Stadium.

Manchester C (From trainee on 1/7/1988)
Oldham Ath (£10,000 on 27/10/1988) FL 60+7/2 FLC 8 FAC 5+4 Others 2
Sheffield Wed (£750,000 on 17/7/1991) F/PL 60+6/6 FLC 9/4 FAC 7+1/5 Others 5/3
Blackburn Rov (£2,700,000 on 17/8/1993) PL 30+27/4 FLC 6+2 FAC 2+1 Others 4+2
Crystal Palace (£1,250,000 on 31/7/1997) P/FL 27/4 FLC 2 FAC 1
Bolton W (£800,000 on 25/11/1998) FL 32+7 FLC 1+3 FAC 1+1 Others 2+2

WARNE Paul
Born: Norwich, 8 May 1973
Height: 5'9" Weight: 11.2

There surely can't have been a more willing runner in last season's Third Division than Rotherham's all-action striker. Paul scored ten times himself and created a multitude of openings for his colleagues with his prodigious workrate. He seemed to specialise in spectacular goals and two in particular stand out as memorable: a cracking volley against Hull and his match-winner at Northampton.

Wigan Ath (£25,000 from Wroxham on 30/7/1997) FL 11+25/3 FLC 0+1 FAC 1 Others 1+2/1
Rotherham U (Free on 15/1/1999) FL 58+4/18 FLC 1+1 FAC 2 Others 4

Tony Warner

WARNER Anthony (Tony) Randolph
Born: Liverpool, 11 May 1974
Height: 6'4" Weight: 13.9

A talented goalkeeper who was denied a chance to prove himself at first-team level at Liverpool by the presence of David James and Brad Friedel in the Anfield squad, Tony joined Millwall at the beginning of 1999-2000 after impressing in pre-season trials. His substantial frame makes him an awesome figure and was used to full effect in his dominance of his goal area last season. Producing a series of inspirational performances, he seized the opportunity to

establish himself as a regular in the side under the expert guidance of Nigel Spink. An excellent shot stopper, which proved invaluable to the Lions on more than one occasion during the campaign, he quickly became a favourite of the Millwall faithful.
Liverpool (From juniors on 1/1/1994)
Swindon T (Loaned on 5/11/1997) FL 2
Glasgow Celtic (Loaned on 13/11/1998) SL 3
Aberdeen (Loaned on 31/3/1999) SL 6
Millwall (Free on 16/7/1999) FL 45 FLC 2 FAC 1 Others 3

WARNER Philip (Phil)
Born: Southampton, 2 February 1979
Height: 5'10" Weight: 11.7
Phil is a right-sided Southampton player who is able to play in defence and midfield. He was loaned to Brentford for the whole of the 1999-2000 season to gain further experience of league football, although he spent most of his time on the subs' bench, managing only two starts. Good in the air, quick and possessing neat ball control, he generally appeared in midfield for the Bees and his experience at Griffin Park should serve him well for the future.
Southampton (From trainee on 23/5/1997) PL 5+1 FLC 1
Brentford (Loaned on 9/7/1999) FL 1+13 FLC 0+1 FAC 1

WARNER Vance
Born: Leeds, 3 September 1974
Height: 6'0" Weight: 13.2
International Honours: E: Yth
Injuries and the outstanding form of others around him prevented Vance from being a regular for the majority of Rotherham's promotion-winning 1999-2000 season, but he epitomised the spirit in the club by producing excellent performances whenever required. A defender who can play in the middle or on the right, he has a tremendous turn of speed, while he also possesses great tackling ability. He was released in the summer.
Nottingham F (From trainee on 14/9/1991) F/PL 4+1 FLC 1+1
Grimsby T (Loaned on 2/2/1996) FL 3
Rotherham U (Signed on 29/8/1997) FL 60+2/1 FLC 1+1 FAC 6 Others 1

WARREN Christer Simon
Born: Weymouth, 10 October 1974
Height: 5'10" Weight: 11.10
Although previously used on the left side of midfield or as a striker, Christer spent the 1999-2000 season as Bournemouth's regular left back. He sometimes seemed uncomfortable in his new role but looked dangerous when coming forward with the ball. A predominantly left-footed player with good pace, he can deliver a fine cross and possesses a powerful shot. Christer was out of contract at the end of last season and at the time of writing appeared to be on the move from Dean Court. Stop Press: He was reported to have signed for Queens Park Rangers in the middle of June.
Southampton (£40,000 from Cheltenham T on 31/3/1995) PL 1+7 FLC 1
Brighton & Hove A (Loaned on 11/10/1996) FL 3
Fulham (Loaned on 6/3/1997) FL 8+3/1
Bournemouth (£50,000 on 8/10/1997) FL 94+9/13 FLC 4+3 FAC 10/1 Others 7

WARREN David John Paul
Born: Cork, 28 February 1981
Height: 5'10" Weight: 11.4
International Honours: RoI: Yth (UEFA-U16 '98)
David came to the Racecourse Ground in the summer of 1999 on the recommendation of Wrexham's Ireland-based scout Tadgh O'Neill and was delighted to join the club's highly successful youth policy (the Robins have now become the first Welsh club to be granted full academy status and are one of only a handful of lower-division outfits to have achieved this). He is a right-sided midfield player who made his bow in senior football last October as a substitute in the FAW Premier Cup tie against Conwy United and went on to receive his Football League debut on Easter Monday in the home match with Colchester. David was a member of the Republic of Ireland squad which won the UEFA U16 title in 1997-98 and made two appearances for the U18s against Germany last season.
Wrexham (Free from Mayfield U on 4/8/1999) FL 1

WARREN Mark Wayne
Born: Clapton, 12 November 1974
Height: 6'0" Weight: 12.2
International Honours: E: Yth
Mark appeared regularly in the Notts County defence throughout the 1999-2000 campaign, contributing a goal in the 4-4 draw with Bristol City last November. He is an uncompromising central defender who has good pace and is strong in the tackle. His wholehearted displays and obvious desire to win made him a big favourite with the Magpies' fans last season.
Leyton Orient (From trainee on 6/7/1992) FL 134+18/5 FLC 8+1/2 FAC 5+1 Others 10+4/1
Oxford U (Loaned on 24/12/1998) FL 4
Notts Co (Signed on 28/1/1999) FL 49+2/1 FLC 4 FAC 1 Others 1

WASSALL Darren Paul James
Born: Birmingham, 27 June 1968
Height: 6'0" Weight: 12.10
Club Honours: FMC '92
This experienced central defender appeared to have recovered from his long-standing achilles tendon problems at the start of the 1999-2000 season. He played several games for Birmingham City reserves and was one of a number of fringe men called up for the Worthington Cup match at Exeter last August. Unfortunately, Darren then spent further time on the injury list with his old complaint, and although he had returned to action with the Blues' second string by the end of the campaign he was released in the summer.
Nottingham F (From apprentice on 1/6/1986) FL 17+10 FLC 6+2 FAC 3+1 Others 4+2/1
Hereford U (Loaned on 23/10/1987) FL 5 FAC 1 Others 1
Bury (Loaned on 2/3/1989) FL 7/1
Derby Co (£600,000 on 15/6/1992) FL 90+8 FLC 9 FAC 4 Others 11
Manchester C (Loaned on 11/9/1996) FL 14+1 FLC 2
Birmingham C (£100,000 on 26/3/1997) FL 22+3 FLC 6

WATERMAN David (Dave) Graham
Born: Guernsey, 16 May 1977
Height: 5'10" Weight: 13.2
International Honours: NI: U21-14
Dave continued to make progress at Portsmouth in 1999-2000, featuring regularly in the starting line-up after Tony Pulis took over as manager in January. A strong and physical midfield player, he showed excellent man-making skills and is now beginning to develop his full potential. Already a regular member of the Northern Ireland U21 team, he won a further four caps last season.
Portsmouth (From trainee on 4/7/1995) FL 40+9 FLC 1 FAC 3

WATKIN Stephen (Steve)
Born: Wrexham, 16 June 1971
Height: 5'10" Weight: 11.10
Club Honours: WC '95; Div 3 '00
International Honours: W: B-2; Sch
Despite failing to get his name on the score sheet for Swansea as regularly as during the previous season, Steve still proved to be a handful for the opposition in 1999-2000 with his ability to hold the ball up and bring his midfielders into play. An ankle ligament injury early in the season at Hull saw him sidelined for four weeks. More worryingly, a fractured cheekbone in the last home match of the campaign against Exeter will probably cause him to miss Swansea's return to Division Two. The Swans' top goalscorer with ten league and cup goals, Steve displayed his ability as a striker when he proved he could forge a good partnership with either a big target man like Julian Alsop or a tricky ball player like Walter Boyd. He also showed his versatility by starting a couple of games in a midfield role. He most deservedly won a Third Division championship winners' medal.
Wrexham (From juniors on 24/7/1989) FL 167+33/55 FLC 11+3/4 FAC 16+6/12 Others 17+5/4
Swansea C (£108,000 on 26/9/1997) FL 100+14/27 FLC 5/1 FAC 5+2/1 Others 2+1/1

WATKINS Dale Andrew
Born: Peterborough, 4 November 1971
Height: 5'8" Weight: 11.12
International Honours: E: SP-2
A key player for Cheltenham during their back-to-back FA Trophy and Nationwide Conference successes in the late 1990s, Dale began 1999-2000 hoping to re-establish himself as a Football League player. He made nine appearances, five of them as a substitute, before deciding to return to the non-league game and making a transfer request. A small but hard-working striker who never gives defenders a minute's peace, Dale moved on to Conference club Kettering Town, for whom he appeared in the FA Trophy final against Kingstonian at Wembley in May.
Peterborough U (From Sheffield U juniors on 23/8/1990) FL 5+5 FLC 0+1 FAC 1 (Free to Peterborough C during 1991 close season)
Cheltenham T (Signed from Gloucester C on 18/7/1997) FL 4+5 FLC 0+2

WATSON Alexander (Alex) Francis
Born: Liverpool, 5 April 1968
Height: 6'1" Weight: 13.0
Club Honours: CS '88
International Honours: E: Yth

Having been written off in some quarters following a bad knee injury, Torquay's player-coach came back as good as ever in 1999-2000. His organisation of the Gulls' defence, and aerial dominance, were first class. Now firmly in the vastly experienced category, Alex looks good for at least another couple of seasons. He is the younger brother of Everton's Dave Watson.

Liverpool (From apprentice on 18/5/1985) FL 3+1 FLC 1+1 FAC 1+1 Others 1
Derby Co (Loaned on 30/8/1990) FL 5
Bournemouth (£150,000 on 18/1/1991) FL 145+6/5 FLC 14/1 FAC 12/1 Others 5
Gillingham (Loaned on 11/9/1995) FL 10/1
Torquay U (£50,000 on 23/11/1995) FL 172/8 FLC 10 FAC 8 Others 6/1

WATSON David (Dave)
Born: Liverpool, 20 November 1961
Height: 6'0" Weight: 12.4
Club Honours: FLC '85; Div 2 '86; Div 1 '87, CS '87, '95; FAC '95
International Honours: E: 12; U21-7 (UEFA-U21 '84)

After more than a decade of defensive excellence at the heart of the Everton rearguard, Dave's outstanding career finally began to draw to a close in 1999-2000. After kicking off the campaign as club captain and in the starting line-up, the 38-year-old's legs finally began to show signs of wear and tear. Injuries he once cheerfully shrugged off began to take longer and longer to heal, and after captaining the Blues at home to Leeds on 24 October he made only fleeting appearances. The last of those was at home to Tottenham, two weeks into the new millennium – and more than 14 years after he first strode out for the Toffees. Such is the esteem in which he is held at Everton that his playing contract has been extended by a further year, but it is more and more likely that he will continue to exert his considerable influence in a coaching capacity. If Dave has pulled on a pair of boots at Goodison for the last time, he will be sorely missed. His reputation as a living legend at Everton has been fully earned. He is the older brother of Torquay's Alex Watson.

Liverpool (From juniors on 25/5/1979)
Norwich C (£100,000 on 29/11/1980) FL 212/11 FLC 21/3 FAC 18/1
Everton (£900,000 on 22/8/1986) F/PL 419+4/23 FLC 39/7 FAC 47+1/5 Others 16+1/3

WATSON Gordon William George
Born: Sidcup, 20 March 1971
Height: 5'11" Weight: 12.9
International Honours: E: U21-2

Gordon joined Bournemouth on a non-contract basis in August 1999 as he sought to rebuild a career shattered by a broken leg suffered back in February 1997. He made a handful of starts and seven appearances from the subs' bench in the first half of the 1999-2000 season but rarely featured in the new year, being troubled by a niggling hamstring injury. He remains a hard-working target man who has good aerial skills.

Charlton Ath (From trainee on 5/4/1989) FL 20+11/7 FLC 2/1 FAC 0+1 Others 1+1
Sheffield Wed (£250,000 on 20/2/1991) F/PL 29+37/15 FLC 6+5/3 FAC 5+2/2 Others 2+2/1
Southampton (£1,200,000 on 17/3/1995) PL 37+15/8 FLC 6+3/5 FAC 5+1/1
Bradford C (£550,000 on 17/1/1997) FL 8+13/5 FLC 1+3
Bournemouth (Free on 23/8/1999) FL 2+4 FLC 0+1 FAC 1+2 Others 0+1

WATSON Kevin Edward
Born: Hackney, 3 January 1974
Height: 6'0" Weight: 12.6

After Kevin moved to Millmoor on a free transfer during the 1999 close season, Swindon's loss proved to be Rotherham's gain as he displayed all his midfield skills to skipper his new team to promotion. A highly accomplished ball player, he is also an excellent passer and was one of the best midfielders in Division Three last season. Kevin netted just one goal in 1999-2000 but it was certainly a memorable strike: playing against Chester at Millmoor last August he returned the 'keeper's clearance from the half-way line and it bounced into the net.

Tottenham H (From trainee on 15/5/1992) PL 4+1 FLC 1+1/1 FAC 0+1
Brentford (Loaned on 24/3/1994) FL 2+1
Bristol C (Loaned on 2/12/1994) FL 1+1
Barnet (Loaned on 16/2/1995) FL 13
Swindon T (Free on 15/7/1996) FL 39+24/1 FLC 2+2 FAC 1+2
Rotherham U (Free on 31/7/1999) FL 44/1 FLC 2 FAC 2 Others 2

WATSON Mark Stewart
Born: Vancouver, Canada, 8 September 1970
Height: 6'0" Weight: 12.6
International Honours: Canada: 58 (Gold Cup 2000); U23-13

Mark had another impressive season in the heart of the Oxford defence in 1999-2000 before suffering from "burn-out" towards the end of the campaign. Due to his international commitments and having joined Oxford from Swedish football (where the season runs from April through to October), Mark has played virtually non-stop for two years and will be looking to recharge his batteries during the close season. Not the tallest of centre backs but good in the air, he has pace and anticipates danger quickly, while he also possesses a useful long throw. A regular with the Canadian national side, he added five caps during the season, being an ever-present in the team that surprisingly defeated Colombia to win the CONCACAF Gold Cup last February. Mark's major contribution was to score the winner in the semi-final tie against Trinidad & Tobago – only his third goal in 58 appearances for his country. Out of contract at Oxford in the summer, he was expected to be offered new terms.

Watford (Signed from Vancouver 86ers, Canada on 19/11/1993) FL 18 FAC 1+2 (Freed during 1995 close season)
Oxford U (Free from Osters IFV, Sweden on 17/12/1998) FL 57+1 FLC 2 FAC 8 Others 1

WATSON Paul Douglas
Born: Hastings, 4 January 1975
Height: 5'8" Weight: 10.10
Club Honours: Div 3 '99

This left-footed right back joined Brighton in July 1999, thus teaming up with Albion boss Micky Adams for the third time in his career, having previously worked with him at Fulham and Brentford. However, he missed the early part of the season owing to a hamstring problem. Paul is Albion's dead-ball specialist and created a number of goals last season with his crosses. This was recognised with selection in Opta Index's "Third Division Team of the Season". He also scored some spectacular goals from free kicks, notably the equaliser at home to Barnet on Boxing Day.

Gillingham (From trainee on 8/12/1992) FL 57+5/2 FLC 4 FAC 6 Others 5+3
Fulham (£13,000 on 30/7/1996) FL 48+2/4 FLC 3/1 FAC 2 Others 2
Brentford (£50,000 on 12/12/1997) FL 37 FLC 2 FAC 2 Others 0+1
Brighton & Hove A (£20,000 on 9/7/1999) FL 40+2/4 FLC 1 FAC 4/1 Others 2

WATSON Stephen (Steve) Craig
Born: North Shields, 1 April 1974
Height: 6'0" Weight: 12.7
International Honours: E: B-1; U21-12; Yth

Steve had a relatively disappointing time in 1999-2000, being in and out of the Aston Villa side and missing out on a place in the FA Cup final squad to youngster JLloyd Samuel. He contested the right-wing-back position with Mark Delaney and struggled to regain his place once he had lost it to the Welsh international. He is a confident right-sided player who can perform equally well in defence or midfield. Calm under pressure and one who always gives 100 per cent effort, Steve is a strong runner with the ball when pushing forward to help out the attack. Stop Press: He was reported to have moved to Everton at the beginning of July.

Newcastle U (From trainee on 6/4/1991) F/PL 179+29/12 FLC 10+6/1 FAC 13+4 Others 18+4/1
Aston Villa (£4,000,000 on 15/10/1998) PL 39+2 FLC 8+1/1 FAC 4

WATTS Julian
Born: Sheffield, 17 March 1971
Height: 6'3" Weight: 13.7
Club Honours: FLC '97

Julian joined Luton at the start of the 1999-2000 season after a frustrating spell with Bristol City but before long it looked as though he had been at Kenilworth Road for years. Having made his debut for the club in the first match of the season, he quickly became a pillar of the defence, playing in all but two of Town's matches. An accomplished central defender with pace who is also authoritative in the air, he makes his task look easy, and his assured and confident displays were a crucial factor in a generally encouraging season for Lenny Lawrence's team.

Rotherham U (Signed from Frecheville CA on 10/7/1990) FL 17+3/1 FLC 1 FAC 4 Others 2
Sheffield Wed (£80,000 on 13/3/1992) PL 12+4/1 FLC 1 Others 1
Shrewsbury T (Loaned on 18/12/1992) FL 9 Others 1

Leicester C (£210,000 on 29/3/1996) P/FL 31+7/1 FLC 6+1 FAC 2+1 Others 4
Crewe Alex (Loaned on 29/8/1997) FL 5
Huddersfield T (Loaned on 5/2/1998) FL 8
Bristol C (Free on 6/7/1998) FL 16+1/1 FLC 3+1
Lincoln C (Loaned on 18/12/1998) FL 2 Others 1
Blackpool (Loaned on 25/3/1999) FL 9
Luton T (Free on 6/8/1999) FL 45/4 FLC 2 FAC 5

WATTS Steven (Steve)
Born: Lambeth, 11 July 1976
Height: 6'1" Weight: 13.7

After winning a national newspaper's "Search for a Striker" competition in 1998, Steve proved that it was not a one-off, and the Leyton Orient forward maintained his progress in 1999-2000. He went on loan to Welling in November but returned in the new year to lead the line well. He added his share of goals to the team's cause, finishing as joint top scorer with seven. Steve will be looking to be a first-team regular in the new season.

Leyton Orient (Signed from Fisher on 14/10/1998) FL 31+29/12 FLC 2+1/1 FAC 1+1 Others 4

WAUGH Warren Anthony
Born: Harlesden, 9 October 1980
Height: 6'1" Weight: 13.5

After spending three months on loan in Finland, Warren returned to England but only made a handful of appearances from the subs' bench for Exeter last season. When he did appear, his height and physical presence proved a handful for opposition defences but in February he was placed on the transfer list. Shortly afterwards he went on loan to Dr Martens League club Dorchester Town, and at the beginning of May he was reported to have signed a two-year deal with Cambridge City.

Exeter C (From trainee on 2/7/1999) FL 0+10 Others 1+1

WEAH George
Born: Monrovia, Liberia, 1 October 1966
Height: 6'1" Weight: 12.10
Club Honours: FAC '00
International Honours: Liberia

Rarely can a player have made such a dramatic arrival at a club as George did when he joined Chelsea on loan from AC Milan last January. Consider the facts: he caught a plane from Milan to London, met his team-mates for the first time at the training ground, waited for his international clearance to arrive, took his place on the substitutes' bench for that evening's fixture against local rivals Tottenham Hotspur and, with the match scoreless, came off the bench to head the only goal of the game three minutes from time – the stuff of which dreams are made! George had joined the Blues on loan until the end of the season after the regime at the San Siro had deemed him to be surplus to requirements; AS Roma and Marseille were keen to sign him but his former team-mate Marcel Desailly extolled the virtues of Chelsea and he decided to move to Stamford Bridge. Blues boss Gianluca Vialli was determined to avoid a repetition of the previous season when a lack of cover for his injured front-line strikers thwarted Chelsea's domestic ambitions. George played a pivotal role in Chelsea's progress to the FA Cup final, scoring the winner in the fifth round against Leicester and looping an impudent header over the Gillingham 'keeper in the quarter-final. George also played in the semi-final against Newcastle, and achieved his lifelong ambition of appearing in a Wembley FA Cup final when Vialli gave him the nod over Tore Andre Flo for the showpiece against Aston Villa. "The Lion King" is one of the greatest footballers to come out of Africa and his achievements are legendary: he was voted World, European and African "Footballer of the Year" in 1995 and is credited with scoring the greatest goal in Serie A history for AC Milan against Verona when he ran the length of the pitch, dribbling past seven players, before scoring. Not content with being a footballing genius, George is a national icon for the long-suffering people of Liberia. He is actively involved with UNICEF, the United Nations fund for underprivileged children, and has virtually kept afloat the cash-strapped Liberian national team by making financial donations and purchasing kit. Stop Press: It was reported at the beginning of July that Chelsea would not be signing him on a permanent basis.

Chelsea (Loaned from AC Milan, Italy on 12/1/2000) PL 9+2/3 FAC 4/2

George Weah

WEARE Ross Michael
Born: Perivale, 19 March 1977
Height: 6'2" Weight: 13.6
Ross is one of Queens Park Rangers boss Gerry Francis's finds from non-league football, having been signed from Essex Senior League club East Ham United. A striker, he has been compared to a young Les Ferdinand in his build and style of play. He did not get a run in the first team last season and made only five appearances, all as a substitute, before sustaining an injury and being forced to miss the rest of the campaign.
Queens Park R (£10,000 from East Ham U on 25/3/1999) FL 0+4 FAC 0+1

WEATHERSTONE Ross
Born: Reading, 16 May 1981
Height: 5'11" Weight: 11.10
Ross showed good form for Oxford's reserves last season and was given his senior debut at centre half in the local derby at Reading in November. He had an impressive game and was rewarded with a couple more outings but his season came to a premature close when he was carried off with damaged knee ligaments at Brentford in an Auto Windscreens Shield tie. He is the younger brother of Simon Weatherstone, also of Oxford.
Oxford U (From trainee on 29/10/1999) FL 3 FAC 1 Others 2

WEATHERSTONE Simon
Born: Reading, 26 January 1980
Height: 5'10" Weight: 11.12
Simon had a mixed time at Oxford in 1999-2000, starting the season as a first-team regular before dropping out of contention, only to return to the side at the end of the campaign under new manager Denis Smith. He appeared in a variety of positions in his second spell of action and scored a vital goal against Colchester. When he lined up with his younger brother Ross for the Auto Windscreens Shield tie with Brentford they became the first siblings to appear in the same team for Oxford since Graham and Ron Atkinson back in the 1960s.
Oxford U (From trainee on 27/3/1997) FL 19+26/3 FLC 1+3/1 Others 1

WEAVER Luke Dennis Spencer
Born: Woolwich, 26 June 1979
Height: 6'2" Weight: 13.2
International Honours: E: Yth; Sch
Carlisle's first-choice 'keeper in 1999-2000, Luke made his debut in the opening-day victory over his first club, Leyton Orient, having moved to Brunton Park from Sunderland, initially on loan, 24 hours earlier. He signed a permanent deal soon afterwards and won plaudits for many of his performances behind a defence that sometimes looked a little suspect. A good shot stopper, he grew in confidence during the season despite a series of injuries that restricted him to 29 league appearances.
Leyton Orient (From trainee on 26/6/1996) FL 9 FAC 1 Others 1
Sunderland (£250,000 on 9/1/1998)
Scarborough (Loaned on 10/12/1998) FL 6
Carlisle U (Free on 6/8/1999) FL 29 FLC 2 Others 1

WEAVER Nicholas (Nicky) James
Born: Sheffield, 2 March 1979
Height: 6'3" Weight: 13.6
International Honours: E: U21-6
Now firmly established as the number one 'keeper at Maine Road, Nicky was an ever-present for Manchester City in 1999-2000 with the exception of the home game against Swindon in December when he was laid low by flu. A great crowd pleaser, he is noted for his forays upfield with the ball but they are not without risk, as was seen against Stockport in December, when he was robbed while a long way outside his area five minutes from time, which resulted in a home defeat. However, he earned the club many more points during the season with exceptional saves, specialising in meeting oncoming forwards, spreading himself and winning the ball, and preventing many certain goals as a result. Still only 21, Nicky has been receiving expert coaching from former Manchester United 'keeper Alex Stepney and is expected to shine in the Premiership during the coming season. Also a regular for England U21s, he added a further six caps last season, appearing for his country in the European Championship finals in Slovakia.
Mansfield T (Trainee) FL 1
Manchester C (£200,000 on 2/5/1997) FL 90 FLC 7 FAC 6 Others 3

Nicky Weaver

WEBB Simon
Born: Castle Bar, Ireland, 19 January 1977
Height: 5'11" Weight: 12.6
After joining Leyton Orient on a free transfer last September Simon found it difficult to break into the Os' first team and was mostly used as cover for injuries and suspensions. In February he was loaned to Chester City, although he failed to make a senior appearance for the Deva Stadium club, and the following month he was off on loan again, this time to Ryman League club Purfleet. Orient later announced that he would not be offered a new contract at the end of the season.
Tottenham H (From trainee on 19/1/1994)
Leyton Orient (Signed on 5/10/1999) FL 3+1

WEBSTER Adam
Born: Leicester, 3 July 1980
Height: 6'1" Weight: 12.5
This promising young Notts County striker spent time on loan with Dr Martens League clubs Grantham and Bedworth in the first half of the 1999-2000 season before returning to Meadow Lane. Adam went on to make his Football League debut last January when he came on as a late substitute at Scunthorpe, and will be aiming to win a regular place in the Magpies' first-team squad during the coming season.
Notts Co (Signed from Thurmaston on 26/2/1999) FL 0+1

WEIR David (Davie) Gillespie
Born: Falkirk, 10 May 1970
Height: 6'2" Weight: 13.7
Club Honours: S Div 1 '94; B&Q '94
International Honours: S: 20
A £250,000 signing from Hearts in February 1999, only defensive partner Richard Gough's free transfer prevented Davie claiming Everton's "bargain buy of the year" award. Tall, calm and commanding, excellent in his reading of and timing of tackles, and precise and thoughtful in his distribution, he enjoyed an outstanding campaign. His quiet and reserved demeanour meant he did not receive the headlines his play deserved at times, but Evertonians were in no doubt as to his value to their cause. Also a linch-pin of the Scotland team, Davie won seven more caps last season. He boasts an astonishing level of consistency and when a rib injury forced him out of action for two games in March, he revealed he had not missed two successive matches through injury for seven years!

Falkirk (From Celtic BC on 1/8/1992) SL 133/8 SLC 5 SC 6 Others 5
Heart of Midlothian (Signed on 29/7/1996) SL 92/8 SLC 10/2 SC 9/2 Others 6
Everton (£250,000 on 17/2/1999) PL 46+3/2 FLC 2 FAC 6

Davie Weir

WELCH Keith James
Born: Bolton, 3 October 1968
Height: 6'2" Weight: 13.7

Keith is a vastly experienced goalkeeper and Northampton felt they had pulled off quite a coup when they signed him from Bristol City during the 1999 close season. He missed the opening matches due to a training injury but soon established himself as first choice and went on to become a key figure in the Cobblers' Third Division promotion team. He brought a new level of stability to the defence and proved to be excellent at handling crosses. Keith deservedly won the club's "Player of the Year" award for 1999-2000.

Rochdale (Free from Bolton W juniors on 3/3/1987) FL 205 FLC 12 FAC 10 Others 12
Bristol C (£200,000 on 25/7/1991) FL 271 FLC 20 FAC 13 Others 14
Northampton T (Free on 7/7/1999) FL 39 FLC 1 FAC 1 Others 1

WELLENS Richard Paul
Born: Manchester, 26 March 1980
Height: 5'9" Weight: 11.6
International Honours: E: Yth

Richard is a hard-tackling young midfielder who was blooded by Manchester United in their Worthington Cup tie against Aston Villa last September, subsequently joining Blackpool on transfer deadline day last March. He soon broke into the first team, making his league debut as a substitute at Stoke and impressing in the final matches of what was a disappointing season for the Seasiders. He subsequently signed a 12-month contract with the Bloomfield Road club and will be looking to extend his first-team experience during the coming season.

Manchester U (From trainee on 19/5/1997) FLC 0+1
Blackpool (Signed on 23/3/2000) FL 5+3

WELLER Paul Anthony
Born: Brighton, 6 March 1975
Height: 5'8" Weight: 11.2

After more than a year on the sidelines with a serious stomach complaint, Burnley's tenacious midfielder finally returned to first-team action last October and featured occasionally in the side from then on. Nothing seems to have been lost from Paul's game, and he was always good value for his place when selected; he made a particularly valuable contribution in scoring the Clarets' last-gasp winner at Oxford as the promotion battle reached its climax. Unfortunately for Paul, Burnley's squad had been strengthened in his absence, and his best chance for progress may now lie elsewhere.

Burnley (From trainee on 30/11/1993) FL 80+23/6 FLC 5+2 FAC 4+2/1 Others 7

WELSH Stephen (Steve) George
Born: Glasgow, 19 April 1968
Height: 6'1" Weight: 12.6

This left-sided central defender joined Lincoln from Scottish club Ayr United on the eve of the 1999-2000 season. Steve initially found it difficult to settle into the team, and was then out for several weeks after suffering a knee injury that required a cartilage operation. He returned to full fitness just before Christmas and soon began to show his true form as an effective stopper. He was also occasionally used as a left back.

Cambridge U (Free from Wimborne T on 22/6/1990) FL 0+1 Others 2
Peterborough U (Free on 8/8/1991) FL 146/2 FLC 20 FAC 8 Others 13
Partick Thistle (£40,000 on 23/12/1994) SL 55 SLC 3 SC 1
Peterborough U (Loaned on 9/7/1996) FL 6 FLC 3
Dunfermline Ath (£65,000 on 8/11/1996) SL 24+2 SC 2
Ayr U (Signed on 4/7/1998) SL 24+1 SLC 4/1
Lincoln C (Free on 5/8/1999) FL 32 FLC 1 Others 1

WEST Colin
Born: Wallsend, 13 November 1962
Height: 6'1" Weight: 14.0

A proven goalscorer whose Nationwide League playing career looked to be over, Colin was appointed assistant manager at Hartlepool in October 1999. He was also registered as a player in case of emergency and, with the Pool strikers struggling, there were calls for him to be given a game. He made brief appearances from the subs' bench against Brighton in the league and Carlisle in the Auto Windscreens Shield before stepping back to concentrate on his managerial role.

Sunderland (From apprentice on 9/7/1980) FL 88+14/21 FLC 13+4/5 FAC 3+1/2
Watford (£115,000 on 28/3/1985) FL 45/20 FLC 2+1 FAC 8/3
Glasgow R (£180,000 on 23/5/1986) SL 4+6/2 SLC 2/1 SC 0+1 Others 0+2
Sheffield Wed (£150,000 on 7/9/1987) FL 40+5/8 FLC 6/3 FAC 6/1 Others 3/1
West Bromwich A (Signed on 24/2/1989) FL 64+9/22 FLC 2 FAC 4/1 Others 2/1
Port Vale (Loaned on 1/11/1991) FL 5/1
Swansea C (Free on 5/8/1992) FL 29+4/12 FLC 0+1 FAC 5/2 Others 3+2/1
Leyton Orient (Free on 26/7/1993) FL 132+10/42 FLC 6/2 FAC 7+1/2 Others 9/4 (Free to Rushden & Diamonds on 4/2/1998)
Northampton T (Loaned on 19/9/1997) FL 1+1
Hartlepool U (Free from Northwich Vic on 2/11/1999) FL 0+1 Others 0+1

WEST Dean
Born: Morley, 5 December 1972
Height: 5'10" Weight: 12.2
Club Honours: Div 2 '97

Dean joined the ex-Bury contingent at Turf Moor shortly before the start of the 1999-2000 season and immediately established himself as Burnley's first-choice right back. A stocky and determined competitor, he always liked to go forward and often linked well with Glen Little on the Clarets' right flank. However, he lost his place following the arrival of Ian Cox, with Stan Ternent thereafter relying increasingly on a very solid back three and opting for more natural attacking players in the full-back roles.

Lincoln C (From trainee on 17/8/1991) FL 93+26/20 FLC 11/1 FAC 6/1 Others 5+2/1
Bury (Signed on 29/9/1995) FL 100+10/7 FLC 6 FAC 3 Others 2+1
Burnley (Free on 26/7/1999) FL 30+4 FLC 1+1 FAC 4 Others 1

WESTERVELD Sander
Born: Enschede, Holland, 23 October 1974
Height: 6'3" Weight: 13.12
International Honours: Holland: 5

Signed from Vitesse Arnhem during the summer of 1999 to replace David James in the Liverpool goal, the Dutchman established himself as a first-class 'keeper last season. A superb shot stopper, Sander is a big man who spreads himself well to deny opposition strikers a chance of hitting the back of the net, but he still needs to work hard to improve his handling of crosses. Still in his mid-twenties, Sander showed he had learned a lot during his first season at Anfield and looks to have the ability to develop into a goalkeeper of the highest calibre. Having made his international debut for Holland against Brazil in June 1999, he won four more caps during the season and is now firmly established as second choice to Edwin van der Sar. A member of the *Oranje* squad for Euro 2000, he featured on three occasions in the tournament, twice appearing from the subs' bench.

Liverpool (£4,000,000 from Vitesse Arnhem, Holland on 18/6/1999) PL 36 FLC 1 FAC 2

WESTHEAD Mark Lee
Born: Blackpool, 19 July 1975
Height: 6'2" Weight: 14.8

Wycombe's number two 'keeper had a run of dreadful bad luck in the 1999 close season, picking up a calf strain, suffering from shin splints trouble and then being knocked out in a collision with a team-mate in a friendly match. Mark was called into action as a substitute for the injured Martin Taylor against Bury last September, but after making the starting line-up for the next game against West Bromwich in the Worthington Cup he too had to be replaced

after he suffered a thigh strain. His only other appearance was against Scunthorpe in January when Taylor was out with flu. Mark has developed into a sound goalkeeper but with his rival in such excellent form at Adams Park he may well have to move elsewhere to get regular first-team football.
Bolton W (Free from Blackpool Mechanics on 23/11/1994. Free to Sligo Rov during 1997 close season)
Wycombe W (Free from Telford U on 6/8/1998) FL 3+1 FLC 2 Others 1

WESTON Rhys David
Born: Kingston, 27 October 1980
Height: 6'1" Weight: 12.3
International Honours: E: Yth; Sch. W: 1
This tall, strong young central defender joined Arsenal during the summer of 1997. A good tackler and strong in the air, Rhys was a regular in the U19 and reserve-team squads at Highbury last season. His big moment came when he made his first-team debut against Newcastle in the final Premiership game of the campaign. He acquitted himself well in the toughest test possible, opposing an in-form Alan Shearer. Having previously been capped by England at U16 level, he was called up to the Wales senior squad in the close season and received his full international debut when he came on from the subs' bench against Portugal at the beginning of June.
Arsenal (From trainee on 8/7/1999) PL 1 FLC 0+1

WESTWOOD Ashley Michael
Born: Bridgnorth, 31 August 1976
Height: 6'0" Weight: 12.8
Club Honours: FAYC '95
International Honours: E: Yth
The 1999-2000 season was a disappointing one for Ashley. He missed Bradford's first three matches through suspension, then suffered a series of injuries to his hamstring, knee and back, and when he was fit he was unable to disrupt the in-form partnership of Andy O'Brien and David Wetherall in the centre of City's defence. He is a good marker, quick in the tackle and with an accurate right foot, and will be looking to put last season behind him as he seeks to win a regular place in the Bantams' first-team squad in 2000-01.
Manchester U (From trainee on 1/7/1994)
Crewe Alex (£40,000 on 26/7/1995) FL 93+5/9 FLC 8 FAC 9/2 Others 10
Bradford C (£150,000 on 20/7/1998) P/FL 18+6/2 FLC 1 FAC 2+1

WESTWOOD Christopher (Chris) John
Born: Dudley, 13 February 1977
Height: 6'0" Weight: 12.2
Chris began the 1999-2000 season as a Hartlepool reserve, but was determined to make the grade. Despite an abundance of central defenders in the Victoria Park ranks, he was able to force his way into the side and over the season he was probably the club's biggest success story. Chris is a hard worker who can also play in midfield; his efforts were much appreciated by the supporters and at the end of the season received some recognition when he was voted the "Away Player of the Year".
Wolverhampton W (From trainee on 3/7/1995) FL 3+1/1 FLC 1+1 (Released during 1998 close season)
Hartlepool U (Signed from Telford U on 24/3/1999) FL 36+5 FAC 2 Others 5

WETHERALL David
Born: Sheffield, 14 March 1971
Height: 6'3" Weight: 13.12
International Honours: E: Sch
David became Bradford City's record buy in the summer of 1999 when he arrived from Leeds for a £1.4 million fee, signing a five-year contract. He established a tremendous partnership with Andy O'Brien in the centre of the defence and was the only ever-present for the Bantams in 1999-2000. Adding steel to the back four, he dominated opponents in the air and showed excellent distribution. He also scored some fine goals when coming up for set pieces, including the header from Gunnar Halle's corner that saw City to victory over Liverpool on the last day of the season and kept them in the Premiership. David was the supporters' club's "Player of the Year".
Sheffield Wed (From trainee on 1/7/1989)
Leeds U (£125,000 on 15/7/1991) F/PL 188+14/12 FLC 19+1/2 FAC 21+3/4 Others 4
Bradford C (£1,400,000 on 7/7/1999) PL 38/2 FLC 2/2 FAC 1

WHALLEY Gareth
Born: Manchester, 19 December 1973
Height: 5'10" Weight: 11.12
Gareth began 1999-2000 as a first choice in Bradford City's midfield but was then dropped last October when the team formation was altered. He returned for a brief spell of first-team action in the new year but was otherwise restricted to reserve-team football. He is a tireless worker, good at keeping possession and accurate with his passing over both short and long distances.
Crewe Alex (From trainee on 29/7/1992) FL 174+6/9 FLC 10+1/1 FAC 15+1/4 Others 24/3
Bradford C (£600,000 on 24/7/1998) P/FL 61/3 FLC 7 FAC 2

WHELAN Noel David
Born: Leeds, 30 December 1974
Height: 6'2" Weight: 12.3
Club Honours: FAYC '93
International Honours: E: U21-2; Yth (UEFA-U18 '93)
The Coventry forward had a frustrating time with injuries in 1999-2000 and missed most of the first half of the season after damaging ankle ligaments against Manchester United in August. On his return he took time to get sharp and for some weeks did not look fully fit. He rarely reached the levels of performance of previous seasons – when he displayed some silky skills and fine ball control – but did give the fans a few glimpses of the old Noel, notably with a superb strike against Burnley in the FA Cup. He scored only one further goal, against Bradford City, and at times it seemed his mind was on new challenges. His contract with the Sky Blues has only one more year to run and after Noel had rejected new terms City placed him on the transfer list.
Leeds U (From trainee on 5/3/1993) PL 28+20/7 FLC 3+2/1 FAC 2 Others 3
Coventry C (£2,000,000 on 16/12/1995) PL 127+7/31 FLC 6/1 FAC 15+1/7

WHELAN Philip (Phil) James
Born: Stockport, 7 March 1972
Height: 6'4" Weight: 14.7
International Honours: E: U21-3
After electing to stay with Oxford in the summer of 1999, Phil forced his way into the United side on a more regular basis last season. Although he managed just four starts under Malcolm Shotton, Phil appeared more often when first Mickey Lewis and then Denis Smith took over the reins at the Manor. A tall central defender who is dominant in the air, he often showed the qualities which had won him England honours earlier in his career and despite a few mistakes will look back on the season as being his best at Oxford. Always dangerous in the opposition penalty area, he scored a couple of goals, with the second being a vital winner at Colchester when he was sitting on the floor. Stop Press: Phil was reported to have moved to Southend during the summer.
Ipswich T (From juniors on 2/7/1990) F/PL 76+6/2 FLC 6+1 FAC 3+1 Others 1
Middlesbrough (£300,000 on 3/4/1995) PL 18+4/1 FLC 5 FAC 3
Oxford U (£150,000 on 15/7/1997) FL 51+3/2 FLC 3/1 FAC 5 Others 3
Rotherham U (Loaned on 12/3/1999) FL 13/4

WHELAN Spencer Randall
Born: Liverpool, 17 September 1971
Height: 6'2" Weight: 12.8
Although he had a frustrating time with injuries in 1999-2000, Spencer had a decent run in the Shrewsbury first team around the turn of the year. He produced some rock-solid performances, forging an excellent partnership with Andrew Tretton in the centre of a Shrews defence that conceded just 13 goals in a run of 14 games. Unfortunately, he then suffered a bad cartilage injury playing against his former club Chester in March and was subsequently ruled out for the remainder of the campaign. If he continues to produce similar form next season he should be a regular once more when he returns to fitness.
Chester C (Free from Liverpool juniors on 3/4/1990) FL 196+19/8 FLC 11+1/2 FAC 9+3 Others 5+2
Shrewsbury T (Signed on 6/11/1998) FL 24+1 FLC 1 FAC 0+1 Others 1

WHITBREAD Adrian Richard
Born: Epping, 22 October 1971
Height: 6'1" Weight: 12.12
Portsmouth captain Adrian led the club through another stormy season in 1999-2000 as they avoided relegation yet again. Dependable and solid in the centre of the defence, he coped admirably with the requirements of three different managers during the campaign and even managed a rare goal when coming up for a corner against Swindon in March. Adrian is an excellent man marker, a good communicator and both reliable and effective as a central defender.

Leyton Orient (From trainee on 13/11/1989) FL 125/2 FLC 10+1 FAC 11/1 Others 8
Swindon T (£500,000 on 29/7/1993) P/FL 35+1/1 FAC 2
West Ham U (£650,000 on 17/8/1994) PL 3+7 FLC 2+1 FAC 1
Portsmouth (Loaned on 9/11/1995) FL 13
Portsmouth (£250,000 on 24/10/1996) FL 133+1/2 FLC 8/1 FAC 3

WHITE Alan
Born: Darlington, 22 March 1976
Height: 6'1" Weight: 13.2

Alan started three early-season games for Luton in 1999-2000 before being loaned to Colchester in mid-November. He made his debut for the U's in a 1-1 draw againstStoke City and retained his place for the duration of the loan period, excepting the game against Luton, from which he was excluded by prior agreement of the two clubs. Back at Kenilworth Road, he showed impressive form and finally established himself as a first-team regular, appearing for the Hatters in the last 12 games of the campaign. A tall central defender, he is powerful in the air, strong in the tackle and comfortable on the ball. However, he was released at the end of the season.

Middlesbrough (From trainee on 8/7/1994) Others 1
Luton T (£40,000 on 22/9/1997) FL 60+20/3 FLC 3+3 FAC 2 Others 4
Colchester U (Loaned on 12/11/1999) FL 4 Others 1

Alan White

WHITE Jason Gregory
Born: Meriden, 19 October 1971
Height: 6'0" Weight: 12.10

A summer 1999 cartilage operation followed by a hernia problem meant it was November before Jason saw any action for Rotherham in 1999-2000. He then found his first-team opportunities very much restricted but whenever he was called upon he could be guaranteed to give maximum effort. A brave and strong striker, he is useful in the air and maintains a good goals-per-game record. Perhaps the highlight of his season came when he netted two goals after coming off the bench to earn the Millers victory over promotion rivals Darlington. He was released at the end of the season. Stop Press: Jason was reported to have signed for Cheltenham during the summer.

Derby Co (From trainee on 4/7/1990)
Scunthorpe U (Free on 6/9/1991) FL 44+24/16 FLC 2 FAC 3+3/1 Others 4+4/1
Darlington (Loaned on 20/8/1993) FL 4/1
Scarborough (Free on 10/12/1993) FL 60+3/20 FLC 2+1 FAC 5/1 Others 1
Northampton T (£35,000 on 15/6/1995) FL 55+22/18 FLC 1+4 FAC 3 Others 5+2
Rotherham U (£25,000 on 9/9/1997) FL 52+21/22 FLC 2 FAC 3+1/1 Others 3/1

WHITE Thomas (Tom) Matthew
Born: Bristol, 26 January 1976
Height: 6'0" Weight: 13.6

After an absence of 20 months due to injury, Tom returned to first-team action in Bristol Rovers' top-of-the-table clash at Preston North End on 27 December. He struggled to show his old form and it was no surprise when he was allowed to spend a three-month loan spell starting in February with Conference club Hereford United, where he was able to play regular first-team football. A dependable central defender, at his best he is an effective man marker who is cool under pressure. However, he was released during the summer.

Bristol Rov (From trainee on 13/7/1994) FL 47+7/1 FAC 5 Others 2+1

WHITEHALL Steven (Steve) Christopher
Born: Bromborough, 8 December 1966
Height: 5'10" Weight: 11.5

Steve finished the 1999-2000 season with a total of 11 league and cup goals for Oldham despite never really performing at his best. Nevertheless, manager Andy Ritchie persevered with him for most of the season as he provided a much-needed experienced figure up front for the Latics. A useful striker with a good goals-per-game record, he will be hoping for a return to form in 2000-01.

Rochdale (£20,000 from Southport on 23/7/1991) FL 212+26/75 FLC 10+3/4 FAC 13+2/3 Others 15+1/10
Mansfield T (£20,000 on 8/8/1997) FL 42+1/24 FLC 2 FAC 2/1 Others 2/1
Oldham Ath (£50,000 on 10/7/1998) FL 55+19/13 FLC 0+2 FAC 6+1/2 Others 2

WHITEHEAD Damien Stephen
Born: St Helens, 24 April 1979
Height: 5'10" Weight: 11.7

Damien joined Macclesfield in the summer of 1999 after scoring 52 goals for North West Counties club Warrington Town in 1998-99. He was introduced to senior football gradually, initially coming on from the subs' bench for the final ten or fifteen minutes. His first goal in the Nationwide League came at Brighton in March and he added two more against Shrewsbury in the following game, when he won the "Man of the Match" award. Although yet to mature fully as a striker, he is already proving a handful for defenders with his speed, agility and eye for goal and looks an excellent prospect for the future. A hero with the fans at Moss Rose, he was rewarded for his progress with a new two-year contract.
Macclesfield T (Signed from Warrington T on 6/8/1999) FL 10+13/6 Others 0+1

WHITEHEAD Dean
Born: Oxford, 12 January 1982
Height: 5'11" Weight: 12.1
This young midfielder made his Oxford United debut as a substitute in the Auto Windscreens Shield tie against Luton last December. Dean came through the trainee ranks and was also on the bench for a number of other games without coming on.
Oxford U (From trainee on 20/4/2000) Others 0+1

WHITEHEAD Philip (Phil) Matthew
Born: Halifax, 17 December 1969
Height: 6'3" Weight: 15.10
A tall, commanding goalkeeper, Phil started last season as Alan Miller's deputy at West Bromwich and made one first-team appearance for Albion, in the Worthington Cup at Halifax, before moving to Reading on a four-year contract in October. He went straight into the side to replace Scott Howie and enjoyed a run of 11 games, during which he added much-needed composure to the Royals' defence, but he then suffered a thigh injury in the 1-1 draw with Scunthorpe. Howie returned and Phil did not get another opportunity until the last two games of the season. He saved the best till last, however, as an acrobatic tip-over from a close-range header ensured Reading's 1-0 victory at home to Stoke City.
Halifax T (From trainee on 1/7/1988) FL 42 FLC 2 FAC 4 Others 4
Barnsley (£60,000 on 9/3/1990) FL 16
Halifax T (Loaned on 7/3/1991) FL 9
Scunthorpe U (Loaned on 29/11/1991) FL 8 Others 2
Scunthorpe U (Loaned on 4/9/1992) FL 8 FLC 2
Bradford C (Loaned on 19/11/1992) FL 6 Others 4
Oxford U (£75,000 on 1/11/1993) FL 207 FLC 15 FAC 13 Others 3
West Bromwich A (£250,000 on 1/12/1998) FL 26 FLC 1 FAC 1
Reading (Signed on 7/10/1999) FL 11 FAC 2

WHITEHEAD Stuart David
Born: Bromsgrove, 17 July 1976
Height: 5'11" Weight: 12.4
Stuart's 1999-2000 season for Carlisle was marked by some assured performances in central defence, although his campaign was not without injury problems. He earned several "star man" accolades in the pre-Christmas period and, apart from two dismissals, the second of which caused him to miss the last four games of the season, he can look back on the campaign with some satisfaction.
Bolton W (Signed from Bromsgrove Rov on 18/9/1995)
Carlisle U (Free on 31/7/1998) FL 65+1 FLC 4 FAC 1 Others 2

WHITLEY James (Jim)
Born: Zambia, 14 April 1975
Height: 5'9" Weight: 11.0
International Honours: NI: 3; B-1
The elder of the two Whitley brothers at Manchester City, Jim was loaned to Blackpool for two months at the beginning of the 1999-2000 season after he found it impossible to break into the City first team. A skilful midfielder, he appeared regularly for the Seasiders without ever featuring in a winning team and returned to Maine Road in October. Jim's only first-team appearance for City last season was as a substitute at Huddersfield in February, when he replaced Ian Bishop in the 90th minute. His approach is a bit more laid back than that of his brother Jeff, but he plays the game with an attractive style. He added a further cap for Northern Ireland when coming on from the subs' bench against Finland in Helsinki last October.
Manchester C (From juniors on 1/8/1994) FL 27+11 FLC 3+1/1 FAC 2+1 Others 0+1
Blackpool (Loaned on 20/8/1999) FL 7+1 FLC 1

WHITLEY Jeffrey (Jeff)
Born: Zambia, 28 January 1979
Height: 5'8" Weight: 11.2
International Honours: NI: 4; B-2; U21-15
Jeff carried on where he had left off for Manchester City in 1999-2000. He had ended the previous season by playing in all three Second Division play-off games and had impressed the manager, Joe Royle, so much that he was selected for the starting line-up at the beginning of the new campaign, playing in 25 of the first 26 league and cup matches. Jeff enjoyed a consistent season in the City midfield, complementing the composed Ian Bishop and helping to supply the strikers. He worked unceasingly, covering the whole pitch during the course of 90 minutes' non-stop endeavour in every game, tackling with great determination throughout. He was understandably delighted with his perfectly executed goal against Blackburn Rovers at Maine Road that secured a 2-0 win: he read the cross from Mark Kennedy on the left and ghosted in to head home at the far post. Although he was briefly out of the side around the turn of the year, Jeff finished the season strongly with some good performances and showed again how his tenacity more than makes up for his occasional lapses in technique. Captain of the Northern Ireland U21 team, he made a further six appearances during the season and now holds the record number of caps for his country at this level. Jeff also appeared in the starting line-up for the senior team for the first time, scoring the only goal in a 1-4 defeat by Finland in October. The younger brother of team-mate Jim Whitley, he signed a new long-term deal with City in November.
Manchester C (From trainee on 19/2/1996) FL 68+22/7 FLC 4+1 FAC 1+2 Others 4
Wrexham (Loaned on 14/1/1999) FL 9/2

WHITLOW Michael (Mike) William
Born: Northwich, 13 January 1968
Height: 6'0" Weight: 12.12
Club Honours: Div 2 '90, Div 1 '92; FLC '97
A solid and dependable defender, Mike appeared regularly for Bolton Wanderers in 1999-2000, mostly featuring at left back but also turning out occasionally as a centre back when required. His skills on the ball and marauding runs down the left flank more than compensated for a slight lack of pace while his experience proved invaluable as the Trotters battled their way to the play-offs. He finally broke his goalscoring duck for the club in the 3-1 victory at Crewe in April and immediately celebrated with a wild performance that itself deserved some sort of award. With his contract due to run out during the summer, the club's supporters are hoping that agreement will be reached on a new deal.
Leeds U (£10,000 from Witton A on 11/11/1988) FL 62+15/4 FLC 4+1 FAC 1+4 Others 9
Leicester C (£250,000 on 27/3/1992) F/PL 141+6/8 FLC 12/1 FAC 6 Others 14
Bolton W (£500,000 + on 19/9/1997) P/FL 75+3/1 FLC 13+1 FAC 7 Others 2

WHITMORE Theodore (Theo)
Born: Jamaica, 5 August 1972
Height: 6'2" Weight: 11.2
International Honours: Jamaica
"Tappa" arrived at Hull along with fellow Jamaican international Ian Goodison in October 1999, bringing a reputation as one of the most talented players to emerge from the Caribbean island in recent years. A veteran of the 1998 World Cup campaign, scorer of both goals in the 2-1 defeat of Japan and with an international career dating back to 1993, he had amassed a substantial number of caps prior to his move. Playing just behind the front two strikers, he impressed with his splendid control, marvellous dribbling skills and thunderous shooting. When his exceptional passing is taken into account, it can be seen that he represents a more than useful midfield operator. Although such skills are perhaps not best suited to the hustle and bustle of Third Division football, he was given the opportunity to perform on a higher stage in the FA Cup tie against Chelsea, when he outshone many of the cosmopolitan London club's more celebrated names. International commitments and niggling injuries reduced his presence in the second half of the campaign, and although there were rumours of strong interest from at least one Premiership club no transfer materialised. However, the possibility of this supremely talented player completing his two-and-a-half-year contract with the Tigers appears to be somewhat remote. A regular for his national team, Theo won further caps against Uruguay, New Zealand, the Cayman Islands and Panama in friendlies and also

Theo Whitmore

appeared for the Reggae Boyz in their highly disappointing CONCACAF Gold Cup campaign.
Hull C (Free from Seba U, Jamaica on 22/10/1999) FL 17/2 FAC 5 Others 1

WHITNEY Jonathan (Jon) David
Born: Nantwich, 23 December 1970
Height: 5'10" Weight: 13.8
One of the heroes of Hull's 1998-99 "Great Escape", Jon negotiated a richly deserved new contract the following summer. He had the misfortune of tearing a calf muscle in the build-up to the 1999-2000 campaign and had to start his pre-season preparation all over again. Showing typical determination, he made an early return in October but he was soon back on the sidelines. It was significant that when he returned to the team in January the Tigers enjoyed their best spell of the season. Essentially a left-sided defender who can play as a wing back or centre back, he is a no-nonsense player who always shows 100 per cent commitment to the cause. With an eye to the future he has recently begun studying to qualify as a physiotherapist.
Huddersfield T (£10,000 from Winsford, via Wigan Ath YTS and Skelmersdale, on 21/10/1993) FL 17+1 FLC 0+1 Others 4/1
Wigan Ath (Loaned on 17/3/1995) FL 12
Lincoln C (£20,000 on 31/10/1995) FL 98+3/8 FLC 9/1 FAC 6+1/2 Others 4
Hull C (Signed on 18/12/1998) FL 40+2/2 FAC 2 Others 3

WHITTAKER Stuart
Born: Liverpool, 2 January 1975
Height: 5'7" Weight: 10.2
This tricky left winger found it difficult to regain form and fitness after an operation on his groin during the 1999 close season and made only a limited number of appearances for Macclesfield in 1999-2000. He did not feature after the home defeat by Hull at the end of January and after being released in February he had a brief trial with Conference club Altrincham.
Bolton W (Free from Liverpool juniors on 14/5/1993) FL 2+1 FLC 0+1
Wigan Ath (Loaned on 30/8/1996) FL 2+1
Macclesfield T (Free on 8/8/1997) FL 49+18/5 FLC 5+1 FAC 5+2/2 Others 2+1

WHITTINGHAM Guy
Born: Evesham, 10 November 1964
Height: 5'9" Weight: 12.2
This experienced striker returned to his first club, Portsmouth, on a free transfer from Sheffield Wednesday in July 1999. Now in his late thirties, he has lost some of his pace but still proved to be a threat up front for Pompey, scoring on the opening day of the 1999-2000 season and adding a further three goals in the autumn. However, manager Alan Ball was sacked in December and Guy found himself limited to a handful of appearances from the subs' bench under new boss Tony Pulis. He always gives 100 per cent effort and his unorthodox style remains effective against opposition defences, suggesting he still has a couple more seasons left in him.
Portsmouth (Free from Yeovil on 9/6/1989) FL 149+11/88 FLC 7+2/3 FAC 7+3/10 Others 9/3
Aston Villa (£1,200,000 on 1/8/1993) PL 17+8/5 FLC 4+1/1 Others 2+1
Wolverhampton W (Loaned on 28/2/1994) FL 13/8 FAC 1
Sheffield Wed (£700,000 on 21/12/1994) PL 90+23/22 FLC 7+2/2 FAC 7+1/1
Wolverhampton W (Loaned on 2/11/1998) FL 9+1/1
Portsmouth (Loaned on 28/1/1999) FL 9/7
Watford (Loaned on 18/3/1999) FL 4+1
Portsmouth (Free on 13/7/1999) FL 15+10/4 FLC 2 FAC 1

WHITTLE Justin Phillip
Born: Derby, 18 March 1971
Height: 6'1" Weight: 12.12
Following his magnificent displays the previous season, Justin gave Hull a tremendous boost by agreeing a new three-year deal on the eve of 1999-2000. Deservedly appointed captain in November following the departure of David D'Auria, he is regarded as one of the Tigers' best buys in recent years. A big and powerful central defender, he had another good season at Boothferry Park, showing the consistent form that has been his hallmark since arriving from Stoke.
Glasgow Celtic (Free from Army during 1994 close season)
Stoke C (Free on 20/10/1994) FL 66+13/1 FLC 3+4 FAC 2 Others 2
Hull C (£65,000 on 27/11/1998) FL 62/1 FLC 4 FAC 4+2 Others 2

WHITWORTH Neil Anthony
Born: Wigan, 12 April 1972
Height: 6'2" Weight: 12.6
International Honours: E: Yth
Neil's only 1999-2000 senior action was the final minute of Hull's last away game of the season at Plymouth. It was a hugely significant minute as he had been sidelined since suffering an ankle injury in an FA Cup tie at Salisbury in November 1998. Following surgery, the joint became infected. That led to another operation and rehabilitation at the National Sports Centre at Lilleshall. He was released at the end of the season but it is to

be hoped that the experienced centre back's courageous recovery will be rewarded with an opportunity to continue his career elsewhere.

Wigan Ath (Trainee) FL 1+1
Manchester U (£45,000 on 1/7/1990) FL 1
Preston NE (Loaned on 16/1/1992) FL 6
Barnsley (Loaned on 20/2/1992) FL 11
Rotherham U (Loaned on 8/10/1993) FL 8/1 Others 2
Blackpool (Loaned on 10/12/1993) FL 3
Kilmarnock (£265,000 on 2/9/1994) SL 74+1/3 SLC 3 SC 4 Others 1
Wigan Ath (Loaned on 11/3/1998) FL 1+3
Hull C (Free on 16/7/1998) FL 18+1/2 FLC 4 FAC 1

WICKS Matthew Jonathan
Born: Reading, 8 September 1978
Height: 6'2" Weight: 13.5
International Honours: E: Yth

This young left-sided central defender was in and out of the Peterborough side in 1999-2000 due to a mixture of injuries and loss of form but has already shown enough to suggest that he has a good future in the game. Strong and competitive, he is not easily knocked off the ball. Matthew is the son of former Chelsea and QPR favourite Steve Wicks.

Arsenal (Free from Manchester U juniors on 23/1/1996)
Crewe Alex (£100,000 on 15/6/1998) FL 4+2
Peterborough U (Free on 3/3/1999) FL 28+3 FLC 2 FAC 1 Others 1

WIDDRINGTON Thomas (Tommy)
Born: Newcastle, 1 October 1971
Height: 5'9" Weight: 11.12

After spending the closing weeks of the 1998-99 campaign on loan at Vale Park, Tommy signed permanently for Port Vale during the summer of 1999. However, he immediately ran into problems at his new club when he was dismissed early on during his debut against Birmingham and it was not until October that he established himself as a regular in the team. A fixture in the line-up from then on, he netted a total of five goals, four of which came from the penalty spot. Tommy is a tough-tackling midfield player adept at breaking up opposition attacks. He won the supporters' "Player of the Year" award.

Southampton (From trainee on 10/5/1990) F/PL 67+8/3 FLC 3+1 FAC 11
Wigan Ath (Loaned on 12/9/1991) FL 5+1 FLC 2
Grimsby T (£300,000 on 11/7/1996) FL 72+17/8 FLC 10+3 FAC 3+1 Others 1
Port Vale (Free on 24/3/1999) FL 46+1/6 FAC 1

WIEKENS Gerard
Born: Tolhuiswyk, Holland, 25 February 1973
Height: 6'0" Weight: 13.4

After showing consistent form for Manchester City the previous season, Gerard made a good start to the 1999-2000 campaign before sustaining a niggling leg injury after just five matches. He bravely made a couple of further appearances before he had fully recovered, which perhaps had the effect of aggravating and prolonging the problem. He then lost his place in the centre of the defence to Richard Jobson, and only when Andy Morrison picked up a long-term knee injury was he restored to the starting line-up. Although he did not progress quite as much as his performances the previous term had suggested he might, Gerard retained his place, Jobson and he complementing each other effectively. With competition for places increasing following the arrival of Spencer Prior from Derby in March, the Dutchman moved into a central midfield position against Bolton and it was soon apparent that this is his best position. Pacy, skilful and with excellent technical skills, he dovetailed neatly with Prior, who took over the organisation of the defence while Gerard was able to play in his more accustomed role as a central provider.

Manchester C (£500,000 from SC Veendam, Holland on 28/7/1997) FL 109+4/8 FLC 8 FAC 7 Others 3

WIGNALL Jack David
Born: Liverpool, 26 September 1981
Height: 6'1" Weight: 11.7

The captain of Colchester's youth team, Jack made his senior debut as a first-half substitute in the Auto Windscreens Shield game at Swansea and also featured for the last five minutes of the Us' visit to Bristol Rovers the following Saturday. A tall and strong central defender, he will be aiming to win a regular place in the first-team squad in the coming season. Jack is the son of the former Colchester and Aldershot centre half Steve Wignall.

Colchester U (Trainee) FL 0+1 Others 0+1

WIJNHARD Clyde
Born: Surinam, 9 November 1973
Height: 5'11" Weight: 12.4

Clive Wijnhard

The lively, burly striker was snapped up by Huddersfield from rivals Leeds United in the summer of 1999 in what proved to be a bargain purchase. With his pace and strength on the ball posing a constant threat to opponents' defences, he struck up a deadly partnership with Marcus Stewart from the outset. Clyde enjoyed a debut goal at QPR on the opening day before producing an outstanding display of goalscoring prowess with his first career hat-trick in the 7-1 demolition of Crystal Palace. Still relatively new to the English game, he led the line tirelessly for the whole season, and even with an assortment of striking partners he still created chances for himself and others.

Leeds U (£1,500,000 from Willem II, Holland, via Ajax, Groningen and RKC Waelwijk, on 22/7/1998) PL 11+7/3 FLC 1 FAC 1+1/1 Others 1+3
Huddersfield T (£750,000 on 22/7/1999) FL 45/15 FLC 6/1 FAC 1

WILBRAHAM Aaron Thomas
Born: Knutsford, 21 October 1979
Height: 6'3" Weight: 12.4

This young Stockport striker drifted in and out of the first team in 1999-2000. Having struggled to score in previous seasons, he did much better, contributing five goals in all, including a double in the last game of the season against Nottingham Forest. Tall and tricky with a good range of skills, Aaron will be looking to win a regular place in the Hatters' starting line-up during the coming season.

Stockport Co (From trainee on 29/8/1997) FL 27+32/5 FLC 3+2/1

Jason Wilcox

WILCOX Jason Malcolm
Born: Farnworth, 15 July 1971
Height: 5'11" Weight: 11.10
Club Honours: PL '95
International Honours: E: 3; B-2

The long-serving midfielder was asked to play tucked in rather than wide on the left by Blackburn manager Brian Kidd in the opening weeks of 1999-2000 and his form suffered. Following Kidd's departure caretaker boss Tony Parkes preferred to use Damien Duff on the left side and shortly afterwards Jason was sold to Leeds United, where he became a valuable addition to the Elland Road squad. He came on as a substitute at Chelsea two days after signing and remained in the match-day squad until the end of the season, scoring his first goal for the club at Sunderland with a superb left-foot strike after being expertly set up by Stephen McPhail. His arrival allowed Harry Kewell to play as a striker, while his wing play gave the side an extra dimension, particularly in the home legs of UEFA Cup ties. Jason's move back to the Premiership coincided with his return to the full England squad and he produced a solid 90 minutes in the friendly with Argentina; however, he was ruled out of the squad for the Euro 2000 finals by injury.

Blackburn Rov (From trainee on 13/6/1989) F/PL 242+27/31 FLC 16+1/1 FAC 18+2/2 Others 7
Leeds U (£3,000,000 on 17/12/1999) PL 15+5/3 FAC 2 Others 3+1/1

WILCOX Russell (Russ)
Born: Hemsworth, 25 March 1964
Height: 6'0" Weight: 12.12
Club Honours: Div 4 '87; Div 3 '96
International Honours: E: SP-3

Now approaching the end of a successful league career, central defender Russ combined a playing role for Scunthorpe United with his new responsibilities as assistant manager during 1999-2000. He was a regular in the side during the first two months of the season, when his experience and organisational skills helped a young team. From the start of the new year he concentrated on his coaching role and only featured once more in the Iron's starting line-up in league games.

Doncaster Rov (Apprentice on) FL 1
Northampton T (£15,000 from Frickley Ath on 30/6/1986) FL 137+1/9 FLC 6 FAC 10 Others 8/1
Hull C (£120,000 on 6/8/1990) FL 92+8/7 FLC 5 FAC 5/1 Others 5+1
Doncaster Rov (£60,000 on 30/7/1993) FL 81/6 FLC 5/2 FAC 3 Others 3
Preston NE (£60,000 on 22/9/1995) FL 62/1 FLC 4 FAC 3/1 Others 2
Scunthorpe U (£15,000 on 8/7/1997) FL 67+6/3 FLC 5+1 FAC 6/2 Others 8

WILDER Christopher (Chris) John
Born: Stocksbridge, 23 September 1967
Height: 5'11" Weight: 12.8

Chris joined Brighton on a short-term contract in July 1999 and soon established himself as a regular in the first team but he elected to return north in October, when he signed for Halifax Town. An experienced right back, he was a key figure in the Shaymen's defence and created a number of goalscoring opportunities with his accurate crosses. Ironically, Chris scored his only goal of the season with a superbly flighted free kick at Brighton.

Southampton (From apprentice on 26/9/1985)
Sheffield U (Free on 20/8/1986) FL 89+4/1 FLC 8+1 FAC 7 Others 3
Walsall (Loaned on 2/11/1989) FL 4 FAC 1 Others 2
Charlton Ath (Loaned on 12/10/1990) FL 1
Charlton Ath (Loaned on 28/11/1991) FL 2
Leyton Orient (Loaned on 27/2/1992) FL 16/1 Others 1
Rotherham U (£50,000 on 30/7/1992) FL 129+3/11 FLC 11 FAC 6+2/1 Others 6+1
Notts Co (£150,000 on 2/1/1996) FL 46 FLC 2 FAC4 Others 1
Bradford C (£150,000 on 27/3/1997) FL 35+7 FLC 2 FAC 1
Sheffield U (£150,000 on 25/3/1998) FL 11+1 FLC 0+1 Others 1
Northampton T (Loaned on 6/11/1998) FL 1
Lincoln C (Loaned on 25/3/1999) FL 2+1
Brighton & Hove A (Free on 30/7/1999) FL 11 FLC 2
Halifax T (Free on 22/10/1999) FL 31/1 FAC 3 Others 1

WILDING Peter John
Born: Shrewsbury, 28 November 1968
Height: 6'1" Weight: 12.12

Peter showed his versatility in the 1999-2000 campaign, appearing at various times as a central defender, sweeper or in midfield as Shrewsbury battled to retain their Nationwide League status. His tremendous determination and will to win were epitomised following the penultimate game of the season against Brighton in which he was stretchered off. Back in action the following week, he played a vital role as the Shrews won 2-1 at Exeter to effect their own version of the "Great Escape". Peter is a real crowd favourite who gets through a huge amount of work in every game.

Shrewsbury T (£10,000 from Telford on 10/6/1997) FL 116+1/3 FLC 6 FAC 6/1 Others 3/1

WILKINS Ian John
Born: Lincoln, 3 April 1980
Height: 6'0" Weight: 12.7

This young Lincoln central defender spent most of his second season as a professional either on the subs' bench or in the reserves. He appeared just six times for the Imps' first team, fitting in well on the right side of a three-man central defensive system. Ian was loaned to Irish League club Ballymena in March and was released by Lincoln in the summer.

Lincoln C (From trainee on 28/3/1998) FL 4+2 FAC 1+1 Others 1+1

WILKINS Richard John
Born: Streatham, 28 May 1965
Height: 6'0" Weight: 12.3
Club Honours: Div 3 '91

Colchester's "Captain Fantastic" fought off the threat to his place over the summer of 1999 with a typically excellent pre-season, and was an automatic selection whenever fit throughout the campaign. Unfortunately, he then sustained a neck injury at Oldham in November; although he made a brief come-back in the new year, he suffered a recurrence of the problem at Scunthorpe and, following medical advice, he announced his retirement from the game. He will be sorely missed at Layer Road, where his valiant efforts were much appreciated by the fans.

Colchester U (Free from Haverhill Rov on 20/11/1986) FL 150+2/22 FLC 6 FAC 7+2/4 Others 9+3/3
Cambridge U (£65,000 on 25/7/1990) FL 79+2/7 FLC 6 FAC 8+1 Others 9

Hereford U (Free on 20/7/1994) FL 76+1/5 FLC 6 FAC 6 Others 8/2
Colchester U (£30,000 on 3/7/1996) FL 125+2/11 FLC 7 FAC 3/1 Others 8

WILKINSON John Colbridge
Born: Exeter, 24 August 1979
Height: 5'9" Weight: 11.0
At first-team level John's 1999-2000 season comprised no more than a six-minute substitute appearance for Exeter in the Worthington Cup at Birmingham. A cruciate knee ligament injury then put him out of action for the remainder of the campaign. This was a big disappointment both for himself and for the club, as he had shown such promise in his first full season. Hopefully John will be raring to go for the start of the new campaign.
Exeter C (From trainee on 9/7/1998) FL 6+13/2 FLC 0+1 FAC 1+1 Others 0+2

WILKINSON Shaun Frederick
Born: Portsmouth, 12 September 1981
Height: 5'8" Weight: 10.13
This young midfielder made his Brighton debut when coming on from the subs' bench for the final 20 minutes at Swansea last December and impressed with his determination and passing. Shaun has been a regular in Albion's successful youth team, and is expected to figure in the first-team squad more often during the 2000-01 campaign.
Brighton & Hove A (Trainee) FL 0+2

WILKINSON Stephen (Steve) John
Born: Lincoln, 1 September 1968
Height: 6'0" Weight: 11.12
Club Honours: Div 3 '96
Steve had a frustrating time at Chesterfield in 1999-2000 for, after missing the opening part of the campaign while recovering from knee surgery, he returned to the team in an unfamiliar midfield role and to compound matters the Spireites were relegated. At his best he is a lively striker who is an intelligent foil for a traditional target man. He was released during the summer.
Leicester C (From apprentice on 6/9/1986) FL 5+4/1 FAC 1
Crewe Alex (Loaned on 8/9/1988) FL 3+2/2
Mansfield T (£80,000 on 2/10/1989) FL 214+18/83 FLC 13+1/4 FAC 10/2 Others 17/1
Preston NE (£90,000 on 15/6/1995) FL 44+8/13 FLC 4/4 FAC 3/1 Others 3
Chesterfield (£70,000 + on 4/7/1997) FL 57+18/13 FLC 3 FAC 4+1 Others 5+1/2

WILLIAMS Adrian
Born: Reading, 16 August 1971
Height: 6'2" Weight: 13.2
Club Honours: Div 2 '94
International Honours: W: 12
After suffering three injury-plagued seasons at Wolves, Adrian recovered fitness last term only to find himself out of favour. In February he rejoined Reading on loan to bolster a defence handicapped by injuries to Andy Bernal and Linvoy Primus but he returned to the Midlands after starting just three games. He subsequently appeared for Wolves for the final 20 minutes at Swindon before going back to the Madejski Stadium for a second loan spell. A powerful, commanding central defender, he showed he had lost none of his aerial ability and contributed the winner for the Royals against Brentford. Adrian was released by Wolves in the summer. Stop Press: He was reported to have joined Reading on a permanent basis in mid-June.
Reading (From trainee on 4/3/1989) FL 191+5/14 FLC 16/1 FAC 16/2 Others 14/2
Wolverhampton W (£750,000 on 3/7/1996) FL 26+1 FLC 3 FAC 2+2 Others 2/1
Reading (Loaned on 15/2/2000) FL 5/1 Others 1
Reading (Loaned on 22/3/2000) FL 10

WILLIAMS Andrew (Andy) Phillip
Born: Bristol, 8 October 1977
Height: 5'10" Weight: 10.10
International Honours: W: 2; U21-9
Andy began 1999-2000 at Southampton but was loaned to Swindon in September and signed permanently shortly afterwards for a £65,000 fee. He featured regularly on the left side of midfield for the Robins and scored his first goal in senior football against Wolves last March. A very fast and tricky winger, he is capable of playing on either flank. Andy made two further appearances for Wales U21s against Belarus and Switzerland last autumn.
Southampton (From trainee on 24/5/1996) PL 3+18 FLC 1+2 FAC 0+1
Swindon T (£65,000 on 8/9/1999) FL 35+1/1 FLC 1+1 FAC 1

WILLIAMS Anthony (Tony) Simon
Born: Bridgend, 20 September 1977
Height: 6'1" Weight: 13.5
International Honours: W: U21-16; Yth

Steve Wilkinson

This young Blackburn Rovers 'keeper was loaned to Gillingham last August to provide competition for first choice Vince Bartram. Tony made four starts for the Gills, including both Worthington Cup ties with Bolton, but returned to Ewood Park when his loan period was over, and was subsequently loaned to Macclesfield in January. Macc needed special dispensation from the Nationwide League to sign him as they were under a transfer embargo and this was only granted because regular 'keeper Lee Martin was out injured. A very capable 'keeper who commands his area well, takes up good positions and inspires confidence in his defence, Tony settled in quickly and thoroughly enjoyed his time at Macclesfield. Although he kept only one clean sheet, this is no reflection on him and was due to the team's indifferent form during his loan spell. He returned to Blackburn at the end of March as he was required as cover, but was released at the end of the season. Tony won a further two caps for Wales at U21 level last autumn. Stop Press: He was reported to have signed for Hartlepool during the summer.

Blackburn Rov (From trainee on 4/7/1996)
Macclesfield T (Loaned on 16/10/1998) FL 4
Bristol Rov (Loaned on 24/3/1999) FL 9
Gillingham (Loaned on 5/8/1999) FL 2 FLC 2
Macclesfield T (Loaned on 28/1/2000) FL 11

WILLIAMS Daniel (Danny) Ivor Llewellyn
Born: Wrexham, 12 July 1979
Height: 6'1" Weight: 13.0
International Honours: W: U21-8

This highly promising youngster joined Wrexham on a two-and-a-half-year contract from Liverpool in March 1999 but did not make his league debut until the opening game of the 1999-2000 campaign. Danny is a strong, hard-tackling midfield anchor man who also has the ability to play in defence. He had the misfortune to suffer a groin injury early on in the FA Cup fourth-round tie against Cambridge after he had begun to stamp his authority on the game and in his absence the Robins went down to a 2-1 defeat. The injury required an operation and he did not return to regular first-team action until last March. Danny also has a cracking shot and netted goals against Kettering in the FA Cup and at Cambridge in the Robins' 4-3 win. He won further caps for Wales U21s against Belarus, Scotland and Northern Ireland during the season.

Liverpool (From trainee on 14/5/1997)
Wrexham (Free on 22/3/1999) FL 24/1 FLC 2 FAC 4/1 Others 1

WILLIAMS Daniel (Danny) Josef
Born: Sheffield, 2 March 1981
Height: 5'9" Weight: 9.13

Danny came into the Chesterfield side during a Saltergate injury crisis last season and won credit with his performances. A youth team graduate, he slotted into a right-back role and played with confidence and self-assurance, while listening to and learning from those around him. Danny has every chance of making the grade in a more successful Chesterfield side.

Chesterfield (From trainee on 2/7/1999) FL 3+2 FLC 0+1 Others 0+1

WILLIAMS Darren
Born: Middlesbrough, 28 April 1977
Height: 5'10" Weight: 11.12
Club Honours: Div 1 '99
International Honours: E: B-1; U21-2

Utility man Darren was widely expected to be pushing strongly for a regular first-team berth at Sunderland last term. However, despite appearing in a variety of positions – right back, midfield and outside right – the former England U21 international's longest run in the side did not materialise until March, when he made six consecutive appearances, reprising his First Division central defensive partnership with Jody Craddock. Quick and a good tackler, Darren made his mark in a side that, having suffered a confidence-battering 2-5 defeat at Leicester, embarked on a five-game unbeaten run which was only ended when they ran into an unstoppable Manchester United side at Old Trafford. Unfortunately, the resultant 0-4 defeat was to cost Darren his place in the team and next term could be an important one for him as he decides whether he is prepared to remain essentially a squad player or must seek regular first-team football elsewhere.

York C (From trainee on 21/6/1995) FL 16+4 FLC 4+1 FAC 1 Others 3/1
Sunderland (£50,000 on 18/10/1996) F/PL 74+23/4 FLC 10/2 FAC 3+1 Others 3

WILLIAMS Eifion Wyn
Born: Anglesey, 15 November 1975
Height: 5'11" Weight: 11.12
International Honours: W: B-1

In his first full season as a professional at Torquay Eifion developed an excellent understanding with his striking partner, Tony Bedeau, and scored a total of nine goals, including several superb strikes. He showed some fine link-up play and worked extremely hard, even when he was having difficulty scoring, and will be looking to find the net more regularly in the coming season.

Torquay U (£70,000 from Barry T on 25/3/1999) FL 45+4/14 FLC 2 FAC 3 Others 1

WILLIAMS Gareth James
Born: Isle of Wight, 12 March 1967
Height: 5'11" Weight: 12.2

Troubled by a thigh injury during the early weeks of the 1999-2000 season, Gareth struggled to re-establish himself at left wing back for Hull, largely due to the consistency of new signing Steve Harper. His versatility makes him a useful squad player, but his up-and-down campaign was typified by City's two league games with York. He put through his own goal to inadvertently help the visitors to a draw at Boothferry Park in September, but netted the Tigers' point-winning equaliser at Bootham Crescent four weeks later. In December he returned to Conference club Scarborough, just 13 months after his move to Hull.

Aston Villa (£30,000 from Gosport Borough on 9/1/1988) FL 6+6 FLC 0+1 FAC 2 Others 0+1
Barnsley (£200,000 on 6/8/1991) FL 23+11/6 FLC 1 FAC 1+1 Others 1+1
Hull C (Loaned on 17/9/1992) FL 4
Hull C (Loaned on 6/1/1994) FL 16/2
Bournemouth (Free on 6/9/1994) FL 0+1
Northampton T (Free on 27/9/1994) FL 38+12/1 FLC 2 FAC 2 Others 5+1
Scarborough (Free on 9/8/1996) FL 102+3/27 FLC 8/1 FAC 6/1 Others 4
Hull C (Free on 27/11/1998) FL 36+2/2 FLC 2 FAC 1 Others 2/1

WILLIAMS Gareth John
Born: Glasgow, 16 December 1981
Height: 5'11" Weight: 11.10
International Honours: S: Yth

Gareth was yet another talented youngster to be promoted to first-team action for Nottingham Forest in the 1999-2000 season. He is a hard-working and skilful midfield player who made his Football League debut as a substitute at Blackburn on Boxing Day. Glasgow-born, he has represented Scotland at U18 level and looks to have a great future in the game.

Nottingham F (From trainee on 23/12/1998) FL 0+2 FAC 1

WILLIAMS James
Born: Liverpool, 15 July 1982
Height: 5'7" Weight: 10.8

This Swindon youngster made steady progress in 1999-2000, taking the move up to senior football in his stride. He was used in a variety of positions, including right back, central defender and in midfield, and it will be interesting to see where he finally settles. James is very quick, strong in the tackle and distributes the ball well. He is expected to stake a claim for a regular place in the Robins' starting line-up in 2000-01.

Swindon T (From trainee on 9/12/1999) FL 15+14/1

WILLIAMS John Nelson
Born: Birmingham, 11 May 1968
Height: 6'1" Weight: 13.12

John joined York early in the 1999-2000 season from Cardiff City. The lively and pacy forward chiefly operated down the right. He always gave 100 per cent effort for his tenth league club and, although he found the net only three times, these were all crucial goals: a headed winner at Carlisle, a last-minute equaliser at Darlington and the first goal in a home win over Hartlepool.

Swansea C (£5,000 from Cradley T on 19/8/1991) FL 36+3/11 FLC 2+1 FAC 3 Others 1
Coventry C (£250,000 on 1/7/1992) PL 66+14/11 FLC 4 FAC 2
Notts Co (Loaned on 7/10/1994) FL 3+2/2
Stoke C (Loaned on 23/12/1994) FL 1+3
Swansea C (Loaned on 3/2/1995) FL 6+1/2
Wycombe W (£150,000 on 15/9/1995) FL 34+14/8 FLC 4+1/2 FAC 5/4 Others 2
Hereford U (Free on 14/2/1997) FL 8+3/3
Walsall (Free on 21/7/1997) FL 0+1
Exeter C (Free on 29/8/1997) FL 16+20/4
Cardiff C (Free on 3/8/1998) FL 25+18/12 FLC 2/1 FAC 5/3 Others 1
York C (£20,000 on 12/8/1999) FL 28+8/3 FLC 1 FAC 0+1 Others 1

WILLIAMS Lee
Born: Birmingham, 3 February 1973
Height: 5'7" Weight: 11.13
International Honours: E: Yth

Although he can also fill a more defensive wing-back role if required, Lee played on the right of the Mansfield midfield in 1999-

2000, when he was an ever-present in the side. He is particularly dangerous when he links with the attack, his excellent crosses from the right causing opposing defenders no end of trouble.
Aston Villa (From trainee on 26/1/1991)
Shrewsbury T (Loaned on 8/11/1992) FL 2+1 FAC 1+1/1 Others 2
Peterborough U (Signed on 23/3/1994) FL 83+8/1 FLC 4+1 FAC 5+1/1 Others 7 (Free to Shamrock Rov during 1996 close season)
Mansfield T (Free on 27/3/1997) FL 113+21/5 FLC 4 FAC 3+1 Others 4+1

WILLIAMS Marc Lloyd
Born: Bangor, 8 February 1973
Height: 5'11" Weight: 12.0
International Honours: W: B-1; SP-1
Having been troubled by pre-season injury and illness, the lively forward was unable to produce his best form for York in 1999-2000. Nevertheless Marc finished the season as second-top scorer for the Minstermen with five goals, these including vital strikes against Chester, Southend and his former club Halifax.
Stockport Co (£10,000 from Bangor C on 23/3/1995) FL 12+6/1 FLC 1+2 Others 0+1 (Free to Altrincham during 1996 close season)
Halifax T (Signed from Bangor C on 3/9/1998) FL 18+6/6 FLC 0+1 FAC 1 Others 2/2
York C (£30,000 on 19/3/1999) FL 22+11/9 FAC 1

WILLIAMS Mark Stuart
Born: Stalybridge, 28 September 1970
Height: 6'0" Weight: 13.0
Club Honours: Div 3 '94
International Honours: NI: 11; B-1
This experienced centre half joined Watford on a free transfer from Chesterfield under the Bosman ruling before the start of the 1999-2000 season and settled down immediately, striking up a good understanding with Robert Page in the heart of the Hornets' defence, However, Mark seemed to lose confidence after being controversially sent off at Old Trafford, and thereafter was not sure of his first-team place. He scored a goal which any striker would have been proud of against Leeds in October and established himself as a regular in the Northern Ireland line-up, winning a further seven caps during the season.
Shrewsbury T (Free from Newtown on 27/3/1992) FL 96+6/3 FLC 7+1 FAC 6 Others 6/1
Chesterfield (£50,000 on 7/8/1995) FL 168/12 FLC 10 FAC 13/1 Others 7/1
Watford (Free on 13/7/1999) P/FL 20+2/1 FLC 2

Marc Williams

WILLIAMS Martin Keith
Born: Luton, 12 July 1973
Height: 5'9" Weight: 11.12
The Reading forward's 1999-2000 season stuttered somewhat, but he will go down in history as the player who converted the first penalty kick in league football of the new millennium when he netted from the spot at Gillingham on 3 January, the game having kicked off at 1 p.m., ahead of other fixtures. He shared the striking position with several other players, but was used mainly as a substitute after the arrival of Martin Butler from Cambridge United. He has lost none of his pace or trickery but he was allowed to leave on a free transfer at the end of the season.
Luton T (Free from Leicester C juniors on 13/9/1991) FL 12+28/2 FLC 1 FAC 0+1 Others 2+1
Colchester U (Loaned on 9/3/1995) FL 3
Reading (Free on 13/7/1995) FL 99+29/26 FLC 10+6/2 FAC 8+2/1 Others 3

WILLIAMS Michael (Mike) Anthony
Born: Bradford, 21 November 1969
Height: 5'10" Weight: 11.6
Released by Oxford in the 1999 close season, Michael went back to Halifax on a trial basis just prior to Christmas but did not do enough to earn a contract. He played in just four full matches before being released. The strong-running midfielder had been at the Shay on loan from Sheffield Wednesday seven years earlier.
Sheffield Wed (Free from Maltby MW on 13/2/1991) F/PL 16+7/1 FLC 3+2 Others 1
Halifax T (Loaned on 18/12/1992) FL 9/1
Huddersfield T (Loaned on 18/10/1996) FL 2
Peterborough U (Loaned on 27/3/1997) FL 6
Burnley (Free on 18/7/1997) FL 15+1/1 FLC 3 FAC 2 Others 1
Oxford U (Free on 25/3/1999) FL 0+2
Halifax T (Free on 21/11/1999) FL 2+1 FAC 1 Others 1

WILLIAMS Paul Darren
Born: Burton, 26 March 1971
Height: 6'0" Weight: 13.0
International Honours: E: U21-6
Paul was a first choice in the centre of Coventry's defence until the arrival of Colin Hendry last March. He is combative in the air and strong in the tackle, and the defence rarely looked uneasy when he was present, while he scored a contender for "Goal of the Month" with a 30-yard effort in the home game with Newcastle. Much to the relief of the club's supporters, it was reported that he had signed a new long-term deal at the beginning of May that should tie him to the Sky Blues until 2003.
Derby Co (trainee on 13/7/1989) FL 153+7/26 FLC 10+2/2 FAC 8/3 Others 14+1/2
Lincoln C (Loaned on 9/11/1989) FL 3 FAC 2 Others 1
Coventry C (£975,000 on 6/8/1995) PL 122+12/5 FLC 12+1/1 FAC 11

WILLIAMS Paul Richard Curtis
Born: Leicester, 11 September 1969
Height: 5'7" Weight: 11.0
Although Paul was generally regarded as Bury's first-choice left back during the first half of the 1999-2000 season, his form

dipped slightly after the turn of the year, which was probably due to a persistent groin injury which he carried for most of the season. Quick and strong in the tackle, he had to contend with considerable competition for his place in the team and was eventually handed a free transfer in May.
Leicester C (From trainee on 1/7/1988)
Stockport Co (Free on 5/7/1989) FL 61+9/4 FLC 3 FAC 4 Others 7+5/1
Coventry C (£150,000 on 12/8/1993) PL 8+6 FLC 1+1 FAC 3
West Bromwich A (Loaned on 19/11/1993) FL 5
Huddersfield T (Loaned on 17/11/1994) FL 2 Others 1
Huddersfield T (Loaned on 17/3/1995) FL 7
Plymouth Arg (£50,000 on 10/8/1995) FL 131/4 FLC 6 FAC 8 Others 7/1
Gillingham (Free on 6/8/1998) FL 9+1 FLC 2
Bury (£50,000 on 5/11/1998) FL 36+5/1 FAC 3+1 Others 1

WILLIAMS Ryan Neil
Born: Sutton in Ashfield, 31 August 1978
Height: 5'5" Weight: 11.4
International Honours: E: Yth
This gutsy young midfielder made an immediate impact after joining Chesterfield on loan from Tranmere in November. Mobile, quick-footed and equally quick-witted, he brought added creativity to the Spireites' midfield and was to remain a fixture in the starting line-up for the rest of the season, the club making his transfer permanent in February. Previously seen as a striker, he proved that he remains an excellent finisher, his sweet left-footed strikes bringing him goals on several occasions. He has made great strides since his move to Saltergate, and Chesterfield will be looking to fashion their midfield around him in the seasons ahead.
Mansfield T (Trainee) FL 9+17/3 FLC 2 FAC 0+1
Tranmere Rov (£70,000 + on 8/8/1997) FL 2+3
Chesterfield (£80,000 on 10/11/1999) FL 30/5 Others 3

WILLIAMSON Lee Trevor
Born: Derby, 7 June 1982
Height: 5'10" Weight: 10.4
The captain of the Mansfield youth team, this talented young midfielder was given some first-team experience when brought on as a late substitute in the home game with Shrewsbury with the Stags 4-0 up. He made three further appearances from the bench towards the end of the season and won the Stags' "Young Player of the Year" award.
Mansfield T (Trainee) FL 0+4

WILLIS Adam Peter
Born: Nuneaton, 21 September 1976
Height: 6'1" Weight: 12.2
Adam was in and out of the Swindon team in 1999-2000 until eventually breaking through to win a regular place in the starting line-up last March. A tall central defender, he is good in the air and distributes the ball effectively. Adam was reported to have been given a new contract by Robins' boss Colin Todd at the end of last season.
Coventry C (From trainee on 1/7/1995)
Swindon T (Free on 21/4/1998) FL 27+7 FAC 1
Mansfield T (Loaned on 25/3/1999) FL 10

WILLIS Roger Christopher
Born: Sheffield, 17 June 1967
Height: 6'1" Weight: 12.0
Club Honours: GMVC '91
International Honours: E: SP-1
"Harry" started the 1999-2000 season on Chesterfield's transfer list but stuck around to offer options to manager John Duncan. He lost his place up front to Jon Howard and became a regular substitute, acquitting himself well when called upon. He usually looked better coming out of the middle of midfield with the ball at his feet, to feed his team-mates or have a pop himself, but a small surplus of such players at Saltergate hampered his chances of regular selection.
Grimsby T (Signed from Dunkirk on 20/7/1989) FL 1+8 FLC 0+1
Barnet (£10,000 on 1/8/1990) FL 39+5/13 FLC 2 FAC 5+1/3 Others 1+4/1
Watford (£175,000 on 6/10/1992) FL 30+6/2 FAC 1
Birmingham C (£150,000 on 31/12/1993) FL 12+7/5 FAC 0+1
Southend U (Signed on 16/9/1994) FL 30+1/7 FAC 1 Others 1
Peterborough U (Free on 13/8/1996) FL 34+6/6 FLC 3 FAC 5+1 Others 5
Chesterfield (£100,000 on 11/7/1997) FL 46+33/12 FLC 9+2/2 FAC 1+2/1 Others 1+2

WILLMOTT Christopher (Chris) Alan
Born: Bedford, 30 September 1977
Height: 6'2" Weight: 11.12
Chris joined Wimbledon in the summer of 1999 and although he had to wait until the new year before he appeared for his new club he then had a decent run in the side. Still very much learning his trade, he is a dependable centre back who is strong in the tackle and always tries to use the ball constructively. He looked at ease in possession and Dons' fans can expect to see a lot more of him in years to come.
Luton T (From trainee on 1/5/1996) FL 13+1
Wimbledon (£350,000 on 14/7/1999) PL 7 FLC 0+1 FAC 1

WILLS Kevin Michael
Born: Torquay, 15 October 1980
Height: 5'8" Weight: 10.7
A product of the Plymouth youth system, Kevin can play either in midfield or up front. He is strong in the tackle, but suffered with injuries in 1999-2000 which restricted him to only two appearances from the substitutes' bench. It was reported that he had been offered month-to-month terms for the coming season.
Plymouth Arg (From trainee on 16/7/1999) FL 0+4

WILNIS Fabian
Born: Surinam, 23 August 1970
Height: 5'8" Weight: 12.6
Fabian was quickly into his stride at Ipswich at the start of the 1999-2000 season and once again demonstrated his ability to support his attack with sorties up the wing and pin-point crosses into the box. It was from such a run and cross that David Johnson headed home the opening goal against Barnsley. The arrival of Gary Croft has provided him with competition but he will be looking to appear regularly in the coming season as Ipswich make their entry into the Premiership.
Ipswich T (£200,000 from De Graafschap, Holland via NAC Breda, on 6/1/1999) FL 47+6/1 FLC 1+1 FAC 2 Others 3+1

WILSON Che Christian Aaron Clay
Born: Ely, 17 January 1979
Height: 5'9" Weight: 11.3
Che found his senior opportunities at Norwich limited in 1999-2000, but whenever called upon he never let the side down. An adaptable defender, he is normally associated with the left-back position, but at reserve level at least he has performed consistently well in the heart of the defence and at right back. He has a calm and measured approach to the game, seldom having to hurry his play due to his good anticipation. Che is solid in the tackle and an accurate passer of the ball, making him a good all-round defender, and he is working at his attacking link-up skills, which are essential for a full back in the modern game. At the end of the season it was announced that his contract would not be renewed for 2000-01.
Norwich C (From trainee on 3/7/1997) FL 16+6 FLC 3

WILSON Clive Euclid Aklana
Born: Manchester, 13 November 1961
Height: 5'7" Weight: 11.4
Club Honours: Div 2 '89
The veteran left back joined Cambridge from Tottenham Hotspur in the 1999 close season. A quality player whose experience and skills shone in a young defence, Clive suffered a knee injury in the second half of the campaign and this eventually prompted him to announce his retirement from the game at the age of 38, after 569 senior appearances.
Manchester C (From juniors on 8/12/1979) FL 96+2/9 FLC 10/2 FAC 2 Others 5
Chester C (Loaned on 16/9/1982) FL 21/2
Chelsea (£250,000 on 19/3/1987) FL 68+13/5 FLC 3+3 FAC 4 Others 10+2
Manchester C (Loaned on 19/3/1987) FL 11
Queens Park R (£450,000 on 4/7/1990) F/PL 170+2/12 FLC 16/1 FAC 8/1 Others 2+1
Tottenham H (Free on 12/6/1995) PL 67+3/1 FLC 7+1 FAC 7+1/1
Cambridge U (Free on 24/8/1999) FL 27 FLC 2 FAC 4 Others 1

WILSON Kevin James
Born: Banbury, 18 April 1961
Height: 5'8" Weight: 11.4
Club Honours: Div 2 '89; FMC '90
International Honours: NI: 42
Northampton's player-manager, Kevin restricted his first-team appearances after taking over the hot seat last October. He still has something to offer, however, as he proved when he netted his 199th first-class goal with a close-range header against Shrewsbury in January. He often named himself as one of the five substitutes, but started several games when the club were struggling with injuries and also turned out quite regularly for the reserve side. With a record of 22 wins from 40 games, he guided the Cobblers to promotion to Division Two and was rewarded with an extended contract to June 2001.

Derby Co (£20,000 from Banbury U on 21/12/1979) FL 106+16/30 FLC 8+3/8 FAC 8/3
Ipswich T (£100,000 on 5/1/1985) FL 94+4/34 FLC 8/8 FAC 10/3 Others 7/4
Chelsea (£335,000 on 25/6/1987) FL 124+28/42 FLC 10+2/4 FAC 7+1/1 Others 14+5/8
Notts Co (£225,000 on 27/3/1992) FL 58+11/3 FLC 3+1 FAC 2 Others 5+1
Bradford C (Loaned on 13/1/1994) FL 5
Walsall (Free on 4/8/1994) FL 124+1/38 FLC 8/3 FAC 13/7 Others 6/1
Northampton T (Free on 28/7/1997) FL 13+12/2 FLC 1+1 FAC 0+2

WILSON Mark Antony
Born: Scunthorpe, 9 February 1979
Height: 5'11" Weight: 13.0
Club Honours: E: Yth; Sch

A young Manchester United midfielder with excellent presence and neat skills, Mark continued to shine in the few games he played for United during the course of the 1999-2000 campaign. In addition to his two full appearances in the Champions' League and a solitary game in the World Club Championship, he also showed up well deputising for David Beckham in the Reds' Premiership match against Watford at Vicarage Road in April. There is every indication that Mark is still very much a part of Sir Alex Ferguson's plans for the coming season.

Manchester U (From trainee on 16/2/1996) PL 1+2 FLC 2 Others 3+2
Wrexham (Loaned on 23/2/1998) FL 12+1/4

WILSON Paul Robert
Born: Forest Gate, 26 September 1964
Height: 5'9" Weight: 12.6
Club Honours: GMVC '91

When experience was needed to steady the ship during Barnet's tumultuous end to the 1999-2000 season, Paul returned to the starting line-up to shoulder responsibility in the middle of the park and helped ensure that the Bees gained a play-off place. His unquestionable loyalty and resolute spirit in the face of adversity had been rewarded in the autumn with a testimonial match against West Ham. For the majority of the campaign the veteran midfielder found himself confined to the reserves. However, with the pressure cranked up, Barnet's form began to wither and Paul was called upon to halt the slump; once again, he did not disappoint. Tackling ferociously, toiling honestly and inspiring his team-mates to follow suit, Paul featured in the concluding nine games of the term, and his penalty against Leyton Orient enabled the Bees to attain a play-off place. It was a fitting end to the season for the most reliable player in Barnet's league history, and he proved that he still has plenty to offer the club.

Barnet (Signed from Barking on 1/3/1988) FL 240+23/24 FLC 13+1/1 FAC 22+1 Others 10+4/1

WILSON Scott Andrew
Born: Radcliffe, 25 October 1980
Height: 5'7" Weight: 9.8

A former Rochdale trainee, Scott broke into the first-team squad at the start of 1999-2000, his second year as a professional, and played in a pre-season game with Raith Rovers. He was selected as a substitute for one early-season match but was then ruled out for a lengthy spell by a dislocated elbow. After a month on loan to Altrincham in January, the young midfielder made his league debut as a substitute in the final game of the season against Barnet. However, he was released by Dale in May.

Rochdale (From trainee on 1/7/1999) FL 0+1

WILSON Stephen (Steve) Lee
Born: Hull, 24 April 1974
Height: 5'10" Weight: 10.12

Although he signed an improved two-year contract in March 1999, the future of Hull's longest-serving player looked bleak when Steve badly damaged a medial ligament in a pre-season game at Goole. In a campaign when Hull equalled a Football League record by using seven 'keepers, it was the new year before he could regain full fitness, but he responded to the challenge in magnificent fashion with a run of eight games in which he conceded only two goals to re-establish his claim to the 'keeper's jersey. Often tagged as too light and too small, Steve continues to prove the doubters wrong. A popular figure whose commitment to the Tigers' cause has never wavered, he will be aiming to complete ten years' service at the close of 2000-01.

Hull C (From trainee on 13/7/1992) FL 180+1 FLC 13 FAC 13 Others 11+1

WILSON Stuart Kevin
Born: Leicester, 16 September 1977
Height: 5'8" Weight: 9.12
Club Honours: FLC '00

Stuart is a promising young Leicester midfielder, whose 1999-2000 season was blighted by injury. He managed only a couple of substitute appearances in the early stages of the Worthington Cup run and was loaned to Sheffield United on transfer deadline day to continue his recuperation and further his league experience. He made his first appearance, as a substitute, the following Saturday, and impressed on his full debut the following week in the 0-5 defeat at Blackburn, where his lively play created several chances. As well as playing wide on the right, he also produced some hard-working performances as a front man alongside Marcus Bent.

Leicester C (From trainee on 4/7/1996) PL 1+21/3 FLC 1+7/1 FAC 0+4
Sheffield U (Loaned on 23/3/2000) FL 4+2

WILSTERMAN Brian Hank
Born: Surinam, 19 November 1966
Height: 6'1" Weight: 13.8

A no-nonsense defender, Brian proved to be a good signing after joining Rotherham during the 1999 close season. He played the majority of his games at right back, although he was equally efficient in the middle. Strong on the ball and sound in the tackle, Brian popped up with three vital goals from set plays in the second half of the season.

Oxford U (£200,000 from Beerschot, Belgium on 28/2/1997) FL 28+14/2 FLC 2 FAC 1
Rotherham U (Free on 1/7/1999) FL 38+4/3 FLC 2 FAC 2 Others 2

WINDASS Dean
Born: Hull, 1 April 1969
Height: 5'10" Weight: 12.6

Dean Windass

Dean spent much of the 1999-2000 campaign battling away in an unfamiliar midfield position for Bradford City but really blossomed when he was moved up to form a striking partnership with Dean Saunders last February. He finished the season as City's top scorer with ten goals including a tremendous first-half hat-trick in the exciting 4-4 draw with Derby County in April. He always gave 100 per cent effort wherever he was played and his determination and hard work were valuable assets for the Bantams in their successful fight against relegation from the Premiership.

Hull C (Free from North Ferriby on 24/10/1991) FL 173+3/57 FLC 11/4 FAC 7 Others 12/3
Aberdeen (£700,000 on 1/12/1995) SL 60+13/21 SLC 5+2/6 SC 7/3 Others 6/1
Oxford U (£475,000 on 6/8/1998) FL 33/15 FLC 2 FAC 3/3
Bradford C (£950,000 + on 5/3/1999) P/FL 42+8/13 FLC 3 FAC 1

WINSTANLEY Mark Andrew
Born: St Helens, 22 January 1968
Height: 6'1" Weight: 12.7
Club Honours: AMC '89

Mark filled a central defensive role for Shrewsbury for part of the 1999-2000 season, but then switched to left back to cover for injury. He added much-needed height to the defence and proved an effective performer, with his wealth of experience a considerable asset. With good cover in the defensive area, Shrewsbury decided not to renew Mark's contract in May.

Bolton W (From trainee on 22/7/1986) FL 215+5/3 FLC 19+1 FAC 19 Others 26/3
Burnley (Signed on 5/8/1994) FL 151+1/5 FLC 13 FAC 8 Others 8+1
Shrewsbury T (Loaned on 17/9/1998) FL 8
Preston NE (Free on 22/3/1999)
Shrewsbury T (Free on 22/7/1999) FL 32+1/1 FLC 2 FAC 1

WINTERBURN Nigel
Born: Nuneaton, 11 December 1963
Height: 5'9" Weight: 11.4
Club Honours: Div 1 '89, '91; PL '98; FAC '93, '98; FLC '93; ECWC '94; CS '98 '99
International Honours: E: 2; B-3; U21-1; Yth

Despite being in his 13th season at Arsenal, Nigel remains as enthusiastic and committed as ever. He is still regarded by a number of critics as being one of the best left-sided defenders in England. Although he started last season as the first choice at Highbury, he picked up an injury early in the campaign which caused him to miss three matches. His place was taken by his intended long-term replacement, Silvinho, and from that point on appearances were shared. Being a true professional, Nigel maintained a high level of fitness and continued to perform consistently when selected, whether starting a game or coming off the bench. He also played on the left side of midfield with great success, providing cover when needed. Stop Press: Nigel was reported to have joined West Ham on a two-year contract in mid-June.

Birmingham C (From apprentice on 14/8/1981)
Wimbledon (Free on 22/9/1983) FL 164+1/8 FLC 13 FAC 12 Others 2
Arsenal (£407,000 on 26/5/1987) F/PL 429+11/8 FLC 49/3 FAC 47 Others 50+1/1

WISE Dennis Frank
Born: Kensington, 15 December 1966
Height: 5'6" Weight: 10.10
Club Honours: FAC '88, '97, '00; FLC '98; ECWC '98
International Honours: E: 19; B-3; U21-1

It was in July 1990 that Dennis, then a chirpy winger from Wimbledon, breezed into a decrepit Stamford Bridge to become Chelsea's record signing. In the ten years since then the winger-turned midfield general has played an instrumental role in Chelsea's transition from perennial under-achievers to one of Europe's strongest clubs. Currently playing under his sixth manager in those ten seasons, Dennis was awarded a prestigious testimonial against Serie A giants Bologna before the start of the 1999-2000 season and the big crowd showed their appreciation of their favourite footballing son. He was determined to erase the memory of the previous campaign's disciplinary problems and certainly began the season in the correct fashion, heading his first league goal for 18 months in the second Premiership match at Filbert Street. His partnership with Didier Deschamps in the

Dennis Wise

Blues' engine room was an instant success as they became the springboard for some outstanding team performances, particularly against AC Milan at Stamford Bridge, where they dominated the Italians' illustrious midfield. Dennis then went from villain to "Hero of the San Siro" in the space of ten days: he received a further red card at Liverpool before scoring a superb equaliser in Milan which virtually assured Chelsea's progress into the second phase of the Champions' League at the expense of the Italians, a moment that Dennis acknowledged was one of the high points of his career. The second half of the season brought further European goals and glory for Dennis: a header against Feyenoord in Rotterdam and the only goal of the game against Marseille at the Bridge helped ease Chelsea through to a quarter-final clash with Barcelona. Although Chelsea lost on aggregate, despite Dennis's imperious display in midfield at Stamford Bridge, where the Blues recorded a memorable 3-1 victory, there was the consolation of another FA Cup triumph to compensate for the Champions' League heartache. Dennis had the privilege of being the last captain to lift the Cup at the original Twin Towers stadium, and he certainly turned it into a family occasion by taking his four-month-old son Henry up to the Royal Box with him. This made it five major trophies in four seasons for Dennis, now Chelsea's most successful captain, who took his first-team appearances through the 400 barrier. On the international front he finally seemed to gain recognition as a regular in the England team, winning seven more caps during the season and featuring in all of his country's games in Euro 2000. Both Dennis and Chelsea have changed beyond recognition in the past ten years: the club and the player have broadened their horizons in tandem under the influence of the overseas contingent and both have benefited immeasurably as a consequence.

Wimbledon (Free from Southampton juniors on 28/3/1985) FL 127+8/27 FLC 14 FAC 11/3 Others 5
Chelsea (£1,600,000 on 3/7/1990) F/PL 287+9/50 FLC 29/6 FAC 35/9 Others 42+1/8

WOAN Ian Simon
Born: Heswall, 14 December 1967
Height: 5'10" Weight: 12.4
Club Honours: Div 1 '98

Ian was very much the forgotten man at Nottingham Forest last season. He started just one game, at Norwich in November, and made a further nine appearances as a substitute. He is still a talented wide-left or central midfield player with good passing and crossing skills who has much to offer. His contract expired in the summer of 2000 and at the time of writing he appeared to be destined to leave the City Ground after failing to agree to a one-year deal.

Nottingham F (£80,000 from Runcorn on 14/3/1990) F/PL 189+32/31 FLC 15+3/1 FAC 20+1/6 Others 13/2

WOLLEASTON Robert Ainsley
Born: Perivale, 21 December 1979
Height: 5'11" Weight: 12.2

Robert is the latest graduate of the prolific Chelsea youth scheme to appear at first-team level. He made two substitute appearances for the Blues last season, against Huddersfield in the Worthington Cup and Sunderland in the Premiership. Robert later spent a month on loan at Bristol Rovers, joining the Second Division club on transfer deadline day. He made his Football League debut for Rovers at Millwall, coming on as a substitute for the second half. He contributed some neat football and made further substitute appearances against Stoke, Reading and Preston. He is a tall, powerfully built attacking midfielder who has earned rave reviews for his performances in Chelsea's reserve team. His outstanding potential earned him a three-year contract with the Blues, and his will be a name to watch out for in the future.

Chelsea (From trainee on 3/6/1998) PL 0+1 FLC 0+1
Bristol Rov (Loaned on 23/3/2000) FL 0+4

WOOD Jamie
Born: Salford, 21 September 1978
Height: 5'10" Weight: 13.0
International Honours: Cayman Islands: 2

Having been coached by Warren Joyce when the Hull boss was involved with Manchester United's U16s, Jamie chose to progress his career with the Third Division club last season. He joined the international ranks in February when appearing for the Cayman Islands in two friendlies against Jamaica, who included his team-mates Ian Goodison and Theo Whitmore, thus giving the Tigers three current internationals for the first time in their history. The link-up came when the Cayman Islands (a British Dependent Territory) took advantage of what they perceived to be a loophole enabling them to select any British passport holder for their team, although this was later outlawed by FIFA. Jamie is a promising striker with good pace who will be looking to win a regular first-team place at Boothferry Park in 2000-01.

Manchester U (From trainee on 10/7/1997)
Hull C (Free on 21/7/1999) FL 13+19/6 FLC 1+2 FAC 3+1/1 Others 1+1

WOOD Steven (Steve) Ronald
Born: Oldham, 23 June 1963
Height: 5'9" Weight: 10.10

This vastly experienced Macclesfield stalwart is still giving good value for money, commanding the midfield and regularly acting as play-maker. A firm favourite with the Macc supporters, Steve reached 100 Football League appearances for the club during the season and in January he stepped up to become joint coach with John Askey after the appointment of Peter Davenport as manager.

Macclesfield T (Free from Ashton U on 22/7/1993) FL 102+19/18 FLC 7+1/1 FAC 5+1/2 Others 3

WOODGATE Jonathan Simon
Born: Middlesbrough, 22 January 1980
Height: 6'2" Weight: 13.0
Club Honours: FAYC '97
International Honours: E: 1; U21-1; Yth

Jonathan is a young centre back who has been nothing short of a revelation since making his Premiership breakthrough with Leeds United. Last season he played with a composure, maturity and skill which belied his 20 years, producing performances of a consistently high quality. In the victory at Chelsea in December, United faced relentless pressure, especially in the first half, but the defence, and Jonathan in particular, were up to the challenge. He is very comfortable on the ball and equally adept playing out of defence, and there have been comparisons with the style of his manager, David O'Leary. Jonathan has also benefited from playing alongside Lucas Radebe. Two surprises of last season were that he didn't add to either his only Premiership goal of the campaign, at Everton, or his single full England cap.

Leeds U (From trainee on 13/5/1997) PL 57+2/3 FLC 4 FAC 8 Others 11

WOODHOUSE Curtis
Born: Beverley, 17 April 1980
Height: 5'8" Weight: 11.0
International Honours: E: U21-4; Yth

Curtis began the 1999-2000 season well and made a further appearance for England U21s against Poland in September. Hamstring problems caused him to miss several games for Sheffield United, however, and were probably the cause of his performances falling below the level of the previous season. Despite playing with the anticipated enthusiasm and commitment, he did not win the ball with the expected regularity and his distribution was not as decisive as before. He was delighted with his headed goal at Port Vale in March and his scoring deflection the following week, and his form improved steadily towards the end of the season. In December, at the age of 19 years and 239 days, he became the Blades' youngest-ever captain when he led the side out against Rushden & Diamonds in the FA Cup. He turned 20 in April, and his total of 89 first-team appearances as a teenager has been bettered by only one player in the Blades' history.

Sheffield U (From trainee on 31/12/1997) FL 69+10/7 FLC 3+2 FAC 9

WOODMAN Andrew (Andy) John
Born: Camberwell, 11 August 1971
Height: 6'3" Weight: 13.7
Club Honours: Div 3 '99

Confident on crosses and a fine shot stopper, Andy was Brentford's first-choice goalkeeper for most of the 1999-2000 season. He lost his place to Jason Pearcey in early March and shortly afterwards went on loan to Peterborough United, only to receive a hasty recall to Griffin Park after Pearcey was injured against Wigan. He himself missed the final game against Colchester after being diagnosed as suffering from viral meningitis and it is hoped he will have made a full recovery in time for the start of the coming season.

Crystal Palace (From trainee on 1/7/1989)
Exeter C (Free on 4/7/1994) FL 6 FLC 1 FAC 1 Others 2

Northampton T (Free on 10/3/1995) FL 163 FLC 13 FAC 8 Others 13
Brentford (Signed on 22/1/1999) FL 61 FLC 1 FAC 2 Others 3

WOODS Matthew (Mattie) James
Born: Gosport, 9 September 1976
Height: 6'1" Weight: 12.13

Although Chester dropped down into the Conference at the end of the 1999-2000 season, Mattie had a solid campaign and only Wayne Brown and Luke Beckett made more league appearances for the club. A competent player with lots of confidence, the former Everton trainee now has the experience of over 150 senior games behind him.

Everton (From trainee on 1/7/1995)
Chester C (Free on 12/8/1996) FL 114+21/4 FLC 8+3/1 FAC 6+1 Others 3+1

WOODS Stephen (Steve) John
Born: Davenham, 15 December 1976
Height: 5'11" Weight: 11.13

Surprisingly released by Stoke last summer, Steve was snapped up by Chesterfield to provide additional options on the left-hand side and in the centre of defence. An intelligent player, he displayed comfort on the ball and had the awareness to link well with his colleagues. A series of minor injuries hampered his progress through the season, though, and the club's fans will doubtless see more of him as he puts these behind him.

Stoke C (From trainee on 3/8/1995) FL 33+1 FLC 2 FAC 2 Others 2
Plymouth Arg (Loaned on 26/3/1998) FL 4+1
Chesterfield (Free on 7/7/1999) FL 22+3 FLC 4 Others 0+1

WOODTHORPE Colin John
Born: Ellesmere Port, 13 January 1969
Height: 5'11" Weight: 11.8

Colin spent much of the 1999-2000 season on the subs' bench for Stockport following the arrival of Shane Nicholson, who took over the left-back position. Restricted to occasional appearances in midfield for the Hatters, he remained a valued member of the first-team squad and never let the side down when called upon. He is strong in the tackle and very effective at breaking forward, making him useful either as a full back or in the middle of the park.

Chester C (From trainee on 23/8/1986) FL 154+1/6 FLC 10 FAC 8+1 Others 18/1
Norwich C (£175,000 on 17/7/1990) P/FL 36+7/1 FLC 0+2 FAC 6 Others 1+1
Aberdeen (£400,000 on 20/7/1994) SL 43+5/1 SLC 5+1/1 SC 4 Others 5+2
Stockport Co (£200,000 on 29/7/1997) FL 78+17/3 FLC 9/2 FAC 2+1/1

WOODWARD Andrew (Andy) Stephen
Born: Stockport, 23 September 1973
Height: 5'11" Weight: 13.6
Club Honours: Div 2 '97

A chest infection prevented the Bury defender from undergoing a hernia operation during the summer of 1999 and he battled against injury throughout last season. His catalogue of woe included a ripped groin muscle in August (five weeks out), a hamstring problem in October, a recurring hamstring injury in November and medial ligament damage in December, and he also lost a stone in weight in January after a severe bout of gastro-enteritis. He eventually resumed light training on 7 March and a little over two weeks later signed for Sheffield United in a £35,000 transfer, rejoining former Bury manager Neil Warnock. Despite being short of match practice he made his debut, as a substitute, the following Saturday, showing his versatility by playing first at right back and then as a central defender. He made the starting line-up for the following week's trip to Blackburn but only featured once more during the season.

Crewe Alex (From trainee on 29/7/1992) FL 9+11 FLC 2 Others 0+3
Bury (Signed on 13/3/1995) FL 95+20/1 FLC 6+2 FAC 6+1 Others 5
Sheffield U (£35,000 on 23/3/2000) FL 2+1

WOOLLISCROFT Ashley David
Born: Stoke, 28 December 1979
Height: 5'10" Weight: 11.2

Ashley started just one game for Stoke, in the FA Cup at Blackpool, in 1999-2000 although he was also used as a non-playing substitute on a number of occasions. The promising young defender, whose tackles have real bite, continues to develop after his rise from the youth-squad ranks and remains a fine prospect, despite the club's surplus of central defenders.

Stoke C (From trainee on 10/2/1997) FL 0+1 FAC 1

Nordin Wooter

WOOTER Nordin
Born: Surinam, 24 August 1976
Height: 5'8" Weight: 11.1
International Honours: Holland: U21-15

This Dutch midfield player arrived at Watford on trial from Real Zaragoza of Spain in September 1999 and soon became the club's record signing at £750,000 – a figure subsequently exceeded by the fee for Heidar Helguson. A mercurial player, small and quick with immaculate control, Nordin proved a handful for several Premiership defences and was always threatening to try something different. His best position was a matter of debate, but he played mainly wide on the right, laying on chances for his strikers and scoring himself against Leicester. Nordin was sidelined for six weeks in December with an ankle injury which recurred in April and disrupted the end of his season.

Watford (£975,000 from Real Zaragoza, Spain on 14/9/1999) PL 16+4/1 FLC 1 FAC 1

WOOZLEY David (Dave) James
Born: Ascot, 6 December 1979
Height: 6'0" Weight: 12.10

Dave is another of the highly promising youngsters at Crystal Palace. A tall left-sided defender, he is solid on the ground and capable in the air. He featured regularly in the Eagles' first-team squad during 1999-2000 despite being in competition with Andy Linighan and Fan Zhiyi, and will be looking to feature regularly in the starting line-up in the coming season.

Crystal Palace (From trainee on 17/11/1997) FL 21+9 FLC 3+1 FAC 0+1

WORRALL Benjamin (Ben) Joseph
Born: Swindon, 7 December 1975
Height: 5'7" Weight: 11.6
International Honours: E: Yth

Ben was signed by Exeter from Scarborough on a short-term basis in July 1999. He displayed tenacity and added a touch of steel to the midfield. Although he made five appearances in total, his contract was not renewed and he was released in January.

Swindon T (From trainee on 8/7/1994) FL 1+2
Scarborough (Free on 2/8/1996) FL 45+22/3 FLC 3+3 FAC 2 Others 2+1
Exeter C (Free on 6/8/1999) FL 1+3 FLC 1

WORTHINGTON Martin Paul
Born: Torquay, 25 January 1981
Height: 6'0" Weight: 12.4

In his first year as a pro at Torquay, Martin was limited to a brief substitute appearance at Gillingham in the Auto Windscreens Shield. He was released in February and finished the 1999-2000 season playing in local non-league football.

Torquay U (From trainee on 1/7/1999) FL 0+1 Others 0+1

WOTTON Paul Anthony
Born: Plymouth, 17 August 1977
Height: 5'11" Weight: 12.0

Paul started the 1999-2000 season on a week-to-week contract with Plymouth, as he was looking for a move to Northampton. He later resolved his differences with his home-town club, and signed a contract until the end of the term. On the field, he became an important member of the team in the second half of the season, always giving 100 per cent. A versatile player who can comfortably play either in midfield or in defence, Paul was offered a new contract for 2000-01.

Plymouth Arg (From trainee on 10/7/1995) FL 94+16/3 FLC 4 FAC 10/1 Others 5+1/2

WRACK Darren
Born: Cleethorpes, 5 May 1976
Height: 5'9" Weight: 12.10

After a tremendous season for Walsall in 1998-99 Darren began 1999-2000 with goals against Sheffield United and Norwich before August was out but after a remarkable run of 89 successive games he lost his place in February and was used mainly as a substitute in the last few weeks of the season. The club's fans will be hoping that back in Division Two his darting runs from midfield will again be a major factor in Walsall's attacking play.

Derby Co (From trainee on 12/7/1994) FL 4+22/1 FLC 0+3 FAC 0+2
Grimsby T (£100,000 + on 19/7/1996) FL 5+8/1 Others 0+1
Shrewsbury T (Loaned on 17/2/1997) FL 3+1 Others 1
Walsall (Free on 6/8/1998) FL 80+10/17 FLC 6 FAC 4 Others 6/1

WREH Christopher (Chris)
Born: Liberia, 14 May 1975
Height: 5'8" Weight: 11.13
Club Honours: PL '98; FAC '98; CS '98
International Honours: Liberia

Christopher is a quick and confident Arsenal striker with the ability to run at defences. He made only one first-team appearance for the Gunners last season, when he came on as a substitute in the Charity Shield match against Manchester United. He spent five weeks on loan with Birmingham City last autumn and made a bright start, scoring a fine goal in a 1-1 draw at Grimsby; however, he dislocated a thumb in early December and chose to return to Highbury for treatment. Christopher ended the season on loan to Dutch side Den Bosch and it seems likely that his long-term future lies away from Highbury.

Arsenal (£300,000 from Guincamp, France, via Monaco, on 14/8/1997) PL 10+18/3 FLC 3+3 FAC 2+4/1 Others 3+2/1
Birmingham C (Loaned on 22/10/1999) FL 6+1/1

WRIGHT Alan Geoffrey
Born: Ashton under Lyne, 28 September 1971
Height: 5'4" Weight: 9.9
Club Honours: FLC '96
International Honours: E: U21-2; Yth; Sch

This consistent full back had another good season with Aston Villa in 1999-2000, culminating in an appearance in the FA Cup final against Chelsea last May. Alan began the campaign as first choice at left back but then suffered a stomach muscle injury early on which brought to an end his run of 97 consecutive Premiership games for the club. Gareth Barry replaced him and performed so effectively that Alan had to wait until October, when Ugo Ehiogu was injured, to win back the position. However, once he had returned he was an ever-present in the Villa team and went on to produce a run of consistent form as Villa recovered from their mid-season dip to finish up in sixth spot. He possesses many of the characteristics of an old-fashioned winger, having pace, ball control, good crossing ability and a powerful shot – all of which make up for his lack of height, for he is one of the smallest Premiership defenders around.

Blackpool (From trainee on 13/4/1989) FL 91+7 FLC 10+2 FAC 8 Others 11+2
Blackburn Rov (£400,000 on 25/10/1991) F/PL 67+7/1 FLC 8 FAC 5+1 Others 3
Aston Villa (£1,000,000 on 10/3/1995) PL 188+3/4 FLC 17 FAC 20 Others 14

WRIGHT Benjamin (Ben)
Born: Leicester, 1 July 1980
Height: 6'0" Weight: 13.7

Since joining Bristol City from Kettering in March 1999, this striker has shown some impressive form in reserve football. He made his first-team debut when coming on as a substitute in the 3-2 win at Bournemouth last January and had a further taste of league football at Millwall in March. Much is expected of this big, strong player with an eye for goal, and he will be looking for further opportunities during the coming season.

Bristol C (£30,000 + from Kettering T on 10/3/1999) FL 0+2

WRIGHT Darren
Born: Warrington, 7 September 1979
Height: 5'8" Weight: 11.2

With more first-team opportunities, Darren attracted more attention in 1999-2000 – especially in his trademark red boots. A player who has worked his way through the Chester ranks, he was primarily employed at centre forward, although Darren can also be used on either wing. A good crosser with plenty of pace who enjoys taking defenders on, he has previously represented Cheshire and England in athletics.

Chester C (From trainee on 8/7/1998) FL 24+24/2 FLC 4+1 FAC 4 Others 0+2

WRIGHT David
Born: Warrington, 1 May 1980
Height: 5'11" Weight: 10.8
International Honours: E: Yth

A former England U18 cap, David has graduated from Crewe's youth development programme and is now firmly established in the first team at right back. An accomplished defender who also enjoys getting forward, he missed only a handful of games in 1999-2000 but was unable to add to his total of one senior goal. He is a fine prospect with a bright future in the game.

Crewe Alex (From trainee on 18/6/1997) FL 64+4/1 FLC 3+1 FAC 1

WRIGHT Ian Edward
Born: Woolwich, 3 November 1963
Height: 5'10" Weight: 11.8
Club Honours: PL '98; FMC '91; FLC '93; FAC '93, '98
International Honours: E: 33; B-3

The veteran striker joined Nottingham Forest on loan from West Ham last August and was an immediate success at the City Ground, keeping up his record of scoring for each of his clubs on his debut and hitting five goals from only ten starts. He showed that he is still a handful for defenders and the crowd took to him immediately but in October he signed for Celtic on a permanent basis after the Scottish giants reportedly made him an irresistible offer. Ian's stay in Glasgow was to be brief, however, and in February he moved to Second Division Burnley. The Lancashire club certainly achieved a publicity coup with their signing of the former England striker, and his arrival sent Turf Moor gates above the 20,000 mark, as well as giving club shop sales a considerable boost. He came into the Clarets' side in place of the suspended Andy Payton but, having failed to score in four starts, dropped to the subs' bench after Payton's return. His value to the playing as well as to the commercial side of the club then became clear as his regular appearances for the last half-hour or so of games produced a display of Premiership skills, excitement and crucial goals, including vital, spectacular, last-ditch strikes against Gillingham and Notts County. It is likely that Ian's Turf Moor career will be a brief one, but one way or another he has certainly left an impression. He is the father of Manchester City's Shaun Wright-Phillips. Stop Press: He announced his retirement from the game during the close season.

Crystal Palace (Free from Greenwich Borough on 2/8/1985) FL 206+19/89 FLC 19/9 FAC 9+2/3 Others 19+3/16
Arsenal (£2,500,000 on 24/9/1991) F/PL 212+9/128 FLC 29/29 FAC 16/12 Others 22/16
West Ham U (£750,000 on 27/7/1998) PL 20+2/9 FLC 2 FAC 1
Nottingham F (Loaned on 27/8/1999) FL 10/5
Glasgow Celtic (Free on 28/10/1999) SL 4+4/3 SLC 1 SC 0+1
Burnley (Free on 17/2/2000) FL 4+11/4

WRIGHT Jermaine Malaki
Born: Greenwich, 21 October 1975
Height: 5'9" Weight: 11.9
International Honours: E: Yth

A speedy midfielder who likes running at defences with the ball, Jermaine joined Ipswich during the 1999 close season after choosing the Suffolk club ahead of Nottingham Forest, but although he started the new campaign in the team his early form was something of a disappointment. A player who can operate either out wide or in a central role, he is particularly effective when moving forward from deep positions. Once Jim Magilton was fit again Jermaine found himself mainly on the substitutes' bench, coming on as fresh legs towards the end of matches. At Crewe he played the whole of the second half and the game was particularly memorable as he scored his first goal for Ipswich in the last minute with a wonderful volley from outside the penalty area which flew into the net via the inside of the post.

Millwall (From trainee on 27/11/1992)
Wolverhampton W (£60,000 on 29/12/1994) FL 4+16 FLC 1+3/1 Others 0+1
Doncaster Rov (Loaned on 1/3/1996) FL 13
Crewe Alex (£25,000 on 19/2/1998) FL 47+2/5 FLC 5 FAC 1

Ipswich T (£500,000 on 23/7/1999) FL 21+13/1 FLC 3 FAC 0+1 Others 1

WRIGHT Mark Stephen
Born: Chorley, 4 September 1981
Height: 5'9" Weight: 9.10

Preston's exciting young forward was on the bench for the opening two league games of 1999-2000, before returning to the reserves. Both a taker and a maker of goals from the left side of the attack, he continued to build his partnership with Mark Beesley away from the spotlight but made his first senior appearance of the season as a substitute against Notts County in November. His only other outing saw the Wright/Beesley combination introduced to the first team late in the win at Oxford, and it will not be long before he warrants a regular place.

Preston NE (From trainee on 16/4/1999) FL 1+2 FAC 0+1 Others 0+1

WRIGHT Nicholas (Nick) John
Born: Ilkeston, 15 October 1975
Height: 5'10" Weight: 11.7

This right-sided midfield player managed only four starts for Watford in 1999-2000 after a season badly affected by injuries. The hero of the 1999 play-off final at Wembley, where he scored a spectacular goal, Nick missed the start of the season with a groin injury, and after a handful of appearances underwent a hernia operation in October. He returned in December, only to sustain a knee injury in the reserves which subsequently required a cartilage operation. Nick's skill, industry and eye for goal were much missed and he must hope for better things next season.

Derby Co (From trainee on 12/7/1994)
Carlisle U (£35,000 on 28/11/1997) FL 25/5 Others 2/2
Watford (£100,000 on 6/7/1998) P/FL 32+5/6 FLC 2 FAC 1+1 Others 3/1

WRIGHT Richard Ian
Born: Ipswich, 5 November 1977
Height: 6'2" Weight: 13.0
International Honours: E: 1; U21-15; Yth; Sch

The 1999-2000 season was another successful one for the goalkeeper talked about in many circles as the natural successor to David Seaman and Nigel Martyn in the full England side. Once again Richard was ever present between the posts for Ipswich and he made an immense contribution to yet another successful season for the club. His double save against Stockport when he parried Tony Dinning's penalty and managed to knock the rebound to safety was voted "Save of the Century" by the fans in a competition sponsored by the Britannia Building Society. In the second leg of the play-off semi-final against Bolton, when Ipswich were 2-3 down, Richard made a crucial save when he managed to block Claus Jensen's shot with his legs. It kept his side in the tie and they went on to win in extra time. He had an eventful game in the play-off final at Wembley. He got off to an unfortunate start when he was credited with an own goal, after Craig Hignett's shot rebounded off the bar, on to his arm and into the net. He was then adjudged to have fouled Hignett in the box but redeemed himself by saving Darren Barnard's penalty and finally, when Barnsley had pulled back to 2-3, made a tremendous reflex save to tip away a close-range header from Georgi Hristov that looked goalbound. His performances during the campaign earned him a place in the PFA award-winning First Division side for the second season in succession. Richard stepped up to the senior England squad during the campaign and made his full international debut against Malta when he saved a late penalty to spare England's blushes and preserve a 2-1 victory. He subsequently made the final 22 for Euro 2000, although as third-choice 'keeper he did not feature in any of his country's matches.

Ipswich T (From trainee on 2/1/1995) P/FL 204 FLC 21 FAC 11 Others 11

WRIGHT Stephen (Steve)
Born: Bellshill, 27 August 1971
Height: 5'10" Weight: 12.2
International Honours: S: 2; B-2; U21-14

Steve found himself mostly restricted to appearances for Bradford City reserves in 1999-2000 after the summer signings of Gunnar Halle and Andy Myers, and he started just three first-team matches, all in the Worthington Cup. He suffered his share of knee and ankle injuries and was generally used by the Bantams' second-string at full back, although he occasionally appeared as a central defender.

Aberdeen (Free from Eastercraigs on 28/11/1987) SL 141+8/2 SLC 11+1 SC 13 Others 3
Glasgow R (Signed on 5/7/1995) SL 7 SLC 5 Others 6+1
Wolverhampton W (Loaned on 20/3/1998) FL 3
Bradford C (Free on 30/7/1998) FL 21+1 FLC 6 FAC 2

WRIGHT Stephen (Steve) John
Born: Liverpool, 8 February 1980
Height: 6'2" Weight: 12.0
International Honours: E: Yth

On the staff at Liverpool, Steve joined Crewe on loan for the whole of the 1999-2000 season and proved to be a popular addition to the squad. A promising defender, he sustained an injury at Norwich in September that kept him out of action until December, but he featured regularly in the Alex first team during the second half of the season and confirmed that he is a talented player with a bright future.

Liverpool (From trainee on 13/10/1997)
Crewe Alex (Loaned on 6/8/1999) FL 17+6 FLC 1

WRIGHT Thomas (Tommy) James
Born: Belfast, 29 August 1963
Height: 6'1" Weight: 14.5
Club Honours: Div 1 '93
International Honours: NI: 31; U23-1

The dependable Manchester City goalkeeper, now in his 37th year, is an excellent professional who would grace many league teams but has few opportunities to show his worth at Maine Road as young Nicky Weaver is in pole position. However, when Newcastle ran into an injury crisis in August, their former 'keeper was brought back on a month's loan to the club he had left over eight years previously and played in three testing games, namely the Sunderland derby in torrential rain, the visit to Old Trafford and the wrong end of a 5-1 hiding, and the narrow defeat at Chelsea, where he had a fine game and was only beaten by a disputed penalty. This last match was Bobby Robson's first at Newcastle, making him the sixth manager for whom Tommy has played at the club. He enjoyed his return to St James' Park and would have relished an extended stay, but the restored fitness of Steve Harper and John Karelse rendered this unnecessary and he went back to Manchester at the end of his loan period, having confirmed that he remains an accomplished performer with safe hands and a reassuring presence. He made one league appearance for City in 1999-2000 at home against Swindon when Weaver was down with flu, keeping a clean sheet, but otherwise he was confined to the substitutes' bench all season. Still very fit and agile, Tommy spends much time giving the benefit of his experience to the club's younger goalkeepers. Still an occasional member of the Northern Ireland squad, he added a further cap when coming on as a substitute against World Champions France in a friendly last August.

Newcastle U (£30,000 from Linfield on 27/1/1988) F/PL 72+1 FLC 6 FAC 4 Others 1
Hull C (Loaned on 14/2/1991) FL 6
Nottingham F (£450,000 on 24/9/1993) P/FL 11 FLC 2
Reading (Loaned on 4/10/1996) FL 17
Manchester C (Loaned on 17/1/1997) FL 5
Manchester C (£450,000 on 3/3/1997) FL 28 FLC 1 FAC 2 Others 1
Wrexham (Loaned on 26/2/1999) FL 16
Newcastle U (Loaned on 25/8/1999) PL 3

WRIGHT-PHILLIPS Shaun Cameron
Born: Greenwich, 25 October 1981
Height: 5'6" Weight: 10.1

Shaun has been with Manchester City for two years, progressing through the youth academy. In 1999-2000 he settled into the reserve team, playing regularly and scoring frequently. Chosen as a substitute for the second leg of the Worthington Cup tie against Burnley, Shaun came on in the second half to make his first-team debut and immediately showed his class with tight ball control and excellent reading of the game for one so young. His next senior appearance was as a substitute at Port Vale at the end of October, and he again breathed life into the City attack with his direct running. His positive approach is all the more impressive given his relatively slight physique. In the Port Vale game he harassed a defender so much that he put through his own goal to pave the way for City's 2-1 win. Shaun started the next two matches without getting on the score sheet but he seems certain to make an impact at first-team level in the near future. Shaun is the son of former Arsenal striker Ian Wright.

Manchester C (From trainee on 28/10/1998) FL 2+2 FLC 0+1

XAVIER Abel
Born: Mozambique, 30 November 1972
Height: 6'2" Weight: 13.6
International Honours: Portugal: 15; Yth (UEFA-U16 '89; U18 '90)

Although he is instantly recognisable by virtue of his shock of multi-coloured hair, the quality of Abel's performances also made him easy to pick out in an Everton jersey last season. Signed from PSV Eindhoven for £1.5 million in September 1999, he quickly established himself as a tall, powerful midfielder, crisp in the tackle and comfortable on the ball. After a career spent at such celebrated clubs as Sporting Lisbon, Benfica, Bari, Oviedo and PSV, Abel settled swiftly into the Goodison scene and at the end of the season professed his liking for Merseyside life. A Portuguese international, he won five more caps during the season and made the final 22 for the Euro 2000 finals. He appeared in the 3-2 victory over England and also in the semi-final with France, when he was controversially deemed to have handled the ball in an incident that led to the deciding penalty. He was later judged to have taken part in the ensuing rumpus and at the time of writing he has a nine-month ban from European competitions, although this may yet be reduced on appeal.

Everton (£1,500,000 from PSV Eindhoven, Holland on 8/9/1999) PL 18+2 FLC 1 FAC 2

YATES Mark Jason
Born: Birmingham, 24 January 1970
Height: 5'11" Weight: 13.2
International Honours: E: SP-2

Mark's central midfield partnership with Lee Howells was a feature of Cheltenham's first season in the Football League in 1999-2000, with his box-to-box running and high level of stamina providing a driving force for the team. Equally at home booting clearances from his own penalty area or making late runs into the opposition box, Mark was unlucky not to contribute more than two league goals during the season. He is unafraid to shoot from distance, and his 25-yarder at Carlisle was one of the goals of the season.

Birmingham C (From trainee on 8/7/1988) FL 38+16/6 FLC 5/1 FAC 0+2 Others 5
Burnley (£40,000 on 30/8/1991) FL 9+9/1 FLC 1 FAC 0+2 Others 2+1
Lincoln C (Loaned on 19/2/1993) FL 10+4
Doncaster Rov (Signed on 30/7/1993) FL 33+1/4 FLC 2 FAC 1 Others 1 (Transferred to Kidderminster Hrs on 13/8/1994)
Cheltenham T (Signed on 28/1/1999) FL 46/2 FLC 2 FAC 2 Others 2

YATES Stephen (Steve)
Born: Bristol, 29 January 1970
Height: 5'11" Weight: 12.2
Club Honours: Div 3 '90

Steve joined Tranmere on trial in the summer of 1999 after being released by Queens Park Rangers and had done enough by September to win a permanent contract. Playing in the centre of defence, he made an outstanding contribution for the Prenton Park club and turned the Worthington Cup final in Rovers' favour when he came on as a substitute. Calm and solid, he has a no-nonsense approach to the game and shows good aerial skills. Steve was also used as a stop-gap right back and is likely to be one of manager John Aldridge's key players during the coming season.

Bristol Rov (From trainee on 1/7/1988) FL 196+1 FLC 9 FAC 11 Others 21
Queens Park R (£650,000 on 16/8/1993) P/FL 122+12/2 FLC 8 FAC 7
Tranmere Rov (Free on 5/8/1999) FL 32+1/2 FLC 6+1/1 FAC 1

YORKE Dwight
Born: Canaan, Tobago, 3 November 1971
Height: 5'10" Weight: 12.4
Club Honours: FLC '96; FAC '99; PL '99, '00; EC '99
International Honours: Trinidad & Tobago

A natural athlete with great balance and a wonderful left foot, Dwight started last season in scintillating fashion, scoring five goals in Manchester United's opening six games, including four in successive matches against Everton, Sheffield Wednesday and Leeds (2). He was combining well with either Andy Cole or Teddy Sheringham up front, and it looked an odds-on bet that he would soon equal or better his tally of 29 goals during the treble-winning campaign. After he had scored his first Champions' League goal against Sturm Graz in September, and a brace in the following Premiership match against Southampton, his "golden" touch mysteriously disappeared, with only one strike against Watford to show for his efforts during the whole of October, and Sir Alex Ferguson decided to sit him on the bench while giving Ole Gunnar Solskjaer a run at the start of December. Despite Ole hitting five goals in successive games, against Everton (4) and Valencia, Dwight celebrated his return to the side in the very next match with a brace against

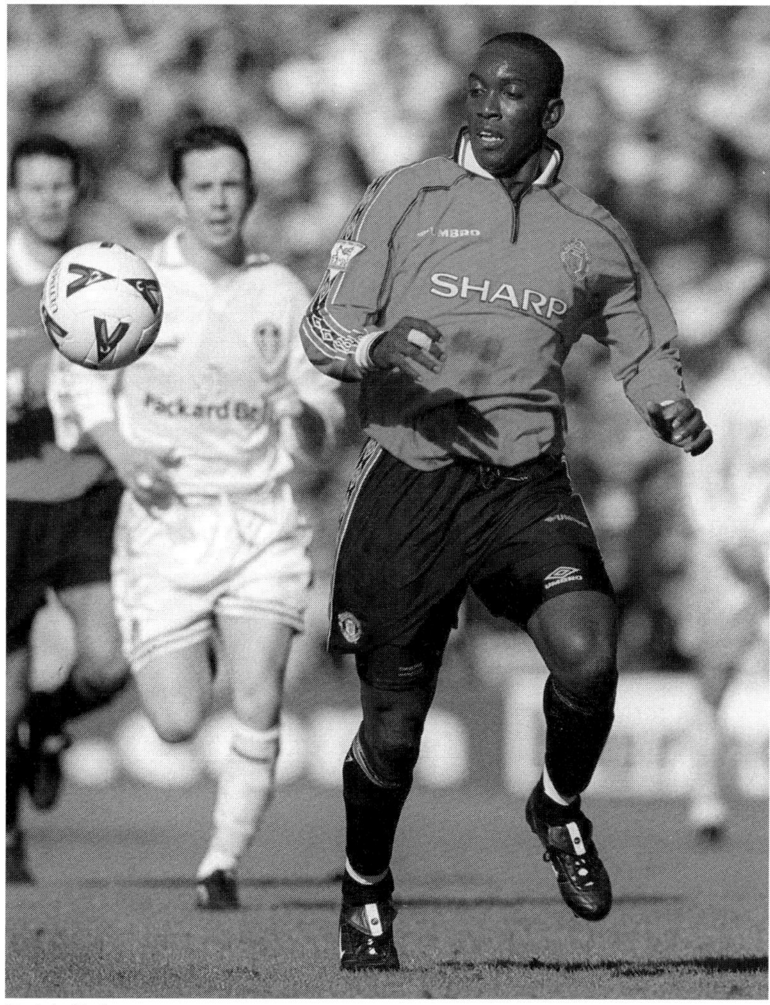

Dwight Yorke

West Ham, six days before Christmas. He was determined to become one of the main "Boys from Brazil" when United travelled to South America for the World Club Championship in January, and a solitary effort in the opening match against Necaxa gave him much cause for optimism. That joy, however, soon turned to disappointment when United were eliminated by Vasco da Gama. Back on home soil, Dwight put the South American trip out of his mind with a hat-trick against Derby at Old Trafford in March. Bang on form with a goal against Leicester and a brace against Bradford City, he was able to put off thoughts of abandoning his international career when Trinidad & Tobago decided not to call upon his services at such a vital stage of United's season. Despite the Reds' disappointment in the European Cup, Dwight's end-of-season form as they retained their Premiership title was good enough to suggest more of the same in 2000-01. A national hero in Trinidad & Tobago, he scored twice in three appearances for his country during the season. Stop Press: Dwight scored both goals in a 2-4 defeat by Jamaica in a rare friendly appearance for the Soca Warriors prior to the next round of World Cup qualifiers in July.

Aston Villa (£120,000 from Signal Hill, Tobago on 19/12/1989) F/PL 195+36/73 FLC 20+2/8 FAC 22+2/13 Others 10/3
Manchester U (£12,600,000 on 22/8/1998) PL 61+3/38 FAC 5+3/3 Others 23+3/11

YOUDS Edward (Eddie) Paul
Born: Liverpool, 3 May 1970
Height: 6'2" Weight: 14.2
Club Honours: Div 1 '00

This tall, commanding central defender started the 1999-2000 season as first choice alongside Richard Rufus in the Charlton Athletic defence but suffered a knee tendon injury at Huddersfield in the last game of 1999 which ruled him out for the rest of the season. Dominant in the air, Eddie loves to get into the opposition penalty area for corners and uses his aerial ability to good effect. He richly deserves his First Division championship medal, having been playing really well before his injury, which Charlton fans are hoping will clear up in time for the coming season.

Everton (From trainee on 10/6/1988) FL 5+3 FLC 0+1 Others 1
Cardiff C (Loaned on 8/2/1990) FL 0+1 FAC 0+1
Wrexham (Loaned on 8/2/1990) FL 20/2
Ipswich T (£250,000 on 15/11/1991) F/PL 38+12/1 FLC 1+2 FAC 5+1
Bradford C (£175,000 on 2/1/1995) FL 85/8 FLC 7/2 FAC 3 Others 4
Charlton Ath (£550,000 on 26/3/1998) P/FL 52+1/2 FLC 4/1 FAC 1+1 Others 3

YOUNG Luke Paul
Born: Harlow, 19 July 1979
Height: 6'0" Weight: 12.4
Club Honours: FLC '99
International Honours: E: U21-5; Yth

The continued development of this promising youngster was a real plus point for Tottenham in 1999-2000. He confirmed his reputation as a strong, reliable defender with great pace and an impressive awareness of his responsibilities in the back four as well as confidence when going forward. Similar in stature to Stephen Carr, Luke still has a great deal to prove at White Hart Lane but has the confidence and tenacity to get his head down and work hard to win a regular spot in the first team. He impressed against such dangerous opposition as Leeds and demonstrated the ability to pick up his defensive responsibilities when returning from his position in the other penalty box at set pieces. He is sure to figure in Tottenham's future plans under George Graham, a manager renowned for developing young talent. Luke also featured regularly in the England U21 squad, winning four more caps and making the squad for the European Championship finals in Slovakia, where he appeared alongside his team-mate Ledley King.

Tottenham H (From trainee on 3/7/1997) PL 25+10 FLC 1+2 FAC 5+2 Others 2+1

YOUNG Neil Anthony
Born: Harlow, 31 August 1973
Height: 5'9" Weight: 12.0

Neil had yet another fine season for Bournemouth in 1999-2000, rarely missing a game and proving to be one of the club's most consistent performers. After six years at Dean Court he is now approaching 250 Football League appearances for the Cherries. A strong, confident right back, he is quick to move up in support of the attack and can deliver a telling cross.

Tottenham H (From trainee on 17/8/1991)
Bournemouth (Free on 11/10/1994) FL 240+2/3 FLC 17 FAC 16 Others 15

Scott Young

YOUNG Scott
Born: Pontypridd, 14 January 1976
Height: 6'2" Weight: 12.6
International Honours: W: B-1; U21-5

Scott had a disappointing season at Cardiff in 1999-2000, being personally affected by injuries and seeing his home-town club relegated after just one season in Division Two. However, he finished the campaign strongly, securing his place at the heart of the Bluebirds' defence, and scored three goals towards the end of the campaign, two of them in the league. A solid central defender, he netted Cardiff's last goal of the campaign to earn his team a 1-0 victory over Bristol Rovers and thus deny their local rivals a place in the play-offs.

Cardiff C (From trainee on 4/7/1994) FL 171+16/7 FLC 12+1 FAC 13 Others 13+3/1

YOUNGS Thomas (Tom) Anthony John
Born: Bury St Edmunds, 31 August 1979
Height: 5'9" Weight: 10.4

This young striker really came of age in 1999-2000. Injuries had previously kept him on the fringes of the Cambridge team but, with nine goals in 24 games, he can now be looked upon as a regular first-teamer. He missed part of the season with a hamstring injury but, with reserve-team manager John Taylor as a mentor, Tom can go from strength to strength in the years ahead.

Cambridge U (From juniors on 3/7/1997) FL 19+16/8 FLC 0+1 Others 2+2/1

ZABEK Lee Kevin
Born: Bristol, 13 October 1978
Height: 6'0" Weight: 12.0

A combative central-midfield ball winner, Lee had to overcome a series of niggling injuries during the first half of the 1999-2000 season which, together with competition from others, restricted his opportunities at Bristol Rovers. If he can remain fit, however, he will soon be pressing for a regular first-team place to justify his early promise.

Bristol Rov (From trainee on 28/7/1997) FL 21+8/1 FLC 2 FAC 2+1/1 Others 4

ZAGORAKIS Theodoros (Theo)
Born: Kavala Greece, 27 October 1971
Height: 5'9" Weight: 11.6
Club Honours: FLC '00
International Honours: Greece: 50

This right-footed midfielder remained very popular with the Leicester fans in 1999-2000 but had to settle for a regular place on the bench for most of the season. Theo became an unlikely emergency goalkeeper in the Worthington Cup opener against Crystal Palace at Selhurst Park after injuries had disposed of both Tim Flowers and Pegguy Arphexad. He netted a neat free kick against Newcastle in December, but was an unused substitute for the Worthington Cup final against Tranmere at Wembley. He still earned a winners' medal, but then elected to return to his native land when his contract expired in the summer and signed a pre-contract agreement with AEK Athens for 2000-01. An experienced international, he added seven more caps for Greece last season.

Leicester C (£750,000 from PAOK Salonika, Greece on 6/2/1998) PL 34+16/3 FLC 6+6 FAC 5+1 Others 2/1

ZAHANA-ONI Landry
Born: Ivory Coast, 8 August 1976
Height: 5'10" Weight: 10.8

This skilful and highly rated midfielder or forward from the Ivory Coast was sadly unable to make the hoped-for breakthrough at Luton last season, having joined the club from non-league Bromley in January 1999. He suffered a knee injury that kept him out of action for much of the campaign and had to undergo keyhole surgery. Landry was restricted to a single first-team appearance, from the subs' bench, against Blackpool in August, and was released in March.

Stirling A (Signed from Ancenis RC, France on 2/10/1997) SL 24+4/5 SC 2 (Freed during 1998 close season)
Luton T (£35,000 from Bromley on 5/1/1999) FL 4+5

ZAMORA Robert (Bobby) Lester
Born: Barking, 16 January 1981
Height: 6'0" Weight: 11.0

This athletic young striker added pace and variety to the Bristol Rovers attack last season. He made his senior debut when coming on from the subs' bench in the Worthington Cup tie against Birmingham City and later featured, also as a substitute, in the FA Cup match with Preston and the league match at Wycombe. Bobby spent a month on loan at Bath City, scoring eight goals in six appearances for the Dr Martens League team before joining Brighton, again on loan, in February. The teenager made a dream start with a goal on his debut against Plymouth and then became Albion's youngest-ever hat-trick hero when scoring three at Chester. Two further goals at home to Halifax meant he left Brighton with the enviable record of six goals in six games. He actually averaged a goal every 84 minutes he was on the pitch. Bobby then returned to Rovers to resume his efforts to force his way into their first team.

Bristol Rov (From trainee on 1/7/1999) FL 0+4 FLC 0+1 FAC 0+1
Brighton & Hove A (Loaned on 11/2/2000) FL 6/6

ZHIYI Fan
Born: Shanghai, China, 6 November 1969
Height: 6'2" Weight: 12.1
International Honours: China

Fan is a quality Crystal Palace defender whose best attributes are his phenomenal workrate and accurate passing. He showed excellent form again in 1999-2000 despite missing the first five games through suspension and then suffering a cracked rib against Birmingham City last October that kept him out for a month. An experienced international, he missed most of January when called up for China's Asian Cup qualifying matches and also appeared for his country in friendlies against Japan and Yugoslavia.

Crystal Palace (£500,000 from Shanghai, China on 10/9/1998) FL 57+1/3 FLC 4/2 FAC 2

ZIEGE Christian
Born: Germany, 1 February 1972
Height: 6'1" Weight: 12.12
International Honours: Germany: 52 (UEFA '96)

Christian arrived at Middlesbrough from Milan last August like a refreshing summer breeze. He initially played in the wing-back role on the left side of the pitch and set up many scoring chances with his deadly distribution. He regularly went forward to preside over set pieces and it didn't take long for Middlesbrough manager Bryan Robson to move him into midfield, where he linked up with Paul Ince and Juninho, a formidable combination when they were all on song together. Christian took the Boro "Player of the Year" award in the face of competition from a number of quality players, and it was well deserved. His lethal left foot redeemed many a seemingly lost cause and, with his creative efforts complemented by his swift, almost ruthless, tackling, he is one of the best players ever to sign for Boro. Christian featured regularly for his country during the season and netted an astonishing hat-trick in the 4-1 defeat of Northern Ireland shortly before his move to the Riverside. He added a further 11 caps

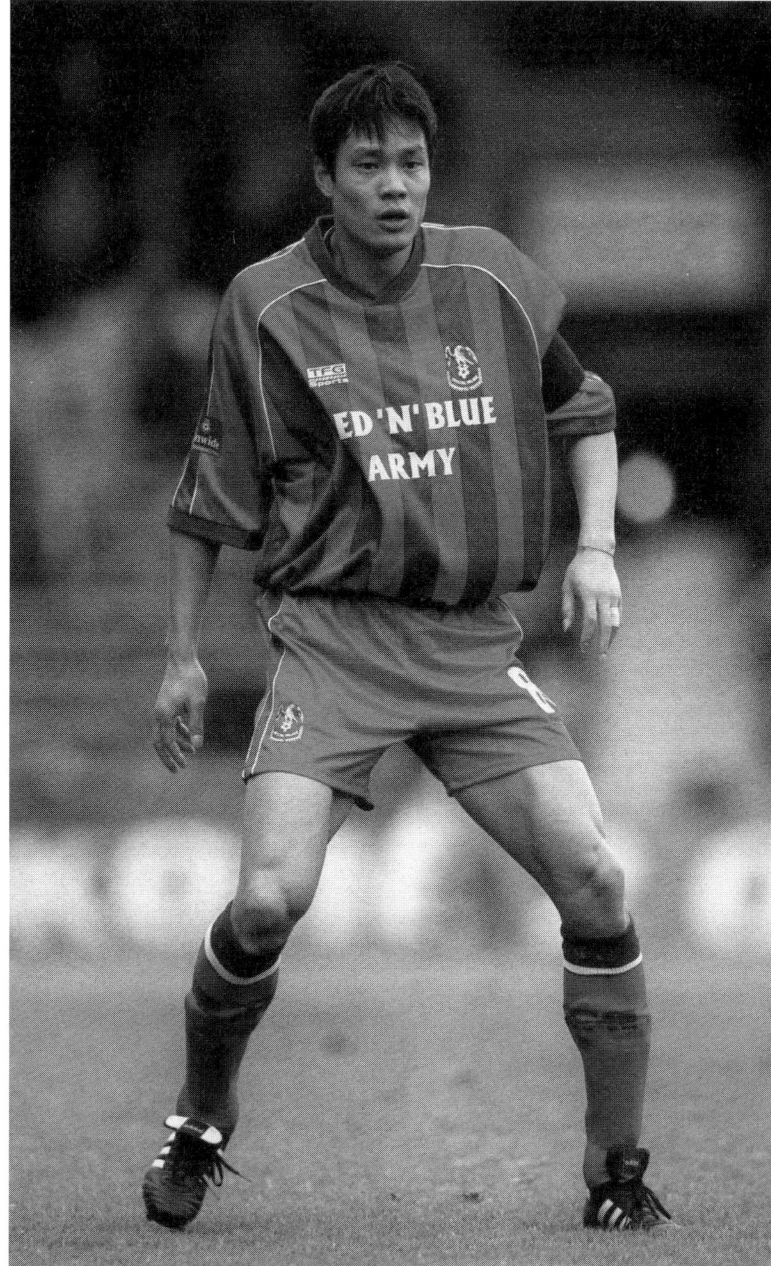

Fan Zhiyi

and appeared against both Romania and England in a very disappointing Euro 2000 campaign for the Germans.

Middlesbrough (£4,000,000 from AC Milan, Italy on 6/8/1999) PL 29/6 FLC 3+1/1 FAC 1

ZOLA Gianfranco (Franco)
Born: Sardinia Italy, 5 July 1966
Height: 5'6" Weight: 10.10
Club Honours: FAC '97, '00; FLC '98; ECWC '98; ESC '98
International Honours: Italy: 35

Gianfranco confirmed his reputation as one of the finest forwards in Europe with some scintillating performances during Chelsea's European Champions' League campaign. Although nearing the veteran stage, he gave one of the outstanding individual displays of the season against Serie A champions AC Milan at Stamford Bridge. His trickery left compatriots Paolo Maldini, Alessandro Costacurta et al chasing shadows as the Blues produced some of their best football for many years. He followed this by scoring one of the most impudent goals of the season in the hostile stadium of Turkish champions Galatasaray, selling the Turks' goalkeeper three dummies in a one-on-one situation before calmly slotting home the third of Chelsea's five goals in a thrilling team performance. Feyenoord were the next to suffer as Zola slammed home a curling drive from the edge of the box to initiate a superb team showing in Rotterdam which resulted in a richly deserved 3-1 victory. But his pièce de résistance in the Champions' League came against Barcelona at the Bridge, Gianfranco first whipping in a trademark free kick from the edge of the penalty area and then creating one of Tore Andre Flo's goals which clinched another 3-1 victory and surpassed even the performance against AC Milan. In the Premiership Gianfranco found goals harder to come by, a total of four being a meagre return for such a richly talented player. Manager Gianluca Vialli's remedy for Chelsea's goalscoring woes was to sign Liberian superstar George Weah on loan and for the first time in his Chelsea career Gianfranco was dropped. In an astute piece of man-management, Vialli immediately reinstated the Sardinian as captain and he regained much of his verve. Although his scoring record was disappointing, Gianfranco was credited with the greatest number of Chelsea "assists" – 24 – the most important coming in the FA Cup final when Aston Villa 'keeper David James could only parry his swerving free-kick to the waiting Roberto Di Matteo, who slammed home the only goal of the game. As the debate rages regarding the impact of foreign players upon the English game, there is no dispute that the Italian wizard has been one of the finest imports; his influence upon the Chelsea success story of the past four years has been immense, a fact recognised by the Chelsea fans, who voted him "Player of the Year" for 1998-99.

Chelsea (£4,500,000 from Parma, Italy, via Napoli, Torres and Nuorese, on 15/11/1996) PL 105+15/33 FLC 4 FAC 18+1/6 Others 29+1/8

Franco Zola

ZUNIGA Yanez Herlin **Ysrael**
Born: Lima, Peru, 27 August 1976
Height: 5'10" Weight: 11.5
International Honours: Peru: 10

With 32 goals in 26 games, Ysrael was the South American "Golden Boot" winner of 1999 and joined Coventry for a relatively cheap £800,000 from Peruvian club Melgar last March. Gordon Strachan stressed that the Peruvian international was an investment for the future and that the fans would initially see little of him, but injuries forced the manager to play him at Leeds when he was far from match fit. There followed four brief substitute appearances, one of which yielded an excellent goal against Bradford City, before his second start in the final home game against Sheffield Wednesday. He now looked a better all-round player and caused the Owls' defence considerable problems before scoring with a diving header after Gary McAllister's shot cannoned off the crossbar. He appears to be a skilful ball player with a very good eye for goal and could be one to watch for in the 2000-01 season. Only introduced to international football in the summer of 1999, he has appeared in all three of Peru's opening games in their qualifying group for the 2002 World Cup since joining the Sky Blues.

Coventry C (£750,000 from FCB Melgar, Peru on 3/3/2000) PL 3+4/2

Where Did They Go?

Below is a list of all players who were recorded in the 1999-2000 *Factfile* as making a first team appearance in 1998-99, but failed to make the current book which covers last season. They are listed alphabetically, and show their leaving dates as well as their first port of call if known. Of course, they may well have changed clubs by now, but space does not allow further reference.

* Shows that the player in question is still with his named club but failed to make an appearance in 1999-2000, the most common reason being injury.

\+ Players retained by the club relegated to the Conference.

Player	Club	Date	Destination
ABRAHAMS Paul	Colchester U	06/99	Kettering T
ADCOCK Tony	Colchester U	06/99	Heybridge Swifts
ALBERT Philippe	Newcastle U	07/99	Charleroi (Belgium)
ALLAN Derek	Brighton & Hove A	06/99	Kingstonian
ALSAKER Paal	Stockport Co	10/98	(Norway)
ALSFORD Julian	Chester C	06/99	Dorchester T
AMSALEM David	Crystal Palace	06/99	Hapoel Haifa (Israel)
ANDERSEN Bo	Bristol C	04/00	Djurgaarden (Sweden)
ANDERSEN Soren	Bristol C	08/99	Odense BK (Denmark)
ANDERSSON Andreas	Newcastle U	08/99	AIK Solna (Sweden)
ANDREASSEN Sven	Portsmouth	01/99	Lillestrom (Norway)
ANDREWS Ben	Brighton & Hove A	*	
ANDREWS Bradley	Bristol Rov	06/99	Mangotsfield U
ANDREWS Wayne	Watford	06/99	St Albans C
ANELKA Nicolas	Arsenal	08/99	Real Madrid (Spain)
ANSAH Andy	Brighton & Hove A	06/99	Farnborough T
ATKINSON Paddy	Scarborough	06/99	
BAARDSEN Espen	Tottenham H	*	
BACQUE Herve	Luton T	01/99	Motherwell
BADDELEY Lee	Exeter C	06/99	*Retired*
BAGSHAW Paul	Barnsley	03/00	Hednesford T
BAILEY Mark	Rochdale	06/99	Winsford U
BAKAYOKO Ibrahima	Everton	07/99	Marseille (France)
BAKER Joe	Leyton Orient	11/99	Sutton U
BARCLAY Dominic	Macclesfield T	06/99	Salisbury C
BARLOW Andy	Rochdale	06/99	Ramsbottom U
BARNARD Mark	Darlington	06/99	Doncaster Rov
BARNES John	Charlton Ath	06/99	*Retired*
BARNES Kevin	Blackpool	05/99	Lancaster C
BARRETT Earl	Sheffield Wed	06/99	*Retired*
BASFORD Luke	Bristol Rov	06/99	Kingstonian
BASS David	Carlisle U	06/99	Scarborough
BEARDSLEY Peter	Hartlepool U	05/99	*Retired*
BENNETT Gary	Chester C	08/99	*Retired*
BENNETT Micky	Brighton & Hove A	06/99	Canvey Island
BERKOVIC Eyal	West Ham U	07/99	Glasgow Celtic
BERNTSEN Robin	Port Vale	11/98	Tromso (Norway)
BERTHE Mohamed	Bournemouth	03/99	Heart of Midlothian
BERTI Nicola	Tottenham H	01/99	Alaves (Spain)
BETTS Simon	Colchester U	06/99	Scarborough
BILIC Slaven	Everton	02/00	
BISHOP Charlie	Northampton T	09/98	Ilkeston T
BJORNEBYE Stig Inge	Liverpool	06/00	Blackburn Rov
BLOMQVIST Jesper	Manchester U	*	
BLUNT Jason	Blackpool	03/99	(Australia)
BODLEY Mick	Peterborough U	03/99	St Albans C
BOLI Roger	Bournemouth	07/99	*Retired*
BORROWS Brian	Swindon T	05/99	*Retired*
BORTOLAZZI Mario	West Bromwich A	05/99	(Italy)
BOS Gijsbert	Rotherham U	12/98	(Holland)
BRACEWELL Paul	Fulham	05/99	*Retired*
BRANCA Marco	Middlesbrough	02/99	*Retired*
BRANNAN Ged	Manchester C	10/98	Motherwell
BRIDGE-WILKINSON Marc	Derby Co	06/00	
BRIGHT Mark	Charlton Ath	06/99	*Retired*

Player	Club	Date	Destination
BRIGHTWELL Stuart	Hartlepool U	06/99	Bishop Auckland
BRODIE Steve	Scarborough	+	
BROWN Jon	Halifax T	06/99	Nuneaton Borough
BROWN Kenny	Gillingham	05/99	*Retired*
BROWN Steve	Macclesfield T	08/99	Dover Ath
BROWN Wes	Manchester U	*	
BROWNE Tony	Brighton & Hove A	06/99	Dover Ath
BROWNE Stafford	Brighton & Hove A	11/99	Welling U
BRUCE Steve	Sheffield U	05/99	*Retired*
BRYSON Ian	Rochdale	06/99	Bamber Bridge
BULL Steve	Wolverhampton W	07/99	*Retired*
BULLIMORE Wayne	Scarborough	06/99	Grantham T
BURNS Alex	Southend U	07/99	Raith Rov
BYRNE Dessie	Stockport Co	02/99	
CABALLERO Fabian	Arsenal	06/99	Atletico Tembet (Argentina)
CADETTE Nathan	Cardiff C	12/99	Inter Cardiff
CARR Graeme	Scarborough	11/99	Workington
CARR-LAWTON Colin	Burnley	06/99	Berwick R
CARRUTHERS Matt	Mansfield T	03/99	Dover Ath
CARTER Jimmy	Millwall	06/99	*Retired*
CARTER Michael	Darlington	06/00	
CARTER Tim	Halifax T	06/99	
CARTWRIGHT Mark	Wrexham	*	
CASIRAGHI Pierluigi	Chelsea	*	
CASTLEDINE Stewart	Wimbledon	06/00	
CHERRY Steve	Oldham Ath	05/99	
CLARK Martin	Rotherham U	06/99	Southport
CLARK Billy	Exeter C	06/99	Forest Green Rov
CLARKE Tim	Scunthorpe U	09/99	Kidderminster Hrs
CLAYTON Gary	Torquay U	03/99	*Retired*
CLEAVER Chris	Peterborough U	05/00	
CLEMENT Philippe	Coventry C	06/99	FC Brugge (Belgium)
CLITHEROE Lee	Oldham Ath	11/99	Lancaster C
CLODE Mark	Swansea C	06/99	Bath C
COBIAN Juan	Sheffield Wed	06/99	(Argentina)
COLLINS Lee	Stoke C	*	
CONNOLLY David	Wolverhampton W	07/99	Excelsior (Holland)
CONROY Mick	Blackpool	08/99	*Retired*
COOK Andy	Millwall	10/99	Salisbury C
COOKSEY Scott	Shrewsbury T	04/00	Hereford U
CORNWALL Luke	Fulham	*	
COSTA Ricardo	Darlington	02/99	Boavista (Portugal)
COX Jimmy	Luton T	06/99	Gloucester C
COYNE Chris	West Ham U	03/00	
CRAVEN Dean	Shrewsbury T	01/00	Merthyr Tydfil
CREANEY Gerry	Notts Co	05/99	
CRITTENDEN Nick	Chelsea	06/00	
CROWE Glen	Plymouth Arg	06/99	
CURCIC Sasa	Crystal Palace	07/99	New Jersey Metros (USA)
DABELSTEEN Thomas	Scarborough	01/99	
DACOURT Olivier	Everton	06/99	RC Lens (France)
DAHLIN Martin	Blackburn Rov	06/99	*Retired*

Player	Club	Date	Destination
DARCHEVILLE Jean-Claude	Nottingham F	06/99	Stade Rennais (France)
DAVENPORT Peter	Macclesfield T	03/99	*Retired*
DAVIES Jamie	Swansea C	06/00	
DAVIES Lawrence	Brighton & Hove A	04/99	Barry T
DAVIS Danny	Brighton & Hove A	*	
DAVIS Kelvin	Wimbledon	*	
DAVIS Neil	Walsall	09/98	Hednesford T
DEAN Michael	Bournemouth	06/00	Weymouth
DELLAS Trianos	Sheffield U	11/99	AEK Athens (Greece)
DEL RIO Walter	Crystal Palace	06/99	Boca Juniors (Argentina)
DE SOUZA Miquel	Peterborough U	12/98	Rushden & Diamonds
DEVENNEY Michael	Burnley	*	
DE VOS Jason	Darlington	10/98	Dundee U
DIAWARA Kaba	Arsenal	07/99	Marseille (France)
DIAZ Izzy	Rochdale	12/98	(Spain)
DICKS Julian	West Ham U	06/99	*Retired*
DOBBIN Jim	Grimsby T	06/99	Gainsborough Trinity
DOHERTY Lee	Brighton & Hove A	06/99	Chesham U
DORNER Mario	Darlington	07/99	
DOUGLAS Andrew	Carlisle U	03/00	
DRYSDALE Leon	Shrewsbury T	*	
DUBLIN Keith	Southend U	06/99	Farnborough T
DUERDEN Ian	Halifax T	10/98	Doncaster Rov
DUNDEE Sean	Liverpool	07/99	VfB Stuttgart (Germany)
DUNGEY James	Plymouth Arg	05/99	Dorchester T
DUNWELL Michael	Hartlepool U	06/00	
DYER Wayne	Walsall	11/98	Hereford U
EASTWOOD Phil	Burnley	06/99	Morecambe
EDINHO	Bradford C	03/99	Porto Menusu (Brazil)
EKOKU Efan	Wimbledon	08/99	Grasshopper Zurich (Switzerland)
ELLIOTT Tony	Scarborough	06/99	*Retired*
ELLISON Lee	Darlington	06/99	Southport
EVANS Nicky	Hartlepool U	09/99	Blyth Spartans
FARLEY Adam	Everton	06/00	
FARRELL Andy	Rochdale	06/99	Morecambe
FENN Neale	Tottenham H	*	
FERNANDES Tamer	Colchester U	06/99	Hemel Hempstead T
FERRARESI Fabio	Aston Villa	07/99	Cesena (Italy)
FERRI Jean-Michel	Liverpool	07/99	Sochaux (France)
FITZHENRY Neil	Wigan Ath	06/00	
FJORTOFT Jan Aage	Barnsley	11/98	Eintracht Frankfurt (Germany)
FLASH Richard	Plymouth Arg	06/99	
FLECK Robert	Reading	02/99	Gorleston
FORD Jon	Barnet	02/99	Kidderminster Hrs
FORD Liam	Plymouth Arg	06/00	
FORD Mark	Burnley	06/99	KFC Lommel (Belgium)
FORSYTHE Mike	Wycombe W	06/99	Burton A
FOSTER John	Bury	06/99	Hyde U
FOSTER Steve	Crewe Alex	*	
FRANCIS Steve	Northampton T	06/99	*Retired*
FRASER Stuart	Stoke C	06/00	
FRY Chris	Exeter C	06/99	Barry T
GAGE Kevin	Hull C	02/99	*Retired*
GARCIA Tony	Notts Co	04/99	
GARDE Remi	Arsenal	06/99	*Retired*
GARDNER Jimmy	Exeter C	06/99	Stirling A
GARRAULT Regis	Walsall	12/98	
GAYLE Brian	Shrewsbury T	06/99	*Retired*
GEORGIADIS George	Newcastle U	07/99	PAOK Salonika (Greece)
GIBSON Neil	Tranmere Rov	06/00	
GILL James	Plymouth Arg	10/99	Liskeard
GIOCCHINI Stefano	Coventry C	05/99	Venezia (Italy)
GLASGOW Byron	Reading	07/99	Crawley T
GOMEZ Fernando	Wolverhampton W	06/99	
GOODMAN Don	Barnsley	03/99	Motherwell
GORAM Andy	Sheffield U	01/99	Motherwell
GOWER Mark	Tottenham H	*	

Player	Club	Date	Destination
GRAHAM Richard	Queens Park R	*	
GRANT Kim	Millwall	08/99	KFC Lommel (Belgium)
GRAY David	Rochdale	06/99	Clitheroe
GREEN Ryan	Wolverhampton W	*	
GREENALL Colin	Wigan Ath	05/99	Retired
GREGORY Neil	Colchester U	02/00	Canvey Island
GRIFFITHS Peter	Macclesfield T	08/99	Winsford
GROBBELAAR Bruce	Lincoln C	01/99	*Retired*
GRONDIN David	Arsenal	*	
GUIVARC'H Stephane	Newcastle U	11/98	Glasgow R
HADLAND Phil	Reading	06/00	
HADLEY Shaun	Torquay U	01/99	Taunton T
HALL Richard	West Ham U	03/99	*Retired*
HAMMOND Nicky	Reading	04/00	
HANDYSIDE Peter	Grimsby T	*	
HANN Matthew	Peterborough U	*	
HANSON Dave	Halifax T	07/99	Nuneaton Borough
HAPGOOD Leon	Torquay U	09/99	Bideford
HARKES John	Nottingham F	02/99	Washington DCU (USA)
HARLE Micky	Barnet	03/99	Welling U
HARRISON Craig	Middlesbrough	*	
HARTFIELD Charlie	Swansea C	06/99	Telford U
HASSELBAINK Jimmy Floyd	Leeds U	08/99	Atletico Madrid (Spain)
HATELEY Mark	Hull C	09/99	Ross Co
HAWES Steve	Hull C	11/99	Altrincham
HAYDON Nicky	Colchester U	06/99	Kettering T
HAYFIELD Matt	Shrewsbury T	09/98	Yeovil T
HAZAN Alon	Watford	08/99	Maccabi Haifa (Israel)
HEBEL Dirk	Brentford	05/99	
HEINOLA Antti	Queens Park R	*	
HENDRIE John	Barnsley	04/99	*Retired*
HENSHAW Terry	Notts Co	06/99	Burton A
HESSEY Sean	Huddersfield T	06/99	Kilmarnock
HEYWOOD Matty	Burnley	*	
HICKS Mark	Millwall	*	
HILL Colin	Northampton T	06/99	*Retired*
HINSHELWOOD Danny	Brighton & Hove A	01/99	Bognor Regis T
HIRST David	Southampton	12/99	*Retired*
HITCHCOCK Kevin	Chelsea	*	
HODGES Glyn	Scarborough	01/99	*Retired*
HODGSON Doug	Northampton T	12/99	*Retired*
HOLLOWAY Ian	Bristol Rov	05/99	*Retired*
HOLMES Matty	Charlton Ath	06/00	
HOLSTER Marco	Ipswich T	05/00	
HORLAVILLE Christophe	Port Vale	01/99	Le Havre (France)
HOUGHTON Ray	Reading	06/99	*Retired*
HOWELLS David	Southampton	03/00	*Retired*
HOYLAND Jamie	Scarborough	+	
HUGHES Danny	Hartlepool U	06/00	*Retired*
HUGHES David	Southampton	*	
HUGHES Paul	Chelsea	03/00	Southampton*
HUMES Tony	Wrexham	06/00	
HUTT Stephen	Hartlepool U	06/99	Bishop Auckland
IFEJAGWA Emeka	Charlton Ath	06/00	
IORFA Dominic	Southend U	02/99	
IROHA Ben	Watford	03/00	*Retired*
IRVINE Stuart	Hartlepool U	06/99	Bishop Auckland
JACKSON Darren	Coventry C	02/99	Glasgow Celtic
JACKSON Elliot	Oxford U	06/99	Bath C
JANSSON Jan	Port Vale	03/99	Norrkoping (Sweden)
JEAN Earl	Plymouth Arg	03/99	West Connection (Trinidad)
JENKINS Jamie	Bournemouth	06/99	Barry T
JENKINSON Leigh	Wigan Ath	12/98	Heart of Midlothian
JERMYN Mark	Torquay U	02/00	
JIHAI Sun	Crystal Palace	07/99	Dalian Wanda (China)
JOHNSON Alan	Rochdale	06/99	
JOHNSON Grant	Huddersfield U	06/00	
JOHNSTON Ray	Bristol Rov	06/00	
JONES Jason	Swansea C	*	

JONES Matthew	Shrewsbury T	*	
JONES Vinny	Queens Park R	03/99	*Retired*

KAAMARK Pontus	Leicester C	06/99	AIK Solna (Sweden)
KAY John	Scarborough	06/99	Workington
KELLER Francois	Fulham	06/99	Strasbourg (France)
KELLER Kasey	Leicester C	07/99	Rayo Vallecano (Spain)
KENNEDY John	Ipswich T	06/00	
KERSLAKE David	Swindon T	06/99	*Retired*
KEY Lance	Rochdale	02/99	Northwich Victoria
KHARINE Dmitri	Chelsea	06/99	Glasgow Celtic
KINDER Vlad	Middlesbrough	12/99	
KING Phil	Brighton & Hove A	05/99	Kidderminster Hrs
KIZERIDIS Nicos	Portsmouth	10/98	(Greece)
KNARVIK Tommy	Leeds U	05/00	
KNILL Alan	Rotherham U	06/99	*Retired*
KONDE Oumar	Blackburn Rov	07/99	SC Freiburg (Germany)
KOORDES Rogier	Port Vale	03/99	TOP Ost (Holland)
KROMHEER Elroy	Reading	08/99	FC Nurnberg (Germany)
KUBICKI Dariusz	Darlington	12/98	*Retired*
KUIPERS Michels	Bristol Rov	06/00	
KVAL Frank	Burnley	06/99	
KVARME Bjorn	Liverpool	08/99	St Etienne (France)

LANDON Richard	Macclesfield T	06/99	Altrincham
LANGAN Kevin	Bristol C	06/00	
LAUDRUP Brian	Chelsea	11/98	Ajax (Holland)
LAW Brian	Millwall	06/00	
LEAH John	Darlington	06/00	
LEESE Lars	Barnsley	06/99	
LEHMANN Dirk	Fulham	07/99	Hibernian
LENAGH Steve	Rochdale	06/00	
LEONARD Mark	Rochdale	01/99	*Retired*
L'HELGOUALCH Cyrille	Mansfield T	04/99	
LINTON Des	Peterborough U	06/99	Cambridge C
LIVETT Simon	Southend U	01/00	Dover Ath
LOMAX Mike	Macclesfield T	08/99	
LOMBARDO Attilio	Crystal Palace	01/99	Lazio (Italy)
LONERGAN Darren	Macclesfield T	04/99	Hyde U
LONGWORTH Steve	Blackpool	06/99	Squires Gate
LOVE Andy	Grimsby T	03/00	Ilkeston T
LOVELOCK Andy	Crewe Alex	06/99	Altrincham
LYDIATE Jason	Scarborough	06/99	Winsford U
LYTTLE Gerard	Peterborough U	*	

McALINDON Gareth	Carlisle U	06/99	Scarborough
McALLISTER Brian	Wimbledon	06/00	
McANESPIE Steve	Fulham	06/00	
McAREAVEY Paul	Swindon T	*	
McARTHUR Duncan	Brighton & Hove A	05/99	Hastings U
McAVOY Larry	Cambridge U	11/99	Ashford T
McCORMICK Steve	Leyton Orient	10/98	Dundee
McDONALD Chris	Hartlepool U	09/98	
McDONALD Martin	Macclesfield T	03/99	Altrincham
McDOUGALD Junior	Leyton Orient	03/99	St Albans C
McFARLAND Andy	Torquay U	06/99	*Retired*
McGILL Derek	Port Vale	11/98	
McGINLAY John	Oldham Ath	01/99	*Retired*
McGINTY Brian	Hull C	06/99	Scarborough
McGORRY Brian	Torquay U	06/99	Telford U
McGOVERN Brendan	Plymouth Arg	08/99	
McGUCKIN Ian	Fulham	06/00	Oxford U
McINNES Derek	Stockport Co	02/99	Glasgow R
MacKENZIE Chris	Leyton Orient	06/99	Nuneaton Borough
McKINLAY Billy	Blackburn Rov	*	
McLEARY Alan	Millwall	05/99	*Retired*
McMAHON Sam	Cambridge U	07/99	Stevenage Borough
McMANAMAN Steve	Liverpool	07/99	Real Madrid (Spain)
McMENAMIN Chris	Peterborough U	03/99	Hitchin T
McMILLAN Andy	York C	10/99	*Retired*
McNAUGHTON Michael	Scarborough	+	
McQUADE John	Port Vale	03/99	Raith Rov
MADAR Mikael	Everton	12/98	Paris St Germain (France)
MALKIN Chris	Blackpool	06/99	Telford U
MANNION Sean	Stockport Co	06/00	
MANUEL Billy	Barnet	06/99	Folkestone Invicta
MARCOLIN Dario	Blackburn Rov	04/99	Lazio (Italy)
MARDON Paul	West Bromwich A	*	
MARGETSON Martyn	Southend U	08/99	Huddersfield T*
MARINKOV Alex	Scarborough	02/99	Hibernian
MARKER Nicky	Sheffield U	11/99	Tiverton T
MARKSTEDT Peter	Barnsley	08/99	Helsingborg (Sweden)
MARSH Simon	Birmingham	*	
MARSHALL Dwight	Plymouth Arg	06/99	Kingstonian
MASKELL Craig	Leyton Orient	06/99	Hampton & Richmond Borough
MASON Paul	Ipswich T	10/98	
MATERAZZI Marco	Everton	07/99	Perugia (Italy)
MATTIS Dwayne	Huddersfield T	*	
MATTSSON Jesper	Nottingham F	*	
MAYBURY Alan	Leeds U	*	
MAYLETT Bradley	Burnley	*	
MENDES Junior	Carlisle U	12/98	St Mirren
MENDES-RODRIGUEZ Alberto	Arsenal	*	
MILBOURNE Ian	Scarborough	+	
MILLS Danny	Brighton & Hove A	06/99	
MIOTTO Simon	Hartlepool U	04/99	
MOLENAAR Robert	Leeds U	*	
MONKHOUSE Andy	Rotherham U	*	
MOORE Alan	Middlesbrough	*	
MOORE Craig	Crystal Palace	03/99	Glasgow R
MORRIS Stewart	Scarborough	+	
MORRISON Owen	Sheffield Wed	*	
MORRISSEY John	Tranmere Rov	06/99	*Retired*
MOUNTFIELD Derek	Scarborough	05/99	Workington
MURPHY Jamie	Halifax T	12/99	

NAISBET Phil	Scarborough	05/99	Barrow
NEVLAND Erik	Manchester U	12/99	Viking Stavanger (Norway)
NILSEN Roger	Tottenham H	06/99	Grazer AK (Austria)
NILSSON Roland	Coventry C	06/99	Helsingborgs (Sweden)

OAKES Andy	Hull C	06/99	Derby Co*
OAKES Scott	Sheffield Wed	06/00	
O'BRIEN Liam	Tranmere Rov	06/99	*Retired*
O'CONNOR Jon	Sheffield U	06/00	
O'GORMAN Dave	Swansea C	02/99	Connahs Quay Nomads
OKAFOR Sam	Colchester U	*	
ONWERE Udo	Barnet	06/99	Aylesbury U
O'REGAN Kieran	Halifax T	04/99	*Retired*
ORLYGSSON Toddy	Oldham Ath	06/99	*Retired*
OTTA Walter	Walsall	01/99	Xerez (Spain)
OVERSON Vince	Halifax T	09/98	Padiham

PADOVANO Michele	Crystal Palace	11/98	
PARKER Garry	Leicester C	06/99	*Retired*
PATTERSON Mark	Southend U	05/99	Leigh RMI
PAYNE Derek	Peterborough U	03/99	Dagenham & Redbridge
PEMBERTON Martin	Hartlepool U	09/98	Harrogate T
PENNEY David	Cardiff C	08/98	Doncaster Rov
PEPPER Carl	Darlington	*	
PEREZ Sebastian	Blackburn Rov	02/99	Bastia (France)
PETERS Mark	Mansfield T	06/99	Rushden & Diamonds
PETRIC Gordon	Crystal Palace	06/99	AEK Athens (Greece)
PETTA Bobby	Ipswich T	07/99	Glasgow Celtic
PIRI	Barnsley	05/99	Deportivo la Coruna (Spain)
PORFIRIO Hugo	Nottingham F	05/99	Benfica (Portugal)
PORTER Gary	Scarborough	06/99	Boston U
PREECE David	Darlington	07/99	Aberdeen
PRENDERGAST Rory	Oldham Ath	07/99	Northwich Victoria
PROCTOR Michael	Sunderland	*	

QUAYLE Mark	Notts Co	06/99	Grimsby T (trial)

RABAT Didier	Notts Co	01/99	(France)

RADIGAN Neil	Darlington	06/00	
RAINFORD David	Colchester U	06/99	Slough T
RAYNOR Paul	Leyton Orient	10/98	Kettering T
REID Brian	Burnley	06/99	Dunfermline Ath
REILLY Mark	Reading	11/98	Kilmarnock
REINELT Robbie	Leyton Orient	10/99	Stevenage Borough
REMY Christophe	Oxford U	06/99	
RENNIE David	Peterborough U	06/99	Boston U
RENNISON Graham	York C	03/00	Whitby T
RENNISON Shaun	Scarborough	+	
RENSHAW Ian	Scarborough	12/98	
RISHWORTH Steve	Wrexham	05/99	Oxford University
RITCHIE Andy	Oldham Ath	05/99	*Retired*
RIZA Omer	Arsenal	12/99	West Ham U*
ROBERTS Tony	Millwall	04/99	St Albans C
ROBERTS Darren	Scarborough	+	
ROBINSON Paul	Leeds U	*	
ROBINSON Liam	Scarborough	06/99	Northwich Victoria
ROCHE Steve	Millwall	02/99	
ROGAN Anton	Blackpool	06/99	*Retired*
ROLLING Franck	Wycombe W	06/99	*Retired*
ROSE Andy	Oxford U	06/99	Harrow Borough
ROSE Karl	Barnsley	*	
ROSENTHAL Ronny	Watford	06/99	*Retired*
ROWE Zeke	Peterborough U	06/99	Welling U
ROYCE Simon	Charlton Ath	06/00	Leicester C
RUSH David	Hartlepool U	05/99	Seaham Red Star
RUSH Ian	Wrexham	06/99	Sydney Olympic (Australia)
RUST Nicky	Barnet	03/99	Cambridge C
RUTHERFORD Mark	Shrewsbury T	09/98	Shelbourne
RYAN Darragh	Brighton & Hove A	06/99	Crawley T
RYDER Stuart	Mansfield T	06/99	Nuneaton Borough
SAHA Louis	Newcastle U	04/99	Metz (France)
SAIB Moussa	Tottenham H	12/99	Al Nasr (Saudi Arabia)
SALE Mark	Colchester U	07/99	Rushden & Diamonds
SALMON Mike	Charlton Ath	07/99	Ipswich T*
SAMUELS Jerome	Notts Co	02/99	
SANETTI Francesco	Sheffield Wed	08/99	
SAVILLE Andy	Scarborough	06/99	Gainsborough Trinity
SCHMEICHEL Peter	Manchester U	06/99	Sporting Lisbon (Portugal)
SCOTT Chris	Burnley	*	
SCOTT Gary	Rotherham U	06/99	Marine
SCOTT Kevin	Norwich C	08/99	*Retired*
SCOTT Martin	Sunderland	06/99	*Retired*
SEAL David	Northampton T	06/99	Sydney Olympic (Australia)
SEDLAN Jason	Mansfield T	06/99	Wisbech T
SEGERS Hans	Tottenham H	06/99	*Retired*
SEGURA Victor	Norwich C	06/99	Getafe (Spain)
SHARPS Ian	Tranmere Rov	*	
SHELIA Murtaz	Manchester C	01/00	
SHEPHERD Paul	Leeds U	09/99	
SHORE Jamie	Bristol Rov	*	
SHOWLER Paul	Peterborough U	*	
SHUTT Carl	Darlington	06/99	Kettering T
SIMPSON Phil	Barnet	02/99	Yeovil T
SINNOTT Lee	Oldham Ath	06/99	Scarborough
SMEETS Jorg	Wigan Ath	06/99	(Portugal)
SMITH Carl	Burnley	06/99	Worksop T
SMITH Jeff	Hartlepool U	10/99	Barrow
SMITH Mark	Bristol Rov	*	
SMITH Peter	Brighton & Hove A	06/99	Woking
SMITH Phil	Millwall	*	
SPARROW Paul	Rochdale	06/99	Lancaster C
SPENCER John	Everton	10/98	Motherwell
STAMP Neville	Reading	*	
STAMPS Scott	Colchester U	06/99	Kidderminster Hrs
STANNARD Jim	Gillingham	06/99	*Retired*

STATHAM Brian	Gillingham	09/99	Chesham U
STEFANOVIC Dejan	Sheffield Wed	06/99	Perugia (Italy)
STENSAAS Stale	Nottingham F	04/99	Glasgow R
STEVENS Keith	Millwall	05/99	*Retired*
STIMPSON Mark	Leyton Orient	06/99	Canvey Island
STOKER Gareth	Rochdale	12/99	Scarborough
STOKOE Graham	Hartlepool U	06/99	Blyth Spartans
STORER Stuart	Brighton & Hove A	06/99	Atherstone U
STUART Mark	Rochdale	06/99	Southport
STURGESS Paul	Brighton & Hove A	06/99	Hereford U
SWEENEY Terry	Plymouth Arg	06/99	Oxford C
TANNER Adam	Peterborough U	06/00	
TEBILY Olivier	Sheffield U	07/99	Glasgow Celtic
THACKERAY Andy	Halifax T	06/99	Nuneaton Borough
THOMAS Tony	Everton	12/98	Motherwell
THOMAS Glen	Brighton & Hove A	03/99	Barking
TODD Andy	Scarborough	05/99	Eastwood T
TOSH Paul	Exeter C	04/99	Hibernian
TOWN David	Bournemouth	06/99	Rushden & Diamonds
TRAMEZANNI Paolo	Tottenham H	01/00	Pistoese (Italy)
TRAVIS Simon	Stockport Co	06/99	Telford U
TSKHADADZE Kakhaber	Manchester C	02/00	
TUCK Stuart	Brighton & Hove A	03/99	*Retired*
TURLEY Billy	Northampton T	06/99	Rushden & Diamonds
TURNER Michael	Barnsley	*	
TWEED Steve	Stoke C	12/98	Dundee
ULLATHORNE Robert	Leicester C	06/99	
UNGER Lars	Southend U	05/99	Bregenz (Austria)
VAN HOOIJDONK Pierre	Nottingham F	06/99	Vitesse Arnhem (Holland)
VIALLI Luca	Chelsea	06/00	*Retired*
WADDLE Chris	Torquay U	11/98	*Retired*
WALKER John	Mansfield T	06/99	Scarborough
WALKER Keith	Swansea C	01/00	Merthyr Tydfil
WALLACE Ray	Stoke C	06/99	Winsford U
WALLEMME Jean-Guy	Coventry C	01/99	Sochaux (France)
WALLING Dean	Lincoln C	08/99	Doncaster Rov
WARBURTON Ray	Northampton T	10/98	Rushden & Diamonds
WARD Peter	Wrexham	06/99	*Retired*
WARNER Mickey	Northampton T	06/99	Farnborough T
WARRINGTON Andy	York C	06/99	Doncaster Rov
WATSON Andy	Walsall	06/99	
WATSON Dave	Barnsley	*	
WATT Michael	Norwich C	06/99	Kilmarnock
WESTCOTT John	Brighton & Hove A	06/00	
WHITE Devon	Shrewsbury T	06/99	Ilkeston T
WHYTE David	Southend U	09/99	
WILDE Adam	Cambridge U	06/99	Cambridge C
WILES Ian	Colchester U	10/99	Heybridge Swifts
WILKINSON Paul	Northampton T	06/00	
WILLIAMS Geraint	Colchester U	06/00	
WILLIAMS Mark	Shrewsbury T	06/99	Shelbourne
WILLIAMS Mark	Rotherham U	06/00	
WILLIAMSON John	Burnley	*	
WILLS David	Halifax T	06/00	
WITTER Tony	Scunthorpe U	05/99	Hayes
WOODS Neil	York C	06/99	Southport
WRAIGHT Gary	Wycombe W	09/99	Stevenage Borough
WRIGHT Andy	Macclesfield T	06/99	Merthyr Tydfil
WRIGHT Andy	Leeds U	07/99	Fortuna Sittard (Holland)
WRIGHT Tony	Oxford U	03/99	Barry T
YATES Dean	Watford	*	
ZWIJNENBERG Clemens	Bristol C	11/98	Aalborg (Denmark)

FA Carling Premiership and Nationwide League Clubs

Summary of Appearances and Goals for 1999-2000.

KEY TO TABLES: P/FL = Premier/Football League. FLC = Football League Cup. FAC = FA Cup. Others = Other first team appearances.
Left hand figures in each column list number of full appearances + appearances as substitute. Right hand figures list number of goals scored.

	P/FL		FLC		FAC		Others	
	App	Goals	App	Goals	App	Goals	App	Goals
ARSENAL (PREM: 2nd)								
ADAMS Tony	21				1	1	11	
BARRETT Graham	0+ 2							
BERGKAMP Dennis	23+ 5	6					11	4
BLACK Tommy	0+ 1		1					
BOA MORTE Luis	0+ 2						0+ 1	
COLE Ashley	1		0+ 1					
DIXON Lee	28	4			3		14	1
GRAY Julian	0+ 1							
GRIMANDI Gilles	27+ 1	2	1		3	1	10+ 1	1
HENRY Thierry	26+ 5	17	2	1	3		7+ 5	8
HUGHES Stephen	1+ 1				0+ 2		0+ 1	
KANU Nwankwo	24+ 7	12	1	1	0+ 2		10+ 6	4
KEOWN Martin	27	1			2		10	
LJUNGBERG Fredrik	22+ 4	6			2		12+ 3	2
LUZHNY Oleg	16+ 5		2		1		6+ 1	
McGOVERN Brian	0+ 1							
MALZ Stefan	2+ 3	1	2	1	2		0+ 2	
MANNINGER Alex	14+ 1		1		1		7	
OVERMARS Marc	22+ 9	7	0+ 1		1	1	11+ 3	5
PARLOUR Ray	29+ 1	1	2		1		10+ 2	4
PENNANT Jermaine			0+ 1					
PETIT Manu	24+ 2	3			3		10+ 1	
SEAMAN David	24		1		2		9+ 1	
SILVINHO	23+ 8	1	2		3		8+ 2	
SUKER Davor	8+14	8	1	1	3		3+10	2
UPSON Matthew	5+ 3		2				1+ 1	
VERNAZZA Paolo	1+ 1		2				0+ 1	
VIEIRA Patrick	29+ 1	2			2		15	
VIVAS Nelson	1+ 4		1				1+ 3	
WESTON Rhys	1		0+ 1					
WINTERBURN Nigel	19+ 9		1				10+ 1	1
WREH Chris			0+ 1					
ASTON VILLA (PREM: 6th)								
BARRY Gareth	30	1	8		6			
BEWERS Jonathan	0+ 1							
BOATENG George	30+ 3	2	7	1	5			
CALDERWOOD Colin	15+ 3		3+ 1					
CARBONE Benito	22+ 2	3			6	5		
CUTLER Neil	0+ 1							
DELANEY Mark	25+ 3	1	1+ 2		4+ 1			
DRAPER Mark	0+ 1							
DUBLIN Dion	23+ 3	12	4	3	2+ 1	1		
EHIOGU Ugo	31	1	7		6			
ENCKELMAN Peter	9+ 1		3		1			
GHRAYIB Naj	1+ 4		1					
HENDRIE Lee	18+11	1	4+ 1	3	0+ 4			
JAMES David	29		5		5			
JOACHIM Julian	27+ 6	6	7+ 1	3	4+ 2			
MERSON Paul	24+ 8	5	5+ 2		6			
SAMUEL Jlloyd	5+ 4		0+ 1					
SOUTHGATE Gareth	31	2	6		6	1		
STONE Steve	10+14	1	3+ 3	1	2+ 4	1		
TAYLOR Ian	25+ 4	5	7+ 1	5	4+ 1			
THOMPSON Alan	16+ 5	2	3+ 2	1	1			
VASSELL Darius	1+10		1+ 4		0+ 1			
WALKER Richard	2+ 3	2	1+ 1					
WATSON Steve	13+ 1		7+ 1	1	2			
WRIGHT Alan	31+ 1	1	5		6			
BARNET (DIV 3: 6th)								
ANSELL Gary	0+ 3		0+ 1					
ARBER Mark	43+ 2	6	2		1		4	1
BARNES Steve	1+ 2				0+ 1			
BASHAM Mike	15				0+ 1		3+ 1	
BELL Leon	0+ 1							
BOSSU Bert							0+ 1	
BROWN Danny	20+ 4	3	0+ 1		1		3	
CHARLERY Kenny	42+ 1	13	2		1		3+ 1	1
CURRIE Darren	44	5	1				4	
D'ARCY Ross	1+ 2						0+ 1	
DAVIDSON Ross	8+ 1						1	
DOOLAN John	44	2	2		1		4	
GLEDHILL Lee	8+ 2				1			
GOODHIND Warren	5+ 4							
HACKETT Warren	34	1	2	1	1		1	1
HARRISON Lee	43		1		1		4	
HEALD Greg	40	5	2		1		3	
KING Marlon	19+12	8	0+ 2				1+ 2	
McGLEISH Scott	30+12	10	2	2	1		4	
NAISBITT Danny	3+ 1		1					
OMOYINMI Manny	1+ 5							
SAWYERS Rob	31+ 1	2	2				3	
SEARLE Stevie	8+11				1		1+ 1	
STOCKLEY Sam	31+ 3	1	2				3	
STREVENS Ben	0+ 6		0+ 1				0+ 1	
TOMS Frazer	27+12	1	2		1		1+ 2	1
WILSON Paul	8+11	1	1				1	
BARNSLEY (DIV 1: 4th)								
APPLEBY Matty	33+ 3	5	2+ 1				3	
AUSTIN Kevin	3		2					
BARKER Chris	28+ 1		4		1		0+ 1	
BARNARD Darren	32+ 9	13	4+ 1	2	1		3	
BASSINDER Gavin			1					
BENGTSSON Robert			1		1			
BROWN Keith	7+ 3						3	
BULLOCK Martin	1+ 3		5					
BULLOCK Tony	5+ 1		2					
CHETTLE Steve	25	2					3	
CURTIS John	28	2					1+ 1	
DYER Bruce	13+19	6	3+ 1		0+ 1		2+ 1	3
EADEN Nicky	38+ 4	1	2+ 2	2	1		2+ 1	
EVANS Andy			0+ 1					
HIGNETT Craig	38+ 4	19	2		1		3	2
HRISTOV Georgi	5+13	4	2+ 3	2			0+ 1	
JACKSON Mark	1							
JONES Scott	20		5	1				
KRIZAN Ales			1					
McCLARE Sean	1+ 9	2	3+ 2					
MILLER Kevin	41		4		1		3	
MORGAN Chris	36+ 1		4	1	1		3	
MOSES Ade	12		4					
PARKIN Jon			0+ 1		0+ 1			
RICHARDSON Kevin	4							
SHERON Mike	28+ 8	9	4	2	0+ 1			
SHIPPERLEY Neil	32+ 7	13	2+ 1	1	1		3	1
THOMAS Geoff	13+14	4	2		1		0+ 2	
TINKLER Eric	28+ 5	4	4+ 1		1		3	
TUTTLE Dave	11+ 1				1			
VAN DER LAAN Robin	23+ 9	3	3+ 1	2			1	
BIRMINGHAM CITY (DIV 1: 5th)								
ADEBOLA Dele	21+21	5	3+ 2	1	0+ 1		0+ 1	
BASS Jon	5+ 3		2		1			
BENNETT Ian	21		1		1			
BERESFORD John	1							
CAMPBELL Stuart	0+ 2							

	P/FL		FLC		FAC		Others	
	App	Goals	App	Goals	App	Goals	App	Goals
CARRICK Michael	1+ 1							
CHARLTON Simon	19+ 1				2			
DYSON James	0+ 2		0+ 1					
FORINTON Howard	0+ 1		1+ 2					
FURLONG Paul	17+ 2	11	2				2	
GILL Jerry	2+ 9		1+ 1		1		1	
GRAINGER Martin	34	5	2	1	2		1	
HAARHOFF Jimmy	0+ 1							
HOLDSWORTH David	43+ 1	5	5	1	1		2	
HOLLAND Chris	2+12		3+ 1		1			
HUGHES Bryan	41+ 4	10	3+ 1		2		2	
HYDE Graham	20+11	1	2+ 1	1	2			
JOHNSON Andy	15+ 7	1	3+ 1	1			1+ 1	
JOHNSON Michael	29+ 5	2	4		2		2	
JOHNSTON Allan	7+ 2		1					
KNIGHT Richard			0+ 1					
LAZARIDIS Stan	26+ 5	2	3		0+ 1		1+ 1	
McCARTHY Jon	21	4	3+ 1					
MARCELO	14+11	5			1+ 1		1+ 1	1
MYHRE Thomas	7						2	
NDLOVU Peter	2+11	1	3+ 1				1+ 1	
NEWTON Eddie	2+ 2		2+ 2		0+ 1			
O'CONNOR Martyn	38+ 1	2	6	3	1		2	
POOLE Kevin	18		5		1			
PURSE Darren	33+ 5	2	5	1	1		2	
RANKIN Izzy	11+ 2	4						
ROBINSON Steve	5+ 1				1+ 1			
ROWETT Gary	45	1	5	1	2	1	2	1
WASSALL Darren			1					
WREH Chris	6+ 1	1						
BLACKBURN ROVERS (DIV 1: 11th)								
BLAKE Nathan	17+11	3	2		4	2		
BROOMES Marlon	13	1						
BURGESS Ben	1+ 1							
CARSLEY Lee	30	10			4	1		
DAILLY Christian	43	4	1		4			
DAVIDSON Callum	28+ 2		1		4			
DAVIES Kevin	2							
DUFF Damien	33+ 6	5	2	1	3	1		
DUNN David	17+ 5	2	3	1	0+ 1			
FETTIS Alan	0+ 1							
FILAN John	16		1		1			
FLITCROFT Garry	18+ 1							
FRANDSEN Per	26+ 5	5			4	1		
GALLACHER Kevin	3+ 2		0+ 1	1				
GILL Wayne			3					
GILLESPIE Keith	11+11	2	2		0+ 1			
GRAYSON Simon	31+ 3		0+ 1		2+ 1			
HARKNESS Steve	17		1+ 1		1			
JANSEN Matt	16+14	4	1+ 1	2	1	1		
JOHNSON Damien	11+ 5	1	2+ 1		1+ 3			
KELLY Alan	29+ 1		2		3			
KENNA Jeff	11		3		2			
McATEER Jason	24+ 4	2			3			
MILLER Alan	1							
OSTENSTAD Egil	21+ 7	8	1		1+ 1			
PEACOCK Darren	15+ 2		2		3			
RICHARDSON Leam			1					
SHORT Craig	17		1					
TAYLOR Martin	4+ 2		2		1			
WARD Ashley	35+ 2	8	2		2			
WILCOX Jason	16+ 4							
BLACKPOOL (DIV 2: 22nd)								
ABLETT Gary	9+ 1	1					2	
ALDRIDGE Martin	0+ 5		0+ 1					
BARDSLEY David	35		2		1		3	
BARNES Phil	12		1				1	
BEESLEY Paul	15+ 3				1		3	
BENT Junior	18+10	1	2		0+ 2		2+ 1	
BRYAN Marvin	14+ 4		0+ 1		2			
BUSHELL Steve	17+ 7	2			3		3	
BYFIELD Darren	3							
CAIG Tony	33		1		3		2	
CARLISLE Clarke	43	4	2		3	1	3	
CLARKSON Phil	34+ 1	3	2	2	3	2	2	1
COID Danny	13+ 8	1			2		1	
CONNELL Darren	1+ 2							
COUZENS Andy	12+ 3		2				1	
DURNIN John	4+ 1	1			1	1		
FORSYTH Richard	10+ 3				0+ 2		0+ 1	
GARVEY Steve	1+ 1							
GILL Wayne	12	7						
HILLS John	32+ 1	2	1		3		1	
HUGHES Ian	31+ 3		2	1	3		1	
JASZCZUN Tommy	19						1	1
JONES Eifion	1							
LAMBERT Rickie	0+ 3							
LEE David	9	1			2		1	
LUMSDON Chris	6	1						
MATTHEWS Rob	5+ 1	2					2	1
MURPHY John	34+ 5	10	1		3		1+ 1	
NEWELL Mike	12+ 1	2						
NOWLAND Adam	5+16	3	1+ 1		2+ 1	1	0+ 2	
ORMEROD Brett	13	5	2					
QUAILEY Brian	1						1	
RACHEL Adam	1							
RICHARDSON Kevin	20	1					2	
ROBINSON Phil	4+ 2				1		0+ 1	
SHUTTLEWORTH Barry	4+ 1		1					
THOMAS James	9	2						
THOMPSON Phil	2+ 1		1					
WELLENS Richard	5+ 3							
WHITLEY Jim	7+ 1		1					
BOLTON WANDERERS (DIV 1: 6th)								
ALJOFREE Hasney	3+ 5		3+ 2		0+ 2			
BANKS Steve	2		4		2			
BERGSSON Gudni	37+ 1	4	7	1	4		2	
BRANAGAN Keith	11		3					
COX Neil	15	2	4	1				
ELLIOTT Robbie	22+ 5	3	3+ 2	1	3		1+ 1	
FARRELLY Gareth	8+ 3	1			0+ 1			
FISH Mark	31		4+ 1	1	4		2	
FRANDSEN Per	7	2	3	2				
GARDNER Ricardo	26+ 3	5	9	1	2+ 2			
GUDJOHNSEN Eidur	40+ 1	13	8	4	4+ 1	4	1	1
HANSEN Bo	15+15	9	4+ 1	1	1	1	0+ 2	
HOLDEN Dean	6+ 6		2		3+ 1			
HOLDSWORTH Dean	22+13	11	3+ 2	1	2		2	3
HOLLOWAY Darren	3+ 1							
JAASKELAINEN Jussi	33+ 1		2		3		2	
JENSEN Claus	41+ 1	6	6		5		2	
JOHANSEN Michael	44+ 1	3	8+ 1	3	5		2	
JOHNSTON Allan	17+ 2	3			2		2	1
KAPRIELIAN Mickael	0+ 1							
NOLAN Kevin	0+ 4							
O'KANE John	7+ 4	1	2		1+ 1			
PASSI Franck	7+ 8		2		2+ 1		0+ 1	
PHILLIPS Jimmy	15+ 8	1	3+ 1				0+ 2	
POTTER Lee			0+ 1					
RITCHIE Paul	13+ 1		1		3+ 1		2	
STATON Luke			0+ 1					
STRONG Greg	6		3+ 1					
TAYLOR Bob	15+12	3	3+ 2	1	3+ 1	2		
TODD Andy	10+ 2		4					
WARHURST Paul	15+ 4		1+ 3		1+ 1		2	
WHITLOW Mike	35+ 2	1	7		5		2	

	P/FL App	P/FL Goals	FLC App	FLC Goals	FAC App	FAC Goals	Others App	Others Goals
BOURNEMOUTH (DIV 2: 16th)								
BAILEY John	0+1		0+1					
BETSY Kevin	1+4							
BROADHURST Karl	16		3		1		1	
COX Ian	28		5		3		1	
DAY Jamie	9+2	1	1+1		2		1	
ELLIOTT Stuart	6+2							
ELLIOTT Wade	6+6	3						
FENTON Nicky	8							
FLETCHER Carl	20+5	3			3		1	
FLETCHER Steve	35+1	7	5		3	2		
FORBES Terrell	3				1			
FORD James	0+2							
HAYTER James	21+10	2	1+1	1	1		2	1
HOWE Eddie	28	1	5					
HUCK Willie	4+13		0+3	1				
HUGHES Richard	20+1	2	2+1				1	
JORGENSEN Claus	34+10	6	4		3		1+1	
KEELER Justin	0+3						0+1	
LOVELL Steve	0+1							
MEAN Scott	26+6	4	5		0+1		2	
O'NEILL John	18+12	3	0+2				1	
O'SHEA John	10	1					1	
OVENDALE Mark	43		5		3		2	
RAWLINSON Mark	2+1		1				1	
ROBINSON Steve	40	9	4		3	1	2	
SHEERIN Joe	3+3	1						
SMITH Danny	0+1							
STEIN Mark	36	11	5	2	3	1	2	1
STEWART Gareth	3							
STOCK Brian	4+1							
TINDALL Jason	4+4						1	
WARREN Christer	39+2	2	4		3	1	1	
WATSON Gordon	2+4		0+1		1+2		0+1	
YOUNG Neil	37		5		3		1	
BRADFORD CITY (PREM: 17th)								
BEAGRIE Peter	30+5	7	2		2			
BLAKE Robbie	15+13	2	2+1	1	2	1		
CADETE Jorge	2+5							
CLARKE Matt	21		1		2			
DAVISON Aidan	5+1							
DREYER John	11+3	1	1					
GRANT Gareth	0+1		1+1					
HALLE Gunnar	37+1		1		2			
JACOBS Wayne	22+2		1+1					
LAWRENCE Jamie	19+4	3			1+1			
McCALL Stuart	33+1	1	2		1+1			
MILLS Lee	19+2	5	1+1	1	2			
MOORE Darren			1					
MYERS Andy	10+3		2		1			
O'BRIEN Andy	36	1	2		2			
RANKIN Izzy	0+9				0+1			
REDFEARN Neil	14+3	1	1+1		2			
RODRIGUEZ Bruno	0+2		1+2					
SAUNDERS Dean	28+6	3	1+1	1	1+1	2		
SHARPE Lee	13+5		0+1		1+1			
SOUTHALL Neville	1							
WALSH Gary	11		2					
WESTWOOD Ashley	1+4		1		1			
WETHERALL David	38	2	2	2	1			
WHALLEY Gareth	16	1	2					
WINDASS Dean	36+2	10	3		1			
WRIGHT Steve			3					
BRENTFORD (DIV 2: 17th)								
AGYEMANG Patrick	3+9							
ANDERSON Ijah	30+1		2				2	
BOXALL Danny	25		2		2		3	
BRYAN Del	5+13	1	1+1		0+1		0+1	1
CHARLES Julian	0+2							
CLEMENT Neil	7+1							
EINARSSON Gunnar	1+2						0+1	
EVANS Paul	33	7	2		1		2	1
FOLAN Tony	1+8	1	1+1		0+1			
GLASS Jimmy	1+1							
GRAHAM Gareth	5+8							
HREIDARSSON Herman	8	2	2					
HUTCHINGS Carl	7+1							
INGIMARSSON Ivar	21+4	1					3	
JAMES Clement	0+1							
JENKINS Steve	2+3				1			
JONES Steve	6+2						2	
KENNEDY Richard	4+5						1	
MAHON Gavin	37	3	2		2		3	
MARSHALL Scott	22	2			2	1		
O'CONNOR Kevin	6						0+1	
OWUSU Lloyd	39+2	12	1		2	1	1+1	1
PARTRIDGE Scott	38+3	6	2		1+1		1+1	
PEARCEY Jason	6		1					
PINAMONTE Lorenzo	5+10	1					0+1	
POWELL Darren	36	2	2		2		3	1
QUINN Robert	42+2		1+1		2	1	3	
ROWLANDS Martin	38+2	6	1+1		1+1		3	
SAROYA Nevin	0+1							
SCOTT Andy	32+4	3	1+1		2		2	1
THEOBALD David	6+4						1	
WARNER Phil	1+13		0+1		1			
WOODMAN Andy	39		1		2		3	
BRIGHTON & HOVE ALBION (DIV 3: 11th)								
ARMSTRONG Paul	0+5		0+1					
ARNOTT Andy	0+1		1					
ASPINALL Warren	19+12	3			3		2	
BROOKER Paul	15	2						
CAMERON Dave	6+11		0+1		2+1		0+1	
CAMPBELL Jamie	22+1	1	2		3		2	
CARR Darren	16+3				3		2	
CROSBY Andy	36	3	2		1		2	
CULLIP Danny	32+1	2			4	1	1	
CULVERHOUSE Ian	1							
FREEMAN Darren	36+2	12	1+1		3	1	1	
HART Gary	42+1	9	1+1		2		2	1
HOBSON Gary	6		2		1+1		1	
JOHNSON Ross	4+5		0+2		1			
LING Martin	2+6	1						
McPHEE Chris	0+4							
McPHERSON Keith	23+2	1	1		3			
MAYO Kerry	25+6	1			0+4	1		
NEWHOUSE Aidan	1+11	2	1		0+1			
OATWAY Charlie	42	4	2		4		2	
ORMEROD Mark	7		2					
PALMER Ryan	1							
PINAMONTE Lorenzo	8+1	2						
RAMSAY Scott	8+16	2			0+2		1	
ROGERS Paul	44+1	8	2		4	1	2	
THOMAS Rod	14+20	1	2		2+1			
WALTON Mark	39				4		2	
WATSON Paul	40+2	4	1		4	1	2	
WILDER Chris	11		2					
WILKINSON Shaun	0+2							
ZAMORA Bobby	6	6						
BRISTOL CITY (DIV 2: 9th)								
AKINBIYI Ade	3	2	1					
AMANKWAAH Kevin	4+1						0+1	
BEADLE Peter	22+3	6			3		4+2	4
BELL Mickey	34+2	5	1		3		4	
BLACK Tommy	4							
BRENNAN Jim	11+1	2	4					
BROWN Aaron	10+3	2	0+2				3+1	
BROWN Marvin	0+2		0+1				0+1	

	P/FL		FLC		FAC		Others	
	App	Goals	App	Goals	App	Goals	App	Goals
BURNELL Joe	15+ 2						3	1
BURNS John	6+ 5						1+ 1	
CAREY Louis	20+ 2		2				5	
CLIST Simon	8+ 1						1+ 2	
COLES Danny	0+ 1							
DOHERTY Tommy	0+ 1		0+ 1					
GOODRIDGE Greg	13+ 8		2+ 1		0+ 1		1	1
HEWLETT Matt	5+ 2						2+ 1	1
HILL Matt	8+ 6						3+ 2	
HOLLAND Paul	22+ 5				3		4	1
HULBERT Robin	1+ 1							
HUTCHINGS Carl	17+ 4	1	2	1	2+ 1		1	
JONES Steve	12+ 2	2	2		2+ 1			
JORDAN Andrew	8		1		1		1	
LAVIN Gerard	18+ 1		1		2		1	
MEECHAN Alex	5+ 7	4	1		0+ 1		1	
MERCER Billy	25				2		5	
MILLEN Keith	28	2			2		6	
MORTIMER Paul	22+ 1		3	1	2			
MURRAY Scott	31 +10	6	4		2+ 1	3	5+ 1	2
ODEJAYI Kayo	0+ 3							
PHILLIPS Steve	21		4		1		1	
PINAMONTE Lorenzo	2+ 4		1+ 2					
SEBOK Vilmos	8+ 3		4					
SHAIL Mark	0+ 1							
SPENCER Damian	6+ 3	1					1+ 2	1
TAYLOR Shaun	25	4	4		3			
TESTIMITANU Ivan	11+ 5	2			2+ 1		3	
THORPE Tony	24+ 7	13	1+ 1	1			5	3
TINNION Brian	42+ 1	3	4		3	2	4	
TORPEY Steve	15+ 5	1	2+ 1	1	1		1+ 1	
WRIGHT Ben	0+ 2							
BRISTOL ROVERS (DIV 2: 7th)								
ANDREASSON Marcus	6							
ASTAFJEVS Vitalis	13+ 3	2						
BENNETT Frankie	0+10		0+ 1				0+ 1	
BRYANT Simon	9+ 6		0+ 3					
BYRNE Shaun	1+ 1						2	
CHALLIS Trevor	36+ 4	1	3		1		1	
CURETON Jamie	46	22	4	1	1		2	1
ELLINGTON Nathan	12 +25	4			0+ 1		1+ 1	
EVANS Rhys	4							
FOSTER Steve	43	1	4		1		2	
HILLIER David	39		4		1		1	
JONES Lee	36		4		1		1	
LEONI Stephane	2+ 6		1					
MAUGE Ronnie	22		4		1		2	
MEAKER Michael	0+ 2		0+ 1					
PARKIN Brian	2+ 1						1	
PENRICE Gary	0+ 3				0+ 1			
PETHICK Robbie	40+ 1	2	4		1		2	
PIERRE Nigel	1+ 2							
PRITCHARD David	21	1	4				1	
ROBERTS Jason	41	22	4	3	1		2	
STEWART Jordan	1+ 3							
TAYLOR Stuart	4							
THOMSON Andy	43	3	4		1		1	
TILLSON Andy	43	1	4		1		1	
TREES Robert	5+ 5	1	0+ 1					
TROUGHT Mike	2+ 2						1	
WALTERS Mark	28+ 2	9					0+ 2	
WHITE Tom	3						1	
WOLLEASTON Robert	0+ 4							
ZABEK Lee	3+ 1				1			
ZAMORA Bobby	0+ 4		0+ 1		0+ 1			
BURNLEY (DIV 2: 2nd)								
ARMSTRONG Gordon	22	1	1		3+ 1			
BRANCH Graham	31 +13	3	2		0+ 3		1	
BRASS Chris	4+ 3		1				0+ 1	

	P/FL		FLC		FAC		Others	
	App	Goals	App	Goals	App	Goals	App	Goals
COOK Paul	44	3	1		4	2		
COOKE Andy	33+ 3	7			4	1		
COWAN Tom	5+ 3		2				0+ 1	
COX Ian	17	1						
CRICHTON Paul	46		2		4		1	
DAVIS Steve	42	7	1		4		1	
GRANT Stephen			0+ 2					
JEPSON Ronnie	1 +30	2	0+ 2		0+ 3			
JOHNROSE Lenny	28+ 7	2	2		0+ 1		1	
LEE Alan	2+13		1+ 1		0+ 2		1	1
LITTLE Glen	36+ 5	3	2		4		1	
MELLON Micky	33+ 9	3	2		4			
MULLIN John	27+10	5			4	1	1	
PAYTON Andy	39+ 2	27	1		4		1	
ROBERTSON Mark	0+ 1		1				0+ 1	
SMITH Paul	17+ 7				1			
SWAN Peter	0+ 2							
THOMAS Mitchell	44		2		4		1	
WELLER Paul	1+ 6	1					1	
WEST Dean	30+ 4		1+ 1		4		1	
WRIGHT Ian	4+11	4						
BURY (DIV 2: 15th)								
AVDIU Kemajl	8+13		0+ 2				0+ 1	
BARNES Paul	13+17	4	0+ 1		2		1	
BARRASS Matt	24+ 1	1					1	
BARRICK Dean	12+ 5		0+ 2		1+ 1			
BHUTIA Bhaichung	6+ 8	2			1+ 3			
BILLY Chris	32+ 4	4	1		3	1	1	
BRYAN Marvin	6+ 3							
BUGGIE Lee	0+ 1							
BULLOCK Darren	22+ 5	2	2		4	1	1	1
CHALLINOR Paul	0+ 1							
COLLINS Sam	19		2		0+ 1			
CONNELL Lee	1+ 1							
CROWE Dean	4	1						
DAWS Nick	43	2	2		4		1	
FORREST Martyn	9+ 6							
HALFORD Steve	1+ 1							
HILL Nicky	4+ 1							
JAMES Lutel	17+ 6	2	2		1+ 2	1		
KENNY Paddy	46		2		4		1	
LAWSON Ian	20+ 5	11	2		3+ 1		1	
LINIGHAN Brian	2+ 1							
LITTLEJOHN Adrian	34+ 8	9	2	1	3	1	1	
PREECE Andy	30+13	12	2		2			
REDMOND Steve	28+ 5	1			4		1	
REID Paul	37+ 2	2	2		2			
RICHARDSON Lee	5	1						
ROCHA Carlos	0+ 3							
SOUTER Ryan	2+ 2							
SWAILES Chris	27	2	2		4		1	
SWAILES Danny	18+ 6	3			1+ 1			
WILLIAMS Paul	22+ 4				2+ 1		1	
WOODWARD Andy	14		1		3+ 1			
CAMBRIDGE UNITED (DIV 2: 19th)								
ABBEY Zema	2+ 6							
ASHBEE Ian	43+ 2	1	2		5			
BENJAMIN Trevor	42+ 2	20	2		5	3		
BUTLER Martin	26	14	2	2	5	2		
BYFIELD Darren	3+ 1							
CASSIDY Jamie	4+ 4		0+ 1				1	
CHENERY Ben	17+ 1		2				1	
CHILLINGWORTH Daniel	0+ 3						0+ 1	
COWAN Tom	4							
DUNCAN Andy	13	1	2					
EUSTACE Scott	34+ 2	1	2		3			
GRAHAM Mark	0+ 1		0+ 1					
GUINAN Steve	4+ 2				0+ 2		1	
HANSEN John	12+ 4	3						

	P/FL App	P/FL Goals	FLC App	FLC Goals	FAC App	FAC Goals	Others App	Others Goals
HUNT Jon	3+ 4	1						
JOSEPH Marc	27+ 6				3		1	
KAVANAGH Jason	19				3			
KYD Michael	12+ 6	3	2		1		1	
LAMEY Nathan	2+ 1							
MacKENZIE Neil	19+ 3				5		0+ 1	
McNEIL Martin	29				4			
MARSHALL Shaun	23+ 1				4			
MILLER Rob	0+ 1							
MUSTOE Neil	28+ 5		2		4			
PATERSON Scott	6							
PEREZ Lionel	9							
PREECE David	1+11						1	
RUSSELL Alex	14+ 1		1		3			
TANN Adam							1	
TAYLOR John	18+22	6	0+ 2	1	1+ 3	1		
VAN HEUSDEN Arjan	14+ 1		2		1		1	
WANLESS Paul	39+ 3	3	1		4+ 1	1	1	
WILSON Clive	27		2		4		1	
YOUNGS Tom	12+ 9	8	0+ 1				1	1

CARDIFF CITY (DIV 2: 21st)

	P/FL App	P/FL Goals	FLC App	FLC Goals	FAC App	FAC Goals	Others App	Others Goals
BOLAND Willie	20+ 8	1	3		1+ 2		1	
BONNER Mark	29+ 2		2		2			
BOWEN Jason	32+ 7	12	4	2	5		1	
BRAYSON Paul	7+ 2	1						
BRAZIER Matt	20+10	1	1+ 3	1	3	1	1	
CARPENTER Richard	28+ 5	1	1+ 1		4+ 1		1	
CORNFORTH John	6+ 4	1	1+ 2					
EARNSHAW Robert	4+ 2	1						
ECKHARDT Jeff	39+ 2	1	4		4			
FAERBER Winston	31+ 2	1	4		4+ 1		1	
FORD Mike	23+ 3		4		5	1		
FOWLER Jason	28	1	3		2+ 1			
HALLWORTH Jon	39		4		5		1	
HILL Danny	12+11	1	1		2+ 1		1	
HUGHES Jamie	0+ 2	1	0+ 3	1				
HUMPHREYS Richie	8+ 1	2					1	
JARMAN Lee	0+ 1		0+ 1					
KELLY Seamus	7+ 1							
LEGG Andy	42	2	4		5			
LOW Josh	12+ 5	2					0+ 1	
MIDDLETON Craig	7+ 3		1		0+ 1		0+ 1	
NOGAN Kurt	4+ 2							
NUGENT Kevin	37+ 2	10	4	1	2	2		
PERRETT Russell	26+ 1	1			5	1	1	
PHILLIPS Lee	0+ 3		0+ 1					
ROBERTS Chris	1+ 7				2+ 1		0+ 1	
SCHWINDENKORF Jorn	5				1			
THOMAS Dai	5+ 2	1			0+ 1			
VAUGHAN Tony	14						1	
YOUNG Scott	20+ 2	2	3		1		1	

CARLISLE UNITED (DIV 3: 23rd)

	P/FL App	P/FL Goals	FLC App	FLC Goals	FAC App	FAC Goals	Others App	Others Goals
ANTHONY Graham	12+ 6		0+ 2		1		2	
BAKER Paul	12+ 5	2						
BARR Billy	28+ 1		1+ 1		1		1	
BLACK Tommy	5	1						
BOWMAN Rob	12+ 3				1			
BRIGHTWELL David	37		2		1		2	
CLARK Peter	42+ 1	1	2		1		1	
CLARKE Adrian	7							
DALTON Paul	3	1						
DIBBLE Andy	2							
DOBIE Scott	25+ 9	7			1		3	
DURNIN John	20+ 2	2					1	
GREGORY Andy	6+ 1	1					0+ 1	
HALLIDAY Steve	16	7					2	1
HARRIES Paul	6+14	2			1	1	0+ 1	
HOPPER Tony	25+ 2		2				1+ 2	
HORE John	1							
INGHAM Michael	7							
KEEN Peter	6							
McKINNON Rob	8						2	1
PITTS Matthew	20+ 9	1	2				2	1
PROKAS Richard	28+ 7	1	2		1		1+ 2	
REID Paul	17+ 2						3	
RODDIE Andy	1+ 1							
SEARLE Damon	14+ 7	1	2				3	
SKELTON Gavin	1+ 6		1					
SKINNER Steve	0+ 2							
SOLEY Steve	35+ 2	8			1		3	1
TEALE Shaun	18						2	
THOMPSON Barry					1			
THORPE Jeff	4+ 9		0+ 2					
TRACEY Richard	25+11	7	2		1		1+ 1	
VAN DER KWAAK Peter	2						2	
WALKER Andy	3		2					
WEAVER Luke	29		2				1	
WHITEHEAD Stuart	29		2					

CHARLTON ATHLETIC (DIV 1: 1st)

	P/FL App	P/FL Goals	FLC App	FLC Goals	FAC App	FAC Goals	Others App	Others Goals
BARNESS Anthony	17+ 2				1			
BROWN Steve	29+11	2	2		4			
HUNT Andy	43+ 1	24	1		4	1		
ILIC Sasa	1							
JONES Keith	16+ 1	1			0+ 1			
JONES Steve	1+ 1							
KIELY Dean	45		2		4			
KINSELLA Mark	38	3	0+ 2		3+ 1	2		
KITSON Paul	2+ 4	1						
KONCHESKY Paul	6+ 2		2		0+ 1			
LISBIE Kevin					0+ 1			
McCAMMON Mark	1+ 3		0+ 1					
MacDONALD Charlie	0+ 3				1	1		
MENDONCA Clive	19	9	1+ 1		1			
NEWTON Shaun	41+ 1	5	2		3+ 1	1		
PARKER Scott	5+10	1	1+ 1		0+ 1			
POWELL Chris	40				4			
PRINGLE Martin	12+20	4	2		2			
ROBINSON John	43+ 2	7	2		3	1		
RUFUS Richard	44	6	2		3			
SALAKO John	4+23	2			2+ 2			
SHIELDS Greg	21	2	2		3			
STUART Graham	33+ 4	7	2		3			
SVENSSON Matt	13+ 5	2						
TILER Carl	4+ 7	1			0+ 1			
TODD Andy	5+ 7				3+ 1			
YOUDS Eddie	23		1		0+ 1			

CHELSEA (PREM: 5th)

	P/FL App	P/FL Goals	FLC App	FLC Goals	FAC App	FAC Goals	Others App	Others Goals
AMBROSETTI Gabriele	9+ 7		1		0+ 1		1+ 4	1
BABAYARO Celestine	23+ 2				1		14+ 1	2
CLEMENT Neil					0+ 1			
CUDICINI Carlo	1		1				0+ 1	
DALLA BONNA Sam	0+ 2						0+ 1	
DE GOEY Ed	37				6		16	
DESAILLY Marcel	23	1			4		16	
DESCHAMPS Didier	24+ 3				6		14	1
DI MATTEO Robbie	14+ 4	2	1		3	2	3+ 6	
FERRER Albert	24+ 1				2		14	1
FLO Tore Andre	20+14	10	1		2+ 4	1	14+ 2	8
FORSSELL Mikael			1				1	
GOLDBAEK Bjarne	2+ 4		1				1+ 1	
HARLEY Jon	13+ 4	2			5		1+ 3	
HOGH Jes	6+ 3		1		2		2+ 3	
LAMBOURDE Bernard	12+ 3	2	1		3		0+ 2	
LEBOEUF Frank	28	2			4	1	13+ 1	1
LE SAUX Graeme	6+ 2		1				3+ 1	
MELCHIOT Mario	4+ 1				1			
MORRIS Jody	19+11	3	1		1+ 3	1	6+ 5	
NICHOLLS Mark			0+ 1				0+ 1	

	P/FL App	Goals	FLC App	Goals	FAC App	Goals	Others App	Goals
PERCASSI Luca					0+ 1			
PETRESCU Dan	24+ 5	4			2+ 1		13+ 2	1
POYET Gus	25+ 8	10			6	6	11+ 3	2
SUTTON Chris	21+ 7	1			3+ 1	1	3+ 4	1
TERRY John	2+ 2		1		2+ 2	1		
THOME Emerson	18+ 2						1	
WEAH George	9+ 2	3			4	2		
WISE Dennis	29+ 1	4			5	2	14+ 1	4
WOLLEASTON Robert	0+ 1		0+ 1					
ZOLA Franco	25+ 8	4			4+ 1	1	15	3
CHELTENHAM TOWN (DIV 3: 8th)								
BANKS Chris	41+ 1		2		2		2	
BLOOMER Bob	1+10		0+ 2				0+ 1	
BOOK Steve	46		2		2		2	
BRISSETT Jason	5+ 3						1+ 1	
BROUGH John	15+22	2	0+ 1		2	1	0+ 1	
DEVANEY Martin	19+ 7	6	2					
DUFF Michael	31	2			2		1	
FREEMAN Mark	36+ 2	2	2		2		2	
FREESTONE Chris	5	2						
GRAYSON Neil	39+ 4	10	2	1	1+ 1		2	
GRIFFIN Antony	14+10		2					
HOPKINS Gareth	0+ 1				0+ 1			
HOWARTH Neil	43+ 1	2	2		2	1	2	
HOWELLS Lee	45	3	2		2		2	
JACKSON Michael	0+ 2		0+ 1					
JONES Mark	3							
McAULEY Hugh	22+17	4	2		1		2	1
MILTON Russell	38	9			2	1	2	1
STEVENS Ian	1							
VICTORY Jamie	46	4	2	1	2		2	
WALKER Richard	6+ 1							
WATKINS Dale	4+ 5		0+ 2					
YATES Mark	46	2	2		2		2	
CHESTER CITY (DIV 3: 24th)								
AGOGO Junior	10	6						
BECKETT Luke	46	14	4	3	4	2	1	
BERRY Paul	0+ 9	1	0+ 2		0+ 1			
BLACKBURN Chris	0+ 1							
BLACKWOOD Michael	9	2						
BROWN Wayne	46		4		4		1	
CARDEN Paul	9+ 2							
CARSON Danny			0+ 1					
CARVER Joe	1+ 1							
CROSS Jon	13+ 4		2		2+ 1	3	1	
DAVIDSON Ross	9		4					
DOUGHTY Matt	19+14	1	2		4			
EVE Angus	9+ 5	4					0+ 1	
EYJOLFSSON Sigi	9	3					1	
FINNEY Steve	4+ 9							
FISHER Neil	34+ 7	1	4		4		1	
HEGGS Carl	11	2						
HEMMINGS Tony	19	2						
HICKS Stuart	13							
HOBSON Gary	20							
JONES Jon	4+ 2		1+ 2	1	0+ 1			
KEISTER John	8+ 2						1	
LAIRD Kamu	2+ 1	1						
LANCASTER Martyn	14+ 3		3		1+ 1		1	
MALONE Steve					1			
MILOSAVLJEVIC Goran	11+ 1		2		3		1	
MOSS Darren	28+ 7		1+ 1		4		1	
NASH Martin	12+ 4				3+ 1			
PICKERING Ally	7	1						
PORTER Andy	16							
REID Shaun	10+ 3		2		2		1	
RICHARDSON Nick	31+ 5	2	4	1	4	1	1	
ROBINSON Jamie	9							
SHELTON Andy	9+ 2		4	1	1+ 2		0+ 1	

	P/FL App	Goals	FLC App	Goals	FAC App	Goals	Others App	Goals
SPOONER Nicky	9				2			
WOODS Mattie	40+ 2		4		2+ 1			
WRIGHT Darren	15+10	1	3		3		0+ 1	
CHESTERFIELD (DIV 2: 24th)								
AGOGO Junior	3+ 1							
ARMSTRONG Joel	3						1	
BARRETT Danny	0+ 2							
BEAUMONT Chris	32+ 1	2	3+ 1		1		3	
BETTNEY Chris	7+ 6		3					
BLATHERWICK Steve	36		2		1		3	2
BRECKIN Ian	37+ 1	1	4		1		3	
CARSS Tony	24+ 7	1	2		1		1+ 1	
CURTIS Tom	17+ 1		3					
D'AURIA David	4+ 1							
DUDLEY Craig	0+ 2							
EBDON Marcus	10+ 1		3	1	1			
GALLOWAY Mick	14+ 1	1					3	
GAYLE Mark	29+ 1		2+ 1		1		1	
HEWITT Jamie	38+ 2		4		1		3	
HOLLAND Paul	4		2+ 1					
HOWARD Jon	19+ 8	2	0+ 1		1		1	
LEANING Andy	6		2					
LEE Jason	3+ 3				0+ 1			
LOMAS Jamie	10+ 7		1+ 1		1	1	1	
MUGGLETON Carl	5							
PAYNE Steve	15+ 3	3	1				0+ 1	
PEARCE Greg	8+ 2							
PERKINS Chris	29+ 2						2+ 1	
POINTON Neil	9+ 1						2	
REEVES David	43	14	4	2	1		3	2
SIMPKINS Mike	8+ 1		2+ 1					
VAUGHAN John	3						1	
WILKINSON Steve	15+ 7	1			1		2+ 1	1
WILLIAMS Danny	3+ 2		0+ 1				0+ 1	
WILLIAMS Ryan	30	5					3	
WILLIS Roger	20+ 8	4	2+ 2		0+ 1		0+ 1	
WOODS Steve	22+ 3		4				0+ 1	
COLCHESTER UNITED (DIV 2: 18th)								
ARNOTT Andy	4+ 8							
ASPINALL Warren	7	2	2					
BRAMBLE Titus	2							
BROWN Simon	38		1		1		1	
BURTON-GODWIN Sagi	9		2					
DOZZELL Jason	38+ 1	5	2	1	1		1	
DUGUID Karl	40+ 1	12	2		1			
DUNNE Joe	19+ 1							
FARLEY Craig	8+ 6				1		1	
FERGUSON Barry	5+ 1							
FORBES Steve	0+ 2							
GERMAIN Steve	1+ 2							
GREENE David	29	1	2		1			
GREGORY David	45		2		1		1	
JOHNSON Gavin	24+ 3							
JOHNSON Ross	17+ 1							
KEEBLE Chris	2+ 3	1						
KEITH Joey	45	1	2	1	1		1	
LAUNDERS Brian	6		2					
LOCK Tony	12+12	2			0+ 1		1	
LUA LUA Tresor	24+17	12	2	1	1	1	1	
McGAVIN Steve	30+ 4	16			1		1	
MORALEE Jamie	20+ 7	1	0+ 1				1	1
OPARA Kelechi	2+14						0+ 1	
PINAULT Thomas	1+ 3		0+ 1					
RICHARD Fabrice	13+ 1		0+ 1		1			
SKELTON Aaron	27+ 6	4			1		1	
SODJE Efe	3							
VAUGHAN John	6							
WALKER Andy	2		1+ 1					
WHITE Alan	4						1	

	P/FL App	P/FL Goals	FLC App	FLC Goals	FAC App	FAC Goals	Others App	Others Goals
WIGNALL Jack	0+1						0+1	
WILKINS Richard	23+1	2	2					

COVENTRY CITY (PREM: 14th)

	P/FL App	P/FL Goals	FLC App	FLC Goals	FAC App	FAC Goals	Others App	Others Goals
ALOISI John	3+4	2						
BETTS Robert	0+2							
BREEN Gary	20+1		1		3			
BURROWS David	11+4		1					
CHIPPO Youssef	33	2	1	2	2	2		
DELORGE Laurent					0+1			
EDWORTHY Marc	10		2					
EUSTACE John	12+4	1	1+1		1+2	1		
FROGGATT Steve	21+5	1	1		3			
GUSTAFFSON Tomas	7+3				0+2			
HADJI Moustapha	33	6	1		2			
HALL Marcus	7+2		1					
HALL Paul	0+1		0+1					
HEDMAN Magnus	35				3			
HENDRY Colin	9							
HUCKERBY Darren	1							
KEANE Robbie	30+1	2			3			
KIRKLAND Chris			1					
KONJIC Muhamed	3+1		1+1					
McALLISTER Gary	38	11	2	2	3			
McSHEFFREY Gary	0+3		2					
NORMANN Runar	1+7				1			
NUZZO Raffaele			1					
OGRIZOVIC Steve	3							
PALMER Carlton	15	1	1		3			
QUINN Barry	5+6							
ROUSSEL Cedric	18+4	6			2+1	3		
SHAW Richard	27+2		2		0+1			
STRACHAN Gavin	1+2		1					
TELFER Paul	26+4		1		3			
WHELAN Noel	20+6	1			1+1	2		
WILLIAMS Paul	26+2	1	1		3			
ZUNIGA Ysrael	3+4	2						

CREWE ALEXANDRA (DIV 1: 19th)

	P/FL App	P/FL Goals	FLC App	FLC Goals	FAC App	FAC Goals	Others App	Others Goals
BIGNOT Marcus	25+2		3		1			
BOERTIEN Paul	2							
CHARNOCK Phil	14+2	1	5					
COLLINS James	8+5		0+1		0+1			
CRAMB Colin	33+4	6	5	1	1			
CRITCHLEY Neil	0+1							
FORAN Mark	11+2		2					
GRANT John	1+3		0+2					
HULSE Robert	0+4	1						
INCE Clayton	0+1							
JACK Rod	21+2	4	2					
KEARTON Jason	46		5		1			
LIGHTFOOT Chris	16+5	1	0+1					
LITTLE Colin	34+3	4	4+1	4	1	1		
LUNT Kenny	39+4	3	5		1			
MACAULEY Steve	35+2	4	4		1			
NEWBY Jon	5+1							
RIVERS Mark	29+3	7	4	2				
SMITH Peter	0+6							
SMITH Shaun	30+1	2	5	1	1			
SORVEL Neil	46	6	5		1			
STREET Kevin	20+8	1	0+2		1			
TAIT Paul	19+14	6			1			
UNSWORTH Lee	3+5		2					
WALTON Dave	8+3							
WRIGHT David	44+1		3		1			
WRIGHT Steve	17+6		1					

CRYSTAL PALACE (DIV 1: 15th)

	P/FL App	P/FL Goals	FLC App	FLC Goals	FAC App	FAC Goals	Others App	Others Goals
AUSTIN Dean	45	2	4		1			
BRADBURY Lee	9+1	2	3+1	1				
CARLISLE Wayne	23+3	3	0+1					

	P/FL App	P/FL Goals	FLC App	FLC Goals	FAC App	FAC Goals	Others App	Others Goals
COLE Ashley	14	1						
DE ORNELAS Fernando	5+4							
DIGBY Fraser	38		4		1			
EVANS Steve	0+1		0+1					
FORSSELL Mikael	13	3						
FOSTER Craig	17+3	1			1			
FRAMPTON Andy	6+3		3		1			
FULLARTON Jamie	13							
FUMACA	2+1		2					
GREGG Matt	6							
HANKIN Sean	0+1							
HARRIS Richard	1+5		1+1					
HIBBURT James	1+3							
HUNT Steve	0+3							
KABBA Steve	1							
LAUNDERS Brian	1+1							
LINIGHAN Andy	44+1	2	2		1			
McKENZIE Leon	24+1	4			1			
MARTIN Andrew	10+9	2						
MAUTONE Steve	2							
MORRISON Clint	28+1	13	4	2				
MULLINS Hayden	45	10	3	1	1			
PHELAN Terry	14							
RIZZO Nicky	2+15		0+3	1	1			
RODGER Simon	34	2	4	1	1			
SHARPLING Chris	1+5							
SMITH Jamie	27		4	2	0+1			
SVENSSON Matt	20+4	9	2		1			
THOMSON Steve	17+4		2+1	1				
TUTTLE Dave	0+1		1					
WOOZLEY Dave	14+9		3+1		0+1			
ZHIYI Fan	29	1	2	1	1			

DARLINGTON (DIV 3: 4th)

	P/FL App	P/FL Goals	FLC App	FLC Goals	FAC App	FAC Goals	Others App	Others Goals
ASPIN Neil	29		1		2		2	
ATKINSON Brian	26+4		2		2		1+1	
BAKER Steve	4+1							
BENNETT Gary	4+1		1					
BRUMWELL Phil	9+9				1+1		3	
CAMPBELL Paul	3+6	2	0+2		1		0+1	
CARRUTHERS Martin	0+6							
COLLETT Andy	13		2		1		3	
DUFFIELD Peter	21+12	12	0+2		2	1	3	
FINCH Keith					0+1			
GABBIADINI Marco	41+1	24	2	1	1	1	4	2
GRAY Martin	40+1		2		2		4	
HEANEY Neil	33+3	5	1		3		3	
HECKINGBOTTOM Paul	44+1	1	2		3	1	4	
HICKEY Ben			0+1					
HIMSWORTH Gary	13+6		2		1+1			
HJORTH Jesper	8+14	6			0+2		2+1	
HOLSGROVE Paul	1+2						0+1	
KILTY Martin	1+1							
LIDDLE Craig	45	1	2		3		4	1
NAYLOR Glenn	8+17	3			0+2		1+3	
NOGAN Lee	19+12	2	2	2	3		1+2	1
OLIVER Michael	35+2	2	1+1	1	3		4	
REED Adam	20+3		2		0+1		1+2	
RUSSELL Craig	11+1	2						
SAMWAYS Mark	33+1				2		1	
TAYLOR Martin	4							
TUTILL Steve	25+2				3	1	3	
WAINWRIGHT Neil	16+1	4						

DERBY COUNTY (PREM: 16th)

	P/FL App	P/FL Goals	FLC App	FLC Goals	FAC App	FAC Goals	Others App	Others Goals
BAIANO Francesco	5+4		2					
BECK Mikkel	5+6	1	2	1	0+1			
BOERTIEN Paul	0+2		0+1					
BOHINEN Lars	8+5		2					
BORBOKIS Vass	6+6		3	1	1			
BURLEY Craig	18	5			1			

	P/FL App	P/FL Goals	FLC App	FLC Goals	FAC App	FAC Goals	Others App	Others Goals
BURTON Deon	15+ 4	4	1+ 1		0+ 1			
CARBONARI Horacio	29	2	1		1			
CHRISTIE Malcolm	10+11	5	0+ 1					
DELAP Rory	34	8	2		1			
DORIGO Tony	20+ 3		3		1			
ELLIOTT Steve	18+ 2		3		1			
ERANIO Stefano	17+ 2		1					
FUERTES Esteban	8	1	2	1				
HARPER Kevin	0+ 5		1+ 2					
HOULT Russell	10		3					
JACKSON Richard	0+ 2							
JOHNSON Seth	36	1	1+ 1		0+ 1			
KINKLADZE Georgi	12+ 5	1			1			
LAURSEN Jacob	36	1	2					
MORRIS Lee	2+ 1							
MURRAY Adam	1+ 7							
NIMNI Avi	2+ 2	1			1			
POOM Mart	28				1			
POWELL Darryl	31	2	1		1			
PRIOR Spencer	15+ 5		3					
RIGGOTT Chris	0+ 1							
ROBINSON Marvin	3+ 5							
SCHNOOR Stefan	22+ 7		0+ 1					
STRUPAR Branko	13+ 2	5						
STURRIDGE Dean	14+11	6	1+ 1	1	1			
EVERTON (PREM: 13th)								
BALL Michael	14+11	1	2		1+ 1			
BARMBY Nick	37	9	0+ 1		5	1		
CADAMARTERI Danny	3+14	1	2	1	0+ 2			
CAMPBELL Kevin	26	12	0+ 2		5			
CLELAND Alex	3+ 6		2		1			
COLLINS John	33+ 2	2	1		4			
DEGN Peter			1					
DUNNE Richard	27+ 4		1		4			
FARRELLY Gareth			1					
GEMMILL Scot	6+ 8	1	2		0+ 1			
GERRARD Paul	34				3			
GOUGH Richard	29	1			3			
GRANT Tony	0+ 2							
HUGHES Mark	9	1						
HUGHES Stephen	11	1						
HUTCHISON Don	28+ 3	6	1		5			
JEFFERS Francis	16+ 5	6	0+ 2		4+ 1			
JEVONS Phil	2+ 1		1					
JOHNSON Tommy	0+ 3							
MILLIGAN Jamie	0+ 1							
MOORE Joe-Max	11+ 4	6			1+ 2	2		
MYHRE Thomas	4				2			
PEMBRIDGE Mark	29+ 2	2			5			
PHELAN Terry	0+ 1		1					
SIMONSEN Steve	0+ 1		2					
UNSWORTH David	32+ 1	6	1		5	3		
WARD Mitch	6+ 4		1+ 1					
WATSON Dave	5+ 1				0+ 1			
WEIR Davie	35	2	2		5			
XAVIER Abel	18+ 2		1		2			
EXETER CITY (DIV 3: 21st)								
ALEXANDER Gary	37	16	1		3	1	4	2
BENNETT Frankie	8+ 1	1						
BLAKE Noel	2+ 5	1					0+ 2	
BOYLAN Lee	3+ 3	1			2			
BRADLEY Shayne	6+ 2	1			1			
BRESLAN Geoff	16+13		2		2+ 1		4	1
BROWN Aaron	4+ 1	1						
BUCKLE Paul	27	1			3+ 1		5	1
CORNFORTH John	12	2						
CURRAN Chris	36+ 2	1			4		4	
DEWHURST Rob	21+ 2	2	2		2+ 1		0+ 1	
ELLINGTON Lee	0+ 1						0+ 1	

	P/FL App	P/FL Goals	FLC App	FLC Goals	FAC App	FAC Goals	Others App	Others Goals
FLACK Steve	19+21	2	2		2+ 2	2	2+ 1	
GALE Shaun	18+ 5	1	1		1	1	2+ 1	
GITTENS Jon	38	2	1		4		4	
HOLLOWAY Chris	20+ 4	1	2		0+ 1		2	
INGLETHORPE Alex	0+ 1						1	
JARMAN Lee	7						0+ 1	
LEE David	3+ 1						2	
LOVELL Steve	4+ 1	1						
McCONNELL Barry	16+ 9	1	2	1	0+ 2		3	
MATTHEWS Jason	11+ 1		0+ 1		0+ 1		4	
NAYLOR Stuart	31		2		4		1	
NYAMAH Kofi	23+12	1	1		1		3+ 1	
POTTER Danny	4							
POWER Graeme	28+ 1		1		3		2	
REES Jason	42+ 1	4	2		4		5	
RICHARDSON Jon	35	1	2		4		4	
ROBINSON Jamie	11+ 1				3		0+ 1	
ROWBOTHAM Darren	13+ 5	2						
SMITH Pete	3+ 4		0+ 1		1			
SPEAKMAN Rob	4+13	3	0+ 2		0+ 1		1+ 3	2
VANNINEN Jukka	3+ 2						1	
WAUGH Warren	0+ 3						1	
WILKINSON John			0+ 1					
WORRALL Ben	1+ 3		1					
FULHAM (DIV 1: 9th)								
BALL Kevin	15+ 3				2			
BETSY Kevin	0+ 2							
BREVETT Rufus	22+ 1		6+ 1		2			
CADAMARTERI Danny	3+ 2	1						
CLARK Lee	42	8	6	1	4			
COLEMAN Chris	40	3	7	1	3	1		
COLLINS Wayne	6+13	1	2+ 1	2	3+ 1	2		
COLLYMORE Stan	3+ 3		1+ 2	1				
DAVIS Sean	15+11		2+ 2	2	1+ 1	1		
FINNAN Steve	35	2	6		4	1		
GOLDBAEK Bjarne	16+ 2	3			1			
HAYLES Barry	21+14	5	3+ 1	2	3+ 1	2		
HAYWARD Steve	34+ 3		5+ 1		2	1		
HORSFIELD Geoff	28+ 3	7	6	6	3	1		
HUGHES Stephen	3		1					
LEWIS Eddie	6+ 2							
MELVILLE Andy	40	3	6		4			
MORGAN Simon	26+ 2		5		2			
NEILSON Alan	4+ 1	1	0+ 1					
PESCHISOLIDO Paul	18+12	4	4	3	1+ 1			
PHELAN Terry	17	2						
RIEDLE Karl-Heinz	15+ 6	5			1			
SYMONS Kit	27+ 2	2	4+ 1		4			
TAYLOR Maik	46		7		4			
TROLLOPE Paul	13+ 9		5+ 1		0+ 2			
UHLENBEEK Gus	11+ 5		1+ 1					
GILLINGHAM (DIV 2: 3rd)								
ASABA Carl	7+ 4	6			0+ 1		2	
ASHBY Barry	41	3	4		8	1	4	1
BARTRAM Vince	43		2		8		3	
BASS Jon	4+ 3							
BROWNING Marcus	0+ 1				1+ 1		0+ 1	
BRYANT Matt	3+ 3		0+ 1		1			
BUTLER Steve	2+ 8	2			2+ 1		0+ 3	1
BUTTERS Guy	38+ 2	2	2		8	1	4	
EDGE Roland	25+ 1	1			7+ 1		3	
GALLOWAY Mick	1+ 1		0+ 1					
GOODEN Ty	15+ 1	4					3	1
HESSENTHALER Andy	41+ 1	5	4	2	6+ 1		3+ 1	1
HODGE John	1+14		2+ 1		3+ 1	1		
LEE Chris	1+ 2		1+ 1					
LEWIS Junior	37+ 5	6	2		5+ 2		4	
McGLINCHEY Brian	6+ 7	1	3+ 1		4	1	1	
MATTHEWS Lee	2+ 3							

	P/FL App	P/FL Goals	FLC App	FLC Goals	FAC App	FAC Goals	Others App	Others Goals
MAUTONE Steve	1							
MILLER Barry	1+ 3		1+ 2					
MITTEN Charlie							1	
NOSWORTHY Nayron	15+14	1	1+ 2		2+ 6		0+ 2	
OMOYINMI Manny	7+ 2	3	2					
ONUORA Iffy	21+ 1	6					3	1
PATTERSON Mark	9		1					
PENNOCK Adrian	34		4		6	1	4	
PINNOCK James	0+ 2		0+ 1				1	
ROWE Rodney	8+14	4					1	
SAUNDERS Mark	20+ 6	1	3		6+ 1	1	1	
SMITH Paul	43+ 1	1	3		7		2+ 2	1
SOUTHALL Nicky	45	9	3	1	7	3	4	
TAYLOR Robert	13+ 2	15	1+ 1	1	2	2		
THOMSON Andy	20+ 8	9	3		5	4	0+ 1	1
WILLIAMS Tony	2		2					
GRIMSBY TOWN (DIV 1: 20th)								
ALLEN Bradley	12+19	8	0+ 4		0+ 2	1		
ASHCROFT Lee	31+ 3	12	5	1	1			
BLACK Kingsley	15+16	2	3		0+ 1			
BLOOMER Matt	0+ 2							
BUCKLEY Adam	8+ 5		0+ 1		2			
BURNETT Wayne	7+ 3		1+ 1					
BUTTERFIELD Danny	21+ 8		4		1+ 1			
CHAPMAN Ben	1				1			
CLARE Daryl	13+ 4	3	0+ 2					
COLDICOTT Stacy	42+ 2	2	5	1	2			
COYNE Danny	44		4		1			
CROUDSON Steve	2+ 1		1		1			
DONOVAN Kevin	41	3	5	1	2			
GALLIMORE Tony	38+ 1		2	1	1			
GROVES Paul	43	3	5	2	1			
HAMILTON Ian	6	1						
LESTER Jack	23+ 3	4	5	3	2			
LEVER Mark	35		0+ 1		2			
LIVINGSTONE Steve	23+ 6		3		2	2		
McDERMOTT John	23+ 3		1+ 1		1+ 1			
NICHOLLS Mark	6							
POUTON Alan	19+16	1	3+ 2		1+ 1			
SMITH David	34+ 2	1	4+ 1	1				
SMITH Richard	19		4		1			
HALIFAX TOWN (DIV 3: 18th)								
ADAMSON Chris	7							
BRADSHAW Mark	17+ 8	1			1+ 1			
BUTLER Lee	38				3		1	
BUTLER Peter	30		2		3			
CLARKE Chris	0+ 1							
CLARKE Matt	8+11				2+ 1		1	
CULLEN Jon	11	5						
FITZPATRICK Ian	2+ 6							
GAUGHAN Steve	29+ 9		2	1	2		1	
HERBERT Robert	1+ 3						0+ 1	
HOLT Grant	0+ 4						1	
HULME Kevin	2+ 1		0+ 1					
JACKSON Justin	0+ 1							
JONES Gary	8	1						
JULES Mark	38+ 4		2		2		1	
KERRIGAN Steve	7	3						
LUCAS Richard	10+ 2		0+ 1		1+ 1		0+ 1	
MIDDLETON Craig	10	1						
MITCHELL Graham	45	2	2		3	1		
MURPHY Stephen	10+ 5	1	2					
NEWTON Chris	4+ 4				0+ 1			
PAINTER Robbie	38+ 4	8	2		3		1	
PARKS Tony	1		2					
PATERSON Jamie	37+ 3	7	2		3	1		
POTTER Lee	13+ 6	2						
POWER Lee	3+ 4	1	0+ 2					
REILLY Alan	15+ 5						1	

	P/FL App	P/FL Goals	FLC App	FLC Goals	FAC App	FAC Goals	Others App	Others Goals
RICHARDS Ian	5+ 1							
ROWE Rodney	7+ 2	2			1			
RUSSELL Matthew	3+ 4		0+ 1					
SERTORI Mark	5		2					
STAMP Darryn	5							
STANSFIELD James	10+ 2				1		1	
STONEMAN Paul	36+ 1	4	2		2		1	
TATE Chris	18	4	2		2	1		
WILDER Chris	31	1			3		1	
WILLIAMS Mike	2+ 1				1		1	
HARTLEPOOL UNITED (DIV 3: 7th)								
ARNISON Paul	5+ 3	1					2	
BARRON Michael	40		2		2		5	
BEAVERS Paul	2+ 5						1	
BOYD Adam	0+ 4	1					0+ 2	
CLARK Ian	34+10	6	1		1+ 1		3+ 2	
COPPINGER James	6+ 4	3					1	
DIBBLE Andy	6		2				2+ 1	
DI LELLA Gustavo	3		1+ 1	1				
FITZPATRICK Lee	16+ 8	2					1+ 1	
FREESTONE Chris	15+12	4	2		2		3	
HENDERSON Kevin	23+12	8	0+ 1		0+ 1		1	1
HOLLUND Martin	40				2		3	
INGRAM Denny	6+ 1		1+ 1					
JONES Gary	30+ 3	6	2		2	1	2+ 2	
KNOWLES Darren	43+ 1		2		2		3	
LEE Graeme	38	7	2		2		4	1
McAVOY Andy	5+11						1+ 3	
MASON Gary	5+ 1				1		1	
MIDGLEY Craig	2+15		0+ 1				2+ 1	1
MILLER Tommy	44	14	2	1	2		4	1
PERKINS Chris	7+ 1		1					
SHILTON Sam	16+ 5	3			2		2	
STEPHENSON Paul	46	5	2	1	1+ 1		5	
STRODDER Gary	28+ 1		1				3	
TENNEBO Thomas	6+ 5		1				1	
VINDHEIM Rune	7				1			
WEST Colin	0+ 1						0+ 1	
WESTWOOD Chris	33+ 4				2		5	
HUDDERSFIELD TOWN (DIV 1: 8th)								
ALLISON Wayne	0+ 3		0+ 1					
ARMSTRONG Alun	4+ 2							
ARMSTRONG Craig	37+ 2		5+ 1		1			
BAKER Steve	3							
BALDRY Simon	5+14	1	0+ 1					
BEECH Chris	34+ 1	9	4	1				
BERESFORD David			0+ 1					
DONIS George	10+10		3+ 1		0+ 1			
DYSON Jon	22+ 6	2	2+ 2					
EDMONDSON Darren	2+ 3							
EDWARDS Rob	1+ 8	1	2					
FACEY Delroy	0+ 2							
GORRÉ Dean	26+ 2	4	3	1	1			
GRAY Kevin	16+ 2	2	2		1			
HAY Chris	2+ 5							
HEARY Thomas	1							
HODOUTO Kwami	1+ 1		1					
HOLLAND Chris	16+ 1	1						
HORNE Barry	6+ 8		3					
IRONS Kenny	39+ 1	3	6	2	1			
JENKINS Steve	33		2		1			
LUCKETTI Chris	26		5	1				
MAY David	1							
MONKOU Ken	19	1	4					
NGONGE Michel	0+ 4							
SCHOFIELD Danny	0+ 2		0+ 2		0+ 1			
SELLARS Scott	23+11	1	1+ 1	1	1			
SENIOR Michael			0+ 1					
SMITH Martin	10+ 2	4						

	P/FL App	P/FL Goals	FLC App	FLC Goals	FAC App	FAC Goals	Others App	Others Goals
STEWART Marcus	29	14	6	1	1			
THORNLEY Ben	16+12	1	4		1			
VAESEN Nico	46		6		1			
VINCENT Jamie	33+ 3	2	1+ 2		1			
WIJNHARD Clyde	45	15	6	1	1			
HULL CITY (DIV 3: 14th)								
ALCIDE Colin	10+ 2	1	3+ 1	2	0+ 2			
BAKER Matt	0+ 2		0+ 1				1	
BETSY Kevin	1+ 1						1	
BOLDER Adam	18+ 1						2+ 1	
BRABIN Gary	37	3	4		3		1	
BRACEY Lee	10		4		3		1	
BRADSHAW Gary	5+ 7							
BROWN David	39+ 6	6	4	2	5	3	2	
BYWATER Steve	4							
CULKIN Nick	4							
D'AURIA David	10+ 2		1+ 2		3			
EDWARDS Michael	36+ 4	1	3		5	2	1+ 1	
EYRE John	24	8	4	2	2+ 1	2	2	
FRENCH Jon							0+ 1	
GOODISON Ian	17+ 1				3+ 1		1	
GREAVES Mark	38	3	2		4	1	2	
HARPER Steve	36+ 2	4	4		5		2	
HARRIS Jason	18+11	4	0+ 3		0+ 1		1+ 1	
HARRISON Gerry	3							
JOYCE Warren	19	1	1		2		2	1
KNIGHT Richard	1							
MANN Neil	2		1					
MORGAN Steve	17+ 2	1			3+ 1		2	1
MORLEY Ben	0+ 1							
PERRY Jason	1						1+ 1	
QUIGLEY Michael	0+ 3						1	
SCHOFIELD John	13+12		4		2+ 2		1+ 1	
SWALES Steve	17+ 3		2+ 1				1	
WHITMORE Theo	17	2			5		1	
WHITNEY Jon	19+ 2	1			2		2	
WHITTLE Justin	38		4		2+ 2		2	
WHITWORTH Neil	0+ 1							
WILLIAMS Gareth	12+ 1	1	2		1		1	
WILSON Steve	27				2		1	
WOOD Jamie	13+19	6	1+ 2		3+ 1	1	1+ 1	
IPSWICH TOWN (DIV 1: 3rd)								
AXELDAHL Jonas	1+15		0+ 3		0+ 1			
BROWN Wayne	20+ 5		2		1		1+ 1	
CLAPHAM Jamie	44+ 2	2	4	2	1		3	1
CLEGG Michael	3							
CROFT Gary	14+ 7	1					2+ 1	
FRIARS Sean	0+ 1							
HOLLAND Matt	46	10	4		1		3	
JOHNSON David	44	22	4	1	1		3	
LOGAN Richard	0+ 1							
McGREAL John	34		4		1		1	
MAGILTON Jim	33+ 5	4	3		1		3	3
MIDGLEY Neil	1+ 3	1						
MOWBRAY Tony	35+ 1	1			1		3	1
NAYLOR Richard	19+17	8	3+ 1		0+ 1		0+ 2	1
REUSER Martijn	2+ 6	2					0+ 3	2
SCOWCROFT Jamie	40+ 1	13	3+ 1	2	1		2	
STEWART Marcus	9+ 1	2					3	3
STOCKWELL Micky	21+14	2	3+ 1		1			
THETIS Manu	15+ 1		3				1	
VENUS Mark	28	2	3	1			3	
WILNIS Fabian	30+ 5		1+ 1		1		1+ 1	
WRIGHT Jermaine	21+13	1	3		0+ 1		1	
WRIGHT Richard	46		4		1		3	
LEEDS UNITED (PREM: 3rd)								
BAKKE Eirik	24+ 5	2	2		3	4	9+ 1	2
BATTY David	16		2				4	

	P/FL App	P/FL Goals	FLC App	FLC Goals	FAC App	FAC Goals	Others App	Others Goals
BOWYER Lee	31+ 2	5	1		3	1	11	5
BRIDGES Michael	32+ 2	19	2		1+ 1		12	2
DUBERRY Michael	12+ 1	1	0+ 1		1		1	
HAALAND Alfie	7+ 6						5+ 1	
HARTE Ian	33	6	1		3	1	12	1
HIDEN Martin	0+ 1							
HOPKIN David	10+ 4	1	1				2+ 1	
HUCKERBY Darren	9+24	2	0+ 1		1+ 2		1+ 8	1
JONES Matthew	5+ 6		0+ 1		0+ 1		3+ 2	
KELLY Garry	28+ 3		2		3		11	
KEWELL Harry	36	10	2		3	2	12	5
McPHALL Stephen	23+ 1	2	1+ 1		3		9	
MARTYN Nigel	38		2		3		12	
MILLS Danny	16+ 1	1	1	1	0+ 1		2	
RADEBE Lucas	31		2		2		11	2
SMITH Alan	20+ 6	4	1		2+ 1	1	2+ 6	1
WILCOX Jason	15+ 5	3			2		3+ 1	1
WOODGATE Jonathan	32+ 2	1	2		3		10	
LEICESTER CITY (PREM: 8th)								
ARPHEXAD Pegguy	9+ 2		3		3+ 1			
CAMPBELL Stuart	1+ 3		0+ 2		0+ 3			
COLLYMORE Stan	6	4						
COTTEE Tony	30+ 3	13	3		2			
DUDFIELD Lawrie	0+ 2							
EADIE Darren	15+ 1				3			
ELLIOTT Matt	37	6	6	3	5	2		
FENTON Graham	1+ 1		0+ 4	1	0+ 3			
FLOWERS Tim	29		5+ 1		2			
GILCHRIST Phil	17+10	1	5+ 1		3			
GOODWIN Tommy	1							
GUNNLAUGSSON Arnar	2		0+ 2		2+ 1			
GUPPY Steve	29+ 1	2	5		2			
HESKEY Emile	23	7	8	1	4			
IMPEY Andy	28+ 1	1	5+ 2		2+ 1			
IZZET Muzzy	32	8	6	1	2	1		
LENNON Neil	31	1	6	1	2			
MARSHALL Ian	2+19		3+ 1	3	0+ 1			
OAKES Stefan	15+ 7	1	7	2	3			
SAVAGE Robbie	35	1	7		5			
SINCLAIR Frank	34		7		3			
STEWART Jordan	0+ 1				0+ 1			
TAGGART Gerry	30+ 1	6	7+ 1	1	5			
THOMAS Danny	0+ 3							
WALSH Steve	5+ 6		2+ 1	1	3+ 1			
WILSON Stuart			0+ 2					
ZAGORAKIS Theo	6+11	1	3+ 4		4			
LEYTON ORIENT (DIV 3: 19th)								
AMPADU Kwame	43		4		2	1	1	
BARRETT Scott	29		2		1			
BAYES Ashley	17		2		1		1	
BEALL Matthew	22+11	1	2		1			
BRKOVIC Ahmet	25+ 4	5			2		1	
CANHAM Scott	1		0+ 1					
CARTER Rob	0+ 2		1					
CHRISTIE Iyseden	22+14	7	2		1+ 1		1	
CLARK Simon	19	1	1		2		1	
CURRAN Danny			0+ 1					
DOWNER Simon	24		1+ 1		1		1	
GOULD Ronnie	0+ 2							
GOUGH Neil	1+ 3		0+ 1					
GRIFFITHS Carl	11	4						
HARRIS Andy	11+ 4		4					
HICKS Stuart	13+ 1		2		1		1	
HOCKTON Danny	1+ 4		1					
HOLLIGAN Gavin	1		1					
IBEHRE Jabo	0+ 3							
INGLETHORPE Alex	12+ 4	2	1	1	0+ 2			
JOSEPH Matt	38+ 3		2+ 1		2		0+ 1	
JOSEPH Roger	0+ 1							

	P/FL		FLC		FAC		Others	
	App	Goals	App	Goals	App	Goals	App	Goals
LING Martin	14	1	3		0+ 1			
LOCKWOOD Matt	41	6	4	2	2			
LOW Josh	2+ 3	1	1					
McELHOLM Benny	3							
McGHEE David	17+ 6	1					1	
McLEAN Aaron	0+ 3						0+ 1	
MARTIN John	8						1	
MORRISON Dave	5+ 8		1+ 2					
MURRAY Jay	0+ 2							
PARSONS David	1							
RICHARDS Tony	9+ 8	2	1+ 1				1	
ROWBOTHAM Darren	4+ 2						0+ 1	
SHOREY Nicky	4+ 3							
SIMBA Amara	8+ 5	3	0+ 2		2			
SMITH Dean	44	4	4		2	1		
WALSCHAERTS Wim	32+ 4	3	2+ 1		1		1	
WATTS Steve	21+11	6	2+ 1	1	1+ 1			
WEBB Simon	3+ 1							
LINCOLN CITY (DIV 3: 15th)								
AGOGO Junior	3	1						
BARNETT Dave	20+ 2	3	1		3	1	1	
BARNETT Jason	17+ 1		1					
BATTERSBY Tony	7+ 9	3					1	
BIMSON Stuart	15+ 5				2		1	
BRANSTON Guy	4		2					
BROWN Grant	25+ 1							
FINNIGAN John	36+ 1	2	2		3		1	
FLEMING Terry	41	5	2	1	3		1	
GAIN Peter	20+12	2	2		2			
GALLOWAY Mick	5							
GORDON Gavin	39+ 2	11	2	1	3	1	1	
HENRY Anthony	14+ 3	1			2		1	1
HOLMES Steve	9	2						
LESCOTT Aaron	3+ 2							
LEWIS Graham	3+ 2							
MARRIOTT Alan	18							
MAYO Paul	19							
MILLER Paul	37+ 3	7	1		3		1	
PEACOCK Richard	16+ 8	3	1+ 1	1				
PHILLIPS David	6+2				1+ 1			
PHILPOTT Lee	18+ 5	3	1+ 1		1+ 1		0+ 1	
POPPLETON David	4+ 1		1+ 1					
RICHARDSON Barry	22				3		1	
SMITH Paul	23+ 4	5	1+ 1		3	1	1	
STANT Phil	3+15	3	0+ 1		0+ 3			
STONES Craig	0+ 3							
THORPE Lee	38+ 4	16	2	1	3			
VAUGHAN John	6		2					
WELSH Steve	32		1				1	
WILKINS Ian	3+ 1				1+ 1			
LIVERPOOL (PREM: 4th)								
BERGER Patrik	34	9	1+ 1		1			
CAMARA Titi	22+11	9	0+ 2		2	1		
CARRAGHER Jamie	33+ 3		2		2			
FOWLER Robbie	8+ 6	3						
FRIEDEL Brad	2		2					
GERRARD Steve	26+ 3	1			2			
HAMANN Dietmar	27+ 1	1			2			
HEGGEM Vegard	10+12	1	1+ 2					
HENCHOZ Stephane	29		2		2			
HESKEY Emile	12	3						
HYYPIA Sami	38	2	2		2			
KIPPE Frode			0+ 1					
MATTEO Dominic	32				1+ 1	1		
MAXWELL Layton			1	1				
MEIJER Erik	7+14		3	2				
MURPHY Danny	9+14	3	2	3	2			
NEWBY Jon	0+ 1		0+ 1		0+ 2			
OWEN Michael	22+ 5	11	2	1	1			
REDKNAPP Jamie	18+ 4	3	1					
RIEDLE Karl-Heinz	0+ 1		1	2				
SMICER Vlad	13+ 8	1	2		2			
SONG Rigobert	14+ 4		2		0+ 1			
STAUNTON Steve	7+ 5		3	1	1			
THOMPSON David	19+ 8	3	3		0+ 1			
TRAORE Djimi			2					
WESTERVELD Sander	36		1		2			
LUTON TOWN (DIV 2: 13th)								
ABBEY Nathan	32+ 1		2		5		1	
AYRES James							1	
BOYCE Emmerson	23+ 7	1	2		0+ 2		1	
DOHERTY Gary	40	6	0+ 2	1	5	2	1	
DOUGLAS Stuart	35+ 5	3	2		5	1	1	
FOTIADIS Andrew	8+15	2	0+ 2					
FRASER Stuart	20	1	1		5		1	
GEORGE Liam	35+ 7	13	0+ 1		5	2	1	
GRAY Phil	28+ 1	11	2		1	1		
JOHNSON Marvin	44				5		1	
KANDOL Tresor	1+ 3		1	1				
LOCKE Adam	27+ 7	3			3+ 1		1	
McGOWAN Gavin	10+ 3							
McINDOE Michael	2+15		2		0+ 2			
McKINNON Ray	0+ 3		1					
McLAREN Paul	25+ 4	1	1		4	1		
MIDGLEY Neil	8+ 2	3						
READ Paul							0+ 1	
ROBERTS Ben	14							
SCARLETT Andre	2+ 1						0+ 1	
SODJE Efe	5+ 4		2		2+ 1		1	
SPRING Matthew	44+ 1	6	1		5	2	1	
TAYLOR Matthew	39+ 2	4	1		5	1		
THORPE Tony	3+ 1	1						
WATTS Julian	45	4	2		5			
WHITE Alan	16+ 3	1	2					
ZAHANA-ONI Landry	0+ 1							
MACCLESFIELD TOWN (DIV 3: 13th)								
ABBEY George	12+ 6		1		0+ 2			
ASKEY John	37+ 3	15	1+ 1		2		1	
BAMBER Mike	0+ 1							
BARKER Richie	35	16	2		2		1	1
BROWN Greg	2+ 3		0+ 1					
BYRNE Chris	5							
COLLINS Simon	37+ 2	3	1		2		1	
DAVIES Simon	30+ 6	1	2		2		1	1
DURKAN Kieran	41+ 1	6	0+ 1		2		1	
HITCHEN Steve	2+ 3							
INGRAM Rae	35+ 1		1		2		0+ 1	
KNIGHT Richard	3							
MARTIN Lee	21				2		1	
MOORE Neil	12+ 3	2					1	
MUNROE Karl	1+ 4							
O'NEILL Paul	0+ 1							
PRICE Ryan	11+ 1		2					
PRIEST Chris	34+ 2	4	2	1	2			
RIOCH Greg	42	5	2		2		1	
SEDGEMORE Ben	31+ 4	1	2		2		1	
TINSON Darren	46	1	2		2		1	
TOMLINSON Graeme	7+11	2	1+ 1		0+ 2			
WARE Paul	9+ 9	2	1					
WHITEHEAD Damien	10+13	6					0+ 1	
WHITTAKER Stuart	2+ 7		1+ 1		0+ 1		0+ 1	
WILLIAMS Tony	11							
WOOD Steve	30+ 6	1	1+ 1		0+ 1		1	
MANCHESTER CITY (DIV 1: 2nd)								
ALLSOP Danny	0+ 4		0+ 4					
BISHOP Ian	25+12	2	2+ 2		2	2		
BROWN Michael			1					

	P/FL App	P/FL Goals	FLC App	FLC Goals	FAC App	FAC Goals	Others App	Others Goals
COOKE Terry	6+7		3+1	1				
CROOKS Lee	9+11	1	3+1					
DICKOV Paul	22+12	5	2	1	1			
EDGHILL Richard	40+1	1	3		2			
FENTON Nicky			0+1					
GOATER Shaun	40	23	3	3	2	3		
GRANT Tony	4+4				1			
GRANVILLE Danny	28+7	2			2			
HORLOCK Kevin	36+2	10	3	1	2			
JOBSON Richard	43+1	3	3		2			
KENNEDY Mark	41	8	4	2	2			
MILLS Lee	1+2							
MORRISON Andy	12		2					
PEACOCK Lee	4+4				1+1			
POLLOCK Jamie	17+7	3	1		1			
PRIOR Spencer	9	3						
TAYLOR Gareth	8+9	5	2+1	1				
TAYLOR Robert	14+2	5						
TIATTO Danny	26+9		3					
VAUGHAN Tony	0+1		0+1					
WEAVER Nicky	45		4		2			
WHITLEY Jeff	41+1	4	3		0+2			
WHITLEY Jim	0+1							
WIEKENS Gerard	32+2	1	2		2			
WRIGHT Tommy	1							
WRIGHT-PHILLIPS Shaun	2+2		0+1					
MANCHESTER UNITED (PREM: 1st)								
BECKHAM David	30+1	6					16+1	3
BERG Henning	16+6	1					14+1	
BOSNICH Mark	23		1				11	
BUTT Nicky	21+11	3					8+2	1
CHADWICK Luke			1					
CLEGG Michael	0+2		1				1+1	
COLE Andy	23+5	19					17	3
CRUYFF Jordi	1+7	3	1				3+5	
CULKIN Nick	0+1							
CURTIS John	0+1		1				0+1	
FORTUNE Quinton	4+2	2					2+4	2
GIGGS Ryan	30	6					14	1
GREENING Jon	1+3		1				2+2	
HEALY David			0+1					
HIGGINBOTHAM Danny	2+1		1				1+1	
IRWIN Denis	25	3					17	
JOHNSEN Ronny	2+1							
KEANE Roy	28+1	5					16	7
MAY David	0+1						1+1	
NEVILLE Gary	22						13	
NEVILLE Phil	25+4						10+4	
O'SHEA John			1					
RACHUBKA Paul							0+1	
SCHOLES Paul	27+4	9					14	3
SHERINGHAM Teddy	15+12	5					4+10	1
SILVESTRE Mikael	30+1						5+2	
SOLSKJAER Ole	15+13	12	1				8+9	3
STAM Jaap	33						18	
TAIBI Massimo	4							
TWISS Michael			1					
VAN DER GOUW Rai	11+3						9	
WALLWORK Ronny	0+5		1				1	
WELLENS Richard			0+1					
WILSON Mark	1+2						3+1	
YORKE Dwight	29+3	20					12+3	3
MANSFIELD TOWN (DIV 3: 17th)								
ALLARDYCE Craig	1+3		0+2					
ANDREWS John	29+1	1					2	
ASHER Alistair	29+6				0+1		1+1	
BACON Danny	6+2	2			0+1			
BASSINDER Gavin	1+3							
BLAKE Mark	40+3	1	1		1	1	2	
BOULDING Michael	16+17	6	1+1		0+1		1	
BOWLING Ian	10				1		2	
BROMBY Leigh	10	1					1	
CAMILIERI-GIOIA Carlo	0+2							
CLARKE Darrell	39	7			1		2	
COWLING Lee	3+5							
DISLEY Craig	2+3				1			
EVANS Andy	4+2							
FORTUNE Jay	4							
GARRATT Martin	4+2							
GREENACRE Chris	31	9					2	
HASSELL Bobby	8+3	1	2		1			
KERR David	10+8		1				0+1	
LAWRENCE Liam	0+2						0+1	
LINIGHAN David	28		2		1		1	
LORMOR Tony	33	9	2		1	1	2	1
MIMMS Bobby	5							
MUGGLETON Carl	9							
PEACOCK Lee	12	7	2	1				
PORTER Andy	5				1			
RICHARDSON Barry	6		2					
RICHARDSON Neil	31		2		1		1	
ROSCOE Andy	29+10	2	2		1		0+1	1
SISSON Michael	24+1	2	2				2	
TALLON Gary	11+2		1				1	
THOMAS Wayne	4+1							
THOMPSON Glyn	16							
WILLIAMS Lee	46		2		1		2	
WILLIAMSON Lee	0+4							
MIDDLESBROUGH (PREM: 12th)								
ARMSTRONG Alun	3+9	1	3					
BERESFORD Marlon	1							
CAMPBELL Andy	16+9	4	0+2					
COOPER Colin	26		4					
CUMMINS Michael	0+1							
DEANE Brian	29	9	3		1	1		
FESTA Gianluca	27+2	2	2		1			
FLEMING Curtis	27		4					
GASCOIGNE Paul	7+1	1	1+1		1			
GAVIN Jason	2+4		2		0+1			
GORDON Dean	3+1							
INCE Paul	32	3	3	1				
JUNINHO	24+4	4	4	1	1			
KILGANNON Sean	0+1							
MADDISON Neil	6+7		2					
MARINELLI Carlos	0+2							
MUSTOE Robbie	18+10		3+1		1			
O'NEILL Keith	14+2		3					
ORMEROD Anthony	0+1							
PALLISTER Gary	21	1	3		1			
RICARD Hamilton	28+6	12	4+1	2	1			
SCHWARZER Mark	37		5		1			
STAMP Phil	13+3		1+1		1			
STOCKDALE Robbie	6+5	1	2					
SUMMERBELL Mark	16+3		0+1					
TOWNSEND Andy	3+2							
VICKERS Steve	30+2		3+1	1	1			
ZIEGE Christian	29	6	3+1	1	1			
MILLWALL (DIV 2: 5th)								
BIRCHAM Marc	22	1	2		1			
BOWRY Bobby	3+2							
BUBB Byron	0+2							
BULL Ronnie	5+4							
CAHILL Tim	45	12	2		1		3	
DOLAN Joe	16+1	1	1					
DYCHE Sean	1							
FITZGERALD Scott	31		1		1		1	
GILKES Michael	26+3	2	0+1					
HARRIS Neil	34+4	25	1+1		0+1		3	

	P/FL App	P/FL Goals	FLC App	FLC Goals	FAC App	FAC Goals	Others App	Others Goals
IFILL Paul	38+ 6	11			1		3	
KINET Christophe	0+ 3						0+ 2	
LAWRENCE Matty	9						2	
LIVERMORE David	29+ 3	2	2				3	
MOODY Paul	24+ 8	11	1+ 1				3	
NEILL Lucas	27+ 4	1	2		1		3	
NETHERCOTT Stuart	37		2		1		3	
NEWMAN Ricky	14							
ODUNSI Leke	1+ 3							
REID Steven	11+10		1		1		1	
RYAN Robbie	33+ 1		2		1		3	
SADLIER Richard	21+ 6	5	1	1	1		0+ 1	
SHAW Paul	17+18	5	2		1		0+ 2	
SPINK Nigel	1							
STUART Jamie	9							
TUTTLE Dave	7+ 1						2	
WARNER Tony	45		2		1		3	
NEWCASTLE UNITED (PREM: 11th)								
BARTON Warren	33+ 1		1		6		5	
BEHARALL David	0+ 2							
CHARVET Laurent	1+ 1				1		2	
DABIZAS Nicos	29	3	1		6	2	6	
DOMI Didier	19+ 8	3	1		1+ 3	1	4	
DUMAS Franck	6						1	
DYER Kieron	27+ 3	3			5+ 1	1	3	
FERGUSON Duncan	17+ 6	6			6	3	2+ 1	1
FUMACA	1+ 4				0+ 1			
GALLACHER Kevin	15+ 5	2			4+ 1	1		
GAVILAN Diego	2+ 4	1						
GIVEN Shay	14		0+ 1		2			
GLASS Stephen	1+ 6	1	1		0+ 1		0+3	
GOMA Alain	14		1				2	
GRIFFIN Andy	1+ 2	1						
HAMILTON Des							0+ 1	
HARPER Steve	18		1		4		6	
HELDER	8	1			4			
HOWEY Steve	7+ 2				1			
HUGHES Aaron	22+ 5	2			3+ 1		2+ 1	
KARELSE John	3							
KETSBAIA Temuri	11+10				0+ 4		2+ 1	1
LEE Rob	30		1		4	1	6	
McCLEN Jamie	3+ 6						0+ 3	
MARCELINO Elena	10+ 1				1+ 1		2	
MARIC Silvio	3+10		1		0+ 1		3	2
PISTONE Alessandro	15	1	0+ 1		3		2	
ROBINSON Paul	2+ 9		0+ 1				0+ 4	1
SERRANT Carl	2						0+ 1	
SHEARER Alan	36+ 1	23	1		6	5	6	2
SOLANO Nol	29+ 1	3	1		3		6	1
SPEED Gary	36	9	1		6	3	6	1
WRIGHT Tommy	3							
NORTHAMPTON TOWN (DIV 3: 3rd)								
BATTERSBY Tony	0+ 3	1						
BYFIELD Darren	6	1	1	1				
CLARE Daryl	9+ 1	3						
CLARKSON Ian	1+ 1		0+ 1					
CORAZZIN Carlo	27+12	14	1+ 1	1	1			
CROWE Dean	3+ 2							
DICKSON Mark							0+ 1	
DOBSON Tony	1							
FORRESTER Jamie	9+ 1	6						
FRAIN John	40	2	2					
GIBB Ally	6+ 8		0+ 1		1		2	
GOULD James							0+ 1	
GREEN Richard	21	2					1	
HENDON Ian	44	2	2		1	1	1	
HODGE John	5+ 3							
HOPE Richard	14+ 3				0+ 1		2	
HOWARD Steve	32+ 9	10	2		0+ 1		1	

	P/FL App	P/FL Goals	FLC App	FLC Goals	FAC App	FAC Goals	Others App	Others Goals
HOWEY Lee	20		2		1		1	
HUGHES Garry	1+ 1						1	
HUNT James	33+ 4	1	2		1		2	
HUNTER Roy	15+ 2	3	1				1	
MATTHEW Damien	0+ 1							
MORROW Andy	0+ 4						2	
O'REILLY Alex	7		1				1	
PARRISH Sean	21+ 4	3					2	1
PEER Dean	6+ 3	1			1		1	
SAMPSON Ian	45	6	2		1			
SAVAGE Dave	43	5	2		1		1	
SPEDDING Duncan	44	1	2		1		2	
STURRIDGE Simon	10+ 8	1			1			
THOMPSON Ryan							0+ 1	
WELCH Keith	39		1		1		1	
WILSON Kevin	4+ 4	1	1+ 1		0+ 1			
NORWICH CITY (DIV 1: 12th)								
ANSELIN Cedric	15+ 4		2		1			
BELLAMY Craig	2+ 2	2						
BRADY Garry	6							
CAREY Shaun	18+ 3		2					
COOTE Adrian	4+ 7	1	1+ 1					
DALGLISH Paul	22+ 9	2	2+ 1		1			
DE BLASIIS Jean	26+ 2		1+ 1		1			
DERVELD Fernando	5							
DE WAARD Raymond	4							
DIOP Pape	2+ 5		1+ 2					
EADIE Darren	12+ 1	1	2					
FLEMING Craig	38+ 1	3	4		1			
FORBES Adrian	15+10	1			0+ 1			
FUGLESTAD Erik	26		1+ 1		1			
GIALLANZA Gaetano	2+ 1							
GREEN Robert	2+ 1							
HAMILTON Des	7							
JACKSON Matt	38		2		1			
KENTON Darren	23+ 3	1	0+ 1		0+ 1			
LLEWELLYN Chris	24+12	3	2+ 1		1	1		
MACKAY Malky	16+ 5		3					
McVEIGH Paul	0+ 1							
MARSHALL Andy	44		4		1			
MARSHALL Lee	21+12	5	2+ 1	1				
MILLIGAN Mike	9+ 2							
MULRYNE Phil	7+ 2		2					
ROBERTS Iwan	44	17	4	2	1			
RUSSELL Darel	28+ 5	4	2		1			
SUTCH Daryl	44+ 1	2	4		1			
WILSON Che	2+ 3		3					
NOTTINGHAM FOREST (DIV 1: 14th)								
ALLOU Bernard	1+ 3	1	2+ 2	1				
BART-WILLIAMS Chris	38	5	2	1	3	2		
BEASANT Dave	27		1+ 1		3			
BECK Mikkel	5	1						
BONALAIR Thierry	10+ 2	2	2+ 2					
BRENNAN Jim	22+ 3				3			
BURNS John	3		1					
CALDERWOOD Colin	6							
CHETTLE Steve	10+ 1	1	4					
COOPER Richard	0+ 1							
CROSSLEY Mark	19+ 1		4					
DAWSON Kevin	4+ 3				1			
DOIG Chris	8+ 3		1+ 1		1			
EDDS Gareth	2							
FREEDMAN Dougie	28+ 6	9	4	1	2+ 1	1		
FREEMAN David	0+ 3							
GRAY Andy	12+10		0+ 2		3			
GUINAN Steve	0+ 1		1					
HAREWOOD Marlon	18+16	4	4+ 1	1	1+ 1			
HJELDE Jon	26+ 7		3		2			
JOHN Stern	13+ 4	3			3			

Kieron Dyer (Newcastle United)

	P/FL App	P/FL Goals	FLC App	FLC Goals	FAC App	FAC Goals	Others App	Others Goals
JOHNSON Andy	24+ 1	2			1			
LESTER Jack	12+ 3	2						
LOUIS-JEAN Matthieu	26+ 1		3+ 1		1			
MANNINI Moreno	7+ 1		1					
MATRECANO Salvatore	11		2					
MELTON Steve	1+ 1		1					
MERINO Carlos	3+ 6		1+ 2					
PALMER Carlton	1+ 2	1						
PETRACHI Gianluca	10+ 3		2					
PLATT David	1+ 2							
PRUTTON David	33+ 1	2	2		3			
QUASHIE Nigel	25+ 3	2	5	1	1			
ROGERS Alan	36+ 1	9	5	1	1+ 1	1		
SCIMECA Ricardo	38		4		3			
TERRY John	5+ 1							
VAUGHAN Tony	10							
WILLIAMS Gareth	0+ 2				1			
WOAN Ian	1+10							
WRIGHT Ian	10	5						
NOTTS COUNTY (DIV 2: 8th)								
ALLSOP Danny	3	1						
ANGELL Brett	6	5						
BEADLE Peter	1+ 7		1+ 3					
BLACKMORE Clayton	21	2	4	2	1		0+ 1	
BOLLAND Paul	18+ 7	1	0+ 3		1		0+ 1	
BROUGH Michael	11							
CROSS David	0+ 1							
DARBY Duane	22+ 6	5	3+ 1	1				
DYER Alex	21+ 9	6			2		0+ 1	
FARRELL Sean	0+ 9							
FENTON Nicky	13	1					1	
FORD Ryan	0+ 1							
GIBSON Paul	1		1					
HEFFERNAN Paul	0+ 2							
HOLMES Richard	38+ 3		3+ 1		2			
HOWELL Dean	0+ 1							
HUGHES Andy	32+ 3	7	4		2		1	
LIBURD Richard	24+ 7	1			1			
LINDLEY Jim	0+ 1							
MURRAY Shaun	4+ 5		1		1			
OWERS Gary	45	4	3+ 1		1		1	
PEARCE Dennis	14+ 6		1+ 1		1		1	
RAMAGE Craig	36+ 4	4	4	2	2			
RAPLEY Kevin	11+18	3			1+ 1	1	1	
REDMILE Matt	39+ 2	1	4		1	1	1	
RICHARDSON Ian	33	4	4		2		1	
ROBSON Mark	0+ 2							
STALLARD Mark	31+ 5	13	4		1		1	
TIERNEY Fran	6+ 7	1	0+ 1		0+ 2	1	1	
WARD Darren	45		3		2		1	
WARREN Mark	31+ 2	1	4		1		1	
WEBSTER Adam	0+ 1							
OLDHAM ATHLETIC (DIV 2: 14th)								
ADAMS Neil	29	2	2		2	1	1	
AGOGO Junior	2							
ALLOTT Mark	28+ 4	10	1+ 1	1	3		1	
BEAVERS Paul	3+ 1		0+ 1				0+ 1	
BOSHELL Danny	4+ 4							
DUDLEY Craig	18+ 7	5			2+ 1	1		
DUXBURY Lee	43	4	1		3	1	1	
FUTCHER Ben	1+ 4				0+ 1			
GARNETT Shaun	32	2	2		2		1	
GRAHAM Richard	14+ 3	2			2			
HOLT Andy	46	3	2		2		1	
HOTTE Mark	34+ 1				2		1	
INNES Mark	15+ 6		2		1			
JONES Paul	16	1					0+ 1	
KELLY Gary	44		1		3		1	
McLEAN Ian	1							
McNIVEN David	3+ 1	1	1					
McNIVEN Scott	45	1	2		3		1	
MISKELLY David	2		1					
RICKERS Paul	40+ 1	3	1		3		1	
SALT Phil	4+ 6		1					
SHERIDAN John	34+ 2	1	1+ 1		3	1	1	
SUGDEN Ryan	3+14	1	1+ 1					
SWAN Iain			1					
TAIT Jordan	0+ 1		0+ 1					
THOM Stuart	9	2	1					
TIPTON Matthew	9+20	3	1		0+ 2		0+ 1	
WALSH Danny	0+ 1							
WHITEHALL Steve	27+11	9			2+ 1	2	1	
OXFORD UNITED (DIV 2: 20th)								
ABBEY Ben	0+10				0+ 1	1	0+ 1	
ANTHROBUS Steve	25+11	2	4		3+ 1		2+ 1	
ARENDSE Andre	13		4		1+ 1			
BANGER Nicky	1+ 2		0+ 1					
BEAUCHAMP Joey	33+ 1	4	5	2	5		1+ 2	
COOK Jamie	11+18	3	1+ 3		1+ 3		3	
DAVIS Steve	20+ 4	1	4		1		0+ 1	
EDWARDS Chris	5	1						
FEAR Peter	13+ 6	1	3		1+ 1		2	
FOLLAND Rob	17+ 6	1	4		4+ 1	1	1	
FRANCIS Kevin	0+ 3				0+ 1		0+ 1	
GILCHRIST Phil	1							
HACKETT Chris	0+ 2							
JEMSON Nigel	13+ 5							
KNIGHT Richard	12+ 1							
LAMBERT Jamie	8+ 5	2			2+ 1			
LEWIS Mickey	3+ 2		2+ 1					
LILLEY Derek	36+ 8	7	3+ 2		5	1	1	
LUNDIN Pal	21+ 1		1		4		3	
McGOWAN Neil	15+ 5		0+ 2		2+1		2	
MURPHY Matt	46	11	5	3	5	3	2	
NEWTON Eddie	7							
POWELL Paul	39+ 1	6	5		3+ 1	3	2	3
ROBINSON Les	46		5		5		3	
RUSSELL Craig	5+ 1							
SHEPHEARD Jon	1+ 1						2	
TAIT Paul	34		5		2		2	
WATSON Mark	34+ 1		2		5		1	
WEATHERSTONE Ross	3				1		2	
WEATHERSTONE Simon	13+ 8	1	1+ 1				1	
WHELAN Phil	31	2	1		5		3	
WHITEHEAD Dean							0+ 1	
PETERBOROUGH UNITED (DIV 3: 5th)								
BROUGHTON Drewe	5+ 5	1	2					
CASTLE Steve	36+ 3	10	2		1		3	
CHAPPLE Phil	15+ 1	1			1		1	
CLARKE Andy	33+ 4	15			2	1	4	2
CONNOR Dan	0+ 1							
CULLEN Jon	12+ 1	3					1	
DAVIES Simon	16	2	2		2			
DRURY Adam	41+ 1	1	2		2		4	
EDWARDS Andy	44	2	2		2		4	
ETHERINGTON Matthew	19	3	1		2			
FARRELL Dave	33+ 2	3	2				3	3
FORINTON Howard	19+ 6	7			2			
FRENCH Daniel	0+ 6				0+ 1			
GILL Matthew	7+13	1			1		1+ 2	
GREEN Francis	8+12	1	0+ 1		1		1+ 2	
GRIEMINK Bart	14							
HALEY Grant	1							
HANLON Richie	9+ 7	1					1+ 2	
HOOPER Dean	28+ 1		2		2		1+ 1	
INMAN Niall	0+ 1		0+ 1					
JELLEYMAN Gareth	14+ 6				0+ 1		3+ 1	
KNIGHT Zat	8							

	P/FL		FLC		FAC		Others	
	App	Goals	App	Goals	App	Goals	App	Goals
KOOGI Andre	0+ 1							
LEE Jason	23	6					2	1
MARTIN Jae	7+ 8	1	1+ 1				1	
MURRAY Dan	2							
OLDFIELD David	9						3	
REA Simon	11+ 3	1	0+ 1				2+ 1	
SCOTT Richard	28+ 6	3					4	
SHIELDS Tony	15+ 9	1	2	1	1		0+ 1	
TYLER Mark	32		2		2		4	
WICKS Matthew	17+ 3		2		1		1	
PLYMOUTH ARGYLE (DIV 3: 12th)								
ADAMS Steve	1							
ASHTON Jon	5+ 3		1		1		1	
BARLOW Martin	1+ 1							
BARRETT Adam	38+ 4	3	2		6+ 1		1	
BASTOW Darren	7+ 6	1	2		3+ 2	1		
BELGRAVE Barrington	2+13		0+ 1		0+ 2			
BESWETHERICK Jon	44+ 1		1		7		1	
ETHERINGTON Craig	4+ 1							
GIBBS Paul	3+ 4							
GRITTON Martin	14+16	6	1	1	0+ 3		1	
GUINAN Steve	8	2						
HARGREAVES Chris	44	3	2		7	2	1	
HEATHCOTE Mick	27+ 2	1	1		7	1		
LEADBITTER Chris	28+ 3	2	1		6		1	
McCALL Steve	14+ 2	1	2		2+ 1			
McCARTHY Sean	21+ 8	6	0+ 1		3			
McGREGOR Paul	44	13	2		7	3		
MIDDLETON Craig	6	2						
MORRISON-HILL Jamie	0+ 1						1	
O'SULLIVAN Wayne	45	2	2		7		1	
PATERSON Scott	5							
PHILLIPS Lee	3+14				0+ 1		1	
ROWBOTHAM Jason	7+ 4	1	1		1			
SHEFFIELD Jon	41		1		5		1	
STONEBRIDGE Ian	27+ 4	9	2	1	7	1	0+ 1	
TAYLOR Craig	41	3			5			
VEYSEY Ken	5+ 1		1		2			
WILLS Kevin	0+ 2							
WOTTON Paul	21+ 2				1		1	
PORTSMOUTH (DIV 1: 18th)								
ALLEN Rory	10+ 5	3	0+ 1					
AWFORD Andy	28+ 6	1	2		1			
BERNTSEN Tommy	1+ 1							
BIRMINGHAM David	1+ 1							
BRADBURY Lee	35	10			1			
BROWN Michael	4							
CLARIDGE Steve	31+ 3	14	0+ 1		0+ 1			
CROWE Jason	21+ 4		3		0+ 1			
CUNDY Jason	9		1		1			
DERRY Shaun	9	1						
DURNIN John	2		1+ 1					
EDINBURGH Justin	11							
FENTON Tony	0+ 1							
FLAHAVAN Aaron	10		3		1			
HARPER Kevin	12	2						
HILEY Scott	4+ 4				1			
HOULT Russell	18							
HUGHES Ceri	15	2						
IGOE Sammy	14+12	1	2+ 1					
KNIGHT Alan	1		0+ 2					
LOVELL Steve	0+ 3		2+ 1	1				
McLOUGHLIN Alan	18+ 1	5	2	1				
MIGLIORANZI Stefan	12+ 1	2	2+ 1		1			
MOORE Darren	25	1			1			
MYERS Andy	4+ 4							
NEWTON Adam	1+ 2		2					
NIGHTINGALE Luke	1+ 6		2	2				
O'NEIL Gary	0+ 1							

	P/FL		FLC		FAC		Others	
	App	Goals	App	Goals	App	Goals	App	Goals
PAMAROT Noe	1+ 1		0+ 1					
PANOPOULOS Mike	18+ 4	1	2		1			
PERON Jeff	9+ 1	2	2					
PETTERSON Andy	17		1+ 1					
PHILLIPS Martin	2+ 5		2					
ROBINSON Matthew	23+ 2		3+ 1		1			
SIMPSON Fitzroy	17		2+ 1					
THOGERSEN Thomas	32+ 3	5	3					
VERNAZZA Paolo	7							
VLACHOS Michail	11+ 1		3		1			
WATERMAN Dave	19+ 1							
WHITBREAD Adrian	38+ 1	1	2					
WHITTINGHAM Guy	15+10	4	2		1			
PORT VALE (DIV 1: 23rd)								
ALDRIDGE Martin	0+ 3							
BARKER Simon	3+ 2		1					
BENT Marcus	7+ 1	1	1					
BOGIE Ian	8+ 1							
BRAMMER Dave	29		2					
BRISCO Neil	11+ 1				1			
BULLOCK Martin	6	1						
BURNS Liam	24				1			
BURTON-GODWIN Sagi	19+ 1	2						
BUTLER Tony	15							
CARRAGHER Matty	36+ 1	1	2					
CORDEN Wayne	0+ 2							
CUMMINS Michael	12	1						
DONNELLY Paul	4							
EYRE Richard	17+13	1	0+ 2		1			
FOYLE Martin	13+ 9	6	1		1			
GARDNER Anthony	26	3	2		1			
GOODLAD Mark	1							
GRIFFITHS Carl	0+ 5		0+ 2	1				
HEALY David	15+ 1	3						
MINTON Jeff	23	3	2	1	1			
MUSSELWHITE Paul	30		1		1			
NAYLOR Tony	25+11	6	2	2	0+ 1			
O'CALLAGHAN George	8+ 3							
PILKINGTON Kevin	15		1					
RIMMER Steve	0+ 2							
ROUGIER Tony	33+ 5	8	2	1	1			
SMITH Alex	9+ 4		2					
SNIJDERS Mark	18+ 3				1			
TALBOT Stewart	6							
TANKARD Allen	31+ 4	1	1		1			
TAYLOR Gareth	4							
VILJANEN Ville	11+ 4	4						
WALSH Michael	10+ 2	1	2					
WIDDRINGTON Tommy	37+ 1	5			1			
PRESTON NORTH END (DIV 2: 1st)								
ALEXANDER Graham	46	6	5	1	6	3	1	
ANDERSON Iain	11+ 1	2						
ANGELL Brett	9+ 6	8						
APPLETON Michael	21+ 5	3	2	1	3		2	
BARRY-MURPHY Brian	0+ 1		0+ 1				1	
BASHAM Steve	11+13	2	1+ 1	1	0+ 1			
BEESLEY Mark	0+ 1						0+ 1	
BERESFORD David	1+ 3				0+ 1		1	
CARTWRIGHT Lee	22+ 8	1	3		2+ 1		0+ 1	
DARBY Julian	2+ 1				2		2	
DIAF Farid	1+ 2				0+ 1		2	
EATON Adam							0+ 1	
EDWARDS Rob	37+ 4	2	5		6		2	1
EYRES David	26+15	7	1+ 2		5	1		
GREGAN Sean	33	3	4		6			
GUNNLAUGSSON Bjarke	12+14	1	0+ 1		3+ 3	1	2	4
JACKSON Michael	46	5	5		6			
KIDD Ryan	28+ 1		3+ 1		3		2	
KING Stuart							0+ 1	

	P/FL App	P/FL Goals	FLC App	FLC Goals	FAC App	FAC Goals	Others App	Others Goals
LUCAS David	6		1		1		1	
LUDDEN Dominic	3		1				1	
MACKEN Jonathan	40+ 4	22	5	2	5+ 1	1	2	
McKENNA Paul	17+ 7	2	5		1+ 1	1	0+ 1	
MATHIE Alex	5+ 7	2	2	2	1+ 2		1	
MOILAINEN Tepi	40+ 1		4		5		1	
MURDOCK Colin	29+ 4	2	3		3+ 1		1	
NOGAN Kurt	16+ 6	4	1+ 2		3+ 2		0+ 1	
PARKINSON Gary	0+ 1							
RANKINE Mark	44		4		5			
WRIGHT Mark	0+ 2							
QUEENS PARK RANGERS (DIV 1: 10th)								
BANKOLE Ade	0+ 1							
BARACLOUGH Ian	45		2		2			
BECK Mikkel	10+ 1	4						
BREAKER Tim	15+ 1	1	2		2			
BRUCE Paul	11+ 1				3			
DARLINGTON Jermaine	34	2	1		3			
DOWIE Iain					0+ 1			
GALLEN Kevin	7+24	4	1+ 1		1			
HARPER Lee	37+ 1		0+ 1		3			
JEANNE Leon	1+ 1							
KIWOMYA Chris	42+ 2	13	2		2	1		
KOEJOE Sammy	5+ 6	1			1+ 1			
KULCSAR George	5+ 8				1			
LANGLEY Richard	36+ 5	3	2	1	3			
McGOVERN Brian	3+ 2							
MADDIX Danny	17	1	2					
MIKLOSKO Ludo	9		2		0+ 2			
MORROW Steve	6+ 1		2					
MURRAY Paul	21+ 9				3			
PEACOCK Gavin	26+ 4	8	2	2				
PERRY Mark	9+ 1							
PLUMMER Chris	17+ 1				3			
READY Karl	32+ 1	2	1					
ROSE Matthew	27+ 2	1	2					
ROWLAND Keith	5+10		0+ 1		0+ 1			
SCULLY Tony	2+ 6		0+ 1		0+ 1			
SLADE Steve	3+ 6	1	0+ 1					
STEINER Rob	24	6	1		2			
TAYLOR Gareth	2+ 4	1						
WARD Darren	14				1			
WARDLEY Stuart	41+ 2	11			3	3		
WEARE Ross	0+ 4				0+ 1			
READING (DIV 2: 10th)								
BERNAL Andy	19+ 4		3+ 1		4	1	3	1
BOWEN Mark							1	
BRAYSON Paul	0+ 7		0+ 1		0+ 1		1	
BREBNER Grant	2	1	1					
BUTLER Martin	17	4					1	
CASKEY Darren	43+ 1	17	4	2	5	3	4	1
CASPER Chris	14+ 1		3		2			
CRAWFORD Jimmy	3+ 1	1	1+ 2				0+ 1	
EVERS Sean	8+ 9		0+ 1		4		2+ 1	
FORSTER Nicky	31+ 5	10	3		2		1+ 1	
GRANT Peter	27+ 2	1	3		0+ 4		2	
GRAY Stuart	13+ 3		4		0+ 1		1	
GURNEY Andy	35+ 3	2	3		5		3	
HADDOW Alex	1+ 1		1					
HENDERSON Darius	2+ 4							
HODGES Lee	15+10	2	1+ 2				0+ 1	
HOWIE Scott	35+ 1		4		3		4	
HUNTER Barry	27+ 4	1	3	1	2	1	3	
IGOE Sammy	3+ 3							
LISBIE Kevin	1+ 1							
McINTYRE Jimmy	15+11	4	1+ 1		2+ 2	1	1+ 1	
McLAREN Andy	2		1+ 1					
MURTY Graham	14+ 3				4+ 1		0+ 2	
NEWMAN Ricky	4+ 3	1						

	P/FL App	P/FL Goals	FLC App	FLC Goals	FAC App	FAC Goals	Others App	Others Goals
NICHOLLS Mark	4+ 1	1					2	2
PARKINSON Phil	22	1			5		2	
POLSTON John	12+ 2	1	1		4		1	
POTTER Graham	4						1	
PRIMUS Linvoy	27+ 1				4		3	
ROBINSON Matthew	19						1	
SARR Mass	0+ 3						0+ 2	
SCOTT Keith	14+11	3	2+ 1	2	2+ 1		1+ 2	1
SMITH Neil	26+10	1	3		1		2+ 1	
TYSON Nathan	0+ 1							
VAN DER KWAAK Peter	0+ 1							
WHITEHEAD Phil	11				2			
WILLIAMS Adrian	15	1					1	
WILLIAMS Martin	22+ 7	5	2+ 1		4+ 1	1	3	
ROCHDALE (DIV 3: 10th)								
ATKINSON Graeme	32+ 8	5	2		3	1	4+ 1	
BAYLISS Dave	26+ 3	3	2		2		3	
BETTNEY Chris	12+12				0+ 1		3+ 2	
CARDEN Paul	3+10		0+ 2		0+ 1			
DOWE Julian	1+ 6				1+ 1	1		
EDWARDS Neil	40		2		3		4	
ELLIS Tony	30+ 1	11			1		4+ 1	
EVANS Wayne	46	1	2	1	3		5	
FLITCROFT Dave	40+ 3	2	2		1+ 2		5	
FORD Tony	28+ 6	2	2		3		3+ 1	
GIBSON Paul	5							
GREEN Richard	6							
HICKS Graham					1			
HILL Keith	37+ 1		2				4	1
HOLT Michael	8+ 6		1+ 1		1+ 1		0+ 2	1
JONES Gary	31+ 8	7			2+ 1		4+ 1	
LANCASHIRE Graham	21+ 8	8	2	1			2+ 1	1
McAULEY Sean	10+ 3							
McCLARE Sean	5+ 4							
MONINGTON Mark	22+ 2	2			3		4	2
MORRIS Andy	1+ 6		1+ 1					
PEAKE Jason	38+ 5	6	2		3	1	3	
PEYTON Warren	1							
PLATT Clive	31+10	9			3	1	4	
PRIESTLEY Phil	1+ 1						1	
SEARLE Damon	13+ 1							
STOKES Dean	18+ 1		2		3		2	
TAYLOR Danny	0+ 1							
WILSON Scott	0+ 1							
ROTHERHAM UNITED (DIV 3: 2nd)								
ARTELL David	0+ 1							
BEECH Chris	5+ 1		2					
BERRY Trevor	18+18	4	0+ 1		2		0+ 2	
BRANSTON Guy	30	4					2	
DILLON Paul	15		2		2			
FORTUNE-WEST Leo	39	17	2		2			
GARNER Darren	33+ 2	9	1+ 1		2	1	1	
GLOVER Lee	0+ 7	1						
HUDSON Danny	3+ 4	1					1	
HURST Paul	25+ 5	2			0+ 2		1	
INGLEDOW Jamie	2+ 2		1				1+ 1	
MARTINDALE Gary	4+ 5	2	1		0+ 2	1	0+ 1	
POLLITT Mike	46		2		2		2	
SEDGWICK Chris	29+ 9	5	1		0+ 2		2	1
SCOTT Rob	33+ 1	1	1+ 1		2		2	
THOMPSON Steve	27+ 4	6			2	1	1	
TURNER Andy	26+ 6	1	2				1	
VARTY Will	26+ 1		2		2		0+ 1	
WARNE Paul	39+ 4	10	1+ 1		2		2	
WARNER Vance	16+ 2		0+ 1					
WATSON Kevin	44	1	2		2		2	
WHITE Jason	8+12	4					2	1
WILSTERMAN Brian	38+ 4	3	2		2		2	

	P/FL App	P/FL Goals	FLC App	FLC Goals	FAC App	FAC Goals	Others App	Others Goals
SCUNTHORPE UNITED (DIV 2: 23rd)								
BARWICK Terry	0+1							
BULL Gary	3+3	1			0+1			
CALVO-GARCIA Alex	18	1	2		1			
CLARKE Richard	1							
CORNFORTH John	2+2	1					1	
DAWSON Andy	40+3	2	2		1		1	
EVANS Tommy	27+1		2		1			
FICKLING Ashley	24+6	1	1		1		1	
GAYLE John	2+10		1					
GRAVES Wayne	9+10		1+1				1	
GUINAN Steve	2+1	1						
HARSLEY Paul	45+1	3	2		1		2	
HODGES Lee	39+1	6	2		1		1	1
HODGSON Richard	1							
HOPE Chris	43+1	3	2		1		1	
HOUSHAM Steve	6+3		0+1					
HUMPHREYS Richie	6	2						
HYLDGAARD Morten	5						2	
IPOUA Guy	28+12	9			1		1	
JACKSON Mark	6							
LOGAN Richard	39	1	1		1			
McAULEY Sean	8						1	
MARCELLE Clint	8+2				1			
MARSHALL Lee	1+4		0+1					
OMOYINMI Manny	6	1					1	
PEREZ Lionel	13							
POUNEWATCHY Stephane							1	
QUAILEY Brian	13+1	5						
SHELDON Gareth	8+14	2	1		0+1		1+1	1
SPARROW Matthew	2+9		0+1				0+1	
STAMP Darryn	5+5		1+1				2	1
STANTON Nathan	27+7		1		0+1		2	
TORPEY Steve	15	1						
TURNER Ross	1							
WALKER Justin	40+2		2		1		1	
WILCOX Russ	13+1		1				2	
SHEFFIELD UNITED (DIV 1: 16th)								
BENT Marcus	32	15			3	1		
BROWN Michael	21+3	3						
BURLEY Adam	0+2	1	0+2					
CRADDOCK Jody	10							
DAVISON Aidan	1+1							
DERRY Shaun	31+3		4		3	1		
DEVLIN Paul	40+4	11	3		2			
D'JAFFO Laurent	6+9	1						
DOANE Ben	0+1		0+1					
FORD Bobby	38+3	2	4		2			
GIJSBRECHTS Davy	9+8		1		1			
HALL Paul	1+3	1						
HAMILTON Ian	3+4		2		0+3			
HUNT Jon	8+6		2+2		3			
JAGIELKA Phil	0+1							
KATCHOURO Petr	8+15	1	3+1	2	0+3			
KOZLUK Rob	36+3		2		2			
LAUNDERS Brian	0+1							
MARCELO	9+1	2	2	2				
MORRIS Lee	0+1							
MURPHY Shaun	42	3	4		2			
NOTMAN Alex	7+3	3						
QUINN Wayne	41+2		3+1		3			
RIBEIRO Bruno	9+11	1			1+1			
SANDFORD Lee	43	1	3		2			
SMEETS Axel	2+3		2		0+1			
SMITH Martin	24+2	10	3+1	4	3	1		
TRACEY Simon	45		4		3			
WILSON Stuart	4+2							
WOODHOUSE Curtis	34+3	4	2		3			
WOODWARD Andy	2+1							

	P/FL App	P/FL Goals	FLC App	FLC Goals	FAC App	FAC Goals	Others App	Others Goals
SHEFFIELD WEDNESDAY (PREM: 19th)								
ALEXANDERSSON Niclas	37	5	4	2	3	1		
ATHERTON Peter	35	1	3		4			
BOOTH Andy	20+3	2	4	1	1	1		
BRISCOE Lee	7+9		2+1					
CARBONE Benito	3+4	2	0+1					
CRESSWELL Richard	2+18	1	1+1	1	0+3			
DE BILDE Gilles	37+1	10	3	1	4			
DONNELLY Simon	3+9	1	1+2		0+3			
HASLAM Steven	16+7		0+1		3			
HINCHCLIFFE Andy	29	1	2		4			
HORNE Barry	7							
JONK Wim	29+1	3	2		4			
McKEEVER Mark	1+1		0+1		0+1			
NEWSOME Jon	5+1							
NOLAN Ian	28+1		3+1		4			
O'DONNELL Phil	0+1							
PRESSMAN Kevin	18+1		2					
QUINN Alan	18+1	3			2+1			
RUDI Petter	18+2	2	4	1	0+1			
SCOTT Phil	2+3				1+1			
SIBON Gerald	12+16	5	1+1		3+1	1		
SONNER Danny	18+9		3+1	1	2+1			
SRNICEK Pavel	20		2		4			
THOME Emerson	16+1		3+1		1			
WALKER Des	37		4		4			
SHREWSBURY TOWN (DIV 3: 22nd)								
AISTON Sam	10							
BERKLEY Austin	27+6		1					
BROWN Mickey	35+9	7	2		3		1	
CULLEN Jon	10	1						
DAVIDSON Ross	9+1							
DUNBAVIN Ian	6+1							
EDWARDS Paul	40		1		3		1	
GAYLE John	17+1	2					1	
HANMER Gareth	31+2		2		3		1	
HERBERT Craig	1+1							
HUGHES David	18+4	1			3		1	
JAGIELKA Steve	14+19	1	0+1		1+1	1	1	1
JOBLING Kevin	25+3	2	2		2+1		1	
KERRIGAN Steve	20+5	3	1+1		2	3		
MURRAY Karl	6+6	1	2		2			
PEER Dean	19							
PREECE Roger	5							
RIGBY Tony	4+4	1			2			
RODGERS Luke	0+6	1			0+1		0+1	
SEABURY Kevin	31+1		2		3		1	
SPINK Dean	1+3							
STEELE Lee	34+3	11	2		3		1	
STURRIDGE Simon	10+1	1						
THOMAS Wayne	11+2	1						
THOMPSON Glyn			1					
TOLLEY Jamie	0+2				0+2			
TRETTON Andy	33	3	1		2		1	
WHELAN Spencer	16		1		0+1			
WILDING Peter	41	2	2		3	1	1	
WINSTANLEY Mark	32+1	1	2		1			
SOUTHAMPTON (PREM: 15th)								
ALMEIDA Marco	0+1							
BEATTIE James	8+10		1+2		0+1			
BENALI Francis	25+1		3		1			
BERESFORD John	0+3							
BOA MORTE Luis	6+8	1	0+2		1			
BRADLEY Shayne	0+1							
BRIDGE Wayne	15+4	1	2		2			
COLLETER Patrick	8		1					
DAVIES Kevin	19+4	6	0+1		1			
DODD Jason	30+1		3+1	1	2			
DRYDEN Richard	1							

	P/FL App	P/FL Goals	FLC App	FLC Goals	FAC App	FAC Goals	Others App	Others Goals
EL KHALEJ Tahar	11	1						
HILEY Scott	3							
HUGHES Mark	18 + 2	1	3		1 + 1			
JONES Paul	31		4		2			
KACHLOUL Hassan	29 + 3	5	4		0 + 1			
LE TISSIER Matt	9 + 9	3	1 + 2					
LUNDEKVAM Claus	25 + 2		4		2			
MARSDEN Chris	19 + 2		0 + 2		1			
MONK Garry	1 + 1							
MOSS Neil	7 + 2							
OAKLEY Matthew	26 + 5	3	4	2	1			
OSTENSTAD Egil	3	1						
PAHARS Marians	31 + 2	13	3		2			
RICHARDS Dean	35	2	4	2	1	1		
RIPLEY Stuart	18 + 5	1	2		2			
RODRIGUEZ Dani	0 + 2							
SOLTVEDT Trond	17 + 7	1	4	1	1 + 1			
TESSEM Jo	23 + 2	4	1		2			
SOUTHEND UNITED (DIV 3: 16th)								
ABIODUN Yemi	1 + 2		1 + 1					
BEARD Mark	38 + 3	1			1			
BOOTY Martyn	28		2		1			
CAMPBELL Neil	6 + 6	1			0 + 1		1	
CAPLETON Mel	40 + 2		2		1		1	
CARRUTHERS Martin	38	19			1		1	
CLARKE Adrian	0 + 4		1 + 1					
COLEMAN Simon	43	5	2		1		1	
CONNELLY Gordon	29 + 4	2	1		1		1	
CROSS Gary	7 + 1		1				1	
FITZPATRICK Trevor	1 + 15						0 + 1	
GOODING Mick	0 + 2							
HAILS Julian	0 + 1							
HOUGHTON Scott	42 + 1	4	2		1			
JOHNSON Leon							1	
JONES Nathan	43	2	1 + 1		1		0 + 1	
JONES Steve	9	2						
KERRIGAN Danny	0 + 4				0 + 1		1	
McDONALD Tom	1 + 2							
MAHER Kevin	18 + 6		1					
MORLEY David	29 + 3		2		0 + 1		1	
NEWMAN Rob	14 + 5							
PEPPER Nigel	9 + 3	2						
PRUDHOE Mark	6							
ROACH Neville	6 + 2	1	1 + 1				0 + 1	
ROGET Leo	28 + 8	2	2		1		1	
TINKLER Mark	41		1		1		1	
TOLSON Neil	29 + 2	10	2		1			
STOCKPORT COUNTY (DIV 1: 17th)								
ALLEN Chris	10 + 6				0 + 1			
ANGELL Brett	5		2 + 1	1				
BAILEY Alan	5 + 9	1	0 + 1		1	1		
BENNETT Tom	8 + 1				1			
BERGERSEN Kent	10 + 7				1			
BRIGGS Keith	4 + 3	1	2	1				
BYRNE Chris	11 + 7	2	1					
CONNELLY Sean	42 + 1	3	3		1			
COOPER Kevin	44 + 2	4	1 + 3	1	1			
DALY Jon	0 + 4							
DINNING Tony	43 + 1	12	2	1	1			
D'JAFFO Laurent	20 + 1	7	2	1				
ELLIOTT Stuart	4 + 1							
ELLIS Tony	1 + 3		1 + 1					
FLYNN Mike	46	1	4		1			
FRADIN Karim	19 + 2	1						
FRANCIS Kevin	4							
GANNON Jim	20 + 9		2 + 1		1			
GIBB Ally	13 + 1							
GIBBENS Kevin	1 + 1		2					
GRAY Ian	8 + 2		1					

	P/FL App	P/FL Goals	FLC App	FLC Goals	FAC App	FAC Goals	Others App	Others Goals
LAWSON Ian	13 + 2	4						
McINTOSH Martin	17 + 3		2 + 1					
MATTHEWS Rob	3 + 1	1						
MONK Garry	2		2					
MOORE Ian	34 + 4	10	4		1	1		
NASH Carlo	38		3		1			
NICHOLSON Shane	42	1	3		1			
ROSS Neil	0 + 2							
SMITH David	7 + 2	1	1					
TAYLOR Martin	7							
WILBRAHAM Aaron	13 + 13	4	3 + 1	1				
WOODTHORPE Colin	12 + 14		3	1	0 + 1			
STOKE CITY (DIV 2: 6th)								
AISTON Sam	2 + 4		1					
BULLOCK Matthew	4 + 3				0 + 1			
CLARKE Clive	39 + 3	1	3 + 1		1		8	
CONNOR Paul	15 + 11	5	2 + 2	1	0 + 1		2 + 3	
CROWE Dean	0 + 6		0 + 2				1	
DANIELSSON Einar	3 + 5	1					1	
DRYDEN Richard	11 + 2						1 + 1	
GISLASON Siggi	4 + 4						2 + 2	
GUDJONSSON Bjarni	7 + 1	1					2 + 3	
GUNLAUGSSON Arnar	10 + 3	2					5	1
GUNNARSSON Brynjar	21 + 1	1					8	1
HANSSON Mikael	24 + 3						9	1
HEATH Robert	0 + 3		0 + 1		0 + 1			
IWELLUMO Chris	0 + 3						0 + 1	
JACOBSEN Anders	29 + 4	2	3		1		6 + 1	
KAVANAGH Graham	44 + 1	7	4	1	1		9	2
KAVANAGH Jason			1					
KEEN Kevin	20 + 3	1	3 + 1	1	1			
KIPPE Frode	15	1					5	
LIGHTBOURNE Kyle	35 + 5	7	3		1		6 + 2	3
MacKENZIE Neil	0 + 2							
MELTON Steve	0 + 5						0 + 2	
MOHAN Nicky	40	5	3				8	
O'CONNOR James	42	6	3	1	1		9	2
OLDFIELD David	7 + 12	1	2 + 1				0 + 1	
PETTY Ben	7 + 6		1				2 + 3	
ROBINSON Phil	14 + 8	1	2		1		1 + 1	
SHORT Chris	14		2 + 1		1			
SIGURDSSON Larus	5	1	2					
SMALL Bryan	5 + 3		1					
TAAFFE Steve	2		1					
THORNE Peter	41 + 4	24	3	1	1		5 + 1	5
WARD Gavin	46		4		1		9	
WOOLLISCROFT Ashley					1			
SUNDERLAND (PREM: 7th)								
BALL Kevin	6 + 5		0 + 1	1				
BICA			0 + 1					
BOULD Steve	19 + 1				2			
BUTLER Paul	31 + 1	1	2		2			
BUTLER Thomas	0 + 1		0 + 1					
CRADDOCK Jody	18 + 1				0 + 1			
DICHIO Danny	0 + 12		3	4				
FREDGAARD Carsten	0 + 1		3	2				
GRAY Michael	32 + 1		2 + 1		2			
HELMER Thomas	1 + 1							
HOLLOWAY Darren	8 + 7		2					
KILBANE Kevin	17 + 3	1						
LUMSDON Chris	1		1					
McCANN Gavin	21 + 3	4	0 + 1		2	1		
MAKIN Chris	34	1	1		2			
MALEY Mark			1					
MARRIOTT Andy	1		3					
NUNEZ Milton	0 + 1							
OSTER John	4 + 6		3					
PHILLIPS Kevin	36	30			2			
QUINN Niall	35 + 2	14			1			

	P/FL App	P/FL Goals	FLC App	FLC Goals	FAC App	FAC Goals	Others App	Others Goals
RAE Alex	22+4	3	3		1			
REDDY Michael	0+8	1	0+1		0+1			
ROY Eric	19+5		3	1	2			
SCHWARZ Stefan	27	1			2			
SORENSEN Thomas	37				2			
SUMMERBEE Nicky	29+3	1	1		2			
THIRLWELL Paul	7+1				0+1			
WAINWRIGHT Neil			2					
WILLIAMS Darren	13+12		3	1				

SWANSEA CITY (DIV 3: 1st)

	P/FL App	P/FL Goals	FLC App	FLC Goals	FAC App	FAC Goals	Others App	Others Goals
ALSOP Julian	29+8	3	2+2		2		1	
APPLEBY Richie	10+10	4	1+2		2		1+1	
BIRD Tony	8+8	1	3+1	1			0+1	
BOUND Matthew	43	2	4	1	2		2	
BOYD Walter	21+6	7			1+1		1	
CASEY Ryan	0+11				0+1		1	
COATES Jonathan	41+1	6	3+1		1		0+1	
CUSACK Nicky	43	7	2		2	1		
DE VULGHT Leigh	0+2						1	
EVANS Kevin	1+1							
FREESTONE Roger	46		4		2		2	
HOWARD Mike	39+1		3		2			
JENKINS Lee	7+9						2	
JONES Steve	34+4		0+1		1		1	
KEEGAN Michael	3+1				1		2	
LACEY Damian	14+2		1		1+1			
MORGAN Bari							0+1	
MUTTON Tommy	1+1		0+1				2	1
O'LEARY Kris	9+11		3		1			
PHILLIPS Gareth	2+1		0+1				1	
PRICE Jason	35+4	6	4	1	1			
ROBERTS Stuart	9+2	1	3				1+1	
SMITH Jason	43	1	4		2		2	
THOMAS Martin	32+8	4	4				2	1
WATKIN Steve	36+3	7	3	1	1+1	1	0+1	1

SWINDON TOWN (DIV 1: 24th)

	P/FL App	P/FL Goals	FLC App	FLC Goals	FAC App	FAC Goals	Others App	Others Goals
CAMPAGNA Sam	1+2							
CARRICK Michael	6	2						
COLLINS Lee	23+1	1			1			
COWE Steve	12+5	1						
CUERVO Philippe	0+6							
DAVIES Gareth	18		1		0+1			
DAVIS Sol	23+5		2		1			
FLANAGAN Alan	0+1							
GLASS Jimmy	8							
GOODEN Ty	8+2				1	1		
GRAY Wayne	8+4	2						
GRAZIOLI Guiliano	11+8	8	2					
GRIEMINK Bart	4							
GRIFFIN Charlie	6+15	1	0+1		0+1			
HALL Gareth	38+1	2	2		1			
HAY Chris	27+4	10	0+1		0+1			
HOWE Steve	24+7	1	1+1					
HULBERT Robin	5+7		1					
LEITCH Scott	28+1		1		1			
McCAMMON Mark	4							
McHUGH Frazer	9+5		0+1					
MEAKER Michael	6							
MILDENHALL Steve	3+2				1			
NDAH George	12	1	2					
ONUORA Iffy	18+6	4	2		1			
QUINN Jimmy	1+6				1			
REEVES Alan	43	1	1					
ROBINSON Mark	40+2		2		1			
SMITH Bryan	0+1							
TALIA Frank	31		2					
TAYLOR Craig	1+1		0+1					
THIRLWELL Paul	12							
WALTERS Mark	11+2	2	2	1				

	P/FL App	P/FL Goals	FLC App	FLC Goals	FAC App	FAC Goals	Others App	Others Goals
WILLIAMS Andy	35+1	1	1+1		1			
WILLIAMS James	14+12	1						
WILLIS Adam	16+7				1			

TORQUAY UNITED (DIV 3: 9th)

	P/FL App	P/FL Goals	FLC App	FLC Goals	FAC App	FAC Goals	Others App	Others Goals
AGGREY Jimmy	22+5		2		2+1		3	
BEDEAU Tony	37+1	16	2		4	1	0+2	
BRANDON Chris	41+1	5	2		4	1	2	
DONALDSON O'Neill	4+11				1+2	1	2	1
FORRESTER Mark	0+1							
GRIFFITHS Michael	8+14	3			0+3		3	2
GUTTRIDGE Luke	0+1							
HEALY Brian	37+1	9	1				1	
HERRERA Robbie	34+1		2		2			
HILL Kevin	39+4	2	0+1		4	1	3	1
HOLMES Paul	30				3		1+1	
INGIMARSSON Ivar	4	1						
JONES Stuart	16							
NEIL Gary	4+3						3	
NICHOLS Jon	1				1		1	
NORTHMORE Ryan	2+1						3	
O'BRIEN Mick	25+5	4	2		4	2	1	
PATTERSON Jamie							0+1	
PLATTS Mark	7+15	1	1+1		0+2		2	
RUSSELL Lee	35		2		4		1	
SIMB Jean-Pierre	1+10		0+2		0+2		0+2	
SOUTHALL Neville	28		2		4			
STOCCO Tom	2+6	2						
THOMAS Wayne	38+2	3			4	1	3	
TULLY Steve	10+3		2		2		3	
WATSON Alex	43	4	2		2			
WILLIAMS Eifion	38+4	9	2		3		1	
WORTHINGTON Martin							0+1	

TOTTENHAM HOTSPUR (PREM: 10th)

	P/FL App	P/FL Goals	FLC App	FLC Goals	FAC App	FAC Goals	Others App	Others Goals
ANDERTON Darren	22	3						
ARMSTRONG Chris	29+2	14	2		0+2		3	
CAMPBELL Sol	29		2		2		2	
CARR Stephen	34	3	1				4	
CLEMENCE Stephen	16+4	1			1		2+1	
DAVIES Simon	1+2							
DOHERTY Gary	0+2							
DOMINGUEZ Jose	2+10		0+1		1+1		0+2	
EDINBURGH Justin	7+1		1		1		1+2	
ETHERINGTON Matthew	1+4							
FERDINAND Les	5+4	2						
FOX Ruel	1+2				1+1		1	
FREUND Steffen	24+3		2		1		4	
GINOLA David	36	3	2	1	2	1	2+1	
IVERSEN Steffen	36	14	1+1	1	2	1	4	1
KING Ledley	2+1							
KORSTEN Willem	4+5							
LEONHARDSEN Oyvind	21+1	4	2	1			4	1
McEWEN Dave	0+1							
NIELSEN Allan	5+9				2		1	
PERRY Chris	36+1	1	2		2		4	1
PIERCY John	1+2		1					
SCALES John	3+1							
SHERWOOD Tim	23+4	8	2	1	1		3	1
TARICCO Mauricio	29		2		1		3	
VEGA Ramon	2+3	1	0+1		1+1			
WALKER Ian	38		2		2		4	
YOUNG Luke	11+9		0+1		2		2+1	

TRANMERE ROVERS (DIV 1: 13th)

	P/FL App	P/FL Goals	FLC App	FLC Goals	FAC App	FAC Goals	Others App	Others Goals
ACHTERBERG John	24+2		6+1		2			
ALDRIDGE Paul	0+4							
ALLEN Graham	21+3		4+2					
ALLISON Wayne	40	16			4	3		
BABB Phil	4		1		2			
BLACK Michael	7+15		1+4	1				

	P/FL App	P/FL Goals	FLC App	FLC Goals	FAC App	FAC Goals	Others App	Others Goals
CHALLINOR Dave	39 + 2	3	8		4			
FRAIL Steve	1 + 2		0 + 3		0 + 1			
GRANT Tony	8 + 1		1	1				
HAZELL Reuben	21 + 2	1	5		3			
HENRY Nicky	28 + 2	1	6	1	4	1		
HILL Clint	28 + 1	5	6	2	1			
HINDS Richard	5 + 1							
HUME Iain	0 + 3							
JONES Gary	27 + 4	3	5		4	1		
JONES Lee	3 + 11		1					
KELLY David	25 + 7	6	9 + 1	8	3 + 1	1		
KOUMAS Jason	9 + 14	2	2 + 3		1			
MAHON Alan	33 + 3	4	10	1	3 + 1			
MATIAS Pedro	1 + 3							
MORGAN Alan	20 + 6		5	1	1 + 2			
MURPHY Joe	21		4		2			
NIXON Eric	1 + 1		0 + 1					
PARKINSON Andy	30 + 7	7	7 + 3	2	4			
ROBERTS Gareth	36 + 1	1	7		3			
SANTOS Georges	9 + 1	1	2					
TAYLOR Scott	23 + 12	3	10	4	1 + 3			
THOMPSON Andy	10 + 5		4 + 1		1 + 1			
YATES Steve	32 + 1	2	6 + 1	1	1			
WALSALL (DIV 1: 22nd)								
ABOU Samassi	7 + 1							
BARRAS Tony	19 + 5	4	4	1	1			
BENNETT Tom	11	3						
BICA	0 + 1							
BRIGHTWELL Ian	9 + 1							
BRISSETT Jason	5 + 2		2	1				
BUKRAN Gabor	33 + 4	2	4	3	0 + 1			

	P/FL App	P/FL Goals	FLC App	FLC Goals	FAC App	FAC Goals	Others App	Others Goals
CARTER Alfie	1		0 + 1					
DALEY Tony	3 + 4		1					
EMBERSON Carl	3 + 2		1					
EYJOLFSSON Sigi	1 + 12	1	1 + 3	3	0 + 1			
FENTON Graham	8 + 1	1						
FORRESTER Jamie	2 + 3							
GADSBY Matthew	1 + 2				0 + 1			
HALL Paul	10	4						
HARPER Kevin	8 + 1	1						
KEATES Dean	27 + 8	1	4	1	2			
KEISTER John	0 + 1		0 + 1					
LARUSSON Bjarne	12 + 11		0 + 1		2	1		
MARSH Chris	40		4		2			
MATIAS Pedro	30 + 3	6			2			
MAVRAK Darko	1 + 3		1 + 2					
PADULA Gino	23 + 2				2			
POINTON Neil	18		3 + 1					
RAMMELL Andy	21 + 9	5	1		1 + 1			
RICKETTS Michael	21 + 11	11	2 + 1		1 + 1			
ROBINS Mark	30 + 10	6	4	1	2	1		
ROPER Ian	32 + 2	1	2 + 1		1			
THOMAS Wayne	0 + 1							
TODD Lee	1		1					
VIVEASH Adrian	41 + 2	1	2		2			
VLACHOS Michail	11	1						
WALKER Jimmy	43		3		2			
WRACK Darren	34 + 10	4	4		2			
WATFORD (PREM: 20th)								
BAKALLI Adrian	0 + 2							
BONNOT Alex	7 + 5							
BROOKER Steve	0 + 1				0 + 1			

Dave Challinor (Tranmere Rovers)

	P/FL App	P/FL Goals	FLC App	FLC Goals	FAC App	FAC Goals	Others App	Others Goals
CHAMBERLAIN Alec	27		3		1			
COX Neil	20+ 1				1			
DAY Chris	11							
EASTON Clint	13+ 4		1+ 1	1				
FOLEY Dominic	5+ 7	1	0+ 1					
GIBBS Nigel	11+ 6		2		0+ 1			
GRAVELAINE Xavier	7	2						
GUDMUNDSSON Johann	1+ 8		0+ 1		0+ 1			
HELGUSON Heidar	14+ 2	6						
HYDE Micah	33+ 1	3	3	1	1			
JOHNSON Richard	20+ 3	3	1		1			
KENNEDY Peter	17+ 1	1	3	1				
LYTTLE Des	11		1					
MILLER Charlie	9+ 5		1		1			
MOONEY Tommy	8+ 4	2	1					
NGONGE Felix	16+ 7	5	2+ 1		1			
NOEL-WILLIAMS Gifton	1+ 2							
PAGE Robert	36	1	3		1			
PALMER Steve	38		3		1			
PANAYI Jimmy	2							
PERPETUINI David	12+ 1	1						
ROBINSON Paul	29+ 3		3		1			
SMART Alan	13+ 1	5	1+ 1					
SMITH Tommy	13+ 9	2	0+ 1					
WARD Darren	7+ 2	1						
WILLIAMS Mark	20+ 2	1	2					
WOOTER Nordin	16+ 4	1	1		1			
WRIGHT Nick	1+ 3		2		1			
WEST BROMWICH ALBION (DIV 1: 21st)								
ADAMSON Chris	9				1			
ANGEL Mark	0+ 3				1			
BURGESS Daryl	23+ 3	1	3		1			
BUTLER Tony	7							
CARBON Matt	33+ 1	2	4+ 1		2			
CHAMBERS James	10+ 2							
CLEMENT Neil	7+ 1							
DE FREITAS Fabian	12+12	1	5	2	1			
EVANS Micky	16+17	3	1+ 3	1	1+ 1	1		
FLYNN Sean	36	4	5	1				
FREDGAARD Carsten	5							
GABBIDON Danny	18		4+ 1		2			
HALL Paul	4							
HUGHES Lee	36	12	5	3	2	1		
JENSEN Brian	12							
KILBANE Kevin	19	5	5	2	1			
LYTTLE Des	8+ 1							
McDERMOTT Andy	10+ 3	1	2		0+ 1			
MARESCA Enzo	19+ 6	3	1+ 3		1			
MILLER Alan	25		4		1			
OLIVER Adam	1+14	1			1			
POTTER Graham	6+ 4		0+ 2					
QUINN Jimmy	30+ 7		1+ 2	1	1			
RAVEN Paul	27+ 5	1	4	1	2			
RICHARDS Justin					0+ 1			
SANTOS Georges	8							
SIGURDSSON Larus	27				1			
SNEEKES Richard	42	3	5		2			
TAYLOR Bob	8	5						
TOWNSEND Andy	15+ 3		2					
VAN BLERK Jason	33+ 2	1	3+ 1		1			
WHITEHEAD Phil			1					
WEST HAM UNITED (PREM: 9th)								
BYRNE Shaun	0+ 1							
BYWATER Steve	3+ 1							
CARRICK Michael	4+ 4	1						
CHARLES Gary	2+ 2		1					
COLE Joe	17+ 5	1	3+ 1	1	1		1+ 2	
DI CANIO Paolo	29+ 1	16	4	1	1		6	1
FERDINAND Rio	33		4		1		5	

	P/FL App	P/FL Goals	FLC App	FLC Goals	FAC App	FAC Goals	Others App	Others Goals
FEUER Ian	3							
FOE Marc- Vivien	25	1	3		1		4+ 1	1
FORREST Craig	9+ 2							
HISLOP Shaka	22		4		1		6	
ILIC Sasa	1							
KANOUTE Frederic	8	2						
KELLER Marc	19+ 4		3+ 1	1			4	
KITSON Paul	4+ 6		0+ 3	1	0+ 1		1+ 3	1
LAMPARD Frank	34	7	4	3	1		6	2
LOMAS Steve	25	1	3	1	1		6	
MARGAS Javier	15+ 3	1	2				2+ 1	
MINTO Scott	15+ 3		1		1		1	
MONCUR John	20+ 2	1					4	
NEWTON Adam	0+ 2						0+ 1	
OMOYINMI Manny			0+ 1					
PEARCE Ian	1							
PEARCE Stuart	8							
POTTS Steve	16+ 1		1		1		5	
RUDDOCK Neil	12+ 3		3+ 1		1		2+ 1	1
SINCLAIR Trevor	36	7	3+ 1		1		6	1
STIMAC Igor	24	1	2				2	
WANCHOPE Paulo	33+ 2	12	3		0+ 1		5+ 1	2
WIGAN ATHLETIC (DIV 2: 4th)								
BALMER Stuart	41	2	4		4		4	
BARLOW Stuart	24+ 9	18	4	2	3	2	1+ 2	1
BOWEN Mark	7		3					
BRADSHAW Carl	21+ 5	1	2	1	2		1+ 1	1
CARROLL Roy	34		3		2		2	
CLEGG Michael	6							
COOKE Terry	10	1						
DE ZEEUW Arjan	39	3	3		3		3	
GREEN Scott	32+ 1	2	3		4		4	
GRIFFITHS Gareth	10+ 6	1			1		2+ 1	
HAWORTH Simon	36+ 4	13	4	3	3	3	5	1
JONES Graeme	1+ 2	1	0+ 2					
KILFORD Ian	18+ 3	1	3		3		4	
LEE David	0+ 4		0+ 3					
LIDDELL Andy	41	8	3		3	1	4	
McGIBBON Pat	30+ 4	2	1+ 1		3		5	
McLAUGHLIN Brian			0+ 1					
McLOUGHLIN Alan	11+ 4	1					2	
MARTINEZ Roberto	14+11	3	1		3+ 1		0+ 3	1
MITCHELL Paul			0+ 1					
MORRIS Andy							0+ 2	1
NICHOLLS Kevin	6+ 2							
O'NEILL Michael	30	2	4		4		1	
PERON Jeff	19+ 4				1		1+ 1	
PORTER Andy	2+ 3		0+ 1					
REDFEARN Neil	12	6					3	
ROBERTS Neil	8+ 1	1						
SHARP Kevin	17+ 4		1		2+ 2		5	
SHERIDAN Darren	25+ 6	3	4		1+ 1		5	1
STILLIE Derek	12+ 1		1		2		3	
WIMBLEDON (PREM: 18th)								
AINSWORTH Gareth	0+ 2	2						
ANDERSEN Trond	35+ 1		2		2			
ANDRESEN Martin	4+10	1	0+ 1		1			
ARDLEY Neal	10+ 7	2	1		0+ 1			
BADIR Walid	12+ 9	1	3		0+ 1			
BLACKWELL Dean	16+ 1		4					
CORT Carl	32+ 2	9	5	5	2	1		
CUNNINGHAM Kenny	37		4		2			
EARLE Robbie	23+ 2	3	3+ 1	2	1			
EUELL Jason	32+ 5	4	5	1	2			
FRANCIS Damien	1+ 8		0+ 3		1			
GAYLE Marcus	35+ 1	7	3		2			
GOODMAN Jon			0+ 1					
GRAY Wayne	0+ 1				0+ 1			
HARTSON John	15+ 1	9	3		1			

	P/FL		FLC		FAC		Others	
	App	Goals	App	Goals	App	Goals	App	Goals
HEALD Paul	1							
HREIDARSSON Herman	24	1			2			
HUGHES Michael	13+ 7	2	1+ 1	1	0+ 1			
JUPP Duncan	6+ 3		2+ 1					
KIMBLE Alan	24+ 4		5	1	1			
LEABURN Carl	5+13		2+ 2		1			
LUND Andreas	10+ 2	2						
PEDERSEN Tore	6							
ROBERTS Andy	14+ 2		5		1			
SULLIVAN Neil	37		5		2			
THATCHER Ben	19+ 1		2					
WILLMOTT Chris	7		0+ 1		1			

WOLVERHAMPTON WANDERERS (DIV 1: 7th)

	P/FL App	P/FL Goals	FLC App	FLC Goals	FAC App	FAC Goals	Others App	Others Goals
AKINBIYI Ade	36+ 1	16			3			
ANDREWS Keith	0+ 2							
BAZELEY Darren	46	3	2		3			
BRANCH Michael	25+ 2	6			2			
CORICA Steve	10+ 5	1	2		1+ 1			
CURLE Keith	44+ 1	2	2	1	2			
EMBLEN Neil	45+ 1	5	2	1	3			
FLO Havard	9+10	4	2		0+ 2			
JONES Mark	0+ 1							
KEANE Robbie	2	2	0+ 1					
LARKIN Colin	1		0+ 1	1				
MUSCAT Kevin	45	4	2		2			
NAYLOR Lee	24+ 6	2	2		3			
NDAH George	3+ 1							
NIELSEN Allan	7	2						
NIESTROJ Robert	0+ 1							
OAKES Michael	28				3			
OSBORN Simon	22+ 3				0+ 1			
POLLET Ludovic	38+ 1	5			3			
ROBINSON Carl	21+12	3	2		3	1		
SEDGLEY Steve	32+ 6	5	2		2	1		
SIMPSON Paul	1+12		1+ 1		0+ 2			
SINTON Andy	31+ 4		1		3			
STOWELL Mike	18		2					
TAYLOR Scott	18+10	3						
WILLIAMS Adrian	0+ 1							

WREXHAM (DIV 2: 11th)

	P/FL App	P/FL Goals	FLC App	FLC Goals	FAC App	FAC Goals	Others App	Others Goals
ALLSOP Danny	3	4						
BARRETT Paul	17+ 1	2			1+ 1		1	
BRACE Deryn	3+ 3						1	
CAREY Brian	43	1	2		5			
CHALK Martyn	10+10							
CONNOLLY Karl	35+ 6	9	2		4+ 1	1	1	
COOPER Steve							1	
DEARDEN Kevin	45		2		5			
EDWARDS Jake	0+ 2	1						
FAULCONBRIDGE Craig	23+12	8	1+ 1		2+ 2	1	1	1
FERGUSON Darren	37	4			5	1		
GIBSON Robin	18+ 6	1			1+ 1	1		
HANNON Kevin	0+ 1							
HARDY Phil	38	1	2		5			
JARRETT Jason	1							
LOWE David	4+ 6	1	1					
McGREGOR Mark	45	1	2		5			
MORRELL Andy	4+ 9	1			0+ 1		1	
OWEN Gareth	35+ 4	3	2		3+ 1		1	
PHILLIPS Wayne	3		1					
RIDLER Dave	22+ 3		2		1+ 2		1	
ROBERTS Neil	18+ 1	6			5	2		
ROBERTS Steve	16+ 3				3	1		
ROGERS Kristian	1							
RUSSELL Kevin	29+ 4	4	1		4+ 1			
RYAN Michael	4+ 3							
SPINK Dean	13+ 2				1+ 1		1	
STEVENS Ian	14+ 2	4	2		1+ 1			
THOMAS Steve	0+ 2		0+ 1					

	P/FL		FLC		FAC		Others	
	App	Goals	App	Goals	App	Goals	App	Goals
WARREN David	1							
WALSH Dave							1	
WILLIAMS Danny	24	1	2		4	1	1	

WYCOMBE WANDERERS (DIV 2: 12th)

	P/FL App	P/FL Goals	FLC App	FLC Goals	FAC App	FAC Goals	Others App	Others Goals
ABLETT Gary	4							
BAIRD Andy	20+10	4	1+ 2	1	3	1	1	
BATES Jamie	30+ 2	1	4		5			
BEETON Alan	10+ 6		2+ 1		4			
BRADY Matt	4+ 3	2					0+ 1	
BROWN Steve	34+ 5	3	3	1	3+ 2	1	1	
BULMAN Dannie	10+19	1			0+ 2		1	
BYWATER Steve	2							
CARROLL Dave	36	2	3+ 1	1	3			
COUSINS Jason	30+ 7	1	2+ 1		3+ 1			
DEVINE Sean	39	23	4	1	5	1		
EMBLEN Paul	12+ 4		1+ 3		1+ 3			
HARKIN Mo	2+15				1+ 2		1	
HOLSGROVE Lee	5+ 4		2					
JOHNSON Roger	0+ 1							
LAWRENCE Matty	29	2	4		4		1	
LEE Martyn	3+ 1							
McCARTHY Paul	21+ 1	1	2	1			1	
McSPORRAN Jermaine	32+ 6	9	4	2	4+ 1		1	1
OSBORN Mark	1		0+ 1					
ROGERS Mark	19+ 6				4		1	
RYAN Keith	38	6	4	1	4	1		
SENDA Danny	5+22	1					0+ 1	
SIMPSON Michael	42+ 1		3+ 1		5	2	1	
TAYLOR Martin	42		3		5		1	
THOMPSON Richard	1+ 5						0+ 1	
TOWNSEND Ben	1							
VINNICOMBE Chris	33+ 2		1		1		1	
WESTHEAD Mark	1+ 1		1					

YORK CITY (DIV 3: 20th)

	P/FL App	P/FL Goals	FLC App	FLC Goals	FAC App	FAC Goals	Others App	Others Goals
AGNEW Steve	20+ 2							
ALCIDE Colin	9+ 6	2					1	
ATKINS Mark	10	2	2					
BOWER Mark	15	1						
BULLOCK Lee	16+ 8		1					
CONLON Barry	31+ 9	11	2		1		0+ 1	
DARLOW Kieran	0+ 2							
DAWSON Andrew	11+ 6		2		1		1	
DIXON Kevin	3		1					
EDMONDSON Darren	7							
FAIRCLOUGH Chris	25+ 1		2		1		1	
FETTIS Alan	13							
FOX Christian	28+ 6	1	1		1		1	
GARRATT Martin	2+ 5		1					
HALL Wayne	23		2		1			
HAWKINS Peter	14							
HOCKING Matt	26+ 6	2	1+ 1		0+ 1		1	
HOWARTH Russell	5+ 1		2					
HULME Kevin	23	4			1		1	
JONES Barry	35+ 2	1	2		1			
JORDAN Scott	26+ 2	2	1		1		1	
KEEGAN John	2+ 1							
MIMMS Bobby	28				1		1	
ORMEROD Anthony	9+ 3						1	
REED Martin	7+ 1							
ROWE Rodney	3+ 4		1+ 1	1				
SERTORI Mark	37+ 3	1			1		1	
SKINNER Craig	1+ 4							
SWAN Peter	9							
TALBOT Paul	5+ 1							
THOMPSON Marc	9+ 1							
THOMPSON Neil	6							
TURLEY James	9+ 2	2						
WILLIAMS John	28+ 8	3	1		0+ 1		1	
WILLIAMS Marc	11+11	5			1			

PFA AWARDS 2000

Player of the Year
ROY KEANE

Young Player of the Year
HARRY KEWELL

Special Merit Award
GARY MABBUTT

DIVISIONAL AWARDS

FA Carling Premiership

Nigel Martyn	Leeds United
Garry Kelly	Leed United
Ian Harte	Leeds United
Jaap Stam	Manchester United
Sami Hypia	Liverpool
Roy Keane	Manchester United
David Beckham	Manchester United
Patrick Vieira	Arsenal
Andy Cole	Manchester United
Kevin Phillips	Sunderland
Harry Kewell	Leeds United

Nationwide League Division 1

Richard Wright	Ipswich Town
Gary Rowett	Birmingham City
Chris Powell	Charlton Athletic
Richard Rufus	Charlton Athletic
Chris Coleman	Fulham
Mark Kinsella	Charlton Athletic
Craig Hignett	Barnsley
Mark Kennedy	Manchester City
John Robinson	Charlton Athletic
Andy Hunt	Charlton Athletic
Marcus Stewart	Ipswich Town

Nationwide League Division 2

Roy Carroll	Wigan Athletic
Graham Alexander	Preston North End
Steve Davis	Burnley
Michael Jackson	Preston North End
Mickey Bell	Bristol City
Sean Gregan	Preston North End
Darren Caskey	Reading
Glen Little	Burnley
Graham Kavanagh	Stoke City
Jason Roberts	Bristol Rovers
Jonathan Macken	Preston North End

Nationwide League Division 3

Mike Pollitt	Rotherham
Ian Hendon	Northampton Town
Matthew Bound	Swansea City
Craig Liddle	Darlington
Matt Lockwood	Leyton Orient
Darren Currie	Barnet
Tommy Miller	Hartlepool
Neil Heaney	Darlington
Nick Cusack	Swansea City
Marco Gabbiadini	Darlington
Richard Barker	Macclesfield Town